Handbook of Research on Improving Learning and Motivation through Educational Games:

Multidisciplinary Approaches

Patrick Felicia
Waterford Institute of Technology, Ireland

Volume I

Information Science
REFERENCE

Senior Editorial Director:	Kristin Klinger
Director of Book Publications:	Julia Mosemann
Editorial Director:	Lindsay Johnston
Acquisitions Editor:	Erika Carter
Development Editor:	Myla Harty
Production Coordinator:	Jamie Snavely
Typesetters:	Michael Brehm and Milan Vracarich, Jr.
Cover Design:	Nick Newcomer

Published in the United States of America by
    Information Science Reference (an imprint of IGI Global)
    701 E. Chocolate Avenue
    Hershey PA 17033
    Tel: 717-533-8845
    Fax: 717-533-8661
    E-mail: cust@igi-global.com
    Web site: http://www.igi-global.com/reference

Library of Congress Cataloging-in-Publication Data

Handbook of Research on Improving Learning and Motivation Through Educational
Games : Multidisciplinary Approaches / Patrick Felicia, editor.
   p. cm.
 Includes bibliographical references and index.
 Summary: "This book provides relevant theoretical frameworks and the latest empirical research findings on game-based learning to help readers who want to improve their understanding of the important roles and applications of educational games in terms of teaching strategies, instructional design, educational psychology and game design"--Provided by publisher.
 ISBN 978-1-60960-495-0 (hardcover) -- ISBN 978-1-60960-496-7 (ebook) 1. Educational games. 2. Simulation games in education. 3. Cognitive learning. 4. Learning, Psychology of. I. Felicia, Patrick.
 LB1029.G3H36 2011
 371.33'7--dc22
                2010054437

British Cataloguing in Publication Data
A Cataloguing in Publication record for this book is available from the British Library.

All work contributed to this book is new, previously-unpublished material. The views expressed in this book are those of the authors, but not necessarily of the publisher.

List of Contributors

Table of Contents

Volume I

Section 1
Introduction to Game-Based Learning

Section 2
Cognitive Approach to Game-Based Learning: Design Patterns and Instructional Design

Section 3
Psychological Approach to Game-Based Learning: Emotions, Motivation and Engagement

Detailed Table of Contents

Volume I

Section 1
Introduction to Game-Based Learning

This section provides introductory material on Game-Based Learning. Readers with little or no prior knowledge of the field will find valuable information to help their understanding of how video games can be appreciated and explained in the light of educational and motivational theories. It also includes two literature reviews on the use of computer games in education that will help the reader to appreciate the evolution of GBL and the challenges that lie ahead. This section also comprises an analysis of the barriers to using video games in the classroom, an overview of the necessary conditions for the successful integration and deployment of video games in instructional settings, and an explanation of the role that teachers can play to support the effective use of video games.

Chapter 1

Gunilla Svingby, Malmö University, Sweden
Elisabet M. Nilsson, Malmö University, Sweden

In this chapter, Svingby and Nilsson present a literature review of projects where Game-Based Learning (GBL) was employed to support science teaching. They classify 50 publications of the last decade, which include empirical data on the use of video games to teach science. This in-depth literature review classifies and assesses each of the publications, based on several criteria, such as type of game, research design, research methodology and topic taught.

Chapter 2

Thomas Hainey, University of the West of Scotland, Scotland
Thomas Connolly, University of the West of Scotland, Scotland
Mark Stansfield, University of the West of Scotland, Scotland
Liz Boyle, University of the West of Scotland, Scotland

In this chapter, Hainey, Connolly, Stansfield, and Boyle provide an introduction to and a literature review of GBL. They define GBL and associated terms, and analyze how video games have been employed to teach computer science, software engineering, and Information Systems. The authors also discuss the advantages and limitations of video games as learning platforms.

Chapter 3

Caroline Kearney, European Schoolnet, Belgium

In this chapter, Kearney reviews and summarizes a study conducted across Europe on the use of video games for learning purposes. During this project, a comprehensive amount of data was collected in order to present a state of play of GBL from many different perspectives (e.g., teachers, experts and policy-makers). An analysis of the data collected has helped the researcher to identify and explain the barriers to using video games in the classroom, the necessary conditions for the successful integration and deployment of video games, and the role that teachers can play to facilitate and support the use of video games in educational settings. Based on her analysis, Kearney provides useful recommendations to teachers and other practitioners.

Chapter 4

René St-Pierre, Université du Québec à Montréal, Canada

In this chapter, St-Pierre explains how video games can be appreciated and analyzed in the light of educational and motivational theories. After a brief introduction that situates the evolution of educational video games within the wider context of multimedia and educational theories, he provides an interesting overview of the instructional theories, often implemented implicitly in video games, which can be used to guide the design, implementation, and deployment of video games. Behavioral, cognitivist, and constructivist approaches to learning are considered. Particular attention is paid to user-centered design, and he explains how individual differences (e.g., personality, learning styles or multiple intelligences) can be accounted for in designing educational video games. St-Pierre also gives designers and instructors a set of specifications for the successful development of video games.

Section 2
Cognitive Approach to Game-Based Learning: Design Patterns and Instructional Design

This section describes GBL solutions that concentrate on the cognitive aspects of learning, with particular emphasis on instructional design, educational theories, and design patterns. The authors address the difficult and complex tasks of identifying, measuring and combining the factors that contribute to both learning and motivation in video games.

Chapter 5

Identifying and measuring factors that contribute to learning and motivation in video games is a difficult task, perhaps due to the complexity involved in accounting for both cognition and motivation. However, in this chapter, Staalduinen, based on a literature review of both video games design and instructional design theories, has singled-out 25 game elements that support deep learning, a state where learners develop a critical understanding of the topic taught. In a study where students used a game called TOPSIM, the author has managed to assess the educational impact of 16 of these elements, and he shares his analysis and results.

Chapter 6

In this chapter, Djaouti, Alvarez and Jessel introduce a classification of video games that they call the G/P/S. This classification can be used to choose and analyze video games, based on their educational and entertaining features. This model might be particularly useful for instructors with little or no prior knowledge of video games. The authors explain the theoretical basis for their model by providing a comprehensive review of existing classifications, identifying their limitations, and explaining in great detail how these limitations have been addressed in their model. The authors also offer a practical example of their methodology, by classifying a sample of different types of serious games with the G/P/S model.

Chapter 7

In this chapter, Ecker, Müller and Zylka address the difficulty of successfully combining educational and entertaining features of video games thanks to design patterns. Their work is based on both game design patterns and pedagogical patterns. The authors explain the background for Game-Based Learning Design Patterns (GBLDPs); they provide examples for such patterns, and discuss the challenges in identifying, recording, and employing adequate patterns for GBL.

In this chapter, Evans explores best practices for the design of effective GBL environments at university-level and for adult learners. Her approach is based on the premise that games are intrinsic learning experiences. She describes seven best practices of entertainment games design that can be adapted to educational content, namely, metaphor, visualization, content as mechanic, self-assessment, achievement, repetition, and multi-linear play. She then explores how these best practices can be employed using Digital Calculus Coach, an online video game that teaches calculus concepts and problem-solving to third-level students.

In this chapter, Schott and Selwyn argue that there is a discrepancy between the literacy employed by digital natives when playing video games and the classification established by digital immigrants. They explain that, contrary to many preconceived opinions among parents and teachers, games also contribute to knowledge, and that more adults should start to learn about video games, and acknowledge their learning benefits. The authors believe that game literacy goes far beyond entertainment; however they also think that game regulations are often guided by beliefs, perception and attitudes. Their chapter offers interesting insights and ideas to change this state-of-mind.

In this chapter, Schwartz and Bayliss offer to bridge the gap between instructional design and game design, by reviewing instructional and game design concepts, and by comparing and contrasting their key aspects. Using three case studies, Schwartz and Bayliss draw parallels between instructional design and game design, and explain how these two fields can be combined successfully.

Chapter 11

In this chapter, Szilas and Acosta, who believe that video games are dynamic systems of signs, introduce a theoretical framework to explain how learning occurs in video games, using a semiotic approach. They then use their model to classify GBL strategies employed in three commercial games.

Section 3
Psychological Approach to Game-Based Learning: Emotions, Motivation and Engagement

This section focuses on a psychological approach to GBL, and explains how emotions and motivation can be harnessed to improve learning in video games.

Chapter 12

Thomas Hainey, University of the West of Scotland, Scotland
Thomas Connolly, University of the West of Scotland, Scotland
Liz Boyle, University of the West of Scotland, Scotland

In this chapter, Hainey, Connolly and Boyle present a study where Alternative Reality Games (ARGs), a popular form of interactive narrative, were employed to motivate secondary school students to learn a modern foreign language. Their chapter explains the rationale for the use of ARGs. It provides a literature review of the utilization of ARGs for educational purposes, with a focus on language learning, and presents both qualitative and quantitative analyses of the motivation of the students who took part in the study.

Chapter 13

Claire Dormann, Carleton University, Canada
Jennifer Whitson, Carleton University, Canada
Robert Biddle, Carleton University, Canada

In this chapter, Dormann, Whitson, and Biddle take a look at how computer games can support affective learning. Their approach, partially based on the activity theory, emphasizes the role of games as effective mediators of learning in the affective domain. They identify and describe design patterns that support affective learning.

Chapter 14

Paul Toprac, Southern Methodist University, USA

Many European countries are experiencing a decline in the number of students embracing a career in science, and GBL is often perceived as an appropriate solution because it provides an open-ended and entertaining environment, where students can experiment and learn-by-doing. In this chapter, Toprac describes his experience of employing a problem-based digital video game called The Alien Rescue

Game (TARG) to teach, and promote an interest in science to middle school students. Throughout this chapter, Toprac defines and explains the theoretical foundations and key motivational factors in video games. He then describes his experiments conducted with TARG. He explains and analyses how this video game has managed to increase students' learning interests and motivation. Toprac also provides newsworthy recommendations for designers and instructors, and identifies future relevant research directions.

Chapter 15
Leonard Annetta, North Carolina State University, USA
Richard Lamb, North Carolina State University, USA
Brandy Bowling, North Carolina State University, USA
Rebecca Cheng, North Carolina State University, USA

In this chapter, Annetta, Lamb, Bowling, and Cheng explore the psychometrics of an engagement observation protocol, based on cognition and learning theories. They explain that learning is strongly linked to involvement and engagement, and they describe how a Student Engaged Learning Technology rich Interactive Classroom protocol (SELTIC) was developed to increase and measure K-12 students' motivation when using a Serious Educational Game (SEG).

Chapter 16
Menno Deen, Fontys University of Applied Sciences, The Netherlands
Ben Shouten, Fontys University of Applied Sciences, The Netherlands

In this chapter, Deen and Shouten propose to address learning and motivation in video games through identified regulations, which can be described as "negotiations with personal valued rules". They explain how identified regulations can motivate players to learn during the game, and even when the game is over. They illustrate their theory through the validation of a beta-version of a second language learning game called CheckOut!, a game designed with identified regulations in mind.

Chapter 17
Nicola Whitton, Manchester metropolitan University, UK

In this chapter, Whitton considers the factors affecting the motivation of adults in the context of Higher Education (HE). She argues that adults' motivations for playing video games differ from those of children and teenagers. She reviews the theoretical explanations for adult motivation, and presents relevant guidelines to harness the educational benefits of motivation for adults.

In this chapter, Voulgari and Komis investigate the use of Massively Multiplayer Online Games (MMOGs) for collaborative learning. They argue that these environments implicitly include a wide range of motivational and instructional features that ought to be harnessed to augment and improve current educational practices. Voulgari and Komis identify and analyze relevant characteristics that may positively impact on learning in MMOGs, and they review learning and psychology theories that could explain how learning and engagement occur in these environments. Following this analysis, they present a framework based on their observations, and provide the reader with recommendations for the effective design, deployment, and use of MMOGs for learning purposes.

Chapter 19

In this chapter Aranda and Sánchez-Navarro describe video games as social activities, in which complexities and intricacies can be understood within sociocultural and educational contexts. They report on three studies that investigated the use of digital gaming in non-formal and informal education: (1) an empirical study on the use and perception of Spanish teenagers in relation to digital technologies as tools for leisure and socialization, (2) an analysis of the introduction of video games in the context of leisure activities, and (3) a workshop for families to discuss the cultural and social significance of the use of video games in the household.

Chapter 20

In this chapter, Haring, Chakinska, and Ritterfield explain serious gaming from a psychological perspective. They focus on the effect of video games on players, and describe the conditions and the significant factors for players' enjoyment, which may in turn influence the extent to which they learn. They also present and describe the Big-Five, a hierarchical model of game enjoyment based on empirical evidence.

Accessibility in video games is an area that demands further attention and investigation from researchers, as there are very few experiments and studies focused on accommodating people with disabilities in video games. Although new standards and regulation have addressed some of these issues, it is very difficult to represent abstract concepts or complex information with inherent spatial attributes (e.g., mathematics) to blind people, who rely predominantly on their tactile and auditory senses to gather information. In this chapter, Neff and Pitt describe and analyze how spatial auditory information can be employed for expressing mathematical problems to blind students in the context of video games. They explain their framework, and illustrate it through the description of a study that examined the representation of trigonometric shapes using surround sound.

Chapter 22

In this chapter, Shin, Norris, and Soloway examine the use of mobile gaming environments for learning, and their effect on students' motivation and attitude toward Mathematics. The authors believe that mobile GBL provides a flexible, interactive and individualized medium for learning, and they explain the need for more empirical evidence on the benefits of mobile GBL. They provide a comprehensive overview of the previous research on mobile GBL, and present the results of a study that they carried-out over a four month period with second grade students. Based on their findings, Shin, Norris, and Soloway provide recommendations and future directions to researchers for the development of effective mobile GBL environments.

In this chapter, Hudlicka emphasizes the importance of using emotions in educational video games. She explains how emotions play a central role in learning, and how they can influence behaviors and the acquisition of new cognitive and motor skills. She focuses particularly on emotions-modeling, which she believes can improve user-modeling and the "believability" of Non-Player Characters (NPCs), and help video games to adapt to players' changing affective states. Hudlicka discusses the creation of an affective game engine, a tool she suggests could improve the design of affect-centered games. Hudlicka also provides interesting recommendations to researchers, practitioners and policy-makers for the advancement of serious affective gaming.

Chapter 24

Emerging game interface designs increasingly incorporate human gestural learning. Electronic gestural games, when effectively designed, offer high levels of user engagement. In this chapter, Danylak presents theatrical practice, an art form that manufactures expressive gestures in set paradigms, as a model for gestural game systems design. A rigorous definition of gesture is first developed from yoga practice as an exercise for performance preparation, emphasizing the gesture as a still form executed within a narrative context. The theatrical model is then refigured into an interactive gestural film game design, To be or not be, based on a section of text from Shakespeare's play Hamlet.

Section 4
User-Centered Approach to Game-Based Learning: Accounting for Users' Differences, Specificities and Disabilities

This section accounts for users' differences, specificities and disabilities in the design of GBL systems. The authors describe theoretical frameworks and guidelines that address issues and challenges such as improving motivation, providing tailored interventions with Intelligent Tutoring Systems (ITSs), accounting for gender differences, applying games to neuro-rehabilitation, or engaging children with attention deficit or intellectual disabilities.

Chapter 25

In this chapter, Marty and Carron propose to increase motivation in GBL environments by improving both the flexibility of the system and users' immersion. They explain the need for adaptive mechanisms to model users. They suggest the use of tailored interventions and scenarios, and describe how immersion can be augmented based on game design considerations. Marty and Carron then illustrate their approach through the description of a GBL environment called Learning Adventure, a management system representing a 3D environment where users are taught basic Unix shell commands, and are provided with an adaptive scenario.

Chapter 26

In this chapter, Ng studies students' different attitudes to GBL and video games based on their gender, as she believes this issue has been overlooked over the past years. She describes a study in which student teachers were taught programming concepts using an educational video game. Ng analyzes their behaviors and achievements in terms of score, strategies, and time spent playing, and she observed interesting and significant differences between genders, notably that male students spent shorter time playing the video game but scored higher, and that female students were inclined to adopt a trial-and-error strategy. She then provides recommendations based on her experience and the results of her study.

Chapter 27

In this chapter, De Byl and Brand present guidelines on the appropriate selection of video game genres in educational settings, based on learners' individual differences, such as learning styles and personality traits. Their comprehensive guidelines help teachers to match appropriate game genres with learning outcomes and students' characteristics, and to maximize educational outcomes and motivation on the part of the students.

Chapter 28

In this chapter, Amon and Campbell focus on serious games for health, and explain how video games can be used to address common attention problems such as Attention-Deficit/Hyperactivity Disorder (AD/HD). The authors focus especially on biofeedback technology, and describe a study where biofeedback video games were used to teach children breathing and relaxation techniques, which helped them to reduce common symptoms of AD/HD.

Chapter 29

In this chapter, Linek analyses educational video games through a psychological perspective. She explains how design recommendations can be derived from the field of media psychology, a discipline that explores how psychology can impact on various media, including radio, television or video games. The author provides an overview of the different fields of media psychology that can be exploited for the creation of effective educational video games. Based on her approach, she identifies key design factors and derives guidelines for the design of educational video games in relation to game items, game mechanics, game characters and game narratives.

Chapter 30

In this chapter, Carr and Blanchfield explore how educational video games can be used to engage children with behavioral disorders (e.g., defiant behaviors or attention deficit). They explain how children, who usually find it difficult to maintain their attention in traditional educational settings, found educational video games more engaging. The authors describe the design and assessment of two prototypes of educational games. They share their experience of creating the game, and guide the reader through the difficult exercise of balancing the educational and entertaining features of the game in order to produce an experience that is both highly engaging and didactic.

Volume II

In this chapter, Maciuszek and Martens explain how Intelligent Tutoring Systems (ITSs), educational systems designed to tailor learning interventions to learners' activities and knowledge, can be employed to seamlessly combine game play and learning. They review game-based ITS architectures, and propose a unified structure partially based on Role-Playing Games (RPGs).

Chapter 32

In this chapter, Perry, Andureu, Cavallaro, Veneman, Carmien, and Keller explain how video games can be effective for neurorehabilitation because they provide motivation and goal-directed exercises and tasks. The authors argue that, for video games to be effectively used for rehabilitation, it is necessary to construct a unified and comprehensive framework that follows user-centered design principles, and that takes into account the needs and viewpoints of all stakeholders. They analyze methods employed in the rehabilitation process, and describe how video games and robotics can be used for rehabilitation. They then identify and outline the requirements for rehabilitation systems, and illustrate them through a prototype they have designed.

Chapter 33

In this chapter, Howel and Veale introduce strategies to facilitate and improve the development and integration of educational video games, and present a process employed in the creation of a video game designed to improve language skills. They describe issues linked to the integration of video games and ITSs, and propose recommendations accordingly. These are partially based on a case study that they carried-out with a serious linguistic casual game called BubbleWords.

Chapter 34

In this chapter Saridaki and Mourlas describe how video games can be successfully employed to motivate students with intellectual disabilities and their educators. They explain the issues and considerations related to teaching students with intellectual disabilities, and emphasize how motivation can play a important role in their learning process, and in changing their attitude towards learning. Based on a thorough literature review and several case studies, the authors show why and how video games can be a powerful educational and motivational medium in Special Educational Needs (SEN) classrooms.

Section 5
Curricular Approach to Game-Based Learning: Integrating Video Games in Instructional Settings

This section describes how video games can be deployed and utilized in different instructional settings. The chapters include experiments on the use of video games to teach law, engineering, physics, leadership and health. The authors explain how these video games can improve current teaching practices. They describe the rationale and theoretical models behind the creation and deployment of their systems, and provide helpful insights and recommendations based on their experiences.

Chapter 35

In this chapter, Bösche and Kattner report on the transformation of a classical seminar course on the psychological impact of violent video games, into a a virtual classroom experience. They explain the shortcomings of traditional methodologies, and how virtual environments can be employed to assess the impact of violence in video games.

In this chapter, Anderson and Courtney describe an educational intervention, based on video games, to introduce and develop design thinking skills to two groups of Australian indigenous high-school students. The authors explain that mainstream education does not always build positive self-perception and self-esteem of Australian indigenous students, and they argue that video games, because they are "food for the soul" and provide a sense of control, are particularly appropriate for this purpose.

Chapter 37

In this chapter, Rossiou argues that Learning Management Systems (LMSs) are predominantly focused on the administration and management of learning resources, but that they place less emphasis on communication, interactivity and cooperation. She investigates how a web-based educational video game, combined with an LMS, can be used to increase interactivity and engagement in the learning process. Rossiou describes a framework to successfully implement such a system. She depicts the integration of a multiplayer game, in the context of a synchronous virtual classroom, and shows how several technologies were combined to produce a GBL system.

Chapter 38

In this chapter, Williamson and Sandford provide an analysis of the use of computer games in authentic classroom settings. They envisage GBL as the result of specific game-based pedagogies that are being developed and employed by increasing numbers of classroom teachers in UK schools. The chapter focuses on the ways in which classroom teachers discuss and describe GBL in relation to their curricular intentions, and their less formal cultural assumptions about the relevance of gaming in learners' new media ecologies outside of school.

Chapter 39

In this chapter, Tan, Johnston-Wilder, and Neill describe the deployment and analysis of a GBL solution at an upper secondary school in the UK, where they conducted a case study on students' perception of the benefits of using a Commercial Off-The-Shelf (COTS) video game to learn about biology. The authors investigate how GBL, combined with a dialogic teaching approach, can support deep learning among students.

Chapter 40
Ryan Flynn, University of Greenwich, UK

In this chapter, Flynn investigates the use of Commercial Off-The-Shelf (COTS) games in educational settings and assesses the practical challenges inherent to their deployment. He describes the issues associated with choosing a COTS game for teaching, and offers practical recommendations that should help instructors and researchers to identify and select appropriate COTS games, based on factors such as customization (e.g., level editors or Software Development Kit), ease of installation and deployment, and ease of empirical data collection.

Chapter 41
Arul Chib, Nanyang Technological University, Singapore

In this chapter, Chib reports on a study that examined the use of an educational interactive game to educate Peruvian youths about sexual and reproductive health. The research design consisted of pre- and post-intervention surveys. The study utilized social cognitive theory to determine the influence of prior knowledge, self-efficacy and game-playing on respondents' attitudes. Chib found that prior attitudes, knowledge, resistance to peer-pressure, and game-playing were significant predictors of attitudes toward sexual health. He also found that health attitudes were influenced by playing video games.

Chapter 42
Vinod Srinivasan, Texas A&M University, USA
Karen Butler-Purry, Texas A&M University, USA
Susan Pedersen, Texas A&M University, USA

In this chapter, Srinivasan, Butler-Purry, and Pedersen present their experience of developing an educational game to teach digital systems design to electrical engineering students. They explain how this approach helped to address the limitations of traditional teaching methods, and to consequently increase learning and motivation on the part of the students. This interesting chapter provides an in-depth overview of their journey from obtaining funding, to implementing and assessing the video game. It describes the challenges faced by instructors who plan to use GBL solutions, and it provides highly relevant and valuable guidelines to researchers and educators engaged in similar endeavors.

In this chapter, Anagnostou and Pappa provide an extensive review of research related to the design and use of GBL solutions for physics education. They explain how learning can occur in video games, based on educational theories and game design (e.g., game mechanics and game genres). Relevant educational theories and game genres are reviewed, and their implications for physics education are analyzed. Based on this review, Anagnostou and Pappa define and describe their framework, which offers a valuable approach for designing effective and engaging video games. The authors also discuss the barriers that impede the widespread adoption of video games for educational purposes, and propose pertinent solutions and guidelines.

Chapter 44

In this chapter, Axe and Routledge share the success stories and lessons learned from the use of serious games, both in formal and informal education. Their goals are to create an increased awareness of GBL among educationalists, and to consequently improve collaboration, engagement and innovation. They explain how attitudes toward the use of video games for education needs to be changed, and emphasize the role of teachers and other educationalists as the key contributors to this change.

In this chapter, Pappa, Dunwell, Protopsaltis, Pannese, Hetzner, De Freitas, and Rebolledo-Mendez focus on GBL for sharing knowledge in the context of intergenerational learning. They explain the challenges of intergenerational learning, and describe how these were addressed by a model that they called e-VITA, which employs a methodology where knowledge creation is envisaged as a spiraling process of interactions between explicit and tacit knowledge. The application of this methodology in the context of the research project e-VITA is discussed, including the implications for pedagogy and game design.

Chapter 46

In this chapter, Akerfeldt and Selander argue that multimodality and didactic design should be considered for a deeper understanding of how information is presented in educational video games. They analyze two educational video games, Rixdax and El Patron, through a semiotic perspective, and they observe how learning goals and the display of on-screen information can be addressed. Their analysis is partially based on Prensky's six structuring factors and Kress and Van Leeuwen's multimodal framework. These models are used to assess video games in terms of information value, information sequencing, and affordance for meta-reflection on the part of the user. Based on their analysis, the authors provide helpful recommendations for game designers.

Chapter 47

Despite evidence of the potential of video games for learning purposes, it seems that few law schools have embraced the use of GBL systems, as many of them essentially use traditional teaching methods. In this chapter, Lettieri, Fabiani, Tartaglia Polcini, De Chiara, and Scarano present an interesting system called Simulex, an online environment for the creation of Role Playing Games (RPGs) that simulate trials. The authors explain how serious games can match the objective of legal education, and how they can provide a more appropriate and effective approach. They review current technology-enhanced teaching solutions for law education, and explain how their project fits within this context. The chapter includes an interesting description of the different stages involved in the design, creation, testing and assessment of the system. Based on their experience, the authors also give pertinent recommendations for the design of effective legal serious games.

Chapter 48

In this chapter, Shabanah describes how and why video games can be employed to teach data structures and algorithms, two topics often perceived as complex and difficult to understand by students. She explains that many algorithm visualization systems are not satisfactory, partly because they are essentially based on graphics and sound, and not on relevant pedagogical or motivational considerations. She describes how algorithm games, which are based on sound educational theories, have inspired students to learn algorithm through active engagement and intrinsic motivation. She explains the rationale behind the use of algorithm games and their attributes in terms of game design and instructional design. She then depicts the design of several algorithm games prototypes.

Chapter 49

Vasiliki Dai, Secondary School Teacher of English, Greece
Vasilis Daloukas, Secondary School Teacher of Informatics, Greece
Spiros Sirmakessis, Technological Institute of Mesolonghi, Greece, & Research Academic
Computer Technology Institute (R.A. CTI), Greece

In this chapter, Dai, Daloukas, Rigou, and Sirmakessis discuss issues related to the design and implementation of effective mobile GBL environments, with an emphasis on games developed for Moodle and Open Source systems. The chapter includes an appreciation of the factors that prevent the integration of games in educational settings. The authors describe how they have incorporated video games into Moodle, and made them available on mobile devices using Java2ME.

Chapter 50

Andrea Corradini, University of Southern Denmark, Denmark

In this chapter, Corradini explores how 2D recreational puzzle games can improve basic spatial skills such as tilting, rotating and flipping. The author describes an experiment with students from high schools and universities, where 2D spatial Maths puzzles were employed to improve students' confidence and problem-solving skills. Corradini explains the practical and theoretical considerations underpinning the design of the games used in the study. Results show that the game, which offered many challenges in terms of forward-planning, decision-making and spatial skills, helped users to visualize the problem mentally, and to elaborate a successful strategy.

Chapter 51

Brent D. Ruben, Rutgers University, USA
Kathleen M. Immordino, Rutgers University, USA
Sherrie Tromp, Rutgers University, USA
Brian Agnew, Rutgers University, USA

In this chapter, Ruben, Immordino, Tromp, and Agnew describe the different approaches to, and critical challenges in, leadership development. They explain how simulations and video games offer a compelling approach because they can be designed to address many dimensions of leadership and integrate the benefits of other instructional approaches. The authors describe LEADER.edu, a scenario-based simulation that is designed to engage participants in strategic leadership learning experiences, using a combination of online access and interactive dialogues and feedback. The authors list, define and explain the theoretical foundations for this software, as well as its structure and content, in terms of pedagogy and interaction. They also provide general recommendations, based on their experience, for those who plan on developing simulation games on a similar topic.

Chapter 52
    Boaventura DaCosta, Solers Research Group, USA
    Angelique Nasah, Solers Research Group, USA
    Carolyn Kinsell, Solers Research Group, USA
    Soonhwa Seok, University of Kansas, USA

In this chapter, DaCosta, Nasah, Kinsell, and Seok identify the gaming propensity of 580 post-secondary school students through a survey. Results suggest that age, gender, and socioeconomic status are composite factors that contribute to gaming. The findings have a number of implications for educators, policy-makers, practitioners, researchers, instructional technologists, and game developers across both the education spectrum and the entertainment industry, for the use and development of video games.

Foreword

In the early days of games and learning scholarship (1980s), academic discussion was largely dominated by essays and treatises on how and why video games had some cognitive benefits.[1] Prevailing popular opinion at the time was that video games were a waste of time and money or even potentially dangerous to developing young minds, like movies, comic books, television, and rock music were in their times. The worry over video games is perhaps no surprise, given their origins in smoke-filled pinball arcades and the fact that few adults played arcade games or video games. As Patricia Greenfield described in her seminal book *Mind and Media: The Effects of Television, Video Games, and Computers* a quarter century ago, it is impossible to understand video games from the outside; you have to play them to understand what is really going on.

These game players grew up and continued to play games in adulthood, carrying gameplay with them into academia, opening the door for consideration of video games as something more than entertainment, and the combined weight of many voices arguing for a reconsideration of this pop culture phenomenon began to wedge that door further open. Articles in the 1990s about the benefits of games began to appear with some regularity in the mainstream press. It seemed the world was ready to hear about games and learning and that we were poised for a generative period of empirical research and practical application of gaming technology in schools and business training.

But a funny thing happened on the way to the promised land. The success of our efforts in changing mainstream opinion created a strong market for publications about games. But research takes time to do (or, at least, to do right), and we were not well prepared for this shift. Having gotten used to the sound of our own voices calling for people to take games seriously, when they finally did, we were perhaps caught short. As any economist will tell you, when demand outstrips supply, you get a lot of people looking to fill that demand any way they can. Works by people who had never specifically studied games were quickly rushed to press. The canon of work on games prior to the mid-to-late 1990s was largely dominated by thought experiments and essays, which many new authors emulated.[2] Many of these authors and researchers entering the arena brought great ideas and unique perspectives from their own disciplines, yet because of differing terminology and academia's propensity for reading and researching only within one's own field, they failed to build on each other's work. And because video games belonged to so many fields, there was no clear academic "leader" for researchers from different fields to read as a basis for considering video games from within their own disciplines. This was an extremely generative period that produced thousands of publications on video games, culture, and learning. But with researchers not reading each other's work, and empirical research proceeding at the slow pace it does, what emerged was more a cacophony than a symphony.

In the last decade, research has begun to catch up to demand. Researchers have begun to sift through the volumes of work, looking for commonality and contradictions and using those to formulate the questions that are necessary to guide this field in the years to come. Scholars have brought their disciplinary rigor to synthesizing existing theory within the context of games and learning. From Mark Wolf and Bernard Perron's *Video Game Theory Reader(s)* in 2003 and 2009 to Jim Gee's seminal work on video games, learning, and literacy, to Ian Bogost's *Persuasive Games and Unit Operations*, to David Williamson-Shaffer's work on epistemic games, to Chris Crawford's work on game design, to the work of Katie Salen, David Michael and Sande Chen, to Joost Raessens, to Jesper Juul, to Kurt Squire, to Constance Steinkuehler, to John Kirriemuir and Angela McFarlane, to Noah Wardrip-Fruin and Pat Harrigan, the field has started to coalesce. This has been matched by rigorous efforts to answer empirically the questions we have only anecdotally addressed in the past. These researchers include Shawn Green and Daphne Bavalier, whose study on visual attention and video game play has definitively answered some of our most pressing questions, opened a whole new avenue of video game research, and set a standard for empirical research on such questions that should be extended to other areas of study of video games. These researchers also include Debbie Denise Reese and her colleagues on CyGaMEs, whose work on measuring flow serves as a model for what is needed in our field as we continue to shift our discussions of such key theories from the anecdotal to the empirical. Works like the meta-analyses of Jennifer and David Vogel, Kathryn Muse, and Michelle Wright are continuing the tradition set by earlier researchers like Josephine Randel, Barbara Morris, Douglas Wetzel, and Betty Whitehill. There are many other researchers who are doing good work in this field but are perhaps not as well known as those mentioned previously. Some of the authors of the chapters you are about to read may not be known to you yet, but combined, all of our voices will help shape the future of games and learning.

This book comes at a critical time for the field. The need for synthesis and evaluation of existing research remains one of our most significant challenges, both for understanding the past, for applying it to the design of learning for today, and for formulating the questions that will guide our field tomorrow. Every one of these chapters presents empirical research; a synthesis of existing research; new ideas, theories, and models; and, in many cases, all three. From practical applications to public education in areas such as science, math, physics, linguistics, reading, and legal education to research and design of serious games for underserved populations such as indigenous peoples, special needs education, and people with disabilities, to the now burgeoning field of biometric research in games and cognition, these chapters differ widely in their disciplinary perspectives. This interdisciplinary breadth is key to the success of our field, yet this can often come at the expense of cohesiveness and generalizability. In this case, thanks to the efforts of the authors and editor, the individual contributions remain accessible to all disciplines and make their connection to future research and practice clear. Together, they represent both the disciplinary and conceptual breadth of the work that is going on in the field of serious games research today.

A volume like this does not come about on its own. Its success is determined by the ability of the editor to survey the field, determine current and future needs, and shape a call for proposals that generates the depth and breadth needed to meet those needs. As proposals come in, s/he must evaluate them for the best fit and provide guidance to help them evolve into chapters that will form a chorus rather than a series of solos. As you read this book, I'm sure you will agree that such has been the case with this text.

This text comes at the start of yet another period of generative research in game-based learning, but this time one that is matched by synthesis and evaluation of prior and current research from a variety of disciplinary perspectives—one which knows how to both ask and answer the right questions AND how to apply what we learn to the real-world problems we will face in the 21st century. Read these chapters carefully and with your mind open to different disciplinary perspectives. Seek to build on them as you add your voice to the chorus of researchers in game-based learning.

Richard Van Eck

Richard Van Eck *is Associate Professor and Graduate Director of the Instructional Design & Technology program at the University of North Dakota (UND). He received his Ph.D. in instructional design and development from the University of South Alabama, where his dissertation examined the use of an original game to promote transfer of mathematics skills in middle school. He was a member of the faculty at the University of Memphis for 5 years, where he was also a member of the Institute for Intelligent Systems. His scholarly work on digital game-based learning includes a cover story for Educause Review, seven book chapters, two edited books, ten referee publications, 25 conference presentations, and 27 invited presentations. He has created five original games for learning, and was elected to the board of directors for the North American Simulation and Gaming Association in 2006. He currently resides in North Dakota with his wife, two cats, and two dogs who think they're people.*

ENDNOTES

[1]   There were certainly notable exceptions, including such well-known names like Thomas Malone, Mark Lepper, and Patricia Greenfield, who were studying games from a cognitive and psychological perspective, but they and their colleagues were more the exception than the rule.

[2]   Again, there were many good researchers producing strong work during this time (e.g. Lloyd Reiber; Yasmin Kafai; Henry Jenkins; Justine Cassel; Randel, Morris, Wetzel, and Whitehill; Seymour Papert; Brian Sutton-Smith; Margaret Gredler), but others who were not.

Preface

INTRODUCTION

Game-Based Learning (GBL) is an emerging educational medium that employs video games to increase students' skills, their level of awareness, and their motivation to learn.

GBL has evolved considerably during the last decades, in terms of theoretical models and applications, and is gaining increasing recognition among a wide range of sectors including formal education and corporate training. This significant change has been supported by new and more accessible gaming technologies, and the advent of educational theories that promote a constructive approach to learning, and acknowledge motivation and personal differences as determining factors for successful learning.

However, despite a growing body of knowledge on educational video games, there is still a need for more rigorous experiments in order to define frameworks that guarantee systematic learning and motivation. Without solid theoretical foundations, and universal guidelines on how to design and use video games in educational settings, it will be difficult to obtain all the benefits that these games can offer.

Several successful GBL solutions have been produced to date, and researchers have made substantial findings which have furthered the understanding of the intricate factors that affect learning and motivation in video games. Nonetheless, many challenges lie ahead:

- More developers need to be informed of best practices pertaining to the design of successful educational games.
- More educators need to be aware of the educational potential of video games. They need to understand how this medium can be used successfully to consistently motivate and instruct learners.
- Stakeholders involved in funding and identifying relevant educational solutions (e.g., company owners, policy-makers, or managers) should be informed accordingly, so that they understand the economical and managerial implications of GBL. This should enable them to make informed decisions, thereby supporting instructors and learners with relevant structures and resources.
- Educational video games should be envisaged through a multidisciplinary approach, and be designed accordingly by multidisciplinary teams including experts in game design, instructional design, and psychology.
- Researchers should avoid the mistakes of the past and create educational applications that truly tap into the motivational and emotional potential of video games; educational games should also account for curricular learning objectives. These two conditions are crucial for the adoption of GBL by both instructors and students.

- More practical recommendations on how to use GBL systems are needed. Whereas many publications on GBL report on experiments and theoretical models, very few manage to provide simple and practical guidelines that designers and instructors can easily follow and apply.
- GBL systems should follow a user-centered approach to learning, and acknowledge personal differences at both cognitive and affective levels. It is only by providing personalized emotional and cognitive experiences to users (e.g., characters, scenarios, or learning interventions) that reproducible and sustainable results will be achieved.

To address some of these challenges and expand the existing body of knowledge on GBL, I decided to launch a publication project involving experts from different fields, all with an interest in designing highly engaging and educational game-based educational systems. The primary objective of this project was to compile current research in GBL, to provide a comprehensive yet practical explanation of GBL, and to analyze the multiple factors, including design, development, integration, and evaluation, that contribute to both learning and motivation in video games.

This project has been an interesting journey and a truly collaborative experience involving the work and contribution of many enthusiastic and dedicated individuals. More than a year after submitting my proposal for this book to IGI-Global, and having collected, reviewed, and compiled the invaluable information submitted by authors and reviewers, it is with great enthusiasm that I am writing the preface of this publication. I believe this book will be instrumental in expanding our understanding of the multiple factors that influence the effective design and use of GBL. I also hope that it will assist teachers, students, policy-makers, and developers, and inspire them to tap into the many possibilities offered by GBL.

This handbook includes chapters from more than 100 experts in instructional design, game design, psychology and educational psychology, who depict their experience of designing and deploying GBL solutions, and reflect on their achievements and shortcomings. These experiences are then employed to inform the reader by providing relevant advice and guidelines accordingly.

All chapters have been evaluated using a thorough review process. In order to recruit authors, a call for chapters was issued, requiring potential contributors to submit a proposal that described the coverage, uniqueness and relevance of their chapter. All proposals were then evaluated based on their relevance, and every effort was made to include a representative range of topics. Selected authors were asked to submit their chapters, which were then assessed through a double-blind review process by three reviewers. Following the double-blind reviews, accepted authors were provided with recommendations from the reviewers and the editor, and asked to submit an amended script. This amended version was then evaluated, and a final notification of acceptance was issued. As a result of this review process, this handbook includes 52 high quality chapters that provide a comprehensive explanation of the issues, solutions, and challenges related to GBL.

BOOK STRUCTURE

The chapters in this book have been divided in five key areas:

- *Introduction to Game-Based Learning.* This section provides introductory material on Game-Based Learning. Readers with little or no prior knowledge of the field will find valuable information to help their understanding of how video games can be appreciated and explained in the light of educational and motivational theories. It also includes two literature reviews on the use of computer games in education that will help the reader to appreciate the evolution of GBL and the challenges that lie ahead. This section also comprises an analysis of the barriers to using video games in the classroom, an overview of the necessary conditions for the successful integration and deployment of video games in instructional settings, and an explanation of the role that teachers can play to support the effective use of video games.

- *Cognitive Approach to Game-Based Learning: Design Patterns and Instructional Design.* This section describes GBL solutions that concentrate on the cognitive aspects of learning, with particular emphasis on instructional design, educational theories, and design patterns. The authors address the difficult and complex tasks of identifying, measuring and combining the factors that contribute to both learning and motivation in video games.

- *Psychological Approach to Game-Based Learning: Emotions, Motivation and Engagement.* This section focuses on a psychological approach to GBL, and explains how emotions and motivation can be harnessed to improve learning in video games.

- *User-Centered Approach to Game-Based Learning: Accounting for Users' Differences, Specificities and Disabilities.* This section accounts for users' differences, specificities and disabilities in the design of GBL systems. The authors describe theoretical frameworks and guidelines that address issues and challenges such as improving motivation, providing tailored interventions with Intelligent Tutoring Systems (ITSs), accounting for gender differences, applying games to neurorehabilitation, or engaging children with attention deficit or intellectual disabilities.

- *Curricular Approach to Game-Based Learning: Integrating Video Games in Instructional Settings.* This section describes how video games can be deployed and utilized in different instructional settings. The chapters include experiments on the use of video games to teach law, engineering, physics, leadership and health. The authors explain how these video games can improve current teaching practices. They describe the rationale and theoretical models behind the creation and deployment of their systems, and provide helpful insights and recommendations based on their experiences.

Section 1: Introduction to Game-Based Learning

In Chapter 1, Svingby and Nilsson present a literature review of projects where Game-Based Learning (GBL) was employed to support science teaching. They classify 50 publications of the last decade that include empirical data on the use of video games to teach science. This in-depth literature review classifies and assesses each of the publications, based on several criteria, such as type of game, research design, research methodology and topic taught. In Chapter 2, Hainey, Connolly, Stansfield, and Boyle provide an introduction to and a literature review of GBL. They define GBL and associated terms, and analyze how video games have been employed to teach computer science, software engineering and information systems. The authors also discuss the advantages and limitations of video games as learning platforms. In Chapter 3, Kearney reviews and summarizes a study conducted across Europe on the use of video games for learning purposes. During this project, a comprehensive amount of data was collected in order to present a state of play of GBL from many different perspectives (e.g., teachers, experts and policy-makers). An analysis of the data collected has helped the researcher to identify and explain the barriers to using video games in the classroom, the necessary conditions for the successful integration and deployment of video games, and the role that teachers can play to facilitate and support the use of video games in educational settings. Based on her analysis, Kearney provides useful recommendations to teachers and other practitioners. In Chapter 4, St-Pierre explains how video games can be appreciated and analyzed in the light of educational and motivational theories. After a brief introduction that situates the evolution of educational video games within the wider context of multimedia and educational theories, he provides an interesting overview of the instructional theories, often implemented implicitly in video games, that can be used to guide the design, implementation, and deployment of video games. Behavioral, cognitivist, and constructivist approaches to learning are considered. Particular attention is paid to user-centered design, and he explains how individual differences (e.g., personality, learning styles or multiple intelligences) can be accounted for in designing educational video games. St-Pierre also gives designers and instructors a set of specifications for the successful development of video games.

Section 2: Cognitive Approach to Game-Based Learning: Design Patterns and Instructional Design

Identifying and measuring factors that contribute to learning and motivation in video games is a difficult task, perhaps due to the complexity involved in accounting for both cognition and motivation. However, in Chapter 5, Staalduinen, based on a literature review of both video games design and instructional design theories, has singled-out 25 game elements that support deep learning, a state where learners develop a critical understanding of the topic taught. In a study where students used a game called TOP-SIM, the author has managed to assess the educational impact of 16 of these elements, and he shares his analysis and results. In Chapter 6, Djaouti, Alvarez, and Jessel introduce a classification of video games that they call the G/P/S. This classification can be used to choose and analyze video games, based on their educational and entertaining features. This model might be particularly useful for instructors with little or no prior knowledge of video games. The authors explain the theoretical basis for their model by providing a comprehensive review of existing classifications, identifying their limitations, and explaining in great detail how these limitations have been addressed in their model. The authors also offer a practical example of their methodology, by classifying a sample of different types of serious games with the G/P/S model. In Chapter 7, Ecker, Müller, and Zylka address the difficulty of successfully combining educational and entertaining features of video games thanks to design patterns. Their work is based on both game design patterns and pedagogical patterns. The authors explain the background for Game-Based Learning Design Patterns (GBLDPs); they provide examples for such patterns, and discuss the challenges in identifying, recording, and employing adequate patterns for GBL. In Chapter 8, Evans explores best practices for the design of effective GBL environments at university-level and for adult learners. Her approach is based on the premise that games are intrinsic learning experiences. She describes seven best practices of entertainment games design that can be adapted to educational content, namely, metaphor, visualization, content as mechanic, self-assessment, achievement, repetition, and multi-linear play. She then explores how these best practices can be employed using Digital Calculus Coach, an online video game that teaches calculus concepts and problem-solving to third-level students. In Chapter 9, Schott and Selwyn argue that there is a discrepancy between the literacy employed by digital natives when playing video games and the classification established by digital immigrants. They explain that, contrary to many preconceived opinions among parents and teachers, games also contribute to knowledge, and that more adults should start to learn about video games, and acknowledge their learning benefits. The authors believe that game literacy goes far beyond entertainment; however they also think that game regulations are often guided by beliefs, perception and attitudes. Their chapter offers interesting insights and ideas to change this state-of-mind. In Chapter 10, Schwartz and Bayliss offer to bridge the gap between instructional design and game design, by reviewing instructional and game design concepts, and by comparing and contrasting their key aspects. Using three case studies, Schwartz and Bayliss draw parallels between instructional design and game design, and explain how these two fields can be combined successfully. In Chapter 11, Szilas and Acosta, who believe that video games are dynamic systems of signs, introduce a theoretical framework to explain how learning occurs in video games, using a semiotic approach. They then use their model to classify GBL strategies employed in three commercial games.

Section 3: Psychological Approach to Game-Based Learning: Emotions, Motivation and Engagement

In Chapter 12, Hainey, Connolly, and Boyle present a study where Alternative Reality Games (ARGs), a popular form of interactive narrative, were employed to motivate secondary school students to learn a modern foreign language. Their chapter explains the rationale for the use of ARGs. It provides a literature review of the utilization of ARGs for educational purposes, with a focus on language learning, and presents both qualitative and quantitative analyses of the motivation of the students who took part in the study. In Chapter 13, Dormann, Whitson, and Biddle take a look at how computer games can support affective learning. Their approach, partially based on the activity theory, emphasizes the role of games as effective mediators of learning in the affective domain. They identify and describe design patterns that support affective learning. Many European countries are experiencing a decline in the number of students embracing a career in science, and GBL is often perceived as an appropriate solution because it provides an open-ended and entertaining environment, where students can experiment and learn-by-doing. In Chapter 14, Toprac describes his experience of employing a problem-based digital video game called The Alien Rescue Game (TARG) to teach and promote an interest in science to middle school students. Throughout Chapter 14, Toprac defines and explains the theoretical foundations and key motivational factors in video games. He then describes his experiments conducted with TARG. He explains and analyses how this video game has managed to increase students' learning interests and motivation. Toprac also provides newsworthy recommendations for designers and instructors, and identifies future relevant research directions. In Chapter 15, Annetta, Lamb, Bowling, and Cheng explore the psychometrics of an engagement observation protocol, based on cognition and learning theories. They explain that learning is strongly linked to involvement and engagement, and they describe how a Student Engaged Learning Technology rich Interactive Classroom protocol (SELTIC) was developed to increase and measure K-12 students' motivation when using a Serious Educational Game (SEG). In Chapter 16, Deen and Shouten propose to address learning and motivation in video games through identified regulations, which can be described as "negotiations with personal valued rules". They explain how identified regulations can motivate players to learn during the game, and even when the game is over. They illustrate their theory through the validation of a beta-version of a second language learning game called CheckOut!, a game designed with identified regulations in mind. In Chapter 17, Whitton considers the factors affecting the motivation of adults in the context of Higher Education (HE). She argues that adults' motivations for playing video games differ from those of children and teenagers. She reviews the theoretical explanations for adult motivation, and presents relevant guidelines to harness the educational benefits of motivation for adults. In Chapter 18, Voulgari and Komis investigate the use of Massively Multiplayer Online Games (MMOGs) for collaborative learning. They argue that these environments implicitly include a wide range of motivational and instructional features that ought to be harnessed to augment and improve current educational practices. Voulgari and Komis identify and analyze relevant characteristics that may positively impact on learning in MMOGs, and they review learning and psychology theories that could explain how learning and engagement occur in these environments. Following this analysis, they present a framework based on their observations, and provide the reader with recommendations for the effective design, deployment, and use of MMOGs for learning purposes. In Chapter 19, Aranda and Sánchez-Navarro describe video games as social activities, in which complexities and intricacies can be understood within sociocultural and educational contexts. They report on three studies that investigated the use of digital gaming in non-formal and informal education: (1) an empirical study on the use and perception of Spanish teenagers in relation to digital technologies as tools for leisure and socialization, (2) an analysis of the introduction of video games in the context of leisure activities, and (3) a workshop for families to discuss the cultural and social significance of the use of video games in the household. In Chapter 20, Haring, Chakinska, and Ritterfield explain serious gaming from a psychological perspective. They focus on the effect of video games on players, and describe the conditions and the significant factors for players' enjoyment, which may in turn influence the extent to which they learn. They also present and describe the Big-Five, a hierarchical model of game enjoyment based on empirical evidence. Accessibility in video games is an area that demands further attention and investigation from researchers, as there are very few experiments and studies focused on accommodating people with disabilities in video games. Although new standards and regulation have addressed some of these issues, it is very difficult to represent abstract concepts or complex information with inherent spatial attributes (e.g., mathematics) to blind people, who rely predominantly on their tactile and auditory senses to gather information. In Chapter 21, Neff and Pitt describe and analyze how spatial auditory information can be employed for expressing mathematical problems to blind students in the context of video games. They explain their framework, and illustrate it through the description of a study that examined the representation of trigonometric shapes using surround sound. In Chapter 22, Shin, Norris, and Soloway examine the use of mobile gaming environments for learning, and their effect on students' motivation and attitude toward Mathematics. The authors believe that mobile GBL provides a flexible, interactive and individualized medium for learning, and they explain the need for more empirical evidence on the benefits of mobile GBL. They provide a comprehensive overview of the previous research on mobile GBL, and present the results of a study that they carried-out over a four month period with second grade students. Based on their findings, Shin, Norris and Soloway provide recommendations and future directions to researchers for the development of effective mobile GBL environments. In Chapter 23, Hudlicka emphasizes the importance of using emotions in educational video games. She explains how emotions play a central role in learning, and how they can influence behaviors and the acquisition of new cognitive and motor skills. She focuses particularly on emotions-modeling, which she believes can improve user-modeling and the "believability" of Non-Player Characters (NPCs), and help video games to adapt to players' changing affective states. Hudlicka discusses the creation of an affective game engine, a tool she suggests could improve the design of affect-centered games. Hudlicka also provides interesting recommendations to researchers, practitioners and policy-makers for the advancement of serious affective gaming. Emerging game interface designs increasingly incorporate human gestural learning. Electronic gestural games, when effectively designed, offer high levels of user engagement. In Chapter 24, Danylak presents theatrical practice, an art form that manufactures expressive gestures in set paradigms, as a model for gestural game systems design. A rigorous definition of gesture is first developed from yoga practice as an exercise for performance preparation, emphasizing the gesture as a still form executed within a narrative context. The theatrical model is then refigured into an interactive gestural film game design, 'To be or not be,' based on a section of text from Shakespeare's play, Hamlet.

Section 4: User-Centered Approach to Game-Based Learning: Accounting for Users' Differences, Specificities and Disabilities

In Chapter 25, Marty and Carron propose to increase motivation in GBL environments by improving both the flexibility of the system and users' immersion. They explain the need for adaptive mechanisms to model users. They suggest the use of tailored interventions and scenarios, and describe how immersion can be augmented based on game design considerations. Marty and Carron then illustrate their approach through the description of a GBL environment called Learning Adventure, a management system representing a 3D environment where users are taught basic Unix shell commands, and are provided with an adaptive scenario. In Chapter 26, Ng studies students' different attitudes to GBL and video games based on their gender, as she believes this issue has been overlooked over the past years. She describes a study in which student teachers were taught programming concepts using an educational video game. Ng analyzes their behaviors and achievements in terms of score, strategies, and time spent playing, and she observed interesting and significant differences between genders, notably that male students spent shorter time playing the video game but scored higher, and that female students were inclined to adopt a trial-and-error strategy. She then provides recommendations based on her experience and the results of her study. In Chapter 27, De Byl and Brand present guidelines on the appropriate selection of video game genres in educational settings, based on learners' individual differences, such as learning styles and personality traits. Their comprehensive guidelines help teachers to match appropriate game genres with learning outcomes and students' characteristics, and to maximize educational outcomes and motivation on the part of the students. In Chapter 28, Amon and Campbell focus on serious games for health, and explain how video games can be used to address common attention problems such as Attention-Deficit/Hyperactivity Disorder (AD/HD). The authors focus especially on biofeedback technology, and describe a study where biofeedback video games were used to teach children breathing and relaxation techniques, which helped them to reduce common symptoms of AD/HD. In Chapter 29, Linek analyses educational video games through a psychological perspective. She explains how design recommendations can be derived from the field of media psychology, a discipline that explores how psychology can impact on various media, including radio, television or video games. The author provides an overview of the different fields of media psychology that can be exploited for the creation of effective educational video games. Based on her approach, she identifies key design factors and derives guidelines for the design of educational video games in relation to game items, game mechanics, game characters and game narratives. In Chapter 30, Carr and Blanchfield explore how educational video games can be used to engage children with behavioral disorders (e.g., defiant behaviors or attention deficit). They explain how children, who usually find it difficult to maintain their attention in traditional educational settings, found educational video games more engaging. The authors describe the design and assessment of two prototypes of educational games. They share their experience of creating the game, and guide the reader through the difficult exercise of balancing the educational and entertaining features of the game in order to produce an experience that is both highly engaging and didactic. In Chapter 31, Maciuszek and Martens explain how Intelligent Tutoring Systems (ITSs), educational systems designed to tailor learning interventions to learners' activities and knowledge, can be employed to seamlessly combine game play and learning. They review game-based ITS architectures, and propose a unified structure partially based on Role-Playing Games (RPGs). In Chapter 32, Perry, Andureu, Cavallaro, Veneman, Carmien, and Keller explain how video games can be effective for neurorehabilitation because they provide motivation and goal-directed exercises and tasks. The authors argue that, for video games to be effectively used for rehabilitation, it is necessary to construct a unified and comprehensive framework that follows user-centered design principles, and that takes into account the needs and viewpoints of all stakeholders. They analyze methods employed in the rehabilitation process, and describe how video games and robotics can be used for rehabilitation. They then identify and outline the requirements for rehabilitation systems, and illustrate them through a prototype they have designed. In Chapter 33, Howel and Veale introduce strategies to facilitate and improve the development and integration of educational video games, and present a process employed in the creation of a video game designed to improve language skills. They describe issues linked to the integration of video games and ITSs, and propose recommendations accordingly. These are partially based on a case study that they carried-out with a serious linguistic casual game called BubbleWords. In Chapter 34 Saridaki and Mourlas describe how video games can be successfully employed to motivate students with intellectual disabilities and their educators. They explain the issues and considerations related to teaching students with intellectual disabilities, and emphasize how motivation can play an important role in their learning process, and in changing their attitude towards learning. Based on a thorough literature review and several case studies, the authors show why and how video games can be a powerful educational and motivational medium in Special Educational Needs (SEN) classrooms.

Section 5: Curricular Approach to Game-Based Learning: Integrating Video Games in Instructional Settings

In Chapter 35, Bösche and Kattner report on the transformation of a classical seminar course on the psychological impact of violent video games, into a a virtual classroom experience. They explain the shortcomings of traditional methodologies, and how virtual environments can be employed to assess the impact of violence in video games. In Chapter 36, Anderson and Courtney describe an educational intervention, based on video games, to introduce and develop design thinking skills to two groups of Australian indigenous high-school students. The authors explain that mainstream education does not always build positive self-perception and self-esteem of Australian indigenous students, and they argue that video games, because they are "food for the soul" and provide a sense of control, are particularly appropriate for this purpose. In Chapter 37, Rossiou argues that Learning Management Systems (LMSs) are predominantly focused on the administration and management of learning resources, but that they place less emphasis on communication, interactivity and cooperation. She investigates how a web-based educational video game, combined with an LMS, can be used to increase interactivity and engagement in the learning process. Rossiou describes a framework to successfully implement such a system. She depicts the integration of a multiplayer game, in the context of a synchronous virtual classroom, and shows how several technologies were combined to produce a GBL system. In Chapter 38, Williamson and Sandford provide an analysis of the use of computer games in authentic classroom settings. They envisage GBL as the result of specific game-based pedagogies that are being developed and employed by increasing numbers of classroom teachers in UK schools. The chapter focuses on the ways in which classroom teachers discuss and describe GBL in relation to their curricular intentions, and their less formal cultural assumptions about the relevance of gaming in learners' new media ecologies outside of school. In Chapter 39, Tan, Johnston-Wilder, and Neill describe the deployment and analysis of a GBL solution at an upper secondary school in the UK, where they conducted a case study on students' perception of the benefits of using a Commercial Off-The-Shelf (COTS) video game to learn about biology. The authors investigate how GBL, combined with a dialogic teaching approach, can support deep learning among students. In Chapter 40, Flynn investigates the use of Commercial Off-The-Shelf (COTS) games in educational settings and assesses the practical challenges inherent to their deployment. He describes the issues associated with choosing a COTS game for teaching, and offers practical recommendations that should help instructors and researchers to identify and select appropriate COTS games, based on factors such as customization (e.g., level editors or Software Development Kit), ease of installation and deployment, and ease of empirical data collection. In Chapter 41, Chib reports on a study that examined the use of an educational interactive game to educate Peruvian youths about sexual and reproductive health. The research design consisted of pre- and post-intervention surveys. The study utilized social cognitive theory to determine the influence of prior knowledge, self-efficacy and game-playing on respondents' attitudes. Chib found that prior attitudes, knowledge, resistance to peer-pressure, and game-playing were significant predictors of attitudes toward sexual health. He also found that health attitudes were influenced by playing video games. In Chapter 42, Srinivasan, Butler-Purry, and Pedersen present their experience of developing an educational game to teach digital systems design to electrical engineering students. They explain how this approach helped to address the limitations of traditional teaching methods, and to consequently increase learning and motivation on the part of the students. This interesting chapter provides an in-depth overview of their journey from obtaining funding, to implementing and assessing the video game. It describes the challenges faced by instructors who plan to use GBL solutions, and it provides highly relevant and valuable guidelines to researchers and educators engaged in similar endeavors. In Chapter 43, Anagnostou and Pappa provide an extensive review of research related to the design and use of GBL solutions for physics education. They explain how learning can occur in video games, based on educational theories and game design (e.g., game mechanics and game genres). Relevant educational theories and game genres are reviewed, and their implications for physics education are analyzed. Based on this review, Anagnostou and Pappa define and describe their framework, which offers a valuable approach for designing effective and engaging video games. The authors also discuss the barriers that impede the widespread adoption of video games for educational purposes, and propose pertinent solutions and guidelines. In Chapter 44, Axe and Routledge share the success stories and lessons learned from the use of serious games, both in formal and informal education. Their goals are to create an increased awareness of GBL among educationalists, and to consequently improve collaboration, engagement and innovation. They explain how attitudes toward the use of video games for education needs to be changed, and emphasize the role of teachers and other educationalists as the key contributors to this change. In Chapter 45, Pappa, Dunwell, Protopsaltis, Pannese, Hetzner, De Freitas, and Rebolledo-Mendez focus on GBL for sharing knowledge in the context of intergenerational learning. They explain the challenges of intergenerational learning, and describe how these were addressed by a model that they called e-VITA, which employs a methodology where knowledge creation is envisaged as a spiraling process of interactions between explicit and tacit knowledge. The application of this methodology in the context of the research project e-VITA is discussed, including the implications for pedagogy and game design. In Chapter 46, Akerfeldt and Selander argue that multimodality and didactic design should be considered for a deeper understanding of how information is presented in educational video games. They analyze two educational video games, Rixdax and El Patron, through a semiotic perspective, and they observe how learning goals and the display of on-screen information can be addressed. Their analysis is partially based on Prensky's six structuring factors and

Kress and Van Leeuwen's multimodal framework. These models are used to assess video games in terms of information value, information sequencing, and affordance for meta-reflection on the part of the user. Based on their analysis, the authors provide helpful recommendations for game designers. Despite evidence of the potential of video games for learning purposes, it seems that few law schools have embraced the use of GBL systems, as many of them essentially use traditional teaching methods. In Chapter 47, Lettieri, Fabiani, Tartaglia Polcini, De Chiara, and Scarano present an interesting system called Simulex, an online environment for the creation of Role Playing Games (RPGs) that simulate trials. The authors explain how serious games can match the objective of legal education, and how they can provide a more appropriate and effective approach. They review current technology-enhanced teaching solutions for law education, and explain how their project fits within this context. The chapter includes an interesting description of the different stages involved in the design, creation, testing and assessment of the system. Based on their experience, the authors also give pertinent recommendations for the design of effective legal serious games. In Chapter 48, Shabanah describes how and why video games can be employed to teach data structures and algorithms, two topics often perceived as complex and difficult to understand by students. She explains that many algorithm visualization systems are not satisfactory, partly because they are essentially based on graphics and sound, and not on relevant pedagogical or motivational considerations. She describes how algorithm games, which are based on sound educational theories, have inspired students to learn algorithm through active engagement and intrinsic motivation. She explains the rationale behind the use of algorithm games and their attributes in terms of game design and instructional design. She then depicts the design of several algorithm games prototypes. In Chapter 49, Dai, Daloukas, Rigou, and Sirmakessis discuss issues related to the design and implementation of effective mobile GBL environments, with an emphasis on games developed for Moodle and Open Source systems. The chapter includes an appreciation of the factors that prevent the integration of games in educational settings. The authors describe how they have incorporated video games into Moodle, and made them available on mobile devices using Java2ME. In Chapter 50, Corradini explores how 2D recreational puzzle games can improve basic spatial skills such as tilting, rotating and flipping. The author describes an experiment with students from high schools and universities, where 2D spatial Maths puzzles were employed to improve students' confidence and problem-solving skills. Corradini explains the practical and theoretical considerations underpinning the design of the games used in the study. Results show that the game, which offered many challenges in terms of forward-planning, decision-making and spatial skills, helped users to visualize the problem mentally, and to elaborate a successful strategy. In Chapter 51, Ruben, Immordino, Tromp, and Agnew describe the different approaches to, and critical challenges in, leadership development. They explain how simulations and video games offer a compelling approach because they can be designed to address many dimensions of leadership and integrate the benefits of other instructional approaches. The authors describe LEADER.edu, a scenario-based simulation that is designed to engage participants in strategic leadership learning experiences, using a combination of online access and interactive dialogues and feedback. The authors list, define and explain the theoretical foundations for this software, as well as its structure and content, in terms of pedagogy and interaction. They also provide general recommendations, based on their experience, for those who plan on developing simulation games on a similar topic. In Chapter 52, DaCosta, Nasah, Kinsell, and Seok identify the gaming propensity of 580 post-secondary school students through a survey. Results suggest that age, gender, and socioeconomic status are composite factors that contribute to gaming. The findings have a number of implications for educators, policy-makers, practitioners, researchers, instructional technologists, and game developers across both the education spectrum and the entertainment industry, for the use and development of video games.

INTENDED AUDIENCE

This book is intended for all stakeholders closely or remotely involved in financing, designing, deploying and using Game-Based Learning solutions. It includes a wide variety of chapters with both theoretical and practical information. Researchers, lecturers, and students will find in-depth literature reviews, theoretical models, and the description and analysis of relevant experiments. Teachers and instructors interested in deploying GBL solutions will be able to learn from the experience of the authors, use guidelines, and appreciate the organizational, technical, and pedagogical requirements for such environments. Developers will find innovative and effective concepts to improve both the educational and motivational aspects of their games. Policy makers will be able to appreciate the changes needed to facilitate the inclusion of GBL.

Each chapter is written with practicality in mind and dedicated to individuals working in different instructional settings such as primary schools, secondary schools, third-level education, or the industry. Different applications are considered, including maths, physics, law, biology, leadership, or language-learning. Particular attention is paid to users' specificities and differences (e.g., gender, age, disabilities, learning difficulties, learning styles, or personalities).

Patrick Felicia
Waterford Institute of Technology, Ireland

Acknowledgment

I would like to thank my colleagues and fellow researchers who have been very supportive, and have shown great interest throughout this project.

I would like to thank all involved in the creation of this handbook, including the advisory board for your valuable suggestions, the authors for your interesting and insightful chapters, and the reviewers for your diligent work and helpful recommendations to the authors.

I would also like to thank the staff at IGI Global, whose contribution and advice were invaluable from the initial idea right through to the final publication. Particular thanks to Mike Killian, Editorial Assistant, who has been very helpful throughout the entire process.

Finally, I would like to thank my wife, Helena, for her support throughout this project.

Patrick Felicia
Waterford Institute of Technology, Ireland

Section 1
Introduction to Game-Based Learning

This section provides introductory material on Game-Based Learning. Readers with little or no prior knowledge of the field will find valuable information to help their understanding of how video games can be appreciated and explained in the light of educational and motivational theories. It also includes two literature reviews on the use of computer games in education that will help the reader to appreciate the evolution of GBL and the challenges that lie ahead. This section also comprises an analysis of the barriers to using video games in the classroom, an overview of the necessary conditions for the successful integration and deployment of video games in instructional settings, and an explanation of the role that teachers can play to support the effective use of video games.

Chapter 1

Research Review:
Empirical Studies on Computer Game Play in Science Education

Gunilla Svingby
Malmö University, Sweden

Elisabet M. Nilsson
Malmö University, Sweden

ABSTRACT

The interest for game-based learning is growing among science educators. A range of research reviews have been published regarding the educational potentials of using computer games as a tool for learning and mediation, but on a general level. This research review focuses on empirical studies conducted on computer game play specifically used to enhance science learning. 50 publications published during the last decade were found that met the criteria of presenting empirical data from students using games for learning science in school contexts. The studies are reviewed and analysed according to: type of game, research design, research interests and research methodology, school subject and content, number and age of students, time spent on the intervention, gender, and teacher roles. The scope and quality of the studies are also discussed.

EDUCATIONAL POTENTIALS OF COMPUTER GAME PLAY

Researchers have long suggested that science instruction should provide students with opportunities to explore the world, and to make connections between these explorations and their personal lives (e.g. Aikenhead, 2007; Linder et al., 2007; Zeidler, 2007). Science educators in many countries have, accordingly, worked for decades to infuse inquiry

into the school, but good scientific inquiry seems to be hard to implement in classrooms (Ekborg et al., 2009; Linder et al., 2007). Evaluations report, that given the constraints of classroom settings, real world data collection and laboratory experiments are difficult to conduct, meaning that there are limited opportunities for teaching higher order inquiry skills in the ordinary classroom (Linder et al., 2007). The contextual clues offered to teachers by textbooks tend to lead away from inquiry (Phelps & Lee, 2003). Game-based learning approaches, on the other hand, are constructed to

DOI: 10.4018/978-1-60960-495-0.ch001

situate learners in complex and authentic tasks. Given the widely acknowledged lack of student interest in school science, and the downward trend in results (e.g. Jidesjö & Oscarsson, 2006; Linder et al., 2007; Osborne, 2007), the educational potential of computer game play (e.g. Aiktin, 2004; Gee, 2003; Klopfer, 2008; Williamson, 2009) might be of interest to science educators. To achieve this, authentic problems, concepts and processes are embedded in the narrative, that provide scope for scientific inquiry (Barab et al., 2007; 2007a, 2007b; Ketelhut, 2007; Magnussen, 2008; Neulight et al. 2007).

When comparing scientific literacy or science education standards (e.g. NRC, 1996; OECD, 2003) with the characteristics of computer games, some striking correspondences can be found. Squire and Jan (2007), for example, identify five core features pertinent to designing computer games for learning. (1) Games ask students to *inhabit roles*. Players are encouraged to create identities that blend the game player role and the role as a scientific professional. All information, experiences and rewards occur within this role, leading to the development of specific skills and competencies mediated by digital tools (e.g. digital lab equipment). (2) The activities in the game are organised around *challenges* and rewards, designed to support engagement, collaboration, and learning. (3) The games offer opportunities to tie goals to particular places, particularly sites of *contested spaces*. (4) The games allow for embedding *authentic resources* and tools that enable acting on higher levels. Digital tools, such as research labs and calculators, both mediate play and provide opportunities for players to interact with the environment in new ways. (5) Playing games is fundamentally social, and produces *social interaction*. After having been met with scepticism at the outset, and seen as "only play", public interest in computer games as learning tools seems to be spreading internationally (Van Eck, 2006, p. 2). On the other hand, even if theoretical assumptions ascribe computer games great poten-

tial for learning, strict empirical research is still lacking, to explain if and why computer games are effective in practice, and if so, under which conditions (e.g. Egenfeldt-Nielsen, 2007; Hanghøj, 2008; Linderoth, 2009; Williamson, 2009; Wong et al., 2007). Aitkin (2004) compares the nature of today's science research with simulation games, and points to simulation as the core of most scientific research today.

To meet the need for more empirical observation on the possibilities gaming can provide, a number of educational computer games have been developed, in various university projects. In these games, researchers have attempted to combine socio-cultural or constructivist approaches to learning, with the affordances of contemporary computer games, with the aim to engage students in authentic, deep forms of inquiry (e.g. Barab et al., 2007a, 2007b; Beckett & Shaffer, 2005; Squire & Jan, 2007). The focus is on offering affordances of making observations, posing questions, gathering data, experimenting, examining books, and so on, as tools for scientific inquiry processes (Ketelhut, 2007). Using educational games, students are invited to explore and negotiate *contested spaces*. Besides the computer games which have specifically been developed for educational purposes in these projects, the possibility of using commercial off-the-shelf (COTS) games for science learning has also been investigated in a few studies (Nilsson & Jakobsson, Accepted; Nilsson & Svingby, Accepted; Steinkuhler & Chmiel, 2006). The aim of the present review is to review computer game projects intended to enhance the teaching and learning of science, also including COTS games.

EARLIER REVIEWS OF COMPUTER GAME PLAY IN RELATION TO LEARNING

Even the first review studies of computer game play and learning (e.g. Van Sickle, 1986; Randel et al., 1992) showed that computer games could promote learning and reduce instructional time, across a row of disciplines. Referring to studies from the eighties and nineties, Van Eck (2006) concludes that, on the whole, these studies report of learning gains. However, he also points to the low number of studies that report empirical studies undertaken according to established research criteria.

In a recent meta-analysis, the effects of computer games on learning and attitudes to learning were summarised for various subject matters (Vogel et al., 2006). The authors evaluated a total of 248 studies, covering the time period 1986–2003, over all sorts of subject content and spanning all ages. They found that only 32 of 248 studies met strict experimental criteria, formulated as "each study must have identified cognitive gains or attitudinal changes, and reported statistics assessing traditional classroom teaching versus computer gaming or interactive simulation teaching" (p. 232). Because of what the authors call "methodological flaws", a majority of the articles could not be included in the meta-analysis. Among the studies included, most involved adults and higher education, and more studies dealt with medicine or similar content, rather than with school subjects. The scientific criteria applied conform to traditional experimental design criteria for certain quantitative research and thus, exclude studies using for example anthropological or ethnological methods. Neither does the meta-analysis include studies developed according to a design-based research tradition (Barab & Squire, 2004; Wang & Hannafin, 2005). Being a recent research field, the study of computer games for science learning still has a focus on the exploration of the tool, and the methodological criteria applied for excluding the majority of studies examined in the meta-analysis are not necessarily entirely relevant to the field. Given these restrictions, however, Vogel et al. (2006) showed that persons using interactive games attained significantly higher cognitive gains and better attitudes toward learning, compared to subjects exposed to traditional instruction.

The authors conclude that "across all situations, games or interactive simulations will most likely instruct subjects with better cognitive outcomes and attitudes toward learning when compared to traditional teaching methods" (p. 235). The results were shown to hold across all age groups.

In a recent meta-study (Boyle, 2009), that included studies of all kinds of content and all types of computer games, but was restricted to studies engaging persons above 16, Boyle found that of more than 2,000 articles published since 2004, only 52 met the criteria of including empirical data on learning, and/or engagement. The outcome of the studies that did include empirical data was reported as positive impacts on learning and engagement. The situation today is similar to the situation in the 1980's: even if much has been written about computer game play, relatively few studies report on empirical data. Van Eck (2006, p. 4) suggests as an explanation the difficulty of measuring effects of computer game play on learning by standardised tests. There is thus the problem of comparing with the effects of traditional school teaching. He argues that the demands in traditional "evidence-based" research of narrowly defined variables and tightly controlled conditions, may lead to narrow claims about learning, that is, the accurate reproduction of facts and simple concepts, whereas computer games embed potentials of more complex learning.

RESEARCH FOCUS OF THIS REVIEW

Several research reviews consider computer game play in relation to learning and motivation to learn (see e.g. De Freitas, 2007; Kebritchi & Atsusi, 2008; Kirriemuir & McFarlan, 2004; Linderoth, Lantz-Andersson & Lindström, 2002; Susi et al., 2007). However, we have not found any study focusing the relations between computer game play and science learning, more specifically.

The present article reviews empirical studies conducted on computer game play specifically used at school to enhance science learning, and to favour more positive attitudes towards science and science learning.

Criteria and Limitations

The studies included in this review meet the following criteria:

1. the computer game is used for science learning in formal school settings, which excludes computer games used only for entertainment, and studies undertaken outside of school contexts,
2. the analytical focus lies on students aged 6–18 (K-12),
3. empirical data is included,
4. the study is peer-reviewed,
5. the study was published between 1999 and 2009.

Studies with strict experimental design using statistical analyses, and studies with a more explorative design using qualitative data are both included.

Search Methods

In order to find publications that met the criteria listed above, several search strategies were used. In a first round, databases and other archive resources were explored. The following databases, and archive resources were used to find relevant articles: Digiplay, DiGRA Digital Library, Games Studies, Google scholar, ERIC, Innovate, Science Direct, SAGE. The following search terms were applied in different combinations: "computer games, video games, digital games, educational games, simulation games, serious games or gaming", and "learning, education, instructional", and "science, physics, chemistry, biology or technology".

The database search was supplemented by searches in conference proceedings, earlier reviews, web sites, and literature lists. In this

way, more than 200 publications were found that related to the use of computer game play at school in science instruction. Of these, 50 publications met the criteria listed above. Many of the publications found in the first search round, dealt with theoretical assumptions concerning the educational potential of computer game play. Since the review had a focus on empirical studies, these publications were sorted out. The most frequent reason for excluding a text from this review, thus, was absence of empirical data. The majority of the articles included were published in peer-reviewed journals. Some were published in peer-reviewed conference proceedings (8 of 50 items), as book chapters (3), or as peer-reviewed but unpublished doctoral theses (4). A majority of the articles selected were published between 2005 and 2008 (43 of 50 items). As the same study in some cases was presented in more than one publication, the number of empirical studies is smaller than the number of articles.

Besides directly applying the criteria listed above, a number of studies were excluded in order to maintain the specific focus of this review. Quite a few articles dealt with the educational potential of letting students design their own computer games. Such studies were excluded, since designing games is a different type of activity than playing games. Articles dealing with ways to improve programming skills through computer game play, or game design activities, or computer games used in computer science/programming courses were also sorted out. Finally, since the analytical focus was on the gaming students, articles dealing solely with pedagogical methods or practical barriers in the classroom were excluded.

Definition of a Computer Game

The definition of *game* presented some problems when choosing studies to be included. The literature on games research provides a range of different definitions of a game. A recent definition views games as a "system in which players engage in artificial conflict, defined by rules, and resulting in a quantifiable outcome" (Salen, 2008, p. 268). Games are further often described as transmedial phenomena, implying that the same game can be transmitted through different kinds of media: on paper, via computers, digital networks, consoles, handhelds, mobile phones etc. (Juul, 2005). Here, only games presented by some sort of digital technology were included.

The demarcation between a game and a simulation also called for reflection. Some of the game applications used in the studies included, may be placed on the borderline, between what would be defined as *computer games* within the games research community, and what may instead be described as a *simulation*. However, with time, this distinction has blurred, as is shown by (Sauvé et al., 2007), and as science simulations and games tend to merge, it may no longer be relevant for this subject area (Aitkin, 2004).

The concept of *multi-user virtual environment* (MUVE) may cause another problem of definition. A MUVE can be described as a computerised environment that enables multiple participants to simultaneously access virtual contexts, to interact with digital artefacts, with other participants, as well as with computer-based agents, and to engage in collaborative learning activities (Dede et al., 2002; Murray, 1997). A MUVE does not necessarily contain gaming activities. The MUVEs included in the review do, however, offer such activities.

We have on the whole solved the dilemma of game definition by accepting the definitions made by the authors, and/or the publishing journals (revealed via key words used, forum for publication, or expressions used in the text). The review, thus, includes empirical studies involving any kind of game sustained by digital technology. Games may in the various articles be signified by the terms: alternate or augmented reality game, immersive game, interactive game, interactive learning environments, multi-user virtual environments (MUVE), simulation game, simulation,

video game, or virtual reality game. Mainly for the sake of simplicity, the term *computer game* is used in the following as an umbrella term for all kinds of games, whatever digital platform they are played on.

Structuring the Article

The studies reviewed are analysed according to the following criteria, which also structure the article.

A. Type of computer game
B. Research design
C. Research interests
D. School subject and content
E. Number and age of students
F. Time spent on the intervention
G. Gender
H. Teacher roles

Publications Included in the Review

FIRST ROUND OF RESULTS: THE RESEARCH SETTING

Computer Game Genre

The studies are categorised according to which of the following types of computer game the students played.

Research-Based Educational Computer Games

The category has three sub-categories: (1) Educational MUVEs (played on PC), (2) Augmented and alternate reality games (played on handhelds or PC), and (3) Educational single-player games (played on PC). In the following, the various computer game genres are presented.

Table 1. Overview of the 50 publications that met the listed criteria, and are included in the review

Author(s)	Year	Computer game	Type of game
Annetta, Mangrum, Holmes, Collazo, Cheng	2009	Dr Friction	MUVE
Barab, Arici, Jackson	2005	Quest Atlantis	MUVE
Barab, Dodge, Tüzün, Job-Sludwer, Jackson, Arici, Job-Sluder, Carteaux, Gilbertson, Heiselt	2007	Quest Atlantis	MUVE
Barab, Ingram-Goble, Warren	2009	Quest Atlantis	MUVE
Barab, Sadler, Heiselt, Hickey, Zuiker	2007	Quest Atlantis	MUVE
Barab, Zuiker, Warren, Hickey, Ingram-Goble, Kwon	2007	Quest Atlantis	MUVE
Beckett, Shaffer	2005	Madison 2200	AR game Epistemic game
Cai, Lu, Zheng, Li	2006	The protein game	Educational single-player game
Cameron, Dwyer	2005	Metalloman	Educational single-player game
Clarke, Dede	2005	River City	MUVE
Colella	2000	The virus game	AR game
Facer, Joiner, Stanton, Reid, Hull, Kirk	2004	Savannah	AR game
Hansmann, Scholz, Francke, Weymann	2005	Simulme	Educational single-player game
Hickey, Ingram-Goble, Jameson	2009	Quest Atlantis	MUVE
Jenkins, Squire, Tan	2004	Supercharged!	Educational single-player game
Kafai	2008	Whyville	MUVE
Kafai, Feldon, Fields, Giang, Quintero	2007	Whyville	MUVE
Kao, Galas, Kafai	2005	Whyville	MUVE
Ketelhut	2006	River City	MUVE
Ketelhut	2007	River City	MUVE
Ketelhut, Dede, Clarke, Nelson, Bowman	2007	River City	MUVE
Klopfer, Yoon, Rivas	2004	The virus game	AR game
Lim, Nonis, Hedberg	2006	Quest Atlantis	MUVE
Magnussen	2005	Homicide	AR game Epistemic game
Magnussen	2007	Homicide	AR game Epistemic game
Magnussen	2008	Homicide	AR game Epistemic game
Marsh, Wong, Carriazo, Nocera, Yang, Varma, Yoon, Huang, Kyriakakis, Shahabi	2005	Metalloman	Educational single-player game
Mathevet, Le Page, Etienne, Lefebvre, Gigot, Proréol, Mauchamp	2007	Butorstar	AR game (RPG game supported by computer simulations)
Mellor	2001	Build your own time machine	Educational single-player game
Miller, Moreno, Estrera, Lane	2004	MedMyst	Educational single-player game
Nelson	2005	River City	MUVE
Nelson	2007	River City	MUVE
Nelson, Ketelhut	2007	River City	MUVE
Nelson, Ketelhut	2008	River City	MUVE
Nelson, Ketelhut, Clarke, Bowman, Dede	2005	River City	MUVE

continued on following page

Table 1. continued

Author(s)	Year	Computer game	Type of game
Neulight, Kafai, Kao, Foley, Galas	2007	Whyville	MUVE
Nilsson, Svingby	2009	Agent O	AR game
Price	2008	Unreal Tournament	COTS game
Rieber, Noah	2008	Computer-based simulation of acceleration and velocity	Educational single-player game
Rosenbaum, Klopfer, Perry	2007	Outbreak @ The Institute	AR game
Squire	2006	Supercharged!	Educational single-player game
Squire, Barnett, Grant, Higgenbotham	2004	Supercharged!	Educational single-player game
Squire, Jan	2007	Mad City Mystery	AR game
Squire, Klopfer	2007	Environmental Detectives	AR game
Svarovsky, Shaffer	2006	SodaConstructor	Educational single-player game
Svarovsky, Shaffer	2007	SodaConstructor	Educational single-player game
Toprac	2008	Alien Rescue III	Educational single-player game
Tüzün	2007	Quest Atlantis	MUVE
Wong, Shen, Nocera, Carriazo, Tang, Bugga	2007	Metalloman	Educational single-player game
Wycliffe, Muwanga-Zake	2007	Zadarh	Educational single-player game

Educational MUVEs

Educational MUVEs are a form of socio-constructivist and situated cognition-based educational software. Educational MUVEs incorporate 2D and 3D virtual worlds, in which learners control characters that represent them in the world (Cobb et al., 2002; Nelson et al., 2005; Nelson & Ketelhut, 2007). The content varies widely; each virtual world can have its own theme.

A growing body of research indicates that based on this relatively new form of technology, educational MUVEs can be designed to support highly interactive scientific inquiry learning, thus offering a safe approach to scientific inquiry (Nelson & Ketelhut, 2007). Advocates of MUVEs argue that they open up new possibilities for creating learning experiences that are authentic, situated and distributed, and also provide a context for changing the standards by which students' accomplishments are assessed (Dieterle & Clarke, 2008).

We have found the following educational MUVEs designed for science learning.

River City

The large-scale project *River City*, at Harvard University (funded by the US National Science Foundation) was created by a team of researchers representing a variety of expertise, and specifically designed for use in formal school settings (Clarke & Dede, 2005; Ketelhut, 2007; Nelson & Ketelhut, 2007). It builds on highly immersive 3D technology. The *River City* virtual world consists of a city with a river running through it. The learners themselves populate the city in teams of three, along with computer-based agents. Students work in teams to develop hypotheses regarding one of three strands of illness in the city. At the end of the project, students compare their research with other teams, to discover the range of potential hypotheses and possibilities to explore. The basic idea is that students "learn to behave as scientists through they collaboratively identifying problems via observation and inference, forming and testing hypotheses and deducing evidence-based conclusions about underlying cause" (Nelson et al., 2005, p. 3). Nearly 10,000 students in the US and internationally are reported to have completed the computer lab-based *River City* curriculum, as part of their middle school science classes.

Quest Atlantis

The Quest Atlantis project at Indiana University focuses on the ability to support authentic scientific inquiry and collaboration in realistic virtual contexts (Barab et al., 2007, 2009). The narrative takes students to a city with a great deal of environmental problems. Students take part in a large number of quests, to save the people of the virtual Atlantis from destruction through environmental, moral and social decay.

Whyville

Whyville is a MUVE designed to support scientific learning and inquiry, but outside the formal school (Kafai, 2008; Kao et al., 2005). It is a 2-dimensional MUVE to be used in informal settings, relating to biology, physics and chemistry. When used in schools, students were confronted with a disease outbreak in the *Whyville* virtual community, which manifested itself as red spots on the faces of the avatars. The "illness" soon spread through the community. Students tracked the spread of the outbreak on charts in their classroom, used an "infection simulator", and gathered information in a virtual "centre for disease control". Galas (2006) found that students could conduct authentic, collaborative scientific inquiry, and got deeply involved in gathering data and forming hypotheses. Neulight et al. (2007) focused on the impact on students' understanding of the causes of real-world diseases. Using pre- and post-surveys showed a significant improvement in the number of students moving from "pre-biological" to "biological" understandings.

Augmented and Alternate Reality Games

One approach to creating stronger connections between students' experience of the real world,

and students' actions in a virtual model of a complex ecological system is to link real and virtual elements, in augmented reality learning environments. In these environments, participants are exposed to both a physical and virtual reality, thus providing students with multiple representations for solving complex problems. While virtual reality attempts to replace the real world, augmented reality seeks only to supplement it (Klopfer, 2008). Augmented reality learning environments enable students to take the technology out of their classrooms, and use it to explore the environment around them (Klopfer & Squire, 2008; Squire & Klopfer, 2007). Learning environments designed with augmented reality technologies are seen as enabling students to participate in the process of scientific investigation, because they provide students with the opportunity to act as scientists, in a situation that blends the real and the virtual. Such learning environments may help to resolve the existing dichotomy between indoor technology environments and outdoor experiences, by using mobile technologies in the context of nature exploration. It is argued that augmented or alternate reality bridges reality and virtual reality by letting students play in the reality or using real data (Beckett & Shaffer, 2005; Klopfer, 2008; Rosenbaum et al., 2007).

Educational Single-Player Computer Games

This kind of computer games are primarily designed for individual play, and do not allow students to interact outside of the game, or online with other gamers. They represent an earlier and less advanced type of educational game, compared to the previous. Mostly, the games of this type are not built on the same stable ground of researchers representing different disciplines, including the learning sciences.

COTS Games

COTS games arc designed to be entertaining, not primarily educational, and not for school use. Teachers say, however, that students are allowed to play such games at school (e.g. Williamson, 2009). Studies reporting empirical results on the use of COTS games for science learning are included among the studies reviewed, but not studies that only write of the potential of a game. In relation to type of game, the publications were distributed as follows in Table 2.

The majority of the games reported of were research-based educational games, most of them developed by researchers in a design-based research process. It is striking that even if COTS games are reported as the type of game most often used in schools (e.g. Williamson, 2009), little research seems to have been conducted on effects of these games on learning and attitudes, judged by the number of publications. The dominance of studies using educational MUVEs, compared with the total number of games, may be explained by the support of grants offered by the US National Science Foundation for this research. The difference between the MUVE and the other games is demonstrated by the number of research articles published on each game. The four MUVE games have resulted in 22 publications, whereas studies of the 7 educational single-player computer games are reported in 15 publications.

Research Design

As mentioned above, some researchers have criticised studies on computer game play for not being undertaken according to certain research criteria, including standardised measurements, control groups and randomisation (e.g.Vogel, 2008). Other researchers argue that to apply such criteria is not adequate, in relation to the complex competences that many of the games are built to promote, and may in fact be counterproductive in the development of a potent tool for science learning (Squire & Klopfer, 2007). In our experience, explorative studies are of great value in the process of developing an educational game. The same is true for the study of students' interactions and explorations when playing. Other measures than standardised tests and standard scales are also needed to investigate the more advanced competences, as defined by the US National Science Standards (NRC, 1996), for example.

As a consequence, we have here categorised the studies as "experimental" or "explorative". A study categorised as experimental includes the use of pre- and post-test, standardised measurements of learning and attitudes, or other types of controlled evaluation, as well as adequate statistical analyses. Some but not all such studies also employ control groups, randomisation and other experimental arrangements. Explorative studies focus on observation of gaming behaviour, and of interactions in and outside of the game. Interview, log book, game activity tracking, and

Table 2. Computer games played in the studies

Computer game genre	Number of publications	Game title
Educational MUVE	22	Dr Friction, River City, Quest Atlantis, Whyville
AR games	11	Agent O, Butorstar,Environmental detectives, Homicide, Mad City Mystery, Madison 2200, Outbreak @ the Institute, Savannah, The Virus game
Educational single-player games	15	Alien Rescue III, Build your own time-machine,, MedMyst, Simulme, SodaConstructor, Supercharged!, Zadarh
COTS games	1	Unreal Tournament 2004

various observation methods are used. Some of the publications combine the two designs.

Experimental and Explorative Design

Table 3 shows the distribution between the two designs.

About half of the publications reported of studies with an experimental design including the use of pre- and post-test. Eleven of these also included explorative data. The assessment tools mostly consisted of both standardised multiple choice/short answer questions and of content related tasks. Control groups were used in a third of the studies. These studies used statistical analyses in order to determine effect sizes and reliability. They were mostly designed according to design-based research methodology, with the aim to introduce innovations into real world classroom contexts, study the activities and interactions emerging, and at the same time scientifically research the impact on learning and derive scientifically grounded claims (Nelson et al., 2005; Hickey et al., 2009).

Another group of studies were designed with an ethnographic, and/or design interest, exploring, for instance, how students related to the computer game, which activities they engaged in, how they collaborated, how the game was included into the classroom, and teachers' roles. In other words, the majority of the experimental studies focused more on the processes of playing the game and less on the strict measuring of effects.

To sum up, roughly two thirds of the studies included in the present review apply one of the standard elements of an experimental study, indicating that published studies on computer games used to enhance science learning meet the expectations and criteria that are usual in quantitative research studies within various scientific disciplines. Taking into account the position of educational computer games for science learning, the amount of studies focusing on students' activities and interactions when playing, as well as the effects of various parallel technical and educational solutions, is promising. The research field is in need, not only of studies undertaken according to strict empirical rules, but also of studies that seek to understand the medium.

Table 3. Research designs

Type of study	Number of studies
Experimental only	16
Explorative only	20
Combining experimental and explorative	11
Pre- and post-test	28
Pre- and post-test plus control group, randomisation	13

Research Interest

The research questions of the experimental studies mainly focused one or more of the variables: learning, engagement, and attitude to the subject content. In addition, the explorative and some of the experimental studies posed questions concerning the relations between playing the game and

Table 4. Research interests of the studies. Some studies take an interest in all or several of these questions, thus the total number of research interests differs from the actual number of studies.

Research interest	Number of studies
Learning	25
Engagement	15
Attitudes to the subject	12
Other aspects	17

the use of inbuilt guidance systems, of continuing motivation, of students' attendance to classes, of collaborative work, of use of representations, of teachers' roles, or other similar issues. Such research interests are summed up by "Other aspects".

Both quantitative and qualitative methods were used to evaluate the research interests. Learning was mostly measured by standardised tests, but in some studies also by other means, aiming to capture more genuine and complex socioscientific qualities. Engagement and attitudes were assessed by surveys, interviews and by observations. The quality of the methodology used and analyses applied corresponded to established methodological practice for these types of research interests.

School Subject and Content

Many of the computer games played in the studies were designed to enhance scientific inquiry and scientific practice, without explicitly implying specific school subjects. Others were more specific about the subject content explored. Our analysis found that the studies had the following focus.

The science content of most of the games can be classified as environmental studies, and health. In combination with such content, a row of studies explored the theoretical assumption that computer games help to make science inquiry attainable at school. Games focusing on chemistry and physics are relatively few. In addition, there is a relationship between the age of the students and content focus, with chemistry and physics primarily included in games for older students.

Number and Age of Students

The studies vary substantially in the number of students involved: from 8 to 1,666. The variation is due to research interest and design with explorative studies involving fewer students, as a rule, and experimental studies involving a moderate to very large number of students. However, as mentioned above, some of the experimental studies with many students also include explorative methods.

We have constructed a variable with four levels: few students (<20), moderate number of students (21–60), many students (61–200), and very many students (201–3 300). The number of students playing the game per study is distributed as shown in Table 6.

The table shows that half of the studies involved more than 60 students and that seven of the studies comprised several hundreds. Half of the publications, on the other hand, report of studies

Table 5. School subjects treated in the studies

School subject	Number of studies
Science inquiry	20
Environmental studies and Health	14
Chemistry	5
Physics	4

Table 6. Number of students. Some of the publications included in the review treated the same studies, thus the number of studies listed in the table are fewer than the number of reviewed publications (50).

Number of students	Number of studies
Few students	16
Moderate number	9
Many	12
Very many	7

Table 7. Age of students. Since some studies include more than one age group the numbers exceed the numbers of reviewed publications (50).

Age of students	Number of studies
<10	9
11–14	21
15–16	11
>16	13

Table 8. Time spend on intervention

Time	Number of studies
1–4 hours	18
1–4 days	13
1–3 weeks	6
4 weeks or more	10

that contained only few students. The number of students involved is largely related to the type of study undertaken, with few students involved in the explorative studies.

The age of the students varies from 9 to 18 years. We have constructed an age variable with four levels: <10, 11–14, 15–16, >16. The studies are distributed on age as shown in Table 7.

With respect to the age of the students, the middle school ages (11–14) are overrepresented.

Time Spent on the Intervention

Students spent from 1 hour (60 minutes) to several months on the intervention. The distribution on four levels is shown here.

In the majority of the studies, students spend relatively little time with the game. 18 publications report of an intervention that takes only a few hours whereas 10 studies report of an intervention that goes on for one or more months. There is another factor involved in this; in the longer studies, game play is integrated more or less into the curriculum and students do not play all the time. It is obvious that the time of exposure to the game play interven-

tion has an impact on what can be learned and experienced. Another aspect is the way the game is played; in groups or alone. In more than half of the studies, the students worked in groups, and in a few other studies the students worked in pairs.

SECOND ROUND OF RESULTS: EFFECTS

We will now turn to the question of possible effects of game play on science learning, attitudes, and engagement.

Science Learning and Engagement

Of the 19 studies that report on learning effects, 16 report positive changes in students' results on tests or other forms of assessment, as a result of the game play. In the eight studies including control groups, all but one showed the experiment group to gain significantly better results than the control group on standardised tests. In a so-called "evidence-based" study, more than 1,000 students played *River City* for three weeks in authentic school settings. Significant gains were demonstrated with respect to scientific inquiry skills (Nelson et al., 2005; Nelson & Ketelhut, 2007). In an experimental study, Squire et al. (2004) showed that the game *Supercharged!* enhanced students' understanding of a complex physics phenomenon. By introducing a virtual disease game in *Whyville*, Neulight et al. (2007) demonstrated that students gained scientific knowledge relating to the causality of natural infectious diseases. The students perceived the game simulations as similar to a natural infectious disease, and used the experiences gained during game play to deepen their understanding of natural diseases. Engagement in the game play was shown to support students' conceptual understanding. The results confirm the theoretical assumptions that when designed in according to the criteria set forward in theories of educational game play, educational computer games do in fact immerse students in activities that help develop deep learning qualities, while practicing skills relevant to scientific inquiry.

The problem of valid assessment of deep learning qualities in science was, however, also illuminated in the studies. General standard assessments do not cover all of the knowledge qualities aimed for by the games. To assess qualities of scientific inquiry defined as "a multifaceted activity that involves making observations; posing questions; examining books and other sources of information to see what is already known; planning investigations; using tools to gather, analyze, and interpret data; proposing answers, explanations, and predictions; and communicating the results" (NRC, 1996) other types of tests are needed (Jönsson, 2008; Jönsson & Svingby, 2008).

In a study reported by Ketelhut et al. (2007), it was shown that on a set of standard questions with multiple-choice/short answers, students playing *River City* got the same results as the control group students. On a content-related task, however, that involved suggesting measures to improve the environment of a city, the experiment group performed far above the control group students. The standard tests were, in other words, shown unable to provide information concerning the inquiry skills developed by the students who had played the game. In consequence, some of the subsequent studies by Ketelhut focused on alternate measures of effects. A number of studies were designed according to the design-based research model. These studies include more specific experimental studies. As part of a US National Science Foundation funded project that implemented *River City* with nearly 3,000 students, Ketelhut (2007) studied the data gathering behaviour of 96 seventh graders. Data gathering behaviour included: (1) making observations by visiting various information sites, (2) using tools, by accessing water sampling and "bug-catching" stations, (3) gathering evidence from book material, from "library books", and "hospital" records, (4) accessing information from other sources, students interacted with guidance messages in the individualised guidance system; and (5) posing questions, students asked for information from virtual agents (p. 104).

Students were randomly assigned to one of two "guidance treatments" (Nelson et al., 2005) that offered one or three guidance hints to help develop students' understanding. Ketelhut (2007) studied students of the "high guidance" group in their second, third and fourth visit to the city. She assumed that students with more knowledge and higher science self-efficacy would be gathering more data, as well as data from different sources, compared to students with less knowledge and lower science self-efficacy. Material concerning students' behaviour was processed using fitted multi-level models, to address the research questions:

- is growth in total scientific inquiry behaviour related to self-efficacy,
- does gender affect this relationship,
- does the data gathering behaviour develop over time?

The results initially confirmed the assumption, showing that self-efficacy and students' content pre-test score both impacted their scientific data-gathering behaviour. Furthermore, students' scientific self-efficacy measured by a Likert scale correlated significantly with students' pre-test score. From the start, there was a significant difference between students with high and low content score/self-efficacy and data-gathering. Boys and girls with high self-efficacy gathered more data than students with low self-efficacy and also data from more different sources. Over time the results changed. During visit four, scientific data gathering was not affected by students' initial content score/self efficacy at all. Girls with initial low self-efficacy showed the strongest positive rate of change. A slightly different pattern was presented for different data sources assessed. To use the information offered by the game leads to better science learning. Initially, girls with high pre-test scores benefitted from the potential sources offered by the game by gathering much more information than girls with low scores. Gradually, this difference disappeared.

The results contradict the argument that novelty was the prime reason why students were engaged in *River City* (Ketelhut, 2007). Had novelty been the reason for student engagement, the engagement would have diminished over time. Ketelhut further argues that the complexity of the game world adapts to all kinds of students, meaning for example, that low self-efficacy regarding science became irrelevant in the game world thus helping such students to engage in science learning. The results, further, suggest that embedding scientific inquiry in the MUVE might act as a catalyst for changing students' self-efficacy and learning processes. The results give support to Lemke's (1990) analysis of science education as being presented as a *difficult* subject resulting in that "[w]hen students fail to master it, they are encouraged to believe it is their own fault: they are just not smart enough to be scientists" (p. 138). Ketelhut (2007) argues, in the same line, that if schools cannot convince students that science is achievable, there is a risk of confirming the idea that science is only for a few elite students. Lack of interest, frequently reported for science teaching, is part of the same problem. In this perspective, the results of the 15 studies reporting on engagement can be seen as encouraging. Twelve of the studies reported positive engagement, or even enjoyment. Students say, for example, that they appreciated "the dynamic nature of the game world, seeing that their actions

had an effect on the outcome of the game in a realistic way" (Rosenbaum et al., 2007, p. 43). Others stress that the inquiry component of the game play was not only experienced as a scientific process, but also "very social and involved understanding people", which "deeply engaged the students and led to rich social negotiations" (Barab et al., 2007a, p. 71). Engagement is in some studies measured by standardised attitude scales, and in other studies by interviews.

Three studies, however, reported negative results on student engagement. Firstly, in a study of 76 students aged 16–18, only half of the students said that they enjoyed playing the physics game *Build your own time machine*, which has a focus on astronomy (Mellor, 2001). Secondly, in a study of 8 students in a Singapore school, who played *Quest Atlantis*, initial interest diminished over time, when students found that the game did not exactly match the assessment test they would be taking (Lim et al., 2006). Students immersed in the game lost focus on the learning task, implying that the game play served as a distracting element. The study points to the dilemma of an educational game built to be almost as interesting as a COTS game, but implemented in school systems that follow quite different principles. Finally, observations of a similar kind are reported by Nelson (2005). The game had an inbuilt guidance system designed to help students learn the embedded scientific formalism. Nelson (2005) showed that the students who used the system performed better. However, only 25 percent of the students, mainly girls, used the teaching help offered. Nelson concludes that for playing the game, the guidance system was not a necessity. To use it was thus a function of student's ambitions to learn, and not primarily to play.

That limited assessment practices may be a problem when assessing engagement was illustrated in a study by Toprac (2008), on the motivation to continue studying science. Students aged 14 years played the game *Alien Rescue III* for nine hours. On a standardised questionnaire, students answered in a way that implied that they were not motivated to further study the subject. However, when observed working with the game and when students were interviewed, they expressed a totally different view. They said that they enjoyed playing the game, and it was observed that they continued to discuss issues from the game in their free time.

Taken as a whole, the studies examined in the present review indicate that game play as part of science education frequently results in positive engagement. Science education through game play appears to be much more enjoyable than traditional science classes.

Gender

It has been assumed that girls are less engaged by gaming technologies than boys (e.g. Krotoski, 2004). A handful of studies report on girls' and boys' engagement in the games, and of learning effects related to gender. Van Eck (2006a) showed that girls' and boys' gaming strategies vary substantially. A simulation game was played differently by the two groups: "the girls tended to discuss and build dwellings complete with bathrooms, hot tubs, and pools; boys, on the other hand, tended to discuss and create swamps, crocodiles, and jaguars to the exclusion of everything else" (p. 5). The assumption of girls being less engaged was not confirmed by these studies. The study by Ketelhut (2007), for example, showed that girls with low self-efficacy gained most by the game, and showed the greatest changes in scientific data gathering behaviour.

The positive impact of games on girls' behaviour was also shown by Mellor (2001), who demonstrated girls to be more "able to approach a physics-based computer game from a less predetermined position and seemed to be happy viewing physics as an imaginative and speculative exercise" (p. 287). The boys, on the other hand, tended to act as collectors of facts, rather than explorers. The researcher concludes that the boys "are vulnerable to feeling patronized and have

difficulty in negotiating situations in which the usual boundaries between the classroom and the home – between education and leisure – have been broken down" (p. 289). The issue of how gender relates to computer game play for science learning is, in other words, far from straightforward. Even if a computer game may appeal equally to girls and to boys, they do not necessarily appreciate the same things about the game.

THIRD ROUND OF RESULTS: RESULTS RELATED TO COMPUTER GAME GENRE

When analysing the studies, some interesting variations in results could be noted, that might depend on the type of computer game played.

Studies Using Educational MUVEs Compared to Studies Using Educational Single-Player Games

Most of the studies using these two types of games are designed as experimental studies, with control groups, pre- and post-tests, and strict statistical analyses. A number of differences are revealed when comparing studies that use these two types of games.

Many more MUVE-based studies report on students' engagement in the game, as well as discussing various aspects of students' interaction with the game, with each other and with the teacher. These interests are related to the overall design of the studies adopted: design-based research. In line with the design, such studies make use of a variety of evaluation measures and methods of analysis in an iterative circle of evaluative and explorative research elements based in real world settings (Barab & Squire, 2004; Wang & Hannafin, 2005).

When the MUVE-based studies are compared to other studies, a range of differences are revealed: number of students involved, the age of the students, the time spent with the intervention, and the subject matter of the game. The educational single-player game studies all involved many students, but on the other hand, lasted over a short period of time. The MUVE-based studies included both experimental studies with very many students (more than 1,000), and explorative studies with a small number of students involved. Six of the studies lasted for two or more weeks. No study based on educational single-player games lasted that long, and the majority lasted only a few hours. The students playing the educational single-player game studies were older than the students playing the MUVEs, and the content of the games was different. A majority of the MUVEs concentrated on general science, specified as scientific inquiry of socio-scientific issues for middle school students. The specific content concerned questions relating to ecological and health issues. The educational single-player game studies, on the other hand, focused on core aspects of the subjects of chemistry, biology and physics for students aged 15–16.

The findings also show different patterns. The effects on learning and engagement reported from the MUVE studies were overwhelmingly positive. When control groups were used, students got better results than the control group students, and when pre- and post-test scores were compared, the gaming students developed more positively. In all but one study, the results hold for standardised knowledge tests as well as for alternative ways of assessing students' learning. By contrast, only half of the educational single-player computer game studies reported learning results, and instead focused on other aspects. In those studies where learning was assessed, the results were positive. Furthermore, the two types of games resulted in different levels of student engagement. All but one of the educational MUVEs demonstrated strong engagement and enjoyment, whereas the educational single-player game studies showed students to be less engaged.

We have found only one exploratory study reported on COTS games (Price, 2008). These studies point to possible learning effects and positive attitudes, but also to problems of keeping students focused on the science content. No experimental studies concerning COTS games were found.

Example of Studies

To illustrate the results we will present a few studies in depth.

Outbreak @ the Institute

A series of augmented reality games played on handheld computers have been developed by researchers at MIT Teacher Education Program (e.g. Klopfer, 2008; Klopfer & Squire, 2007). An example of an exploratory study of such a game is *Outbreak @ the Institute* (Rosenbaum et al., 2008). The players are presented to a fictional scenario: the outbreak of a new form of bird flu that has become transmissible between humans. Players may encounter both bird flu, as well as the common seasonal flu. Some students are already exhibiting symptoms. Players worked as a team to gather information, using the tools available to them in order to try to stop the outbreak. Players joined the game in one of three possible roles, each having specific competences and tools. As there are no specific criteria for "winning" the game, players must decide what their goals should be throughout the game. No teachers were involved in the game play. The study involved twenty one students aged 17 years, playing for two hours. Data included observations, as well as a pre- and post-survey. The survey asked for a list of five factors in the game that would influence the number of sick people. Students appeared to perceive the game as authentic, in several ways. Observations demonstrated that students behaved in ways suggesting that they felt personally embodied in the game. The roles felt authentic, and the possibilities of communication and collaboration were seen as important. During the course of the game, students' goals shifted from initially knowledge-based, to more personal and team-based. The results were used to re-design the game.

Mad City Mystery

The augmented reality game *Mad City Mystery* was developed by researchers at the University of Wisconsin-Madison. They explored students' development of scientific argumentation skills when were playing a location-based augmented reality game on handheld computers (Squire & Jan, 2007).The study is an example of studies that adopt an ethnological type of qualitative research design. These studies concentrate on exploration, using ethnographic methods, with mostly qualitative measures. The research focus is not on learning effects, but on understanding how and why learning may occur.

The game story is about a person found dead in a lake close to the University campus. The task of the player is to investigate the case, and to piece together an explanation. This is done in groups. Players interview virtual characters, gather data, and examine documents. Playing the game takes 90–120 minutes. The study reports of 28 students, aged 9–16 years, playing the game with no teachers involved. The study aims to explore the hypothesis that a game designed according to established principles of contemporary computer games can be a useful tool, for supporting students in developing scientific argumentation skills (Squire & Jan, 2007). The study investigated whether the game could engage students in scientific thinking, in specific hypothesis formation, as well as reasoning from evidence. Qualitative methods were used, including observations and interviews, but also a questionnaire on students' attitudes toward science and gaming. All student groups were observed to engage in argumentation cycles, similar to those advocated by science educators, and thought to be difficult to produce in classrooms. The research-

ers concluded that playing the game required students to weigh evidence, develop hypotheses, test them against evidence, and generate theories based on the evidence, thus engaging students in the practice of scientific argumentation.

Quest Atlantis

The educational MUVE *Quest Atlantis* exemplifies the high quality of the research-based projects funded by the US National Science Foundation. The game was developed by a team of researchers and designers at Indiana University. *Quest Atlantis* is intended to engage children aged 9–12 in a form of dramatic play. At the core is the narrative about Atlantis, a world in trouble. Sheltered within a digital game, *Quest Atlantis* introduces students to inquiry processes, as well as to practices of social commitment. Through the *Quest Atlantis* community, students can complete quests, talk with other children, and build their virtual persona. Completing quests requires children to participate in academically meaningful activities, either in the real world, or through simulation. Two-week curricula composed of 5–8 quests with a common focus (e.g. water quality) are presented to teachers as unit plans. Teachers may also create their own quests, through a "Teacher Toolkit" (Barab et al., 2007, p. 158). *Quest Atlantis* has more than 3,500 registered members, from all over the world.

The project has a well developed theoretical and educational basis. *Quest Atlantis* is described as a "situationally embodied curriculum", that relates scientific formalisms to contexts (Barab et al., 2007b). The researchers underline their interest to use gaming principles to embed standards-based science concepts, without undermining the situative embodiment. The project group has designed a context for learning, in the intersection of education, entertainment, and social action. The authors refer to it as a "context for participation" (Barab et al., 2007, p. 159), underlining that this form of learning context is not to be seen simply as a technological innovation (Barab et al., 2005,

2007). The project was developed using design-based research methodology. A team of researchers and other experts, representing various disciplines and expertise, progressively refined the project in ongoing cycles of research, design, tests, and experiments. A series of mainly explorative studies have been reported from the project. Data were derived from students from Australia, Denmark, China, Malaysia, Singapore, and the US. The interventions mostly lasted two weeks, but one study went on for two years, calculating various data from 3,279 students (Barab et al., 2005, 2007). Among the 3,279 registered users, approximately 2,500 were elementary school children, aged 9–12 (in public and private schools), 450 undergraduate students, and 50 teachers.

By means of the computerised records of children's choices and accomplishments in the quests, as well as by participant observation and interviews, students' participation has been in focus. In building qualitative interpretations, the researchers used multiple raters, and whenever possible, calculated inter-rater reliabilities. Learning gains were assessed by pre- and post-tests (Tüzün, 2007). The research design also included experimental studies on sub-samples, where students were randomly assigned to either the *Quest Atlantis* condition, or to a worksheet control condition, to test the effectiveness of the *Quest Atlantis* context (Barab et al., 2009). Statistically significant learning gains were documented for science. For example, elementary students taking part in a unit on plant and animal cells demonstrated significant gains in their understanding of the cell (Barab et al., 2007).

Simulme

Hansmann et al. (2007) report of two experimental studies using the educational single-player computer game *Simulme*. This game is built to develop students' knowledge of ecological and economic effects of food consumption, and give them the opportunity to reconsider their own consumption patterns. During the game play, the gamers had to make six virtual "purchases" of meat and vegetables. Each purchase represented the player's typical consumption pattern. Within the game, the player's choices were said to influence the national and global ecological and economic situation. After each purchase, the player received feedback on the consequences of his or her consumption pattern. To achieve good performance, the player should increase the consumption of food that was produced according to organic farming standards, regionally produced, and decrease the share of meat. The game involved answering questions on the origin, type of cultivation, and mode of production of various provisions. The study reports of a 90 minutes intervention, with six experiment classes, and six control classes (aged 17 years), as part of biology curriculum. The same teachers taught in both conditions. Both students and teachers judged the lessons using the game more favourably, than the lessons not using the game. Statistical analysis showed that, regardless of teacher, students profited more from instruction using *Simulme* compared to instruction without the game. In a second experiment with the same game, 212 students were randomly assigned to the experiment (98) and control situations (114). The experiment group played *Simulme* before shopping in an online store, whereas the control group made their shopping at once. The experimental group's purchasing behaviour significantly differed from the control group, in the sense that the students who had played the game bought more organic products and more regionally produced food than the control group. No differences were found in the buying of meat.

As is shown above, the design, scope and focus of research varies substantively with game genre. The most consistent and varied research involves the educational MUVEs (e.g. *River City*, *Quest Atlantis*). Extensive research is also reported on the augmented reality games (e.g. *Mad City Mystery*, *Outbreak @ the Institute*). Each of the rest of the games included in this review (close to ten games) has only been subjected to one or two studies, many which represent the exploratory phase. Nevertheless, even if the number of studies is limited, certain tendencies related to type of game may be noted.

The research studies published on the MUVEs *River City* and *Quest Atlantis* undoubtedly show that carefully designed computer games can successfully support real world inquiry practices, that are equally compelling for girls and boys. The games are characterised by the use of most of the characteristics of COTS games that make such games immersive. They build on a storyline which appeals to the age group. The narrative unfolds as a result of students' activities. Alone or together, students have to solve a row of issues and tasks, using tools, skills and processes typical of scientific practice. The student acts via an avatar, representing her/himself in the game, and can also interact with virtual agents. Attempts are made to imbed scientific formalisms into the issues that students work with. The games are effective as tools for learning, because learning takes place within a meaningful context, and is applied in this context. Feedback is integrated into the game play.

The designers of some games attempted to cross the border between the virtual and the real world, by locating the game in a real place, and having students play the fictional story in a place in the physical world. These so-called augmented reality games were played on handheld computers, in teams of students who had to collaborate in order to gather data, and find plausible solutions to the problem at hand. Two games *Madison 2200* and *Homicide*, referred to as "alternate reality games" and "epistemic games", used real data, as well as the epistemology of professionals in the real world. The games thus put students in a fictional story, working according to the practices of the real profession, and with data belonging to the profession. The games were studied in small exploratory studies, mostly using ethnographic data. Very positive results on learning and engagement were reported.

COTS Games for Science Learning

In contrast to the above studies, that all report on educational computer games, carefully developed by researchers and teachers, the review can say little about the possibilities for science learning embedded in COTS games. Amazingly, very few studies have reported results of this kind of games used in school contexts. Even though such games are reported to be most frequently played in classrooms (e.g. Williamson, 2009), few researchers have studied learning outcomes, and/or interactions with teaching. The few studies available report of some possible learning benefits, but also of many problems that emerge from the way the games treat science content and processes. Still, as other researchers have suggested (e.g. Gee, 2003) it might be possible to integrate some COTS games in the science curriculum, taking advantage of their immersive qualities and potentials for inquiry and problem solving. To realise this, teachers need to occupy a much more central position.

SUMMARY AND CONCLUSION

It has been argued that computer games can afford learning contexts where students are supported in the practice of scientific inquiry and experimentation. This is achieved by providing scientific tools (authentic resources) that are used in the game play, a process that is claimed to be similar to the process of scientific inquiry. The review confirms the theoretical assumptions, that when designed in according to the criteria set forward in theories of educational game play, educational computer games do offer students the possibilities of practicing skills relevant to scientific inquiry.

The review is based on 50 publications published during the last decade (1999–2009) that were found to meet the criteria of presenting empirical data from students using games for learning science in school contexts. Compared to the overall amount of studies reporting of empirical studies of science education and learning, this is a surprisingly small number, and illustrates the limited interest in computer games for science learning. The majority of the games in the studies were developed by researchers, mostly at universities in the US. The number of games developed and reported on, for example, by European researchers is strikingly low (9 out of 50). The number of publications that report on COTS games used for science learning is extremely low. It can thus, be concluded that reports on computer games used for educational purposes in the science curriculum are likely to be based on games that were from the start designed to be educational, since so little research on COTS games exists.

The studies reviewed apply either one, or a mixture of the following two research designs. (1) A type of evidence-based design which is carried out in authentic school settings. These studies applied standard methodology including control groups, pre- and post-test and conformed to experimental criteria, such as having identified cognitive gains/attitudinal changes, using standardised assessment scales and analysing the data by adequate statistics, in some studies even on advanced level. (2) An ethnographical field study design, focusing on observations and recordings of what happens in the interactions between students and the game, as well as between students and teachers or other students.

Many of the studies combined elements of the two designs. Only a small number of studies met the criteria adopted by Vogel et al. (2006) of comparing traditional classroom teaching without the game to teaching with the game (e.g. Ketelhut, 2007; Hansmann, 2007; Toprac, 2008). Most of the games were designed for elementary and middle school students. The analysis revealed that the games built for these age groups focused more on enhancing general science inquiry skills, and less on developing the use of formal science concepts. Specific content addressed was further, more often ecology and biology than physics and chemistry. Specific science concepts and rigid scientific simulations were more often addressed by studies aimed for older students.

When learning effects were assessed, playing the computer game was found to contribute positively to students' science learning. In studies including control groups, the gaming students got better results, both on standardised and content-based tasks, compared to the non-gaming students. The importance of using various types of assessment and evaluation methods and the advantages in combining quantitative and qualitative data were also effectively demonstrated. An important aspect is the enjoyment and engagement in science learning that the games brought about. On the whole, the studies reviewed indicate that educational games for science learning have the potential to favourably influence students' attitude towards science learning and, as a consequence, to accelerate students' learning. Even if almost all studies report on positive effects and experiences, it is, as pointed to by Egenfeldt-Nielsen (2007, p. 8) unrealistic to expect the computer games to always facilitate a desired educational outcome, since such outcomes seldom is a part of the game culture. Computer game play is an activity of great variation that can take many directions, and outcomes may therefore correspond to teachers' expectations in some cases, while leading to quite different outcomes in others.

An important notion, thus, is the situatedness of game play. Playing computer games in an institutionalised setting is clearly a different activity, compared to playing computer games in times of leisure (Linderoth, 2009). To solve problems in a computer game as a part of an assignment in a school context, is a different matter compared to playing the game outside school.

Learning processes are intertwined with the surrounding culture, and constitute a situated practice that cannot be extracted from the context in which they occur (Lave & Wenger, 1991; Säljö, 2005). Computer games brought into a school setting are thus cultural product, associated to expectations based on students' previous experiences of game play outside school. When computer game play is actively situated in a regular school situation and made part of it, it can be shown that students bring forth, and make use of scientific concepts and theories (Barab et al., 2007a, 2007b; Svingby & Jönsson, 2007).

The ethnographical studies allowed for analysis of what was going on when students used the games for learning. Observation revealed that, even when they attained good results on the scientific standard tests, students only occasionally applied domain formalism while playing (Barab et al., 2007a, 2007b; Rosenbaum et al., 2007; Squire et al., 2004). It was further observed that when students applied scientific reasoning skills, they sometimes displayed inconsistency between conclusions and solutions, made inaccurate scientific assumptions, and underestimated social impacts (Barab et al., 2007b; Squire et al., 2004). Rosenbaum et al. (2007) report, for example, that students understood the dynamics of the game, but misunderstood some of the details of the scientific matter at stake in the game (that is, disease transmission mechanism). It seemed as if students drew this mental model of disease from their everyday experiences, and that the game did not provide enough feedback to challenge it (Nelson, 2007).

Lack of clear connection to the curriculum, or of follow up by the teacher in the classroom, seems to result in students not reaching the potentials for learning offered (Nelson, 2005; Rehn et al., 2007). Such results suggest that students need to consciously relate the game play to a learning purpose. Most of the studies reviewed, accordingly, take an interest in the part played by the teacher in the intervention. Game development has followed two main paths in designing educational computer games: (1) to include the support, structure and help by the game itself, or/and by other players (which may include a teacher). In the educational MUVEs, teachers are mostly not built into the game. Instead, virtual "agents" play the role of helping, structuring and giving feedback. Teachers may in any case take advantage of the game. (2) Designing a game to be administered, controlled and supplemented by the teacher. The designers have thus either from the outset calculated with teachers' active participation, and given them adequate training; or the studies showed that teachers integrated the game into the curriculum by adding data, gathering students to reflect on activities and solutions suggested by the students in the game, or other similar initiatives.

In studying the game *Homicide* Magnussen (2005, 2008) clearly demonstrates the importance of the mediating activities brought forward by the teacher. In this game the teacher is further, given a specific role, by acting as chief detective. As such, s/he can contribute new information, as well as gather teams of students for briefing and reporting. In a physics game, where students were acting as electronic particles, Squire et al. (2004) further noticed that by prompting deeper reflection, the teacher added qualities to the game play. In still another study, Rieber and Noah (2007) showed that the teacher played a significant role in helping students to make sense of and learn about the science content. It was observed that in the absence of such help, boys focused too much on the competitive parts of the game. Teachers' low gaming competence and lack of computer game play experiences were in some studies shown to be an obstacle to involvement.

According to the studies reviewed, both the two strategies outlined above may work, suggesting that the role of the teacher is a promising area for further research. This conclusion is strengthened by recent studies of teachers' attitudes to using computer games at school. Teachers were reported to hold mainly positive attitudes towards games, but also feelings of not knowing where to find "good" computer games, and what to do with them (e.g. Williamson, 2009).

This implies the importance for teachers and schools to consciously strive to integrate the game into the curriculum and for game developers to either integrate educational guidance systems into the game, or/and integrate the game as part of the curriculum. Close collaboration between developers, designers and teaching experts are recommended. If computer games are to be used in the classroom appropriate instructional actions are required. The studies suggest that use of information, guidance etc. needs to be guaranteed.

To sum up, computer games hold a promise for engaging students in science education and to hold their interest. To do so, the game play need to be integrated in the curriculum in a way that guarantees that students are both engaged by the game and made to stop and discuss and reflect on the experiments, concepts and theories relevant to solve the problems presented in the game world.

REFERENCES

Aikenhead, G. (2007). Expanding the research agenda for scientific literacy. In Linder, C., Östman, L. & Wickman, P.-O. (Eds.), *Promoting scientific literacy: Science education research in transition. Proceedings of the Linnaues Tercentenary Symposium, Uppsala University.* Uppsala: Geotryckeriet.

Aitkin, A. L. (2004). *Playing at reality: Exploring the potential of the digital game as a medium for science communication.* Unpublished doctoral dissertation, Faculty of Science, The Australian National University.

Annetta, L., Mangrum, J., Holmes, S., Collazo, K., & Cheng, M.-T. (2009). Bridging reality to virtual reality: Investigating gender effect and student engagement on learning through video game play in an elementary school classroom. *International Journal of Science Education, 31*(8), 1091–1113. doi:10.1080/09500690801968656

Barab, S., Ingram-Goble, A., & Warren, S. (2009). Conceptual Play Spaces. In Ferdig, R. E. (Ed.), *Handbook of Research on Effective Electronic Gaming in Education.* Hershey, PA: IGI Global publications.

Barab, S., Zuiker, S., Warren, S., Hickey, D., Ingram-Goble, A., & Kwon, E.-J. (2007b). Situationally embodied curriculum: Relating formalisms and contexts. *Science Education, 91*(5), 750–782. doi:10.1002/sce.20217

Barab, S. A., Arici, A., & Jackson, C. (2005). Eat your vegetables and do your homework: A design-based investigation of enjoyment and meaning in learning. *Educational Technology, 65*(1), 15–21.

Barab, S. A., Dodge, T., Tüzün, H., Job-Sludwer, K., Jackson, D., & Arici, A. (2007). The Quest Atlantis Project: A socially responsive play space for learning. In Shelton, B. E., & Wiley, D. (Eds.), *The educational design and use of simulation computer games.* Rotterdam: Sense Publishers.

Barab, S. A., Sadler, T. D., Heiselt, C., Hickey, D., & Zuiker, S. (2007a). Relating narrative, inquiry, and inscriptions: Supporting consequential play. *Journal of Science Education and Technology, 16*(1), 59–82. doi:10.1007/s10956-006-9033-3

Barab, S. A., & Squire, K. (2004). Design-based research: Putting a stake in the ground. *Journal of the Learning Sciences, 13*(1), 1–14. doi:10.1207/s15327809jls1301_1

Beckett, K. L., & Shaffer, D. W. (2005). Augmented by reality: The pedagogical praxis of urban planning as a pathway to ecological thinking. *Journal of Educational Computing Research, 33*(1), 31–52. doi:10.2190/D5YQ-MMW6-V0FR-RNJQ

Boyle, L. (2009). *Keynote lecture at the 3rd European Conference on Games Based Learning.* University of Applied Sciences, Graz, Austria.

Cai, Y., Lu, B., Zheng, J., & Li, L. (2006). Immersive protein gaming for bio edutainment. *Simulation & Gaming, 37*(4), 466–475. doi:10.1177/1046878106293677

Cameron, B., & Dwyer, F. (2005). The effect of online gaming, cognition and feedback type in facilitating delayed achievement of different learning objective. *Journal of Interactive Learning Research, 16*(3), 243–258.

Clarke, J., & Dede, C. (2005). *Making learning meaningful: An exploratory study of using multi-user environments (MUVEs) in middle school.* Paper presented at American Educational Research Association Conference, Montréal, Québec.

Cobb, S., Neale, H. R., Crosier, J. K., & Wilson, J. R. (2002). Development and evaluation of virtual learning environments. In Stanney, K. M. (Ed.), *Handbook of virtual environments: Design, implementation, and applications.* Mahwah, NJ: Lawrence Erlbaum Associates, Inc.

Colella, V. (2000). Participatory simulations: Building collaborative understanding through immersive dynamic modeling. *Journal of the Learning Sciences, 9*(4), 471–500. doi:10.1207/S15327809JLS0904_4

De Freitas, S. (2007). *The learning in immersive worlds: A review of game based learning report.* UK: JISC e-Learning Programme, Higher Education Funding Council for England (HEFCE).

Dede, C., Ketelhut, D. J., & Ruess, K. (2002, October). *Motivation, usability, and learning outcomes in a prototype museum-based multi-user virtual environment.* Paper presented at The Fifth International Conference of Learning Sciences, Seattle.

Dieterle, E., & Clarke, J. (2008). Multi-user virtual environments for teaching and learning. In Pagani, M. (Ed.), *Encyclopedia of multimedia technology and networking.* Hershey, PA: Idea Group, Inc.

Egenfeldt-Nielsen, S. (2007). *Educational potentials of computer games.* New York: Continuum.

Ekborg, M., Ideland, M. & Malmberg, C. (2009) Science for life-a conceptual framework for analysis and construction of socio-scientific cases. *NorDiNa, 10*(1).

Facer, K., Joiner, R., Stanton, D., Reid, J., Hull, R., & Kirk, D. S. (2004). Savannah: Mobile gaming and learning? *Journal of Computer Assisted Learning, 20*(6), 399–409. doi:10.1111/j.1365-2729.2004.00105.x

Galas, C. (2006). Why Whyville? *Learning and Leading with Technology, 34*(6), 30–33.

Gee, J. P. (2003). *What video games have to teach us about learning and literacy.* New York: Palgrave Macmillan.

Hanghøj, T. (2008). *Playful knowledge: An explorative study of educational gaming.* Unpublished doctoral dissertation Copenhagen: Institute of Literature, Media and Cultural Studies, University of Southern Denmark.

Hansmann, R., Scholz, R. W., Francke, C.-J. A. C., & Weymann, M. (2005). Enhancing environmental awareness: Ecological and economic effects of food consumption. *Simulation & Gaming, 36*(3), 364–382. doi:10.1177/1046878105279116

Hickey, D. T., Ingram-Goble, A. A., & Jameson, E. M. (2009). Designing assessments and assessing designs in virtual educational environments. *Journal of Science Education and Technology, 18*(2), 187–208. doi:10.1007/s10956-008-9143-1

Jenkins, H., Squire, K., & Tan, P. (2004). You can't bring that game to school! Designing supercharged! In Laurel, B. (Ed.), *Design research: Methods and perspectives.* Cambridge, MA: MIT Press.

Jidesjö, A., & Oscarsson, M. (2006). Student's attitudes to science and technology–first results from the ROSE-project in Sweden. In Janiuk, I. R. M., & Samonek-Miciuk, E. (Eds.), *Science and technology education for a diverse world. Dilemmas, needs and partnerships.* Lublin, Poland: Marie Curie-Sklodowska University Press.

Jönsson, A. (2008). *Educative assessment for/of teacher competency. A study of assessment and learning in the interactive examination for student teachers*. Unpublished doctoral dissertation, Malmö University, Malmö.

Jönsson, A., & Svingby, G. (2008). The use of scoring rubrics: Reliability, validity, and educational consequences. *Educational Research Review, 2*(2), 130–144. doi:10.1016/j.edurev.2007.05.002

Kafai, Y. B. (2008). Understanding Virtual Epidemics: Children's Folk Conceptions of a Computer Virus. *Journal of Science Education and Technology, 17*(6), 523–529. doi:10.1007/s10956-008-9102-x

Kafai, Y. B., Feldon, D., Fields, D., Giang, M., & Quintero, M. (2007). *Life in the times of Whypox: A virtual epidemic as a community event*. Paper presented at The Third International Conference on Communities and Technology, New York.

Kao, L., Galas, C., & Kafai, Y. (2005). *A totally different world: Playing and learning in multiuser environments*. Paper presented at DIGRA 2005 Conference: Changing Views – Worlds in Play, Vancouver.

Kebritchi, M., & Hirumi, A. (2008). Examining the pedagogical foundations of modern educational computer games. *Computers & Education, 51*(4), 1729–1743. doi:10.1016/j.compedu.2008.05.004

Ketelhut, D. J. (2007). The impact of student self-efficacy on scientific inquiry skills: An exploratory investigation in River City, a multi-user virtual environment. *Journal of Science Education and Technology, 16*(1), 99–111. doi:10.1007/s10956-006-9038-y

Ketelhut, D. J., Dede, C., Clarke, J., Nelson, B., & Bowman, C. (2007). Studying situated learning in a multi-user environment. In Baker, E., Dikieson, J., Wulfeck, W., & O'Neil, H. (Eds.), *Assessment of problem solving using simulations*. New York: Lawrence Erlbaum Associates.

Kirriemuir, J., & McFarlan, A. (2004). *Literature review in games and learning*. Bristol: FutureLab series.

Klopfer, E. (2008). *Augmented learning: Research and design of mobile educational games*. Cambridge, MA: MIT Press.

Klopfer, E., & Squire, K. (2008). Environmental detectives–the development of an augmented reality platform for environmental simulations. *Educational Technology Research and Development, 5*(2), 203–228. doi:10.1007/s11423-007-9037-6

Klopfer, E., Yoon, S., & Rivas, L. (2004). Comparative analysis of palm and wearable computers for participatory simulations. *Journal of Computer Assisted Learning, 20*(5), 347–359. doi:10.1111/j.1365-2729.2004.00094.x

Krotoski, A. (2004). Chicks and joysticks: An exploration of women and gaming. Entertainment and Leisure Software Publishers Association. Retrieved January 31, 2010, from www.elspa.com/assets/files/c/chicksandjoysticksanexplorationofwomenandgaming_176.pdf

Lave, J., & Wenger, E. (1991). *Situated learning: Legitimate peripheral participation*. New York: Cambridge University Press.

Lemke, J. (1990). *Talking science: Language, learning, and values*. Norwood, NJ: Ablex.

Lim, C. P., Nonis, D., & Hedberg, J. (2006). Gaming in a 3D multi-user virtual environment: Engaging students in science lesson. *British Journal of Educational Technology, 37*(2), 211–231. doi:10.1111/j.1467-8535.2006.00531.x

Linder, C., Östman, L., & Wickman, P.-O. (Eds.). (2007). *Proceedings of the Linnaues Tercentenary Symposium, Uppsala University*. Uppsala: Geotryckeriet.

Linderoth, J. (2009). Hur datorspelande kan ge en illusion av lärande. In Selander, S., & Svärdemo-Åberg, E. (Eds.), *Didactic designs in digital environments: New learning opportunities*. Stockholm: Liber.

Linderoth, J., Lantz-Andersson, A., & Lindström, B. (2002). Electronic exaggerations and virtual worries: Mapping research of computer games relevant to the understanding of children's game play. *Contemporary Issues in Early Childhood*, *3*(2), 226–250. doi:10.2304/ciec.2002.3.2.6

Magnussen, R. (2005). *Learning games as a platform for simulated science practice*. Paper presented at DiGRA 2005 Conference: Changing Views – Worlds in Play, Vancouver.

Magnussen, R. (2007). *Teacher roles in learning games–when games become situated in schools*. Paper presented at DiGRA 2007 Conference: Situated Play, Tokyo.

Magnussen, R. (2008). *Representational inquiry in science learning games*. Unpublished doctoral thesis, Danish School of Education, University of Aarhus, Copenhagen

Marsh, T., Wong, W. L., Carriazo, E., Nocera, L., Yang, K., Varma, A., et al. (2005). *User experiences and lessons learned from developing and implementing an immersive game for the science classroom*. Paper presented at The 11th International Conference on Human-Computer Interaction, Portland, Oregon.

Mathevet, R., Le Page, C., Etienne, M., Lefebvre, G., Gigot, G., & Proréol, S. (2007). BUTORSTAR: A role-playing game for collective awareness of wise reedbed use. *Simulation & Gaming*, *38*(2), 233–262. doi:10.1177/1046878107300665

Mellor, F. (2001). Gender and the communication of physics through multimedia. *Public Understanding of Science (Bristol, England)*, *10*(3), 271–291. doi:10.1088/0963-6625/10/3/302

Miller, L., Moreno, J., Estrera, V., & Lane, D. (2004). Efficacy of MedMyst: An Internet teaching tool for middle school microbiology. *Journal of Microbiology & Biology Education*, *5*, 13–20.

Murray, J. H. (1997). *Hamlet on the Holodeck: The future of narrative in cyperspace*. New York: The Free Press.

National Research Council. (1996). *National science education standards*. Washington, DC: National Academy Press.

Nelson, B. (2007). Exploring the use of individualized, reflective guidance in an educational multi-user virtual environment. *Journal of Science Education and Technology*, *16*(1), 83–97. doi:10.1007/s10956-006-9039-x

Nelson, B., & Ketelhut, D. J. (2007). Scientific inquiry in educational multi-user virtual environments. *Educational Psychology Review*, *19*(39), 265–283. doi:10.1007/s10648-007-9048-1

Nelson, B., & Ketelhut, D. J. (2008). Exploring embedded guidance and self-efficacy in educational multi-user environments. *International Journal of Computer-Supported Collaborative Learning*, *3*(4), 413–427. doi:10.1007/s11412-008-9049-1

Nelson, B., Ketelhut, D. J., Clarke, J., Bowman, C., & Dede, C. (2005). Design-based research strategies for developing a scientific inquiry curriculum in a multi-user virtual environment. *Educational Technology*, *45*(1), 21–34.

Neulight, N., Kafai, Y. B., Kao, L., Foley, B., & Galas, C. (2007). Children's participation in a virtual epidemic in the science classroom: Making connection to natural infectious disease. *Journal of Science Education and Technology*, *16*(1), 47–58. doi:10.1007/s10956-006-9029-z

Nilsson, E. M., & Jakobsson, A. (in press). Simulated sustainable societies: Students' reflections on creating future cities in computer games. *Journal of Science Education and Technology*.

Nilsson, E. M., & Svingby, G. (2009). Gaming as actions: Students playing a mobile educational computer game. *Human IT*, *10*(1), 26–59.

Nilsson, E. M., & Svingby, G. (In press). Simulating a real world or playing a game? Students playing a COTS game in the science classroom. In Cai, Y. (Ed.), *IDM and VR for education in virtual learning environment*. New York: Nova Sciences Publishers.

OECD. (2003). *The PISA 2003 assessment framework*. Paris: Organisation for Economic Co-Operation and Development.

Osborne, J. (2007). Engaging young people with science: Thoughts about future direction of science education. In C. Linder, L. Östman & P.-O. Wickman (Eds.), *Promoting scientific literacy: Science education research in transition. Proceedings of the Linnaues Tercentenary Symposium, Uppsala University*. Uppsala: Geotryckeriet.

Phelps, A. J., & Lee, C. (2003). The power of practice: What students learn from how we teach. *Journal of Chemical Education, 80*(7), 829–883. doi:10.1021/ed080p829

Price, C. B. (2008). Learning physics with the unreal tournament engine. *Physics Education, 43*(3), 291–337. doi:10.1088/0031-9120/43/3/006

Randel, J. M., Morris, B. A., Wetzel, C. D., & Whitehill, B. V. (1992). The effectiveness of games for educational purposes: A review of recent research. *Simulation & Gaming, 23*(3), 261–276. doi:10.1177/1046878192233001

Rehn, A., Persson, S., & Svingby, G. (2007). *Lasaurs–a computer game about the human body, health, and health care played by students in grades 3-7*. Report, School of Education, Malmö University, Malmö.

Rieber, L. P., & Noah, D. (2008). Games, simulations, and visual metaphors in education: Antagonism between enjoyment and learning. *Educational Media International, 45*(2), 77–92. doi:10.1080/09523980802107096

Rosenbaum, E., Klopfer, E., & Perry, J. (2007). On location learning: Authentic applied science with networked augmented reality. *Journal of Science Education, 16*(1), 31–45.

Salen, K. (2008). *The ecology of games: Connecting youth, games, and learning*. Cambridge, MA: MIT Press.

Säljö, R. (2005). *Learning and cultural tools: About learning processes and the collective memory*. Stockholm: Norstedts akademiska förlag.

Sauvé, L., Renaud, L., Kaufman, D., & Marquis, J.-S. (2007). Distinguishing between games and simulations: A systematic review. *Journal of Educational Technology & Society, 10*(3), 247–256.

Shaffer, D. W. (2007). *How computer games help children learn*. New York: Palgrave Macmillan.

Squire, K. (2006). From content to context: Videogames as designed experience. *Educational Researcher, 35*(8), 19–29. doi:10.3102/0013189X035008019

Squire, K., Barnett, M., Grant, J. M., & Higgenbotham, T. (2004). *Electromagnetism supercharged! Learning physics with digital simulation games*. Paper presented at the International Conference of the Learning Sciences 2004, Santa Monica.

Squire, K., & Jan, M. (2007). Mad city mystery: Developing scientific argumentation skills with a place-based augmented reality game on handheld computer. *Journal of Science Education and Technology, 16*(1), 5–29. doi:10.1007/s10956-006-9037-z

Squire, K., & Klopfer, E. (2007). Augmented reality simulations on handheld computers. *Journal of the Learning Sciences, 16*(3), 371–413.

Steinkuehler, C. A., & Chmiel, M. (2006). *Fostering scientific habits of mind in the context of online play*. Paper presented at The 7th International Conference of the Learning Sciences, Bloomington, IN.

Susi, T., Johannesson, M., & Backlund, P. (2007). *Serious games–an overview. (Technical report HS-IKI -TR-07-001). Skövde: School of Humanities and Informatics.* University of Skövde.

Svarovsky, G. N., & Shaffer, D. W. (2006). *SodaConstructiong an understanding of physics: Technology-based engineering activities for middle school students.* Paper presented at 36th ASEE/IEEE Frontiers in Education Conference, San Diego.

Svarovsky, G. N., & Shaffer, D. W. (2007). Soda-Constructing knowledge through exploratoids. *Journal of Research in Science Teaching, 44*(1), 133–153. doi:10.1002/tea.20112

Svingby, G., & Jönsson, R. (2007). *Simulation games and learning.* Paper presented at the Game in Action conference, Gothenburg.

Toprac, P. K. (2008). *The effects of a problem based learning digital game on continuing motivation to learn science.* Unpublished doctoral dissertation, Faculty of the Graduate School of The University of Texas at Austin.

Tüzün, H. (2007). Blending video games with learning: Issues and challenges with classroom implementations in the Turkish context. *British Journal of Educational Technology, 38*(3), 465–477. doi:10.1111/j.1467-8535.2007.00710.x

Van Eck, R. (2006). Digital game-based learning: It's not just the digital natives who are restless. *EDUCAUSE Review, 41*(2), 16–30.

Van Eck, R. (2006a). Using games to promote girls' positive attitudes towards technology. *Innovate, 2*(3).

Van Sickle, R. (1986). A quantitative review of research on instructional simulation gaming: A twenty year perspective. *Theory and Research in Social Education, 14*(3), 245–264.

Vogel, J. J., Vogel, D. S., Cannon-Bowers, J., Bowers, C. A., Muse, K., & Wright, M. (2006). Computer gaming and interactive simulations for learning: A meta-analysis. *Journal of Educational Computing Research, 34*(3), 229–243. doi:10.2190/FLHV-K4WA-WPVQ-H0YM

Wang, F., & Hannafin, M. J. (2005). Design-based research and technology-enhanced learning environments. *Educational Technology Research and Development, 53*(4), 5–23. doi:10.1007/BF02504682

Williamson, B. (2009). *Computer games, schools, and young people.* Bristol: FutureLab series.

Wong, W. L., Shen, C., Nocera, L., Carriazo, E., Tang, F., & Bugga, S. (2007). Serious video game effectivenes. *ACM International Conference Proceeding Series, 203,* 49–55.

Wycliffe, J., & Muwanga-Zake, F. (2007). Evaluation of an educational computer programme as a change agent in science classrooms. *Journal of Science Education and Technology, 16*(6), 473–490. doi:10.1007/s10956-007-9078-y

Zeidler, D. (2007). An inclusive view of scientific literacy: Core issues and future directions. In C. Linder, L. Östman & P.-O. Wickman (Eds.) *Promoting scientific literacy: Science education research in transition. Proceedings of the Linnaues Tercentenary Symposium, Uppsala University.* Uppsala: Geotryckeriet.

KEY TERMS AND DEFINITIONS

Empirical Studies: Studies presenting results that are based upon empirical data, and not on theoretical assumptions.

Formal School Settings: Learning activities in school.

Game-Based Learning: Learning settings involving computer game play.

K-12 Students: Students aged 6-18 years.

Research Review: An overview and analysis of the publications found that met the set criteria.

Science Education: Science learning in school, including the physics, chemistry, biology.

Chapter 2
The Use of Computer Games in Education:
A Review of the Literature

Thomas Hainey
University of the West of Scotland, Scotland

Thomas Connolly
University of the West of Scotland, Scotland

Mark Stansfield
University of the West of Scotland, Scotland

Liz Boyle
University of the West of Scotland, Scotland

ABSTRACT

Games-based learning has captured the interest of educationalists as it is perceived as a potentially highly motivating approach for learning in a diverse number of areas. Despite this, there is a dearth of empirical evidence in the GBL literature, and confusion as to where games-based learning fits in relation to games, simulations, and serious games. This chapter will present a review of the current state of the GBL empirical literature, but will particularly focus on the fields of software engineering, Information Systems, and computer science. This chapter will also take into account the advantages and disadvantages that have to be considered when selecting a GBL approach.

INTRODUCTION

This chapter will discuss the definition of 'Games-Based Learning' (GBL) and its associated terms and will suggest a position for GBL in terms of its relation to games and simulations. A brief review of the use of some computer games in education will then be performed to show the diversity of the use of GBL outside of computer science. The chapter will then review the use of computer games in computing education and will summarise the empirical evidence associated with the relevant games. Finally there will be a brief discussion on the advantages and disadvantages of games-based learning.

DOI: 10.4018/978-1-60960-495-0.ch002

WHAT IS GAMES-BASED LEARNING?

This section will provide a definition of Games-Based Learning and some of the cognate terms surrounding it in the literature such as: games, simulations, computer games, simulation games, computer simulations, computer simulation games and serious games. Taking these definitions and distinctions into account, a diagram will be produced to illustrate the position of GBL to situate these terms within the literature.

The term "game" covers a very wide range of activities but, as Juul (2003) and others (e.g. Crawford, 2003) have observed, it is difficult to define in terms of necessary and sufficient features, and there is no real consensus on shared terms and their definitions. Several definitions of games have been proposed. For example, Dempsey, Haynes, Lucassen and Casey (2002) define a game as "... *a set of activities involving one or more players. It has goals, constraints, payoffs, and consequences. A game is rule-guided and artificial in some respects. Finally, a game involves some aspect of competition, even if that competition is with oneself.*" Grendler (1996, pp. 523) defines games as "*consisting of rules that describe allowable player moves, game constraints and privileges (such as ways of earning extra turns) and penalties for illegal (non permissible) actions. Further the rules may be imaginative in that they need not relate to real world-events.*" On the other hand, Caillois (1961) defines a game as "*an activity that is voluntary and enjoyable, separate from the real world, uncertain, unproductive (in that the activity does not produce any goods of external value), and governed by rules.*" The main characteristics of games are that they are voluntary, and typically enjoyable, physical or mental activities; they involve goals and ways of achieving these goals usually through "moves" or actions within the game that can be subject to constraints or rules; they are in some way separate from real life. Games can be played singly, in pairs

or in teams. Smed and Hakonen (2003) define a computer game as "*a game that is carried out with the help of a computer program.*"

The term "simulation" generally refers to a representation of a real system, an abstract system, an environment or a process that is electronically generated. Crookall and Saunders (1989) view a simulation as a representation of a real world system that may focus on a specific aspect of reality. Thavikulwat (1999) defines the term "simulation" as "*a replicable representation of a process. The representation can be phenotypical or genotypical. If phenotypical, it is a reflection of the process; if genotypical, it is a subset. Thus, a phenotypical representation of employment would have participants employ fictitious persons; a genotypical representation would have them employ each other. Computer animation might make the phenotypical representation realistic, but it cannot make it real. Genotypical representation, however, is real.*"

The term "computer simulation" has many definitions. Pritsker (1979) compiled an inventory and found twenty-one different definitions. In the largest possible sense, McLeod (1986) defines a computer simulation as "*the use of computers to model things*" whereas Laurillard (2002) defines it as an "*artefact that embodies some model of an aspect of the real world, allows the user to make inputs to the model, runs the model and displays the results.*"

There is both a distinction and an overlap associated with the terms "simulation" and "game", which gives rise to the terms "simulation game" and "computer simulation game." Heinich, Molenda, Russell and Smoldino (1996) provide the following distinction between a game and a simulation: "*a game is an activity in which participants follow prescribed rules that differ from those of real life as they strive to attain a challenging goal. The distinction between play and reality is what makes games entertaining...A simulation is an abstraction or simplification of some real-life situation or process. In simulations, participants usually play a role that involves them in interactions with other people or with elements of the simulated environment."*

To complicate matters, simulation games are defined by Kriz (2003) as *"representing dynamic models of real situations (a reconstruction of a situation or reality that is itself a social construction). Simulation games help to mimic processes, networks, and structures of specific existing systems. In addition to mirroring real-life systems, simulation games incorporate players who assume specific roles."* He distinguishes between two kinds of simulation games that are generally used: closed (rigid rule) and open (free form). In rigid rule simulation games, the players receive clear instructions based on well-defined rules. The problem is presented to the player(s) in a well-defined framework, and they are expected to solve it in a target-oriented manner as precisely as possible by making decisions in line with the instructions. In free-form games, the simulation model, rules, and flow of the gaming simulation are not given a priori. On the basis of an initial scenario, models of systems are co-constructed by the players themselves (facilitated by experienced gaming simulation designers).

Zyda (2005) defines a 'serious game' as: *"a mental contest, played with a computer in accordance with specific rules, that uses entertainment to further government or corporate training, education, health, public policy, and strategic communication objectives."* Sawyer and Smith's (2008) taxonomy of serious games includes games for health, advergames, games for training, games for education, games for science and research, production and games as work in the areas of government and NGOs, defense, healthcare, marketing and communications, education, corporate and industry. Games-based learning is a sub-category of Serious Games, however, it should be noted that the terms are sometimes used synonymously as mentioned by Corti (2006). Tang, Hanneghan and El-Rhalibi (2009) define games-based learning as: *"games-based learning refers to the innovative learning approach derived from the use of computer games that possess educational value or different kinds of software applications that use games for learning and education purposes such as learning support, teaching enhancement, assessment and evaluation of learners."* Figure 1 shows where GBL could potentially fit in relation to games, simulations and serious games.

Figure 1. Position of GBL in relation to simulations, games and serious games

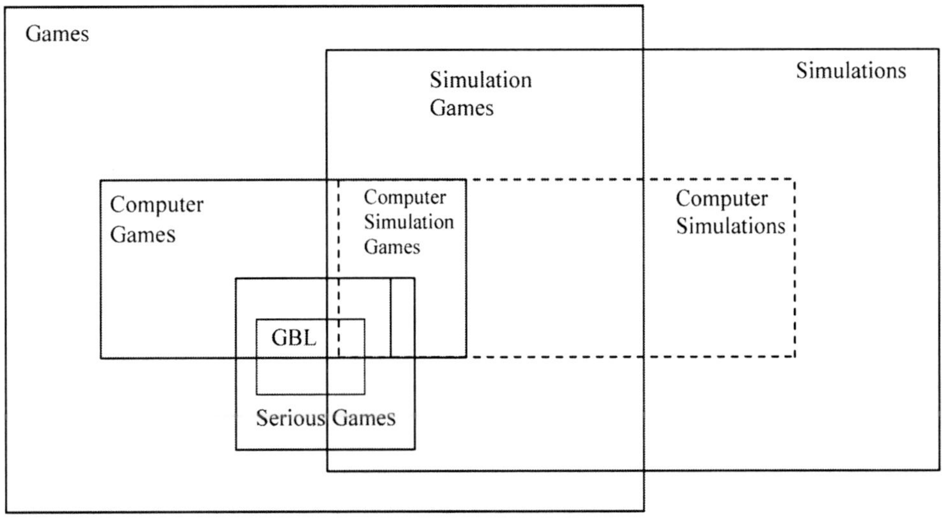

GAMES-BASED LEARNING EMPIRICAL EVIDENCE

One of the primary concerns associated with the GBL literature is the dearth of empirical evidence supporting the validity of the approach (Connolly, Stansfield and Hainey, 2007; de Freitas, 2006). O'Neil, Wainess and Baker (2005) believe that an essential element missing is the ability to properly evaluate games for education and training purposes. If games are not properly evaluated and concrete empirical evidence is not obtained in individual learning scenarios that can produce generalisable results, then the potential of games in learning can always be dismissed as unsubstantiated optimism. In the O'Neil study, a large amount of literature was collected and analysed from the PsycINFO, EducationAbs, and SocialAciAbs Information Systems. Out of several thousand articles, 19 met the specified criteria for inclusion and had some form of empirical evidence that was either qualitative, quantitative or both. The literature was then viewed through Kirkpatrick's four levels for evaluating training and the augmented CRESST (Center for Research on

Evaluation, Standards, and Student Testing) model. The majority of the studies reviewed analysed performance on game measurements. Other studies included observation of military tactics used, observation, time to complete the game, transfer test of location (in the context of a maze game), flight performance and a variety of questionnaires including exit, stress and motivation questionnaires.

The review of empirical evidence on the benefit of games and simulations for educational purposes in the past 10 or 20 years is a recurring theme in the literature and can be traced even further back. For example, Randel, Morris, Wetzel and Whitehill (1992) examined 68 studies from 1963 comparing simulations/games approaches and conventional instruction in direct relation to student performance. Some of the following main discoveries were made:

- 38 (56%) of the studies found no difference; 22 (32%) of the studies found a difference that favoured simulations/games; 5 (7%) of studies favoured simulations/games however control was questionable; 3 (5%) found differences that favoured conventional instruction.
- With regards to retention, simulations/games induced greater retention over time than conventional approaches.
- With regards to interest, out of 14 studies, 12 (86%) showed a greater interest in games and simulations over conventional approaches.

Dempsey, Rasmassen and Lucassen (1994) performed a literature review ranging (but was not limited to) 1982 to 1994 and discovered 91 sources (most of them journal papers). The main findings of this study were that the majority of the articles discovered were discussion articles ($n = 43$) i.e. "articles which state or describe experiences or opinions with no empirical or systematically presented evidence." Thirty-three research articles were discovered, nine literature review, seven theoretical articles and four development articles. It should be noted that the papers discovered could fit into more than one of the categories, for example a paper may be both a literature review and a discussion article. The study acknowledges that it has unsystematically sampled a very small amount of the literature as a whole but expects the literature to follow the trend of being dominated by discussion articles.

Hays (2005) conducted a review of 48 empirical research articles and summarised 31 theoretical articles and 26 review articles on the effectiveness of instructional gaming, leading to the following five conclusions:

- The empirical evidence is 'fragmented'. The literature contains research on different types of games, age groups and tasks and has methodological flaws and ill-defined terms.

- Despite the fact that research has shown that games can provide effective learning; this does not indicate to an instructor whether to use a game for a specific instructional task. It is also not advisable to generalise from the effectiveness of one game to the effectiveness of all games.
- No evidence exists to indicate that games are the preferred method of instruction in every situation.
- Games should be embedded in instructional programs, include debriefing and feedback to allow the learners to understand what is happening in the game and how these events support instruction.
- Instructional effectiveness of the game increases with instructional support to help learners understand how to use the game.

The lack of empirical evidence supporting GBL is not a new issue, the growing popularity of computer games in conjunction with recent advances in games and hardware technology, the emergence of virtual worlds and massively multiplayer online games (MMOGs), reinforces the need for the generation of empirical evidence. The following section will review some of the games in education and will critically evaluate the associated empirical evidence.

GAMES IN EDUCATION

This chapter will primarily focus on computer-based or digital GBL environments, however it should be noted that board games and trading card games exist for educational purposes in some of the fields discussed, for example, programming (Baker, Oh Navarro & Van der Hoek, 2003) and a trading card game to teach about pathogens (Steinman & Blastos, 2002).

Games Outside Computer Science

Games are a very versatile medium and have been used for educational purposes in a number of different areas outside of computer science including: medicine, business, military training, science, mathematics, biology, writing and geography and language education.

Medicine

Games have been used in medicine primarily because of their ability to teach without any real consequences beyond the boundary of the game (Lennon, 2006; Roubidoux, Chapman & Piontek 2002; Roubidoux, 2005). Thus medical students can learn safely to a respectable standard without putting the lives of patients at risk. Games in medicine are not restricted solely to medical students and can be used for rudimentary medical education and also as a mechanism to understand and accept treatments. Beale, Kato, Marin-Bowling, Guthrie and Cole (2007) performed a study with 375 young adult and adolescent cancer patients from 34 cancer treatments centers in the US, Canada and Australia. The participants either received a copy of Re-Mission (a third person action psycho-educational game to increase cancer related knowledge of adolescent and young adult cancer patients) or the commercial game: *Indiana Jones and The Emperor's Tomb* (a third person action game). Participants were asked to play the game for one hour a week for up to three months. A knowledge test for cancer was administered prior to contact with the game (baseline) and then again after one month (follow-up group) and again after three months (long term follow-up group). The Re-Mission group was also required to rate the acceptability and credibility of the game. Both of the participant groups increased their knowledge significantly, however the Re-Mission group scored significantly higher.

Prior to performing the main study performed by Beale, Kato, Marin-Bowling, Guthrie and Cole (2007), Kato and Beale (2006) performed a study to make sure that an action video game about cancer would be acceptable to young and adolescent cancer patients. The study uses a control group to draw comparisons with the experimental group; a number of statistical techniques are utilised including a multiple regression test assessing whether changes in baseline knowledge scores were predictable from different factors such as age, gender and gaming experience. The study is one of the few in the literature to use a long-term follow-up group to assess if the game promotes sustained knowledge. As well as a knowledge test, the study performs a credibility and acceptability test due to the delicate nature and content of the game. The results of the study was an increase in cancer related knowledge in both groups but higher in the Re-Mission group. The participants sustained the heightened knowledge scores over time.

Business

Virtual U (http://www.virtual-u.org/) is a computer-based simulation game that is modelled after the highly popular SimCity series. The game uses situated learning (Gee, 2003) by challenging the player to act as the president of a university and manage the affairs of the institution. While Virtual U is a simulation, it is grounded in authentic data from 1,200 universities and colleges in the US. No empirical evidence associated with Virtual U was found in this literature review; however the Virtual U website (2009) indicates that as of 2005 the game has been used in over 800 institutions in 90 countries and that 25% of respondents to an installation survey are using it as part of formal training or a classroom exercise. This indicates that while GBL is being used in education on a large scale, empirical evidence may not always be collected.

Virtual Leader (http://www.simulearn.net) is a 3D educational simulation game developed by SimuLearn (co-founded by Clark Aldrich) to allow the player to practise and apply appropriate skills associated with effective leadership. Virtual Leader is currently in use by thousands of undergraduate students, postgraduate students and the US military. Fortune 500 companies such as Coca-Cola and Johnson & Johnson are also using it. The empirical evidence associated with Virtual Leader is available online at http://www.simulearn.net/pdf/practiceware_works.pdf where four case studies have been performed. The case studies results are that Virtual Leader was significantly better than traditional approaches with regards to leadership skills, cognitive change, memorisation, application of knowledge and positive behaviours. One important issue this raises is that empirical evidence is not restricted to academic articles and can be located in the grey literature or websites for both research and commercialisation purposes.

Military Training

America's Army (http://www.americasarmy.com/) was developed by the American Army to aid its recruitment process and to explain/describe military life by introducing them to key military skills such as collaboration, communication and navigation of challenges. America's Army was launched in 2002 and consists of the following two realistic simulations:

- Soldiers – A RPG where players navigate various challenges to achieve goals.
- Operations – A first-person action game allowing up to 32 players to enter "virtual service" with the US Army on the same unit mission.

The empirical evidence associated with America's Army is available online at: http://www.casos.cs.cmu.edu/projects/americas_army/publications.

php. The majority of these publications focus on factors affecting team success, movement and communication and team structures. One publication directly compares America's Army to a Unit of Action simulation (Schneider, Carley & Moon, 2005). The results of this study are inconclusive and further development and experimentation with Unit of Action simulations is required for better insight.

Science

Squire, Barnett, Grant and Higginbotham (2004) performed a study that was part of a larger study examining the pedagogical potential of Super-Charged! performed at Chamberlain middle school. SuperCharged! is a simulation game to assist learners to build stronger intuitions of electromagnetism concepts developed in consultation with MIT physicist John Belcher. Players must place charged particles and control a ship (by altering its charge) to explore and navigate through electromagnetic mazes. Two classes served as the control group with a total of 32 students and another three classes served as the experimental group with a total of 58 students. In general the experimental group outperformed the control group in the conceptual electromagnetism exam (Mean experimental = 5.4, SD = 0.20, Increase = 1.2; Mean control = 4.7, SD = 0.27, Increase = 0.6). A two-way ANOVA using post-test scores as the dependent variable with gender and intervention as between subject variables indicated that the difference in knowledge levels was significant ($F(2,89) = 4.8$, $p < 0.05$), however there was no significant difference due to gender indicating that the GBL application was equally effective for males and for females.

Mathematics

The SMILE project (http://www2.tech.purdue.edu/cg/i3/SMILE/index.html) is centered on developing an immersive virtual learning environment for deaf and hearing children (age 5–10). Adamo-Villani and Wright (2007) describe smile as "*the first bilingual immersive VLE (Virtual Learning Environment) for deaf and hearing students combining key elements of successful computer games, emotionally appealing graphics, and realistic real-time 3D signing, with goal-oriented, standards-based learning activities that are grounded in research on effective pedagogy*". A formative evaluation of the second version of SMILE has been carried out with children showing that the application is fun and easy to use. The second version of SMILE embraces 'constructivism' and 'constructionism' learning theories to extend the user interaction giving the participant the opportunity to build new content and dynamically change the virtual environment. The empirical evidence associated with SMILE is a formative evaluation during the preliminary development stages and focuses on usability and not pedagogy.

Zombie Division (Baker, Hadgood, Ainsworth & Corbett, 2007) is an educational third person action game with adventure game elements and was designed to teach elementary school students about division. The player assumes the role of an Ancient Greek hero who must engage skeleton enemies in hand-to-hand combat to progress in the game environment. Each of the skeleton enemies has a number on their chest. The player is equipped with a number of weapons linked to keys on the keyboard. Each weapon corresponds to a particular divisor number. If the player attacks a skeleton with an appropriate divisor weapon then the number on the skeleton decrements. Zombie Division is the main game associated with doctoral dissertation by Habgood (2007).

The empirical evidence associated with Zombie Division discusses four studies conducted to empirically evaluate the effectiveness of extrinsic and intrinsic approaches to game development. The intrinsic approach integrated the mathematical content into the game play. The extrinsic version had the same game play and mathematical content, but the two components were separated as the mathematical problems were presented to the player at the completion of each level rather than during the game play. In each of the studies a control group is utilised, the dissertation particularly focuses on learning outcomes and uses a wide variety of statistical analysis techniques. The results show that intrinsic approaches to designing games have the potential to create improved learning outcomes and higher motivational appeal than extrinsic approaches to designing games. One primary factor that has become apparent during the literature review is that the highest concentration of high quality empirical evidence is located in the grey literature.

Biology

The River City Project (http://muve.gse.harvard.edu/rivercityproject/index.html) is a computer simulation for middle grade science students supported by the National Science Foundation. The objective of River City is for students to learn 21st century skills, scientific enquiry, hypothesis formation and experimental design conveyed by means of standard-based Ecology and Biology content. River City is a Multi-User Virtual Environment (MUVE) where students gain knowledge through "participatory" historical situations, immersive simulations and virtual museums. The virtual world itself consists of a city that has a river running through it, there are various industries; neighbourhoods, institutions and terrains influencing the course of the water runoff. The students can explore the city encountering digital objects including audio and visual clips, instructor avatars and computer-based agents. Dede, Clarke, Ketelhut, Nelson and Bowman (2005) performed a study regarding motivations and learning in MUVEs to ascertain if a guided social-constructivist model of learning was preferable to students in terms of motivation and acquisition of Biology and inquiry knowledge. The results of the study showed an increase in Biology knowl-

edge in the test group by 32% to 35%, and the control group increased by 17%. Inquiry content improved in the control group by 20% while the guided social constructivist group increased by 18% and the expert modelling and coaching group increased by 16%. Nelson (2007) performed a study using River City to ascertain what volume of guidance was preferable in MUVEs (no guidance, moderate guidance or extensive guidance). The result of this study was the level of advice was ineffective, however there was a knowledge gain. The no guidance group had a gain of 0.14 and the extensive guidance had a gain of 0.13, which was nearly identical to the control group.

Writing and Geography

Quest Atlantis (http://atlantis.crlt.indiana.edu/) is a learning and teaching project designed to immerse children (ages 9–15) in a 3D MUVE while performing educational activities or Quests. Quests are engaging curricular tasks structured to be entertaining as well as educational. Quest Atlantis has four core elements: (1) a 3D MUVE, (2) learning quests and unit plans, (3) a storyline that is centered around a mythical council and set of social commitments presented to the player by a comic book, an introductory video and novella and (4) a community of globally-distributed participants. Quest Atlantis is structured around a set of seven social commitments: compassionate wisdom, creative expression, environmental awareness, personal agency, healthy communities, social responsibility and diversity affirmation. The philosophy of Quest Atlantis is based on incorporating the medium of story in computer game form. The narrative is set around Atlantis, a fictional world run by leaders whose leadership decisions and practices are questionable. The narrative allows the participants to reflect on and share real world experiences to bridge the gap between the virtual experience and the real world experience. Due to the diverse nature of Quest Atlantis it has been used to teach various subjects, two examples are writing (Barab, Warren and Ingram-Goble, 2006) and Geography (Tüzün, Yılmaz-Soylu, Karakuş, İnal & Kızılkaya, 2008).

The empirical evidence associated with Quest Atlantis discovered in the literature review is more qualitative in nature and very little quantitative material was discovered. Lim, Nonis and Hedberg (2006) performed a study involving 4 participants, where the majority of the information collected was qualitative, there was no appropriate form of control used and the study was not sufficiently extensive to draw any generalisable conclusions.

Language Education

Games for language education such as Tactical Iraqi, EverQuest II and Second Life have been discussed in a previous publication (Connolly *et al.,* 2008). This study showed that games have also been used successfully for language learning with positive empirical evidence being collected. The study also formulated the high level objectives for an Alternate Reality Game (ARG) for language learning which was positively evaluated in a large scale pilot across Europe in 2009 (Hainey *et al.,* 2009).

Games in Computing

Connolly, Stansfield and Hainey (2007) performed an extensive literature search specifically looking at games to teach software engineering concepts and their associated empirical evidence from 1996 onwards in the first half of 2006. The search highlighted four reasonably mature games:

- KM Quest in the area of knowledge management (Leemkuil, de Jong, de Hoog and Christoph, 2003; Leemkuil & de Hoog, 2005);
- Open Software Solutions (Sharp and Hall, 2000);
- The Incredible Manager (Dantas, Barros & Werner, 2004, 2005) and

- SimSE (Oh, 2001; Oh Navarro, 2006; Oh Navarro & der Hoek, 2001b, 2004, 2005a, 2005b; Oh Navarro, Baker & Van der Hoek, 2003).

Two further more extensive literature reviews were performed in 2008 and 2009: One focusing on developing an evaluation framework for GBL (Connolly, Stansfield and Hainey, 2009), and another focusing on learning value and skill enhancement of gaming and methods of measuring the resultant outcomes and impacts (Connolly *et al.,* in press). The additional searches highlighted three additional games.

- SimVBSE (Jain & Boehm, 2006);
- RPG-SE (Zhu, Wang & Tan, 2007);
- Antiphising Phil (Sheng *et al.,* 2007).

The seven relatively mature games have been discussed in detail in a previous study (Hainey, 2009). The main findings on the evaluation of the impact of the GBL approach were that empirical evidence supporting GBL is severely limited. There is also a distinct lack of longitudinal studies, which is surprising and worrying, given the fact that .GBL is not a new method of learning. The 2007 study (Connolly, Stansfield & Hainey, 2007) was not looking outside the fields of computer science, software engineering and Information Systems, however the 2008 and 2009 studies were looking at all disciplines and managed to confirm the fact that the lack of longitudinal studies is not isolated to the these fields but is a prominent problem across a much larger proportion of the GBL literature. Although not all disciplines are discussed in this chapter the results of the 2008 literature review will be discussed in chapter 6. This section will provide descriptions of the relevant games relating to computer science, software engineering and Information Systems and will critically review the associated empirical evidence.

Literature Review Summary

The summary of the empirical evidence associated with the games discovered in the literature reviews in the fields of computer science, software engineering and Information Systems is listed in Table 1.

24 studies were identified in the literature search in the fields of computer science, software engineering and Information Systems. 14 (58%) of these studies had no evaluation associated with them. 4 (17%) of the studies performed either a small quantitative or qualitative evaluation with a small number of participants or a small number of questions. 1 study performed a pre-post knowledge test to see if the game improved knowledge, however this was not compared to an appropriate form of control. 1 study evaluated acceptability and usability of a game. 1 study performed a small usability analysis and then a larger analysis, however this was not compared to a method of control and the results indicated that only 7% of the respondents found the software useful. Out of the 24 studies identified, 3(13%) used a larger sample size with an appropriate method of control. 2 of these studies were attempting to assess whether a GBL approach outperformed a traditional approach. The results of this literature search have show that the majority of the studies found in the fields of computer science, software engineering and Information Systems, have no empirical evaluation evidence or have a small evaluation performed. Only a small number of studies (3) used an appropriate form of control with larger samples and no longitudinal studies were discovered.

Advantages and Disadvantages of Games-Based Learning

Advantages

There are a number of advantages and disadvantages cited in the literature for or against the use of computer games for learning. Some of these advantages are related to motivation, the ability of computer games to provide risk free environments, self esteem, versatility, emotional purification and suitability of computer games for learning.

Motivation

Computer games are extremely motivating and engaging because they include features that are extremely compelling, even addictive (Griffiths and Davies, 2002). Malone and Lepper (1987) present a framework of intrinsic motivation in relation to computer games encompassing four individual factors and three interpersonal factors. On an individual level computer games can provide:

- **challenge:** an appropriate level of difficulty and challenge, multiple goals for winning, constant feedback and sufficient randomness;
- **fantasy:** an appropriate level of immersion by assuming a particular role and dealing with related responsibilities;
- **curiosity:** providing sensory stimulation to ensure prolonged participation;
- **and control:** the ability to select choices and observe the consequences of these choices.

On an interpersonal level computer games can provide:

- **cooperation:** Assist others to achieve common goals;
- **competition:** Compare their performance to the performance of other players;
- **recognition:** A sense of satisfaction when accomplishments are recognised.

Garris, Ahlers and Driskell (2002) present six dimensions that computer games can provide for educational purposes that are based on the work

Table 1. Games-based learning empirical evidence in computing science/software engineering/information systems

Authors	Area	Evaluation
Connolly and Stansfield (2007)	Requirements Analysis	No evaluation
Shaw and Dermoudy (2005)	Project management of software development process	Small quantitative evaluation (n = 11).
Wang (2005)	"Cyber War" – a multi-step cyber attack or cyber defense protection	No evaluation
Chua (2005)	Knowledge management	Pre-post test (n = 32); small increase in knowledge, skills and attitude.
Veronese, Barros and Werner (2005)	Framework to support the development of educational games based on simulation models	No evaluation
Waraich (2004)	Teach binary arithmetic and logic gates	Quantitative; pre/post testing (n = 15 control group, n = 22 experimental group). Showed improved performance using games approach.
Ford and Minsker (2003)	Tree traversal techniques and iterative and recursive traversal algorithms.	No evaluation
Martin (2000)	Information Systems Development	No evaluation
Open Software Solutions		
Sharp and Hall (2000)	Interactive multimedia simulation of a software house Open Software Solutions (OSS)	First run: MUMMS usability analysis (n = 31) Second run: questionnaire (n = 354; 36% response). Only 7% thought software useful.
KM Quest		
Leemkuil, de Jong, de Hoog and Christoph (2003)	Knowledge management (KM QUEST)	Evaluated usability, behaviour of players/models and acceptability (n = 41: 18 managers and 23 students). However, no statistics provided.
Leemkuil and de Hoog (2005)	Investigation of effectiveness of several learning support tools in gaming environment (KM QUEST)	Pre-post test analysis (n = 29). Tested importance of advice (n = 15 with advice, n = 14 without advice) rather than any increase in learning brought about by game. The players appreciated the advice functionality, however the effectiveness of the advice was low.
The Incredible Manager		
Dantas, Barros and Werner (2005)	Software Project Management	Small qualitative evaluation (n = 24)
Dantas, Barros and Werner (2004)	Software Project Management	Small (5 questions) survey (n = 15)
SimSE		
Birkhölzer, Oh Navarro and Van der Hoek (2005)	Proposal for students to build a new software process simulation model using SimSE	No evaluation
Oh Navarro and Van der Hoek (2005a)	Describes the different constructs in a SimSE process model	No evaluation
Oh Navarro and Van der Hoek (2005b)		Small (8 questions) questionnaire (n = 29)
Oh Navarro and Van der Hoek (2004)	Describes SimSE, which simulates software engineering processes	No evaluation
Oh Navarro, Baker and Van der Hoek (2003)		No evaluation
Oh and Van der Hoek (2001a)	Discusses basis for economic cost model for software engineering	No evaluation

continued on following page

Table 1. continued

Authors	Area	Evaluation
Oh and Van der Hoek (2001b)	Proposal to develop SimSE	No evaluation
Oh (2001)	Proposal to develop SimSE	No evaluation
SimVBSE		
Jain and Boehm (2006)	Describes the theory behind and the constructs of SimVBSE	No evaluation
RPG-SE		
Zhu, Wang and Tan (2007)	Describes the environment of RPG-SE within Second Life	No evaluation
Anti-Phishing Phil		
Sheng *et al.* (2007)	Describes the development and evaluation of Anti-Phishing Phil – Anti-Phishing techniques	Evaluation with 3 groups (n = 14 in all conditions). Existing materials group, tutorial group and game group. The game group produced greater scores.

of Malone and Lepper (1987). These dimensions are: fantasy - imaginary themes, characters or contexts; rules/goals - clear rules, goals and feedback; sensory stimuli - novel auditory and visual stimuli; challenge - optimal level of difficulty and goal attainment uncertainty; mystery - similar to curiosity providing optimal level of complexity of information; and control - active learner control.

Thiagarajan (1996) suggests five critical characteristics of computer games: conflict - similar to challenge (Malone and Lepper, 1987) and encompasses the attainment of goals in both cooperation and competition with other players or the computer; control - the rules that regulate play; closure - the game has some form of 'end point'; contrivance - the game is not taken too seriously by the players and they are offered motivation to continue; and competency - the players experience growth in their problem solving, skill level and knowledge. Cordova and Lepper (1996) discovered that students learning by traditional methods were outperformed by students learning with instructional games and that control, context, curiosity and challenge increased.

Teachers are always eager to find ideas that will attract and retain the attention of their students and

educationalists have considered whether it might be possible to exploit the absorbing features of computer games and use them to engage students more effectively in learning (Garris, Ahlers & Driskell, 2002).

Risk Free Environment

Computer games can provide risk-free environments (Griffiths 2002; Crookall, Oxford & Saunders, 1987) when consequences are too costly or dangerous in real life (Berson, 1996; Kirriemuir & MacFarlane, 2004; Oh & Van der Hoek, 2005b), for example, in medical education. Kriz (2003) points out that mistakes are normal and expected, and that these mistakes have no consequences within the simulated reality, as it is possible for the player to begin all over again. Thus, computer games can produce "errot-tolerant" learning environments where players learn through trial and error with immediate feedback making it possible for newly acquired abstract knowledge to be used in new domains, stimulating curiosity and increasing experimentation and exploration.

Fripp (1993) emphasises the following advantages of simulations: motivation, teamwork, risk free environments, variety and experiential learning. According to Fontana and Beckerman (2004), with computer games *"students can instruct themselves, repeating simulations as often as they wish without the embarrassment of addressing somewhat sensitive issues."*

Self Esteem

Learners' confidence and interest in a particular topic can be improved (Dempsey, Rasmussen & Lucassen, 1994), possibly as a result of games accommodating different learner types (Becker, 2007) and modes (Haughland & Slade, 1988) such as individualistic, competitive, cooperative and encouraging self-paced learning (Ke, 2006; Ke & Grabowski, 2007; Zaphiris, Ang & Law, 2007).

Versatility

Griffiths (2002) identifies some of the benefits of computer games education. Computer games can be used to measure a very wide variety of tasks, as they are adaptable and easily standardised. They can be used as research tools due to their great diversity. They are appealing to a large number of individuals and can assist children in setting goals by providing feedback, goal rehearsal, and maintaining records of behavioural change. Computer games can be useful when examining individual characteristics such as goal setting, self-esteem, self-concept and individual differences. They can provide elements of interactivity and have the ability to hold an individual's attention for long periods of time. The participants are allowed to experience curiosity, challenge, novelty and fun, possibly stimulating learning. Children can have access to technology that may help overcome technophobia and may assist in the development of transferable IT skills. Players are allowed to engage in "extraordinary" activities as computer games can act as simulations and allow adolescents to regress to childhood as reality is suspended.

Emotional Purification

Catharsis theory indicates that "purification" and purging of negative emotions such as aggression is psychologically positive (Bushman, 2002). This suggests that playing violent computer games may be a useful mechanism for releasing pent-up aggression and diffusing anger (Emes, 1997). Evidence in the GBL literature shows that computer games have been used to prevent violent behaviour and improve attitudes about conflict resolution (Fontana & Beckerman, 2004).

Suitability of Computer Games for Learning

Connolly, Stansfield, McLellan, Ramsay and Sutherland (2004) suggest that computer games should build on theories of motivation, constructivism, situated learning, cognitive apprenticeship, problem-based learning, and learning by doing. By creating virtual worlds, computer games integrate *"…not just knowing and doing. Games bring together ways of knowing, ways of doing, ways of being, and ways of caring: the situated understandings, effective social practices, powerful identities, and shared values that make someone an expert"* (Shaffer, Squire, Halverson & Gee, 2004). Games and simulations fit well into the constructivist paradigm and "generally advocate the active acquisition of knowledge and skills, collaboration and the use of authentic and realistic case material" (Christoph, Sandberg & Wielinga, 2003). The use of computer games can be linked to the display of "expert" behaviours such as: superior long and short-term memory, pattern recognition, qualitative thinking, pattern recognition, principled decision-making and self-monitoring (Van Deventer & White, 2002).

O'Neil, Wainess and Baker (2005) highlight that computer games are perceived as useful for instructional purposes and are *"hypothesised to provide multiple benefits: (a) complex and diverse approaches to learning processes and outcomes;*

(b) interactivity; (c) ability to address cognitive as well as affective learning issues, and perhaps most importantly, (d) motivation for learning." Gee (2003) identifies thirty-six different learning principles as to why games are good for learning. Some of these learning principles are:

- **identity:** how a game immerses and captures the player,
- **interaction:** appropriate feedback providing additional problems based on the players decisions,
- **production:** the players seeing the decisions they make as helping to "write" the world, possibly leading to prolonged participation,
- **risk taking:** decrease the consequences of failure allowing the player to experience a minimal of real world consequences or no consequences at all,
- **customisation:** players are allowed to customise their own desired attributes such as character customisation or difficulty setting, agency - the player has a sense of ownership over what they are doing.

Disadvantages

The negative aspects associated with computer games in the *"empirical"* literature nearly *"always involve people who were excessive users"* of computer games (Griffiths, 2002). Connolly and Stansfield (2007) point out that the majority of the disadvantages cited in the literature revolve around the *"long-term effects of violence on game players, however there is no consensus on this"*. Some of the disadvantages cited in the GBL literature are focused on the lack of empirical evidence, destructive behaviour such as violent aggressive behaviour and attitudes, logistics, costs disagreements and misconceptions.

Lack of Empirical Evidence

The primary disadvantage that is being discussed in this chapter is that there is a dearth of empirical evidence supporting GBL (Connolly, Stansfield & Hainey, 2007; de Freitas, 2006; Bredemeier & Greenblatt, 1981; Druckman, 1995). There is a distinct lack of longitudinal studies and a lack of evaluation frameworks (O'Neil, Wainess & Baker, 2005). Squire (2002) states *"the pedagogical potential of games and social contexts of gaming have been woefully unexamined"* and points out that previously performed reviews of games and learning have not highlighted any large benefit associated with the use of a GBL approach. Leemkuil (2005) points out that there are very few studies comparing the effectiveness of computer games to other forms of instruction such as role-playing, paper-based case-studies, lectures, tutorials and labs etc.

de Freitas and Oliver (2006) point out that earlier studies investigated in (de Freitas, 2004) of computer games in education found that more specialised methods of evaluation are necessary for educational computer games and there has been no distinction drawn between educational games and leisure time games meaning that educational game evaluation has typically rested on leisure-based games. Griffiths (2002) identifies some of the disadvantages of the application of computer games in education as: computer games can cause participants to become over enthusiastic during play resulting in the production of a wide array of confounding variables associated with individual skill and motivation. In terms of evaluation, it is highly difficult to assess educational impact across studies due to the rapid advancement of computer game technology. Results may be skewed when evaluating particular GBL interventions as the participants practice and experience may enhance performance on particular games. Shaffer, Squire, Halverson and Gee (2004) point out that most educational computer games have been developed with no underlying body of research or coherent learning theory. Virvou, Katsionis and Manos (2005) point out that *"the marriage of education and game-like entertainment has produced some not-very-educational games and some not very-entertaining learning activities."*

Destructive Behaviour and Attitudes

Provenzo (1991, 1992) claims that computer games: "(a) can lead to violent, aggressive behaviour (Emes, 1997); (b) employ destructive gender stereotyping; (c) promote unhealthy 'rugged individualist' attitudes and (d) stifle creative play" (as cited in Squire, 2003). Other negative aspects of gaming that researchers emphasise include gaming addiction (Griffiths & Hunt, 1998); poor sleep patterns (Higuchi, Motohashi, Liu & Maeda, 2005); obesity (Vandewater, Shim & Caplovitz, 2004); the prevalence in computer games of violent imagery (Smith, Lachlan and Tamborini, 2003); and problematic cultural ideologies (Gottschalk, 1995). Rosas *et al.* (2003) highlights that the most commonly studied negative effects of computer games are: aggression, gender bias and an immersion effect causing an alienation effect resulting in an 'electronic autism' which hinders academic and social development.

Logistics, Costs Disagreements and Misconceptions

Prensky (2001) identifies some of the disadvantages of computer games in education associated with logistics, high cost and disagreements and misconceptions about the place of games and fun in learning. Logistically, educational computer game environments require distribution, installation and support. Software installed must be compatible with hardware and software that is already present in the organisation or educational setting (Foreman, 2004). Rosas *et al.* (2003) also highlights some of the issues associated with implementation in a school system as: coverage

(which is particularly problematic in developing countries), teachers resistance towards the technology-centered learning approach and complexities associated with edutainment in terms of being entertaining but still lacking those attractive attributes for children since the primary focus is the pedagogical activity. Development of a fully interactive, engaging, immersive GBL environment can be very costly and time consuming requiring planning, design and implementation. This also means that only certain organisations are able to afford a GBL application and it may prove difficult to implement in institutions with limited resources. There are organisations that specifically develop GBL applications for other organisations; however this is not an inexpensive process in itself. The process requires an entire team of developers consisting of graphics designers, programmers, and scriptwriters etc. There is still resistance to the incorporation of GBL into training or education, as "traditionalists" believe that learning is serious and the introduction of fun will mean that learning is no longer engaging or taken seriously, hence reducing retention.

SUMMARY OF EMPIRICAL REVIEW OF GAMES IN EDUCATION

This literature review has attempted to explore the place of GBL and serious games in relation to games and simulations. The two primary purposes of the literature review were: firstly, show the diversity of the application of GBL in a number of different areas and secondly to provide a critical review of the empirical evidence associated with the reviewed computer games but with an emphasis on empirical evaluation of computer games used in the education of computer science, software engineering and Information Systems. The advantages and disadvantages of GBL were then summarised from the literature review. The main findings of the review are as follows:

- GBL environments have been used in a wide variety of subjects suggesting that it is a highly adaptable form of learning with many different potential applications that have not yet been fully explored and validated.
- There is a dearth of empirical evidence in the fields of computer science, software engineering and Information Systems to support the use of GBL. The additional literature reviews performed in 2008 and 2009 have identified three additional games and no significant improvement to the state of empirical evidence, as rigorous evaluations of current mature games have not been carried out. There still remains an absence of longitudinal studies.
- The problem of the dearth of empirical evidence is not isolated specifically to computing science, software engineering and Information Systems, and it is in fact a problem in all the areas encountered in the literature review.
- With the exception of a few examples in the literature, the majority of which are located, in unpublished doctoral dissertations, when evaluation is carried out it is not necessarily attempting to address the question of "does the GBL condition provide a better platform for learning than traditional methods of teaching?" The evaluation may have been carried out to assess issues such as aspects of usability, acceptability, attitudes toward computer games, attitudes to the taught subject and technical aspects of the software.
- Empirical evidence is not restricted to electronic databases and can be located at websites for particular games, for example three unpublished doctoral dissertations containing a large amount of empirical evidence have been retrieved from websites. Two of these doctoral dissertations concern KMQuest (Leemkuil, 2005; Christoph,

2007) and one concerns Zombie Division (Habgood, 2007).

REFERENCES

Adamo-Villani, N., & Wright, K. (2007). SMILE: An immersive learning game for deaf and hearing children. In *ACM Proceedings of SIGGRAPH 2007*- Educators, 5-10 August 2007, San Diego, ACM Digital Library. New York: ACM Publications.

Baker, A., Oh Navarro, E., & Van der Hoek, A. (2003). Problems and programmers: An educational software engineering card game. In *Proceedings of the 25th International Conference on Software Engineering*.

Baker, S. J., Hadgood, J., Ainsworth, S. E., & Corbett, A. T. (2007). Modeling the acquisition of fluent skill in educational action games. In *Proceedings of User Modeling*, (pp. 17-26).

Barab, S., Warren, S., & Ingram-Goble, A. (2006). *Academic play space: Designing games for education*. Paper presented at the meeting of the American Educational Research Association, April 2006, San Francisco, CA.

Beale, I. L., Kato, P. M., Marin-Bowling, V. M., Guthrie, N., & Cole, S. W. (2007). Improvement in cancer-related knowledge following use of a psychoeducational video game for adolescents and young adults with cancer. *The Journal of Adolescent Health, 41*, 263–270.

Becker, K. (2007). Pedagogy in commercial video games. In Gibson, D., Aldrich, C., & Prensky, M. (Eds.), *Games and simulations in online learning: Research and development frameworks*. INFOSCI Information Science Publishing.

Berson, M. J. (1996). Effectiveness of computer technology in the social studies: A review of the literature. *Journal of Research on Computing in Education, 28*(4), 486–499.

Birkhölzer, T., Oh Navarro, E., & Van der Hoek, A. (2005). Teaching by modeling instead of by models. In *Proceedings of the 6th International Workshop on Software Process Simulation and Modeling, St. Louis, MO, May 2005*.

Bredemeier, M. E., & Greenblatt, C. E. (1981). The educational effectiveness of games: A synthesis of findings. *Simulation & Gaming, 12*(3), 307–332.

Bushman, B. J. (2002). Does venting anger feed or extinguish the flame? Catharsis, rumination, distraction, anger, and aggressive responding. *Personality and Social Psychology Bulletin, 28*, 724–731.

Caillois, R. (1961). *Man, play, and games*. New York: Schocken Books.

Christoph, N. (2007). *The role of metacognitive skills in learning to solve problems.* Unpublished doctoral thesis, the University of Amsterdam. Retrieved 28th November, 2007 from http://dare.uva.nl/document/22568

Christoph, N., Sandberg, J., & Wielinga, B. (2003). *Added value of task models and use of metacognitive skills on learning.* Retrieved December 10, 2008, http://www.cs.ubc.ca/~conati/aied-games/christophetal.pdf

Chua, A. Y. K. (2005). The design and implementation of a simulation game for teaching knowledge management. *Journal of the American Society for Information Science and Technology, 56*(11), 120–1216.

Connolly, T.M., Boyle, E., MacArthur, E., Hainey, T., Hancock, F., & Boyle, J. (In press). *A literature review of research conducted on the learning value and skill enhancement of gaming and methods of measuring the resultant outcomes and impacts.*

Connolly, T.M. & Stansfield, M.H. (2007). From e-learning to games-based e-learning: Using interactive technologies in teaching an IS course. *International Journal of Information Technology Management*.

Connolly, T. M., Stansfield, M. H., & Hainey, T. (2007). An application of games-based learning within software engineering. *British Journal of Educational Technology, 38*(3), 416–428.

Connolly, T. M., Stansfield, M. H., & Hainey, T. (2009). Towards the development of a games-based learning evaluation framework. In Connolly, T. M., Stansfield, M. H., & Boyle, E. (Eds.), *Games-based learning advancement for multi-sensory human computer interfaces: Techniques and effective practices.* Hershey, PA: Idea-Group Publishing.

Connolly, T. M., Stansfield, M. H., Hainey, T., Josephson, J., Lázaro, N., Rubio, G., et al. (2008). Arguing for multilingual motivation in Web 2.0: Using alternate reality games to support language learning. In *Proceedings of the 2nd European Conference on Gamesbased Learning (ECGBL)*, 16-17 October 2008, Barcelona, Spain.

Connolly, T. M., Stansfield, M. H., McLellan, E., Ramsay, J., & Sutherland, J. (2004). Applying computer games concepts to teaching database analysis and design. In *Proceedings of the International Conference on Computer Games, AI, Design and Education*, Reading, UK, November 2004.

Cordova, D. I., & Lepper, M. R. (1996). Intrinsic motivation and the process of learning: Beneficial effects of contextualization, personalization, and choice. *Journal of Educational Psychology, 88*(4), 715–730.

Corti, K. (2006). *Games-based learning: A serious business application.* PIXELearning Limited. Retrieved 29 November, 2009, from www.pixelearning.com/docs/games_basedlearning_pixelearning.pdf

Crawford, C. (2003). *Chris Crawford on game design.* New Riders Publishing.

Crookall, D., Oxford, R. & Saunders, D. (1987). Towards a reconceptualization of simulation: From representation to reality. *Simulation/Games for Learning, 17*(4), 147-171.

Crookall, D., & Saunders, D. (1989). Toward an integration of communication and simulation. In Crookall, D., & Saunders, D. (Eds.), *Communication and simulation: From two fields to one of them.* Clevedon, UK: Multilingual Matters.

Dantas, A. R., Barros, M. O., & Werner, C. (2004). A simulation-based game for project management experiential learning. In *Proceedings of the Sixteenth International Conference on Software Engineering and Knowledge Engineering (SEKE'04)*, Alberta, Canada, June 2004, 19-24.

Dantas, A. R., Barros, M. O., & Werner, C. (2005). *Simulation models applied to game-based training for software project managers.* Process Simulation and Modeling Workshop (ProSim), St Louis, USA, May 2005, 110-116.

de Freitas, S. (2004). *Learning through play. Internal report.* London Learning and Skills Research Centre.

de Freitas, S. (2006). *Learning in immersive worlds.* Joint Information Systems Committee.

de Freitas, S., & Oliver, M. (2006). How can exploratory learning with games and simulations within the curriculum be most effectively evaluated. *Computers & Education, 46*(3), 249–264.

Dede, C., Clarke, J., Ketelhut, D. J., Nelson, B., & Bowman, C. (2005). *Students' motivation and learning of science in a multi-user virtual environment.* Paper presented at the meeting of the American Educational Research Association, Montréal, Quebec.

Dempsey, J. V., Haynes, L. L., Lucassen, B. A., & Casey, M. S. (2002). Forty simple computer games and what they could mean to educators. *Simulation & Gaming, 33*(2), 157–168.

Dempsey, J. V., Rasmussen, K., & Lucassen, B. (1994). *Instructional gaming: Implications for instructional technology.* Annual Meeting of the Association for Educational Communications and Technology, 16–20 February 1994, Nashville, TN.

Druckman, D. (1995). The educational effectiveness of interactive games. In Crookall, D., & Arai, K. (Eds.), *Simulation and gaming across disciplines and cultures: ISAGA at a watershed* (pp. 178–187). Thousand Oaks, CA: Sage.

Emes, C. E. (1997). Is Mr. Pac-Man eating our children? A review of the impact of video games on children. *Canadian Journal of Psychiatry, 42*(4), 409–414.

Fontana, L., & Beckerman, A. (2004). Childhood violence prevention education using video games. *Information Technology in Childhood Education Annual*, 49–62.

Ford, C. W., & Minsker, S. (2003). TREEZ-an educational data structures game. *Journal of Computing Sciences in Colleges, 18*(6), 180–185.

Foreman, J. (2004). Game-based learning: How to delight and instruct in the 21st century. *EDUCAUSE Review, 39*(5), 50–66.

Fripp, J. (1993). *Learning through simulations.* London: McGraw-Hill.

Garris, R., Ahlers, R., & Driskell, J. E. (2002). Games, motivation, and learning: A research and practice model. *Simulation & Gaming, 33*(4), 441–467.

Gee, J. P. (2003). *What video games have to teach us about learning and literacy.* New York: Palgrave/St. Martin's.

Gottschalk, S. (1995). Videology-video-games as postmodern sites, sights of ideological reproduction. *Symbolic Interaction, 1*(1), 1–18.

Grendler, M. E. (1996). Educational games and simulations: A technology in search of a research paradigm. In Jonassen, D. H. (Ed.), *Handbook of research for educational communications and technology* (pp. 521–540). New York: Simon & Schuster, Macmillan.

Griffiths, M., & Hunt, N. (1998). Dependence on computer games by adolescents. *Psychological Reports, 82*(2), 475–480.

Griffiths, M.D. (2002). The educational benefits of videogames. *Education and Health, 20*(3).

Griffiths, M. D., & Davies, M. N. O. (2002). Excessive online computer gaming: Implications for education. *Journal of Computer Assisted Learning, 18*, 379–380.

Habgood, M. P. J. (2007). *The effective integration of digital games and learning content.* Unpublished doctoral dissertation, the University of Nottingham. Retrieved 27th October, 2008, from http://zombiedivision.co.uk/

Hainey, T. (2009). Games-based learning in computer science, software engineering and Information Systems. *Computing and Information Systems, 13*(3).

Hainey, T., Connolly, T. M., Stansfield, M. H., Boyle, L., Josephson, J., O'Donovan, A., et al. (2009). Arguing for multilingual motivation in Web 2.0: An evaluation of a large-scale European pilot. In *Proceedings of the 3rd European Conference on Games-based Learning (ECGBL)*, October 2009, Graz, Austria.

Haughland, S. W., & Slade, D. D. (1988). Developmentally appropriate software for young children. *Young Children, 43*(4), 37–43.

Hays, R. T. (2005). The effectiveness of instructional games: A literature review and discussion. Retrieved September 6, 2009, from http://adlcommunity.net/file.php/36/GrooveFiles/Instr_Game_Review_Tr_2005.pdf

Heinich, R., Molenda, M., Russell, J. D., & Smoldino, S. E. (1996). *Instructional media and technologies for learning* (6th ed.). Upper Saddle River, NJ: Merrill.

Jain, A., & Boehm, B. (2006). SimVBSE: Developing a game for value-based software engineering. In *Proceedings of 19th Conference on Software Engineering Education and Training (CSEET).* Turtle Bay Resort, Oahu, Hawaii. 103–114.

Juul, J. (2003). The game, the player, the world: Looking for a heart of gameness. In Copier, M., & Raessens, J. (Eds.), *Proceedings of Level-Up: Digital games research Conference* (pp. 30–45). University of Utrecht.

Kato, P. M., & Beale, I. L. (2006). Factors affecting acceptability to young cancer patients of a psychoeducational video game about cancer. *Journal of Pediatric Oncology Nursing, 23*(5), 269–275.

Ke, F. (2006). Classroom goal structures for educational math game application. In *Proceedings of the 7th International Conference on Learning Sciences ICLS '06.* International Society of Learning Sciences.

Ke, F., & Grabowski, B. (2007). Gameplaying for maths learning: Cooperative or not? *British Journal of Educational Technology, 38*(2), 249–259.

Kirriemuir, J., & McFarlane, A. (2004). *Literature review in games and learning.* Bristol: NESTA Futurelab.

Kriz, W. C. (2003). Creating effective learning environments and learning organizations through gaming simulation design. *Simulation & Gaming, 34*(4), 495–511.

Laurillard, D. (2002). *Rethinking university teaching: A conversational framework for the effective use of learning technologies.* London: Routhledge Falmer.

Leemkuil, H. (2005). *Is it all in the game? Learner support in an educational knowledge management simulation game.* Unpublished doctoral thesis, University of Twente, Enschede, The Netherlands.

Leemkuil, H., & de Hoog, R. (2005). Is support really necessary within educational games? In Conati, C., & Ramachandran, S. (Eds.), *Educational games as intelligent learning environments* (pp. 21–31). Amsterdam.

Leemkuil, H., de Jong, T., de Hoog, R., & Christoph, N. (2003). KM QUEST: A collaborative Internet-based simulation game. *Simulation & Gaming, 34*(1), 89–111.

Lennon, J. L. (2006). Debriefings of Web-based malaria games. *Simulation & Gaming, 37*(3), 350–356.

Lim, C. P., Nonis, D., & Hedberg, J. (2006). Gaming in a 3D multi-user virtual environment: Engaging students in Science lessons. *British Journal of Educational Technology, 37*(2).

Malone, T. W., & Lepper, M. R. (1987). Making learning fun: A taxonomy of intrinsic motivations for learning. Aptitude, learning and instruction: *Vol. 3. Co-native and affective process analysis* (pp. 223–253). Hillsdale, N.J: Lawrence Erlbaum.

Martin, A. (2000). The design and evolution of a simulation/game for teaching Information Systems development. *Simulation & Gaming, 31*(4).

McLeod, J. (1986). Computer modelling and simulation: The changing challenge. *Simulation,* 114–118.

Nelson, B. C. (2007). Exploring the use of individualized reflective guidance in an educational multiuser virtual environment. *Journal of Science Education and Technology, 16,* 83–97.

O'Neil, H. F., Wainess, R., & Baker, E. L. (2005). Classification of learning outcomes: Evidence from the computer games literature. *Curriculum Journal, 16*(4).

Oh, E. (2001). Teaching software engineering through simulation. In *Proceedings of the 2001 Workshop on Education and Training (WET), Santa Barbara, CA, July 2001.*

Oh, E., & Van der Hoek, A. (2001a). Challenges in using an economic cost model for software engineering simulation. *Projects & Profits, 4*(8), 43–50.

Oh, E., & Van der Hoek, A. (2001b). Adapting game technology to support individual and organizational learning. In *Proceedings of the 13th International Conference on Software Engineering and Knowledge Engineering, Buenos Aires, Argentina, June 2001.*

Oh Navarro, E. (2006). *SimSE: A software engineering simulation environment for software process education* Unpublished doctoral thesis, University of California, Irvine.

Oh Navarro, E., Baker, A., & Van der Hoek, A. (2003). Teaching software engineering using simulation games. In *Proceedings of the 2004 International Conference on Simulation in Education, San Diego, California, January 2003.*

Oh Navarro, E., & Van der Hoek, A. (2004). SimSE: An interactive simulation game for software engineering education. In *Proceedings of the 7th IASTED International Conference on Computers and Advanced Technology in Education, Kauai, Hawaii, August 2004.*

Oh Navarro, E. & Van der Hoek, A. (2005a). Software process modeling for an educational software engineering simulation game. *Software Process Improvement and Practice.*

Oh Navarro, E., & Van der Hoek, A. (2005b). Design and evaluation of an educational software process simulation environment and associated model. In *Proceedings of the Eighteenth Conference on Software Engineering Education and Training,* Ottawa, Canada, April, 2005.

Prensky, M. (2001). *Digital games-based learning.* New York: McGraw-Hill.

Pritsker, A. A. B. (1979). Compilation of definitions of simulation. *Simulation, 33*(2), 61–63.

Provenzo, E. F. (1991). *Video kids: Making sense of Nintendo.* Cambridge, MA: Harvard.

Provenzo, E. F. (1992). What do video games teach? *Education Digest, 58*(4), 56–58.

Randel, J. M., Morris, B. A., Wetzel, C. D., & Whitehill, B. V. (1992). The effectiveness of games for educational purposes: A review of research. *Simulation & Gaming, 23*(3), 261–276.

Rosas, R., Nussbaum, M., Cumsille, P., Marianov, V., Correa, M., & Flores, P. (2003). Beyond Nintendo: Design and assessment of educational video games for first and second grade students. *Computers & Education, 40,* 71–94.

Roubidoux, M. A. (2005). Breast cancer detective: A computer game to teach breast cancer screening to Native American patients. *Journal of Cancer Education, 20*(1), 87–91.

Roubidoux, M. A., Chapman, C. M., & Piontek, M. E. (2002). Development and evaluation of an interactive Web-based breast imaging game for medical students. *Academic Radiology, 9*(10), 1169–1178.

Sawyer, B., & Smith, P. (2008). *Serious games taxonomy.* Retrieved 26 March, 2008, from http://www.dmill.com/presentations/seriousgames-taxonomy-2008.pdf

Schneider, M., Carley, K., & Moon, I. (2005). *Detailed comparison of America's Army game and unit of action experiments.* Carnegie Mellon University, School of Computer Science, Institute for Software Research International, (Technical Report CMU-ISRI-05-139).

Shaffer, D. W., Squire, K. T., Halverson, R., & Gee, J. P. (2004). *Video games and the future of learning.* Phi Delta Kappa. Retrieved 6th December, 2008 from http://www.academiccolab.org/resources/gappspaper1.pdf

Sharp, H., & Hall, P. (2000). An interactive multimedia software house simulation for postgraduate software engineers. In *Proceedings of the 22nd International Conference on Software Engineering.* Limerick, Ireland.

Shaw, K., & Dermoudy, J. (2005). Engendering an empathy for software engineering. In *Proceedings of the 7th Australasian Computing Education Conference (ACE2005),* Newcastle, Australia, *42,* 135–144.

Sheng, S., Magnien, B., Kumaragurg, P., Acquisiti, A., Cranor, L. F., Hong, J., et al. (2007). Anti-phishing Phil: The design and evaluation of a game that teaches people not to fall for phish. In *Proceedings of the 3rd Symposium on Usable Privacy and Security SOUPS '07.* ACM Press.

Smed, J. & Hakonen, H. (2003). *Towards a definition of a computer game.* Turku Centre for Computer Science TUCS, (Technical Report No 553).

Smith, S. L., Lachlan, K., & Tamborini, R. (2003). Popular video games: Quantifying the presentation of violence and its context. *Journal of Broadcasting & Electronic Media, 47*(1), 58–76.

Squire, K. (2002). Cultural framing of computer/video games. *Game Studies, 2*(1). Retrieved 22nd December, 2008 from http://www.gamestudies.org/0102/squire/.

Squire, K. (2003). Video games in education. *International Journal of Intelligent Simulations and Gaming, 2*(1), 49–62.

Squire, K., Barnett, B., Grant, J. M., & Higginbotham, T. (2004). Electromagnetism supercharged! Learning physics with digital simulation games. In. *Proceedings of the International Conference on Learning Sciences, 6,* 513–520.

Steinman, R. A., & Blastos, M. T. (2002). A trading-card game teaching about host defense. *Medical Education, 36,* 1201–1208.

Tang, S., Hanneghan, M., & El Rhalibi, A. (2009). Introduction to games-based learning. In Connolly, T. M., Stansfield, M. H., & Boyle, E. (Eds.), *Games-based learning advancement for multisensory human computer interfaces: Techniques and effective practices*. Hershey, PA: Idea-Group Publishing.

Thavikulwat, P. (1999). Developing computerized business gaming simulations. [Sage Publications, Inc.]. *Simulation & Gaming, 30*(3), 361–366.

Thiagarajan, S. (1996). Instructional games, simulations, and role-plays. In Craig, R. L. (Ed.), *The ASTD training & development handbook* (pp. 517–533). New York: McGraw-Hill.

Tüzün, H., Yilmaz-Soylu, M., Karakuş, T., İnal, Y., & Kizilkaya, G. (2008). *The effects of computer games on primary school students' achievements and motivation in geography learning*. Paper presented at the meeting of the American Educational Research Association, New York.

Van Deventer, S. S., & White, J. A. (2002). Expert behaviour in children's video game play. *Simulation & Gaming, 33*(1), 28–48.

Vandewater, E. A., Shim, M. S., & Caplovitz, A. G. (2004). Linking obesity and activity level with children's television and video game use. *Journal of Adolescence, 27*(1), 71–85.

Veronese, G., Barros, M., & Werner, C. (2005). *Model support for simulation-based training games: From behavioral modeling to user interactions*. In Software Process Simulation and Modeling Workshop (ProSim), St Louis, USA, May 2005, 9-15.

Virtual, U. (2009). *Virtual U*. Retrieved November 28, 2009, from http://www.virtual-u.org/

Virvou, M., Katsionis, G., & Manos, K. (2005). Combining software games with education: Evaluation of its educational effectiveness. *Journal of Educational Technology & Society, 8*(2), 64–65.

Wang, A. (2005). Web-based interactive courseware for information security. In *Proceedings of the 6th Conference on Information Technology Education SIGITE '05*.

Waraich, A. (2004). Using narrative as a motivating device to teach binary arithmetic and logic gates. In *Proceedings of the 9th annual SIGCSE Conference on Innovation and Technology in Computer Science Education*. (pp. 97–101). Leeds, UK.

Zaphiris, P., Ang, C.S. & Law, D. (2007). Individualistic vs. competitive game-based e-learning. *Advanced Technology for Learning, 4*(4).

Zhu, Q., Wang, T., & Tan, S. (2007). Adapting game technology to support software engineering process teaching: From SimSE to Mo-SEProcess. In *Proceedings of Third International Conference on Natural Computation (ICNC)*, (pp. 777–780).

Zyda, M. (2005). From visual simulation to virtual reality to games. *IEEE Computer Society Press, 38*, 25–32.

Chapter 3
European Schoolnet[1]'s Games in Schools Study:
The Current State of Play in European Schools and the Game Ahead

Caroline Kearney
European Schoolnet, Belgium

ABSTRACT

This chapter summarizes the main results of the comparative study, How are digital games used in schools? (European Schoolnet, April 2009), representing the most recent and comprehensive attempt to understand the current situation regarding games-based learning in schools across Europe. The study's various elements are described, including: a literature review, teachers' survey, case studies, and interviews with educational policy makers and experts. It concludes that some teachers do indeed use digital games (educational as well as commercial) in schools regardless of their gender, age, number of years in the profession, familiarity with games, age of their pupils, or the subject they teach. However, the use of games-based learning in schools across Europe remains limited. The study sheds some interesting light on the facilitators and barriers to using digital games in the classroom, the necessary conditions for their successful integration into the school context, and the role of the teacher. Recommendations for the education sector and industry are put forward, and new projects at European level aimed at further integrating games-based learning in schools are documented.

INTRODUCTION

Why investigate the learning potential of digital games? Considering their increased popularity as a leisure activity amongst young people, and the skills, knowledge and values young people inevitably assimilate through gaming, it is time education systems seriously reflected on their educational potential. In a digital age many have professed the need to transform education to make it more relevant to students' needs and those of the

DOI: 10.4018/978-1-60960-495-0.ch003

labour market. Equipping schools with information and communication technologies (ICT) and training teachers to use them has been a starting point for the modernization of pedagogical processes, however it has certainly not been sufficient. We now know from the latest educational and psychological research that learner empowerment, personalized learning, trans-disciplinary approaches and meta-cognitive development are very important for successful learning. These criteria are not automatically guaranteed simply by providing schools with ICT. New ICT tools, such as digital games, need to be understood and used in an informed and conscious way in order to have the potential to produce good results. The study described in this chapter, *How are digital games used in schools?* (European Schoolnet, April 2009), investigated whether digital games, if used in the right way, do have the potential to contribute to successful learning.

This chapter summarizes the main results of the study which represents the most recent attempt at European level to better understand in what ways and to what extent digital games could contribute to improving teaching and learning in schools. The study is a good starting point in an area that has seen an increasing amount of research on the learning benefits of digital games, but far less reporting and monitoring of how they are actually being used in educational settings. In this context the study provides a valuable pool of evidence which can be built on to better understand the facilitators and barriers of integrating digital games in schools.

European Schoolnet is active in this area, having previously been a partner in a project called *eMapps.com*[3], which focused on games and mobile technology in formal and informal learning contexts. It is also currently involved as a partner in new projects related to games-based learning, described in the final section of this chapter. The current study in question was perceived as a chance to deepen the knowledge arising from these projects, and to obtain answers to the following questions: why do teachers use

digital games in their lessons?; how do they do this?; what pedagogical objectives do they aim at?; what is the impact on their pupils' learning?; what approach do European education systems currently use with regards games-based learning, and is there potential for collaboration between the education sector and the games industry? The study approaches these specific questions within a larger framework of reflection on the major challenges education faces today. Namely; at a time when students have never felt more disaffected, demotivated and alien to the education system, and the latest research in the cognitive sciences tell us that traditional teaching methods are not the most effective for learning, can digital games offer a partial solution? Can they contribute to the learning of key skills which education systems across Europe are increasingly prioritizing above the acquisition of knowledge? All these questions were considered objectively, without any preconceptions for or against the use of digital games as learning tools.

The study comprised of several elements: a preliminary literature review of the academic research in this area, a teachers' survey, case studies, interviews with educational policy makers and experts, an online community of practice, and a handbook for teachers. This mixed methodology using quantitative but mostly qualitative approaches was considered most appropriate to get a comprehensive as possible first overview of the situation at European level. Eight countries were targeted in particular, in order to get enough in-depth information to provide thorough analysis. These countries included: Austria, Denmark, France, Italy, Lithuania, the Netherlands, Spain (Catalonia), and the United Kingdom. The selection was made with the intention of covering a range of situations, including countries where games-based learning is known to be taking place in schools, and other countries where this is rare, so as to better understand the facilitators and barriers. To facilitate the study's organization of information gathering, a national coordinator from each focus country was selected on the basis of being in a good position to carry out the following tasks: promote the teachers' survey at national level, identify an interesting case study from their country, provide information and organize interviews with policy makers and experts to contribute to the analysis of the national context in this area, and promote and contribute to the study's community of practice for teachers and other stakeholders. Because this study was undertaken with the aim of giving a first overview of the situation regarding games-based learning across Europe, it was considered important to keep the definition of 'digital games' as open as possible, in order to be inclusive of all the practices currently going on in this area. Digital games were therefore defined in a broad sense, covering video games and online games, games that run on consoles, computers or mobile phones, whether they be adventure games, role plays, strategy games, simulations, racing games or puzzles.

This chapter is divided into the following sections devoted to the main elements of the study: the literature review, the teachers' survey, the case studies, the approaches of education systems, and recommendations for policy makers and games producers. While the study's main objective was simply to establish the status quo in eight European countries, the results nevertheless shed some interesting light on the facilitators and barriers to using digital games in the classroom, the necessary conditions for their successful integration into the school context, and the role of the teacher.

LITERATURE REVIEW

The first step of the study was to produce a review to summarize the available literature in the area of games-based learning, and specifically analyse how it relates to teaching in the classroom. It was produced by Maja Pivec, Professor of Games-based Learning and e-Learning at the

University of Applied Sciences FH Joanneum in Austria, together with Paul Pivec. The literature review concluded that digital games can be a supportive pedagogical tool in the classroom, given the right environment, the correct choice of game and the central role of the teacher for moderation and debriefing purposes. The review highlighted that digital games are only one of many useful tools, and can be used to supplement traditional teaching and learning methods, but not replace them. Teachers currently do not have sufficient knowledge or skills required to successfully incorporate games-based learning into their lessons. Teacher support in this area is therefore an issue which needs to be addressed on a wide scale, if games-based learning is to be integrated into the curriculum of schools across Europe.

The examples of games-based learning highlighted in the literature review illustrate that when a digital game is used in the classroom for research purposes, it is often an educational game developed by a researcher specifically for the purposes of the experiment. When on the other hand a game is used by a teacher as part of a lesson, it is often a commercial off-the-shelf (COTS) game, which is sometimes modified to match a certain desired learning outcome. The review points out that because digital games can easily be used outside of the classroom, they provide an ideal platform for study aids to be used at home and to assist students with learning difficulties. The review concludes that despite digital games being in existence for roughly 40 years and research into their learning potential enjoying a tradition of over 20 years, the uptake of games-based learning in schools has been slow. The main reason for this is the lack of teacher support, in terms of resources and training in this area, without which digital games will remain an untapped resource in schools. The lack of time available to teachers to adapt digital games for curriculum use, and the lack of adequate technology in schools were also identified as barriers. Other issues to be addressed

Figure 1. (Wastiau, P., Kearney, C., & Van den Berghe W. (Final Report, 2009), pp. 64)

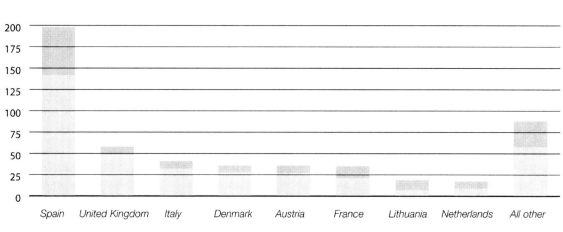

Distribution of respondents by country and use of games at school

Use of games at school   No use of games at school

include technical requirements, licensing policies and sustainability.

THE TEACHERS' SURVEY

A survey for teachers was made available online in 9 languages (English, French, German, Spanish, Italian, Danish, Dutch, Lithuanian and Estonian[4]) between October 2008 and February 2009, to identify and explain the opinions and practices of both teachers who do and do not use digital games in their teaching. The survey was announced at the European level through European Schoolnet's websites and newsletters, which reach teachers interested or involved in using ICT and/or European projects. The study's 8 focus countries also publicized the survey through national channels, usually connected to the ICT departments in ministries of education and/or agencies responsible for education at national or regional level. No type of school (whether public or private, or providers of general or vocational education etc.) were particularly targeted or excluded. In all countries, the survey was answered on a voluntary basis.

Context and Profile of Respondents

The survey aimed to investigate how teachers use digital games for pedagogical purposes, including the type of games they use, the subject learning and skills they are used to develop, the objectives they are intended to meet, and the category of learners they are targeted at. Teachers were asked about the impact they considered the use of digital games to have had on their pupils' motivation and learning, and other aspects of the pedagogical process. Attention was also given to identifying the various obstacles faced by teachers who use and do not use digital games in the classroom. A total of 528 responses were collected from 27 European countries. The majority of responses were collected from the study's 8 focus countries, in addition to 88 responses from other countries[5].

The questionnaire consisted mainly of closed questions, where respondents were asked to select one or more answers from a list, in addition to some open questions, allowing the respondent to express his/her opinion freely. A frequency distribution of the answers to all closed questions was calculated, and in a number of cases the re-

Figure 2. (Wastiau, P., Kearney, C., & Van den Berghe W. (Final Report, 2009), pp. 66)

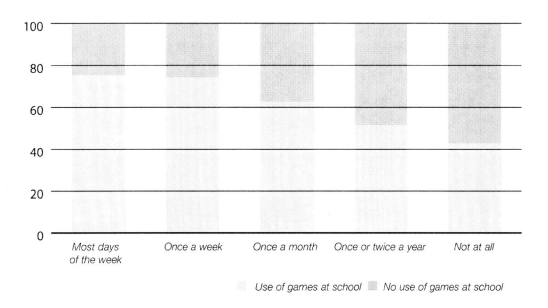

➡ Relation between the frequency of use of ICT and the use of games at school

Use of games at school ▨ No use of games at school

lationship between the answers to different questions was cross-analysed in order to reveal interesting results.

The majority of teachers who responded to the survey claimed to be familiar with ICT. 70% rated themselves as having "good" or "moderate" ICT skills, and 23% considered themselves to be "expert" users. About half of the respondents said they use ICT most days of the week in the classroom, and another quarter roughly once a week. The graph below clearly shows that teachers who use games in their teaching are also more frequent users of ICT in teaching than their colleagues who do not use games in their lessons for learning.

This ICT-familiar profile is not surprising considering that the survey was mainly promoted to teachers with an interest and experience in using ICT, and therefore somewhat affected the results. Although the websites and newsletters where the survey was announced were ICT-focused they were not particularly digital games-

oriented. This ensured the possibility of collecting the views of teachers who were not necessarily already convinced of the educational potential of digital games, or perhaps simply do not use them, as the study was as interested in their views as much as those of the already 'converted'.

Teachers' Interest in Using Digital Games and the Profile of Those Who Do

373 out of 528 respondents stated they used digital games in their teaching. Whether or not they use digital games in their teaching, the teachers surveyed expressed a real interest in their potential. Almost 85% of teachers already using games in their lessons wanted to know more and roughly the same percentage of teachers not yet using games said they were also interested. Less than 10% of respondents who said they do not use digital games in their teaching, claimed they had no place

Figure 3. (Wastiau, P., Kearney, C., & Van den Berghe W. (Final Report, 2009), pp. 67)

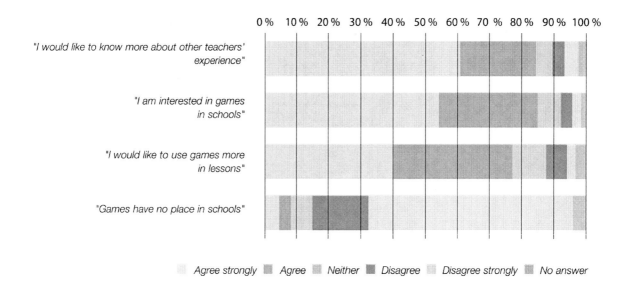

Opinion of teachers using games in schools (N=373)

in schools, compared to 60% who expressed an interest in starting to use them in their lessons. Therefore, these results demonstrate that there is real potential and willingness to increase the use of digital games in schools, both on the part of teachers already using them and wanting to know more, as well as novices.

58% of the survey respondents who claimed they use digital games in their lessons were female teachers, reflecting Europe's predominantly female teaching population. Teachers claiming to use games were mainly in the 20-35 age group, but the 36-45 and 46-55 age groups were also well represented with 30% and 26% of respondents falling within these categories.

Almost 50% of respondents were secondary school teachers (fairly evenly distributed between lower and upper secondary level), and 40% were primary school teachers. The remaining respondents included teaching staff in vocational training, adult education and higher education institutions, outside of the study's scope. How long they

have been teaching was not a decisive factor, except among those who have been teaching for more than thirty years, very few of whom said they use digital games in their lessons.

Expert games skills does not appear to be a requirement for using games in schools, as 85% of the teachers who claimed they use them said they had "moderate" games skills (57%) or even those of a "beginner" (28%).

Teachers' use of Digital Games in the Classroom

The games teachers mentioned using pedagogically varied greatly from commercial simulation and adventure games, to educational games targeted at specific subject teaching or skill development. Teachers were asked to list the name of the games they use, and the result was a majority of commercial off-the-shelf games suggesting that the educational use of such games is more widespread than commonly thought[6]. The word

Figure 4. (Wastiau, P., Kearney, C., & Van den Berghe W. (Final report, 2009), pp. 67)

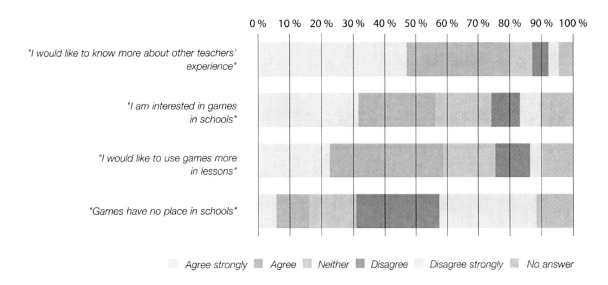

➡ Opinion of teachers not using games in schools (N=155)

Figure 5. (Wastiau, P., Kearney, C., & Van den Berghe W. (Final report, 2009), pp. 69)

➡ Distribution by age and gender

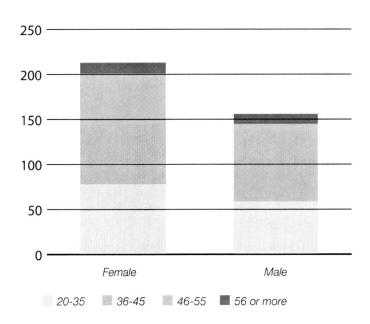

Figure 6. (Wastiau, P., Kearney, C., & Van den Berghe W. (Final report, 2009), pp. 71)

➡ Distribution by years of teaching and predominant student group

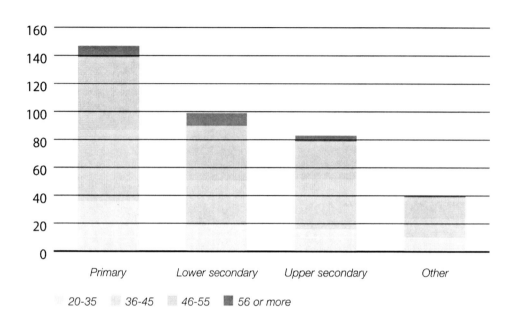

Figure 7. (Wastiau, P., Kearney, C., & Van den Berghe W. (Final report, 2009), pp. 72)

➡ Game skills level (N = 220)

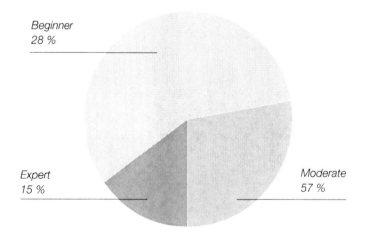

Figure 8. (Wastiau, P., Kearney, C., & Van den Berghe W. (Final report, 2009), pp. 83)

cloud in Figure 8 gives an idea of the games cited by teachers.

Teachers claimed that they mainly get the information and training they require to use digital games in the classroom from the internet and colleagues. Of the teachers surveyed, the highest rated expectation of digital games was that they should increase the motivation of their pupils, and be useable in a flexible way, allowing for a didactical approach, particularly in providing rapid feedback. With regards to the game's content, teachers expected it to be relevant to the curriculum and contain valid information (with no factual errors), as well as be suited to the age and ability range of students. Teachers also expressed that games should promote positive values, develop social skills, be fun to play, and to a lesser extent, promote creativity. Teachers emphasized the importance of the games being easy to use, and some mentioned the need for them to have a professional and appealing look and feel (to captivate students), be inexpensive, and not take too long to play (to fit timetable restraints).

Teachers use digital games in the classroom first and foremost to facilitate learning certain subjects and developing particular skills. Additionally, teachers claim they use games to increase their pupils' motivation, and make learning more enjoyable and relevant by reflecting their pupils' everyday environment. Other reasons put forward included games being useful for test and revision activities, and for accommodating different learning paces, as well as being a popular reward for pupils. From the survey results digital games appeared to be used most in national and foreign language lessons. Other subjects frequently cited were geography, mathematics and history. Teachers claimed they also use digital games to develop certain skills, particularly social, intellectual, ICT and motor skills.

Only 13% of teachers said they used games with specific groups of learners, suggesting that the majority think that they can be used with all students (as indeed some specified). The categories of learners most mentioned were boys, competitive pupils, pupils with special needs (academic, behavioural etc.) and demotivated pupils. Teachers confirmed the above reasons for, and

Figure 9. (Wastiau, P., Kearney, C., & Van den Berghe W. (Final report, 2009), pp. 73)

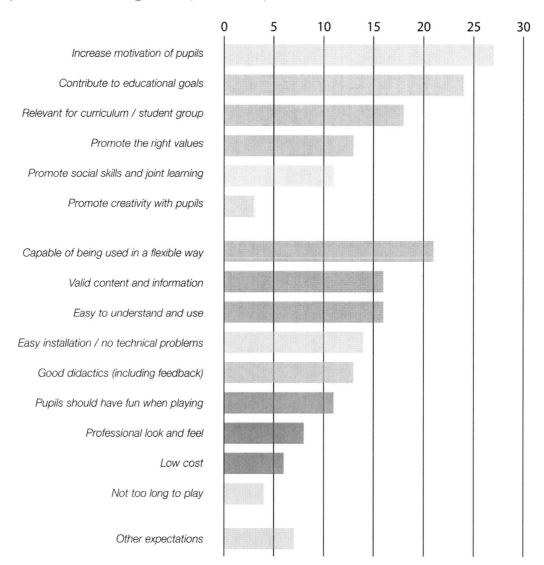

ways of, using games in the classroom, by rating their impact most highly in terms of increasing their pupils' motivation, and having a positive effect on personal, spatial, motor, intellectual, ICT and social skills. Some teachers also mentioned the positive impact the games had on social co-operation between pupils. Teachers were less convinced about digital games' ability to contrib-ute to the development of critical skills and impact on the performance in the subject taught.

The cost and licensing of digital games was most often cited by teachers as an obstacle to using them in class, with most also specifying that there were insufficient computers available at schools, and lack of resources to purchase new ones. The school's timetable was also listed as

Figure 10. (Wastiau, P., Kearney, C., & Van den Berghe W. (Final report, 2009), pp. 76)

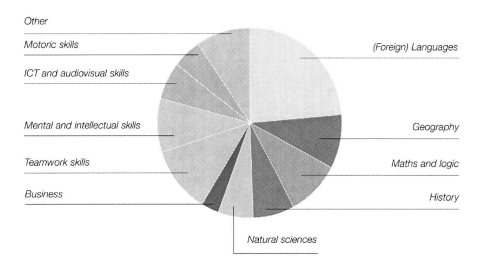

➡ Approximate distribution of subjects and skills for which games are used

Figure 11. (Wastiau, P., Kearney, C., & Van den Berghe W. (Final report, 2009), pp. 85)

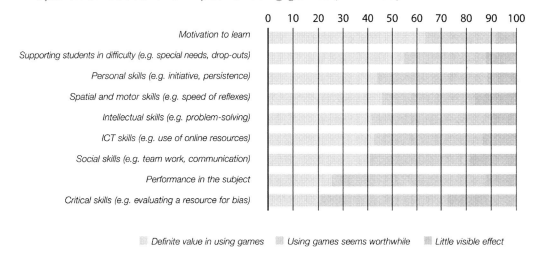

➡ Opinion on educational impact of using games (N = ± 200)

one of the main barriers to implementing the use of games in the classroom, for a number of reasons: the timetable is already overcrowded as it is, teachers do not have the time to plan and prepare the use of games in class, and often the computer laboratory is not available or the games last longer than the length of a lesson. Another significant barrier is the problem of integrating digital games into the curriculum, because the level of skill required and the specific terminology used do not correspond to the aims and structure of the course being taught. The cross disciplinary approach of games is also often not compatible with the division of subjects, especially at secondary level.

Figure 12. (Wastiau, P., Kearney, C., & Van den Berghe W. (Final report, 2009), pp. 78)

Main obstacles to using games in teaching	
1	Cost and licensing
2	Timetable of the school
3	Finding suitable games
4	Attitudes of other teachers
5	Training and support
6	Inappropriate content
7	Worries about negative aspects
8	Insufficient evidence of value
9	Examinations

Also mentioned by respondents, is the lack of available evidence evaluating the educational impact of digital games, which can be seen to be tightly linked to another barrier noted by teachers; namely, the negative attitudes of colleagues and parents. Figure 12 shows the overall result of the ranking made by teachers when asked a closed question on the obstacles they encounter, and Figure 13 shows the results of an open question on the same topic.

CASE STUDIES

In order to get a better idea of what is happening on the ground in games-based learning in Europe, the study collected a variety of proposals for case studies from each of the focus countries' national

Figure 13. (Wastiau, P., Kearney, C., & Van den Berghe W. (Final report, 2009), pp. 79)

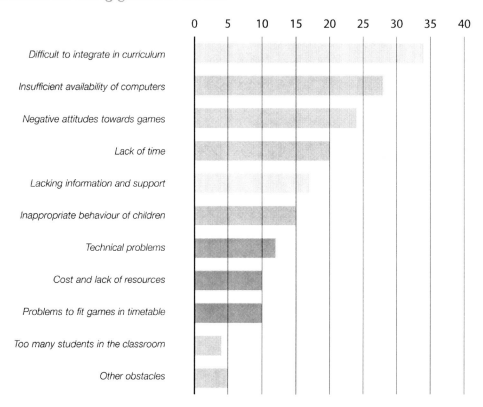

➥ Obstacles for using games in school

coordinators. Finally, 6 examples from Denmark, the Netherlands, Italy, the United Kingdom France and Austria were showcased, having been selected for illustrating a mixture of commercial and educational games, used in a range of subjects, and aimed at different age groups and educational objectives. The case studies were mostly drafted by teachers or researchers who were involved in the projects or experiments themselves. All the schools involved in the case studies are in the state sector[7], and are providers of compulsory education, either at primary or secondary level. This section describes the common observations made across the 6 case studies, and provides some details of individual case studies where relevant[8].

Scale and Support of Practices

The study analyses three small-scale case studies of the use of digital games in schools in Denmark, France, and Austria, and three medium to large scale experiments which took place in Italy, the United Kingdom and the Netherlands. The *DANT* (*Didactics Assisted by New Technologies*) project in Italy brought together teachers, experts and technicians to develop, test and use educational games in teaching mathematics and Italian language. It involved a thousand teachers from primary and lower secondary schools, and more than 10,000 pupils aged 6-14. It was first deployed in the Trentino region and then expanded to cover almost the whole of Italy. Another fairly large scale project described is the Scottish *Consolarium* project which tested the impact of several commercial games, such as *Dr. Kawashima's Brain Training* and *Nintendogs*, on various skills. It involved more than 500 primary school teachers and over 30 local authorities. In the Netherlands, the *Games Atelier* project, following a pilot phase to develop a tool for mobile games-based learning, was made available in 2009 to all secondary schools in the country. These three projects also benefited from the support of local, regional or central education authorities, including financial backing. Even in

the smaller case studies reported in Austria and Denmark, the ministries of education purchased and distributed the necessary licenses and games to schools. However, the involvement of education authorities remains limited.

The Use of a Structured Pedagogical Framework

All the case studies emphasize the importance teachers give to planning the use of digital games within a structured pedagogical framework. The game is carefully selected and the conditions in which it is played are made to be conducive to developing new skills and/or build on those previously learned by the pupil. The case studies show examples of teachers planning to use the game in a collective fashion, either for whole class teaching or group work, or alternatively individually, depending on the pedagogical objective. A strong feature of all the cases described is the follow-up discussions following the game play, organized between pupils and with the teacher to evaluate the strategies used for example, or discuss solutions to problems that arose.

The Italian, Scottish and Dutch case studies are all examples of medium to long term experiments carried out over a period of roughly 3-4 years, allowing for the evaluation of the games' impact on pupils' skills in the target subjects. At the start of the DANT project in Italy, participating teachers set up an experimental group with which to use the educational games they had developed, in addition to a control group. At the end of the project a test was given to all pupils in the experimental and control groups, to assess the impact on attainment in the subjects concerned, complimented by questionnaires used to evaluate qualitative aspects[9]. Similarly, a randomized controlled trial was carried out to test the commercial game *Dr. Kawashima's Brain Training* in Scottish schools[10], involving pre and post tests to measure the impact on attainment levels of primary level pupils in mathematics[11]. Rigorous research methodologies were employed in the cases of Scotland, Italy and the Netherlands, the latter two also involving the collaboration of university researchers.

The positive impact of digital games on pupils' motivation and various skills mentioned by teachers in the survey, are confirmed in the evaluation reports of each of the case studies. Similarly, the importance of feedback which is an integral and not separate part of the game, and the increased retention of knowledge by pupils, are commonly observed by the teachers involved in the case studies. Interestingly, while the survey results indicated teachers' uncertainty regarding a game's ability to impact positively on subject-specific knowledge and skills, the Scottish, Dutch and Italian case studies demonstrated scientifically a rise in attainment in mathematics, history and Italian respectively. Although introducing digital games in schools was mainly aimed at improving academic performance in the Italian and UK case studies, other case studies had a different focus. In the French case study, digital games were introduced as a tool to help with remedial learning, while in Austria and the Netherlands the development of team-learning was pursued as the main goal.

Combining the Use of Digital Games with Traditional Teaching Aids

The case studies demonstrate that digital games are often combined with traditional teaching aids, before, during and/or after playing the game. For example, the Danish case study describes how the *Harry Potter and the Prisoner of Azkaban* game was used to teach genre awareness and media literacy. The secondary level pupils were asked to read the book, watch the film and then play the game, in order to compare the genres. Similarly, in the other case studies examples are given showing increased knowledge retention and motivation of pupils to engage with more traditional teaching aids (such as factual documents), when their content is linked to the theme of the complimentary game used. Moreover, the Scot-

tish case study shows how playing digital games can encourage pupils to produce their own work, as a result of the high levels of engaged learning during the game play. The other case studies also testify to how pupils show greater enthusiasm for recording what they have learned through writing blog entries or essays for example, as a result of playing a digital game. Pupils were observed as being keen to communicate what they had learned through the game to other pupils and the wider community.

Support from Collaborative Experiences

Due to games being an innovative teaching tool in the classroom, they often give rise to many exchanges between teachers about their practices. These can be offline exchanges or online exchanges which take place within a community of practice. Novices to the pedagogical use of games seek the advice of more experienced teachers, and those who already use them compare their experiences with other users to overcome difficulties or exchange useful ideas. The *DANT* project in Italy illustrates the setting-up of a teachers' community of practice on a relatively large scale. Firstly, a small group of teachers gathered to develop some educational games, and invited technical experts and researchers to collaborate with them, before inviting a larger group of teachers to test the games so that the final versions could be made available online for a large audience of teachers nation-wide. Moreover, the Danish case study provides an example of how teachers using digital games in their lessons often are involved in fruitful cooperation with other staff members, such as ICT coordinators and librarians.

The case studies also demonstrate how the success of implementing the use of digital games in the classroom in part depends on informing school management, parents, and the rest of the school community, and obtaining their support from the start. This is particularly illustrated by the

Austrian and Danish case studies, where parents' agreement was sought before the games were used by the teachers in class. Furthermore, the teachers were careful to inform all stakeholders of the pupils' progress being made throughout the project, and to share the results with them at the end. This regular briefing before, during and after the project on how the games were being used and the learning outcomes being aimed at, was considered to have curbed any cautious or negative attitudes from parents or other stakeholders.

THE APPROACHES OF EDUCATION SYSTEMS

To better understand the national context of each of the study's focus countries with regards to games-based learning, interviews were undertaken with national policy makers and experts[12]. The section below draws out the main analysis from the interviews, focusing on the extent of involvement of education authorities and the main approach used at national level.

Involvement of Education Authorities

As is made clear from the teachers' survey and case studies, games-based learning in European schools is currently a new, limited and mainly grassroots initiative, usually involving isolated teachers motivated to experiment with innovative tools. Considering this early stage of development, it is understandable that the involvement of education authorities at the national or regional level is generally rather limited, even though to what extent varies from country to country. In Denmark, the Netherlands and the United Kingdom explicit support is given to the development of games-based learning at systemic level, and research in this area is also quite advanced in these countries. In the Netherlands for example, Kennisnet[13] has taken an active role in research and pilot projects on games-based learning, particularly targeted

at re-engaging disaffected learners. In 2006 in particular, the Netherlands invested considerably into exploring the educational potential of digital games. National initiatives to promote the use of digital games in schools include the Ministry of Economics "Maatschappelijke Sectoren & ICT" action programme which has funded seven games projects[14], and the 'Make a Game'[15] annual national competition for pupils to design and build a computer game for use in schools.

Denmark also has a fairly long tradition of research on the potential of games-based learning for teaching at university level, notably through the work done by the Centre for Games Research at Aarhus University. Moreover, the Ministry of Education has been interested in the potential of digital games for learning in the school context for a number of years. Digital games are considered part of the Danish ICT strategy for education, as well as the media education strategy. A group of experts composed of the Ministry of Education, university researchers, teachers and industrialists is currently working on identifying the challenges the Danish education is facing. One of the recommendations to emerge from this expert group's work is the need to develop more 'serious games' (in line with the curriculum, in which the teachers' role before, during and after playing is integrated into the game's design) to make learning more attractive and motivating. As a result of this recommendation the Ministry of Education is supporting further research in the field of serious games and a collaborative partnership between industry and academia has been established for this purpose.

Similarly in the United Kingdom, there is a solid interest in the potential of games-based learning at policy level, in particular in relation to digital safety, the enhancement of learner-parent collaboration[16], and the development of higher-level skills for creativity and innovation[17]. Furthermore, the British government commissioned a report commonly known as the Byron Review[18], on the effects of computer games and the internet on young people. The Review calls for more evidence of demonstrated learning outcomes on which to develop an independent accreditation scheme for games-based learning software, to help teachers and parents make informed choices about using games in the classroom and at home. Scotland is particularly advanced in this area, as its new Curriculum for Excellence (2009)[19] explicitly mentions playing and learning with 'electronic games', both to develop specific skills and to learn game design[20]. Games-based learning in Scotland can already be considered as mainstream.

Despite the notable interest in and support of games-based learning in the Netherlands, Denmark and the United Kingdom at systemic level, it is important to note that the use of games for learning in these countries remains limited. Isolated examples of innovative schools experimenting with the use of games for learning can be said to characterize the study's other focus countries (France, Italy, Spain, Lithuania and Austria) to an even greater extent, where there is little or no interest or activity at the level of national policy. Moreover, in these countries there also seems to be less interest in games-based learning from teachers themselves, often because they have low ICT skills and/or are sceptical about digital games which they might associate with violence or other negative aspects.

The following paragraphs describe the four main conceptions of games-based learning which emerge from the study's analysis of eight education systems. The first systemic approach to games-based learning the study identifies is the understanding of digital games as a tool for modernizing education. The Netherlands is particularly representative of this approach, followed by Denmark and the United Kingdom, which however also pursue other objectives. Italy and Austria also follow this model to a lesser extent. In this approach education authorities support the use of digital games in the classroom to a certain extent, and research centres develop projects in this area. Teachers believe that school culture needs to more closely reflect young peoples' everyday reality. By engaging them through a tool that speaks their language, students can be motivated to take control of their own learning.

The second systemic approach views digital games as a tool to prepare young citizens for the virtual worlds present in society. This approach is very representative of Denmark and the Netherlands. Digital games are considered as a phenomena to be dealt with in media education. This approach not only teaches through games by using them as a tool for teaching curricular subjects, but also examines digital games as a type of media in comparison to others. Digital games are therefore treated critically and the world of digital games is explored in itself. For example, issues concerning marketing strategies, the risks involved in excessive gaming, and target groups are discussed openly and debated. A third approach identified by the study considers digital games as a tool to encourage innovation and the development of advanced skills. This conception of games-based learning is particularly evident in the United Kingdom. Digital games are seen to be of value in so far as they can help develop the necessary skills for creativity and innovation, including initiative, self-confidence, ability to explore and investigate, and a high sense of enterprise. In view of this, institutional support for digital games in the United Kingdom emanates from the Ministries more directly responsible for the development of enterprise and innovation, rather than education. The final approach which emerged from the contextual analysis of the study's focus countries views digital games as a tool to support students in difficulty. France currently uses this approach by valuing digital games for their potential to help students experiencing difficulties in academic learning or behavioural and social problems. Digital games are used in this context because of their ability to deal with students' mistakes in a non-traumatizing way, and to allow students to progress at their own pace and repeat exercises as often as necessary.

RECOMMENDATIONS

The Games in Schools study concludes by putting forward some recommendations on the basis of the teachers' survey, case studies, and analysis of national contexts discussed earlier. The recommendations are addressed to policy makers, the education sector and the games industry.

Evaluation of Practices

As the study shows, examples of games-based learning are taking place across Europe, however in a limited manner. To encourage the widespread practice of games-based learning, teachers and policy makers express the need to develop evaluations of the impact of digital games on students' learning. This is not only to convince them of their learning potential, but also to change the possibly sceptical opinions of fellow colleagues, senior school management and parents. Without their support, the integration of games-based learning into classroom practice cannot become a reality. To move the discussion forward, it would be important to explore specific areas of analysis, rather than remain at the level of generalities. For example, specific questions of interest for the purposes of evaluation might include: how can different learning styles be managed through the use of digital games in the classroom? What elements within the game itself are responsible for the impact on certain skills?

Examining the Potential of Digital Games in Light of Cognitive Research

Considering that today's modern school curricula increasingly defines learning outcomes in terms of key skills rather than content to be learned, we need to ask whether traditional teaching methods and tools are adequate for developing skills for innovation or interpersonal and civic skills. Traditional teaching material and methods have not necessarily been designed with such key skills in mind. Digital skills should therefore be considered as a possible answer to the need to address the development of these skills. The study demonstrates how the features and qualities of digital games closely correspond to the latest knowledge we have regarding modes of learning, gained from research on cognitive processes. Digital games support many of the principles of learning that have been recognised as most effective by recent research. For example, digital games enable personalized learning by allowing repetition and choice of pace or level of difficulty. The feedback given when using digital games is essential for learning as it allows for meta-cognition. Learning by doing is also incorporated into the experience of playing a digital game, as the player is actively involved in a role. Collaborative learning is also encouraged by digital games, as they often lend themselves to collective use and act as a stimulus for interaction between players. We know from research that intelligence is dynamic and not divided into subject disciplines, in the way school curricula is usually organized. Digital games reflect our multiple intelligences by implementing a pluridisciplinary approach, requiring a wide range of skills from the player. Finally, precisely because intelligence is diverse, students learn in different ways. In this context digital games can be proposed as a complimentary or alternative teaching tool to traditional methods.

Supporting Innovation at Grassroots Level and Building Communities of Practice

Further support is needed from local, regional, or central education authorities for in-depth research, pilot projects, and the dissemination of case studies and evaluation reports in this area. Likewise, it is important that digital games become recognized as one of other types of ICT tools which are often the subject of specific initiatives and trainings supported by education authorities, with the objective of modernizing the education system. The development of grassroot initiatives in the area of games-based learning should be encouraged. The study also identified the need for and benefits of supporting communities of practice where teachers can share information, tools and practices. Such communities are invaluable for disseminating good practice and encouraging the integration of digital games in the classroom. In addition to communities of practice at the national, regional or local level, the development of a European community of practice would bring substantial benefits. This would allow teachers, researchers and policy makers to have access to a much larger and richer range of information on current games-based learning practices. It would also facilitate communication between these groups and encourage possible cooperation on cross-country projects.

Such a community would also enable the development of large-scale projects in collaboration with industry. In this way, teachers and pupils could contribute to the challenges we face in relation to the need for creativity, innovation and multiculturalism.

Developing Cooperation between the Education Sector and Games Industry

As the teachers' survey shows, teachers who use digital games for learning often have precise expectations regarding the necessary qualities of the games and the skills they should develop. Industry should benefit from the knowledge of these requirements in order to create digital games that have a maximum impact on learning. As the case studies illustrated, teachers already do cooperate with researchers and experts in the development and testing of digital games. It could only be fruitful for them to cooperate in the same way with game developers. There are also many significant current issues of concern that schools need to teach students about, such as climate

change, which could be addressed by digital games. These current issues could be treated in an effective, pluridisciplinary way, by attractive digital games of a high quality technical standard.

FUTURE DEVELOPMENTS

The study identifies two main emerging trends, defining the direction of the development of games-based learning in the European school context. The first is a growing interest from policy makers in 'serious games', notably in Denmark and France. The definition of 'serious games' can vary from country to country. For example Danish research in this area defines them in terms of the central role of the teacher at the design stage, as well as during and after game play. In France and other European countries however, the emphasis is more on their relevance to the curriculum. If countries would like to see a larger take-up of games-based learning in their classrooms it would seem important to encourage teachers to be involved in the design of digital games themselves. By taking into consideration their pedagogical requirements and giving them a certain ownership of the initiative, it is likely this would have a decisive impact on the use of digital games in classrooms across Europe. More in-depth comparative research on serious games is needed to explore the role of the teacher in games-based learning more thoroughly.

The second pathway for future development in this field concerns policy makers' interest in investigating the possibilities for the participation of pupils in game design, through pilot projects. The study showed how Denmark and particularly the Netherlands have gone one step further by realizing the added value of getting students to design as well as play digital games. Learning through playing games can of course be beneficial as has already been demonstrated, but designing a game requires students not only to familiarize themselves thoroughly with the subject content in question, but also master the principles of game design. The pilot experiments documented in the study's Dutch case study testify to the learning gains made in terms of motivation, development of key skills and knowledge of the subject being taught. Moreover, involving students in game design may moderate their high expectations in terms of the game's level of technology.

CONCLUSION: THE GAME AHEAD

The *Games in Schools* study was launched at a major European conference, hosted at the Council of Europe in Strasbourg, in May 2009[21]. The conference brought together 100 participants, including key experts in the area of digital games and/or education, researchers, policy makers at national and European level, as well as teachers and representatives from industry. In this way the conference implemented one of the study's recommendations, by facilitating possible future collaboration between the various stakeholders of games-based learning. The event was opened by the European Commissioner for Education and Culture at that time, Jan Figel, followed by a welcoming address from Elda Moreno (the Council of Europe's Programme Director for 'Building a Europe for and with children'), and a keynote speech by Toine Mander, (MEP and rapporteur of the draft resolution on the protection of consumers, in particular minors, in respect of the use of video games[22]). The high calibre and number of participants, as well as the willingness of the Council of Europe to host the event, testify to the notable interest now apparent in the potential of digital games for learning. It is a topic which is being taken seriously at national and European level, as evidenced by the increasing frequency of seminars, round tables and conferences, and the number of academic and other articles published on the subject. It is significant that these developments are beginning to be organized in a framework which directly addresses teachers, and

are sometimes initiated by education authorities themselves.

For example, since the publication of the study, European Schoolnet has been invited by various education authorities in Europe, including in Austria[23] and Sweden[24], to present the study's results and particularly promote the accompanying handbook at teachers' conferences organized at national level. The teachers' handbook[25] is a practical guide for teachers explaining how to integrate games-based learning effectively in the classroom. As such it answers a concrete need expressed by teachers in the study's survey, and aims to facilitate the integration of games-based learning in schools across Europe on a wider scale. The issues addressed in the handbook correspond to concerns and questions raised by teachers in the online community of practice[26], which was also set up within the framework of the *Games in Schools* project. The project also provided stakeholders with a regularly updated blog[27], documenting the progress of the study and other games-related news. Both the community of practice and the blog are still active and will continue to be fora where interested stakeholders can debate and exchange information in this area.

Furthermore, European Schoolnet is continuing its contribution to knowledge building in the area of games-based learning through its involvement in various European level projects concerned with this topic. One such project is *IMAGINE*[28] (*Increasing Mainstreaming of Games In Learning Policies*) which aims to have an impact on games-based learning at policy level, through valorizing the outcomes of projects and initiatives in this field. Another relevant project European Schoolnet is a partner in is *PING*[29] (*Poverty Is Not a Game*). This project aims to develop an educational role play game about poverty, in an attempt to address the topic of this year's European Year[30], using a pedagogical and engaging approach for teaching young people aged between 12 and 14.

A recent report[31] undertaken as desk research for the *IMAGINE* project identifies games-based learning projects in Europe, providing a description of good practice case studies spread across all levels of education. The report usefully categorizes the projects in this area by target audience, the specific technology they focus on, and the main output they have produced. 57% of the projects surveyed (including IL GRECO, Europa Eureka and SITCOM) produce resources for games-based learning, while 36% are aimed at developing methodology in this area (e.g. ELEKTRA, ARGuing and 80Days), and very few produce literature (the Games in Schools study being one of the rare examples cited). The report concluded that unfortunately many of the projects identified in this area have not produced sustainable results, and outputs and resources are often only available throughout the project's lifetime, when funding is available. This means valuable knowledge and resources to forward the games-based learning movement in the school context are being lost and not exploited.

European Schoolnet and its partners are currently working on meeting a related need for a central place to store, share, build, update and evaluate knowledge regarding games-based learning, through its new *LINKED*[32] project. This project aims to develop an online interactive platform where knowledge about games-based learning (as well as other topics relevant to ICT in education) will be brokered in user-friendly forms to policy makers and practitioners respectively, to ensure maximum impact. The game therefore is clearly not over, and there is much still to be done to make games-based learning a reality in schools across Europe. The process however is clearly in place, and this publication is a fruitful contribution to it.

REFERENCES

Department for Children. Schools and Families. (2008). *Safer vhildren in a digital world-the report of the Byron review.* Nottingham: DCSF. Retrieved February 11, 2010, from http://www.dcsf.gov.uk/byronreview/

European Parliament. (2008). *Draft resolution on the protection of consumers, in particular minors, in respect of the use of video games.* Retrieved February 11, 2010, from http://www.europarl.europa.eu/oeil/file.jsp?id=5666002

Felicia, P. (2009). *Digital games in schools: A handbook for teachers.* Brussels: European Schoolnet. Retrieved February 10, 2010, from http://games.eun.org/upload/GIS_HAND-BOOK_EN.PDF

Learning and Teaching Scotland. (2009). *Curriculum for excellence.* Retrieved February 11, 2010, from http://www.ltscotland.org.uk/curriculumforexcellence/index.asp

Nesler, R. (2007) *Imparando giocando: Videogiochi e apprendimento - rapporto di ricerca sul quadriennio di sperimentazione.* Trento: IPRASE del Trentino. Retrieved February 5, 2010, from http://www.iprase.tn.it/prodotti/materiali/download/07_10_17_Rapporto_imparo_giocando.pdf

Pivec, M., & Pivec, P. (2009). *Imagine LLP KA4. Work package 2: Final report.* Retrieved February 11, 2010, from http://www.imaginegames.eu/eng/Reports

Robertson, D. (2009). *The games in schools community of practice.* Brussels: European Schoolnet. Retrieved February 11, 2010, from http://games.eun.org/2009/06/the_games_in_school_community_1.html#more

Robertson, D., & Miller, D. (2008). *Using Dr. Kawashima's brain training in primary classrooms: A randomised controlled study. A summary for the BBC.* Retrieved February 5, 2010, from http://ltsblogs.org.uk/consolarium/files/2008/09/lts-dr-kawashima-trial-summary.pdf

Wastiau, P., Kearney, C., & Van den Berghe, W. (2009). *How are digital games used in schools. Complete results of the study. Final report.* Brussels: European Schoolnet. Retrieved February 5, 2010, from http://games.eun.org/upload/gis-full_report_en.pdf

Wastiau, P., Kearney, C., & Van den Berghe, W. (2009). *How are digital games used in schools. Main results of the study. Synthesis report.* Brussels: European Schoolnet. Retrieved February 5, 2010, from http://games.eun.org/upload/gis-synthesis_report_en.pdf

ENDNOTES

[1]   European Schoolnet (EUN – www.eun.org) is a network of 31 ministries of education in Europe and beyond. EUN was created in 1997 to bring about innovation in teaching and learning for its key stakeholders: ministries of education, schools, teachers, and researchers.

[2]   European Schoolnet (EUN – www.eun.org) is a network of 31 ministries of education in Europe and beyond. EUN was created in 1997 to bring about innovation in teaching and learning for its key stakeholders: ministries of education, schools, teachers, and researchers.

[3]   *eMapps.com* was a project funded under the European Commission's 6th Framework Programme for Research and Technologocial Development, and ran from 2006-2008. See http://emapps.info/.

[4]   These are the 8 languages of the study's focus countries, with the addition of Estonia, which was originally selected as a focus country, but then replaced by the Netherlands due to lack of information and contact points.

[5]   From these 88 responses, 21 were from Romania, 16 from Belgium and 12 from Portugal.

[6]   This result should be interpreted with care as the respondents are not a representative sample of European teachers, and some educational software such as simulation games, may not be considered by a teacher as a game but rather as an educational tool.

[7]   One exception is a private school in the Netherlands, the Montessori Comprehensive School Amsterdam, which was involved in the pilot of the game *Frequency 1550*, which was later developed into the *Games Atelier*.

[8]   For a detailed description of each case study please refer to Wastiau, P., Kearney, C., & Van den Berghe W. (2009). *How are digital games used in schools. Complete results of the study. Final report* (pp. 10-59). Brussels: European Schoolnet, or Wastiau, P., Kearney, C., & Van den Berghe W. (2009). *How are digital games used in schools. Main results of the study. Synthesis report* (pp.22-34). Brussels: European Schoolnet

[9]   See Nesler, R. (2007) *Imparando giocando: videogiochi e apprendimento - rapporto di ricerca sul quadriennio di sperimentazione.* Trento: IPRASE del Trentino [Italian]: http://www.iprase.tn.it/prodotti/materiali/download/07_10_17_Rapporto_imparo_giocando.pdf

[10]   For this particular experiment, 32 schools in the lowest quartile in terms of socio-economic status (as measured by entitlement to free school meals) from four local authorities in Scotland (The Western Isles, Aberdeenshire, Dundee City and East Ayrshire) were selected.

[11]   Robertson, D, & Miller, D. (2008). *Using Dr Kawashima's brain training in primary classrooms: a randomised controlled study. A summary for the BBC.* See http://ltsblogs.org.uk/consolarium/files/2008/09/lts-dr-kawashima-trial-summary.pdf

[12]   For full descriptions of the national context for games-based learning in each of the study's 8 focus countries see Wastiau, P., Kearney, C., & Van den Berghe W. (2009). *How are digital games used in schools. Complete results of the study* (pp. 86-117). Brussels: European Schoolnet

[13]   Kennisnet is a public organization that supports the implementation of ICT in

education in the Netherlands. Kennisnet aims at national and regional cooperation with schools, branch organizations and (municipal-)governments to provide tailor-made ICT support for primary, secondary and vocational education. See http://corporate.kennisnet.nl/international

[14] For a list of all the education projects funded under this call for proposals from the Ministry of Economics see http://www.m-ict.nl/index.php?option=com_content&task=category&sectionid=27&id=55&Itemid=212.

[15] See http://www.surfnetkennisnetproject.nl/resultaten/mag [Dutch] and http://www.surfnetkennisnetproject.nl/internationalvisitors/resultssofar [English]

[16] See Futurelab's Gaming with Familities project: http://www.futurelab.org.uk/projects/gaming-in-families.

[17] See Futurelab's Games and Learning project: http://www.futurelab.org.uk/projects/games-and-learning.

[18] Department for Children, Schools and families (2008) *Safer Children in a Digital World- The Report of the Byron Review.* Nottingham: DCSF. See http://www.dcsf.gov.uk/byronreview/

[19] *Curriculum for Excellence* (2009). Scotland: Learning and Teaching Scotland. See http://www.ltscotland.org.uk/curriculumforexcellence/index.asp

[20] *Curriculum for Excellence* (2009) *Experiences and Outcomes, Technologies Area* (pp. 7). Scotland: Learning and Teaching Scotland. See http://www.ltscotland.org.uk/Images/technologies_experiences_outcomes_tcm4-539894.pdf

[21] See http://insight.eun.org/ww/en/pub/insight/thematic_dossiers/articles/games_in_schools/games_in_schools_final.htm and http://games.eun.org/conference/.

[22] European Parliament (2008) Draft *resolution on the protection of consumers, in particular minors, in respect of the use of video games.*

See http://www.europarl.europa.eu/oeil/file.jsp?id=5666002

[23] The study was presented at the national Austrian eLearning teaching symposium, *eLearning Didaktik Fachtagung*, in Vienna on October 21, 2009. See http://edidaktik.tgm.ac.at/.

[24] The study was presented at the national Swedish teachers' congress, *Skolforum 2009*, in Stockholm, October 21, 2009. See http://www.skolforum.com/common/category.aspx?id=2440.

[25] Felicia, P. (2009). *Digital Games in schools: A handbook for teachers*, Brussels: European Schoolnet

[26] See http://gamesinschools.ning.com. The Games in Schools community of practice was launched on a Ning platform on March 23rd 2009, and moderated by an experienced educator in this field up until the end of May 2009. Its main purpose was to encourage debate and the sharing of knowledge between teachers presently using digital games as learning tools in schools, and those who are not yet doing so. The community of practice currently has 886 members coming from almost every European country and others beyond. For the *Games in Schools Community of Practice* report see http://games.eun.org/2009/06/the_games_in_school_community_1.html#more.

[27] See http://games.eun.org.

[28] See http://www.imaginegames.eu/eng. *IMAGINE* is a project which started in 2008 and will run until the end of 2010, funded by the European Commission's Lifelong Learning Programme.

[29] See http://www.nefic.org/projects-data.php?id=38. The *PING* (Poverty *Is Not* a *Game*) project is coordinated and financed by the Network of European Foundations, and supported by the Belgian Presidency of the European Union due to take up its position in the second half of 2010. The project has

also been awarded the label for contributing to the European Year for Combating Poverty and Social Exclusion.

30   2010 is the European Year for Combating Poverty and Social Exclusion. See http://ec.europa.eu/social/main. jsp?langId=en&catId=637.

31   The report can be downloaded from http:// imaginegames.eu/eng/Reports.

32   *LINKED* (*L*everaging *I*nnovation for a *N*etwork of *K*nowledge on *E*ducation) is a new one-year project (2010-2011) funded under the European Commission's Lifelong Learning Programme, aimed at developing a system to broker knowledge to policy makers and practitioners on the use of digital games in schools and pupils' and teachers' digital skills.

Chapter 4
Learning with Video Games

René St-Pierre
Université du Québec à Montréal, Canada

ABSTRACT

Playing video games stimulates affective, cognitive, and communicational processes, thus facilitating the emergence of knowledge. In order to support this idea, this chapter first historically contextualizes the evolution of educational video games and provides some basic classification of genres. Then it identifies the major theoretical currents that may inspire teachers and designers to develop learning scenarios adapted to educational video games. It also describes some interesting examples of the educational usage of video games by the general public and of video games specifically created for a particular pedagogical context. Several arguments are presented to stimulate discussions around motivation, evaluation, and learning aspects of educational video games usage and design. With the intention of supporting an approach that responds to user needs, some models identifying user profiles are also described. Finally, this chapter presents general design specifications for successful development of educational video games projects.

INTRODUCTION

This chapter is part of a research and design methodology about Educational Video Game Design. This method is intended to assist artists and designers in the complex process of educational video game design. It is for professionals working in the areas of culture, education, science,

art, communication, research and experimentation but also for people who would like to grasp the overall concept behind Educational Video Game Design. The methodology is comprised of four capsules describing the potential of educational video games while presenting the theoretical and practical concepts necessary for the understanding and practice of multimedia design. The capsules are accompanied by examples of educational games to try out, a glossary to expand understand-

DOI: 10.4018/978-1-60960-495-0.ch004

ing of the subject and a list of websites dealing with educational game design issues.

CAPSULE 1: THE MULTIMEDIA FIELD

Multimedia applications come in many forms and meet a variety of user needs. This capsule defines the concept of interactive multimedia and describes the major types and end users of its applications. It also defines the multimedia application development process, including work functions, the designer/writer role and software and hardware aspects useful for the design, production and dissemination of multimedia projects.

CAPSULE 2: NARRATIVE AND HYPERMEDIA

The practice of hypermedia design implements new ways of playing, communicating and learning. Interactors are at the centre of a dynamic system in which they become active participants working with the elements of a narrative space. This capsule is meant to make designers/writers aware of some aspects of cinematographic language that may be used in multimedia writing projects. It also defines hypermedia characteristics, the forms they can take and the different operating procedures via which users can interact with hypermedia content.

CAPSULE 3: LEARNING THROUGH VIDEO GAMES

The practice of video games promotes some affective, cognitive and communicational processes that pave the way for the emergence of knowledge. First, this capsule puts the changing trends in educational video games in historic perspective. Then it identifies the major theoretical currents that may inspire teachers and designers to develop

learning scenarios adapted to educational video games. Last, this capsule describes an emerging area of research concentrated on learning via already-existing video games used by the general public and video games specifically created with particular pedagogical contexts in mind.

CAPSULE 4: EDUCATIONAL VIDEO GAME DESIGN MODEL

Out of the complexity of forms, methods, techniques and procedures emerges a model designed to simplify the work of multimedia design. This capsule describes a systemic model that brings the purpose of an educational video game design project together with all the information, interface and interactivity components needed. It also presents the indispensable elements that must be part of multimedia design specifications.

The methodology and examples can be found at: http://www.clikmedia.ca/CM/

Brief History of Educational Games

Educational video games are inscribed in the historical continuity of a long tradition associated with the dissemination of pedagogical games. From the doll to the toy soldier, the puzzle to the role play, the presence of these artifacts indicates educational situations apparently far removed from the school context. Often the conveyors of sociocultural stereotypes, these games and toys reflect evolving techniques and mentalities; they illustrate the growing impact of scholarly knowledge on recreational learning activities.

First Mass Recreational Productions

The progress associated with the appearance of the printing press led to a sixteenth century abundance of card games dealing with the divinatory arts (e.g., astrology and tarot), lottery and [art de mémoire]. The iconography associated with these card games encouraged the development of the masses' visual awareness despite their underdeveloped literacy[1]. Playing cards gave people who could not read the ability to count, recognize symbols and develop new cognitive skills (Frété, 2002, citing Meggs, 1992).

One of the main metamorphoses of seventeenth, eighteenth and nineteenth century educational games was snakes and ladders. Snakes and ladders is played with a pair of dice, a dice cup and a game board composed of 63 spiral staircases. Each staircase has a number and an image. Players take turns rolling the dice. The first to reach the grove wins, but that is not easy to do because there are many obstacles along the way! Inspired by reality, literature, religion, politics, science and geography, devoted to personalities, love, the theatre, industry and fashion and illustrated with animals or plants, snakes and ladders boards are often real lessons presenting great pedagogical, historical and documentary interest. (Le Musée du Jouet de Moirans-en-Montagne, France). During this period, the educational game entered the restricted circle of the aristocracy and several productions demonstrate that the game was used in the education of princes and the elite.

The nineteenth century was marked by a huge increase in the output of the means of production[2]: it was the beginning of the Industrial Revolution. The appearance of factories and long-run rotary presses, coupled with progress in transportation and communication methods, fostered the mass distribution[3] of games and toys. The first half of the nineteenth century saw the appearance of games and toys for developing the aesthetic and artistic senses and interest in science, technology and domestic affairs. Those educational games seem to be truly analogous precursors of contemporary virtual simulation models such as *The Sims®* (management and development of social avatars) and *SimCity®* (construction of cities).

Hochet (2005) identifies several forms of games specifically designed for the virtuous, moral and political education of princes and elites:

...the moral purpose of snakes and ladders was learning to be a good king. Emblem recognition and genealogical games taught players to recognize reigning families, lead or cardboard soldiers prepared them for conducting wars, historical and mythological games instilled identification with edifying role models and geography games taught them to know their kingdoms and the new lands discovered in the world. On the other hand, we also find few math, reading, scientific or foreign language games and no games for girls either. All of the games were of rather plain workmanship and were more instructive (knowledge-based) than educational (understanding-based). However, their existence indicates a new acceptance of pleasure and gentleness in pedagogical thought.

There was a multitude of doll models designed for girls, and girls from the more comfortable classes were more likely to have dollhouses as well. Boys had assembly and construction games. Boys from middle-class families played with their Meccanos® (patented in 1901 by Franck Hornby) while boys from upper-class families built networks of electric trains. Both boys and girls seem to have been somewhat conditioned to learn to amuse themselves according to the stereotypical roles promoting a division of labour determined by gender and social class.

General Characteristics of Games

For games of action, strategy or simulation, some invariables must be considered to structure game design specifications (Crawford, 1984). In fact, games are defined by their territories that limit players with a system of playing rules. Furthermore, games inevitably send players on a quest or objective to be met, and they will be rewarded or punished by a system of gains and losses.

Space and territory: games are defined by their territories

For example, Monopoly's ® territory is a playing board, dice and cards used to determine players' movements in that territory. In video hockey games, the territory is the rink and its zones. Players move by directly manipulating the joystick.

Rules and instructions: games' rule systems control players

To win, players must follow certain rules and instructions that form part of their strategies and allow them to progress in the plot of the game within that framework. Game rules and instructions control and manage the competition or cooperation along the way to the final objective, which is to complete the quest victoriously while having fun.

Competition or cooperation: games direct players toward an objective to be reached

The desire to compete demonstrates a willingness to defeat and win, but it is also the accepted manifestation of the personal worth in establishing some superiority over oneself or others. Cooperation may express the desire to belong to a group but also the need for mutual aid and sharing to ensure one's evolution or survival. To encourage players in their quests, games must offer systems that reward successful task completion or problem resolution (e.g., point system, skill development, etc.)

Pedagogical Classification of Games

Educational video games develop psychomotor[4], intellectual[5], identity and relational[6] skills and support several pedagogical objectives, including introduction to academic subjects, problem resolution and simulation of emergent dynamic systems (Kahn, 2004).

1. **Games that teach academic subjects:** There are many games designed to teach academic subjects such as living languages, mathematics, science, art, culture, geography and history. Several pedagogical models have been developed to support teaching and learning of those subjects. The *Where in the World is Carmen Santiago?*® game (1985) is a classic example of an educational adventure game for teaching history and geography. *Math Blaster*® (1986) was also a forerunner of a drill and practice game, fostering the understanding of basic math rules (addition, subtraction, division, multiplication and percentage).

2. **Problem-resolution games:** Classic problem-resolution games use the labyrinth metaphor based on physical principles (force, resistance, movement, gravity, acceleration, deceleration, etc.) allowing users to develop their problem-solving abilities. For example, *The Strange Case of Professor Scientifix*® (CREO interactive) game uses the five phases of the scientific method (observation, formulation of hypothesis, testing hypothesis through experimentation, data analysis/conclusion and confirmation of hypothesis). Players must, by using objects' current or emergent properties, coordinate the interface elements so that a chain reaction is produced.

3. **Emergent dynamic system simulation games:** Simulation games attract players' attention because of the freedom that is offered to them: the playing rules are not defined, but the system has its laws instead. Like Lego's ® blocks or Meccano's® parts, such games offer a wide range of possibilities. The game only ends when the player decides, and there are no other objectives than the ones the player decides (Falgas, 2004). For example, *SimCity*® makes players the managers of cities, and they have to respect certain basic rules of urbanism and

manage the human, material and financial resources. As in real life, players must also accommodate and satisfy everyone's interests: for example, the residents of a city neighbourhood to which the player has not paid enough attention will possibly rebel against the power in place.

Learning Models

Not everyone responds the same way in learning situations. Learners assimilate and retain material and knowledge better when several teaching strategies, models or situations are used (Isabelle citing Ritchie and Baylor, 1997).

Behavioural Learning Models

According to behaviourist theories, the scientific study of psychological phenomena and human behaviour can only be based on external, observable behavioural data. The origin of these theories is attributed to J. B. Watson, who wanted to model psychology on the other physical sciences, the laws of which are discovered based on the analysis of observable data. According to this concept, human functioning may be explained by laws stemming from the observation of behaviour in the form of stimuli and responses (Source: http://www.granddictionnaire.com Original French consulted December 25, 2005).

Thorndike's Behavioural Learning Model

The two greatest principles of Edward Thorndike's theories (1874-1949) rely on the concepts of effect and exercise. The law of effect is based on the fact that repeating a behaviour bringing a satisfactory result (reward and gratification) will become a natural or automatic response to that situation, while the law of exercise tends to demonstrate that the repeated practice of a behaviour that brings positive reinforcement will bring that positive reinforcement increasingly faster in successive trials (Balmer, 2005).

In his doctoral dissertation completed in 1898 (*Animal Intelligence: An Experimental Study of the Associative Processes in Animals*), Thorndike laid out the basis of his learning theory. His famous experiment went as follows: he locked a hungry cat in a cage with a door equipped with a latch and put a little food outside the cage. If the cat managed to move the latch effectively, the door would open, and it could reach the food. Put in this situation, the animal demonstrated various "exploratory" behaviours before accidentally moving the latch enough to get out and eat the food. The repeated trials of the experiment made the time required for the cat to open the latch decrease exponentially. Learning was believed to have occurred when the cat successfully opened the latch as soon as it was put in the cage (Depover, 2004).

Application of these Principles to Educational Video Game Design

Several adventure games comply with Thorndike's trial-and-error principle. A classic is *Myst®* (Cyan), in which players have to develop a group of cognitive strategies (law of effect) to unlock access points allowing them to explore the game's higher levels. The law of exercise can be verified in all exerciser-type applications (sometimes called "drill & practice games") in which participation and reflection levels are low, questions often being presented in the form of repetitive tasks to be executed, such as answering multiple-choice questions, completing sentences or putting objects in the right places.

Pavlov's Behavioural Learning Model

At the beginning of the twentieth century, Ivan Pavlov (1849-1936) conducted a series of experiments[7] on dogs to understand what associations could be made between a series of stimuli and the physiological responses produced in their nervous, vascular and digestive systems. His most remarkable experiment was based on the finding that it is possible to produce a conditioned response to a stimulus (through a learning process).

Application of this Principle to Educational Video Game Design

All games using visual or sound signals to indicate when players must perform an action, avoid an obstacle or hit a target are applying this principle.

Skinner's Behavioural Learning Model

Based on Pavlov's work, B.F Skinner (1904-1990) conducted experiments that helped him to develop a behavioural theory stipulating that the learning experience may by induced by the subject's own activity. Skinner's operant conditioning principle is differs from Pavlov's respondent conditioning in that the subject animal is active and must obtain the food itself through its own activity and thereby establish the connection between a stimulus and a response.

The basic protocol of Skinner's cage experiment (Skinner box) is simple: a rat was placed in a cage; the rat actively explored its environment and accidentally pushed a lever designed to present food to the rat. The rat then pushed the lever more and more frequently. After a while, the food was not presented, and the rat continued to push on the lever. The object of this procedure was to construct a new conduit through which a connection could be established between a stimulus (lever) and a response (pushing on the lever) with the introduction of a reinforcement agent (food). The conduit was acquired when the stimulus-response connection became independent of the presentation of the food (Depover, 2004). Skinner also created a negative reinforcement device. The rat in the box received a small electric shock if it did not push the lever in a certain amount of time.

This type of negative reinforcement was designed to regulate the behaviour with a certain form of preventive coercion, which aims to demonstrate that, as long as the subject behaves in accordance with what a system expects the subject to do, the subject will change and progress normally in the system. There are several examples today that use this control model to get us to adopt a conduit, such as the sounds, lights or even computer "vocal" messages that remind us to buckle our seat belts in cars.

Application of this Principle to Educational Video Game Design

Most video games operate on Skinner's token economy[8] principle in which it is necessary to collect resources continuously (point and inventory system) to adapt adequately in the virtual environment. Furthermore, Skinner's principle of negative reinforcement is used widely in life simulation games like *The Sims*® (Electronic Arts). In fact, if players let their *Sims* characters do as they like, they will adopt anti-social and self-destructive behaviours. It is necessary to regulate their life cycle to keep them reasonably satisfied with certain basic necessities.

According to Maslow's human needs theory, human motivation is conditioned by the progressive satisfaction of a group of needs organized into a hierarchical pyramid in which, at the base, there are the basic physiological needs, and, at the top, there are the highest psychological and emotional needs. The first level of the pyramid begins with the satisfaction of physiological needs related to survival (hunger, thirst, sexuality, rest, absence of pain). Then follows the satisfaction of the need for protection (safety), which must be met before the need for love (belonging) and then the need for self-esteem (recognition); finally, at the summit of the pyramid, is the need for self-realization and spirituality (Mias, 2005).

Although the progressive nature of this theory may be questioned (for example, if a need for personal esteem drives a subject to neglect personal safety: e.g., in competitions, contests or risky challenges), players of *The Sims®* who do not respect certain essential needs of their Sims characters could be the victims of reproach and social stigmatization.

Gagné's Behavioural Learning Model

What are the elements facilitating a learning situation? Are there steps to follow to acquire knowledge more effectively? According to Gagné and Briggs (1974), the acquisition of knowledge should be done in a learning context that allows nine successive stages to be followed in the order below (adapted from Hoffman, 2005):

- **Attract attention:** show an image of a chocolate cake, and describe how delicious it must be;
- **Announce learning objectives:** announce that the course objective will be to make a chocolate cake;
- **Remember the acquired knowledge:** question subjects on their knowledge about making a chocolate cake;
- **Explain the new knowledge:** show how a chocolate cake is made;
- **Assist the learning process:** show media elements helping subjects to understand the cake-making process (images, illustrations, video, narration, etc.);
- **Proceed with the experiment:** provide the ingredients for making the cake;
- **Provide feedback:** observe the performance of the task, and correct as needed;
- **Evaluate the performance:** allow subject to eat cake if it has been made successfully;
- **Encourage retention and knowledge transfer:** ask them to repeat the experiment by creating cakes with other ingredients.

Cognitive Learning Model

Similar to the way a computer operates, the human thought process consists of processing information in the form of abstract symbols that represent the reality on which we perform logical operations (Depover, 2004). Learners are active information-processing systems similar to computers: they perceive information that comes from the sensory register system (5 senses), recognize it, store it in the memory and then recover it when needed to understand their environment or resolve problems (Henri, 1997).

Sensory Register System

The sensory register system is the place in the human body where one receives via the five senses (sight, hearing, taste, smell and touch) stimuli coming from the external environment. Complex processes of the recognition of information forms and filters are implemented (Henri, 1997). Information filtering allows, for example, the voice of a person talking to us to be heard among ambient noises (Depover, 2004).

Example

It is sufficient to focus intensely on an object for several seconds and then close the eyes. Then there will be a phenomenon of persistence or consecutive images presented in the memory. The visual organ thereby has this capacity for memorization. Another example is to focus on a colourful object and then turn the gaze toward a grey piece of paper.

Working Memory

Working memory (or short-term memory) is the place in the brain where information perceived by the sensory register is transferred to a memory that has a very limited duration and capacity (Henri, 1997). The principle of the limited psy-

chological capacity of the working memory has been demonstrated by Miller (1956). The results of his study, *The Magical Number Seven, Plus or Minus Two,* demonstrate that, in the presence of non-structured elements (figures and syllables), we can remember seven of them. To increase that retention capacity, it is an issue of structuring the elements in distinct groups (Depover, 2004).

Example

Instead of memorizing the sequence of numbers, 51498730008237, we break it into short, easier to remember groups: 514 987 3000 8237. In the case of this figure, the technique thus reduces the effort of memorization to four instead of ten elements.

Information Retention Capacity

According to Dempster (1981), there is a relation between age and the ability to retain information. At about 11-12 years of age, the magical 7 plus or minus 2 is attained. Consideration of this relation is important during the design of educational games for younger children.

Long-Term Memory

Long-term memory is where information is stored in a memory with, technically, an unlimited capacity and retention. Long-term memory is the outcome of any information lasting more than a few dozen seconds (Henri, 1997). We perceive information based on what we already know, that is, on what is available in the long-term memory. The capacity to recall information is thereby connected with its context (Depover, 2004).

Example

A good way to activate the long-term memory for facilitating recollections is to return to the places where we spent our childhood, look at photographs or repeat a story from our own experience.

Application of these Principle to Educational Video Game Design

We can encourage the learning process with scenarios and learning materials. There are a certain number of techniques that improve the encoding and structuring of information in the memory (Depover, 2004). (Table 1)

Constructivism Learning Model

Constructivism emphasizes the notion of cognitive evolution in which specific stages may be observed in the course of the intellectual development of children. Inherited from psychologist Jean Piaget's work (1896-1980), constructivist pedagogy is concerned with the process of the genesis of cognitive structures called "schemes," which are observable behaviours and mental organizations involved in the acquisition or organization of knowledge. Those schemes grow, develop and change over time through assimilation or accommodation. Assimilation is the integration of new knowledge with an existing scheme, and accommodation is the readjustment of already existing schemes in response to knowledge that is foreign to or incompatible with those existing schemes. Major changes of children's cognitive capacities are called "stages of cognitive development" (Schäfer-Altiparmakian, 2005).

Hypermedia design must therefore take account of the target audience by translating and adapting the multimedia environment to children's cognitive modalities, depending on the stage of cognitive development corresponding to their age group.

Application of these Principles to Educational Video Game Design

The components effectively reinforcing learning are the close connection between the action and the area of learning domain, the possibility of exploring knowledge from different points-of-view,

Table 1.

Design element or technique	Pedagogical rule or usage in video games
Metacognitive variables	Focus on emphasizing all elements encouraging assimilation, such as previous structuring (objectives, posed questions, recall of previous structuring) and future structuring (syntheses, generalization, expansion, research perspectives). In video games you can see this in the back story, cut-scenes, maps or in the promotional trailer.
Self-questioning, problematization	Facilitates habituation of subjects to asking themselves questions about material to be learned. In video games you can see this with the tutorial mode, in fan sites or game communities.
Distributed learning	Focuses on spreading learning out over time instead of concentrating all of into the last minute (cramming). In video games you can see this with the ability to pause and resume a game sequence.
Latent information reactivation	Focuses on reactivating the memory through usage of a retrieval cue (ex.: information access path). In video games you can see this in game replays, back story and maps.
Overlearning	Pursues learning beyond the moment in which one has the impression of knowing, thus allowing the construction of more stable and enduring learning. Review via exercises or a research activity between two learning modules (or levels in games) are good examples. In video games you can see this with the sandbox or tutorial mode.
Tables, diagrams and graphics	These tools may be useful in several stages of a pedagogical project: at the beginning to provide a plan, a synopsis; during teaching to illustrate a concept visually, a relation; or even presented as a synthesis after learning. In video games you can see this with maps or H.U.D (Heads Up Display).
Flow charts	Allow the graphic representation of a process. Each form represents a stage or specific function (processing, making a decision, starting a sequence, acquiring of distributing information, etc.). In video games you can see this with mission maps.
Visual emphasis	Uses graphic language elements to communicate more effectively. All games using visual or sound signals to indicate when players must perform an action, avoid an obstacle, hit a target or is surrounded by a protection field are applying this design technique.

social interaction (competition or collaboration), learning through a buddy system, self-managed learning (metacognition), problem-resolution and management of complex resources. It seems important here to stress the contribution of Lev Vygostky's work (1896-1934) on learning through peer collaboration, more specifically the zone of proximal development. The results of his experiments verified the hypothesis that the mediation of a higher authority of knowledge, an adult, more specifically, encourages the acceleration of learning (Balmer, 2005). This principle can be applied to video games in which the presence of a help system is required. The spectrum of support possibilities is very wide: it can be as simple as frequently asked questions (FAQ) but can also be an intelligent agent or even a real tutor working from a distance. Support, assistance and accompaniment may be provided through multiple forms of agents called "online assistants." According to the constructivist view, they encourage the acquisition of knowledge and facilitate the system user's learning path.

Metacognition means both learners' knowledge of their own and others' cognitive processes and how individuals manage their own cognitive processes during problem resolution or the execution of a cognitive task that involves planning, supervising and evaluating their own cognitive processes. Therefore, students develop a learning strategy by taking notes and summarizing concepts. In preparation for exams, they develop metacognitive strategies by questioning themselves about the quality of their notes and on the need to add to them with additional readings (Basque, 2003).

Simulation, role and strategy games are very good examples of constructivist environments because they allow participants to manage resources, the maintenance and development of which require mathematical calculation and the management of a complex inventory of human, material and financial resources (Facer, 2005).

Learning with Video Games

Concurrently with media education,[9] there is a growing interest in the use of video games as learning tools. Current research in the area is focused on usage in schools of titles marketed to the general public and of video games created specifically for the school context (Facer, 2005).

For example, in 2001-2002, the Games-to-Teach Project presented 10 conceptual prototypes of next-generation educational games to support learning in math, science, and engineering at the advanced high school and introductory undergraduate levels (Squire, 2002). Among these prototypes are: *The Jungle of the Optics*, a game where players use a set of lenses, telescopes, cameras, optical tools and optics concepts to solve optics problems within a role-playing environment. *Hephaestus*, a massive multiplayer resource management game in which players learn physics and engineering through designing robots to colonize a planet. *Replicate!*, an action game in which players learn virology and immunology through playing a virus attempting to infect a human body and replicating it so that the virus may spread through a population. *Supercharged!*, a flying/racing game in which players learn about electromagnetism by flying a vessel, which has adopted the properties of a charged particle, through electric and magnetic fields.

As in the medieval times when playing cards allowed illiterate people to learn how to count, recognize symbols and develop cognitive skills, the usage of video games today allows the development of certain skills, such as hand-eye coordination (visio-haptic coordination), analysis and management of complex data, interpersonal communication, problem-resolution and literacy (Frété, 2002, citing Meggs, 1992).

Literacy concerns all reading and writing knowledge that allows a person to function in society. The level of knowledge needed to be functional changes over time and varies among societies. All the acquired knowledge must allow a person to read and understand three types of texts: narratives (e.g., newspaper articles), schematic texts (e.g., road maps) and quantitative texts (e.g., loan interest calculations). (Office québécois de la langue française. http://w3.granddictionnaire.com Original French consulted December 25, 2005).

Introduction: Can Video Games be Used for Learning?

According to Marshall (1964) "We shape our tools, and afterwards our tools shape us". Today, young people[10] subjected to the universe of the media, computer technology and video games are developing new cognitive and relational skills, and a growing number of teachers and researchers believe that video games facilitate the development of children's abilities and so, in that sense, shape them as well (Facer citing Tapscott, Greenfield and Prensky). Prensky (2000) has summarized these new cognitive or behavioural skills as:

- Accelerated and simultaneous information processing;
- Ability to process and distinguish several types of information from various sources rapidly and simultaneously;
- Prevalence of image over text;
- Preference for searching for meaning via visual content and then spending time on text to refine, expand and explore understanding of the subject;
- Random and distant access instead of step-by-step and local;
- Ability to jump from one kernel of information to another by creating connections rather than following an information narrative or hierarchy ;
- Familiarity with the concept of synchronous and asynchronous modes of access to scattered and distant resources;
- Activity and play rather than passivity and work;

- Tendency to prefer an active learning model (trial-and-error method) rather than learning in order to be able to act ;
- The game is valued and becomes relevant because it is played on the computer;
- Gratification and fantasy instead of patience and reality;
- Expectation of gratification based on effort ;
- Computer universe as a metaphorical space of fantastic and entertaining discovery;
- Technology as a motivational factor;
- The computer is a tool for play and discovery, and it is often via video games that young people become familiarized with new technologies.

Video games can be used in the school environment[11] to fulfill certain pedagogical functions, such as tutoring, exploration, entertainment, attitudinal change and the practice of certain personal and social competencies or skills (Mitchell and Savill-Smith, 2004). Furthermore, video games have demonstrated an interesting potential for the treatment of some cognitive and behavioural problems Griffiths (1997).

Competence and skill development

- **Ability to communicate and work collaboratively:** kids playing the games have to communicate with other players to describe what is happening, share resources and debate and discuss certain issues.
- **Ability to resolve problems:** children are faced with challenges or mysteries they have to resolve if they want to complete the game.
- **Ability to use numbers:** several simulation games require players to manage resources, the maintenance and development of which require mathematical calculation and budget planning.

Cognitive and behavioural problems

- Treatment of attention deficit disorder resulting in improved scanning and tracking (Larose et al. 1989; Pope and Bogart, 1996)
- Treatment of pain via distraction of cognitive attention: several tests have been conducted on patients suffering from pain, nausea, infarct, burns and even on kids undergoing chemotherapy (Vasterling et al., 1993).
- Treatment of schizophrenia (Samoilovich et al., 1992) and psychomotor abilities (Sietsema et al., 1993)
- Analysis of the development of children's ability to focus: some games on PlayStation 2 showed potential for assessing the ability to process visual information (Kirriemuir, 2002).

Evaluation of Video Game Learning

To solve problems and get around the obstacles in video games, players usually proceed in an exploratory, trial-and-error manner, which is a learning method that encourages the development of logical thought and, more broadly, the ability to solve problems (Inkpen et al. (1995). Furthermore, the familiarity with and interest in[12] video games may favourably influence the confidence kids will have when they use more common computer applications, such as office, communication and multimedia editing software (Mackereth, 1998).

Educational video games may encourage the acquisition of basic skills that, ideally, any learner must have mastered before leaving the school system (Frété (2002) citing the work of Jacques Henry and Jocelyne Cormier of DISCAS). Furthermore, it may be useful to identify the specific skills that can be developed via the usage of different educational video games (adapted from Frété, 2002).

Basic and Specific Skill Development

Ability to Equip Oneself Effectively

This skill involves the mastery of content, languages, structures and procedures while being able to develop positive attitudes toward oneself and others.

- **Mastery of content and languages:** people's bases of declarative knowledge allow them to identify, describe and generalize, with the assistance of organized systems, signs and conventions that in turn allow them to represent the real world and describe, manipulate and transmit information. These languages may be of several types: gestural, verbal, graphic, mathematic, artistic, etc. Some examples of game types: question-answer, memory and trial-and-error, matching, detective, quest and adventure, iconic interface, visual memory, reading of maps, plans and relational or presentational tables.
- **Mastery of structures, systems and procedures:** comprehension and management of dynamic and complex systems with a significant number of parameters, variables and interrelated processes. Some examples of game types are games of reflex and action, life simulation, ecosystems, conceptual models and dynamic systems.

Ability to Interact with the World

Acting on the world involves the ability to communicate (through the interpretation, choice and production of acts of communication) and to make decisions in a context of problem-resolution or even project realization.

- **Development of attitudes, communication and cooperation:** these include acquisition of open-mindedness, critical faculty, solidarity, independence, creativity and responsibility;
- **Comprehension of sender-receiver roles** and how to adapt own mode of communication depending on various contexts;
- **Knowledge of how to evaluate different types of discourse, communication situations, media, message content and sender-receiver intentions:** e.g., online games, virtual, practice and learning communities, role-playing, media ethics education and chatterbots;
- **Decision-making:** these include effective use of information in the context of a problem to be resolved or an action or project to be carried out;
- **Ability to analyze a context, anticipate results, define strategies for carrying out/managing a project:** e.g., life or ecosystem simulators, conceptual models and dynamic systems.

Motivational Factors of Video Games

To develop a motivating educational video game environment, some qualitative criteria should be observed in order to adopt players' or teachers' points-of-view.

An important study of 40 educational video games (Dempsey et al., 1997) presented a series of players' recommendations. Nearly eighty percent of the respondents said they used an exploratory trial-and-error method. That method is defined as the absence of a planned action strategy and involves actions/reactions depending on the circumstances, consequences and feedback of the interface or the system. Learning about the way to play the game is acquired through accumulation, that is, observation and active participation in the game rather than reading the instructions and rules. The reasons justifying this approach are the lack of clear instructions and objectives and a desire to explore the object of the game freely. Players often begin their exploration with the trial-and-error method and then possibly will look for a form of support, assistance or guidance by reading the instructions or hints appearing on the screen. Therefore, learning games must be presented in the form of an exploratory space for discovery with help functions that can be consulted in context as needed. The announcement of a purpose or objectives to be attained seems important for encouraging more commitment to this type of game.

General Recommendations for Educational Video Game Design

From the players' point-of-view, the following elements should be considered:

- Need for clear instructions;
- Need for sufficient level of motivation and challenge;
- Possibility of controlling certain game options: speed, level of difficulty, visual and sound effects and type of feedback;
- Importance of aesthetic quality of graphic and sound interface;
- Strong points: positioning, help, hints, integration of familiar scenarios or narratives;
- Weak points: lack of objectives, instructions, control and interactivity.

From the teachers' perspective, the following elements should be considered:

- Applications should include a clear pedagogical objective;
- Development teams should include teachers and kids throughout the project development cycle;
- Projects should entail a wide range of learning objectives;
- The role of the onsite/classroom teacher should be considered;
- Pedagogical scenarios should facilitate effective discussions between students and teachers.

Csikszentmihalyi's Flow Concept

Csikszentmihalyi's theory of Flow is the basis of all criteria promoting involvement and motivation[13] in video games. Flow is the physical and mental immersion people experience when they are involved in an activity so deeply that nothing around them seems to matter. In the flow state (being in the "zone") the proposed problem and the skill to resolve it are in balance (Malone 1980; Jones, 1998; Prensky, 2001).

The flow state involves the following:

- Activity is structured so that participants can increase or reduce the proposed challenge's level of difficulty to be in synch with the requirements of the [project] and their current skill level;
- Activity is isolated from other external and internal stimuli, at least on the perceptual level;
- Activity gives concrete feedback to users in a way that shows them how to meet performance criteria successfully;
- Activity offers a range of challenges or objectives and possibly several levels of difficulty for each, thus providing users with an increasingly complex understanding of a problem;
- Clear performance criteria that let users know their progress toward an objective at all times.

Jones (1998) has identified links between the components of the flow state and its possible usages in educational video games, and Crawford (1984) on the idea of learning needs as an essential motivational factor of games.

Flow State Components and Their Usage in Educational Video Games

The following should be considered to induce a state of flow:

- **Task with clear objective:** collection of elements, artefacts or points, resolving a mystery or problem or completing a quest
- **Achievable task:** usage of game levels: distribution of the task into small sections leading to the success of the quest in several stages
- **Possibility of concentrating on the task:** use of immersive and engaging metaphor
- **Task with immediate feedback:** tools allowing users to interact with on the environment as if the content were real
- **Profound yet effortless involvement:** environment functionally, aesthetically and cognitively stable point-of-view that keeps users in a coherent universe
- **Impression of control over actions:** direct manipulation and immediate feedback with mouse and keyboard
- **Sensation of immersion:** feeling of involvement in which nothing else seems to matter
- **Suspension of time:** usage of significant temporal jump cuts to advance in the storyline. A game extending over several years/centuries can be played in a few hours.
- **Need to prove oneself:** high scores facilitate entry into competition with other players. Some types of players who value competition are more motivated when their adversaries are worth the trouble of beating.
- **Need to transgress social restrictions:** players can be violent without feeling guilty. Extremely anti-social behaviour is possible within the safety provided by the virtual space of the game.
- **Need for real social connections:** players can, for example, organize game parties.
- **Need for exercise:** may be mental, physical or a combination of both
- **Need for recognition:** interaction allows players to be recognized and learn to know each other better.

Constraints on the Implementation of Video Games in Learning

(BECTA, 2001; McFarlane et al., 2002; Kirriemuir, 2002)

- It is difficult for teachers to identify what is pedagogically relevant (possible connections between game and curriculum)
  - It is difficult to promote educational potential of video games in the teaching profession
- There's a lack of time and resources needed to become familiarized with the game environments and to develop pedagogical scenarios adapted to the curriculum
  - It is difficult to concentrate exclusively on the relevant elements of a game due to number of functions that can distract users
- It takes considerable effort that teachers should deploy to ensure that students are in step with game instructions
  - There's a technical access and usage problems of hardware/software.

User-Centred Design

A user-centred environment takes players' psychomotor, cognitive and relational profile into account. Design consists of suggesting pedagogical scenarios adapted to the learning needs of each student. The concept of the user profile can then be considered in terms of learning styles, multiple intelligences and psychological types. However, applying user profiling specifically to Game Based Learning is outside of the scope for this article. This discussion is more about what are the basic parameters that could be observed in focus groups or when it's time develop a course outline with skill development objectives (psychomotor, cognitive and relational).

Analysis of Learning Styles

Barbara Prashnig worked with Rita Dunn to produce a research protocol for evaluating the learning, teaching and working styles of several types of people (Maaløe, 2004). This work was conducted after the development of *Learning Style Analysis*. This analytical method is represented in the form of a pyramid in which the first four layers correspond to the individual's innate traits or biological and genetic characteristics. The last two layers correspond to the acquired traits: conditioned or experiential learning produced through the person's life and through the sociocultural and emotional context in which s/he has grown up and evolved. The six layers of the pyramid model (Prashnig, 1998), including their main characteristics with regard to learning preferences, are the following:

1. **Asymmetry of the cerebral cortex** (dominance of the left brain or right brain): Reflective thinkers like time to consider everything before they make a decision, whereas impulsive thinkers make quick decisions based on little information. Analytic (left-brain dominant) people prefer logical, step-by-step information, concentrate well on details and are highly sequential in taking in new information. Holistic (right-brain dominant) people prefer to see the "big picture" when learning new things, are not interested in details and process information simultaneously.

2. **Sensory perception:** In learning situations, some people (auditory type) remember things they hear, are good listeners, like verbal instructions and/or prefer to discuss new information. Some people (visual type) remember much of what they read and prefer instructions to be written while others remember and understand best when shown pictures. Others use their imagination and many a combination of these modali-

ties. People with a tactile preference have a strong need to manipulate things and use their hands while listening or concentrating. Some people (kinesthetic type) like to be actively, physically involved in work projects and remember best through their own experiences; others have a strong intuition and need to feel good to understand and remember easily.

3. **Physical aspects:** Some people find it hard to sit still and need to move around a lot, especially when they are working or concentrating hard. Others prefer to stay put and avoid getting up when they work on something difficult. Some people work better when they nibble, eat or drink while concentrating, while others find it distracting when working on difficult tasks. People reach optimal cognitive performance when their brains are most active and so they can concentrate most easily. For some it's the early or late morning, for a few it's the afternoon and for many others it's the evening. The amount of time people can spend on cognitive effort varies, so some can concentrate for several hours while others need to take regular breaks to refresh their minds.

4. **Environment:** Several environmental (workplace) factors can affect the learning experience favourably or negatively. Some people need a to be in a quiet envieonment when working on something difficult, while others prefer backgound sound or music. Some people prefer bright light while others work far better in low light situations: too much light disrupts their concentration. Some people like warm temperatures when working, but others concentrate better when it's cool. Straight back chairs with desks suit a formal working style. Lounge chairs or lying on the floor when concentrating suits people with an informal working style.

5. **Social context:** Some people concentrate best when allowed to work on their own

while others prefer to have to work in a team. Some people perform best when they can share their ideas and work within a group of like-minded people who are all at a similar level. Some people love to be part of a team (sometimes as leader) and work most easily with others. Some people accept authority and need very regular feedback, while others prefer not to have authority figures present and don't need supervision.

6. **Personal attitudes:** Some enjoy work, are self-starters and high achievers. Others can lose motivation easily, like incentives and need all other preferences matched to improve the motivation for their work. Some people always finish what they begin while others stop when they lose interest and need frequent breaks and lots of encouragement to complete tasks. Some people need rules and regulations and always like to do what's "right"; others follow their own rules and like doing unconventional things, often going "against the current." People who take on responsibility do what's expected of them and consider the consequences of their actions carefully. Others don't consider work the most important thing in their lives, can be easily distracted from their duties and often forget what they promised. Some people need clear guidelines and a framework to work within; others prefer to work independently without needing instructions. Some like variety and do better when they have the chance to take on new challenges while others like the stability of a familiar and routine context on which they can depend every day.

Multiple Intelligences

The theory of multiple intelligences is based on the fact that human beings all possess an intelligence that can be manifested in several forms, as illustrated by all the human aptitudes and so all the possible crafts and professions. Each type of intelligence may be encouraged or valued by personal predispositions, specific situations or even the current values of the society in which the subject lives (Gardner, 1983). The following definitions are adapted from Isabelle (2002) and connect the forms of intelligence with the use of information technologies. The following table describes how computer systems might match people's multiple intelligences. Video games designer could want to develop one's specific form of intelligence by adding software functionalities listed in the computer programs column. (Table 2)

Myers-Briggs Psychological-Type Indicator

The theory[14] behind the psychological-type indicator is that the behavioural variations observed among individuals are not accidental but the consequence of spontaneous preferences related to four fundamental human dimensions: interaction with others, perception of the world, decision-making and life style. The combination of these preferences is manifested by various behaviours and allows for the delineation of 16 different psychological types.

Interaction with others:
- **Extraversion:** People who belong to this category prefer to draw energy from others, outside themselves; prefer to learn by doing, have people skills, verbalize and express themselves well in social situations
- **Introversion:** People who belong to this category prefer to get energy from own inner world of ideas, emotions and impressions; prefer to observe before acting; independent workers

Perception of the world:
- **Sensing:** People who belong to this category prefer to collect information via five

Table 2.

Form of intelligence	Definition/Skills	Computer programs
Linguistic	Deep knowledge of a language, ability to articulate expression and thought itself; **Profession types:** journalist, radio or TV broadcaster, storyteller, student, salesperson, writer	Word-processing, word games or matching, interactive history books, learning of languages, encyclopedias, text generators
Logical-mathematical	Ability to use figures to resolve concrete or abstract problems; **Profession types:** scientist, accountant, programmer, mathematician	Spreadsheets and databases; problem-resolution, quest or mystery games; games of strategy or logic; scientific discovery, experimentation and simulation
Visual-spatial	Ability to perceive, think about or recreate the visible world in three dimensions; **Profession types:** artist, sculptor, sailor, pilot, engineer, architect, film director, painter, sculptor.	Graphic creation in two and three dimensions; palette, shooting and steering games.
Musical	Ability to perceive and appreciate sounds, melodies and rhythms; **Profession types:** musician, dancer, orchestra leader	Sound editor and musical sequencer, karaoke, teaching music or an instrument
Corporal and kinesthetic	Ability to control movements of own body and manipulate objects (note: also the ability to create, i.e., go into action and update his/her different forms of understanding); **Profession types:** surgeon, athlete, artisan, clown, dancer	Software with data acquisition devices or peripherals (gloves, board, motion/pressure detector, etc.)
Interindividual or interpersonal	Ability to understand others, work with them, guess their moods, temperaments, intentions and desires and use them to own advantage, motivating others, listening to them attentively, finding the best in them; **Profession types:** business leader, theatre director, educator	Game networks, instant messaging, online discussion boards, life simulators
Introspective or intrapersonal	Ability for reflection, meditation, contemplation, spiritual quest; more individualistic, the person with this form of intelligence prefers to work alone and practice self-discipline.	Intelligence tests, tutorials, courseware, self-teaching software
Naturalistic	Ability to recognize and classify repetitive motifs (patterns) in nature; **Profession types:** naturalist classifying animals, plants or minerals into taxonomies	Spreadsheets and databases
Global or existentialistic	Ability to generalize and use several forms of intelligence to bring a morality and spirituality to her life	History, anthropology, social science, psychology. CD-ROMs.

senses and note the factual; realistic and pragmatic; like routine and order

- **Intuition:** People who belong to this category prefer to collect information via a sixth sense and note what could be; imaginative et abstract thought; like new challenges and the unknown

Decision-making:

- **Feeling:** People who belong to this category prefer to organize and structure information based on decisions made with values and feelings; more interested by people than by ideas; prefers conciliation to conflict; empathic, sensitive to the feelings of others; warm and enthusiastic

- **Thinking:** People who belong to this category prefer to organize and structure information based on logical and objective decisions; more interested in concepts, ideas and visions

Life style:

- **Perceiving:** People who belong to this category prefer to lead spontaneous and flexible lives; They are curious, flexible, adaptable, tolerant and it is difficult for them to form opinions

- **Judging:** People who belong to this category prefer to lead planned and organized lives; have clear ideas and strong opinions; rapid judgement and decision-making

Design Specifications for Successful Development of Educational Video Games

Designers/screen writers must formulate their designs by preparing and illustrating a group of preliminary documents articulating the project's orientation. Depending on the scope or progress of the project, several types of design and technical specifications[15] may be produced. The form of specifications in this capsule is a preliminary proposal that must later be supported by mapping illustrating the aesthetic that makes the project's essential functions operational. It is an issue of benchmarks allowing design/screen writing work to begin. Downloadable examples of each preliminary document can be found under "Preparation of specifications" in the "Design model" capsule of the following Web site: http://www.clikmedia. ca/CM

Purposes (One Page Suggested)

Definition of expected project objective: purposes must determine the target audience and the needs the project meets. They include a general description (paragraph of less than 200 words summarizing the design) and an abridged description comprised of a promotional hook serving as the communication aspect. When it is a recreational-educational project, the skills it focuses on are described. Furthermore, a summary description of the game system must help us to imagine the game universe (e.g., setting, atmosphere and characters). The idea of the game, the role of players and the overall quest of the game must be explained. It is also important to identify the minimum technological configuration required to use the application adequately.

The idea of the game may be inspired by the concept of a film, with the difference being that the outcome is directed by players and not by a predetermined purpose. The idea of a film is a one-sentence summary of the film's direction: its theme, point-of-view, story and outcome. The idea

must contain the main character and her action that exposes her desire or need (Ziolkowski & Barzman, 1999). For example: after a homicide, two police detectives look for a psychopathic killer who murders his victims based on which of the seven deadly sins they have committed. *Sooner or later, one of the detectives will be confronted with his own avenging morality*. This is the idea of the film *Seven*. In this example, the underlined sentence presents a summary of the story's quest. The main idea of the film (the theme) is expressed by the sentence in italics: the drama of an individual that will lead to him committing one of the seven deadly sins. The point-of-view is that of the main character, the detective who tries to solve this vile case (*Seven*, 1997: Directed by David Fincher and starring Brad Pitt, Morgan Freeman, Gwyneth Paltrow and Kevin Spacey).

Synopsis (Two Pages Suggested)

General description of the application: in the case of a recreational-educational application, the synopsis may revolve around two distinct but complementary axes: pedagogical[16] and recreational. Description of the game story line, i.e., the progression of the action in space and time: above all, that progression includes key events in the story (dramatic turning points) that allow the location of points for going on to higher game levels. They also include the list of obstacles that players will have to confront and the means at their disposal to circumvent them. For all quests (overall and secondary quests), there must be a list of the main elements of which they are comprised: playing and non-playing characters (NPCs), game rules, territory, setting and props, point-of-view, point and inventory system, time lock, help system, connectivity and interface customization.

Competition Research (One Page Suggested)

Comparison and analysis of a minimum of three similar projects: analysis of the competition highlights the strong and weak points of each application and fosters your proposal's novelty and innovation. The evaluation report may be done with the aid of the multimedia production evaluation grid located at: http://www.clikmedia.ca/CM/B_Analyse_Grille.pdf

Specific Functionalities
(One Page Suggested)

Description of interactivity mechanisms: for example, the interface elements allowing parameter control or validation, manipulation, magnification, selection, assembly, passage to a higher level, saving data, networking updating and a direct messaging system.

Graphical User Interface Prototyping
(Three Pages Suggested)

Interfaces broadly illustrate the project aesthetic and display formatting. They must be accompanied by a legend describing the content and functionalities associated with each interface zone. Some interfaces are enough to give an overview of the whole: e.g., navigation summary interface (main menu), inventory system or game instructions interface and problem-solving interface (game obstacle or learning validation).

Information and Process Mapping
(One to Three Pages Suggested)

These documents are communication tools circulating in the development team and then with external project agents (client, donor, etc.). They enable the diagrammatic visualization of the connections unifying the components of a complex system. Those diagrams (flow chart, modelization, data flow, etc.) make the hierarchical organization and program input functionalities (e.g., login interface, alert box) and output functionalities visible (e.g., sending of e-mail, saving data). They must be designed with the idea in mind

that non-programmers have to be able to interpret them easily.

Fact Sheet (One Page Suggested)

This illustrated document synoptically presents and defines a project's main characteristics. It is a tool for marketing and promoting the product during informal meetings in specialty shows, business fairs. exhibits, etc.

FUTURE RESEARCH DIRECTIONS AND CONCLUSION

In this chapter, we first saw that video game play encourages the development of psychomotor, cognitive and interpersonal skills. Observation of certain trends in development has shown us that contemporary educational video games fall on a historic continuum that began before the advent of the computer era and they seem, in their way, to commission certain political, economic and sociocultural values.

This chapter has outlined the pedagogical trends inspiring the development of learning scenarios adapted for video games. In addition, we also present the work of researchers who are interested in learning using "commercial" video games, or games specifically for pedagogical contexts. This is a relatively new field of research the intention of which is to respond to a certain negative perception of playful learning environments. Several play-based educational applications were developed to validate specific competencies or skills. They often featured marketing approaches that dazzled parents, who were relatively uninformed with respect to pedagogical usability, with potentially innumerable learning opportunities for their children. Yet experience has shown that children who want to play quickly lose interest if they perceive a game as cover for a pedagogical project. When they are at home, children do not necessarily want to recreate the school environment.

For the educational video game designer, the secret lies in developing an activity that carries the pedagogical project yet appears first and foremost as play and free from all formal, academic constraints. Since young people are already very attached to their digital leisure activities, it seems that role-playing and strategy games, as well as the emerging dynamic systems (for example, *Starcraft®*, *SimCity®*, and *Civilization®*), may be a springboard, a new approach for learning several concepts such as resource management, the dynamics of complex systems, designing data bases and object modelling. As a matter of fact, role-playing and strategy games, by abstracting the logical models to which they give form, make it possible to create and manage complex resource inventories. In this way, they represent a model that is particularly well-adapted to teaching principles of design and object modelling. Concepts related to the creation of classes make it possible to define attributes and methods for each object eventually instantiated by the player or the game system. Interpersonal skills may also be enhanced through the use of network technology, which connects several people at a distance from one another in order to share information or cooperate on common projects.

Several research questions related to learning using video games are on hold. These include investigation of the long-term effects certain types of video games may have on cognitive, identity and social development for younger generations. The study of adaptive learning systems is only in its early stages, opening the way for several types of experimentation, especially with clients who have cognitive deficits or learning disabilities. In parallel, the all-digital paradigm has encouraged the emergence of social and cultural practices that emphasize visual and iconic thought as well as social connection. This has led to the birth of a new perception of space and fragmented time, and the actual sensation of presence even when at a distance. Finally, the emergence of social networks (Web 2.0) bears the seed of a collaborative intelligence that is wide-spread and very dynamic. These knowledge aggregators, by virtue of the phenomenal quantity not only of information but also of individuals whom they connect, put a much finer point on the issues of cognitive overload and the disorientation that results from virtually infinite hypermedia navigation. What will be the long-term effects on learning of these new ways of perceiving, being and acting?

REFERENCES

Balmer, B. (2009). *Home page*. Retrieved December 18, 2009, from http://www2.uqtr.ca/hee/site_1/index.php?no_fiche=2287

Crawford, C. (1984). *The art of computer game design. Chapter one. What is a game?* Emeryville, CA: Mcgraw-Hill/Osborne Media.

Csikszentmihalyi, M. (1990). *Flow: The psychology of optimal experience*. New York: Harper and Row.

Dempsey, J., Lucassen, B., Haynes, L., & Casey, M. (1997). *An exploratory study of forty computer games. (COE technical report no. 97-2)*. University of South Alabama.

Depover, C. (1998). *Les environnements d'apprentissage multimédia, analyse et conception*. Paris: l'Harmattan.

Depover, C., De Lièvre, B., Quintin, J.-J., Porco, F., & Floquet, C. (2004). *Partie IV.1: Modèle centré sur le traitement de l'information*. Retrieved December 18, 2009, from http://ute.umh.ac.be/dutice/uv6a/module6a-4a.htm

Depover, C., Giardana, M., & Marton, P. (1998). *Les environnements d'apprentissage multimédia–analyse et conception: Le concept clé: L'interactivité*. (pp. 94-96). Paris: L'Harmathan.

DISCAS. (2005). *Home*. Retrieved December 18, 2005, from http://www.csrdn.qc.ca/discas/tdm.html

Downes, T. (1998). *Children's use of computers in their homes*. Unpublished doctoral thesis, University of Western Sydney Macarthur.

Esculier, A. (2009). *Le wondergraphe*. Retrieved December 18, 2009 from http://www.dma.ens.fr/culturemath/maths/html/juel/juel.html

Facer, K. (2005). *Computer games and learning. Why do we think it's worth talking about computer games and learning in the same breath?* Bristol, UK: NESTA Futurelab.

Facer, K. (2005). *Could computer games help to transform the way we learn?* Bristol, UK: NESTA Futurelab.

Falgas, J. (2004). *Toile Ludique, Vers un conte multimédia*. Université de Metz, UFR des sciences humaines et arts.

Frété, C. (2002). *Le potentiel du jeu vidéo pour l'éducation*. Mémoire du DESS STAF, Université de Genève.

Gagne, R. M., & Briggs, L. J. (1974). *Principles of instructional design*. New York: Holt, Rinehart, & Winston.

Gardner, H. (1983). *Frames of mind: The theory of multiple intelligences* (2nd ed.). London: Fontana.

Henri, F. (1997). *Le multimédia permet-il d'apprendre?* Module T213: Support pédagogique au cours TEC 6205. Environnements d'apprentissages multimédia. Montréal: Télé-université et École de technologie supérieure.

Henri, F. (1997). *L'ingénierie pédagogique*. Module T211: Support pédagogique au cours TEC 6205. Environnements d'apprentissages multimédia. Montréal: Télé-université et École de technologie supérieure.

Hoffman, B. (Ed.). (2009). *Gagne's nine events of instruction*. Retrieved December 18, 2009, from http://coe.sdsu.edu/eet/articles/gagnesevents/index.htm

Isabelle, C. (1987). *Étude de facteurs influençant l'utilisation par les filles des micro-ordinateurs*. Université de Montréal.

Isabelle, C. (2002). *Regard critique et pédagogique sur les technologies de l'information et de la communication*. Montréal: Chenlière/McGraw-Hill.

Jones, M. G. (1998). *Creating engagement in computer-based learning environments*. Retrieved December 18, 2009, from http://itech1.coe.uga.edu/itforum/paper30/paper30.html

Kirriemuir, J., & McFarlane, A. (2002). *Report 8: Literature review in games and learning*. NESTA FuturLab Series.

Malone, T. (1980). *What makes things fun to learn? A study of intrinsically motivating computer games*. Palo Alto, CA: Xerox.

Mathonière, J.-M. (2009). *L'art de mémoire*. Retrieved December 18, 2009, from http://www.compagnonnage.info/ressources/tarot.htm

McFarlane, A., Sparrowhawk, A., & Heald, Y. (2002). *Report on the educational use of games*. TEEM (Teachers Evaluating Educational Multimedia). Retrieved December 18, 2009, from http://www.teem.org.uk/publications/teem_games-ined_full.pdf

Miller, G. A. (1956). The magical number seven, plus or minus two: Some limits on our capacity for processing information. *The Psychological Review, 63*, 81-97. Retrieved December 18, 2009, from http://www.musanim.com/miller1956/

Prashnig, B. (1998). *The power of diversity: New ways of learning and teaching*. Auckland, New Zealand: David Bateman. Retrieved December 18, 2009, from http://WWW.CLC.CO.NZ/learningstyles.asp?page=styles&sub=pyramid

Prensky, M. (2001). *Digital game-based learning*. New York: McGraw-Hill Education.

Rabecq-Maillard, M. (1969). *Histoire des jeux éducatifs*. Paris: Nathan.

Schäfer-Altiparmakian, M. (2005). *Les stades piagétiens*. Institut de Recherche et de Conseil dans le domaine de la famille. Retrieved December 18, 2009, from http://www.unifr.ch/

Skinner, B. F. (1971). *L'analyse expérimentale du comportement, un essai théorique*. Bruxelles: C. Dessart.

Squire, K. (2002). Cultural framing of computer/video games. *Games Studies- the International Journal of Computer Game Research*. Retrieved december 18, 2009, from http://www.gamestudies.org/0102/squire/

Thorndike, E. (1898). Animal intelligence: An experimental study of the associative processes in animals. *Psychological Review, 2*(8), 1–109.

ENDNOTES

[1] Literacy is all the reading and writing knowledge a person needs to function in society. The knowledge necessary to be functional changes over time and varies from one society to another. All acquired knowledge must allow a person to read and understand three types of texts: narratives (e.g., newspaper articles), maps and texts with quantitative content (e.g., calculation of interest on a loan) (http://w3.granddictionnaire.com Retrieved December 25, 2005).

[2] That century was also marked by better access to basic education and by major scientific discoveries in physics, mathematics, electromagnetism and visual imagery techniques. The fad created by the promises of technological, cultural and social transformation was a powerful vector of capitalization in the development of the educational game industry.

[3] Several large companies, such as Milton Bradley (1860) and Parker Brothers (1883), were founded in this era; today Hasbro, world leader of the game industry, owns both of them.

[4] Psychomotor skills: through the manipulation of various types of prostheses (mouse, keyboard, joystick, etc.) or the active participation in multi-sensorial spaces. These skills may be substantially developed in action games.

[5] Identity and relational skills: through the development of characters in role, action or strategy games. These skills may be equally developed in action games, adventure and strategy games and resource-management games.

[6] Intellectual skills: through analysis, strategic planning and problem resolution. These skills may be substantially developed in adventure and strategy games.

[7] Pavlov's dog experiment consisted of ringing a bell at the same time the dog was given food. After repeating this association between the sound and the food several times, Pavlov noticed that the dog salivated at the sound of the bell alone (Depover, 2004). Pavlov received the Nobel Prize in medicine in 1904 for the discoveries about conditioned responses he made during his experiments.

[8] The application of intermittent reinforcement programs to people has had great success, specifically in the development of certain behaviours for intellectually-deficient subjects. On this basis, token economy systems have been developed that consist of providing subjects with so-called secondary reinforcements in the form of tokens that allow them to obtain treats, watch a video, be told a story, etc. (Depover, 2004).

[9] Media education in schools greatly encourages kids to appropriate information and

communication technologies (ICT) through the production of video reports, web pages and multimedia presentations. This tendency is part of the larger context of the response to ICT usage requirements by primary and secondary educational programs in Quebec, Canada and all of the industrialized countries, where ICT usage is prevalent.

10 People born since the computer revolution began in the general public have grown and changed their cultural consumption habits with video games at home or in arcades, music videos (MTV) and more recently, the Internet. Therefore, among the young, technology has accentuated and reinforced certain cognitive or behavioural capacities.

11 The TEEM project (McFarlane et al, 2002) reports how teachers were taught how to use video games in the classroom setting. In the study, more than 700 parents and kids were questioned about the educational potential that could come from that usage. The report stresses that the classroom usage of certain video games for the general public, such as *Sim City*, *Age of Empires*, *Rollercoaster Tycoon* and *Championship Manager*, can help in the development of some personal and social skills (Facer, 2005).

12 In this vein, two studies on kids using computers at home contend that their early interactions with the computer universe, more specifically in the video game context, encourage them to develop a recreational approach to computers (Downes, 1998). Therefore, this validates the idea that the trial-and-error method is valuable and that traditional earning models associated with reading instructions and textbooks are often less effective ways of introducing kids to the world of information and communication technologies (Facer et al., 2003).

13 Motivation is one of the key concepts of most learning theories because it provides the possibility of creating intentions and goals without which no learning can really take place (Frété, 2002).

14 Descriptions were adapted from Gaëtan Boisvert (2000), professor at the Public Administration University, Quebec (ENAP). Designers of all role games and life simulators in which characters or roles are developed are likely to benefit by using the Myers-Briggs Type Indicator (MBTI) as a tool for analyzing psychological profiles. For example, in the game *The Sims* (Electronic Arts), players can create their Sims (avatars) according to several traditional personality traits.

15 The method presented in this capsule is intended for anyone who wants to interest a producer or subsidizing organization in an educational video game design. It does not concern the material, human and financial resources needed for development. Also, this method does not concern the preparation of the production bible either, the production bible completely documenting the design, process and evolution of a creative project (see glossary for more details).

16 Description of the abilities, skills and knowledge that must be acquired to attain the skills that the application targets: this section includes a description of the skills to be attained (and the required steps for doing so), action instructions and learning and evaluation strategies.

Section 2
Cognitive Approach to Game–Based Learning:
Design Patterns and Instructional Design

This section describes GBL solutions that concentrate on the cognitive aspects of learning, with particular emphasis on instructional design, educational theories, and design patterns. The authors address the difficult and complex tasks of identifying, measuring and combining the factors that contribute to both learning and motivation in video games.

Chapter 5
A First Step towards Integrating Educational Theory and Game Design

Jan-Paul van Staalduinen
Delft University of Technology, The Netherlands

ABSTRACT

As of yet, there is no clear relationship between game elements and deep learning. This chapter used a literature review to create an overview of 25 game elements that contribute to learning. The TOPSIM game, by TATA Interactive Systems, was used in a case study to delve into the educational impact of 16 of these game elements. Using pre-game and post-game tests, it was concluded that the students learned from the game, and that they considered the following elements to contribute to their learning: 'action-domain-link', 'adaptation', 'debriefing', 'conflict', 'control', 'fantasy', 'goals/objectives', 'mystery', and 'safety'. These results will be used in the construction of a game-based learning model that also incorporates theory on education game design, research on educational elements and principles in games, and theory on core elements that make up all games, whether educational or entertaining.

INTRODUCTION

For years games have been used to teach about a wide variety of fields, such as business, military, and policy analysis (Gredler, 2004). Although much is known about games and learning in general, little is known about what components of these games (i.e., game attributes) influence learning outcomes (Wilson, Bedwell et al. 2009).

DOI: 10.4018/978-1-60960-495-0.ch005

Kebritchi and Hirumi (2008) argue that synthesis of information on how established learning theories and instructional strategies are being applied to design educational games to guide research and practice, has been limited. Pedagogy and game design currently seem to be two separated worlds.

Concurrently, a growing body of literature emphasizes the importance of applying established instructional strategies and theories to design educational games and to facilitate game-based learning (Quinn, 1994; Squire, 2004; Dickey,

2005; Egenfeldt-Nielsen, 2005; Kiili, 2005; Amory, 2006; Dickey, 2006; Egenfeldt-Nielsen, 2006; Dickey, 2006b; Bots & Daalen, 2007; Kebritchi & Hirumi, 2008; Hong, Cheng et al. 2009). This, apparently, is a general problem with regards to both level of education and type of game: Egenfeldt-Nielsen's and Squire's work focuses on secondary education, whereas Amory, Bots & Daalen, and Kiili are rooted in higher education; and while authors studied different kinds of games, they reached the same conclusions about design.

Insight into the learning process of games is limited: it is still unclear why, when, how and what participants learn from which phase in a game, or what influence individual facilitators have on the learning outcomes of a game (Peters, Vissers et al. 1998; Squire, 2004; Dickey, 2005; Kiili, 2005; Dickey, 2006; Leemkuil, 2006; Dickey, 2006b; Burgos, van Nimwegen et al. 2007; Oliver & Carr, 2009). If we wish to improve the quality of the learning that occurs while playing these games, we first need to know which elements in games contribute to learning. Game 'elements' are the components that make up the game; in some research these are also called the game 'attributes'.

This chapter describes the outline and results of our literature research into game elements that contribute to learning. We have combined three lines of thinking to construct an initial overview of elements in games that relate to deep learning. These three lines of thinking are theory on serious game design, research on educational elements and principles in games, and theory on core elements that make up all games, whether educational or entertaining. This overview of game elements can serve as a first step in creating a game-based learning model, which would combine theories on game elements, engagement, and learning organization. We used the TOPSIM game, by TATA Interactive Systems, as a case study to delve into the educational impact of some of these game elements.

BACKGROUND

Games and Learning

Gredler (1996) argued that insight in the connection, between educational games and disciplinary theories of learning and knowing, has been limited. Lack of understanding of the learning process of games prohibits structured implementation of instructional design, and control of desired learning outcomes, in game design (Egenfeldt-Nielsen, 2005).

This problem is encountered in the full spectrum of the field of game design. Egenfeldt-Nielsen (2006) points out that overviews of the broader field of learning from video games are limited, because of:

- Underdeveloped theory on facilitating learning through video games, and weak theoretical knowledge of video games (Kirriemuir & McFarlane, 2003).
- Further work still needs to be done to bring the games development and education communities closer together in order to build shared vocabularies and expectations, as well as to inform new learning designs to support effective game-based learning experiences (Freitas, 2006).
- Incomplete use of previous literature owing to the variation in terminology, place of publication, and researcher backgrounds (Squire, 2002).

Egenfeldt-Nielsen (2005) concludes that the inherent learning features of computer games should be maintained when designing and thinking about educational game titles. But the current inability to structure and control learning within games, makes valid statements about the expected effectiveness of a game impossible.

In the past years numerous games have been designed and best practices have come forth from the design processes (Quinn, 1994; Mayer

& Veeneman, 2002; Kirriemuir & McFarlane, 2003). These best practices, combined with current theories on game design and instructional design, provide a solid theoretical and practical foundation. Educational games that are built on sound educational theories could be seen as instruments that promote the use of modern educational theories in the classroom (Amory & Seagram, 2003).

Gee (2003) states that games nowadays are mostly classified as entertainment. The educational framing may be alien to many, even though players learn the relevant actions in a given game in order to acquire the wished for game outcome (e.g. 'winning'). But games do not automatically facilitate a wished for educational outcome, as this is seldom part of either the game universe or the game culture. Egenfeldt-Nielsen (2005) states that it is necessary to either make educational interventions through the surrounding context of the computer game experience, or to design games that support an educational framing.

Gee (2005) argues that a good instructional game would pick its domain of authentic professionalism well, intelligently select the skills and knowledge to be distributed, build in a related value system as integral to gameplay, and clearly relate any explicit instructions to specific contexts and situations.

Early work on using an educational framework in game design has been done by Quinn (1994; 2005). Both Amory (Amory & Seagram, 2003; Amory, 2006) and Kiili (Kiili, 2005; Kiili, 2005b; Kiili, 2005c; Kiili, 2006; Kiili, 2007) expanded on this and developed their own game design models, which drew heavily on constructivist theory. Other important components of the game design models were instructional design theory and Kolb's experiential learning cycle (Kolb, 1984).

Deep Learning

Educational research states that learners adopt either deep or surface learning strategies (Newman, Johnson et al. 1997; Biggs & Tang, 1999). When

people are 'surface learning', they skim texts and information, memorize it, and 'regurgitate' their knowledge for tests. When people are 'deep learning', they try to develop a critical understanding of the material, underlying meanings, main ideas, themes, principles, and successful applications. When surface learning, un-interpreted information transfer occurs from information source, to brain, to examination paper. But deep learners integrate new learning into their knowledge; thus critical thinking is a key skill that is required in deep learning. Newman, Johnson et al. (1997) state that deep learning is promoted by active learner participation. Learner participation flows forth from interaction, which takes place in a social context, such as group learning. So Newman, Johnson et al. argue that there are relationships between deep learning, critical thinking, and group learning. Similarly, Anderson, Krathwohl et al. (2001) consider three learning outcomes:

1. **No (intended) learning:** the learner does neither possess, nor is able to use the relevant knowledge.
2. **Rote learning:** the learner possesses the relevant knowledge, but cannot use that knowledge to solve problems; the knowledge cannot be transferred to a new situation.
3. **Meaningful learning:** the learner possesses the relevant knowledge, but can also use that knowledge to solve problems; the knowledge can be transferred to new problems and new learning situations. The learner has attended to relevant information and has understood it.

Thus, 'meaningful learning' provides learners with the knowledge and cognitive processes they need for successful problem solving (Anderson, Krathwohl et al. 2001). We argue that 'meaningful learning' and 'deep learning' are the same concept, both emphasizing *retention* and *transfer* of relevant knowledge. For the sake of simplicity, only the term 'deep learning' will be used in our research.

We use the term retention to talk about learning that persists beyond the learning situation and can be applied at appropriate opportunities on an ongoing basis. We use the term transfer to characterize learning applied to appropriate situations not covered in the learning situation. Our goals of learning, then, are to foster retention and transfer of knowledge and skills. [...] Retention is fostered by comprehension and practice. [...] Transfer is developed through practice across contexts (Quinn 2005).

Surface and deep approaches to learning are not personality traits, as is sometimes thought, but are most usefully thought of as reactions to the teaching environment (Biggs & Tang, 1999), e.g. in our research: games. Games provide an environment where learners can exercise in problem solving, in a way that allows for mistakes and failures from which they can learn (Gee, 2003; Veen & Vrakking, 2006; Veen & Staalduinen, 2009).

Intrinsic Motivation in Games

Intrinsic motivation comes from rewards inherent to a task or activity itself. Lepper argues that intrinsic motivational orientation may have significant instructional benefits (Lepper, 1988). Malone (1981) has argued that the following characteristics are common to all intrinsically motivating learning environments: challenge, fantasy, and curiosity. Malone and Lepper later added 'control' to the list of characteristics (Malone & Lepper, 1987; Lepper, 1988). Rieber (1996) argues that games represent the instructional artifact most closely matching these characteristics. Garris, Ahlers et al (2002) built upon this and other research, to expand the list of key gaming features necessary for learning:

Although many have noted the potential benefits that may be gained from incorporating game characteristics into instructional applications, there is clearly little consensus regarding how

these essential characteristics are described. This suggests that either the characteristics of games are so varied and diffuse that attempts to categorize them are likely to be futile or that different researchers are using different approaches and terms to describe similar game dimensions. We believe the latter is the case. Based on a review of the literature, we conclude that game characteristics can be described in terms of six broad dimensions or categories: fantasy, rules / goals, sensory stimuli, challenge, mystery, and control (Garris, Ahlers et al. 2002).

Games are designed to generate a positive affect in players and are most successful and engaging, thus intrinsically motivating, when they facilitate the flow experience (Gee, 2003; Salen & Zimmerman, 2004; Kiili, 2005; Schell, 2008). Flow describes a state of complete absorption or engagement in an activity and refers to the optimal experience (Csikszentmihalyi, 1975; Csikszentmihalyi, 1990). During optimal experience, a person is in a psychological state where he or she is so involved with the goal driven activity that nothing else seems to matter.

A game can facilitate the flow experience if the challenges that the game offers are up to par with the skills of the player. If a game provides not enough challenge, the player eventually gets bored. If a game provides too much challenge, the player might experience anxiety, or quit after endless defeats. If the challenges of a game are equal to the player's skills, the player enters the flow channel (Csikszentmihalyi, 1990), shown in Figure 1. As part of meeting a challenge is knowing what the challenge is, presenting clear goals and providing feedback are an important component of game design (Bateman & Boon, 2006).

The flow state has a positive impact on learning (Webster, Klebe Trevino et al. 1993; Brockmyer, Fox et al. 2009) and thus should be the desired outcome of a game. If the system can offer the learner challenges that are in correspondence with his or her skills, the possibility of

Figure 1. Two axes (challenges and skills) and the flow channel (Csikszentmihalyi 1990)

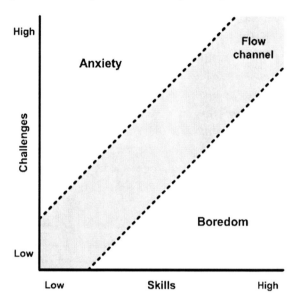

experiencing flow is higher. Generally, the aim of an educational game is to provide students with challenges related to the main task so that flow experience is possible (Kiili, 2005). Important flow antecedents in games are clear goals, active player feedback, and the (sense of) control that players have over the game (Kiili, 2006).

A Constructivist Approach to Games

An important, but sometimes complicating factor, is the relationship between 'games' and 'play'. Salen and Zimmerman (2004) conclude that there are two ways to frame the relationship of play and games:

1. **Games are a subset of play:** The category of play represents many kinds of playful activities. Some of these activities are games, but many of them are not. In this sense, games are contained within play.
2. **Play is a subset of games:** Games are complex phenomena and there are many ways to frame them and understand them. *Rules,*

play and culture are three aspects of the phenomena of games. In this sense, play is contained within games.

One design artifact consistent with 'play', is the constructivist idea of a 'microworld' (Martens, Diener et al. 2008). Rieber (1996) therefore suggests that games might be understood within a constructivist framework of learning. The concept of 'microworlds' was introduced by Papert (1981). Microworlds are given domains or environments which may be explored in a non-linear way by users or learners. Microworlds thus describe a situation where learners do not study a particular domain but become part of the scenario, thus stimulating interest and motivation, and are able to interact with and explore complex ideas within such spaces (Rieber, 1996). Rieber believes games may provide a meaningful way to present microworlds to learners. For learning to be effective a relationship needs to be made between what is learnt and how it is applied in practice. This broadly follows Kolb's experiential learning cycle, although connections are not always made between what is learned and how it is applied in practice (Freitas, 2006).

Constructivism is the psychological theory which argues that humans construct knowledge and meaning from their experiences (Piaget, 1955; Bruner, Jolly et al. 1976; Vygotsky, 1978). Constructivism is not a particular pedagogy; it is the theory of describing how learning happens, and which suggests that learners construct knowledge out of their experiences. Constructivist educational theory focuses on concept development and deep understanding, rather than behaviors or skills, as the goals of instruction (Amory & Seagram, 2003). This concept development and deep understanding are constructed by the learner itself, instead of transmitted directly from one person (the teacher) to another (the learner). The fundamental principle of constructivism is that knowledge is actively built up by the learner (Siemen, 2004). Learning involves individual constructions of knowledge that come about through interactions with one's environment or culture (Rieber, 1996). Therefore learners are viewed as constructing their own knowledge of the world.

For effective learning, knowledge should be uniquely constructed by people through play, exploration and social discourse with others. Learning objectives presented in constructivist learning environments should be firmly embedded in context, and should, at least in some way, represent every day life situations. Learners should also accept responsibility for their own learning and be self-motivated to explore different knowledge domains (Amory & Seagram, 2003).

TOWARDS A GAME-BASED LEARNING MODEL

Identifying Game Elements: A Literature Review

Researchers on game design have argued that an 'ultimate' design method for educational games cannot be constructed, and thus focus on providing suggestions for design (Amory & Seagram, 2003; Kiili, 2005c; Amory, 2006; Becker, 2006; Kiili, 2006; Becker, 2008). At the same time, educationalists have constructed overviews of educational elements and principles in games (Gee, 2003; Gee, 2005; Wilson, Bedwell et al. 2009). A third line of researchers has identified core elements that make up all games, whether educational or entertaining (Salen & Zimmerman, 2004; Juul, 2005). These three lines of thinking can be combined to construct an initial overview of elements in games that relate to deep learning. This overview of game elements can serve as a first step in creating a game-based learning model. For this literature review, which was carried out in August 2009, we used the taxonomy as presented by Cooper (Cooper, 1985), which can be found in appendix A.

The focus, or central interests of our review were: theories on the educational value of games, models of educational elements in games, and educational analyses of (commercial) games. The goal of this literature review was to make an overview of elements in games that relate to deep learning. This means integrating and synthesizing past literature related to our research focus, through both generalization, and linguistic bridge-building. This naturally implies a judgmental approach to the literature found, as decisions have to be made about the inclusion of literature, and the comparative qualities of definitions.

The aim of this review was to be exhaustive in its coverage, and to include all (or most of it) of the literature on serious games and (serious) game design, within respect to our literature keywords and search boundaries. Thesis, anti-thesis and synthesis were based on this all-inclusive information base.

Several sources were used for the literature search. First of all, a list of relevant scientific journals, from both the gaming-simulation and the educational disciplines. Although ideally these journals were ISI-rated, we recognized that games research has really taken of in the last decade, resulting in numerous journals that haven't existed long enough to be ISI-rated. Excluding these journals would most likely put serious limitations on our literature review. For this reason we included journals in our review that are younger than ten years old, as long as they are peer-reviewed. As our research takes place on the intersection of game design and education, journals used for our literature review included the following keywords in their title: *education (educational), higher education, game(s) (gaming), learning, computer, technology,* and *multi-media*. The journals that we used for our literature review can be found in Appendix B.

The second source for our literature review were (scientific) search engines and other (online) archival databases. These search engines were also used to find further material by authors that describe specific sets of elements in games. The search engines that we used for our literature review can be found in Appendix B. Keywords that were used in the literature search are: *game attributes, learning, learning outcomes, pedagogical issues, educational effectiveness, educational goals, game elements, game properties, games and learning, learning principles, game-based learning, serious games, educational games, instructional games,* and *edutainment.* To exclude non-game related publications, the words *games, gaming,* or *game design* were added to further specify the search requests.

Significant research on games has been carried out for the last 40 years (Duke, 1974; Shubik, 1975a; Shubik, 1975b). Even in the early days of games research, the educational impact of games has been discussed and described. Even though computer technology may have made great leaps in the past 20 years, causing great changes in the way we think about computer games, the essentials of board games have remained more or less the same. Therefore, we incorporated the full 40 years (or so) of research into our literature review.

Results from the Literature Review

Using the described research approach and search parameters, 85 articles (journal and conference), and six books / dissertations were found. Of the articles that were found, 13 described game design methods or aspects of game design. Another 16 described learning theories or instructional strategies used to design games. These articles were also reviewed to find recommended guidelines for game design. A further 15 articles focused on game elements that relate to learning, or that optimize the learning effect of a game. The remaining articles that did not discuss specific learning theories or instructional strategies were excluded from this review, including 18 articles that focused on the uses, effectiveness and advantages of game-based learning, 20 articles that focused on case studies of using games to teach students, and three ar-

ticles that focused on design of non-game-related instructional methods. Interestingly, the majority (73%) of these sources was written after 1999, even though we looked through the full last 40 years of publishing.

Game Elements that Contribute to Learning

Our aim is to construct an overview of game elements that are assumed to increase the learning effect of serious games, based on the sources we found in our literature review. This overview of game elements can serve as a first step in creating a game-based learning model. Using the articles found in our literature review, we ultimately identified 25 game elements that related to learning. These elements are listed and described in Table 1. Due to space restrictions, these 25 elements are only given short descriptions, but readers are referred to the selected references in which the elements are more fully studied and explained. Of particular note are the works of Gee (2003), Juul (2005) and Salen and Zimmerman (2004), that seem to be fundamental to nearly all of the selected references. Usage of these game elements in a game is tied to game type and game subject. Games often use only a selection of the available game elements; even good games are not required to use all the elements.

A FIRST CASE STUDY: THE TOPSIM GAME

Many authors have identified important game elements that relate to learning, but whether they all increase the learning effect of serious games is still unknown. To determine whether there is an actual connection between a game element and learning, we use case studies. For our first case study, we used the TOPSIM game. "TOPSIM - General Management II," built by TATA Interactive Systems, is a business management

Table 1 Game elements, definitions, and selected references for those elements

Game element	Short description	Selected references
Action-Domain Link	The story of the game consists of situations where the learner really needs to apply the knowledge that he gains from playing the game. This includes a close enough link to reality so that learners easily see how to apply knowledge to the real world.	Gunter, Kenny et al. (2007); O'Connor and Menaker (2008); Quinn (2005)
Adaptation	The level of difficulty of the games gradually increases, or adjusts to the skill level of the player.	Wilson, Bedwell et al. (2009)
Assessment / Feedback	The measurement of achievement within game (e.g., scoring). The game gives the learner feedback on the outcomes of his actions. This provides users with opportunities to learn from previous actions. Scoring also compares performance among (competing) players.	Chin, Dukes et al. (2009); Dempsey, Haynes, et al. (2002); Elverdam and Aarseth (2007); Houser and Deloach (1997); Kiili (2006); Quinn (2005); Wilson, Bedwell et al. (2009)
Challenge	The amount of difficulty and probability of obtaining goals a player has within the game. A challenging game possesses multiple clearly specified goals, progressive difficulty, and informational ambiguity. Challenge adds fun and competition by creating barriers between current state and goal state. Combined with feedback, it provides a systematic balance of difficulty that changes as the learner progresses.	Amory and Seagram (2003); Amory (2006); Dempsey, Haynes, et al. (2002); Elverdam and Aarseth (2007); Garris, Ahlers et al. (2002); Moser (2000); Quinn (2005); Wilson, Bedwell et al. (2009)
Conflict	Solvable problems that the player is confronted with within the game and that usually drive the game's plot or in-game action by providing interaction. Conflict can be provided by the game itself (e.g. puzzles), by autonomous game agents (e.g. enemies) and by other players.	Amory and Seagram (2003); Amory (2006); Wilson, Bedwell et al. (2009)
Control	The player's possibilities for active and direct manipulation of specific aspects the game. In order to exert control, the learner needs to be active in making decisions in the story. Abundant learner control gives the player a sense of unrestricted options.	Amory and Seagram (2003); Amory (2006); Dempsey, Haynes, et al. (2002); Garris, Ahlers et al. (2002); Kiili (2006); Moser (2000); O'Connor and Menaker (2008); Quinn (2005); Wilson, Bedwell et al. (2009)
Debriefing / Evaluation	To utilize opportunities for learning, an evaluative session (the debriefing) is held after the game. In the evaluation the players and the facilitator / teacher talk about the experiences and outcomes of the game. The individual player can be evaluated, the players can be evaluated as a team, or they can be evaluated both as a team and as individual players.	Elverdam and Aarseth (2007); Peters and Vissers (2004); Peters, Vissers, et al (1998)
Fantasy	The make-believe aspects of the game; environment, scenario's (narrative), the role(s) of the player, non-player characters (game agents) that can be interacted with. "Exogenous fantasy is a direct overlay on learning content. It is dependent upon the skill, but the skill does not depend on the fantasy. Endogenous fantasy is related to learning content. It is an essential relationship between the learned skill and the fantasy context (engaging and educational) (Habgood, Ainsworth, et al. 2005)."	Dickey (2006); Garris, Ahlers et al. (2002); Gunter, Kenny, et al. (2007); Habgood, Ainsworth, et al. (2005); Moser (2000); O'Connor and Menaker (2008); Wilson, Bedwell et al. (2009)
Goals / Objectives	Goals and objectives describe the game's win conditions. In this capacity the provide motivation for actions within the game. The game's objectives can either be absolute (unchanging), or subject to change, depending on specific circumstances, scenario's and player actions.	Amory and Seagram (2003); Amory (2006); Elverdam and Aarseth (2007); Garris, Ahlers et al. (2002); Houser and Deloach (1997); Kiili (2006); O'Connor and Menaker (2008); Quinn (2005); Wilson, Bedwell et al. (2009)
Instructions / Help / Hints	Helpful comments, tutorials, and other hints that the game provides in order to get a player started with quickly, to get him / her out of a difficult situation, or to get him acquainted quickly with newly introduced aspects of a game.	Dempsey, Haynes, et al. (2002); Houser and De-loach (1997); Kebritchi and Hirumi (2008)

continued on following page

Table 1. continued

Game element	Short description	Selected references
Interaction (Community)	"Interpersonal activity that is mediated by technology, which encourages entertaining communal gatherings by producing a sense of belonging (Wilson, Bedwell et al. 2009)."	Amory and Seagram (2003); Amory (2006); O'Connor and Menaker (2008); Wilson, Bedwell et al. (2009)
Interaction (Game equipment)	"The adaptability and manipulability of a game. The game changes in response to player's actions (Wilson, Bedwell et al. 2009)."	Dempsey, Haynes, et al. (2002); O'Connor and Menaker (2008); Wilson, Bedwell et al. (2009)
Interaction (Interpersonal)	"Face-to-face interaction, relationships between players in real space and time. It provides an opportunity for achievements to be acknowledged by others, and challenges become meaningful, which induces involvement (Wilson, Bedwell et al. 2009)."	Amory and Seagram (2003); Amory (2006); O'Connor and Menaker (2008); Wilson, Bedwell et al. (2009)
Language / Communication	Specific lingual or communication rules of the game.	Wilson, Bedwell et al. (2009)
Location	The physical or virtual environment in which the game takes place; thus linked to 'fantasy'. Location influences rules and solution parameters.	Dickey (2006); Westera, Nadolski, et al. (2008); Wilson, Bedwell et al. (2009)
Mystery	The gap between available information and unknown information. Mystery provides puzzlement and complexity, and triggers curiosity, and is enhanced by surprise and unpredictability (random elements).	Amory and Seagram (2003); Amory (2006); Garris, Ahlers et al. (2002); Moser (2000); Wilson, Bedwell et al. (2009)
Pieces or Players	The game pieces (objects) or people that are included in the game scenario. This includes game items, player characters (avatars) and real life human participants.	Dempsey, Haynes, et al. (2002); Dickey (2006); O'Connor and Menaker (2008); Wilson, Bedwell et al. (2009)
Player Composition	The organization of players in a game; individual, as a team, multiple individuals (multiplayer), or multiple teams.	Elverdam and Aarseth (2007)
Problem-Learner Link	The way in which the game's location, theme and story relate to the learner's interests. It makes the game relevant to the player.	Amory and Seagram (2003); Amory (2006); Corbeil (1999); Gunter, Kenny, et al. (2007); Quinn (2005)
Progress	The measure of how the player progresses in achieving the goals (win conditions) of the game.	Quinn (2005); Wilson, Bedwell et al. (2009)
Rules	Rules constitute the inner, formal structure of games. Rules impose limits on player action. The rules also set up potential actions, actions that are meaningful inside the game, but meaningless outside. Rules specify limitations and affordances. Rules established criteria for how to win.	Amory and Seagram (2003); Amory (2006); Elverdam and Aarseth (2007); Garris, Ahlers et al. (2002); Quinn (2005); Wilson, Bedwell et al. (2009)
Safety	The lack of real world consequences that actions within the game have; the only consequence is a possible loss of dignity when losing. This provides players with a safe way to experience the reality, as presented in the game. It allows for risk-taking and experimentation, thus providing players with more learning opportunities.	Grammenos (2008); Houser and Deloach (1997); O'Connor and Menaker (2008); Wilson, Bedwell et al. (2009)
Scope	The player's perception of the game's reality, that the game allows; a more narrow scope of representation provides a player with focus, a broader scope of representation provides a player with distractions.	Elverdam and Aarseth (2007); Houser and Deloach (1997); Wilson, Bedwell et al. (2009)
Sensory Stimuli	The game's presentation stimulate player's senses and tap into the player's emotions, allowing for a (temporary) acceptance of the game's reality (fantasy, location, theme) by the player.	Dempsey, Haynes, et al. (2002); Garris, Ahlers et al. (2002); O'Connor and Menaker (2008); Wilson, Bedwell et al. (2009)
Theme	The setting or context of the game. A game is a thematically driven experience.	Amory and Seagram (2003); Amory (2006); Corbeil (1999); Dickey (2006); Quinn (2005)

game that establishes a link between business management theory and business management in practice. In TOPSIM, student teams play a company that produces and sells copiers. Together with other teams, the students form the copier market in which they compete against each other. As a company, students have to make decisions about important business factors, such as the acquisition of production lines, marketing budgets, human resource management, research & development and environmental impact. As part of a course, this game was played game with 59 students, divided into 12 groups. The game was played for a full study week (40 hours), during which the students played several consecutive rounds of the game.

Setup of the Case Study

The case study is limited to the TOPSIM game. This means that we can only study the relationship between learning and the game elements that are in the TOPSIM game. Game elements that were found in the literature review, but are not in the TOPSIM game, thus cannot be studied. For future research this has some implications; it means that we have to study different games to get a clear picture of the learning impact of all game elements.

For this case study, as part of playing the game, students were presented with three questionnaires:

1. The first questionnaires was a pre-game questionnaire, in which students were asked about their previous experience with games. Also, students were asked to self-rate their knowledge, of 17 subjects taught in the TOPSIM game, on a five point Likert scale.

2. The second questionnaire was held post-game, in which students were asked about their experiences with / during the TOPSIM game. Also, students were asked again to self-rate their knowledge, of 17 subjects taught in the TOPSIM game, on a five point Likert scale, to check if playing the game had had any impact on this.

Table 2. Game elements in the TOPSIM game

Action-Domain Link	Goals / Objectives
Adaptation	Instructions / Help / Hints
Assessment / Feedback	Interaction (Interpersonal)
Challenge	Location
Conflict	Mystery
Control	Pieces or Players
Debriefing / Evaluation	Safety
Fantasy	Scope

3. The third questionnaire was another post-game questionnaire, held one week after playing the game. In this questionnaire, students were asked to reflect back on playing the TOPSIM, and indicate which of the 16 game elements in Table 2 they thought contributed to their learning experience. Descriptions of these elements were tailored to the way they were implemented in the TOPSIM game. They were asked to indicate this on a five point Likert scale.

The results of the questionnaires were entered in SPSS. The first and second questionnaires were compared to each other to establish whether actual learning had taken place, according to the students. Because this was a self-rated test, the exact scores of the students before and after were not relevant. But the difference in scores (the actual increase or decrease) was considered indicative of the students' learning experiences. Our assumption is that students are capable of indicating whether they have learned something, although we acknowledge that using student opinions in our study has certain limitations. For our case study it is less important how much has been learned, but more important to conclude that learning has taken place.

Case Study Outcomes

To see whether the students rated themselves as having learned from playing the game for a full week, their pre-game and post-game scores on the

17 subjects taught through the game, were compared. A paired-samples t-test was conducted to evaluate the impact of the intervention on students' scores on their self-rating. All post-game scores for the 17 subjects were higher than the pre-game scores, but there was a statistically significant increase for 9 of the 17 subjects. The eta squared statistic with these 9 subjects was larger than 0.14 (0.32 on average), indicating a large effect size. Given the fact that the students spent the entire week working on these subjects, we conclude that this large effect size was caused by playing the game. Although these results do not indicate anything about the use of game elements, they do lead us to conclude that the students learned from playing the game, which is important for further results from the case study.

With regards to the educational contribution of game elements, the questionnaires produced the following results:

- There were no conclusive negative scores for any game element students were asked about. Only one element had a mean score below 3 ('Scope'), but with high kurtosis, indicating more evenly spread out answers, implying no consensus.
- There was general consensus on the positive learning impact of 'Adaptation' and 'Conflict'. Both game elements score a mean well above 4.00, with a negative kurtosis, indicating more evenly spread out answers, indicating in this case that most students scored either a 4 or a 5 (the lowest score given on both elements was a 3).
- Students indicated a high positive impact for 'Action-Domain-Link', 'Debriefing', 'Mystery', and 'Safety'. These game elements had means well above 4.00, and a skewness lower than -0.200, indicating answers leaning towards one extreme. A kurtosis > 0.100 indicated that the scores approached a Bell curve shape, indicating consensus among the students' answers.

- Students indicated a somewhat positive impact for 'Control', 'Fantasy', and 'Goals / Objectives'. These game elements had means well above 3.50, and a skewness lower than -0.200, indicating answers leaning towards one extreme. A kurtosis > 0.100 indicated that the scores approached a Bell curve shape, indicating consensus among the students' answers.
- No significant results were found for 'Assessment / Feedback', 'Challenge', 'Instructions / Help / Hints', 'Interaction (Interpersonal)', 'Location', 'Pieces or Players', and 'Scope', with statistics leading to inconclusive outcomes.

CONCLUSION AND FUTURE RESEARCH

In this chapter we have presented an overview of game elements that is based on current insights, ideas and theories on educational games. This overview consists of 25 game elements that increase the learning effect of serious games. Additionally, this overview can enhance educational game design, by providing insight into the educational impact of a specific design.

In a case study, students indicated that at least 9 of these game elements, 'Action-Domain-Link', 'Adaptation', 'Debriefing', 'Conflict', 'Control', 'Fantasy', 'Goals / Objectives', 'Mystery', and 'Safety', contributed to their learning while playing the game. Other game elements require more research before definitive conclusions can be drawn. Currently none of the 16 tested game elements has been indicated as negatively contributing to learning. The limitation of this case study is that we currently do not have a valid method to truly objectively study the impact of individual game elements, as they are too interconnected within a specific game. This is why we rely on student experiences to determine which game elements have an impact on learning. Future research will address distinguishing between individual game elements.

For the foreseeable future, more research is required on this overview. Serious games (incorporating different elements) need to be observed through case studies, before we can draw conclusions about the entire overview. Also, experiments are needed to test the specific kind of impact of game elements; not just whether there is a positive or negative impact. This will require different research methods and instruments. The overview of game elements that contribute to learning will then be adapted according to research outcomes.

Once those conclusions are drawn, the overview will become part of a game-based learning model. Although early educational game design models by Garris, Ahlers et al (2002) and Wilson, Bedwell et al (2009) touch upon instructional design, they do not take the larger questions of learning alignment and the impact of specific learning theories into account. Important aspects, such as engagement and 'flow' are also left out. Future work will be aimed at constructing a model that incorporates these different aspects, including learning organization theory (Bloom, Englehart et al. 1956; Anderson, Krathwohl et al. 2001), Flow-theory (Csikszentmihalyi 1990), and Engagement-theory (Moser 2000). This framework of game elements would explore the relationship between individual game elements and expected learning outcomes. This proposed hybrid framework can be used to design games, or to map out the design of existing games. It can be used both as a design aid and an evaluation tool. Ultimately, this framework could assist game designers in constructing their own game design methods that lead to more effective serious games.

ACKNOWLEDGMENT

The authors would like to thank TATA Interactive Systems GmbH for their input and support on the TOPSIM case study.

REFERENCES

Amory, A. (2006). *Game object model version II: A theoretical framework for educational game development*. Educational Technology Research and Development.

Amory, A., & Seagram, R. (2003). Educational game models: Conceptualization and evaluation. *South African Journal of Higher Education, 17*(2), 206–217.

Anderson, L. W., & Krathwohl, D. R. (Eds.). (2001). *A taxonomy for learning, teaching, and assessing: A revision of Bloom's taxonomy of educational objectives*. New York: Addison Wesley Longman, Inc.

Bateman, C., & Boon, R. (2006). *21st century game design*. Hingham, MA: Charles River Media, Inc.

Becker, K. (2006). Pedagogy in commercial video games. In Gibson, D., Aldrich, C., & Prensky, M. (Eds.), *Games and simulations in online learning: Research and development frameworks*. Hershey, PA: Idea Group Inc.doi:10.4018/9781599043043. ch002

Becker, K. (2008). *The invention of good games: Understanding learning design in commercial video games*. Calgary, Alberta: University of Calgary.

Biggs, J., & Tang, C. (1999). *Teaching for quality learning at university*. Berkshire, UK: Open University Press.

Bloom, B. S., & Englehart, M. D. (Eds.). (1956). *Taxonomy of educational objectives. The classification of educational goals: Handbook 1: Cognitive domain*. New York: Longmans.

Bots, P. W. G., & v. Daalen, C. E. (2007). Functional design of games to support NRM policy development. *Simulation & Gaming, 38*(4), 512–532. doi:10.1177/1046878107300674

Brockmyer, J. H., & Fox, C. M. (2009). The development of the game engagement questionnaire: A measure of engagement in video game-playing. *Journal of Experimental Social Psychology, 45,* 624–634. doi:10.1016/j.jesp.2009.02.016

Bruner, J. S., & Jolly, A. (1976). *Play-its role in development and evolution.* New York: Basic Books, Inc.

Burgos, D., van Nimwegen, C., et al. (2007). Game-based learning and the role of feedback. A case study.

Chin, J., & Dukes, R. (2009). Assessment in simulation and gaming: A review of the last 40 years. *Simulation & Gaming, 40*(4), 553–568. doi:10.1177/1046878109332955

Cooper, H. (1985). *A taxonomy of literature reviews.* Annual Meeting of the American Educational Research Association. Chicago.

Corbeil, P. (1999). Learning from the children: Practical and theoretical reflections on playing and learning. *Simulation & Gaming, 30*(2), 163–180. doi:10.1177/104687819903000206

Csikszentmihalyi, M. (1975). *Beyond boredom and anxiety.* San Francisco: Jossey-Bass Publishers.

Csikszentmihalyi, M. (1990). *Flow: The psychology of optimal experience.* New York: Harper Perennial.

Dempsey, J. V., & Haynes, L. L. (2002). Forty simple computer games and what they could mean to educators. *Simulation & Gaming, 33*(2), 157–168. doi:10.1177/1046878102332003

Dickey, M. D. (2005). Engaging by design: How engagement strategies in popular computer and video games can inform instructional design. *Educational Technology Research and Development, 53*(2), 67–83. doi:10.1007/BF02504866

Dickey, M. D. (2006). Game design narrative for learning: Appropriating adventure game design narrative devices and techniques for the design of interactive learning environments. *Educational Technology Research and Development, 54*(3), 245–263. doi:10.1007/s11423-006-8806-y

Dickey, M. D. (2006b). *Game design and learning: a conjectural analysis of how massively multiple online role-playing games (MMORPGs) foster intrinsic motivation.* Educational Technology Research and Development.

Duke, R. D. (1974). *Gaming: The future's language.* New York: Sage Publications.

Egenfeldt-Nielsen, S. (2005). *Beyond edutainment: Exploring the educational potential of computer games.* Copenhagen: IT-University of Copenhagen.

Egenfeldt-Nielsen, S. (2006). Overview of research on the educational use of video games. *Digital kompetanse, 1*(3), 184–213.

Elverdam, C., & Aarseth, E. (2007). Game classification and game design: Construction through critical analysis. *Games and Culture, 2*(3), 3–22. doi:10.1177/1555412006286892

Freitas, S.d. (2006). Learning in immersive worlds: A review of game-based learning. *Journal of the International Society of Computing.* London.

Garris, R., & Ahlers, R. (2002). Games, motivation, and learning: A research and practice model. *Simulation & Gaming, 33*(4), 441–467. doi:10.1177/1046878102238607

Gee, J. P. (2003). *What video games have to teach us about learning and literacy.* New York: Palgrave Macmillan.

Gee, J. P. (2005). *What would a state of the art instructional video game look like?* Innovate - Journal of Online Education.

Grammenos, D. (2008). *Game over: Learning by dying. CHI 2008.* Florence, Italy: ACM.

Gredler, M. E. (1996). Educational games and simulations: A technology in search of a research paradigm. In Jonassen, D. H. (Ed.), *Handbook of research for educational communications and technology* (pp. 521–539). New York: MacMillan.

Gredler, M. E. (2004). Games and simulations and their relationships to learning. D.H. Jonassen (Ed.), *Handbook of research on educational communications and technology.* Mahwah, NJ: Association for Educational Communications and Technology.

Gunter, G. A., & Kenny, R. (2007). Taking educational games seriously: Using the RETAIN model to design endogenous fantasy into standalone educational games. *Educational Technology Research and Development, 56,* 511–537. doi:10.1007/s11423-007-9073-2

Habgood, M. P. J., & Ainsworth, S. E. (2005). Endogenous fantasy and learning in digital games. *Simulation & Gaming, 36*(4), 483–498. doi:10.1177/1046878105282276

Hong, J.-C., & Cheng, C.-L. (2009). Assessing the educational values of digital games. *Journal of Computer Assisted Learning, 25,* 423–437. doi:10.1111/j.1365-2729.2009.00319.x

Houser, R. & Deloach, S. (1997). Learning from games: Seven principles of effective design. *Technical Communication,* 319-329.

Juul, J. (2005). *Half-real: Video games between real rules and fictional worlds.* Cambridge, MA: MIT Press.

Kebritchi, M., & Hirumi, A. (2008). Examining the pedagogical foundations of modern educational computer games. *Computers & Education, 51,* 1729–1743. doi:10.1016/j.compedu.2008.05.004

Kiili, K. (2005). Digital game-based learning: Towards an experiential gaming model. *The Internet and Higher Education, 8*(1), 13–24. doi:10.1016/j.iheduc.2004.12.001

Kiili, K. (2005b). Content creation challenges and flow experience in educational games: The IT-Emperor case. *The Internet and Higher Education, 8*(3), 183–198. doi:10.1016/j.iheduc.2005.06.001

Kiili, K. (2005c). *Educational game design: Experiential gaming model revised.* Pori, Tampere University of Technology.

Kiili, K. (2006). Evalutions of an experiential gaming model. *Human Technology, 2*(2), 187–201.

Kiili, K. (2007). Foundation for problem-based gaming. *British Journal of Educational Technology, 38*(3), 394–404. doi:10.1111/j.1467-8535.2007.00704.x

Kirriemuir, J., & McFarlane, A. (2003). *Literature review in games and learning.* Futurelab Series.

Kolb, D. A. (1984). *Experiential learning.* Englewood Cliffs, NJ: Prentice-Hall, Inc.

Leemkuil, H. H. (2006). *Is it all in the game? Learner support in an educational knowledge management simulation game.* University of Twente.

Lepper, M. R. (1988). Motivational considerations in the study of instruction. *Cognition and Instruction, 5*(4), 289–309. doi:10.1207/s1532690xci0504_3

Malone, T. W. (1981). Toward a theory of intrinsically motivating instruction. *Cognitive Science, 5*(4), 333–369. doi:10.1207/s15516709cog0504_2

Malone, T. W., & Lepper, M. R. (1987). Making learning fun: A taxonomy of intrinsic motivations for learning. In R.E. Snow & M.J. Farr (Eds.), *Aptitude, learning, and instruction: Vol. 3. Conative and affective process analyses.* (pp. 223-253). Hillsdale, NJ: Lawrence Erlbaum.

Martens, A., & Diener, H. (2008). *Game-based learning with computers–learning, simulations, and games. Transactions on Edutainment*. Berlin, Heidelberg: Spinger-Verlag.

Mayer, I., & Veeneman, W. (2002). *Games in a world of infrastructures: Simulation-games for research, learning and intervention*. Delft, The Netherlands: Eburon.

Moser, R. (2000). *A methodology for the design of educational computer adventure games. Computer Science & Engineering, Faculty of Engineering. South-Wales*. UNSW.

Newman, D. R., & Johnson, C. (1997). Evaluating the quality of learning in computer supported co-operative learning. *Journal of the American Society for Information Science American Society for Information Science, 48*(6), 484–495. doi:10.1002/(SICI)1097-4571(199706)48:6<484::AID-ASI2>3.0.CO;2-Q

O'Connor, D. L., & Menaker, E. S. (2008). Can massively multiplayer online gaming environments support team training? *Performance Improvement Quarterly, 21*(3), 23–41. doi:10.1002/piq.20029

Oliver, M., & Carr, D. (2009). Learning in virtual worlds: Using communities of practice to explain how people learn from play. *British Journal of Educational Technology, 40*(3), 444–457. doi:10.1111/j.1467-8535.2009.00948.x

Papert, S. (1981). Computer-based microworlds as incubators for powerful ideas. In Taylor, R. (Ed.), *The computer in the school: Tutor, tool, tutee* (pp. 203–210). New York: Teachers College Press.

Peters, V., & Vissers, G. (2004). A simple classification model for debriefing simulation games. *Simulation & Gaming, 35*(1), 70–84. doi:10.1177/1046878103253719

Peters, V., & Vissers, G. (1998). The validity of games. *Simulation & Gaming, 29*(2), 20–30. doi:10.1177/1046878198291003

Peters, V., Vissers, G., et al. (1998). Debriefing depends on purpose. J.L.A. Geurts, C. Joldersma, & E. Roelofs (Eds.), *Gaming/simulation for policy development and organizational change*. Tilburg, The Netherlands: Tilburg University Press.

Piaget, J. (1955). *The child's construction of reality*. Wellingborough, Northants, Weathery Woolnough.

Quinn, C. N. (1994). Designing educational computer games. In Beattie, K., McNaught, C., & Wills, S. (Eds.), *Interactive multimedia in university education: Designing for change in teaching and learning* (pp. 45–57). Amsterdam: Elsevier Science.

Quinn, C. N. (2005). *Engaging learning: Designing e-learning simulation games*. San Francisco: Pfeiffer.

Rieber, L. P. (1996). Seriously considering play: Designing interactive learning environments based on the blending of microworlds, simulations, and games. *Educational Technology Research and Development, 44*(2), 43–58. doi:10.1007/BF02300540

Salen, K., & Zimmerman, E. (2004). *Rules of play: Game design fundamentals*. Cambridge, MA: The MIT Press.

Schell, J. (2008). *The art of game design: A book of lenses*. Burlington, MA: Morgan Kaufmann.

Shubik, M. (1975a). *Games for society, business, and war*. Amsterdam: Elsevier Scientific Publishing.

Shubik, M. (1975b). *The uses and methods of gaming*. Amsterdam: Elsevier Scientific Publishing.

Siemens, G. (2004). *Connectivism: A learning theory for the digital age*. Retrieved August 4, 2008, from http://www.elearnspace.org/Articles/connectivism.htm

Squire, K. (2002). *Cultural framing of computer/ video games*. Game Studies.

Squire, K. (2004). *Replaying history: Learning world history through playing Civilization III*.

Veen, W., & Staalduinen, J. P. v. (2009). *Homo zappiens and its impact on learning in higher education*. Algarve, Portugal: IADIS Press.

Veen, W., & Vrakking, B. (2006). *Homo zappiens: Reshaping learning in a digital age*. London: Network Continuum Education.

Vygotsky, L. S. (1978). *Mind in society-the development of higher psychological processes*. Cambridge, MA: Harvard University Press.

Webster, J., & Trevino, L. K. (1993). The dimensionality and correlates of flow in human-computer interactions. *Computers in Human Behavior, 9*, 411–426. doi:10.1016/0747-5632(93)90032-N

Westera, W., & Nadolski, R. (2008). Serious games for higher education: A framework for reducing design complexity. *Journal of Computer Assisted Learning, 24*(5), 420–432. doi:10.1111/j.1365-2729.2008.00279.x

Wilson, K. A., & Bedwell, W. L. (2009). Relationships between game attributes and learning outcomes. *Simulation & Gaming, 40*(2), 217–266. doi:10.1177/1046878108321866

ADDITIONAL READING

Abt, C. C. (1970). *Serious games*. New York, NY: The Viking Press, Inc.

Adams, E., & Rollings, A. (2007). *Game Design and Development: Fundamentals of Game Design*. Upper Saddle River, New Jersey: Pearson Education, Inc.

Amory, A., & Seagram, R. (2003). Educational Game Models: Conceptualization and Evaluation. *South African Journal of Higher Education, 17*(2), 206–217.

Avedon, E. M., & Sutton-Smith, B. (1971). *The Study of Games*. New York: John Wiley & Sons.

Becker, K. (2007). Digital game-based learning once removed: Teaching teachers. *British Journal of Educational Technology, 38*(3), 478–488. doi:10.1111/j.1467-8535.2007.00711.x

Björk, S., & Holopainen, J. (2004). *Patterns in Game Design*. Boston: Ma, Charles River Media.

Blow, J. (2004). Game Development: Harder Than You Think. *Queue, 1*(10), 28–37. doi:10.1145/971564.971590

Caluwé, L. d., & Hofstede, G. J. (Eds.). (2008). *Why do games work?* Deventer: Kluwer.

Crawford, C. (1984). *The art of computer game design*. Berkely, California: Osborne / McGraw-Hill.

Duke, R. D., & Geurts, J. L. A. (2004). *Policy games for strategic management: Pathways into the unknown*. Amsterdam: Dutch University Press.

Freitas, S. d. (2006). Using games and simulations for supporting learning. *Learning, Media and Technology, 31*(4), 343–358. doi:10.1080/17439880601021967

Harteveld, C., & Guimaraes, R. (2009). *Balancing Play, Meaning and Reality: The Design Philosophy of LEVEE PATROLLER*. Simulation & Gaming OnlineFirst.

Juul, J. (2005). *Half-real: Video Games between Real Rules and Fictional Worlds*. Cambridge: MIT Press.

Kirriemuir, J., & McFarlane, A. (2002). *Use of Computer and Video Games in the Classroom*. Coventry: Becta.

Klabbers, J. H. G. (2003b). Gaming and simulation: Principles of a science of design. *Simulation & Gaming, 34*(4), 569–591. doi:10.1177/1046878103258205

Mayer, I., & Veeneman, W. (2002). *Games in a world of infrastructures: simulation-games for research, learning and intervention*. Delft: Eburon.

Mitchell, A., & Savill-Smith, C. (2004). *The use of computer and video games for learning: A review of the literature*. London: Learning and Skills Development Agency.

Oblinger, D. G., & Oblinger, J. L. (Eds.). (2005). *Educating the Net Generation*. Washington: Educause.

Papert, S. (1981). *Computer-based microworlds as incubators for powerful ideas. The computer in the school: Tutor, tool, tutee. R. Taylor* (pp. 203–210). New York, NY: Teachers College Press.

Peters, V., & Vissers, G. (1998). The Validity of Games. *Simulation & Gaming, 29*(2), 20–30. doi:10.1177/1046878198291003

Prensky, M. (2001). *Digital game-based learning*. New York: McGraw-Hill.

Simons, I. (2007). *Inside Game Design*. London: Laurence King Publishing Ltd.

Squire, K. (2005). Toward a Media Literacy for Games. *Telemedium, 52*(1-2), 9–15.

Squire, K., B. DeVane, et al. (2008b). "Designing Centers of Expertise for Academic Learning Through Video Games." Theory Into Practice.

Zin, N. A. M., & Jaafar, E. (2009). Digital Game-based learning (DGBL) model and development methodology for teaching history. *TRANSACTIONS on COMPUTERS, 8*(2), 322–333.

KEY TERMS AND DEFINITIONS

Business Management Game: Business management games are serious game that establish a link between business management theory and business management in practice, by providing learners a environment in which they can act as business leaders.

Educational Game Design: The design of serious games; games intended for educational use. The key to good educational game design is having a clear understanding of the educational impact of a specific game design.

Flow Experience: Flow describes a state of complete absorption or engagement in an activity and refers to the optimal experience (Csikszentmihalyi, 1990).

Game Elements: Game elements are the components that make up a game. In some research these are also called game attributes.

Intrinsic Motivation: Intrinsic motivation comes from rewards inherent to a task or activity itself. Characteristics of games that provide intrinsic motivation are: fantasy, rules / goals, sensory stimuli, challenge, mystery, and control (Garris, Ahlers et al 2002).

Meaningful Learning: Meaningful learning has occurred when a learner has gained the relevant knowledge, and can also use that knowledge to solve problems; the knowledge can be transferred to new problems and new learning situations.

Microworld: Microworlds are environments which learners can explore in a non-linear way. They describe a situation where learners do not study a particular domain, but become part of the scenario and are able to interact with and explore complex ideas within such spaces (Rieber, 1996).

APPENDIX A: TAXONOMY OF LITERATURE REVIEWS (COOPER 1985)

Characteristic	Categories
Focus	Research Outcomes Research Methods Theories Practices or Applications

Goal	Integration
	      a) Generalization
	      b) Conflict Resolution
	      c) Linguistic Bridge-building
	Criticism
	Identification of Central Issues

Perspective	Neutral Representation Espousal of Position
Coverage	Exhaustive Exhaustive with Selective Citation Representative Central or Pivotal
Organization	Historical Conceptual Methodological
Audience	Specialized Scholars General Scholar Practitioners or Policy Makers General Public

Appendix B: Journals and Search Engines used in the Literature Review

Table 1. Journals used in the literature review

Journal	Rating
Active Learning in Higher Education	
American Educational Research Journal	JFIS 3.07
British Educational Research Journal	JFIS 1.22
British Journal of Educational Studies	JFIS 0.66
British Journal of Educational Technology	JFIS 0.78
Computers & Education	JFIS 1.24
Education and Information Technologies	
Educational Technology Research and Development	JFIS 1.30
Educational Technology & Society	JFIS 0.62
Games and Culture, A Journal of Interactive Media	
Game Studies, International Journal of Game Research	
Higher Education: The International Journal of Higher Education and Educational Planning	JFIS 1.12
Innovative Higher Education	
Interactive Learning Environments	JFIS 0.38
International Journal of Computer Games Technology	
Journal of Computer-Assisted Learning	JFIS 1.37
Journal of Educational Computing Research	
Journal of Educational Technology & Society	
Journal of Higher Education	JFIS 1.09
Research in Higher Education	JFIS 1.26
Review of Educational Research	JFIS 4.81
Review of Higher Education	JFIS 0.98
Review of Research in Education	JFIS 4.40
Simulation & Gaming	
Studies in Higher Education	JFIS 0.95
Teaching in Higher Education	JFIS 0.54

Appendix C: Additional Reading

Table 2. Search engines used in the literature review

Search Engine	URL
Abi info	http://proquest.com/
Education Resources Information Center	http://www.eric.ed.gov/
Google Scholar	http://scholar.google.nl/
JSTOR	http://www.jstor.org/
Narcis	http://www.narcis.info/
Scopus	http://www.scopus.com/

Chapter 6
Classifying Serious Games:
The G/P/S Model

Damien Djaouti
IRIT – University of Toulouse, France

Julian Alvarez
IRIT – University of Toulouse, France

Jean-Pierre Jessel
IRIT – University of Toulouse, France

ABSTRACT

The purpose of this chapter is to introduce an overall classification system for Serious Games. The intention of this classification is to guide people through the vast field of Serious Games by providing them with a general overview. For example, it may appeal to teachers who wish to find games with strong educational potential though they may be outside the "edugames" field. This chapter will start by discussing the definition of Serious Games, and define them as having a combination of "serious" and "game" aspects. This theoretical framework will be used to review previous classification systems and discuss their limitations. It will then introduce a new classification that addresses a number of these limitations: the G/P/S model. This classifies games according to both their "serious-related" and "game-related" characteristics, and combines the strengths of several previous classification systems.

INTRODUCTION

During the last 10 years, an increasing number of Serious Games have been released which relate to a wide range of fields: healthcare, defense, education, communication, politics, etc. When any topic becomes suddenly available with a wide variety of options, it encourages a natural desire to classify it. And there are several studies that propose classifying Serious Games, but classification is not an all-purpose tool. And where several classification systems exist, it is usually because each system is able to fulfill only one specific need. As the focus of this book is Education, the first question is: what educational-related needs can be addressed with a classification system suited to Serious Games?

DOI: 10.4018/978-1-60960-495-0.ch006

Several answers come to mind. The most obvious is to assist teachers by classifying games according to the cognitive skills they support (e.g. repetitive task, memory, exploration, etc.). Such systems are closely related to Instructional Design, as illustrated by the work of O'Neil (2005). In addition to the classification of games already identified as "educational", classification systems may also be used to discover games featuring an educational potential without being explicitly labeled as "educational". For example, in the vast field of Serious Games, many games that were not designed for "education" could be used in a classroom (Gee, 2003). Indeed, as defined by Chen & Michael (2005), Serious Games are *"Games that do not have entertainment, enjoyment or fun as their primary purpose"*. The "seriousness" of these games refers to a content that may well be used as teaching material by teachers. These games could also be used to teach media literacy, by showing people that video games are not "neutral" and that they could include a "serious" content (Matteas, 2008). For teachers or educators who wish to use games in this way, the question is: how can we identify games with an educational potential if they are not labeled as "educational?"

In this case, the use of an overall classification system for Serious Games may well be of assistance. Unlike systems that are focused solely on one field, such as education, overall classifications are designed to classify any Serious Game by the same set of criteria. As they provide a "broad view", they can help teachers to identify games that are not labeled "educational" despite the fact that they may be relevant to classroom use.

Therefore, the aim of this chapter is to propose an overall classification system that teachers can use to identify easily and analyze Serious Games. After a brief discussion about the definition of Serious Games, we will explore several previous classifications. This analysis will highlight the clues that may be used to create a new system designed to analyze Serious Games: the G/P/S model. Finally, to illustrate this, a sample set of Serious Games will be classified using the G/P/S model. And in order to help teachers find games with a strong potential for education outside of the "edugames" field, classified examples will be taken from a wide range of the Serious Games markets.

DEFINING SERIOUS GAMES

A Definition of Serious Games

There are several definitions of "Serious Games". The first formal definition of the concept would appear to have been introduced by Abt (1970). In his book, Abt presents simulations and games to improve education, both in and outside of the classroom. The examples he provides are either "mainframe computer" or "pen-and-paper" based games, as the video game industry was not yet established. Abt's book influenced other teachers, like Jansiewicz (1973) who published a book describing a game he invented to teach the basics of US politics. Several years later, the concept of the "Serious Game" was redefined in a white paper written by Sawyer (2002). His updated definition of Serious Games is based on the idea of connecting a serious purpose to knowledge and technologies from the video game industry. In association with Rejeski, Sawyer helped to shape the current "Serious Games" industry through the *Serious Game Initiative*, and conferences like the *Serious Game Summit* and *Games For Health* (Sawyer, 2009). Nowadays, most recent definitions, like those of Chen & Michael (2005) and Zyda (2005), appear to stem from Sawyer's influence. Although the general definition of "Serious Game" appears to be shared by many people, the domain boundaries of the Serious Games field are still subject to debate. As discussed by Corti (2007), the "Serious Game" industry brings together participants from a wide range of fields, such as Education, Defense, Advertising, Politics, etc. who do not always agree on what is and what is not a part of the Serious Games industry. To reflect these differences, some "domain-specific" definitions are used to force a limited view of the nature of "Serious Games" (Sawyer & Smith, 2008). However, a common line may still be drawn across all professional fields despite these territorial debates. Serious Game designers use people's interest in video games to capture their attention for a variety of purposes that go beyond pure entertainment. Therefore, although the main focus of this book is Education, throughout the chapter we will rely on a broader definition of "Serious Games": any piece of software that merges a non-entertaining purpose *(serious)* with a video game structure *(game)*.

Differences between Serious Games and Entertainment Games

In the light of the previous definition, we can try to differentiate "Serious Games" from "Entertainment Games". Just as we defined a Serious Game as being a piece of software combining both "serious" and "game" dimensions, we can define an entertainment video game as a piece of software featuring only a "game" dimension. For example, the game *Trauma Center: Under the Knife*[1] casts players as surgeons and asks them to operate on patients. However, aside from the hospital theme and certain references to real-life surgical equipment and techniques, the game was not designed with an explicit "serious-purpose" scenario. In this game, healthcare is used only as a background to build an entertaining game scenario. On the other hand, *Pulse!!* [2] is very different, even though the players are also cast as doctors. The designers of *Pulse!!* have introduced a doctor-training scenario into the game scenario, in order to provide a serious purpose for the game. The differences are even more evident when playing these two games. Whilst *Trauma Center: Under the Knife* asks players to use a laser on their patients' hearts to kill dragon-shaped viruses, *Pulse!!* provides

them with real-life cases that have to be solved using current medical techniques.

However, there is nothing to prevent players from using *Trauma Center: Under the Knife* with a serious intention in mind. And the same goes for any commercial "off the shelf" game that is subsequently used to serve a serious purpose. This kind of "purpose-shifting" is very common in education where some teachers use entertainment video games as teaching materials. Comprehensive examples of such "purpose-shifting" for Education are detailed and discussed in (Gee, 2003) and (Shaffer, 2006). A similar example, related to Healthcare, is given by the psychologist Michael Stora (2005) in his book "Healing through virtual worlds". During therapy sessions with children, he uses the game *ICO*[3] by "shifting" its original entertainment purpose. At some point in this game, the player must hold the hand of a princess *(by keeping a button pressed down on the gamepad)*, and guide her to the exit. In order to finalize his task, the player must then release the button and let the princess go away. The therapist observes the reaction of children when they have to perform this task. Some children become confused and refuse to abandon the princess. Then, Stora begins a dialogue with these children, using the game as a metaphor for their own familial experience.

Nevertheless, there remains a major difference between those games used to perform "purpose-shifting" and games crafted by the "Serious Games" industry. Video games used for "purpose-shifting" were not designed to serve a serious purpose, but purely for entertainment. This argument might be cited by some designers in order to exclude the "purpose-shifting" of commercial "off the shelf" games from the "Serious Game" movement. However, when teachers use entertainment video games for their lessons, to an extent they create their own "serious scenario" which they introduce alongside the play sessions of their students. This "serious" dimension is not directly embedded in the game, but the teacher uses it to influence the way his/

her students might play. Thus, we can consider that the "serious" and the "game" dimensions are both present in the "purpose-shifting" approach, and that the real difference between a "Serious Game" and a game used for "purpose-shifting" lies in the design process. Teachers are obliged to take a game scenario previously designed and adapt it to their "serious" goals, whilst designers from the Serious Games industry have full control over the content of their games.

Halfway between "purpose-shifting" and games that are designed from scratch to serve a serious purpose, there are some Serious Games that are built as software modifications *(called "mods")* of entertainment video games. For example, *Escape from Woomera*[1] is a software modification of the video game *Half-Life*[5]. The "game" scenario of *Half-life,* which originally referred to fighting an alien invasion, was transformed to give "serious" information about the difficult living conditions in an Australian immigration centre. The main difference between "mods" and Serious Games designed from scratch is the relationship between the designers of both the "game" and the "serious" dimensions. Whilst the designers of *Pulse!!* had full creative control over the design of both the "serious" and the "game" dimensions, the designers of *Escape from Woomera* designed only the "serious" dimension which they then had to fit into a pre-existing "game" scenario not originally crafted by them.

To summarize, we can still define entertainment video games as software applications featuring only a "game" dimension. In addition to the "Serious Games" designed from scratch by the "Serious Games" industry, there are two alternative methods that can be used to add a "serious" dimension to a pre-existing game. Both "purpose-shifting" and "mods" seem relevant to the spirit of "Serious Games". However, as "purpose-shifting" can be applied to virtually any piece of software, we will draw a line between software designed with both "serious" and "game" dimensions and software designed solely with a "game" dimension. To be relevant to the "Serious Game" category, software must be designed with both "serious" and "game" dimensions. These two dimensions can be designed from scratch by the same team or by a number of other unrelated people through the use of "mods". When a game that is designed for entertainment is used with "purpose-shifting" to serve a serious purpose, no software modification is involved. Referring to Jenkins (2009), to emphasize the difference between "purpose-shifting" and the other approaches, we propose the creation of a broader category called "Serious Gaming". This category brings together "purpose-shifting" and "Serious Games". Whereas "Serious Games" is a label that refers to applications featuring both a "serious" and a "game" dimension within the software, "Serious Gaming" is a label that refers to any video game used for "serious" purposes, whether the "serious" dimension is or is not designed within the software.

As an aside, it can be argued that the presence of the "serious" dimension depends on the subjective assessment of the game by the player. For example, players of a Serious Game can fail to identify the serious purpose that the game intends to serve. In such cases, when the "seriousness" of a game appears unclear, we suggest referring to the intention of its designers rather than to the perception of the players.

Classifiying Serious Games

Since 2002, several methods and tools have been introduced to classify Serious Games. Each of these methods endeavours to address the issues of its predecessors. However, no classification system has yet achieved a level of general acceptance. In this section, we will present some of these systems, and attempt to highlight their respective limitations.

From a chronological point of view, the first classification systems were based on a single criteria. As pointed out by Sawyer & Smith (2008), these models can be divided into two categories:

Figure 1. The relationship between video games, serious games and serious gaming

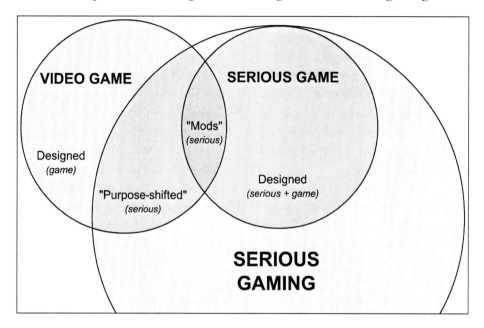

market-based classifications and purpose-based classifications.

Market-Based Classifications

These classification systems are designed to index games according to the "markets" which use them (i.e. the kind of people who play them). Here are some examples of market-based classifications:

- In a 2005 article, Zyda (2005) divided Serious Games into five domains: *Healthcare, Public policy, Strategic Communication, Defense, Training & Education.*
- In their 2005 book, Chen & Michael (2005) classified Serious Games according to markets, in eight different categories: *Military Games, Government Games, Educational Games, Corporate Games, Healthcare Games, Political Games, Religious Games, Art Games.*
- In a 2008 study, Alvarez & Michaud (2008) identified seven Serious Games markets, quite similar to those mentioned

above: *Defense, Training & Education Games, Advertising, Information & Communication, Health, Culture, Activism.*

Albeit very useful, these market-based classifications suffer from two limitations. First, due to the discovery of new markets for Serious Games, their boundaries continue to expand. Secondly, these classifications are based solely on the applications of Serious Games rather than on the games themselves. In other words, market-based classifications are able only to inform about the uses of Serious Games, not about their content.

Purpose-Based Classifications

Alongside the classifications based on the uses of Serious Games, there are systems based on the intention that each Serious Game was designed to satisfy: the "purpose". Some examples of such classifications include:

- In his 2006 book, Bergeron (2006) presented seven "purpose" categories: *Activism games, Advergames, Business Games,*

Exergaming, Health and Medicine Games, News Games, Political Games.

- In a 2008 article, Despont (2008) proposed a typology of four Serious Games "purposes": *Advert Games, Institutional Serious Games, Business Games, Learning Games.* This typology is based on another typology by the same author, which identified six "serious intentions": *to increase awareness, to simulate, to train, to inform, to teach* and *to influence*[6.]

- In our own previous work, we (Alvarez & al., 2007) also introduced six "purpose" categories for Serious Games: *Edugames, Advergames, Newsgames, Activism games, Edumarket games, Training & Simulation games.*

While they are still based on a single criteria, purpose-based classifications are harder to use than market-based ones. In each of the above models, categories seem heterogeneous. For example, *"Health and Medicine Games"*, *"Institutional Serious Games"* and *"Business Games"* are tied to the "targeted market" of the game, while categories such as *"Edugames"*, *"Learning Games"* and *"Exergaming"* are clearly based on the "purpose besides entertainment" and are features of the game. Overall, these systems are an interesting step towards understanding the purpose of Serious Games. They encourage separating "purposes" from "markets", which at first is not an obvious distinction. Unfortunately, they suffer from heterogeneous categories that prevent them from being a reliable source for general classification. Hopefully, these systems opened a path for multiple criteria classifications by introducing models that went further than a simple market analysis of the game. More importantly, they helped to shift the classification focus onto the "contents" instead of the "uses".

A Multiple Criteria Classification

The complementary nature of the criteria used in the market-based and purpose-based classifications inspired a system based on multiple criteria: the "Serious Game Taxonomy". Introduced by Sawyer & Smith (2008), this global taxonomy indexes Serious Games according to two criteria:

- **Market:***Government & NGO, Defence, Healthcare, Marketing & Communication, Education, Corporate, Industry.*
- **Purpose:***Games for Health, Advergames, Games for Training, Games for Education, Games for Science and Research, Production, Games as Work.*

Each "purpose" category also comes with a "sub-taxonomy" whose complexity varies greatly from one "purpose" to another. At first glance, this global taxonomy uses 49 categories, plus many additional sub-categories. This taxonomy cleverly analyzed and merged previously available classification systems. It is more complex to use than single-criterion systems, but it provides a better understanding of Serious Games through a more precise categorization. Shaped as a table, this "Serious Game Taxonomy" is also useful to detect "empty fields", i.e. a combination of "market + purpose" that lacks any Serious Game reference.

Nevertheless, this system also suffers from certain issues. For example, the "purpose" criterion appears not to be sufficiently accurate, as a game such as *September 12th* falls outside of its scope. Furthermore, some "market" and "purpose" categories overlap. These issues appear to be inherited from previous single criterion classifications, especially the "purpose-based" ones which suffer from similar limitations.

In Addition to "Purposes" and "Markets"

Either based on one or two criteria, all of these classifications focus on two aspects of Serious Games: the purpose they are designed to serve and the kind of market that uses them. Overall, these systems are a simple way to present an overview of the Serious Games field. However, they all suffer from a major limitation of their scope - none of these systems classifies "Serious Games" as "games". Indeed, no classification presented in this section can provide relevant information about the game structure of the games it classifies.

As discussed in the previous section, Serious Games are defined by the combination of a "serious" dimension and a "game" dimension. The systems we have just reviewed are solely focused on the analysis of the "serious" side and disregard the "game" aspect. It may be just that the "game" dimension is not relevant to classify games. But since the beginning of the entertainment video game industry, video games have had a strong impact on the general public and have led to the birth of a rich video-gaming culture, with several game styles, genres and design approaches. Moreover, several classifications of entertainment video games have been introduced since the early 80's. Therefore, can these classifications that focus on the "game" dimension help classify Serious Games?

Classifications of Entertainment Video Games

Systems designed to classify entertainment video games come from various sources such as academics, designers, editors, the gaming press or even experienced players. The most common approach to classify video games is to categorize them into "genres".

The first kinds of such genre-based classifications originate from players and the gaming press, and are called "freeform classifications". As their name implies, they are crafted from a subjective and empirical analysis. They led to the emergence of numerous classifications that share similar structures, but rely on different definitions[7] and different genres[8]. Although they are an important part of the global video game culture, these classifications are too numerous and too focused to be used as a reference. Looking at this wild group of "freeform classifications", several designers and academics tried to refine them through critical thinking, in order to produce more reliable "genre-based" classifications. We can for example refer to Crawford (1982), Myers (1990), LeDiberder (1993), Wolf (2002), Rollings & Adams (2003) and Natkin (2006), among others. While these studies resulted in improved classification systems, unfortunately they failed to create a consensus, essentially because each system was different from its predecessor... Nevertheless, as these classifications are established and explained, unlike the "freeform classifications", they provide an interesting historical resource for the evolution of video game genres.

After a review of these "genre-based" classification systems, studies like Letourneux (2005) and Apperley (2006) highlighted their flaws, and called for a new approach to video game classification. As a result, a few recent classifications are not based on "genres". For example, Strange Agency (2006) introduced a system which classifies games according to the analysis of what the player does during play. This classification defines forty-nine possible activities such as *Driving, Collecting, Management, Building, Puzzling...* These categories are then quantified for each game, in order to create an "activity profile" that provides a high level of detail on how the game feels from a player's perspective. Elverdam & Aarseth (2007) proposed a classification built on a typology of video games with 17 dimensions, such as *Goals, Challenge, Synchronicity, Savability...* Each of these dimensions is a criterion with a finite set of values, and can be used to classify game mechanics in a detailed manner. This classification is an update of the multi-dimensional typology of video games introduced by Aarseth (2003). However, such complex and accurate systems are more suited for in-depth analysis of the game structure than overall classification.

To summarize, the analysis of the game structure is possible and indebted to many different approaches, from free-form "genre classifications" to "mechanics analysis" systems. Because the video game culture continues to spawn new kinds of games, several studies continue to be conducted on the classification of video games. As an unfortunate consequence, the large choice of available tools makes it impossible to refer to just one classification system. For our current study, not all of these systems can be used directly but they do offer interesting alternatives. Classifying a set of Serious Games with any system referred to in this section will generate a very different result from that which can be obtained by classifying those same games with the systems presented in the previous section. On one hand, it will bring together games that share similar play principles and on the other it will bring together games with similar purposes or uses. But, in both cases, there is one area of information that is lacking: Serious Games are defined by both a "serious" and a "game" dimension, and all the systems we have presented so far focus on one single dimension at a time. In order to build an overall classification system for Serious Games, we should try surely to try to define a classification system that uses both dimensions at the same time.

A Classification of Both "Serious" and "Game" Dimensions

From an overall perspective, to classify Serious Games with more precision, we propose a new classification model that combines the analysis of both "serious" and "game" dimensions: the G/P/S model

The Gameplay / Purpose / Scope (G/P/S) Model

Referring back to our observations concerning definition, a Serious Game is composed of both a "serious" and a "game" dimension. To combine both dimensions, the G/P/S model extends the "Purpose & Market" paradigm by the addition of a "Gameplay" related criterion. More specifically, the G/P/S model relies on three aspects:

- **Gameplay,** which refers to the type of gameplay used. This aspect is intended to provide information about the game structure of the Serious Game: how it is played.
- **Purpose,** which refers to the designed purpose. This aspect accounts for the eventual purpose(s) apart from entertainment intended by the designer of the Serious Game.
- **Scope,** which refers to the targeted application(s) of the title. This aspect suggests the actual use(s) related to the Serious Game: the kind of market, the audience… who uses it.

These three aspects, defined in the G/P/S model, can be used to build criteria suitable for the classification of any video game. The model places serious and entertainment games on the same footing (i.e.) any video game can be defined by a gameplay structure, a targeted scope of use, and an optional "purpose" apart from entertainment. These criteria are detailed below.

Gameplay

As observed above, the notion of "genre" is an important part of the video-gaming culture, but is used mainly in subjective free-form classifications. Therefore, instead of relying on empirical "genre-based" analysis, we will try a different approach to the "game" side of Serious Games.

125

This approach will focus on a fundamental notion of the "game dimension": the **gameplay.**

Defining gameplay is a complex task. Among academics, game designers, the gaming press and even players, no single definition of this concept has yet reached a state of consensus. Historically, the word is assumed to derive from the expression *"How the game plays?"*, which was the title of instructions written on early arcade cabinets. From an empirical point of view, this concept seems tied to the way the game is played. But it may also be used to talk about the general play experience of some players. From the various definitions available, we will refer to the one proposed by Portugal (2006), a Serious Game designer. He defines "gameplay" as the combination of five components: *Rules, Input methods, Space-related setup, Time-related setup, Drama-related setup⁹*.

To build a classification based on gameplay, we will try to define a criterion based on one of these components: *Rules*. The "Rules" component is very interesting for classification tasks because its "logical" nature makes it eligible for formal deconstruction. In some studies of "Ludology"¹⁰[10], a distinction is made between several "kinds" of rules. We will begin to define a standard from these "different kinds of rules".

An initial distinction can be made between two forms of "play", as introduced by Caillois (1962): a play form framed by a defined set of rules, called *ludus*, and a more freeform kind of play called *paidia*. In fact, these two forms are related to the definition of the words "game" (ludus) and "play" (paidia), and apply to any kind of play/game structure (board game, card game, toys, etc.).

Both of these forms of play also exist in video games and are tied to the kinds of rules used to design the games. *Sim City¹¹* is a common example of a "play-based" (or "videotoy") type of game, whereas *Pac-Man¹²* is "game-based". The main difference between the rules of these two titles is that *Sim City* lacks any rule defining "goals": it cannot be "won" or "lost". Furthermore, as it

has no goals to aim for, the performance of the player will not be appraised by this video game, whereas *Pac-Man does* incorporate goals *(eat all the pills and avoid the ghosts)* and these are used to provide a positive *(score increment)* or negative *(life loss)* feedback to the player. Hence, a video game lacking "goals" will be considered as "Play-based", whereas a video game featuring "goals" will be considered as "Game-based". In the examples detailed in the last section of this chapter, *September 12ᵗʰ* is "Play-based", while all the others are "Game-based".

This information on the nature of gameplay appears to be quite relevant to several cases of Serious Game applications. For example, in the first part we discussed the "purpose-shifting" conducted by some teachers to add a virtually "serious" dimension to entertainment based "off-the-shelf" commercial video games. Though it is not always the case, "purpose-shifting" might be easier to perform with "Play-based" titles than with "Game-based" ones. Because this type of video game does not feature stated goals, a teacher can propose his own goals quite freely when he introduces the game to the classroom. With "Game-based" titles, a teacher must react to goals designed previously, which means he has to adapt his teaching to the game, or choose a different video game.

A more detailed discussion on the *paidia/ludus* duality is presented by Frasca (2003), which expands his analysis by proposing a typology of the rules found in video games. Additionally, several studies deal extensively with different kinds of video game rules, such as Salen & Zimmerman (2003), Juul (2005), Djaouti & al. (2008) and Järvinen (2008). These studies feature relevant information on the nature of rules, and provide clues that can help to build a more detailed criterion based on them.

In 2006, we introduced such a criterion to build a video game classification according to gameplay. Briefly, we conducted a formal breakdown of "Rules", in order to find recurrent structures that could lead to a viable standard. After analysing the rules of 600 video games, we were able to highlight a set of "primary rule patterns" that could be combined to represent the fundamental rules of video games. For convenience, each of these "rule patterns" was shaped into a "GamePlay brick", named after verbs.

For example, the two games *Pac-Man* and *Space Invaders*[13] feature the following rules:

- *"If Pacman collides with Ghost, then destroy Pacman"*.
- *"If Spaceship collides with Enemy's shot, then destroy Spaceship"*.

We observe a very strong similarity between these rules and therefore are able to consider that they are built on the following pattern: *"If the player element collides with a hostile element, then there is a negative feedback towards the player element"*. For simplicity, this "rule pattern" is then shaped into a "gameplay brick" named "Avoid". This summarizes the rule into a single verb. As discussed above, the rule patterns identified through bricks are of two kinds: *"Game bricks"*, which state the goals to achieve, and *"Play bricks"*, which define the means and constraints for reaching these goals. Currently, a set of 10 combinable bricks have been identified:

- **Stated Goals**: Avoid, Match, Destroy.
- **Means & Constraints**: Create, Manage, Move, Select, Shoot, Write, Random. (See Figure 2)

A detailed presentation of the 10 bricks and the "rule patterns" that define them can be found in (Djaouti & al., 2008). Concisely, these "Game-Play bricks" are able classify the basic rules used in a video game and provide an overview of how the game plays. Note that there are more complete systems referred to in the section about entertainment games, but their high level of detail makes them difficult to use in a classification suited for a general overview.

To summarize, the analysis of gameplay "rules" provides several ways to classify video games, with differing levels of accuracy. An initial distinction can be made between "Game-based" and "Play-based" video games, according to their use/lack of rules stating the goals. A more detailed analysis of these rules can be made with the "GamePlay" bricks, to provide information about the basic rules used that shape the gameplay. A third level of analysis could be made through the use of in-depth rule analysis tools, such as the *Ludemes* (Koster 2005), the *Game Design Patterns* (Bjork & Holopainen, 2005), or the *Game Grammar* (Bura, 2006). However, these tools provide such a high level of accuracy that their results would be difficult to use in a classification. They appear more suited to an extensively detailed analysis of just a few games. The G/P/S Model therefore relies on two levels of gameplay analysis: the difference between "Game" or "Play" types and a general overview of the basic rules thanks to "GamePlay bricks".

Figure 2.

Purpose

The purpose-based classifications presented earlier suffer from several limitations. We have observed already that some of these classifications are based on heterogeneous categories, because some of them are more related to the "market" than to the "purpose" of the game. But the boundaries of several "purpose-related" categories can also be discussed. More specifically, some categories seem to suffer from overlapping boundaries, and could be merged into a single category.

By way of example, of the four purpose classifications presented earlier, we will compare the purposes of *"Edugames"* / *"Games for Education"* / *"Learning Games"* with those of *"Advergames"* / *"Advert Games"*.

The purpose of *Edugames* is to transmit educational knowledge. The purpose of *Advergames* is to broadcast advertising, which can be understood as some kind of a commercial product-related knowledge. Hence, though their intentions are different (commercial or educational), these two categories of games appear to share the same "purpose" - **to broadcast a message**.

The same observation applies to other categories: *"News Games"* deliver news-related messages; *"Political Games"* deliver political messages; *"Business Games"* deal with business messages... Thus, the "purpose" of these categories is used to differentiate between the nature of the messages broadcast by the games. In order to produce a simple result, we will deal with the four "less specific" characteristics of the messages that can be broadcast by games: educative *(Edugames)*, informative *(Newsgames)*, persuasive *(Advergames, Political Games* – see Bogost 2007*)* and subjective *(Military games, Art games)*.

However, not all Serious Games are based on message delivery. Indeed, games that fall into purpose categories such as *"Training and Simulation Games"* or *"Games for Health"* are aimed at a slightly different "purpose" from communication: **training**.

For example, *Pulse!!* is used to train medical professionals on how to handle health emergency situations, while other titles such as *Mosbe* are simulators used to train soldiers for military operations. The main "purpose" of these games is not to broadcast a message but to improve the player's cognitive and/or motor skills for precise tasks or applications.

Moreover, if we look more closely at some "purpose" categories, we can observe that they actually group both "training" and "message-broadcasting" games. For example, *"Games for Health"* feature both training games such as *Pulse!!* and message-broadcasting games such as *Re-mission*. Such a "purpose" category as this, that makes no distinction between these two types of game, appears to be quite limited. In the case of a game that combines both "commercial message broadcasting" and another "purpose", for example in a "message broadcasting" or in a "training" category, we propose that it should be regarded as an *Edumarket game*.

We also propose introducing a third "purpose" category related to the **exchange of data**. At the time of writing, few examples of these Serious Games exist. *Foldit* is a Serious Game in which players must find the best way to fold proteins. The solutions thought up by the players are used to extend knowledge in the scientific research field. *Google Image Labeller* uses a similar approach to improve the image searching technology created by *Google*. Whilst these two games are dedicated to a one-way exchange, from the players to the publisher of the game, other titles are designed to simplify the exchange of information between players. For example, *Lure of the Labyrinth* is designed to support the teaching of the basics of mathematics and geometry in the classroom. The teacher sets up an online game session for the students to join and they can then solve mathematics-based puzzles by helping each other. Players are rewarded with score points for helping other players and, as a consequence students are obliged to practice their math skills to a point at which they are able to help. *PowerUP[14]* uses a similar concept to deal with ecological topics.

As a result, we propose classifying the "purpose" according to the following list. A single video game can be designed for one, several or none of these purposes:

- **Message-broadcasting:** the game is designed to broadcast a message. This message can be of several types: educative *(Edugames)*, informative *(Newsgames)*, persuasive *(Advergames)* and/or subjective *(Military games, Art games)*.
- **Training:** the game is designed to improve cognitive performance or motor skills. *Exergames* (related to brain training or fitness) are typical examples of this purpose.
- **Data exchange:** the game is designed as support for exchanging data. Games collecting information from their players or encouraging them to exchange data are examples of this purpose.

Scope

Our analysis of market-based classifications has already highlighted the main limitations of this standard: the ever-increasing number of available markets. The best approach to this standard seems to be to merge the previously identified markets into one single list, whilst leaving it possible to add new markets when necessary. For the G/P/S model, this list will contain the following items: *State & Government, Military & Defense, Healthcare, Education, Corporate, Religious, Culture & Art, Ecology, Politics, Humanitarian, Advertising, Scientific Research.* A precision with respect to the *Corporate* market: this should be used only to classify games designed to be used within a company, and not for any game that was released by a corporation. Indeed, the "market"

criterion solely reflects the targeted domains that will "use" the game.

Also note that *Entertainment* should be included as a market in this list: whilst most entertainment games are used only in the entertainment market, some Serious Games are used in both entertainment and non-entertainment markets (for example, *America's Army[15]* is used both in military training courses and in gaming tournaments[16]).

However, the professional field(s) for which a game is designed is not the only example that can define the "scope" dimension of a video game. For example, a more detailed analysis of the targeted audience (age-range, type, gender, etc.) would enable the classifying of video games with more precision. These kinds of criteria were already used in "rating systems", such as ESRB (1994) and PEGI (2003), but they were designed solely for the prevention of content that shocks. We propose using a more general approach to the audience targeted by game designers. For now, we will classify the target audience from two aspects: its "age" and its "type". To classify "age" we will define several ranges *(0 to 3 years old, 4 to 7 years old, etc...)* inspired by both ESRB and PEGI rating systems. The "type" will simply differentiate between *General Public*, which refers to anybody, *Professionals* which represents workers from the targeted market, and *Students* which groups the people who are studying to join the professionals. For example, in the *Healthcare* market, *Professionals* will refer to medical practitioners, *General Public* to their patients, and *Students* to medical school students.

Summary

The plan below summarizes the G/P/S classification model on a single page. By ticking the boxes on this page, it is possible to classify a video game very rapidly, see Figure 3.

Figure 3. A "printable page" representation of the G/P/S model

Using G/P/S to Identify Games for Education

Now that we have described this overall classification system, how can it be used in the field of Education?

As discussed in the introduction, this system is not intended to provide a detailed analysis of the cognitive skills that Serious Games support, a task that only a system sharply focused on Education could perform. The G/P/S model is intended to provide common ground with which to browse the whole field of Serious Games. Teachers are able to use it to identify games not labeled as "educational" but which, due to their "serious" purpose, may be relevant for classroom use. Using the "printable page" (Figure 3) games can be classified easily by ticking boxes. However, classifying games is a time-consuming task as is that of identifying games designed for a "serious" purpose. Therefore, to emphasize the fact that the G/P/S model can be used to discover new Serious Games, we have built a collaborative online database around it. This database assembles the classification information for a large range of Serious Games originating from a wide array of sources. At the time of writing, this tool hosts

"classification pages" for 2200 Serious Games. Thus teachers are now able to go to http://serious. gameclassification.com/ and use the G/P/S model to browse quickly through games designed for a serious purpose. If someone identifies a game missing from the database, its collaborative nature allows him/her to add the game reference directly and classify the game.

As an example, we provide a small selection of Serious Games chosen from this database. These games are associated with different "markets" but their "serious" content makes them potentially interesting within an educational context:

- *Lure of the Labyrinth*[17], is an educational multiplayer online game created by MIT's 'The Education Arcade' and is supported by Maryland Public Television. Designed for classroom use in middle schools, this game enables teachers to prepare "game sessions" for their students. Each student can then create an avatar to join an online adventure in a fantasy world full of puzzles. To solve these puzzles, players will have to be aware of basic mathematical concepts like proportionality, graphing, geometry, variables and rational numbers.

This Serious Game also encourages writing, as players can earn points by helping teammates. Indeed, the content of the built-in help system for each play session is written solely by the students. Each player faces puzzles that are based on the same principles but with different solutions. Therefore, in order to help each other students have to write down problem-solving strategies instead of sharing answers.

- ○ Gameplay:
  - ▪ Type: *Game-based.*
  - ▪ Goals: *Avoid, Match.*
  - ▪ Means: *Create, Manage, Move, Select, Write.*
- ○ Purpose:
  - ▪ Purposes: *Educative message broadcasting, Data Exchange.*
- ○ Scope:
  - ▪ Markets: *Education.*
  - ▪ Target audience: *11 to 15 year olds, Students.*

- *Fatworld[18]*, is a game about the politics of nutrition, released by the Corporation for Public Broadcasting (a corporation which funds public television and radio in the US). This game starts by allowing players to customize an avatar, from its appearance to its eating-related disorders (obesity, diabetes etc...). They then enter a virtual world in which they must take care of their avatar and organize its daily life. In addition to finding a job to earn money and making social contact with other avatars, the players will have to take extra care about what their avatars eat. This game illustrates the complexity of nutrition policies from the perspective of 'daily life'.

- ○ Gameplay:
  - ▪ Type: *Game-based.*
  - ▪ Goals: *Avoid, Match.*
  - ▪ Means: *Move, Manage, Select.*
- ○ Purpose:

  - ▪ Purposes: *Educative message broadcasting, Informative message broadcasting.*
  - ○ Scope:
    - ▪ Markets: *Healthcare.*
    - ▪ Target audience: *8 to 25 year olds, General Public.*

- *Re-Mission[19]*, a game about cancer released by HopeLab, a non-profit association. This game enables players to assume the role of chemotherapy, pictured as futuristic nano-soldiers. These soldiers can enter the bodies of patients and eradicate cancer by shooting drug molecules. Based on real medical cases, this game is used inside clinics to present how chemotherapy works to young patients, and also is distributed to the general public to raise their consciousness about cancer.

- ○ Gameplay:
  - ▪ Type: *Game-based.*
  - ▪ Goals: *Avoid, Match, Destroy.*
  - ▪ Means: *Move, Shoot.*
- ○ Purpose:
  - ▪ Purposes: *Educative message broadcasting, Informative message broadcasting.*
- ○ Scope:
  - ▪ Markets: *Healthcare.*
  - ▪ Target audience: *8 to 25 year olds, General Public.*

- *September 12[th20]*, a news-related game created by video game researcher Gonzalo Frasca. This game presents the player with an unnamed village in the Middle East. The village is inhabited by a number of terrorists and many innocent people. The player is able to shoot missiles into the village, but the delay between pulling the trigger and hitting the target, and the area effect of the explosion, makes it very hard to kill a specific target. If the player kills innocent people their virtual relatives will mourn their loss and become terrorists to avenge them. This game provides no goals or judgment of a player's choices. It shows players only the consequences of their actions. This military game is a type of "interactive essay" about "military response" that was chosen by the US government after the 9/11 tragedy.

- ○ Gameplay:
  - ▪ Type: *Play-based.*
  - ▪ Goals: *(none).*
  - ▪ Means: *Shoot.*
- ○ Purpose:
  - ▪ Purposes: *Subjective message broadcasting.*
- ○ Scope:
  - ▪ Markets: *Politics.*
  - ▪ Target audience: *17 to more than 60 year olds, General Public.*

- *Stop Disasters![21]*, a game about natural disaster prevention released by the United Nations. This game enables players to take control of several villages that are facing imminent disaster, such as a tsunami, a giant fire or an earthquake. Players are able to build and organize preventative procedures in order to limit casualties in the best way possible. This game provides a great deal of educational information about the methods used in natural disaster prevention and shows a glimpse of the way of life of people living in different countries often threatened by disaster.
  - ○ Gameplay:
    - ▪ Type: *Game-based.*
    - ▪ Goals: *Avoid, Match.*
    - ▪ Means: *Create, Manage, Select.*
  - ○ Purpose:
    - ▪ Purposes: *Educative message broadcasting, Informative message broadcasting.*
  - ○ Scope:
    - ▪ Markets: *Healthcare, Ecology, Humanitarian & Caratative*

- ▪ Target audience: *12 to more than 60 years old, General Public.*

All these games are freely distributed on the Internet, and whilst they address different issues, they all fit into the definition of Serious Games as discussed at the beginning of this chapter. For the G/P/S model, video games that are designed solely for entertainment will be characterized by a lack of any qualification within the "purpose" criterion and *"Entertainment"* will be the only targeted market within the "Scope" criterion. According to our definition, a video game classified with any other "purpose" and "market" can be considered as a "Serious Game".

Of these example games from the G/P/S database, none was designed for the "Education" market, with the exception of *Lure of the Labyrinth*. However, some of them were designed to broadcast an educational or informative message, and that gives them some potential for being used as teaching material. Serious Games that lack such an educational dimension yet that broadcast a subjective message, such as *September 12th*, can also be of interest if used in the classroom. In such cases, the teacher should be fully aware of the "subjective" nature of the game and this particular aspect should be drawn to the attention of the student. So again, the use of the G/P/S model and its database can help teachers to make a selection of Serious Games for educational use.

CONCLUSION

At first the wide variation of Serious Games may be confusing. With the aim of introducing some order into this confusion, there exist a number of bids to develop a system of classification. The Serious Games medium brings together participants with many different perspectives and from many differing fields such as communication, simulation, training etc. Yet, despite all these differences, they appear to agree on the basic components of

Serious Games: having a "serious" dimension combined with a "game" dimension.

According to this definition therefore, it is surprising to observe that all currently available classifications of Serious Games are focused solely on the "serious" side. In parallel with these classifications, were a larger set of classifications created for entertainment games, but they focus only on the "game" side and disregard any purpose other than entertainment. A review of both types of systems reveals that they are "incomplete", as they both provide equally relevant but very different information.

Considering the dual nature of Serious Games, we propose the introduction of a system that classifies Serious Games according to both the "serious" and the "game" dimensions. The G/P/S model defines a set of criteria that encapsulates these aspects of Serious Games: Gameplay (for the "game" side), and Scope+Purpose (for the "serious" side). These criteria are presented on printable pages with checkboxes to enable a rapid classification of games. However, to guide teachers through the vast field of Serious Games, the system is also embedded in an online database of Serious Games. Here, the G/P/S model provides a general overview of how each game is played and for what purpose it is designed. Using this information, teachers can browse quickly through a vast array of Serious Games in order to choose those that are relevant to their teaching. For example, in games dealing with ecology, different gameplay (shooting, management...) and purposes (information, training...) are available. It is the ability to differentiate and identify games quickly, compared with previous classifications, that is the main improvement that the G/P/S model provides.

However, as with any classification system, the G/P/S model does have certain limitations. As a classification model designed intentionally to provide a general overview, the system is not able to provide detailed information concerning a specific area of the Serious Games field. For example, for games associated with the Education market, the classification is unable to differentiate between those dealing with mathematics and those with linguistics. It can only differentiate between games according to the criteria shared by all application domains of Serious Games. However, as stated before, it can assist teachers to discover those Serious Games not designed for the Educational market, but interesting for classroom use. The system can also help to identify those video games designed for entertainment that can be "shifted", to serve an educational purpose. Such "purpose-shifting" of entertainment games is an extremely promising method of using games as teaching tools. We call it "Serious Gaming".

REFERENCES

Aarseth, E. (2003). *A multi-dimensional typology of games.* Paper presented at the Level Up Conference, Utrecht, Netherlands.

Abt, C. (1970). *Serious games.* USA: Viking Press.

Alvarez, J., & Michaud, L. (2008). *Serious games: Advergaming, edugaming, training, and more.* France: IDATE.

Alvarez, J., Rampnoux, O., Jessel, J.-P., & Methel, G. (2007). Serious game: Just a question of posture? In *Proceedings of Artificial and Ambient Intelligence Convention (Artificial Societies for Ambient Intelligence) - AISB (ASAMi) 2007,* (pp. 420-426). UK, University of Newcastle.

Apperley, T. (2006). Genre and game studies: Toward a critical approach to video game genres. *Simulation & Gaming, 37*(1), 6–23. doi:10.1177/1046878105282278

Bergeron, B. (2006). *Developing serious games.* USA: Charles River Media.

Bjork, S., & Holopainen, J. (2005). *Patterns in game design.* USA: Charles River Media.

Bogost, I. (2007). *Persuasive games*. USA: MIT Press.

Brougères, G. (2005). *Jouer/Apprendre*. France: Economica.

Bura, S. (2006). *A game grammar*. Retrieved March 8, 2009, from http://www.stephanebura.com/diagrams/

Caillois, R. (1961). *Man, play and games*. USA: Free Press of Glencoe.

Chen, J., & Ringel, M. (2001). *Can advergaming be the future of interactive advertising?* Retrieved February 24, 2007, from http://www.locz.com.br/loczgames/advergames.pdf

Chen, S., & Michael, D. (2005). *Serious games: Games that educate, train and inform*. USA: Thomson Course Technology.

Corti, K. (2007). *Serious games-are we really a community?* Retrieved March 8, 2009, from http://www.seriousgamessource.com/item.php?story=15832

Crawford, C. (1982). *The art of computer game design*. USA: Osborne/McGraw-Hill.

Despont, A. (2008). *Serious Games et intention sérieuse: typologie*. Retrieved March 8, 2009, from http://www.elearning-symetrix.fr/blog/index.php?post/2008/02/15/Serious-Games-et-intention-serieuse-%3A-typologie

Diberder, A., & Diberder, F. (1993). *Qui a peur des jeux vidéo?* France, La découverte.

Djaouti, D., Alvarez, J., Jessel, J.-P., & Methel, G. (2008). Play, game, world: Anatomy of a videogame. *International Journal of Intelligent Games & Simulation, 5*(1), 35–39.

Djaouti, D., Alvarez, J., Jessel, J.-P., Methel, G., & Molinier, P. (2008). A gameplay definition through videogame classification. *International Journal of Computer Games Technology, 2008*(1).

Egenfeld-Nielsen, S. (2006). Overview of research on the educational use of video games. *Digital Kompetanse, 2006*(3), 184-213.

Elverdam, C., & Aarseth, E. (2007). Game classification and game design: Construction through critical analysis. *Games and Culture, 2*(1), 3–22. doi:10.1177/1555412006286892

Entertainment Software Rating Board. (1994). *Game ratings & descriptor guide*. Retrieved March 8, 2009, from http://www.esrb.org/ratings/ratings_guide.jsp

Frasca, G. (2003). Simulation versus narrative: Introduction to Ludology. In Wolf, J. P., & Perron, B. (Eds.), *The video game theory reader*. USA: Routledge.

Gee, J. P. (2003). *What video games have to teach us about learning and literacy*. USA: Palgrave Macmilan.

Henriot, J. (1989). *Sous couleur de jouer*. France: Jose Corti.

Hunicke, R., LeBlanc, M., & Zubek, R. (2004). *MDA: A formal approach to game design and game research*. Paper presented at the Nineteenth National Conference on Artificial Intelligence, San Jose, USA.

Jansiewicz, D. (1973). *The new Alexandria simulation: A serious game of state and local politics*. USA: Canfield Press.

Järvinen, A. (2008). *Games without frontiers: Theories and methods for game studies and design*. Unpublished doctoral dissertation, University of Tampere, Finland.

Jenkins, H., Camper, B., Chisholm, A., Grigsby, N., Klopfer, E., & Osterweil, S. (2009). From serious games to serious gaming. In Ritterfeld, U., Cody, M., & Vorderer, P. (Eds.), *Serious games: Mechanisms and effects*. USA: Routledge.

Juul, J. (2005). *Half-real-videogames between real rules and fictional worlds*. USA: MIT Press.

Koster, R. (2005). *A theory of fun for game design*. USA: Paraglyph Press.

Letourneux, M. (2005). La question du genre en jeu vidéo. In S. Genvo (Ed.), *Le game design de jeux vidéo – approches de l'expression vidéoludique*. France: L'Harmattan.

Matteas, M. (2008). Procedural literacy: Educating the new media practitioner. In Davidson, D. (Ed.), *Beyond fun: Serious games and media*. USA: ETC Press.

Myers, D. (1990). Computer game genres. *Play & Culture, 1990*(3), 286-301.

Natkin, S. (2006). *Video games and interactive media: A glimpse at new digital entertainment*. UK: A.K. Peters.

O'Neil, H., Wainess, R., & Baker, E. (2005). Classification of learning outcomes: Evidence from the computer games literature. *Curriculum Journal, 16*(4), 455–474. doi:10.1080/09585170500384529

Pan-European Game Information. (2003). *About PEGI–what do the labels mean?* Retrieved March 8, 2009, from http://www.pegi.info/en/index/id/33/

Portugal, J.-N. (2006). *Le Rapprochement du Jeu et de l'Apprentissage*. Paper presented at the Serious Games Summit Europe 2006, Lyon, France.

Rollings, A., & Adams, E. (2003). *Andrew Rollings and Ernest Adams on game design*. USA: New Riders.

Salen, K., & Zimmerman, E. (2003). *The rules of play*. USA: MIT Press.

Sawyer, B. (2002). *Serious games: Improving public policy through game-based learning and simulation*. USA: Woodrow Wilson International Center for Scholars.

Sawyer, B. (2009). Foreword. In U. Ritterfeld, M. Cody, &. P. Vorderer (Eds.), *Serious games: Mechanisms and effects*. USA: Routledge.

Sawyer, B., & Smith, P. (2008). *Serious game taxonomy*. Paper presented at the Serious Game Summit 2008, San Francisco, USA.

Shaffer, D. W. (2006). *How computer games help children learn*. USA: Palgrave Macmilan. doi:10.1057/9780230601994

Stora, M. (2005). *Guérir par le virtuel*. France: Presses de la Renaissance.

Strange Agency. (2006). *Strange analyst activity groups definitions*. Retrieved March 8, 2009, from http://www.strange-agency.com/downloads/ActivityGroupDefinitions.pdf

Tricot, A., & Rufino, A. (1999). Modalités et scénarii d'interaction dans des environnements informatisés d'apprentissage. *Revue des Sciences de l'Education, 25*(1), 105–129.

Wikipedia. (2009). *Video game genres*. Retrieved March 8, 2009, from http://en.wikipedia.org/wiki/Video_game_genres

Wolf, M. (Ed.). (2002). *The medium of the video game*. USA: University of Texas Press.

Zyda, M. (2005). From visual simulation to virtual reality to games. *Computer, 38*(9), 25–32. doi:10.1109/MC.2005.297

ENDNOTES

[1] http://www.gameclassification.com/EN/games/1248-Trauma-Center-Under-the-knife/index.html

[2] http://serious.gameclassification.com/EN/games/1017-Pulse/index.html

[3] http://www.gameclassification.com/EN/games/3206-Ico/index.html

4 http://serious.gameclassification.com/EN/games/1222-Escape-From-Woomera/index.html

5 http://gameclassification.com/EN/games/1223-Half-Life/index.html

6 Personal translation from French: "*sensibiliser, simuler, former, informer, éduquer et influencer*".

7 A common example is the definition of the "simulation" category. A game like "Gran Turismo" might either be considered as "simulation" or not, depending on the player who classify it.

8 Some classifications will dig deeper into details than others. For example, the "shoot'em up" category can be used as is, can be merged into a larger "action" category, or can be divided in several "sub-genres" such as "run n' gun", "manic shooter", "cute them up", etc.

9 Personal translation from French: "*un ensemble de règles, des modes de commandes, l'organisation spatiale, l'organisation temporelle, l'organisation dramaturgique*".

10 Ludology is an interdisciplinary academic field dedicated to the study of games. See Frasca (2003) for more details.

11 http://www.gameclassification.com/EN/games/580-Sim-City/index.html

12 http://www.gameclassification.com/EN/games/501-Pac-Man/index.html

13 http://www.gameclassification.com/EN/games/597-Space-Invaders/index.html

14 http://serious.gameclassification.com/EN/games/12111-PowerUp/index.html

15 http://serious.gameclassification.com/EN/games/758-Americas-Army/index.html

16 More information on e-sports tournament related to America's Army: http://www.gotfrag.com/aa/

17 http://serious.gameclassification.com/EN/games/11511-Lure-of-The-Labyrinth/index.html

18 http://serious.gameclassification.com/EN/games/1018-Fatworld/index.html

19 http://serious.gameclassification.com/EN/games/1041-Re-Mission/index.html

20 http://serious.gameclassification.com/EN/games/734-September-the-12th/index.html

21 http://serious.gameclassification.com/EN/games/1334-stop-disasters/index.html

Chapter 7
Game-Based Learning Design Patterns:
An Approach to Support the Development of "Better" Educational Games

Manuel Ecker
University of Education Weingarten, Germany

Wolfgang Müller
University of Education Weingarten, Germany

Johannes Zylka
University of Education Weingarten, Germany

ABSTRACT

The application of computer games in the field of learning has gained increasing interest lately. Research in this area has been enforced and more, and more computer games have appeared on the market. However, only a few of these educational games can convince and fulfill the high expectations. A major reason for this is that it is not easy to integrate game play with learning elements without interfering both in a negative way.

This chapter introduces an approach to use best-practice experiences in terms of Design Patterns to support the development of high-quality and successful educational games. These Game-based Learning Design Patterns draw from previous work on Game Design Patterns and Pedagogical Patterns. The chapter provides background on the Design Pattern approach and explains the structure of the new pattern type based on selected examples. It also illustrates that existing patterns, e.g., from Game Design, may provide first evidence, while the identification of Game-based Learning Design Patterns is not straightforward.

DOI: 10.4018/978-1-60960-495-0.ch007

INTRODUCTION

Since Marc Prensky introduced the term Game-based Learning (Prensky, 2001), the development and application of computer games has received increasing interest, and a number of quite successful examples of learning games and serious games have been introduced (for a more detailed classification of these genres cf. Tang, 2009). The idea to utilize the highly motivating aspects of games and the inherent possibility to create situated learning contexts, and even the potential to initiate stealth learning is indeed fascinating. Yet, progress in this field isn't actually satisfying. The vast majority of learning games does not match the high expectations (cf. Jantke, 2006; for a recent comprehensive study Ritterfeld, 2009; and for a detailed analysis of specific examples Weiß, 2008). In fact, it has been argued that the same problems can be found in edutainment titles since the 1980s (Egenfeldt-Nielsen, 2008).

Still the question, how the development of educational games can be supported and the quality of content and design can be increased, remains. In this chapter we describe the approach of collecting best practices in this field in terms of so called Game-based Learning Design Patterns (GBLDPs). Those patterns support authors developing Game-based Learning applications and may probably improve the quality and educational integration in teaching and learning scenarios. We provide some background on Design Patterns and their application to combine know-how and best practices, as well as on the application of Design Pattern approaches in both, the domain of computer games and in the educational field. Based on existing approaches in these domains we describe and discuss a structure for GBLDPs. Moreover, we provide three examples for such patterns and their description utilizing the proposed structure as well as we discuss challenges in identifying and recording adequate patterns and best practices in the field of Game-based Learning which may be caused by the wide spectrum of possible applications of educational games and the corresponding instructional decisions.

BACKGROUND

The Design Patterns Approach: Theory and History

The introduction of Design Patterns and the notion of a pattern language can be attributed to the architect Christopher Alexander (cf. Alexander, 1977). Alexander's main motivation was actually to provide a toolbox containing solutions to common problems that designers face when designing and creating buildings and cities. The result was a document of established solutions and common knowledge in architectural design in the form of a collection of patterns. Alexander pictured this collection as a language – a pattern language –, which combines elements following certain rules.

Later, Alexander's concept of Design Patterns was successfully adapted to the domain of software development (Gamma et al., 1995), providing a means to describe best practices in software design in a structured and well-defined way. Today, the Design Pattern approach is well accepted and is widely applied to identify and describe solutions for design problems in a semi-formal way. Well-known examples relate to fields such as human-computer interaction (cf., e.g., Borchers, 2001; Tidwell, 2005; or Schümmer and Lukosch, 2007), web programming (cf., e.g., Wallace, 2000; and Vora, 2009) and others.

Design Patterns have also been proposed in the field of computer games as an approach to document best practices. Björk and Holopainen (2005) presented a collection of patterns in Game Design, describing elements of and approaches to computer games that can be found regularly. The focus of this pattern collection is clearly on the gameplay as a core aspect of computer games, examples for named Game Design Patterns are Role Playing, Social Dilemma, Exploration or

Collection. Educational aspects do not occur in the given descriptions of Game Design Patterns explicitly.

Design Patterns have also been adopted in the educational domain. For instance, several approaches related to Design Patterns were applied to describe best practices in instructional design (cf., e.g., Vogel &7 Wippermann, 2003; and Kolfschoten et al., 2009 for more general discussions). Following this idea, different initiatives started developing collections of patterns, for example by describing their structure as well as experiences with specific learning designs (e.g., The pedagogical patterns project, 2009; TELL project, 2005). Thus, a number of such patterns have been published recently (e.g., Bescherer et al., 2008; Retalis & Kohls, 2008). These different initiatives employed differing terms, such as Educational Patterns, Didactical Design Patterns, Learning Patterns or Pedagogical Patterns. Though these items indicate differences in the respective approaches, they usually depict similar structures and overlap typically.

However, Design Patterns are not intended to be standard components, which can merely be applied and connected to other elements to create new solutions or applications without a careful adaptation to a specific application domain and problem. Therefore, the implementation of these patterns is hardly possible without design experience and appropriate skills.

In this context, there have been few approaches to capture experiences using games in context of learning within the scope of projects (e.g., Kaleidoscope Project, 2009). If these project's outcomes contain patterns, they mostly remain restricted to the application of learning games, and particularly do not provide any explicit information on the design of successful learning games. Moreover, these elements are limited to very specific application domains, which may become essential, because Design Patterns in general should represent solutions to one or more reoccurring problems. Empirical evidence on the relevance and reoccurrence of both, problem and solution, are indispensable for applicable Design Patterns (cf. Buschmann et al., 2007 for a more detailed discussion). Thus, a detailed discussion of the context in which the solution is valid, is necessary to provide an insight into respective conditions.

Inferentially, an appropriate formalism to describe Design Patterns in context of Game-based Learning, including a standardized structure and layout, is absolutely needed. This standardization shall fulfill several purposes: First of all, it shall ensure that the documentation of a pattern is outright and contains all necessary aspects to determine possible benefits and requirements for the application of a pattern. For an author of a pattern, the structure therefore represents a guideline to provide all necessary information and helps to avoid ambiguities. Moreover, the standard presentation layout shall support users to compare patterns and to identify possible candidates to solve a specific design problem.

Additionally, the point of introducing such a formal structure seems to be very reasonable, because the domain of Game-based Learning itself is manageable at the moment, and – as mentioned above – there are just a few approaches concerning Design Patterns in context of Game-based Learning (e.g. Zhen Zeng, 2009).

GAME-BASED LEARNING DESIGN PATTERNS

As aforementioned, the development of 'good' educational games is very challenging. A major problem in this field is the appropriate integration of gameplay and learning objectives (cf. Weiß, 2008 for a more detailed discussion). However, the majority of educational games also falls short to meet the requirements with respect to sufficient quality of technological functionality, good game design, quality of visuals and audio, story line, and appropriate interaction as well as participation (Ritterfeld, 2009). Since well-accepted and evaluated models and methods for developing high-quality applications in the field of Game-based Learning are missing, collecting and providing best practices currently seems the most promising approach to further development in this field.

Pattern Identification

In context of collecting best practices in terms of such patterns, the procedure can be divided into a top down and a bottom up approach. The top down approach means an analysis of existing patterns, such as Game Design Patterns (Björk & Holopainen, 2005) or Educational Game Design Patterns (see Zhen Zeng, 2009). The bottom up approach leads to the identification of GBLDPs in educational games, or in beta-versions of these games.

The top down approach is very important at this point, because by analyzing existing Design Patterns, interesting aspects can possibly be found. The second approach can be subdivided into two methods: Structural analysis and play-testing. "Analysis requires an existing game – or a prototype or a design document describing a game – so one can study what Game Design Patterns exist within the game. Design can refer to the creation of an idea, concept, or description of a game by using Game Design Patterns, or of formalizing a game idea or concept into a more structured description." (cf. Björk & Holopainen, 2005, p. 41 ff.). Therefore, identifying GBLDPs in educational games or prototypes can be done by test-playing educational games, doing it stand-alone or by observing others. According to Björk and Holopainen (2005), structural analysis is usually quicker and more ordered than test-playing, because test-playing causes a conflict of interests when doing it by oneself, since the analyzing person wants to study the game on the one hand, and has to play it on the other hand. Besides, the observation of other players may generate a vast amount of data.

These named approaches is supposed to lead to an extensive and coherent library of GBLDPs that may help to communicate experiences on developing educational games and may enable the exchange between developers, practitioners, and researchers in the application of games for learning purposes. At the same time, collections of Game-based Learning Design Patterns will be a good base for further research and development, either in terms of technological solutions, or new learning designs. The comparability and possibility of analysis between different designs could be another assignment of such a collection.

Patterns in general can be used in many different ways. It is possible to employ GBLDPs to generate new educational game ideas, to support developing new game concepts, to solve problems, and furthermore, may support communication on different levels. Using this pattern structure in communication allows to structure descriptions of designs, motivations, and learning objectives plus it offers advantages in presenting the educational game design to other people.

Problems of Existing Patterns

One may ask whether a new type of pattern – e.g., GBLDP – is really needed, and whether it may not be sufficient to utilize existing pattern types. For instance, one might argue that in-game aspects, such as game-technology and game-design, can easily be captured by the means of Game Design Patterns, while out-of-game aspects such as learning context and specific learning objectives could be described in terms of Educational or rather Pedagogical Patterns. However, such an approach will have to fail due to the lack of an integrative view of in-game and out-of-game aspects.

For instance, Game Design Patterns, such as *Puzzle Solving* (Björk & Holopainen, 2005) or Educational Game Design Patterns, such as *Ask-a-friend* (Kiili, 2009) or *Constructing things is fun and helps learning* (Zhen & Zeng, 2009) may comprise both: prove a good solution and, depending on the learning objectives and its context (cf. Ecker, 2009 for a more detailed analysis), also become inappropriate. Therefore, patterns may even become anti-patterns, what shall be explained based on an example. In the math-game DimensionM, the pattern *Puzzle-Solving* is being applied frequently, and corresponding scenes and scenarios play the predominant role in the whole game design. While the *Puzzle-Solving* pattern can be considered useful in general, it is not suitable to support learning with respect to all possible learning objectives (cf. Bloom, 1956; and Krauthwohl, 1973 for a more detailed discussion). In the consistent lasting form, the pattern is being applied in this game regardless of it's well-known restrictions, it mutates into an anti-pattern. To prevent this sort of misuse of patterns, it is necessary to add information concerning these relevant limitations and possible risks to the patterns.

Thus, the development of a GBLDP library as well as the integration of Game Design Patterns and Educational Patterns leads to the construction of a template that has to be founded in educational and pedagogical categories. These educational and pedagogical issues have – at least compared to Game Design Patterns – a great significance in our pattern structure, because these aspects are supposed to be very important to achieve the goals of educational games. Therefore, we will describe the structure of GBLDPs in the following subchapters as well as give some examples afterwards.

Pattern Template

The necessary pattern structure resembles the well-accepted, generic template that can be found in Game Design Patterns, but gets amended with aspects of learning objectives and the corresponding context. Coming back to the GBLDPs, we have to describe gameplay and learning aspects briefly in a corresponding way.

As all patterns, GBLDPs come with their specific meta-pattern (cf., e.g., Wippermann, 2008), their own well-defined structure. This structure includes pre-defined slots, ensuring the coverage of all important aspects and dimensions of the pattern, especially regarding their instantiation and application. This structure also provides authors with a guideline for documenting own patterns. Common to all Design Patterns, essential elements are: (1) Name of pattern, (2) Section of problem, (3) Section of solution, (4) Section of consequences. According to Wippermann (2008), each pattern needs these elements to be described in a usable way. Below, we want to define a template for GBLDPs based on these layers in terms of a consistent formal description mask.

Generally, most available pattern templates have a very similar layout that mostly simply differs in details and specification, based on their respective context. The following figure (see Figure 1) shows a collection of frequently used structure elements in Design Patterns.

The next list is based on these elements, reduces some of these aspects and shows the structure of the pattern template for Game-based Learning Design Patterns, which gets supplemented by some detailed comments.

Figure 1. Structure elements in design patterns

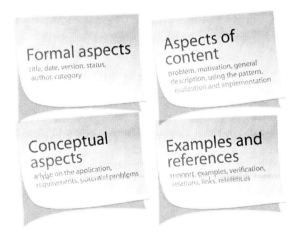

- **Formal Aspects (category, author(s), version, date):** The elements of this first section are supposed to find, to use, and to categorize appropriate patterns. By naming them, version numbering, and dating changes, it should be possible to get additional information about the presented pattern's history, to contact the writer(s) of the patterns if necessary, or to advance it without running the risk of losing the pattern's background or build number.

- **Aspects of Content (basic problems, approach, general description):** In this section the given problem as well as the approaches of solving it should be described. Some further information should be given in the general description of the pattern.

- **Conceptual Aspects (educational concept, learning objectives, activated cognitive skills, potential problems in using, requirements, advice on application and scenario):** This chapter describes important details that have to be considered during the development of educational games. For instance, it is elementary to know, which specific educational concept lies at the bottom of the pattern. The concrete learning objectives and the level of comprehension should be named to externalize the pattern's pedagogical background. Some advice on application, a declaration of requirements and some hints to potential problems as well as providing some information on restrictions can be helpful.

- **Examples and references (related patterns, application example(s), references):** It may be useful to know which patterns are related to each other and to name exemplary applications to understand the pattern. If there already exist any publications about the described pattern, these should be mentioned.

The named aspect 'category' will not be mentioned in the following examples, because we cannot provide detailed and valid information at this point. Even if some categories of educational games are presented, for instance, by Kiili (2009), this aspect has to be further investigated in future research approaches.

A general problem when working with Design Patterns is to achieve an adequate level of semi-formal description in order to compare them to patterns for the technical field and providing a good base for an implementation in different relations, e.g., in context of educational games. Besides, it is also crucial that enough space is provided to cover the aspects of a specific application context, which will also be explained by means of vivid examples of such patterns.

To solve this given gap and in addition to the semi-formal description of the patterns, we amend the presented table in each of the following examples with a case story, which describes a concrete application of the respective pattern. It should offer some further information on the basis of a summary that includes a declaration of the author and contributors as well as a discussion of the pattern used in an educational game. Because of the classification in task, actions, conclusion, and lessons learned it should be traceable for readers.

EXAMPLES OF GAME-BASED LEARNING DESIGN PATTERNS

In the chapter above, we introduced a template for Game-based Learning Design Patterns. In order to remain comprehensible at this point, we provide some detailed samples for the use of the pattern template described above. Two of these samples originate from the fields of Game Design Patterns as well as Pedagogical Patterns, one was created by the authors on the basis of educational games in terms of an bottom up approach.

Table 1.

GBLDP: Constructive Play	
Formal Aspects	
Category	
Author(s)	Zylka, J., based on Björk, S. and Holopainen, J. (2005)
Version	1.0
Date	2010-02-01
Aspects of Content	
Basic Problem	Patterns like *Puzzle Solving* are used quite often in the context of learning games. These cannot communicate all necessary competencies in phases of practicing or exploring contents in a reasonable way. Accordingly, if used in these game phases, they can possibly become anti-patterns if not combined with other patterns in an adequate way.
Approach	*Constructive Play* seems to be an applicable pattern in these phases.
General description	As mentioned above, this pattern is characterized through putting game elements together to construct new game element configurations. Imagination and experimental problem solving is trained.
Conceptual aspects	
Educational concept	The pattern offers an inductive form of playing that might cause an interesting gaming experience within the corresponding gaming phase, which is a very important element in the context of GBLDPs.
Learning objectives	Particularly self-determination, planning, and developing.
Activated cognitive skills	This pattern includes the five dimensions of Bloom's taxonomy. It contains actions of knowledge, comprehension, application, analysis, and synthesis.
Requirements	At least, there has to be a framework as well as some goals for the use of the pattern, because it could very easily become an anti-pattern without this framework.
Potential problems in using	As already mentioned above, there might be an affinity to endless gaming, what possibly causes this pattern to get an anti-pattern. It offers lots of possibilities to be combined with other patterns, above all, it should be used in phases of practicing or exploring.
Advise on the application/scenario	The application of this pattern should be framed by other phases and should leastwise be used in context of following goals.
Examples and references	
Related patterns	e. g., Randomness, Predictable Consequences, Stimulated Planning
Application sample(s)	Making History, games of the Sim series (e. g. Sim City)
References	Björk, S. and Holopainen, J. (2005)

Game Design Patterns as Game-Based Learning Design Patterns

As an example for a Game-based Learning Design Pattern we firstly present a pattern introduced by Björk and Holopainen (2005, p. 255f) called *Constructive Play*. This pattern can be used, when different game elements get assembled to construct new kinds of game element configurations. Usually they are requiring and enhancing imagination as well as training experimental problem solving. (see Table 1)

It gets clear that some well-known Game Design Patterns can very well be used as GBLDPs, because of their similar use in context of Game-based Learning. Other Game Design Patterns like *Roleplaying*, *Social Dilemma* or *Collection* (see Björk & Holopainen, 2005) have to be analyzed in further investigations. This Game-based Learning Design Pattern will be exemplified in the following case story. (see Table 2)

This Game-based Learning Design Pattern is not only used in Serious Games or Educational Games. It is hardly possible to find any strategy

Table 2.

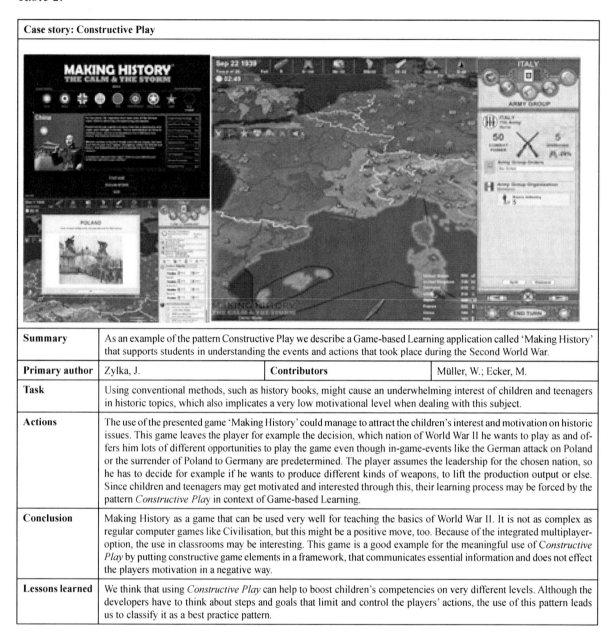

Case story: Constructive Play			
Summary	As an example of the pattern Constructive Play we describe a Game-based Learning application called 'Making History' that supports students in understanding the events and actions that took place during the Second World War.		
Primary author	Zylka, J.	**Contributors**	Müller, W.; Ecker, M.
Task	Using conventional methods, such as history books, might cause an underwhelming interest of children and teenagers in historic topics, which also implicates a very low motivational level when dealing with this subject.		
Actions	The use of the presented game 'Making History' could manage to attract the children's interest and motivation on historic issues. This game leaves the player for example the decision, which nation of World War II he wants to play as and offers him lots of different opportunities to play the game even though in-game-events like the German attack on Poland or the surrender of Poland to Germany are predetermined. The player assumes the leadership for the chosen nation, so he has to decide for example if he wants to produce different kinds of weapons, to lift the production output or else. Since children and teenagers may get motivated and interested through this, their learning process may be forced by the pattern *Constructive Play* in context of Game-based Learning.		
Conclusion	Making History as a game that can be used very well for teaching the basics of World War II. It is not as complex as regular computer games like Civilisation, but this might be a positive move, too. Because of the integrated multiplayer-option, the use in classrooms may be interesting. This game is a good example for the meaningful use of *Constructive Play* by putting constructive game elements in a framework, that communicates essential information and does not effect the players motivation in a negative way.		
Lessons learned	We think that using *Constructive Play* can help to boost children's competencies on very different levels. Although the developers have to think about steps and goals that limit and control the players' actions, the use of this pattern leads us to classify it as a best practice pattern.		

or simulation game published in the last years that do not leastwise contain some elements relating to this pattern. Also, games from other areas, for instance persuasive games like Geocaching (cf., e.g., Björk, 2007), mobile games like Spore or online games such as Farmville use this pattern quite often.

Nevertheless, this pattern is very useful especially in context of Game-based Learning, what can be imagined when talking about the framework of educational games below. But first, we mention an example that originates from the field of Educational and accordingly Pedagogical Patterns.

Table 3.

GBLDP: Early Bird	
Formal Aspects	
Category	
Author(s)	Zylka, J., based on Bergin, J. (1998)
Version	1.03
Date	2010-02-01
Aspects of Content	
Basic Problem	In progress of a tutorial, the students or pupils loose their attention or do not get the essential ideas of the course. Speaking of educational games, quite similar problems probably exist.
Approach	Generally, a seminar is designed for its important ideas, so these become the basic principles in context of the course's framework. Those ideas are taught at the beginning and over and over again throughout the tutorial.
General description	Exactly the same aspects can be found in educational games. If one wants to convey mathematical issues with focus on a special algebraic formula, this one will be mentioned consistently. Thus, this is important in nearly every educational game that wants to allow Game-based Learning. This way the pattern can be used in very different contexts.
Conceptual aspects	
Educational concept	Because the concentration of educational gamers decreases during a gaming session or during the game in general, it is advised to put the most important facts to the beginning of the game, and to repeat them once in a while.
Learning objectives	The goals can basically be described as learning or practicing basic and respectively important content.
Activated cognitive skills	This pattern corresponds predominantly on the dimensions knowledge and comprehension, but is at least transferable to the other dimensions such as exercises.
Requirements	Constitutionally, some essential ideas or contents, which should get conveyed, have to exist. Otherwise there is no reason for applying this Pedagogical Pattern, and likewise, GBLDP.
Potential problems in using	One can imagine that a unwise use of this pattern may lead to unintentional effects, for example a vast damage to motivation.
Advise on the application/scenario	This pattern should be applied with caution because of the described addiction to become an anti-pattern if used inappropriately.
Examples and references	
Related patterns	e.g., Spiral, Lay of the Land, Fix Upper, Toy Box, Larger than Life
Application sample(s)	Dimenxian, DimensionM, MathEvolver, Ice Ice maybe
References	http://csis.pace.edu/~bergin/PedPat1.3.html

Educational and Pedagogical Patterns as Game-Based Learning Design Patterns

Educational Patterns as well as Pedagogical Patterns try to convey information about the practice of teaching and learning to structural knowledge. Each pattern should be capable to problems that appear in different contexts from time to time. This can relate to education and training planning or different other educational aspects.

From a pedagogical point of view, these patterns are supposed to motivate students, to evaluate them, to provide them appropriate material or to give some general advices to lecturers. The planning of a seminar for instance occurs by considering content, time range, learner's background and other important factors. While designing educational games, some of these points can possibly get very useful, because the aspects that have to be considered are at least very similar. Due to this fact, they can also be found in approaches to develop online learning (cf., e.g., Jones, 1999) or

Table 4.

Case story: Early Bird	

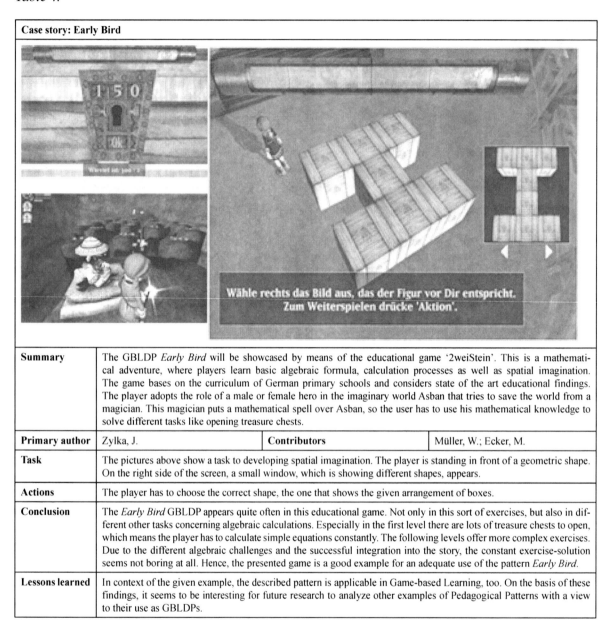

Summary	The GBLDP *Early Bird* will be showcased by means of the educational game '2weiStein'. This is a mathematical adventure, where players learn basic algebraic formula, calculation processes as well as spatial imagination. The game bases on the curriculum of German primary schools and considers state of the art educational findings. The player adopts the role of a male or female hero in the imaginary world Asban that tries to save the world from a magician. This magician puts a mathematical spell over Asban, so the user has to use his mathematical knowledge to solve different tasks like opening treasure chests.		
Primary author	Zylka, J.	**Contributors**	Müller, W.; Ecker, M.
Task	The pictures above show a task to developing spatial imagination. The player is standing in front of a geometric shape. On the right side of the screen, a small window, which is showing different shapes, appears.		
Actions	The player has to choose the correct shape, the one that shows the given arrangement of boxes.		
Conclusion	The *Early Bird* GBLDP appears quite often in this educational game. Not only in this sort of exercises, but also in different other tasks concerning algebraic calculations. Especially in the first level there are lots of treasure chests to open, which means the player has to calculate simple equations constantly. The following levels offer more complex exercises. Due to the different algebraic challenges and the successful integration into the story, the constant exercise-solution seems not boring at all. Hence, the presented game is a good example for an adequate use of the pattern *Early Bird*.		
Lessons learned	In context of the given example, the described pattern is applicable in Game-based Learning, too. On the basis of these findings, it seems to be interesting for future research to analyze other examples of Pedagogical Patterns with a view to their use as GBLDPs.		

to advance cognitive learning efficiency (cf., e.g., Kolfschoten, 2010).

In the following template, we present the GBLDP *Early Bird* that derives from the Pedagogical Patterns (see Bergin, 1998) and therefore represents an example for this section. (see Tables 3 and 4)

Like the Game Design Pattern before, the Educational and Pedagogical Pattern *Early Bird* also is

applicable in context of GBLDPs. At this point, one has to ask whether other Pedagogical or Educational Patterns are transferable to GBLDPs as well.

Bergin (1998) describes at least 14 Pedagogical Patterns. Reading and carefully analyzing them leads us to the assumption that nearly all of these patterns can be used in context of Game-based Learning. For instance, the pattern *Spiral* means

Figure 2. The Sandwich GBLDP

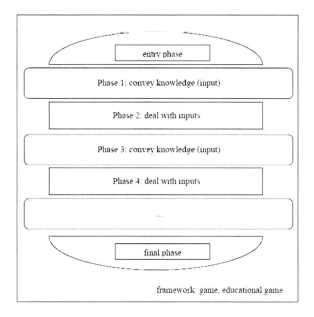

that the contents of a seminar should be at a basic level at the beginning and get challenging throughout the course, what can be adopted very well on Educational Games. The Pedagogical Pattern *Consistent Metaphor* implicates that the students learn by using known metaphors, which might also become a very interesting GBLDP. The pattern *Gold Star* actually gets used in lots of educational games: good solutions or good work in general should be rewarded.

The following chapter offers a new Game-based Learning Design Pattern that was developed in an inductive way from different educational games. As were the previous examples, it will be demonstrated by an example application.

Game-Based Learning Design Pattern Extracted from Educational Games

Looking on games in general as well as on most meaningful educational games, there are different merging game-phases. For instance, these can be a phase of *Puzzle Solving* combined with a sequence of practicing the acquired knowledge.

This leads us to the classification of a *Sandwich* GBLDP, that points to the general practice of combining different patterns respectively phases within a game or a level. As implicated above, it has to be mentioned that this GBLDP may consist of different subordinate patterns.

Figure 2 shows the basic configuration of a Sandwich Game-based Learning Design Pattern, in general it can be amended as well as reduced by some phases. (see Tables 5 and 6)

These examples showed three GBLDPs, arising different areas of research. They showed that the approach of creating a specific structure of patterns in context of Game-based Learning actually works. Compared to Game Design Patterns or Educational Game Design Patterns, this approach does not just allude relations between patterns, it includes these relations as substantial elements of GBLDPs.

FUTURE RESEARCH DIRECTIONS

For improving learning and motivation through educational games, an extensive collection of

Table 5.

GBLDP: Sandwich	
Formal Aspects	
Category	
Author(s)	Zylka, J., based on Wahl, D. (2005)
Version	1.00
Date	2010-02-01
Aspects of Content	
Basic Problem	There has to be a switch of phases (not only but especially) in educational games, because if it just consists of one phase it might become a not very useful educational game. To mention an example: depending on the version, even the well known game Tetris consists at least of two phases. One phase of gaming, and one that shows the results.
Approach	The majority of interesting and good educational games uses this switching of phases as a matter of course.
General description	This pattern means the switching of phases conveying content, e.g., knowledge, to phases of subjective examination with this content or other stages.
Conceptual aspects	
Educational concept	The switching between two phases (e.g., conveying content, subjective examination) can be seen as smallest element of an educational game that actually makes sense. As already mentioned above, a game that consists of just one phase hardly makes sense.
Learning objectives	The goals of this GBLDP depend on the used phases, but in general they can be described as learning, using and exploring content with a view to the continuous preservation of motivation.
Activated cognitive skills	Due to the flexible form of this pattern the comprehension level can reach from basic to advantage knowledge.
Requirements	At least two different game phases that necessarily are related to each other.
Potential problems in using	Problems can occur, e.g., if too many phases get applied or if the used phases are not adjusted to each other in an adequate way. The pattern consists of at least two phases, but it is hardly possible to conclude, that every combination of 2 phases can be seen as meaningful *Sandwich* GBLDP from an educational point of view.
Advise on the application/scenario	Whether the use of this GBLDP makes sense, strongly depends on the respective context. For instance, it seems not very applicable to put two incoherent phases of knowledge transfer after each other.
Examples and references	
Related patterns	e.g., Randomness, Stimulated Planning, Constructive Play, Puzzle Solving
Application sample(s)	Dimenxian, Ice Ice Maybe, MathEvolver, Making History
References	Wahl, D. (2005)

GBDLPs as a first step is necessary. Developers and researchers as well as evaluators may benefit from a basic guideline at their disposal, what hopefully leads to a significant better quality of educational games, since authors will be supported by empirical values through information about dependencies and exercisable educational applications. Of course, in context of this GBLDP library especially expert knowledge on pedagogical aspects and structural game aspects with a view to motivational level of players has to be included, but information on the development of Educational games as well as other aspects can be of value, too.

Thus, a suitable categorization of GBLDPs has to be developed. This may be helpful to develop Game-based Learning applications. Some similar elements already exist, e.g., as Educational Game Design Pattern categories (Kiili, 2009) or as pattern classification in object-oriented software (cf.

Table 6.

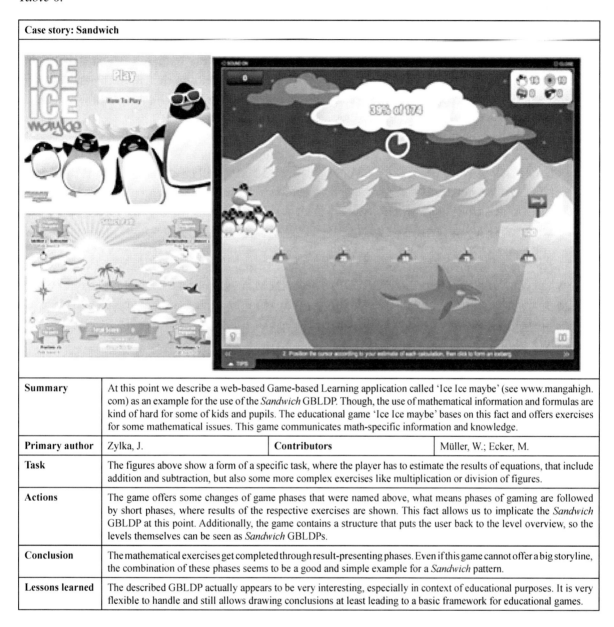

Summary	At this point we describe a web-based Game-based Learning application called 'Ice Ice maybe' (see www.mangahigh. com) as an example for the use of the *Sandwich* GBLDP. Though, the use of mathematical information and formulas are kind of hard for some of kids and pupils. The educational game 'Ice Ice maybe' bases on this fact and offers exercises for some mathematical issues. This game communicates math-specific information and knowledge.		
Primary author	Zylka, J.	Contributors	Müller, W.; Ecker, M.
Task	The figures above show a form of a specific task, where the player has to estimate the results of equations, that include addition and subtraction, but also some more complex exercises like multiplication or division of figures.		
Actions	The game offers some changes of game phases that were named above, what means phases of gaming are followed by short phases, where results of the respective exercises are shown. This fact allows us to implicate the *Sandwich* GBLDP at this point. Additionally, the game contains a structure that puts the user back to the level overview, so the levels themselves can be seen as *Sandwich* GBLDPs.		
Conclusion	The mathematical exercises get completed through result-presenting phases. Even if this game cannot offer a big storyline, the combination of these phases seems to be a good and simple example for a *Sandwich* pattern.		
Lessons learned	The described GBLDP actually appears to be very interesting, especially in context of educational purposes. It is very flexible to handle and still allows drawing conclusions at least leading to a basic framework for educational games.		

Gamma et al., 1995; Bescherer et al., 2008; & Wippermann, 2008). Björk und Holopainen (2005) divide their catalogue in different topics, which may be useful as basal categories, too.

Even if our approach clearly is a big step and needs a lot of preparatory work, especially an early start of the pattern mining process is absolutely necessary to allow further investigation on this approach, for instance, to help getting a better understanding on where certain patterns are applicable or to be the substructure for empirical evidence. At least, there are two essential points for the development of a GBLDP library: a co-operation between and coordination of different researchers.

Researchers in the context of starting a GBLDP catalogue may consider the following advices:

1. It's not necessary to present all new patterns. Look at Design Patterns, Game Design Patterns, Educational Game Patterns (or else) first, these may provide a good basis.
2. When you analyze existing patterns, do not just search for a specific name. Different names can actually mean very similar things.
3. When you have an idea of a GBLDP, even an existing one, think about the category your GBLDP belongs to. Maybe it belongs not just to one category?
4. Be sure to describe your GBLDP in an adequate way, including one or more examples – only a good analysis provides useful data to other readers and developers.
5. When you have one or more new GBLDPs, try to connect with other researchers in this field. Only by communicating with each others, scattered approaches may succeed.

Is a categorization of GBDLPs possible and can it prove itself usable? Is it possible to picture Educational Patterns using GBLDPs respectively to look for a sensible and workable link? Does it succeed, to assemble complex applications on the basis of Game-based Learning Design Patterns? These and other questions remain to be clarified in the course of further research.

CONCLUSION

In the first part of this chapter, an overview and some basic information on the use of Design Patterns in different contexts, such as game design or in educational fields, was given. We introduced a new approach concerning Design Patterns that uses elements from both, patterns in game design as well as Educational and Pedagogical Patterns: The Game-based Learning Design Patterns.

Furthermore, the structure of a pattern template was discussed. The most important conclusion is that Game-based Learning Design Patterns have to connect two different approaches: One that originates from gameplay and one that picks up educational contexts. The combination of these two aspects might be extensive at an early stage, but – in our opinion – might also become a reasonable and particularly a practicable way for developing games in context of Game-based Learning.

The three named examples showed that Game Design Patterns as well as Pedagogical Patterns can be very well used as GBLDPs. Although the concept of Design Patterns is widely accepted and established in many areas of research, the approaches in this paper must prove themselves exercisable. This must be shown in the course of additional studies on these aspects and additionally in an appropriate evaluation and discussion by representatives of the involved branches.

REFERENCES

Alexander, C. (1977). *A pattern language. Towns, buildings, construction*. New York: Oxford University Press.

Bergin, J. (1998). *Pedagogical patterns*. New York: Pace University. Retrieved January 26, 2010, from http://csis.pace.edu/~bergin/PedPat1.3.html

Bescherer, C., Spannagel, C., & Müller, W. (2008). Anti pattern and pattern for introductory mathematics tutorials. *Proceedings of 13th European Conference on Pattern Languages of Programs*. Irsee, Germany.

Björk, S., & Holopainen, J. (2005). *Patterns in game design*. Hingham, MA: Charles River Media.

Björk, S., & Peitz, J. (2007). *Understanding pervasive games through gameplay design patterns*. Tokyo: University of Tokyo.

Bloom, B. S. (1956). *Taxonomy of educational objectives. Handbook I: The cognitive domain*. New York: David McKay.

Borchers, J. (2001). *A pattern approach to interaction design.* New York: John Wiley & Sons.

Buschmann, F., Henney, K., & Schmidt, D. C. (2007). *Pattern oriented software architecture: On patterns and pattern languages.* San Francisco: John Wiley & Sons.

Ecker, M., Weiß, S. A., & Müller, W. (2009). *Aspekte von Interactive Digital Storytelling Technologien im Bereich Game-based Learning.* Paper presented at the 11. Workshop Sichtsysteme – Visualisierung in der Simulationstechnik. Wuppertal, Germany.

Egenfeldt-Nielsen, S., Heide Smith, J., & Tosca, S. P. (2008). *Understanding video games: The essential introduction.* New York: Routledge.

Gamma, E., Helm, R., Johnson, R., & Vilissides, J. (1995). *Design patterns: Elements of reusable object-oriented software.* Reading, MA: Addison-Wesley.

Jantke, K. P. (2006). Games that do not exist: Communication design beyond the current limits. *Proceedings of 24th Annual ACM International Conference on Design of Communication.* Myrtle Beach, SC: ACM.

Jones, D., Stewart, S., & Power, G. (1999). Patterns: Using proven experience to develop online learning. *Proceedings of ASCILITE'99 Responding to Diversity,* (pp. 155-162). Retrieved February 1, 2010, from http://www.ascilite.org.au/conferences/brisbane99/papers/jonesstewart.pdf

Kaleidoscope Project. (2009). *Learning patterns for the design and development for mathematical games.* Retrieved January 26, 2010, from http://lp.noe-kaleidoscope.org/outcomes/patterns/

Kiili, K. (2009). *Educational game design patterns.* Retrieved May 15, 2010, from http://www.pori.tut.fi/~krikii/patterns/

Kohls, C., & Windbrake, T. (2008). Where to go and what to show: More patterns for a pattern language of interactive information graphics. *Proceedings of the 2006 conference on Pattern languages of programs,* (pp. 1-11). Portland: ACM.

Kolfschoten, G., Lukosch, S., Verbraeck, A., Valentin, E., & Vreede, G.-J. (2010). Cognitive learning efficiency through the use of design patterns in teaching. *Computers & Education, 54.*

Prensky, M. (2001). *Digital game-based learning.* New York: McGraw-Hill.

Retalis, S., & Kohls, C. (2008). Patterns for tools and pedagogies for higher education. *Proceedings of 13th European Conference on Pattern Languages of Programs.* Irsee, Germany.

Ritterfeld, U., Cody, M., & Vorderer, P. (Eds.). (2009). *Serious games: Mechanisms and effects.* New York: Routledge.

Schümmer, T., & Lukosch, S. (2007). *Patterns for computer-mediated interaction.* West Sussex, UK: John Wiley & Sons.

Tang, S., Hanneghan, M., & El Rhalibi, A. (2009). Introduction to games-based learning. In T. Connolly, M. Stansfield, & L. Boyle (Eds.), *Games-based learning advancements for multi-sensory human computer interfaces: Techniques and effective practices,* (pp. 1-17). Retrieved January 29, 2010, from http://www.igi-pub.com/downloads/excerpts/33410.pdf

TELL Project. (2005). *Design patterns for teachers and educational (system designers).* Pattern book. Output of WP3 TELL project. Retrieved January 26, 2010, from http://cosy.ted.unipi.gr/images/stories/design-patterns/TELL_pattern_book.pdf.

Tidwell, J. (2006). *Designing interfaces–patterns for effective interaction design.* Sebastopol, CA: O'Reilly Media.

Vogel, R. & Wippermann, S. (2003). Einsatz neuer Lehr-Lernformen an Hochschulen mit Hilfe Didaktischer Design Patterns. *Ludwigsburger Beiträge*, 4/2003.

Vora, P. (2009). *Web application design patterns*. Burlington, Canada: Morgan Kaufman.

Wahl, D. (2005). *Lernumgebungen erfolgreich gestalten: Vom trägen Wissen zum kompetenten Handeln*. Bad Heilbrunn, Germany: Klinkhardt.

Wallace, N. (2000). *Design patterns in Web programming*. Retrieved January 31, 2010, from http://www.e-gineer.com/v1/articles/design-patterns-in-web-programming.htm

Weiß, S.A. & Müller, W. (2008). The potential of interactive digital storytelling for the creation of educational computer games. *Proceedings of Edutainment 2008*, Nanjing, China.

Wippermann, S. (2008). *Didaktische Design Patterns zur Dokumentation und Systematisierung didaktischen Wissens und als Grundlage einer Community of Practice*. Saarbrücken, Germany: Dr. Müller.

Zhen Zeng, H., Plass, J. L., & Homer, B. D. (2009): *Educational game design pattern candidates*. New York: Games for Learning Institute. Retrieved May 14, 2010, from http://g4li.org/wp-content/uploads/2009/12/1_Game-Design-Patterns.pdf

ADDITIONAL READING

Holopainen, J., & Björk, S. (2007). Design patterns are Dead - Long Live Design Patterns. Borries, F. von, Walz, S. P., Böttger, M. (eds.) (2007). *Space Time Play. On the Synergy Between Computer Games, Architecture, and Urbanism*, Basel, Switzerland: Birkhäuser Publishing.

Holopainen, J., & Björk, S. (2008). *Gameplay Design Patterns for Motivation*. Paper presented at the ISAGA 2008 Conference on Games: Virtual Worlds and Reality, Kaunas, Lithuania.

Krathwohl, D. R., Bloom, B. S., & Masia, B. B. (1973). *Taxonomy of Educational Objectives: The Classification of Educational Goals. Handbook II: Affective Domain*. New York: David McKay Co.

Vogel, R., & Wippermann, S. (2004). Communicating didactic knowledge in university education. In: Cantoni, L. and McLoughlin, C. (Ed.). *Proceedings of ED-Media 2004. World Conference on educational multimedia, hypermedia, telecommunications* (pp. 3231-3235). Chesapeake, VA: AACE.

KEY TERMS AND DEFINITIONS

Game-Based Learning: An innovative learning approach derived from the use of computer games that possess educational value or different kinds of software applications that use games for learning and education purposes such as learning support, teaching enhancement, assessment and evaluation of learners. (cf., e.g., Tang et al., 2009).

Design Patterns: A semi-formal way of documenting a solution to a design problem in a particular field of expertise.

Pedagogical Patterns: A semi-formal way of documenting a solution in the field of learning and instruction.

Educational Patterns: A semi-formal way of documenting a solution in the field of learning and instruction.

Game Design Patterns: A semi-formal way of documenting a solution in the field of game-design.

Game-Based Learning Design Patterns: A semi-formal way of documenting a solution in the field of Game-based Learning.

Chapter 8
I'd Rather Be Playing Calculus:
Adapting Entertainment Game Structures to Educational Games

Monica Evans
The University of Texas at Dallas, USA

ABSTRACT

Educational games often implement educational theory, but rarely implement the best practices of entertainment game structures. Currently, many educational games have difficulty engaging and immersing players to the same degree as entertainment games without diminishing the level and complexity of the educational content. This chapter discusses seven best practices of entertainment game design: metaphor, visualization, content as mechanic, self-assessment, achievement, repetition, and multi-linear play–as adapted to meaningful educational content in a variety of fields, with a particular focus on university-level and adult learners. This chapter explores these best practices as utilized in the development of the Digital Calculus Coach, an online game intended to teach calculus concepts and problem solving at the university level.

INTRODUCTION

A favorite reference among game studies and educational technology scholars is a line often attributed to Marshall McLuhan, that "anyone who tries to make a distinction between education and entertainment doesn't know the first thing about either." In a traditional classroom setting, a compelling and fun educational experience is a fond hope but not necessarily a requirement. For developers of educational games, this aphorism represents the best possible case for nearly an entire field of research: that computer games, now a multi-billion dollar entertainment industry and a mainstream pastime for most of North America, Europe, and Asia, can be harnessed to become the 21st century's greatest teaching tool, and that the millions of gaming-literate students can directly

DOI: 10.4018/978-1-60960-495-0.ch008

apply their love of gaming to meaningful educational content.

This desire is not limited to academia or to primary and secondary education, but applies to multiple industries in which education and training play a major part, including the military, medical and health fields, business development, and others. In the military, for example, educational games and game structures are already used to teach a variety of skills and strategies to both soldiers and civilians. The first-person shooter America's Army has been in operation for nearly a decade as both a realistic combat simulation and a recruitment tool (Bossant, 2010). At the University of Texas at Dallas, the First Person Cultural Trainer uses living world scenarios to teach cultural norms, non-verbal and gestural communication skills, and situational awareness in graphically-immersive environments created in the Unreal 3 engine (Zielke. et. al., 2009). Numerous on-going projects at the Institute for Creative Technologies at the University of Southern California explore post-traumatic stress disorder therapy, speech and language training, disaster-response training, and other forms of virtual training through the use of high-end game engines (2010). In medicine, Virtual Heroes has developed Zero Hour: America's Medic, a true-to-life gaming simulation that trains first-responders in handling real-life natural disasters and potential terrorist attacks, and HumanSim, a healthcare education simulation which provides game-based training in rare, complicated or otherwise error-prone tasks for physicians, nurses, and students in realistic, immersive environments (Virtual Heroes, 2010). These projects and others exemplify the growing interest in and application of educational games in complex training situations.

For primary, secondary, and university education, gaming technology would seem to be a natural fit. There has been a marked rise in research into the potential for educational games in the last few decades, both in and out of the classroom, and for a wide variety of games, genres, and media. From work on intrinsic learning motivation through games (Malone, 1981; Malone & Lepper, 1987; Garris et. al., 2002), to studies on active learning through play (Bonwell & Eison, 2000; de Weck et. al. 2005); play as primary concern for educators (Barab et. al., 2009); the psychological aspects of games and play through computers (Reiber, 1996); and even ways of preventing learners from gaming a play-based educational system (Baker et. al. 2008), there is clearly both an interest and a need for research in the area of games and education. Significant work on games, cognition, and learning is also being pursued, most recently by Bavelier and Green (2004; 2006; 2009), and by Baker and others (2010). This rise in research may be partially attributed to the growing acceptance of game studies as an academic field with strong ties to numerous disciplines.

In terms of development, we can perhaps also attribute this growing interest in educational games to significant changes in the commercial game industry. With the rise of the independent game movement, we have seen that small teams of developers can create polished, sophisticated game experiences with far fewer resources than big-budget, AAA commercial titles. Development tools and engines are easier to acquire and use than ever before. And gaming as a pastime is now clearly mainstream, at least in the United States. The most recently released set of facts from the Entertainment Software Association (2009) states that sixty-eight percent of all American households play computer games; the average game player is 35; forty percent of game players are women; twenty-five percent of Americans over the age of 50 play games; and, perhaps most importantly, sixty-three percent of parents believe that games are a positive part of their children's lives. The leap to games as a positive part of education is not a great one. Why is it that games are not yet a major part of primary, secondary, and university education?

Primarily, there are a number of logistical hurdles to overcome, not the least of which is adapting various kinds of technology to existing school systems and curriculum (Halverson & Smith, 2009). From a design standpoint, a potentially solvable hurdle is what I have begun to call the "magic bullet" problem: the idea that squeezing any kind of learning content into any popular game structure will create an instantly successful educational game. We have learned that not all game structures are suited to all kinds of learning, and that creating a successful educational game depends a great deal on applying the correct gaming methodologies to the desired educational content. Additionally, the fun of an educational game must be balanced or merged with meaningful educational content. A game that places too much emphasis on entertainment and not enough on education might be well received by students, but have little to show in terms of a meaningful learning experience.

To solve the "magic bullet" problem, aspiring educational game developers must look at educational game design as separate from entertainment game design, subject to the same complexities of form, structure, and immersion but with an entirely new agenda: to teach through engagement. For students to actively seek out and enjoy educational games as much as those created solely for entertainment – for a student to feel, for example, that they would honestly "rather be playing calculus" – educational game designers have a great deal of research to do in designing a variety of game types for a variety of teachers, environments, and content, and for students at all levels, learning styles, and literacies. The objective of this chapter is to begin this process by looking at the best practices of entertainment game design as they can be applied to educational games, to specify which of those practices are most pertinent to the challenges of educational game design, and to explore how those best practices can be applied by looking at an educational game currently in development, The Digital Calculus Coach.

LEARNING GAMES AND ENTERTAINMENT GAMES: RELATIONSHIPS BETWEEN STRUCTURES

All games, regardless of content, are educational experiences. As developer Filament Games notes, this does not mean that all games teach something of value in the real world (2010). There is a great deal of available research in educational theory, for both formal and informal learning structures, much of which can be directly applied or adapted to game design. The balance between challenge and skills, for example, in Csikszentmihalyi's theory of flow (1991) has a direct application in the creation of well-paced game spaces. In educational psychology, numerous attempts have been made to link the structure and immersive qualities of digital games with specific learning styles, outcomes, or classifications, including work on perspective-making and constructivism (Lainema, 2009), player motivation (Garris et. al., 2002; Medina, 2005), and multiple ways to break down the elements of games (Garris et. al., 2002; Juul, 2003) into useful components for educators. Recent work by Katherine Wilson and others looks for relationships between learning attributes and specific game attributes, particularly which components of games are most useful for particular kinds of learning (2009). It is also worth noting that, while much of this research focuses on the potential applications and advantages of game-based learning, there are also potential limitations to the medium, some of which are technological or logistical (Halverson & Smith, 2009). Additional limitations in terms of content and structure may also be discovered, in the sense that – to reiterate the "magic bullet" problem – some forms of education may be less effective when taught through digital games of a particular genre or type.

There has also been significant work by both scholars and industry developers on the nature of game design, ranging from defining core philosophies to lists of specific "dos and don'ts" of game design. One of the most useful texts is Raph Koster's *A Theory of Fun for Game Design* (2005), a lighthearted discussion that ultimately defends both games and fun as important for children and adults alike. Koster's design philosophy is based on pattern-recognition and pattern-mastery: in simple terms, human beings enjoy creating order out of chaos and games create a space for us to do that. Koster's definition of a good game, in fact, is "one that teaches everything is has to offer before the player stops playing… Fun is just another word for learning" (p. 46). The question that follows, of course, is what do games teach? Koster's answers range from spatial relationships, exploration, and precision to learning valuable life skills, but always come back to things that, in his words, "were useful to us when our species was first evolving" (p. 67). Koster's challenge to future designers is to create games with more complex, less easily perceived patterns and sophisticated challenges, "as sophisticated as the best stories give [to readers]" (p. 215). His definition of current games as puzzles to be solved lends itself to a number of educational fields, particularly those in the sciences: the puzzles of organic chemistry or physics, by Koster's description, would fit very nicely in the right game structure.

Another highly useful text for exploring the specifics of good game design is Jesse Schell's *The Art of Game Design: A Book of Lenses* (2008). More practical than Koster's text, Schell's discussion of game design explores not only how to conceptualize new game ideas but how to put those ideas into production and development with a team. Schell focuses on game design as a collaborative experience. He lists the most important skill of a game designer, in fact, as listening: to one's team, one's client, one's audience, one's game, and finally to oneself (p. 4-6). The core of Schell's design philosophy is in creating experiences for players. He discusses a number of game types, including those that are educational, as transformative experiences that can change players for better or for worse. In education, he also notes that it isn't that learning isn't fun, but that too many educational experiences are "poorly designed," specifically that "traditional educational methods feature a real lack of surprises, a lack of projection, a lack of pleasures, a lack of community, and a bad interest curve" (p. 443). Rather than recreate these educational experiences in digital games, it would be wise to look at how games create engagement and interest in players, and adapt those structures to educational content. Schell also argues that games would be better used as tools, not as complete educational experiences, and that the medium of games is particularly suited for lessons that define facts, center on problem solving, explore systems of relationships, explore insights, and promote curiosity (p. 445).

One cannot discuss educational games without discussing James Gee's *What Video Games Have to Teach Us About Learning and Literacy* (2003). The work is not a design text, but includes thirty-six learning principles that, Gee argues, are built into good video games, among them principles of identity, active learning, critical learning, semiotic domains, social and cultural models, achievement, and situated meaning (pp. 207-212). Gee primarily discusses commercially-released entertainment games, but his principles could certainly be applied to the development of educational games, particularly in terms of how the player's experience and identity are constructed. Digital games, Gee says, have great potential to inspire active and critical learning in players, more so than most common ways of classroom teaching (p. 46), regardless of the content being taught. Like Koster and Schell, Gee points out that kinds of content most effectively taught by doing – how to play basketball, for example – can be more easily taught through interactive game structures than other kinds of learning content. Gee also touches on the "problem of content": that games may be seen as a waste of time when they don't appear to be directly teaching educational content, regardless of what the player is indirectly learning from the experience (p. 19). This is one of the major issues faced by educational game developers: that they must appeal to students with engaging and entertaining content, but are often expected to directly point out or "hang a lantern" on learning content in a way that, while reassuring to teachers or parents, is likely unappealing to students.

Beyond defining a core philosophy or a set of principles for good game design, educational game designers face additional issues of genre, interaction, scenario, and development. What kinds of current game structures, for example, would make for excellent learning environments? Is there something specific to the design of a first-person-shooter or a traditional console-based role-playing game that would lend itself to excellent interactive tools for teaching a particular set of concepts? Conversely, what kinds of academic or classroom learning might be improved by the application of well-designed educational games? Questions of formal or informal learning, in-classroom versus at-home or leisure game time, design considerations for games for children as opposed to those for adolescents or adults, and the level and quantity of educational content included in a given game must eventually be answered, either through scholarship or through experiments in design and development by educational game makers.

While many educational games fail to engage students in a meaningful way, often by falling into one of the many design pitfalls described above, there are a few that have successfully avoided the stigma of "edutainment" to create worthwhile learning experiences for students, primarily by adapting entertainment game structures. Quest Atlantis, an online educational game developed partially at Indiana University and currently intended for 9-16 year old students, combines "strategies used in the commercial gaming environment with lessons from educational research on learning and motivation" (Quest Atlantis, 2010). Providing children with lessons in "transformational play" (Barab, Gresalfi, & Arici, 2009),

Quest Atlantis has nearly 50,000 student learners at the time of this writing. Filament Games, the creators of numerous successful educational games including Resilient Planet and Argument Wars, combines "best practices in commercial game development with key concepts in the learning sciences" (Stone, Norton, & White, 2010). Filament's core philosophies include numerous ideas supported by both educational theory and commercial game design, including the idea that "all games are learning games... but games are not a good fit for all learning goals. Good games leverage the affordances of digital interactions" (Stone, Norton, & White, 2010). Both Filament Games and the developers of Quest Atlantis have managed to capture the attention and engagement of thousands of learners without losing sight of educational goals or diluting educational content, and can be looked at as models for aspiring educational game developers.

BEST PRACTICES OF ENTERTAINMENT GAMES

The next step for educational game studies is to define the specific aspects of entertainment game design that are most applicable to educational games, as well as the ways they might be used. Many scholars have categorized the elements or components of digital games, often in relation to educational theory (Garris et. al., 2002; Juul, 2003; Wilson et. al., 2009). During development of several game research projects at the University of Texas at Dallas, we have found the need to categorize those development practices, objectives, or outcomes of entertainment games that best create an engaging and meaningful game experience. We have noted the following seven best practices as directly applicable to educational game design, particularly when designing games that are focused on math or science education. Each of these best practices includes an example of an entertainment game that successfully implements this aspect, as well as a description of how it might then be adapted to fit a variety of educational game structures and learning content.

It must be noted that engagement is the focus of these seven best practices, although it is not listed itself. Entertainment games use these practices and others to more fully engage the player in the game world. Continual engagement is key to a game's success, as the player's potential interest and eventual investment determine how well the game will sell, not to mention how well it will be critically received. The computer game is still a primarily interactive medium, and the only major artistic medium that the audience must earn their way through. Any lessening of engagement endangers the player's actually continuing to play or completing the game. Engagement therefore is not a best practice, but rather the desired result of these best practices. Engagement by this definition has a direct link to what Malone and others describe as "fantasy" or "imaginative context" (1987), and shares many qualities with what the entertainment game industry often describes as "immersion." For educational games, engagement with a game's learning content is equally as important as engagement with the game's structure and mechanics. The following seven best practices provide ways in which entertainment game structures may be used to capture that same engagement with educational content.

Metaphor

One of the most important skills a game designer has is the ability to break down the complexities of human existence into metaphors that a computer can interpret in a measurable way. Some of the most common systems in games deal with life, death, movement, combat, experience, and ownership. While hit points have little relation to any real measures of health or life span, and in-game combat has even less to do with real-world combat, these things have been successfully reduced to base parts in order that we can reinterpret them

through the game. This becomes more difficult with systems that we as humans disagree on, don't fully understand, or contain huge gray areas, such as love, ethics, truth and justice, religion, poetry, and philosophy. Future research in this area is of course both necessary and fascinating, and may determine the next major design structures for games as a medium.

Metaphor is not quite the same thing as the literal adaptation of an existing real-world system, which is a more common structure for games in the simulation genre. When creating a flight simulator, for example, it is in the designer's best interests to accurately represent the real cockpit as closely as possible. Designing a system to accurately represent a character's declining mental health, as well as an underlying simulation to describe that decline, is a different problem altogether, primarily because the real world system does not directly translate into a computer system. The design principles, however, are similar.

Describing a prime example of the use of metaphor in commercial games is difficult to put one's finger on, as the majority of digital games depend on the idea. Additionally, many of these metaphorical constructs have become industry standards, such as health points, to the point that choosing one representational game is nigh impossible. An individual mechanic that displays metaphor quite well, however, is the insanity bar from the survival-horror game Eternal Darkness, released for the GameCube in 2002. The game, which involved a set of thirteen related characters exploring the same four areas during multiple periods in history, included a standard health and magic bar for all characters, but also a bar that represented the current character's mental status. If the bar filled too quickly, characters would quite literally hallucinate, representing their loosening grip on reality. Given that many of the encounters in Eternal Darkness were inspired by the fiction of H.P. Lovecraft, it is no surprise that most characters fought for their state of mind over the course of the game. The insanity meter was notable for affecting not only the character's mental state but the player's; in particular, one of the hallucinations caused a "glitch" that apparently erased the player's saved games (often ten or twenty hours worth of play) and turned off the player's GameCube console, before returning to the character's pre-hallucinatory state. As a system, the insanity bar is an effective metaphor for the character's declining mental health, representing both the mechanics and the feeling of mental breakdown during the game experience. Of course, the game's description of mental illness is in no way accurate, but a similar system could be utilized to, for example, raise awareness among students about a particular illness by putting players in those digital shoes.

Visualization

Games are excellent at helping players visualize the abstract. Computer games are primarily an interactive medium, but a highly visual and graphical one as well, and their ability to help players visualize is one that merits further exploration. In its simplest form, visualization can be as expressed in terms of interface design: the idea that the player needs to see the most amount of information in the most efficient and meaningful way possible, with the least amount of graphics on the screen, and in the shortest amount of time. This kind of visualization is not unique to games, but the sophistication of current game interfaces deserves mention, and can be utilized for other kinds of visualization that are more complex than abstracted or condensed visual data. It should also be noted that visualization in games occurs in both 2D, 3D, and hybrid 2D-3D environments, and that the differences between these kinds of visualization, while fascinating, are of less significance to this particular discussion.

In terms of curriculum, visualization could be as simple as presenting graphical representations of difficult-to-imagine curves or shapes in mathematics, or as complex as allowing players to see themselves walking on the surface of Mars or the bottom of the ocean. An entertainment game that exemplifies the use of visualization is World of Goo, a physics puzzle game in which players create structures by connecting sticky, somewhat sentient gooballs together in a variety of mechanical structures. The game does not include any descriptions of physics concepts, equations, or word problems. By playing with the gooballs and solving puzzles, players gradually learn about stress, torque, and other physics concepts in an informal way, primarily by observing what happens to their structures as they build them. It is no great leap to imagine the mechanics and underlying simulation of World of Goo as applied to classroom physics equations and experiments; or, given the right teacher and lesson plan, to see World of Goo itself as a classroom example.

A slightly different definition of visualization deals with player identity: that playing a particular game experience might help a student to visualize the character, or themselves, as a particular kind of person. Seeing yourself as the world's chosen savior, the sports hero, the rock star, or the unstoppable action hero is common in entertainment games. The action role-playing game Fable uses visualization as both an indicator of identity and graphical feedback, in that characters that have behaved heroically are gradually surrounded by sparkling light, butterflies, and even a halo, where characters that have acted in a villainous way eventually emit a dark red haze, grow horns, and are surrounded by flies. In education, this kind of visualization is less about feeling strong, wicked, cool, or special as it is about feeling smart, socially conscious, or full of potential. Specifically, a game in which students could visualize themselves in the future as someone who might become a scientist – or at least someone who knew a little bit about physics, and was better for it – would be a powerful use of this design structure.

Content as Mechanic

One of the major issues in educational game design is that learning content and gaming content are too often separated. If players are treated to a fun game that suddenly presents multiple-choice questions or long blocks of textbook reading, not only is immersion broken, but the learning content appears to players as an impediment to gameplay, not part of it. Likewise, presenting a fun game as a reward for slogging through uninspired interactive learning content will more likely inspire the student to trade the educational game for an entertainment game. A more useful practice is to structure the learning content as the core mechanic of the game: to make what the player *does* the same as what the player *learns*.

A similar issue has been addressed in interactive narrative and game narrative research. Stories that are best told through games, rather than films or novels, must arguably be conveyed through the actions and experience of the player, rather than depending on cinematics or eternal dialogue. As a medium, computer games are primarily interactive systems, not narrative systems, but their potential for storytelling experiences can be found through meaningful narrative-based interaction (Evans, 2007). The same argument might easily apply to learning content: that a game's potential to teach must be seen in the creation of meaningful learning interactions. Consider also that computer games, as noted before, are the only major artistic medium in which the audience must earn their way through the experience, which requires an experience that is consistently engaging. An educational experience should also strive to be consistently teaching, meaning that the learning content and the engagement of the game would be well served to be as similar as possible.

One of the best recent examples of content as mechanic is Jonathan Blow's Braid, a platforming puzzle game in which the player's manipulation of time directly relates to the player's understanding of the game content, in this case a narrative about mistakes, forgiveness, redemption, and past relationships. Another example is Portal, a short science fiction game in which the player moves through nineteen 3-D test chambers with the use of the portal gun, an item that allows the player to teleport between any two flat planes, including walls, floors, and ceilings. Additionally, the narrative experience of Portal is entirely conveyed through the player/character's actions, to the point that the story of Portal could not be told effectively in a non-interactive medium.

It should be noted that both Gee and Koster discuss the "problem of content", in which the mechanics of a game are considered educational but the content is not. Gee uses the example of Pikmin as a game that teaches sophisticated, active learning and critical problem solving to children as young as six years old, although the game's content concerns a two-inch-high spaceman exploring an Earth backyard (2003, p. 39-43). Koster uses the infamous Grand Theft Auto III example, in which players can pay a prostitute for sex to regain health points, kill her, and reclaim their money. Koster points out that, while an observer sees a horrendous crime, the actual player of the game sees a loophole in the system by which they can gain one resource without expending any of another: in short, "they see a power-up" (Koster, 2005, p. 85). Both games teach the player skills that are not immediately obvious given the apparent content of the game. At some point, the problem of content will have to be addressed by game makers and educators, but at the moment there is room for both games that directly address learning content, such as describing content through core mechanics, and games that use entertainment-based content over educational mechanics for learning purposes.

Self-Assessment

The idea of self-assessment as presented by entertainment games is a simple one: players should have at their fingertips at every instance of the game a simple way to see how well they are doing. One of the tenets of good game design is the constant presentation of instant, real-time feedback for players. For entertainment games, this feedback primarily represents whether or not the player is on the path to succeeding at the game, often defined as reaching the game's win state. Feedback can be as simple as a health-point bar that drops every time the player's character is damaged, or as complex as the character, equipment, inventory, party, faction, and quest statistics of role-playing games or the resource- and unit-management systems of real-time strategy games. These systems are often quite sophisticated in terms of the presentation and clarity of this data, as discussed under the visualization best practice.

In educational game design, adapting these feedback systems to present real-time, in-game assessment in individualized ways to students is, from a technical standpoint, not difficult. When properly constructed, an educational game could easily present feedback of this kind to students both in-game and out of game, as well as teachers, parents, and others. Entertainment games, particularly those with large, persistent player bases like massively-multi-player role playing games (MMORPGs), often contain a great deal of data mining, so that developers can continue to create the most entertaining, least boring or frustrating experience possible. Pairing these feedback structures with educational research on data-mining, assessment, and learning outcomes to present in-game self-assessment for players would be quite powerful, and is not out of our reach.

As with metaphor, it is difficult to pinpoint one game that exemplifies self-assessment, as it is essentially an industry standard at the time of this writing. The interface and assessment systems of the MMORPG World of Warcraft are worth mentioning, particularly given that players are expected to create and evolve multiple characters with numerous skills, professions, and reputation factions over long periods of time, such as months or years. Additionally, players at all skills levels can choose very different styles of play and switch between them at will. World of Warcraft players need to see the current status of their character essentially at a glance, as well as personalize the placement and usage of each character's vast numbers of individual skills, particularly in combat-based and communication-based situations. Between experience and reputation bars, profession advancements by skill, talent trees, macros, interface and keystroke options, and a heavily graphical instant feedback system, not to mention the overwhelming number of player-created interface modifications that can be downloaded, players can see at a glance a huge amount of information on their current progress in multiple areas, which helps them reach whichever end-state of the game they prefer.

Another industry standard worth mentioning is the prevalence of embedded tutorials in entertainment games. While most commercial games still include paper manuals, nearly all games include systems that teach new players, in real time, how to play the game. Many tutorials become optional on a second playthrough, as players have already mastered the necessary skills. Especially complex or massive games such as World of Warcraft often include tutorial-like sections through the entire game experience, so that each new facet of gameplay is introduced to the player in as seamless a way as possible. Good tutorial design is its own art form, as well as a major part of guiding the player to a fully-engaging game experience, and should be taken advantage of by educational game designers.

Achievement

As an external game mechanic, the "achievement" has come into its own in the last five years. In common parlance, achievements are game-specific goals that earn points, where points are collected external to individual games and tagged to a player's specific online identity, most clearly exemplified by the Gamerscore on XBOX Live.

The 2005 implementation and subsequent success of the Gamerscore has changed the landscape of commercial games, so much so that numerous developers now go out of their way to include achievements in their designs, with the understanding that well-implemented achievements will improve overall sales (Hicks, 2009). That said, the Gamerscore itself may not be as significant as what it highlights: the psychological need to achieve in games, as applied to players at all levels of gaming literacy. Game designers have depended for years on the idea that, given a set of goals, subgoals, or even optional, difficult-to-achieve goals, most players will strive to attain them for bragging rights, completion, or simply for the added challenge, extending the gameplay experience and adding to replay value. Achievement designer Greg McClanahan notes that when "players are presented a goal, their first inclination is to devise the most efficient (not necessarily the most fun) means of reaching that goal" (2009), which says a great deal about the hold achievements have on many players.

This idea of achievement might be well-implemented in educational games. As Gee notes, children and adults alike are often willing to commit huge amounts of time and effort towards the mastery of a computer game, which we as players often prefer to be longer, more varied, and more challenging experiences. "Wouldn't it be great," he asks, "if kids were willing to put in this much time on task on such challenging material in school and enjoy it?" (2003, p. 5) In particular, those subjects that are often seen as overwhelming or impossible challenges, such as algebra or trigonometry for students who claim that they have always been "too dumb to do math", would be well-served not only by good game design, in particular good pacing and tutorial sections, but by the additional psychological drive of achievement. The feeling of always being just a few minutes away from getting a reward, opening a new area, or seeing something new and interesting, not to mention the drive to keep up with or beat out one's classmates

in terms of in-game progress, can be a powerful driving force for students at all levels. McClanahan lists a high skill component and perfection of a core game mechanic as good design constraints for creating engaging, worthwhile achievements. If the mechanics of an educational game are also the learning content being taught, this emphasis on improving one's skill in numerous difficult areas might improve both the in-game learning experience and the educational outcome of that experience.

While the XBOX Live Gamerscore is the clearest example of achievements in games, a single game that represents the impact achievements have had on the industry is Borderlands, whose development team first stated that achievements were a way to increase sales. It is also interesting to note that, at the time of this writing, an online search for achievements does not result in lists of the most fun, best-designed, or most interesting achievements, but in lists of those that are most easily achieved, often in games that are considered badly designed or overly simple themselves. This desire to collect achievements, regardless of the perceived worth of the game experience, might be very useful in educational games – at the very least, as a way to inspire students who seemingly don't care about a particular learning subject, regardless of game design, to get caught up in it.

Repetition

The misperception of games as "mindless" entertainment has already been addressed, by Gee and others, but this misperception stems from a fundamental truth about games as a medium: that often the course of a game experience involves players repeating the same gameplay actions over and over in a variety of scenarios and situations, until those actions are perfected. To the outside observer, this emphasis on repetition may seem problematic. For particular kinds of learning, however, the idea of pleasurable repetition might certainly be used to beneficial effect. Repetition has already been explored as one of the ways in which humans learn and perfect new skills, particularly in psychomotor and lower-level cognitive skills, and as a way to enhance memory for rote learning (Bloom, 1956; Anderson & Krathwohl, 2000). As immersive experiences, in which the repetition of actions and problem-solving puts the player "in the zone," games are more clearly informed by Csikszentmihalyi's theory of flow: the idea that a person can be completely mentally focused and immersed in a particular activity, and that this focusing of all mental and emotional attributes onto a single task leads to a pleasurable, even rapturous state (1991). Meditation, athletic performance, musical performance, and numerous practices in the martial arts can be explored from the standpoint of "optimal experience." The integration of flow principles into game design is a natural fit, and has been explored by both game studies scholars and industry developers as a way to enhance player enjoyment and engagement, particularly as it relates to continual problem-solving with ever-changing tools, obstacles, and constraints.

The pleasurable repetition of actions in games is perhaps most exemplified by two of the best-known casual games, Tetris and Bejeweled. Players of Tetris must fit falling geometric shapes together to form lines, which disappear and clear more working space on the game board. As the game continues, shapes fall at a gradually increasing speed, providing a gradually increasing challenge for players. Bejeweled, arguably the most famous example of the "match-three" game type, presents players with a grid of multi-colored gems in which adjacent gems can be flipped in position. Players must flip numerous gems to form lines where three or more adjacent gems are the same color, at which point those gems disappear and are replaced. The goal of both games is to continue the game experience for as long as possible, while collecting as many points as possible. For learning content in which repetition of actions or problem-solving is particularly important, such

as mathematics, finding ways to present that repetition as both pleasurable and educational is of primary importance for educational games.

Multi-Linear Play

Currently, computer games depend on an ordered, structured, and deterministic system that can be controlled and interpreted by a computer. The most immersive, engaging games are those that make players feel as if they can go anywhere and do anything. This is particularly true in those games in which players are severely constrained in their choices, due to current technological limitations. While all individual game experiences are effectively linear in the moment of playing, subsequent playthroughs of a well-constructed multi-linear game are likely to be vastly different, depending on the choices the player makes. The core of multi-linear gameplay is in making the player feel as if they are in complete control, while guiding players into particularly interesting, challenging, or meaningful experiences.

Design structures that allow a player to determine a personalized path through a game experience are highly useful in creating educational games. When discussing how learners are introduced to complex systems, for example, Jesse Schell defines the problem with lectures and textbooks as linearity: "A linear medium," he argues, "is a very difficult way to convey a complex system of relationships. The only way to understand a complex system of relationships is to play with it and to get a holistic sense of how everything is connected" (2008, p. 446). Schell lists traffic patterns, ecologies of endangered species, and the workings of the human circulatory system as examples of systems that might be taught well with games. There are determined aspects, for example, to the way the circulatory system works that can be coded into a computer, but the way in which each student might explore that system can be effectively guided freeform.

In entertainment games, there are a number of ways in which games present multi-linear experiences, including interactive narrative, multiple endings, character creation systems, user-create content, and others. A game that exemplifies multi-linear play through a sandbox structure is The Elder Scrolls IV: Oblivion, a fantasy role-playing game in which the player creates a personalized hero and explores the world of Cyrodil. The linear story-driven part of this game involves a cult attempting to open a gateway between Cyrodil and a demonic realm, but the player's involvement in this story is entirely optional. Saving the world can be indefinitely postponed in favor of exploration, pursuing missions and side quests, buying houses, interacting with numerous non-player characters, taking over the Thieves' Guild, and any number of other actions. A sandbox game like this one, in which players have the benefit of a structured experience within an open world, would be well suited for educational games in the area of history or science, or for any game in which complex systems or societies might be explored.

APPLIED PRACTICES: THE DIGITAL CALCULUS COACH

The previous section explored seven best practices of entertainment game design that might be best adapted to educational games. This section explores those best practices as applied to the Digital Calculus Coach, an educational game currently in development at the University of Texas at Dallas.

University-level mathematics, including calculus, is seen by some as one of the fields most in need of improved or modernized teaching methods, particularly in the United States (Wilson, 1997; Committee on Science, Engineering, and Public Policy, 2007). The usefulness of using computers to teach mathematics has long been established (Kulik & Kulik, 1986; Rinaldi, 1997), but computer-aided learning does not necessarily include games or game-like structures; and while numerous educational games or game-like software teach mathematics at primary or secondary school levels, very few games tackle university-level math. And while some commercial games can help students engage with mathematics in an informal but meaningful way (Steinkuhler, 2008), there are again few digital games that directly teach or review university-level mathematics through game mechanics. The Digital Calculus Coach is created as a research prototype in part to discover whether digital games could successfully teach calculus and other university-level math concepts, as well as to further explore how the above best practices of entertainment games might be adapted to educational game development and design. At the time of this writing, only preliminary tests have been completed; full testing of the prototype game will occur in the summer and fall of 2010, and a detailed evaluation of learning effectiveness will be pursued based on collected data.

The Digital Calculus Coach is an online, modular educational game that teaches introductory calculus concepts at the university level through concept exploration, practice and test preparation, review of concepts, and player engagement. The game is intended to increase student access to self-paced, individualized calculus instruction, and to appeal to students accustomed to multiple media and technologies and who have high expectations for their sophistication, interactivity, and ease of use. The game is also intended to supplement the best practices of current calculus education, and can be used as a tool by instructors in both university and high school classrooms, as well as directly by the students themselves. The Digital Calculus Coach is intended to be "classroom agnostic", a structure made possible by the fact that calculus instruction has not changed significantly in terms of the order of and complexity of concepts, and that in general the same set of problems and concepts will be helpful to high school students, university students, and returning students. For the initial round of testing in June and July 2010, the Digital Calculus Coach will be used external to the classroom by students simultaneously enrolled in one of the introductory calculus courses. Later tests may include high-school students who are preparing for pre-university exams, such as the AP test, and tests in which the coach is used by teachers within the classroom as an educational aid.

Structurally, the Digital Calculus Coach is a platforming game with both role-playing and puzzle elements. The prototype in development covers roughly the first half of a traditional calculus course, specifically limits and derivatives, and pulls from a large database of problems that can be used to supplement a course using any textbook. As a classroom tool, the Digital Calculus Coach is intended to help address the high drop/fail/withdraw rate in university calculus courses, and to improve the understanding and retention of calculus concepts by students. To do this, one of our development goals is to present calculus, often seen as an overwhelming difficult subject, in a non-threatening, engaging way, and to reach out to those students who feel, incorrectly, that calculus is simply beyond their reach as a subject.

Our solution is to present a humorous game world with rich graphics, sound, and narrative that appeals to players in the same ways as entertainment games, while explaining calculus concepts with direct, engaging mechanics. The game is set in a fantasy steampunk world in which mathematicians are treated like rock stars, calculus is seen as a spiritual, almost magical force that drives the world, and citizens live on fantastic floating islands and travel by means of flying airships, captained only by those who can do calculus. The player begins as sub-captain of a somewhat rickety airship owned by Admiral Newton, who is in competition with Vide-Admiral Leibniz to discover a magical object known only as the Fundamental Theorem of Calculus. Newton, obsessed with other experiments, has sent the player to look for it in his stead. He has also sent a somewhat-functional mechanical assistant named Robot Newton to guide the player, through which Newton will sometimes speak to assist with the solving of calculus problems. Over the course of the game, the player flies to many islands looking for the Fundamental Theorem, and meets numerous characters that require assistance, often in the form of calculus problems. Solving these problems, both conceptually and as worked problems, is the core mechanic of the game.

The world of the Digital Calculus Coach is admittedly a silly one, but takes enough of its inspiration from the real world to lend it an air of believability. Many of the non-player characters are re-envisioned versions of famous mathematicians, and in fact L'Hopital, Galois, Maria Agnesi, and Muhammad ibn Musa al-Khwarizmi make appearances in the prototype as rival ship captains, all looking for their own individual solutions to theoretical problems. The world, narrative, and atmosphere all serve as support systems for presenting calculus as a fun, engaging experience. The game is developed in Flash with 2D graphics to increase accessibility to the game and to better display graphs and concepts that are most often presented in two dimensions in current traditional calculus instruction. The following sections discuss in more detail how the best practices of entertainment games have been applied towards that goal.

Figure 1. One of the opening screens of the digital calculus coach, in which players select and customize their character

Adapting Best Practices: Metaphor, Repetition, Content as Mechanic

When learning calculus, there comes a point where students simply have to do the math. Repetitive problem-solving is often the way in which students are expected to understand calculus, both in homework sets and on quizzes and tests. For the Digital Calculus Coach to succeed, solving calculus problems must be engaging; likewise, for students to understand calculus on a basic level they must be able to successfully work the problems themselves. Our challenge, then, is to make doing calculus the core mechanic of the game, and to find metaphors for expressing the mental interaction students have with calculus problems within the mechanics of the game. In terms of specific cognitive challenges, at its most basic level the Digital Calculus Coach is intended to assist students with calculus comprehension, as well as improved retention of the general steps and techniques necessary to solve individual types of problems. At a more ambitious level, the game is intended to inspire students to further analyze these concepts, primarily through the processes of in-game discovery and engagement.

Our first step was to discover how calculus appealed to mathematicians. When asked, most instructors and math students who enjoyed calculus said either "Because it's beautiful" or "Because it's fun." If presented not as homework problems but as elegant, logical puzzles - as well as paced correctly with the right kind of embedded tutorials – the fun of calculus might be expressed more clearly to students. Within the Digital Calculus Coach, each calculus problem is presented as a challenge to overcome with particular constraints, rules, and a win state, as well as a piece of a larger, intricate language that may eventually be understood. Much of the player's interaction with calculus problems is mental, rather than physical, which adds a secondary challenge: that the mechanics of the game must inspire the right kind of mental interaction with a given calculus problem. For example, solving limits using tables requires the student to read the table and know what to look for. In the Digital Calculus Coach, players interact with tables according to particular game-like constraints that guide the player to look for the right sorts of information in the table.

Another way to increase engagement is to add an element of strategy that is external to the calculus problems. In the game node dealing with the power rule, one of the basic rules of derivation, players are presented with thirty functions at varying levels of difficulty in a grid. To cross the grid, players must make a path by solving adjacent problems. The problems are arranged in such a way that doing the more difficult problems will make a shorter path, but players can choose to do easier problems and take a longer time crossing the grid. This kind of strategy provides players with a more engaging goal than simply doing thirty homework problems in a row, primarily by providing players with interesting choices. As with Koster's discussion of pattern-recognition, players are expected to play with two types of patterns: the over-arching strategy of the grid, and the individual strategies necessary to solve a variety of calculus problems.

Adapting Best Practices: Self-Assessment, Achievement

The Digital Calculus Coach is supported by a sophisticated database that tracks a wide variety of player data, including how long a player has been logged into the game; how many times a particular problem has been attempted, successfully solved, or failed; the percent success rate for a given problem as attempted by all users; and other data that will be used primarily to evaluate the learning effectiveness of the game. As with entertainment games, the difficulty is not in collecting data from the system, but in filtering and interpreting that data in a meaningful way. While playing the Digital Calculus Coach, players are provided with a great deal of information on their

Figure 2. An image from one of the numerous grid-games in progress; this one involves the placement of gears in a particular pattern, and helps players review the delta-epsilon definition of the limit

current progress using the same kinds of complex interfaces used for entertainment, primarily in the areas of progression and collection. In World of Warcraft, for example, a player who has chosen the Alchemy profession might see that they have 167 points out of a possible 450 of mastery, a list of the potions they can create given certain ingredients, and which potions are most likely to increase their skill. With the Digital Calculus Coach, a player might similarly see that they have completed 45 out of a possible 75 unique problems using the power rule, that they must solve five more problems to achieve competency but not mastery of the power rule, that they have completed approximately 65% of the content on Derivaria, and the specific nodes and areas that are suggested as the next problem nodes to attempt. By allowing the player to track their progress, as well as receive instant feedback on their particular strengths and weaknesses in calculus,

we aim to increase player engagement not only with calculus but with an evaluation of their own learning progress. We believe this adaptation of an entertainment structure will also allow players to track their improvements as related to a given class or other learning environment, while still keeping the game itself "classroom agnostic."

To increase engagement and affinity, the main player character of the Digital Calculus Coach can be customized in terms of gender, appearance, airship preference, and choice of hat. There are numerous hats scattered throughout the world of the Digital Calculus Coach that can be collected and worn by the player, from pirate bandannas and newsboy caps to more fanciful creations such as a top hat containing a working cuckoo clock and a literal stovepipe hat that spews calculus equations. The inclusion of collectible hats is where our work in self-assessment and achievement comes together: hats are collected by completing certain

Figure 3. Characters from the digital calculus coach illustrating both the whimsical nature of the game world and some of the numerous hats available for collection

criteria in calculus problem solving, and therefore the number and kind of hats collected by a player is a visual indication of how well that player is progressing in the game. For players engaged in the game, hats are essentially an achievement, proving an impetus for players to continue playing the game as well as attempt some of the more difficult challenges, many of which go above and beyond simple mastery of calculus concepts. We have begun calling this measurement the "hat metric", and hope that further research will show that including achievements of this kind can lead to successful educational engagement. Among players, we hope to show also that increased desire to collect achievements, in this case hats, leads to a faster progression of improvement in calculus, as multiple factors will be pulling the player through educational content.

Adapting Best Practices: Multi-Linear Play

Approaching calculus as our game content has provided the game design with some interesting fundamental features. Unlike other subjects at the university level, calculus has right answers, as well as some standard procedures for solving certain kinds of problems. Calculus is also extremely hierarchical, and nearly all calculus courses introduce concepts in the same linear order. The initial design of the Digital Calculus Coach was multi-linear in nature and much more open-ended than the current build; we quickly discovered that calculus is taught in order for good reason, and that each concept must be mastered in a specific place in the sequence. Our challenge, then, is to make the player feel as if they can move through the gamespace in an open-ended way while guiding them towards a linear hierarchy of skills and concepts. The Digital Calculus Coach is also intended for students at multiple levels, which means there must be a mechanism for more advanced students to move quickly through or bypass beginning material if they choose.

Our solution is to divide the game world into hubs by content, but to allow the player to move freely between those hubs. Each hub is represented as a floating island with a different theme, such as Limit Island, a mining station; Derivaria, a tiered city with a lower, middle, and upper class; and Chain Island, a rocky highland held together by thick chains. Players can enter any hub and attempt to solve problems, but players who attempt to explore Chain Island, for example, before Derivaria will likely have a difficult time solving Chain Island problems. The denizens of Chain Island, while happy to let players play with the problems, will gently suggest the player return to particular other portions of the game to prepare themselves. Likewise, the calculus concepts covered by each island are broken into a series of nodes in which different problems can be learned and attempted.

Limit Island, for example, is separated into two parts by Epsilon Bridge, with introductory concepts placed on the left side, and intermediate and advanced concepts placed on the right side. The player's first major task is to repair and cross the bridge, which requires a proved understanding of the epsilon-delta definition of the limit. To complete this task, the player must work different kinds of calculus problems for every miner on the left side of the island. Miners can be approached in any order, but are placed in such a way that the player encounters them in roughly the right correct order. Players are also encouraged to solve problems in a particular order by the non-player characters, but are not forced to do so or limited in which problems they can attempt by the game.

Adapting Best Practices: Visualization

Visualization occurs in the Digital Calculus Coach in a number of ways. The most obvious is

Figure 4. The player moving between game nodes on Limit Island, one of many game spaces to explore

that calculus is represented as a major part of the game's art style. Steam clouds vent equations, the buildings and bridges of Limit Island contain asymptotic curves, and the tiered structure of Derivaria references the hierarchy of functions as they are derived and simplified. Some representations are quite direct: for example, the curve that Maria Agnesi was famous for studying, known as the Witch of Agnesi, is clearly represented in the shape and decoration of her game character's hat. Another use of visualization is the literal graphical representation of the calculus problems. There are numerous problems in which the player either draws or is presented with the graph of a function, and can sometimes interact with it. One such problem involving derivatives requires the player to graph a course for an airship through a field of floating rocks. Another problem, intended to teach the epsilon-delta definition of the limit, involves the player convincing every member of a shift of miners that Epsilon Bridge is in fact free of holes – proved by taking the limit of the function at a variety of values for delta and epsilon – and safe to cross.

More importantly, players are encouraged to visualize themselves as people who can, in fact, do calculus. The game's scenario, as well as the language used in character dialogue and in the review and help functions, are intended to inspire players not to fear failure but to play with the concepts, as well as to take pride in each individual concept they come to understand. Much like playing Guitar Hero makes players feel cool, the Digital Calculus Coach should make players feel smart, as well as able to succeed in all aspects of the game.

Finally, the Digital Calculus Coach encourages players to visualize calculus as an important aspect of education. The motto of the game, as well as the unofficial motto of the development team, is a quote by Niloo Jalilvand, the calculus instructor at Booker T. Washington High School for the Performing and Visual Arts in Dallas: "Why study calculus? Because calculus is the study of change, and everything changes" (personal communication, October 25, 2009). This quote is also the first line the player sees upon starting a new game experience. The idea that calculus is more than a class but an important part of understanding the world around us is something we would like to impart to players of the Digital Calculus Coach, in the hopes that they might then see themselves as people for whom knowledge of calculus is an important and meaningful skill.

NEW DIRECTIONS FOR EDUCATIONAL GAMES

The first line of James Gee's *What Video Games Have to Teach Us About Learning and Literacy* is, "I want to talk about video games – yes, even violent video games – and say some positive things about them." In 2003, this might have been a controversial statement. At the time of this writing, it seems instead that games are accepted as a medium deserving of further study, one that has a great deal of potential in educational fields. The next steps for educational games research is not in proving games have an effect on learners, but in specifying the exact nature and usefulness of certain game genres and mechanics to certain kinds of educational content, in addition to introducing new kinds of games into classrooms, homes, and educational programs and systems. As with entertainment games, educational game designers must discover the exact structures that will best facilitate meaningful learning for a variety of students, environments, and educational content. The best practices discussed in this chapter – metaphor, visualization, content as mechanic, self-assessment, achievement, repetition, and multi-linear play – are not the only such practices, but those that perhaps are the most clearly understood in entertainment games, as well as those that are most easily adapted to educational game content. As technology, entertainment, and the complex processes and standards of education change over the next decades, design, mechanics, structures, and even the potential for immersive experiences in educational games will change as well.

For educational game researchers and developers, the future holds both potential and limitations, as the changing nature of the medium will further define not only what games are possible, but what kinds of learning and education we consider most important and most valid for future generations. In the short term, new research on the Digital Calculus Coach will take the shape of a full and ongoing assessment of the success or failure of each individual mechanic and aspect in the game, and the iteration of game types and structures to improve the game's quality as an educational tool. In the long term, and looking beyond this single project, the design, development, and production of educational games in a wide variety of complex, ambiguous, or even developing fields will help characterize both the nature of games and the nature of learning, as well as the numerous ways in which games are changing us are players, students, and teachers. It is my hope that new educational game designers will further demonstrate not just the potential but the ability of the medium to make significant, lasting changes on the ways in which we teach our most important lessons.

ACKNOWLEDGMENT

Special thanks to the students and faculty whose work on the Digital Calculus Coach continues to inspire: Michael Andreen, Samantha Bratton, Lee Brown, Noel Byrd, Chris Evans, Spencer Evans, Bobby Frye, Niloo Jalilvand, Karin Khoo, Steven Kirtzic, William Lemons, David Lewis, Jacob Naasz, Lily Ounekeo, Susan Ounekeo, Rex Ounekeo, Jainan Sankalia, Skylar Rudin, and Sarah Wells. Thanks also to Tim Christopher, who patiently listened to each and every one of these ideas, and then improved them.

REFERENCES

Anderson, L. W., & Krathwohl, D. R. (Eds.). (2000). *A taxonomy for learning, teaching, and assessing: A revision of Bloom's taxonomy of educational objectives*. Boston: Allyn & Bacon.

Baker, R. S. J. d., Corbett, A. T., Roll, I., & Koedinger, K. R. (2008). Developing a generalizable detector of when students game the system. *User Modeling and User-Adapted Interaction, 18*(3), 287–314. doi:10.1007/s11257-007-9045-6

Baker, R. S. J. d., D'Mello, S. K., Rodrigo, M. M. T., & Graesser, A. C. (2010). Better to be frustrated than bored: The incidence, persistence, and impact of learners' cognitive-affective states during interactions with three different computer-based learning environments. *International Journal of Human-Computer Studies, 68*(4), 223–241. doi:10.1016/j.ijhcs.2009.12.003

Barab, S. A., Gresalfi, M., & Arici, A. (2009). Transformational play: Why educators should care about games. *Educational Leadership, 67*(1), 76–80.

Bavelier, D. & Green, C.S. (2009). Video game based learning: There is more than meets the eye. *Frontiers in Neuroscience, special issue on Augmented Cognition, 3*(1), 109.

Bloom, B. S. (1956). *Taxonomy of educational objectives, handbook I: The cognitive domain.* New York: David McKay Co., Inc.

Bonwell, C. C., & Eison, J. A. (2000). *Active learning: Creating excitement in the classroom.* ASHE-ERIC Higher Education Report No. 1, The George Washington University, School of Education and Human Development, Washington, D.C.

Bossant, P. (2010). *Then and now: A review of the last eight years.* Retrieved January 28, 2010, from http://www.americasarmy.com/aa/about/makingof.php

Committee on Science, Engineering, and Public Policy, Committee on Prospering in the Global Economy of the 21st Century. (2007). *Rising above the gathering storm: Energizing and employing America for a brighter economic future.* Washington, DC: The National Academies Press.

Csikszentmihalyi, M. (1991). *Flow: The psychology of optimal experience.* New York: Harper Collins Publishers.

de Weck, O., Kim, I. Y., & Hassan, R. (2005). Active learning games. *Proceedings from* CDIO Annual Conference, Kingston, Ontario.

Entertainment Software Association. (2009). *ESA: Industry facts.* Retrieved January 29, 2010, from http://www.theesa.com/facts/

Evans, M. (2007). *Computer games and interactive narrative: A structural analysis.* Unpublished doctoral dissertation, University of Texas at Dallas, Richardson.

Garris, R., Ahlers, R., & Driskell, J. (2002). Games, motivation, and learning: A research and practice model. *Simulation & Gaming, 33*(4), 441–467. doi:10.1177/1046878102238607

Gee, J. P. (2003). *What video games have to teach us about learning and literacy.* New York: Palgrave Macmillan.

Green, C. S., & Bavelier, D. (2006). Enumeration versus object tracking: Insights from video game players. *Cognition, 101,* 217–245. doi:10.1016/j.cognition.2005.10.004

Green, C. S., & Bavelier, D. (2006). The cognitive neuroscience of video games. In Messaris, P., & Humphreys, L. (Eds.), *Digital media: Transformations in human communication* (pp. 211–224). New York: Peter Lang.

Halverson, R. & Smith, A. (2009). How new technologies have (and have not) changed teaching and learning in schools. *Journal of Computing in Teacher Education.*

Hicks, J. (2009). *Gearbox: Easy achievements mean 40,000 extra sales.* Retrieved January 28, 2010, from http://www.oxm.co.uk/article.php?id=14388

Institute for Creative Technologies. (2010). *What we do.* Retrieved January 30, 2010, from http://ict.usc.edu/about

Juul, J. (2003). The game, the player, the world: Looking for a heart of gameness. In M. Copier & J. Raessens (Eds.), *Proceedings at the Level Up: Digital Games Research Conference, November 4-6,* (pp. 30-45). Utrecht, the Netherlands: Utrecht University.

Koster, R. (2005). *A theory of fun for game design.* Scottsdale, AZ: Paraglyph Press.

Kulik, C. C., & Kulik, J. A. (1986). Effectiveness of computer-based education in colleges. *AEDS Journal, 19,* 81–108.

Lainema, T. (2009). Perspective making: Constructivism as a meaning-making structure for simulation gaming. *Simulation & Gaming, 40,* 48–67. doi:10.1177/1046878107308074

Malone, T. W. (1981). Toward a theory of intrinsically motivating instruction. *Cognitive Science, 4,* 333–370. doi:10.1207/s15516709cog0504_2

Malone, T. W., & Lepper, M. R. (1987). Making learning fun: A taxonomy of intrinsic motivations for learning. In R.E. Snow & M.J. Farr (Eds.), *Aptitude, learning and instruction: Vol. 3. Cognitive and affective process and analyses.* (pp. 223-253). Hillsdale, NJ: Lawrence Erlbaum.

McClanahan, G. (2009). *Achievement 101.* Retrieved January 28, 2010, from http://www.gamasutra.com/blogs/GregMcClanahan/20091202/3709/Achievement_Design_101.php

Medina, E. (2005). Digital games: A motivational perspective. *Proceedings from DiGRA 2005 Conference: Changing View - Worlds in Play.* June 16-25, Vancouver, B.C.

Quest Atlantis Design Team. (2010). *Quest Atlantis.* Retrieved January 28, 2010, from http://atlantis.crlt.indiana.edu

Rieber, L. P. (1996). Seriously considering play: Designing interactive learning environments based on the blending of microworlds, simulations, and games. *Educational Technology Research and Development, 44*(2), 43–58. doi:10.1007/BF02300540

Rinaldi, I. L. (1997). *A study of the effects of computer assisted instruction and teacher instruction on achievement in mathematics.* MA thesis, Eastern Michigan University.

Schell, J. (2008). *The art of game design: A book of lenses.* New York: Morgan Kaufman Publishers.

Steinkuehler, C. (2008). Massively multiplayer online games as an educational technology: An outline for research. *Educational Technology, 48*(1), 10–21.

Stone, M., Norton, D., & White, D. (2010). *Filament Games: About us.* Retrieved January 28, 2010, from http://www.filamentgames.com/about

Virtual Heroes. (2010). *Advanced learning technology: Healthcare.* Retrieved January 28, 2010, from http://www.virtualheroes.com/healthcare

Wilson, K. (2009). Relationships between game attributes and learning outcomes: Review and research proposals. *Simulation & Gaming, 40*(2), 217–266. doi:10.1177/1046878108321866

Wilson, R. (1997). A decade of teaching reform calculus has been a disaster, critics charge. *The Chronicle of Higher Education, 43*(22), A12–A13.

Zielke, M., Evans, M., & Dufour, F. (2009). Serious games for immersive cultural training: Creating a living world. *IEEE Computer Graphics and Applications, 29*(2), 49–60. doi:10.1109/MCG.2009.30

ADDITIONAL READING

Barab, S. A., Arici, A., Jackson, C. (in press). Eat your vegetables and do your homework: A design-based investigation of enjoyment and meaning in learning. *Educational Technology 65*(1), 15-21.

Barab, S. A., Gresalfi, M., & Arici, A. (2009). Why educators should care about games. *Educational Leadership, 67*(1), 76–80.

Barab, S. A., Thomas, M., Dodge, T., Carteaux, R., & Tuzun, H. (in press). Making learning fun: Quest Atlantis, a game without guns. *Educational Technology Research and Development.*

Bavelier, D. & Green, C.S. (2009). Video game based learning: there is more than meets the eye. *Frontiers in Neuroscience, special issue on Augmented Cognition, 3*(1), 109.

Bogost, I. (2006). *Unit operations: an approach to video game criticism.* Cambridge, MA: The MIT Press.

Bogost, I. (2007). *Persuasive games: The expressive power of video games.* Cambridge, MA: The MIT Press.

Caillois, R. (2001). *Man, play, and games* (Barash, M., Trans.). Chicago, IL: University of Illinois Press. (Original work published 1958)

Castronova, E. (2005). *Synthetic worlds: the business and culture of online games.* Chicago, IL: University of Chicago Press.

Clark, R. E. (2007, May-June). Learning from serious games? Arguments, evidence, and research suggestions. *Educational Technology, 47*(3), 56–59.

Csikszentmihalyi, M. (1991). *Flow: the psychology of optimal experience.* New York: Harper Collins Publishers.

Davidson, D. (Ed.). (2009). *Well played 1.0: video games, value, and meaning.* Pittsburgh, PA: ETC Press.

Driscoll, M. (2005). *Psychology of learning for instruction* (3rd ed.). Boston, MA: Pearson Education, Inc. Frasca, G. Videogames of the oppressed: critical thinking, education, tolerance, and other trivial issues. In Wardrip-Fruin, N., & Harrigan, P. (Eds.) *First person: new media as story, performance, and game.* (85-94). Cambridge, MA: The MIT Press.

Garris, R., Ahlers, R., & Driskell, J. (2002). Games, motivation, and learning: a research and practice model. *Simulation & Gaming, 33*(4), 441–467. doi:10.1177/1046878102238607

Gee, J. P. (2003). *What video games have to teach us about learning and literacy.* New York: Palgrave Macmillan.

Gee, J. P. (2007). *Good video games + good learning: Collected essays on video games, learning, and literacy.* New York: Peter Lang.

Halverson, R. (2005). What can K-12 school leaders learn from video games and gaming? *Innovate* 1(6). Retrieved from http://www.innovateonline.info/index.php?view=article&id=81

Holland, W., Jenkins, H., & Squire, K. (2003). Theory by design. In M. Wolf & B. Perron (Eds.), *The Video Game Theory Reader* (25-46). New York: Routledge.

Huizinga, J. (1950). *Homo ludens: a study of the play element in culture.* Boston, MA: Beacon Press.

Kafai, Y. B. (2006). Playing and making games for learning: Instructionist and constructionist perspectives for game studies. *Games and Culture, 1*(1), 36–40. doi:10.1177/1555412005281767

Koster, R. (2005). *A theory of fun for game design.* Scottsdale, AZ: Paraglyph Press.

Lainema, T. (2009). Perspective making: constructivism as a meaning-making structure for simulation gaming. *Simulation & Gaming, 40,* 48–67. doi:10.1177/1046878107308074

Medina, E. (2005). Digital games: A motivational perspective. Proceedings from *DiGRA 2005 Conference: Changing View - Worlds in Play.* June 16-25, Vancouver, B.C.

Nielsen, S. E., Smith, J. H., & Tosca, S. P. (2008). *Understanding video games.* New York: Routledge.

Rollings, A., & Adams, E. (2003). *Andrew Rollins and Ernest Adams on game design.* Indianapolis, IN: New Riders.

Rouse, R. (2005). *Game design: theory and practice* (2nd ed.). Plano, TX: Wordware Publishing, Inc.

Salen, K., & Zimmerman, E. (2004). *Rules of play: game design fundamentals.* Cambridge, MA: The MIT Press.

Schell, J. (2008). *The art of game design: a book of lenses.* New York: Morgan Kaufman.

Squire, K. (2008). Open-ended video games: A model for developing learning for the interactive age. In K. Salen (Ed.) *The John D. and Catherine T. MacArthur Foundation series on digital media and learning* (167-198). Cambridge, MA: The MIT Press.

Squire, K. D., Giovanetto, L., DeVane, B., & Durga, S. (2005). From users to designers: Building a self-organizing game-based learning environment. *TechTrends, 49*(5), 34–42. doi:10.1007/BF02763688

Taylor, T. L. (2006). *Play between worlds: exploring online game culture.* Cambridge, MA: The MIT Press.

Van Eck, R. (2006). Digital game-based learning: It's not just the digital natives who are restless.... *EDUCAUSE Review, 41*(2).

Virvou, M., Katosionis, G., & Konstantinos, M. (2005). Combining software games with education: Evaluating its educational effectiveness. *Journal of Educational Technology & Society, 8*(2), 54–65.

KEY TERMS AND DEFINITIONS

Content: What is presented to the player through game mechanics; what the game is about. Content often includes the graphics, story, and sound of the game, and is expressed through interaction.

Educational Game: A game created with the express purpose of teaching a particular set of concepts, either formally or informally, in or out of the classroom, for learners of any age.

Engagement: The compelling, interesting, immersive, or meaningful quality of a game; the fun of the game. A player who is engaged with a game will continue playing voluntarily out of enjoyment.

Entertainment Game: A game created for the express purpose of entertainment, either in the commercial or independent gaming industry. Some entertainment games, such as Civilization IV, can be used by educators for teaching purposes.

Game Design: The process of defining the idea, concept, structure, rules, and content of a game. Also the iterative process of improving upon those things during game development.

Game Development: The process of creating and producing a game with a team of people, often including artists, animators, programmers, sound designers, writers, producers, and game designers.

Mechanics: The rules, structures, systems, and interactions that allow the player to interact with the game; how the game is played. Core mechanics are those that are most central to the experience of the game.

Chapter 9
Game Literacy:
Assessing its Value for Both Classification and Public Perceptions of Games in aNew Zealand Context

Gareth Schott
University of Waikato, New Zealand

Neil Selwyn
London Knowledge Lab, UK

ABSTRACT

Game playing is made possible by players' engagement in configurative practices that work in conjunction with interpretive practices, referring to how a viewer's semiotic work on the text (when reading and interpreting it) is taken directly from the semiotic resources that are put to use and made available by the text itself. That is, games are dynamic entities that remain 'in potentia' until actualised by the player. In doing so, the player is involved in recursive actions that produce polysemic performances and readings. The literacy demands of games support the argument that it is a 'mistake' to consider that [they] offer only one type of experience and foster one type of engagement (Newman, 2002). Yet, when applied to the processes of media regulation and classifying game content (which guides the general publics' understanding of games), the competencies required to engage successfully with interactive texts fail to receive accurate representation or acknowledgment. This chapter addresses how the rise of new forms of literacy, has created a discrepancy between the literacy employed by digital natives when playing games and the way digital immigrants classify games by attributing greater meaning to the 'screen' as the major carrier of information. The central thesis of this chapter is to present an argument for classification processes to account for the contributions to knowledge from theory and research examining game based learning.

DOI: 10.4018/978-1-60960-495-0.ch009

INTRODUCTION

A great deal of attention is currently being lavished on identifying and promoting the learning principles involved in engaging with interactive games and its broader participatory culture. As a result new forms of cultural, technological and communicative competencies have been observed and outlined (Gee, 2003; Shaffer, 2007; Squire, 2005; Steinkuehler, 2006). Such work examines learning within an extremely diverse medium capable of offering players vastly different experiences and engagement with contemporary trans-media storytelling (Jenkins, 2004). Indeed, games constitute cultural artefacts that occupy a place in a broader cultural context that demands understanding of how they exploit different technological platforms, diverge amongst titles and genres and the degree and nature of the relationships they possess with other mediums. This chapter seeks to examine the extent to which the above factors contribute to the process of game regulation in a New Zealand context. This context-specific approach reflects the dialogue currently taking place between the academy and the government agency responsible for fulfilling censorship legislation in New Zealand, The Office of Film and Literature Classification (OFLC). At the heart of these discussions, is an argument for the need to acknowledge a broader range of scholarly discussions on games, including game based learning. In particular, the notion of game literacy that promotes how game players possess more developed message analysis and interpretation skills than has previously been acknowledged. This perspective on users of interactive games currently fails to penetrate the process of game regulation, which in turn plays a crucial role in determining public perception and understanding of games. Theory and research advocating game based learning currently trails behind a more powerful and influential discourse that guides regulation of game content which promotes the idea that games require examination for their deterministic ability to foster anti-social

behaviors and attitudes (Anderson & Bushman, 2001; Anderson & Dill, 2000; Gentile *et al.*, 2004).

The process of regulating game content characteristically entails administering a legally enforceable system of classification that assigns age-restriction labels for interactive games based upon its content. In doing so, it shares with approaches to 'game based learning' a fundamental interest in how games are *understood* by those who play (Zagal, 2008). Additionally, the process of game regulation in New Zealand is *informed by* public perception, attitudes and beliefs as it regularly monitors the social mores and taste boundaries of its population. This process often serves to validate the existing classification system, and therefore how the focus of public understanding is shaped by the classification systems' emphasis upon language, violence and sexual content. It is argued here that the manner in which the classification process is both fashioned and preserved (via commissioned research, discussed below) creates a de-stabilising force for the acknowledgment and effectiveness of theory and research that present gaming technologies as beneficial learning experiences. Absent from its processes is information on how knowledge is acquired *about* games within wider society. That is, to what degree are games critically and analytically engaged via play, or assessed using different criteria? Such an approach would serve to examine the underlying assumption associated with the concept of media regulation, that those who assess and judge the appropriateness of game content for younger generations of players (either in classifying or subsequent management of, and access to media content) possess a clearer understanding of the nature and function of games compared to sections of the population deemed either less savvy and/or more vulnerable.

For Gee (2003) literacy, as it is applied to games, not only entails the ability to decode and understand meanings with respect to the semiotic domain of games but also the ability to produce meanings. Likewise, Espen Aarseth (1997) has highlighted how games constitute a mode of textuality and activity that demand the player work with the materiality of the text and participate in the construction of its structure. In acknowledging the nature of the medium as interactive, understanding has therefore becomes analogous with the ability to access the content, i.e. play. These treatments of literacy reflect a shift from the more traditional and narrow conceptualizations of literacy that have previously guided formal education practices. In the midst of a digital age, the concept of 'media literacy' has come to represent and acknowledge the expectation that individuals are required to access, analyse and evaluate the power of images, sounds and messages with which they are being confronted on a daily basis within *contemporary culture*. Educational literature is often divided in the manner it promotes media literacy more generally as, on the one hand *enabling* students to 'become more knowledgeable, aware and active participants in a democratic society' (Mihailidis & Hiebert, 2006, p. 1) and, on the other hand, empowering students through mutual respect, acknowledging and repositioning their media use from 'passive to active, from recipient to participant, from consumer to citizen' (Livingstone, 2004, p. 20). Rather than offering new content for educators to cover, the latter conceptualisation of the learner provides educators with a new set of resources and tools to utilise and employ in the classroom – the student. Seeman (2004) has cited educator Chris Worsnop's comments that good media education is not about 'propagandising students into a single way of thinking' but to support them to 'make their own choices and decisions about the ideological and political messages surrounding them in 21st century culture.' Returning to game regulation, the 'parental guidance' label is the closest equivalent that the classification system possesses for promoting discretion, contextual decision making or dialogue around access to media content and experiences.

In the US the 1994 *Video Game Rating Act* stipulated that the game industry establish its own ratings and regulatory system (or the government would step in) which eventually heralded the Entertainment Software Ratings Board (ESRB). Sara Grimes (2009) argues that, 'One of its founding principles, as well as a key argument for keeping the system voluntary, was the promise that by enabling them to make informed choices, the ESRB system put parents back "'in charge'" of their kids' media.' While New Zealand's Office of Film and Literature Classification (OFLC) is an Independent Crown Entity, like its UK counterpart the British Board of Film Classification (BBFC) it supports a legally enforceable system, meaning that it is illegal for anyone to supply age-restricted games to anyone under the stipulated age on the classification label (13, 15, 16 & 18). In the UK the BBFC has handed over responsibility for games to the Video Standards Council (VSA) who apply the Pan European Game Information (PEGI) framework in assessing game content. While the PEGI system does not comment on game difficulty or the skill required to play, it has standardised classification into a single European system that comprises of five age categories (3,7,12,16 & 18) based upon an expanded range of content descriptors (addressing profanity, discrimination, drugs, fear, sex, violence and gambling). For the majority of the 31 European countries that use the PEGI system, it remains advisory and voluntary, legally enforceable only in the Netherlands, Finland, Poland as well as the United Kingdom.

It is argued that discordant treatments of games discussed here can be traced, in part, to the initial assimilation of games into systems of regulation designed to assess representational content within linear mediums. Indeed, in New Zealand videogames currently fall under the definition of 'film' on the basis of their moving image content, as outlined in its *Film, Videos and Publications Classification Act 1993*. Subsequent media-blindness (Hausken, 2004) to the unique properties of the medium, fails to acknowledge or treat interactive games as the distinct form of expression and discrete category of cultural activity they are. Games constitute a complex hybrid medium, at once unique and inter-textual, a mode of textuality and activity. The process employed in classifying games, which steers public perception, remains detached from the *experience of play* and how games are unmade and disseminated under the agency of players once they enter life and culture (Dovey & Kennedy, 2006). The specific configuration of gaming technologies and the experiences they invite has produced new theorisation but still demands applied research and progressive legislation. This chapter therefore considers the differing responses to the lasting influence of games, which on the one hand, asks for the application and influence of gaming technologies to be expanded (e.g. into education), while on the other, inevitably fuels concerns and pessimism. We examine the potential impact that the latter might be having on the former and how regulation might benefit from acknowledging the contribution of games as learning literature.

"ITS EDUCATIONAL"

Mainstream media is rife with depictions of games as a medium that should be despised and distrusted. Galarneau (2009) cites the example of Canadian radio presenter Pia Shandel's broadcast statement that gaming is 'a waste of time for boys, like 40-year old men wearing golfing pants' thus highlighting the nature of 'expert' opinions that parents often receive that cast 'a negative light on digital games that is counter-productive within the larger imperative of cultivating media literacy across a variety of interactive platforms' (p. 19). Initially, resistance to the disdain aimed at games came from citing studies that identified benefits as increased improved manual dexterity or hand-eye coordination (Egenfeldt-Nielsen, 2003; Mamei & Zambonelli, 2004; Rosenberg, Landsittel & Averch, 2005). This progressed to enthusiasm and attention being paid towards the use of gaming environments to support con-

structivist forms of learning through exploration, problem solving and reflection on experience. In particular, some educationalists are now arguing that 'realistic' simulations offer a particularly appropriate means of supporting exploratory spaces for constructivist learning. As Pelletier (2009) describes, "ludic simulations like *The Sims*, *SimCity*, or *Railroad Tycoon* are understood to have the greatest potential for teaching educationally desirable and generic skills" (p.85). Much interest has also been shown in the socio-cultural learning potential of participating in 'virtual worlds' and 'massively multiplayer online games' such as *Second Life* and *World of Warcraft*. Indeed, it is now recognised that a number of learning activities and processes are associated with inhabiting and exploring such online environments. For example, these applications are based on large groups of users encountering, interacting and engaging with other users. These processes are often seen to lead to informal and formal communities of practice where users will work together in groups with hierarchies of expertise and learning. As Oliver and Carr (2010) reason, participating in virtual worlds can involve a range of learning practices – from ongoing processes of developing expertise, to learning socially-produced conventions relating to identity, etiquette and trust. Perhaps most significantly, much of what takes place in a virtual world involves collaborative activities between users (such as pursuing collective 'quests') all of which involve creative and collaborative learning practices. Whether one is operating a virtual shop or learning to be a warrior-king on an alien planet, virtual worlds and online gaming can support the 'social dynamic' that many people now feel is at the heart of effective learning. As Chatfield (2010) concludes:

We are deeply and fundamentally attracted, in fact, to games: those places where efforts and excellence are rewarded, where the challenges and demands are severe, and where success often resembles nothing so much as a distilled version of the worldly virtues of dedicated learning and rigorously co-ordinated effort (p.28).

Games have long been perceived as both a benefit *and* threat to young people. On the one hand, a number of advantages are felt to accrue from engaging with digital media - not least enriched and expansive forms of learning; social and cultural empowerment; and increased choice over the form, time, place and pace of one's activities. Yet many commentators contend that such benefits are tempered by an attendant set of *risks*. These fears are often centred around the notion of the 'child-in-danger' (Oswell 1998); i.e. the risk of children being exposed to undesirable violent or sexual content. The threatening nature of games is also reflected in fears over the 'dangerous child' (Oswell 1998); i.e. children who 'knowingly' use games to harm both themselves and others by actively engaging in illicit experiences away from the regulation of adults. Aspects of these arguments are currently being rehearsed more broadly within the UK education technology community in terms of 'e-safety'. Whilst often used by commentators in a somewhat nebulous manner, official definitions of 'e-safety' that acknowledge that "children and young people are vulnerable and may expose themselves to danger – knowingly or unknowingly – when using ... digital technologies" (BECTA 2006, p.10). In the UK policy context these concerns with vulnerability, danger and appropriateness have been expressed in terms of specific 'e-safety' risks and dangers centred around 'four Cs' of online content, contact, commerce and culture. From this perspective children are felt to require protection from a host of online risks, such as cyber-bullies, paedophiles, violent games, illicit downloading of copyrighted and/or inappropriate material, disclosure of personal information and commercial exploitation.

Whilst there are initiatives in the UK that constitute a comprehensive policy response to a fast-changing set of problems (e.g. *Child Ex-*

ploitation and Online Protection Centre & UK Council on Child Internet Safety), the nature of the UK e-safety agenda has attracted criticism from some commentators - not least in terms of its alarmist representation of the risks that young people encounter when using ICTs more generally. These arguments derive in part from the mixed conclusions of recent investigations of the *actual* levels of risk encountered by young people. Such research literature appears to lend some support to Livingstone's (2003) contention that while one should not deny the real dangers that can exist in some exceptional circumstances, the relation between risk, danger and incidence of harm implied in much of the official safety and protection rhetoric is 'genuinely tenuous'. As such, a disjuncture between the implication of risk, as articulated within say official e-safety agendas, and the far lower incidence of risk within young people's engagement with ICTs, suggests increased discussion needs to take place between adults and young people with regards to the issues connected to the negotiation and comprehension of digital content, configurative environments and participatory cultures.

SURMISING GAME CONTENT

Burn and Willett (2005) have argued, the present tone of much of the broader 'e-safety' agenda configures listeners as objects of instruction and acts to close down rather than stimulate discussion. Likewise, in contrast to efforts that unearth the educational value fused into the way games operate and invite engagement, legislative-driven categorisation of games also serves to uphold the long-standing agenda evident in the large volume of literature disseminating experimental 'media effects' research. Under this model of research, social betterment is sought through establishing videogames as the root of 'causation,' which in turn endorses and fuels the viewpoints of 'moral entrepreneurs' (Becker, 1963). Furthermore, this model has established a pervasive belief in the capacity of scientific methods to 'derive obdurate truths about the nature of the subject matter and the casual networks in which it is embedded' (Gergen, 1992, p. 20) – a trait presumably shared with research seeking to establish games as learning tools. In the case of effects research, it is the capacity of media content to engender associations such as 'the impetus for aggressive acts' (Geen, 1994, p. 158) that is relentlessly pursued.

In New Zealand, the OFLC (2009) openly acknowledges that its chief obligation is to consider the 'impact of the medium' when classifying games, signifying that its practices are directly aligned with, and informed by media effects theory. In doing so, the classification process shares reason with a research paradigm that has thus far failed to demonstrate any understanding of the properties of the particular games or the medium it denigrates, or a broader awareness of the social dimensions of play or the productivity inherent in the practices of its surrounding cultures. In its earliest discussions Game Studies scholars obviously debated how the medium should be studied. This produced warnings against the lack of neutrality of framing games as other mediums such as film, 'as it emphasises some traits and suppresses others' (Juul, 2001). Similarly, media effects research has developed and refined its methodological approach whilst seamlessly shifting its object of study from film and television to games. In doing so, there exists an inherent failure to articulate the particular relationship and interactions between games and their players, the way meaning in games is emergent and play is a situated practice (Carr, 2009). Too greater emphasis is still being placed on the textual properties of games, over its structural properties. Games are instead activated making them a configurative as well as an interpretative practice. Should models of the underlying strategies driving choice and meaning-making during play pervade the regulation of games, a shift might occur, from classification as an assessment of the likely

reception of representational content, toward an understanding of game experiences as real events capable of generating meanings both in conjunction with, and independently from, the particular fictional universes in which they take place.

Textual and Structural Analysis

Typically, in making the argument for the need to consider games in terms of literacy there is an implication that 'games can be analyzed in terms of a kind of language … It also implies that there is a competency in using that language" (Buckingham and Burn, 2007). Research conducted in *Aoteroa* New Zealand by the first author (2008, 2009ab) has critiqued the social science effect models guiding classification by beginning to unearth the complexity of players' understanding and relationship with the function and articulation of 'violence' in interactive digital games. Despite forming the readership of popular culture, Schott drew on arguments that stipulate how young people are commonly denied a voice by the very 'authorities and opinion makers' (Thompson, 1998) that chastise their media interests and practices. By prioritizing the experiences and perspectives of young people on the nature and function of what is commonly understood as 'violent' content within games, he was able to demonstrate how game players actively perceived games as a fusion of ludic, narrative and representational forces that continually fold, unfold and refold as play is activated. This layered appreciation of game content, activity and intent contrasts with commonly articulated perceptions of game players as 'unintelligible' 'teenage zombies' that waste their time playing games – 'time that could be spent engaging in more constructive activities' (Griffiths, 1997, p. 233). Such viewpoints are attributable, in part, to the language that players have at their disposal to articulate their experiences. In working with players to encourage more personal, contextual, textual and structural accounts of game playing the research was able to highlight the richness of players' tastes in terms of what they were capable of taking from their experiences with game texts. This stood in a stark contrast to initial conclusions produced from time spent with the projects' participants, in which they demonstrated the extent to which their viewpoints were initially wedded to dominant public discourse surrounding gaming. Players initially appeared to be ill equipped to express the content, nature, and scope of their gaming experiences. In asking players to articulate what constitutes a game experience, it invited the frequent and unqualified use of inadequate words such as 'people', 'kill', 'shoot', and 'violence'. This was perceived as a ritual of exchange that found players automatically employing the restricted vocabulary made available to them.

During the course of the research, players demonstrated their preference for the historical revisionism of First Person Shooter *Resistance: Fall of Man* (Insomniac Games), a game that received attention for the Church of England's objection to Sony's recreation of both the exterior and interior of Manchester Cathedral for the game. Bishop of Manchester, the Right Reverend Nigel McCulloch, was quoted on the BBC stating: 'For a global manufacturer to re-create one of our greatest cathedrals with photo-realistic quality and then encourage people to have gun battles in the building is beyond belief and highly irresponsible'. The argument extended to an accusation that Sony were also directly contributing to the city's 'gun crime problem.' Sony's response, inevitably privileged the fictional quota of the game as they responded with the argument that they 'do not accept that there is any connection between contemporary issues of 21st century Manchester and a work of science fiction in which a fictitious 1950's Britain is under attack by aliens.' (e-mail correspondence posted on the Church of England's web-site). News media coverage of the debate confounded matters further with misleading accounts of the game, describing it as a 'computerized scene of mass murder' reinforced by the Bishop of Manchester's comments that: 'for any house of God,

to be used as a context for a game about *killing people* is offensive' (emphasis added).

When presented with the active discourses that have an impact upon how games are perceived, players subsequently sought to distinguish themselves more clearly in terms of the depth of their understanding and grasp of how game texts function and provoke thought. Literacy and nuanced appreciation became hallmarks of players' discussions as they attempted to illustrate a deeper awareness of what the medium offers. Institutional objections to *Resistance: Fall of Man* were deemed to have 'missed the point.' Players instead claimed to have interpreted the locale and the inability of the structure to uphold its role as a sacred site, as signifying the demise of faith and the downfall of civilized society and its values (irrespective of New Zealand players' failure to recognize the space as Manchester Cathedral). Players perceived their contribution and participation in the game as morally defensible, powerful and meaningful, with their avatar ascribed with a high moral stature, put into action in defense of rational values and envied for being indefatigable in the face of powerful antagonists. Finally, these viewpoints were coupled with views that prioritized the flow and generic structure of play; 'it's a church, awesome, a stronghold.' The reading of the game produced by players proved to be far more logically sound, representative and composed, offering context and insight into the game as an engagement with the symbolic resources contained within the game text.

New Zealand is in the enviable position of still being able to respond to the social mores and taste boundaries of its population through its protective framework and legislative obligations. Thus, in response to Schott's (2008, 2009ab) critique of legislative treatment of games, the OFLC (2009) acknowledged their capacity to be able to give weight to other criteria under Section 3(4) of the 1993 Classification Act, such as 'dominant effect', 'merit' and 'purpose' when classifying games. As complex as achieving more accurate representation of play and player experience gained from game software is, these qualities are required to be applied in the process of classifying game content in order to educate the public and acknowledge the meaningful experiences on offer within games. As the OFLC themselves conclude:

further research needs to explore the extent to which the public's perception of causal links between game playing and various social ills is moderated or even undermined by [knowledge of] how players actually respond to and negotiate their way through the content and characteristics of the medium (2009, p. 24).

Little is currently understood on degree to which public perception of age-restriction labels also fosters or promotes any understanding of the multiple ways games invite, demand and permit the player to act when engaging in play. While games clearly represent further evidence of the 'transposability of the story' (Chatman, 1978) into any medium, a key difference that renders games distinct from more traditional media is its ludic constituents. Competing with the interpretive demands of film and literature, is a basic perceptual act that demands that a game player picks up affordances in the game environment that indicate possibilities for how to interact with, and in the game space. New Zealand government funded research into games has thus far been unsuccessful in encouraging the public to offer viewpoints that are play-derived or textually evaluative. Instead, existing research, like the players in Schott's (2008, 2009ab) research, show a propensity for rehearsing the arguments of dominant interpretive frameworks that serve to eclipse the specific conditions, value and experiences offered by game texts.

DEMONSTRATING PUBLIC PERCEPTION

As New Zealand's censors, the OFLC (like the BBFC) show continued commitment to ascertain-

ing the populations' understanding and perceptions of the classification system, by commissioning research that observes the degree of knowledge, and attention paid to, the age-restriction categories put into practice to protect the public from possible injury. What is less understood however is the degree to which public perception of age-restriction includes understanding of the qualities designed and embedded into the game system, such as:

- the basic affordances of any object with a physical presence or
- agents in the environment which posses some form of artificial intelligence.

The research design employed by the OFLC (2009) in their examination of the public perception of *X-Men Origins: Wolverine* provides a useful insight into how regulators continue to approach games. In this research a perception-analysis methodology was employed to record participants' comfort levels when viewing (not playing) short audio-visual clips from the game that required participants to evaluate; (1) player-activated gameplay footage and (2) non-interactive cut-scenes, typically designed to either move the narrative plot of the game forward or bridge game levels. Squire (2008) has already argued that: 'Choosing a single set of inter-actions in a game for scrutiny is unproductive and disingenuous although it is a common tact of mainstream media reporting of games' (p. 644). He reports research that has demonstrated how gamers do wildly different things with the worlds available to them and, conceptualizes the worlds and themselves within them according to their own lived histories (Squire & DeVane, 2006; Vargas, 2005). When examined in the context of play, emotion research also highlights a certain predictability associated with emotion types that produces *action tendencies,* that is, likely courses of action triggered by a particular emotion in a particular situation (Drake & Myers, 2006). It is therefore logical to assume that games are designed precisely to provoke action responses from the player that are not possible when viewed and evaluated solely as a moving-image clip. Furthermore, unlike film, where *looking* is choreographed for the audience, the observation of game-play is typically unprocessed, characterized by a largely rigid world-view (1ˢᵗ or 3ʳᵈ person perspective) through which the drawn out execution of a limited range of actions in a repetitive sequence of encounters is evident. Indeed, participants in the OFLC research described the game as so repetitive that it became 'boring' and 'mindless' to watch. When classifying and assessing the impact of games, the OFLC (like other regulators) similarly opt to watch game play rather than engage directly in it. Should context also be 'central to the question of acceptability' (BBFC, 2009, p.10), the distinction between watching and playing becomes crucial in terms of the perceived acceptability and understanding of 'game states'. Repetition occurs in games as they function as pedagogic texts (Oliver & Pelletier, 2005), preparing players to engage competently with the experiences contained ahead. Indeed, players' goals and oppositional structures iteratively evolve as games progress, with earlier levels serving to prepare the player to face more worthy, difficult and challenging opposition in the subsequent stages of the game. The qualitative distinction in effect between watching and playing games, not only holds implications for the process of how games are classified and adjudged but also the dual presence of game software in households as both played experiences and viewed experiences - games are not only watched by the players, but also onlookers and peripheral players during collaborative play, it would seem producing different impressions.

Trans-Media Storytelling

Overlooking these limitations in the research, crucial in restricting public perception and understanding of the effect of games, the OFLC report how the research verified the appropriateness of the assigned classification label - R18. In their assessment of the simulated violent content contained within this game, participants however made little reference to the role of the interactive text (and its appropriateness) as it relates to the authorial original of the comic book and/or consistency with its filmic counterpart (Rated M). Verbatim quotations provided by the report did not address any expectation set up by the character's pre-existence, which not only defines the parameters and nature of the players behavior as anti-hero Wolverine, once play is activated in a game, but also crucially for parents and guardians, creates a potentially incompatible position regarding dependents access to film, literature, game and merchandising containing the same fictional character. As an R18 game text *X-Men Origins: Wolverine* potentially contradicts the popular preconception of superhero narratives and comic and games mediums as children's culture. Of interest, is whether the intensification of the character's violence through its game translation (as illustrated by the classification label) is more commanding than its lengthy presence within popular culture as part of pervasive trans-media superhero industry. For parents to answer this question, and/or make such judgments, requires knowledge of how games function, and how in turn they are likely to change the nature of an audiences' engagement with the same fictional universe. Games more than any other medium, translate well-known narratives into playable immersive experiences.

Engaging Parents

Thirty eight per cent of the 331 young people surveyed in OFLC's (2005) *Underage Gaming Research* indicated their games were purchased by parents or received as gifts, but public perception appears to be effected by a 'digital divide' that exists between *Video Nations* and subsequent *iGenerations*. Despite persistent warnings of the 'holding power' of games, examination of early research purporting disruption to parent-child communication reveals that it is not always children that determine that they are 'bowling alone,' (Putnam, 2000) but often parents, as a result of their own insufficient understanding of, and unwillingness to partake in the game cultures (Green et al., 1998). In *Toward a Precautionary Risk Management of TV Violence* (2004), Ellen Wartella, a principal researcher for a major US *National Television Violence Study* (NTVS), argued that research is required on how 'child audiences perceive, appropriate, and negotiate media messages through the variety of social groups to which they belong, such as the family' (cited in King & Bridgman, 2003, p.53). A potential implication associated with the rise of new forms of literacy (Gee, 2003), is that generations preceding 'digital natives' (Prensky, 2001) may be placing more emphasis on the 'screen' as the major carrier of information being processed from games. While the concept of media and multi-literacies has achieved value within contemporary education, discussions rarely promote consideration of the manner in which parents are responding to technological and economic changes. That is, the extent to which parents feel equipped to negotiate a fast-changing consumer culture that regularly serves to merge children and adult culture in its creation of new markets (e.g. the tweenager). As a mediator of public understanding and bastion of what is acceptable, the narrow focus of classification processes are failing to support transitions what and how learning takes place and the blurring of boundaries sparked by informal often spontaneous learning cultures.

In an interesting and related online discussion thread, players (age unknown) were noted discussing 'can you teach parents to game?' Comments included:

My parents hate videogames [but] they only played them like once EVER

I tired to teach my Mum Guitar Hero. I had to go Beginner on Slowest Speed, and even then she missed tones of notes. It's truly pitiful =D

I tried and succeeded my mom likes Fable 2 and Kirby on DS. She's not very good but she will learn. But my dad will not even touch the controller

http://forums.sarcasticgamer.com/showthread. php?t=15973

Returning to Prensky's (2001) label 'digital natives,' the term was coined precisely to describe an innate confidence witnessed in the use of new technologies such as the internet, videogames, mobile telephony and "all the other toys and tools of the digital age" (p.1) by our most recent generations. His work also typifies a fast-growing body of commentary from around the world that seeks to make sense of the distinct technological cultures and lifestyles of current generations of children and young people. Rather than using these technologies merely as part of their everyday lives, Prensky like others has reasoned that digital technology is essential to these young people's existence. Digital natives are therefore depicted as being constantly 'surrounded' and 'immersed' by new technologies in ways that older generations could never be. Other authors have elaborated upon the digital native definition – identifying the phenomenon across most (if not all) sections of society and everyday life. Such descriptions are certainly compelling and often presented in an extremely slick and seductive manner. Indeed, much of the language used to describe digital natives is closer to the branding that would be employed in advertising or marketing campaigns than serious academic debate. For example, readers are informed that 'generation digital' were 'born to be wired' (Montgomery 2007) and 'grew up bathed in bits' (Tapscott & Williams, 2008, p.47). A host of commentators write persuasively of computer-games obsessed 'homo-zappiens' (Veen and Vrakking 2006) and 'net savvy' youth (Levin & Arafeh, 2002). These are young people who are described as living 'digital childhoods' (Vandewater *et al.* 2007) ensconced within 'media families' (Rideout & Hammel, 2006). From an educational viewpoint, these are the new 'millennial learners' (Greenhow *et al.* 2009). All of these popular accounts neatly depict a distinct but common step-change in the ways in which contemporary forms of childhood, adolescence and young adulthood are now centred on digital technology and media. These differences imply a series of 'disconnects' between the ways that digital natives go about their business and the manner in which the world is still controlled largely by older generations. Disconnects, frictions and clashes are especially apparent when it comes to focus and nature of the assessment of games.

As these last points suggest, the idea of the digital native carries a range of implications for institutions and organisations that seek to address young people's engagement with contemporary media. In this sense, many of the structures of the digital immigrant world are felt to be increasingly incompatible with the needs and demands of young people. Amongst more direct institutions such as schools, libraries, universities, museums there is a growing 'legitimacy crisis' with younger generations (Kenway & Bullen, 2005). Classification as a process of regulation and constraint appears even more poorly placed to accommodate the social, cultural and economic changes associated with young people's digital technology use. It could be argued that it is more realistic to seek out opportunities for change that engage directly with the micro-politics of the home. The form these 'subtler,' 'less disruptive' approaches may take to digital technology use could arise from altering the processes and practices surrounding play within the home. That is, involving the home in a re-configuration of the 'formality-informality span,' addressing the varying "extent and strictness of the social rituals which bind the behaviour of people" in their dealings with technology and each other (Miszta,l 2000, p.8). Individual digital technology use in domestic settings has the advantage of being characterised as rather more informalised. As Misztal (2000) argues:

Although the process of formalisation is the dominant trend in modern social life, informality is the essential element in constructing trust relationships and, thus, in any cooperative arrangement aimed at improving the quality of life ... only a society that achieves an optimal balance between the informality and formality of interactional practices is in a position to create the conditions for cooperation and innovation (p.229).

As the ultimate 'end users' of gaming technology it would also seem self-evident that parents also accommodate and pay more attention to the views, opinions, ideas and expertise of their children as players. As Mimi Ito et al. (2008) conclude:

Although youth are often considered early adopters and expert users of new technology, their views on the significance of new media practice are not always taken seriously. Adults who stand on the other side of a generation gap can see these new practices as mystifying and, at times, threatening to existing social norms and existing standards. Although we do not believe that youth have all the answers, we feel that it is crucial to listen carefully to them and learn from their experiences of growing up in a changing media ecology (p.35).

Encouraging inter-generational conversations and shared experience of games in order to establish digital technology use as a site for meaningful negotiation and collaboration between household members is not however considered a straightforward task. This is why the classification process is imperative, as relations surrounding gaming technology would need to be moved on from the 'climates of unease' that presently surround them. While regulators, advocacy groups and parents that share concerns over game content may see increasing trust in players as a potentially problematic step to take, Schott's (2008, 2009ab) research suggests otherwise, that with support young people are able to show a capacity to be trusted when it comes to reaching sensible and realistic assessment of game content. Such logic might do well when incorporated in the assessment of games. There are few reasons to suggest that allowing the understanding and logic displayed by players to play an increased part in the governance of games would result in a slew of unreasonable or unrealistic demands. Digital technology could well be an area where increased trust in the opinions and actions of young people is merited. Indeed, given the affinity and expertise that young people are presumed to have with gaming technologies, interactive home entertainment is surely a conducive site for the development of "warmer, more interactive relationships" between parents and children (Deuchar, 2009, p.30).

CRITICAL REFLECTION

Beyond the ability of games texts to teach the player how to perform isolated skills, sequenced skills, and finally produce mastery (Gee, 2005), little is known about how players learn to read games more broadly, thus recognizing and reflecting upon the moral and ethical frameworks governing particular game ecologies. As Zagal (2009) argues, actions considered unethical in an out-of-game context may be expected or even demanded while playing a game. A good player may be one that best exploits his opponent's weaknesses or deceives his fellow players most effectively. Does this make games unethical? Furthermore, do they pose a challenge to the current social order by encouraging players to operate in these ways? These questions reflect the enduring need to *ensure* that players become informed about their choices and actions when using games - what could be termed 'critical digital literacies'. This involves supporting young people in developing the critical understandings required to make best use of games. As Kay Withers and Ruth Sheldon (2008) note, 'the success of self- and co-regulation relies on users themselves being able to make informed decisions: being "media literate"' in the way they

access and use content and information' (p.51). In this sense, it should be possible for parents to help their children question and challenge the place of games in their everyday lives. A critical thinking approach would be an ideal means, for example, of helping pupils reflect on games, moving understanding away from what Atkinson (cited in Nightingale, 2009) recently called the unhelpful and seemingly ineffectual 'hard-hitting messages' that merely serve to add 'to a culture of fear that doesn't help our young people.' Critical thinking could also help children to get to grips with the many non-technical challenges and issues associated with engaging with games, as noted in the example of players' readings of *Resistance: Fall of Man*. These additional complex aspects are all addressed by having a critical conception of what it means to be literate and skilled in the twenty-first century.

CONCLUSION AND RECOMMENDATIONS

Advancing arguments for the negotiated adjustment of game technology use is certainly not intended to propose a complete relaxation of the formal aspects of game classification. Instead, it is an acknowledgment that regulators (as mediators of public perception) can and do play a valuable authoritative role in educating, informing and directing the activities of children and young people – in particular allowing parents to be informed about their choices than they may otherwise and determining the status of games in immediate social contexts. From this perspective we ask:

- Further thought should be given to the way regulators go about helping players and parents learn *about* (as opposed to learn with) digital games.

Parents are perfectly placed to better support players to develop forms of 'critical' digital literacy – i.e. "cultivat[ing] the habit of uncovering and critiquing both [players'] own constructed and contingent experiences and resulting worldviews, particularly those that influence society's relation with technology" (Duffelmeyer 2001, p.243).

- Digital games need to be introduced to players in a questioning and challenging, rather than passively accepting manner – thus introducing "a reflective and critical discourse" (Muffoletto, 2001, p.4).

Although differing in substantive focus, the case of science education, for example, proponents of the public understanding of science have long argued for education that "helps citizens make informed decisions [about science and technology], particularly those which involve social responsibility" (Power, 1987, p.5) and therefore informs "citizen thinking - i.e. everyday thinking" about scientific issues (Jenkins, 1998, p.704). Like Jane Kenway and Elizabeth Bullen (2005) have reasoned, there is a pressing need for spaces to be provided for young people to develop a sense of critical agency that goes beyond that made available by consumer–media culture (see also Steinberg & Kincheloe, 1997). These authors talk of giving young people the time to 'look between the scenes' of the technological cultures they live within, and consider the many social, ethical and political issues which surround technology consumption and use.

- Increased parental knowledge and game literacy could help young people reach a better understanding of the processes and power relations involved in 'why they want what they want' (Walkerdine 1991, p.89) and even, it could be argued, why they get what they get.

Such arguments are not only concerned with supporting the population to become more effective and 'savvy' consumers of technology, but are also intended to establish governance as a supporting and guiding presence that can help parents and young people develop into effective digital age citizens. In this way, the notion of school-based critical digital literacy is fed into wider contemporary concerns over the need for all technology users to be able to understand the coded mechanics of how digital tools and applications actually work rather than merely understanding what they are programmed to do. For writers such as Kirkpatrick (2004), for example, a 'deep understanding' of digital technology is seen to be a crucial element of an individual's empowerment, agency and equal citizenship in the digital age. Conversely, exclusion from such understanding is seen as leading to an almost inevitable marginalisation if not disenfranchisement. Within the context of domestic technology use, for example, parents should play important roles in managing players' experiences of using digital technologies and supporting their attempts to apprehend the structures and meanings of digitally-based information (Ljoså, 1998).

REFERENCES

Aarseth, E. (1997). *Cybertext: Perspectives on ergodic literature*. London: John Hopkins University Press.

Anderson, C. A., & Bushman, B. J. (2001). Effects of violent games on aggressive behaviour. Aggressive cognition, aggressive affect, physiological arousal and prosocial behaviour: A meta-analytic review of the scientific literature. *Psychological Science*, *12*, 353–359. doi:10.1111/1467-9280.00366

Anderson, C. A., & Dill, K. E. (2000). Videogames and aggressive thoughts, feelings and behaviour in the laboratory and in life. *Journal of Personality and Social Psychology*, *78*(4), 772–790. doi:10.1037/0022-3514.78.4.772

Atkinson, S. (2009). *Don't panic*. Retrieved from http://www.guardian.co.uk/resource/jan-panic

British Board of Film Classification. (2009). *BBFC: The guidelines*. London: BBFC.

Buckingham, D. (2000). *The making of citizens: Young people, news and politics*. London: Routledge.

Buckingham, D., & Burn, A. (2007). Game literacy in theory and practice. *Journal of Educational Multimedia and Hypermedia, 16*(3), 323–349.

Chatman, S. (1978). *Story and discourse: Narrative structure in fiction and film*. Ithaca, NY: Cornell University Press.

Dovey, J., & Kennedy, H. (2006). *Game cultures: Computer games as new media*. Maidenhead, UK: Open University Press.

Drake, R. A., & Myers, L. R. (2006). Visual attention, emotion, and action tendency: Feeling active or passive. *Cognition and Emotion, 20*, 608–622. doi:10.1080/02699930500368105

Duffelmeyer, B. (2001). Using digital technology to augment a critical literacy approach to first-year composition. In Muffoletto, R. (Ed.), *Education and technology: Critical and reflective practices*. Creskill, NJ: Hampton Press.

Egenfeldt-Nielsen, S. (2003). Keep the monkey rolling: Eye-hand coordination in Super Monkey Ball. In Copier, M., & Raessens, J. (Eds.), *Level up: Digital game research conference*. Utrecht: University of Utrecht Press.

Galarneau, L. (2009). *Spontaneous communities of learning: Cooperative learning ecosystems surrounding virtual worlds*. Retrieved from http://adt.waikato.ac.nz/public/adt-uow20100324.100734/index.html

Gee, J. P. (2003). *What video games have to teach us about learning and literacy*. New York: Palgrave Macmillan.

Gentile, D. A., Lynch, P. J., Linder, J. R., & Walsh, D. A. (2004). The effects of violent video game habits on adolescent aggressive attitudes and behaviours. *Journal of Adolescence, 27*, 5–22. doi:10.1016/j.adolescence.2003.10.002

Grimes, S. (2009). Obsolescence pending: Rating the ESRB. Retrieved from www.escapistmagazine.com/articles/view/issues/issue_223/6647-Obsolescence-Pending-Rating-the-ESRB

Hausken, L. (2004). Textual theory and blind spots in media studies. In Ryan, M.-L. (Ed.), *Narrative across media: The language of storytelling*. Nebraska: University of Nebraska Press.

Ito, M. (2008). *Living and learning with new media: Summary of findings from the digital youth project*. Illinois: The McArthur Foundation.

Jenkins, E. W. (1999). School science, citizenship and the public understanding of science. *International Journal of Science Education, 21*(7), 703–710. doi:10.1080/095006999290363

Jenkins, H. (2004). Game design as narrative architecture. In Wardip, N., & Harrigan, P. (Eds.), *First person: New media as story performance*. Cambridge, MA: MIT Press.

Juul, J. (2001) Games telling stories? A brief note on games and narrative. *Game Studies, 1*(1). Retrieved from http://www.gamestudies.org/0101/juul-sts/

Kenway, J., & Bullen, E. (2005). Globalising the young in the age of desire: Some educational policy issues. In Apple, M., Kenway, J., & Singh, M. (Eds.), *Globalising public education: Policies, pedagogies and politics*. New York: Peter Lang.

Kincheloe, J. L., & Steinberg, S. R. (1997). *Changing multiculturalism*. Buckingham: Open University Press.

King, D., & Bridgman, G. (2003). *Television violence in New Zealand: A study of programming and policy in international context*, (p. 53).

Kirkpatrick, G. (2004). *Critical technology: A social theory of personal computing*. Aldershot, UK: Ashgate.

Livingstone, S. (2004). What is media literacy? *Intermedia, 32*(3), 18–20.

Ljoså, E. (1998). *The role of university teachers in a digital era*. Retrieved from http://www1.nks. no/eurodl/shoen/eden98/Ljosa.html

Mamei, M., & Zambonelli, F. (2004). *Motion coordination in the Quake 3 arena environment: A field-based approach*. Environments for Multi-agent Systems-First E4MAS Workshop, New York, July 19.

Mihailidis, P., & Hiebert, R. (2006). Media literacy and student/teacher engagement. *Academic Exchange Quarterly, 10*(3), 1–6.

Misztal, B. A. (2000). *Informality: Social theory and contemporary practice*. London: Routledge.

Muffoletto, R. (Ed.). (2001). *Education and technology: Critical and reflective practices*. Creskill, NJ: Hampton Press.

Newman, J. (2002). The myth of the Ergodic videogame, *Game Studies, 2*(1).

Office of Film and Literature Classification. (2009). *Public perception of a violent videogame: X-Men origins: Wolverine*. Wellington, New Zealand: OFLC.

Oliver, M., & Pelletier, C. (2005). The things we learned on Liberty Island: Designing games to help people become competent game players. In de Castell, S., & Jensen, J. (Eds.), *Changing views: Worlds of play*. Vancouver: Simon Fraser University Press.

Prensky, M. (2001). *Digital game-based learning*. New York: McGraw Hill.

Putnam, R. (2000). *Bowling alone: The collapse and revival of american community*. New York: Simon & Schuster.

Rosenberg, B. H., Landsittel, D., & Averch, T. D. (2005). Can video games be used to predict or improve laparoscopic skills? *Journal of Endourology, 19*(3), 372–376. doi:10.1089/end.2005.19.372

Schott, G. (2008). Language-GAME-players: Articulating the pleasures of violent game texts. *Loading, 1*(3). Retrieved from http://journals.sfu. ca/loading/index.php/loading/issue/view/4

Schott, G. (2009a). I like the idea of killing but not the idea of cruelty: How New Zealand youth negotiate the pleasures of simulated violence. In T. Kryzwinska, B. Atkins, & H. Kennedy (Eds.), *Breaking new ground: Innovation in games, play, practice and theory. Proceedings of DiGRA 2009*. Retrieved from http://www.digra.org/dl/db/09287.36489.pdf

Seeman, N. (2004). *Beware the media police* (pp. 19–20).

Shaffer, D. W. (2007). *How computer games help children learn*. New York: Palgrave Macmillan.

Squire, K. (2005). Changing the game: What happens when videogames enter the classroom. *Innovate, 6*(1).

Squire, K. (2008). Video-game literacy: A literacy of expertise. In Coiro, J., Knobel, M., Leu, D., & Lankshear, C. (Eds.), *Handbook of research on new literacies*. New York: Macmillan.

Squire, K. D., & DeVane, B. (2006). Pimping my ride and representing my hood: GTA as a sandbox for constructing identity and representing race. *Keynote presentation to the Media, Culture, and Communications Special Interest Group at the Annual Meeting of the American Educational Research Association*, April 8-12.

Steinkuehler, C. (2006). Massively multiplayer online video gaming as participation in a discourse. *Mind, Culture, and Activity, 13*(1), 38–52. doi:10.1207/s15327884mca1301_4

Turkle, S. (1984). *The second self: Computers and the human spirit*. New York: Simon and Schuster.

Vargas, J. A. (2005). *Gamers' intersection-Grand Theft Auto: San* Andreas plays to a generation from the streets to suburbia. Retrieved from http://www.washingtonpost.com/wp-dyn/content/article/2005/09/26/AR2005092601697_pf.html

Walkerdine, V. (1991). *School girl fiction*. London: Verso.

Withers, K., & Sheldon, R. (2008). *Behind the screen: Hidden life of youth online*. Institute for Public Policy Research.

Zagal, J. P. (2008). A framework for games literacy and understanding games. *Future Play: Proceedings of the 2008 Conference on Future Play: Research, Play, Share*. Toronto, Ontario, Canada.

Zagal, J. P. (2009). Ethically notable videogames: Moral dilemmas and gameplay. *Breaking New Ground: Innovation in Games, Play, Practice and Theory. Proceedings of DiGRA 2009*. Retrieved from http://www.digra.org/dl/db/ 09287.13336.pdf

KEY TERMS AND DEFINITIONS

Classification: A classification is a statement about who is eligible to view a publication. In New Zealand, the Classification Office is responsible for classifying all publications that may be harmful and need to be restricted (e.g. R18) or banned.

Digital Natives: Mark Prensky is acknowledged to have coined the term digital native in 2001 in his work *Digital Natives, Digital Immigrants*. In his seminal article, he assigns it to a new breed of student entering educational establishments who have grown up using digital technology. These students take technology for granted compared to digital immigrants who adapt to technological developments. A native will refer to their 'new camera' whereas an immigrant would more often than not describe it as a 'digital camera'.

Game Literacy: Entails the ability to decode and understand meanings with respect to the semiotic domain of games but also the ability to produce meanings. In acknowledging the interactive nature of the games, understanding has therefore becomes analogous with the ability to access content, i.e. play.

Ratings: Rating labels provide consumer advice relating to the most appropriate age categories for which a game is suitable. Ratings differ between rating systems, but commonly include G (General), PG (Parental Guidance), M (Mature or 15+), R16 and R18 (Restricted for persons under 16 years of age and 18 years of age respectively).

Structural Analysis: Refers to an analysis of a game's constituting units and the ways in which these units inter-relate in time and space. Falling within the realm of structural analysis are aspects of game design, typologies (rules or genre), temporality, spatial navigation and the study of event types (ludic or narrative) Games are understood as systems, as 'a set of parts that interrelate to form a complex whole'.

Textual Analysis: Is conceptualized as the meaning that emerges when the text is actualized or practiced (*read*, in the case of a novel, *played*, in the case of a game). Textual analysis expresses how text 'is unmade, how it explodes, disseminates – by what coded paths it goes off' (Barthes, 1977) under the control of the player.

Chapter 10
Unifying Instructional and Game Design

David I. Schwartz
Rochester Institute of Technology, USA

Jessica D. Bayliss
Rochester Institute of Technology, USA

ABSTRACT

Games have impacted education, research, and industry in multiple ways, altering notions of interaction. Traditionally, instructional design and educational research have dominated academic studies of pedagogy, teaching, and training. There are many parallels between the fields of game design and education, as both draw inspiration from the study of engagement, interaction, and motivation. State-of-the-art research and trends show great potential to cross-pollinate and uplift each area. This chapter synthesizes instructional and game design concepts based on current research, comparing and contrasting key elements. Towards the goal of providing a road map for readers, the chapter demonstrates three active case studies that illustrate how both fields greatly influence each other, leading to positive outcomes. These cases demonstrate that many concepts in both fields have direct parallels. The chapter concludes with a discussion of potential future directions and trends.

INTRODUCTION

Angelo and Cross (1993) indicate two main questions regarding education:

1.   How well do students learn?
2.   How effectively do teachers teach?

DOI: 10.4018/978-1-60960-495-0.ch010

Instructional design matters heavily in answering both of these questions, but first, we give a few definitions. Gagné, Briggs, & Wager (1992) refer to instruction to encompass the multitude of ways a person learns. Instructional design is the "systematic and reflective process of translating plans" for the variety of material used for learning and teaching (Smith & Ragan, 2005). Thus, instead of teaching, we tend to focus on learning, which we define more formally later. To motivate the focus on learning, consider that significant learning experiences entail process and outcomes (Fink, 2003):

- Process hopefully involves student engagement and "high-class energy."
- Outcomes hopefully provide significant and lasting change for the students. Ideally, the course somehow enhances the lives of students through individual life enhancement, preparation for participation in multiple communities, or work preparation.

Games often provide significant learning experiences in a similar manner. Time magazine ran an article on "The Future of Work" that included the World of Warcraft© massively multiplayer online game as an example of the future of how people will work:

Rob Carter, chief information officer at FedEx, thinks the best training for anyone who wants to succeed in 10 years is the online game World of Warcraft. Carter says WoW, as its 10 million devotees worldwide call it, offers a peek into the workplace of the future. Each team faces a fast-paced, complicated series of obstacles called quests, and each player, via his online avatar, must contribute to resolving them or else lose his place on the team. The player who contributes most gets to lead the team — until someone else contributes more. (Goldberg et al., 2009)

This sort of comparison is not an accident, as many of formalisms found in games also affect our lives—we follow rules, seek goals, and attempt to overcome challenges, just as in education. In the above example, the article claims individuals obtain significant learning experiences both in terms of work preparation and preparation for participation in the communities of the future. Continuing the comparison, note that games have numerous benefits over "reality." For example, unlike real life, a game may be restarted and played again, often encouraging the player to try new ideas, which helps motivate the study presented in this chapter.

Hypothesis

Given the established commonality and relationships of learning and game environments, game design warrants study as a mechanism for influencing instructional design (Bayliss & Schwartz, 2009). To increase learning and motivation in the classroom, cross-pollination between the two areas is promising. In this chapter, we demonstrate explicit connections between the two areas, forming the hypothesis that instructional and game design share common approaches and can elevate each other's implementation. For example, what happens when the classroom becomes a questing place and a game becomes an achievement system?

Three examples of recent research projects will frame and test the hypothesis:

1. Current research on perceptual learning through action video games.
2. Development of an active learning introductory programming pedagogy that uses games as a context for learning.
3. Game design applied to game theory to teach the ethics of sustainability.

These projects cover a relatively complete range of forms of games and learning, starting from perceptual learning and leading to higher levels of cognitive activities. The common elements of these projects are discussed along with practical advice on instructional design from the perspective of game design. The chapter concludes with a discussion of future areas that remain open problems, with a suggestion of various targeted projects.

BACKGROUND

What do scores, grades, and points have in common? Depending on the context, a score can qualify and/or quantify an entity or action, representing a measurement. In fact, an abstraction called a metric has "meandered" from mathematical and scientific parlance into general academic vernacular. Outside of experimentation and research, academics embrace a multitude of measurements, evaluating our students, our writing, our performance, and more. We find it interesting that a score/point can be so many things—established measurements for biology, statistics, education, and others. Yet, measurement also involves games. Classic arcade games used points to report performance, which drove many players to surrender more coins to achieve greater mastery. Modern day competitions still relish this quest (e.g., GameBattles, 2010). Although many modern videogames have since abandoned points, popular genres continue to display scores, especially in music-rhythm games (e.g., Guitar Hero©/Rock Band©).

Playing a game to win differs little from a student competing to get an "A"—this connection between points/scores/grades is not a coincidence. We initially posed a question about connections between games and education. Are there other connections besides points? We return to scoring systems later in this chapter, but for now, we need to present some fundamental concepts from a variety of fields to draw our comparisons.

Play and Games

Professionals and academics do not agree upon the most fundamental definitions for games and play (Salen & Zimmerman, 2004). Nevertheless, many definitions share fundamental notions and, if anything, further demonstrate connections to instructional design. Given the lack of universal agreement, we choose to focus on aspects and accepted definitions that draw these connections.

According to Huizinga (1955), play follows certain rules and is interesting from the viewpoint that even animals appear to play. It may be defined as having the following elements:

- Play must be voluntary and superfluous—it can be suspended and/or deferred at a moment's notice.
- Play differs from ordinary life in terms of duration and location, creating a "magic circle" property, where play and special rules for play are in effect. For example, the playground is special because play happens there, and it may stop when players leave.
- Play creates order and has rules, though play should not be work.
- Play promotes the formation of social groupings—people play with each other.

This definition of play is not globally agreed upon, but it provides an interesting backdrop for a comparison with classroom learning.

With what we consider reasonable components of play defined above, we could facetiously define a game as just "what people play." However, in their seminal book, Salen & Zimmerman (2004) summarize, compare, and contrast numerous definitions. Others continued this work (e.g., Malaby, 2007), but with a reasonable definition of play already established, we seek a formalism that helps inform instructional design. For this work, we define a game as a system of rules/constraints, conflicts/contests, challenges, and goals, which educational systems already exhibit. Note that other aspects tabulated in *Rules of Play* (Salen & Zimmerman, 2004) include art, culture, volition, and "fun," which still relate to education. For example, many exercises in elementary school involve art, music, and other activities as part of the classroom environment.

Game Design

Given these definitions of play and game, we adopt Salen & Zimmerman's (2004) definition of game design: "the process by which a game designer creates a game, to be encountered by a player, from which meaningful play emerges." With this view, we see the seeds of a formal connection between game and instructional design. For example, the rules of a game and the rules of a class should hopefully constrain, guide, and motivate a learner/player to certain goals. As we demonstrate later in this chapter, perhaps an educator is akin to a game designer, laying out the rules for tasks and interactions with a system in which students engage to learn.

Learning and Instruction

Smith & Ragan (2005) define education as "all experiences in which people learn," which helps to distinguish instruction (i.e., the delivery of education). They further distinguish teaching from learning—learning can happen through a variety of sources, but a teacher is a live person providing instruction.

Some research focus specifically on learning, as quoted from Schunk (2008): "Learning is an enduring change in behavior, or in the capacity to behave in a given fashion, which results from practice or other forms of experience." Schunk expands the definition, as summarized below:

- Learning involves doing different things.
- Learning is inferential: we can only witness and observe the outcomes.
- Learning may not be permanent (e.g., students forgetting what they "crammed").
- Learning involves practice. Some say, "practice makes perfect," though the authors have heard a modification: "practice makes permanent." Either way, action will usually reinforce lessons.

We now expand upon instruction's definition: instruction provides a means by which a learner learns. The processes and course material could include assignments, exams, class time, tutoring, and more, all functioning according to a course's rules/syllabus.

Instructional Design

Smith & Ragan (2005) summarize relevant concepts with respect to instructional design. They borrow Driscoll's definition of instruction as "the deliberate arrangement of learning conditions to promote the attainment of some intended goal" (Driscoll, 2000).

As a further demonstration of connections with instructional and game design, we can expand the definition of instructional design given in the introduction, above. According to Smith and Ragan (2005), an instructional designer must address three questions: goals, strategy/medium, and outcomes/assessment. These notions should seem strikingly familiar. In fact, the authors even distinguish between instructional design (i.e., planning) and developing (i.e., making), which is akin to game design and development and has parallels in a multitude of other fields.

To draw further connections, we refer to Gustafson & Branch (2007), who note six key aspects of instructional design, which we summarize below:

1. Learner centered
2. Goal oriented
3. Meaningful performance
4. Assessable outcomes
5. Empirical, iterative, and self-correcting
6. Team effort

The above aspects should seem familiar based on the definition of play—just replace "learner" with "player" and "performance" with "play." We are now ready to draw formal connections between all of these fundamental concepts.

CORE RELATIONSHIPS

Consider the following analogies:

Playing ↔ Learning

Games ↔ Instruction

Game Design ↔ Instructional Design

Many researchers have tapped into these ideas (e.g., Schaffer et al., 2004; Bayliss & Schwartz, 2009). In this section, we expand upon the core definitions and principles that we presented in the background to draw these connections.

Playing as Learning

Rothwell & Kazanas (2004) present a wide range of contentious research about learning into various "camps," which we summarize below:

- Reception learning: instructors deliver material, give assignments to apply it, and then test it.
- Discovery learning: instructors create experiences, guide and observe reactions, and create opportunities for application.
- Action learning: instructors guide teams through real-world examples that require experimentation.

Other forms of learning involve ongoing work, e.g., informal learning (Rossett & Hoffman, 2007) and others (Schunk, 2008). Regardless of approach, these researchers try to guide instructional designers to guide learning. For example, Rothwell and Kazanas (2004) suggest planned/unplanned discovery, summarized from earlier work by Romiszowski (1981).

Thus, a classroom and class provide experiences for the learners. We expand upon the instructor's roles later in this section. But now we can make the connection that the rules of a classroom closely follow Huizinga's rules:

- Just as play is voluntary, interaction and participation in the classroom is also voluntary. Within modern classrooms that provide computers and internet access, students (for better or for worse) can freely explore.
- Learning in the classroom is superfluous– it *usually* suspends the moment students leave a classroom for the day. However, as pointed out by instructional designers, informal learning happens outside of class, e.g., "hallway conversations."
- Just as play distinguishes from "normal life," a class's duration and location provides a "magic circle" for the learner/player.
- A classroom environment has rules and order, just as a game provides.

Although play promotes the formation of social groupings, traditional classroom education focuses on the individual learner. However, as noted above, modern philosophies, like action learning, promote team-based problems, which we address later in Case Study 3.

Games as Instruction

Above, we hinted at a classroom's rules. Educators provide syllabi for students, but, what does instructional design "say" about a syllabus? Rothwell and Kazanas (2004) define an instructional syllabus as usually referring to a "sequence of objectives [as] the basis for an instructional outline." Consider one of the many components that define a game: the rules. Regardless of definition, when playing a game, the player needs to know "what to do" (and often, where to go, what to get, how to win, and so forth). Koster (2005) demonstrates in an excellent fashion how a player can react to a game's system of rules, and as we believe, makes an exceptionally strong case for a game relating to instruction.

Although we have focused on rules, educational games provide direct applications of learning experiences and are especially studied in terms of the Serious Games Initiative (2010). Instructional designers are well aware of the motivation that games provide, e.g., (Schunk, 2008; see pp. 313-314). Our second and third case studies explore two instances of a content-driven application of games, though we will defer conversation about serious games to other sources.

However, we can relate content and rules—and pretty much everything else—in a game in terms of immersion, agency, and transformation (Murray, 1997), which we summarize below (Bayliss & Schwartz, 2009);

- **Immersion:** Consider the notion of "losing oneself" in an experience, as in focusing on a project, a conversation, or even writing a book chapter. Games are well-known for providing environments and experiences in which players lose track of time, become engaged, and to which they return to replay.
- **Agency:** Apart from game controls and user-interactions, a game should provide the ability for players to make meaningful choices, which usually result in changes to the world/environment in which the game occurs. For example, even in chess, a single move not only alters the board/game state, but can vastly change the outcome of the game (especially considering opening strategies).
- **Transformation:** The ability of an individual to turn a game playing experience into a personal and potentially life changing series of experiences.

While these aspects help to explain instruction and games, not all games, and certainly not all education, guarantees these things. Educators and educational research strive to provide these aspects, and in an ideal world, every game and every course would immerse, engage, and transform the players/learners in positive, productive ways. Nevertheless, knowing that a "common ground" exists in these fields should help to improve professional practice in both, as we believe our case studies demonstrate later in this chapter.

Game Design as Instructional Design

In the above discourse, we delayed the discussion of the *process* of designing instructional material. Previous work (Bayliss & Schwartz, 2009) draws a number of comparisons with respect to rules and mechanics of a classroom experience. Here, we expand upon these connections and past work, drawing a closer connection to a formal process with a model of the instructional design extracted and adapted from Rothwell and Kazanas (2004). For each step, we relate corresponding actions that a company might consider to fund and produce a game:

- **Conduct a needs assessment:** conduct a business case. What do learners/players need/want?
- **Assess learner characteristics:** assess consumer market. Who will learn/play?
- **Develop course outcomes and assessment:** develop goals for the game. What core experiences will the learners/players have?
- **Organize the performance objectives:** organize the game's "flow." What sequence of actions do the learners/players perform/play? In a way, a game's level design should not seem far apart from course topics that progress from start to end.
- **Make and run the course:** build and sell the game. In both, collect learner/player feedback during and following the release to improve the current (and future) experiences.

Akin to education seeking more efficient means to teach better, if designers can find an ideal, "guaranteed" process, production costs would decrease, and profits would increase. A multitude of guides, articles, books, and industry presentations provides guidance for excellence in game design (e.g., Salen & Zimmerman). What we feel is missing, however, is the connection between instructional and game design research.

Reconsider the six key aspects of instructional design from Gustafson and Branch (2007) with respect to game design. As stated previously, if we replace "learner" with "player" (as we have done in several places above), it seems that instructional design research and practice provides guidelines for game design. Technically, since instructional design itself is "unsolved" (though constantly improving), we cannot say we have indeed "solved" game design, as well. However, as we demonstrate in the subsequent sections, specific aspects of learning and instructional research directly apply to game design.

LEVELS AND LEARNING

In Bayliss and Schwartz (2009), we draw initial comparisons with instructional and game design based on the core elements of games: feedback, aesthetics, and mechanics. As we have conducted and expanded this initial effort, we have pursued a variety of research projects that help broadly define the comparisons at different "levels." Akin to Bloom's taxonomy, in which course materials can address a range of learning from simple memory to abstract reasoning, learning itself can occur biologically, psychologically, and socially (Schunk, 2008). Using this abstraction of low-to-high levels of learning, we can explain a powerful synergy between instructional and game design:

- **Low-level:** perceptual learning.
- **Mid-level:** common (and core) elements of both games and courses.

- **High-level:** designing "meta-games," where games and instruction merge.

In the following sections, we present three case studies to provide a "roadmap" for other researchers. The projects cover a relatively complete range of forms of games and learning, starting from cognitive science and leading to instructional design. We extract and generalize the common elements of these projects, which will provide practical advice for other researchers and developers seeking to incorporate either or both fields.

We start with biology. Although numerous texts on education provide guidance on "best practices," educators rarely discuss the biological and cognitive implications of learning. However, the game industry is quite aware and interested in biological and psychological feedback given profit motives. For example, through pattern recognition and repetition, most players simply get better at playing a game. Performing a repeated action has a biological effect. In fact, funding for "educational games" via serious games often involves training and not education given the appeal of games to encourage drilling. The first case study delves further into the processes by which researchers can explore this level.

When considering more traditional models of learning theory and instructional design, educators consider studies on cognitive models and instructional practice. Our previous work demonstrated a number of strong connections with game design, which is also often studied in this "medium-level" fashion. By summarizing and extending this work in the second case study, we demonstrate an even greater connectivity to instructional design.

Combining and extending this work involves even greater abstractions in the third case study. What if the grade students get in playing a game ties directly into their course score? And what if the game they play teaches the principles intrinsic to the course? This work also involves changing the way engineering ethics is taught to engender engineering students with a motivation to consider sustainability throughout their career. As we demonstrate, this work ties into a social context, as well.

CASE STUDY 1: PERCEPTUAL LEARNING

Modern technology provides an increasing access (and bombardment) of information, resulting in multi-tasking. Appelbaum et al. (2008) refer to multi-tasking as a paradox in the business world—individual task completion is harmed, but overall productivity seems to have increased over the years. Gonzalez & Mark (2004) studied information workers and discovered that they spend an average of three minutes per task with an overarching hierarchy of tasks that they called working spheres. Even the spheres were disjointed in that workers spent an average of twelve minutes working in a single sphere.

Are modern workers getting inundated? The field of education actively debates the harm multi-tasking may have on learning. Bauerlein (2009) inspected the argument from the positions that multi-tasking should always be eschewed to a more "middle ground." Multi-tasking is neither terrible nor wonderful—it is a necessary human activity with some positive benefits. Since mult-tasking requires split attention, a central theme of the article is perceptual learning—where greater attentional powers can be trained. This view departs from typical representations of learning, but it has much potential.

Perceptual Learning

To explain perceptual learning, we turn to biology and neuroscience. Using actual biology as a basis for education research has had profound effects. For example, taking short breaks during a traditional lecture has been shown to improve student engagement (Felder, 2010)—such work is fundamentally biological in nature. By understanding how the human brain receives, translates, and transmits information, we might challenge established views of learning.

Schunk (2008) devotes an entire chapter to the neuroscience of learning as part of his discourse on learning theory, focusing on the central nervous system. We only briefly review a few basics and leave further study to the reader. We start with the brain as an information processing system. As information arrives, the input translates to a perception of the input and matches to information in memory. In essence, by repeatedly receiving sensory input, a human forms and strengthens neural connections, resulting in perceptual learning.

Action Video Games and Perceptual Learning

Playing action video games can lead to long-term perceptual learning. *Action video games* are those that require fast and accurate actions with regards to potentially multiple, unpredictable targets, and have an emphasis on peripheral visual processing. Both first- and third- person shooters commonly fall into this category.

Perceptual learning via action video games has great potential. Li et al. (2009) found that playing action videogames can increase the contrast sensitivity function (CSV), a primary limiting factor in how well one sees. Given this result, a follow-on experiment has devised an Unreal Tournament 2004© modification (or just, mod) to help patients with Amblyopia, or a "lazy eye." The experiment's mod splits a screen, whereby one side shows special gabor filters to the patient's lazy eye. A gabor filter is a linear filter image used in image processing for edge detection. Patients must shoot this image when it appears, or else an enemy will pop up and shoot at them. The main instructional outcome is to enable patients to train their lazy eye by making them select a gabor filter image within a time limit.

Two additional studies show positive, long term biological effects from action videogames:

- Dye et al. (2009) demonstrate evidence that playing action video games reduces reaction times without sacrificing accuracy.
- Green et al. (2006) demonstrate that action videogame players have enhanced attentional resources when compared with non-gamers.
- Of particular note, non-action video games, like Tetris, do not show this type of perceptual learning. These findings are relevant for education as they indicate the following:
- Different students have different abilities due to playing action video games.
- Students playing these games may task-switch more quickly.

It is unknown whether or not students perform better in a multi-tasking environment—the performance likely depends on the degree to which the task-switches are predictable.

Relating to Instructional Design

Why do action videogames cause long-lasting perceptual learning? And what does this mean for instructional design? The answer likely lies in the design of action videogames. Green et al. (2009) specified the necessary design constraints necessary to qualify as an action video game:

- Quick reactions to transient events and the velocity of moving objects are needed.
- Multiple items need to be tracked.
- The necessity of considering and deciding among multiple action plans quickly.
- Precise and timely actions are needed.
- Temporal unpredictability.
- Spatial unpredictability.
- Important items often appear away from the center of the screen.

The main attributes of a game that would be necessary for the types of perceptual learning indicated above are as follows:

- Aiming at rapidly changing items to accomplish a task in a timely manner: first-person shooters require a primary task of shooting and killing an enemy. Using any item would likely have the same effect as long as the item was moving, and the player had to target it precisely.
- A rich environment where real-time multitasking is necessary: such an environment would need spatial and temporal unpredictability, multiple items, and task switching to accomplish goals. For example, a first-person shooter game would need multiple, unpredictable enemies and rewards.

Thus, action videogames exhibit many of the required features—and they also connect with notions of play/learning. For example, the necessity to aim precisely within a certain time period gives players a very goal-centered approach to learning. Moreover, since experiments show that the playing of these games affects perceptual learning, we see a direct connection between neuroscience, learning theory, and games. Even more impressive, two key aspects of the connections directly map from games to learning:

- **Agency:** although agency involves more than control schemes, the actual interactions of the game have a direct effect on perceptual learning.
- **Transformation:** playing action videogames literally transforms the players!

These games meet the criteria for play set by Huizinga (1955), although social interaction and team effort still need study. It will be interesting to see if teamwork enhances perceptual learning over long periods of time as it commonly does in both play and instruction.

With respect to game design, the performance of players over time should, however, also be meaningful lest the player quit playing before achieving learning. First-person shooters can keep players engaged through events, like competitive player kill-scores or unlocking of achievements and/or new items.

CASE STUDY 2: INTRODUCTORY COMPUTER PROGRAMMING EDUCATION

This case study summarizes and expands upon initial work presented in Bayliss & Schwartz (2009), which involves an ongoing project on using games to teach an introductory programming course sequence. The instructional design follows modern principles in terms of defining the learning outcomes for each course and then assessing those outcomes. The courses focus heavily on using active learning in the classroom through the use of games, since they are an area of study in programming that has broad applicability to the interests of students in the courses. We discuss how the sequence has handled these different elements over time and what has, and has not, worked.

The Classroom as a "Magic Circle"

The primary location for teaching at an academic institution is the classroom—it is often unappreciated as a place to bend and redefine ordinary rules. Huizinga refers to such a place where play can happen as a magic circle. We believe that the classroom has its own rules and regulations that can suspend upon exiting the room. Students voluntarily enter the classroom and may choose whether or not to learn, as learning is a voluntary activity.

The special properties of the classroom mean that the very notion of it as a place for learning separates it from ordinary life. The Quest2Learn (2010) school in New York city has taken advantage of this separation in that many of their current learning materials appear to be quest-based and involve an active role playing component.

We have taken advantage of the properties and rules of the classroom in several ways throughout the introductory programming courses. Sometimes, changing the rules of the classroom leads to better immersion in learning materials. Some common rules for the classroom include the following:

- Sit quietly while the instructor lectures.
- Follow whatever the instructor says to do.

Both active and cooperative learning methodologies essentially "stomp" on these rules. In the introductory programming courses, we explicitly try to encourage active student participation in our sections. As an example, one exercise requires that students analyze program fragments and then act out stories generated from the fragments. We also encourage group work, whereby groups may not agree with each other or the instructor.

Since a classroom is a magic circle, artificial constraints may be used to affect learning. As an example, competition among students can limit a resource, e.g., grading on a curve, which limits available letter grades. Not only are such measures counterproductive (Guskey, 1994), studies show that this approach is gender biased–men are more likely to succeed and thrive in this type of environment than women (Kirk & Zander, 2002). Interestingly, not all competition is bad–competition between different groups may *enhance* student motivation.

Much as the different levels of a game often provide unique experiences, it is important that course materials vary. According to Koster (2005), a game holds a player's interest only until the player recognizes the pattern behind the game. Thus, Tic-Tac-Toe (also called Noughts and Crosses) becomes boring after the player determines the patterns. For the classroom, too many exercises or activities of the same type may reduce interest in course materials. We, and likely many other instructors, constantly experiment with new "mixes" of material to encourage classroom participation.

Contextualization and Agency

Regardless of language, computer programming involves a tremendous amount of rules—what you can and can't type/do, akin to a written language. Not that every rule system is a game (let alone a course), but with digital games and programming, students immediately do recognize the connection. Thus, several researchers documented the success of contextualizing introductory programming (e.g., Bayliss, 2007). But as stated above, we believe that influence of games extends beyond courses that teach how to make them.

Application-driven examples, or contextualized problems, tend to motivate students as evidenced by changes to STEM (science, technology, engineering, and math) education. In fact, the notion of action learning that we introduced previously seems to encompass the same idea: motivate students by relevance. Though the fields of learning theory and instructional design still debate the variety of ideas, this notion of application-driven work seems to have been widely adopted, at least in the technical domains. With games, however, the motivation seems "built-in" because of popularity. It should be no surprise that the connection between programming and videogames can entice students immediately. Consider the notion of rule systems: game design seems to inform instructional design automatically in this particular case.

How does agency factor in? In our courses, we simultaneously adopt several notions of learning theory and game design:

- Make each assignment domain specific to games (application-driven/ contextualization).

- Provide opportunities for creative computer program development (discovery learning).
- Make classroom exercises active in terms of promoting both individual student involvement and group work.

Not only do students follow specifications, but the assignments allow students to extend/refine/customize the work to be creative. Since game design does involve creating and planning experiences, the students experience programming in the service of their field. Consequently, the game design opportunities create mini-instructional design moments for students, as they define their own problems to solve. In a way, the freedom to design in multiple ways furthers the "cause" of agency.

This approach has yielded excellent results. Initially, the *Reality and Programming Together* (RAPT) program succeeded with a student retention rate (~93%) that exceeded the regular computer science sequence (~70%), which lacked a specific context (Bayliss, 2007).

Feedback and Scoring

One of the core examples of Bayliss & Schwartz (2009) considered the initial motivation of relating scores, grades, and points. Most games use summative feedback for users, rewarding the user for achieving goals. The scoring system in games and classes are both metrics, and as previously demonstrated, are strikingly similar. Guskey (1994) provides an extensive study of scoring systems.

We show a graph of a student's potential grade over a particular course in the sequence below in Figure 1.

The pattern in Figure 1 relates to numerous courses. This pattern may be compared to the original Dungeons and Dragons (D&D)© role-playing game leveling curve shown in Figure 2. Modern massively multiplayer online games, like

Figure 1. Graph of the potential grade in the introductory programming course (CS1)

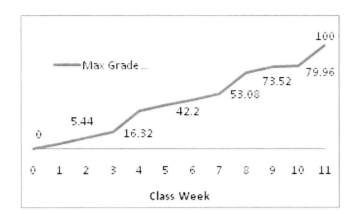

Figure 2. Approximate leveling curve for the original Dungeons and Dragons© roleplaying game

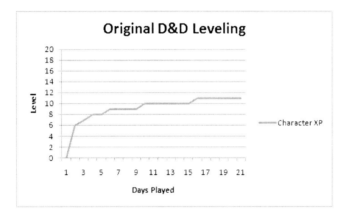

World of Warcraft©, show similar leveling curves to the original D&D© game.

We did try to perform a direct conversion between a course system and a leveling system for two quarters in a row in the introductory programming courses. The direct conversion failed because it did not motivate students more or less than the initial points system did. It appears that the underlying reason is that a game leveling system has a different "trending rate" when compared to the course system. Also, the final result (i.e., a grade) has a very specific meaning throughout a course.

The trends differ because a game tends to reward players early, essentially to "hook" them once they get past initial learning of rules. However, a course doles out points in a roughly linear fashion, except for larger "spikes" around exams and major projects. It is interesting to note that with respect to total accrued points, a student is already failing a course until a later period in which course material has provided greater "investment." Were education to adopt game design's early-reward system, perhaps courses would benefit from more smaller (but high-yield) assignments earlier. Regardless of approach, the connection between points and grades does indicate a connection between the player/learner relationships frequently mentioned throughout this chapter.

Relating to Instructional Design

Above, we express many of the core relationships between instructional and game design. Now that our programming sequence is composed of only game design and development majors, our research has shifted towards understanding and refining our processes. As explained before, having games already embedded in the classes immediately provides contextualized and motivated learning. The newest challenges have been breaking out of traditional paradigms to adopt further game design techniques.

Koster (2005) discusses the different types of fun, which are equivalent to Gardner's multiple intelligences:

1. Linguistic: games such as crossword puzzles and Scrabble©.
2. Logical-mathematical: strategy games such as Chess.
3. Bodily-kinesthetic: sports games and rhythm/dancing games.
4. Spatial: spatial puzzle games such as Tetris©.
5. Musical: music games such as Guitar Hero©.
6. Interpersonal: social games such as massively multiplayer online games; intrapersonal (self-motivated): games with formative feedback such as WiiFit©.

The fact that Koster suggests there are different games for different folks is important—as instructors, we need to better appeal to a wider variety of learners through the design of instructional materials. Doing so is a very difficult problem, although in our course sequence we are beginning to tackle it through the use of different assignments and exercises that may appeal to different types of intelligence.

For example, in the second introductory programming course, one assignment requires students to program a sound symphony from different sound components, which would appeal to those with musical intelligence. We also teach different sorting techniques in programming by having students stand at the front of the room and figure out how to sort themselves using a particular technique, which relate to a bodily-kinesthetic exercise.

Our group has become a cohort of budding game designer/developers. In a small way, the unified group seems to provide an immersive environment, given the focus on, and shared interest in, games. Even without games, the notion of learning communities (i.e., groups of students with common/shared interests and beliefs) has shown success in academia (e.g., Malone, 2009). In this respect, perhaps the relationship to leveling in a game may not seem arbitrary—a class can resemble a guild, questing through a particular level trying to achieve a goal.

Through shared experience, we believe we can engender immersion. For example, in the final course, teams of students spend the term building a game. Even though the course focuses on data structures, the project provides a "taste" of action learning, application, and game design. To date, a majority of the projects finish and run, albeit with some bugs. Many students spend time after the conclusion of the course finishing and refining their game project. The project itself tends to encourage the formation of friendships between students.

We also believe that transformation occurs—transformation in the classroom is essentially a "teaching moment," just as a light bulb turning on over a student's head. Once a teacher can establish immersion and agency, transformation will more likely occur, as engaged students will more likely learn. Other kinds of transformation happen in our sequence, as well. Unlike most other introductory courses, students often have never programmed—even students who have prior experience will often relate that college programming greatly exceeds the demands of past experiences. Consider biology, chemistry, math, language, and so forth.

For example, even though a student may take calculus for the first time, they certainly have had some form of math beforehand. Until programming and computer science become standard curricula, this field has a unique challenge. The single cohort and separate sequence of courses has brought to light an intriguing idea. That a population of students who (on the whole) lack any knowledge of programming can produce their own games within a year indicates transformation.

The RAPT program has additional pieces of evidence for transformation, as follows:

- A signed letter from the first student group (all but two signed the letter) lobbying for the RAPT program to continue beyond the first year.
- The 93% retention rate in the major (whether students failed the course or not).
- All students who have shown their resumes to the RAPT program instructor have explicitly put down RAPT on their resume.
- An extremely high number of students in RAPT became assistant lab instructors.
- 100% of the students surveyed said that RAPT should continue for future students.

Most of the above items are not goals in an introductory computer programming sequence. Instead, they indicate how much the sequence changed students' affective state towards the computer science discipline. Since we have identified a variety of interesting connections, much work remains.

CASE STUDY 3: MOTIVATING LEARNING ABOUT SUSTAINABILITY ETHICS

Our final case study demonstrates how game and instructional design completely converge, whereby the game is the course, and the course is a game. Similar efforts are under way, i.e, Quest2Learn

(2010), in which 6-12th grade children learn using games and game-design principles. This convergence derives from the parallels in instructional and game design summarized at the beginning of this chapter. In fact, the emergence of "games-based education" derives from numerous sources, though many refer to serious games as one motivation. If a designer could map "real" rules into a game's rules, then a player should theoretically learn—and enjoy doing so, thus increasing further motivation to master the material.

One area that traditionally "de-motivates" students is engineering ethics. Entire educational programs and professional organizations strive to improve this area (ASEE, 2010). Traditionally, ethics material focuses on design and professional practice, especially in the light of the Challenger disaster and other horrific events—we suggest searching the Internet for "Engineering Disasters." By presenting these real cases, educators hope to convince future engineers to be "good." However, as indicated by Bucciarelli (2008), not many students actually think that they would intentionally make mistakes to hurt anyone! Without providing an immersive environment so that a student might make such mistakes (thus also losing agency), it is no wonder such material lacks transformation.

But, the demands for expanded ethics education continue. In particular, engineering ethics has expanded focus to include sustainability (i.e., sustainability ethics), given political and global trends/pressures (e.g. O'Neill-Carrillo et al., 2008). As Rothwell and Kazanas (2004) indicate, this thorny, real-world problem can provide action learning. Moreover, Schunk (2008) relates a series of interesting games and simulations that engage students and encourage learning. But if the instructional material cannot "reach" the students in the first place, the recent expansion will likely also lack appeal.

In this section, we demonstrate how games that apply game theory can become instructional material to explain and motivate sustainability ethics with an ongoing research project (Seager et al., 2009). In the games, students generate "products" (their desired grades), resulting in "pollution" (grade penalties). Students must overcome competition via collaboration to learn how to balance personal and collective goals (higher profit/grades) with outcomes (greater pollution/penalties). The games and game playing *are* the course materials.

Game Theory

We start with traditional economic game theory, in which "players" compete for goals/resources, trying to maximize their gain. Not only does game theory involve competition for resources, but in fact, game theory occurs in "everyday life" (Fisher, 2008). For example, one of the authors of this paper continually takes multiple coupons supplied by a local supermarket for particular item—after all, how can one resist the appeal of $1-off coupons? However, the supply of coupons recently—and rapidly—depleted. Thus, that author essentially maximized her/his gain at the expense of "everyone else." (We leave to the reader to guess which author was the "cheapskate.")

A common question for "game educators" is the connection between game design and game theory (Wolfire Blog, 2010). In reality, although the academic and professional *domains* differ greatly, definite connections exist, especially those seen in traditional board games, like Tic Tac Toe, Chess, and so forth. Government, military, and industrial funding continues to explore larger-scale examples with research and development in wargames (Shubik, 2009; Smith, 2010).

Externalities and the Coase Theorem

The notion that industries will likely compete (and negotiate) for resources and produce externalities hints at an important connection to simulations and games. A wide-variety of research and applications has applied this field, especially in computer networking, the military, and business

(Coase, 1960). To motivate the need for a game that applies game theory, we look to ethics education.

Engineering students are taught to analyze and design a wide variety of products and services, all consuming materials and generating waste. However, with economies driven by production and consumption, what happens to the waste? Economists speak externalities, which are comprehensive effects of this process (Cornes & Sandler, 1996). People can benefit from production while damaging others (including themselves) with pollution.

Coase attempted to address this issue—if transaction costs are low and property rights are determined, resources have optimal allocations without government intervention (Coase, 1960). For example, a factory polluting nearby water used by farmers would negotiate a transfer of payments between them to accept reduced farm yields or reduce factory production, depending on the profitability of either industry. Although numerous debates and advances to these concepts continue, the core question remains the same for engineering students: the external effects of what they will design/make.

Sustainability Ethics Game Design

We introduce on ongoing research project that involves developing games to teach engineering students sustainability ethics (Seager et al., 2009). Unlike educational games, these "ethics games" map directly into course material by making the games *be* the course material. The hypothesis is that if students do not feel "distant" from the ethical decisions, they will not passively ignore an ethical lesson. So, instead of instructing "don't be like this bad example," teachers can provide classroom activities that provide choices for students.

How? Students act as industries that produce points—real grade points. For example, in the first game, a student might react, "well, I guess I just got 100!" As discussed above, production also causes externalities (assumed as primarily negative, e.g., pollution). So, what externalities could "production points" generate? Penalties! So, when a student produces points (simply by choice), every student in the "world" (including the student who chose the points) receives a penalty. This game's rules actually involve a mathematical formula derived from various "fiddling" with values and parameters, as shown below:

$$E = \frac{\left[\Sigma_i (P_i - 70)^x\right]}{Nk} \qquad (1)$$

where E=externalities, P_i=points for the ith player, and N=number of players. Constants k and x are arbitrary constants found during the "fiddling" process. Given all the player-chosen points from Equation 1, the game (which is essentially a spreadsheet) can calculate the actual grade for each player using Equation 2, below:

$$G_i = P_i - E \qquad (2)$$

Figure 3 shows a qualitative view of the mathematical model.

Game Balance and Gameplay

A consequence of choosing a mathematical model abstracted from game theory is that game balancing primarily consists of mathematical parametric analysis of Equations 1 and 2—what we referred to as "fiddling" above. For example, N and k can be "tuned" for a certain number of students in class and an optimal grade of 93 to let everyone potentially get an A. Gameplay for this particular game has options, whereby an instructor could hide/reveal the model, prevent/allow student collaboration, and offer no/multiple replays.

Initial results with focus groups demonstrate that players will try to uncover the underlying model and collaborate to avoid penalties. For fairness (and to avoid scaring potential students), the games include reflective, written essays and class discussions following a more traditional model, especially to provide additional grading to "make up" for lost game-points.

Figure 3. Grades for Student-Chosen Points with Applied Externalities

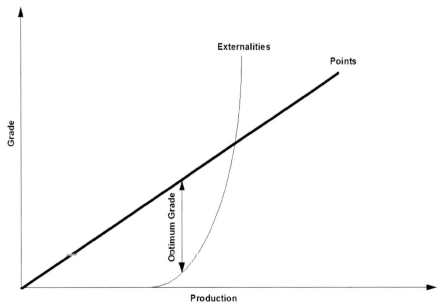

Extending the Model

The sustainability ethics game is only an initial, highly abstracted version of the full suite of four games described in the research (Seager et al., 2009). For example, if players take on roles (i.e., luxury, intermediate, and subsistence producers), a more granular model provides multiple plots to determine a variety of optimal conditions. Figure 4 shows an example interface in which player classes in different regions negotiate production levels.

Relating to Instructional Design

Recall the various fundamental principles of instructional and game design from earlier in the chapter. This project seeks to provide agency, immersion, and transformation literally through games taking place as classroom exercises:

- **Agency:** students must make meaningful choices, as their own grades depend on their initial choices and subsequent negotiations. Unlike other educational games, the students/players must engage—even students who choose to "tune out" still have made a choice (i.e., grade of zero with resulting global penalties).
- **Immersion:** although the "production" and "pollution" may seem distant (i.e., too abstract for a student), connecting these concepts to points and penalties seems to immerse the students in the model—an abstracted economy that has immediate, and perhaps, severe consequences.
- **Transformation:** as stated before, the research seeks to remove passive learning. By motivating the students with real choices and real consequences, the play sessions should facilitate the learning process.

Figure 4. Example Coase-Theorem Game

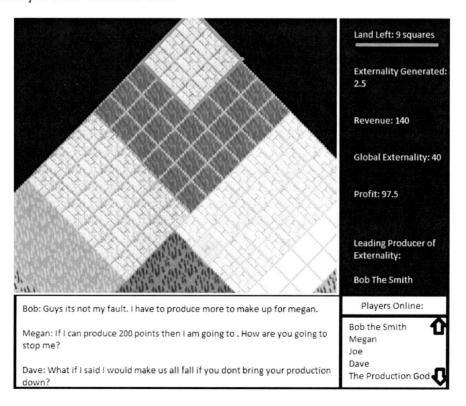

The above relationships should not be surprising given that the course material itself is a game. The applied game theory taps into an idea we introduced at the beginning—points as forms of measurement. By connecting game points to modeled production and academic grades, the sustainability ethics games demonstrate a specific case where instructional design is game design.

Although the work is ongoing, initial results are promising. Ultimately, the goal is to create an active in-class discussion to *engage* the students to consider sustainability ethics.

SOLUTIONS AND RECOMMENDATIONS

Each of the above cases demonstrated that game design can indeed inform instructional design in multiple ways. To extend our original work (Bayliss & Schwartz, 2009), we have pursued a variety of more targeted research problems to address a variety of "levels" of learning. In essence, the way game design seems to generally inform instructional design happens with respect to designing material to maintain agency, immersion, and transformation. These aspects arise over and over again.

More specifically, identifying the core components of the instructional experience, especially in terms of game components provides a framework for considering the experience. For example, rules, interface, interactions, and scoring especially help draw the connection between the fields. Throughout this process, we suggest a variety of practices from the field of game design, asking a variety of questions:

- Is this experience fun/engaging? Can the designer test it with a focus group?
- Do the participants have meaningful decisions?
- Does the experience provide objectives? Does the designer use some form feedback/scoring to assess and/or alert the player/learner?
- What level of engagement exists? Does the designer look to neuroscience, educational research, group dynamics, or some other field?

In a way, we suggest finding the common connections, as many will exist—as we have shown, starting by substituting "play" for "learn" and "game" for "class". The results are somewhat surprising with how close the fields lie.

FUTURE RESEARCH DIRECTIONS

Although we feel that we have presented a solid case for the common ground and connections of both instructional and game design, much work remains. Numerous resources exist that explain established learning theories and research trends, but such literature makes little mention of games. Whereas serious games literature and games education does explore the burgeoning field, it seems that partnerships need to emerge to bridge the gaps and rigorously test each of the connections.

The action videogame research is ongoing and provides a fertile testing ground for a variety of game genres. Can we improve other forms of perceptual learning, perhaps even through all human senses? Even for the current research, understanding how multi-tasking is truly affected will greatly inform a large number of instructional and industrial environments.

Many of the open problems stated by Bayliss & Schwartz (2009) still offer many avenues. For example, as we explained in Case 2, our programming courses could relate to small groups "questing" for knowledge. Perhaps a course modeled after fantasy roleplaying game (e.g., Dungeons & Dragons©) with the instructor as a "game master" would greatly test the concepts and certainly extend the ideas much further. Capitalizing on the extensive body of work already vetted, game theory has long since employed its own notion of role playing (Green, 2002). This combination would not only incorporate roles, but because of the game theory connection, extend the work presented in Case 3.

With regard to the leveling that would occur, game scoring systems (whether visibly apparent or embedded) strongly suggest ways to reconsider educational points/grades. The sustainability ethics research is essentially tackling one aspect of this area, but the work focuses on the specific in-class education games, not the scoring systems. Given the reluctance to adopt experimental grading systems, this area might be difficult to approach, and thus, makes an intriguing opportunity. There also seems to be a connection to epistemic game research, e.g., Epistemic Games (2010).

CONCLUSION

We are very excited to lay the groundwork for these connections. In this chapter, we demonstrated a variety of ways that instructional design and game design correlate from a variety of levels. Learning can happen in multiple ways, ranging from perceptual learning to social groups. By considering core aspects of the field of games (play, game design, agency, immersion, and transformation), we hope that educators continue this work to adopt successful notions for instruction to improve learning. Much work remains in this field, especially with drawing together more specialists from the various domains.

ACKNOWLEDGMENT

A Microsoft Computer Gaming Curriculum grant and Microsoft Course Assessment Grant supported the RAPT program. Students working on Case Study 1 were partly funded by the Office of Naval Research (MURI Award 00140710937) through the University of Rochester's Brain and Vision Lab. The Air Force Research Laboratory (AFRL) in Rome, New York sponsored a summer faculty research fellowship that inspired the exploration of scoring systems. Last, but not least, the NSF grant with RIT colleagues Tom Seager and Evan Selinger helped to generate additional funds through an additional RIT grant. Our student researcher, Dan Whiddon, developed and tested the initial set of sustainability ethics games, including interfaces that we demonstrate in this chapter. We gratefully acknowledge the support of all these grants, colleagues, and students.

REFERENCES

ACM. (2010). *Welcome to SIGCSE*. Retrieved February 8, 2010, from http://www.sigcse.org

Angelo, T. A., & Cross, K. P. (1993). *Classroom assessment techniques: A handbook for college teachers* (2nd ed.). San Francisco: Jossey-Bass Publishers.

Appelbaum, S. H., Marchionni, A., & Fernandez, A. (2008). The multi-tasking paradox: Perceptions, problems and strategies. *Management Decision, 46*(9), 1313–1325. doi:10.1108/00251740810911966

ASEE. (2010). *Engineering ethics division by-laws*. American Society for Engineering Education. Retrieved February 8, 2010, from http://www.asee.org/activities/organizations/ divisions/bylawsEthics.cfm

Bauerlein, M. (2009). Life in the tech lane. *Chronicle of Higher Education Brainstorm*. Retrieved February 8, 2010, from http://chronicle.com/blogPost/Life-in-the-Tech-Lane/9160/?sid=at&utm_source=at&utm_medium=en

Bayliss, J. D. (2007). The effects of games in CS1-CS3. *Journal of Game Development, 2*(2), 7–18.

Bayliss, J. D., & Schwartz, D. I. (2009). Instructional design as game design. In *Proceedings of the 4th International Conference on Foundations of Digital Games,* (pp. 10-17). New York: ACM. Retrieved February 8, 2010, from http://doi.acm. org/10.1145/1536513.1536526

Bucciarelli, L. (2008). *Ethics and engineering education.* Retrieved February 8, 2010, from http:// dspace.mit.edu/handle/1721.1/40284

Coase, R. H. (1960). The problem of social cost. *Journal of Law and Economics.* Retrieved February 8, 2010, from http://www.sfu.ca/~allen/ CoaseJLE1960.pdf

Cornes, R., & Sandler, T. (1996). *The theory of externalities, public goods, and club goods.* Cambridge, MA: The MIT Press.

Driscoll, M. P. (2000). *Psychology of learning for instruction* (2nd ed.). Needham Heights, MA: Allyn & Bacon.

Dye, M. W. G., Green, C. S., & Bavelier, D. (2009). Increasing speed of processing with action video games. *Current Directions in Psychological Science, 18*(6), 321–326. doi:10.1111/j.1467-8721.2009.01660.x

Epistemic Games. (2010). *Home page.* Retrieved February 8, 2010, from http://epistemicgames.org

Felder. R. (2010). *Resources in science and engineering education.* Retrieved February 8, 2010, from http://www4.ncsu.edu/unity/lockers/users/f/ felder/public

Fink, L. D. (2003). *Creating significant learning experiences.* San Francisco: Jossy-Bass.

Fisher, L. (2008). *Rock, paper, scissors: Game theory in everyday life.* New York: Basic Books.

Gagné, R. M., Briggs, L. J., & Wager, W. W. (1993). *Principles of instructional design* (4th ed.). Belmont, CA: Wadsworth/Thompson Learning.

Goldberg, S., Villano, C., & Villano, M. (2009). The future or work: The way we'll work. *Time Magazine.* Retrieved February 8, 2010, from http://www.time.com/time/specials/packages/ article/0,28804,1898024_1898023_1898169,00. html

González, V. M., & Mark, G. (2004). Constant, constant, multi-tasking craziness: Managing multiple working spheres. In *Proceedings of the SIGCHI Conference on Human Factors in Computing Systems, CHI '04,* (pp. 113-120). New York: ACM. Retrieved February 8, 2010, from http:// doi.acm.org/10.1145/985692.985707

Green, C. S., & Bavelier, D. (2006). Effect of action video games on the spatial distribution of visuospatial attention. *Journal of Experimental Psychology. Human Perception and Performance, 32*(6), 1465–1468. doi:10.1037/0096-1523.32.6.1465

Green, C.S., Li, R. & Bavelier, D. (2009). Perceptual learning during action video games. *Topics in Cognitive Science,* 1-15.

Green, K. C. (2002). Forecasting decisions in conflict situations: A comparison of game theory, role-playing, and unaided judgment. *International Journal of Forecasting, 18*(3), 321–344. doi:10.1016/S0169-2070(02)00025-0

Guskey, T. R. (1994). Making the grade: What benefits students? *Educational Leadership, 2*(52), 14–20.

Gustafson, K. L., & Branch, R. M. (2007). What is instructional design? In Reiser, R. A., & Dempsey, J. V. (Eds.), *Trends and issues in instructional design and technology* (pp. 10–16). Upper Saddle River, NJ: Pearson.

Huizinga, J. (1955). *Homo ludens: A study of the play element in culture.* Boston: Beacon Press.

Kirk, M., & Zander, C. (2002). Bridging the digital divide by co-creating a collaborative computer science classroom. *Journal of Computing Sciences in Colleges, 18*(2), 117–125.

Koster, R. (2005). *A theory of fun*. Phoenix: Paraglyph Press.

Li, R., Polat, U., Makous, W., & Bavelier, D. (2009). Enhancing the contrast sensitivity function through action video game playing. *Nature Neuroscience, 12*, 549–551. doi:10.1038/nn.2296

Malaby, T. M. (2007). Beyond play. *Games and Culture, 2*(2), 95–113. doi:10.1177/1555412007299434

Malone, M. (2009). Learning communities on college campuses. *The Everything College Survival Book, 3*, 45–65.

Murray, J. H. (1997). *Hamlet on the holodeck: The future of narrative in cyberspace*. New York: The Free Press.

O'Neill-Carrillo, E., Frey, W., Jiménez, L., Rodriguez, M., & Negrón, D. (2008). Social, ethical and global issues in engineering. In *Proceedings of the 38th ASEE/IEEE Frontiers in Education Conference*. New York: ASEE/IEEE.

Quest to Learn. (2010). *Quest to learn*. Retrieved February 8, 2010, from http://q2l.org

Romiszowski, A. (1981). *Designing instructional systems: Decision making in course planning and curriculum design*. New York: Nichols.

Rothwell, W. J., & Kazanas, H. C. (2004). *Mastering the instructional design process: A systematic approach* (3rd ed.). San Francisco: Pfeiffer.

Salen, K., & Zimmerman, E. (2004). *Rules of play: Game design fundamentals*. Cambridge, MA: The MIT Press.

Schunk, D. H. (2008). *Learning theories: An educational approach* (5th ed.). Upper Saddle River, NJ: Pearson.

Seager, T., Allenby, B., & Selinger, E. (2009). An experiential pedagogy for sustainability ethics. Retrieved February 8, 2010, from http://www.nsf.gov/awardsearch/showAward.do?AwardNumber=0932490

Serious Games Initiative. (2010). *SGI*. Retrieved February 8, 2010, from http://www.seriousgames.org

Shaffer, D. W., Squire, K. D., Halverson, R., & Gee, J. P. (2004). Video games and the future of learning. *Phi Delta Kappan, 87*(2), 105-111. Retrieved February 8, 2010, from http://www.academiccolab.org/resources/gappspaper1.pdf

Shubik, M. (2009). It is not just a game! *Simulation & Gaming, 40*(1), 587–601. doi:10.1177/1046878109333722

Smith, P. L., & Ragan, T. J. (2005). *Instructional design* (3rd ed.). Hoboken, NJ: Wiley.

Smith, R. (2010). The long history of gaming in military training. *Simulation & Gaming, 41*(1), 6–19. doi:10.1177/1046878109334330

The 400 Project. (2006). *The inspiracy*. Retrieved February 8, 2010, from http://www.theinspiracy.com/ 400_project.htm

Think Services. (2010). *Game career guide*. Retrieved February 8, 2010, from http://gamecareerguide.com

Unreal Tournament. (2010). *Game play*. Retrieved February 8, 2010, from http://www.unrealtournament.com

Wolfire Blog. (2010). *Game theory applied to game design*. Retrieved February 8, 2010, from http://blog.wolfire.com/2009/01/game-theory-applied-to-game-design

ADDITIONAL READING

Adams, E. (2010). *Fundamentals of game design* (2nd ed.). Berkeley, CA: New Riders.

Ames, C., & Archer, J. (1988). Achievement Goals in the Classroom: Students' Learning Strategies and Motivation Processes. *Journal of Educational Psychology, 80*(3), 260–267. doi:10.1037/0022-0663.80.3.260

Anderson, L. W., Krathwohl, D. R., & Bloom, B. S. (2000). *A taxonomy for learning, teaching, and assessing: a revision of Bloom's taxonomy of educational objectives, complete edition*. New York, NY: Longman Publishing Group.

Bayliss, J.D. (2009). Using Games in Introductory Courses: Tips from the Trenches, *SIGCSE 2009*.

Bayliss, J. D., & Bierre, K. (2008). Game Design and Development Students: Who are They? *Microsoft Academic Days Conference on Game Development in Computer Science Education*.

Beaubouef, T., & Mason, J. (2005). Why the high attrition rate for computer science students: some thoughts and observations. *SIGCSE Bulletin, 37*(2), 103–106. doi:10.1145/1083431.1083474

Brathwaite, B., & Schreiber, I. (2009). *Challenges for Game Designers*. Boston, MA: Charles River Media.

Chen, J. (2006). Flow in games. Retrieved February 8, 2010, from http://www.jenovachen.com/flowingames/introduction.htm.

Dick, W., Carey, L., & Carey, J. O. (2008). *Systematic design of instruction* (7th ed.). Upper Saddle River, NJ: Allyn & Bacon.

Dickey, M. D. (2005). Engaging By Design: How Engagement Strategies in Popular Computer and Video Games Can Inform Instructional Design. *Educational Technology Research and Development, 53*(2), 67–83. doi:10.1007/BF02504866

Fullerton, T. (2008). *Game design workshop: a playcentric approach creating innovative games* (2nd ed.). Burlington, MA: Morgan Kauffman.

Gredler, M. E. (2008). *Learning and instruction: theory into practice* (6th ed.). Upper Saddle River, NJ: Prentice Hall.

Gunter, G., Kenny, R., & Vick, E. (2006). A Case for Formal Design Paradigm for Serious Games. In *CODE - Human Systems; Digital Bodies. The International Digital Media and Arts Association and the Miami University Center for Interactive Media Studies*.

Hodell, C. (2009). *ISD from the ground up: a nononsense approach to instructional design* (2nd ed.). Alexandria, VA: ASTD Press.

Jacobs, S. (2008). Games For Learning: Perlin, Salen On The Future Of Educational Games. Retrieved February 8, 2010, from http://www.seriousgamessource.com/item.php?story=20965.

Kapp, K. M. (2007). *Gadgets, games, and gizmos for learning*. San Francisco, CA: Pfeiffer.

LaChapelle, N. (2008), Game Design as Instructional Design. Retrieved February 8, 2010, from http://connect.educause.edu/blog/HiredEd/gamedesignasinstructional/44703.

Law, C.-K. (1996). Using fuzzy numbers in educational grading system. *Fuzzy Sets and Systems, 83*, 311–323. doi:10.1016/0165-0114(95)00298-7

Mertler, C. A. (2001). Designing scoring rubrics for your classroom. *Practical Assessment. Research Evaluation, 7*(25).

Olson, M., & Hergenhahn, B. R. (2008). *Introduction to the theories of learning, eight edition. Upper Saddle River*. NJ: Prentice Hall.

Rajagopalan, M. & Schwartz, D. I. (2005). Game Design and Game-Development Education, *Phi Kappa Phi Forum, 85*.

Reigeluth, C. M., & Carr-Chellman, A. A. (Eds.). (2009). *Instructional-design theories and models, volume III: building a common knowledge base*. London: Routledge.

Schell, J. (2008). *The art of game design: a book of lenses*. Burlington, MA: Morgan Kaufmann.

Schwartz, D. I. (2008). Motivating Engineering Mathematics Education with Game Analysis Metrics, In *Proceedings of the ASEE Zone I Conference*. Retrieved February 8, 2010, from http://www.asee.org/activities/organizations/zones/proceedings/zone1/2008Professional.cfm.

Whittington, K. (2004). Infusing active learning into introductory programming courses. *Journal of Computing Sciences in Colleges, 19*(5), 249–259.

Wolz, U., Barnes, T., Parberry, I., & Wick, M. (2006). Digital gaming as a vehicle for learning. In *Proceedings of the 37ᵗʰ SIGCSE technical symposium on Computer Science Education.*

KEY TERMS AND DEFINITIONS

Agency: The ability for players to make meaningful choices in a game, which usually result in changes to the "game world" (Murray, 1997).

Game: A type of play that include rules/constraints, conflict/contest, challenges, and goals (as defined by the authors).

Game Design: The process by which a game designer creates a game, to be encountered by a player, from which meaningful play emerges (as defined by the authors).

Immersion: The notion of "losing oneself" in an experience (Murray, 1997).

Instruction: The multitude of ways a person learns including all course materials, assignments, exams, class time, tutoring, etc. (adapted by the authors from Gagné, Briggs, & Wager, 1992).

Instructional Design: The "systematic and reflective process of translating plans" for the variety of material used for learning and teaching (Smith & Ragan, 2005).

Learning: An enduring change in behavior, or in the capacity to behave in a given fashion, resulting from practice or other forms of experience (Schunk, 2008).

Magic circle: A place to bend and redefine ordinary rules (Huizinga, 1955).

Play: An experience that must have the following features: it must be voluntary, it must be superfluous (it can be suspended/deferred at a moment's notice), it creates order and has rules, it promotes the formation of social groupings, and it differs from ordinary life in terms of duration and/or location (Huizinga, 1955).

Transformation: The ability of an individual to turn a game playing experience into a personal and potentially life changing series of experiences (Murray, 1997).

Chapter 11
A Theoretical Background for Educational Video Games:
Games, Signs, Knowledge

Nicolas Szilas
University of Geneva, Switzerland

Martin Acosta
Universidad Industrial de Santander, Colombia

ABSTRACT

The potential of video games for learning is now widely accepted among the community of Educational Technology. However, there is a critical lack of guidance for the design of educational games. In order to provide such guidance, there is a need for a solid theoretical basis regarding the nature of learning in games. This chapter redefines what a game is, in semiotic terms, enabling four groups of strategies to be formally identified, depending on how the knowledge to be acquired is inserted into the game. These four groups are: systemic learning, when knowledge is embedded in the game mechanics; winner strategies, when the game provides an environment in which knowledge is required to reach the game's goal; loose coupling, when knowledge is arbitrarily required to unblock the progression towards the game's goal; and contextual coupling, in which the game serves as a context for the exposition of static learning material.

This theory is then put into practice by analyzing three commercial educational games. It constitutes a first step towards Instructional Game Design.

INTRODUCTION

The potential of video games for learning is now widely accepted among the community of Edu-

DOI: 10.4018/978-1-60960-495-0.ch011

cational Technology (Quinn, 1997; Jones, 1998, Amory, 2001; Rieber, 1996; Prensky, 2001; Gee, 2003). Contrary to common belief, play and games are not specific to children, but constitute an essential activity for adults too (Huizinga, 1938; Rieber,

1996). Play is not frivolous but can be quite serious (Rieber, 1996). The recent explosion of computer and video games in modern culture makes it even more obvious that games are to be considered as a new medium, with unique properties.

Among the most cited advantages of video games over other instructional technologies are their motivational appeal and their compatibility with modern pedagogy (Kirriemuir & McFarlane, 2004, p. 19).

In terms of motivation, it is argued that games are intrinsically motivating; players are motivated to play regardless of the consequences of the learning activity (Malone & Lepper, 1987; Jones, 1998). This is related to one fundamental characteristic of a game: the fact that it has no perceived utility for the player (Huizinga, 1938). Games are played because they provide a multitude of emotions, such as fear, surprise, pride, relief, etc. and have other motivational aspects such as challenge and fantasy. Given this intrinsic motivation to play, several educational games have been developed, including all the games considered as "edutainment". While it has been shown that games in certain contexts provide higher levels of motivation of engagement than traditional education (Wishart, 1990 in Hays, 2005), the level of engagement or "gameplay" of these titles seems lower than in pure entertainment games (Hagbood, 2005), as if adding pedagogical constraints to a game diminished the motivation. In other terms, "making learning fun", as stated by Malone & Lepper (1987) remains a difficult task (Hays, 2005).

In terms of pedagogy, the active nature of games encourages learner-centered pedagogy. As described by Rieber (1996), play is a natural learning strategy for children according to the Piagetian theory; this makes video games suitable for computer-based learning. Game-based learning is usually associated to the situated learning theory (Brown, Collins & Duguid, 1989), because in many games, especially 3D games, any action has a meaning within a situation in the game

(Gee, 2003, p. 84). However, in many educational games, the player's actions are not used to promote situated learning. Indeed, among players' actions, some are dedicated to learning while others are purely for the game play, resulting in a dissociation between game and learning which is contrary to situated learning. This insufficient integration between game and learning is also reported by several research studies (Malone & Lepper, 1987; Kirriemuir & McFarlane, 2004; Habgood, et al., 2005; Szilas & Sutter-Widmer, 2009).

Besides, using existing games for educational purposes is very difficult, since the games were not designed for that purpose. For example, several practical difficulties are reported when using commercial history strategy games to learn history in a classroom environment (Egenfeldt-Nielsen, 2004; Connoly & Stansfield, 2006).

This short overview leads to the conclusion that there is a need to design educational games that better exploit the pedagogical potential of computer games, but also that we lack guidance for such design. As far as learning is concerned, the field of Instructional Design (in the broad sense of the term) is dedicated to providing guidelines on tools/methods for organizing learning content and activity, should the tools/methods use computer or not (Reigeluth, 1999). On the game side, the field of Game Design provides more and more established methods to design games with a good gameplay, in terms of balancing for example (Salen & Zimermann, 2003). Each of these two design-oriented fields fails however in providing relevant methodology for educational games. Instructional Game Design (IGD) should emerge to improve the quality of current educational games. More specifically, the goal of IGD is to find a methodology making it possible to produce an efficient learning game from any given knowledge domain, if such a game is possible. Very few attempts towards IGD can be found so far, and they remain preliminary (Dickey, 2005; Kiili, 2005; Amory, 2007). These attempts tend to share elements between methodologies; this leads to a relatively shallow integration of Game Design and Instructional Design, without sufficiently taking into account the specificity and the difficulty of using games for learning. Questions related to this definition of IGD are:

- How to assess the quality of an educational game, in terms of learning?
- What can be learned with games, and what cannot?
- How to adapt existing instructional design methods to educational game design?

We consider that in order to provide further guidance in the design of educational games, there is a need for a solid theoretical basis regarding the nature of learning in games. To date, the connection between learning and game playing is not clearly established. More precisely, it is admitted that game playing promotes learning, but the exact nature of the articulation between these two activities remains unknown. Our position is that this articulation must be better understood before proposing more efficient guidance for educational game design.

This paper aims to contribute to such a theoretical base. We raise the fundamental issue: what are the relations between games and knowledge and how can this relation inform the design of educational games that promote efficient learning?

The chapter is structured as follows. First we propose a definition of games that is relevant within the domain of learning. Then, from this definition, some fundamental principles regarding games and knowledge are listed. In particular, four educational game types are distinguished, depending how the relation between game and learning is underlined. Then, three video games are analyzed according to the theoretical principles of games and knowledge. Finally, recommendations and future research direction are proposed.

REDEFINING GAMES

Why a New Definition?

The difficulty in providing necessary guidance for the design of educational games is due to a very vague and extensive concept of games that is usually adopted. If one needs to understand, from a theoretical point of view, how learning and gaming can work together, it is necessary to rigorously define what a game is. Then, learning being the acquisition of knowledge, it will be possible to precisely identify how knowledge and games are potentially related, opening the way to a better understanding of the various possibilities of learning by game playing.

In order to limit the scope of this study, which still remains wide, only games with game-defined goals and rules will be studied here. Games where the player defines his/her own goals or rules, such as when children engage in free play or pure simulation games (i.e. Sim City), despite their potential benefit for learning, are outside the scope of this paper. Only single player games are discussed here, but to some extent, results of this paper can be extended to the multi-player case.

There have been several definitions of games, starting with the pioneer work of Johann Huizinga (Huizinga, 1938). More recently, academic interest for video games has raised updated definitions based on an overview of existing definitions (Salen & Zimmerman, 2003, p. 71; Juul, 2003). Despite these efforts, all proposed definitions lack precision or miss important features of games, as will be demonstrated below.

Games as Signs

Some of the main features of games are the fact that the activity occurs outside ordinary life, in a separate time and space, and the activity is unproductive (Huizinga, 1938, p. 35). This notion of separation is difficult to defend since some current games, in particular pervasive games, are deeply interlaced with everyday life (Juul, 2003). Juul proposed to replace the notions of separation and non-productivity by the notion of "negotiable consequence": the fact that a game "can be played with or without real-life consequences". However, this latter notion, not only remains imprecise itself (who is negotiating with whom?), but is also based on the assumption that because one can earn money in a game, then the goal of the game is to earn money. However, the goal of the game is still to win the game, which by itself is not productive, even if the game is sometimes embedded in a larger context where there are consequences.

The difficulties in understanding/addressing the notion of what Salen and Zimermann (2003) call "artificiality" can be solved if the focus is shifted from the objects themselves to their interpretation. The "arena" where the game takes place (Huizinga, 1938) is not necessarily a delimited physical space, but becomes separated from the real world through players' interpretations. For example, even if someone plays chess by e-mail (Juul, 2003), the game occurs in a separate world, not a world of physical objects but a world of interpretations. This brings us to the notion that games are made of signs (Salen & Zimmerman, 2003, p. 42). In the field of semiotics, which is concerned with the study of signs, a sign is considered a link between a physical configuration of the world and an interpretation (or representation) in the mind of the interpreter, the player in our case (Klinkenberg, 2000, p. 42). For example, the bottom left square in a chess board is a sign with a certain meaning in the context of the game. No matter the size of this square its precise color or material, the meaning of this square in chess comes from the rules of the game which provide specific relations between this sign and other signs in the game.

Games as Dynamical Systems

This example illustrates an important feature of signs: a sign in isolation does not mean anything because signs are organized into systems of signs. Salen and Zimmerman (2003) acknowledge the systemic nature of games, without explicitly stating that games are systems of signs. Furthermore, we want to be more specific in asserting that games are dynamical systems, by analogy with the dynamical systems formalization in mathematics. In other words, games are defined by an initial state and a function that describes its evolution, according to its inputs, including the players' action. This dynamical nature of games differentiates them from other semiotic systems such as languages: languages are static, and their rules (the grammar) define the set of correct sentences of the system. Games are temporal, and their grammar not only defines the correct states in the game but also correct temporal evolution of those states.

The resulting definition that we propose is the following:

A game is a dynamical system of signs in which the player acts, independently of any consequence outside the system, in order to reach a goal assigned by the game.

This definition does not use the term "rules", as in almost all other definitions, because it is included into the notion of dynamical system. Let us enter into the details of game dynamics.

A game contains two components: the game mechanics and the playing rules (see Figure 1). The game mechanics – equivalent to the constitutive rules discussed by Salen and Zimmerman (2003) – describe how the game evolves, according to the player's inputs. The mechanics itself is composed of a *specific component* designed for the game and of an *environmental component*, which is ruled by the physical environment. For example, in the board game "Connect Four", the fact that the discs fall into the grid because of gravity, is a law of the environment, not of the game, but it has consequences for the game: one cannot put the discs in any position (as it is possible when playing with a grid on paper). Within the specific component of the game mechanics, the dynamics (the rules) can be automatically executed by the game itself or manually executed by the player (or another person). A particularity of video games is that their mechanics only have a specific component and are automated.

The playing rules – equivalent to the operational rules discussed by Salen and Zimmerman (2003) – define what the players are allowed to do in the game. That is, which inputs they are allowed to provide to the game mechanics. The playing rules act as a filter between all the possible actions of the player and the allowed actions provided to the game mechanics. In classical games, this filter is usually controlled by the player himself and by the other players when possible. Voluntarily not applying this filter is called cheating (which is not part of the game). A specificity of video games is that the player cannot easily provide an input that is not allowed, because the game can control the validity of the input. This makes it possible to avoid mentioning the playing rules.

Note that this definition is centered on one given player because the multiplicity of players is not a mandatory feature of games. In other words, a game only requires the point of view of one player to be considered a game. To include multi players' case into this definition, other players are part of the dynamical system, more precisely in the environmental component in the figure 1 below.

There exists a classic distinction between games and toys, between *Ludus* and *Paidia* (Caillois, 1958). *Ludus* relates to rule based playing, where the player is constrained to follow rules. *Paidia* denotes free play, without precise goals and rules, as when playing with toys. The above definition clearly enters into the *Ludus* category, following the scope of the paper defined above. We are aware of this limitation, since *Paidia* games should be included in the scope of learning games in general, but this restriction allows us to draw stronger theoretical conclusion.

Note that the concept of fiction or diegesis (de Freitas & Oliver, 2006), although not necessary, is

Figure 1. Formal architecture of a game

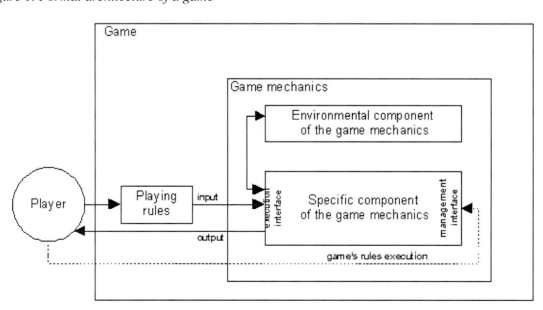

often associated to games, especially educational games. The system of signs related to the fictional game world should however be distinguished from the system of signs mentioned above. Fictional games add a level of complexity because the entities of the game not only constitute the game system mentioned in the definition above but also refer to our own world, as does any representational media (feature film, novel, etc.). Thus, in fictional games, two semiotic systems are superimposed.

THE PARADOX OF EDUCATIONAL GAMES

In this section and the following, we discuss the use of games for pedagogical purposes using the above definition of games.

First of all, one can observe a fundamental paradox when games are used for learning.

On the one hand, games are artificial: one plays for the sake of playing, regardless of the consequence of the playing activity outside the game (see previous section). On the other hand, learning is useful and must be perceived as such in order to be efficient: "there is now a wide consensus that effective, meaningful learning is facilitated by explicit awareness of and orientation towards a goal" (De Corte, 1995). It is considered important that the student understands the structure of what is to be learned (Merrill, 2002). In particular, it helps students reflect of their own learning activity. This paradox is also observed by Becker (2006): "If education is deliberate, and being *made* to play a game causes that object to cease being a game, then the whole notion of educational games would constitute a paradox." To solve the paradox, either the first or the second assertion has to be disproven.

Let us first disprove the first assertion and consider educational games as special types of games which are not artificial because they have a goal within ordinary life. In this case, the activity of playing an educational game would satisfy both

the artificial goal of the game and the utilitarian learning goal.

The double goal hypothesis: The learner-player could maintain during his/her playing activity the two goals in mind, with two types of motivation. The learner-player would be motivated both by the game's goals (game-intrinsic motivation) and by the learning outcome. According to this hypothesis, the attention of the player would shift between the two goals. Designing a good game is already a tricky task, so designing a good game that manages to add learning goals and motivations to learn in the mind of the player without diminishing the interest of the game appears to be quite a challenging task, if not impossible. A more reasonable hypothesis consists in assuming that while both goals are present, one is more conscious than the other, at a given moment of the user experience. More precisely, the main goal is the game's goal, but the player is aware that s/he is learning something while playing, and pretends s/he is only playing. This attitude would be analogous to what is called the "suspension of disbelief" in film: the viewers know perfectly well that what happens on the screen is not true, but they suspend this belief in order to get immersed and feel various emotions (Tan, 1996, p. 228). In this case, the player would alternate between periods where s/he would suspend their disbelief that the game has only a gaming goal with periods in which s/he would take the opportunity to think of the learning goal and reflect on it (e.g. debriefing periods).

Let us now disprove the assertion that educational games are played with the intention to learn. Two cases can be distinguished.

Implicit learning: In this case the learners do not know they have learned, since educational games can be based on implicit learning. Ciavarro, Dobson and Goodman (2008) used a hockey game to train hockey players to behave properly during a match. A hidden rule gave advantage to players who did not use violent actions. As a result players did improve their in game behavior, without even

noticing they had learned. They only played the game as a usual game, for the sake of winning the match. With implicit learning, a game can be used without interference between learning and playing.

Unsaid goal: In some situations, with children in particular, it is possible to omit mentioning the learning goal. Still, contrary to implicit learning, by the nature of the game or its context, players might guess that the game is dedicated to learning. In this case, the player experience switches to the "double goal" case. It remains possible for the learner to feel fooled because s/he was proposed a game that ends up being a pretext for learning. Note that there is also an interesting case where the learner is aware that learning content is targeted by the game, but does not know what exactly.

Among these solutions to the paradox of educational games, none constitutes a unique general solution to be applied in any situation. It appears that for the educational game to be a game, learning has to be considered a "side effect". By this, we mean that, to benefit from the advantage of games, the learners should have the artificial goal of the game as a primary goal, and that his/her primary activity should be oriented towards that goal.

EPISTEMIC COMPONENTS OF GAMES

In this section, our goal is to identify where learning could take place in a game. More precisely, our goal is to identify various strategies for embedding an educational goal into a learning game, that is various articulations between the educational goal and the game's components. The result we are after is a classification of strategies of using games for learning and not a classification of educational games. Many educational games would use several methods, as will be shown in the next section. Furthermore, our intention is not to pick up common game characteristics that are relevant for learning (Garris, Ahlers & Driskell,

2002; Wilson et al., 2009) but to deduce from a formal definition of games how the fundamental (or necessary) characteristics of games can combine with knowledge and its acquisition. For example, many authors, following Malone and Lepper (1981) mention fantasy as a game characteristic relevant for educational games. While we are not denying this assumption, we simply note that fantasy (or fiction) is not a necessary feature of games (see above) and that fantasy is also used in books, movies and simulations. Thus to understand why and how games should be used for learning, one needs to understand and focus on what games fundamentally are.

To establish a basis for IGD, a theoretical categorization of the strategies for mixing learning and games is essential. Starting with an educational goal, the learning game designer has to be aware of the various existing methods for inserting educational goals into the game. The game designer also has to understand the relative advantages and drawbacks of each method, in order to be able to choose the most appropriate ones to focus on.

As stated above, our approach consists in starting from the necessary and essential features of a game, described in the definition above and refined in Figure 1. First, from the game's general architecture depicted in Figure 1, one can straightforwardly locate two places where knowledge could be embedded: playing rules and game mechanics. We could not find any examples of a learning game whose learning content is located within the playing rules (operational rules) themselves. In a first person shooter for example, knowledge to be acquired would be that once there are no munitions with a weapon, one cannot shoot with this weapon; in order to go from one place to another, one needs to walk or run, etc. Learning at this level is equivalent to learning "prescriptive" knowledge, in a context where only correct knowledge effects the system. It seems more interesting to focus on the game mechanics (constitutive rules), a case that is studied below, as the learner has more freedom to explore the domain and observe the consequences of not following the rules to be learned. Therefore, we will not further elaborate the option of learning at the level of the playing rules in the rest of the article.

From the definition of a game, we can distinguish two types of learning in games: goal driven learning and mechanics driven learning. In goal driven learning, learning occurs because knowledge is required to reach the goal of the game. By arranging goals of various types and difficulty, games can be seen as a series of problems or exercises related to various knowledge to be used and acquired. This type of learning is then divided into two subtypes: *winner strategies* and *loose coupling*, depending on the level of integration between learning and gaming.

In mechanics driven learning, what is learned comes from the mechanics itself, the game's goal being an external factor in the learning. This type is further divided into two subtypes: In *systemic learning*, what is learned is the mechanics itself, that is the relation between the input and the output (see Figure 1), while in *contextual coupling*, what is learned is only an output of the mechanics (see Figure 1), regardless of the input.

In the following sections, these four types are presented in decreasing order of value from most valuable to less valuable types of articulations in terms of exploiting fundamental characteristics of games.

Articulation Around the Game Mechanics: Systemic Learning

When players interact with the game, they learn its game mechanics. After having played, they acquire a certain knowledge of the system's behavior. To a variable extent, they can, for example, anticipate the system's behavior and adapt their actions accordingly. Such learning happens in most games, and at various levels. In a first person shooter for example, the players could learn how to handle the mouse, how to move the character in a corridor, how to orient in space, how to anticipate

non playing characters' actions, etc. The player progressively acquires the part of the rules that constitute the game mechanics. This acquisition is neither automatic nor guaranteed, and it depends on the design of the game. If the educational goal is directly related with learning the game mechanics, we can use the game to obtain this goal.

From a pedagogical point of view, learning a system makes sense if the system shares similarities with an existing system of reference, so that the competencies acquired during play can be transferred to the system of reference. This learning strategy is applied instructional design when using simulations (Gokhale, 1996) and microworlds (Rieber, 2004) - a microworld is an engaging learning environment that students explore in a playful way, such as *LOGO*.

Games, in the sense of the goal-oriented games covered by this paper add a new dimension to simulations and microworlds by adding a goal structure to the simulation system itself. The benefits of this goal structure are twofold:

Firstly, the goal structure increases motivation for interacting with the simulated system. Even if microworlds are designed as toys to play with (Rieber, 1996), difficulties are reported getting learners engaged in the system (Gokhale, 1996; Rieber, 2002; Rieber, 2004, p. 599). The explicit goals attached to the game provide a solution to this issue.

Secondly, the goal structure allows a progressive exposure to the complexity of the game. The goal structure, of both goals and subgoals, initially exposes players with easy problems exposing them to only a subset of the game mechanics. Instead of letting the user interact with a complex system without guidance, the goal structure allows for the problem complexity to be smoothly increased, using a scaffolding strategy.

While the distinction between games and simulation is recognized (Prensky, 2001, p. 210; Gredler, 2003), the terms are often used almost interchangeably (see for example (de Freitas & Oliver, 2006)), as also observed in (Hays, 2005,

p. 9) and the benefits of the former are often assimilated with the benefits of the latter. In fact, for the type of articulation we are discussing in this section, simulations and their benefits constitute a subpart of the game. Such "in-game" simulations can take various forms, from realistic simulations to simplified simulations (Horwitz, 2000) to imaginary worlds like microworlds (see for example *Cabri-Géomètre* (Laborde & Capponi, 1994), an abstract mathematical world).

The notion of fiction that was introduced above is particularly relevant in systemic learning. When creating an artificial world of places and characters that evoke real places and real characters, games provide the ability for a learner to rehearse a behavior that is relevant in real life, in the game world.

Articulation Around Winner Strategies

The mechanics of games can also be used to produce learning, if it supports certain strategies and dismisses others in the pursuit of the game's goal. In which case, what is learned is not the dynamical system itself, but the winner strategies, which are reinforced by playing the game. Therefore, the goal of the game must be carefully designed in order to promote these winner strategies.

Such a game was used and analyzed by Brousseau to study the learning and teaching of mathematics, and resulted in the "Theory of Situations" (Brousseau, 1998). The theory was inspired by Piaget's "learning by adaptation", according to which, individuals learn by interacting with the world and adapting their actions in order to reach a goal (Piaget, 1959). The term "game" in the Theory of Situation is used by reference of the game theory, rather than video or child games; nevertheless, this theory is relevant for our purpose. For Brousseau, a game proposes a goal to be reached, defines the means that may be used, and (implicitly or explicitly) the actions that may be performed in order to reach the goal.

If the goal is clearly understood and accepted, the subject will use a trial and error process, mobilizing his/her mental schemas, and will receive feedback that enables him either to confirm the validity of these schemas, or to adapt them in order to reach the goal.

Brousseau describes three types of situations in which mathematics learning is promoted at three different levels: action, formulation and validation. For our purpose, the action situation is relevant for the design of educational games. It defines a practical goal to be achieved within a given 'milieu'. At this level, the knowledge is embedded in the actions that pupils do in order to reach the goal. The game is played with the world as an opponent. The game is organized so that the subjects do something to win. The rules and the 'milieu' (the game mechanics) grant that all actions produce a consequence that can be interpreted by subjects in terms of success or failure.

In this situation individuals learn by experimentation: they are confronted with a problem to be solved or goal to be reached, are provided with opportunities to perform certain actions (material, verbal or symbolic), and receive feedback from the 'milieu'. The feedback is as natural as possible (avoiding an authority evaluation: false/correct), and enables the subjects to evaluate their strategies by themselves, in order to correct themselves and reach the goal.

The most important factor in these games is what Brousseau calls the 'milieu', which we could assimilate to the game mechanics. According to the Theory of Situations, the most relevant feature of the 'milieu' is that "it has no pedagogical intention"; this means that the learner can assimilate its reactions to the natural reactions of the material world, in contrast with the reactions of a teacher, which could (voluntarily or not) give hints towards the correct actions to perform. In terms of the game mechanics, feedback in the form of judgments (true/false, correct/incorrect) should be avoided, and replaced by natural consequences of actions.

What subjects learn from this type of activity is the strategy that enables them to reach the goal. Therefore, an important aspect is to control all the possible strategies subjects could use spontaneously, and to ensure that the goal cannot be reached using a 'wrong' strategy (or a strategy that is not important to be learned). For example, if the objective is to learn to use a compass and ruler to draw a reflection about a line, it is important not to use a grid, which would enable reaching the goal without using a compass and ruler.

Applying these ideas to our definition of games, we could say that we can articulate the educational goal around the winner strategies if the game mechanics enforces three conditions:

- the player can enact different spontaneous strategies,
- only strategies that support the targeted knowledge objectives are successful,
- the feedback to the player's actions should avoid judgment and be presented as a natural consequence of the actions.

Therefore, this type of strategy only applies to domains where there exists some didactic knowledge regarding good or bad strategies and solutions, such as mathematics for example, in contrast with domains where there might be no right or wrong answer.

Articulation Around the Obstacles: Loose Coupling

In both categories above, the educational goal is embedded in the game mechanics. In many educational games however, certainly most of them, the game mechanics is composed of two almost dissociated parts, one dedicated to the learning goal and the other dedicated to gaming itself. The only link is the following: succeeding or failing to solve a task related to the educational goal changes a parameter in the gaming part of the mechanics. Typically, succeeding a task opens a new possibility in the game. This is a loose coupling because even if there is an interaction between the educational goal and the game, the structure of the learning task does not have any impact on the design of the rest of the game mechanics. As in winner strategies, knowledge is required to reach the goal of the game, but this is achieved at the price of a clear separation between learning and gaming components.

The articulation between learning and playing occurs via a component that is central to both activities: obstacles. On the learning side, several instructional strategies use problems or tasks that learners have to solve (Merriënboer, Clark, de Croock, 2002; Merril, 2008). These problems or tasks constitute obstacles, because they are not immediately solvable by the learner, otherwise there would be no learning. On the gaming side, the notion of conflict is considered as a core component of games (Crawford, 1982; Salen & Zimmerman, 2003). The conflict can occur between the player and the game rules, between players or within a player. It is related to the notion of competition which is one of the four categories of play identified by R. Caillois (1958). Thus the wide use of obstacle-based coupling between learning and playing can be explained because obstacles constitute the most obvious way to connect the two apparently separate fields.

Furthermore, it should be noted that obstacles are also basic components of narrative and drama. This notion is widely used in the domain of screen writing (McKee, 1998; Vale, 1972), where it is often termed "external conflict". It is also discussed in narratology. According to U. Eco for example, a narrative sequence needs actions which are difficult to perform (Eco, 1985, §6.4). In the theories of Greimas and Souriau, one of the actants is the opponent, which acts against the protagonist (Greimas & Courtes, 1979; Souriau, 1950). With many modern games being based on stories, obstacles are naturally used as the locus of integration between games, narrative and learning.

Loose coupling however meets several limitations. First, contrary to previous approaches, the systemic nature of games is not exploited. The game is used as a "motivational recipient" of activities that would be considered less motivating otherwise. The problem with such games is twofold. On one hand we wonder whether the recipient effectively motivates the learner or not and on the other hand if it does not just distract the learner and impede learning.

Second, the pedagogy behind the use of obstacles is often very limited. The obstacles are often questions asked to the learner (quiz) which departs from the active and constructive nature of learning that should be supported in game-based environments. An extreme example, outside of the computer realm, is the game *TRIVIAL PURSUIT®*. It is definitely a good game, in terms of entertainment, but the player does not learn much with it despite its heavy relying on players' knowledge. The part of the game related to an educational goal consists of a series of unrelated anecdotal questions in various domains, an approach that cannot be supported by any learning theory. In other words, some educational games are a "sugar coating of 'fun'" (Kirriemur & McFarlane, 2004) on top of an irrelevant pedagogy.

However, the obstacle-based coupling approach should not be rejected. It is the lack of pedagogical thinking in the design of the obstacles that provides a poor learning product in the end. Obstacle-based coupling is still a valid approach in various contexts, in particular, in the context of low level learning of recurrent tasks (Merriënboer, Clark, de Croock, 2002). Games can provide a relevant environment by exposing the learner to repetitive tasks, a strategy which is suitable for this kind of learning. For example, the game *TYPERSHARK* uses a fictional setting in which sharks are dangerously moving towards the player character. In order to remove these obstacles (the sharks), the player has to type the word that is written on the shark. The learner automatizes his/her typing skills by repeatedly typing words to remove sharks.

To sum-up, obstacle-based coupling between games and learning is a straightforward approach for learning with games which does not exploit all potentialities of games but which can be appropriate if the obstacles are designed in a pedagogically meaningful way.

Articulation Around the Context: Contextual Coupling

In this last category, the educational goal does not interfere with the game mechanics. The educational goal is fulfilled by delivering information during the game, and the way the user processes this information has no effect on the game. We call this type of articulation contextual coupling, because while the educational information does not advance the game, it can be considered as context for the core game.

Several edutainment games are based on this principle. For example, in French historical games such as *VERSAILLES* or *CHINE*, the plot happens within a historical context. The visual environment teaches about the culture and society related to the game. Encyclopedic information is also provided within the game, by clicking on the game's elements (a character, a building, etc.). At last the player is sometimes faced with documents which also contain information to learn. All this content is usually not relevant for solving the game, but it is provided in a narrative context that could help memorization. Note that all these instructional strategies are not equivalent. When information is provided via a separate encyclopedic hypertext or within a separate document, the relation to the context is weaker than when information is transmitted in dialogs, which are a more integral part in the fiction of the game.

Fiction again is quite useful in this type of articulation. If an educational goal is related to a specific place or time, setting a game within a fiction in that place provides the player with plenty of information that is relevant to the educational goal.

This example illustrates that there exists a variety of configurations where learning-related information can accompany a game mechanics, while not being part of it. These various configurations are not all equivalent. The most valuable are the ones which manage to integrate smoothly into the games, so that learning is not completely separated from the playing activity.

Contextual learning however does not fully exploit the characteristics of games. In particular, the user's action has no role in learning. Typically, contextual learning could be used similarly within non interactive media, such as movies or comics.

Contextual learning in games is often used in combination with more integrated learning strategies. While other strategies above such as *systemic learning* or *winner strategies* typically promote meaningful and situated learning, it should be accepted that such learning has to be reinforced by declarative knowledge. It has been shown that when learning occurs only by interacting with an environment, following a situated approach, learners tend not to be able to use their knowledge in other contexts (Rieber, 2002). Thus contextual coupling can be used to support situated learning with classical content.

ANALYSES OF GAMES

In order to illustrate our formal classification of game-based learning strategies, this section analyses in more detail three educational games. For each game, the goal is to identify which components make it belong to one or the other category.

Such analysis is difficult since all games are themselves complex and composite interactive products. The choice of the granularity level at which our analysis should be performed is not obvious. It is to some extent arbitrary.

The selection criteria for the three games were:

- being purely educational games rather than typical games adapted to learning, such as

CIVILIZATION for History, *SEGA RALLY* for driving, *SIMCITY* for city management, etc.

- being different from eachother, possibly covering different types of games according to our classification,
- having good gaming qualities (this criteria is subjective, but the idea was to avoid game with obvious flaws),
- available for free via Internet.

Dimenxian

Description

DIMENXIAN is a commercial game published by Tabula Digita, designed to teach algebra at high school. It proposes four different missions. Only the first activity of the first mission is analyzed here, available as a demo on the publisher's web site (Dimenxian, 2010). It concerns the use of coordinates in Mathematics.

The fiction: The game uses a science fiction scenario, in which the player takes the role of a commando member in charge of detecting and neutralizing a virus introduced by enemies on an island. The player has to obtain data in different locations and introduce them on computers to analyze them. In the first mission, Kep (the hero) is teleported on the island to collect data from five meteorological stations located at different points. A voiceover is used for communication between "the base" and the player's character.

The mechanics: The player is presented with two representation systems of the island (see Figure 2):

- A tridimensional (realistic) system, with all characteristics of the landscape where the character must evolve (objects, plants, water, etc.). The character is represented at the center, as a body seen from behind (third person perspective).

Figure 2. Screenshot of the game DIMENXIAN (© Tabula Digita. Used with permission)

- A bidimensional (formal) system, in the form of a 10x10 grid, with coordinates of rows and columns at left and bottom. The character is at the center and is represented as an arrow.

The player can move the character around using the keyboard. Also, the mouse controls the direction of the eyes (look to the floor, to the sky or in front, to the left or to the right).

The tridimensional representation system also has lines that represent the grid of the bidimensional system, and coordinates of some points.

In some cases, it is sufficient to look at the bidimensional system, but in others cases there are physical obstacles to avoid that are only represented on the tridimensional system. This forces the player to quit his/her trajectory temporarily to avoid the obstacle.

In some other cases, enemies come to kill the hero, and s/he must shoot them. This forces the player to quit his/her trajectory temporarily and concentrate on enemies.

Finally, when the player moves too far away from the target, two types of guidance aids are proposed:

- The environment itself is bound, so the player cannot move further away from the target.
- A head-up display is proposed to guide the movements of the player until s/he begins to follow the right direction for a certain duration.

The goal: Station locations are given as coordinates. The player must determine his/her own location in the coordinate system and move in the appropriate direction to reach the various stations.

Educational objectives: Learning to use coordinates to locate a point on a grid (pointing to the place on a grid represented by a pair of numbers), and determining the relative location of one point with respect to another given two sets of coordinates – left or right, up or down).

Articulation between the Educational Goal and the Game

The game is a good illustration of the winner strategy articulation. To succeed the missions, the strategy is:

- If my abscissa is greater than the abscissa of the station, then I must move to the left of the grid, otherwise to the right.
- If my ordinate is greater than the ordinate of the station, then I must move to the bottom of the grid, otherwise up.

The game mechanics ensures that only this strategy will enable the player to find the stations. Wrong strategies, for example going to the right if the own ordinate is greater than the ordinate of the station, will not produce a judgment feedback, but simply not reach the station. And other possible strategies, for example 'visually' guiding the movement, are unusable because the target objects do not appear on the representation systems until they are very close.

The goal of the game (finding a station) and the educational goal (using coordinates to guide movement) are embedded in the game mechanics in such a way that the goal of the game can only be reached if one reaches the educational goal. Using the coordinate system is not only a condition for the educational goal, but also for the goal of the game. The player can use different strategies, but only one of them will succeed, and strategies that get around the educational goal are unusable.

In the general case, in DIMENXIAN, the feedback of the system is not given in the form of judgments, but as natural consequences of the actions: getting lost, or reaching the stations. Exceptionally, when the player gets lost for too long, the heads-up display provides a more explicit and less natural feedback. This feedback attempts to reestablish a proper gaming situation in which the player makes effective use of the natural feedback from the environment, that is the 10x10 bi-dimensional grid.

Trivia Machine

Description

TRIVIA MACHINE is a trivia game published by *HIPsoft*, available through various game websites (Trivia Machine, 2010). The version evaluated here is the free demo download. The game consists of asking players questions in several domains.

The fiction: contrary to DIMENXIAN, the fictional elements are limited in TRIVIA MACHINE; no characters or tridimensional worlds. The game contains however an imaginary machine, represented in 2D (see Figure 3), which asks questions to the player.

Figure 3. Screenshot of the game TRIVIA MACHINE (© HipSoft. Used with permission)

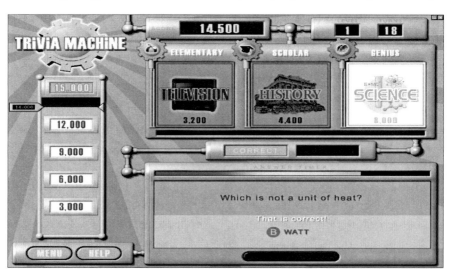

The mechanics: At each turn, the game generates a new set of three questions. Each question is associated to a domain and a level: easy, medium and hard (having more than three domains, these change at each turn). Each level is associated with points; the more difficult the question, the more points to be won. The player chooses a question according to its domain and level, receives the question, and then has one minute to pick the right answer from a possible four. If the answer is correct, the player wins the points. If it is wrong (or not given in one minute), the correct answer is given and some points are lost. A threshold mechanism in the scoring is implemented: when one threshold is reached, the player's score can never go below this threshold. Thus, at maximum the player looses the amount of the question, but often s/he is just set back to the previous threshold. The player can also simplify the task by limiting the number of choices to two, in which case it halves the score. When the player reaches a certain score, s/he moves to the next level.

The goal: gathering points and reaching the last level.

Educational objectives: Learning facts.

Articulation between the Educational Goal and the Game

As all trivia games, *TRIVIA MACHINE* is a typical case of an articulation between the educational goal and the game based on obstacles. The players get points depending on their ability to answer questions.

From a game perspective, *TRIVIA MACHINE* is a good game. It provides the player with a choice for the level and domain of questions, with an engaging dilemma between a difficult but rewarding question versus an easy but less rewarding one. Furthermore, this dynamic is combined with the choice of the domain, which depends on the player's self perception of expertise in the domain. Finally, suspense is created as the player approaches a threshold.

From a pedagogical perspective however, the product consists of a series of questions for the player, with a feedback limited to "right" or "wrong". No strategy is proposed to either understanding his/her mistakes or improving his/her skills. In terms of learner control, the mechanics of the game doesn't allow for players to deepen their study of a subject.

The metaphor of the machine, which increases the playfulness of the experience, does not however support the learning. The educational goal is not related to the machine in any manner.

In short, *TRIVIA MACHINE* manages to make learning fun, but fails to make learning efficient. It would be interesting to explore whether this game could be improved from a pedagogical point of view, without altering its gameplay. Would the addition of feedback be of any interest from a ludic point of view? Could the game memorize successes and failures in order to guide the player towards certain questions?

Energyville

Description

ENERGYVILLE is a *SIMCITY*-like game created by The Economist media organization and presented by Chevron, a global energy company. It is freely available on the Internet (Energyville, 2010). It aims to demonstrate that choices made in developing a global energy strategy has various impacts on the economy, environment, and energy security, and that this choice is not trivial.

The Fiction: ENERGYVILLE is based on a simulation of an imaginary city, inspired from the classical game *SIMCITY* (see Figure 4). The player plays the role of the "owner" of the city and in this role s/he has to make various choices regarding the energy supply of the city. Choices regarding energy sources visibly modify the fictional environment.

The mechanics: Two types of choices are performed by the user: choices of energy sources and global strategic decisions (favoring economy over environment for example).

According to the choices, the system determines events that occur until 2030 (a terrorist attack on a gas pipe, an innovation on wind production technology, etc.). The impact of the user's choices and the events on economy, environment and security is then calculated and displayed.

Contrary to a usual simulation, the player does not intervene when time goes on but only at two distinct instants: in 2007 and in 2015. The player is given two sets of feedbacks after these two interventions.

During the game, the player is given plenty of information on various energy sources such as solar, nuclear, gas, petroleum or biomass. S/he is also given the impact of these energy sources on economy, environment and security.

Goal of the game: At the end of the game, three curves are displayed, showing the evolution of impact on economy, environment and security over the whole period (2007-2030). A final score is also given, and compared with scores from other players. Although no explicit goal is given, this score appears to be the implicit goal: maximizing the global score and appearing in the top ten scores.

Educational objectives: Raising awareness on energy strategic management.

Articulation between the Educational Goal and the Game

As a simulation, *ENERGYVILLE* is primarily based on the first type of articulation: around the game mechanics. Indeed, the educational goal of the game is to teach the users the impacts of various choices on the evolution of a city. The knowledge is located in the mechanics itself, for example: adding more nuclear power is dangerous for security; dependence on oil and gas presents risks in case of terrorist attacks; wind and solar energy are better for the environment, etc.

Figure 4. Screenshot of the game ENERGYVILLE (© 2007-2010 Chevron Corporation. Used with permission)

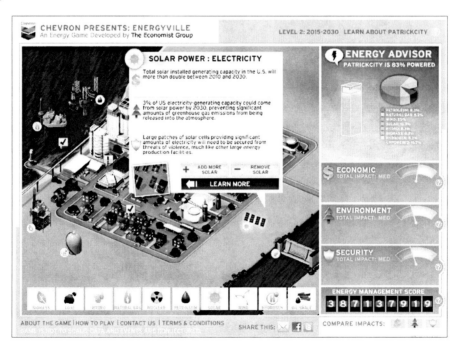

In *ENERGYVILLE*, the articulation between the educational goal and the game also occurs around the context. A significant amount of information is given via text bubbles and information screens, which are accessible only in the context of the game. For example, when the user is about to choose between wind and oil, s/he can access factual data related to these types of energy. Providing such information in the context of the game, when it is needed by the player or at least when it is related to what the player has in mind, increases the chance of memorization. This is similar to the concept of "just in time information", promoted by some pedagogical strategies in Instructional Design (Merriënboer, Clark, de Croock, 2002).

TOWARDS INSTRUCTIONAL GAME DESIGN

Given the four types of game-knowledge articulations discussed and illustrated above, that stem from our definition of a game, the next step consists in deriving useful guidelines for designing educational games.

As a preliminary remark, the theoretical discussion above illustrates the fact that an educational game is a very complex learning object. As a game, it contains at least one specific system of signs that is dynamic (the game mechanics) and often several systems of signs superimposed to it (e.g. the fictional word, the iconic language, the language included in the texts, etc.). The adding of pedagogical goals to a game adds another layer of complexity. This complexity of educational games tends to be overlooked, but if the goal is to be able to optimally convert a learning objective into a game, this complexity must be understood.

It is certainly too preliminary to derive a whole Instructional Game Design model, from our theoretical approach. However, some recommendations can already been proposed, which are direct outcomes of the theoretical discussion above.

Recommendation 1: First Choose an Articulation between the Game and the Knowledge

The way the knowledge is embedded within the game should constitute the initial design step. One type of articulation must be chosen by the designer as the main design principle. This choice depends of course of the type of knowledge included in the instructional goal, but also on the time and effort available for the project. Starting from an existing game is, most of the time, suboptimal, because, as we discussed above, if the knowledge is specific, the game must be specific as well. But designing a totally new game requires much more time and effort, which is not always available. Although we recommend integrated types of articulations (see next recommendation), other articulations might be an alternative for some projects.

Recommendation 2: Try to Invent Relevant Game Mechanics

Any process of Instructional Design relies on an analysis of the learning goals and the set of knowledge targeted by these goals. This being accomplished, if one wants to use a game for an educational goal, one should first try to fit into one of the first two categories above (systemic learning, winner strategies). Indeed, only these two categories really exploit the systemic nature of games, and their ability to really situate learning in a relevant activity in context.

Such a game mechanics is thus quite specific to the educational goal. Even if a lot of games have been invented so far, it is probable that existing game mechanics do not really fit the educational goal, hence the necessity to invent a specific game's mechanics, whenever it is possible.

In some cases, this game mechanics can be naturally derived from the idea of simulating the domain itself. For example, learning Newtonian laws would involve objects (e.g. spaceships) moving in a space according to these laws. In others cases, it might seem difficult to find a system of rules that is relevant to the domain. Note however that the rules of the game do not need to be the strict model of the domain itself. For example, suppose you want to teach the duration of various notes in music, that a time span of the quarter-note is half of the time span of the half-note. Starting from the shooting gameplay, so popular in videogames, one can imagine a game where a player should shoot on a half note in order to decompose it into two quarter-notes in order to produce the desired rhythm. The game mechanics would implement the fact that "two quarter notes make a half note" as a dynamical system which is not musical but still relevant.

Applying the "winner strategy" approach is different. We are not directly looking for a game mechanics but we are searching for a problem that can be solved (the game's goal) within an environment governed by a mechanics where:

- A large choice of actions and strategies is available;
- Finding the set of actions that reach the goal requires having the knowledge specified by the educational goal;
- It is not possible to reach the game's goal without this knowledge;
- Whenever possible the feedback for wrong actions should appear as natural consequences of the actions, rather than judgments; and
- Learning can be scaffolded from easy goals to more complex ones otherwise learning could be too difficult.

It is not an easy task to design such an environment. A key stage is to identify the wrong knowledge and strategies used by learners and design the environment such that these wrong strategies are inefficient (Margolinas, 1993). This requires certain knowledge of both the field and the didactics of the field.

Recommendation 3: Analyze the Learning Tasks Independently from the Game Mechanics (in Some Types of Educational Games)

In the case of an educational game where the educational goal and the game mechanics are articulated around obstacles or around the context (categories 3 and 4 above), how can the validity of different propositions formulated during the design phase be assessed? According to the theoretical analysis above, if knowledge is not embedded into the game mechanics, the game component of the software can be considered as an additional layer on top of a learning strategy existing by itself. This additional layer is meant to improve the receptivity of the learner, in terms of motivation and context. However, the designer has to be aware that this additional layer does not substitute a learning strategy. In other words, one has to analyze a design by considering only the learning events, and determining whether they constitute a valuable learning organization or not. The Trivia Machine above is a trivial (!) negative example: once the game mechanics is withdrawn, only a very poor learning organization and strategy remains. The game TyperShark, also discussed above is a more positive example, since repeatedly training a learner to type words is not a bad strategy, given the motor nature of the task. However, it does not reach the pedagogical quality of a real typing instructional design, which includes teaching proper hand and finger positions on the keyboard.

Furthermore this additional layer can be resource consuming, resources being time or effort. Regarding time, games are often acclaimed for their potential for learning, but efficiency is rarely questioned. A game that teaches equally well than another multimedia product but that takes two or three times more time is not necessarily interesting from an instructional point of view. This aspect is rarely discussed in the literature on game and learning. Regarding effort, the game mechanics itself can require considerable attention and effort to the learner, at the expense of the learning itself. In that case, the game is a distraction from the main educational goal. The designer must be sure that the ratio between the player's attention/effort to play and the player's attention/effort to learn is not too high.

Recommendation 4: Define the Status of the Player Regarding Learning

Given the paradox discussed above, the status of the learner must be decided beforehand. We believe that in general, the "willing suspension of learning goals" hypothesis is the most valuable strategy because it enables the learner to keep his/her general motivation to learn (if any…) while concentrating his/her effort on the game itself, and being engaged in it. In terms of design, it means that the educational goal has to be announced before the active gaming session itself. During the learner's/player's activity, the educational goal does not need to be regularly restated.

In term of motivation, we are not making the claim that "learning is boring" to justify that learners should forget about learning during play. Rather, we are claiming that the motivation to learn is not necessarily correlated to the motivation to play and that for the game to be efficient, both in terms of learning and pleasure, it has to be intrinsically motivating. Thus, when assessing the quality of an educational game, the only motivation that must be measured is the motivation to play. In other words, a question such as "did you like learning mathematics with this game" is biased, because only learners who like mathematics will tend to answer positively. A better question is "did you have fun with this game?" The assessment regarding learning can then be based on acquired knowledge.

Recommendation 5: Do Not use Games in Isolation

We have stressed that what makes games particularly relevant for learning is their systemic nature and the fact that the user can act on the dynamical system underlying the game. Therefore, as for simulations (Fanning and Gaba, 2007), debriefing is needed as games are not good for reflexive learning and conceptualization. A single active learning session requires an additional stage, where learners are encouraged to verbalize and assess their contextual skills in order to build stable and transmittable knowledge. As reported by Rieber (2002), "the use of games generally interferes with explicit learning (ability to answer test questions), but improves participants' tacit learning (ability to perform other tasks embedded in the simulation)".

In Didactics, as explained above, the active learning phase is followed by two additional phases: formulation – verbalization of learner's strategy – and validation – assessment of the validity of the strategy – (Brousseau, 1998). The importance of debriefing in instructional games is also reported by Hays (2005): "Debriefing gives the learners the opportunity to reflect on their experience with the game and understand how this experience supported the instructional objectives of the course or program of instruction."

The necessity of a classical debriefing is problematic as it often required a specific expertise from the teacher. Therefore, designing a larger software that includes game sessions and debriefing sessions is a promising direction to explore. How to alternate these two kinds of sessions is an important issue, that has been experimented recently (Sutter-Widmer, 2010).

FUTURE RESEARCH DIRECTIONS

This research is still preliminary. We intend to extend it in at least three directions.

First, the above discussion remained at a general level. In order to provide more specific guidelines to the design of educational games, one needs to take into account the type of skill that is targeted by the learning objective. Starting from an existing classification of knowledge types (Carson, 2004; Paquette, 2005, p. 196), we expect to be able to precisely inform design choices according to each knowledge type concerned by the game. Such a classification will resemble existing attempts to match knowledge types to learning games types (Garris, Ahlers & Driskell, 2002; Wilson et al., 2009; Wouters, van der Spek & Van Oostendorp, 2009), but with stronger theoretical foundations.

Second, in order to empirically verify the principles that have been enunciated, we need to design a cognitive model of educational game playing. According to this model, predictions related to the relative efficiency of one design choice versus another could be made and empirically tested. Currently, experimental research has found little evidence regarding the benefits of games for learning (Hays, 2005; Egenfeldt-Nielsen, 2006). We expect that such a model could greatly help guide experimental investigation towards more precise comparisons between conditions.

Third, a better knowledge of the fundamentals of educational games should form the basis of new authoring tools for educational game making. Existing tools for making educational games are oriented either towards games but do not include any pedagogical principles (e.g. *Game Factory, Game Maker, Neverwinter Night* toolset, etc.) or towards multimedia tools (*Authorware, Adobe Captivate*, etc.). With a specialized authoring tool, we both expect to decrease development time, and improve the quality of the final result, because the tool will naturally foster proper use of games for learning. The ability to design such an authoring tool will be an indicator of the feasibility of Instructional Game Design, as a general strategy for improving current university and professional curricula.

CONCLUSION

Despite the large amount of research and development that use, promote and analyze games for learning, there exists limited experimental or theoretical work that supports the hypothesis that games are beneficial for learning, beyond general considerations. This lack is also correlated to a lack of understanding of what a game is. Therefore, this paper attempted to establish some fundamental principles of the utilization of games in instruction.

From a formal redefinition of games and a careful examination of pedagogical principles currently in use in instructional theory and practice, we found some answers to our initial question (the relation between game, knowledge and learning):

- Game playing always involves learning, but this statement does not inform us how to design a game for a given learning objective.
- At the level of user intention, gaming and learning are fundamentally incompatible, a phenomenon that we term the paradox of educational games.
- Within an educational game, we distinguished four types of articulation between the educational goal (target knowledge) and the game itself. These articulations are around: the game mechanics, the winner strategy, obstacles, and context.
- Even if some of these articulations exploit games more efficiently than others, they may be combined to improve learning.

These considerations have been put in practice into the analysis of existing games and have been used to enunciate some recommendations.

Our findings constitute premises of a yet to be invented methodology, that we have termed "Instructional Game Design". While (good) games are easy to play, they are very hard to design. Instruction as well is quite difficult to design.

Combining the two still adds other constraints which make IGD a very challenging task. This challenge is usually underestimated, leading to a weak integration between learning and playing.

REFERENCES

Amory, A. (2001). Building an educational adventure game: Theory, design and lessons. *Journal of Interactive Learning Research, 12*(2/3), 249–263.

Amory, A. (2007). Game object model version II: A theoretical framework for educational game development. *Educational Technology Research and Development, 55,* 51–77. doi:10.1007/s11423-006-9001-x

Becker, K. (2006). *Design paradox: Instructional games.* Paper presented at the Future Play, The International Conference on the Future of Game Design and Technology, The University of Western Ontario, London, ON, Canada, October 10 - 12 2006.

Brousseau, G. (1998). *Théorie des situations didactiques.* Grenoble, France: La Pensée Sauvage.

Brown, J. S., Collins, A., & Duguid, P. (1989). Situated cognition and the culture of learning. *Educational Research, 18*(1), 32–42.

Caillois, R. (1958). *Les Jeux et les Hommes.* Paris: Gallimard Editions.

Carson, R. N. (2004). A taxonomy of knowledge types for use in curriculum design. *Interchange, 25*(1), 59–79. doi:10.1023/B:INCH.0000039020.49283.90

Ciavarro, C., Dobson, M., & Goodman, D. (2008). Implicit learning as a design strategy for learning games: Alert hockey. *Computers in Human Behavior, 24*(6), 2862–2872. doi:10.1016/j.chb.2008.04.011

Connolly, T. M., & Stansfield, M. H. (2006). Using games-based e-learning technologies in overcoming difficulties in teaching Information Systems. *Journal of IT Education, 5,* 459–476.

Crawford, C. (1982). *The art of computer game design.* Retrieved January 29, 2010, from http://www.vancouver.wsu.edu/fac/peabody/game-book/Coverpage.html

De Corte, E. (1995). Learning theory and instructional science. In Reimann, P., & Spada, H. (Eds.), *Learning in humans and machines: Towards an interdisciplinary learning science* (pp. 97–108). Oxford: Elseiver Science Ltd.

de Freitas, S., & Oliver, M. (2006). How can exploratory learning with games and simulations within the curriculum be most effectively evaluated? *Computers & Education, 46*(3), 249–264. doi:10.1016/j.compedu.2005.11.007

Dickey, M. (2005). Engaging by design: How engagement strategies in popular computer and video games can inform instructional design. *Educational Technology Research and Development, 53,* 67–83. doi:10.1007/BF02504866

Dimenxian (2010). *Dimenxian.* Retrieved June 4, 2010, from http://www.dimensionu.com/dimu/home/dimugames.aspx

Eco, U. (1979). *Lector in Fabula.* Milan: Bompiani.

Egenfeldt-Nielsen, S. (2004). Practical barriers in using educational computer games. *Horizon, 12*(1), 18–21. doi:10.1108/10748120410540454

Egenfeldt-Nielsen, S. (2006). Overview of research on the educational use of video games. *Digital Kompetanse, 1*(3), 184-213. Retrieved January 29, 2010, from http://www.itu.dk/~sen/papers/game-overview.pdf

Energyville. (2010). *Will you join us?* Retrieved June 4, 2010, from http://www.willyoujoinus.com/energyville/

Fanning, R., & Gaba, D. (2007). The role of debriefing in simulation-based learning. *Simulation in Healthcare, 2*(2), 115–125. doi:10.1097/SIH.0b013e3180315539

Garris, R., Ahlers, R., & Driskell, J. E. (2002). Games, motivation, and learning: A research and practice model. *Simulation & Gaming, 33*(4), 441–467. doi:10.1177/1046878102238607

Gokhale, A. A. (1996). Effectiveness of computer simulation for enhancing higher order thinking. *Journal of Industrial Teacher Education, 33*(4), 36–46.

Gredler, M. E. (2003). Games and simulations and their relationships to learning. In Jonassen, D. (Ed.), *Handbook of research for educational communications and technology* (2nd ed., pp. 571–581). Mahwah, NJ: Lawrence Erlbaum Associates.

Greimas, A.-J., & Courtès, J. (1982). *Sémiotique. Dictionnaire raisonné de la théorie du langage.* Paris: Hachette.

Habgood, M. P. J. (2005). *Zombie Division: Intrinsic integration in digital learning games.* Paper presented at the 2005 Human Centred Technology Workshop, Brighton, UK.

Habgood, M. P. J., Ainsworth, S. E., & Benford, S. (2005). Endogenous fantasy and learning in digital games. *Simulation & Gaming, 36*(4), 483–498. doi:10.1177/1046878105282276

Hays, R. T. (2005). *The effectiveness of instructional games: A literature review and discussion.* (Technical Report 2005-004). Orlando, FL: Training Systems Division, Naval Air Warfare Center.

Horwitz, P. (2000). Designing computer models that teach. *@CONCORD Newsletter, 4*(1). Retrieved January 29, 2010, from http://www.concord.org/publications/newsletter/2000winter/comp-models.html

Huizinga, J. (1938). *Homo ludens. Essai sur la fonction sociale du jeu.* Paris: Gallimard.

Jones, M. G. (1998). *Creating engagement in computer-based learning environments.* Paper presented at the Instructional Technology Forum. Retrieved January 29, 2010, from http://it.coe.uga.edu/itforum/paper30/paper30.html

Juul, J. (2003). The game, the player, the world: Looking for a heart of gameness. In M. Copier & J. Raessens (Eds.), *Level up: Digital Games Research Conference Proceedings,* (pp. 30-45). Utrecht: University of Utrecht.

Kiili, K. (2005). *Educational game design: Experiential gaming model revised. Research report 4.* Pori, Finland: Tampere University of Technology.

Kirriemuir, J., & McFarlane, A. (2004). *Literature review in games and learning.* Nesta Futurelab Series. Report 8. Retrieved January 29, 2010, from http://www.futurelab.org.uk/resources/documents/lit_reviews/Games_Review.pdf

Klinkenberg, J.-M. (2000). *Précis de sémiotique générale.* Paris: Le Seuil.

Laborde, C. & Capponi, B. (1994). Cabri-géomètre constituant d'un milieu pour l'apprentissage de la notion de figure géométrique. *Recherches en Didactique des Mathématiques, 14*(1.2), 165–210.

Malone, T. W., & Lepper, M. R. (1987). Making learning fun: A taxonomy of intrinsic motivations for learning. In Snow, R. E., & Farr, M. J. (Eds.), *Aptitude, learning, and instruction III: Cognitive and affective process analysis* (pp. 223–253). Hillsdale, NJ: Lawrence Erlbaum Associates.

Margolinas, C. (1993). *De l'importance du vrai et du faux dans la classe de mathématiques.* Grenoble, France: La Pensée Sauvage.

McKee, R. (1997). *Story: Substance, structure, style, and the principles of screenwriting.* New York: HarperCollins.

Merrill, M. D. (2002). First principles of instruction: A synthesis. In Reiser, R. A., & Dempsey, J. V. (Eds.), *Trends and issues in instructional design and technology*. Columbus, OH: Merrill Prentice Hall.

Merrill, M. D. (2008). Converting e sub3-learning to e 3rd power-learning: An alternative instructional design method. In Carliner, S., & Shank, P. (Eds.), *The e-learning handbook: Past promises, present challenges* (pp. 359–400). San Francisco: Pfeiffer.

Paquette, G. (2005). *L'ingénierie pédagogique. Pour construire l'apprentissage en réseau*. Sainte-Foy, QC, Canada: Presse de l'université du Québec.

Piaget, J. (1959). *La naissance de l'intelligence chez l'enfant*. Neuchâtel: Delachaux et Niestlé.

Prensky, M. (2001). *Digital game-based learning*. New York: McGraw Hill.

Quinn, C. N. (1997). *Engaging learning*. Instructional Technical Forum. Retrieved January 29, 2010, from http://itech1.coe.uga.edu/itforum/paper18/paper18.html

Reigeluth, C. M. (1999). What is instructional design theory and how is it changing? In Reigeluth, C. M. (Ed.), *Instructional design theories and models: A new paradigm of instructional theory* (pp. 5–29). Hillsdale, NJ: Lawrence Erlbaum Associates.

Rieber, L. P. (1996). Seriously considering play: Designing interactive learning environments based on the blending of microworlds, simulations, and games. *Educational Technology Research and Development, 44*(2), 43–58. doi:10.1007/BF02300540

Rieber, L. P. (2002). *Supporting discovery-based learning within simulations*. Paper presented at the International Workshop on Dynamic Visualizations and Learning, Tübingen, Germany. Retrieved January 29, 2010, from http://www.iwm-kmrc.de/workshops/visualization/rieber.pdf

Rieber, L. P. (2004). Microworlds. In Jonassen, D. (Ed.), *Handbook of research for educational communications and technology* (2nd ed., pp. 583–603). Mahwah, NJ: Lawrence Erlbaum Associates.

Salen, K., & Zimmerman, E. (2003). *Rules of play: Game design fundamentals*. Cambridge, MA: MIT Press.

Souriau, E. (1950). *Les Deux-cent-mille situations dramatiques*. Paris: Flammarion.

Sutter-Widmer, D. (2010). *Se plonger dans un jeu pour mieux apprendre? Théorie, conception et expérimentation*. Unpublished doctoral dissertation, TECFA, FPSE, University of Geneva, Switzerland.

Szilas, N., & Sutter-Widmer, D. (2009). *Mieux comprendre la notion d'intégration entre l'apprentissage et le jeu*. Paper presented at the Workshop. Jeux Sérieux: conception et usages, in conjunction with the 4ème Conférence francophone sur les Environnements Informatiques pour l'Apprentissage Humain (EIAH), Le Mans, France.

Trivia Machine. (2009). *Trivia machine*. Retrieved January 29, 2010, from http://www.hipsoft.com/tm.jsp

Vale, E. (1973). *The technique of screenplay writing (3rd ed.)*. New-York: Universal Library Edition.

Van Merrienboer, J., & Clark, R. & de Croock. (2002). Blueprints for complex learning: The 4C/ID-model. *Educational Technology Research and Development, 50*(2), 39–64. doi:10.1007/BF02504993

Wilson, K. A., Bedwell, W. L., Lazzara, E. H., Salas, E., Burke, C. S., & Estock, J. L. (2009). Relationships between game attributes and learning outcomes: Review and research proposals. *Simulation & Gaming, 40*, 217–266. doi:10.1177/1046878108321866

Wouters, P., van der Spek, E., & Van Oostendorp, H. (2009). Current practices in serious game research: A review from a learning outcomes perspective. In Connolly, T. M., Stansfield, M., & Boyle, L. (Eds.), *Games-based learning advancements for multisensory human computer interfaces: Techniques and effective practices* (pp. 232–250). Hershey, PA: IGI Global.

KEY TERMS AND DEFINITIONS

Contextual Coupling: Articulation between game and knowledge in which knowledge to be learned lies outside the game mechanics.

Game: A game is a dynamical system of signs in which the player acts, independently of any consequence outside the system, in order to reach a goal assigned by the game.

Instructional Game Design (IGD): The goal of IGD is to find a methodology making it possible to produce an efficient learning game from any given knowledge domain, if such a game is possible.

Loose Coupling: Articulation between game and knowledge in which rules that involve the knowledge to be learned are loosely connected to the main rules of the game mechanics.

Paradox of Educational Games: Games are played for the sake of playing, regardless of the consequences of the playing activity outside of the game while learning is useful and must be perceived as such in order to be efficient.

Systemic Learning: Articulation between game and knowledge in which knowledge lies in the rules of the game mechanics.

Winner Strategies: Articulation between game and knowledge in which learning occurs when the game proposes a non didactical system in which knowledge is required reach the game's goal, and in which this goal cannot be reached without the knowledge.

Section 3
Psychological Approach to Game−Based Learning:
Emotions, Motivation and Engagement

This section focuses on a psychological approach to GBL, and explains how emotions and motivation can be harnessed to improve learning in video games.

Chapter 12
ARGuing for Multilingual Motivation in Web 2.0:
An Evaluation of a Large-Scale European Pilot

Thomas Hainey
University of the West of Scotland, Scotland

Thomas Connolly
University of the West of Scotland, Scotland

Mark Stansfield
University of the West of Scotland, Scotland

Liz Boyle
University of the West of Scotland, Scotland

ABSTRACT

While there are some teachers who are dubious about the benefits of gaming in education, language teachers make great use of simulation/gaming methodologies, and there are many supporting textbooks. While many of the simulations/games used are non-computer based, during recent years, the computer game has become an important development in popular culture. During the same period, there has been an appreciation that computer games can play a significant role in education. This chapter explores the use of one particular type of computer game called an Alternate Reality Game (ARG), a form of interactive narrative, often involving multiple media and game elements. The chapter has developed an ARG to motivate secondary school students to learn a modern foreign language and has piloted this game across Europe in 2009. This chapter will review the empirical literature associated with the utilisation of ARGs for educational purposes and will focus on language learning. The chapter will then present a quantitative and qualitative analysis of student motivation in the pilot study using a developed evaluation framework for games-based learning. The evaluation will focus on learner motivations, aspects of the ARG, player perceptions, skills acquired, attitudes and qualitative data. The chapter will reflect on this analysis and provide directions for future research.

DOI: 10.4018/978-1-60960-495-0.ch012

INTRODUCTION

As noted by Crookall (2007), language teachers make great use of simulation/gaming methodologies and there are many supporting textbooks and research papers that present various forms of role-play, games, simulations, and other exercises. (e.g. Gaudart, 1999; Garcia-Carbonell, Rising, Montero, & Watts, 2001; Halleck, 2007).

Over the last 40 years computer games have become an increasingly popular form of entertainment and have replaced some traditional leisure activities (Connolly, Stansfield & Hainey, 2007). Games-based learning has captured the interest of educationalists as it is considered to be a potentially motivational approach for learning even at a supplementary level. Games-based learning has been applied in a wide variety of different fields including medicine (Beale, Kato, Marin-Bowling, Guthrie & Cole, 2007; Lennon, 2006; Roubidoux, 2005), business and knowledge management (Christoph, 2007; Virtual University Website, 2010; Virtual Leader Website, 2010), military training (America's Army Website, 2010), science and mathematics (Squire, Barnett, Grant, and Higginbotham, 2004; Young and Upitis, 1999; Habgood, 2007; Nelson, 2007; Barab, Warren & Ingram-Goble, 2006) promotion of language education (Johnson and Wu, 2007; Rankin, Gold and Gooch, 2006), software engineering, computer science and information systems (Waraich, 2004; Oh Navarro & Van der Hoek, 2005; Shaw & Dermoudy, 2005; Ford & Minsker, 2003; Jain & Boehm, 2006; Zhu, Wang & Tan, 2007). However, two of the current issues with games-based learning are the dearth of empirical evidence to support the approach and the lack of frameworks to use for evaluating games-based learning applications. We were very conscious of these problems at the outset of the project and carried out research to ensure that we had an appropriate framework for evaluation. In this chapter, we explore the use of one particular type of computer game called an Alternate Reality Game (ARG), a form of inter-active narrative, often involving multiple media and game elements, to tell a story that may be affected by participants' ideas or actions (Connolly *et al*, 2008). We have developed an ARG to motivate secondary school students to learn a modern foreign language and have piloted this game across Europe in 2009.

This chapter presents the developed evaluation framework used to evaluate the ARG, some of the problems teaching modern foreign languages (MFLs), and some examples of the use of games in language education. We then discuss ARGs and the use of ARGs within an educational context. We then describe the evaluation study of the *Tower of Babel* ARG that was piloted from 22 April to 30 April 2009 involving 328 students and 95 teachers from 28 schools across 17 countries and provide both a quantitative and qualitative analysis of student motivation in the pilot. We complete the chapter with a discussion of the findings and directions for future research.

PREVIOUS RESEARCH

In this section, we briefly discuss the utilised evaluation framework to evaluate the ARG, intrinsic motivation, the problems and importance of teaching modern foreign languages before discussing previous use of computer games in teaching second languages.

Utilised Evaluation Framework

Connolly, Stansfield and Hainey (2009) reviewed the literature and formulated a new evaluation framework for GBL (Figure 1). The purpose of the framework is to identify the main potential evaluation categories of games-based learning available in the scientific literature. The categories do not necessarily have to be viewed in isolation but as a collective whole depending on what is to be evaluated. The framework can be used in both a developmental sense to inform design during the

Figure 1. Evaluation framework for effective games-based learning

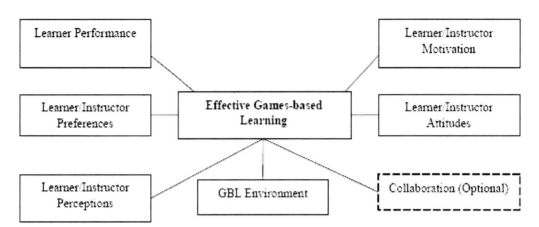

implementation and embedding a games-based learning environment into curricula in a formative evaluation sense and also points to examples of individual analytical measurements already present in the literature for focusing on an evaluation at the end of development in a summative evaluation sense.

A brief description will be provided of each category: *Learner Performance*– Encompasses pedagogy from the perspective of the learner and is to evaluate aspects of learner performance. It is primarily concerned with whether there is an improvement in learner performance. *Motivation*– The particular motivations of the learner using the intervention, the level of interest in participating in the intervention, participation over a period of time and determining what particular motivations are most important. *Perceptions* – Encompasses perceptions associated with the learner such as overview of time, how real the game is, it's correspondence with reality, whether the games-based learning intervention represents a holistic view of a particular organisation or process, game complexity, advice quality and level of self reported proficiency at playing games etc. *Attitudes*– Learner and instructor attitudes towards various elements that may alter the effectiveness of the games-based learning intervention. Elements include: learner attitudes towards

the taught subject, learner attitudes towards games, instructor attitudes towards the incorporation of games into the curricula etc. *Preferences* – This category is designed to consider learner and instructor preferences during a games-based learning intervention. There are different learning styles (Kolb, 1984) therefore it stands to reason that different learners have different preferences, for example, preference for medium used when teaching the material. *Collaboration* – Collaboration is optional when considering games-based learning as it is dictated by whether the game is played on an individual level, cooperative group level, competitive group level etc. The main ways of evaluating collaboration are through log files monitoring interaction, mapping team aspects to learner comments, measuring the regularity and level of collaboration and learner group reflection essays. *Games-Based Learning Environment category* – This category encompasses all aspects that could potentially be evaluated about the games-based learning environment. It is one of the most complicated categories as it can be divided into five subcategories: environment, scaffolding, usability, level of social presence and deployment. The framework was highly instrumental in formulating the pre-tests and post-tests for the evaluation of the ARG. The framework has also been used to evaluate a different type of game to teach requirements collection and analysis at tertiary education level (Hainey, Connolly & Boyle, 2009a)

Intrinsic Motivation

Probably the best known distinction in motivation research is that between intrinsic and extrinsic motivation (Deci an&d Ryan, 2000). Intrinsically motivated behaviours are carried out because they are rewarding in themselves, while extrinsically motivated behaviours are carried out because of the desire for some external reward, such as money, praise or recognition from others. Intrinsic motivation is thought to be more successful in engaging students in effective learning because intrinsically motivated students want to study for its own sake, they are interested in the subject and want to develop their knowledge and competence. This distinction has been used by designers of educational computer games, notably Malone and Lepper (1987) who argued that intrinsic motivation is more important in designing engaging games. They suggested that intrinsic motivation is created by four individual factors: challenge, fantasy, curiosity and control and three interpersonal factors: cooperation, competition, and recognition. Interestingly these factors also describe what makes a good game, irrespective of its educational qualities.

The primary purpose for the discussion of intrinsic motivation in this study is due to the fact that an adapted version of Malone and Lepper's 1987 framework of intrinsic motivation is utilised to gain measurements. The framework uses the original interpersonal and individual factors. On an individual level:

- **Challenge:** an appropriate level of difficulty and challenge, multiple goals for winning, constant feedback and sufficient randomness;

- **Fantasy:** an appropriate level of immersion by assuming a particular role and dealing with related responsibilities;
- **Curiosity:** providing sensory stimulation to ensure prolonged participation; and
- **Control:** the ability to select choices and observe the consequences of these choices.

On an interpersonal level:

- **Cooperation:** assist others to achieve common goals;
- **Competition:** compare their performance to the performance of other players;
- **Recognition:** a sense of satisfaction when accomplishments are recognised.

Additional factors were included based on qualitative answers from previous studies (Connolly, Boyle, Stansfield & Hainey, 2006; Connolly, Boyle, Stansfield & Hainey, 2007; Connolly, Boyle & Hainey, 2007) including the following: pleasure, feel good, prevented boredom, relaxation, escape stresses of life, leisure, release tension, avoid other activities and emotional stimulation.

There has been a number of previous questionnaire/survey studies performed to find out peoples, reasons and motivations for playing computer games. Gibson, Halverson and Riedel (2007) performed a survey of 228 "pre-service" students to ascertain perceptions and attitudes in relation to simulations and games. 80% of respondents were white females. 46% believed that simulations and games could be a very important learning tool and 19% believed that they could be an important learning tool. Only 7% believed that they were of little or no importance. Males were more negative about the potential of games in learning. 53% or males were positive where 70% of females were positive. There was no notable generation gap between the respondents. Whitton (2007) performed a study with 200 participants to examine gaming preferences, attitudes towards games in HE and motivations. 63.1% reported that they would find games positively motivating for learning, 28.3% not motivating either way and 8.6% demotivating. Eglesz, Fekete, Kiss, and Izsó (2005) performed a study with two surveys, one online survey with 843 participants and a second with 102 participants. The studies found that woman play computer games significantly less than men and prefer RPG games while men prefer action, adventure simulation and sports games. Yee (2006) performed a study of 30,000 participants over a 3 year period particularly focusing on motivations and experiences of users of MMORPGs and found significant differences between males and females in relation to relationship, manipulation, immersion, escapism and achievement factors. The results of this study were later used to formulate an empirical model of player motivations in online games (Yee, 2007).

Problems Teaching MFL

According to figures obtained by one of the political parties in the UK, only 48% of pupils in England took a modern European language at GCSE level in 2007, down from 83% in 2000. There is also a significant drop off in students who then progress to A-level and an even smaller number who move on to university to study languages (Connolly *et al*, 2008). This decline has been recognised for some time despite a number of initiatives to reverse this trend. Among other proposals, the UK government is now proposing to make languages compulsory in primary schools. This is an unfortunate situation that has developed as modern foreign languages can provide an enhanced learning experience. MFL teaching promotes young people's cultural development by providing them with insights into cultural differences and with opportunities to relate these to their own experience and to consider different cultural and linguistic traditions, attitudes and behaviours. Effective teaching in MFLs can make a significant contribution to young people's ability to value diversity and challenge racism. Students

who are learning a second language can struggle with developing conversational proficiency for a variety of reasons; for example, lack of confidence and inhibitions, particularly in front of peers (Hudson & Bruckman, 2002). To overcome this, language teachers attempt to engage students in target language conversations to help build their confidence and develop language competency.

GAMES IN LANGUAGE EDUCATION

There is a dearth of empirical evidence supporting the approach of games-based learning (GBL) throughout the GBL literature (Connolly, Stansfield & Hainey, 2007; de Freitas, 2006). This problem is particularly apparent and exacerbated when focusing in on a particular area such as language education. A highly extensive literature review was carried out by Connolly *et al* (in press) particularly focusing on the learning value and skill enhancement of gaming and methods of measuring the resultant outcomes and impacts. This literature review returned approximately 7,000 articles, 127 were considered relevant to the primary research criteria of providing some form of empirical evidence. Two of these studies used a computer game and were considered relevant in the discipline of language learning.

1. Yip and Kwan (2006) compared vocabulary learning for a group who played online vocabulary games versus a group who learned vocabulary via conventional activities. They found that the GBL group performed significantly better. Three different types of puzzle games were used including tile moving games (similar to the well-known 8 puzzle game) and crossword puzzles; games that require good motor skills, such as 'space invaders'; games such as card matching that required a good memory. All three are of the drill and practice type games.

2. Miller and Hegelheimer (2006) performed a study to show how the popular authentic simulation, The Sims, can be adapted to enhance vocabulary learning through supporting materials. 18 participants were divided into three conditions: a group that received mandatory supplementary materials, a group with voluntary access to supplementary materials and a group with no access to supplementary materials. The results showed that when support for the game is properly structured then the game can be effective for vocabulary acquisition. There was a statistically significant increase in vocabulary acquisition for the first group.

We now briefly describe in some detail three different types of computer games that have been used for language education.

Tactical Language and Culture Training System

The Tactical Language and Culture Training System (http://www.tacticallanguage.com/) by Alelo Inc. provides self-paced foreign language training programs focusing on verbal communication, non-verbal communication and cultural protocols such as: awareness and sensitivity, politeness, gestures and etiquette. The technology uses immersive, interactive 3D lessons and games to teach what to say, how to say it and when to say it. This has interesting military applications in terms of enabling military personnel to adapt more quickly to foreign cultures when serving abroad and has the potential of equipping them with the knowledge to diffuse potentially violent situations peacefully. There are currently three different versions of the system including: Tactical Iraqi for Iraqi Arabic, Tactical Pashto for Afghanistan and Tactical French for Sahel Africa.

Tactical Dari for Afghanistan is scheduled for release soon. Each of the courses consists of three main learning modules: the skill builder, the arcade game and the mission game. The skill builder focuses on task-oriented communication skills (vocabularies, pronunciation, grammar and cultural knowledge) using exercises and quizzes involving listening and speaking to the computer in a one-to-one interactive tutoring environment. The arcade mode allows the player to learn a variety of topics in an interactive 3D environment including: direction, colours and numbers. The player earns points by successfully navigating through a maze with two modes supported, one where the player is listening and the other where the player is speaking. AI techniques process the learners' speech to evaluate actions and allow the NPCs to provide hints when necessary. The mission mode is an immersive, interactive 3D environment simulating authentic social and military situations. The player has to use the dialogs, gestures and non-gesture cultural interactions with intelligent virtual characters. For example, in Tactical Iraqi the player must utilise the skills learned to perhaps search the home of a local resident. The mission game does not follow a narrow script and the outcome is dependent on what the player says and does.

Johnson and Wu (2008) report on a study that suggests strong evidence for the effectiveness of Tactical Iraqi and examines the experience of the 2nd and 3rd Battalion, 7th US Marine Regiment (2/7 and 3/7 Marines) who trained with the game prior to a tour of duty in Iraq. 3/7 Battalion did not suffer any combat casualties and officers believed that the game increased operational capacity in terms of increased language proficiency and an increased understanding of the situation resulting in better relationships with the local people. 49 participants from regiment 2/7 took part in the initial assessment of Tactical Iraqi; the marines from regiment 3/7 have been re-stationed to Afghanistan where they will be participating in a similar experiment with Tactical Dari. Figure 2 shows two screen shots of Tactical Iraqi.

Figure 2. Screen shots of Tactical Iraqi

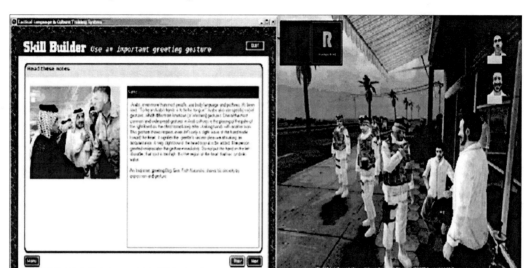

EverQuest II

Rankin, Gold and Gooch (2006) performed a "highly preliminary" study using EverQuest II to support the teaching English as a second language. EverQuest II is a Massively Multiplayer Online Role Playing Game (MMORPG) and was preferable to World of Warcraft as the environment has everything in it labeled providing visual reinforcement. It also has the quests in the game documented on screen meaning that by completing the quests the learners gain an appreciation for colloquial meanings, verbs and adverbs. The preliminary study was performed over an 8 week period with 6 learners – four males and two females. The participants were either Northwestern graduate students or the spouses of Northwestern graduate students. Two of the subjects spoke Korean, two Chinese and two Castilian. The results suggest that EverQuest and possibly MMORPGs in general reinforce language acquisition as the players must become active learners and engage with other learners within the environment.

Second Life

Second Life (SL) (www.secondlife.com) is a persistent online 3D world or "metaverse" created by its users or "residents". SL can also be described as an online Multi-User Virtual Environment (MUVE). It opened to the public in 2003 and is now inhabited by millions of residents from all around the world. Thousands of new residents join each day and the size of land within SL, which originally began as 64 acres, is currently over 65,000 acres and rapidly expanding. Residents access SL by means of a freely downloadable client program called the SL Viewer and interact with other residents and objects through a customisable avatar. As in the real world, SL has museums, beaches, parks, shops, schools and universities in it, for example, Coventry University in the UK, has its own island within SL (launched in 2007) where students and staff can meet virtually to socialise or attend lectures and seminars. Coventry University has effectively been reproduced architecturally in SL by members of staff and students who are residents and members of the Serious Games Institute.

Figure 3. Screen shots of Second Life (the entrance to Coventry University on the left and an exhibition hall in Instituto Cervantes on the right)

SL is supported by its own economy and a virtual currency called the "Linden" dollar, which can be converted into US dollars at online Linden dollar exchanges. Residents can buy land, buy houses, explore the virtual world, and interact with other residents in either a socialising capacity or a conventional capacity, for example, business deals take place within SL as it is sometimes far more efficient than meeting in person. SL provides scripting tools for interactive content and tools for construction of 3D objects. SL has been used in many colleges and universities for educational purposes, for example, Imperial College London and Lulea University of Technology have developed a region in SL with the aim of delivering GBL activities associated with the care of virtual patients that can drive experiential, role-playing activities concerned with the selection of treatment and investigations concerning diagnosis (Toro-Troconis, Mellstrom, Partridge & Barret, 2008). In terms of MFL education, Connolly *et al* (2008) give the example of Spain's language and cultural institute having an island in Second Life and point out that, depending on the approach, students can practice their language skills in a closed environment or in the public part of

Second Life with other residents. Figure 3 shows two screen shots of Second Life.

The studies presented in this section show that games-based learning can be a novel, motivational approach for learners to learn and practise MFLs.

Alternate Reality Games

Alternate Reality Games (ARGs) or "immersive gaming" is a blend of online narrative and puzzle solving (similar to an online scavenger hunt). The narrative is gradually revealed through a series of media such as websites, Instant Messenger conversations, text messages, emails and in some cases, TV and newspaper adverts and telephone calls. Central to the development and running of an ARG is the *puppetmaster*, who is simultaneously an ally and adversary to the player base, creating obstacles and providing resources for overcoming them in the course of telling the game's story. Fundamental to the solving of the game is collaboration – players must work together to solve the puzzles and ultimately the game. One further technological area that has been identified as having strong impact on learning is the emergence of social networking. Interestingly, not only are

ARGs a form of computer game they are also heavily built around social networking.

One of the earliest ARGs was developed in 2001 to market the film *A.I.: Artificial Intelligence* and a series of Microsoft computer games based on the film. It was based on an elaborate murder mystery played out across hundreds of websites, email messages, faxes, fake ads, and voicemail messages. At its height it involved over three million active participants from all over the world; in essence, it was a type of massively multiplayer online game (MMOG). Due to the size of the assets involved in the early stages of development, the game became known as "The Beast". Microsoft also used this type of game to create significant market hype around the launch of the XBox game *Halo 2*. Called "I Love Bees", the game wove together an interactive narrative set in 2004 and a War of the Worlds-style radio drama set in the future, broken into 30-60 second segments and broadcast over telephones worldwide.

USE OF ARGS IN AN EDUCATIONAL CONTEXT

While there are a number of well-known ARGs in the non-educational field, very few ARGs have been implemented in the educational field, and little empirical evidence of their effectiveness exists. One of the earliest examples of their use in education appears to have been the eMapps project, which aimed to demonstrate how online games and mobile technologies could be combined to provide new and enriching experiences for children (9-12 year olds) in the school curriculum and beyond (Davies, Kriznova & Weiss, 2006). Some of the main objectives of the project were:

- to build communities of creative, networking children in the New Member States (NMS) of the EU, generating their own cultural content and communicating with peer groups in other countries;

- to contribute to the growth of a community of teachers who are aware of the potential for change through 'schools without walls' and who exchange knowledge and experience through communication with counterparts in other NMS countries;
- to develop adaptable interactive tools (primarily games played on a mobile platform) with which to deliver learning objectives and which help to integrate the use of ICT in the delivery of the school curriculum. The project developed a game platform based on the concept of a map with embedded objects, which teachers could adapt and use in their own local setting, to create a pedagogically sound online game mapped around a defined territory (for example, a school's city centre, a local nature reserve, a historical site or a tourist attraction).

The players were teams of pupils, divided into two groups:

- one group controlled and managed the "game desktop" from a PC or laptop based within the school, sent "challenges" to the players in the field to guide their activities, and received information back from the players in the form of photo, audio or video evidence as proof that they had met the challenge;
- the other group used a range of mobile handheld devices such as smartphones, GPS devices, PDAs and laptops to navigate the game territory while completing the tasks and challenges, which made up the game.

During this time, the teacher monitored and controlled the activities of both groups by releasing instructions and feedback via the desktop. In the evaluation of the pilot of the platform, teachers reported that children had learned new facts across a range of curriculum subjects (one of the strengths of the game being that it could be cross-curricular), new technology skills with handhelds, and transferable ICT skills. The teachers also reported improved generic skills especially: teamwork and cooperation, analytical appraisal, collaborative decision-making, negotiating, independent decision-making, self-reliance, planning, navigating in real and virtual spaces and self-confidence.

Teachers also reported that:

- in four schools game playing stimulated other work such as artwork, acting, writing and video making;
- in six schools children remembered what they learned (although this wasn't universal across all schools);
- in all schools children achieved their intended learning outcomes;
- parents were generally supportive of the actuality of playing educational games.

Some unexpected outcomes were that passive children emerged as leaders in some games and shy children, especially girls, spoke up in the games (Brophy, 2008). The project did find though that there were significant barriers at to the use of such games within school education around issues like ICT facilities, teacher training, health and safety, cultural and language barriers, linking games to the curriculum, and lack recognition of social skills in assessment (Balanskat, 2008). More recently, the JISC (Joint Information Systems Committee) funded the Alternate Reality Games for Orientation Socialisation and Induction (ARGOSI) project to use an ARG to support the student induction process in a Higher Education institution with the aim of providing an engaging and purposeful alternative to traditional methods of introducing students to university life. The ARGOSI project had four key objectives (http://playthinklearn. net/argosi.htm):

- to enable students to meet the intended learning outcomes of the library and information skills at a first level at HE;
- to create social networks during the induction period;
- to improve student confidence in navigating the city and university campus;
- to encourage students to engage in, and enjoy, the induction experience.

The ARGOSI project attempts to overcome many of the weaknesses in the 'traditional' induction process for new students. Induction is typically an extremely intensive first few weeks where students are overloaded with information from across the University. This information often lacks any real context because their studies have not really begun. Induction also appears to provide a distinct lack of city orientation and instead merely focuses on the social aspects. An ARG provides an alternative forum for students not only to study serious learning outcomes but also to create networks and familiarise themselves with the city and university campus. The ARGOSI project delivers induction information over a gradual time period avoiding information overload. It encourages students to establish friendships and work within communities in order to accomplish challenges within the game and discover the secrets that underlie the story.

THE TOWER OF BABEL ARG

The *Tower of Babel* was developed as part of the ARGuing project supported by the EU Comenius Programme. The storyline that was developed for the ARG is based on a set of characters who, through a collective effort, plan to build a contemporary *Tower of Babel*, a place where people understand the interconnectedness of themselves to other people, animals, the planet, and the rest of the universe. The characters, along with the game participants, discover throughout the game how to build the foundations of the tower. These foundations, based on the principles and values of Europe, include: democracy, tolerance and respect, freedom and the rule of law, and access to education. By building the foundations and the tower, step by step, the intention is that the students will gain an understanding of other languages and cultures.

From an implementation perspective, the tower was to be designed as an ever-growing wiki (visually and in content) where students and teachers could add their own building blocks. The "building blocks" for the tower would be puzzles, assignments and quests in multiple languages and in different subjects. Quests can be puzzles, assignments and questions. Sometimes this may require answering multiple choice questions, translating languages, uploading files, searching on the Internet or simply trying to solve puzzles that present the player with information, an interface or a situation that lacks context. These were to be delivered through forums, blogs, websites, short video clips, and emails. Participants would not be able to access the next clue until they had completed the current assignment. Participants would be able to communicate with one another through forums, guilds and IM.

Multi-Lingual Capability

The game had to be multi-lingual. For the initial pilot, English, French, Spanish, German, Dutch and Bulgarian would be supported.

Profiles

Players have profiles and can browse other players' profiles. The profiles hold some basic information about each participant, such as specialist areas, interests, skills, completed quests, languages spoken and how many points they have, both "building blocks" and "empathy" points. The empathy system is the average rating given by other players based on their experience collaborating with the player in question – very similar to the eBay rating system and player rating scores on Microsoft's Xbox Live platform. The profiles are essential to aid the process of player collaboration – players can browse the profiles looking for someone with an adequate skill set to collaborate with.

Supported Media

As we have already mentioned, ARGs are a cross media game and therefore the platform should support the following media:

Blogs: Key characters from the ARG story have their own blogs. Some of the character blogs would be translated into multiple languages while others would be provided in a limited selection of languages – participants are expected to collaborate with one another to interpret the blogs. The blogs tie in with plot development of the storyline and occasionally play parts in quests, such as providing clues or hints. The blogs also provide a mechanism for puppetmasters to intervene with the game if the community is struggling with a specific quest.

Wiki: The wiki, named "Tower of Babel", is the heart of the game space, where quests are uploaded. Solutions to quests will also be uploaded to the wiki – this provides an opportunity for participants to reflect on their and other players' contributions, hopefully further enriching their understanding and appreciation of the quest's learning outcomes. The content being uploaded could contain several media types – images, text, video clips, audio clips, mini games (such as flash or java games) and links to other sites.

Forum: While the wiki may be the heart of the game space, providing the community with quests to complete, the forums are the essence of the ARG. The forums are employed as a means of facilitating communication and collaboration amongst participants. It is on here that the concept of collective intelligence should be evident – players seeking out guidance on quests from other players with specific knowledge and skills. The forums should also promote the discussion of quest related topics amongst community members, where participants can share views and opinions – similarly to the wiki this should enrich the learning as students' appreciation of discussion topics increase.

Guilds: Players should be able to form themselves into guilds to work collaboratively together to solve quests. The guild concept would be similar to the clan/guild structures in MMOGs.

Video and Audio: Part of the storyline would be presented to players in the form of short video clips (in English with subtitles)

Mini Games: Some quests could employ the use of mini games (e.g. in Java or Flash). A basic example would be a puzzle game that participants would need to complete to unlock a hint to a quest. The learners were expected to solve these mini-games and then appropriately communicate with each other to assist other learners who were having any degree of difficulty with any of the games.

Email: Email would mostly be used by puppetmasters to inform participants of important game related events. Messages also include the addition of new quests and, at the request of players, hints and tips to quests.

SMS: Similarly to email, SMS could be used for quest updates, hints and tips. It could also be used as part of a quest – send a SMS text with a key phrase or string of characters to a mobile number which would generate an automatic response with the answer or hint. Due to time and funding constraints, this was not implemented for the pilot.

IM: While the forum provides a means of communication, an IM interface allows participants to communicate in real time. Perhaps playing a less important role than the forum and more geared towards socialising, it still presents participants with another opportunity to network with other players.

Assessment

An aim of this project is to provide a learning environment that the students feel they truly own. To achieve this sense of ownership, the level of assessment should remain informal. The assessment of players' solutions, and the allocation of points, should remain as simple and informal as possible so as to not make players feel they are ultimately being controlled by their teachers. Players will have the opportunity to reflect on their work while comparing their solution to other players' work on completion of a quest. The game uses two scoring systems – building blocks awarded for the completion of a quest and an empathy score which rates the player's collaboration as voted by other players. While the allocations of the building block points are to be informal, these could be used as a means of assessing how well a player is doing within the ARG and also the games effectiveness with regards to the project objectives.

Security

The platform had to be secure and only allow registered students and teachers to access it.

Puppetmasters and Teachers

Puppetmasters (ARG project members for the pilot) would have complete control over the game, although eventually the hope is that teachers would assume this role. Puppetmasters would be able to monitor how the community is coping with quests and provide hints and tips through the various communication channels supported. Teachers will also have a degree of control, lower than that of the puppetmasters, as they will be mostly monitoring their own pupils. The teachers from the participating schools will be asked to help moderate content, both player designed quests and individual answers to quests, from their students. The ARG, from the teachers' perspective, mainly relies around monitoring their own students who are participating. For the pilot, puppetmasters created the quests, while teachers helped assess student work and decided if "building block" points were to be awarded. Puppetmasters and teachers were also be at hand to provide guidance to their pupils. Once the main quests are complete, it was intended that teachers and students would be able to generate their own quests for other participants to attempt. Teachers could use the themes discussed in their class and create new quests with their own content to fit their educational programme. Figure 4 shows the Tower of Babel theme.

EVALUATING THE TOWER OF BABEL ARG

This section will discuss the evaluation of the ARG in terms of methodology selected, particular categories of the evaluation framework used, procedure and an initial results discussion.

Methodology

The general experimental designs of studies evaluating games-based learning are experimental as opposed to quasi-experimental and are typically based on the pre-test/post-test approach (Maguire *et al*, 2006). Despite the fact that the most impressive pedagogical results in the literature have a pre-test/post-test experimental/control group design it should be noted that a control group is not always producible or appropriate. In the case of the distributed nature of the ARG study, multiple control groups would be required which is not realistic. The ARG study is primarily interested in student motivation, engagement, skills, technical aspects and attitudes. Therefore the experimental design selected for this study is pre-test → ARG intervention → post-test. The particular categories of interest from the devised evaluation framework discussed in the earlier section are learner motivations, learner attitudes, learner preferences, perceptions and a section from the GBL environment category concerned with the technical aspects of the ARG. Learner motivations

Figure 4. Theme of the Tower of Babel

were adapted from Malone and Lepper's (1987) framework on intrinsic motivation.

Procedure

Each participant was sent a pre-test designed to: collect some demographic and learner type information, information on foreign languages being learned, skills that participants' believe can be obtained from computer games, how important reasons and motivations are for playing computer games, how important technical aspects of a game are and general attitudes towards playing computer games. Participants were then given the opportunity to play the *Tower of Babel* Alternate Reality Game in classroom situations and at home for a period of approximately 10 days. Participants were then sent a post-test collecting information on how much time they got to play the game in class, how much time they played the game in their own time, how reliable internet access was to the game, what particular motivations were present in the game that was important to the player, technical aspects, skills acquired from the game and attitudes. Additional questions were asked about realism, confusion and complexity. The two questionnaires were developed and sent through SurveyMonkey.com and all initial results obtained were transferred into SPSS version 15 for further detailed analysis.

Results

105 of the participants completed the pre-test, 92 participants completed the post-test and 45 completed both the pre-test and the post-test. As a result of this the pre-test and post-test results can be analysed in isolation and comparisons can be made between the two tests with the 45 participants. This section will firstly discuss the pre-test results, the post-test results and then perform a comparison between the pre and post-tests.

Table 1. Reasons for playing computer games

Reasons	Rank	Mean	SD
Challenge	1st	3.74	1.08
Cooperate	2nd	3.64	1.24
Fantasy	3rd	3.60	1.30
Curiosity	4th	3.51	1.30
Pleasure	4th	3.51	1.20
Competition	5th	3.48	1.10
Feel Good	6th	3.38	1.17
Prevented Boredom	7th	3.38	1.28
Relax	8th	3.27	1.47
Escape Stresses of Life	9th	3.24	1.31
Leisure	10th	3.23	1.38
Release tension	11th	3.12	1.37
Control	12th	3.11	1.50
Avoid Other Activities	13th	2.85	1.43
Recognition	14th	2.85	1.38
Emotional Stimulation	15th	2.79	1.38

Pre-Test

Of the 105 participants who completed the pre-test, 34.3% of the respondents were male and 65.7% were female with a mean age of 14.22 (Standard Deviation (SD) = 0.85) with a range of 12 to 15. Participants spent an average of 4.58 hours (SD = 5.47) a week playing computer games which is significantly different from computer game participation observed in a higher education institution were participants played games for approximately 7.72 hours a week (Hainey, Connolly and Boyle, 2009b). The foreign languages being studied by participants were: 94 (89.5%) learning English, 27 (25.7%) learning German, 25 (24%) studying French, 12 (11.4%) studying Russian, 8 (7.6%) studying Spanish, 8 (7.6%) studying Italian and 7 (6.6%) Bulgarian. Other languages mentioned were Polish, Latin and Portuguese.

In terms of skills that participants believed could be obtained from computer games: 66 (63.8%) creativity, 54 (51.4%) collaboration/ teamwork, 51 (49%) problem solving, 39 (37.1%)

reflection, 37 (35.2%) critical thinking, analyzing/classifying, leading/motivating and 30 (28.5%) management skills. The majority of the participants (66.7%) preferred cooperative learning – learning by working with other students. Due to the collaborative nature of the ARG game, this particular learning preference was expected. Table 1 shows the mean rating for each reason for playing computer games along with the order of importance for its rating and Table 2 shows the mean rating for the importance of aspects in a game with the order of importance of its rating.

Post-Test

92 participants completed the post-test. The mean amount of time that participants got to play the game in class was 1.94 hours a week (SD = 2.41) with a range of 0 to 10.33 hours indicating that different time allowances for playing the game in class may have been a factor. Participants played the game for a greater amount of time in their own time (3.66 hours, SD = 3.82, range 0 to 17.5) possibly indicating that the game was more intrinsically enjoyable outside of a classroom structure.

The reliability of Internet access to the game was generally good with 32 (35%) of participants indicating that it was very good, 42 (46%) of students indicating that it was good and 11 (11.9%) indicating that it was medium.

78% of the participants indicated that the game was what they expected. Those who indicated that the game was not what they expected gave some of the following reasons:

"I was expecting it to be more interesting and for more people to take part in the game facilities."

"It was more like a website and forum than a 'game' in 3d."

"The story of the game wasn't much connected with the quizzes."

"It was much better than I was expected!"

61% of participants indicated that they did not experience confusion while playing the game. Those who did gave a number of reasons why that was the case including:

"There were some misunderstandings on my side as I skipped some instructions in order to save more time on playing the game."

"I found some of the quests hard to understand. I mean the questions were unclear."

"I was confused when I couldn't find where those diaries of the characters were and I didn't know where to look for information on their personalities."

78% of participants indicated that the level of realism and the complexity of the ARG were adequate. Table 3 shows the mean ratings of motivations for playing the ARG game along with the order of importance while Table 4 shows the mean rating for the importance of aspects in the ARG with the order of importance of its rating.

In terms of skills that students believed they obtained from the ARG, 49.4% believed that they obtained problem solving skills, 37.6% believed they obtained reflection skills, 45% analyzing and classifying skills, 55% collaborative and team work skills, 43% leading and motivating skills,

Table 2. Importance of aspects of computer games

Aspect	Rank	Mean	SD
Narrative	1st	4.08	0.99
Help and Support	2nd	3.97	1.03
Story	3rd	3.95	1.18
Solving Quests	4th	3.88	1.14
Realism	5th	3.84	1.09
Characters	6th	3.80	1.02
Collaboration	7th	3.70	1.31

Table 3. Reasons for playing the ARG

Reasons	Rank	Mean	SD
Control	1st	3.70	1.27
Curiosity	2nd	3.63	1.19
Fantasy	3rd	3.45	1.16
Pleasure	4th	3.41	1.34
Leisure	5th	3.39	1.26
Cooperation	6th	3.34	1.27
Avoid Other Activities	7th	3.31	1.41
Emotional Stimulation	8th	3.30	1.19
Feel Good	9th	3.21	1.19
Escape Stresses of Life	10th	3.15	1.31
Release Tension	11th	3.14	1.26
Relax	12th	3.09	1.28
Recognition	13th	3.08	1.30
Challenge	14th	3.08	1.32
Competition	15th	2.91	1.33
Prevented Boredom	16th	2.88	1.30

Table 4. Importance of aspects of the ARG

Aspect	Rank	Mean	SD
Realism	1st	3.71	1.13
Help and Support	2nd	3.62	1.26
Solving Quests	3rd	3.62	1.12
Collaboration	4th	3.6	1.16
Narrative	5th	3.56	1.43
Story	6th	3.54	1.23
Characters	7th	3.46	1.39

31% critical thinking skills, 31% management skills and 54% creativity.

The attitudes towards the ARG were generally very positive. 29% strongly agreed and 35% agreed that the ARG was a social activity. Only 5% strongly agreed and 13% agreed that playing the ARG was a waste of time. 13% strongly agreed and 38% agreed that the ARG helped them to develop new skills. 19% strongly agreed and 54% agreed that playing the ARG was an interesting activity. 14% strongly agreed and 34% agreed that the game was a worthwhile activity. 18% strongly agreed and 41% agreed that playing the ARG was an enjoyable activity. 15% strongly agreed and 41% agreed that playing the ARG was a valuable activity. 19% strongly agreed and 32% agreed that the ARG was an exciting activity.

Comparison of Pre- and Post-Tests

Due to the fact that 45 participants completed both the pre and post tests the data can be analysed in two different ways. Within sample tests can be performed for the 43 participants as one group and between sample tests can be performed on the remaining participants as independent groups i.e. 60 participants remaining in the pre-test group and 47 remaining in the post-test group.

In terms of motivations the pre-test asked the participants what motivations they considered to be important in games and the post-test asked them what motivations they considered to be important in the *Tower of Babel*. This means that we can assess if important motivations have been sufficiently incorporated into the ARG. A Wilcoxon matched pairs signed ranks test between the 45 pre and post test participants only showed a significant difference with regards to fantasy (Z = -2.842, p < 0.04). The mean score for fantasy in the pre-test (3.71, SD = 1.24) was greater for fantasy in the post-test (3.14, SD = 1.30). The lower mean suggests that while fantasy is considered important in games in general, it can be an area of improvement in the ARG. The important aspect of the results is that out of 16 motivations only 1 had a significant reduction and indicates that the ARG is acceptably motivational for the participants.

In the independent groups comparison, a Mann-Whitney *U* test indicated that the only motivation that had a significant difference was recognition (Z = -2.146, p < 0.03). The mean in the pre-test is significantly lower than the mean in the post-test indicating that the ARG provided participants with more recognition than they initially expected from computer games in general. Although the groups are treated as independent, the fact that the majority of the motivations for playing games and the motivations for playing the ARG are not significantly different indicates that the ARG is sufficiently motivating.

In terms of technical aspects of the ARG, the independent groups showed a significant difference in relation to story ($Z = -2.981$, $p < 0.003$) and characters ($Z = -2.946$, $p < 0.003$). The mean in the pre-test is significantly higher than the post-test indicating that the ARG story or characters did not meet the participants' expectations. In the group of 45 who completed both the pre and post-tests a Wilcoxon matched pairs signed ranks test showed that there was no significant differences with regards to narrative, characters, help and support, solving quests and collaboration, however there was a significant reduction with regards to story and realism. This indicates that the ARG did not meet the participants' expectations of these technical aspects in comparison to what they expect of computer games in general.

DISCUSSION

This chapter has discussed the evaluation of a pilot of the *Tower of Babel* ARG that ran from 22 April to 30 April 2009 involving 328 students and 95 teachers from 28 schools across 17 countries. Overall, the students' reaction to the ARG was very positive. Expected motivations in general computer games and motivations for playing the ARG were on the whole not statistically different indicating that the ARG has managed to deliver the motivational experience expected by the students. In terms of the technical aspects the results indicate that the ARG did not manage to reach student expectations with regards to story and characters, which have been identified as a possible area for future enhancement. The ARG did manage to reach learner expectations with 5

of the aspects which were narrative, characters, help and support, solving quests and collaboration

Curiosity, cooperation and pleasure were rated as important expected motivations for playing computer games and for playing the ARG - a finding which is consistent with three studies performed in Higher Education (Hainey, Connolly, & Boyle, 2009b) indicating that the expectations of using computer games in education are similar regardless of age group and educational context.

The majority of the students who completed the post test either agreed or strongly agreed that they would be willing to play the game over a prolonged period of time and that they would play it as part of a foreign language course. Again the majority of students reported that the game was engaging and that it motivated them to learn and use foreign languages. Interestingly participants played the game for a greater amount of time in their own time (3.66 hours, SD = 3.82, range 0 to 17.5) possibly indicating that the game was more intrinsically enjoyable or more suitable and accessible in a home environment.

The students believed that they obtained a number of skills from playing the ARG and the results suggest that the ARG is very encouraging in terms of cooperation, collaboration and team work. Cooperation was ranked as one of the higher motivations for playing the ARG. Also a higher percentage of students believed that they obtained collaborative skills from the ARG than would have been expected from the pre-test results. The obtained skills result was more than 10% higher.

CONCLUSION AND FUTURE DIRECTIONS

While the results are very encouraging, we have identified a number of enhancements that we would like to make to the game. We would like make these changes and then repeat the pilot across Europe, potentially with more students and teachers than the pilot. We would use a similar evaluation framework to determine whether the results of the pilot still hold. After that, we would like to use the underlying ARG platform but produce a different narrative and quests to evaluate the ARG in a different subject area, for example, history, modern studies or personal and social education (PSE) and again determine whether the results from the pilot still apply.

ACKNOWLEDGMENT

This work is supported by the EU Comenius Programme under contract 133909-2007-UK-COMENIUS-CMP.

The images of Tactical Iraqi were provided by Alelo Inc.

REFERENCES

America's Army Website. (2010). *Homepage information.* Retrieved April 28, from http://www.americasarmy.com

Balanskat, A. (2008). *eMapps.com–impact on policy and recommendations for policy makers.* Learning through Games and Mobile Technology Conference eMapps.com final event, 12 February 2008, Prague.

Barab, S., Warren, S., & Ingram-Goble, A. (2006). *Academic play space: Designing games for education.* Paper presented at the meeting of the American Educational Research Association, San Francisco, CA.

Beale, I. L., Kato, P. M., Marin-Bowling, V. M., Guthrie, N., & Cole, S. W. (2007). Improvement in cancer-related knowledge following use of a psychoeducational video game for adolescents and young adults with cancer. *The Journal of Adolescent Health, 41,* 263–270. doi:10.1016/j.jadohealth.2007.04.006

Brophy, P. (2008). *Learning impact.* Learning through Games and Mobile Technology Conference eMapps.com final event, 12 February 2008, Prague.

Christoph, N. (2007). *The role of metacognitive skills in learning to solve problems.* PhD Thesis submitted to the University of Amsterdam. Retrieved 28th November, 2007, from http://dare.uva.nl/document/22568

Connolly, T. M., Boyle, E., & Hainey, T. (2007). A survey of students' motivations for playing computer games. In *Proceedings of the 1ˢᵗ European Conference on Games – Based Learning* (University of Paisley), 25 - 26 October 2007, Paisley, Scotland.

Connolly, T.M., Boyle, E., MacArthur, E., Hainey, T., Hancock, F. & Boyle, J. (In press). *A literature review of research conducted on the learning value and skill enhancement of gaming and methods of measuring the resultant outcomes and impacts.*

Connolly, T. M., Boyle, E., Stansfield, M. H., & Hainey, T. (2006). Can computer games help next generation learners? A survey of students' reasons for playing computer games. In *Proceedings of the 3ʳᵈ International Conference of the Association of Learning and Teaching ALT-C 2006: The next generation,* 5-7 September 2006, Edinburgh, Scotland.

Connolly, T.M., Boyle, E.A., Stansfield, M.H. & Hainey, T. (2007). The potential of online games as a collaborative learning environment. *Journal of Advanced Technology for Learning.*

Connolly, T. M., Stansfield, M. H., & Hainey, T. (2007). An application of games-based learning within software engineering. *British Journal of Educational Technology, 38*(3), 416–428. doi:10.1111/j.1467-8535.2007.00706.x

Connolly, T. M., Stansfield, M. H., & Hainey, T. (2009). Towards the development of a games-based learning evaluation framework. In Connolly, T. M., Stansfield, M. H., & Boyle, E. (Eds.), *Games-based learning advancement for multisensory human computer interfaces: Techniques and effective practices*. Hershey, PA: Idea-Group Publishing. doi:10.4018/978-1-60566-360-9.ch015

Connolly, T. M., Stansfield, M. H., Hainey, T., Josephson, J., Lázaro, N., Rubio, G., et al. (2008). Arguing for multilingual motivation In Web 2.0: Using alternate reality games to support language learning. In *Proceedings of the 2nd European Conference on Games-based Learning (ECGBL)*, 16-17 October 2008, Barcelona, Spain.

Crookall, D. (2007). Second language acquisition and simulation. *Simulation & Gaming, 38*(6).

Davies, R., Kriznova, R., & Weiss, D. (2006). eMapps.com: Games and mobile technology in learning. In *Proceedings of First European Conference on Technology Enhanced Learning*, EC-TEL 2006 Crete, Greece, October 1-4, 2006.

de Freitas, S. (2006). *Learning in immersive worlds*. Joint Information Systems Committee.

Deci, E. L., & Ryan, R. M. (2000). The what and why of goal pursuits: Human needs and the self-determination of behavior. *Psychological Inquiry, 11*, 227–268. doi:10.1207/S15327965PLI1104_01

Eglesz, D., Fekete, I., Kiss, O. E., & Izsó, L. (2005). Computer games are fun? On professional games and players' motivations. *Educational Media International, 42*(2). doi:10.1080/09523980500060274

Ford, C. W., & Minsker, S. (2003). TREEZ-an educational data structures game. *Journal of Computing Sciences in Colleges, 18*(6), 180–185.

Garcia-Carbonell, A., Rising, B., Montero, B., & Watts, F. (2001). Simulation/gaming and the acquisition of communicative competence in another language. *Simulation & Gaming, 32*(4), 481–491. doi:10.1177/104687810103200405

Gaudart, H. (1999). Games as teaching tools for teaching English to speakers of other languages. *Simulation & Gaming, 30*(3), 283–291. doi:10.1177/104687819903000304

Gibson, D., Halverson, W., & Riedel, E. (2007). Gamer teachers. In Gibson, D., Aldrich, C., & Prensky, M. (Eds.), *Games and simulations in online learning: Research and development frameworks* (pp. 175–188). Information Science Publishing.

Habgood, M. P. J. (2007). *The effective integration of digital games and learning content*. Thesis submitted to the University of Nottingham. Retrieved 27th October, 2008 from http://zombiedivision.co.uk/

Hainey, T., Connolly, T. M., & Boyle, L. (2009a). Development and evaluation of a game to teach requirements collection and analysis in software engineering at tertiary education level. In *Proceedings of the 3rd European Conference on Games-based Learning (ECGBL)*, 12-13 October 2009, Graz, Austria.

Hainey, T., Connolly, T. M., & Boyle, L. (2009b). A survey of students' motivations for playing computer games: A comparative analysis of three studies in higher education. In *Proceedings of the 3rd European Conference on Games-based Learning (ECGBL)*, 12-13 October 2009, Graz, Austria.

Halleck, G. B. (2007). Second language acquisition and simulation. *Simulation & Gaming, 38*(1), 31–34. doi:10.1177/1046878106298466

Hudson, J. M., & Bruckman, A. S. (2002). IRC Francais: The creation of an Internet-based SLA community. *Computer Assisted Language Learning, 15*(2), 109–134. doi:10.1076/call.15.2.109.8197

Jain, A., & Boehm, B. (2006). SimVBSE: Developing a game for value-based software engineering. In *Proceedings of 19th Conference on Software Engineering Education and Training (CSEET)*. (pp. 103–114). Turtle Bay Resort, Oahu, Hawaii.

Johnson, W. L., & Wu, S. (2008). Assessing aptitude for learning with a serious game for foreign language and culture. In *Proceedings of the 9th International Conference on Intelligent Tutoring Systems*, Montreal, April 2008.

Kolb, D. (1984). *Experiential learning*. New Jersey: Prentice-Hall Inc.

Lennon, J. L. (2006). Debriefings of Web-based malaria games. *Simulation & Gaming, 37*(3), 350–356. doi:10.1177/1046878106291661

Maguire, M., Elton, E., Osman, Z., & Nicolle, C. (2006). Design of a virtual learning environment for students with special needs. *Human Technology. An Interdisciplinary Journal on Humans in ICT Environments, 2*(1), 119–153.

Malone, T. W., & Lepper, M. R. (1987). Making learning fun: A taxonomy of intrinsic motivations for learning. Aptitude, learning and instruction: *Vol. 3. Conative and affective process analysis* (pp. 223–253). Hillsdale, NJ: Lawrence Erlbaum.

Miller, M., & Hegelheimer, V. (2006). The Sims meet ESL: Incorporating authentic computer simulation games into the language classroom. *International Journal of Interactive Technology and Smart Education, 3*(4).

Nelson, B. C. (2007). Exploring the use of individualized reflective guidance in and educational multiuser virtual environment. *Journal of Science Education and Technology, 16*, 83–97. doi:10.1007/s10956-006-9039-x

Oh Navarro, E., & Van der Hoek, A. (2005). Design and evaluation of an educational software process simulation environment and associated model. In *Proceedings of the Eighteenth Conference on Software Engineering Education and Training*, Ottawa, Canada.

Rankin, Y., Gold, R., & Gooch, B. (2006). Gaming as a language learning tool. *Proceedings of the ACM SIGGRAPH Educators Program*, 2006.

Roubidoux, M. A. (2005). Breast Cancer Detective: A computer game to teach breast cancer screening to Native American patients. *Journal of Cancer Education, 20*(1), 87–91. doi:10.1207/s15430154jce2001s_17

Shaw, K., & Dermoudy, J. (2005). Engendering an empathy for software engineering. In *Proceedings of the 7th Australasian Computing Education Conference (ACE2005),* Newcastle, Australia, 42, 135–144.

Squire, K., Barnett, B., Grant, J. M., & Higginbotham, T. (2004). Electromagnetism supercharged! Learning physics with digital simulation games. *Proceedings of the International Conference on Learning Sciences, 6,* 513–520.

Toro-Troconis, M., Mellstrom, U., Partridge, M., & Barrett, M. (2008). *An architectural model for the design of games-based learning activities for virtual patients in Second Life.* Paper presented at the 2nd European Conference on Games-Based Learning (EC-GBL), 16-17 October 2008, Barcelona Spain.

Virtual Leader Website. (2010). *Simulearn.* Retrieved April 28, from http://www.simulearn.net

Virtual University Website. (2010). *Virtual U.* Retrieved April 28, from http://www.virtual-u.org

Waraich, A. (2004). Using narrative as a motivating device to teach binary arithmetic and logic gates. In *Proceedings of the 9th Annual SIGCSE Conference on Innovation and Technology in Computer Science Education.* (pp. 97–101). Leeds, UK.

Whitton, N. J. (2007). *An investigation into the potential of collaborative computer game-based learning in higher education.* Unpublished doctoral thesis. Retrieved 30th April, 2007, from http://playthinklearn.net/?page_id=8

Yee, N. (2006). The demographics, motivations and derived experiences of users of massively-multiuser online graphical environments. *Presence (Cambridge, Mass.)*, *15*, 309–329. doi:10.1162/pres.15.3.309

Yee, N. (2007). Motivations of play in online games. *Journal of Cyber Psychology and Behavior*, *9*, 772–775.

Yip, F. W. M., & Kwan, A. C. M. (2006). Online vocabulary games as a tool for teaching and learning English vocabulary. *Educational Media International*, *43*(3), 233–249. doi:10.1080/09523980600641445

Young, J., & Upitis, R. (1999). The microworld of Phoenix Quest: Social and cognitive considerations. *Education and Information Technologies*, *4*(4), 391–408. doi:10.1023/A:1009600528811

Zhu, Q., Wang, T., & Tan, S. (2007). Adapting game technology to support software engineering process teaching: From SimSE to Mo-SEProcess. In *Proceedings of Third International Conference on Natural Computation (ICNC)*, 777–780.

Chapter 13
Computer Games for Affective Learning

Claire Dormann
University of Ottawa, Canada

Jennifer R. Whitson
Carleton University, Canada

Robert Biddle
Carleton University, Canada

ABSTRACT

This chapter addresses how computer games can support affective learning, taking specific focus on learning for the affective domain. It first explores this domain, describes the issues that can arise in support, and makes connections to the strengths of computer games. The chapter uses activity theory to highlight the role of a game as an effective mediator of learning in the affective domain. These studies of how games support the affective domain involve the observation of game-play and identification of recurring design elements that can be identified as patterns. The chapter describes several patterns, first in larger commercial games, and then in smaller serious games. Finally, it reflects on its findings, and surveys the general nature of game support for learning in the affective domain. Clear evidence is given that games can and do provide such support, with indications of even greater potential with better understanding of the nature of the game-play.

INTRODUCTION

Computer games are now ubiquitous, and their role and value for learning has been substantiated in many areas. Similarly to Durkin and Barber (2002), we are using "computer game" in this article as a generic term independent of platform (PCs, laptops, consoles, etc.). Playing computer games has been shown to have substantial cognitive worth. Educational researchers have documented how computer games can improve practical reasoning skills and heighten levels of continuing motivation, and complex problem solving (De Aguilera & Mendiz, 2003). Indeed, as Gee (2007) highlights, computer games challenge players to strategize, to solve problems,

DOI: 10.4018/978-1-60960-495-0.ch013

and to acquire a range of skills that can transfer over to other domains. This mostly applies to the cognitive side of learning and development.

The importance of the affective domain, dealing with the emotions and social values that shape one's behavior, has often been overlooked. And despite some related research on affective gaming and research regarding the role of emotions in games, this area is not well documented. Emotional involvement typifies computer games because we care about our avatar's fate, we feel for them, we identify with their needs and desires, and thus grow with them, demonstrating important features for affective learning (Gros, 2003; Pohl, 2008). Computer role-play games create the opportunity to act out and experiment with different roles, and thus can support affective development in a specific way: they allow easy exploration of different perspectives, patterns of behaviour, and resulting consequences. Thus, we propose in this chapter to focus on affective learning, especially learning in the affective domain.

The use of computer games for education and life-long learning has increased drastically in a variety of contexts, including universities, workplaces and other specific domains. Games are becoming an important form of interactive rhetoric and an educational tool. Serious games such as social change games attend to a complex range of socio-emotional issues involving the promotion of social awareness, emotional competencies, and behaviour changes. We thus need to better understand the ways in which affective learning can be supported through games, and develop a critical understanding of the affective learning potential of computer games.

We are interested in understanding how computer games can effectively support affective learning and the acquisition of affective competencies for training, leisure and life-long learning. In this chapter we focus on learning in the affective domain and the design of games for adults (including young adults). We first define affective learning and situate learning in the affective domain. We

then introduce activity theory and discuss how we apply it to understand support for affective learning in games. We go on to discuss the conceptual tools that can support affective learning through the identification of reusable game design patterns. To illustrate game design patterns, we present two case studies: the first relates to commercial games and the representation of socio-emotional interaction; and the second relates to social change games and how they support affective learning. To conclude, we address the wider context of game-play and suggest future development. We hope this chapter will constitute a call for action for further research in this promising area.

BACKGROUND: AFFECTIVE LEARNING

Perhaps the most well-known aspect of affective learning involves supporting cognitive leaning. Affective learning includes sustaining positive attitudes toward the course content, subject material or the teacher (Russo & Benson, 2005). Teachers provide emotional assistance and so help students to manage their emotions, therefore reducing anxiety and stress generated by learning tasks, and thus facilitating immediacy. It can also involve support for the joy of learning, inspiring a persistence to accomplish the desired goals even in the face of difficulty (Schlechty, 2001).

This aspect of affective learning is not our focus in this chapter, but we acknowledge its importance as a particularly relevant factor for serious games, as these games have to be engaging and fun to motivate play. Fun and enjoyment are well known to be effective in development, both in supporting and deepening learning as well facilitating engagement and motivation (Bowen, 2005). How computer games can motivate players has been well documented in the work of many, especially including Malone (1981) and Squire (2003).

Our focus is on another aspect of affective learning, specifically, learning in the affective domain as defined by Martin and Reigeluth (1999) and Payton et al. (2000). Our concerns relate to the positive aspects of games and how games stimulate affective learning and, more particularly, social and emotional learning in the affective domain. Anti-drug campaigns and health education (Lin & Hullman, 2005), tolerance and social inclusion, corporate diversity training, and social justice are all examples of learning in the affective domain. In this context, affective learning outcomes involve attitudes, motivation, and values. Related affective reactions and characteristics include feelings of self-confidence, self-efficacy, advocacy, and social emotions such sympathy, showing concern for the well-being of others, and empathy.

Educators can assist in the development of emotional literacy, self-awareness, and social awareness, as well as work toward building better interpersonal skills and promoting ethical decision-making. Emotional literacy, the ability to recognize, understand and appropriately express our emotions, is a fundamental component of affective learning, as is establishing interactions and maintaining relationships with others. Social awareness is instantiated as empathy and the development of pro-social attitudes, such as caring and social justice. Empathy is a complex process involving both cognition (perspective, role taking) and emotion (experiencing somebody else's emotions) which helps to develop socially and emotionally responsible action (Coplan, 2004). Emotion theories suggest that in challenging situations, one might need to practice emotional perspective-taking and the sharing of emotional experiences, so vicariously learning how to feel.

When affective learning is the central focus, different instructional strategies may be used than is typical for cognitive learning. Typical affective learning strategies would include the following, which also provide guidance relating to potential support through games (Orey, 2001):

- Display of the desired behavior, for example by a role model
- Practice and experience of the required behavior through role playing
- Creation of strong persuasive messages, and facilitation of emotional engagement
- Providing discussion around affective learning or opportunities to critique the material
- Implicating the learner in the production of the message and material

Social learning theory suggests that an individual learns attitudes by observing the behaviors of others, and this can also be supported through stories, films or games. Social television drama allows for possibilities of role modeling, identification, empathy, and efficacy (Wang & Singhal, 2009). For example, FearNot© (Aylett, Louchart, Dias, Paiva, & Vala, 2005) is a digital drama constructed using synthetic characters about bullying, and aiming at creating empathy between the player and the victimized character. To take the perspective first of an aggressor and then of a victim is a didactic technique that activates sympathy and empathic engagement, aiming at changing subsequent socio-emotional behaviour. Moreover, characters that elicit strong emotional connections with the viewer/player have a greater affective impact (McKee, 1997). Stories often engage people by means of their empathy with the protagonist and demonstration of behaviors including selfless deeds, sacrifices, caring, and rescuing others, resulting in value changes and thus embedding a lesson that can be learned: the "moral of the story". Such mechanisms can be created in games.

Affective learning is often related to cognitive engagement in the learning process, and we acknowledge other connections between emotion and cognition. Dirkx suggests that "Emotions and our imaginative appraisal of them are integral to the process of meaning making, to the ways we experience and make sense of ourselves" (2001, p.

66). Picard (1997) outlines how emotional experiences lend us the ability to better comprehend and regulate our activities, to understand our motivation and how to fulfill our needs, while Ratner argues that cognition and affect are intrinsically linked: "Objective thinking gives rise to feelings, and non-objective thinking gives rise to cognition" (2000, p. 6). Vygotsky (1978) also considered that affect cannot be separated from cognition.

It therefore has to be noted that learning in the affective domain also involves cognitive strategies, such as solving social problems and responding to social dilemmas, or resolving cognitive dissonance to stimulate attitude and behavior change. Reflexivity and dissonance can create compelling educational opportunities for learners as they contend with multiple viewpoints, values and affective perspectives presented (Pedretti, 2004). Learners should be challenged to explore topics from many points of view and to communicate their learning creatively. It is important in our context to suggest that learning in the affective domain involves dealing with conflicting interests and emotions while solving problems and reflecting on the socio-cultural 'appropriateness' of solutions.

GAME SUPPORT FOR AFFECTIVE LEARNING

Learning and games is a topic that has garnered much academic interest, yet this interest is focused largely on the cognitive domain and neglects the affective domain. There has been little work on how games might support affective learning, either as a formal and primary aim, or even as an informal or secondary aspect of their design intent. The controversy about whether games can support learning is complex, as we must consider a range of ways in which games can help, rather than taking any narrow focus on subject matter transfer. In particular, as Gee (2007) shows, games are good at supporting various kinds of informal learning, regardless of their intent about formal educational content.

Supporting affective learning is an important topic for education that impacts a variety of domains from health to environmental education as well as enhancing affective competencies in the work place. For example, research has shown that games can influence attitudes (Garris, Ahlers, & Driskell, 2002), Thomas, Cahill, and Santilli (1997) demonstrate that an adventure game could successfully enhance students' confidence in safe sex negotiations, and Delwiche (2007) maintains that computer games have affordances that can model attitude and behavior. Moreover, games can create vicarious emotional experiences from which we can learn, and spaces in which ethical or moral dilemmas are embedded (Zagal, 2009). However, negative aspects of games such as addiction and violence have received increasing media attention. Violent computer games have been linked with aggressive behavior, but this has not received compelling academic support (Fergusson, 2007). Moreover, Durkin and Barber (2002) evidence that, contrary to this negative perception, computer games can play a positive role in development. Accordingly, it certainly seems that games have features and mechanisms that can be used to support learning in the affective domain.

In the sections below, we present two approaches to address affective learning in games. First, we propose an activity theory framework to understand how games support learning and how it might relate to affective learning. In this framework, games are seen as simulacra in which human activities can be situated to reflect socio-emotional strategies that we wish to address. Second, we outline our study of existing games, both commercial games and serious games, and our identification of game design patterns, constituting conceptual tools that will enable designers to identify and implement affective learning strategies.

Activity Theory and Learning through Games

The theoretical framework that we use is cultural-historical activity theory, stemming from the work of Vygotsky (1962), and described using the models suggested by Leontiev (1978). This framework provides insight and structure for understanding affective learning and how it can be supported. Activity theory is especially informative about the role of tools in learning, and we focus on computer games as tools for learning in the affective domain.

The fundamental structure in activity theory is that subjects use mediating artifacts as tools to transform objects and thus accomplish goals. In the primary model suggested by Leontiev this structural relationship is shown as the top triangle in Figure 1: the subject acts via a tool on an object. While mediating artifacts might be physical tools such as hammers or pens, they can also be more conceptual tools such as contracts or meetings – or games. Moreover, the structure also applies to the affective domain, where accomplishing affective goals can also be supported by using tools. For example, expression of sympathy can be shown by a self-revealing anecdote or a supportive gesture. The activity structure is seen to support learning

by a process of externalization, then a process of internalization. The first stage is externalization, which involves the identification of the tool as a reified means to accomplish the intent. This is effective because it substitutes an abstract intent with a concrete and operationalizable tool. The second stage is internalization, the tool usage becoming bound with the intent. This is effective because is reduces the load on the subject, which then allows greater availability and capacity for the subject to pursue other goals. Both processes apply to the affective domain, where externalization can guide behaviour, and internalization allows repeatability and progress.

In the context of workplace behaviour, Leontiev's original triangular model was extended, and has since been widely applied by Engeström (1987). While activity still involves an individual subject, it is seen in the context of a broader group. This approach is in accord with ideas dating back to Vygotsky, who saw both the cultural and historical context as essential to understanding human activity. The expanded model is shown in Figure 1 as the full triangle of triangles, with the original model of Leontiev at the top. The larger model identifies, in addition to the subject, tool, and object, now also the wider group, the rules of the group, and the division of labour in

Figure 1. Activity system model of Leontiev (1978)

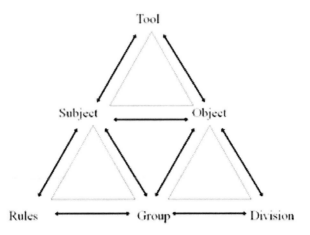

the group. This larger model allows the perspective on process to be larger too: instead of considering activity as an individual process, we can see it within the context of groups, their rules, and the roles within the group. These relationships can be seen as similar to tools, and also involving elements of externalization and internalization. In Engeström's work on organizational activity systems, there is a focus on growth from aggregation and combination of activities by resolving contradictions between the component elements. Resolving conflicts in such rich social and organizational settings involves learning in both cognitive and affective domains.

The activity theory perspective on learning and the nature of games combine together especially well. Vygotsky suggested that support for learning and the externalization/internalization processes must be done within the "Zone of Proximal Development" (ZPD): "the distance between the actual developmental level as determined by independent problem solving and the level of potential development as determined through problem solving under adult guidance, or in collaboration with more capable peers" (Vygotsky, 1978, p. 86). We suggest that by integrating the affective lessons within the game-play, the structure and constraints of the game itself can position the lessons within the ZPD, ensuring that players are given the support necessary to learn without or boredom or frustration before moving on. This kind of careful structure resembles that provided by a teacher.

In applying this framework to understanding how computer games might support learning in the affective domain, we use both the smaller and larger models of activity as described above. We wish to leverage conceptual tools, externalization and internalization, and specifically within a social context. We focus on one broad category of games: those that depict situated human behaviour. This is not any precise game genre, although it would include many games in genres such as role-play,

action-adventure, and even some first or third-person shooters, as well as many serious games. It would not, however, include more abstract games such as Tetris©, or many simulation games such as flight simulators, car racing games, or even political-economy games such as SimCity©. What we focus on are games that depict human or human-like characters, interacting with other such characters, within appropriate settings for understandable human or human-like behaviour. While learning about the affective domain principally involves human behaviour, we also allow some breadth in characterization both to allow metaphorical and allegorical devices, and also to address affective relationships with regard to the natural environment.

The idea is that the game-world, the world of activity within the game, is a simulacrum in which activities can be situated, and that the player engages by proxy and by observation, and relates what happens in these game-world activities to themselves and their own (real) world. This suggests that affective tools can be supported within the game-world activity systems for observation and engagement by the player, with the intent of transfer to the players themselves in their activities in the real world. This combines the activity theory structures we outlined above together with the nature of game-play. Within the game-world, situations can be designed or amended to relate to the affective domain, and the game-play can then influence behaviour. As an activity theory basis for affective learning, the game-play should include various affective domain intents and goals, then conceptual tools that externalize attempts at their accomplishment, and the results that ensue. The nature of games, however, means that more than mere depiction is available. Of course, there are the narrative aspects of the game, which with character design, mise-en-scène, and other devices can support storytelling. Moreover, there are also the ludic aspects of the game, where game-mechanics and in-game economic models can be used to influence player interpretation of the various elements as an implicit value system (Barr, Noble, & Biddle, 2007).

Game Design Patterns as Conceptual Tools for Affective Learning

Originating from the field of architecture (Alexander, Ishikawa, & Silverstein, 1977), design patterns describe and document recurring design decisions. They describe best practices and problem-solving techniques in a format that allows others to learn from, re-use and apply the patterns to new and different contexts. Kreimeier (2002) makes the case for design patterns for computer games. Specific patterns are the result of consistent application, leading to collections of design patterns that are assigned names and documented by both anecdotal and formal abstract descriptions. Pattern methods provide semi-formal tools for problem domains in which rigorously formal methods cannot easily be applied, or are simply not available or even conceivable.

Design patterns have already become popular in object-oriented software design (Gamma, Helm, Johnson, & Vlissides, 1994), and interaction design (Tidwell, 2005). Generally, each pattern is a three-part rule, which expresses a relation between a certain context, a problem and a solution. According to Alexander, "…each pattern is a relationship between a certain context, a certain system of forces which occurs repeatedly in that context, and a certain spatial configuration which allows these forces to resolve themselves" (Alexander et al., 1977). In game design, patterns create a shared design vocabulary and are advocated as a method of codifying design knowledge (Church, 1999; Falstein & Barwood, 2006), and describing game elements related to interaction (Björk & Holopainen, 2005).

In particular, game design patterns have been used to describe the representation of social in-

teraction and how emotional elements can sustain immersion. Lankoski and Björk (2007) propose several patterns relating to social interaction, such as *Competing For Attention, Social Dilemma* and *Social Maintenance.* We suggest that game design patterns can be used to identify, classify, and examine design structures that support affective learning. Building on these ideas, we can discuss how existing game design patterns relate to social interaction and emotional representation could be adapted and refined for affective learning. We will present affective game patterns in relation to two case studies from computer games and from serious games, describing the patterns formally, and giving examples of such patterns in games, showing how they can be articulated to support socio-emotional learning. We believe that commercial games (such as role-play games), and educational games (such as those dedicated to social change) will provide complementary insights for the design of affective learning.

Lankoski and Björk (2007) argue that the social interactions between game characters are an important aspect of game-play. While complex social relations are typically part of game storylines (i.e. morality tales of brotherhood and romance, allegiances and betrayal), most games do not let players directly interact with and influence these relationships. Instead, players passively watch these relationships change and develop through static cut-scenes and animation sequences. Jesper Juul argues that complex interactions such as friendship, love and deceit are difficult to incorporate into actual game-play because "emotions are hard to implement in rules" (2005, p. 20). The suggested consequence is that it is much easier to create violent games. Just as in film and television, violence is easy to plot, requires a minimum of creative scripting and design, and translates well across cultures (Kline, Dyer-Witheford, & De Peuter, 2005). As a solution, Lankoski and Björk (2007) suggest that by utilizing game design patterns that prioritize social interaction and making

267

social relations a core game-play feature, game designers may "expand the possible game-play space and put stronger focus upon social actions rather than physical (or violent) ones". Unlike Lankoski and Björk, we are not focused on providing design patterns to promote the creation of games with increased socio-emotional components, but instead are interested in how these specific patterns – especially the ones relating to social interaction – can be identified in existing games and leveraged to assist *learning* of socio-emotional skills. The patterns identified by Lankoski and Björk accordingly have considerable utility because they provide a vocabulary for discussing games in general, and highlighting how specific components of both mainstream and serious games can be used for affective learning.

To support their position, Lankoski and Björk focus on single player games and the relationship between the player and the non-player characters (NPCs) in the game. To keep this chapter within a manageable scope, our analysis follows their lead and focuses largely on player/NPC relationships, although the patterns we discuss can be applied to the relationships between players themselves, such as in multiplayer games. Lankoski and Björk draw from established game patterns (Björk & Holopainen, 2005) and highlight those patterns they believe contribute to rich social interactions, providing numerous examples of games that utilize one or more patterns. They identify a number of new game design patterns that specifically provide for richer socio-emotional engagement in games (e.g. *Competing for Attention, Gain Allies, Internal Conflict,* and *Social Maintenance*). Due to space requirements, they do not describe complete design patterns, but instead list the pattern names and the context in which they were identified. In the following case study we elaborate on one of the patterns suggested by Lankoski and Björk and offer two complementary patterns that can be leveraged to support affective learning.

CASE STUDY ONE: COMPUTER GAMES AND DRAGON AGE

Our research strategy has been to examine games through inspection and game-play, identifying and documenting examples of the conceptual tools and supporting game-play as design patterns. We performed an affective walkthrough of one mainstream role-play game (RPG) to conduct a preliminary assessment of the utility of game patterns for affective learning. Affective walkthroughs have been utilized by Dormann and Biddle (2008), and are adapted from the user interface inspection methodology for cognitive walkthroughs (Wharton, Rieman, Lewis, & Polson, 1994). The steps of a walkthrough are an iterative process that consists of the following steps: form goals, execute actions, evaluate the effects of these actions, and repeat; much like Norman's "human action cycle" (Norman, 2002). Affective walkthroughs emphasize the affective learning elements involved in the cycle of forming goals, taking action, and evaluating results. Our walkthrough consisted of forty hours of game-play and included video recording of important game sequences, and well as extensive note-taking throughout. During the walkthrough we asked: How would the affective experiences above influence the experience and goals in game-play?

Dragon Age: Origins© (2009), developed by BioWare and published by Electronic Arts, was selected specifically for our walkthrough because of its positive reception by critics and fans, as well as its claims to provide an emotionally rich environment. Set in a mythical world and often dealing with mature themes, players set off on a quest to unite the different races (human, dwarf, elf, etc.) in a battle against the rising horde of Darkspawn. Game-play alternates between exploration of the game world, social interaction (collecting information and forming alliances with NPCs via complex conversation trees) and strategy (determining how the player's character and the NPCs in the party respond in the event of attack). Designers of the game prioritized social interaction, especially in terms similar to *Social Maintenance,* a pattern discussed by Lankoski and Björk (2007). While Lankoski and Björk do not find extant examples of *Social Maintenance* in their own study, they suggested the pattern could be leveraged to redesign existing games and create new ones that provided richer interactions between characters. It seems that BioWare, whether knowingly or not, fulfilled Lankoski and Björk's suggestion.

Game Pattern:Social Maintenance

Definition:*Social Maintenance* can be simply described as performing actions to redefine and refine the relationships of an individual with others and within a group.

Problem/Goal: In the real world, it is often necessary to put thought and effort into creating relationships. These relationships require maintenance to sustain, and will deteriorate if not enough effort is put into them. In games, relationships are often static, only changing during cut scenes. Players are not able to change, develop or even cause deterioration in these relationships. This negatively impacts the ability of players to learn from or experiment with social relationships through the game.

Solution: Require the player to perform and sustain actions that mimic the real world behaviours that go into relationship formation and maintenance, and prioritize *Social Maintenance* as a main function of game-play. Allow the player to experiment with different actions to maintain relationships, as well as show meaningful and realistic consequences of allowing relationships to deteriorate.

Example: In Dragon Age©, *Social Maintenance* plays an important role. Each NPC character travelling in the player's party has a meter that measures their 'approval' of the player. This rating fluctuates in relation to the players' decisions. The NPC's opinion of the player is not an objective grade of how the player is faring in the game, but rather a reflection of the NPC's own background and personality. For example, if the player steals a holy relic in order to complete a quest, the approval rating of devout NPCs decreases. Decisions often take place in a moral grey space and will please one NPC in the party while angering another. Pleasing all party members is a difficult task that can only be achieved through careful decision-making, continued conversations, and gift-giving. High approval ratings reward the player with new quests, increased abilities, and the possibility of 'intimate' relationships. Low approval ratings can result in abandonment or betrayal.

While many of the other design patterns suggested by Lankoski and Björk could be found in *Dragon Age*, the affective walkthrough highlighted new patterns as well. We identified one new pattern in particular, *Sacrificial ACTION,* which supports emotional engagement and affective learning.

Game Pattern: Sacrificial Action

Definition:*Sacrificial Action* is the action of prioritizing others' well-being (NPCs and, in multiplayer games, other players) ahead of the player's own character's well-being and advancement.

Problem/Goal: Games encourage self-mastery, skill building, and individual advancement. In games that allow for team play, the goals of the team are generally aligned with individual player goals, thus team members work together for their mutual benefit. This is an over-simplistic rendering of true social relations. Beyond games, individual goals and desires sometimes conflict with the well-being of others and the well-being of the community. It is a sign of emotional maturity to prioritize the needs of others over one's own personal needs and desires. Yet, within games, self-interest and personal advancement is prioritized over sacrifice.

Solution: Allow players the freedom of choice to place the advancement of NPCs and other players over their own. Create situations wherein the player is forced to choose between the needs of others and personal needs and ensure that there are both negative and positive consequences for any decision. In other words, increase the complexity of decision-making by avoiding outcomes that would benefit all involved and thus negate the need for *Sacrificial Action*. Any *Sacrificial Action* should be meaningful in terms of its cost and impact.

Example: In Dragon Age© there are multiple instances of *Sacrificial Action*, with differing levels of impact. Most often, personal sacrifice is superficial, as it benefits other NPCs that are travelling with and aiding the player, and accordingly advances the well-being of the team and indirectly rewards the player. For example, armaments and weapons can be used by the player, or can be given to NPCs travelling with the player, or can be sold for a profit. Giving weapons and armor to NPCs directly benefits the player, as NPCs are made more valuable by being able to assist the player in battle. However, real instances of *Sacrificial Action* are evident, especially at the end of the game where the player must choose between sacrificing their own life, allowing one of their companions to die, or permitting a demon spirit to enter an innocent baby. This is a difficult decision that has direct ramifications for how the game ends. The choice to sacrifice oneself, while altruistic, is especially challenging given the considerable amount of time spent developing the abilities of the character (which often amounts to more than 50 hours of game-play).

The ability of players to learn about actions and consequences online though wikis and fan sites points to another pattern for affective learning, *Shared Learning*. *Shared Learning* extends Björk and Holopainen's original pattern of *Co-operation* to include *Collaborative Actions* that extend beyond the instance of a single game. While *Co-operation*, as defined by Björk and Holopainen (2005), is restricted to players interacting within a game, *Shared Learning* includes a broader range of activities, and can be applied to single player games as well as multiplayer games.

Game Pattern: Shared Learning

Definition: *Shared Learning* is the opportunity for players to share lessons from the game with other players. Through direct and indirect cooperation, players work together to master the game.

Problem/Goal: Progress may be halted when players encounter difficult challenges and lack the knowledge on how to proceed. In single player games, NPCs can provide hints and strategies to the player, yet this knowledge is by necessity pre-defined and limited in scope and number, and thus may not aid the player.

Solution: Players may communicate with other players and share knowledge on strategy and challenges. Together, players can identify a range of possible alternative solutions, thinking prospectively about the probable consequences of each, and make a more informed choice on how to proceed.

Example: *Shared Learning* is closely tied to the pattern *Meta Game*, which Björk and Holopainen define as "features that can support player, and non-player, participation outside the play of a single game instance" (2005, p. 401). Important parts of the *Meta Game* for Dragon Age© are the fan sites and wikis that promote direct co-operation between players. Players may pose questions on these sites, receive advice from more experienced players, and debate the merits of the potential actions. Written tips, strategy guides and game walkthroughs are also available. A more indirect form of shared learning is built into the single-player game Demon's Souls© (2009). When a player dies, a bloodstain appears on the ground in the location of the player's death in the games of other players. When interacted with, the bloodstain presents a replay of the original player's death, providing clues as to traps and hazards. Players can also leave runes for others that include tips and hints. Other players rate the utility of each message, and health points are awarded to those players that leave the most helpful messages. Although in this context players do not directly interact with each other, and only inhabit their own distinct game worlds, *Shared Learning* is directly facilitated by the design of the game itself.

Our theoretical foundation of Activity Theory provides a deeper understanding of how the patterns work to support affective learning in games. Dragon Age© offers social problems that the player must solve. Each of the patterns illustrates a particular social problem and provides a solution in terms of a game-play mechanism or strategy. In terms of Activity Theory, each strategy is a tool that allows the subject (player) to act on an object (the game) in order to solve a social problem and accomplish in-game goals. In *Social Maintenance*, the game-play tool of approval ratings encourages repeated social contact and the exhibition of social caring in order for the player to gain allies. *Sacrificial Action* is a strategy prioritizes the needs of others and promotes the welfare of groups over individuals. This strategy breaks the norms of expected game-play (winning at all costs) and instead prioritizes less individualistic norms. The pattern of *Shared Learning* encourages individuals to help others and enhances the bond between communities of players. In all these cases, the possibility for transferring these prosocial strategies to the real world would involve vicarious learning. When we can identify with characters, we can learn from their actions and the consequences that result, and learn from both positive and negative examples.

We have presented here only a very limited number of game patterns as possibilities to support affective learning. Existing patterns indentified by Lankoski and Björk (2007), such as *Identification:* "the characters or parts of the game with which players identify" or *Emotional Immersion:* "being emotionally affected by the events that occur in a game." can be used and refined for affective learning. In particular, emotional identification with the player's avatar or main character can

become a powerful tool for affective learning. Other patterns for social interaction, such as *Competing for Attention* and *Social Dilemma,* as we have mentioned, can also be refined socioemotional learning. Of particular importance are game patterns that represent group dynamics and the interaction between characters and social groups. Furthermore, other forms of games, such as educational and serious games such social change games, utilize game patterns of their own and offer unique opportunities for affective learning, some of which we discuss in the next section.

CASE STUDY TWO: SOCIAL CHANGE GAMES

Bogost (2007) debates how digital games can question or transform existing social structures and values. Social change games attempt to raise awareness of important social issues by delivering powerful statements and inspiring new thinking with the aim of transforming players' views or attitudes as well as real-world behavior (Schreiner, 2008). These have also been called "activism games" and can be seen as fostering a critical type of play (Flanagan & Lotko, 2009). Many such games are created through student projects, while others are supported by research funding from various agencies including corporate/public-sector partnerships, activist groups, and non-profit organizations such as the United Nations Refugee Agency (UNHCR), Amnesty International, and United Nations Children's Fund (UNICEF). Most social change games offer only brief game-play, and require a small downloaded program or are played from the web. However, some role-play games such as Peacemaker© (2007) or Global Conflicts: Latin America© (*GC:LA*) (2008) can be more complex. These games deal with socioemotional or cultural issues related to various global issues including human rights (Pictures for Truth©), ethnic conflicts (Darfur is Dying©), and endemic poverty (Ayiti©), while others concern the margins of "modern" society such as home-lessness, unemployment, or new migrants. As in the Dragon Age© case study, we performed an affective walkthrough of a number of social change games and examined many others through inspection and game-play.

Game Pattern: Call to Action

Definition:*Call to Action* provides functions within the game framework that inspire players to step beyond the game and actively participate in social activism.

Problem/Goal: Social change games are de-signed to enhance awareness of social issues, and to make intentional statements or actions to bring about change. To achieve this, games often utilize the social network of players to reach a broader audience. Moreover, social change games also intend to inspire players to reflect more deeply on social issues and to act, that is for players to become proactive and participate as informed citizens in debates, protests, and so on. Thus for players to truly engage, they must step beyond mere game-play.

Solution: Most social change games are Inter-net based games and run in a web browser. Links to related web sites should be provided within the games and integrated with the game functions. These links will motivate players to distribute games, as well as offer opportunities to take fur-ther action such as writing letters, joining activist groups, or supporting non-profit organizations.

Example: This game pattern is found in many social change games, including Darfur is Dying© (2006) and 3rd World Farmer© (2006). Darfur is Dying© has perhaps the most extensive approach that we have seen so far. The game aspires to in-crease the awareness of the genocide taking place in Darfur by simulating the experiences of people living in the refugee camps. The game is embedded in a website giving players the choice to send the game link to a friend. Moreover, within the game proper, players can choose the option "Sudan: take

action". On doing so, players are offered different choices including "Send a message to president Obama", which helps the players get involved in a activist group, "Ask your representative to support the people of Darfur" which allows the player to send an email to elected officials, or "Start a divestment movement on your campus" which aids the player to participate in changing investment practices.

The game 3rd World Farmer© aims at simu-lating the real-world mechanisms that cause and sustain poverty in 3rd world countries. Players have to take care of a farm, including raising crops and dealing with events such as weather and war. The game supports *Call to Action* by demonstrating the challenges facing third world farmers, confronting the player with extremely difficult game challenges, and then providing links to explanations, for example: "Rules unfair? Game rigged? Think about the people to whom this isn't a game, but everyday life. Please visit the relief agencies on this page to learn more about how you can help." The tactic seems less power-ful than in Darfur, as it is more passive and less immediate. We believe that the more immediate the *Call to Action*, the more satisfying it will be for the players (and a greater chance that they follow through).

Call to Action is particularly appropriate for social and humanitarian organizations as they rely on support and involvement from many people. It is expected that more innovative solutions link-ing games to the real-world issues will appear as social games continue to develop. Besides, from an affective learning perspective, *Call to Action* also suggests another pedagogical dimension, cor-responding to a higher degree of engagement and learning, as we will see in the discussion below.

Game Pattern: Sympathy for Victims

Definition:*Sympathy for Victims* involves support for feeling concern and compassion for victims. Sympathy has been defined as social affinity in which one person understands and is affected by another's feelings or emotions. In experiencing sympathy, we recognize the emotions of another, but we do not – as in empathy– experience the other person's feelings, but instead feel sympathy for them.

Problem: Social change games are very carefully designed to deliver a strong message about real people facing different types of hardships (e.g. poverty, homelessness). Players should understand the situations in which characters find themselves and how it makes them feel and react. As a result, players should be moved by the plight of those people depicted in the game, feeling concern and compassion for them as victims.

The issue is related to *Call to Action,* because sympathy incites players to take action in favour of the victims. It is also related to the pattern *Emotional Immersion* (Björk & Holopainen, 2005) and more general affective strategies.

Solution: Players, through resolving dilemmas and making important decisions relating to character welfare, are confronted with some of the anxiety, uncertainty, disempowerment and hardships faced by real people. Moreover, by "talking" with the characters, they will better understand the characters; situations, their sorrow and joy, the way they feel, and how their situations affect them.

Example: In Ayiti© (2006), 3rd World Farmer© (2006), and Darfur is Dying© (2006), similar structure and game-play generate sympathy. In these games, players follow the day-to-day life of an immigrant teen, a third-word farmer, or an impoverished inhabitant. To survive, the game characters (i.e. usually a family) must accumulate enough wealth to provide food, remain healthy, and improve their living conditions. The consequences are shown over time through simple game actions (e.g. making choices and collecting things) while impaired by adverse conditions (crises of various kinds), which can even result in the death of a family member.

Role-play games have even more complex game mechanics that afford new possibilities.

In games like GC: LA (2008), whose game-play revolves around factories (maquiladoras) and their abuses in the context of poor Latin-American countries, the player encounters different victims (and tormentors) and gradually attunes to the victims' plights, thus developing compassion toward those victims.

Limitations: Social games succeed partly in stimulating sympathy through demonstrating social dilemmas and exposing the needs and problems faced by people. However, it seems that a lack of depiction of affective aspects is typical, with a too-heavy reliance on cognitive game-play strategies, and this seems detrimental in achieving sympathy. For example, in Ayiti© and Darfur is Dying©, the characters never seem to react to the death of family members, which seems somewhat strange and contradictory to the game aims. Social change games need a better balance between the cognitive and affective learning strategies, especially including some form of emotional representation and affective feedback that would stimulate sympathy and make the game more immersive.

Again, Activity Theory provides a deeper understanding of how the patterns work to support affective learning in games. In contrast to the first study, social change games explicitly aim to change attitudes and behaviours beyond the context of the game. This is reflected in the patterns, and is well-situated within the context of social groups and their rules. *Sympathy for Victims* acts as a game-play mechanism (tool) that presents a need and an emotional appeal, and at the same time positions the player effectively with respect to the people involved so as to suggest an activity structure. *Call to Action* not only provides the suggestion for action, but explicitly provides tools to act, such as built-in mechanisms that link to petition signing and letter writing campaigns. The structure is established: the victims need help, the player *can* help, and the tool is at hand. The result therefore is not only practical action, but also affective development in terms of generating socio-emotional responsibility, acting upon it, and in doing so, developing a feeling of shared belonging.

The domain of serious games, including social change games and games for health, has more recently emerged than that of mainstream games and is so far smaller in scale, thus leading to a more limited set of game patterns, two of which that we have discussed here. However, we see more possibilities for design. Empathy can be defined as the identification with and vicarious experiencing of feelings, thoughts, or attitudes of another. The small casual games that we discussed cannot truly accommodate empathy. They lack the emotional richness and depth for players to be truly immersed and experience the character's lives as their own. Most of all, as we highlighted above, the characters do not often express or experience any feelings, an important component in generating empathy. However, more complex socio-emotional role-play games, like the virtual drama *FearNot* about bullying, or those inspired from computer games such as Black & White 2© (2005) have greater power for creating empathy. Thus new patterns such as *Empathy with Victims* will emerge as serious games continue to develop.

SUPPORTING AFFECTIVE LEARNING IN GAMES

In the sections above we have given a few examples of game patterns for socio-emotional learning that we have found in our in-depth study of Dragon Age© and of a set of serious games. Even in these particular games, there are more patterns that can be identified, and there are many other games worthy of study, and also much potential for supporting affective learning in new ways that have not yet been used in any game.

The role of patterns, and how they might work, seems well supported by the activity theory framework we described earlier. The way the patterns support learning is related to Vygotsky's ZDP and the more specific mediation strategy called "scaffolding" as identified by Bruner and colleagues (Wood, Bruner, & Ross, 1976). The key idea is that mediation – either via assistance or with tools – can be temporary, and facilitate learning that later will no longer require such assistance. "Although the teacher assumes much of the control during scaffolded instruction, the ultimate goal of instruction is covert, independent self-regulatory learning" (Ellis, Worthington, & Larkin, 1994, p. 12). Nardi, Ly, & Harris (2007) explore how game players ask for and receive support through game-play conversation involving cognitive and affective elements. Most importantly, while scaffolding in conventional learning typically requires explicit identifiable support, in the world of a computer game it can be designed as part of the game-play. Situations in game-play can be limited in the choices they offer in order to support player exploration, and the appreciation of the consequences and relationships between different paths of action. More generally computer games can begin with more limited challenges and only progress to a more difficult scope when the play demonstrates that they are ready. The control implicit in game design, together with the potential to show varying perspectives, offers rich possibilities for learning from experience. Finally, to support affective learning through games, we suggest that a debriefing and reflection step is critical in order to filter, to shape, and to reinforce the lessons within the game design.

In managing the kind of support that the patterns provide, a key characteristic of game-play is the nature of player engagement. In a game-world with human or human-like characters, the player can play the role of in-game characters, either specifically in role-play games, or less formally in third-person games or god games. Gee (2007) has pointed out that the relationship between player and avatar or character is often different than strict role-play, and resembles more a parent-child relationship where the player attempts to guide the character to greater experience and success, in a process that Gee calls "projective identity". We should thus consider the effect on the players themselves. Aarseth (1997) claims than games, by contrast to traditional media, have *ergodic* character: players must make decisions that lead to consequences, together with the anticipation and the reflections that follow the consequences, all with the knowledge the player's actions influenced the outcomes.

At the level of interaction between characters and within groups, there are many challenges for representation that are necessary to underpin support for affective learning. Character personalities, moral systems, and background may need depiction or allow discovery, and to model the affective learning challenges of the real work, the depiction and discovery may need to involve non-verbal dynamics such as facial expressions and body language. The interaction design might need to involve exploration and experimentation, and foster the development of moral problem solving skills. There will be a need for immediate decisions, such as trust or dependence, and also need for longer term effects, such as reciprocity or revenge. How such interactions are managed and evolve in the real world can show what might work in games. For example, we suggest that knowledge about the mediating role of humour can work in similar ways within games (Dormann & Biddle, 2009). Ultimately, even truly difficult moral decisions may need to be addressed, where grey areas do not have clear-cut answers, and the consequences of decisions need to be demonstrated for consideration of difficult choices. Situations involving a number of characters become even more complex, as affective learning must address group dynamics, including the effects of peer pressure, conflict within groups, and split allegiances.

It is also important to consider such games within a wider context, to forge links between game experience and learning, and to make connections between the game world and the real world. The analysis of events that occur in the game itself, and identification of feelings that the game evokes and what was experienced during game-play, are essential didactic practices necessary for affective learning (Garris et al., 2002). Allowing players time to reflect on their emotions, decisions and choices they made, helps them to analyze the situation and put everything in perspective (Petranek, 2000). To stimulate deeper reflections still, players can be asked, for example, to keep a journal of their game activities and experiences.

The game-play experience can then be further used to deepen and strengthen the affective learning experience. As Frasca suggests in Videogames of the Oppressed, players can re-design game characters according to their knowledge and understanding of specific socio-emotional problems (2001). We can embrace the power of creativity, imagination and willingness of game players to become authors. This can be seen as a specific form of the *Call to Action* pattern but also relates to other patterns involving communication between player, and the strength of participatory culture. Border Games©, a project by Spanish media activists, was conceived as a collaborative process in which young migrants describe and express their experiences by translating them into game narratives (Zehle, 2008).

By going through this process, players can reach a deeper level of engagement and affective learning, by moving from receiving (playing with the game), to responding (criticizing game viewpoints) and valuing (producing games or participating in activist activities, as we discussed in game patterns) (Krathwohl, Bloom, & Masia, 1964). Ultimately, the game experience should take the players on a journey of personal evolution. Social change games are important in that they aim to transform players' intellectual views and real-world behaviors by "engaging them on a deep, and meaningful level around an important social issue." (Games for Change Awards, 2007).

SOLUTIONS AND RECOMMENDATIONS

This chapter has outlined and illustrated our proposed approach to game support for affective learning, especially meaning learning for the affective domain. In essence, we propose that we adopt an activity theory framework, where we focus on games that depict situated social human behaviour. These games can then become, both themselves at a larger level, and in their design elements at a smaller level, conceptual tools that scaffold operational understanding of the affective domain. We suggest that these conceptual tools can be identified, and made reusable as design patterns.

The patterns we have identified in this chapter cover a range of possibilities. To begin with, our two case studies involve quite different contexts. Dragon Age© is a commercial role-playing game with a context of engagement and entertainment featuring interactive narrative. Our patterns address problems of social interaction, and highlight solutions by illustrating behaviour that can solve these problems. *Social Maintenance* illustrates how bonds between people are kept strong by continuing engagement and care; *Sacrificial Action* foregrounds how individual behaviour must sometimes put the needs of others, or a group, foremost for the common good; and *Shared Learning* shows how a little effort in relaying discoveries can provide significant help to others in similar situations and can ground reciprocity. The key outcome is the juxtaposition of these problems with their solutions, so that the linkage becomes clear, leveragable, and transferable beyond the games. The social change games we studied (Ayit*i*©, 3rd World Farmer©, Darfur is Dying©, *etc.)* involve a context of advocacy and an intent to influence attitudes and behaviour. Our patterns in this context involve the affective elements that can assist this effort, helping to bridge the gap between the subject matter and audience (*Sympathy for Victim*) and the gap between the audience and actual involvement (*Call to Action*). The key outcome is the resulting change itself: whether the intervention is successful.

Game design patterns can help us to further both the study of affective learning in games, and the inclusion of affective learning in new games. In particular, we suggest that we need more understanding about how to structure character and group interaction within games to support affective learning, and we need to learn more about how to manage engagement while providing scaffolding. We must be cautious, however, as pattern practice in both architecture and software design has illustrated: design structures should not be regarded as proven patterns until they have been shown to work effectively in a variety of contexts. We must also consider the wider scope of affective learning through critical and reflective engagement beyond the game-play itself and how real-world attitudes and behaviour are affected.

Beyond these specifics, there are important implications for various stakeholders. For players, the benefit is a richer vicarious experience in game-play. Cinema, theatre, and storytelling have strategies that enthrall their audience on a deeper level— touch their hearts—and games can do the same. For game developers, this ability needs to be understood and explored through actual usage leveraging the strengths of this new interactive medium. Game patterns provide tools for design, for generating new game-play, and address new areas of learning. For others, such as teachers and policy-makers, the key implication involves broadening the scope and possibilities of games. Beyond the negative aspects of games that have received increasing media attention, preparing people to function and grow in a global, connected world demands new ways of learning. Games can help us to support affective learning, developing socio-emotional skills or civic engagement, but also to re-invent and imagine new ways of thinking about teaching and training.

FUTURE RESEARCH DIRECTIONS

The role of games in learning is multifaceted and involves much more than support of transfer of curricular content. In this chapter we have concentrated on learning in affective domain, and how an activity theory framework can inform the identification and discovery of appropriate conceptual tools. The immediate future work is the further identification and exploration of new patterns, which needs to be followed with evaluation of the effectiveness of the patterns in varying contexts. The wider scope also indicates work is needed on facilitation and the role of the teachers, especially in supporting critical and reflective engagement about the affective learning experience of game-play.

We also need to consider a variety of broader issues involving learning, games, affect, and how they might be related. These are all broad areas and the potential for interaction is great. In each case, however, we see a particular line of current research that shows promise for the area of affective learning. In learning, the work of Fogg (2003) on "persuasive technology" deserves attention because of its focus on psychological principles for changing attitudes and behaviour with technological interaction. In games, the work of Bogost (2007) on "persuasive games", and especially his conception of "procedural rhetoric" has great potential in linking narrative connection between cause and effect that can support affective decision-making. Finally, the work by Picard (1997) on mapping out "affective computing" must also be considered.

CONCLUSION

In this chapter we have addressed the potential for affective learning in computer games. As we discussed, affective learning has a number of aspects, and our focus was especially on socio-emotional learning, being learning for the affective domain, and so including topics such as emotional literacy, self-awareness and social awareness, as well as related interpersonal skills and the ability to make ethical decisions. We outlined a theoretical framework of activity theory for understanding how games can support affective learning. The framework fits well because it features exactly the kind of tools, constraints, and progression that are common in game-play. We then introduced our method for exploration, identification, and transfer. We study games using an affective walkthrough method, and document supporting structures in game-play as design patterns for further study and reuse.

We have shown that there is a distinct agenda for learning in the affective domain, that there is a good theoretical framework for understanding how it might be supported, and have documented some patterns we have identified in existing commercial and serious games. There is much work yet to be done, both in study and in design. We need to continue the study of existing games to identify current design patterns that serve affective learning, and we need to explore new design to support affective learning situations, first between individuals and within groups, and then in larger social and organizational settings. We also need to explore supporting structures, both within games, so as to support engagement, and externally with human mentorship, so as to support reflection and consolidation of learning.

ACKNOWLEDGMENT

The authors acknowledge support from the Social Sciences and Humanities Research Council (SSHRC) of Canada under the Research Development Initiatives program.

REFERENCES

Aarseth, E. J. (1997). *Cybertext: Perspectives on ergodic literature*. Baltimore: Johns Hopkins University Press.

Alexander, C., Ishikawa, S., & Silverstein, M. (1977). *A pattern language: Towns, buildings, construction.* New York: Oxford University Press.

Ayiti: The Cost of Life. [computer game for web browser]. (2006). Developed for UNICEF by Gamelab. Available for download at: http://costoflife.ning.com

Aylett, R. S., Louchart, S., Dias, J., Paiva, A., & Vala, M. (2005). *FearNot!: An experiment in emergent narrative* (pp. 305–316). London: Springer-Verlag.

Barr, P., Noble, J., & Biddle, R. (2007). Video game values: Human-computer interaction and games. *Interacting with Computers, 19*(2), 180–195. doi:10.1016/j.intcom.2006.08.008

Björk, S., & Holopainen, J. (2005). *Patterns in game design.* Boston: Charles River Media.

Black & White 2. [computer game]. (2005). Electronic Arts.

Bogost, I. (2007). *Persuasive games: The expressive power of videogames.* Cambridge, MA: The MIT Press.

Bowen, E. R. (2005). *Student engagement and its relation to quality work design: A review of the literature.* Retrieved January 25, 2010, from http://teach.valdosta.edu/are/ebowenLitReview.pdf

Church, D. (1999). *Formal abstract design tools.* Gamasutra. Retrieved January 5, 2010, from http://www.gamasutra.com/view/feature/3357/formal_abstract_design_tools.php

Coplan, A. (2004). Empathic engagement with narrative fictions. *The Journal of Aesthetics and Art Criticism, 62*(2), 141–152. doi:10.1111/j.1540-594X.2004.00147.x

Darfur is Dying. [computer game for web browser]. (2006). mtvU. Available for download at: http://www.darfurisdying.com

De Aguilera, M., & Mendiz, A. (2003). Video games and education: Education in the face of a parallel school. *ACM Computers in Entertainment, 1*(1), 1–14.

Delwiche, A. (2007). From the green berets to America's army: Video games as a vehicle for political propaganda. In Williams, J. P., & Smith, J. H. (Eds.), *The players' realm: Studies on the culture of video games and gaming.* London: McFarland & Company, Inc.

Demon's Souls. [Playstation 3 console game]. (2009). Atlus.

Dirkx, J. M. (2001). The power of feelings: Emotion, imagination, and the construction of meaning in adult learning. *New Directions for Adult and Continuing Education, 89,* 63–72. doi:10.1002/ace.9

Dormann, C., & Biddle, R. (2008). Understanding game design for affective learning. In *Proceedings of the 2008 Conference on Future Play: Research, Play, Share,* (pp 41-48). New York: ACM.

Dormann, C., & Biddle, R. (2009). A review of humor for computer games: Play, laugh and more. *Simulation & Gaming: An Interdisciplinary Journal, 40*(6), 802–824.

Dragon Age. (2009). *Origins* [Playstation 3 console game]. Electronic Arts.

Durkin, K., & Barber, B. (2002). Not so doomed: Computer game play and positive adolescent development. *Journal of Applied Developmental Psychology, 23*(4), 373–392. doi:10.1016/S0193-3973(02)00124-7

Ellis, E. S., Worthington, L. A., & Larkin, M. J. (1994). Executive summary of the research synthesis on effective teaching principles and the design of quality tools for educators. Retrieved January 20, 2010, from http://idea.uoregon.edu/~ncite/documents/techrep/tech06.html

Engeström, Y. (1987). *Learning by expanding: An activity-theoretical approach to developmental research.* Helsinki: Orienta-Konsultit.

Falstein, N., & Barwood, H. (2006). The 400 project. Retrieved January 22, 2010, from http://www.theinspiracy.com.

Ferguson, C. J. (2007). Evidence for publication bias in video game violence effects literature: A meta-analytic review. *Aggression and Violent Behavior, 12,* 470–482. doi:10.1016/j.avb.2007.01.001

Flanagan, M., & Lotko, A. (2009). Anxiety, openness, and activist games: A case study for critical play. In *Breaking New Ground: Innovation in Games, Play, Practice and Theory.* Presented at DiGRA 2009.

Fogg, B. J. (2003). *Persuasive technology: Using computers to change what we think and do.* San Francisco: Morgan Kaufmann Publishers.

Frasca, G. (2001). *Videogames of the oppressed: Videogames as a means for critical thinking and debate.* Unpublished doctoral thesis, Georgia Institute of Technology, Georgia.

Games for Change Awards. (2007). *Games for Change.* Retrieved January 29, 2010, from http://www.gamesforchange.org/conference/2007/awards.php

Gamma, E., Helm, R., Johnson, R., & Vlissides, J. M. (1994). *Design patterns: Elements of reusable object-oriented software.* Reading, MA: Addison-Wesley Professional.

Garris, R., Ahlers, R., & Driskell, J. E. (2002). Games, motivation, and learning: A research and practice model. *Simulation & Gaming: An Interdisciplinary Journal, 33*(4), 441–467.

Gee, J. P. (2007). *What video games have to teach us about learning and literacy.* New York: Palgrave Macmillan.

Global Conflicts. *Latin America.* [computer game]. (2008). Serious Games Interactive. Available for download at http://www.globalconflicts.eu/

Gros, B. (2003). The impact of digital games in education. *First Monday, 8*(7). Retrieved January 20, 2010, from http://firstmonday.org/issues/issue8_7/gros/index.html

Juul, J. (2005). *Half-real.* Cambridge, MA: The MIT Press.

Kline, S., Dyer-Witheford, N., & De Peuter, G. (2005). *Digital play: The interaction of technology, culture, and marketing.* Montréal, QC: McGill-Queen's University Press.

Krathwohl, D., Bloom, B. S., & Masia, B. B. (1964). *Taxonomy of educational objectives: The classification of educational goals.* New York: McKay, Longman.

Kreimeier, B. (2002). *The case for game design patterns.* Gamasutra. Retrieved January 5, 2010, from http://www.wattpad.com/93567

Lankoski, P., & Björk, S. (2007). *Gameplay design patterns for social networks and conflicts.* Presented at the Fifth International Game Design Technology Workshop and Conference, Liverpool. Retrieved January 20, 2010, from http://www.mlab.uiah.fi/~plankosk/blog/?p=105

Leontiev, A. N. (1978). *Activity, consciousness and personality.* New York: Prentice Hall Press.

Lin, C. A., & Hullman, G. A. (2005). Tobacco-prevention messages online: Social marketing via the Web. *Health Communication, 8*(22), 177–193. doi:10.1207/s15327027hc1802_5

Malone, T. W. (1981). Toward a theory of intrinsically motivating instruction. *Cognitive Science, 5*(4), 333–369. doi:10.1207/s15516709cog0504_2

Martin, B. L., & Reigeluth, C. M. (1999). Affective education and the affective domain: Implications for instructional-design theories and models. In Reigeluth, C. M. (Ed.), *Instructional-design theories and models* (pp. 485–510). Hillsdale, NJ: Lawrence Erlbaum Associates.

McKee, R. (1997). *Story: Substance, structure, style and the principles of screenwriting.* New York: Regan Books.

Nardi, B. A., Ly, S., & Harris, J. (2007). Learning conversations in World of Warcraft. *Proceedings of the 40th Annual Hawaii International Conference on System Sciences.* (pp.79-88). New York: IEEE Computer Society Press.

Norman, D. A. (2002). *The design of everyday things.* New York: Basic Books.

Orey, M. (2001). *Emerging perspectives on learning, teaching, and technology.* Retrieved from http://projects.coe.uga.edu/epltt

Payton, J. W., Wardlaw, D. M., Graczyk, P. A., Bloodworth, M. R., Tompsett, C. J., & Weissberg, R. P. (2000). Social and emotional learning: A framework for promoting mental health and reducing risk behavior in children and youth. *The Journal of School Health, 70*(5), 179–185. doi:10.1111/j.1746-1561.2000.tb06468.x

PeaceMaker. [computer game]. (2007). Impact-Games. Available for download at http://www.peacemakergame.com/

Pedretti, E. G. (2004). Perspectives on learning through research on critical issues-based science center exhibitions. *Science Education, 88,* S34–S47. doi:10.1002/sce.20019

Petranek, C. F. (2000). Written debriefing: The next vital step in learning with simulations. *Simulation & Gaming: An Interdisciplinary Journal, 31*(1), 108–118.

Picard, R. (1997). *Affective computing.* Cambridge, MA: The MIT Press.

Pictures for Truth. [computer game]. (2008). Amnesty International. Available for download at: http://www.picturesfortruth.com

Pohl, K. (2008). Ethical reflection and emotional investment in computer games. In S. Günzel, M. Liebe, & D. Mersch (Eds.), *Conference Proceedings of the Philosophy of Computer Games,* (pp. 92 - 107). Potsdam: University Press.

Ratner, C. (2000). A cultural-psychological analysis of emotions. *Culture and Psychology, 6*(1), 5–39. doi:10.1177/1354067X0061001

3*rd* World Farmer. [computer game for web browser]. (2006). 3rd World Farmer Team. Available for download at: http://www.3rdworldfarmer.com

Russo, T., & Benson, S. (2005). Learning with invisible others: Perceptions of online presence and their relationship to cognitive and affective learning. *Journal of Educational Technology & Society, 8*(1), 54–62.

Schlechty, P. (2001). *Shaking up the schoolhouse: How to support and sustain educational innovation.* San Francisco: Jossey-Bass Publications.

Schreiner, K. (2008). Digital games target social change. *IEEE Computer Graphics and Applications, 28*(1), 12–17. doi:10.1109/MCG.2008.4

SimCity. [computer game]. (1989). Maxis.

Squire, K. (2003). Video games in education. *International Journal of Intelligent Games & Simulation, 2*(1). Retrieved January 20, 2010, from http://www.scit.wlv.ac.uk/~cm1822/absij21.htm

Tetris. [computer game]. (1986). Alexy Pajnitov.

Thomas, R., Cahill, J., & Santilli, L. (1997). Using an interactive computer game to increase skill and self-efficacy regarding safer sex negotiation: Field test results. *Health Education & Behavior, 24*(1), 71–86. doi:10.1177/109019819702400108

Tidwell, J. (2005). *Designing interfaces: Patterns for effective interaction design.* Sebastopol, CA: O'Reilly Media.

Vygotsky, L. S. (1962). *Thought and language*. Cambridge, MA: The MIT Press. doi:10.1037/11193-000

Vygotsky, L. S. (1978). *Mind in society: The development of higher psychological processes*. Cambridge, MA: Harvard University Press.

Wang, H., & Singhal, A. (2009). Entertainment-education through digital games. In Ritterfield, U., Cody, M., & Vorderer, P. (Eds.), *Serious games: Mechanisms and effects* (pp. 271–292). New York: Routledge.

Wharton, C., Rieman, J., Lewis, C., & Polson, P. (1994). The cognitive walkthrough method: A practitioner's guide. In Nielsen, J., & Mack, R. L. (Eds.), *Usability inspection methods* (pp. 105–140). New York: Wiley.

Wood, D., Bruner, J., & Ross, G. (1976). The role of tutoring in problem solving. *Journal of Child Psychology and Psychiatry, and Allied Disciplines*, *17*, 89–100. doi:10.1111/j.1469-7610.1976.tb00381.x

Zagal, J. P. (2009). Ethically notable videogames: Moral dilemmas and gameplay. In *Breaking new ground: Innovation in games, play, practice and theory*. Presented at DiGRA 2009. Retrieved January 20, 2010, from http://www.digra.org/dl/db/09287.13336.pdf

Zehle, S. (2008). Border games: Migrant media changes terrain. In M. Ghosh-Schellhorn & R. Marti (Eds.), *Playing by the rules of the game*. (pp. 287-296). Münster: LIT. Retrieved January 20, 2010 from http://orgnets.cn/wp-content/uploads/2009/02/zehle_bordergames_2008.pdf

ADDITIONAL READING

Carr, D. (2005). Contexts, gaming pleasures, and gendered preferences. *Simulation & Gaming: An Interdisciplinary Journal*, *36*, 464–482.

Chen, M. (2005). Addressing social dilemmas and fostering cooperation through computer games. In *Changing Views – Worlds in Play*. Presented at DiGRA 2005.

Davidson, D. (2003). Interactivity in ico: Initial involvement, immersion, investment. In R. Smith (Ed.), *Second International Conference on Entertainment Computing, Vol. 38*, (pp 1-21), Pittsburgh, PA: Carnegie Mellon University.

Egan, K., & Gajdamaschko, N. (2003). Some cognitive tools of literacy. In Kozulin, A., Gidis, B., Ageyev, V. S., & Miller, S. M. (Eds.), *Vygotsky's educational theory in cultural context* (pp. 83–98). Cambridge, UK: Cambridge University Press.

Ellis, A. K., & Fouts, J. T. (1996). *Handbook of educational terms and applications*. Princeton, NJ: Eye on Education.

Fien, J. (1997). Learning to care: A focus for values in health and environmental education. *Health Education Research*, *12*(4), 437–447. doi:10.1093/her/12.4.437

Fullerton, T., Chen, J., Santiago, K., Nelson, E., Diamante, V., Meyers, A., et al. (2006). That cloud game: Dreaming (and doing) innovative game design. *ACM SIGGRAPH Symposium on Videogames*, (pp. 51 – 59). New York, NY: ACM.

Gilleade, K., Dix, A., & Allanson, J. (2005). Affective videogames and modes of affective gaming: assist me, challenge me, emote me. In *Changing Views – Worlds in Play*. Presented at DiGRA 2005.

Jelfs, A., & Whitelock, D. (2001). Presence and the role of activity theory in understanding: How students learn in virtual learning environments. In Beynon, M., Nehaniv, C. L., & Dautenhahn, K. (Eds.), *Cognitive technology: Instruments of mind* (pp. 123–129). Berlin: Springer-Verlag. doi:10.1007/3-540-44617-6_12

Losh, E. (2005). In country with tactical Iraqi: trust, identity, and language learning in a military video Game. Heirich, A. & Thomas D. (Eds.) *Digital Arts and Culture Conference* (pp. 69-78). Copenhagen: University of Copenhagen.

Martin, B., & Briggs, L. (1986). *The affective and cognitive domains: Integration for instruction and research*. Englewood Cliffs, NJ: Educational Technology Publications.

McCrary, N. (2000). *Expanding a model for affective development: Implications for an activity component. Presented at 22nd Annual Proceedings, Research & Theory Division*. Denver, CO: AECT.

Michael, D., & Chen, S. (2005). *Serious games: Games that educate, train, and inform*. New York, NY: Muska & Lipman/Premier-Trade.

Oliver, M., & Pelletier, C. (2004). Activity theory and learning from digital games: implications for game design. Buckingham, D. & Willet, R. (Eds.) *Conference on Digital Generations: Children, young people and new media*, (pp. 329-342) London: London University.

Pivec, M. (2007). Games for learning and learning from games. *Informatica, 31*, 419–423.

Rusch, D. (2009). Mechanisms of the soul: Tackling the human condition in videogames. In *Breaking New Ground: Innovation in games, play, practice and theory*. Presented at DiGRA 2009. Retrieved January 20, 2010, from http://www.digra.org/

KEY TERMS AND DEFINITIONS

Social Change Games: Games that directly attempt to raise awareness of important social issues by delivering powerful statements. These games aim to transform players' views or attitudes about social issues as well as inspire real-world behavior.

Game Design Pattern: A convention for describing and documenting recurring game design decisions, generally documented as a three-part rule, which expresses a relation between a certain context, a problem and a solution.

Social Maintenance: A game design pattern that promotes affective learning. *Social Maintenance* is described as performing actions to redefine and refine the relationship with a group.

Sacrificial Action: A game design pattern that promotes affective learning. *Sacrificial Action* is the ability to prioritize others' well-being (NPCs and, in multiplayer games, other players) ahead of the player's own character's well-being and advancement.

Shared Learning: A game design pattern that promotes affective learning. Players share lessons from the game with other players. Through direct and indirect cooperation, players work together to master the game.

Call to Action: A game design pattern that promotes affective learning, *Call to Action* refers to the functions within the game framework that inspire players to step beyond the game and actively participate in social activism.

Sympathy for Victim: A game design pattern that promotes affective learning by promoting feelings of concern and compassion for victims.

Chapter 14
Motivating by Design:
Using Digital–Game Based Learning Techniques to Create an Interesting Problem–Based Learning Environment

Paul Toprac
Southern Methodist University, USA

ABSTRACT

This chapter describes how to design a motivating educational game for middle school students using digital-game based learning techniques in a problem-based learning environment. Specifically, The Alien Rescue Game (TARG), a problem-based digital-game based learning program, is compared to commercial digital games to determine how to design a motivating educational game. Results showed that students believed that their interest in learning science was influenced by their self-efficacy, attainment value, intrinsic value, utility value, cost perceptions, and knowledge. Furthermore, these same influences affected players' perceptions of and experience with commercial digital games. Thus, these motivational constructs should be considered when developing educational games, with self-efficacy, intrinsic value, knowledge, and cost being the most important based. Intrinsic motivation sources were found to be control, challenge, immersion, and socializing. Considerations and implications for the design of motivating digital game-based learning programs, recommendations, and future research directions are presented.

INTRODUCTION

Computer and video games (digital games) have increasingly captivated the minds of our youth (Malone, 1981; Randel & Morris, 1992; Rosas, Nussbaum, & Cumsille, 2003; Ryan, Rigby, & Przybylski, 2006). The significance of digital

DOI: 10.4018/978-1-60960-495-0.ch014

games in our society is evidenced by the fact that more than two-thirds of all American households play games and 42% of households have video game consoles (Electronic Software Association, 2010). The youth, those under 18 years old, are major players of digital games accounting for 25% of the most frequent game players with nearly 50% of these players being female. Furthermore, parents are playing with their children, identifying "fun for the entire family" as the top reason to participate in this activity (Electronic Software Association, 2010). Finally, adult gamers have been playing digital games for an average of 12 years. Clearly, digital games are a major form of entertainment in the 21st century because they are fun and engaging.

Beyond just entertaining, most digital games require extensive learning in order to succeed. Digital game players must plan and execute strategies, problem solve, manage resources, and adapt rapidly to changing circumstances. In many ways, digital game players learn skills that can be useful in everyday life. The combination of fun and engagement in digital games with the potential of learning useful skills has made digital games a promising opportunity as an educational media and interactive learning environment.

Unfortunately, the design for and the use of digital games in classroom settings to leverage their motivational power have not been extensively studied (Dickey, 2005; Hoffman & Nadelson, 2006). This chapter investigates whether a digital game could be designed to enhance motivation to learn academic subject matter while playing, and promote continuing interest to learn after playing has ended.

The aim of this chapter is to provide insight on how to design digital games for the purposes of engaging middle school students and developing interest in academic subject matter. That is, this chapter describes the theoretical model of how to design a digital game to engage students in solving complex problems, such as those required in mathematics and science. In particular, a problem-based learning (PBL) digital game, *The Alien Rescue Game (TARG)*, that was designed specifically to promote students' learning, motivation, and interest in a middle school science class will be described and assessed, along with findings from motivational studies of commercial digital games. Furthermore, this chapter attempts to determine if students can be motivated by playing *TARG* to become interested in academic subjects and

toward the development of a personal interest in the academic subject matter.

BACKGROUND

Theoretical Framework: Model of Motivation

To understand how to design motivating digital games, one must understand motivation and the sources of motivation. Motivation is the psychological construct driving an individual's choice of behavior, intensity of behavior, latency of behavior, and persistence of behavior (Graham & Weiner, 1996). Furthermore, motivation both influences and is influenced by cognition, such as goal setting, and emotional reactions, such as the feeling of fun. Motivation is often considered to promote learning (Gottfried, 1985; Lepper, Corpus, & Iyengar, 2005).

Currently, the expectancy-value motivational theory is the predominant theory of achievement motivation, which posits that motivation increases with the expectation of reaching the goal and the goal's value (Graham & Weiner, 1996; Liberman & Forster, 2008). Furthermore, extensive research on motivation for classroom academic achievement has been performed using the Eccles' expectancy value model of motivation (Schunk, Pintrich, & Meece, 2007). According to Wigfield and Eccles (2000), achievement motivation influences the choice, engagement, and performance of individuals. A simplified version of this complex and elaborate model is shown in Figure 1.

In this model, expectancy and subjective task value predicts achievement behavior, which is the intention to approach or avoid engaging a task, and, once engaged, the quality of effort and persistence. Though expectancy and subjective task value are often independently measured, they influence each other and build reciprocally together for a subject or activity (Eccles & Wigfield, 2002). That is, an individual is willing to expend

Figure 1. Simplified version of Eccles' expectancy-value model of motivation

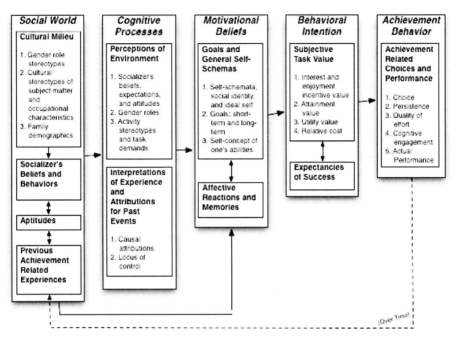

Note: Adapted from (1) *Motivation in Education: Theory, Research, and Applications*, 2nd ed., p. 61 by P. Pintrich and D. Schunk, 2002, Upper Saddle River, NJ. Copyright 2002, 1996 by Pearson Education, Inc. (2) Eccles, J. S., & Wigfield, A. (2002) "Motivational Beliefs, Values, and Goals," by J. S. Eccles and A. Wigfield, 2002, *Annual Review of Psychology*, 53(1), p. 119. Copyright 2002 by Annual Reviews. (3) "Expectancy--Value Theory of Achievement Motivation", by A. Wigfield and J, S, Eccles (2000) *Contemporary Educational Psychology*, 25(1), p. 69.

more effort on something that is he or she values, which can lead to success, and being successful at a task can lead to the task becoming more valued.

According to Eccles (2009; Eccles & Wigfield, 2002), expectancy is a person's self-evaluation of his or her ability and beliefs about the probability of success in upcoming tasks. These expectancy beliefs are analogous to ability self-concept (Brookover, Thomas, & Paterson, 1964), perceived competence (Harter, 1992), and Bandura's (1996) self-efficacy expectations. Though Bandura may not believe that expectancy and self-efficacy are similar, "empirical work has shown that children and adolescents do not distinguish between these two different levels of beliefs" (Eccles & Wigfield, 2002, p. 19). Thus, theoretically, these two constructs are different; but in real world achievement situations they are indistinguishable. Therefore,

we can consider self-efficacy, expectancy, ability self-concept, perceived competence, and other competency-related beliefs as the same basic construct.

Subjective task value is the other reason why an individual are motivated to engage in an undertaking. Subjective task value—beliefs about value of doing the task—comprises of the sum of the components of attainment value, the utility value, and the intrinsic value, minus the cost value component (Schunk, et al., 2007). The attainment value is the individual's assessment about whether the task is congruent with the core aspects of the person's identity. For example, a child who is striving for the identity of being a "writer" will likely resolve that a writing project has a high attainment value for him- or herself to successfully achieve. The utility value is the individual's evaluation of whether performing well

285

on a task will be useful for achieving future goals, such as career goals. For instance, a student may strive to perform well in a mathematics course in mathematics because she wants to become an engineer to attain a good standard of living. The future reward of a good wage is an extrinsic motivator that is influencing the student's perception of value of mathematics. Thus, utility value captures some of the extrinsic motivators, which are external rewards and punishments that affect the individual's tendency to respond a certain way (Greeno, Collins, & Resnick, 1996).

The intrinsic value is the individual's appraisal of whether a task is enjoyable and/or interesting (Schunk, et al., 2007). Eccles and Wigfield (2002) argue that intrinsic value is similar to flow (Csikszentmihalyi, 1990), and situational interest (Hidi & Renninger, 2006; Krapp, 2005; Schiefele, 1991), where flow is the emotional and psychological state that occurs when an individual is fully engaged and immersed in an activity (Eccles & Wigfield, 2002) and situational interest is the situation or context that individuals find interesting (see below for more details on situational interest). According to Malone and Lepper (1987), intrinsically motivation can be described as interesting, enjoyable, and fun. For example, the intrinsic value in doing a history project occurs when he or she determines that the project is "fun" to do.

There are many different perspectives on intrinsic motivation because it varies over time, circumstances, and how people view what they are doing (Schunk, et al., 2007). One prominent perspective of intrinsic motivation is self determination theory (Ryan & Deci, 2000), which hypothesizes that individuals are motivated to seek out activities that meet the innate needs of autonomy, competence, and relatedness. The autonomy need is the need to feel in *control* of one's environment. Thus, environments that provide choices and self-direction support the feeling of autonomy, which promotes intrinsic motivation. The competence need is fulfilled when individuals

feel challenged, yet maintain a sense of efficacy over their environment. The experience of competence is enhanced when individuals acquire new skills or abilities, are optimally *challenged*, and receive positive feedback (Ryan, Rigby & Przybylski, 2006). The relatedness need is the need to feel secure and connected to others. The need for security and connectedness is highly congruent with Maslow's (1955) concepts of needs for safety and belongingness. In support of the existence of this need, numerous studies have shown that cooperative learning and group activities have positive effects on students' interest, engagement, and motivation (Shernoff, Csikszentmihalyi, Schneider, & Shernoff, 2003). The importance of development and maintenance of *interpersonal* relations, including the sense of belonging to and participating in a social group or community, is also highly congruent with the social constructivist view of motivation (Greeno, et al., 1996).

However, other researchers have found that different aspects of intrinsic motivation. Malone (1981) determined that *fantasy* promotes intrinsic motivation and Berlyne (1978) posited that individuals are innately *curious*. Malone and Lepper (1987) proposed a set of heuristics and principles for designing intrinsically motivating instructional environments that include five sources in a learning environment: challenge, curiosity, control, fantasy, and interpersonal as described in Table 1.

Finally, the fourth component of Eccles' model of subjective task value is the cost component, which is the perceived negative side of engaging a task. Cost is relative to the other opportunities because when individuals engage in one task, it means that they are not engaged on other tasks (Eccles & Wigfield, 2002). The cost of an activity can be considered the "opportunity cost" of doing the activity, and includes the perceived amount of effort and pain for engaging the activity. "For example, a college student might not choose to continue in science or math because

Table 1. Sources of intrinsic motivation

Source	Implications
Challenge	**Learners as problem solvers:** learners are presented with the optimal level of challenge so that learner masters challenge and feels competence/self-efficacy
Curiosity	**Learners as information processors:** learners enjoy resolving mysteries or incongruent pieces of information (disequilibrium), as well as novel activities
Control	**Learners as voluntary actors:** providing choices and a sense of control over their environment promotes the feeling of autonomy and self-direction
Fantasy	**Learners as players:** fantasy using characters, graphics, sound, and story promotes the feeling of playing that suspends the player from everyday life
Interpersonal	**Learners as socializers:** working with colleagues in a collaborative environment that develops and maintains social relations in a peer group and with the instructor

he perceives that the costs in terms of effort required are too much for him to bear at this time" (Pintrich & Schunk, 2002, p. 73). Unfortunately, Eccles and colleague have not explained the cost component in great detail and it has been studied very little (Anderson, 2000).

Interest

Researchers have three general approaches on interest: personal/individual interest (disposition of the person), interestingness (characteristics of the context and situation), and the resulting psychological state of the individual due to the interaction with the context and situation (Schunk, et al., 2007). The psychological state of experiencing an interesting activity is considered to be either actualized personal interest or situational interest.

The features of a situation or context that individuals find interesting evoke situational interest. That is, different characteristics of the context and content can generate short-term interest in the student to engage the learning task. A few frequent features that are found to be interesting include novelty, surprise, complexity, ambiguity, and certain types of themes, such as death and sex (Schunk, et al., 2007). These features are similar to the fantasy, curiosity, and challenge sources of intrinsic motivation. In fact, some interest researchers theorize that situational motivation is analogous to intrinsic motivation.

Researchers have suggested that situational interest may have two phases: one where interest is triggered and another where interest is further maintained (Hidi & Harackiewicz, 2000). That is, if a situation succeeds to trigger and catch the individual's interests then there is an opportunity for that interest to hold and maintain. Holding interest for longer than the situational experience requires learning conditions that are meaningful for and valued by the students (Mitchell, 1993).

Besides situational interest, interacting with the appropriately interesting context and content may actualize the student's personal interest. Personal (individual) interest is considered to be a relatively enduring and stable disposition toward an object, content, or task (Schunk, et al., 2007). An individual's personal interest can be specific to certain domains and academic subjects or a general orientation toward the desire to learn new information (Ainley, Hidi, & Berndorff, 2002). More than fifty studies have shown that interest in learning a subject and achievement are positively correlated (Krapp, 2002). Specifically for science, researchers have found that interest in science contributed to performance by students (Shernoff & Hoogstra, 2001)

Personal interest has feeling-related and value-related components, and it is intrinsic in nature (Krapp, 2002). The feeling-related component refers to the positive feeling associated with an object and/or activity, especially enjoyment and engagement. The value-related component is the personal significance attributed to the object and/or activity, such as personal values and goals toward the object of interest (Krapp, 2002).

In addition to these two psychological constructs, research has shown that there is a stored-knowledge component of personal interest that represents the individual's knowledge and understanding of subject content (Ainley, et al., 2002). This knowledge not only leads the individual to seek challenges and answers to his or her piqued curiosity, but also "informs his or hers developing sense of possible selves" (Renninger, 2000, p. 379), which shapes a person's identity.

A comparison of Eccles' model of motivation to personal interest indicates several highly related, if not directly overlapping, constructs. The intrinsic value component of the Eccles' subjective task value has similar attributes as the feeling-related valence of interest theory. Moreover, Eccles' attainment value has similar attributes as the value-related valence of personal interest since both are defined as cognitive components related to personal value and goals toward an object. Only stored-knowledge in interest theory is not addressed directly by Eccles' theory of motivation.

In summary, situational interest occurs when the interestingness of a task initially triggers the student's engagement leading to maintained engagement on the task until completion. Over time, if the student's engagement with the content continues beyond the immediate task, the student may develop a personal interest for a subject matter. Once an individual already has an identity structured around an interest on a subject, changing the person's interest or lack of interest is difficult and seldom happens (Krapp, 2002). Thus, it is imperative to start the process of promoting long-term engagement with academic subjects by providing students with interesting related tasks at an early age.

CHARACTERISTICS OF EDUCATIONAL DIGITAL GAMES

There is little consensus by philosophers and researchers on the definition of games (Martens, Gulikers, & Bastiaens, 2004). One of the most influential philosophers of the 20th century, Ludwig Wittgenstein, argued that there are no common characteristics among all games and that games only bear a 'family resemblance' to one another. After reviewing attempts by educational researchers, such as Lepper, Malone, and others, to define educational games, Garris and Ahlers (2002) concluded that digital based learning games have six broad dimensions: fantasy, rules/goals, sensory stimuli, challenges, mystery, and control, as shown in Table 2.

Non-educational game and play researchers provide another perspective on the definition of games. Salen and Zimmerman (2004) compared game definitions from notable play and game historians, designers, and researchers, such as David Parlett, Clark C. Abt, Johann Huizinga, Roger Caillois, Bernard Suits, Chris Crawford, Greg Costikyan, Elliot Avedon, and Brian Sutton-Smith, and found no consensus, though all of them, except Costikyan, include rules as a key aspect of games (see Table 3). Ultimately, Salen and Zimmerman defined games as "a system in which players engage in artificial conflict, defined by rules, that results in quantifiable outcome" (p.

Table 2. Digital learning game dimensions

Source	Implications
Challenge	Optimal level of difficulty and uncertain goal attainment
Mystery	Optimal level of informational complexity
Control	Active learner control
Fantasy	Imaginary or fantasy context, themes, or characters
Rules/ Goals	Clear rules, goals, and feedback on progress toward goals
Sensory Simuli	Dramatic or novel visual and auditory stimuli

80). In their definition, artificial refers to the artificial space that separates games from "real life." Conflict is considered a contest of some kind between players or players and the game. That is, there is a challenge from other players or the game, or both, that must be overcome. And quantifiable outcome means the player has either won or lost, or received a numerical score.

Comparing the game dimensions identified by educational game researchers to those identified by non-educational game and play researchers, the following concepts overlap:

- Fantasy/make-believe/artificial context/safe
- Constricting rules
- Goal/outcome oriented with feedback
- Challenge/conflict/contest/complexity (optimized for players)

- Uncertainty of the outcome
- Active control/decision-making activity
- Inefficient processes for gathering information/mystery

In addition, because of the unique affordances of the computer technology used in digital games, a final dimension to add is sensory stimuli, which includes both visual display and sound. If a digital game successfully combines these dimensions, then, under the right context, the player should become engrossed and absorbed in the activity. Additionally, if the digital game endogenously supports educational objectives, then these may be attained while providing a positive (affective) experience for the student.

Table 3. Non-educational game dimensions

Dimensions of Games	Game and Play Researchers							
	Parlett	Abt	Huizinga	Caillois	Suits	Crawford	Costikyan	Avedon/Sutton-Smith
Constricting rules	X	X	X	X	X	X		X
Conflict or contest	X					X		X
Goal/outcome oriented	X	X			X		X	X
Activity, process, event		X			X			X
Decision-making		X				X	X	
Playful and absorbing			X					
No extrinsic reward			X	X				
Artificial/Safe			X	X		X		
Creates social groups			X					
Voluntary				X	X			X
Uncertain				X				
Make believe				X		X		
Inefficient					X			
System of parts						X	X	
A form of art							X	

Note: Adapted from *Rules of Play: Game Design Fundamentals* (p. 79) by K. Salen and E. Zimmerman, 2004, Cambridge, MA: The MIT Press.

DESIGNING FOR MOTIVATION CASE STUDY: *THE ALIEN RESCUE GAME*

Design Considerations

Egenfeldt-Nielsen (2007) identified three different generations of educational games. The first generation of educational games corresponds to what is commonly called "edutainment." The predominant underlying learning theory of edutainment games is behaviorist in nature. Edutainment games typically consist of drill-and-practice routines and tutorials, along with a strong dose of sensory stimuli, such sounds and animated graphics, to "sugar coat" the learning content. Edutainment games are not immersive because the learning content is not integrated with the sensory stimuli and fantasy. That is, the motivational elements of edutainment games are exogenous, as extrinsic rewards, from the game-play elements. Moreover, edutainment games are not immersive because freedom of movement in space is not provided or permitted (Paras & Bizzocchi, 2005) due to being grounded on linear and didactical sequencing (Denis & Jouvelot, 2005). Unfortunately, by relying heavily on exogenous fantasy and sensory stimuli to engage the player/learner rather than intrinsically motivating techniques, students soon lose interest playing these games and players become disappointed. For these reasons, behaviorist based edutainment games have not been considered successful for learning complex concepts (Denis & Jouvelot, 2005).

In contrast to first generation educational games, the second generation educational games are grounded in cognitivist learning theory. Cognitivists emphasize the natural inclination for students to consciously engage and learn given certain learning environments (Greeno, et al., 1996). These learning environments—ones that are more student-centered than edutainment programs—can evoke the innate desire of individuals to learn, i.e. intrinsic motivation. In second generation educational games multimedia supports the player's desire for his or her own progression and exploration, and provides scaffolding to support different learning abilities (Egenfeldt-Nielsen, 2007). Second generation games immerses the player by not interrupting the flow of the game while providing endogenous fantasy, feedback, and sensory stimuli that is woven into the learning content of game (Gunter, Kenny, & Vick, 2008; Paras & Bizzocchi, 2005). Rather than providing right or wrong feedback as in 1st generation educational games, 2nd generation games provide constructive feedback to scaffold the learner while he or she attempts to problem solve. Second generation educational games are still popular today when the learning objective is problem-solving, analyzing, perceiving, and spatial ability (Egenfeldt-Nielsen, 2007).

Finally, third generation educational games are grounded in social constructivist learning theory. Social constructivist theories of motivation are concerned with the individual's interaction with others in a context or social milieu in which an activity occurs. Social constructivists believe that motivation is the engagement to maintain interpersonal relationships and identity in a person's communities (Greeno, et al., 1996). The existence of an appealing social group, including possibly a classroom work group, that plays digital games provides motivation for players. This social group can be friends, relatives, colleagues, or other game players. The super-motive is the reciprocal process of valuing the social group and the development of one's identity within the social group through the collective playing of the educational digital game. That is, individuals have the need to belong to a social group where they can develop their self-esteem and attain esteem (via social recognition) from others through participation in that social group while playing a digital game (see Hickey, 2003; Maslow, 1955; Ryan & Deci, 2000). Third generation educational games engage students by requiring them to work in groups, either in person or online, to complete the game, and by changing the role of the teacher to facilitator and mediator between the game and real world practices (Egenfeldt-Nielsen, 2007). Third generation educational digital games are the avant-garde of educational uses of digital games.

Yet, each new generation of educational games carries forward some of the features of the past generation while de-emphasizing other features (Egenfeldt-Nielsen, 2007). Rewards and punishments for certain actions within the game, as advocated by behaviorist, are still used in next generation games. However, the rewards and punishments have more meaning in next generation games because they are part of the gameplay and endogenous fantasy. Likewise, constructive feedback, scaffolding, and endogenous fantasy are often still used in the 3rd generation educational digital games, but the new generation adds social interaction as an important aspect of the game. Thus, when designing an educational digital game, it is important to determine how the learning content of the game will be best provided along with fantasy and gameplay.

Designing *the Alien Rescue Game*

The Alien Rescue Game is a third generation educational digital game that is based on the problem-based learning (PBL) approach. Savery and Duffy (1995) consider PBL environments to have the three primary underlying cognitivist and social constructivist propositions: (1) understanding is in our interactions with the environment, (2) cognitive conflict is the stimulus for learning and determines the organization and nature of what is learned, and (3) knowledge evolves through social negotiation and by the evaluation of the viability of one's understanding. An early proponent of PBL, Barrows (1996), proposed the following as the main characteristics of PBL:

- Learning is student-centered as students assume a major responsibility for their own learning;
- Learning occurs in small groups;

- Teachers are facilitators or guides;
- Problems form the organizing focus and stimulus for learning;
- Problems, similar to those one would face in future professions, are a vehicle for the development of problem-solving skills;
- New information is acquired through self-directed learning (pp. 5-6).

According to Mann, Eidelson, Fukuchi, Nissman, Robertson, and Jardines (2002), game-based learning can be considered a kind of PBL, because games and PBL share in the characteristics of an unknown outcome, multiple paths to a goal, construction of the problem context, and, when there are multiple players, collaboration. They found that students learned not only from the content of a PBL-based surgical management game, but also from the dialogue and sharing of knowledge while they participated in the activity. This type of learning through social interaction is consistent with the social constructivist perspective of learning that is exemplified by Lave and Wenger's (1991) theory of situated learning.

The benefits of PBL, according to Barrows, Barzak, Ball, and Ledger (2002), are that PBL promotes activation of prior learning, self-directed learning, and motivation. PBL environments promote intrinsic motivation and motivation from participation in a social group that includes the teacher and fellow students. Thus, a PBL approach to designing educational digital games may be advantageous to learning, motivation while playing, and interest in the content after playing the game has stopped.

The Alien Rescue Game (TARG) is a digital game based on the stand-alone multimodal hypermedia problem-based learning (PBL) environment, called *Alien Rescue* (see http://alienrescue.edb.utexas.edu/). *TARG* is designed to fulfill the astronomy unit of the science curriculum for 6th grade in Texas, USA and it complies with the U.S. National Science Education Standards (Liu, Williams, & Pedersen, 2002). *TARG* presents a complex problem for scientific investigation and decision-making by middle school children. *TARG* has a science fiction premise that allows students to take on the role of a scientist in charge of finding habitats, i.e. planets or moons, in our solar system for six endangered aliens. In order to find habitats for the aliens, students must learn, using a rich set of cognitive tools, about the planets and moons in our solar system. The learning objectives include increasing knowledge of our solar system and improving problem-solving skills. The following is a description of *Alien Rescue II* by Liu, Williams, and Pederson (2002, pp. 259-260):

The science fiction premise of Alien Rescue takes students to a newly operational international space station where they become a part of a worldwide effort to rescue alien life forms. Students are informed that a group of six species of aliens, fleeing their own planetary system, have arrived in Earth orbit....Students, acting as scientists, are asked to participate in this rescue operation, and their task is to determine the most suitable relocation site for each alien species. To solve this problem, students must engage in a variety of activities. They must learn about the aliens and identify the basic needs of each species. They must then investigate the planets and moons of our solar system, searching them for possible matches with the needs of the aliens. Students gather this information by performing searches in the databases and launching probes that they have constructed to gather the additional information not available through the existing databases. They must also engage in collaborative planning and decision-making as they determine how to use the resources of the solar system effectively. In the course of developing a solution plan, students learn about both our solar system and the tools and procedures scientists use to gather that information. The hypermedia program allows students to have access to all the tools and information needed to develop a solution plan, but the program is structured in such a way as to not suggest what that solution should

be. Students are encouraged to explore the virtual space station as they determine for themselves the information they need and the process they will use to develop a solution plan.

As part of the design of *The Alien Rescue Game*, several digital game-based learning (DGBL) features were added to the PBL *Alien Rescue* environment, including the following:

1. Three levels that the student is challenged to complete to solve the whole problem. Each level is progressively more difficult to scaffold the student cognitively and to enhance self-efficacy and self-esteem. There is clear indication of success between levels.
2. A guided activity, also called a game tutorial, where an expert solves a simple problem to show the student the process and then the student solves another simple problem, on his or her own. This is accomplished at the beginning of the game in order to enhance the student's feelings of competency and self-efficacy before being presented with the more complex problem.
3. Information about a malicious alien character in the narrative is revealed over time in order to provide a mystery element and promote fantasy.
4. The inclusion of surprising outcomes based on student's actions, including some very powerful effects, and intrigue in the narrative to promote curiosity.
5. Endogenous formative feedback and summative feedback on performance by evaluating students' recommendations for viability and by showing the consequences of students' decisions on habitats.
6. True three dimensional (3D) environment promotes curiosity and the feeling of control because of the perspective of a first-person agent within the game, which creates a more engaging experience (Dickey, 2005).

The design of *The Alien Rescue Game* can be compared to what is considered to be a educational digital game (see the previous section on Characteristics of Educational Digital Games). The following characteristics of an educational digital game can be identified in the design of *TARG*:

- Fantasy/Make believe/artificial context/safe: science fiction narrative where students play the role of a scientist to rescue aliens with no negative endogenous consequences
- Constricting rules: affirmative
- Goal/outcome oriented with feedback: goal of finding homes for endangered aliens with feedback on decisions
- Challenge/conflict/contest/complexity: challenge is progressively more complex (with levels) and endogenous conflict with a malicious alien
- Uncertainty of the outcome: outcome with malicious alien is unknown and is based on quality of decision-making by students
- Active control/decision-making activity: student makes choices of what information to gather and analyze to make a decision
- Inefficient processes for gathering information/mystery: information is spread amongst databases and must be consolidated in a notebook for analysis and information regarding the malicious aliens is progressively revealed in order to provide mystery

Malone and Lepper's (1987) set of heuristics and principles for designing intrinsically motivating instructional environments was used, as shown in Table 4, to ensure that the DGBL techniques would be intrinsically motivating, and to determine if any further features needed to be included.

METHODOLOGY

The current study was held in two seventh grade classrooms in a suburban parochial private middle school in Texas, USA. Each science class had 22 students, with a total of 44 participating students in the study, who were predominately White (89%) and evenly split between females and males. The same teacher taught both classes. *The Alien Rescue Game* required six class sessions of approximately 90 minutes each for a total of 9 hours of playing time to complete plus total class discussion time of approximately one hour devoted to *TARG* and space science.

In order to measure the students' knowledge and understanding of scientific concepts in *TARG*, the Science Knowledge Test (Liu, 2004) was administered pre- and post-test. The Science Knowledge Test (SKT) instrument comprised of twenty multiple-choice questions that measures factual (n=15) and applied (n=5) knowledge of astronomy concepts introduced by *TARG* (Liu, 2004). Content validity of SKT has been assured by pilot-testing the instrument numerous times with classroom teachers and university faculty in astronomy education (Liu, 2004).

In total, fifteen students were interviewed using the Continuing Interest Interview Guide, which required 8-15 minutes to complete. The Continuing Interest Interview Guide was used to explore students' indications of interest in learning science, and students' view of how their self-efficacy, intrinsic motivation, attainment value, knowledge, and utility value influenced their interest in science. Five students were interviewed four weeks before playing *TARG*. Furthermore, these students were asked to check the transcribed answers and interviewer's interpretation of the answers for accuracy between two days and two weeks after finishing the *TARG* treatment to enhance credibility of the data and results. These students were also asked if they had changed their opinion since playing *TARG*. Two more samples of students

Table 4. Intrinsically motivating features of The Alien Rescue Game

Sources of Intrinsic Motivation	Features	Sub-Features	Design and Comments
Challenge	Goals	*Clear & fixed*	Introductory video states the problem
		Short-term goals	Level design provides short-term goals. Not typically part of PBL.
		Long-term Goals	Long-term goal of situating 6 aliens in our solar system.
	Uncertain Outcomes	*Variable Difficulty Levels*	Groups of students are assumed to have similar competency within the classroom. Not typically considered in PBL designs.
		Multiple Goals	Level design with increasing difficulty scaffolds player. Not typically part of PBL designs.
		Hidden Information	Information regarding the antagonist is revealed over time.
		Randomness	No randomness included.
	Performance Feedback		Feedback by showing the consequences of decisions.
	Self-Esteem		Easy problem is presented to student after observing expert tutorial.
Curiosity	Sensory		3D environment.
	Cognitive		Surprise when antagonist initially attacks and intrigue about conflict between aliens.
Control	Contingency		Game responds to any action taken by the player.
	Choice		Player/student can take many different pathways to solve the problem.
	Power		Powerful effect of battle at the end due to student's decisions.
Fantasy	Emotional		Empathy for the aliens is promoted by providing extensive graphics and information about them.
	Cognitive		The science fiction narrative does not interfere with the cognitive tasks.
	Endogeneity		Problem-solving activity is contained within and integral to science fiction narrative.
Cooperation			Players/students are expected to work in small teams because of the complexity of the problem.
Competition			Not typically part of PBL and not included in the game.
Recognition			Not typically part of PBL and not included in the game.

were interviewed after the *TARG* treatment. One sample of five students was interviewed within two days of completing *TARG*. Another five students were interviewed approximately two weeks after the treatment.

In addition, every student group, which consisted of two students each (total of 22 groups), was interviewed but not all the students were interviewed because of absenteeism. Questions focused on students' perceptions of the affective outcome from playing *The Alien Rescue Game*, possible influences on their desire and interest to

learn science, and behavioral intention to continue learning science after finishing *TARG*.

Moreover, observations of the classroom provided further evidence of motivation. The focus was to observe the engagement of students with *TARG* and their interactions with fellow students and the teacher, as well as the researcher as facilitator.

Often opportunities emerge while performing research in the classroom that can provide additional evidence for analysis. In this study, one class was nearer completion of *TARG* than the other class, and the opportunity arose to divert some of the time for class discussion so that the faster class would not complete the program prematurely. At the end of this discussion, the students were asked to write their responses to questions regarding their experience with *TARG*.

Finally, the science teacher for both classes was interviewed. The purpose of this interview was to obtain his perspective on the students' reactions to *TARG* and the researcher's preliminary interpretation of results.

After gathering the qualitative evidence, the constant comparative method was used to obtain pertinent information from the students' utterances or incidents using systematic methodological procedures (Lincoln & Guba, 1985). Focused coding (Charmaz, 2006) was used to concisely describe relevant incidents in the transcripts. At a higher level of abstraction, categories emerged by comparing codes to each other and integrating codes that "look/feel" (Lincoln & Guba, 1985, p. 347) the same. Categories are compared to codes and incidents hermeneutically (Gadamer, 1977; Warnke, 1987). The resulting categories were used to assist in the finding, sorting, and extraction of relevant qualitative findings.

Dickey (2005) states that despite indications that commercial games are highly motivating, research into educational games has often ignored commercial games. To rectify this shortcoming in previous research, this study's findings are compared to findings in two commercial digital game studies. The study by Ryan, Rigby, and Przybylski (2006) selected two commercial digital games from the 3D adventure genre: *Zelda: The Ocarina of Time* (1998) and *A Bug's Life* (1999). These two games were selected because one game (*Zelda*) received very high ratings (97.8% favorable) and the other game (*A Bug's Life*) received a low rating (56.6% favorable). In fact, *Zelda: The Ocarina of Time* for the Nintendo 64 is still, in 2010, the highest ranking game on gamerankings.com. In the adventure game genre the player assumes the role of a character in a fictional world where gameplay is focused on exploration and puzzle-solving rather than challenges such as combat. Comparison of *TARG* to the selected commercial games is productive because *The Alien Rescue Game* can be classified as a 3D adventure game. *Zelda* and *A Bug's Life* were played by 50 undergraduates (36 female, 14 male) for 40 minutes on the *Nintendo 64* (1996-2002). Furthermore, evidence of motivation and its sources relied on post-play 7-point Likert-type questionnaires measuring in-game autonomy, in-game competence, presence, intuitiveness of game controls, game enjoyment (intrinsic motivation), and preference for future play.

In contrast, the study by Hoffman and Nadelson (2006) had students from undergraduate and master degree-level education courses self select strategy or problem-solving video games to play. These 25 participants (9 females and 16 males) were highly engaged video game players who played regularly five or more hours per week (2.7 hours during the experimental week). Both qualitative and quantitative empirical methods were used. The qualitative method comprised of collecting and analyzing interview data to discover the attributes of gaming motivation and engagement. The quantitative method included the Video Game Play survey collected data from 7-point scale to measure subjective assessment of flow and engagement.

RESULTS

The findings in this section discuss how both *TARG* and the commercial games affect learning interest and motivation, including self-efficacy, attainment value, intrinsic interest, utility, and cost.

Evidence of Engagement and Motivation

During the break, when the students were allowed about five minutes of free time, which included the opportunity to leave the classroom, many students remained in the classroom working on *TARG*. As the teacher explained, "They were seriously engaged during the activity. As I mentioned to you previously, during the break [mid-class] I never had to tell them to go sit back down to go back to work. They would do that on their own and they never do that." Thus, students were engaging space science subject matter when not required, a clear indication that students were motivated.

For commercial games, the study by Hoffman and Nadelson (2006) determined that the three main reasons that players engage in games are: fun, social connectivity, and feeling of achievement through control of the game, with the fun objective being the highest reported reason for playing video games.

Development of Interest

Of the ten students who addressed the question of changes in interest in space science during interviews, six stated that their interest had increased and four stated that it was the same. For instance, during the member check session with Rafe, he indicated his change in interest: "I want to learn more astronomy." The five other students interviewed did not express a clear opinion. No student claimed a decrease in interest for space science from before using to after using *TARG*.

In the written response questionnaire there were 11 responses out of 22 that indicated students talked about *TARG* outside of class, which in an indication of interest development. It would be reasonable to assume that during discussions of *TARG* there was some dialogue about science, as well as on gameplay and progress.

Many other students developed an interest in space science but were explicit about the limits of their interest. Of the twenty-nine students who provided responses to the question of learning more in or out of classroom in interviews (classroom and individual), and in written responses, there were nine who desired to learn more inside and outside of the classroom, eight who wanted to

learn more inside the classroom, four who either wanted to learn a little more or who answered with "maybe inside", and seven who did not wish to learn any more about space science.

Similarly in commercial games, the designer's goal is for players to develop an interest in the game beyond the first encounter, which can be measured as the preference for future play. In Ryan, Rigby, and Przybylski (2006) study, players scored *Zelda* significantly higher than *A Bugs Life* on preference for future play [Zelda $M = 3.2$, Bugs $M = 2.8, p < 0.001$]. For preference for future play, both autonomy/control [$B = 0.41$, p < 0.01] and competence/challenge [$B = 0.54$, $p < 0.01$] were significant predictors of the difference between the scores of the two games. That is, players indicated the preference to play *Zelda* in the future more than *A Bug's Life* because *Zelda* fulfilled more of their autonomy and competence needs.

Self-Efficacy

Of the fifteen interviews, five students stated in interviews that their perceived ability to learn space science had increased while playing *The Alien Rescue Game*. For example, Blanche answers the question of whether she was better at learning and doing space science since using *Alien Rescue*: "I know more about space and stuff. I think it helped me a lot." One student mentioned that her perceived ability was about the same, and the remaining nine students did not clearly provide an opinion one way or the other. No student mentioned a decrease in self-efficacy. Eight out of the fifteen interviewees stated that self-efficacy does influence interest; three interviewees said that it did not, and the remaining four did not clearly state one way or the other.

In the study by Hoffman and Nadelson (2006) participants indicated that motivation to continue playing commercial video games was influenced by self-efficacy: "It's worthwhile to keep going because I know I am getting better and I see progression." Additionally, there was indication that the design of the video game should promote self-efficacy by the gradual progression in task difficulty as stated by this participant: "If it's an adaptive game and I have confidence- my confidence gets better."

Attainment Value

Two students stated in interviews that their personal importance of space science had increased; three stated that it was about the same, and ten did not answer the question with a clear opinion one way or the other. No student claimed a decrease in personal importance of space science from using *TARG*. Nine out of the fifteen interviewees thought that personal importance of science was an influencer of interest. Four students did not think importance influenced interest in science, and two did not express an opinion. However, there seemed to be some confusion as to what it meant for science to be important. A few students had an extrinsic perspective on importance. For instance, Darryl considers importance to be about grades: "Umm..it is only important that I get good grades." All three students who thought attainment value was not an influencer on interest did not have a science identity. For instance, when Darryl was asked if he was a science person, he answered "No."

Intrinsic Value

Seven students in the interviews stated that their enjoyment of space science had increased while playing *TARG*. For instance, Sally indicated that she enjoyed playing *TARG* in the classroom: "I think it is fun but I wouldn't do it outside of the classroom." Another seven students mentioned that their enjoyment or liking of space science was about the same. No student answered that his or her liking of science/space science had decreased while using *Alien Rescue*. Nine out of the fifteen students stated that enjoyment of science influenced their interest in science; two students did not think enjoyment of science influenced their interest in science, and four did not express a clear opinion.

As would be expected, players of commercial video games enjoy playing them and the games that players prefer are more fun. This is evidenced by the significant difference between the enjoyment of playing *Zelda* [$M = 4.6$] and *A Bug's Life* [$M = 3.6$]. Furthermore, there were significant differences of the sources of intrinsic motivation, autonomy/control and competence/challenge, between the two games. For game enjoyment, both autonomy/control [$B = 0.35$, p < 0.01] and competence/challenge [$B = 0.54$, $p < 0.01$] were significant predictors of the difference between the scores of the two games. That is, players enjoyed *Zelda* more than *A Bug's Life* because *Zelda* fulfilled more of their autonomy and competence needs.

A unique source of intrinsic motivation hypothesized by Ryan, Rigby, and Przybylski (2006) in gaming contexts is *presence*, which is the sense that one is *immersed* in the game world, as opposed to the experience of externally manipulating the game. Presence is enhanced by making the game feel real and authentic, which are supported by a compelling story and graphics environments, as well as making the controls as user-friendly as possible. In the study by Ryan et al, players were significantly more immersed playing *Zelda* [$M = 3.2$] were than playing *A Bug's Life* [$M = 2.4$]. Also, for presence, both autonomy/control [$B = 0.45$, p < 0.01] and competence/challenge [$B = 0.40$, $p < 0.01$] were significant predictors of the difference between the scores of the two games. Immersion was also reported in the study by Hoffman and Nadelson (2006) with participants expressing "engrossment," and a "degree of separation" from the real world when playing engaging video games, losing a sense of time - "zone out", and "forgetting about the other stuff I have to do." Participants of this study described vividness, stimulating brightly colored graphics, and intriguing story line with elements of spontaneity as important influencers of their engagement and motivation to continue playing. Moreover, participants became disengaged when they perceived the game to have poor game design, inferior graphics, and predictability. These results suggest that presence or immersion in the game is a source of intrinsic motivation and that presence is supported by high quality production value and game design.

The study by Hoffman and Nadelson (2006) also indicated that challenge, control, and socializing as important sources of intrinsic motivation to play commercial video games. Their interview data indicated that participants perceived challenge to be motivating. For example, one participant stated. "It is a recreation, but, um, I enjoy—I enjoy thinking. I enjoy thinking, I enjoy learning, I like strategy-type games that let me really think my way through something." Conversely, if the game was too challenging or too easy then players would lose motivation and avoid engagement, as indicated by these participants: "if it's too complicated to pick up on fairly quickly I get disinterested," and "if the game is too easy, I mean, I don't even play it" and "I'll have to find a way to increase the challenge or I'll start to lose interest in the game."

Control was also indicated as an important source of motivation to play commercial video games. The interview data in the Hoffman and Nadelson study suggested that the ability to control the game characters, game environment, and handheld controls were important motivators, as stated by this participant: "You control the pace and you kind of decide where to go and what to do, so, um, it's kind of like acting it out."

Yet, the single most important intrinsic motivator for playing commercial video games may be socializing (interpersonal/relatedness/belongingness) with nearly two-thirds of participants playing with others and socializing was a significant predictor of motivation to play video games. As one participant stated, "It is a fun social way to interact with people." The interview data in

the Hoffman and Nadelson study indicated that some participants fostered relationships with acquaintances, friends, and family by playing video games together, as this participant states that games "…brings communities together, with young and old playing alike." Interestingly, some participants admitted that they only played video games when persuaded by others to play together as a social group.

Utility Value

No student mentioned a decline in their opinion of the usefulness of science/space science in the interviews. Rather, three students stated that their opinion of the usefulness of space science had increased; seven students claimed it was about the same, and the remainder did not express clearly any changes in their opinion on space science usefulness. Five students said that usefulness influenced interest; five said that it did not, with the remainder not clearly vocal one way or the other.

Cost

In interviews two students stated that they thought space science was harder than expected, three students said it was easier than expected, two students claimed that the cost was about what they expected, and eight did not state a clear opinion on this. However, some students did not conceptualize an activity being difficult—taking time and effort to complete—as a detractor to interest, but rather as a challenge that is positive in nature. Nine students believed that cost influenced interest, whereas four students did not, and the remaining two students did not mention their perspective on whether cost was an influencer on interest or not.

In the study by Ryan, Rigby, and Przybylski (2006), they hypothesized that the degree to which game controls are intuitive or user-friendly influences the player's experience. They developed the Intuitive Controls scale to assess the interface between the player and the gameplay taking place. Results from their study indicated that intuitive controls were related to presence, which was correlated with intrinsic motivation. However, intuitive controls acted more as a gatekeeper to the game experience, rather than the game experience itself. Once the controls were clear enough or hurdled a cost threshold ("price of admission") then other sources of motivation were important. For example, though *Zelda* was found to be more enjoyable and immersive than *A Bug's Life*, there was not a significant difference in scores of intuitiveness of controls because both games had simple controls.

Knowledge Acquisition

Scores on the Science Knowledge Test showed a significant ($p < 0.05$) increase with the overall mean scores improving by 50%. All but two students scored higher in the post-test than pre-test. This finding confirms previous research that indicates that games for learning can improve performance (Wilson, et al., 2009). In interviews, ten students stated that they thought that the amount of knowledge on a subject influenced interest, while four students did not think it did, and one student was not clear one way or the other. For Madeleine, as with most of the students, the relationship between science knowledge and enjoyment is clear and positive: "I think I know a lot of science and that helps me understand it more and the more I understand it the more I get. The more I get it the more I like it, I guess."

In the study by Hoffman and Nadelson (2006), none of the video game players who participated indicated that learning was a goal. However, some video game players did indicate that they learned something from playing: "Like as much as you might learn something when you go to a movie" and "So, whether or not I can learn anything I'm not sure, but it is—it's not a mindless process. You have to really be thinking about some of the things you're doing. I guess I'm saying that just

in improving your critical thinking skills, really." Interestingly, many participants indicated interest in only one genre and were not interested in games outside of that genre. Perhaps, this is analogous to becoming interested in an academic subject because of stored-knowledge.

Summary

Many students stated that their interest in space science increased from playing *The Alien Rescue Game*. Table 3 shows the number of students who responded to how much their motivation to learn science changed due to playing *TARG* and whether or not they believed a given motivational construct affected their interest. Furthermore, Table 3 show the relative importance of the influence of a motivational construct on interest in science by multiplying the responses of "increase" since playing *TARG* to the responses stating "yes" to affect on interest in science. As shown in Table 3, students' responses suggest that the changes in self-efficacy and all of the task value constructs, as well as knowledge, influence interest to learn science, though not for all the students, all the time. That is, some students thought that self-efficacy, attainment value, affect, utility value, and cost influenced their continuing interest in science, but others would mention only some of these constructs as influencing interest. Overall, self-efficacy, attainment value, affect, cost, and knowledge were mentioned as influencers of interest by approximately the same number of students (8-10 students out of 15 interviewed), whereas utility value was mentioned by about half as many students (5 students). Also, students stated that some of these motivational constructs influenced them more strongly than others. Furthermore, the calculation of the relative importance of the motivational constructs indicate that the biggest influencers on interest in space science are self-efficacy, intrinsic value, and knowledge, whereas attainment value, utility, and cost were relatively not as important to contributing to interest due to playing *TARG*. Interestingly, results suggested that knowledge was the most important influencer on interest. However, it is not clear whether students interest increases with increasing knowledge or if students interest increases when first encountering a new subject matter, i.e. situational interest driven by curiosity and/or novelty or both.

Similarly, results suggested that motivation to play commercial video games were mainly influenced by self-efficacy, intrinsic value, and cost, with cost being the "price for admission" and not a motivator once the game controls were considered "good enough." Findings suggested that the design of video games should promote self-efficacy through gradual progression in task difficulty, such as with increasing difficulty when the player progresses to the next level.

Since the primary reason that students play commercial video games is to experience fun, the main focus of motivational research on commercial video games is concerning intrinsic motivation. The findings show that the most important contributors to intrinsic motivation were autonomy/control, competence/challenge, presence/immersion, and relatedness/socializing. The findings that autonomy/control, competence/challenge, and relatedness/socializing influenced intrinsic motivation corroborate with many previous studies (Eccles & Wigfield, 2002; Krapp, 2005; Oginsky, 2003; Ryan, et al., 2006; Wu, 2003). However, the socializing aspect of digital games appears much more prominently than these other studies. Perhaps games afford many more enjoyable social interactions than found in non-game situations. Interestingly, two important sources of intrinsic motivation found in previous studies, fantasy and curiosity, were not found in the studies directly described in this chapter. It may be that fantasy is included in the presence/immersion component since this is supported by the use of sensory engagement and story, which also defines fantasy. That is, fantasy is an intrinsic motivator because it affords immersion. Likewise, perhaps curiosity was experienced as part of the other contributors to intrinsic motivation.

DISCUSSION

Results showed that students found *The Alien Rescue Game* to be motivating. Students reported during interviews and in written responses that they talked about *The Alien Rescue Game* outside of class. Moreover, the most compelling evidence of students exhibiting motivation to learn science was from observing students during the break, when the students were allowed about five minutes of free time, which included the opportunity to leave the classroom. During this time, many students remained in the classroom working on *TARG*. Students were exhibiting motivation to learn space science by continuing to play *TARG* and engaging space science subject matter when not required.

Table 3. Summary of motivation and interest to learn science

Motivational Constructs	Since Engaging *TARG*				Affect on Interest in Science			Relative Importance
	Increase	Same	Unknown	Decrease	Yes	No	Unknown	
Self-Efficacy	5	1	9	0	8	3	4	40
Attainment Value	2	3	10	0	9	4	2	18
Intrinsic Value	7	7	1	0	9	2	4	63
Utility Value	3	7	5	0	5	5	5	15
Cost	2	2	8	3	9	4	2	18
Knowledge	38	0	0	2	10	4	1	380

Results also suggest that students' self-efficacy and task value, including all task value's positive motivational constructs improved. Moreover, results suggest that cost perceptions decreased. However, the results of attainment value and cost perceptions were somewhat unclear because of some students' alternative meanings from the questions' original intent.

Many students stated that their interest in space science increased from playing *TARG*. Students' responses also suggest that self-efficacy, task value (including all of its components), and knowledge influence continuing interest to learn. Students stated that some of these motivational constructs influenced them more strongly than others, with self-efficacy, intrinsic value, and knowledge being the biggest influencers on interest to learn science. An analysis of studies of commercial digital games corroborated with these results; self-efficacy, intrinsic motivation, and cost are the most important contributors for player motivation, with cost requiring a minimum threshold of usability of game controls to overcome, after which it does not contribute to motivation to play.

Recommendations for Educational Game Designers

The results imply the need for educational game designers to consider all aspects of Eccles' model of achievement motivation—self-efficacy, attainment value, intrinsic value, utility value, and cost—when designing educational digital game-based learning environments. The creation of educational games that build students' confidence (self-efficacy) in solving interesting problems while enjoying (intrinsic value) the process seems intuitively obvious. This approach to designing educational digital games would most likely also reduce students' perceptions of cost regarding the activity. Concerning cost, educational digital game designers need to ensure that the game controls are intuitive and user-friendly. What is less obvious is the promotion of attainment value

and utility value to enhance students' experience and achievement. Unfortunately, a digital learning game cannot accommodate all of the different idiosyncratic attainment values/identities of students. Rather, the goal of the educational game designer should be to create an environment where the student can participate in an authentic role with meaningful activities. As stated by Liu, Toprac, and Yuen (2009). "the best way to accomplish the inclusion of meaningful activities is to present them in a way that convinces students that the processes employed are authentic in nature." If the student enjoys the role then the student could start developing an identity around the academic subject matter, i.e. increased attainment value.

Also, it is important to show students using a digital learning game that what is learned can be useful and applied to everyday life. Students value academic concepts that are useful in their everyday lives. For instance, one participant valued the usefulness of science as he stated, "Science has been pretty useful because, umm, mostly when I see something odd I can usually explain it. I'm not like duh." Whereas for another participant, usefulness could be a motivator to learn, "If I knew I would use it a lot then I would probably study it more." Digital educational game designers should connect academic subjects to students' ordinary life-experience to enhance engagement and motivation. In summary, if all of the discussed motivational enhancements are considered in the design of digital game-based learning environments, it is likely students' situational interest will not only be enhanced but also many students may begin the path of developing a personal interest in academic subject matter.

Design Considerations and Recommendations

According to Mann, Eidelson, Fukuchi, Nissman, Robertson, and Jardines (2002), game-based learning can be considered a kind of problem-based learning (PBL), because games and PBL share in the characteristics of an unknown outcome, multiple paths to a goal, construction of the problem context, and, when there are multiple players, collaboration. However, I found that there is a tension between the PBL approaches and digital game based learning (DGBL) approaches to designing a computer based learning environment. In particular, feedback and structure of the learning environment differ between the two approaches, as described below.

Tension between DGBL Feedback and PBL

The PBL approach often focuses on providing feedback on the problem-solving processes of the student. That is, feedback is provided regarding the quality of the student's decision-making process, which affects the student's recommendation. Ultimately, in a strictly PBL environment the focus is on the process and not the product (i.e. recommendation or decision). The theory is that striving for good decision-making processes will lead to good decisions.

In contrast, a DGBL approach provides feedback on the decisions (products) that the player makes, regardless of the player's decision-making process. Digital games typically provide immediate feedback on decisions to show the player his or her current status and progress toward the goal. In PBL learning environments, the teacher should provide feedback on students' decisions, though some teachers fail to do this. Using DGBL approaches, the *TARG* provided feedback after each student's recommendation of habitat for an alien species. *TARG* would either approve or reject the student's recommendation. Although some worlds were more optimal than others for each alien species, *TARG* only provided feedback regarding whether or not the selected world was acceptable.

Unfortunately, there were unintended consequences to providing immediate feedback on students' recommendations. Students appeared to use *TARG* as the way to test their hypothesis. Thus, students were focused on making recommendations that the program would approve instead of attempting to find the most optimal worlds for the alien species. This response to *TARG* would be a form of satisficing (Krosnick, 1991; Simon, 1957) in that students were not interested in finding optimal solutions to the problem but rather they were focused on finding the first solution that was satisfactory and sufficient to obtain approval from the game.

Furthermore, *TARG's* feedback appeared to both heightened motivation to complete the game and demotivated students to engage in the decision-making process and space science content. Students quickly grasped that in order to progress through the game, they needed to provide satisfactory, not necessarily optimal, recommendations that were approved by the game. After the program approved a recommendation or series of recommendations, *TARG* rewarded the student with surprising and/or seductive multimedia effects. Furthermore, *TARG* introduced a conflict between an alien species and Earth early in the game. Consequently, students may have not only been motivated to see the multimedia effects, but also learn the resolution of the conflict. Again, this motivation would have focused the students on playing the game, and not on learning the content and the decision-making process. The ultimate result was that students appeared to rush to complete the game instead of trying to provide the most optimal solutions.

Another unintended consequence of *TARG's* feedback was the lower than expected amount of conversation between students in groups and between classmates outside of class. Typically, in PBL environments, students within groups are heavily engaged in conversations about solving the problem. However, in the current study, students did not engage in lengthy conversations amongst each other. This lack of conversations between students may have impacted motivation to learn space science/astronomy. Studies have shown that often students enjoy working with each other and the conversations between students was not only fun but moved the student's knowledge through the zone of proximal development (Vygotsky, 2006; Wells, 2000). The DGBL approach to feedback appeared to motivate students to complete the game but may have reduced motivation to learn space science/astronomy because the DGBL approach did not promote conversations between students on the pros and cons of habitats for aliens in comparison to the PBL approach.

Tension between DGBL Mechanics and PBL

The other major tension between PBL approaches and DGBL approaches is the structure of how the problems are presented. In PBL environments, "students are presented with a complex, ill-structured problem that they are expected to resolve" (MacKinnon, 1999, p. 50). Students then solve the problem in groups. The solution path and management of the workload between students in a group are self-directed. PBL environments are typically open in that students are able to choose whichever path they desire to attain a solution.

In comparison, DGBL environments often are more closed in the structure of pathways to solving problems than PBL environments. For instance, *TARG* presented a sequential series of increasingly difficult scenarios, called "levels" in DGBL terminology. The first level had to be solved correctly before the student could advance to the next level. Presenting the problems on ever increasingly levels of difficulty was a way to scaffold students learning while they gained self-efficacy to learn and use science content to solve for habitats. *TARG* presented one alien species to solve on the first level, two alien species to find habitats on the second level, and three alien species on the third level. The alien species were predetermined for each level. Thus, all the students worked on the same alien species within each level. Furthermore, the level in which the students were

working on was made salient by displaying this information at the top of the screen. Whenever a student correctly solved for all alien species within a level then the program would advance the student onto the next level and the screen display of the level number, e.g. Level 2, would change appropriately. After solving for all the aliens, there were three possible outcomes for students to watch that provided summative feedback on the quality of the student's recommendations.

There were two major unintended consequences of the DGBL mechanics: (1) students were focused on moving up levels, and (2) information on acceptable habitats was easily shared. Once students understood that there were levels, they appeared to be motivated to move up the levels. Moving up levels is called "leveling up" by players of digital games. The students in the current study were probably familiar with the concept of leveling up because the use of levels in digital games is pervasive. Once students recognized that the game had levels they may have been motivated to level up while playing *TARG*. Unfortunately, this could have encouraged students to complete levels with satisficed recommendations instead of optimal recommendations. Furthermore, because all the students found out that they were working on the same aliens on the same levels, and at least at first, at the same time, they quickly shared information regarding their recommendations for aliens. This information sharing was made easy because *TARG* provided immediate feedback as to whether or not a recommendation was acceptable. Consequently, on the first level, when one student group found that Pluto was an acceptable recommendation, almost all the other groups in that class selected Pluto, as well. Only one student, who was very interested in space science/astronomy, found the most optimal solution—Charon.

In conclusion, the combination of the type of feedback and mechanics of the problem presentation of *The Alien Rescue Game* appeared to focus students to finish the game, which discouraged taking the time to find the most optimal solutions, i.e.

best choices for habitats. The consequence of this focus was that students did not discuss as much the pros and cons of habitats as expected. In addition, students may have not been adequately motivated to engage and learn the necessary space science to provide optimal recommendations, but rather students may have been motivated to learn just enough to provide satisfied recommendations.

FUTURE RESEARCH DIRECTIONS

Interest and motivation are complex constructs and no one classroom based study is sufficient to provide conclusive results. Multiple studies need to be performed in different contexts to assist in our understanding of how motivation and interest can be promoted.

Larson's (2000) found that adolescents rarely feel intrinsically motivated and intensely engaged at school. This is disturbing because the adolescent years are the years where students are developmentally ready to form habits of self-regulation (Zimmerman, 1989), initiative (Larson, 2000), and volition (Corno, 2004; Kuhl & Kazén, 1999). Thus, future research should be focused on understanding how to develop interventions that promote intense, intrinsically motivating engagement for students using digital game based learning techniques. To initially understand game-based motivation a qualitative approach using a naturalistic inquiry (Lincoln & Guba, 1985) research design is recommended. Using this approach, the participant-researcher gathers data from classroom observations and interviews before, during, and after the intervention. The researcher collects and analyzes data from a substantial number of cases, in terms of different contexts, classrooms and students, until no new categories emerge and existing categories are saturated so that any new information no longer informs them. Using grounded theory, perhaps an understanding on how students become engaged, how their interest develops, and how continuing motivation is

promoted using a particular intervention can be attained.

From the results of this naturalistic inquiry, quantitative measures could be developed to measure engagement, motivation, and interest. These new instruments, instead of being generic, could be limited in their use to contexts and interventions that are close to the ones that were researched. Indeed, I have trouble believing that a generic instrument that can be used to measure differences in teaching approaches could also be used, with the same validity, to measure differences from an intervention using a computer game. Using the developed context specific instruments, there could be more studies performed at a larger scale to show viability of massive adoption of the intervention in schools. In the current study, I did not attempt to find grand theories of motivation or interest but focused more on creating useful, as in can be used in the classroom, interventions that inform motivational theory with the intention of developing *petite generalizations* (Stake, 1995). I believe that this approach is fruitful for both improving education and informing theory. Future research should continue using this approach.

CONCLUSION

Results suggest that some students found space science more interesting than they had anticipated and that many students were interested in learning more space science in the classroom, if not outside of the classroom. Whether *The Alien Rescue Game* was the cause of this increase in interest or whether the cause was the engagement with space science content alone, regardless of the medium, awaits further study. I concur with the recommendation of Hidi and Harackiewicz (2000) for educators to create interventions that promote students' interest to learn academic subjects. Indeed, an important goal of educators should be to provide interventions that promote students' interest to pursue activities and learning goals related to academic subjects, and to promote interest to learn outside of the classroom. One approach promising approach to developing interventions, as indicated in this study, is the use of educational digital games.

REFERENCES

Ainley, M., Hidi, S., & Berndorff, D. (2002). Interest, learning, and the psychological processes that mediate their relationship. *Journal of Educational Psychology*, *94*(3), 545–561. doi:10.1037/0022-0663.94.3.545

Anderson, P. N. (2000). *Cost perception and the expectancy-value model of achievement motivation.* Paper presented at the Annual Meeting of the American Educational Research Association, New Orleans, LA.

Bandura, A., Barbaranelli, C., Caprara, G. V., & Pastorelli, C. (1996). Multifaceted impact of self-efficacy beliefs on academic functioning. *Child Development*, *67*(3), 1206–1222. doi:10.2307/1131888

Barrows, H. S. (1996). Problem-based learning in medicine and beyond: A brief overview. *New Directions for Teaching and Learning*, *68*(3), 3–12. doi:10.1002/tl.37219966804

Barzak, M. Y., Ball, P. A., & Ledger, R. (2002). The rationale and efficacy of problem-based learning and computer assisted learning in pharmaceutical education. *Pharmacy Education*, *1*(2), 105–113. doi:10.1080/15602210210329

Berlyne, D. E. (1978). Curiosity and learning. *Motivation and Emotion*, *2*(2), 97–175. doi:10.1007/BF00993037

Brookover, W. B., Thomas, S., & Paterson, A. (1964). Self-concept of ability and school achievement. *Sociology of Education*, *37*(3), 271–278. doi:10.2307/2111958

Charmaz, K. (2006). *Constructing grounded theory: A practical guide through qualitative analysis.* Thousand Oaks, CA: Sage Publications.

Corno, L. (2004). Introduction to the special issue work habits and work styles: Volition in education. *Teachers College Record*, *106*(9), 1669–1694. doi:10.1111/j.1467-9620.2004.00400.x

Csikszentmihalyi, M. (1990). *Flow: The psychology of optimal experience.* New York: HarperCollins Publishing.

Denis, G., & Jouvelot, P. (2005). *Motivation-driven educational game design: Applying best practices to music education.* Paper presented at the Proceedings of the 2005 ACM SIGCHI International Conference on Advances in computer entertainment technology.

Dickey, M. (2005). Engaging by design: How engagement strategies in popular computer and video games can inform instructional design. *Educational Technology Research and Development*, *53*(2), 67–83. doi:10.1007/BF02504866

Eccles, J. S. (2009). Who am I and what am I going to do with my life? Personal and collective identities as motivators of action. *Educational Psychologist*, *44*(2), 78–89. doi:10.1080/00461520902832368

Eccles, J. S., & Wigfield, A. (2002). Motivational beliefs, values, and goals. *Annual Review of Psychology*, *53*(1), 109–132. doi:10.1146/annurev.psych.53.100901.135153

Egenfeldt-Nielsen, S. (2007). Third generation educational use of computer games. *Journal of Educational Multimedia and Hypermedia*, *16*(3), 263–281.

Electronic Software Association. (2010). *Industry facts.* Retrieved May, 2010, from http://www.theesa.com/facts/index.asp

Gadamer, H. (1977). *Philosophical hermeneutics.* Berkely, CA: University of California Press.

Garris, R., & Ahlers, R. (2002). Games, motivation, and learning: A research and practice model. *Simulation & Gaming: An Interdisciplinary Journal, 33*(4), 441–467.

Gottfried, A. E. (1985). Academic intrinsic motivation in elementary and junior high school students. *Journal of Educational Psychology, 77*(6), 631–645. doi:10.1037/0022-0663.77.6.631

Graham, S., & Weiner, B. (1996). Theories and principles of motivation. In Berliner, D., & Calfee, R. (Eds.), *Handbook of educational psychology* (pp. 63–84). New York: Simon & Schuster, Macmillan.

Greeno, J. G., Collins, A. M., & Resnick, L. B. (1996). Cognition and learning. In Berliner, D., & Calfee, R. (Eds.), *Handbook of educational psychology* (pp. 15–46). New York, NY: Simon & Schuster, Macmillan.

Gunter, G., Kenny, R., & Vick, E. (2008). Taking educational games seriously: Using the RETAIN model to design endogenous fantasy into stand-alone educational games. *Educational Technology Research and Development, 56*(5), 511–537. doi:10.1007/s11423-007-9073-2

Harter, S. (1992). The relationship between perceived competence, affect, and motivational orientation within the classroom: Processes and patterns of change. In Boggiano, A. K., & Pittman, T. S. (Eds.), *Achievement and motivation: A social-developmental perspective* (pp. 77–114). Cambridge: Cambridge University Press.

Hickey, D. T. (2003). Engaged participation versus marginal nonparticipation: A stridently sociocultural approach to achievement motivation. *The Elementary School Journal, 103*(4), 401–429. doi:10.1086/499733

Hidi, S., & Harackiewicz, J. M. (2000). Motivating the academically unmotivated: A critical issue for the 21st century. *Review of Educational Research, 70*(2), 151–179.

Hidi, S., & Renninger, K. A. (2006). The four-phase model of interest development. *Educational Psychologist, 41*(2), 111–127. doi:10.1207/s15326985ep4102_4

Hoffman, B., & Nadelson, L. (2006). Motivational engagement and video gaming: A mixed methods study. *Educational Technology Research and Development, 58*(3), 245–270. doi:10.1007/s11423-009-9134-9

Krapp, A. (2002). Structural and dynamic aspects of interest development: Theoretical considerations from an ontogenetic perspective. *Learning and Instruction, 12*(4), 383. doi:10.1016/S0959-4752(01)00011-1

Krapp, A. (2005). Basic needs and the development of interest and intrinsic motivational orientations. *Learning and Instruction, 15*(5), 381–395. doi:10.1016/j.learninstruc.2005.07.007

Krosnick, J. A. (1991). Response strategies for coping with the cognitive demands of attitude measures in surveys. *Applied Cognitive Psychology, 5*(3), 213–236. doi:10.1002/acp.2350050305

Kuhl, J., & Kazén, M. (1999). Volitional facilitation of difficult intentions: Joint activation of intention memory and positive affect removes Stroop interference. *Journal of Experimental Psychology. General, 128*(3), 382–399. doi:10.1037/0096-3445.128.3.382

Larson, R. W. (2000). Toward a psychology of positive youth development. *The American Psychologist, 55*(1), 170–183. doi:10.1037/0003-066X.55.1.170

Lave, J., & Wenger, E. (1991). *Situated learning: Legitimate peripheral participation*. New York: Cambridge University Press.

Lepper, M. R., Corpus, J. H., & Iyengar, S. S. (2005). Intrinsic and extrinsic motivational orientations in the classroom: Age differences and academic correlates. *Journal of Educational Psychology, 97*(2), 184–196. doi:10.1037/0022-0663.97.2.184

Liberman, N., & Forster, J. (2008). Expectancy, value and psychological distance: A new look at goal gradients. *Social Cognition, 26*(5), 515–533. doi:10.1521/soco.2008.26.5.515

Lincoln, Y. S., & Guba, E. D. (1985). *Naturalistic inquiry*. Thousand Oaks, CA: Sage Publications, Inc.

Liu, M. (2004). Examining the performance and attitudes of sixth graders during their use of a problem-based hypermedia learning environment. *Computers in Human Behavior, 20*(3), 357–379. doi:10.1016/S0747-5632(03)00052-9

Liu, M., Toprac, P., & Yuen, T. (2009). What factors make a multimedia learning environment engaging: A case study. In Zheng, R. (Ed.), *Cognitive effects of multimedia learning*. Hershey, PA: IGI Global.

Liu, M., Williams, D., & Pedersen, S. (2002). Alien rescue: A problem-based hypermedia learning environment for middle school science. *Journal of Educational Technology Systems, 30*(3), 255–270. doi:10.2190/X531-D6KE-NXVY-N6RE

MacKinnon, M. M. (1999). CORE elements of student motivation in problem-based learning. *New Directions for Teaching and Learning, 78*, 49. doi:10.1002/tl.7805

Malone, T. W. (1981). Toward a theory of intrinsically motivating instruction. *Cognitive Science, 4*, 333–369. doi:10.1207/s15516709cog0504_2

Malone, T. W., & Lepper, M. R. (1987). Making learning fun: A taxonomy of intrinsic motivations for learning. In Snow, R. E., & Farr, M. J. (Eds.), *Aptitude, learning and instruction: Cognitive and affective process analysis* (*Vol. 3*, pp. 223–253). Hillsdale, NJ: Lawrence Erlbaum Associates.

Mann, B. D., Eidelson, B. M., Fukuchi, S. G., Nissman, S. A., Robertson, S., & Jardines, L. (2002). The development of an interactive game-based tool for learning surgical management algorithms via computer. *American Journal of Surgery, 183*(3), 305–308. doi:10.1016/S0002-9610(02)00800-0

Martens, R. L., Gulikers, J., & Bastiaens, T. (2004). The impact of intrinsic motivation on e-learning in authentic computer tasks. *Journal of Computer Assisted Learning, 20*(5), 368–376. doi:10.1111/j.1365-2729.2004.00096.x

Maslow, A. H. (1955). *Deficiency motivation and growth motivation*. Paper presented at the Nebraska Symposium on Motivation.

Mitchell, M. (1993). Situational interest: Its multifaceted structure in the secondary school mathematics classroom. *Journal of Educational Psychology, 85*(3), 424–436. doi:10.1037/0022-0663.85.3.424

Oginsky, T. (2003). *Supporting the development of intrinsic motivation in the middle school classroom*. Michigan, U.S.

Paras, B., & Bizzocchi, J. (2005). *Game, motivation, and effective learning: An integrated model for educational game design*. Paper presented at the Digital Games Research Association (DiGRA)

Pintrich, P., & Schunk, D. H. (2002). *Motivation in education: Theory, research, and applications* (2nd ed.). Upper Saddle River, NJ: Merrill Prentice Hall.

Randel, J. M., & Morris, B. A. (1992). The effectiveness of games for educational purposes: A review of recent research. *Simulation & Gaming: An International Journal, 23*(3), 261–276. doi:10.1177/1046878192233001

Renninger, K. A. (2000). How might the development of individual interest contribute to the conceptualization of intrinsic motivation? In Sansone, C., & Harackiewicz, J. M. (Eds.), *Intrinsic motivation: Controversies and new directions* (pp. 375–407). San Diego: Academic Press.

Rosas, R., Nussbaum, M., & Cumsille, P. (2003). Beyond Nintendo: Design and assessment of educational video games for first and second grade students. *Computers & Education, 40*(1), 71–94. doi:10.1016/S0360-1315(02)00099-4

Ryan, R., & Deci, E. L. (2000). Self-determination theory and the facilitation of intrinsic motivation, social development, and well-being. *The American Psychologist, 55*, 68–78. doi:10.1037/0003-066X.55.1.68

Ryan, R., Rigby, C., & Przybylski, A. (2006). The motivational pull of video games: A self-determination theory approach. *Motivation and Emotion, 30*(4), 344–360. doi:10.1007/s11031-006-9051-8

Salen, K., & Zimmerman, E. (2004). *Rules of play: Game design fundamentals*. Cambridge, MA: The MIT Press.

Savery, J. R., & Duffy, T. M. (1995). Problem based learning: An instructional model and its constructivist framework. In Wilson, B. (Ed.), *Constructivist learning environments: Case studies in instructional design* (*Vol. 35*, pp. 31–38). Englewood Cliffs, NJ: Educational Technology Publications.

Schiefele, U. (1991). Interest, learning, and motivation. *Educational Psychologist, 26*(3-4), 299–323. doi:10.1207/s15326985ep2603&4_5

Schunk, D., Pintrich, P., & Meece, J. (2007). *Motivation in education: Theory, research, and applications* (3rd ed.). Upper Saddle River, NJ: Prentice Hall.

Shernoff, D. J., Csikszentmihalyi, M., Schneider, B., & Shernoff, E. S. (2003). Student engagement in high school classrooms from the perspective of flow theory. *School Psychology Quarterly, 18*(2), 158–176. doi:10.1521/scpq.18.2.158.21860

Shernoff, D. J., & Hoogstra, L. (2001). Continuing motivation beyond the high school classroom. *New Directions for Child and Adolescent Development*, (93): 73–88. doi:10.1002/cd.26

Simon, H. A. (1957). *Models of man: Social and rational. Mathematical essays on rational human behavior in society setting*. New York: Wiley.

Stake, J. (1995). *The art of case study research*. Thousands Oaks, CA: Sage Publications, Inc.

Vygotsky, L. S. (2006). *Mind in society: Development of higher psychological processes*. Cambridge, MA: Harvard University Press.

Warnke, G. (1987). *Gadamer: Hermeneutics, tradition, and reason*. Stanford, CA: Stanford University Press.

Wells, G. (2000). Dialogic inquiry in education: Building on the legacy of Vygotsky. In Lee, C. D., & Smagorinsky, P. (Eds.), *Vygotskian perspectives on literacy research: Constructing meaning through collaborative inquiry. Learning in doing: Social, cognitive, and computational perspectives* (pp. 1–21). New York: Cambridge University Press.

Wigfield, A., & Eccles, J. S. (2000). Expectancy-value theory of achievement motivation. *Contemporary Educational Psychology, 25*(1), 68–81. doi:10.1006/ceps.1999.1015

Wilson, K. A., Bedwell, W. L., Lazzara, E. H., Salas, E., Burke, C. S., & Estock, J. L. (2009). Relationships between game attributes and learning outcomes: Review and research proposals. *Simulation & Gaming, 40*(2), 217–266. doi:10.1177/1046878108321866

Wu, X. (2003). Intrinsic motivation and young language learners: The impact of the classroom environment. *System, 31*(4), 501. doi:10.1016/j.system.2003.04.001

Zimmerman, B. J. (1989). A social cognitive view of self-regulated academic learning. *Journal of Educational Psychology, 81*(3), 329–339. doi:10.1037/0022-0663.81.3.329

KEY TERMS AND DEFINITIONS

Digital-Game Based Learning (DGBL): An instructional approach that emphasizes engagement on educational content using techniques commonly found in successful commercial digital games.

Educational Games: An instructional approach that presents educational content in a game format.

Individual (aka Personal) Interest: A relatively stable, enduring positive disposition toward a content or object that influences a student to desire to learn more about a content over an extended time.

Middle School (also known as Junior High): A school that bridges students between elementary and high school. In the U.S., middle school often contains grades 6 through 8 (Junior High is often considered 7 through 8) and where students typically ranges from 11 years old to 14 years old.

Problem-Based Learning (PBL): An instructional approach that exemplifies authentic learning and emphasizes solving complex problems.

Self-Efficacy: An individual's competency-related beliefs concerning his or her ability to successfully complete an action, also known as *expectancy*, *ability self-concept*, and *perceived competence*.

Subjective Task Value: An individual's beliefs about value of doing the task, and comprises of the sum of the components of attainment value, the utility value, and the intrinsic value, minus the cost value component.

The Alien Rescue Game (TARG): A digital educational game that middle school students play to engage middle school space science using PBL and DGBL techniques.

Chapter 15

Assessing Engagement in Serious Educational Games:
The Development of the Student Engaged Learning in a Technology Rich Interactive Classroom (SELTIC)

Leonard A. Annetta
North Carolina State University, USA

Richard Lamb
North Carolina State University, USA

Brandy Bowling
North Carolina State University, USA

Rebecca Cheng
North Carolina State University, USA

ABSTRACT

The critical nature of engaging students in authentic learning tasks is not a new concept, but as 21st century technologies become more pervasive in K-20 settings, it is emerging as a significant indicator of learning. This chapter will ground itself in cognition and learning theory, describe the creation and psychometrics of an engagement observation protocol, and provide practical examples of implementation of the SELTIC.

INTRODUCTION

In a 2008 edited book, Annetta, et.al. designated a sub-category of Serious Games. The term Serious Educational Games came to pass as the category of Serious Games that are created for educational purposes. One could argue that all Serious Games are educational in nature but this book focused on K-12 educational settings and thus Serious Educational Games (SEG) were those games for K-12 teachers and students. One important

DOI: 10.4018/978-1-60960-495-0.ch015

justification for integrating SEGs into the educational environment is that these environments are innate to many K-12 students. However the school -educational environment- is void of the digital tools and thus the common interactions the students have with technology. The lack of availability of digital tools creates a digital void which is formed due to the discrepancy between the in school digital tool availability and out of school digital tool availability. Thus, there is a need to fill the void found in these educational environments during school hours. A long understood common indicator of all learning environments has been the notion of students being engaged in the content and spending more time on task. As SEGs begin to become more commonplace during school hours, a need for a valid, reliable protocol to assess student engagement in a technology rich classroom also becomes more critical. Although there are many teacher centered observation protocols in the literature, there are no valid and reliable instruments currently focusing on students using technology; especially SEGs.

Educational games cover a wide variety of game models to include console-based games, computer based games, simulations, first-person and third person games. Serious Educational Games by contrast are a specific genus within the educational game community. Serious Educational Games are characterized by their immersive nature and authentic problem-based teaching mode. In addition, SEGs foster a critical thinking components combined with open-world, architecture and game play. This creates a more realistic and authentic experiences for the game player and differentiates them from other modes of educational games and warrants a separate category.

Operationally, student engagement can be defined as a sense of belonging, level of teacher supportiveness, presence of good friends, engagement in academic progress, fair and effective disciple in, participation in school activities (Libbey, 2004). Understanding and agreeing that engagement is a prerequisite to learning, there is also a distinction between superficial, or procedural, engagement and substantive, or cognitive, engagement. It is only through the latter that learning actually occurs (McLaughlin, et al., 2005). Examples of cognitive engagement are the use of self-regulated learning processes which showing a high level of sophistication in the students' engagement level (Mandinach, 2004). Meaning that students shift cognitive load and vary engagement levels due to the feedback responses found in the game.

The literature regarding student engagement is well beyond the aim and scope of this chapter. Instead we will focus only on the intersection of educational games and student engagement with the understanding that this instrument –SELTIC rubric - can possibly be used with all computer-based educational activities.

The degree to which a student learns and personally develops in any educational program is directly proportional to the quality and quantity of student involvement (e.g. Heath, Herman, Lugo, Reeves, Vetter, & Ward, 2005). *Flow Theory* has been used to examine student engagement (Jones, 1998; Shernoff, Csikszentmihalyi, Schneider, and Shernoff, 2003). The cognitive state of *Flow* is the highest level of engagement one can reach. Shernoff concluded that high school students experienced increased engagement and often reached *Flow* when the challenge of the task and their own skills were high and in balance. Indications of *Flow* can be evidenced by complete cognitive immersion in a task to a point where outside distracters are not a factor during learning and connection processes which are occurring in the working memory (Grow, 1996).

The more problem-based an educational activity, the higher the engagement (Ahlfeldt, Mehta, and Sellnow, 2005). When we make the problem a competition, the motivational to succeed and thus the engagement in the content increases. Although some educators argue against competition on the basis that structural completion (institutionalized) created mutually exclusive goal attainment resulting in the degradation of self worth, competency beliefs, cooperation and interpersonal relationships within the classroom (Kohn, 1986). Contrary to this view there is a body of evidence, which shows that competition motivates students to participate in uninteresting or routine educational activities and has been seen to stimulate involvement and interest (Yu, 2001). For example the military has used commercial games to increase eye-to-hand abilities, simulators are used to train pilots for flight and simulations for other crewed vehicles. Further evidence is the use of products in the classroom such as the historical simulation games *Gettysburg* and *Rail Tycoon* have been used in the classroom to good effect as students are engaged (Squire, 2000).

Jayakanthan (2002) concluded that putting two or more children in the same game, participation and achievement improve as well as motivation; due in part to the competitive nature of games. Therefore, another relationship with engagement is created. These may be reasons why educational games are often couched in a problem-based environment. Author (in press), stated that playing is developmentally appropriate for children and when children are actively engaged in play, they are learning.

SEGs have the potential to reach students who do not do well academically with traditional teaching and learning strategies. Because the current generation of learner had almost everything at the touch of a button, their attention span has become arguable become shorter. This change in attention is impacting teachers and classrooms in every subject (deCastell & Jenson, 2004). SEGs led to increases in active engaged time and decreases in off-task behaviors relative to independent seatwork in a study on math understanding for children with attention deficit hyperactive disorder (Ota, 2002). A similar result has been reported on students with emotional and behavioral disorders (Wilder, 2001). Regardless of the disability, games seem to have potential to engage the seemingly unengaged and unreachable.

This chapter will give some background about time-on-task and student engagement, explain how the Student Engaged Learning in a Technology rich Interactive Classroom (*SELTIC*) protocol was developed and the metrics derived from testing the instruments effectiveness. Finally, the chapter will conclude with a rich description of future directions and the variables that impact student engagement in a technology rich environment.

BACKGROUND

Student Engagement

The term student engagement encompasses behavioral, affective, academic, and cognitive aspects of meaningful student involvement within the learning environment (Appleton, Christenson, Kim, & Reschly, 2006; Chapman, 2003; Goldspink, Winter, & Foster 2008; Wikipedia, 2010). Chapman (2003) defined student engagement as "students' cognitive investment, active participation, and emotional engagement with specific learning tasks" (p. 3). Student cognitive engagement is a prerequisite of learning and academic success (Cummins, 2001; McLaughlin et al., 2005). Additionally, the condition for learning has two dimensions that include both internal factors (defined as things residing within the student) and external factors (defined as the contexts in which learning occurs) (Hall & Bissell, 2006). Specific characteristics of student behavior that serve as evidence of student engagement include internal factors such as students' self-efficacy such as making "I can statements" (Linnenbrink & Pintrich, 2003), students' motivation such as task completion and discipline such as self-regulating behaviors. (Brewster & Fager, 2000; Voke, 2002), and students' socio-emotional readiness and level of academic skills (Walqui, 2000). According to Hickey and Zuiker (2005), while it is difficult to measure these intrinsic states of student engagement, these factors provide crucial insights into increasing students' learning outcomes. In addition to these internal factors, cognitive engagement is also dependent on external factors such as overall school environment and teacher behavior (de Frondeville, 2009; Walqui, 2000). Teachers' pedagogical content knowledge base and their knowledge of how to teach specific content areas can influence students' willingness and ability to stay focused and engaged in the learning process (University of Northern Iowa, 1999; Walqui, 2000). Furthermore, Naffziger, Steele, and Varner (1998) incorporated both cooperative learning and alternative assessments, which resulted in improved student enjoyment and feelings of competency leading to greater student engagement. Finally, Heath et al. (2005) emphasized that the effectiveness of any educational policy or practice is directly related to its capacity to increase student involvement in learning.

Time on Task

Another important factor in measuring student engagement involves students' time spent completing academic tasks, or time-on-task (TOT). Moore (1983) asserted that TOT research data was necessary in order to improve classroom instruction. Furthermore, Karweit and Slavin (1980) found that the methodologies for collecting data regarding the effect of TOT behavior on student achievement is quite sensitive to the number of students sampled, the number of observation days, and the use of alternative definitions of TOT. Spanjers, Burns, and Wagner's (2008) research supported Karweit and Slavin's (1980) results. Spanjers et al. (2008) found that the methodology of Systematic Direct Observation (SDO) was not a sensitive measure of TOT. Finally, Echevarria, Vogt, and Short (2004) described allocated time, engaged time, and academic learning time as three aspects of efficient and rigorous instruction that are important for student engagement.

Educational Technology in the Classroom

It is important to determine how the increased use of technology in the classroom is affecting the many factors of student learning; including engagement, motivation, TOT, academic outcomes. Wilder and Black (2001) asserted that educational technology motivates students to learn, increases student engagement, and improves academic outcomes while Appelbaum and Clark (2001) showed that the concept of fun is often used to motivate students to learn science. Thus, among educational technologies currently being used in the classroom, SEGs, computer games, and virtual learning environments are becoming more popular. Ota and DuPaul (2002) showed that using computer software with a game format led to increases in active engaged time and decreases in off-task behaviors when compared to independent seatwork. Martens, Gulikers, and Bastiaens (2004) found that students with high intrinsic motivation did not do more in an electronic learning environment designed as a game-like realistic simulation, but rather tended to do different things such as engaging in more explorative behavior. Furthermore, de Castell and Jensen (2004) identified the impact of student attention on learning and advocated the use of online computer games as an educational tool to sustain the attention of the learner.

Identity

Recently, in a study of high school genetics students, participants showed much higher engagement (time on task, concentration, etc.) during game play than a similar class conducting traditional genetics laboratory experiments indicating student engagement was due to students feeling present and having a unique identity (Annetta, Minogue, Holmes, & Cheng, 2009). This unique identity was developed through an immersive and interactive environment in which the student takes on the shell of a scientist's identity and complete set of authentic tasks as if they are the scientists themselves. Thus each student provides their own unique sets of prior knowledge, problem-solving ability and cultural moderators to the simulation providing for unique identity. Thus, when game players have a sense of identity and are immersed, they become motivated to proceed through the obstacles and objectives of the game. Gamers prefer to be immersed in a digital world where they become the main character and/or empathize with other characters in a game's narrative. Yee (2006) established that games clearly motivate users in ways that conventional instruction, including online non-routine challenge problems, do not. Players find themselves immersed in the games they play because they find games inherently satisfying. When people are motivated intrinsically they become more engaged in the task at hand. Video games are the 21st century medium comparable to losing oneself in a book that could be read for hours or in a movie where the consumer empathizes and identifies with the main character.

Creation and Sustainment of Flow

Players immersed in a video game or virtual learning environment reach a state of *Flow* when they become engaged and motivated to continue the game's challenge. D. Shernoff, Csikszentmihalyi, Schneider, and E. Shernoff (2003) examined student engagement within the context of *Flow Theory*. They found that high school students experienced increased engagement when the challenge of the task and their own skills were high and in balance, instruction was relevant, and the learning environment was under their control. *Flow Theory* is based on Csikszentmihalyi's (1990) definition of *Flow* as "the state in which people are so involved in an activity that nothing else seems to matter; the experience is so enjoyable that people will do it even at great cost, for the sheer sake of doing it" (p. 4). An example of

student in flow is a student who is so engrossed in completion of an assignment that the student does not hear the dismissal. Thus, *Flow* is a highly energized state of concentration and focus. It can further be described as a psychological state, based on concrete experiences, which acts as a reward by producing intrinsic motivation and active engagement. In order to achieve *Flow*, the level of game challenge must increase as the individual's skill level increases so a dynamic tension remains between the states of boredom and frustration within the student. Finneran and Zhang (2005) stated that *Flow* represents a state of consciousness in which the person is so absorbed in an activity that he shows high performance without being aware of his environment.

When designing an educational game, it is important to consider Csikszentmihalyi's (1990) eight characteristics that describe a person in the *Flow* state. These characteristics include a sense that the activity can be completed successfully, high player concentration, clearly outlined goals, quick feedback, deep player involvement, sense of player control, disappearance of player self-awareness, and an altered sense of time. These occurrences commonly happen while the student is engaged in video game play outside of the educational environment. Hence, the educational game should mimic video games outside of the educational environment and be created to increase student engagement with the learning activities to the level in which the student seems to "flow" along within the game in a spontaneous and almost automatic manner.

Measures of Engagement

Given the different challenges in the design and implementation of SEGs and virtual learning environments, instruments are needed to assess various aspects of student engagement including students' involvement in the lesson, students' intrinsic motivation to learn, and students' interaction with the technology as a source of challenge in order to maintain students' attention and focus on improving critical thinking skills while increasing student initiation of student-to-student exchanges. Currently, there are many teacher characteristic based engagement protocols, such as the revised Stallings' Observation System (Knight, 2001), but few reliable instruments that focus solely on the student. Ahlfeldt, Mehta, and Sellnow (2005) developed a survey, adapted from the National Survey of Student Engagement (NSSE), that measures student engagement at the post-secondary level. Salient features of an observational instrument show allowance for direct observation, creation of a manageable subset of discrete behaviors and allow for the ability of the observer to accurately and easily record activities (O'Malley et. al, 2003).

Their results showed engagement was higher in higher-level classes, classes with fewer students, and in classrooms with more problem-based learning. Carle, Jaffee, Vaughan, and Eder (2009), developed and validated three new surveys, also adapted from the NSSE, which measured student engagement with faculty, community based activities, and transformational learning opportunities. Other surveys to measure student engagement include the Multimedia Project survey (Penuel & Means, 1999), STROBE (O'Malley et al., 2003), and Student Engagement Instrument (Appleton et al., 2006). As preciously stated, what is missing is an instrument or protocol to measure the level of SEG player engagement. This is the focus of this chapter.

MAIN FOCUS OF THE CHAPTER

Through our work in SEGs over the last seven plus years and as our research interests became for focused on the learning sciences, the need to align student engagement with other indicators of learning became critical to our endeavors. Reviewing the aforementioned instruments and modifying them to meet our needs led us to create the Student Engaged Learning in a Technology rich Interactive Classroom (*SELTIC*). The *SELTIC* consists of four subscales evaluated by each rater. The four subscales are: *Affective, Academic, Behavioral* and *Cognitive*. Each subscale is further broken down into several, specific, item or qualitative statements that are rated from *0* (never) to *2* (very descriptive). The lower the rating, the less the characteristics were thought to be present by the rater. As seen in the appendix, the *SELTIC* also provides an area for items that might not be applicable and thus do not impact the total score of the protocol. As the entire rubric represents a measure of engagement, no one question specifically addresses engagement. However each question does a address a portion of the construct of engagement as indicated by the subscale header show on rubric in the appendix. The combination of measures and the resulting coefficient of engagement show engagement levels.

The presented protocol in this chapter is the work of several iterations. Based on the literature on student engagement, key concepts were noted. Such concepts as *activities encouraging students to seek and value multiple modes of investigation or problem solving* and *ensuring course materials relate to students' lives and highlight ways learning can be applied in real-life situations directly impact engagement* were listed and the categorized into similar groups. From these groups, experts worked with the researchers to categorize the *SELTIC* into three broad areas: motivation, competition and problem-based learning. The original SELTIC was tested and the results suggested a need for these broad areas to be more specific. The four more specific categories became: Affective, academic, behavioral and cognitive engagement. Discussed later in this chapter, Figure 7 illustrates the relationship between the original three broad areas with the final four more specific areas that were validated by a panel of experts on student engagement, cognitive psychology, and psychometrics.

Upon completing what we believed was a valid instrument, we measure content and construct validity through expert validation. Once the protocol was agreed upon by all expert raters, it was used with three SEGs constructed in our research projects and those data were exposed to reliability testing.

Three different SEGs were used to test the *SELTIC*. We will operational define these games as STIMULATE (a science laboratory safety training SEG), RACING GAME (an off road racing game designed to teach physics concepts), and OUTBREAK (an SEG to teach biotechnology and ethical decision making).

Kappa Coefficient

Two variation of the Kappa Coefficient were used to calculate the inter-rater reliability. The first equation is the Cohen's Kappa using equation 1.

$$K = \frac{\bar{P} - \bar{P}_e}{1 - \bar{P}_e} \qquad (1)$$

[pbar] is defined as the observed agreement between two raters. [pbar$_e$] is defined as the probability fo the agreement as occurs by random chance. The second Kappa coefficient was used to calculate the inter-rater reliability associated with multiple raters (more than two). The primary differences between the two Kappa Coefficients is the manner in which [pbar] and [pbar$_e$] are calculated [pbar] and [pbar$_e$] are calculated using equations 2 and 3.

$$\bar{P} = \frac{1}{Nn(n-1)} \left(\sum_{i=1}^{N} \sum_{j=1}^{k} n_{ij}^2 - Nn \right) \qquad (2)$$

$$\bar{Pe} = \sum_{j=1}^{k} p_j^2 \qquad (3)$$

Result of the calculation of [pbar$_e$] and [pbar] are inserted into the Kappa equation and a standard Kappa coefficient equation is obtained. Kappa Coefficients range from -1.00 to +1.00. A negative Kappa value indicates that the agreement between raters is worse than would be expected by chance. A 0.00 rating indicates that agreement has occurred by chance and at +1.00 rating indicates perfect agreement. The larger the positive value the closer to non-chance perfect agreement the results are.

Figure 1. STIMULATE gauge attribute chart showing percentage agreement across factors

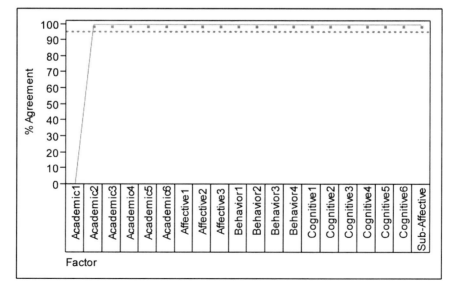

Figure 2. STIMULATE percent agreement for each rater agreement

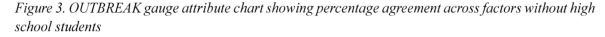

Data analysis was completed using Cohen's Coefficient Kappa for double blind raters for all three SEGs and Fleiss's Coefficient Kappa for multirater rubrics (more than two raters) for the OUTBREAK assessments. The subsections within the rubric sections were treated as a single unit and the Kappa Coefficient was calculated for each rubric as a whole. Fleiss Kappa Coefficient used for the OUTBREAK assessment is weighted based on the number of raters as opposed to the Cohen Kappa Coefficient, which is not as there are only two raters.

By its nature the Fleiss Coefficient Kappa takes the number of raters into account. The three coefficient values (one for each session) for each section of the rubric were then compared using an independent t-test, testing for statistically significant differences between the values. A independent t-test is indicated for the analysis of the Coefficients of Engagement as the coefficients of engagement represent a numerical quantifica-

Figure 3. OUTBREAK gauge attribute chart showing percentage agreement across factors without high school students

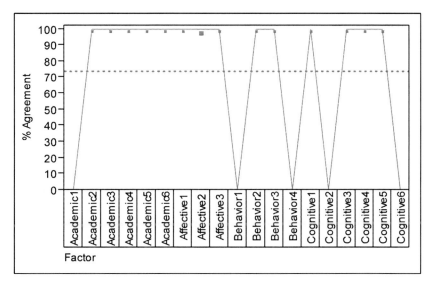

Figure 4. OUTBREAK percent agreement for each rater without high school students

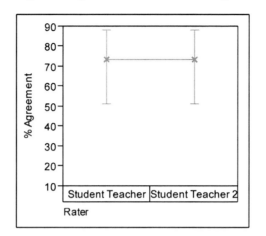

tion of the level of engagement. An average value for the three coefficients in each section was calculated and that value was reviewed using the Landis & Koch Kappa Benchmarks. The Kappa values were then assigned a rating for each section of the rubric ranging from "No Agreement" to "Complete Agreement". From each section and individual rating, an overall rating of the rubric was established.

Figures 1-6 show the relative agreement between raters and the agreement of the raters across the measured factors. Figures 1 and 5 show

almost complete agreement across factors with only one measured factor in Figure 1 (Academic 1) showing variation among the raters. Figure 3 shows variations across the assessed factors, but figure 4 shows little variation among the raters. This increase in variation across factors may be due to the complexity of the game. Assessment of the game using the rubric maybe better accomplished through a periodic rating of stages of play allowing for more user interaction as opposed to impressions as a whole.

Figure 5. RACING GAME gauge attribute chart showing percentage agreement across factors

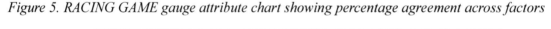

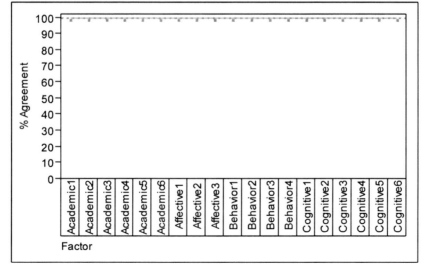

Figure 6. RACING GAME percent agreement for each rater with agreement between & within raters

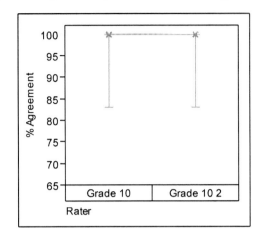

Table 1. Agreement comparisons between and within raters

Rater	Compared with Rater	Kappa Coefficient	Standard Error	Interpretation	
STIMULATE Student Teacher	STIMULATE Student Teacher 2	0.89	0.11	Almost Perfect Agreement	
OUTBREAK Student Teacher	OUTBREAK Student Teacher 2	*0.52	0.18	Moderate Agreement	
OUTBREAK All Raters		*0.33	0.23	Fair Agreement	
RACING GAME Grade 10	RACING GAME Grade 10 2	1.00	0.00	Almost Perfect Agreement	

Note. Outbreak Student Teacher and Outbreak Student Teacher 2 comparison uses Cohen's Coefficient Kappa and the OUTBREAK All Raters uses Fleiss's Kappa Coefficient.

Even numbered figures show the agreement between raters using the rubric. Figures 2 and 6 show almost complete agreement with ratings of over 90% agreement, figures 4 show less agreement across raters with mean agreement levels of 75% which is still a significant level of agreement.

Table 1 shows comparisons of Kappa Coefficients across games using the same rubric. The RACING game shows the highest agreement with a Kappa Coefficient of 1.00 while OUTBREAK showed the lowest level of agreement with a coefficient of 0.52. However it should be noted that OUTBREAK is a far more complex and longer game when compared to the other two SEGs and rater fatigue may play a role in the level of agreement.

Table 2 shows the Landis and Koch Kappa Benchmarks established in 1977. Each rating is tied to a range of values for the Kappa Coefficient. Notice the overlap between the 0 and 0.0 categories. Given this overlap, the interpretation of the

Table 2. Landis & Koch Kappa benchmarks

κ Coefficient	Interpretation
0	No agreement
0.0 — 0.20	Slight agreement
0.21 — 0.40	Fair agreement
0.41 — 0.60	Moderate agreement
0.61 — 0.80	Substantial agreement
0.81 — 1.00	Almost perfect agreement

0.0 is actually >0.0 will result in a slight agreement (Landis, 1977; Annetta, 2009).

Analysis of the Kappa values shows on average, substantial agreement with a mean Kappa Coefficient of 0.69 among the raters for each portion of the rubric and across rating sessions. As no statistically significant differences were found in the Kappa Coefficients across sessions, this further lends itself to the reliability of the rubric. Given the high agreement between raters it can be stated that the reliability of the *SELTIC* is high. By design the ratings of each portion of the game was independent and was not otherwise confirmed or denied by another rater; thus mitigating any inflation of the Kappa Coefficient.

The use of the rubric across multiple sessions, different games and different raters lends creditability to the multi-purpose use of the *SELTIC*. When we reduce the three separate sessions to Kappa Coefficients we are now comparing similar measures. Thus, the game choice does not matter so long as the rubric is the same. This was the goal of the *SELTIC* construction. It can measure engagement regardless of the game but it can inform the immersion of the game. If the *SELTIC* score is low, then the game is not as immersive as the developed might have hoped and vice-versa.

Variation found among raters of the OUTBREAK game may be due to the complex nature of the game. Given the epistemic nature of the SEG with its complex story line and increased numbers of tasks of OUTBREAK, a rating system in which the raters are given multiple opportunities to rate the game throughout stages of play would be warranted. Often time players in a game may forget small details from the beginning of the game, which would help to increase agreements amount the raters. It is similar to asking individuals to relate the portions of a large novel after reading the entire book rather than chapter by chapter. While the overall details would be remarkably similar the smaller details would most likely vary greatly due to recall differences.

The level of agreement is based on the Landis and Koch (1977) standards of strength. The choice of such benchmarks, however, is inevitably arbitrary and the effects of prevalence and bias on Kappa must be considered when judging its magnitude (Brennan & Silman, 1992; Dunn, 1999; Sim & Wright, 2005). Due to the large number of raters for each session and the conservative nature of the (Fleiss) Kappa coefficient which can result in underreporting of the level of agreement (Fleiss, 1971), the level of agreement descriptor is adjusted one level in the positive direction. Therefore the Landis and Koch benchmarks are modified (Table 3). Engagement is accessed via the Coefficient of Engagement using the criteria for scoring found on the SELTIC measure as noted in the appendix.

FUTURE RESEARCH DIRECTIONS

Clearly, engagement is a crucial indicator of learning. As this book is focused on learning and motivation in SEGs it is important to share not only the results of the *SELTIC* but also to illustrate the relationships that inform engagement. Learning and motivation are key components to the development of student engagement understanding. In what has become known in our research group as the "Len Diagram" Figure 7 revisits the relationship between competition, motivation and problem-based learning (PBL) with engagement. Further, the categories derived from the *SELTIC* (affective, academic, behavioral, and cognitive)

Table 3 Shows the engagement rating for each game based on rater rubric scores

Game	Engagement Coefficient (E)
Stimulate	0.842
Outbreak	0.746
Racing Game	0.447

*Note. Student engagement is rated as the Coefficient of Engagement (E) developed through scoring of the SELTIC. The coefficient is calculated using the following equation: E= case (i-j)/n(yi-yj)/k are included as well. It is our contention that the factors in blue (PBL, competition and Motivation) are the essence of SEGs and the factors from the *SELTIC* (in yellow) have overlap in many areas and the area in which all seven factors overlap is where engagement occurs at its highest.

The visual representation of the theory as depicted by the Len diagram can inform the theory by illustrating the connections and overlaps for the integration of the factors of engagement. With the informative nature of the Len diagram it can be used to drive the development of the theory by showing areas and factors of interaction where research can take place.

The Len Diagram suggests that the development of a SEG can be accomplished through the proper blending and overlap of the characteristics shown to make up engagement. Through movement of the engagement circle, appropriate measure using the SELTIC and use of the elements motivation, competition and PBL it is possible to create a proper "mix" resulting in the proper placement of the engagement circle.

Future research on this topic needs to enlighten and inform the *SELTIC*. Although the metrics of this protocol are solid, the *SELTIC* needs to be used and measured with varying age groups at different levels in school and with different populations of learners. If in fact learning disabled students, for example, are more engaged playing SEGs in school then the *SELTIC* can inform the research as to what level of engagement the students reach. These results could suggest the importance of whether or not to infuse learning through SEGs in the future. With a keen eye on reliability, each modification of the *SELTIC* needs to go through more rigorous testing and the subsequent validation needs to be reported as well.

Further, the Len Diagram has gone through much iteration over time but future research needs to help modify the graphic to include other factors that inform what engages students in a technology rich environment. This author team is very interested in how this protocol and diagram is used. We look forward to reading more about this topic; especially as it pertains to SEGs.

Figure 7. The len diagram on engagement and the factors that influence it

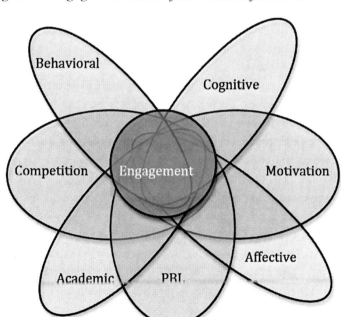

CONCLUSION

In this study, we reported on the initial development of this protocol. However, we believe that on-going testing with larger groups of students is needed to confirm these analyses. In addition the inclusion of confirmatory factor analysis will help to define the factors that make up the construct of engagement.

It is well documented that students drop out of school because they are not engaged. A student not engaged is a student not learning. If video games are a vehicle for engaging students then we need to use them more in educational settings. One of the reasons SEGs are not yet widely accepted is because there have not been enough empirical evidence to suggest they work. We contend that the difficulty is making data driven decisions on learning in SEGs because it is nearly impossible to isolate the game and to make claims it is the sole reason learning occurs. There are plenty of pretest-posttest designs but those research designs are not authentic in that they don't suggest how students assimilate the content in the game. Further, the conceptual change by the teacher is often not accounted for either. This is why such indicators of learning, as those presented in this chapter and throughout this book, are important factors for future research. The key element is the affordance of valid and reliable instrumentation to measure these factors.

The use of emerging technologies, such as SEGs, applies principles well understood by the entertainment industry to engage students in their own learning. Once students are engaged, they can be challenged with more complex material. We hope that this development of a valid and reliable measure of engagement is a first step in that process. The results of the SELTIC study are in line with previous studies suggesting that the use of CAI, video games and other forms of instructional technology aids in student engagement. Literature also suggests that the factors that make up the construct of engagement can be manipulated to find the correct mix of factors and thus allow creation of the highly engaging and educational games.

RECOMMENDATIONS

The use of SELTIC is indicated for an educator who would like to assess and quantify levels of engagement in order to understand the impact of specific programs of instruction using SEGs and other types of computer assisted instruction. Additionally the quantification of the engagement construct allows for comparison of levels of engagement though standard inferential statistics.

In an era where user-created content is becoming more mainstream (i.e., Web 2.0) there continues to be a need for assessing that content. SELTIC can be the driving force behind user-created content as it pertains to Serious Educational Game construction. Whether teachers or students develop a game or a game studio is charged to create a game for you, the SELTIC could be the framework by which the design document and resulting game is conceptualized.

LIMITATIONS

SELTIC loses reliability as the number of unanswered questions increase. This is due to an inherent limitation of the Kappa Coefficient. As the number of items reviewed decrease the probability of chance agreement increases thus inflating the engagement coefficient. The inflation of the Kappa coefficient becomes significant when the number of answered items decreases to 50% within the subscale. However removal of one subscale does not invalidate the coefficient of engagement. Secondary limitations of SELTIC become apparent in longer games, as rater fatigue seems to play a role in calculated outcomes as evidenced by the outcomes associated with OUTBREAK.

REFERENCES

Ahlfeldt, S., Mehta, S., & Sellnow, T. (2005). Measurement and analysis of student engagement in university classes where varying levels of PBL methods of instruction are in use. *Higher Education Research & Development, 24*(1), 5–20. doi:10.1080/0729436052000318541

Annetta, L. A., Lamb, R., & Stone, M. (2010In press). Assessing serious educational games: The development of a scoring rubric. In Annetta, L. A., & Bronack, S. (Eds.), *Serious educational game assessment: Practical methods and models for educational games, simulations and virtual worlds.* Amsterdam: Sense Publishers.

Annetta, L. A., Minogue, J. A., Holmes, S., & Cheng, M. T. (2009). Investigating the impact of video games on high school students' engagement and learning about genetics. *Computers & Education, 54*(1), 74–85. doi:10.1016/j.compedu.2008.12.020

Appelbaum, P., & Clark, S. (2001). Science! Fun? A critical analysis of design/content/evaluation. *Journal of Curriculum Studies, 33*(5), 583–600. doi:10.1080/00220270010023812

Appleton, J. J., Christenson, S. L., Kim, D., & Reschly, A. L. (2006). Measuring cognitive and psychological engagement: Validation of the student engagement instrument. *Journal of School Psychology, 44*, 427–445. doi:10.1016/j.jsp.2006.04.002

Brennan, P., & Silman, A. (1992). Statistical methods for assessing observer variability in clinical measures. *BMJ (Clinical Research Ed.), 304*, 1491–1495. doi:10.1136/bmj.304.6840.1491

Brewster, C., & Fager, J. (2000). *Increasing student engagement and motivation: From time-on-task to homework.* Portland: Northwest Regional Educational Laboratory.

Carle, A. C., Jaffee, D., Vaughan, N. W., & Eder, D. (2009). Psychometric properties of three new national survey of student engagement based engagement scales: An item response theory analysis. *Research in Higher Education, 50*(8), 775–794. doi:10.1007/s11162-009-9141-z

Chapman, E. (2003). Alternative approaches to assessing student engagement rates. *Practical Assessment. Research Evaluation, 8*(13). Retrieved from http://PAREonline.net/getvn.asp?v=8&n=13.

Csikszentmihalyi, M. (1990). *Flow: The psychology of optimal experience.* New York: Harper Row.

Cummins, J. (2001). *Negotiating identities: Education for empowerment in a diverse society* (2nd ed.). Los Angeles: California Association for Bilingual Education.

de Castell, S., & Jenson, J. (2004). Paying attention to attention: New economies for learning. *Educational Theory, 54*(4), 381–397. doi:10.1111/j.0013-2004.2004.00026.x

de Frondeville, T. (2009). Ten steps to better student engagement. *Edutopia.* Retrieved from http://www.edutopia.org/project-learning-teaching-strategies

Dunn, G. (1989). *Design and analysis of reliability studies: The statistical evaluation of measurement errors.* London: Edward Arnold.

Echevarria, J., Vogt, M., & Short, D. (2004). *Making content comprehensible for English learners: The SIOP model* (2nd ed.). Boston: Pearson, Allyn, and Bacon.

Finneran, C. M., & Zhang, P. (2005). Flow in computer-mediated environments: Promises and challenges. *Communications of the Association for Information Systems, 15*, 82–101.

Fleiss, J. L. (1971). Measuring nominal scale agreement among many raters. *Psychological Bulletin, 76*(5). doi:10.1037/h0031619

Goldspink, C., Winter, P., & Foster, M. (2008). *Student engagement and quality pedagogy.* Conference presentation at Annual Meeting of European Conference on Education Research. Göteborg, Sweden. Retrieved from http://www.earlyyears.sa.edu.au/files/links/Student_Engagement_and_Qua.pdf

Hall, D. M., & Bissell, A. N. (2006). *Who are we trying to help? A framework for understanding the nature of academically vulnerable college learners and implications for practice.* Conference presentation at Enriching the Academic Experience of College Science Students. Ann Arbor, MI: University of Michigan.

Heath, B., Herman, R., Lugo, G., Reeves, J., Vetter, R., & Ward, C. (2005). Developing a mobile learning environment to support virtual education communities. *Technological Horizons in Education Journal Online, 32*(8), 33–36.

Hickey, D. T., & Zuiker, S. J. (2005). Engaged participation: A sociocultural model of motivation with implications for educational assessment. *Educational Assessment, 10*(3), 277–305. doi:10.1207/s15326977ea1003_7

Karweit, N. L., & Slavin, R. E. (1980). *Measuring time-on-task: Issues of timing, sampling and definition.* Baltimore, MD: The Johns Hopkins University. Retrieved from http://www.eric.ed.gov/ERICDocs/data/ericdocs2sql/content_storage_01/0000019b/80/3f/36/b3.pdf

Knight, S. L. (2001). *Using technology to update traditional classroom observation instruments.* Conference presentation at Annual Meeting of the American Educational Research Association. Seattle, WA.

Kohn, A. (1987). *The case against competition.* New York: Vanderbilt Press.

Landis, J. R., & Koch, G. G. (1977). The measurement of observer agreement for categorical data. *Biometrics, 33.*

Libbey, H. (2004). Measuring student relationships to school: Attachment, bonding, connectedness, and engagement. *The Journal of School Health, 74*(7). doi:10.1111/j.1746-1561.2004.tb08284.x

Linnenbrink, E. A., & Pintrich, P. R. (2003). The role of self-efficacy beliefs in student engagement and learning in the classroom. *Reading & Writing Quarterly, 19*(2), 119–137. doi:10.1080/10573560308223

Martens, R. L., Gulikers, J., & Bastiaens, T. (2004). The impact of intrinsic motivation on e-learning in authentic computer tasks. *Journal of Computer Assisted Learning, 20*(5), 368–376. doi:10.1111/j.1365-2729.2004.00096.x

McLaughlin, M., McGrath, D. J., Burian-Fitzgerald, M. A., Lanahan, L., Scotchmer, M., Enyeart, C., et al. (2005). *Student content engagement as a construct for the measurement of effective classroom instruction and teacher knowledge.* Washington, DC: American Institutes for Research. Retrieved from http://www.air.org/news/documents/AER-A2005Student%20Content%20Engagement.pdf

Moore, J. E. (1983). *Assessing time-on-task: Measurement problems and solutions.* Conference presentation at Joint Meeting of the Evaluation Network and Evaluation Research Society. Chicago, IL. Retrieved from http://www.eric.ed.gov/ERICDocs/data/ericdocs2sql/content_storage_01/0000019b/80/2e/87/3e.pdf

Naffziger, S. C., Steele, M. M., & Varner, B. O. (1998). *Academic growth: Strategies to improve sudent engagement in their learning.* Master's thesis, Saint Xavier University, 1998. Retrieved from http://www.eric.ed.gov/ERICDocs/data/ericdocs2sql/content_storage_01/0000019b/80/15/c3/a3.pdf

O'Malley, K. J., Moran, B. J., Haidet, P., Seidel, C. L., Schneider, V., & Morgan, R. O. (2003). Validation of an observation instrument for measuring student engagement in health professions settings. *Evaluation & the Health Professions, 26*(1), 86–103. doi:10.1177/0163278702250093

Ota, K. R., & DuPaul, G. J. (2002). Task engagement and mathematics performance in children with attention deficit hypcractivity disorder: Effects of supplemental computer instruction. *School Psychology Quarterly, 17*(3), 242–257. doi:10.1521/scpq.17.3.242.20881

Penuel, W. R., & Means, B. (1999). Observing classroom processes in project-based learning using multimedia: A tool for evaluators. Retrieved from http://74.125.155.132/scholar?q=cache:hg 3JY0wURnIJ:scholar.google.com/&hl=en&as_sdt=2000

Shernoff, D. J., Csikszentmihalyi, M., Schneider, B., & Shernoff, E. S. (2003). Student engagement in high school classrooms from the perspective of flow theory. *School Psychology Quarterly, 18*(2), 158–176. doi:10.1521/scpq.18.2.158.21860

Sim, J., & Wright, C. (2005). The kappa statistic in reliability studies: Use, interpretation and sample size requirements. *Journal of Physical Therapy, 85*(3), 257–268.

Spanjers, D. M., Burns, M. K., & Wagner, A. R. (2008). Systematic direct observation of time on task as a measure of student engagement. *Assessment for Effective Intervention, 33*, 120–126. doi:10.1177/1534508407311407

University of Northern Iowa. (1999). *Technology as a facilitator of quality education model: A component of integrating new technologies into the methods of education* (in time). Cedar Falls, Iowa: University of Northern Iowa, College of Education. Retrieved from http://www.intime. uni.edu/

Voke, H. (2002). Student engagement: Motivating students to learn. *ASCD Infobrief, 28*. Retrieved from http://www.ascd.org/publications/newsletters/infobrief/feb02/num28/Motivating_Students_to_Learn.aspx

Walqui, A. (2000). *Access and engagement: Program design and instructional approaches for immigrant students in secondary school*. McHenry, IL: Delta Systems.

Wikipedia. (2010). *Student engagement*. Retrieved from http://en.wikipedia.org/wiki/Student_engagement

Wilder, L. K., & Black, S. (Eds.). (2001). *Integrating technology in program development for children/youth with E/BD*. Retrieved from http://www.eric.ed.gov/ERICDocs/data/ericdocs2sql/content_storage_01/0000019b/80/19/6c/87.pdf

Yee, N. (2006). The demographics, motivations, and derived experiences of users of massively multi-user online graphical environments. *Presence (Cambridge, Mass.), 15*, 309–329. doi:10.1162/pres.15.3.309

ADDITIONAL READING

Adamo-Villani, N., & Wright, K. (2007). *SMILE: an immersive learning game for deaf and hearing children*. Paper presented at the International Conference on Computer Graphics and Interactive Techniques.

Annetta, L. A. (2008). *Serious Educational Games: From Theory to Practice* (p. 83). Amsterdam, The Netherlands: Sense Publishers.

Annetta, L. A. (2008). Designing and evaluating educational video games. *Learning and Leading with Technology, 36*(2).

Annetta, L. A. (2008). Why and how video games should be used in education. *Theory into Practice, 47*(3), 229–239. doi:10.1080/00405840802153940

Annetta, L. A. (in press August 25, 2009). Building Community in 21st Century Graduate Classes Through Synchronous Online Research Presentations: A Case for 3-Dimensional Learning Environments. International Journal of Web Based Communities.

Annetta, L.A. (in press August 16, 2009). The "I's" have it: A framework for educational game design. Review of General Psychology

Annetta, L. A., Cheng, M. T., & Holmes, S. (in press). Assessing 21st century skills through a teacher created video game for high school biology students. *Research in Science & Technological Education.*

Annetta, L.A., Klesath, M. J., & Holmes, S. (2008). How gaming and avatars are engaging online students. Innovate, 4 (3). http://innovateonline. info/index.php?view=article&id=485&action=synopsis

Annetta, L. A., Mangrum, J., Holmes, S., Collazo, K., & Cheng, M. (2009). Bridging reality to virtual reality: Investigating gender effect and student engagement on learning through video game play in an elementary school classroom. *International Journal of Science Education, 31*(8), 1091–1113. doi:10.1080/09500690801968656

Bransford, J. D., Brown, A. L., & Cocking, R. R. (Eds.). (1999). *How people learn: Brain, mind, experience, and school.* Washington, DC: National Academy Press.

Carr, D. (2007). Computer games in classrooms and the question of 'cultural baggage'. *British Journal of Educational Technology, 38*(3), 526–528. doi:10.1111/j.1467-8535.2007.00717.x

Dede, C., Salzman, M., & Loftin, B. (1999). Multisensory immersion as a modeling environment for learning complex scientific concepts. In Feurzeig, W., & Roberts, N. (Eds.), *Modeling and simulation in science and mathematics education.* New York: Springer Verlag.

DeKanter, N. (2005). Gaming redefines interactivity for learning. *TechTrends, 49*(3), 26–31. doi:10.1007/BF02763644

Fulford, C. P. (1993). Can learning be more efficient? Using compressed speech audio tapes to enhance systematically designed text. *Educational Technology, 33*(2), 51–59.

Garris, R., Ahlers, R., & Driskell, J. E. (2002). Games, motivation, and learning: A research and practice model. *Simulation & Gaming, 33*(4), 441–467. doi:10.1177/1046878102238607

Graves, W. H. (2005). Improving institutional performance through IT-enabled innovation. [executive summary]. *EDUCAUSE Review, 40*(6), 78–98.

Grow, G. (1996) Serving the Strategic Reader: Reader Response Theory and Its Implications for the Teaching of Writing," an expanded version of a paper presented to the Qualitative Division of the Association for Educators in Journalism and Mass Communication. Atlanta, August, 1994. Available on-line at: <http://www.longleaf.net/ggrow>. Original paper available as Eric Documentation Reproduction Service No. ED 406 644.

Hickey, D., & Zuiker, S. J. (2005). Engaged participation: A sociocultural model of motivation with implications for educational assessment. *Educational Assessment, 10*(3), 277–305. doi:10.1207/s15326977ea1003_7

Hidi, S. R., K. A. (2006). The four-phase model of interest development. *Educational Psychologist, 41*(2), 111–127. doi:10.1207/s15326985ep4102_4

http://www.ed.gov/technology/1999/whitepapers

Jaipal, K., & Figg, C. (2009). *Factors Impacting the Effectiveness of Using Video Games to Teach Grade 8 Science: A Thematic Case Study.* Paper presented at the Society for Information Technology & Teacher Education International Conference 2009, Charleston, SC, USA.

Kirrirmuir, J. (2002). Video gaming, education, and digital learning. *D-Lib Magazine,* •••, 8.

Ma, Y., Williams, D., Prejean, L., & Richard, C. (2007). A research agenda for developing and implementing educational computer games. *British Journal of Educational Technology, 38*(3), 513–518. doi:10.1111/j.1467-8535.2007.00714.x

Mandinach, E., & Corno, L. (2004). Cognative engagment variations among students of differnet ablity level and sex in a computer problem solving game. *Sex Roles*, *13*(3-4), 241–251. doi:10.1007/BF00287914

Mayer, R. (2002). Cognitive Theory and the design of multimedia instruction: An example of the two-way street between cognition an distruction. *New Directions for Teaching and Learning*, •••, 55–71. doi:10.1002/tl.47

Meyers, C., & Jones, T. B. (1993). *Promoting active learning: Design and implementation*. Columbus, OH: Bell & Howell.

Oblinger, D. G. (2006). The next generation of educational engagement. *Journal of Interactive Media in Education, Special Issue on the Educational Semantic Web, 8*. Retrieved from http://www-jime.open.ac.uk/2004/8/oblinger-2004-8-disc-paper.html

Penuel, W. R., & Means, B. (2005). Observing classroom processes in project-based learning using multimedia: A tool for evaluators. Retrieved from http://www.riverdeep.net/for_teachers/pro_development/iowa3/sessions

Pintrich, P. R., & De Groot, E. V. (1990). Motivational and self-regulated learning components of classroom academic performance. *Journal of Educational Psychology*, *82*(1), 33–40. doi:10.1037/0022-0663.82.1.33

Roberts, D. F., Foehr, U. G., & Rideout, V. (2005). *Generation M: Media in the Lives of 8-18 Year Olds*. Menlo Park, CA: Kaiser Family Foundation.

Salomon, G., Perkins, D. N., & Globerson, T. (1991). Partners in Cognition: extending human intelligence with intelligent technologies. *Educational Researcher*, *20*(3), 2–9.

Spellings, M. (2007). *Report of the Academic Competitiveness Council*. from http://www.ed.gov/about/inits/ed/competitiveness/acc-mathscience/report.pdf.

Squire, K. (2000). *Video games in education*. Comparitive Media Studies Department, Massachuetts Insittute of Technology.

Squire, K. (2002). Cultural framing of computer/video games. *Interantional journal of computer game research, 2*(1).

Verenikina, I., Harris, P., & Lysaght, P. (2003). *Child's play: Computer games, theories of play and children's development*. Paper presented at the IFIP Working Group 3.5 Conference, UWS Paramatta.

APPENDIX

Student Engaged Learning in a Technology rich Interactive Classroom (*SELTIC*)

Teacher: _____ Grade _____ Location_____

Observer: _____ Date: _____ Start Time _____End Time _____

# of students_____

Criteria	Never Observed 0	Observed sometimes 1	Very Descriptive 2	Not Applicable	Total	Average Subscale Score
Affective						
Activity related to students real lives (tapped prior knowledge)						
Communication is encouraged by teacher						
Small groups were used effectively						
Academic						
Technology challenged students, particularly to exhibit critical thinking skills						
Students had control over their learning (choices in the task)						
Activity progressive challenges from easy to very difficult						
Activity had a reward system built in or teacher provided reward for success						
Teacher closes technology lesson through tying into lesson objective						
Technology provides content and pedagogical feedback						
Behavioral						
There was productive student-student communication (conversations among students who are constructing knowledge together)						
Students were focused on the activity						
Goals expectations were clearly stated (either in the technology and/or from teacher)						
Students were able to communicate their ideas to peers and/or teacher						
Cognitive						
This activity encouraged students to seek and value multiple modes of investigation or problem solving.						
Students were reflective about their learning.						

Criteria	Never Observed 0	Observed sometimes 1	Very Descriptive 2	Not Applicable	Total	Average Subscale Score
Reached Flow state						
Students were intellectually engaged with the content related to the lesson activities.						
The lesson challenged most students to think at high cognitive levels.						
The lesson was effective at intrinsically motivating students to learn by appealing to students' interest, addressing a relevant topic, creating a desire to resolve a discrepancy, creating cognitive dissonance, or employing other intrinsic motivators.						

Low scores suggest low engaging technology and/or teacher facilitation of integrating the technology

Chapter 16
Games that Motivate to Learn:
Design Serious Games by Identified Regulations

Menno Deen
Fontys University of Applied Sciences, The Netherlands

Ben A.M. Schouten
Fontys University of Applied Sciences, The Netherlands

ABSTRACT

It is commonly acknowledged that intrinsically motivated learning makes for better students. Yet, facilitating students to become intrinsically motivated to learn is difficult, if not, impossible to accomplish. As every student has different and personal intrinsic needs, the design of regulations that satisfy intrinsic needs may seem an unfruitful approach to serious game design. Inspired by research to the beta-version of the second language game CheckOut!, this chapter proposes a different approach to serious game design, based on identified regulations.

Identified regulations are negotiations with personal valued rules. The regulations can be positioned between external regulations (based on punishments and rewards) and intrinsic regulations (based on a personal willingness to act). To develop identified regulations, game designers should create a correspondence between the game regulations and the student's perceptions about the educational instruction.

To accomplish this fit, game designers could not conceal the learning within a game, but explicitly communicate the constructed knowledge to the player. Progressive feedback, the availability of various learning styles in the game, and the embedding of the game in a social environment, might satisfy students' needs for competence, autonomy and relatedness to significant others. When these needs are satisfied within the context of the educational instructions, students might become motivated to learn during play, and even when the game is over.

DOI: 10.4018/978-1-60960-495-0.ch016

INTRODUCTION

'Hello! I am Stella, your tour guide for *DreamBox Learning K-2 Math*', Stella, a red-haired girl welcomes us to the world of sums and equations. We are 'playing' *DreamBox*, an internet application designed by DreamBox Learning Ltd. (2009a) for middle school students. By solving equations and other math exercises, students can explore an imaginary world of dinosaurs and fairies. *DreamBox* is an example of e-learning applications that uses game-elements to make 'serious learning, serious fun' (Dreambox Learning, 2009b).

There are many motivational features that can enhance the initial enjoyment for equating in *DreamBox*. These features consist of scoring points and unlocking mini-games or cinematics[1]. Educational applications like *DreamBox* rely excessively on punishments and rewards. As research shows, these external regulations may diminish motivations for learning (Arnold, 1976; Lepper, Corpus, & Iyengar, 2005)[2]. Furthermore, external regulations may obscure the learning content; they may change the player's focus from learning to scoring points and avoiding failures.

Many of today's serious games are based on external regulations. Players are often encouraged to (learn or) play by the prospect of gaining victory over a classmate, increasing one's high score or receiving a particular award. We propose a different regulation to motivate learning, called identified regulation. Identified regulations are defined by Ryan & Deci (2000) as the negotiations with personally important-, and consciously valued rules and goals. We argue that identified regulations are a more feasible approach to serious games than external regulations. Identified regulations may motivate learning during play, *and* after the game is over.

This hypothesis is inspired by Deen's (2009) validation of the second language learning game *CheckOut! (Beta Version)* (Ranj Serious Games & ROC West-Brabant, 2010). The game is designed with identified regulations in mind. Deen found a change in students' motivation towards traditional[3] second language instruction. Although not fully implemented, certain identified regulations may account for this motivational change.

We argue that games can change students' motivations to learn for the better. By designing a game trough identified regulations and by satisfying three basic human needs (competence, autonomy, and relatedness), students may become motivated to play and learn, even when the game is over.

NEED THEORY: COMPETENCE, AUTONOMY, AND RELATEDNESS

Game theorist Sutton-Smith assumes that 'psychological factors operate internally to determine the range of gratifications that the players will get from the activity and the needs that it will meet' (1959, p. 24). The psychological factors that determine motivations are researched in what is called *Theory of Needs,* a part of cognitive psychology. According to Need Theory, (possible) need satisfaction is an essential condition to act. Specific goals, rules and activities (called regulations) may satisfy a particular need and in turn motivate to act.

It remains difficult to pinpoint which needs are satisfied through which regulations. People in different circumstances have different needs. The personal character of needs is stressed by Reiss' theory of sixteen basic human desires (2004, 2009), for example needs for vengeance, eating, and romance are circumstance dependent. Most likely, these needs are not always of main importance to learning processes, nor are other basic human needs, like physiological needs or needs for safety (Maslow, 1943).

The needs and regulations described by self-determination theory (Ryan & Deci, 2000) fit an educational environment better. Ryan & Deci defined three types of motivation: *amotivation, extrinsic motivation* and *intrinsic motivation,* as

Figure 1. The self-determination matrix (Adapted from Ryan & Deci 2000). Three types of motivation (first row), their corresponding regulation (second row), and their style descriptions in the third row

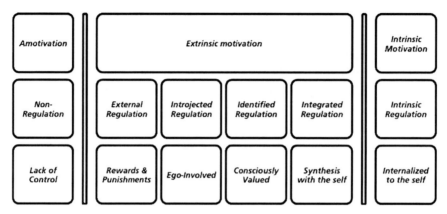

well as three basic human needs and their associated regulatory styles, see Figure 1. In general, the more intrinsic a motivation is, the more the user acts in an autonomous manner. Furthermore, every motivational type is regulated differently.

Ryan and Deci (2000) emphasize that intrinsic motivation cannot be regulated by the use of rewards and punishments. These external regulations need to be integrated to the self. This means, the regulations have been evaluated and brought into congruence with one's other values and needs. Like a judo-practitioner does not enjoy doing push-ups, but the jūdōka may value them as an important part of his training schedule and daily life. In fact, when not exercising, he may miss these 'former' external regulations. The jūdōka evaluated the push-ups and brought them in congruence with his personal values and needs. If integration to the self is successful, the jūdōka can be intrinsically motivated to do push-ups, and may miss his them when they are skipped.

In order to integrate regulations into one's self, one should be able to identify these regulations first. Identified regulations describe the negotiations with personally important-, and consciously valued goals or regulations. We will elaborate on this in the next section. A shift from extrinsic motivation to intrinsic motivations, which are autonomous and more self-determined is called

integration. Integration, 'refers to internalization in which the person identifies with the value of an activity and accepts full responsibility for doing it' (Deci, Eghrari, Patrick, & Leone, 1994, p. 121). We like to emphasize that internalization should be better stimulated in learning environments, as intrinsic motivated learning makes for better students.

According to self-determination theory, the internalization only occurs when specific needs are satisfied, which will be central to our theory of how to design games that motivate to learn. These needs are feelings of *competence*, *autonomy*, and *relatedness* (C.A.R) (Ryan & Deci, 2000). Regulations that satisfy these basic needs can be better related to educational settings than the basic needs described earlier. According to Deci (Deci et al., 1994), if needs for competence, autonomy, and relatedness are all satisfied, a person may internalize the regulations and become intrinsically motivated.

IDENTIFIED REGULATIONS

Identified regulations take 'the best of both worlds', as they can be positioned between external regulations and intrinsic regulations. Identified regulations are consciously valued rules, procedures, and goals. They present students with goals and rules that are external but at the same time intrinsically valuable. To consciously value a regulation, students *identify*, as in understanding, the learning regulations first. Then, students can *identify with* the learning regulation as something personally important. In other words, students do not have to enjoy the activity. Instead it is important that students value the learning regulations as personally relevant (Keller, 1999; Gunter, Kenny, & Vick, 2006).

Opportunity to Identify with the Learning Regulations

To get students to value regulations as personally relevant, the concept of regulatory fit can help. According to Bianco et.al. (2003) and Higgins (2000), if the learning regulations and game regulations fit the theory that students' hold implicitly about the particular subject of instruction, students are more motivated to learn. If students think that something is important, teachers may be less inclined to change students' mind, but if students think that a subject is dull, teachers might feel obliged to enliven a tedious learning exercise. Teachers may try to turn something boring into something fun. Enlivening a boring exercise makes it more difficult for students to integrate regulations to the self and it therefore may result in a decline of motivation. In a way, the task instruction should make sense to the student. If regulations make sense to students, they may think about the learning regulation as something personal relevant. In turn, they may become motivated to learn more.

The Ability to Identify Learning Regulations

Students can only identify with regulations if they can perceive these regulations first. One way of achieving this is to explicitly communicate the learning regulations, which is not always easy to do. In *DreamBox*, for example, the learning regu-

lations are easily recognized. As such, *DreamBox* should be considered a well-designed serious game. The regulations however are based on punishments and rewards and do not make equating less tedious or boring. Reviewing *DreamBox*, a journalist explains: 'kids who already believe they dislike math, or aren't good at it, won't be fooled by the playful nature of the site. It's very clearly math' (Matte, 2009).

While *DreamBox* explicitly communicates the math assignments, it uses fairies, pirates and dinosaurs to embellish the learning content. Moreover, players are rewarded with extra mini-games that do not relate to the learning content. The mini-games amplify the failing attempt to engage players in the game itself. Clearly, the problem is that the game regulations do not relate to the learning regulations. For example, students are first asked to find some missing dinosaur's eggs. By finishing equation exercises, they are awarded with additional eggs.

A mismatch between learning and game regulations is common in educational games and is described by Michael Bas as *The Closed Door Syndrome*. Bas, CEO of a major Dutch serious game development studio, describes an educational game 'suffering from the syndrome' as follows. Players are invited to visit an imaginary world, while exploring the environment, players stumble onto a closed door, when the door is clicked, the player must solve an equation to open it. The game world is only designed to navigate between problems, instead of relating to the learning content. While the game is based on finding hidden objects (visual recognition), the learning content is about equating[4]. The Closed Door Syndrome describes a mismatch in game regulations and learning regulations.

Matching Basic (Cognitive) Activities

To avoid the Closed Door Syndrome, designers can match the basic activities of the learning regulations to the gameplay. It is difficult, however, to accomplish this match without embellishing the learning exercise with game elements only. That is why we present a four-layered model. The model is inspired by the MDA model (Hunicke, LeBlanc, & Zubek, 2004) distinguishing *mechanics*, *dynamics* and *aesthetics*.

In our model, the mechanics are the rules and goals of the game, much like the core mechanics of Salen & Zimmerman (2003). The dynamics are the actual activities emerging from the rules and goals, i.e. emergent play. The aesthetics are the 'surface-level elements of the game, including thematic and narrative elements as well as the player's emotional responses' (Hullet, Kurniawan, & Wardrip-Fruin, 2009, p. 2). We added *core concepts* to this interpretation of the MDA model.

A core concept is not a manual, a blueprint, a narrative or a genre, instead it is the most basic activity needed for gameplay. The core concept is what all the mechanics, dynamics, and aesthetics are about. All the game rules and all the learning regulations relate to the core concept. The core concept answers the question: what the learning is really about? Designers may abstract the mechanics, dynamics, and aesthetics to the basic activity of the gameplay. After the abstraction of the learning activity, designers can either design new regulations, or seek out games with a similar core concept. This will make it easier to translate educational contexts to a game.

For example, the core concept of *Super Mario Bros.* (Nintendo EAD, 1985) is not about rescuing the Princess. The narrative is only part of the aesthetics. The game is not about throwing fireballs, collecting every coin, or finding the warp-zone (dynamics). Nor is the game about time constraints or receiving scoring-points (mechanics). Players overcome obstacles by skillfully manipulating the forces of an artificial gravity, players learn how to jump across a small fissure and how to accelerate Mario's pace to overcome greater ravines. The mechanics, dynamics, and aesthetics of the game all relate to playing with gravity[5]. This is the most

basic activity of the game, all other regulations favor this core concept.

In *Super Mario Bros.* players learn to play with artificial gravitational forces. Edugames like *Mario is Missing!* and *Mario's Time Machine* (The Software Toolworks, Inc., 1992, 1993) did not change the core concept of *Super Mario Bros.* but changed the aesthetics and some mechanics to relate to geography and history lessons. As a consequence, there is a mismatch between the game's core concept and the educational context.

Matching the core concepts of the educational instruction and a game can enhance the instructive value of a game, because players can actually play with the instructional content. If accomplished, the mechanics, dynamics and aesthetics (in short: regulations) can be changed to help students identify them as personally valuable.

Matching the basic cognitive activities (e.g. the core concepts) is only the first step in the development cycle of a serious game. The second step is to create identified regulations (mechanics, dynamics and aesthetics) that satisfy needs for competence, autonomy and relatedness. How this can be accomplished will be discussed in the next section.

SATISFYING COMPETENCE, AUTONOMY AND RELATEDNESS

We discussed how players could identify with learning regulations if game designers create a regulatory fit, and by choosing a core concept that is identical to both the learning regulation and the gameplay. The next step is to create regulations that help players to internalize the regulations. Regulations that engage players satisfy needs for *competence*, *autonomy*, and *relatedness*.

Competence: Scaffolding

There are many ways to satisfy needs for competence. Feelings of competence typically address the perceived ability of (possible) successful engagement, or 'the beliefs in one's capabilities to organize and execute the courses of action required to manage prospective situations' (Bandura, 1997, p. 4).

When students play a game, they negotiate with the game's rules, goals and activities. These regulations can be designed to satisfy students' need for competence. For example, if a student wishes to outshine in a specific knowledge domain, the game's regulations can be structured to enable students to construct the knowledge and be aware of his/her knowledge growth.

The structuring of the learning difficulty and the feedback style are two important ways to satisfy students' need of competence. The structure of knowledge can be characterized as a learning curve, in which knowledge builds forth on former knowledge. Vygotsky (1978) argues that all students have their personal knowledge level, or zone of development. According to Vygotsky students learn best when new knowledge is presented a little outside the boundaries of their knowledge zone.

Wood, Bruner and Ross (1976 in Verenikina, 2003) elaborated on the zone of proximal development by describing a method for knowledge construction called *scaffolding*. Within a scaffolded curriculum the difficulty of the learning content is raised step-by-step. By breaking the content into manageable pieces that are only a little above students' cognitive level (Verenikina, 2003), students may actually construct knowledge every time they negotiate with the content.

The scaffolding principle can be described with [i + 1], in which i stands for the current knowledge zone, and 1 represents the manageable piece of knowledge that is only a little above students' cognitive level. By scaffolding the learning process, students' actual competence might grow, satisfying the need for competence. Learning can therefore be seen as a process of progression.

Progression in games often follows a scaffolded growth of difficulty as well. Shigeru Miyamoto is credited for many well scaffolded games. One

of them is *Super Mario Bros*. The first level of *Super Mario Bros.* illustrates how scaffolding can be subtly integrated into gameplay.

In Figure 2 a typical *Super Mario Bros.* scenario is portrayed that illustrates the process of scaffolding play. The player needs to overcome a small cleft of two slightly different pyramids constructed by two facing triangles. At pyramid 1 (the left pyramid), the player will probably drop Mario in the space between the opposing triangles. Falling in the cleft has no huge consequences; it only slows the pace of the game. At the second pyramid falling into the cleft results in immediate death. At the first pyramid, the player develops a skill to jump across small and save spaces (marked with [i]). At the second pyramid the stakes are higher, so the skill will be mastered [i + 1]. These skill developments are highlighted in figure 3 with [i], indicating new skills, and with [i + 1], indicating skill development. *Super Mario Bros.* is not a game of balancing challenges, but it is a game of subtle progression.

Super Mario Bros. offers progression in skill development and competence. The player can only progress if the skill is mastered. This means that the skill is educated by the game. By subtle scaffolding, games can satisfy the need for competence. The scaffolding principle [i + 1] raises the actual competence in negotiating with the game procedures.

However, the abilities trained in games or other media are seldom transferred to other activities or domains (Clark, 2001). The reason for the lack of knowledge transfer may be caused by players' ignorance of knowledge construction during play. The construction of specific abilities may go unnoticed. For example, players of *Medal of Honor: Heroes 2* (EA Canada, 2007) may unconsciously pick up military strategies of World War II, while players of MMORPGS may enhance their leadership capabilities as guild leaders (Reeves & Malone, 2007; DeMarco, Lesser, & O'Driscoll, 2007). Some serious game developers call this accidental learning. Johnson (2005) depicts ac-

Figure 2. Super Mario Bros., an example of scaffolding

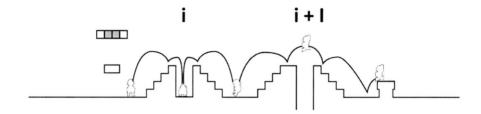

Figure 3. Several learning points in level 1-1 of Super Mario Bros

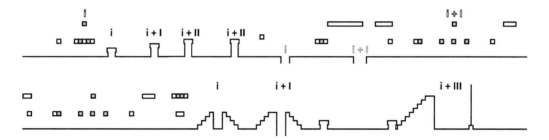

cidental learning in what he calls the *Sleeping Curve*. The learning curve 'sleeps', because gamers are not aware of constructing knowledge during gameplay.

Competence: Progressive Feedback

One way to make players aware of their educational progress is by giving them feedback. One common feedback style is marking. Marks praise the learners' level of competence. These external regulations can 'provide useful information about competence and mastery' (Lepper et al., 2005, p. 191). Still, some students fail to understand how marks communicate progression, or students simply do not care for marks. Within Dutch education, marking is a declining practice. Instead, *profile matrixes*[6] are emerging. Profile matrixes communicate students' ability more specifically than an abstract mark does.

Research on instructive feedback suggests that teachers give positive and constructive feedback, and focus on the learning activity, instead of on the students' self. For example, exclaiming 'the

summarizing is done inaccurately,' is perceived as a correct way to give feedback. Proclaiming that '*you* cannot summarize' is incorrect.

The feedback can communicate progress and it could outline prospective progression. This means that *progressive feedback* has a reflecting and activating role. It describes both 'the learned' and the 'to be learned'. This way the reward of successfully accomplishing a learning goal is not finite, but opens the gate to new learning experiences.

Engaging players with relevant progressive feedback has been a major achievement of the game industry since its early days. Gamers are rewarded with new and more challenging problems after completing an initial level. When players successfully finish the first game world of *Super Mario Bros.*, Mario stumbles upon a sack containing a Mushroom Kingdom's citizen exclaiming: 'Thank you Mario! But our princess is in another castle!' E.g. you have done a great job, now you can learn something more in the next level. Continuous progression is very common in games, and progressive feedback is very important in education. Both motivate the subject for a prolonged experience instead of a finite goal[7].

Autonomy: The Ability and Opportunity to make Significant Decisions

Needs for autonomy can be satisfied by gameplay as well. Autonomy is the *ability*, and the *opportunity* to make decisions that are of significance to the gameplay and the person's self. The ability to make significant decisions equals the actual competence to understand the regulations and the possible results of a decision.

The opportunity to make significant decisions is comparable to freedom of choice. However, presenting an individual with several alternatives does not satisfy the need for autonomy. A choice between life and death is not an autonomous option, as a healthy individual will seldom choose death. Autonomous persons perceive a particular freedom of choice, as well as the feeling that their own choices/actions have significant impact.

To present individuals with significant alternatives, the individuality of a person should be taken into account. The individuality of students is prominent in the manner students approach learning objectives. Researchers like Kolb (A. B. Kayes, D. C. Kayes, & Kolb, 2005; Kolb, Boyatzis, & Mainemelis, 2001), Silver, Strong and Perini (2000), Felder and Spurlin (2005), describe various learning styles in accordance to students' personality. These learning styles are considered tools to 'help instructors achieve balanced course instructions and to help students understand their learning strengths and areas for improvement' (Felder & Spurlin, 2005, p. 111). Knowledge of learning styles and the ability to learn, in accordance with a specific learning style, might raise the feeling of autonomous actions.

Empirical research has seldom found a significant learning gain, retention rate or motivation change, by *imposing* learning styles on students after signifying a students' learning style (Cof-

field, Moseley, Hall, & Ecclestone, 2004). In contrast to other researchers, Katz (in Coffield et al.) does not impose the learning styles on students but presents students with several exercises that were designed with Kolb's learning styles in mind. Katz argues that the 'better match between students' individual characteristics and instructional components, the more effective or efficient the learning program was [in relation to higher-order cognitive outcomes]' (Coffield et al., 2004, p. 68). Silver, Strong & Perini (2000) argue for a similar approach to personalize the learning experience. It is arguable that needs for autonomy can be satisfied, when students are given the opportunity to educate themselves in several ways.

Incorporating various playing styles in one game can enhance players' autonomy. The research done on playing styles (Canossa, 2005, 2007, 2008; Canossa & Drachen, 2009; Bartle, 1996; Deen, 2007) imply the importance of players' autonomy and present how one game can offer more than one playing style. Canossa describes how specific game environments and certain game features can offer players personal styles of play. For example, a gamer of the *Hitman*-series (IO Interactive, 2007) may play in an area with many hiding spots and open areas. The Hitman-player is able to equip the game-character with a machine gun and a dimmed sniper rifle. In this setting, players can play as a stealthy murderer or through brute power. Instead of designing four different exercises, one game can offer various learning styles and even give players the opportunity to blend styles into a personal one.

The works of Canossa (2005, 2007, 2008) and Bartle (1996) are deduced from specific game genres and might not directly be applicable to all games. However, both researchers indicate the importance of a personal play experience. An understanding of playing styles and learning styles may help game designers to create an environment in which subjects can choose their personal style.

Autonomy: Playing Styles

Playing styles and learning styles are very similar to one another (Deen, 2007). Deen found a correspondence between playing styles and learning styles. By bringing together developmental psychology and game theory, Deen described a *theoretical*-style, *pragmatic*-style, *interpersonal*-style and *self-expressive*-style of development.

People with a theoretical style of development tend to be a little apprehensive. They first analyze the data on the screen and supported media, after which they compile the data into a conceptual model. Theoretical players enjoy fast amounts of data streams to crunch through and elaborate background information. In *Pokémon Red / Blue* (Game Freak, 1996), theoretical players might enjoy the Pokédex (an in-game encyclopedia of every monster in the game world), a fast number of attacks and attributes in the game, and online databases like serebii.net. This is in contrast to pragmatic players, who learn and play by 'bricolage' or a trial-and-error strategy. Players enjoy a hands-on experience and do not mind making mistakes. These are the players who enjoy the repetitive gameplay of *Pokémon*.

Other people learn / play by cribbing or discussing their problems with fellow gamers. They enjoy the multiplayer possibilities of *Pokémon* and they tend to grow quite attached to their virtual pet. These interpersonal players can be commonly found on forums or game-related websites. Another style of interpersonal play is exhibited by self-expressive players. This is the most creative style. Self-expressive players often try to work their way around the formal game rules by cheating, hacking, griefing, or just by playing. They enjoy setting their own goals and agenda, and they like to have the possibility to communicate their distinctiveness to others. Instead of playing with others, you will find self-expressive gamers playing for / against others. They are the comedians, the artists, of play. In *Pokémon* they enjoy naming their Pokémon, creating absurd Pokémon-teams and finding loopholes or glitches[8] in the game.

Pokémon incorporates all four playing/learning styles. In so, *Pokémon* offers gamers a pallet of styles to color their play sessions and satisfy needs of autonomy. This may account for the huge and diverse fan base of the small creatures, and what is more, for some serious cognitive activities. Players memorize 150 to 493 Pokémon names, discover new ways to communicate, and learn new ways to solve and approach a problem.

Like Katz's imbedding of various learning styles in educational practice, the incorporation of various playing styles in a game might enhance the higher cognitive learning outcomes of a game. These higher cognitive learning outcomes are amongst others, problem solving (Gee, 2003) and approaching activities from a specific epistemology (Shaffer, 2008). In the case study we will explain how various playing styles are made possible in *CheckOut!*, and how this satisfies the need of autonomy.

Relatedness: The Need to Relate to Significant Others

So far, we discussed how needs for competence and autonomy may be satisfied by game regulations. The last need presented by self-determination theory is relatedness. This may come as no surprise, as feelings of competence and autonomy can only exist in relation to an 'other'. People only feel competent when the can relate their ability to the ability of others. The needs of competence and autonomy can thus only be satisfied in a social environment. This social environment can satisfy needs for relatedness.

Needs of relatedness are the perceptions of social support for/against persons' performances of the behavior. Relatedness can be divided in the belief that others think the behavior should be performed, and the motivation to comply with others. Relatedness does not suggest a relation with everyone but describes an attachment with people of certain significance to the subject. These *significant others* contextualize feelings of autonomy and competence.

Educators, aligned with the social constructivist movement, state that learning is first and foremost a social negotiation (Duffy & Tobias, 2009). By definition, gaming is a social act as well. According to Copier (2005, 2007), players negotiate with other players and game developers in order to formulate (new) game rules and forms of play. These social negotiations are also eminent during non-play. Players negotiate with others in the modding community (Sihvonen, 2009), through fan-culture (Jenkins, 2008), in the cheater scene (Consalvo, 2009), on casual game portals, and in social networks (Deen & Korsman, 2010).

Social negotiations are not always related to the learning content or game rules. Players of *Ultima Online* (Origin Systems, 1997) for example, did not use spare time (time not spend on game related exercises) for planning a game-strategy. Instead, players exchanged real life recipes and talked about family, friends and lovers. These social negotiations enhance the feelings of relatedness.

The mere possibility of social negotiations may suffice in the need for relatedness as well. In the online game *FarmVille* (Zynga, 2009) players cannot actually play together simultaneously. Instead, players can visit and post messages on friends' farms. Players can give and receive *FarmVille*-gifts, and players can fertilize friends' crops in exchange for experience points and virtual currency. Although players are not actually playing together in the same space at the same time, there is still a strong feeling of relatedness. People do not have to be in the same (virtual) space to satisfy a need for relatedness.

In many online games, social bonding or feelings of relatedness are facilitated by a certain social interdependence (Ventrice, 2009). This interdependence is obvious in MMORPGs[9] like *World of Warcraft* (Blizzard Entertainment, 2004). Players need the help of other players, to fully explore all facets of these games. While most MMORPGs are designed to create *new* relationships, other online games like *FarmVille* and *MafiaWars* (Zynga, 2008) strengthen *existing* relationships. Games, like *FarmVille* and *MafiaWars*, are played within online social networks like *Facebook* or *MySpace* and use existing connections, outside the game context, to strengthen feelings of relatedness. To expand a farm field in *FarmVille*, players either need to pay real money or invite friends to become their respective 'neighbors'. A player needs to invite at least eight friends to unlock the first farm expansion. In *MafiaWars* 'friends' become assets to strengthen an attack on another player. Players rely on their connections to win a battle. Social interdependence is of uttermost importance to play the game successfully, and in turn may satisfy the need for relatedness.

CASE STUDY: IDENTIFIED REGULATIONS MAY CHANGE MOTIVATION

The implementation of identified regulations during a game design process will be discussed by a case study of a second language learning game called *CheckOut!*. The game is developed by Ranj Serious Games in the Netherlands and targets students'[10] uncertainty about their ability to speak English. This uncertainty results in the avoidance of English. The game encourages students to (dare to) communicate. The didactic approach to second language learning was derived from the works of Sciarone (1984, 2004; Sciarone & Meijer, 1993). According to Sciarone, a language is best learned by active use and immersion in texts that fit students' zone of development.

The zone of development of *CheckOut!*'s texts are based on level A1 of the Common European Framework of Reference (CEFR) for language learning, teaching and assessment (Baten et al., 2008; Europe, 2004; Hest, Jong, & Stoks, 2001).

A1 students possess the most rudimentary English skills, such as reading and writing simple sentences. The game's content and context is based on level A2 of CEFR. According to level A2, students can relate casual (often used) expressions with issues of immanent importance, like family, shopping, personal information, work and geographical data. An A2 student can understand and explain people's relationships to each other, and students are able to give and understand directions.

Ranj Serious Games designed a multiplayer variant of the classic point-and-click adventures. The core concept of the game is linking knowledge within a conditional structure. Like all point-and-click adventures, a particular condition is only accessible if another condition is. Players are asked to remember what a character needs, in order to bring the person the proper items and need to textually communicate in English to establish this. By walking around in the game world, players actively connect characters to items and visa versa.

In the game, clues to the conditional structure are hidden in the texts. Students are presented with a fragmented storyline that is scattered around a virtual environment. Together with their classmates they are invited to make a coherent structure of these small bits of information, by linking new and old knowledge into a whole.

The game designers of *CheckOut!* successfully created a match between the core concept of an existing game genre, point-and-click adventures, and the core concept of writing an essay / understanding spoken English. The core concept of the game could best be described as 'linking knowledge'. Players are not only playing a point-and-click adventure, but the game regulations are all about linking new and old knowledge into a whole; therefore students are actually constructing knowledge while playing the game. Despite this knowledge construction, players may not be aware of their cognitive development, which may hinder the satisfaction of needs for competence.

Effectively Satisfy Needs for Autonomy and Relatedness

Still, the regulations designed from the core concept may satisfy needs for relatedness. Two regulations foster interdependence among players: a scarcity of items, and a complex game world. *CheckOut!* is played online, in cooperation with classmates. Four players can play simultaneously and are invited textually coordinate the distribution of items. Some items can be acquired only once.

For example, if a player buys a dress for the game character Beatrice, a second player is unable to buy the dress. In turn, players coordinate the scarcity of items. The game world is mazelike, so players get lost easily. When lost, players do not hesitate to ask their classmates for directions via the chat-channel. The chat-channel scrambles Dutch words, so students are encouraged to communicate in English. The channel is buzzing with English chats. The design of scarcity, and maze-like environments fosters a social interdependence; students, however, are still able to make individual decisions.

Autonomy is satisfied by the active role of players as well. Without their participation nothing happens. Students actively link various texts into a coherent story to accomplish specific objectives. In this way, the game encourages active negotiations with language construction instead of passive assimilation.

The game regulations made sense to students. This was especially true for students of the Tourism Faculty. In the game players where stranded on a foreign party island. This setting may fit the implicit theory students have about working abroad in the tourist sector. Thus, there is a regulatory fit between players' implicit theory and the instruction.

The game regulations offer multiple playing styles. By doing so, students can make a (autonomous) choice in the way they play the game. Some players are very *pragmatic* in their learning/playing style. They hit every clickable attribute in the game, and if one conversation circle ends in failure, they try again. Not all players have a trial-and-error style of playing. Some like to consider various options first, create a theoretical or conceptual model of the situation, and then test their hypothesis. The game presents these players with a mission log. Thanks to the mission log, players can deduce an optimal strategy by carefully reading the log.

A third group of players like to learn from others, by following others' lead or by reading walkthroughs on the internet. In *CheckOut!* players can help each other by using the chat channel. We often observed two players following each other through the game world. Although this is not the fastest strategy, it certainly was the most social playing style.

Lastly, some players try to work their way around the formal game rules. These *self-expressive* players are often demonized as cheaters (Consalvo, 2009), killers (Bartle, 1996; Lindley, 2005), or griefers. Other scholars tend to describe self-expressive media users in a more positive way as hackers (Scheäfer, 2008) or modders[11] (Sihvonen, 2009). *CheckOut!* does not promote self-expressive play. Although the language filter in *CheckOut!* is easily bypassed by using slang, leet[12], erroneous Dutch spelling, or another second language, the rigid and formal structure of other game regulations do not offer much creativity.

Meagerly Addressing Needs for Competence

The beta version of *CheckOut!* 'scores' high on relatedness and autonomy satisfaction, it does however, seem to fail to satisfy needs for competence. The beta version of *CheckOut!* lacks a well scaffolded game regulation and progressive feedback. Students find themselves struggling with unfamiliar[13] gameplay, without any introduction to the concept of point-and-click adventures. Even more, the game presents the player with a

meager amount of feedback on game progression and language development.

Still students reported to learn appropriate greetings. *CheckOut!*-players are forced to greet a game character (in short: NPC[14]) before a conversation cycle can start. After clicking an NPC a pop-up asks the player to enter a greeting. If the greeting is mistyped, the NPC will complain and ask the player to spell it properly. Players are forced to type 'excuse me officer' before asking the game's police officer for directions. The greeting sequence resulted into discussions around the NPC Beatrice. Beatrice has the looks of a hippopotamus and is to be greeted with 'excuse me gorgeous'. Obviously, this sparks a lot of comments as being an inappropriate greeting for ugly Beatrice.

This greeting sequence felt relevant to students as it caricatures a socio-cultural rule. It makes sense to use appropriate greetings to get help. If mistyped, the students were told how to properly address the NPC. In this way, the player was presented with feedback that related to both the learning and gaming at the same time. While *CheckOut!* meagerly addresses the need for competence, the game excels in satisfying needs for autonomy and relatedness.

Validation

In 2008 one of the authors started to gather empirical data to test the hypothesis that playing *CheckOut!* changes students motivations towards traditional second language learning for the better. The experimental research was both quantitatively, and qualitatively tested. A pre-test and post-test was conducted for both a control group (N=33), and an experiment group (N=44) of MBO-students[x] from ROC-West Brabant. Qualitative material was assembled through in-class observations, screen capturing and interviews with students and teachers.

The Self-Determination Questionnaire of Ryan & Connel (1989a, 1989b) was translated to Dutch and rewritten to focus on second language learning. The experimental group played (for approximately 1.5 hours) the beta-version of *CheckOut!*, while the control group followed the standard curriculum program.

A significant (p=.03) motivational change was reported for both the control, and experimental groups. While the control group reported an increase of externally regulated experiences, the experimental group reported that the same feeling decreased. The decline in external regulated experiences concerned the self-regulation towards traditional second language learning programs. Thus, students felt less forced to learn English by rewards or punishments after they played the game.

The motivational change may be related to a (partly) successful regulatory fit design, and successfully satisfying needs for autonomy and relatedness. We wonder if a thorough scaffolded process, and a larger amount of progressive feedback would have a greater motivational change.

The questionnaire's results remained inconclusive for motivational regulations such as identified regulations, and intrinsic regulations[15]. The interviews with students, teachers, and the observations of play sessions showed high commitment to game goals and extensive use of English in the chat channel. Two observations illustrate this.

During one play session, the fire alarm was malfunctioning, and remained sounding. Still, students played the game for two hours while the claxon was deafening everyone. Students did not seem to care about the klaxon while playing the game. On another occasion, a teacher expressed to be surprised about his students' ability to write complete English sentences in the chat-channel. Normally his group was not keen on writing, while in the game, communicating in a foreign language seemed to come naturally. While not 'bulletproof', both teachers and students expressed the value of the language filter. It seemed appropriate to chat in English when immersed in a foreign environment during an English course.

Still, students had difficulties in identifying the learning regulation of the game. The same was true for teachers who played the game[16]. While they expressed an understanding of the learning value of reading English texts, the procedural (meta) knowledge of linking knowledge remained unnoticed and difficult to identify. The lack of progressive feedback on learning regulations and a non-thorough scaffolded learning process might account for this problem.

DISCUSSION: METHODS FOR SERIOUS GAME DESIGN

Based on the previous sections we propose six principles for serious game design in order to heighten players' motivation towards learning a specific subject or skill, not only during play, but also when the game is over.

1. Create a regulatory fit between the implicit theory of students about the educational instruction.
2. Design from a core concept that is identical for both the educational instruction and the game.
3. Explicitly communicate the learning regulations to player.

4. Use progressive feedback (satisfy needs for competence).
5. Implement various playing styles into one game (satisfy needs for autonomy).
6. Create a social interdependence (satisfy needs for relatedness)

Creating a Regulatory Fit

To identify with the learning content, the game designer could design a regulatory fit. Serious games are often designed to make tedious exercises more fun. Instead of making it more fun, the games should make the learning more engaging. This is a significant difference, as an engaging experience is not a 'fun experience' by definition. An engaging experience can be unpleasant, or of importance as well. Students can become motivated when the task instruction fits the implicit theory students have about the task instruction. If students think a subject is of importance to their further development and the instruction signifies this importance, students may become engaged.

E-learning applications like *NikoLand* (Intelliga Publishing, 2008) and *DreamBox* try to 'fun-up' the learning experience but could instead 'importance-up' the learning regulations. Knowledge construction can become a useful tool in the game instead of a mere necessity. The greeting sequence in *CheckOut!* illustrates this well. In 'real life' it is important to use a proper greeting when approaching a particular person. If you do not start a conversation in the right manner, some people might feel offended or even unwilling to talk. The game caricatures this social rule by making it impossible to speak to a game character using improper greetings. There is no 'fun' in greeting characters (especially not in greeting ugly Beatrice). Still, students reported that they found the greeting sequence the most educational worthwhile part of the game.

More over, the setting of a holiday island worked very well for students of the Tourism Faculty. During play sessions at beautician or hair-dressing school, students exclaimed that they would have found the game more interesting and educational if the setting was not a party island, but a saloon or wellness centre instead.

Match Core Concepts of Game and Knowledge Construction

What is the game or instruction really about? That is the question a designer can ask when matching the core concepts of a game with the core concept of an instructional practice. Matching the most basic cognitive activities may be the most difficult and abstract part of designing a serious game. An in-depth explanation about this process is therefore out of scope for this chapter. Still, an examples may illustrate the process.

In *CheckOut!*, the core concept 'linking knowledge' is both applicable to writing an essay and playing a point-and-click adventure. Players actively link various knowledge sources into a coherent story. This cognitive skill is used when writing an essay as well. Students need to search in libraries and other knowledge sources, to bring together all this fragmented information into a structured writing. The matching of core concepts makes players actually perform the same cognitive activity in the game as in a writing class.

Explicitly Communicate the Learning Regulations

The visuals of feedback may help students to understand how the knowledge developed during game-play may help them outside the game. For example, to encourage players to read more books by playing a game, the player probably reads various texts during the play session. The designer could connect the difficulty of the game-texts to the difficulty of actual books. A novice player will earn a 'Jip & Janneke[17] - children's book' trophy, while an advanced player receives a Shakespearean award. The designer communicates that a player is competent enough to read an adult book. This way, the designer relates game knowledge to 'out of game abilities'.

Progressive Feedback

Progressive feedback is reflective and activating. Players can be made aware that they *have learned* something, and that they *will learn* more. This can be designed with cumulative scoring systems (concerning learning and gaming progress) and by implementing high-score lists. Both will give players insight in the average scorings, the high-end achievements and their own progress. Another way to communicate further development is the design of various difficulty settings or using the 'advent calendar' method. The advent calendar method may be most discernable by its implementation in *Super Mario Bros. 3* (Nintendo R&D4, 1988). Every game level is visible on the world-map. After succeeding at one level the next level becomes available to the player. Like an advent calendar, players can already perceive the coming events. This way, the game explains what is accomplished, and what should be accomplished next.

Implementing Various Play Styles in One Game

Several learning styles can be implemented in one game as well. Silver, Strong and Perini (2000) describe four learning styles that can shortly be described as: a *pragmatic* (trial and error), a *theoretical* (conceptualizing – optimal strategy), an *interpersonal* (co-op - competitive), and *a self-expressive* (creative – cheater - generator) learning style. While Silver, Strong & Perini argue for freedom in four different assignments by offering all learning styles, a game can offer all four styles in one game, giving players the opportunity to develop blended learning styles.

Most games already offer several learning styles. Games rely for a great extent on trial and error play by offering several *lives* or *tries*[18] to beat a game level. Tries invite players to try the game again if they fail in their first attempt. Real-Time-Strategy games like *StarCraft* (Blizzard Entertainment, 1998) and *Command & Conquer* (Westwood Studios, 1995) offer players extensive data to crunch through and help them to conceptualize a model of optimal strategy. By adding multiplayer capabilities to the game, players can co-operate or fight each other on a social level. Lastly, the

Figure 5. Super Mario Bros.3 the advent calendar method

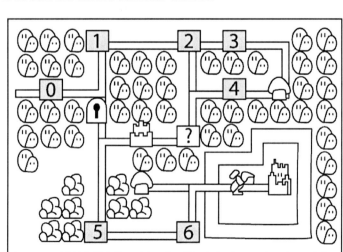

adding of cheat codes, level editors and possibilities to construct teams, bases or characters adds to the creative use of the regulations. In other words, designers can personalize the game experience[19], which may enhance players' motivation to play.

Relatedness

Relatedness is often accomplished by designing social interdependence. As described earlier, interdependence is created for *World of Warcraft* and *FarmVille* in various ways. Interdependence emerges from item scarcity, the use of friends' relations as commodity/asset/resource, the creation of interdependence among game characters (rock-paper-scissors formations in classes), combative scenarios, and a shared goal/enemy. Some games offer players an asynchronous way to battle their friends called a *ghost-run/ghosting*. In *Mirror's Edge Pure Time Trial Pack* (EA Digital Illusions CE, 2009), players can play a time trial. Their fastest play performance will be recorded and stored. Players can review their own jumping and running, and battle their own recording. Players hunt a 'ghost' of themselves. In some games players can send their ghost to friends, so they can try to beat it.

Social negotiations are often mediated by chat channels, forums, voice over internet protocol[20], social networks, and real life conferences. Without these tools the social inclusion may be almost impossible to attain.

CONCLUSION

To enhance the learning outcome of serious games, games can get students motivated to learn. To accomplish this, identified regulations can enable students to identify (to comprehend) and to identify with the learning regulation. If students are able (partly) internalize the learning regulations that are embedded in the negotiation with the game, they can become more motivated to learn. To achieve this internalizing, the game regulations can satisfy students' needs of competence, autonomy and relatedness to significant others.

Gaming can stimulate these feelings, but today's educational game developers tend to focus more on embellishments and external regulations, instead of focusing on motivations to learn in general. The creation of a regulatory fit, progressive feedback, and various playing styles may

Figure 6. Mirror's edge pure time trial pack: beating the player's ghost

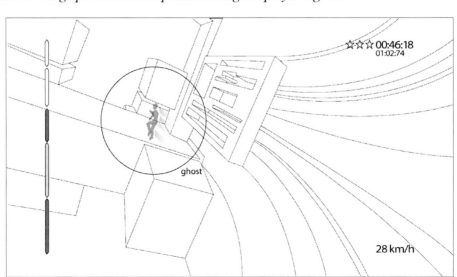

enable students to consciously value the learning regulations as personally important. In turn, this may stimulate the internalization of the external regulations presented by the game.

Thus, by designing identified learning regulations, players may become motivated to learn, not only in the game, but also when the game is over. To motivate student to learn, the game can clarify students what they *can* and that they are *making progress*, not only their ability to play, but also in the construction of new knowledge.

The surplus value of games is found in their ability to construct an environment in which players are invited to personally negotiate with regulations, where players are given immediate feedback on their actions, and where feelings of relatedness can be enhanced by social interdependence. Enliven learning exercises with rewards and praising might not be the way to go: communicating progression and agency within a safe and social environment might.

REFERENCES

Arnold, H. J. (1976). Effects of perfomance feedback and extrinsic reward upon high intrinsic motivation. *Organizational Behavior and Human Performance*, *17*, 274–288. doi:10.1016/0030-5073(76)90067-2

Bandura, A. (1997). *Self-efficacy in changing societies*. Cambridge University Press.

Bartle, R. (1996). Hearts, clubs, diamonds, spades: Players who suit MUDs. *Journal of MUD Research*, *1*(1).

Baten, L., Coutuer, M., Goethals, M., Raes, N., Gysen, S., & Liemberg, E. (2008). *Gemeenschappelijk Europees Referentiekader voor Moderne Vreemde Talen: Leren, Onderwijzen, Beoordelen* (Meijer, D., & Noijons, J., Eds.). Nederlandse Taalunie.

Bianco, A. T., Higgins, E. T., & Klem, A. (2003). How fun/importance fit affects performance: Relating implicit theories to instructions. *Personality and Social Psychology Bulletin*, *29*(9), 1091–1103. doi:10.1177/0146167203253481

Bordewijk, J. (Ed.). (2009). *Bachelor of ICT, domeinbeschrijving*. Amsterdam: HBO-I stichting.

Canada, E. A. (2007). *Medal of Honor: Heroes 2*. Medal of Honor. Electronic Arts.

Canossa, A. (2005). *Designing levels for enhanced player experience cognitive tools for gameworld designers*. IO Interactive / Denmark's School of Design.

Canossa, A. (2007). *Weaving experiences, values, modes, styles, and personas*. IO Interactive / Denmark's School of Design.

Canossa, A. (2008). *Towards a theory of player: Designing for experience*. IO Interactive / Denmark's School of Design.

Canossa, A. & Drachen, A. (2009). *Play-personas: Behaviours and belief systems in user-centred game design*.

Clark, R. E. (2001). *Learning from media: Arguments, analysis, and evidence*. Information Age Publishing.

Coffield, F., Moseley, D., Hall, E., & Ecclestone, K. (2004). *Learning styles and pedagogy in post-16 learning: A systematic and critical review*. London: Learning and Skills Research Centre. Retrieved from www.LSRC.ac.uk

Consalvo, M. (2009). *Cheating: Gaining advantage in videogames*. The MIT Press.

Copier, M. (2005). Connecting worlds. Fantasy role-playing games, ritual acts and the magic circle. *Proceedings DiGRA 2005 Conference: Changing Views - Worlds in Play*, (pp. 16-20). Retrieved from http://citeseerx.ist.psu.edu/viewdoc/summary?doi=10.1.1.97.2637

Copier, M. (2007). *Beyond the magic circle: A network perspective on role-play in online games.* Utrecht University.

Deci, E. L., Eghrari, H., Patrick, B. C., & Leone, D. R. (1994). Facilitating internalization: The self-determination theory perspective. *Journal of Personality, 61*(1).

Deen, M. (2007). *Versnelde Kennisontwikkeling in Games.* Utrecht University.

Deen, M. (2009). *Onderzoeksrapport validatie CheckOut!*Ranj Serious Games & ROC West-Brabant.

Deen, M., & Korsman, N. (2010). *Casual games. Contact! Children & New Media.* Bohn Stafleu van Loghum.

DeMarco, M., Lesser, E., & O'Driscoll, T. (2007). *Leadership in a distributed world.* IBM Corporation.

Duffy, T. M., & Tobias, S. (2009). *Constructivist instruction* (1st ed.). Routledge.

EA Digital Illusions CE. (2009). *Mirror's Edge Pure Time Trial Pack.* Electronic Arts.

Entertainment, B. (1998). *StarCraft.* Blizzard Entertainment.

Entertainment, B. (2004). *World of Warcraft.* Blizzard Entertainment.

Europe, C. O. (2004). *Common European framework of reference for languages: Learning, teaching, assessment (CEFR).* University Press.

Felder, R. M., & Spurlin, J. (2005). Applications, reliability and validity of the index of learning styles. *International Journal of Engineering Education, 21*(1), 103–112.

Freak, G. (1996). *Pokémon Red & Blue.* Nintendo.

Games, R. S., & West-Drabant, R. O. C. (2010). *Check Out!*Game Factory Online.

Telltale Games. (2006). *Sam & Max Save the World.* Sam & Max. JoWooD Productions.

Games, T. (2009). *Tales of Monkey Island.* Telltale Games.

Gee, J. P. (2003). *What video games have to teach us about learning and literacy* (1st ed.). Palgrave Macmillan.

Gunter, G., Kenny, R., & Vick, E. (2006). A case for a formal design paradigm for serious games. *The Journal of the International Digital Media and Arts Association, 3*(1), 93–105.

Habgood, M. P. J. (2005). Zombie Division: Intrinsic integration in digital learning games. *Cognitive Science Research Paper-University of Sussex CSRP, 576,* 45.

Habgood, M. P. J. (2007). *The effective integration of digital games and learning content.* Unpublished Dissertation, University of Nottingham, Nottingham, UK.

Habgood, M. P. J., Ainsworth, S. E., & Benford, S. (2005). Intrinsic fantasy: Motivation and affect in educational games made by children. *Simulation & Gaming, 36*(4), 483–498. doi:10.1177/1046878105282276

Hest, E. V., Jong, J. H. D. & Stoks, G. (2001). *Nederlandse taalkwalificaties in Europees verband.* Cito groep & SLO Specialist in Leerprocessen.

Higgins, E. T. (2000). Making a good decision-value from fit. *Journal of Personality and Social Psychology, 62,* 676–687.

Hullet, K., Kurniawan, S., & Wardrip-Fruin, N. (2009). *Better game studies education the Carcassonne way.* In DiGRA 2009. Presented at the Breaking New Ground: Innovation in Games, Play, Practice and Theory. London: Digital Games Research Association.

Hunicke, R., LeBlanc, M., & Zubek, R. (2004). *MDA: A formal approach to game design and game research*. Retrieved from http://www.cs.northwestern.edu/~hunicke/MDA.pdf

Id Software. (1992). *Wolfenstein 3D*. Apogee Software.

Id Software. (1996). *Quake*. GT Interactive.

Intelliga Publishing. (2008). *Nicoland*.

Interactive, I. O. (2007). *Hitman (Series)*. Eidos Interactive.

Jenkins, H. (2008). *Convergence culture: Where old and new media collide* (Revised edition). New York University Press.

Johnson, S. (2005). *Everything bad is good for you: How today's popular culture is actually making us smarter* (1st ed.). Riverhead Hardcover.

Kayes, A. B., Kayes, D. C., & Kolb, D. A. (2005). Experiential learning in teams. *Simulation & Gaming, 36*(3), 330–354. doi:10.1177/1046878105279012

Keller, J. M. (1999). Using the ARCS motivational process in computer-based instruction and distance education. *New Directions for Teaching and Learning, 78*, 39–47.

Knapp, B. (2010). *Ventrilo*. Flagship Industries, Inc. Retrieved from http://www.verntrilo.com

Kolb, D.A., Boyatzis, R.E. & Mainemelis, C. (2001). Experiential learning theory: Previous research and new directions. *Perspectives on Thinking, Learning, and Cognitive Styles*, 227–247.

Dreambox Learning. (2009a). *DreamBox*.

Learning, D. (2009b). *DreamBox Learning partners with Computers for Youth to help young children excel at math*. EarthTimes. Retrieved October 8, 2009, from http://www.earthtimes.org/articles/printpressstory.php?news=971018

Leet. (2010). In *Wikipedia, the free encyclopedia*. Wikipedia. Retrieved from http://en.wikipedia.org/wiki/Leet

Lepper, M. R., Corpus, J. H., & Iyengar, S. S. (2005). Intrinsic and extrinsic motivational orientations in the classroom: Age differences and academic correlates. *Journal of Educational Psychology, 97*(2), 184–196. doi:10.1037/0022-0663.97.2.184

Lindley, C.A. (2005). *Story and narrative structures in computer games*.

Ludwig, R., Kirk, P., Werensteijn, N., & Strempel, P. (2010). *TeamSpeak*. TeamSpeak Systems GmbH. Retrieved from http://www.teamspeak.com

Malone, T. W. (1981). Toward a theory of intrinsically motivating instruction. *Cognitive Science, 5*(4), 333–369. doi:10.1207/s15516709cog0504_2

Maslow, A. H. (1943). A theory of human motivation. *Psychological Review, 50*, 370–396. doi:10.1037/h0054346

Matte, C. (2009). Math Websites for kids-DreamBox learning K-2 math. Retrieved October 8, 2009, from http://familyinternet.about.com/od/websitesforkids/fr/dreamboxlearning_k2_math.htm

Maxis. (2000). The Sims. Electronic Arts.

Nintendo, E. A. D. (1985). *Super Mario Bros.* Super Mario Bros. Nintendo.

Nintendo R&D1. (1983). *Mario Bros.* Nintendo.

Nintendo R&D4. (1988). *Super Mario Bros. 3.* Super Mario Bros. Nintendo.

Nintendo. (1981). *Donkey Kong*. Nintendo.

Reeves, B., & Malone, T. W. (2007). *Leadership in games and at work: Implications for the enterprise of massively multiplayer online role-playing games*. Seriosity. Retrieved from http://www.seriosity.com/downloads/Leadership_In_Games_Seriosity_and_IBM.pdf

Reiss, S. (2004). Multifaceted nature of intrinsic motivation: The theory of 16 basic desires. *Review of General Psychology, 8*(3), 179–193. doi:10.1037/1089-2680.8.3.179

Reiss, S. (2009). *The normal personality: A new way of thinking about people* (1st ed.). Cambridge University Press.

Rigby, C. S., Deci, E. L., Patrick, B. C., & Ryan, R. M. (1992). Beyond the intrinsic-extrinsic dichotomy: Self-determination in motivation and learning. *Motivation and Emotion, 16*(3), 165–185. doi:10.1007/BF00991650

Ryan, R. M., & Connell, J. P. (1989a). Perceived locus of causality and internalization: Examining reasons for acting in two domains. *Journal of Personality and Social Psychology, 57*(5), 749–761. doi:10.1037/0022-3514.57.5.749

Ryan, R. M., & Connell, J. P. (1989b). *Academic Self-Regulation Questionnaire* (SRQ-A). Retrieved from http://www.psych.rochester.edu/SDT/measures/SRQ_academic.php

Ryan, R. M., & Deci, E. L. (2000). Self-determination theory and the facilitation of intrinsic motivation, social development, and well-being. *The American Psychologist, 55*(1), 68–78. doi:10.1037/0003-066X.55.1.68

Salen, K., & Zimmerman, E. (2003). *Rules of play: Game design fundamentals (illustrated edition)*. MIT Press.

Scheäfer, M. (2008). *Bastard culture! User participation and the extension of cultural industries*. Unpublished doctoral dissertation, Utrecht University, Utrecht.

Sciarone, A. G. (1984). *Hoe leer je een taal?: De Delftse methode*. Boom. A.G. Sciarone (Ed.). (2004). *De Delftse methode nader bekeken*. Boom.

Sciarone, A. G., & Meijer, P. (1993). How free should students be? A case from CALL: Computer-Assisted Language Learning. *Computers & Education, 21*(1/2), 95–101. doi:10.1016/0360-1315(93)90052-K

Sega AM7. (1990). *Castle of Illusion Starring Mickey Mouse*. Sega.

Shaffer, D. W. (2008). *How computer games help children learn*. Palgrave Macmillan.

Sihvonen, T. (2009). *Players unleashed! Modding The Sims and the culture of gaming*. University of Turku.

Silver, H. F., Strong, R. W., & Perini, M. J. (2000). *So each may learn: Integrating learning styles and multiple intelligences*. ASCD.

Sonic Team. (1991). *Sonic the Hedgehog*. Sega.

Studios, W. (1995). *Command & Conquer*. Virgin Interactive.

Sutton-Smith, B. (1959). A formal analysis of game meaning. *Western Folklore, 18*(1), 13–24. Retrieved from http://www.jstor.org/stable/1496888. doi:10.2307/1496888

Systems, O. (1997). *Ultima Online*. Electronic Arts.

Technos Japan Corp. (1988). *Double Dragon II: The Revenge*. Technos Japan Corp.

5th Cell. (2007). *Drawn to Life*. THQ.

5th Cell. (2009). *Scribblenauts*. Warner Bros. Interactive Entertainment.

The Software Toolworks, Inc. (1992). *Mario Is Missing!* The Software Toolworks, Inc.

The Software Toolworks, Inc. (1993). *Mario's Time Machine*. The Software Toolworks, Inc.

Ventrice, T. (2009). *Building the foundation of a social future*. Gamasutra - Features. Retrieved December 10, 2009, from http://www.gamasutra.com/view/feature/4210/building_the_foundation_of_a_.php?print=1

Verenikina, I. (2003). *Understanding scaffolding and the ZPD in educational research*. Australian Association of Educational Research Conference, Auckland, New Zealand.

Vygotsky, L. S. (1978). *Mind in society: Development of higher psychological processes (New edition)*. Harvard University Press.

Wikipedia. (2009). *Vocational education*. Retrieved from http://en.wikipedia.org/wiki/Vocational_education

Zynga. (2008). *Mafia Wars*. Zynga.

Zynga. (2009). *FarmVille*. Zynga.

ENDNOTES

[1] Cinematics are small movies that often explain the story behind the game.

[2] Extrinsic motivation does not necessarily diminish intrinsic motivation. They are not antagonistic or dichotomous (Rigby, Deci, Patrick, & Ryan, 1992).

[3] Traditional instruction is learning with schoolbooks, lectures and role-plays.

[4] The Closed Door Syndrome may have originated from the idea that 'fantasy' was considered an intrinsically motivating feature (Malone, 1981). Jacob Habgood (2005, 2007) researched the motivational effect of various fantasy forms and concludes that a (endogenous) fantasy layer, in itself, does not have any motivational value. Instead Habgood argues to embody the learning material 'within the structure of the gaming world and the player's interactions with it, providing an external representation of the learning content that is explored through the core mechanics of the gameplay' (Habgood, Ainsworth, & Benford, 2005, p. 10).

[5] At first glance, the aesthetics of *Super Mario Bros.* do not relate to gravity in any way. A fat and mustached plumber who should jump for coins (miraculously floating in the air) and avoiding mushroom-like foes does not seem related to gravity at all. However, the cultural history of Mario explains many of today's representations of the Super Mario landscape and the emotions it steers.

Mario is introduced in the game scene as a character called *Jumpman*. Featuring in the arcade-classic *Donkey Kong* (Nintendo, 1981), Jumpman must climb a scaffold-like structure and jump over falling and rolling barrels. Climbing a scaffold and avoiding rolling and falling barrels does relate to gravity. Moreover, the name '*Jump*man' signifies gravity as well.

Due to technical (graphical) constrains of the early 80s, Jumpman was designed to be a recognizable character. The Jumpman character was later transported to the multiplayer-platform-game *Mario Bros.* (Nintendo R&D1, 1983). He was given a name, Mario, and a counterpart Luigi. The game was not situated on a skyscraper, but in a sewer. The barrels of *Donkey Kong* where changed into sewer-like animals (turtles, flies and crabs). Still, *Mario Bros.* is essentially the same game as *Donkey Kong*: playing with artificial gravity. When Mario surfaced from the sewers, many references to *Mario Bros.* where kept in place to communicate that the game was still about playing with gravity. Pauline became Princess Toadstool/Peach, Donkey Kong became a supersized-sewer-creature called Bowser and the world was decorated with green-sewer-pipes. This means that Mario's cultural legacy communicates it core concept in a very profound way.

[6] In Bordewijk (2009) the Bachelor of ICT's profile matrixes can be found.

[7] In the 90s, gamers where often rewarded with a new difficulty setting after completing a game. Difficulty settings are given colorful names like 'nightmare' in *Quake* or 'I am Death incarnate!' in *Wolfenstein 3D* (Id Software, 1996, 1992). Gamers can replay games with more and tougher enemies. Another example is the final level of the beat-

um up *Double Dragon II* (Technos Japan Corp., 1988). This level is only available on the hardest difficulty setting. By doing a harder job, players are not rewarded with a trophy, but with a prolonged game experience instead.

8   In *Pokémon Red / Blue* there are many glitches or 'faults' in the game mechanics. For example, the 'duplicate trick' lets players duplicate an item infinitely: http://cheats.ign.com/ob2/068/009/009846.html

9   MMORPG stands for Massively Multiplayer Online Role Playing Game, these games are played in cooperation and competitively on the net.

10   The students followed the Dutch Mbo-education, which is similar to vocational education, 'also called Career and Technical Education (CTE), CTE prepares learners for jobs that are based in manual or practical activities, traditionally non-academic and totally related to a specific trade, occupation or vocation, hence the term, in which the learner participates. It is sometimes referred to as technical education, as the learner directly develops expertise in a particular group of techniques or technology' ("Vocational education," 2009).

11   Modding refers to the act of modifying a game (or other cultural artifact) to perform a function not originally conceived or intended by the designer.

12   'Leet, also known as eleet or leetspeak, is an alternative alphabet for the English language that is used primarily on the Internet. It uses various combinations of ASCII characters to replace Latinate letters. For example, leet spellings of the word leet include 1337 and l33t; eleet may be spelled 31337 or 3l33t' ("Leet," 2010).

13   Point-and-click adventures seemed a dying genre, but are recently revitalized in episodic manner by TellTale Games in *Sam & Max Save the World* (2006) and new episodes of Monkey Island: *Tales of Monkey Island* (2009).

14   NPC means Non Playable Characters. It is often used to describe the game's characters that are controlled by the computer.

15   See Ryan & Deci (2000) for an explanation of these regulations forms.

16   On November 27th 2009 more than 700 teachers played *CheckOut!* during a workshop serious games for approximately two hours.

17   Jip en Janneke are two characters from a Dutch children's book series, written by Annie M.G. Smith.

18   *Lives/Ups* are known in the *Super Mario* series, while *tries* can be found in *Castle of Illusion Starring Mickey Mouse* (Sega AM7, 1990)

19   Personalizing can be done in many games, like creating a personalized team and character names in *Pokémon Red / Blue* (Game Freak, 1996), personalized home-bases in *Command & Conquer*, playing with personal drawings in *Drawn to Live* (5th Cell, 2007), use every noun imaginable in *ScribbleNauts* (5th Cell, 2009), or create your own character and level in *Little Big Planet*.

20   VOIP lets players communicate verbally through the internet. VOIP applications are *TeamSpeak* (Ludwig, Kirk, Werensteijn, & Strempel, n.d.) and *Ventrilo* (Knapp, n.d.)

Chapter 17
Theories of Motivation for Adults Learning with Games

Nicola Whitton
Manchester Metropolitan University, UK

ABSTRACT

This chapter considers motivation from the adult learning perspective, specifically in the context of Higher Education. It is common for the findings of research carried out on children in this area to be used as a justification for game-based learning in university settings. However, adults' motivations for playing games are unlike those of young people, and motivations to play games for leisure and learning also differ. This chapter considers these differences by first examining the literature on motivation and games, and secondly by presenting and critically discussing two recent theories of adult motivation. It aims to provide an overview of motivations for game-playing outside the post-compulsory education sector, and to present guidelines to better understand how adult motivations can improve learning.

INTRODUCTION

This chapter examines motivation with games and learning from the perspective of adults, particularly focusing on the context of Higher Education. It provides an overview and critique of relevant theoretical frameworks of games and motivation, and it also considers some of the latest empirical research findings in the area. The chapter

examines the ways in which university students approach educational gaming, and discusses the two motivational frameworks that emerged from these projects.

Much of the use of games for learning is inspired by the assumption that games are motivational for the majority of people. Throughout the literature on game-based learning, in the case of both adults and children, it is commonly assumed that the rationale for using games for learning is that games are intrinsically motivat-

DOI: 10.4018/978-1-60960-495-0.ch017

ing for most people (e.g. Alessi & Trollip, 2001; McFarlane et al, 2002; Miller & Robertson, 2010). This hypothetical motivation is then used as an argument for using games to learn, the argument being that if the motivational factors associated with games can be transferred to learning, then the learning will be more effective (e.g. Oblinger, 2004; Prensky, 2007). However, it is evident that not all people (and particularly adults) find games motivational; while they may motivate some, for others they will be extremely off-putting, and there must be a convincing argument for using games before some learners (particularly at university level where time is precious) will engage. In the context of formal education, the majority of research on games and learning in formal settings has been undertaken with children (as opposed to learners in Higher Education) although it is acknowledged that there is also considerable research with adults in the military, training and medical arenas. It is when the assumptions and findings of the research undertaken with children are applied to adult learning in Higher Education that problems arise, when in fact adult motivations for playing games often differ significantly from those of children. This chapter highlights adult motivations for playing games, and considers how these motivations might be harnessed for learning purposes.

There are several possible explanations for the widely held assumption that games are intrinsically motivating for most people. It could also be hypothesised that games researchers may be motivated to play games themselves, and perhaps do not consider that playing games is not motivating, or indeed is actually demotivating, for some individuals. It is also self-selecting enthusiasts who elect to participate in many educational gaming studies, which only serves to propagate these assumptions.

Adults and children typically play computer games for different reasons. Play is a fundamental part of a child's development (Colarusso, 1993; Koster, 2005) and is generally seen as an appropriate way for children to learn. For most adults, game playing is more closely associated with leisure time than with learning or work, and it is not an activity in which all adults engage (Whitton, 2007). While some adults will happily play computer games for fun or relaxation, others prefer alternative ways of spending their free time. When faced with limited time, playing games is not an appealing option for everyone.

The ways in which the concepts of *play* and *fun* are perceived in relation to learning differs from early years to primary and tertiary education and beyond. While fun and games may be seen as appropriate within the context of children's learning, they are seen by some adults as a frivolous distraction and inappropriate in the context of formal learning (Whitton, 2009). Games, and in particular computer games, also have many negative associations, such as leading to aggressive or antisocial behaviours (Sandford & Williamson, 2005) or promoting gender discrimination (Becta, 2001). These connotations further limit the potential acceptability of games for learning with adults.

Children and adults have different reasons for engaging in formal learning. In formal education, children typically learn because something is on a curriculum or required to meet an assessment requirement; they may also have an interest in the subject but this is not the primary reason they learn about it formally. Adults have a range of different reasons for taking part in further education and training, whether to further their careers or simply out of interest. While children may be interested in playing games regardless of what they might be learning, simply because they are fun and novel, older learners may be more strategic (particularly those who are paying for their education) and games may be seen as 'dumbing down', 'frivolous' or simply a 'waste of time'. These perceptions may be held by teachers and lecturers as well as students, so it is important that games are seen to have a value beyond that of simply being motivating, and that the true potential of games as robust learning environments is understood, in the case of older learners as well as children.

Adult learning theory (Knowles et al, 2005) provides a theoretical basis to explain the differences in motivation between adults' and children's learning. This theory argues that adults need to know why they need to learn something before they are willing to invest time and energy in learning it, they are motivated to take responsibility for their own learning, and that they are task-oriented and learn best when they achieve meaningful goals or learn transferable skills. It could be argued that adult motivations for learning are very similar to those that children and young people exhibit when learning through choice or in informal settings rather than in the formal setting of the classroom.

Knowles and colleagues (2005) also argue that adult learners typically have a greater understanding of the learning process itself, and develop more mature and self-reflective attitudes to learning. Concepts such as 'stealth learning' (Prensky, 2007) have been applied to games, where learners are motivated to play a game and incidentally learn from it without necessarily understanding what or how they are learning. It is doubtful whether these models of learning are appropriate for adults, who may seek greater control over the meta-cognitive aspects of learning (if indeed it is even appropriate for children). For adult learners, greater relevance of any learning to the real world may be needed to motivate, and ways in which learning from games can be transferred to authentic contexts may not always be apparent.

Even as regards children, the oft-cited hypothesis that exposure to technology from an early age has changed the way in which young people think and the way they approach learning (e.g. Oblinger, 2004; Prensky, 2007) has not been backed up by empirical evidence. While young people may be more confident with technology, there is evidence (e.g. IPSOS MORI, 2007; CIBER, 2008) that the majority skill lack critical reflection and information literacy skills.

When considering the intrinsic motivation potential of games for learning, it is crucial to recognise that different types of games exist. Game preferences differ among players, and it is unlikely that a person will find all equally motivational. For example, while an individual may be happy playing a board game in a social gathering, he or she may be less interested when faced with a solo computer game. There are a variety of different types of digital game, from which players can learn different things, but not all are necessarily appropriate for school or university curricula. The types of game commonly played for leisure, such as first-person shooters and platform games, may have little relevance to formal learning.

While it might also be assumed that people who play games in their leisure time will be motivated to use them for learning, this assumption cannot be left unchallenged. Reasons for playing games differ depending upon the context, as well as the types of game selected. In a study by Whitton (2007) a survey of 200 computing students, all but three of whom played games recreationally, only 66% said that they would be positively motivated to use games to learn. There was also no statistical link between motivation to play games recreationally (based on levels of play) and inclination to use games as a medium for learning.

The motivational aspects of games are not as apparent with adults in formal education as with children and it cannot be assumed that because students like to play games for recreation they will be motivated to learn using them. This chapter aims to investigate some of the issues around adults in formal education and consider what is known about motivation, games and learning. First, the background section provides a theoretical overview of some of the key theories in the field of games and motivation as it pertains to learning. The second section presents and compares theories that have emerged from two recent studies on adults, games and motivation. This is followed by a discussion of the implications of this research, and the chapter finishes with a brief conclusion that highlights areas for further research in the field.

BACKGROUND

This section provides an overview and critique of some of the key theoretical approaches that consider motivation to play games, and the aspects of games that make them motivational. First, the different types of motivation that exist are considered in relation to games, and the relationship between motivation and engagement is explored. Finally, the section concludes by examining the concepts of fun and pleasure and their relationship to motivation.

The term 'motivation', when used in the context of computer games (and perhaps other activities) tends to be used in two different ways. The first being the initial motivation to play a game, what Salen and Zimmerman (2004) refer to as the 'seduction' into the 'magic circle' that is necessary before a player is willing to take part. The second element is sustained motivation after the initial participation, or engagement. Much of the literature on motivation does not differentiate between these two types of motivation, but it is worth recognising that a difference does exist and that different authors are actually referring to different types of motivation.

Crawford (1984) distinguishes between motivation to play games in the first place, and motivations to play a specific game. Motivations for game playing he describes as fantasy fulfilment, overcoming social restrictions, demonstrating prowess, social lubrication, mental or physical exercise, and a need for acknowledgement. In terms of motivations to play a specific game, he describes two: the game play and sensory gratification. While Crawford's observations were made at a time when computer games were in their infancy and are applied primarily to skill-and-action games, many of these insights are still relevant today.

Some of the seminal work on computer games and motivation was carried out in the 1980s by Malone (1980) and later revised (Malone & Lepper, 1987). While this work is clearly dated, it is still regularly cited by researchers in the field and still highly relevant today. This work was carried out with children at a time when computer games were still a novelty, and while the motivational factors may be similar for adults there is no actual research evidence of this. Malone originally hypothesised that there are three aspects of games that motivate players: challenge, fantasy and curiosity. He said that appropriate challenge can be created by the use of goals, which should be obvious, compelling and adaptable, coupled with an uncertainty of whether these goals can be met but a belief that they are achievable. Fantasy is described as either intrinsic, where the learning outcomes are closely related to, and dependent on, the fantasy, while in extrinsic fantasies the fantasy is irrelevant to the learning (for example being rewarded by some game play after a learning objective has been achieved). Malone states that intrinsic fantasies are better for learning, and this is supported by more recent work (Habgood et al., 2005). The motivational aspect of curiosity is described as an environment that offers the opportunity to arouse and then satisfy sensory or cognitive curiosity (i.e. stimulating the senses or the brain). Malone and Lepper (1987) extended Malone's original theory to include an additional motivational factor of control, which they broke down into three elements: the notion that actions have logical reactions (contingency), that a large number of options are available (choice), and the idea that any decision has a strong effect (power).

Malone is not the only researcher to focus on goals as being highly motivational in creating appropriate challenges. Grodal (2003) describes a hierarchy of higher-order to lower-order goals, from objectives such as becoming a king to fighting a dragon to acquiring the appropriate weapon. While games typically include these sub-quest goals, he argues that overarching game stories have the advantage of bringing these smaller elements together to provide higher-order goals (e.g. a number of smaller tasks are required in order to save the world), and that these higher-level narrative-led goals are very emotionally motivating.

A concept that is similar to motivation, and in fact often used interchangeably in relation to computer games, is engagement. Motivation to play games includes the reasons for playing in the first place, as well as the motivation for continued and sustained interaction, engagement. Flow theory (Csikszentmihalyi, 2002) provides a framework for understanding this type of sustained motivation, which is particularly relevant to the field of computer games. He hypothesises that there are eight components that lead to the optimal enjoyable experience, or state of 'flow', described as "the state in which people are so involved in an activity that nothing else seems to matter; the experience itself is so enjoyable that people will do it even at great cost, for the sheer sake of doing it" (p4). These elements are: (a) an activity that is challenging, requires skills and has a chance of being completed; (b) complete concentration; (c) clear goals; (d) immediate feedback; (e) deep involvement that makes everyday worries forgotten; (f) a sense of control over actions; (g) loss of self-consciousness; (h) the transformation of time.

While flow theory is easy to understand, its application is sometimes difficult because of the nature of the components described, some being objectively discernible (e.g. goals and feedback), others entirely dependent on the participant's subjective experience of the activity (e.g. concentration, loss of worries). Draper (1999) extends the theory, arguing that flow is not a single concept but is comprised of u-flow – a smooth but unconsciously managed flow of actions such as driving a car – and c-flow, which requires the total conscious attention of the individual. He also argues that engagement only occurs where there is a "connection to the person's deepest values and goals" (Draper, 1999). Salen and Zimmerman

(2004) make a similar point saying that flow may be intrinsic to a game but depends on the player's state of mind.

Prensky (2001) describes twelve elements that make games engaging, and for each of these elements he describes the outcome.

- Games are a form of fun. That gives us *enjoyment and pleasure*.
- Games are a form of play. That gives us *intense and passionate involvement*.
- Games have rules. That gives us *structure*.
- Games have goals. That gives us *motivation*.
- Games are interactive. That gives us *doing*.
- Games have outcomes and feedback. That gives us *learning*.
- Games are adaptive. That gives us *flow*.
- Games have win states. That gives us *ego gratification*.
- Games have conflict/competition/challenge/opposition. That gives us *adrenaline*.
- Games have problem-solving. That sparks our *creativity*.
- Games have interaction. That gives us *social groups*.
- Games have representation and story. That gives us *emotion*.

(Prensky, 2001, p106.)

While this model might seem to oversimplify the elements of engagement, particularly as regards the notion of one-to-one cause-and-effect from game characteristic to outcome (e.g. it is debatable whether enjoyment and pleasure can simply be attributed to fun alone), it does however provide some insights both into the range of characteristics of games that can enhance engagement and their possible reasons for doing so.

The notion that games are motivational because they are fun, pleasurable or enjoyable is often used in the games-based learning literature without really exploring what is meant by these terms or considering *why* a game is fun or enjoyable. Koster (2005) describes the notion of 'fun' simply as "the act of mastering a problem mentally" (p90), which, he says, can have aesthetic, physical or social elements. Hunicke and colleagues (2004) attempt to deconstruct 'fun' by creating a taxonomy of experiential pleasure that players derive from playing games, which consists of: sensation, fantasy, narrative, challenge, fellowship, discovery, expression and submission. Koster (2005) describes six factors that he says will not guarantee that a game is fun, but the absence of which will guarantee that it is not. These are: preparation where the player makes choices that can affect the chance of success; a sense of space; a solid core game mechanic, usually a fairly small rule; a range of challenges; a range of in-game abilities required to solve the challenges; skills required in using the abilities.

Csikszentmihalyi (2002) explains the difference between the concepts of 'pleasure' and 'enjoyment' saying that pleasure is "a feeling of contentment that one achieves whenever information in consciousness says that expectations set by biological programs or by social conditioning have been met" (p45) while enjoyment is characterised as going beyond pleasure to the point where the individual has "achieved something unexpected, perhaps something even unimagined before" (p46). He argues that while pleasure can be passive, enjoyment requires deep attention and concentration.

As well as there being a variety of theories surrounding engagement and motivation, there are also a number of practical lessons to be learned from games in relation to increasing motivation with any activity. Oxland (2004) suggests the following devices for increasing motivation and engagement: the use of progressive sub-quests with clear goals and worthwhile rewards that lead towards the overall objective; ensure that the player always knows what the next sub-quest is, can get started on it and believes it is achiev-

able; use intrigue and curiosity to keep the player engaged; make sure everything in the game has a reason for being there; provide hidden secrets that the player is aware exists; teasing the player with future rewards that are currently unattainable; set pieces that provide a break from repetitive game play; and the use of integrated sound for more than simple rewards.

This section has explored some of the literature on games and motivation, looking at ways in which different individuals have defined the concepts of motivation including seduction, engagement, fun and enjoyment. There are a variety of reasons why people chose to play a game in the first place, including fulfilling fantasies, social reasons, mental or physical exercise, and a need for acknowledgement or to demonstrate skill. Players' interest can be maintained through a number of factors such as a sense of curiosity and mystery, appropriate challenge, a feeling of being in control, immersion in a fantasy or narrative, or complete concentration and transformation of time. Devices to support these are implemented in games using techniques such as layered goals and challenges, feedback, rules, interactivity, puzzles and storytelling.

Both empirical and anecdotal evidence to explain the reasons why people play games have has been published. However, much of this evidence does not differentiate between motivation in adults and children. The following section examines two pieces of original research undertaken to better understand the motivations of adults in Higher Education for initially playing and continuing to engage in games.

ADULTS, GAMES AND MOTIVATION

In this section, two pieces of recent research are presented, each of which examines adult motivations to play and to continue to engage with games. The first study investigated the reasons that adults play games in their leisure time and presents the primary motivations that were given for game playing, considers the factors that were considered to be universally motivational and de-motivational and presents a number of factors that can positively or negatively motivate different individuals (Whitton, 2007).

The second area of work that will be presented is the findings of the recent ARGOSI project, which used an alternate reality game (ARG) to motivate students to engage in university induction. The project is described briefly and a model presented that highlights six reasons why the players engaged in this type of game (Whitton, 2009). In the final part of this section the findings of the two studies are considered together, looking at commonality and differences in order to gain insights into the nature of motivation with games.

Motivations for Game Playing

This sub-section describes the results of a small exploratory study that was carried out to discover what the primary adult motivations for game playing were. Adults have different motivations for learning than children (Knowles et al, 2005) and this study aimed to investigate whether this impacted on their motivations to learn with games. A series of twelve in-depth interviews were conducted, the main objective of which was to develop a wider understanding of the range of attitudes toward, and perceptions of, games and computer gaming. These interviews also investigated the veracity of the assumption that a majority of people find games intrinsically motivating, and sought to discover whether people who were not intrinsically motivated by games were open to the potential of game-based and computer-based learning.

Methods

The method for data collection and analysis of these interviews was based upon the phenomenographic methodology, a research approach designed to answer questions about how different people perceive different aspects of reality. It is interested in categorising the different conceptions people have about the object of interest, and does not try to characterise reality, but how reality is perceived by an individual (Marton, 1981). This methodology provides a structured approach to the analysis of interviews, and focuses on categorisations of description as a way of understanding the different ways in which different people view the world. The phenomenon of adult game playing and how it is viewed by different people was thought to be an appropriate topic for the use of phenomenographic methods, but for practical reasons was not carried out with the large number of participants normally used for this type of study. It was felt that a small number of participants would be adequate in this instance to get a feel for the subject, and the initial work was backed up with a quantitative survey with a larger population.

Twelve interviews were conducted with interviewees recruited by word of mouth, all of whom either were studying in Higher Education or had previously studied to at least first degree level. This was a sufficient number to allow a range of opinions to be explored while still being practically achievable. There were an equal number of male and female participants, with ages covering all categories from 20–29 to 60+ years. Half of the individuals who took part in the study considered themselves 'game players' and half considered themselves to be 'non-game players' (i.e. people who play games by choice in their leisure time and those who do not).

Each of the twelve interviews lasted between 30 and 90 minutes and although there were set questions, the format was as unstructured and open as possible, so the actual questions and lines of discussion varied from interview to interview as different themes and topics were brought up by the participants. The interviews were transcribed so that data would not be lost during the analysis, and so that there would be less reliance on the memory and initial interpretations of the researcher. The interview transcripts were analysed iteratively, initially examining them to draw out themes and hypothetical categories of description, then re-analysing to test statements in the interviews against the proposed framework, until a coherent set of categories were arrived at that accounted for the perceptions of all individuals interviewed.

Results

It was apparent, even from this small number of interviews, and perhaps unsurprising, that the interviewees who considered themselves to be game players had different motivations for playing games than those who did not. Five primary motivations for playing games emerged, which led to five categories of description. All of the people who considered themselves game players appeared to fall predominantly into one of the first three categories, although they are not mutually exclusive: mental stimulation, social interaction, and physical challenge. The participants who did not consider themselves to be game players, did, however, sometimes play games. There appeared to be two circumstances in which they would play games: killing time and social facilitation. In the case of both of the latter two motivations, the game was seen as a means to achieving another end (i.e. passing time or making a social occasion easier) rather than being motivational in itself.

Mental stimulation is a motivation to play predominantly for the intellectual challenge. Players may prefer to solve puzzles, problem-solving games and other types of game that are mentally challenging. For example:

"I enjoy games with problem-solving in them mainly, quests, finding things, solving mysteries."

Social interaction is a motivation to play with other people and to interact with other people, either in competition, collaboration or simply in the same social gaming space. People with this primary motivation may prefer multi-user games and team games. For example:

"...I would play with my friends whereas I wouldn't play with other people."

Physical challenge is a motivation to play to achieve physical goals, which could include exercise, physical exertion, as well as computer games that involve dexterity or hand-eye co-ordination. For example:

"...it's good exercise and at the same time you're getting something out of it."

Games can also be used to kill time, as something to fill time when the person has nothing better to do. For example:

"Solitaire, yeah, I've done that when I'm bored on a rainy day."

Or games can be used as a form of social facilitation, as a way to alleviate awkwardness during social situations or as a way to get to know other people. For example:

"...this was a way that kids and Grandparents got together on a Saturday evening, we played card games."

As well as these five primary motivations, the interviews also highlighted a range of other factors that affected motivation for different individuals. There emerged two factors that seemed to be motivating for all those who mentioned them, four that were universally de-motivational, and a further fifteen factors that were either motivational or de-motivational depending on the individual. The two motivating factors were:

- **Continual improvement:** being able to see swift and steady advances.

- **Perceived proficiency:** a feeling of being skilled and adept.

The four factors that were considered by all to be demotivating were:

- **Difficulty starting:** problems beginning to play, understanding the concept or mastering the rules
- **Getting stuck:** reaching a dead end and being unable to make progress.
- **Unfairness:** a lack of trust in the game, where it is seen as being inequitable or unjust.
- **Boredom:** intrinsic lack of interest with the subject matter or game itself.

Being able to continually see improvement in one's skills while playing a game was seen as an important motivational factor for adults, which is consistent with some of the key research on what makes games motivating for children (Malone, 1980). For example:

"[It is good when you can] keep getting your score higher and getting up the levels..."

"I do like the challenge of being able to eventually play something that previously I couldn't."

As well as a perception of improvement, a feeling of being good at something was seen as motivating. This may be associated with a feeling of being in control of the activity (Malone & Lepper, 1987; Csikszentmihalyi, 2002). For example:

"I'm good at it ... so I like that 'cause I can do it."

"[I played the game] because I was good at it."

The importance of being able to start a game quickly without having to spend too long learning the rules, etiquette and parameters was highlighted. This may also be the case for children but is

particularly true for adults who may have more limited free time and do not want to feel that it is being wasted (Knowles et al, 2005). When people undertake an activity for the first time they are more likely to perform poorly (which is demotivating in itself) so it is of crucial importance that they can get started quickly and see a swift initial improvement. For example:

"I've never got round to actually playing it 'cause it takes a long time to get into and it's probably a bit dull to start off with."

"I don't like the ones where I can't start, I like to at least have some chance of getting somewhere in the game."

Getting stuck for a long time at a certain point, for instance plateauing in skill level or being unable to solve a puzzle, and not being able to progress, was seen as frustrating and highly demotivating, although there was often a fine line between getting stuck because something is difficult (and then feeling satisfaction when it was finally achieved) and getting stuck to the point where the player wants to give up. Again, balancing appropriate challenges for adults, who place an extremely high value on their time and do not want to waste it by going over the same ideas or repeating the same actions, may be different than for children. For example:

"I kept getting chucked back to the beginning and I'd have to go through the whole lot again."

"I felt I reached a plateau at a very early point and never seemed to get very much better..."

Another demotivating factor occurred when an individual felt that he or she had lost trust in the environment of the activity or game itself, that it was perceived as being unfair, inequitable, or incorrect. Again, this may be closely linked to the need for players to feel that they have control over the gaming environment, or at least some ability to influence it. For example:

"[Regarding online gambling] I think it'd be fixed for a start."

"I'm not convinced that the answers in Trivial Pursuit are entirely correct."

The final demotivating factor, and perhaps one that cannot be addressed or countered by any amount of intrinsic motivating factors is a simple lack of interest in the game itself. This last finding is directly contrary to some of the assertions made in the literature that games-based learning is ideally suited for teaching material that is boring (e.g. Prensky, 2001). For example:

"I find racing games on computer really, really boring ... partly 'cause I'm really bad at them partly because they're just so pointless ... it's like having to watch sports on telly, they're so boring they make you queasy."

"...a lot of it's about statistics and about, like organising all these things, like how much food the city gets, I don't really care."

As well as the six positive or negative factors, there were fifteen additional factors that were found to be motivating for some of the participants, but demotivating for others. Clearly in such a small sample it is impossible to draw any conclusions from this other than to highlight that the elements may have different motivational effects on different people and are worthy of further research. The fifteen additional elements are:

- **Cerebral activity:** the extent to which the game is intellectually challenging.
- **Chance:** the degree of random input into the game.
- **Collaboration:** whether the activity is undertaken collaboratively or individually.
- **Competition:** the importance of playing against others and winning.
- **Complexity:** the degree to which the rules are hard or easy to master.
- **Difficulty:** whether the games is easy or hard to play.
- **Involvement:** the degree of active participation required.
- **Length:** whether the game is quick or time-consuming.
- **Open-endedness:** whether the game has a fixed end or could continue indefinitely.
- **Playfulness:** whether the game is serious or light-hearted.
- **Physical activity:** the extent to which the game requires physical exertion.
- **Realism:** whether the game is realistic or fantastic.
- **Sociability:** whether the game is played alone or with others.
- **Speed-dependence:** the degree to which speed of action is important.
- **Stimulation:** whether the game is relaxing or stimulating.

It is hypothesised that each individual will find each of these factors motivating or demotiving to different degrees. Some preferences may be static or change little for an individual, and others will be more fluid depending on the particular circumstances and context of the game play (e.g. mood, purpose, other players, etc.). A person's preferences will determine whether they are generally more likely to play games (as opposed to other leisure activities) as well as influencing the types of games played.

This was a small study and it does not purport to have identified all of the factors that can be motivational and demotivational in games. However, what it has aimed to highlight is that the factors that contribute to the design of a game are complex and that – for the adults interviewed in this study at least – it is not a straightforward as games being motivational and different individuals find different aspects motivating.

Alternate Reality Games for Orientation, Socialisation and Induction

This sub-section describes a recent project that examined the use of an alternate reality game (ARGs) as part of a university student induction process, and presents some of the findings from the research activities, which examined the students' motivations for engaging (or otherwise) with the game.

Alternate reality games are a relatively recent type of game where an underlying narrative unfolds over time as players complete a range of collaborative challenges, which take place both online and in the real world. Martin and colleagues (2006) highlight the intertwined nature of real and fantasy worlds, saying that ARGs 'take the substance of everyday life and weave it into narratives that layer additional meaning, depth, and interaction upon the real world. The contents of these narratives constantly intersect with actuality, but play fast and loose with fact, sometimes departing entirely from the actual or grossly warping it' (p6).

ARGs are generally played over several weeks or months and consist of an ongoing storyline that the players assemble as the game progresses. They can use many different media formats including web sites, email, social networking sites, television, radio, telephone and printed media and it is not always clear what is real and what is part of the game. A key feature of ARGs is that players work together to build communities to solve the puzzles and build up the storyline interactively, often by setting up their own web sites or blogs to chronicle the story or creating artefacts such as books or videos. As the game unfolds over a longer period of time, it is possible for the players to influence the game as it progresses (Stewart, 2006).

Alternate reality games are interesting from an educational perspective because they provide an authentic context and purpose for activity; they are fundamentally collaborative in nature; and by presenting a series of challenges and an unfolding narrative they create puzzlement and mystery – therefore providing challenge, curiosity and fantasy to support motivation (Malone, 1980). The fact that they take place over an extended time period also provides the space for reflection. A common feature of ARGs is also their ability to create self-sustaining communities with established players supporting and guiding new players – this feature has potential within Higher Education to provide a framework for peer mentoring. A further advantage of ARGs over other types of computer game is, because they rely predominantly on existing web technologies, they do not require the same high production values, technical ability, time, or expense to produce as conventional computer games. This makes them a much more practical and feasible game-based option for education. In addition, because players experience a number of different types of media there is the potential additional outcome of familiarising them with a range of internet technologies.

The Alternate Reality Games for Orientation, Socialisation and Induction (ARGOSI) project, a joint JISC-funded project between Manchester Metropolitan University and the University of Bolton, provided an alternative to traditional student induction by developing an ARG framework for mapping learning objectives to game challenges (Whitton et al, 2008). A game called *ViolaQuest* was developed in which players had to solve a variety of challenges to find pieces of a map that would provide a clue to a 'hidden machine'. Solving these challenges would also help the players find their way around a new city, meet other people, and develop their information literacy skills. The game was designed to engage learners by presenting a range of challenges at different levels (Malone, 1980; Grodal, 2003), problems that need to be solved creatively within a compelling narrative (Prensky, 2001), and hidden secrets that need to be discovered (Oxland, 1984).

Methods

The overall game was developed and tested in stages as a series of pilots, which allowed for ongoing feedback and modification during the development process. As part of this piloting process, a version of the game with limited challenges was condensed into the course of a single week (the final version ran for ten weeks). Twelve people were recruited through word-of-mouth to take part in the game and ten of these were interviewed by telephone at the end of the pilot. It is recognised that because they were a self-selecting group of 'gamers' taking part in this pilot, their responses may not be representative of the student population. In order to gather data on the game mechanics and the gaming experience, as well as the players' perceptions and motivations, each player took part in a 30-minute telephone interview after the game was complete at the end of the week. These interviews were analysed to draw out themes and areas of commonality and disagreement between participants.

Results

The majority of players said that they played for around three hours in total during the week, although two played for less than an hour and one reported playing for over eight hours. The amount of free time available appeared to be an important factor in determining how much time was spent on the game.

All players said that it was easy to get started, they knew what they had to do and that the user interface was very easy to navigate and interact with. Reactions to the difficulty of the first challenge were, however, polarised with some players finding it extremely easy and others finding it impossible to solve without considerable help. The importance of making this entry point to the

game accessible was highlighted, as two players dropped out at this stage when they could not progress.

In general, there was a more positive reaction to the challenges that involved physically exploring the city rather than simply working at a computer screen. Attitudes towards competition in the game and the perceived value of the game community were again mixed with some players seeing these elements as very important and others viewing them as peripheral. All players said that the narrative was good to hold the challenges together but not a crucial element of the game. Overall, it appeared that there were six elements that motivated the different players to different extents:

- **Completion:** some players simply wanted to complete the game and achieve all the tasks or challenges.
- **Competition:** some players were motivated by competing against others.
- **Narrative:** the ongoing story, and uncovering the mystery, was seen as more integral by some players.
- **Puzzle-solving:** the ongoing puzzles, riddles and challenges were seen as motivational for their own sake by many players.
- **Community:** the community elements and discussion boards were important for some players.
- **Creativity:** the opportunity for players to be creative, either through creative problem-solving or the creation of artefacts was important for some.

These elements were not mutually exclusive, or even necessarily the primary motivations for the individuals taking part, but for each person one or more of these elements were key to their participation. They also show the range of factors that motivated players to engage with the game. Competition was mentioned in the previous study as a factor that motivated some people and put others off, and this finding was replicated here, which links to the ideas of demonstrating prowess and a need for acknowledgement (Crawford, 1984). Completion and puzzle-solving may be closely linked with both the curiosity motivation (Malone, 1980) and the primary motivation of mental challenge (Koster, 2005). The taxonomy of fun, developed by Hunicke and colleagues (2004) mentions both narrative and expression, which could be considered to be akin to creativity, as motivating factors. The community motivation for playing links closely to the primary social motivation highlighted in the previous study.

Again, this research was carried out with a small sample, which was self-selecting so contained an inbuilt bias towards people who would chose to play a game in their leisure time, so may be more enthusiastic about the notion of using a game to learn. This study does not aim to be all-encompassing, but simply aims to highlight additional elements that may be motivational to certain adult game players in certain situations, which are considered to be worthy of further consideration.

The following section draws together the findings from this study and the one described in the previous sub-section. They are considered in the context of the literature on motivation and games, to present practical guidance on designing game-based learning for an adult audience.

DISCUSSION

From the previous section, it appears that although adult and children's motivations to play games differ in some respects, there is also much in common. While some adults are intrinsically motivated to play games for their own sake, others will play them for varied reasons, one of which may be to learn. So, while many adults may be willing to play games to learn, it should be recognised that the primary motivation for playing is to learn something, and not to play the game for its own sake. Adults may be more selective about how they spend their time and the games they chose to play, and games as a learning tool may be less acceptable to adults than to children, so careful selection of the type of games used in any particular learning situation, and a clear articulation of purpose, is essential for adults to feel that its use is appropriate and that they are not wasting time.

Malone and Lepper (1987) presented a model of motivation based on four areas: challenge, fantasy, curiosity, and control. These areas were elicited from work undertaken with children, so it is interesting to consider their appropriateness for adults, based on the findings from the previous section. Challenge also appears to be a motivator for adults, be it mental or physical, although adults may be less inclined to work on something after they have become 'stuck' if they perceive it as wasting time, so gauging the level of challenge to the player is perhaps of greater importance. Fantasy may not be motivating to all adults, although the use of storytelling may provide context and help relate learning from a game to the real world. If storytelling is going to be used in a Higher Education context, it is essential (although not easy) to select of an appropriate narrative that is attractive to this audience and is not perceived to be frivolous or childish. Curiosity is still an important motivational factor for some adults, for example finding hidden elements or uncovering a mystery, and control, if anything, may be more crucial in an adult context, where learners need to feel that they are making their own decisions about learning and not wasting time (Knowles et al, 2005).

So while this model may be largely applicable to adults, two areas it does not examine are the social element or creativity, both highlighted as important motivators from the original research described in this chapter. It could be hypothesised that their exclusion from Malone's model is not related to the differences between adults and children, but to the fundamental changes in the nature of computer games over the past thirty years. Technological advances mean that online collaboration and creative development are possible in a way that simply wasn't even countered when Malone undertook his research on games.

The findings of the two studies described in the previous section are different, but complementary. The motivation to play a game in the first place may also be different from the reasons for continuing to engage with it after the initial 'seduction' (Salen & Zimmerman, 2004) and for a prolonged time period. The first study presented five primary motivations for game playing – three intrinsic, two extrinsic – and 21 elements that could affect motivation while playing the game (although the factors that impact on ongoing motivation would also affect initial motivation because they would influence the expectation of the player). The second study presented six elements of alternate reality games (that are also present in other game forms) that encouraged sustained engagement and were motivational for different people who played the game. One of the clear points from both studies is that different people have varied preferences, and that it would be very difficult to design a game that would appeal to all. The two key factors to consider when designing games must be customisation and choice, so that players can customise the game environment to suit their motivational needs and chose which elements of the game to engage with (e.g. undertaking puzzles but not following a story).

A greater understanding of why people play games, as well as of the factors that may impact on motivation once they are playing, enables game designers and educators to make informed choices when developing games as learning experiences. Purposefully designing customisability into a game as much as possible allows players to tailor their preferences to those that are most motivational for them, as well as increasing the amount of perceived control over the game, one of the motivational factors mentioned earlier.

These studies have looked at motivation to play games, and it is also important to consider how these motivational factors might be used to improve the design of game-based learning and educational experiences in general. It has already been highlighted that simply using a game 'because it is a game' or using game-based learning to make something less boring may not work for adult learners in a Higher Education context, but it may be possible to transfer elements of game design that are motivational to more generic educational contexts. The framework below has taken seven elements from the previous two pieces of research, and was based on the literature described in the background, to highlight the factors that appear to be motivating for many adult learners in games, and to consider how to apply them to learning environments in order to create more engaging learning experiences.

Goals. Having a compelling overarching goal, sub-divided into smaller sub-goals (or sub-quests) that are clear, gradually increasing in difficulty and perceived to be achievable. Presenting the higher-order long-term goals as well as lower-order short-term ones. The motivation to 'complete the set' can be exploited if all the sub-goals are made apparent from the start and are linked to an overarching quest or narrative (this could be as simple as being given check marks when sub-goals have been achieved). Other motivational features include building (ideally intrinsic) rewards into the achievement to sub-goals, and provision of appropriate and timely feedback and support (such as hints) to insure that learners don't get stuck for more than a reasonable time.

Challenge. Designing activities that are of an appropriate difficulty and type to engage learners is one of the most difficult problems in learning design. Using game devices such as hints, levels, or customisation can allow increasingly difficult levels of challenge to be attempted, with the learner being able to progress quickly though the easier levels and gaining a sense of being good at the activity as well as making swift and steady initial progress. Different types of challenge, for example mental or physical, will motivate different people so, if possible, it is good to try and provide variety (even if it is not strictly relevant to the overall learning a different type of challenge can act as a break or 'cut-scene').

Curiosity. The creation of suspense and intrigue, or simply stimulating the learner to find out more, is a way of supporting continued motivation. Using the game model, this can be done through the use of surprises, hidden clues, creation of mysteries that need to be solved, or secrets to be discovered.

Narrative. Use of characters, setting and storyline can help add motivation for some people as well as providing context to learning. It is important to ensure that the type of narrative is appropriate for the type of learner (e.g. is perhaps not too fantastic). Narrative also allows events to unfold over time and presents a way of providing an overarching picture and rationale for learning.

Control. Adults need to feel that they are in control of the environment is important to adult learners, so being able to customise the environment, undertake activities in a range of orders and have a choice in what to do, when, is crucial. Being able to see that actions taken actually have and effect is also important for motivation.

Community. Player community, either working with others or in competition, is a good way of harnessing motivation for some, although it is important to be wary of competition as this can be equally de-motivating for others. Also be careful when linking competition with assessment or reward as this can actually detract from the intended learning as learners may strive to 'win' by any means without actually learning, or may be de-motivated if they feel that they are unable to 'win'. Creation of social space and group working activities, and publicly linking achievement to tasks completed (e.g. using a leaderboard to graphical representation of tasks completed) can be motivational. There is a fine balance between rewarding individual behaviour and collaborative behaviour, especially in an educational setting.

Creativity. The ability to create and share items in the game, and input into the game itself through the creation and sharing of artefacts or game levels is very motivational for some. In terms of learning, this translates to enabling learners to plan their own learning, design activities for others, develop artefacts such as stories, videos, web resources, music, for example, that can be shared with others and contribute to the learning experience, (where the creation of artefacts is relevant to the intended learning outcomes).

This framework is not intended to be a comprehensive analysis of all the factors that might lead to motivation with games, but simply to provide a guide of elements to consider when designing any learning experience, game-based or otherwise. The two studies described in this chapter highlight that the motivations of university students (or any learners) to engage with games cannot be assumed and by creating experiences that cater flexibly to different preferences there is more chance of creating games that motivate and engage. By understanding the factors that make games motivational, and focusing on those that do not de-motivate people it may be possible to create learning activities that are not games in themselves, but are inspired by games, and share some of their dynamic, and are more acceptable in an adult learning context. It is also important to be aware that motivations for playing vary between individuals, but it is useful to understand what they are in order to create a balance that provides something for everyone.

CONCLUSION AND FUTURE RESEARCH DIRECTIONS

This chapter examined the research on games and motivation, particularly investigating how adult motivation might differ from that of children, and the implications this might have for the design of adult learning experiences. As well as looking at some of the existing research in the area, it presented two pieces of recent research that specifically focus on adults and their motivations to play computer games.

It is accepted that one of the major limitations of both of these pieces of research is their scale, with small numbers of interviews carried out and analysed in an in-depth fashion. The generalisability of what can be drawn from these studies is severely limited. However, what is presented here does not claim to make statements about the predominance of different motivations or to provide a complete categorisation of motivations, merely to highlight that a range of motivations that exist and to suggest what some of these might be.

The transferability of these motivations from games to learning is also not proven, and the practical suggestions given in the previous section are simply ideas or reflections on how motivational elements found in games could be applied to learning. Further research would be needed to determine the effectiveness of an approach based on this model.

To conclude, it is important to recognise that there are a wide variety of motivations for adults to play games and to learn. A better understanding of what these motivations might be, and an appreciation of the fact that what might be motivational for one person may be de-motivational for another, can help to improve the design of learning, both in terms of initial motivation and continued engagement.

REFERENCES

Alessi, S. M., & Trollip, S. R. (2001). *Multimedia for learning*. Boston: Allyn and Bacon.

Becta. (2001). *Computer games in education project: Findings report*. Retrieved from http://partners.becta.org.uk/index.php?section=rh&rid=13595

CIBER. (2008). *Information behaviour of the researcher of the future*. Bristol: JISC.

Colarusso, C. A. (1993). Play in adulthood. *The Psychoanalytic Study of the Child, 48*, 225–245.

Crawford, C. (1984). *The art of computer game design*. Berkeley, CA: Osborne/McGraw Hill.

Draper, S. (1999). Analysing fun as a candidate software requirement. *Personal and Ubiquitous Computing, 3*(3), 117–122. doi:10.1007/BF01305336

Grodal, T. (2003). Stories for eye, ear, and muscles: Video games, media and embodied experiences. In Wolf, M. J. P., & Perron, B. (Eds.), *The video game theory reader*. New York: Routledge.

Habgood, M. P. J., Ainsworth, S. E., & Benford, S. (2005). Endogenous fantasy and learning in digital games. *Simulation & Gaming, 36*(4), 483–498. doi:10.1177/1046878105282276

Hunicke, R., LeBlanc, M., & Zubek, R. (2004). *MDA: A formal approach to game design and game research*. Retrieved from http://cs.northwestern.edu/~hunicke/pubs/MDA.pdf

IPSOS MORI. (2007). *Student expectations study*. Bristol: JISC.

Knowles, M., Holton, E., & Swanson, R. (2005). *The adult learner* (6th ed.). Houston: Butterworth-Heinemann.

Koster, R. (2005). *A theory of fun for game design*. Scottsdale, AZ: Paragylph Press.

Malone, T., & Lepper, M. R. (1987). Making learning fun: A taxonomy of intrinsic motivations for learning. In Snow, R. E., & Farr, M. J. (Eds.), *Aptitude, learning and instruction, III: Cognitive and affective process analysis*. Hilldale, NJ: Erlbaum.

Malone, T. W. (1984). Heuristics for designing enjoyable user interfaces: Lessons from computer games. In Thomas, J. C., & Schneider, M. L. (Eds.), *Human factors in computer systems*. Norwood, NJ: Ablex.

Martin, A., & Chatfield, T. (2006). Introduction. In A. Martin, B. Thomson, & T. Chatfield (Eds.) *2006 alternate reality games White Paper*. Mt Royal, NJ: International Game Developers Association.

Marton, F. (1981). Phenomenography–describing conceptions of the world around us. *Instructional Science*, *10*, 177–200. doi:10.1007/BF00132516

McFarlane, A., Sparrowhawk, A., & Heald, Y. (2002). *Report on the educational use of games*. TEEM. Retrieved from http://www.teem.org.uk/resources/teem_gamesined_full.pdf

Miller, D. J., & Robertson, D. P. (2010). Using a games console in the primary classroom: Effects of Brain Training programme on computation and self-esteem. *British Journal of Educational Technology*, *41*(2), 242–255. doi:10.1111/j.1467-8535.2008.00918.x

Oblinger, D. (2004). The next generation of educational engagement. *Journal of Interactive Media in Education*, *8*. Retrieved from http://www-jime.open.ac.uk/2004/8/oblinger-2004-8.pdf.

Oxland, K. (2004). *Gameplay and design*. Harlow, UK: Addison-Wesley.

Prensky, M. (2001). *Digital game-based learning*. New York: McGraw Hill.

Salen, K., & Zimmerman, E. (2004). *Rules of play: Game design fundamentals*. Cambridge, MA: The MIT Press.

Sandford, R., & Williamson, B. (2005). *Games and learning*. Bristol: Nesta Futurelab.

Stewart, S. (2006). *Alternate reality games*. Retrieved from http://www.seanstewart.org/interactive/args/

Whitton, N. (2007). An investigation into the potential of collaborative computer game-based learning in Higher Education. Unpublished doctoral thesis, Edinburgh: Napier University. Retrieved from http://playthinklearn.net/

Whitton, N. (2009). *ARGOSI evaluation report*. Retrieved from http://argosi.playthinklearn.net/evaluation.pdf

Whitton, N., Wilson, S., Jones, R., & Whitton, P. (2008). Innovative induction with alternate reality games. In *Proceedings of the 2nd European Conference on Game-Based Learning*. Reading, MA: ACI.

ADDITIONAL READING

ARGOSI web site. Retrieved from http://argosi.playthinklearn.net/

Bateman, C. (Ed.). (2007). *Game Writing: Narrative Skills for Videogames*. Boston, MA: Charles River Media.

de Freitas, S., Savill-Smith, C., & Attewell, J. (2006). *Computer games and simulations for adult learning: case studies from practice*. London: Learning and Skills Network.

Egenfeldt-Nielsen, S., Smith, J. H., & Tosca, S. P. (2008). *Understanding video games: the essential introduction*. New York: Routledge.

Habgood, M. P. J. (2007) The Effective Integration of Digital Games and Learning Content. PhD Thesis. Retrieved from http://www.zombiedivision.co.uk/

Hon, A. (2005). The rise of ARGs. *Gamasutra*. Retrieved from http://gamasutra.com/features/20050509/hon_01.shtml

Krawczyk, M., & Novak, J. (2006). *Game Development Essentials: Game Story and Character Development*. Clifton Park, NY: Delmar Learning.

Rieber, L. P., Smith, L., & Noah, D. (1998). The value of serious play. *Educational Technology*, *38*(6), 29–37.

Wolf, M. J. P., & Perron, B. (Eds.). (2003). *The Video Game Theory Reader*. New York: Routledge.

KEYWORDS AND DEFINITIONS

Alternate Reality Game: Game that spans both the online and real-world environments with a story that unfolds over time, and creative and puzzle-solving challenges that are completed by the player community.

Engagement: The motivation to take part in an activity in a sustained way.

Enjoyment: A feeling beyond pleasure, created by unexpected or novel achievement and requiring deep concentration.

Fun: A sense of immediate pleasure and/or ongoing and retrospective enjoyment.

Extrinsic Motivation: Motivation to undertake an activity for some external goal.

Intrinsic Motivation: Motivation to undertake an activity for its own sake.

Pleasure: A passive feeling of contentment brought about by biological function or social conditioning.

Seduction: The initial motivation to take part in an activity in the first place.

Chapter 18

Collaborative Learning in Massively Multiplayer Online Games:
A Review of Social, Cognitive and Motivational Perspectives

Iro Voulgari
University of Patras, Greece

Vassilis Komis
University of Patras, Greece

ABSTRACT

In this chapter a theoretical framework is proposed for the investigation of Massively Multiplayer Online Games (MMOGs) as environments for the emergence of collaborative learning. Elements and features of MMOGs such as the integrated tasks, the interactions among players, the groups, the members' characteristics, and the environment are examined through the perspective of their motivational, cognitive and social potential, based on literature review, interviews with players and participant observation. It is argued that MMOGs are environments that can integrate a wide range of motivational features, opportunities for social interactions and for the emergence of cognitive processes, into a meaningful context. Implications for the educational practice are also reviewed.

INTRODUCTION

Why should we review Massively Multiplayer Online Games (MMOGs) in a handbook oriented towards educational games, learning and motivation? MMOGs constitute a flourishing industry, attracting and sustaining the interest of millions of players. Their "massively multiplayer" aspect entails a large number of players logging in the same environment and interacting with each other through their virtual representations, their avatars. Although they are often criticized for aggression, violence, addiction and sensitive to gender and race discrimination issues, with stereotypes describing the typical gamer as socially deviant or

DOI: 10.4018/978-1-60960-495-0.ch018

marginalized, addicted, usually young and male (Soper & Miller, 1983; Fisher, 1994; Anderson, 2004; Wallenius & Punamäki, 2008, Anderson et al., 2010), this debate is still ongoing: the stereotypes have been debunked (Williams et al., 2008) and research on the impact of video games on aggressive behavior and addiction is being challenged, either in relation to the selection of the sample, the statistical methods used, or the interpretation of results (Castronova, 2010). Linking of aggressive behavior with video games does not suggest causality; aggression does not always entail violent behavior; excessive playing does not necessarily qualify as addiction (Griffiths & Davis, 2005; Charlton & Danforth, 2007) or should be attributed exclusively to the medium rather than to individual or social factors. In response to this criticism, and although they are mainly commercial games aiming at the entertainment of the players, far from the formal objectives of the curriculum, a number of studies have discussed their learning potential, focusing on areas such as collaborative problem-solving, the acquisition of expertise, their employment in educational settings, digital media literacy, collaboration skills, informal scientific reasoning, computational literacy, and cultural mechanisms for learning (Griffiths, 2002; Steinkuehler et al., 2007; Schrader & McCreery, 2008).

McGrenere (1996) reviewed multi-player games for education, from the perspective of CSCL and CSCW. Although MMOGs were not directly addressed in this study, since they were at that time at their initial stages, the educational benefits of children's co-operation and social interactions within a gaming environment were recognized. Garris et al. (2002) examined instructional games from the perspective of their motivational features and proposed a model where the instructional content and motivational characteristics of games, such as fantasy, rules, and challenge, trigger the game cycle (user judgments, user behavior, system feedback), and after a debriefing phase (i.e. the instructional support)

may produce learning outcomes. Kiili (2005a) presented a model linking educational theory and flow theory with game design. In this model the challenges based on educational objectives form the heart of the model; design decisions on the gameplay, the storytelling, the game balance, the optimization of cognitive load and appropriate challenges sustain and support motivation, engagement and learning outcomes. de Freitas and Oliver (2006) proposed a framework for the evaluation of games and simulations in relation to curriculum objectives. This framework involved learner or learner group preferences and requirements, the context within which play and learning take place, the representation of the environment, and the relevant learning processes and frameworks. These approaches though did not address the highly social aspect of MMOGs and the role of the spontaneous social interactions of players in motivation and learning. On the other hand, in research on MMOGs involving the social interactions and in-game group dynamics, there is limited review of the learning aspects. The complexity and the dynamics of these environments require novel models and tools for the investigation of the cognitive processes emerging. Our article is situated within this context, attempting to combine aspects of learning, motivation and social interactions into one conceptual framework, and view MMOGs through this interconnection of factors.

Single Player Games, MMOGs and Virtual Worlds

Although MMOGs present many similarities to single-player, stand-alone games and virtual worlds, they also present inherent structural characteristics which may positively impact learning. Virtual Worlds such as "Second Life"©, "There" ©[1], and "Active Worlds"© are being used over the past few years as environments to support learning and training (de Freitas, 2008). Although they present many similarities to MMOGs, such as the 3D space, the graphical representations, the flexibility of user navigation within the environment, the avatars as representations of the players, they also present certain structural differences with MMOGs, such as the different levels of flexibility of the environment, the integrated goal-oriented activities and the predominant role of collaboration and competition, which are considered determinant for the emergence of specific user activities and for learning, as will be discussed in the section on the emergence of opportunities for collaborative learning in MMOGs. In an MMOG the players have to accomplish specific tasks designed in the environment and they have to progress their virtual character. The game rewards them for their efforts. Many of the designed tasks require the formation of groups and the collaboration and coordination with other players.

Interaction -social or task-oriented- among players, is apparently the main difference between MMOGs and single-player games. MMOGs are persistent worlds. Even if the player logs out, there are still other players in the environment, the environment continues to function and in some MMOGs, mainly browser-based, the player may even be attacked by other players. In MMOGs there is not a single goal to be attained or a story to be uncovered, as in single-player games, but rather the player has to accomplish a number of different tasks, situated within a narrative context and a general story background. They don't follow a linear, pre-structured story, or have a single hero, but rather the player is the hero of his or her own story, intersecting with the stories of other players, and selects his or her own tasks and activities.

These features of MMOGs, features such as motivation, collaboration, player-control, interaction with others, goal-oriented tasks, progress in the environment, individualized navigation based on the level of the player and his or her choices, very often come up as features of an effective collaborative learning environment. It seems, therefore, that collaborative learning in MMOGs constitutes an area of research that may provide useful insights for education and for the develop-

ment of effective educational collaborative and networked environments.

RESEARCH FRAMEWORK

Research in the area of learning has emphasized the significance of collaboration and interaction among peers not because of any failure of individual learning but because collaborative learning triggers specific cognitive mechanisms and processes in addition to the individually performed learning cognitive processes. During individual learning activities, cognitive processes such as induction, deduction and compilation emerge. When a group has to collaborate in order to perform an activity, additional activities and cognitive mechanisms are triggered because of this requirement for team working, such as argumentation, disagreement, explanation, adjustment of mental schemata, knowledge elicitation, internalization, reduced cognitive load (Dillenbourg, 1999). Learning theories such as the Situated Learning Theory (Lave & Wenger, 1991) view learning as an activity within the framework of socio-cultural interactions and the engagement in community practices. Collaboration and interaction with others does not necessarily mean, though, that learning will occur. A major concern for collaborative learning research is therefore the investigation of the factors that positively influence the emergence of collaborative learning activities and cognitive mechanisms, in addition to the cognitive mechanisms that emerge through individual learning, and the conditions under which collaborative learning is optimally effective (Slavin, 1996).

Problem-solving is being situated at the core of learning, either through the acquisition of problem-solving skills (Jonassen, 2000) or as a method for attaining specific learning objectives, through constructivist based educational approaches such as problem-based learning and inquiry based learning. Group dynamics and group communication processes are being identified to be among the most important factors that influence the effectiveness and efficiency of group problem solving (Hirokawa & Pace, 1983; Jonassen & Kwon, 2001). Taking a step back, we may want to ask "What, in turn, are the variables that influence group dynamics?" McGrath (1984, p. 287) proposed a conceptual framework for the study of group interactions: the structure of the group, the environment where the group interactions are taking place, the characteristics of each member, the task or the situation the members are trying to cope with are the factors affecting the group processes. These group processes, in turn, affect the characteristics of the members. Problem-based learning approaches also discuss the impact of the design of the task, the activity or the problem on the internal schemata of the students and the cognitive processes evoked (Jonassen, 2000).

Motivation is another significant factor involved both in individual and in collaborative learning (Dillenbourg et al., 2009). Research in the area of motivation and learning provides empirical evidence that not only the cognitive component but also the motivation component and affective aspects have an impact on learning and the cognitive strategies employed by the students (Boekaerts, 2001; Järvelä and Volet, 2004). Positive emotions such as "happiness, eagerness, fun or excitement" (Volet, 2001) may increase motivation for engagement in a learning environment. Motivation may derive either from the individual interest of the learner or from the situational interest emerging from the environment and the task (Mayer, 1998). Deci and Ryan (1985) defined a number of factors in a learning environment that support intrinsic motivation, the motivation inherent in the activity, while Csikszentmihalyi (1992) also described the common features of flow activities that trigger positive emotions and engagement in the task, such as the built-in goals, the feedback, the rule-bound action system, and the challenges that correspond to the level of the individual's skills (p. 71). Motivation may also derive from the sense of self-efficacy of a learner, in relation

to the task; the sense of self-control and of having the knowledge and skills required to solve the problem. Self-beliefs of efficacy impact on the engagement and perseverance on a task and the knowledge and skills acquisition. Success or failure in a task is a critical determinant for the development of beliefs of individual capability to succeed in subsequent tasks (Bandura, 1978; 1991). Motivation is also being situated within the environment and the social context and not only investigated at the level of individual cognitive and psychological processes. It does not only constitute a variable that influences learning but it is also influenced by the social and cultural environment (Zimmerman, 1989; Järvelä and Volet, 2004; Dillenbourg et al., 2009).

When collaboration and collaborative learning take place through the mediation of a computer and a specific computer program, additional factors are involved in the activities that promote effective interactions for learning. The setting and affordances of the environment define the types of actions and activities the participants may perform, while computer mediated communication (CMC) presents intrinsic differences from naturally occurring communication among a collaborating group, such as anonymity and absence of nonverbal and real life cues.

Having sketched an outline of the framework for the investigation of collaborative learning in MMOGs (Figure 1), we will describe the opportunities for collaborative learning in existing MMOGs, as emerging from the literature and our own research through virtual ethnography immersion and interviews with players of MMOGs (Voulgari & Komis, 2010)[2]. In the next sections we will review the components involved in collaborative learning and collaborative problem solving in MMOGs, through the perspective of motivation, sociability and cognition. We will not focus specifically on the impact of computer mediation. This aspect will be rather described in relation to the other three constructs.

Figure 1. Framework for the investigation of collaborative learning in MMOGs

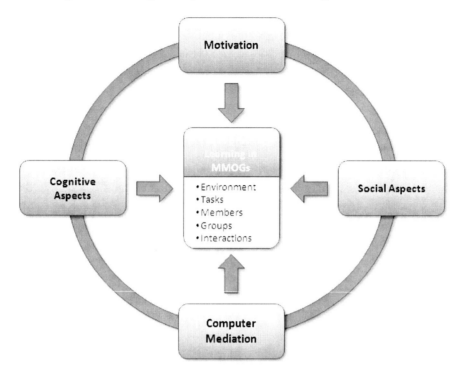

OPPORTUNITIES FOR COLLABORATIVE LEARNING IN MMOGs

One of the main reasons, for engaging in an MMOG, as opposed to a stand-alone single player game, is the interaction with other people. MMOGs are described as the new "third places", spaces for socialization and interactions among players (Kolo & Baur, 2004; Steinkuehler, 2005). The social experience of playing has been reported by almost 40% of the players in Seay and co-authors' study (2004) as the primary reason for playing. Even if the player is engaged in individual activities, other players constitute a context for his or her actions either as a constant "background chatter" in the general communication channels of the game or as an audience for his or her achievements and performances, as a spectacle or a "source of information and chitchat" (Ducheneaut et al., 2006a). Players who select an MMOG seem to rely on this massively multiplayer aspect.

Types of Collaborative Interactions

These social interactions and the social context, though, are not merely a semantic difference to single-player games. Interactions among players in MMOGs are an integral part of the attainment of the goals of the game, the progress of the player, and the general gaming experience. Players are directed by the environment to co-operate and collaborate with others, to interact, to communicate and to form smaller or larger and more structured groups. Players gain more experience points and progress faster when they play as part of a group. Specific content such as areas of the environment or quests and tasks are only accessible to groups of players. Furthermore, the separation of the virtual characters, or avatars (mainly in Massively Multiplayer Online Role-Playing Games) into different races, such as humans, elves, dwarves, orcs, minmatar or callente and different classes such as fighters, priests, mages, knights, mystics, brutors, or even different professions such as blacksmiths, tailors or miners, depending on the game[3], and the character inter-dependency, promote meaningful and task-oriented interactions. The different classes and races complement each other so that fighters, for example, with the skill to cause damage need the company of a mage with the ability to restore lost health points, and a mage needs the interaction with a crafter for the provision of materials and potions.

Interactions in MMOGs are "complex", "nuanced" and "multi-modal" (Steinkuehler, 2004a). They range from misbehavior of players against other players, such as the repeated killing of a virtual character, to informal and unplanned helpful interactions among passing strangers, and from random acts of fun, such as flirting, dancing, drinking, hugging, smiling, to structured collaborations with friends and the formation of smaller and ephemeral groups, or more structured and long-term such as guilds, and battlegrounds where teams play against other teams (Nardi and Harris, 2006). This variety of interaction types adds to the motivation of the players, the fun and the emergence of rich learning opportunities.

Apprenticeship and peer-mentoring as spontaneous acts of help or as a designed function of the game also constitute a significant part of the gaming experience (Ducheneaut & Moore, 2004a; Steinkuehler, 2006; Schrader & McCreery, 2008). Novice players very often rely on more advanced players for help, in the form of advice, resources, or co-participation in a difficult task (Huang et al., 2009). They ask questions through the chat channels or the fora, they search for information in external websites, and they observe the practices of expert players. Knowledge is distributed and shared among players and is easily accessible. Many of the players we interviewed admitted that they would not have been able to progress in the game as efficiently and effectively, without the support of other players and mainly the support of the group they were members of, while as experts they were willing to provide help to members of their group as well, in return for the help they once received. Yee (2009) attributed the emergence of acts of help to the design of the environment, to functions such as the severe penalties or the inter-dependence of the characters. In his article on social architectures in MMOGs (2008) he reports "Some players felt that the severe death penalties increased the general willingness of players to help each other, because all players understood the burden of death and, more importantly, all players knew that they too would need help one day". Players learn and advance in the game through their interactions with other players. Achievement, progress and learning the game seem to be the result of both design decisions of the environment as well as the social practices emerging from the community of players. Learning mechanisms, therefore, cannot be viewed only as a "designed object" but also as a "social practice" (Steinkuehler, 2004a).

The Quests as Designed Tasks for Learning

MMOGs, though, do not only rely on the social practices of players for the emergence of learning mechanisms. The environment provides designed tasks and activities the players may engage in, either individually or collaboratively. These tasks constitute the problems-to-be-solved having the two critical attributes described by Jonnasen (2000): an "unknown entity in some situation" and the social, cultural, or intellectual value to the community the problem is situated in. These tasks help the players learn the game, acquire experience and advance. Although MMOG environments present a variety of goal-oriented tasks and problem opportunities, such as designed tasks, tasks imposed by social pressure, or goals the players set for themselves, the easier discernible and investigated problem unit is the quest. The quests or questing system is one of the main distinctive, embedded functions of MMOGs (Schrader & McCreery, 2008). Through the quests the players learn the mechanics of the game in an active, participatory mode.

A number of studies have focused on in-game quests, mainly for examining and defining their features and their role in the game context, viewed from the perspective of ludology or the perspective of narratology[4]. Quests are structured and structural components of the game and the game story, guiding and defining the personal growth and the spatial expansion of the player-avatar (Juul, 2002; Jenkins, 2004; Aarseth, 2004; Ashmore & Nitsche, 2007). They fulfill the definition of well-defined and well-structured problems as those "for which there are absolutely correct and knowable solutions" (Kitchener, 1983), with an initial state, a goal, the challenges, the tasks, the rules, and the success or failure conditions.

Although quests are distinguished based on variables such as their linearity, the duration, or whether they are single or multiplayer (Tosca, 2003), or based on what the player is required to do, such as bounty quests, collection quests, escort quests, goodwill quests (Dickey, 2007), they mainly involve the search for an item or an NPC (Non-Player Character), the collection of items, or killing a large number of computer generated monsters, processes which are particularly time-consuming and repetitive and are often criticized by players and referred to as "grinding" (Ducheneaut et al., 2006b; Huffaker et al., 2009). One of our interviewees (male, 26 years old) insightfully suggested that when the tasks require a predefined strategy there is no motivation for the players to discuss, negotiate, plan and make decisions. They just go ahead and do the task.

The Social Environment as a Dynamic Context for Learning

MMOGs, thought, do not lack opportunities for critical thinking, planning of strategies, negotiation and discussion. These opportunities mainly involve the dynamic content of the environment and the interaction with other people: co-operative, where a consensus and a collective decision has to be made among the members of a group, or competitive where the players have to fight against other players. Although, concerning the Player versus Player (PvP) aspect of the game, the level, the class, the gear and the items of the avatar indicate the odds for winning (Steinkuehler, 2006) there are a number of additional variables defining the final outcome. Some of our interviewees admitted that when they have to duel with another player, the outcome cannot always be guaranteed, since the reaction of the other player or group of players is not always predictable. Different strategies and group dynamics may bring the battle to an unexpected outcome. In the web-based strategy MMOG "Tribal Wars" ©, we had the opportunity to observe players resisting multiple attacks by stronger enemies, due to their skills and experience, the tactics and strategies they employed. The formal group of players, discussed later, very often has to make decisions concerning, for example, a group task, the election of a new leader, acceptance or ban of a member, the negotiation of pact or war terms with other groups of players or the planning of a strategy for a raid or a battle against another group. Such situations present rich opportunities for negotiation, explanation, argumentation, agreement, disagreement, revision of ideas, adaptation, accommodation of different viewpoints, processes which are valuable for the development of collaborative problem solving cognitive skills (Cho & Jonassen, 2002).

Do players actually learn something, though, in an MMOG? If we want to examine MMOGs as learning environments we have to investigate the knowledge and skills that the players exhibit in the game and whether this knowledge may be transferable to other domains. In the next section we will review the types of knowledge and skills emerging.

Cognitive Perspective: The Expert Player

What is the definition of "expertise" in an MMOG? Who is the expert player? Overview of research in the area of problem-solving in games indicates that the key for the acquisition of expert knowledge and the development of high level problem-solving skills is the meaningful encoding of game-related information in memory and the integration of new knowledge into coherent schemata (Frensch and Sternberg, 1991). Chess players could search through internal representations of current and anticipated game situations and be able to select the most appropriate move in the game. The skills, the domain specific knowledge and the metaskills, the knowledge and strategies for the selection, the organization and coordination of the appropriate for each task skills, seem to be the main features of an expert problem solver (Mayer, 1998).

Huffaker and co-authors (2009) identified two dimensions of expertise in MMOGs: achievement and performance, with achievement referring to the level of the player and performance referring to how efficient the player is. Wang and co-authors (2009) also linked expertise to the measurable, through logs and achievement records, performance of the player. Knowledge of the game mechanics and high achievement scores do not seem, though, to address the highly social aspect of MMOGs. Players may only function within the players' community and they may only reach higher levels with the co-operation of other players. Social skills such as communication and collaboration skills seem, therefore, to be linked to the progress in the game and the acquisition of expertise. Furthermore, achievement may not always be a reliable indicator of player expertise for two main reasons: (a) cheating behaviors often observed in MMOGs. Players may exchange game accounts with friends, they may buy high level characters, or hire companies to level up their characters (Yee, 2006a; Dibbell, 2007) and (b) a player with a very good knowledge of the game may spent more time on supporting other players or leveling up the group, than in leveling up his or her own character, behavior which was also reported by players we interviewed.

Skills and Knowledge of the Expert MMOG Player

During our interviews a wide range of answers came up in the question "What do you think are the features of a good player?", answers such as "the one with the most extensive knowledge of the game", "the one who has explored the content", "the one who acts efficiently with respect to his or her gear", "the one with a good real-life personality", "the one with the best behavior towards other players", "the one who reaches his or her objective more efficiently", "the one that plays for the game and not for winning". It was interesting to observe that age was related to the orientation of these answers. Younger players tended to consider achievement as the predominant feature of a good player, while older players (above 30) highlighted maturity and social skills as more essential. Features of the good player seem to combine knowledge and efficiency in the game mechanics, internalized strategies involved in the game-play, inter-personal skills such as collaboration, leadership, coordination, co-operation, effective communication, competition, persuasion, diplomacy or strategy planning skills, and real-life personality traits. Gee also linked the skills of the virtual character with the skills and knowledge of the real player in an effective unit (Gee, 2007, p. 77).

The trends which emerged in our interviews were also supported by research in the area. A number of studies have examined the strategies of expert players, the skills they exhibit, their motivations and social practices in the game. A good player is not only the player who "mindlessly" gains experience points but also the player who has developed a holistic perception of his or her actions as well as a sense of the actions of others in the environment (Reeves et al., 2009) and also the player who has acquired a "social capital", who has communication skills and has been accepted by the community of players (Ducheneaut & Moore, 2004b). There seems to be a positive relation between socialization and expertise, either as a motivation for engagement in the game or through the formation of groups for coping with difficult tasks (Wang et al., 2009). The consideration of both game-related knowledge and achievement as well as social and interpersonal skills in the investigation of expertise in MMOGs would, therefore, provide a more holistic approach of MMOGs as environments for collaborative and not only individual learning.

The Acquisition of Expertise

From this perspective, what are the skills emerging from an MMOG and how does a player practice these skills and acquire expertise? The easy and short answer is: by playing, by spending hours in front of the computer screen, which is not far from the truth. Players learn the game by spending time on it, through repeated and effortful practice, by trying out small variations of the "same" response to the enemy, by completing the game tasks, by seeing each game relative to previous games, by approaching other players, talking to them and establishing relations, by selecting the appropriate group or group members, by telling jokes, coordinating combat actions, being sensitive to the needs of other players, distributing loot to team members (Ducheneaut & Moore, 2005; Wang et al., 2009; Reeves et al., 2009). They learn the game by playing, by referring to external resources such as websites, and by conversing with others (Nardi et al., 2007). The player is actively engaged in the exploration of the environment and the construction of knowledge, in accordance to principles of exploratory and constructivist based learning approaches (Ma et al., 2006; Gratch & Kelly, 2009).

Through these practices players seem to develop both domain-specific knowledge as well as interpersonal and social skills (schematized in Figure 2): how to effectively play their role in the group, how to coordinate a group combat, how to be a good teammate, they practice leadership skills such as reinforcement of good behavior and addressing coordination problems, they learn how to respect and empathize with the needs of other players, they learn that they have to attract the interest of other players, how and when to use humor, how to approach strangers and form relationships, how to ask and answer questions (Ducheneaut & Moore, 2005), they learn the facts, the strategies and the ethos of the game (Nardi et al., 2007). Despite the strong indications, though, empirical evidence relating engagement in the game with the acquisition or not of these skills and their transfer to other contexts and to real life is still limited. Players do develop context specific knowledge, they learn the content of the game and they have to interact successfully with other players, but do they learn these interpersonal skills in the game? And if so, can these be transferred to other domains and to real life? This could probably be an interesting research direction, with valuable implications for the employment of MMOGs in the educational practice.

MOTIVATIONAL AND AFFECTIVE PERSPECTIVE: THE FUN OF THE GAME

The exponential growth of player population, the time the players spend in the game, and the emergence of an online games culture has led a considerable part of research on MMOGs to focus on their motivational elements. The motivation of the players, the "fun" of the game, is one of the strongest aspects of MMOGs. The immersion of the players in the game environment, their passion and enthusiasm identifies with what is described as "flow experience" (Csikszentmihalyi, 1992;

Figure 2. Summary of the opportunities for learning and relevant skills emerging in an MMOG

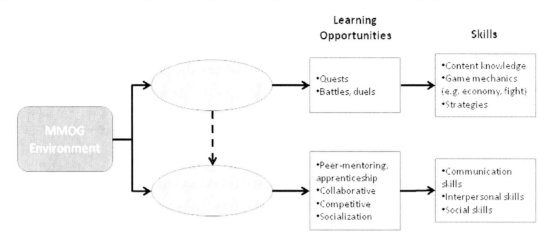

Stapleton, 2003; Kiili, 2005b) at which state the users concentrate and are deeply involved in the activity. During our interviews, a number of interesting responses came up to questions relevant to the motivations for play. These responses referred mainly to the social aspect of the game, the sense of freedom of choices, mode and pace of playing, the graphic representation of the environment, the game rewards, the personalization of the virtual characters, and the narrative and story background of the game. These responses were consistent with research in the area of motivation in MMOGs.

Bartle (1996) set the foundation for research on player motivation in MMOGs by proposing a typology of players: (a) achievers, players interested mainly in attaining goals and accumulating valuable in-game items, (b) explorers, players interested in exploring and experimenting with the environment, (c) socialisers, players mainly interested in role-playing and communicating with others, and (d) killers, players more inclined in acquiring weapons and cause distress to other players. Later research verified Bartle's typology or enhanced it; escapism, immersion to the environment, the genre of the game, relationships, manipulation of the game, rewards, choice, control, collaboration, challenge, and interactions with real people, seem to be strong motivators for playing, with achievement and the social aspect

being the most prominent among them (Yee, 2005, 2006b, 2006c; Dickey, 2007; Williams et al., 2009). Different motivators relate to players of different age, gender, usage patterns and in-game behaviors indicating that MMOGs may address a wide spectrum of player types and individual preferences. Further on, we elaborate on these motivational components as a result of environment design elements:

- **Fantasy and Background Story:** Rieber (1996) distinguished fantasy in games into endogenous or exogenous. Endogenous fantasy is inseparably linked to the learning content of the game and not merely the "sugar coating". The endogenous fantasy and the narrative environment seem to support intrinsic motivation of players (Dickey, 2007). They provide a context for the tasks, the virtual characters, and the representation of the game environment. They also address players' individual preferences. Interestingly, some of our interviewees related aspects of their real life ideology to specific game and virtual character background story aspects.
- **Graphic Representation:** The representation of the virtual environment, the 3D graphics, the audio, the music and the ani-

mation add to the immersion of the players. The external representation of a problem or a task seems, furthermore, of particular importance for the problem solving procedure. It determines the perceived information and structures and the processes to be activated, and affects the cognitive processes during problem-solving (Jonassen, 2004).

- **Virtual Character Design:** In MMORPGs players may select and customize the appearance and skills of their virtual character; they relate to it, they exhibit it for attracting the admiration of other players and it partially defines their role within a team (real life personality traits and expertise are also considered for the assumption of a role in the team). The representation of an avatar also seems to have an impact on the behavior of the players. Yee and Bailenson (2007) positively linked the attractiveness of an avatar to the intimacy with strangers, and height to the confidence of the player. The design of the virtual character also adds to the intrinsic motivation of the environment.

- **Design of Quests:** Well designed quests as designed tasks and as components of the game narrative, may contribute to the "emotional engagement" of the players as they can be "the *glue* where world, rules and themes come together in a meaningful way" (Tosca, 2003); they provide challenge, context and purpose for the tasks, and reward. The difficulty of the tasks corresponds to the level of the player, adding to the players' sense of control and manipulation. Quests may be either individual or collaborative. As described earlier, the format of quests seems to be standardized and some of the players we interviewed admitted that they only take up quests if the reward is worth the time spent on them.

- **Rewards:** In-game tasks and actions provide immediate reward to the player: with every computer generated monster killed, with every task completed, the player gains in-game currency, experience and skill points that help him or her progress in the game; the more difficult the quest or the task, the more rare and valuable the items gained. The player is rewarded even after a few minutes of play, even after a few minutes after logging in the game for the first time, and continuous to be rewarded throughout the game. These rewards increase play time, engage the players, and render games into "virtual Skinner boxes drawing the players deep into the game" (Ducheneaut et al., 2006a).

- **Flexibility and Adaptability of the Environment:** Except of the pre-designed tasks and quests of the game, the players may also select their own goals depending on their playing style, their individual preferences and their level (Juul, 2007). They may decide that they want to gain more in-game currency, through trade, or explore the environment, or they may decide which quests to accept and how much time to spend on them. Progress through the tasks and quests of the game is incremental. This flexibility and adaptability provides them with a sense of control and of freedom.

- **Social Relationships:** Design decisions such as the communication channels available and their features, the interdependence of characters and the necessity to group, the dependence on other players, the severe penalties and the crisis scenarios, increase the opportunities for meaningful relationship formation, altruism and trust. Through meaningful interactions with other real people, players derive memorable and salient emotional experiences (Yee, 2006c). These relationships often extend to real life as well. Both in our interviews and in game-related fora a large number of testimonies of real life relationships, friendships or even marriages originating from the game, were reported.

Although motivation may have a positive impact on learning, the content of knowledge in MMOGs is mainly focused on the acquisition of game-specific information relevant to the goals of the game. Hoffman and Nadelson (2009) suggested that for the transfer of games into a pedagogical context, a direct relationship should be established between the game and the learning context. For the employment of an MMOG in an educational setting, the aforementioned motivating features should be coupled with the appropriate educational and academic content.

SOCIAL PERSPECTIVE: FORMATION AND PROCESSES OF IN-GAME GROUPS

So far, we have reviewed the social aspect of the game as a strong motivator for play and as a context within which social skills can be practiced and collaborative learning may occur. The social aspect of gaming involves two main components: the features and affordances of the environment and the social interactions that emerge in the player community. The design of the environment may support or prevent co-operation and communication among players. Peaceful in-game areas, for example, dedicated to sociability and exchanges among players, may favor playful and casual interactions (Koster, 2009). Furthermore, the rules and social practices of the game are also shaped by the community of the players. Myers describes a case where the rules set by the community of the players, were sometimes considered more important than the objectives of the game, and players deviating from these rules were marginalized and even rejected (Myers, 2008).

For the investigation of collaborative learning, collaborative problem solving and group dynamics in particular, we need to define a group within which we could be able to study the variables involved, such as the characteristics of the members and the interaction processes described in the theoretical framework. The most prominent group type may have different names in different MMOGs - the guilds in the "World of Warcraft" ©, the clans in "Lineage II" ©, the tribes in "Tribal Wars" ©, the Corporations in "EVE Online" © - but it presents certain indentifying features, distinguishing it from the casual, goal-oriented groups: it constitutes a structured and formal group, defined by the game mechanics, it is of a more permanent and long term nature and it presents specific rules, formal practices, orientation and hierarchies. Most of our interviewees identified this type of group as the most important. Research on group dynamics in MMOGs has mainly focused on this type of groups, which we will call for purposes of conciseness "formal groups".

Group Processes and Practices

Most MMOGs provide mechanisms for the formation of either ephemeral, casual groups or for structured, formal groups. Casual groups are task and combat-oriented and they disband after the completion of the task. Although there is usually a limit in the number of players that may join a casual group, it is up to the players to decide on its optimal structure and size, in order to effectively attain their goal. The goal, the orientation and the size of the formal groups also depend on the decisions of participating members. Williams and co-authors (2006) proposed a typology of guilds in the "World of Warcraft", based on their goals and orientation: (a) social guilds, (b) PVP guilds, (c) raiding guilds, and (d) role-play guilds. They also linked the size of the guilds to their goals: smaller guilds were more social-oriented, while large and huge guilds were mainly goal, achievement and performance-oriented.

Successful and effective formal groups in MMOGs present specific characteristics such as the balanced representation of different classes with different skills, complimenting each other, the number of members, so as for the group to be sufficiently active, a wide character level spread, effective organizational processes, interdependence of members, group cohesion, the sense that the group may help the members achieve their goals, fair distribution of game rewards, matching of self identity and personal objectives with group identity and goals, effective leadership, time spent on collaborative tasks, and strong social relations and bonds among members (Ducheneaut et al., 2007; Pisan, 2007; Malone, 2009; Ho & Huang, 2009). Chen (2008) described the collaborative practices of his guild in the "World of Warcraft" © in relation to task-oriented activities: planning strategies for the task, performing the task together, coordinating, learning through trial-and-error, reflecting on any failures, re-assessing their approach and performance, communicating, and developing trust among group members. When socially constructed goals, such as friendship and having fun, were valued more than game mechanics goals or individual achievement goals, such as completing the task and gaining reward items, then survival of the group after a failure was more probable. Failure to address these characteristics usually entails the withdrawal of members or the failure of the group.

Interactions may be distinguished in (a) actions and (b) discussions or (a) nonverbal and (b) verbal (Manninen, 2001). Players communicate through their gestures, the virtual body language, their actions but also through text-based or audio-based communication via the different communication channels integrated in the environment: chat windows for private messages, messages to a specific group, messages to the general population within a specific area or within the whole game world (e.g. the server), fora integrated or external to the environment or voice communication through tools integrated in the environment or third-party

applications (e.g. Skype©, TeamSpeak©, Ventrilo©). MMOGs provide communication channels exclusively for the members of a group, through voice or text. Rich media for CMC were found to have a strong impact on the affective state, on community and friendships (Rauterberg, 2006; Williams et al., 2007). Communication through voice (VoIP) and text have positive effects on joint task coordination, on problem solving and on dealing collectively with dynamic situations, while the integration of tools to support the complex social and managerial tasks involved in group management are necessary for the development of positive and trusting groups (Steinkuehler, 2004b; Halloran, 2009).

An extended part of the communication among players also takes place beyond the game, through external websites, official or player-developed. Through these sites players post their questions, their answers, their perceptions of the game, tips and advice, their experiences, they argue, they coordinate their actions in the game, they publicize their achievements and they recruit new members. A large part of the game content spills over outside the game environment, it is user-created, and it was considered by players we interviewed as an essential resource for success in the game.

Summarizing this short review of research in the area of MMOGs formal groups, in relation to the scaffolding of collaborative processes and learning, factors such as the communication channels available, the size of the group, the goals of the group, the characteristics of the members, appropriate tasks for each group, the distribution of rewards, and the social goals and bonds among group members positively affect both task-oriented performance and collaborative problem solving, as well as the affective and motivational state of the group members. As argued by most of the researchers examining group dynamics in MMOGs, design decisions have a direct impact on the formation, the survival and the success of in-game groups and consequently the learning occurring within these groups. Furthermore, the flexibility of the environment gives the opportunity to the groups of players to select their own goals, set their own rules and define their in-group interactions.

In Table 1, we summarize features of the designed (DE) and the social environment (SE) in relation to specific guidelines emerging from research in the area of collaborative learning and collaborative problem solving, relevant to research in group interactions in MMOGs.

MMOGs IN THE EDUCATIONAL PRACTICE

Although single-player games are being used for learning and in school settings, MMOG employment is rather limited, and mainly within the framework of research. Further on we will present some indicative examples of MMOG employment in the educational practice (for more comprehensive reviews of game application in

Table 1. Summary of MMOG features relevant to the support of collaborative learning interactions, as emerging from the Designed (DE) and the Social (SE) environment

		MMOG Environment Features	Requirements for Collaborative Learning
DE		Environment affordances for the formation of different types of groups (casual, formal)	Mechanisms for the formation of the groups according to the given problem, support collaborative problem solving and learning (Hoppe & Ploetzner, 1999).
SE		Players decide on the structure and the synthesis of group	
DE		Environment affordances of different group sizes	The size of the group is relevant to the nature of the task and the background of the members of the group (Dillenbourg, 1999; 2000).
SE		Players decide on the size of their groups	
DE		Skills are distributed among virtual characters For attaining a goal, co-operation of different characters or multiple players is required.	Shared goals and distributed knowledge, which increases inter-dependence among students, seem to positively influence collaboration (Hoppe & Ploetzner, 1999).
SE		Knowledge and experience is distributed among players Attainment of group goals also helps members progress and acquire rewards	
DE		Different virtual characters and different character levels have access to different in-game areas and resources (equipment, materials, etc)	Heterogeneity of resources available to the students positively affects the quality and quantity of interactions (Fidas, 2005).
SE		Players are of different cultural and cognitive backgrounds, of different age, experiences, skills, and personalities	
DE		A variety of different and complimentary character types, with different skills, abilities, and role in the group Affordances of the environment define hierarchy in groups (e.g. group leader)	Different and complimentary roles assumed by the collaborating parties constitute an important cognitive dimension for the collaborative problem solving activities and for learning (Hoppe & Ploetzner, 1999).
SE		Real life personality and skills of the players are also considered for assignment of a role in group	
DE		MMOGs may support both co-operation and competition for addressing the preferences of different players	Productive interactions and co-operation rather than competition should be promoted (Dillenbourg, 1999).
SE		Players may select a competitive or a collaborative style of playing	
DE		Verbal communication is mainly channeled through text or audio (e.g. chat, forum, VoIP) Nonverbal communication in MMORPGs through avatar animations and actions Mainly support of *comcon* communication network (all members communicate with all other members), but also possibility for one-to-one communication	Communication structures supporting high level questions and explanations constitute factors with a positive impact on collaborative problem solving and learning (Webb, 1989; Hoppe & Ploetzner 1999).
SE		Players select the communication channels to use They resort to external, third party software for enhancing their communication (e.g. VoIP)	

education and learning, see also de Freitas, 2009, and Ke, 2009). In the following examples MMOGs designed specifically for education were used, with the exception of one commercial game. "Quest Atlantis" ©, an educational MMOG developed by the Indiana University School of Education, is one of the most commonly used educational MMOGs. It was specifically designed for educational purposes and presents the students with the challenge to save Atlantis from imminent ecological distraction. "River City Project" ©, a Multi-User Virtual Environment, was developed by Harvard University and aims at promoting information and communication, scientific inquiry, thinking, problem-solving, interpersonal and self-directional skills. "eScape" © was developed with the collaboration of the University of Oulu and the University of Jyväskylä. The learning activities applied in the cases summarized below were mainly based on exploratory, inquisitory, and problem-based learning strategies. Students were given a problem and they were required to explore within and beyond the game environment (e.g. in web sites) in order to collect the appropriate data and information, and plan the most appropriate approach for solving the problem, in co-operation with their peers[5]:

Cases of Educational MMOGs Application

- Ketelhut and co-authors (2006) implemented "River City Project" in approximately 2000 middle school students. Their findings indicated that students learned the content, they were highly motivated and engaged, and inquiry learning was facilitated.

- Research on the use of "eScape" on university students showed that the game allowed the students to engage in constructive collaborative activity, and multiplayer games could be used to promote group cohesion and development, when employed in a pedagogically meaningful manner (Bluemink and Järvelä, 2010).

- Kim et al. (2009) investigated social problem solving in controlled settings using the commercial MMORPG "Gersang" ©. They concluded that meta-cognitive strategies that require interaction with peers, such as "think-aloud" and "modeling" had a stronger positive impact on problem solving ability and learning.

- "Quest Atlantis" was used in a fourth grade gifted class for supporting socio-scientific inquiry in the curriculum (Barab et al., 2007). The study suggested that multi-user virtual worlds can support academic content learning. The role of external resources and teacher facilitation was also highlighted.

- "Quest Atlantis" was also used in after school sessions for 11 months on academically at-risk students. The environment attracted, motivated and engaged students but constant negotiation was required among the student-centered approach, the goals and activities the students selected, the curriculum objectives, and the role of the teacher (Tay & Lim, 2010).

Despite the potential of MMOGs as environments for collaborative learning, their implementation in educational settings still requires extensive design and planning. Commercially available MMOGs lack the educational content appropriate for formal education objectives. Although MMOGs do not seem to be appropriate for the school setting, due to time and curriculum constraints, their design, integrating motivational, cognitive and social features, conveyed through and exploiting the advantages of the computer mediated environment, may provide useful insights for the design of collaborative learning environments, as well as of the practices that promote student engagement in learning activities. Players in MMOGs, supported by the game environment, willingly and spontaneously form groups, collaborate, interact and learn the game, in order to achieve both game goals as well as their own objectives. Similar engagement and effective involvement in the activities and content are the ultimate goal of any educational collaborative learning environment.

During our interviews, we conducted a focus group of 6 16-year old students (3 boys and 3 girls) in the presence of their teacher. What started as a 1 hour long focus group ended up a 2.5 hour passionate talk, from the part of the students, on their achievements in the game, their progress, their interactions with other players, and their knowledge of the game content. After the end of the focus group, the teacher confessed that she hadn't imagined that MMOGs would be so much more than mere mindless and superficial interaction with the computer, and she admitted that she felt as if she had found a code of communication with her students. She observed that one of the most talkative and passionate students in the focus group, was actually a student who barely talked and participated in class activities and tasks. It is possible that the sense of freedom and of control on their own pace provide to the students the opportunity to assume responsibility of their own progress, within the context of their own objectives as well as the recognition of the player community. The players balance between their own freedom of choice and the constraints and rules of the social and the designed environment.

Although, so far we have discussed the ways learning theories and learning context could apply to MMOGs, the reverse, the employment of MMOG design features and practices in educational approaches, could possibly produce positive, for the students, effects. For games, learning occurs even beyond the environment, in online or real life communities, where players talk about the game, they share their achievements, and discuss their problems and solutions with peers and experts. Williamson and Facer (2004) examined these practices, and proposed that such a model of learning could inspire educational practices.

Applying the Framework

In Table 2 we summarize the features of MMOG as examined in this chapter, through the perspective of our framework. This schematization though is indicative and could possibly be expanded including more features and elements, as there is a strong interdependence among the constructs of the framework: motivation, cognitive aspects and social aspects interact with each other, while features and elements of the tasks, the members, the group structure and processes seem to overlap; the fantasy background is relevant not only to the environment but also to the tasks and the avatars, and group cohesion is not only motivating for players but also impact team learning behaviors and the construction of shared meaning (Van Den Bossche et al, 2006). Furthermore, factors relevant to the quality of interactions have to also be considered. Collaborative learning depends on the quality and content of communication among players (Barron, 2003). Groups are more effective, and collaborative and individual learning are favored when the members listen to each other and build on each other's suggestions and ideas. The table below though, as applied in the examination of positive features of MMOGs, could be of use to educators for the identification and exploitation of these features and possibly their transfer to other contexts, such as classroom practices or the design of similar networked educational environments.

Summary of Key Points for the Educational Design and Implementation

Summarizing some general directions for the educational design and implementation of multiplayer game environments, as emerging from this chapter, we are highlighting the interconnection of motivational, cognitive and social factors and their functional integration into a meaningful context within and beyond the game environment:

Table 2. Mapping elements and features of MMOGs on framework constructs

	Motivational Aspects	Cognitive Aspects	Social Aspects
Environment	• Fantasy, background story • Graphic representation • Freedom of choices and playing style	• Content	• Social architectures for the promotion of interactions among players
Tasks	• Goal-oriented • Challenge • Reward, feedback • Purpose • Matching to individual preferences and skills • Sense of control	• Require planning and strategy • Well structured and ill-structured problems	• Require collaboration
Members	• Avatar selection and personalization	• Distribution of knowledge	• Interdependence of players
Groups	• Group cohesion • Help to members • Group identity matching individual identity • Fair rewards distribution • Wide range of classes and levels of members	• Socially constructed goals • Groups appropriate for tasks (size, structure)	• Rich communication channels • Group management tools • Social bonds among members
Interactions	• Sharing of achievements with other players • Support for social interactions • Communities in and beyond the game for support and discussion	• Support of collaborative problem solving practices and discourse	• Multiple channels for verbal and nonverbal communication

- The availability of opportunities for a variety of interaction types, ranging from social interactions to goal-oriented and from co-operative to competitive, provides the players with the possibility to engage in their preferred activities as well as to practice different social skills.

- Multiple communication channels, through voice, audio, text, or gestures, supporting these different types of interactions, facilitate and promote socialization, co-operation, discourse and discussions among players.

- Functions such as the interdependency of the players, the distribution of knowledge and skills within the community, the difficulty of the tasks, and the link of the success of the individual with the success of the team, promote and support group formation and co-operation among the participants. Co-operation emerges as an integral part of the attainment of the objectives.

- The availability of a wide range and variety of tasks and activities provides a motivation for engagement to different player or group types and requirements and players of different cognitive styles.

- Furthermore, for the promotion of discussion, planning, negotiation, argumentation, and decision making in groups, tasks (e.g. quests) should allow for a variety of approaches and strategies. One single dominant effective strategy for the solution of a problem would direct the players to blindly adopt this strategy.

- The design of the environment should provide some degree of control and freedom to the players and to the player community, through features such as the customization of the virtual characters, the emergence of socially constructed goals, the freedom to select or not specific tasks and activities, and the possibility to adopt different playing (or learning) styles and player behaviors.

- The meaningful integration of the motivational elements of the designed environment, such as the representation of the environment, the audio, the music, the virtual characters, the fantasy background, the rules, the challenges, the goals and the feedback, into the appropriate educational content and context, could facilitate the implementation of MMOGs into formal education. The balance, though, between the curriculum objectives, which have to be attained within a specific time-frame, and the freedom of action of the players-learners has to be carefully considered, even at the level of the design of the environment.

- For an educational MMOG, the role of the educator has to also be considered at the design level, possibly through the development of virtual characters specifically for the teachers, with specific abilities, responsibilities and role within the environment. From within the environment, it could be easier for the teacher to interact with the players-learners, rather than as an outside observer, and provide the appropriate instructional support and assessment of players' actions, knowledge, achievements and behavior.

CONCLUSION AND FURTHER RESEARCH

In this chapter we reviewed factors involved in collaborative learning processes such as the types of interactions, the learning processes and outcomes, the group dynamics, the size and structure of the group, the characteristics of the members, the tasks, the environment, the group communication processes, motivation, and emotion. We presented a framework for the investigation of the learning potential of MMOGs and applied it in the examination of existing MMOGs through literature review and data collected from interviews and participant observation in different MMOGs.

Research in MMOGs has highlighted the importance of appropriate mechanisms for the support of different forms of interactions and effective communication among players, the significance of co-operation through mechanisms such as the interdependence of players and the shared knowledge, and the impact of motivation, task-oriented activities and social bonds among players. The large disparity of players requires the implementation of a wide range of motivational components, with achievement and socialization being the most prominent. Players of different gender, age and behavior are motivated by different aspects of the environment. In this chapter it is argued that MMOGs are environments that have the potential to meaningfully integrate such a diversity of motivators, as well as opportunities for cognitive and social processes, into a functional context, where learning of the content and practice of social and interpersonal skills are supported.

Even younger children and adolescents become experts in MMOGs, they commit to the game, they learn its mechanisms and processes, and they interact, very often in equal terms, in relation to their knowledge of the game, with adults. Research though and empirical data on the skills acquired and developed through MMOG playing is still limited. Are the social and interpersonal skills practiced in the environment existing characteristics of the player's personality? Can they be developed in the game and transferred to other contexts, and under which conditions? This could be an interesting direction of research with valuable implications for the educational practice.

REFERENCES

Aarseth, E. (2004). Beyond the frontier: Quest games as post-narrative discourse. In Ryan, M. (Ed.), *Narrative across media: The languages of storytelling*. University of Nebraska Press.

Anderson, C. (2004). An update on the effects of playing violent video games. [Elsevier.]. *Journal of Adolescence, 27*(1), 113–122. doi:10.1016/j.adolescence.2003.10.009

Anderson, C. A., Shibuya, A., Ihori, N., Swing, E. L., Bushman, B. J., & Sakamoto, A. (2010). Violent video game effects on aggression, empathy, and prosocial behavior in eastern and western countries: A meta-analytic review. *Psychological Bulletin, 136*(2), 151–173. doi:10.1037/a0018251

Ashmore, C., & Nitsche, M. (2007). The quest in a generated world. In *Situated Play, Proceedings of DiGRA 2007 Conference.* (pp. 503-509).

Bandura, A. (1978). Self-efficacy: Toward a unifying theory of behavioral change. *Advances in Behaviour Research and Therapy, 1*(4), 139–161. doi:10.1016/0146-6402(78)90002-4

Bandura, A. (1991). Social cognitive theory of self-regulation. *Organizational Behavior and Human Decision Processes, 50*(2), 248–287. doi:10.1016/0749-5978(91)90022-L

Barab, S., Sadler, T., Heiselt, C., Hickey, D., & Zuiker, S. (2007). Relating narrative, inquiry, and inscriptions: Supporting consequential play. *Journal of Science Education and Technology, 16*(1), 59–82. doi:10.1007/s10956-006-9033-3

Barron, B. (2003). When smart groups fail. *Journal of the Learning Sciences, 12*(3), 307–359. doi:10.1207/S15327809JLS1203_1

Bartle, R. A. (1996). Hearts, clubs, diamonds, spades: Players who suit MUDs. *Journal of MUD Research, 1*(1). Retrieved from http://www.mud.co.uk/richard/hcds.htm.

Bluemink, J. & Järvelä, S. (2010). Elements of collaborative discussion and shared problem-solving in a voice-enhanced multiplayer game. *Journal of Interactive Learning Research.*

Boekaerts, M. (2001). Context sensitivity: Activated motivational beliefs, current concerns and emotional arousal. In Volet, S., & Järvelä, S. (Eds.), *Motivation in learning contexts: Theoretical and methodological implications* (pp. 17–31). Pergamon, Elsevier.

Castronova, E. (2010). *MediaFX sound and fury.* Terra Nova weblog. Retrieved April 2010 from: http://terranova.blogs.com/terra_nova/2010/03/mediafx-full-of-sound-and-fury.html#more

Charlton, J. P., & Danforth, I. D. W. (2007). Distinguishing addiction and high engagement in the context of online game playing. *Computers in Human Behavior, 23*(3), 1531–1548. doi:10.1016/j.chb.2005.07.002

Chen, M. G. (2008). Communication, coordination, and camaraderie in World of Warcraft. *Games and Culture, 4*(1), 47–73. doi:10.1177/1555412008325478

Cho, K., & Jonassen, D. H. (2002). The effects of argumentation scaffolds on argumentation and problem solving. *Educational Technology Research and Development, 50*(3), 5–22. doi:10.1007/BF02505022

Csikszentmihalyi, M. (1992). *Flow: The classic work on how to achieve happiness.* New York: Harper Perennial.

de Freitas, S. (2008). *Serious virtual worlds. A scoping study. A scoping guide.* The JISC e-Learning Programme.

de Freitas, S. (2009). Massively multiplayer online role-play games for learning. In Ferdig, R. E. (Ed.), *Handbook of research on effective electronic gaming in education* (p. 51). Hershey, PA: IGI Global.

de Freitas, S., & Oliver, M. (2006). How can exploratory learning with games and simulations within the curriculum be most effectively evaluated? *Computers & Education, 46*(3), 249–264. doi:10.1016/j.compedu.2005.11.007

Deci, E. L., & Ryan, R. (1985). *Intrinsic motivation and self-determination in human behavior*. New York: Plenum.

Dibbell, J. (2007, June 17). The life of the Chinese gold farmer. *New York Times Magazine*. http://www.nytimes.com/2007/06/17/magazine/17lootfarmers-t.html.

Dickey, M. D. (2007). Game design and learning: A conjectural analysis of how massively multiple online role-playing games (MMORPGs) foster intrinsic motivation. *Educational Technology Research and Development*, *55*(3), 253–273. doi:10.1007/s11423-006-9004-7

Dillenbourg, P. (1999). Introduction: What do you mean by collaborative learning? In Dillenbourg, P. (Ed.), *Collaborative learning: Cognitive and computational approaches* (*Vol. 1*, pp. 1–15). Oxford: Elsevier.

Dillenbourg, P. (2000). *Virtual learning environments*. In EUN Schoolnet Conference 2000. Learning in the new millenium: Building new educational strategies for schools. Brussels.

Dillenbourg, P., Järvelä, S., & Fischer, F. (2009). The evolution of research on computer-supported collaborative learning. In Balacheff, N., Ludvigsen, S., Jong, T. D., Lazonder, A., & Barnes, S. (Eds.), *Technology-enhanced learning principles and products* (pp. 3–19). Dordrecht, The Netherlands: Springer.

Ducheneaut, N., & Moore, R. (2005). More than just XP: Learning social skills in massively multiplayer online games. [Emerald Group Publishing Limited.]. *Interactive Technology and Smart Education*, *2*(2), 89–100. doi:10.1108/17415650580000035

Ducheneaut, N., & Moore, R. J. (2004a). The social side of gaming: A study of interaction patterns in a massively multiplayer online game. In *Proceedings of the 2004 ACM Conference on Computer Supported Cooperative Work*, (pp. 360-369). New York: ACM.

Ducheneaut, N., & Moore, R. J. (2004b). Gaining more than experience points: Learning social behavior in multiplayer computer games. *In CHI 2004 Workshop on Social Learning Through Gaming*.

Ducheneaut, N., Yee, N., Nickell, E., & Moore, R. J. (2006a). Alone together? Exploring the social dynamics of massively multiplayer online games. In *Proceedings of the SIGCHI conference on Human Factors in computing systems - CHI '06,* (p. 407). New York: ACM Press.

Ducheneaut, N., Yee, N., Nickell, E., & Moore, R. J. (2006b). Building an MMO with mass appeal. A look at gameplay in World of Warcraft. *Games and Culture*, *1*(4), 281–317. doi:10.1177/1555412006292613

Ducheneaut, N., Yee, N., Nickell, E., & Moore, R. J. (2007). *The life and death of online gaming communities: A look at guilds in World of Warcraft*. Conference on Human Factors in Computing Systems.

Fidas, C. (2005). Heterogeneity of learning material in synchronous computer-supported collaborative modelling. *Computers & Education*, *44*(2), 135–154. doi:10.1016/j.compedu.2004.02.001

Fisher, S. (1994). Identifying video game addiction in children and adolescents. *Addictive Behaviors*, *19*(5), 545–553. doi:10.1016/0306-4603(94)90010-8

Frensch, P. A., & Sternberg, R. J. (1991). Skill-related differences in game playing. In Sternberg, R. J., & Frensch, P. A. (Eds.), *Complex problem solving: Principles and mechanisms* (pp. 343–381). Hillsdale, NJ: Lawrence Erlbaum Associates.

Garris, R., Ahlers, R., & Driskell, J. E. (2002). Games, motivation, and learning: A research and practice model. *Simulation & Gaming*, *33*(4), 441–467. doi:10.1177/1046878102238607

Gee, J. P. (2007). *Good video games and good leaning: Collected essays on video games, learning and literacy. New literacies and digital epistemologies.* New York: Peter Lang Publishers.

Gratch, J., & Kelly, J. (2009). MMOGs: Beyond the wildest imagination. *Journal of Interactive Learning Research, 20*(2), 175–187.

Griffiths, M. (2002). The educational benefits of videogames. [Mary Ann Liebert, Inc.]. *Education and Health, 20*(3), 47–51.

Griffiths, M., & Davis, M. (2005). Does video game addiction exist? In Raessens, J., & Goldstein, J. (Eds.), *Handbook of computer game studies.* Cambridge, MA: The MIT press.

Halloran, J. (2009). It's talk, but not as we know it: Using VoIP to communicate in war games. *Proceedings of Conference in Games and Virtual Worlds for Serious Applications.* (pp. 133-140).

Hirokawa, R., & Pace, R. (1983). A descriptive investigation of the possible communication-based reasons for effective and ineffective group decision making. *Communication Monographs, 50*(4), 363–379. doi:10.1080/03637758309390175

Ho, S. H., & Huang, C. H. (2009). Exploring success factors of video game communities in hierarchical linear modeling: The perspectives of members and leaders. *Computers in Human Behavior, 25*(3), 761–769. doi:10.1016/j.chb.2009.02.004

Hoffman, B. & Nadelson, L. (2009). Motivational engagement and video gaming: A mixed methods study. *Educational Technology Research and Development.*

Hoppe, H. U., & Ploetzner, R. (1999). Can analytic models support learning in groups? In Dillenbourg, P. (Ed.), *Collaborative-learning: Cognitive and computational approaches* (pp. 147–169). Advances in Learning and Instruction Series. Pergamon, Elsevier.

Huang, Y., Zhu, M., Wang, J., Pathak, N., Shen, C., Keegan, B., et al. (2009). The formation of task-oriented groups: Exploring combat activities in online games. *Proceedings of the 2009 International Conference on Computational Science and Engineering,* (pp. 122-127). IEEE.

Huffaker, D., Wang, J., Treem, J., Ahmad, M. A., Fullerton, L., Williams, D., et al. (2009). The social behaviors of experts in massive multiplayer online role-playing games. In *Proceedings of the 2009 International Conference on Computational Science and Engineering,* (pp. 326-331). IEEE.

Järvelä, S., & Volet, S. (2004). Motivation in real-life, dynamic, and interactive learning environments: Stretching constructs and methodologies. *European Psychologist, 9*(4), 193–197. doi:10.1027/1016-9040.9.4.193

Jenkins, H. (2004). Game design as narrative architecture. In Wardrip-Fruin, N., & Harrigan, P. (Eds.), *First person: New media as story, performance, game* (pp. 1–15). Cambridge, MA: MIT Press.

Jonassen, D. H. (2000). Toward a design theory of problem solving. *Educational Technology Research and Development, 48*(4), 63–85. doi:10.1007/BF02300500

Jonassen, D. H. (2004). *Learning to solve problems: An instructional design guide.* Pfeiffer.

Jonassen, D. H., & Kwon, H. (2001). Communication patterns in computer mediated versus face-to-face group problem solving. *Educational Technology Research and Development, 49*(1), 35–51. doi:10.1007/BF02504505

Juul, J. (2002). The open and the closed: Games of emergence and games of progression. In *Computer Game and Digital Cultures Conference Proceedings,* (p. 323–329).

Juul, J. (2007). Without a goal: On open and expressive games. In Krzywinska, T., & Atkins, B. (Eds.), *Videogame/player/text.* Manchester, UK: Manchester University Press.

Ke, F. (2009). A qualitative meta-analysis of computer games as learning tools. In Ferdig, R. E. (Ed.), *Handbook of research on effective electronic gaming in education* (p. 1759). Information Science Reference.

Ketelhut, D., Dede, C., Clarke, J., & Nelson, B. (2006). A multi-user virtual environment for building higher order inquiry skills in science. *Proceedings of the American Educational Research Association Conference*, (pp. 1-11).

Kiili, K. (2005a). Digital game-based learning: Towards an experiential gaming model. *The Internet and Higher Education, 8*(1), 13–24. doi:10.1016/j.iheduc.2004.12.001

Kiili, K. (2005b). Content creation challenges and flow experience in educational games: The IT-emperor case. *The Internet and Higher Education, 8*(3), 183–198. doi:10.1016/j.iheduc.2005.06.001

Kim, B., Park, H., & Baek, Y. (2009). Not just fun, but serious strategies: Using meta-cognitive strategies in game-based learning. *Computers & Education, 52*(4), 800–810. doi:10.1016/j.compedu.2008.12.004

Kitchener, K. S. (1983). Cognition, metacognition, and epistemic cognition: A three-level model of cognitive processing. *Human Development, 4*, 222–232.

Kolo, C. & Baur, T. (2004). Living a virtual life: Social dynamics of online gaming. *Game Studies, 4*(1).

Koster, R. (2009). *Ways to make your virtual space more social*. Retrieved from http://www.raphkoster.com/2009/01/28/ways-to-make-your-virtual-space-more-social/#more-2486

Lave, J., & Wenger, E. (1991). *Situated learning: Legitimate peripheral participation (Learning in doing: Social, cognitive and computational perspectives)*. Cambridge University Press.

Ma, Y., Williams, D., Richard, C., Prejean, L., & Liu, M. (2006). *Integrating video games with problem-based learning: A conceptual model.* (pp. 2364-2368).

Malone, K. (2009). Dragon kill points: The economics of power gamers. *Games and Culture, 4*(3), 296–316. doi:10.1177/1555412009339731

Manninen, T. (2001). Rich interaction in the context of networked virtual environments-experiences gained from the multi-player games domain. In A. Blanford, J. Vanderdonckt, & P. Gray (Eds.), *Joint Proceedings of HCI 2001 and IHM 2001 Conference,* (pp. 383-398).

Mayer, R. E. (1998). Cognitive, metacognitive, and motivational aspects of problem solving [Netherlands: Kluwer Academic Publishers.]. *Instructional Science, 26*(49), 49–63. doi:10.1023/A:1003088013286

McGrath, J. E. (1984). *Groups: Interaction and performance*. Prentice-Hall, Inc.

McGrenere, J. L. (1996). *Design: Educational electronic multi-player games: A literature review.* Vancouver, BC, Canada: Department of Computer Science, The University of British Columbia.

Myers, D. (2008). Play and punishment: The sad and curious case of Twixt. In *The Player Conference Proceedings,* (pp. 1-25). Copenhagen: The Center for Computer Games Research, The IT University of Copenhagen.

Nardi, B., & Harris, J. (2006). Strangers and friends: Collaborative play in World of Warcraft. In *Proceedings of the 2006 20th anniversary conference on Computer supported cooperative work - CSCW '06,* (p. 149). New York: ACM Press.

Nardi, B. A., Ly, S., & Harris, J. (2007). Learning conversations in World of Warcraft. In *Proceedings of the 2007 40th Annual Hawaii International Conference on System Sciences (HICSS '07),* (pp. 79-79). IEEE.

Pisan, Y. (2007). My guild, my people: Role of guilds in massively multiplayer online games. In *Proceedings of the 4th Australasian Conference on Interactive Entertainment,* (Vol. 305). Melbourne, Australia: RMIT University.

Rauterberg, M. (2006). Determinantes for collaboration in networked multi-user games. In Nakatsu, R., & Hoshino, J. (Eds.), *Entertainment computing-technologies and applications* (pp. 313–321). Kluwer Academic Press.

Reeves, S., Brown, B., & Laurier, E. (2009). Experts at play: Understanding skilled expertise. *Games and Culture, 4*(3), 205–227. doi:10.1177/1555412009339730

Rieber, L. P. (1996). Seriously considering play: Designing interactive learning environments based on the blending of microworlds, simulations, and games. *Educational Technology Research and Development, 44*(2), 43–58. doi:10.1007/BF02300540

Schrader, P. G., & McCreery, M. (2008). The acquisition of skill and expertise in massively multiplayer online games. *Educational Technology Research and Development, 56*(5-6), 557–574. doi:10.1007/s11423-007-9055-4

Seay, A. F., Jerome, W. J., Lee, K. S., & Kraut, R. E. (2004). Project Massive: A study of online gaming communities. In *Extended Abstracts of the 2004 Conference on Human Factors and Computing Systems - CHI '04,* (pp. 1421-1424). New York: ACM Press.

Slavin, R. (1996). Research on cooperative learning and achievement: What we know, what we need to know. *Contemporary Educational Psychology, 21*(1), 43–69. doi:10.1006/ceps.1996.0004

Soper, W. B., & Miller, M. J. (1983). Junk-time junkies: An emerging addiction among students. *The School Counselor, 31*(1), 40–43.

Stapleton, A. J., & Taylor, P. C. (2003). *Why videogames are cool and school sucks!* Paper presented at Australian Game Developers Conference, Melbourne, Australia, 20-23 November.

Steinkuehler, C., Duncan, S., & Simkins, D. (2007). Massively multiplayer online games and education: An outline of research. In C. Chinn, G. Erkins, & S. Puntambekar (Eds.), *Proceedings of the Eighth Conference of Computer Supported Collaborative Learning,* (Vol. 48, pp. 674-684). New Brunswick, NJ: Rutgers University.

Steinkuehler, C. A. (2004a). Learning in massively multiplayer online games. In Y.B. Kafai, W.A. Sandoval, N. Enyedy, A.S. Nixon, & F. Herrera (Eds.), *Proceedings of the 6th International Conference on Learning Sciences,* (pp. 521-528). Mahwah, NJ: Erlbaum.

Steinkuehler, C. A. (2004b). *Providing resources for MMOG guild leaders.* In MUD Developers Conference. San Jose, CA.

Steinkuehler, C. A. (2005). The new third place: Massively multiplayer online gaming in American youth culture. *Tidskrift Journal of Research in Teacher Education, 3*(3), 17–32.

Steinkuehler, C. A. (2006). Why game (culture) studies now? *Games and Culture, 1*(1), 97–102. doi:10.1177/1555412005281911

Tay, L. Y., & Lim, C. P. (2010). An activity theoretical perspective towards the design of an ICT-enhanced after-school programme for academically at-risk students. *Educational Media International, 47*(1), 19–37. doi:10.1080/09523981003654951

Tosca, S. (2003). The quest problem in computer games. In *Proceedings of Technologies for Interactive Digital Storytelling and Entertainment conference,* (pp. 1-16).

Van Den Bossche, P., Gijselaers, W. H., Segers, M., & Kirschner, P. A. (2006). Social and cognitive factors driving teamwork in collaborative learning environments: Team learning beliefs and behaviors. *Small Group Research, 37*(5), 490–521. doi:10.1177/1046496406292938

Volet, S. (2001). Emerging trends in recent research on motivation in learning contexts. In Volet, S., & Järvelä, S. (Eds.), *Motivation in learning contexts: Theoretical and methodological implications* (pp. 319–334). Pergamon, Elsevier.

Voulgari, I., & Komis, V. (2010). Elven elder LVL59 LFP/RB. Please PM me: Immersion, collaborative tasks and problem solving in massively multiplayer online game. *Learning, Media and Technology, 35*(2), 171–202. doi:10.1080/17439884.2010.494429

Wallenius, M., & Punamäki, R. (2008). Digital game violence and direct aggression in adolescence: A longitudinal study of the roles of sex, age, and parent-child communication. *Journal of Applied Developmental Psychology, 29*(4), 286–294. doi:10.1016/j.appdev.2008.04.010

Wang, J., Huffaker, D., Treem, J., Fullerton, L., Ahmad, M., Williams, D., et al. (2009). *Focused on the prize: Characteristics of experts in virtual worlds*. Presented to the Annual Meeting of the International Communication Association (ICA). Chicago, IL.

Webb, N. (1989). Peer interaction and learning in small groups. *International Journal of Educational Research, 13*, 21–39. doi:10.1016/0883-0355(89)90014-1

Williams, D., Caplan, S., & Xiong, L. (2007). Can you hear me now? The impact of voice in an online gaming community. *Human Communication Research, 33*(4), 427–449. doi:10.1111/j.1468-2958.2007.00306.x

Williams, D., Consalvo, M., Caplan, S., & Yee, N. (2009). Looking for gender: Gender roles and behaviors among online gamers. *The Journal of Communication, 59*(4), 700–725. doi:10.1111/j.1460-2466.2009.01453.x

Williams, D., Ducheneaut, N., Xiong, L., Zhang, Y., Yee, N., & Nickell, E. (2006). From tree house to barracks: The social life of guilds in World of Warcraft. *Games and Culture, 1*(4), 338–361. doi:10.1177/1555412006292616

Williams, D., Yee, N., & Caplan, S. E. (2008). Who plays, how much, and why? Debunking the stereotypical gamer profile. *Journal of Computer-Mediated Communication, 13*, 993–1018. doi:10.1111/j.1083-6101.2008.00428.x

Williamson, B., & Facer, K. (2004). More than just a game: the implications for schools of children's computer games communities. *Education Communication and Information, 4*(2-3), 255–270. doi:10.1080/1463631041233 1304708

Yee, N. (2005). Motivations of play in MMORPGs. *Proceedings of DiGRA 2005 Conference.*

Yee, N. (2006a). The labor of fun: How video games blur the boundaries of work and play. *Games and Culture, 1*(1), 68–71. doi:10.1177/1555412005281819

Yee, N. (2006b). Motivations for play in online games. *Cyberpsychology and behavior: The Impact of the Internet. Multimedia and Virtual Reality on Behavior and Society, 9*(6), 772–775.

Yee, N. (2006c). The demographics, motivations and derived experiences of users of massively-multiuser online graphical Environments. *Presence (Cambridge, Mass.), 15*, 309–329. doi:10.1162/pres.15.3.309

Yee, N. (2008). *Social architectures in MMOs*. Retrieved from http://www.nickyee.com/daedalus/archives/print/001625.php.

Yee, N. (2009). Befriending ogres and wood-elves: Relationship formation and the social architecture of Norrath. *Game Studies. The International Journal of Computer Game Research, 9*(1).

Yee, N., & Bailenson, J. (2007). The Proteus effect: The effect of transformed self-representation on behavior. *Human Communication Research, 33,* 271–290. doi:10.1111/j.1468-2958.2007.00299.x

Zimmerman, B. (1989). A social cognitive view of self-regulated academic learning. *Journal of Educational Psychology, 81*(3), 329–339. doi:10.1037/0022-0663.81.3.329

KEY TERMS AND DEFINITIONS

Computer Supported Collaborative Learning (CSCL): Scaffolding of collaborative and distance learning through the mediation of a computer system, usually via the internet, through appropriate computer software or e-learning platforms.

Computer Supported Collaborative Work (CSCW): Support of collaborative work via the use of relevant computer systems.

Flow Theory: A theory, in psychology, proposed by Mihály Csíkszentmihályi. Flow describes a mental state where the individual is focused, motivated and fully immersed in an activity or a task.

Intrinsic Motivation: Individual motivation that derives from the activity or the task rather than from external rewards.

Massively Multiplayer Online Games (MMOGs): Sometimes referred also as MMOs, they are video games, played over the internet and capable of supporting hundreds of thousands of players simultaneously.

Massively Multiplayer Online Role Playing Games (MMORPG): A genre of Massively Multiplayer Online Games where the players assume virtual characters (avatars) and interact with other virtual characters, often within a fantasy context.

Persistent Worlds: Virtual worlds, such as MMOGs, which exist and evolve even after the player has logged out.

Virtual Worlds: Computer simulated 3D environments, accessed through the internet, supporting interactions among users, through their virtual characters, as well as between user and environment.

ENDNOTES

[1] "There.com" has closed down since March 2010: http://www.there.com/info/announcement

[2] As part of our research, we conducted 15 semi-structured interviews of MMOGs players and 1 focus group, participated in immersive virtual ethnography in the games "Lineage II" and "Tribal Wars", and looked into MMOG-related fora and websites. It is not within the scope of the paper to extrapolate findings from this part of our research, due to the size and the selection of our sample. All volunteers to participate were interviewed.

[3] These examples are taken from three different games, namely "Lineage II", "World of Warcraft" and "EVE Online".

[4] There is a debate between narratology and ludology in game studies. Narratology views games as novel forms of narrative, while ludology supports that games should be viewed as systems in their own terms.

[5] For examples of educator resources and learning activities in "Quest Atlantis" and "River City Project" see also http://atlantis.crlt.indiana.edu/site/view/Educators, and http://muve.gse.harvard.edu/rivercityproject/curriculum_teachers.htm respectively.

Chapter 19
How Digital Gaming Enhances Non-Formal and Informal Learning

Daniel Aranda
Universitat Oberta de Catalunya, Spain

Jordi Sánchez-Navarro
Universitat Oberta de Catalunya, Spain

ABSTRACT

This study presents the results of three investigations on the use of digital gaming in non-formal (leisure institutions) and informal (household context) education. These are: (1) an empirical enquiry on the uses and perceptions of Spanish teenagers in relation to digital technologies as tools for leisure and socialization, (2) an intervention in a public school in Barcelona, in which this chapter analyzes the introduction of video games in the context of leisure activities, and (3) a workshop for families to discuss the cultural and social significance of the use of video games in the household. The results of these experiences have allowed for observation of the youth in their environment and verification that their uses of technology and attitudes towards digital gaming have a great potential for non-formal and informal learning.

INTRODUCTION

The debate over the use of video games is one of the most lively and omnipresent in our public discussions regarding contemporary media, especially in those areas where entertainment and educational practices converge. When most parents and teachers think about video games, they show an obvious concern about the dynamics of use among the younger population in issues, such as excessive consumption or overuse of violence in some games.

Schools, as the formal education institution of reference, have long reflected and investigated the possibilities of introducing different digital resources into the classroom, including video games. The aim of these interventions, without going into too much detail, is to improve the quality and effectiveness of school educational practices and processes.

With respect to educational institutions that work in the field of non-formal or leisure educa-

DOI: 10.4018/978-1-60960-495-0.ch019

tion, this reflection and experimentation with digital leisure resources has not yet been carried out. Despite the fact that these institutions use the traditional game as an educational tool, digital gaming is still seen as the enemy they have to fight against.

In relation to informal learning, the family and household context is one of the most important settings where informal learning takes place, and at the same time, is also the primary location where the activity of playing video games occurs. On most occasions, the conversations around video games in the household revolve around the time spent on them or the kind of games that the youngsters play. On the contrary, the conversations regarding how to play or the ways of achieving some of the goals of the game are not common.

This study provides some conclusions of three activities or research projects in the field of leisure education and informal learning related to children, teens, and parents regarding video games (or better stated, digital gaming and tinkering with digital technologies) as tools that can potentially enrich their institutional or family activities and relationships. Taking into account that aiding access to Information and Communication Technologies (ICTs) is a primordial aim in any contemporary educational project, this study states that it is necessary to go one step beyond, thus using and reinforcing ICTs as significant personal and social objects. We need to integrate new digital technologies, which obviously include video games, into our daily lives, involving education and family context, as video games can be powerful tools in the sense that they can be used to work on group social cohesion as well as to reflect about effort, frustration, and pleasure. Thus, three activities are presented in this study on the use of video games in non-formal (leisure institutions) and informal (household context) education: (1) an empirical research embedded in a larger project funded by the Spanish Ministry of Industry, which aims to integrate resources and digital tools, including video games, in the space of non-formal educa-

tion in collaboration with the Catalan Esplai Foundation – an organization that mobilizes more than 15,000 children and youngsters; (2) a digital classroom in a public school in Barcelona in the context of leisure activities; and (3) a set of workshops for families on the cultural and social significance of the use of video games, funded by the autonomous administration of Catalonia.

With regard to the nature of the cultural and social transformation in a digital environment, it is obvious that the new generations are growing up in a social and cultural context in which sharing is associated with social networks like ©Facebook or peer-to-peer networks; buying or selling is related to Ebay© or Amazon©; creating is linked to blogging; and collecting information is associated with using Google© or the Wikipedia©. Beyond labels and stereotypes, most of the studies on the activities of youth in these digital environments state that these activities profoundly affect the way they work, study, collaborate, communicate, and solve problems. Common sense seems to assume that the so-called digital natives are completely immersed in the world of video games. In contrast, the results of our quantitative research in Spain show that only 42.4% of the young people from 12 to 18 years of age usually play video games.

Given that the cultural context that surrounds us is increasingly digital, the digital game might play an important role in the leisure context of individuals in our society. It is now widely accepted that for any culture to be reproduced, it needs to be played. There is no culture without game, because culture is not merely a compilation of texts, works, and images, but a whole set of processes that allow us to think, relate, and be entertained. Culture cannot be developed without a playful context because "culture is [and developed] in the shape of a game," as claimed by Huizinga (1994, p. 67). There is no doubt at this point that (traditional) gaming is a tool for social and cultural learning, in particular in the stages related to childhood. However, there are still many who see digital game as a stranger, as a threat that promotes violence or social isolation.

In order to explore the potential of video games is undoubtedly helpful to establish a definition that allows structural analysis. By picking up the definitions that have been constructed historically, we have offered one of our own. We understand videogame as the rule-based systems with goals that must be overcome with the effort and interaction of the players and their emotional bond, which are implemented through software and through computers, game consoles, and other platforms.

With regard to the practical proposals, in recent years, our research group SPIDER (Smarter People through Interactive Digital Entertainment Resources) has been working to explore the tools and devices related to digital entertainment (video games, social networks, mobile phones, and other portable devices) as potential resources for education. The various research projects in which we work are aimed at studying the technology in entertainment, and their use and application in the leisure space for children, young people, and parents, in both non-formal educational institutions and household context.

THE MEANING OF DIGITAL GAMING

Before tackling the description of the landscape shaped by the uses of digital game technologies and the depiction of the experiences above mentioned, in this section we outline a reflection on the meaning of gaming and tinkering with digital media within contemporary culture. To frame the subject, we must first analyze how young people are building their relationships with digital technologies in general and video games in particular.

Video games, like any other cultural resource, are basic tools for learning and socialization, which provide the player with social and instrumental skills. From our point of view, video games are communication products that respond to the desire and need of many children, youngsters, and

adults to be entertained, and above all, to enhance different aspects of their social identity. We also suggest that video games generate contexts that foster digital literacy, problem-solving, and decision-making skills among young people. As stated by Gee (2004a), video games are particularly good learning tools in which people learn to situate meanings through experience. The games promote learning in the player (which could be a student), seducing him/her to try to overcome a problem, devote effort, and finally, achieve some significant success. There is no doubt, at this point, that game (traditional) is a learning tool for social and cultural development, especially during child-related stages. However, there are still many who see digital game as a stranger and as a threat that promotes violence or social isolation. This is, in fact, a part of a larger debate in which the young constitutes a fundamental concern in relation to the broader field of ICT use and consumption. These kinds of contributions are built around the heralding of the young as "the digital generation," which "is claimed to represent the future, being 'in the vanguard'; yet it is also vulnerable, at risk from new information and communication technologies" (Livingstone, 2003, p.148).

The Young and Digital Technologies

Indeed, with regard to research that tackles the relationships between the young and digital technologies, the outcome of the reports easily falls, and all too often, into the youth-as-digital-generation heralding trend. Arguably, this effect is due to the plain fact that people appropriate these technologies, just as any other, in straightforwardly natural ways according to the needs, obligations, interests, and preferences that are significant of their everyday lives and contexts. Thus, notwithstanding the complexity of the factors involved in these processes (Lin, 2003), it seems altogether logical that the young, upon having access to these technologies at an early age than other media technologies, try to make the most of their technical traits and possibilities insofar as they can (or are allowed to) afford a minimum time to tinker with them. Within this framework, children and adolescents are usually regarded "as a special object of study, as a homogenous category" (Livingstone, 2003, p. 148) with the capability to appropriate digital technologies in completely different and innovative ways, when compared with their elders. The images thus range from the natural child computer user, i.e., the perceived "transformative capabilities of the use of IT when in the hands of children" and the adult child computer user, i.e., children as teachers for adults with regard to the use of digital technologies, to the child computer addict, i.e., the victimized child computer user and the "needy" child, i.e., children lacking the necessary skills to make the most, as conceived by adults, of these technologies (Selwyn, 2003).

Accordingly, we may consider one aspect that is essential concerning the debate over the young's access to digital technologies. We must indeed pay special attention to the household, because "the family plays a key role in [children's] introduction to […] technologies" (McMillan & Morrison, 2006, p. 88), within what is usually a media-saturated environment, at least in places where ICT use is becoming thoroughly widespread, and thus, a primary site for people's appropriation of media and ICTs. Interestingly, the terms of the discussion very often come down to time-related issues concerning the frequency and total amount of time spent by children and adolescents with media and technology (Dickinson et al., 2001; Hagen, 2007), which, in turn, even though are apparently value-free, carry a significant sociocultural weight. Nevertheless, the values underlying these domestic generational negotiations constitute a projection of the larger cultural, institutional, corporate, and academic debate, because they deal precisely with the wonder-and-concern perception of technological developments and their sociocultural significance, and thus, with the combination between advocacy and warnings regarding the use

of digital technologies by children and teens. These opposing values are often summarized within the notions of "hedonic/instrumental dichotomy" or "work/play dichotomy" (McMillan & Morrison, 2006, pp. 80–83).

The Young and Video Games

In the case of video games, we suggest that playing (and playing video games) is, as claimed by Goldstein, Buckingham, and Brougére (2004), an activity that strengthens social bonds and self-esteem. Video games and gaming, in general, improves the quality of our social relations by allowing spaces of relaxation and pleasure. Play is, in short, a way to minimize the consequences of our actions, and thus, a way of learning in less risky situations. The idea that has guided our research and intervention proposals is that video games not only satisfy the need for recreational pleasure, but they become experimental laboratories for emotional and social development, as evidenced by Williamson and Facer (2004) and Jansz and Marten (2005), among others.

Video games not only allow young (and not so young) people to strengthen social bonds with their peers, and at the same time, enhance their networks for material exchange (videogame copies, magazines, and consoles), but also aid in knowledge exchange (walkthroughs, tricks, or passwords). Understanding what playing video games means obviously requires thinking about what happens in the hardware—software—player interaction, as well as, more importantly, thinking about a bunch of processes related to discussion, evaluation, comparison, exchange, social relations, and identity construction of players. Mia Consalvo (2007), by collecting the concept of *cultural capital* as coined by Bourdieu, developed the idea of *gaming capital,* to understand individuals' interaction with games, information about games, the game industry, and other players. Becoming a member of the gaming community does not mean just playing, or even playing well, but mastering the secrets of the game and being able to disseminate this knowledge among peers. Furthermore, the gaming experience is a complex phenomenon that takes place in a social context (Mäyrä, 2007). There are many reasons to support the notion that it is necessary to have a more comprehensive view of the player's experience as something that occurs not only during the play session, but as a broader phenomenon. The gaming experience is predefined and postmodified by multiple dimensions that are a part of several networks of meaning. To focus the research on what playing a videogame means, we advocate for a better understanding of the sociocultural extension of these structures of meaning. We honestly presume that we cannot investigate the gaming experience in laboratory conditions, detached from the experiences and social networks that are the real testing ground in which the game experience takes place.

We have developed our interventions from this conceptualization of video games as tools for situated learning, as social acts, as social and emotional laboratories, and from the consideration of gaming capital as an observable phenomenon. On the one hand, these interventions are boosting activities in themselves, and hence, have been submitted to the educational project of leisure-based educational institutions. On the other hand, it is an ongoing research, guided by the certainty that only participant observation can thoroughly map out how the young use video games and connect them with their lives. Therefore, though several theoretical approaches may be useful to reveal some aspects of our research, we consider that it is, at this point, grounded on empirical observation.

YOUTH AND DIGITAL ENTERTAINMENT IN SPAIN

A necessary second step in order to observe the complexity of the relationship of young people with video games is effectively determine their uses and perceptions by obtaining a set of quantitative data. This data would eventually reveal the big picture in which the research on the potential of video games for non-formal and informal learning makes sense.

The everyday life of adolescents takes place in contexts characterized by the increasing presence of different kinds of media involving digital technologies. Computers, video games, the Internet, digital cameras, or mobile phones are basic in their lives, being essential tools to communicate, share, consume, participate, and create. In fact, as has been argued in recent years (Tabernero et al., 2008, 2009), the number of teens who actively create and maintain spaces for communication, self-presentation, and contribution is growing. In this context, it is clear that such activities are necessarily associated with the ways of adoption of these technologies, tools, and services for youth, having a significant effect on the dynamics of production and skills development with regard to social, cultural, and educational aspects. In this sense, some argue that it is precisely the young who are contributing in a particularly eloquent way in developing a participatory culture, characterized by a greater ease of expression and civic engagement. In this new culture, knowledge, whether it is social, cultural, or technical, is shared informally. This sharing constitutes one of the main factors in peer recognition (Jenkins et al., 2008). Thus, youth acquires network capital, i.e., knowledge associated with the contribution to the community by sharing their experiences and views on new spaces of support, sociability, and recognition that they generate and develop (Rheingold, 2002). Thus, the activity articulated through the tools and services of digital technologies, such as online social networks, can be understood as collaborative non-formal learning spaces, sustained by relations of friendship and/or interest (Ito et al., 2008). The social use of video games has a prominent place in this emerging digital culture (Gee, 2004b).

An Empirical Observation

Our research made an attempt to explore the communicative practices and cultural consumption of adolescents related to the use of digital technologies through a nationwide survey conducted in Spain. The objective of this survey was to establish the actual uses that young people make of these technologies, and thereby, to have more arguments to analyze their potentialities as informal learning spaces. For the purposes of the case being analyzed here, we were particularly interested in gathering data about video-game uses as well as the perceptions and opinions about them. In this sense, the survey is primarily a tool to get a picture of the social context in which digital gaming is employed in our surroundings.

According to the ideas commonly expressed in popular informal discussions on video games, one would think that they represent a serious public health problem. Thus, in this debate, it is not uncommon to hear or read that: (1) All young people play video games and spend much of their time on this activity, (2) Video games are targeted only at boys, while girls do not play because the contents are sexist and prevent them for feeling comfortable, (3) The activity of playing video games prevents young people to do other things traditionally considered healthier, like going out with friends, (4) Video games promote youth isolation and alienation, and (5) Young people are not aware of the risks that come with playing video games. Even though academic research has debunked these myths (Jenkins, 2004), the above-mentioned statements are a part of many public discourses that often underlie the debate on video games. Our intention was, first, to determine to what extent the image that data drew corresponded to these popular intuitions, and, second, to draw a context that would allow us to better understand the current relationship of youth with technologies, in this case, the video games. Consequently, it should be stated that the survey design and approach to the resulting data

did not pursue the goal of validating the results or intuitions clearly defined in advance, but tried to obtain empirical data on the forms and determine the factors of the relationship between young people and technologies.

Procedure and Sample

The results of this survey were based on telephone interviews among a sample of Spanish teenagers. The population consisted of all teenagers between 12 and 18 years of age living in Spain (a total of 3,044,131 inhabitants, excluding those living in the Canary Islands, Ceuta, and Melilla). Overall, this population generated a final sample of 2,054. The number of telephone interviews followed a distribution proportional to the Spanish population both by gender and age. From this premise, 51.7% of the interviews were conducted with men and 48.3% with women. With respect to age, 53.9% of the interviews were conducted with boys and girls between 12 and 15 years of age, and 46.1% were conducted with those between 16 and 18 years of age. Additionally, the sample was also segmented by the size of the place of residence. The sampling procedure followed a multistage selection of persons according to the following scheme: (a) primary sampling units: municipalities, randomly selected, (b) secondary sampling units: households, by random selection of phone numbers, and (c) the ultimate sampling units: individuals, by selection of person between 12 and 18 years of age. Besides the segmentation variables of the sample, a set of additional variables such as place of birth or extracurricular or leisure activities that characterize the profile of this population group were also included.

The questionnaire consisted of 85 questions divided into several sections. The first section was conducted with parents to obtain the sociodemographic data. At the end of this section, the interviewer requested the consent of the parents to carry out interview with the boy or girl living in the house. The second section was designed to gather data on the characteristics of boys and girls, with regard to their current level of education and extracurricular activities, to determine the constraints for the interviewee's management of time. The third section consisted of questions concerning the use, perception, and parental control of the Internet and tools, such as instant messaging and social networks. The fourth section consisted of questions concerning the use, perception, and parental control of video games.

A pilot test was carried out between 5 and 6 March 2009, in which a total of 51 consultations were conducted in the region of Catalonia. The results obtained were used to reorder, reformulate, and adapt some of the questions, a factor that led to gather more reliable data through the improvement of the questionnaire. Finally, the fieldwork was carried out between 16 March and 1 April 2009 by the reputable market research company Instituto Opina.

Results and Discussion

As mentioned earlier, the use of video games among teenagers is often one of the key points of debate about the relationship between youth and consumption of new media. Aspects such as access to relevant content regarding the age of the players and matters related to addiction and alienation of social life in adolescents are standard arguments that are discussed at all levels (academic, administrative, public). Overall, according to the data obtained in this study, only 42.4% of the adolescents in Spain usually play video games.

Table 1. Do you usually play video games?

Total	42.4
Male from 12 to 15 years	67.1
Male from 16 to 18 years	56.6
Female from 12 to 15 years	27.1
Female from 16 to 18 years	14.1

Table 1 reports the data by gender and age group. In this respect, there are significant differences in relation to gender and age (confirmed by preliminary regression analysis): first, boys (62.3% of total) are found to play more than girls (21.0%); second, younger teen players, between 12 and 15 years of age (47.9%), are observed to be more common than those between 16 and 18 years of age (35.9%). The average age at which teens begin to play is found to be 9.3 years.

For most who do not play video games (57.6%), the main argument, so far, is the lack of interest (I'm not interested, 79.2%) and the next argument is the lack of time (12.2%) (see Table 2).

The average time that young people spent playing games was observed to be 5.2 hours per week, and the most common playing place was their own room (49.0%) and the living room (40.8%). While younger teens tended to play more in the evenings and at weekends and in the common living spaces of the home, older teens played more at night and in the private environment of their room. In relation to the average time spent, there were differences with regard to age and gender: 6.3 hours per week for those between 16 and 18 years of age, when compared with 4.4 hours for those between 12 and 15 years of age, and 5.9 hours for boys, when compared with 2.8 hours for girls.

Moreover, a large majority of the players (72.6%) personally decided on the kind of games

Table 2. Which is the main reason why you do not usually play?

I have not got a console	4.6
I am not allowed to by my parents	2.0
I am not interested	79.2
Lack of time	12.2
I prefer to spend my time in the Internet	0.9
Video games cause addiction	0.3
I prefer to spend my time with my friends	0.5
Refuse to answer	0.2

Table 3. Who do you usually talk about video games with?

Parents	36.2
Relatives	56.8
Friends	85.5
Classmates	77.9
Teachers	6.9
People I have met online, but not in person	27.1
Friends' friends	50.5

that they acquired. In this context, it is not surprising that a majority (51.3% of the adolescent boys and girls) claimed to have no rules at home about the use of video games. When there are parent rules, they are primarily related to the time spent (time, days of the week that they can play). Only 14.4% reported that parents had some kind of control on the type of games they could or could not play.

An interesting question to examine video games as a cultural resource capable of generating the above-mentioned gaming capital, which could be used by young people in their social relations in particular contexts, is: Who do you usually talk about video games with? Table 3 shows the answers to this question.

Friends and classmates were the people with whom they mostly talked about video games, while parents were much less common partners. The preliminary regression analysis confirmed that girls, in general, but especially those between 12 and 15 years of age, have significantly closer relationships with parents when playing or talking about video games. With regard to the social habits associated with the use of video games, 66.3% of adolescent boys and girls usually played alone in Spain. However, 52.2% played with friends and 43.3% played with siblings. Fathers and mothers, in contrast, appeared just as companions and playmates in 7.8% of the responses.

With regard to their perceptions, and contrary to what one might expect, the majority of the teen population recognized that they "prefer to go out with friends than playing video games" (89.2%), which is a proof of the fact that video games do not necessarily become substitutes of their everyday social life. Moreover, they preferred playing video games to watching television (49.9%), which illustrates the strong competition between the different modes of technologies available at home. It might be strange, but significant numbers of videogame players attributed some openly positive characteristics associated with sociability, their welfare, and notably, learning, to video games: 31.6% of the players said that video games allow them to make friends; 39.3% said that they were more relaxed after playing; and 45.3% said that video games allow them to learn things.

In summary, the findings of this survey reveal that young people do not play as long as stated by those who defend the idea of video games as a sort of epidemic. The findings also show that gaming activity is just one among a set of activities consistent with their socialization and learning processes, and that the risks associated with digital gaming does not seem to be as many as some may presume. Moreover, young people themselves are aware of the numerous possibilities with regard to socialization and learning that video games have.

THE DIGITAL CLASSROOM

As mentioned earlier, one of our practical proposals was to create a digital classroom in a public school (32 boys and girls in their last year of primary school, 11 and 12 years of age) in Barcelona in the context of what we call in Spain, an Esplai Center. An Esplai center is an educational and nonprofit organization working for the comprehensive education of children and young people outside the formal educational system. In these sort of non-formal educational facilities, children and teens learn by doing and playing values of equality, democracy, peace, cooperation, or friendship (among others) through a set of activities (conceived as educational tools), such as drama, music, nature, sport, game, craft, or trip. In this educational methodology context, we created a digital classroom where we endeavored to provide the first impetus to those working in the field of leisure education centres (Esplais) to see video games as a tool that could potentially enrich their educational project. The project's aim was to explore and document the results of introducing digital games as educational tools in non-formal education.

Although we had mentioned earlier that the debate on video games is biased by some prejudices unproven empirically, i.e., video games promote the isolation of young people and, therefore, they are a waste of time, we must state that professionals of non-formal education are not strangers to these preconceptions. On the contrary, we propose that quotidian culture or everyday culture, which is not valued but which we live each day, including those resources that form a part of young people's digital leisure, needs to be a part of the educational toolkit for all those proposals that see leisure as an opportunity for investment. In the explained case, rather than denouncing the existence of violence or socially undesirable cultural models and extrapolating the effects in terms of antisocial behavior and consequences, we wanted to study the meaning of the social uses of these artifacts, bearing in mind that, as stated by Salen and Zimmerman (2004), playing video games is related to experience, meaning, pleasure, or simulation.

Hence, the classroom was set up in the school's computer room, which had 16 computers connected to the Internet. Alongside the room's own infrastructure, we also installed a PlayStation 2©, a PlayStation 3©, a Nintendo Wii©, two Nintendo DS Lite©, and an Xbox 36©0. Plans were made for 14 workshop sessions on Mondays and Wednesdays from 1:30 pm to 2:30 pm, under supervision from an instructor responsible for the classroom and two members of the research group. Our presence was aimed, on the one hand, to offer support to the instructor and to ensure that the strategies and dynamics agreed to by the research group were met; and, on the other hand, to act as participants and observers, and to take charge of the proper audiovisual recording of each of the sessions.

The first session was dedicated to presenting the proposal to the 32 boys and girls who were signed up for the school dinner service. Given the need to have a small number of participants in the digital classroom, the decision was taken to create two groups of around 15 to take turns. The first turn involved observation by the research group, the second, during the month of June, allowed the other children to take part and not be left out of the project that was so exciting for them, as is the prospect of playing cutting-edge video games in a non-formal educational context.

The choice of turns and the make-up of the groups were decided by lottery. The name of each child was placed in a bag and the first 16 names pulled out entered the first group, and the rest, the second. The boys and girls celebrated enthusiastically, with cries of joy and embraces, not because fortune saw them form a part of the first group, from April 20 to June 6, but for the fact that the groups of friends were not broken up. The vast majority of the children chosen to form a part of the first group had sufficient friends with them to feel happy about the result. The group of boys and girls who were to form a part of the second group were equally satisfied with the results, despite having to wait another month to take part in the activity. It should also be pointed out that three girls decided, voluntarily, not to take part in the video games workshop, even before the draw was made; however, they were not the only ones; two more girls turned down the chance to take part as one of their friends who had already pulled out asked them to.

In short, this shows that video games are not, on their own, exciting enough to break up a group of friends. The gaming experience has to be enjoyed as a group. In other words, the pleasure, in this case associated with video games, is greater and more desirable when enjoyed socially.

Likewise, this fact reinforces the need to overcome the myth of the asocial and solitary game player, which is very much rooted among educators and their non-formal methods. Newman (2004, p. 146), citing the work of Carsten Jensen (1995), stated that "the suspicion about the content is however only one side of the widespread scepticism about computer games. Another, far more serious criticism is levelled at the influence of the medium on children's social relations. It is a common assumption that computer games lead to children becoming socially isolated, all in their separate rooms where they engage in a lone struggle in the artificial universes of the games. In other words, the computer destroys social relations and playing."… As Jensen follows: "Fortunately that is not so. In fact children rarely play alone, and computer games are about more than the actual game. Contrary to appearances, the computer and the games are absorbed into the existing children's culture." (Jensen, 1999, p. 158).

Cultural consumption, and the consumption of video games, has to be understood as a participative, social, and cooperative activity, similar to traditional play. As stated by Vigotski (quoted by Delval, 1994), playing is a social activity where, owing to the cooperation with others, we can take on roles that are complementary to our own. Playing is a social activity, a shared activity that forms a part of a network made up of people, tools, and technologies. Notable examples of this configuration of playing as a social activity were seen throughout the activity. The session dedicated to the Space Invaders© game was, for example, the quietest and most productive of all. The fact that each player had their own position, but, at the same time, were playing in a competition involving all of them created a very special feeling of communal participation.

The following sessions were organized to present the video games that were to form a part of the proposals for the workshop. Nine proposals were presented: four by the participants themselves and the other five chosen by the workshop's instructors. The list of games presented was as follows: Wii Sports©, the PS3's© MotorStorm©, Space Invaders© and King Kong© for PC, Rayman© for the Wii©, Pro Evolution Soccer© and Guitar Hero© for the Xbox 360©, and finally, Dance Factory© and MotoGP 4© for the PS2©.

The first half an hour of each session was spent explaining the characteristics of the games, the group's reasons for presenting the proposal, and its interest. The second half an hour was devoted to playing freely. It should be pointed out that the definitive list of games presented was to be voted on and only four from the total chosen, and only these four formed a part of the list of games to be used during the workshop.

The results, with respect to the competences, know-how, knowledge, or cultural capital that they had acquired, whether because they were videogame players, or because they had read about them in magazines or on websites, was virtually nonexistent. They were not able to offer reasons or justification for their proposals, or the pleasure they gained as players, beyond obvious factors or those highlighted by the games' advertising campaigns. In MotorStorm's© presentation, they valued the spectacular graphics and spatial simulation, as well as the spectacular simulation of the physical behavior of the vehicles or the represented crashes. In this case, the element valued was simply the spectacular nature, which is, similarly, the main argument used in the advertising campaign for this product, one of the first latest generation games to appear on the PlayStation 3©. In another case, in the presentation of Pro Evolution Soccer 6©, the focus was again on the fidelity of the graphic representation and its playability (a concept which they used without really knowing what it meant) being better or worse than FIFA 07©; likewise, discussion centred on the licenses required representation of the actual teams and players, i.e., all those debates that are to be found in the magazines or on the internet.

The time spent playing freely allowed us to see that there was no fear in terms of putting their skills to the test in public, in front of schoolmates. There was no fear of failure. The classroom was a safe haven where mistakes formed a part of the playing, and their aim was to improve and dominate a range of skills including coordination, rhythm, or strategy. While in real life, mistakes are penalized, in the context of playing video games, mistakes are the dynamic strategy that allows players to practice, try new strategies, and eventually progress. Likewise, mistakes generated collaboration dynamics between boys and girls. Those who were well versed in the basic routines and skills offered their know-how to the rest with the aim of improving the group's competence. Social spaces were established where the game was the object of discussion and evaluation, given that, as Frith (1996) stated, part of the pleasure of popular culture is talking about it; part of its meaning is this talk.

One of the signs from this initial stage of the research was that "there is no support for some of the common beliefs about the possibilities of computer games as educational media, at least when educational outcome is supposed to be the learning of specific curricular topics represented in the theme of the game" (Linderoth et al., 2004) However, the one which is strengthened by video games is the catalyzing and building of social structures that encourage discussion and sharing of knowledge. For example, in the case of the session on Space Invaders, the players acquired competences in the use of computers for playing games and finding resources for casual play (quick games), and found out about a virtual community of players. In the case of Wii© and Dance Factory©, the players acquired technological skills in the use of alternative controllers, such as using their own body at the same time as using the game's remote controller. Other know-how worked on in the presentations included knowledge of the physical simulation in games (in MotorStorm©: acceleration and simulation of impact; or in Virtual

Tennis: direction, rebounds, and force of impact). Thus, players quickly became familiar with the aspects of physical simulation increasingly used in game design.

The research, despite still being in an embryonic stage, has highlighted that video games, contrary to the common beliefs (Jensen, 1995; Jenkins, 2004), are tools that could enhance some educational objectives in the context of non-formal education systems such as Esplais Centers.

Thus, the main results from the pilot can be summarized in three statements:

1. The pleasure associated with video games is greater and more desirable when enjoyed socially, and is not directly related to social isolation.
2. No fear of failure. Mistakes are the dynamic that allows learning the rules of the game, and thus, effort, concentration, and communication are required.
3. The know-how, the cultural capital regarded with video games, is very poor at these ages, and Esplais Centers can be the place where this capital cultural can be enriched.

In summary, children and teens have to be in contact with playful contexts with regard to the so-called Information or Digital Society. Digital gaming is one of the practices, as traditional games, that help us to a better understand our current digital society. Non-formal education has a key role in transforming the negative myths of video games into an opportunity to work with values, senses, or tools that are, and will be, a part of our culture.

THE FAMILY WORKSHOPS

Over the last months of 2008 and early 2009, SPIDER developed, together with the media cooperative Drac Magic, a series of workshops funded by the Department of Family Policies and Citizens Rights of the Generalitat de Catalunya, to promote responsible use and a more complete understanding of the complexity of the cultural phenomenon of video games. In these workshops, we observed and talked to the participants (families with children) about the numerous possibilities of interaction that a videogame offers, emphasizing proactive demands and social requirements of video games with the intention of providing alternative viewpoints to the common assumptions seeded in the collective imagination, such as player addiction or isolation. As Ito states, the "instances of families' spending time together in and around new media, (is) a practice not commonly discussed in much of the literature on the generation gap" (Ito et. al., 2010). Second, in these workshops, we proposed an analysis of the imagery of video games, connecting their symbolic strategies with the logic of communication and the contemporary entertainment industry. Factors such as the spectacular and the sensational attraction of violent representation were treated as complex communication phenomena, observing and discussing the way video games, just like the media, in general, deal with fiction in a challenging, sometimes disturbing, way, both to provide information and establish their own and specific entertainment dynamics. With this proposal, we tried to give some clues to address the use of video games as a responsible and creative activity within family life and household environment.

The need to generate a dynamic of family work is given by two certainties: the first is that there is no doubt that video games are nowadays the most significant part of the whole young leisure toolkit. The second is that there is a noticeable gap between what children and young people know (or want to) about video games and the knowledge that parents can give to their children. Thus, what is important in an experience, like in these workshops, is to provide a framework to establish discussions that generate knowledge about the game, to promote a proactive use.

In general, we described the proposed activity as an exercise for 2 hours in two parts. In the first part, a simulation of a game was used. In this case, the simulation was a complete game previously played and recorded. The person in charge of the workshop, sometimes a member of the research team, commented on the game, stopping the recording at the proper moments to facilitate reflection on the game and its demands. With this exercise, we were able to discuss how concentration and engagement were key factors, not only to play, but to optimize the strategies and skills of the players in relation to the challenges proposed by the game system.

In the second part of the exercise, the person responsible for the workshop provided the opportunity to parent–children teams to play together with one of the leading game consoles: the Nintendo Wii©. The objective of this second part, and the purpose of the overall experience, was not only the achievement of the objectives of the game, but to explore the relational dynamics that emerge when dealing with a game, such as organization, responsibility, coordination, playing according to standards and rules, or reinventing the game itself, dynamics that were evident in the gameplay. Finally, the workshops ended with the screening of a short documentary used as a guide for further reflection on the representational and narrative orders proposed by video games. By means of comparing the internal logic of videogame storytelling with those of other media content, the participants were able to outline the significant practices of gamers, paying particular attention to the critical analysis of the similarities and differences between games and other media content consumed through film and television.

The game that held the design of the workshops was *Lego Star Wars The Complete Saga©*, a game that shows that one of the main traits of contemporary popular culture is what Henry Jenkins (2006) called as transmedia storytelling. Briefly, transmedia storytelling is a process in which the integral elements of fiction are systematically dispersed by multiple distribution channels to create a unified and coordinated entertainment experience. Despite neither being a canonical example nor a particularly significant example, a relatively close reading of *Lego Star Wars©* was a good starting point that allowed us to introduce the concept into the debate to very young people and parents who were not used to think critically about the entertainment industries. In the field of transmedia storytelling, *Lego Star Wars©* is a worthy case study because of its double position in two streams of entertainment experiences. On the one hand, the game is obviously just one of the many pieces in the transmedia discourse of the Star Wars© universe, because, together with films, animated series, comic books, toys, and other video games, it is a part of the complex set of products in which the franchise is deployed. On the other hand, the game is clearly integrated into the Lego© universe, not only because the product Lego Star Wars© is an established part of the supply of the toy company, but mainly because it incorporates into the gameplay procedures and tactics derived from the experience of mounting Lego blocks. However, understanding Lego Star Wars© as a transmedia piece involves paying more attention to its potential than to that offered in the first instance, because it is possible to complete the game without drawing a greater knowledge of the plot and the world of Star Wars when, paradoxically, it is played in the *story mode.* In that case, what we have is a playable adaptation of the main action sequences of the films in the series, and the player's success depends less on the prior knowledge of the films, owing to the strict adherence to the rules of each of the genres and specific codes in which the gameplay is embodied. In essence, playing the story mode in Lego Star Wars© is like stepping into the highlights of each of the motion pictures to solve the different challenges for the sole purpose of progressively progressing in the events predetermined by the plot of the films already known. This is, without doubt, the immediate and easy way to dive into the gaming and narrative experience that the game offers.

For example, to complete the Episode V – *The Return of the Jedi* – the player has to overcome two levels – *The Battle of Hoth* (1) and *Persecution in the asteroids* (3) – which are pure shooters that must be solved through the use of different ships, weapons, and combat strategies. The other four levels are action adventures that include cooperative puzzles. As each character has its own characteristics —the robots can open doors, while the human (or humanoid) characters can shoot, jump, push blocks, and drive or ride animals— the problem-solving strategies must take into account the proper selection of characters to perform tasks in a sort of dynamic that should ideally be played by two players. Nevertheless, a single player can, and have to, run dozens of different actions to solve all the problems that the game unfolds: run, jump, shoot, connect remotely to control mechanisms through robots, capturing, drag and firing torpedoes, get through obstacles with the help of a hook, drag blocks, ride different animals, trigger several mechanisms, and even dress up in costumes to unlock certain doors. By being a Jedi character, the player can enter melee combats with the lightsaber, use the weapon to deflect enemy fire, and above all, use the Force to solve puzzles. All these comprise a maximum guideline to be followed: pick up pieces and assemble Lego blocks. The rest of the levels follow the same outline design: genres and codes are combined and the player is allowed to discover the internal logic of each of them. In addition, the game offers the chance to go collecting hidden objects such as Lego Minikits and increase power. All the rewards that the game offers are helpful to progress and conclude the story, which is, at the same time, the way to unlock new characters that delves into one of the most utilized strategies in contemporary game design: the collector eagerness. The unlockable stuff and second-best rewards improve, by far, the gaming experience, because they manifest potentialities, i.e., enrich the game with promises of future.

Returning to the dynamics of the workshops, we can say that the first subject discussed by the instructors of the workshops was the narrative nature of the game and its association with a transmedia discourse. More specifically, topics for discussion were the links between the six films and the game, as well as the link between the knowledge needed to play the game and the knowledge about the specific movie the game is based on. In this sense, the main question was: Is it essential to know the plot and conflicts of the movie in order to play, or can players discover the rules of the game by themselves? Another important issue is the link between the Lego toy and the game. As a part of the gameplay is based on assembling Lego bricks, a further reflection on the use of specific bricks for specific purposes emerges. The point here is to establish the skills that the player must develop to solve these kinds of puzzles. In short: What are the relations, if any, between gameplay in Lego Star Wars© and the previous experiences defined by the consumption of the film and toy-industries products?

In short, the purpose was to promote responsible use and a more complete understanding of the complexity of a cultural phenomenon like video games. In these workshops, the families had the chance to see so many opportunities for interaction offered by game to provide a certain level of nuance to assumptions installed in the collective imagination, such as addiction or waste of time. Knowing how to explain their own cultural consumption is essential, as is knowing how and what they play.

Family videogame play, similar to traditional gameplay, can provide a frame for informal socialization, and thus can enhance family communication. However, this will happen only if families jointly learn what a videogame is, or what play does mean. Promoting this kind of workshops is a way to minimize the common sense that links video games to isolation, violent behavior, or addiction, giving the parents a context to experiment the possibilities of being involved in their children's digital leisure.

However, the goal of these workshops was not only to share gaming experiences, but to reflect on the acquirement of some (gaming) capital cultural, in this case, derived from the consideration of video games as a complex set of rules that develop organization, responsibility, or coordination.

CONCLUSION

The main objective of the experiences described earlier is to thoroughly develop a background for the forthcoming phases of our project "Rethinking Digital Entertainment: a project in young people's digital socialization in leisure time." This project aims to build up methodologies, dynamics, and effective training to enable educators and leisure-time associations to integrate the current and future digital screens as an educational tool, which have become common in teenage leisure. To do so, our research group is currently carrying out a qualitative enquiry on the usage and meanings of the digital devices used within the spare time of the teenagers, as well as the practices of leisure-time educators involving these devices. In this sense, qualitative research, comprising analysis of 16 focus groups, in-depth interviews with adolescents, and participant observation of 28 new activities through pilot classrooms, will allow us to further describe and understand the processes of foundation of a symbolic space for personal expression and identity creation, and to analyze the discourses made by young people on these technologies and ways of sociability. In this future research, we would examine the concept of transfer in depth, by understanding transfer as the phenomenon of taking what youth learn in the context of digital gaming and transferring it to broader social contexts. We suggest that a fruitful research direction would be not only to study what causes transfer or what prevents it from happening, but also to indentify what counts as transfer in the context of digital gaming and how to assess when it might be taking place, bearing in mind that we are reflecting on the field of non-formal and informal learning. One final goal of this future research will be to establish the suitable methodological criteria for the use of digital media in the context of leisure education through the development of a white paper.

Recommendations

It is important to note that, according to our study, teenagers associate digital technologies primarily for entertainment and not for learning, even though it is certain that youth, through the use of these technologies, are generating spaces of sociability and recognition that are also collaborative learning spaces, though certainly not formal, sustained by everyday social circles. Sharing their experiences, concerns, and opinions through alternative spaces and leisure participation is an important vehicle for learning.

This is exactly what we wanted to highlight by using video games in non-formal learning activities. By introducing video games in leisure-based education, our intention has been to go one step further from considering these products, moving away from the superficial analysis of what games show or how they influence young people, to finding what young people do when they play. Our concluding remarks in this regard are that videogame consumption has to be understood as a participative, social, and cooperative activity, similar to that of traditional play. Digital gaming is a social activity where, owing to cooperation with others, we can take on roles that are complementary to our own. Gaming is a shared activity that forms a part of a network made up of people, tools, and technologies. In our participant observations of children and youngsters gaming freely, we could see that there was no fear in terms of putting their skills to the test in public, in front of schoolmates. There was no fear of failure. The digital classroom was a safe haven where mistakes formed a part of

the playing. The aim of those who played was to improve and to dominate a range of skills including coordination, rhythm, or strategy. Besides, the gaming experience has to be enjoyed as a group. In other words, the pleasure associated with video games was found to be greater and more desirable when enjoyed socially.

All these issues demonstrate that the activity of play cannot be understood by observing 20 or 30 minutes of a game session. The game experience has to be put in sociocultural and educational context to be understood in all of its complexity. Besides, promoting a responsible use of video games in non-formal and informal education implies a more complete understanding of the complexity of the cultural phenomena in which they are involved.

REFERENCES

Ang, I. (1985). *Watching Dallas. Soap opera and the melodramatic imagination*. London: Routledge.

Aranda, D., Sánchez-Navarro, J., & Tabernero, C. (2009). *Jóvenes y ocio digital. Uso de herramientas digitales por parte de adolescentes en España*. Barcelona: Editorial UOC.

Consalvo, M. (2007). *Cheating. Gaining advantage in video games*. Cambridge, MA: MIT Press.

Dickinson, R., Murcott, A., Eldridge, J., & Leader, S. (2001). Breakfast, time, and breakfast time: Television, food, and the organization of Cconsumption. *Television & New Media, 2*(3), 235–256. doi:10.1177/152747640100200304

Frith, S. (1996). *Performing rites*. Cambridge, MA: Harvard University Press.

Gee, J. P. (2004a). *What video games have to teach us about learning and literacy*. New York: Palgrave MacMillan.

Gee, J. P. (2004b). *Situated language and learning: A critique of traditional schooling.* New York: Routledge.

Goldstein, J., Buckingham, D., & Brougére, G. (Eds.). (2004). *Toys, games and media.* London: Lawrence Erlbaum Associates.

Hagen, I. (2007). We can't just sit the whole day watching TV: Negotiations concerning media use among youngsters and their parents. *Young, 15*(4), 369–393. doi:10.1177/110330880701500403

Huizinga, J. (1955). *Homo Ludens: A study of the play-element in culture.* Boston: The Beacon Press.

Ito, M., Horst, H. A., Bittanti, M., Boyd, D., Herr-Stepehnson, B., & Lange, P. G. (2008). *Living and learning with new media: Summary of findings from the digital youth Project.* Chicago: The MacArthur Foundation.

Ito, M., Horst, H. A., Bittanti, M., Boyd, D., Herr-Stephenson, B., & Lange, G. L. (2010). *Hanging out, messing around and geeking out: Living and learning with new media.* New York: MIT Press.

Jansz, J. (2005). The emotional appeal of violent video games for adolescent males. *Communication Theory, 3,* 219–241. doi:10.1111/j.1468-2885.2005.tb00334.x

Jansz, J., & Marten, L. (2005). Gaming at a LAN event: The social context of playing video games. *New Media & Society, 7*(3), 333–355. doi:10.1177/1461444805052280

Jenkins, H. (2004). *Reality bytes: Eight myths about video games debunked.* Retrieved from http://www.pbs.org/kcts/videogamerevolution/impact/myths.html

Jenkins, H. (2006). *Convergence culture: Where old and new media collide.* New York: New York University Press.

Jenkins, H., Purushotma, R., Clinton, K., Weigel, M., & Robison, A. J. (2008). *Confronting the challenges of participatory culture: Media education for the 21ˢᵗ century.* Chicago: The MacArthur Foundation.

Jensen, C. (1999). *Children's computer culture: Three essays on children and computers.* Retrieved from http://www.sdu.dk/~/media/Files/Information_til/Studerende_ved_SDU/Din_uddannelse/Kultur_og_formidling/WorkingPapers/08_ChildrensComputerCulture%20pdf.ash

Lin, C. A. (2003). An interactive communication technology adoption model. *Communication Theory, 13*(4), 345–365. doi:10.1111/j.1468-2885.2003.tb00296.x

Linderoth, J., Lindström, B., & Alexandersson, M. (2004). Learning with games. In Goldstein, J., Buckingham, D., & Brougére, G. (Eds.), *Toys, games and media* (pp. 157–178). London: Lawrence Erlbaum Associates.

Livingstone, S. (2003). Children's use of the Internet: Reflections on the emerging research agenda. *New Media & Society, 5*(2), 147–166. doi:10.1177/1461444803005002001

Mäyra, F. (2007). The contextual game experience: On the socio-cultural contexts for meaning in digital play. *Proceedings of DiGRA 2007 Conference: Situated Play,* (pp. 810-814). Retrieved from http://www.digra.org/dl/db/07311.12595.pdf

McMillan, S., & Morrison, M. (2006). Coming of age with the Internet. *New Media & Society, 8*(1), 73–95. doi:10.1177/1461444806059871

Newman, J. (2004). *Video games.* London: Routledge.

Rheingold, H. (2002). *Smart mobs. The next social revolution.* Cambridge, MA: Perseus Publishing.

Selwyn, N. (2003). Doing IT for the kids: Re-examining children, computers and the information society. *Media Culture & Society, 25*(3), 351–378.

Tabernero, C., Sánchez-Navarro, J., Aranda, D., & Tubella, I. (2009). Media practices, connected lives. In Cardoso, G., Cheong, A., & Cole, J. (Eds.), *Worldwide Internet: Changing societies, economies and cultures* (pp. 331–355). Macau, China: University of Macau.

Tabernero, C., Sánchez-Navarro, J., & Tubella, I. (2008). The young and the Internet: Revolution at home. When the household becomes the foundation of socio-cultural change. *Observatorio Journal, 6*, 273–291.

Williamson, B., & Facer, K. (2004). More than just a game: The implications for schools of children's computer games communities. *Education Communication and Information, 4*(2/3), 255–270. doi:10.1080/1463631041233130470 8

ADDITIONAL READING

Buckingham, D., & Scanlon, M. (2002). *Education, edutainment, and learning in the home.* Cambridge: Open University Press.

Cassell, J., & Jenkins, H. (1998). *From Barbie to Mortal Kombat: Gender and computer games.* Cambridge, MA: MIT Press.

De Certeau, M. (1984). *The Practice of Everyday Life.* Berkeley: University of California Press.

Dovey, J., & Kennedy, H. (2006). *Game cultures: Computer games as new media.* Glasgow: Open Univ. Press.

Ermy, L., & Mäyra, F. (2005). Fundamental Components of the Gameplay Experience: Analysing Immersion. *Proceedings of DiGRA 2005 Conference: Changing Views - Worlds in Play* (pp. 15-27). Retrieved from http://www.digra.org/dl/db/06276.41516.pdf

Feike, K. M., & Nicholson, M. (2001). Divided by a Common Language: Formal and Constructivist Approaches to Games. *Global Society, 15*(1), 7–25. doi:10.1080/13600820124575

Gee, J. P. (2007). *Good video games and good learning: Collected essays on video games, learning and literacy.* New York: Peter Land Publishing.

Greenhow, C., & Robelia, B. (2009). Informal learning and identity formation in online social networks. *Learning, Media and Technology, 34*(2), 119–140. doi:10.1080/17439880902923580

Grossberg, L. (1992). Is There a Fan in the House?: The Affective Sensibility of Fandom. In Lewis, L. A. (Ed.), *The Adoring Audience: Fan Culture and Popular Media* (pp. 50–65). London: Routledge.

Ito, M. (2009). *Engineering Play: A Cultural History of Children's Software.* Cambridge, MA: MIT Press.

Johnson, L., Levine, A., Smith, R., & Smythe, T. (2009). *The 2009 Horizon Report: K-12 Edition.* Austin, Texas: The New Media Consortium. Available from http://wp.nmc.org/horizon-k12-2009/

Juul, J. (2005). *Half-Real. Video games between real rules and fictional worlds.* Cambridge: MIT Press.

Livingstone, S. (2007). The challenge of engaging youth online. *European Journal of Communication, 22*(2), 165–184. doi:10.1177/0267323107076768

Livingstone, S., & Helsper, E. (2007). Gradations in digital inclusion: children, young people and the digital divide. *New Media & Society, 9*(4), 671–696. doi:10.1177/1461444807080335

Newman, J. (2008). *Playing with video games.* London: Routledge.

Perron, B. (2005). A Cognitive Psychological Approach to Gameplay Emotions. *Proceedings of DiGRA 2005 Conference: Changing Views - Worlds in Play.* Retrieved from http://www.digra.org/dl/db/06276.58345.pdf

Prensky, M. (2001). *Digital game-based learning.* New York: McGraw-Hill.

Prensky, M. (2005). *Don't Bother Me Mom – I'm learning!* St. Paul: Paragon House.

Salen, K., & Zimmerman, E. (2003). *Rules of play: Game design fundamentals.* Cambridge, MA: MIT Press.

Sherry, J. (2004). Flow and media enjoyment. *Communication Theory, 4,* 328–347. doi:10.1111/j.1468-2885.2004.tb00318.x

Sutton-Smith, B. (1979). *Play and learning.* New York: Gardner Press.

Taylor, T. L. (2006). *Play between worlds: Exploring online game culture.* Cambridge, MA: MIT Press.

Willianson, B., & Facer, K. (2004). More than 'Jus a Game': the implications for schools of children's computer game communities. *Education Communication and Information, 4*(2/3), 255–270. doi:10.1080/1463631041233304708

Wilson, K. A., Bedwell, W. L., Lazzara, E. H., Salas, E., Burke, C.S., & Estock, J.L.,… & Conkey, C. (2009). Games, Motivation, and Learning: A Research and Practice Model. *Simulation & Gaming, 40*(4), 441–467.

KEY TERMS AND DEFINITIONS

Cultural Consumption: According to a more complex theory about the interaction between producers and consumers – a theory that goes beyond the absolute figures of consumption in economic terms – we are neither the passive victims portrayed by the "critique of mass culture" school, nor are we the liberated consumers reported by many other authors. We are creative, active individuals, working with a range of cultural materials, and through a range of consumption practices, constructing and making sense of our everyday life.

Digital Gaming: In a broad sense, digital gaming includes, but is much more than, playing using software running on PCs, consoles, or portable devices. It not only encompasses a wide range of cultural and media practices, including those designed specifically to be played, but also comprises other practices that provide pleasures derived from playful tinkering with digital technologies.

Informal learning: It is defined as learning resulting from daily-life activities related to work, family, or leisure. It is often referred to as experiential learning, and can, to a certain degree, be understood as accidental learning. It is not structured in terms of learning objectives or learning time. Informal learning may be intentional, but in most cases, it is nonintentional.

Non-Formal Learning: Refers to activities that are explicitly designated as learning, which are embedded in the leisure-time associations as a part of their curricula and objectives. Non-formal learning is intentional for the educator, but not from the learner's point of view.

Social Use: Through their social use, cultural resources, such as TV programs, fashion, music, and others including video games, have become more than tools for knowledge. They have become powerful mechanisms for building our own world structure, providing us with tools for identity construction, status negotiation, and peer-to-peer sociality.

Chapter 20
Understanding Serious Gaming:
A Psychological Perspective

Priscilla Haring
VU University Amsterdam, The Netherlands

Dimitrina Chakinska
VU University Amersterdam, The Netherlands

Ute Ritterfeld
Technical University of Dortmund, Germany

ABSTRACT

This chapter argues the importance of understanding the process of serious gaming, i.e. playing a game with a purpose other than solely entertainment. Taking a psychological perspective, it focuses on the effects of the game rather than the game itself. Emphasis is put on the experience of enjoyment as a core element of a successful entertainment gaming experience, which, in turn, is a prerequisite for a successful learning experience. To identify enjoyment factors in gaming, a hierarchical model is presented which is based on empirical evidence. Based upon the Entertainment-Education theory, the authors propose a paradigm shift from motivation for game playing to implicit educational goals in serious games. A successful blending of entertainment experiences with educationally enriched content is assumed to be mediated by the experience of presence within media. Furthermore, storytelling and character development as well as socially shared experiences are identified as valuable areas for future serious game development.

INTRODUCTION

From a social science or, more specifically, a psychological perspective "serious games" do not exist. The seriousness of a game must be determined by the experience of the user instead.

DOI: 10.4018/978-1-60960-495-0.ch020

The notion that a distinct category of applications would exist outside a user's experience is not consistent with a social science philosophy. In fact, a commercial game that enriches a player's knowledge of any valuable content can no doubt be serious and desirable in its effect. We hereby argue that in principle any game can be a serious game. In contrast, an acclaimed serious game does not necessarily result in educational impact at all. The genre itself is mainly driven by design purposes or content advocates. But the development intention does not necessarily match the effect of the game play. The effects, however, may be more or less educational or entertaining, or possibly even both. Consequently, social scientists do not investigate serious games but the processes, mechanisms, and experiences involved in serious gaming.

This chapter starts with a definition of play and games and elaborates on the key factors that define them, e.g. free, separate, uncertain, unproductive, governed and make-believe (Caillois, 1957). Next we will touch upon the seeming contradiction of being playful and serious at the same time, building on the assumption that enjoyment is at the core of an entertaining gaming experience and needs to be harvested if serious gaming is to be successful. As enjoyment itself is a complex construct it requires differentiating between various qualities associated with serious gaming. The "Big Five", a hierarchical model of game enjoyment developed on the basis of empirical evidence, is presented. In the following section we turn to the educational component embedded in games and how this component is linked to the entertainment experience. A summary of several theoretical models of Entertainment-Education is given that describe how to connect enjoyment with education. In these models, the gaming experience becomes the explicit motivation for playing the game, while the educational goals remain rather implicit. However, even an enriched blend of meaningful content with enjoyable game play may fail to elicit the desired learning response in some players. Special emphasis will therefore be given to the limitations of motivation for learning, learning goals, competing contexts and selection. We hypothesize that the key to a successful blend of entertainment with education lays in the experience of non-mediation and intrinsic motivation, facilitated by the experience of presence. The most commonly found forms of presence, spatial, social and self presence, are briefly discussed. Finally,

two valuable areas for future game development are put forward: (1) storytelling and character development, and (2) socially shared experiences. A short elaboration on the relevance of narrative structures and character development in serious gaming will be given.

BACKGROUND

When the revenue of digital entertainment games passed the revenue in film production in the United States of America in 2004 and games became the fastest growing segment in the entertainment industry (ESA, 2004), advocates, teachers, and politicians alike were wondering how the interest in games could be channelled into educational domains. The enthusiasm in game play observed particularly in younger users could, so the assumption goes, be harvested for more serious purposes than merely entertainment. Academic education, language skills, health related knowledge or appropriate attitudes and behaviours may be better and more efficiently taught using game technology. Game-based learning seemed to be the ultimate pathway not only to counteract any detrimental effects of "non-serious" games, but also to reach out to populations on whom rather traditional educational efforts were lost, to facilitate the educational impact in general or to enhance it in providing, for example, opportunities for deeper learning. The U.S. military was one of the first agencies recognizing the inherent potential of games and invested significant funds for new developments, which have been tremendously successful (e.g., America's Army). At the same time, education for children within and outside the curriculum was targeted by less economically powerful agencies such as schools, museums, or small companies devoted to enriching learning experiences for children and adolescents. Their attempts resulted in much less sophisticated games than developed by the US military that often did not fulfil the promise of an engaging learning experience (Shen, Wong, & Ritterfeld, 2009). So far, the development of games with serious purposes, such as educational or health enhancement has had some, limited, success.

The genre of serious games emerged with the intention to harvest these essentials of game play for educational purposes. Often a game is classified as a serious game because it has been developed to have certain well-intended effects on the player that go beyond entertainment (cf., Ritterfeld, Cody, & Vorderer, 2009). Unfortunately, by no means do the intentions of game developers guarantee that these effects will manifest themselves. Whether or not these intended effects occur can only be determined by empirical research. In the past decade a multitude of such effect studies have been successfully completed (for an overview see: Durkin, 2006; Lee & Peng, 2006; Lieberman, 2006; Ritterfeld & Weber, 2006). Several of these studies have shown that intended effects do occur. However, these studies are limited in their generalizability (Watt, 2009). First, because of obvious differences in game design and content, making every game different from others. The fact that games share some features (such as interactivity or multi modality) is not sufficient to conclude universal principles of gaming effects. Moreover, as every game is interactive, each gaming experience is unique and research results cannot easily be transferred from one experience to another (Klimmt, Vorderer, & Ritterfeld, 2007). Individuals may have different experiences and even the same individual can have very different gaming experiences with the very same game.

It has therefore been proposed that the term serious games should be replaced by the concept of serious gaming (Jenkins et al., 2009). This shift in perception recognizes that serious gaming should not be approached as a finished product but as a complicated process, of which the outcome is uncertain until the results are actually obtained. The psychological perspective on "serious gaming" instead of the genre "serious games" also allows for inclusion of unintended effects of serious gaming. As stated earlier in this chapter, any game has the potential to result in serious effects. Several games which were developed without any serious game-intent have prompted the advancement of sensory, cognitive or social skills and even real world knowledge (Ritterfeld & Weber, 2006). Whether or not a game is serious cannot be determined beforehand, as is done in the serious game perspective. It can only be determined based on the process and its results, as is done within the serious gaming perspective.

UNDERLYING PSYCHOLOGICAL PROCESSES

Motivation to Play

In the first half of the last century psychologists discovered 'play' as an area of interest (e.g., Caillois, 1957; Huizinga, 1938). Play or playful activities were considered a facilitator of child development and viewed as a valuable cultural transference. The definition that Caillois (1957) and Huizinga (1938) both use, defines play as a domain that is within society yet different from it and that has no merit beyond itself. Within this domain chance is always of influence and a set of rules govern the fantasy of which the domain is created. The domain in which play takes place is the game arena or simply: the game. Any game will take place in and outside of our physical reality. The game will provide limitations by adhering to the physical limitations of the medium (e.g., a board game; the game ends at the edges of the board) and a structure of rules keep the play within the domain. It is of utmost importance that a player enters the domain voluntarily. Any prescription of play will change the quality of the activity and experience. In addition, play has a repetitive nature: If the play is enjoyable it is repeated over and over again, resulting in high redundancy of the experience. These two elements combined, deliberate and repetitive activity, provide a unique combination of features that are also essential to any educational process.

The deliberate nature is therefore an essential component of game play: A player chooses to play a game. If the activity is mandatory the playful nature would be diminished. Whether and to which extent game play (or any other behaviour) is self-determined is the main focus of the so called Self-Determination Theory (Deci & Ryan, 1985; Deci & Ryan, 2000; Ryan & Deci, 2000). This is a macro-theory of human motivation which is relevant to the development and functioning of an individual's personality within different social contexts. Self-Determination Theory (SDT) is based on the assumption that people are active organisms, driven by natural tendencies toward psychological growth and development. People attempt to deal with everyday challenges without losing a coherent sense of self. This process depends mainly on continuous support and affirmation from their social environment along with the behavioural context of their actions. In light of SDT, personal health and well-being depend on the satisfaction of basic psychological needs, which are innate, universal, and essential to all people, regardless of gender, group, or culture. If those psychological needs are repeatedly satisfied, one's effective functioning and well-being are guaranteed. Conversely, if their satisfaction is frustrated this will result in dysfunctional behaviour and psychological ill-being.

Research guided by SDT has focused on examining the social environmental conditions that facilitate or frustrate the natural processes of healthy psychological development and self-motivation (Ryan & Deci, 2000). Specific factors that benefit or hinder self-motivation and self-regulation have been examined, leading to the establishment of three basic psychological needs – competence, autonomy and relatedness. These, when satisfied, provide for enhanced self-motivation and psychological well-being; and when thwarted lead to lower self-motivation and reduced general mental health. Need satisfaction

in terms of SDT applies to player motivation in gaming contexts (Ryan, Rigby, & Przybylski, 2006). Specifically, games are motivating to the extent in which players experience competence, autonomy, and relatedness while playing. The satisfaction of these primary needs leads to the motivation to continue playing. If however, these needs are not satisfied involvement and persistence will be lacking, and game play might be ended altogether. The need for competence is fulfilled by a task that is challenging, but not too challenging. If one feels achievement in completing such a task, and not frustrated because one is unable to the need for competence is fulfilled (Graesser, Chipman, Leeming & Biedenbach, 2009). The need for autonomy is met by one of the 'ground rules' of play, namely, that it is purely voluntary. The player autonomously decides to play. The need for relatedness is met in the social aspects of play: Most playing is done within social interactions; be it between players, between a player and an audience, or even between a player and computer generated characters. The research by Ryan et al. (2006) also validated the idea that having 'fun' during game play can contribute to the satisfaction of the above mentioned needs. Again, we recognize here the importance of enjoyment beyond entertainment itself.

However in non-mediated ("real") life, people are often quite flexible with these self-determination processes. They usually do not regulate their actions in a strictly conscious and intentional way, but in harmony with their inner needs, motives, and life experiences. This *implicit* mode of self-regulation and motivation is rather intuitive and not mediated by explicit intentions (Baumann & Kuhl, 2002). Implicit self-regulation is more advantageous than explicit self regulation when people face challenging and more complex situations, where common sense is not a necessary and sufficient condition to solve a certain problem. Under such circumstances, implicit self-regulation uses the support of a wide range of inner psychological resources, such as implicit self-esteem (Koole,

Figure 1. The Big Five in game enjoyment

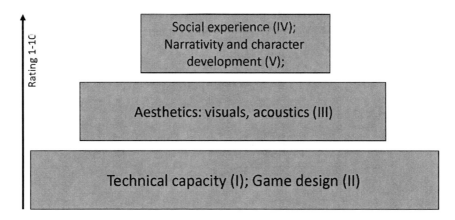

Wang, Shen & Ritterfeld, 2009

2004), intuitions (Baumann & Kuhl, 2002), and positive affect (Koole & Jostmann, 2004). Applying these resources allow people to function in a flexible and efficient way. In situations that are more easily solved intuitively rather than analytically, such as multi-tasking environments (Jostmann & Koole, in press), emotional conflicts (Koole, 2009), or existential problems (Koole & van den Berg, 2005) implicit self-regulation proves to be the superior approach.

Most of the time, certain actions happen in a less self-regulated, non purposeful manner. When a player goes about playing a serious game, s/he does not necessarily have to do this with the explicit intention to learn something. In fact, the processing of the educational content of the game is possibly more successful if it happens implicitly, whilst simply enjoying the game.

Enjoyment in Games

In most studies of digital media the term enjoyment is used to describe the positive reactions towards media and its content. Vorderer, Klimmt, and Ritterfeld (2004) conceptualize this phenomenon as the core experience of entertainment and postulate that game enjoyment is mainly driven by three distinct sets of causes that have the potential to elicit cognitive, affective or conative responses in the player: (1) sensory delight; (2) suspense thrill, and relief; and (3) achievement, control, and self-efficacy. But how does enjoyment through media entertainment products manifest itself on the physiological, cognitive and affective levels? Most common manifestations of enjoyment, as studied by psychological and communication research, are laughter as expression of enjoyment in comedy; experience of suspense through the unfolding of dramatic events; or the occurrence of a sense of achievement, control, and self-efficacy. The game genre offers ample opportunities for these kinds of experiences. Often it is the character featured or, more precisely, the audience's interactions and personal relationships with the character that creates enjoyment. The enjoyment, as the firmament of the entertainment experience, is a product of numerous interactions between various motives to be entertained and conditions of this experience on both the user's and the media application's side (Vorderer et al., 2004).

However, gaming enjoyment does not exclusively imply positive emotions, but could also be based on experiences that we might consider unpleasant such as sadness or fear. The common observation that some gamers are particularly attracted to fearful content may cause a paradox for entertainment research at first glance. Why would one deliberately choose to immerse him- or herself in unpleasant emotions? The concept of meta-emotion suggested by Oliver (1993) provides an explanation for this paradox. Meta-emotion, or meta-enjoyment, results from evaluating an emotional experience, e.g. 'I enjoyed being scared by the monsters in the game'. Ritterfeld (2009) argues that emotion elicitation during game play can be one of the main driving forces behind it. Many gamers enjoy being in an emotionally intense situation that challenges their ability to cope with the emotion. Similar to cognitive challenges which require development and/or application of problem solving strategies (e.g., Gee, 2009; Graesser, 2009; Lieberman, 2006), the elicitation of strong negative emotion within game play calls for successful coping, or, in other words, emotion regulation (Gross & Thompson, 2007). According to Ritterfeld (2009) emotion regulation episodes may be considered educational if they support development and fine tuning of coping strategies in high intensity emotional states. This argumentation is in line with Jansz (2005) who claims that games are a private and safe laboratory to practice self-relevant experiences. Representation by one or even multiple avatars offers, for example, an opportunity to explore possible selves. Thus, the gaming environment provides a stage for self exploration (Probehandeln) that may go beyond the physical world. Consequently, experiencing mastery and control during game play may elicit feelings of potency that contribute to self-enhancement and, in the long run, to the development of positive self-esteem (Ritterfeld, 2009). No doubt, an increase in self-esteem is a highly enjoyable experience.

Wang, Shen, and Ritterfeld (2009) identified 27 fun factors based on a comprehensive literature review and a content analysis of 60 professional game reviews. They proposed the so called Big Five in game enjoyment (i.e., technological capac-

ity, game design, aesthetic presentation, entertainment game play experience, and narrativity) and a three-level threshold perspective (i.e., playability threshold, enjoyability threshold, and super fun boosting factors). One of their major findings is that when basic gaming requirements are met, narrative elements can significantly contribute to a pleasant game play experience (Wang et al., 2009). The Big Five in game enjoyment are shown in a hierarchical model below. At the left side of the model we can see the ratings on game enjoyment going up as more of the elements are incorporated in a game.

Although most of the serious games on the market do not yet provide the complex quality necessary for full enjoyment, some authors believe that they can be developed (Shen, Wang & Ritterfeld, 2009). A general guideline is that such games should use entertainment features with educational experience in order to let learning unfold its potential rather incidentally, not explicitly.

Narrativity and Character Development

Despite the debate about the role of narrative in digital games (e.g., Harrigan & Wardrip-Fruin, 2007; Jenkins, 2006; Wardrip-Fruin & Harrigan, 2004) the model of The Big Five with narrative in the top threshold, is consistent with the philosophies of several expert game designers (e.g., Fullerton, Swain, & Hoffman, 2004; Fullerton, Swain, & Hoffman 2008). Many scholars have acknowledged the important role of the narrative in serious games research (Baranowski, Buday, Thomson, & Baranowski, 2008; Lee, Park & Jing, 2006; Peng, in press a; Schneider, Lang, Shin, & Bradley, 2004; Wang et al., 2009; Wang & Singhal, 2009). At the core of the narrative aspect of digital games are virtual characters. Many games allow or even require players to control an avatar as their self-representation in the gaming world.

Role playing is another powerful aspect in gaming because players develop emotional bonds with their avatars. They have to feel what the avatars feel and think what the avatars think, in order to accomplish the missions and advance in the game. Thus, it is likely that players have to at least temporarily adopt the attitude and perceptions that could be pre-planned and incorporated as options for the virtual characters in the game designing process. Through strong identification with these characters players may achieve significant change in their own knowledge, attitude, and behaviour (Peng, in press b).

Enjoyment through Presence

For the blending of entertainment and education to be able to occur, the player should be 'grasped' by the game in such a way that the learning can take place implicitly. This idea of being grasped by a game is known as the concept of presence. Presence is the illusion of being there, that is needed to interact and play within media. "Presence can be understood as a psychological state in which the person's subjective experience is created by some form of media technology with little awareness of the manner in which technology shapes this perception" (p.226, Tamborini, 2006). Presence is a multidimensional concept; the three dimensions that are most often cited in the literature are spatial presence, social presence and self presence. Spatial presence, or 'being in', has a very high impact on the effect the game will have on the user and is mainly determined by two qualities: involvement and immersion. Involvement relies on mental vigilance and depends on the meaningfulness of an environment, while immersion depends on the environments ability to isolate people from other surrounding stimuli. Social presence, or 'being with', is the sense of being in a social environment. Self presence, or 'being, is the presentation of oneself in the virtual world. This sense of presence allows for interaction with the media, the content and social entities.

Social Experiences

According to Social Cognitive Theory, social learning entails that people can learn from their own experience or the observed behaviour of others. This can be applied to learning from the interactions in a game; "People can learn many complicated behaviours, attitudes, expectations, beliefs and perceptual schemata through observation and participation in video games" (p. 368, Buckley, 2006). The Massively Multi player Online (MMO) genre has the potential to induce such learning through a strong sense of social presence as most of the other players are actual humans. There is enormous potential for serious gaming development in allowing for stronger social experiences in the MMO genre. Both the virtual world and the avatar (digital representation of self) are persistent meaning that they exist without stop or pause, even without the individual player present. This continuity of an avatar creates a persistent identity which allows for communication and social interaction on a deeper level. This connection to the avatar allows for a deeper learning process over time. Physicality refers to the similarity of the virtual world to the physical world. It is largely similar to the physical laws and manifestations of the reality. The MMO-platform allows players to experience a real connection with other players, in real-time while in a virtual world. These experiences allow for meaningful social interactions. A MMO environment would allow a player to experience certain behaviour or observe certain behaviour of other players from which he/she could learn.

ENTERTAINMENT-EDUCATION

Engaged Learning

For children, learning is a playful activity. Initially, children do not experience a distinction between learning and fun (Ritterfeld, 2008). Growing up,

Figure 2. Model of engaged learning (Ritterfeld, 2008)

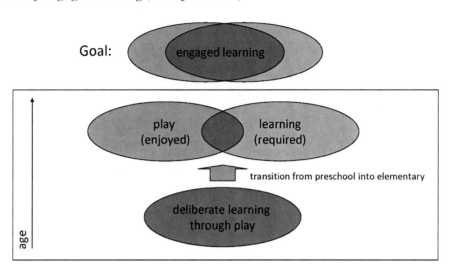

however, the two entities will slowly drift apart and eventually establish two distinct sets of experiences: Fun is seen to exclude learning and learning is seen to exclude fun (c.f., Figure 2). This distinction is mainly supported by the educational system and reinforced when a child experiences learning as difficult and painful. Designing serious games is motivated by the intention to reunite these processes: learning with fun or even better, learning because of fun. It is fascinating to watch gamers overcome frustration if they encounter impasses and explore alternatives or try again and again to reach their game goal without any external encouragement. Most interestingly, the experience itself, although potentially frustrating, is enriched with enjoyment. As shown in the model below, the goal of serious gaming is to overcome the gap between education and entertainment by providing the learner with a playful educational experience, called 'engaged learning'. We hereby assume that this merger of learning and fun is independent from age and can be applied to any educational activity.

Paradigms of Entertainment-Education

If the motivation to be educated is lacking, there are three Entertainment-Education paradigms (i.e. motivation paradigm, reinforcement paradigm and blending paradigm), that are generally used to enhance motivation by adding an entertainment component with games (Ritterfeld & Weber, 2006). These three models are shown below, their development set out over time.

In the motivation paradigm, an entertainment component is used to make the overall learning experience more attractive for unmotivated learners. Here it is assumed that the educational content in itself is not sufficiently attractive to stimulate the learning process. Therefore the entertainment component is meant to draw the user's attention, which is subsequently shifted to the educational content, providing for a more implicit way to motivate the user to learn. This approach has already proven successful for linguistic (Ritterfeld, Klimmt, Vorderer, & Steinhilper, 2005), science (e.g., Ritterfeld, Weber, Fernandes, & Vorderer, 2004; Ritterfeld, Wang, Shen et al., 2009) and health (e.g., Ritterfeld & Jin, 2006) content.

Figure 3. Paradigms of entertainment-education (Ritterfeld & Weber, 2006, p. 407)

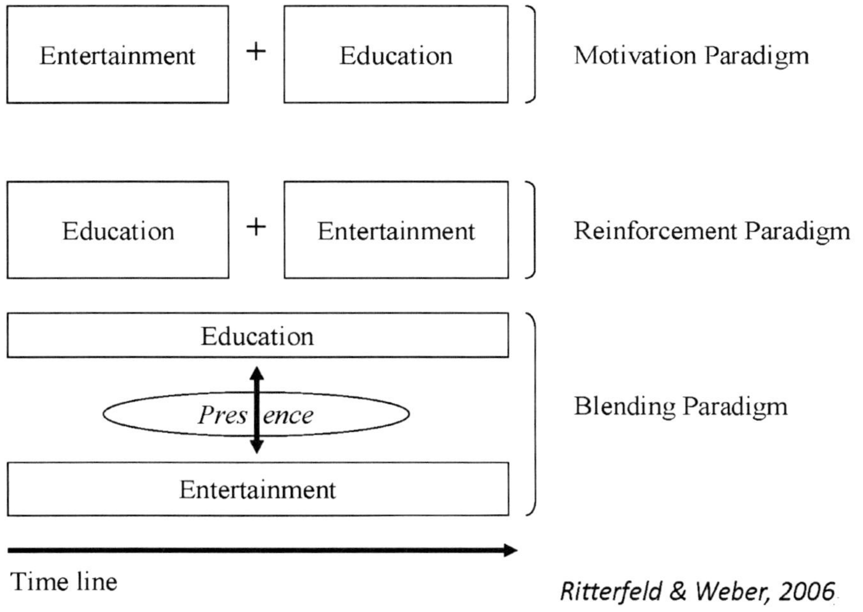

The reinforcement paradigm, contrary to the motivation paradigm, inverts the order of the entertainment and education components, and uses the entertainment part as a motivational incentive (Ritterfeld & Weber, 2006). The entertainment component is usually offered as reinforcement after the completion of the educational part and may be incorporated as an expected reward or a surprise. In the example of educational games incentives can vary from appointed scores, earned virtual money, fun animations, or accomplishing different levels in a video game (Ritterfeld & Weber, 2006).

The concept of motivation can be subdivided into intrinsic and extrinsic motivation. Intrinsic motivation entails that motivation comes from inside the person, whereas extrinsic motivation entails that the person is motivated because of factors outside of the explicit goal of the behaviour itself. For example, one could donate money to a beggar because one genuinely wants to help the beggar (intrinsic motivation), or one could donate money to a beggar in order to make him go away (extrinsic motivation). The first two paradigms for entertainment-education discussed here, the motivation paradigm and the reinforcement paradigm, both apply to explicit motivation.

The third paradigm discussed, the blending paradigm, aims to merge entertainment with education by using the concept of 'presence'; which is the illusion of being in the game. The blending must occur in such a way that entertainment is no longer complementary to education, but they are blended into one experience. By doing so, learning becomes incidental and implicit, rather than an explicit goal. The explicit goal has become the overall experience of game play, the blend of entertainment and education, where the education part has now become only one of the components to reach the goal. Hence, the explicit motivation to play the educational game has been shifted from the direct educational purpose to the new goal that encompasses both educational and entertainment components. This way, the purely educational component has become an implicit, rather than explicit motivation.

A longitudinal study by Schneider and Stefanek (2004) describes three necessary components for above average learning performance: practice, interest, and intrinsic motivation. By blending the education and entertainment components together to a new enjoyable experience, two of Schneider and Stefanek's (2004) components for good learning performance, intrinsic motivation and interest, can be facilitated. The third, practice, can be achieved by playing the game. The third paradigm for entertainment-education, the blending paradigm, applies to implicit motivation.

Psychological Mechanisms

Ratan and Ritterfeld (2009) identified four underlying psychological mechanisms embedded in serious games: (1) skill practice, (2) knowledge gain through exploration, (3) cognitive problem solving, and (4) social problem solving. According to their findings, skill practice is the primary underlying psychological mechanism for the majority of all serious games. Practice is undoubtedly important for learning and it involves the repetition of the learned content or skill. Nevertheless, this finding implies that most serious games do not target a more sophisticated, deeper learning. In this respect, the potential of digital games is not yet fully explored. It is therefore not surprising that most of these skill-focused games, that have been demonstrated to effectively facilitate learning, are not deliberately selected nor deliberately played over a longer period of time by their users. Instead they were prescribed by a research team. In some studies, incentives were given to impose the necessary game play, which triggers extrinsic motivation (e.g., Moore, Rosenberg, & Coleman, 2005). In those cases, the expectation to harvest the potential for intrinsically motivating game play is clearly not fulfilled. Models, used in the discussion of Entertainment-Education, assume the successful blending of two very different game play experiences; the entertaining experience and the educational experience (Ritterfeld & Weber, 2006; Wang & Singhal, 2009). Entertainment makes a manifold contribution on game selec-

tion and persistence of game play. The deliberate selection of a game (in contrast to prescribed use) as well as enduring and repeated gaming will provide the motivational basis for sustained skill practice, educational content processing or problem solving and will, consequently, result in deeper learning. One of the main challenges posed for Entertainment-Education in game play is how to sustain enjoyment despite an enrichment of content.

Limitations of Entertainment-Education

In order for serious gaming to be successful both an enjoyable experience and meaningful processing of content must occur. The enjoyable experience of gaming is the explicit motivation, while the learning episode remains implicit. However, this model of Entertainment-Education is not applicable to all learners or situations. We will now look at some of the limitations of Entertainment-Education through serious gaming. Special attention will be paid to the motivation to learn, the level of both entertainment and education, and context.

Entertainment-Education may not work for learners who have no interest in, or even aversion to, the offered educational content. If a learner is not motivated to learn about a certain subject or to master a certain skill, providing the undesired educational content in a gaming environment will decrease the enjoyment of the gaming experience. On the other hand, if a learner is already explicitly motivated to learn about a certain subject or to master a certain skill, providing the desired educational content in a gaming environment could demotivate the player. In this case the entertainment component may be perceived as an unnecessary detour or even a distraction. Consequently, the application of Entertainment-Education is especially suitable for the segment of learners, who have some or a latent motivation to grasp the content, but are not yet determined to do so. This idea is further elaborated on by examining some of the assumptions that models in Entertainment-Education often carry. These assumptions and the Moderate Entertainment Hypothesis are visualized in a graph below (Figure 4).

The line representing the Facilitation Hypothesis, assumes the educational value will rise along with heightened entertainment value. This means that the more entertained learners are, the more opportunities for processing of meaningful content. The line representing the Distraction Hypothesis assumes the opposite; the educational value will decrease with heightened entertainment value. Following this logic it would mean that the more entertained learners are, the more they are distracted from any meaningful content. Ritterfeld and Weber (2006) propose that the more accurate assumption is indicated by the line representing the Moderate Entertainment Hypothesis; where there is an optimum level of entertainment for an optimal level of education. If the level of entertainment is heightened the education value will decrease but if the entertainment level is lowered the education value will also decrease. The challenge is to find this optimum entertainment level.

Another element that provides limitations on Entertainment-Education is the context outside of the game play. This context may significantly interfere with game play experiences. Individuals are unlikely to select serious gaming if it competes with other leisure activities. Also, actual experiences compete with virtual ones. Furthermore, some experiences will be avoided completely, even if they are virtual. Being bored, in pain or generally unhappy are experiences that will be avoided in a real and a virtual environment. These considerations may apply less to a school context, where games may be a welcome alternative to more traditional pedagogy.

FUTURE DIRECTIONS

Enjoyment of digital games is critical to serious gaming, perhaps even more than to game play for pure entertainment (Ritterfeld & Weber, 2006). Yet, the complexity of this concept creates a real challenge for evaluation (Wang, 2010). There has not yet been a standard validated set of measures

Figure 4. Model of assumptions on the entertainment-education link (Ritterfeld & Weber, 2006, p. 406)

Theoretical Assumptions on the Entertainment-Education-Link

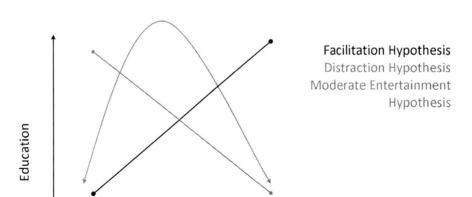

of game enjoyment. Scale items that are commonly used tend to be general statements with variations of synonyms (fun, enjoyable, interesting, etc.). Other factors for measuring enjoyment in games are often derived from specific types of games and game players, or adapted from intrinsic motivational approaches (e.g., Malone & Lepper, 1987; Ryan, Rigby, & Przybylski, 2006; Yee, 2007). The development of a multi-dimensional measurement of game enjoyment may be a useful direction for future research.

Parasocial interactions have been studied for decades since the term was coined by Horton and Wohl (1956) to describe an imaginary relationship between television or radio audience members and a media persona (e.g., Giles, 2002; Rubin, Perse, & Powell, 1985; Schiappa, Allen, & Gregg, 2007). Given the popularity and prevalence of digital game play, perhaps it is time to extend the research of parasocial interaction to this new entertainment media format. Young scholars have just started to investigate the parasocial communication between players and their avatars (Hartmann, 2008; Klimmt, Hartmann, & Schramm, 2006), but their thinking remains largely at the conceptual level. There is obviously much room for further theoretical, methodological, and empirical advancement into to the underlying mechanisms for emotional involvement, feeling of presence, agency, and consequences carried from the virtual worlds to real life (e.g., Peng, in press a; Ritterfeld, 2009; Ritterfeld & Weber, 2006).

The development of serious gaming is rapidly progressing to meet the standard of the development of commercial games, although it is not always of the same quality. However, in order for presence and explicit enjoyment to occur simultaneously with implicit learning, serious gaming has progressed sufficiently. Different aspects could be developed even further, but serious games are already of such a quality to allow these important psychological processes to occur. Significant progress might still be achieved in the development of narrativity and character development, as well as the social experience of serious gaming. The attentive reader will notice that these are the top-two levels in the model of the Big Five in game enjoyment, as elaborated above (Figure 1).

CONCLUSION

Although the concept of serious games or gaming has been around for a while, there is still some dispute on what the term does and does not mean. From a social science perspective it entails the process of playing a (digital) game, after which the player is left with more than just an enjoyable experience. Games have the ability to carry educational content in an implicit manner, which means that serious-game designers can teach without overtly teaching. The enjoyable media experience is also the explicit motivation for selection and repetition of game play, which reinforces the learning process. The Big Five are the key-features that determine whether or not a game is enjoyable. These are technological capacity, game design, aesthetic presentation, entertainment game play experience, and narrativity. In this order they represent a hierarchy of threshold processes. The more sophisticated each of these features is incorporated in the game, the more enjoyable the game play becomes. However, there is a limit to the amount of educational content that enjoyment can carry. If there is too much entertainment in a game the educational content may get lost; if there is too much educational content in a game there may be no more room left for entertainment. The goal is to reach for the optimum level of education and entertainment so that they complement each other. Even if this optimum is reached there are still limitations on the type of learner this is suited for. The completely unmotivated learners cannot be compelled by adding entertainment while the already motivated learners will be demotivated by the distraction that the entertainment provides. In order for any game to accomplish enjoyment it is vital that the player realizes 'presence' within the gaming environment. When presence is established the blending paradigm of Entertainment-Education can come into play. The authors urge serious game development to look towards social experiences, narrativity and character development as gaming-elements that could be further developed. Meanwhile, social sciences will strive for a standard, validated, multidimensional measurement of enjoyment in games.

RECOMMENDATIONS

Researchers

*   Evaluation of serious gaming should be based solely on effects of game play, not on the intention of the designers
*   A robust measurement set of entertainment in gaming is very much needed, the development of such a tool could be based on the Big Five
*   When evaluation (serious) gaming the researcher must be mindful that the interactive nature of game play creates a unique experience and generalizability is limited

Developers

*   Blending entertainment with education must remain focused on the entertainment aspect
*   The experience of presence (self, spatial and social) is an important facilitator for the blending of entertainment and education
*   Keep in mind that when competence, autonomy and relatedness are addressed by the game play, the player will be motivated to continue playing
*   Aspects that can be better utilized to enhance game play are
    *   Narrativity
    *   Socially shared experiences
    *   Character development

Instructors

*   Utilizing serious gaming as didactic tool has a (motivational) target group and does not provide an overall solution
*   Serious gaming is a very effective mediated learning tool, regardless of content
*   Educators must be weary not to push serious gaming too much, when the game play turns into a task it loses the entertainment element

REFERENCES

America's Army - Vision and Realization. (2004). *MOVES Institute & U.S. Army*. Retrieved January 31, 2010, from http://www.americasarmy.com/

Baranowski, T., Buday, R., Thomson, D., & Baranowski, J. (2008). Playing for real. Video games and stories for health-related behavior change. *American Journal of Preventive Medicine, 34*, 74–82. doi:10.1016/j.amepre.2007.09.027

Baumann, N., & Kuhl, J. (2002). Intuition, affect, and personality: Unconscious coherence judgments and self-regulation of negative affect. *Journal of Personality and Social Psychology, 83*, 1213–1223. doi:10.1037/0022-3514.83.5.1213

Buckley, K. E. A., & Craig, A. (2006). A theoretical model of the effects and consequences of playing video games. In Vorderer, P., & Bryant, J. (Eds.), *Playing video games: Motives, responses, and consequences* (pp. 363–378). Mahwah, NJ: Lawrence Erlbaum.

Caillois, R. (1957). *Man, play and games*. University of Illinois press.

Chan, E., & Vorderer, P. (2006). Massively multiplayer online games. In Vorderer, P., & Bryant, J. (Eds.), *Playing video games. Motives, responses, and consequences* (pp. 77–90). Mahwah, NJ: Lawrence Erlbaum.

Deci, E. L., & Ryan, R. M. (1985). *Intrinsic motivation and self-determination in human behavior*. New York: Plenum.

Deci, E. L., & Ryan, R. M. (2000). The what and why of goal pursuits: Human needs and the self-determination of behavior. *Psychological Inquiry*, *11*, 227–268. doi:10.1207/S15327965PLI1104_01

Durkin, K. (2006). Game playing and adolescents' development. In Vorderer, P., & Bryant, J. (Eds.), *Playing video games: Motives, responses, and consequences* (pp. 415–428). Mahwah, NJ: Lawrence Erlbaum.

Fullerton, T., Swain, C., & Hoffman, S. (2004). *Game design workshop: Designing, prototyping, and playtesting games*. New York: CMP Books.

Fullerton, T., Swain, C., & Hoffman, S. (2008). *Game design workshop: A playcentric approach to creating innovative games* (2nd ed.). Boston: Elsevier Morgan Kaufmann.

Gee, J. P. (2009). Literacy, video games, and popular culture. In Olson, D. R., & Torrance, N. (Eds.), *The Cambridge handbook of literacy* (pp. 313–325). New York: Cambridge University Press. doi:10.1017/CBO9780511609664.018

Giles, D. (2002). Parasocial interaction: A review of the literature and a model for future research. *Media Psychology*, *4*, 279–305. doi:10.1207/S1532785XMEP0403_04

Graesser, A., Chipman, P., Leeming, F., & Biedenbach, S. (2009). Deep learning and emotion in serious games. In Ritterfeld, U., Cody, M., & Vorderer, P. (Eds.), *Serious games: Mechanisms and effects* (pp. 83–102). Mahwah, NJ: Routledge/LEA.

Gross, J. J., & Thompson, R. A. (2007). Emotion regulation: Conceptual foundations. In J.J. Gross (Ed.), *Handbook of emotion regulation*. (pp. 3-24). New York: Guilford Press. Retrieved from http://www-psych.stanford.edu/~psyphy/pdfs/2007

Harrigan, P., & Wardrip-Fruin, N. (2007). *Second person: Role-playing and story in games and playable media*. Cambridge, MA: The MIT Press.

Hartmann, T. (2008). Parasocial interactions and paracommunication with new media characters. In Konijn, E. A., Utz, S., Tanis, M., & Barnes, S. B. (Eds.), *Mediated interpersonal communication* (pp. 177–199). New York: Routledge.

Horton, D., & Wohl, R. R. (1956). Mass communication and para-social interaction. *Psychiatry*, *19*, 215–229.

Huizinga, J. (1938). Homo Ludens – A study of play element in culture. In E.L.B., et al. (Eds.), *Verzamelde werken V. Cultuurgeschiedenis III.* (pp. 26-146). Haarlem: H.D. Tjeenk Willink & Zoon N.V.

Industry Facts. (2004). *ESA industry facts*. Retrieved May 25, 2004, from http://www.theesa.com/facts/index.

Jansz, J. (2005). The emotional appeal of violent video games for adolescent males. *Communication Theory*, *15*, 219–241. doi:10.1111/j.1468-2885.2005.tb00334.x

Jenkins, H. (2006). Game design as narrative architecture. In Salen, K., & Zimmerman, E. (Eds.), *The game design reader: A rules of play anthology* (pp. 670–689). Cambridge, MA.

Jenkins, H., Camper, B., Chisholm, A., Grigsby, N., Klopfer, E., & Osterweil, S. (2009). From serious games to serious gaming. In Ritterfeld, U., Cody, M., & Vorderer, P. (Eds.), *Serious games: Mechanisms and effects* (pp. 448–469). New York: Routledge/LEA.

Jostmann, N. B., & Koole, S. L. (2009). When persistence if futile: A functional analysis of action orientation and goal disengagement. In Moskowitz, G., & Grant, H. (Eds.), *The psychology of goals* (pp. 337–361). New York: Guilford Press.

Klimmt, C., Hartmann, T., & Schramm, H. (2006). Parasocial interactions and relationships. In Bryant, J., & Vorderer, P. (Eds.), *Psychology of entertainment* (pp. 291–314). Mahwah, NJ: Erlbaum.

Klimmt, C., Vorderer, P., & Ritterfeld, U. (2007). Interactivity & generalizability: New media, new challenges? *Communication Methods & Measures*, *1*(3), 169–179.

Koole, S. L. (2004). Volitional shielding of the self: Effects of action orientation and external demands on implicit self-evaluation. *Social Cognition*, *22*(1), 100–125. doi:10.1521/soco.22.1.100.30985

Koole, S. L. (2009a). The psychology of emotion regulation: An integrative review. *Cognition and Emotion*, *23*, 4–41. doi:10.1080/02699930802619031

Koole, S. L., & Jostmann, N. B. (2004). Getting a grip on your feelings: Effects of action orientation and external demands on intuitive affect regulation. *Journal of Personality and Social Psychology*, *87*, 974–990. doi:10.1037/0022-3514.87.6.974

Koole, S. L., & Van den Berg, A. E. (2005). Lost in the wilderness: Terror management, action orientation, and nature evaluation. *Journal of Personality and Social Psychology*, *88*(6), 1014–1028. doi:10.1037/0022-3514.88.6.1014

Lee, K. M., Park, N., & Jing, S.-A. (2006). Narrative and interactivity in computer games. In Vorderer, P., & Bryant, J. (Eds.), *Playing video games: Motives, responses, and consequences* (pp. 259–274). Mahwah, NJ: Erlbaum.

Lee, K. M., & Peng, W. (2006). What do we know about social and psychological effects of computer games? A comprehensive review of the current literature. In Vorderer, P., & Bryant, J. (Eds.), *Playing video games: Motives, responses and consequences* (pp. 325–346). Mahwah, NJ: Lawrence Erlbaum Associates, Inc.

Lieberman, D. A. (2006). What can we learn from playing interactive games? In Vorderer, P., & Bryant, J. (Eds.), *Playing video games. Motives, responses, and consequences* (pp. 379–397). Mahwah, NJ: Lawrence Erlbaum Associates.

Malone, T., & Lepper, M. (1987). Making learning fun: A taxonomy of intrinsic motivations in learning. In Snow, R. E., & Farr, M. J. (Eds.), *Aptitude, learning and instruction: Conative and affective process analyses* (*Vol. 3*, pp. 223–253). Hillsdale, NJ: Erlbaum.

Moore, D. R., Rosenberg, J. F., & Coleman, J. S. (2005). Discrimination training of phonemic contrasts enhances phonological processing in mainstream schoolchildren. *Brain and Language*, *94*(1), 72–85. doi:10.1016/j.bandl.2004.11.009

Oliver, M. B. (1993). Exploring the paradox of the enjoyment of sad films. *Human Communication Research*, *19*, 315–342. doi:10.1111/j.1468-2958.1993.tb00304.x

Peng, W. (in press). Is a computer game an effective medium for health promotion? Design and evaluation of the RightWay Café game to promote a healthy diet for young adults. *Health Communication*.

Peng, W. (in press). The mediational role of identification in the relationship between experience mode and self-efficacy: Enactive role-playing versus passive observation. *Cyberpsychology & Behavior*.

Rigby, C. S., & Przybylski, A. (2009). Virtual worlds and the learner hero: How today's video games can inform tomorrow's digital learning environments. *Theory and Research in Education*, *7*(2), 214–223. doi:10.1177/1477878509104326

Ritterfeld, U. (2008). *Serious gaming: Assumptions and realities*. Invited address Meaningful Play Conference, Michigan State University.

Ritterfeld, U. (2009). Identity construction and emotion regulation in digital gaming. In U. Ritterfeld, M. Cody, & P. Vorderer (Eds.), *Serious games: Mechanisms and effects.* (204-218). Mahwah, NJ: Routledge/LEA.

Ritterfeld, U., Cody, M., & Vorderer, P. (Eds.). (2009). *Serious games: Mechanisms and effects.* New York: Routledge.

Ritterfeld, U., & Jin, S.-A. (2006). Addressing media stigma for people experiencing mental illness using an entertainment-education strategy. *Journal of Health Psychology, 11,* 247–267. doi:10.1177/1359105306061185

Ritterfeld, U., Klimmt, C., Vorderer, P., & Steinhilper, L. K. (2005). Play it again, Pupunga! Narrative audio tapes and preschoolers' entertainment experience. *Media Psychology, 7,* 47–72. doi:10.1207/S1532785XMEP0701_3

Ritterfeld, U., & Weber, R. (2006). Video games for entertainment and education. In Vorderer, P., & Bryant, J. (Eds.), *Playing video games: Motives, responses, and consequences* (pp. 399–413). Mahwah, NJ: Lawrence Erlbaum.

Ritterfeld, U., Weber, R., Fernandes, S. & Vorderer, P. (2004). *Think science! Entertainment education in interactive theaters. Computers in entertainment: Educating children through entertainment.*

Rubin, A. M., Perse, E. M., & Powell, R. A. (1985). Loneliness, parasocial interaction, and local television news viewing. *Human Communication Research, 12,* 155–180. doi:10.1111/j.1468-2958.1985.tb00071.x

Ryan, R. M., & Deci, E. L. (2000). Self-determination theory and the facilitation of intrinsic motivation, social development, and well-being. *The American Psychologist, 55,* 68–78. doi:10.1037/0003-066X.55.1.68

Ryan, R. M., Rigby, C. S., & Przybylski, A. (2006). The motivational pull of video games: A self-determination theory approach. *Motivation and Emotion, 30,* 347–364. doi:10.1007/s11031-006-9051-8

Schiappa, E., Allen, M., & Gregg, P. B. (2007). Parasocial relationships and television: A meta-analysis on the effects. In Preiss, R. W., Gayle, B. M., Burrell, N., Allen, M., & Bryant, J. (Eds.), *Mass media effects research: Advances through meta-analysis.* New York: Routledge.

Schneider, E. F., Lang, A., Shin, M., & Bradley, S. D. (2004). Death with a story: How story impacts emotional, motivational, and physiological responses to first-person shooter video games. *Human Communication Research, 30,* 361–375. doi:10.1093/hcr/30.3.361

Schneider, W., & Stefanek, J. (2004). Developmental changes of general cognitive abilities and school related skills in children and adolescents: Evidence of a widening gap? *Zeitschrift für Entwicklungspsychologie und Pädagogische Psychologie, 36*(3), 147–159. doi:10.1026/0049-8637.36.3.147

Shen, C., Wang, H., & Ritterfeld, U. (2009). Serious games and seriously fun games: Can they be one and the same? In Ritterfeld, U., Cody, M., & Vorderer, P. (Eds.), *Serious games: Mechanisms and effects.* New York: Routledge.

Tamborini, R. S. P. (2006). The role of presence in the experience of electronic games. In Vorderer, P., & Bryant, J. (Eds.), *Playing video games: Motives, responses and consequences* (pp. 225–240). Mahwah, NJ: Lawrence Erlbaum Associates, Inc.

Vorderer, P., Klimmt, C., & Ritterfeld, U. (2004). Enjoyment: At the heart of media entertainment. *Communication Theory, 14*(4), 388–408. doi:10.1111/j.1468-2885.2004.tb00321.x

Vorderer, P., & Ritterfeld, U. (2009). Digital games. In Nabi, R., & Oliver, M. (Eds.), *The SAGE handbook of media processes and effects*. Thousand Oaks, CA: Sage.

Wang, H. (2010). *Digital games for health promotion: What we know and what we would like to know*. Unpublished manuscript, University of Southern California.

Wang, H., Shen, C., & Ritterfeld, U. (2009). Enjoyment of digital games: What makes them seriously fun? In Ritterfeld, U., Cody, M. J., & Vorderer, P. (Eds.), *Serious games: Mechanism and effects* (pp. 48–61). New York: Routledge.

Wang, H., & Singhal, A. (2009). Entertainment-education through digital games. In Ritterfeld, U., Cody, M. J., & Vorderer, P. (Eds.), *Serious games: Mechanisms and effects* (pp. 271–292). New York: Routledge.

Wardrip-Fruin, N., & Harrigan, P. (Eds.). (2004). *First person: New media as story, performance, and game*. Cambridge, MA: The MIT Press.

Watt, J. H. (2009). Improving methodology in serious games research with elaborated theory. In Ritterfeld, U., Cody, M. J., & Vorderer, P. (Eds.), *Serious games: Mechanisms and effects* (pp. 374–388). New York: Routledge/LEA.

Yee, N. (2007). Motivations of play in online games. *Cyberpsychology & Behavior, 9*, 772–775. doi:10.1089/cpb.2006.9.772

ADDITIONAL READING

Bryant, J., & Vorderer, P. (2006). (Eds.), *Psychology of entertainment*. Mahwah NJ: Lawrence Erlbaum Associates.

Csikszentmihalyi, M. (1990). *Flow: The psychology of optimal experience*. New York: Harper and Row.

Gee, J. P. (2007). *Good digital games and good learning*. New York, NY: Lang.

Nabi, R., & Oliver, M. B. (Eds.). (2009). *Handbook of media effects*. Thousand Oaks, CA: Sage.

Prensky, M. (2001). *Digital game-based learning*. New York: McGraw-Hill.

Reeves, B., & Nass, C. (1996). *The media equation: How people treat computers, television, and mew media like real people and places*. New York: Cambridge University Press.

Ritterfeld, U., Cody, M., & Vorderer, P. (Eds.). (2009). *Serious games: Mechanisms and effects*. New York, N.Y.: Routledge/LEA.

Singhal, C., Cody, M. J., Rogers, M. E., & Sabido, M. (2004). *Entertainment-education and social change: History, research, and practice*. Mahway, NJ: Lawrence Erlbaum Associates.

Vorderer, P., & Bryant, J. (Eds.). (2006). *Playing video games: Motives, responses, and consequences*. Mahwah, N.J.: Lawrence Erlbaum Associates.

Zillmann, D., & Vorderer, P. (2000). *Media entertainment: The psychology of its appeal*. Mahwah, NJ: Lawrence Erlbaum Associates.

KEY TERMS AND DEFINITIONS

Entertainment-Education: Simultaneous enjoyment and processing of meaningful content.

Explicit Motivation: An action motivated by a process that you are aware of.

Extrinsic Motivation: An action motivated by something other than the action itself.

Meta-Enjoyment: To enjoy having a particular emotional state.

Implicit Motivation: An action motivated by a process that you are unaware of.

Intrinsic Motivation: An action motivated by the action itself.

Parasocial Interactions: Interactions with a mediated/fictional character creating an affective relationship.

Presence: The feeling of being immersed in a game/media environment.

SDT: Self Determination Theory

Serious Gaming: The process of playing a game which has merit beyond the enjoyment of the game itself.

Chapter 21
Using Spatial Audio in Game Technology for Expressing Mathematical Problems to Blind Students

Flaithrí Neff
Limerick Institute of Technology, Ireland

Ian Pitt
University College Cork, Ireland

ABSTRACT

Game technology often offers solutions to problems that are difficult or impossible to solve in traditional educational settings. Maturing spatial audio technology being developed to enhance the playing experience of gamers is increasingly recognized as a promising method for relaying complex educational scenarios to blind students. The subject of mathematics is a prime example of complex information in education that has challenged teachers of blind students, the students themselves, and researchers for many years. This is especially prevalent in relation to mathematics with inherent spatial attributes or complex sequences that are most effectively portrayed in the traditional medium using visual diagrams or spatially organized symbols on a page. This chapter discusses the alternative uses of spatial sound in gaming industry for overcoming some of the problems associated with presenting some of these complex attributes in mathematics to blind students. The authors also present a theoretical framework designed to offer guidelines to audio game designers focused on presenting complex information to blind students using spatial sound technology. Furthermore, the authors present results of a pilot study examining the presentation of trigonometric shapes using game surround sound tools.

DOI: 10.4018/978-1-60960-495-0.ch021

INTRODUCTION

We live in a society that is fundamentally dependent upon what is frequently regarded as our primary sensory apparatus – vision. However, for many members of our society, their sense of vision is either impaired or completely absent. For a blind person, the sense of hearing and touch plays an extremely important role in how he/she gathers information about the world around them. They have overcome many difficulties in an environment that relies almost predominantly on the visual presentation of data and that presumes one must 'see' data in order to interact with it. Digital technology and the digitization of data have made information accessible to the visually disabled that was previously out of reach and difficult to acquire. For example, instead of depending on others to relay text content from a book or waiting for a Braille print version, thousands of books now have a digital equivalent that can be easily accessed using standard Text-To-Speech (TTS) software. However, there remains a significant amount of data that is exclusively available only to those who are sighted, and even though there is increased recognition that information should be available to all members of our society, progress in this regard remains slow in some areas. In many cases this is down to either the unwillingness or lack of awareness of those disseminating the information, but in other instances it remains technically difficult to efficiently and comprehensively represent certain types of information in a non-visual format.

An example of information that is difficult to comprehend without some form of visual representation is certain forms of mathematics. Some mathematics is, of course, easily translatable to standard non-visual formats, such as TTS output. However, other forms consist of abstract elements, spatial composition and structural organization that are incompatible with the linear nature of speech output or Braille. This represents a serious problem when it comes to mathematics education for blind students. A lack of access to mathematics eventuates to problems with subjects such as science, engineering and technology, since many topics in these areas rely on sound mathematical knowledge. The kinds of mathematical elements that pose most problems for blind students when using Braille devices or TTS are those that traditionally rely on key visual elements, such as diagrammatic aids (e.g. trigonometry), spatial association (e.g. matrices), or particular structural arrangement that influences the problem's outcome (e.g. algebra). Representing these non-linear visual elements using either TTS output or a digital Braille device is very difficult, perhaps due to the fact that TTS output and Braille output is linear in nature. Furthermore, even when the mathematical content is purely linear, speech presentation of complicated equations can easily become overwhelming for the listener, given the transient nature of speech (Edwards & Stevens, 1993). Furthermore, in the case of sighted users, the screen display allows them to review elements that occurred at the beginning of the equation, but blind users lack this form of external memory. Without an external memory facility in speech output systems, the listener can only rely on their own internal memory, which may be incomplete (Edwards & Stevens, 1993).

Although speech output is one of the richest and successful methods for presenting digital information to visually disabled computer users (especially for relaying precise information), it is not the most ideal method for representing an overview of complex content. The importance of an overview, or glance, in mathematics is fundamental to understanding and tackling the problem. For example, algebraic equations displayed in a visual format present key syntactic elements in its notation (Stevens et al, 1994). For a sighted user, this relational structure is immediately recognized, even before examining the precise content of the equation itself. An overview, therefore, relays information to the user that is fundamental to the planning and decision-making process of tackling an equation (Ernest, 1987; Stevens et al, 1994). As a consequence of the difficulties pertaining to obtaining an overview of a mathematical problem via speech, researchers in the field have looked to using non-speech sound (Stevens et al, 1996; Stevens et al, 1994; Brewster et al, 1994).

Another feature available to sighted students when presented with mathematical problems in a visual format is the opportunity to tackle the problem at their own pace, review past changes and interact with different stages of the problem. For the blind student using speech output, such a facility is non-existent (or at the very least, much more cumbersome), once again due to the temporal nature of speech output and the lack of external memory. User-interface control is, therefore, an important issue in this regard. Indeed, user-interface control is also a major topic for complex data presented in the visual domain and is being increasingly employed in the area of data visualization (Mazza, 2009)

Therefore, if the problems associated with mathematics education for blind students are to be solved, new approaches, as well as the enhancement of current technology, is required. One of the main aims of any new approach should include a system that empowers the blind student to learn mathematics incidentally (like sighted students do in their visual environment), rather than systematically, which is slow, cumbersome and cognitively tasking (Tanti, 2007; Dick & Kubiak, 1997). We have identified three primary issues that need to be addressed in this regard. The first relates to representing non-linear and structural elements of the mathematical problem, such as spatial attributes in trigonometry and matrices, or relational structures in algebra. The second relates to presenting the blind student with an effective overview of the problem, so that they can plan out their strategy for tackling it. The third relates to user-interface control, allowing the student to step progressively (forward and backward) through the mathematical problem, obtain more precise information about certain elements, and

have control over the rate of information output. We believe that game technology can provide a solution to all three of these issues.

Not only is game technology being extensively employed in the general education arena, it is also increasingly recognized as a significant way of making education accessible to disabled groups. Video game technology directly focused on the issue of accessibility has already had a profound effect on the perception and integration of blind students into mainstream education (Sánchez & Sáenz, 2009). However, more work is required in terms of effectively using the technology for complex mathematics education. Gaming technology is one of the few technologies that already package the required tools to allow researchers to tackle the three primary issues mentioned above. Because of intense competition in the industry for market-share, a lot of innovative research has propelled the development of spatial audio technology. Although the main drive and purpose of this development is to offer a better overall gaming experience for the general gaming population, it has also provided researchers in other areas valuable tools for implementing advanced spatial audio environments. There are also other tools and services that have seen significant technological advances in the gaming industry that may also play a vital role in providing solutions to current issues in education for blind students. These include a huge variety of input devices, including wireless gyroscopic hardware, and advanced in-game 3D navigation facilities.

Spatial audio may allow for a far more accurate representation (or mapping) of non-linear mathematical content. The spatial structure of geometric shapes, for example, could be directly represented, giving the blind student an equivalent aural diagrammatic aid. Elements of a matrix may be spatially ordered like they would in the visual domain, again providing the blind student with a direct mapping of spatial organization. The advantages seen with using non-speech sound for portraying an overview of mathematical problems may be enhanced within a spatial context. Finally, user-interface control, which is an inbuilt feature of game technology, can be incorporated so that students can 'navigate' the mathematical problem, activate speech output only when precise information is required, and interactively step in or out of each stage of the problem. Therefore, gaming technology may be perhaps the most innovative and promising solution to the issue of mathematics education for blind students.

In this chapter, we will present an overview of recent approaches to the problem of presenting mathematical content to blind students. We will also discuss the human hearing system and how both physiological and perceptual evidence supports a spatial sound approach to this issue. Furthermore, we will present and explore a user interface model we have devised to outline the cognitive processes involved when presenting complex auditory data to a listener. The goal of the model is to help audio game designers and developers who are utilizing game-related technology, to build perceptually compliant interfaces capable of presenting complex information to blind people. We will also describe a pilot study based on some of the model's guidelines that examines spatial audio rendition in relation to trigonometric problem solving. A glossary of terms has also been provided for readers unfamiliar with some of the terminology and acronyms used in sound related technology.

TOOLS FOR RENDERING SPATIAL AUDIO ENVIRONMENTS IN GAMES

There are an abundance of tools available to developers for generating spatial audio environments on both desktop and mobile platforms. The game industry has played an extremely important role in pushing spatial audio forward, both in terms of consumer awareness and technological advancement. Significant innovations in the area

of spatial audio continues to grow rapidly, and it is an exciting time for researchers who want to use spatial audio for relaying complex mathematical scenarios to blind students. Technical restrictions to developing high quality spatial audio renditions are becoming less of an issue, but one of the key elements in ensuring sustainable and successful solutions to the problems outlined in this chapter are the perceptual and cognitive considerations. However, before exploring the perceptual and cognitive issues involved, we will first summarize some of the spatial audio technologies used in the game industry, from audio APIs and audio middleware to spatial sound encoders and decoders.

For the purpose of simplifying the wide spectrum of spatial audio tools and formats available, we will broadly and loosely categorize them as being either multichannel or virtual binaural. In this case, the category of multichannel will be used to refer to spatialized audio content that is rendered for discrete speaker output. Currently, the most common setup is 3/2 or 5.1 (Left, Center, Right, Left Rear, Right Rear, LFE), but 3/4 or 7.1 and 10.2 arrangements are emerging configurations. 22.2 is also being evaluated for use with the experimental Ultra High Definition Video format (Sugawara et al, 2004). The category of virtual binaural indicates spatialized audio content that is rendered for headphone output or stereo speakers incorporating acoustic crosstalk cancellation. These can include technologies utilizing generic HRTF (Head Related Transfer Functions) filters obtained from databases (Algazi et al, 2001) and other psychoacoustic elements such as Interaural Time and Level Differences or binaural recording. This area of spatial sound reproduction continues to mature, with head-tracking technology introducing a new dimension. Some technologies mentioned here are not exclusive to gaming technology, and also serve related areas such as virtual reality, the film industry and the music industry.

Multichannel Audio

The idea and understanding of multichannel reproduction is not a new development, and researchers have experimented with various configurations since the 1930s (Toole, 2008). The 5.1 Dolby® Digital configuration is currently very popular in the film and game industry, and maintains six discrete channels during storage and transmission. In order to fit that number of channels onto various storage media, some form of perceptual compression is required, which usually involves using lossy techniques. In relation to content that is rendered using Dolby® Digital, the codec is called AC-3 and is scalable depending on the storage and transmission format. The AC-3 bitrate for audio on DVD is 448 kbps but on Blu-ray™ this can be as high as 640 kbps. Blu-ray™ discs may also contain lossless discrete channels.

Another significant player in the multichannel arena is DTS® (Digital Theater Systems). It is also implements a lossy-based perceptual encoder but at higher bitrates than AC-3 in general (Toole, 2008). It is not as popular on video game media as Dolby® Digital.

DTS®-ES Discrete 6.1 implements seven discrete digital signals, incorporating a back surround channel. Dolby® Digital EX and THX® Surround EX are also 6.1 configurations but implement a matrixed back surround.

Another commercially available surround configuration is 7.1. Blu-ray™ players usually support 7.1, which includes discs that contain eight discrete, lossless audio channels (Dolby® True HD and DTS®-HD Master Audio). DTS®-HD (High Resolution) and Dolby® Digital Plus are encoded using lossy compression, while the Sony® SDDS™ format interprets the configuration as 5/2 rather than 3/4.

Although not commercially competitive with Dolby® or DTS® systems, Ambisonics is technologically a significant multichannel audio method. It is a spatial recording technique and spatial reproduction system using a multi-speaker configuration. The recording process involves capturing a soundfield (encoded as B-format™) using a particular microphone configuration, or via a special four capsule microphone called the Soundfield™ microphone (Gerzon, 1975). Although Ambisonic decoders are far and few between, the technique is often viewed as producing a superior spatial experience to its more commercial counterparts, and is being enhanced and hybridized, particularly in the area of virtual reality research (Ahrens & Spors, 2007; Ahrens & Spors, 2008; Chapman, 2008; Santala et al, 2009; Furse, 2009).

Binaural Audio

In broad terms, binaural audio relates to the reproduction of sound based on the influence of the pinnae, head and shoulder structures. Essentially, these structures impose a filter and delay mechanism on sound entering the listener's ear canal. The folds and contours of the pinna are extremely influential on the auditory mechanisms that process elevated sound sources and high frequencies (> 5kHz). There are two mainstream theories in relation to how the pinna affects the sound entering the human auditory system. The first (Batteau, 1967; Kahana & Nelson, 2000) considers the pinna is a time-domain filter, whereby the folds produce a secondary (reflected) path in conjunction with the direct path reaching the auditory canal (see Figure 1). These concurrent paths, with miniscule time latency between them, produce a high probability of some destructive interference (Long et al, 2005), with the most noticeable effect occurring when the wavelength of the secondary path is 180° degrees out of phase with the wavelength of the direct path. Two wavelengths of the same frequency, but with one that is 180° degrees out of phase, cancels each other out. In the context of a complex sound, only some of the frequencies within the complex wave will cancel out, resulting in a final complex wave that is notch filtered. Typically, this filtering (the pinna notch) occurs

Figure 1. The pinna. Folds and contours reflect sound from an elevated (+ and -) source. This means that a combination of the direct path and a secondary path of the same source exist. Some of the higher frequencies in the secondary path are delayed by a half wavelength compared to those in the direct path, thereby being canceled in the final mix when reaching the auditory canal. This produces a pinna notch (notch filter effect)

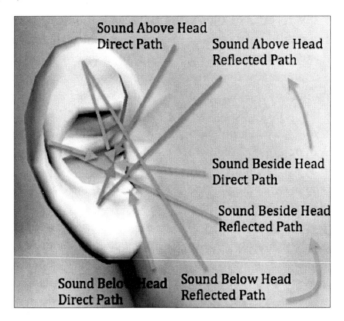

primarily between 5kHz/6 kHz and 16 kHz (Long et al, 2005).

Dynamic movement of an elevated source aids the localization processes immensely as the affected frequencies and the depth of the notch filter changes with source elevation. The depth of the notch is more pronounced with elevated sources in the frontal area.

The second view is that the pinna is a frequency-domain filter, promoting spectral peaks due to the excitatory properties of various areas of the pinna structure (Shaw & Teranishi, 1968; Kahana & Nelson, 2000; Blauert, 1997; Han, 1991). The pinna's transfer function (filter profile) is linearly dependant upon the distance and direction of the sound source. This is the only portion of the human auditory system that is linear in function, and by the time frequency spectra are coded at the basilar membrane stage, the coding properties are logarithmic. It is also important to note that because every person's pinna shape and structure

is unique, their transfer functions are unique. This is a trait that makes virtual binaural simulation so difficult to render on mass. A generic HRTF, therefore, only works on a portion of the general population.

Another important factor to consider when describing the above system is the acoustically rigid structure to which the pinnae are attached – the head. This aspect of the hearing system primarily relates to binaural hearing (comparing the input of both ears) on the azimuth. The head shadows auditory content on the far side of the sound source, creating a signal intensity level difference when comparing input of both ears and is referred to as Interaural Intensity Difference (IID), or Interaural Level Difference (ILD) when specified in dB (Moore, 2003) – see Figure 2. Also produced are phase differences in relation to low frequency content and timing differences of entire wavelengths in relation to high frequency

Figure 2. The head and shoulders interfere with energy of an approaching sound-waves as it passes these structures, causing differences of intensity levels between each ear (IID or ILD)

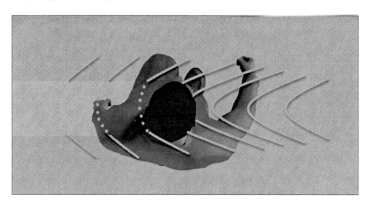

Figure 3. Sound approaching the listener from directly in front means that the sonic event reaches both left and right ears at the same time. Sound slightly off to the right means that the sonic event will reach the right ear c. 0.3msec before the left. Sound coming from the far right means that the sonic event will reach the right ear c. 0.6msec before the left

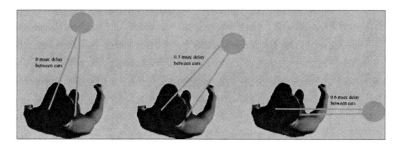

content. The timing differences are referred to as Interaural Time Difference (ITD) – see Figure 3.

Interaural Time Delay is most functional for frequencies between 20 Hz and 2 kHz. The human auditory system is very accurate at locating sounds based on ITD. Studies (Bear et al, 2007) show that humans can discrimination sound-source location to an angle as minute as 1° or 2°. In terms of a time value equivalent, this works out at about 11 µsec.

Interaural Intensity, or Level, Difference (IID/ILD) entails the difference in intensity between sound arriving at one ear compared to the other. Essentially, the head absorbs and reflects some of the energy of the sound-wave before it has a chance of reaching the ear at the 'shadowed' side

(see Figure 2). The combination of both IID/ILD and ITD is known as the duplex theory.

Spatial Audio in DirectX Audio

DirectX® is a set of APIs associated with multimedia entertainment and game-play on Windows® machines. Many of the features outlined in this section are also fundamental features of other APIs implementing spatial audio for games. DirectX® Audio consists of two primary elements – the Buffer (the element that creates the sound) and the Listener. Both elements have two fundamental properties, position and velocity, but some other properties are also included. The correlation between sound intensity and distance between Buffer and Listener is based on two Buffer-only properties called Maximum Distance and Minimum Distance (see Figure 4). If the listener is outside Maximum Distance, then he/she cannot hear the sound source (Turcan & Wasson, 2004). If the Listener is between Maximum Distance and Minimum Distance, then the sound volume gradually increases as the Minimum Distance threshold is reached, and gradually fades as the Maximum Distance threshold is reached. Once

Minimum Distance is reached, the sound volume is capped (McCuskey & Boer, 2003).

Sound Cones are also a Buffer-only property in DirectX®. An inner and outer cone is defined and is similar in implementation to the Maximum Distance and Minimum Distance properties. However, Sound Cones express the Buffer's sound directionality (see Figure 4). The Sound Cone default setting is 360°, which means the Buffer

Figure 4. The Buffer outputs sound. A Maximum Distance and Minimum Distance are specified. When a Listener is inside the Minimum Distance (L1), the Buffer is heard at full volume. If the Listener is between Minimum Distance and Maximum Distance (L2 & L3), the sound fades in or out depending on whether they are moving toward Minimum Distance or Maximum Distance. If the Listener is outside Maximum Distance (L4), then they cannot hear the Buffer. A Sound Cone can also be set for the Buffer's sound, giving it directionality. A Sound Cone is made up of two parts, the Inside Cone and the Outside Cone. A Listener that is directly in front of the Buffer (L1 and L2) will experience a louder sound than a Listener that is off angle (L3). Sound Cones and Max/Min Distance are used in conjunction. Therefore, L1 will experience the loudest sound from the Buffer because L1 is both in the Inside Cone and within Minimum Distance. Although L2 is also in the Inside Cone, L2 is further away (between Minimum and Maximum Distance) and therefore will experience a slightly softer sound. L3 will experience a softer sound again, even though L3 is the same distance from the Buffer as L2. This is because L3 is in the Outer Cone

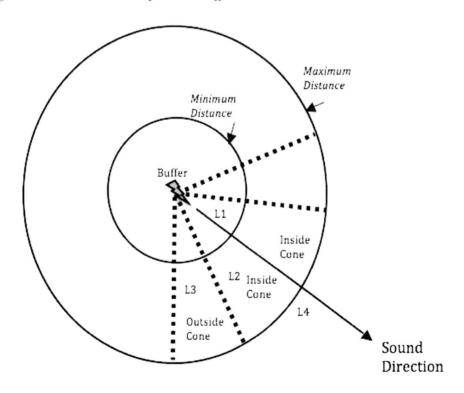

sound output is omni-directional, but this can be altered by the audio programmer.

Some Listener only properties in DirectX® Audio include Orientation. This allows for the audio engine to dampen sounds coming from the rear of the Listener. Rolloff Factor allows the Listener to experience appropriate fading attributes as they move towards or away from the Buffer. This is especially useful in relation to Minimum and Maximum Distance properties associated with the Buffer. The Doppler Factor is again a Listener-only property that simulates the Doppler Shift from the game-player's viewpoint (i.e. Buffers that have a fast velocity and pass quickly by the Listener).

Spatial Audio in OpenAL

The OpenAL™ API is a cross-platform, cross-collaborative audio library specializing in 3D audio. It is related to OpenGL™, the 3D graphics API. It is a significant audio component of games on Mac OS® X and the iPhone® OS systems, as well as other major platforms such as Windows®, Linux® varieties, Xbox®, BDS®, Solaris® etc. Many of its underlying features are similar to those outlined in the previous section (DirectX® Audio).

There are three primary objects in OpenAL® – Sources, Buffers and Listeners (McCuskey & Boer, 2003) (Hiebert et al, 2007). The Buffer refers to the actual PCM file, while the Source references the Buffer (the audio file) and adds positional attributes. More than one Source can reference the same Buffer (McCuskey & Boer, 2003). A Buffer contains properties such as the sample-rate of the PCM file, bit-depth, channels (for spatial sound implementation, this should be mono) and file size.

A Source has a significant number of properties, some of which are very similar to DirectX® Audio. These refer to elements such as pitch changes, min and max volume changes, maximum distance, inner and outer cone gains, sound-source position and velocity, sound-source direction and roll-off

factors. The Listener properties are also familiar such as Listener position, velocity and orientation.

Spatial Audio in XNA

Microsoft® announced their .NET™ Framework-based computer game development suite, XNA®, in 2004. It is a more 'user-friendly' implementation of Microsoft® DirectX® components for game programming. Using the XNA® toolset, one can develop games using the C# programming language for the Xbox® and Windows® platforms. Audio is implemented using 5.1 surround sound or stereo output. Unfortunately, although 5.1 is by far the most popular spatial speaker arrangement in the mainstream market, it presents quite a coarse spatial representation compared to other spatial renditions. Implementing spatial attributes to the audio in XNA® is a relatively simple procedure, and some very intuitive tools are provided for the sound designer. Using XACT®, a tool that is central to XNA's audio API, a sound designer can easily render spatial sonic attributes to sprites, characters and other elements in the game. The XACT™-rendered audio (with associated spatial attributes) can be accessed from within the main XNA® project through the Content Pipeline, much like any other external game element (for example, images, sprites, and textures). XACT's GUI is what makes the process so easy and the sound designer can graphically implement spatial attributes such as Doppler Shift, Distance Attenuation etc. and apply them to a game character or sprite (the emitter) in the main XNA® project. XACT™ will dynamically update the spatial audio output of the emitter in the game as it moves around, based on the criteria set in its GUI.

Spatial Audio in the Unreal Engine

Some spatialization cues are also present in the Unreal™ Audio System by Epic Games®. A sonic asset in Unreal™, is called a SoundCue, which is more than just a raw audio file. A SoundCue may include several separate WAV files grouped together (for example, a series of hammering sounds), as well as node instructions relating to cue information. During any one random loop rendition, one or more of the hammering sounds may be output, ensuring that the loop is not repetitive. SoundCue node instructions can include elements such as volume attenuation or pitch adjustment. These instructions can be implemented in the SoundCue Editor, which also give the designer an overview of how node instructions are connected. For example, the Attenuation node can be given a MaxRadius value and a MinRadius value. As the listener progresses away from the emitter, the sound will fade out as he/she travels from the MaxRadius to MinRadious, and will be silent once the listener goes beyond the MaxRadius value. The DistanceCrossFade node allows for a similar environment, but with multiple emitters in the scene.

Spatial Audio in JSR-234

A number of spatial audio solutions have been present for several years in the mobile phone industry, but have not been fully commercially developed. The Advanced Multimedia Supplements (AMMS, JSR-234) is a Nokia® initiative that brings spatial audio to J2ME™ supporting devices, such as the Symbian™ OS (Li & Knudsen, 2005). It is developed and maintained by the Java Community Process. JSR-234 significantly enhances the Mobile Media API (MMAPI, JSR-135) and offers the implementation of generic binaural audio output for mobile games. JSR-234 is based on a model comprising source-medium-receiver (Goyal, 2006) and incorporates functions such as sound-source directivity, distance attenuation, receiver orientation, velocity, Doppler, location, reverberation etc. These are implemented using Java classes in the J2ME™ environment.

Spatial Audio in OpenSL-ES

Another interactive spatial audio solution for mobile phones is OpenSL-ES™, developed by Khronos® Group as an open standard. It expands on the services offered in OpenMAX™ AL (an open multimedia API for embedded systems). Three auditory profiles are implemented – Phone, Music and Game. The Game profile is the most sophisticated of the three, offering advanced spatial audio features not present on the other two profiles. The implementation is again binaural and offers features much like that offered in JSR-234.

Spatial Audio in MPEG-4

MPEG® (Motion Picture Experts Group) is a working group of an ISO/IEC subcommittee dedicated to forming multimedia standards. One of the main original goals of MPEG® was the definition and multiplexing of low bitrate video and audio bit streams. However, MPEG-4™ has significantly expanded the scope of MPEG®, and now includes a wide variety of both natural and synthetic multimedia objects, producing a dynamic, interactive, platform-independent format. This means that MPEG-4™ has many potential benefits for the online gaming industry (Wang et al, 2001).

MPEG-4™ multimedia scenes have inherited a lot from VRML/X3D™. However, extra scene nodes have been added. Sound nodes in MPEG-4™ have also been significantly extended and incorporate sound spatialization, implemented using the Environmental Spatialisation of Audio (ESA) architecture. The ESA model has two distinct elements – physical and perceptual. The physical element enables sound sources to contain spatial attributes, such as directivity, velocity, location, intensity etc., and also simulates environmental factors such as reverb, diffusion, transparency etc. The ESA also enacts perceptual elements incorporating descriptive fields such as Liveness, RoomPresence, Warmth etc. (Rault et al, 1998; Pereira & Ebrahimi, 2002; Murphy & Rumsey, 2001; Väänänen, 1998).

Spatial Audio in MPEG-Surround

MPEG Surround™ technology enables the transmission of multichannel audio over a network with bit rate efficiency and mono/stereo backward compatibility. In addition, the specification allows for the decoding of the surround data into binaural stereo output on MPEG Surround™-enabled mobile devices via headphones (see figure 5). MPEG Surround™ is based on Spatial Audio Coding (Breebaart, 2006), which exploits inter-channel irrelevance during the compression process. The spatial cues are extracted from the multichannel audio and down-mixed to mono, stereo or another number of channels that is less than the original number of channels. These down-mixed audio files are compressed and transmitted using standard MPEG® encoders, while the spatial information is transmitted as ancillary data along with the audio. On a multichannel-receiving end, an up-mix regenerates the multichannel output. However, if the output device is legacy stereo, MPEG Surround™ will render the spatial cues as 3D binaural sound (binaural decoding mode) for headphones (see Figure 5). For more in-depth information on MPEG Surround™, consult (Breebaart et al, 2006; Breebaart, 2007; Breebaart et al, 2005). This technology may have a significant impact on network-based games for mobile applications.

Design Options: New Choices for Developers of Math Education Tools

The background description of some of the tools capable of rendering spatial audio environments shows that there is ample choice for developers who seek to explore the potential of using spatial sound in mathematics education for blind students. The initial decision lies in whether to present the material binaurally or via discrete multi-channel speakers. This decision will inevitably cut down the choice available. There are several differences between binaural and multi-channel that the designer needs to first consider.

Advantages to Multi-Channel

- A multi-channel setup, most notably 7.1 or more, provides excellent spatial imaging when seated in the sweet spot.
- A multi-channel setup does not suffer from trying to 'externalize' the sounds. A problem with many binaural renditions is that sound can feel like it is inside the head, or confined to the dimensions of the headphones.
- In a multi-channel setup, the listener's ears are not covered, allowing him/her to remain aware of other sound sources around them, or to interact with others in the environment.
- If trends continue, 22.2 configurations built into the room spec will provide excellent spatial resolution both on the azimuth and on the vertical plane.

Advantages to Binaural

- Binaural presentation of spatial sound information has the distinct advantage of allowing the system to be mobile and light, providing the opportunity to be easily implemented on mobile devices.
- The setup time and simplicity of a binaural system provides an advantage over multi-speaker setups. Typically, a binaural system only requires the user to plug in a pair of headphones.
- The binaural system is more robust in terms of improper placement by the end-user. A multi-channel setup needs to conform to the correct configuration or speaker placement standards. This fact is often ignored by the end-user, resulting in a very poor spatial image experience.

Figure 5. MPEG Surround. Multichannel audio is encoded by down-mixing to stereo and abstracting spatial cues as ancillary data. On the receiver side, audio is decoded and combined again with spatial cues

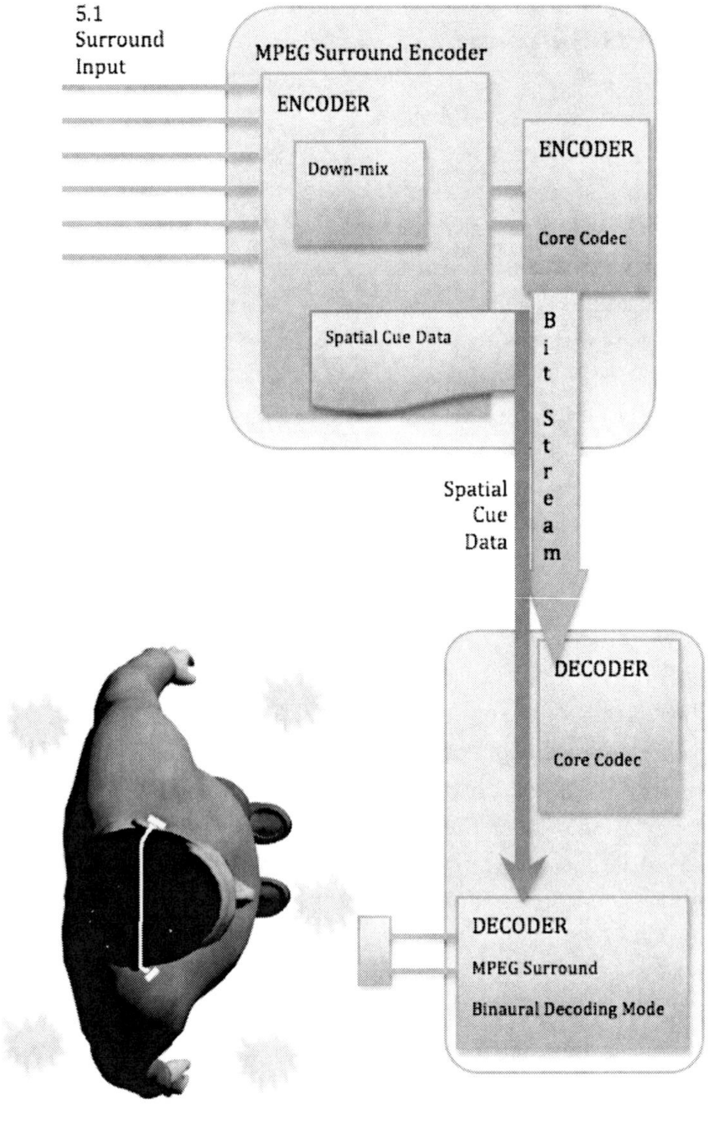

- The binaural system is a tidy solution in terms of cabling, lessening the hazard of falling over cables or knocking speakers.

If a multi-channel system has been chosen, then DirectX® Audio, XNA/XACT®, OpenAL®, MPEG-Surround™ and Unreal™ Audio System are some obvious choices. If the binaural approach is required, then OpenAL® and MPEG-Surround™ cater for this, but so too do JSR-234, OpenSL-ES™ and MPEG-4™.

Another decision that will curb the designer's choice of tools is the preferred platform. For example, if the developer requires the mathematical software to be cross-platform, then XNA/XACT® and DirectX® Audio are obviously sided with Microsoft® platforms. Other fundamental choices in this domain are whether the education software needs to be implemented on a mobile or desktop platform. Environments such as J2ME™ have been designed from the ground-up to cater for hardware limitation associated with mobile devices, offering extremely efficient spatial sound rendering. However, distinct differences exist between the libraries of J2SE™ (Java environment for desktop machines) and J2ME™, forcing some re-coding if the education software is to be implemented on both desktop and mobile devices. In this vain, MPEG-4™ and MPEG-Surround™ offer solutions to both the cross-platform desktop-only issue and the cross-platform desktop to mobile device issue. Although MPEG-4™ and MPEG-Surround™ have yet to be fully implemented and exploited, it is an attractive solution for this issue alone.

Included in all of these implementations is the ability for the listener to virtually navigate the spatial environment. This is an important feature if blind students are to get the most out of the education tool. The ease at which both the spatial sound environment and virtual-listener-navigation can be welded together in all of the above-mentioned tools is impressive. This is of a huge advantage over the systems currently employed by blind students for mathematics education (see section Current State of Mathematics Education for the Blind). The ability to explore content in an interactive, non-linear manner and to allow users to zoom in and out of content detail has yet to be properly exploited. The software environments mentioned above inherently cater for this approach due to a strong gaming design. However, the primary method of relaying mathematics to the blind student remains linear-speech, limited haptics and an array of unconventional, restricted methods.

CURRENT STATE OF MATHEMATICS EDUCATION FOR THE BLIND

Access to high quality education for blind students varies considerably from country to country. Some provide dedicated schools, others provide dedicated classes within mainstream education, others provide no dedicated stream at all for the blind, and other countries provide a mix of all the above. For more information on related statistics, refer to (OECD, 2005). It is debatable which approach is best in this regard, and although students with visual disabilities generally attain high grades (Blackorby et al, 2004), what is evident is that an improvement is required in the way mathematics, engineering, science and technology are taught to blind students.

Prior to the proliferation of digital technology, a variety of systems prevailed for relaying mathematics to blind students. These included special Braille code, German Film, Fuzzy Felt and some other unorthodox approaches. Braille is a reading and writing system for the visually disabled invented in the early half of the 19th Century. In its most fundamental form, it consists of cells incorporating up to 6 dots (2x3 matrix) to represent a character. Like spoken language, different codes exist in Braille, with variations used by different nationalities (even of the same spoken language) and for alternative scripts. Codes are also used for music, computer notation and mathematics. Nemeth code facilitates the linear presentation of mathematical and scientific notation using six-dot Braille. 8-dot Braille (2x4 matrix) has also been developed, primarily in Europe, to accommodate more character possibilities and is common in refreshable computer Braille devices.

Several other 'non-digital' forms of representing mathematical elements have been utilized in education, and in some cases continue to play a significant role in early math learning. Embossed rulers, corkboard and pushpins, embossed graph paper etc. are tools that are still utilized for early learners, but their use is limited when it comes to managing and interpreting more complex and advanced mathematical scenarios.

Tactile Devices

In contrast to expert opinion that learning Braille is of significant importance to young blind students, Braille literacy has fallen dramatically over recent decades (Jernigan Institute, 2009). Precise reasons for this are sometimes difficult to ascertain, but the integration of TTS into core operating systems as standard, as well as the cost of purchasing peripheral digital Braille devices may be significant factors. Considered as specialist devices, refreshable Braille displays are extremely expensive when compared to the standard mouse and keyboard, reaching up to $12,000 for an 80-character display. Although we believe that Braille is an extremely important skill for a blind student to have, it still does not solve the problem relating to the transcription of spatial oriented mathematics or complex equations (Chapman & Stone, 1988; Tanti, 2007).

Some other tactile form factors have also been explored. Tactile graphics tablets incorporate raised surfaces in order to relay non-textual information to the user and are commonly employed for graphic intensive website browsing. However, problems with the effectiveness of tactile tablets when used as the sole presentation tool have led investigators to explore the possibility that congenitally blind users do not accurately match the dimensions of real-world 3D objects obtained via touch with their 2D representations on the flat tablet surface (Noordzij et al, 2007). This suggests that visual experience of 3D objects in space, even if only briefly acquired in early life, is necessary for accurately recognizing its 2D representation. Without the experience of actually visually witnessing details such as the convergence of lines with distance, or the diminishing of objects with distance, one's mental imagery is different if relying solely on gathering spatial data via touch. However, in contrast, other studies show examples where congenitally blind individuals actually do possess accurate mental images of 3D objects and can represent these accurately on a 2D plane

(Kennedy & Juricevic, 2006). Therefore, more research is required from a perception point of view to establish the exact circumstances, but what is clear is that tactile tablets, in their current design, still require Braille and/or speech support in order for them to be effective. Examples of this multimodal approach are the NOMAD project (Parkes, 1991) and the IVEO® touchpad.

In addition to tactile tablets, a more advanced form of haptic/force-feedback technology in the form of virtual surface property simulators are also used. The potential use of these devices in providing blind users with tactile feedback of simple geometric shapes and textures has been explored for over a decade (Jansson et al, 1999; Magnusson et al, 2002; Sjöström, 2001). Although the current form factor restricts the user to only one-point-contact, the benefits of this kind of research will be seen more readily when mass-produced force-feedback gaming devices become more advanced, allowing for a more dexterous haptic experience using standard, mainstream equipment.

Mathematics Software for the Blind

Perhaps one of the most significant undertakings in the area of providing interactive mathematical content to blind users is LAMBDA (Linear Access to Mathematics for Braille Devices and Audio-synthesis) (Edwards et al, 2006), a EU-IST funded project active from 2002 to 2005. It is a system consisting of an advanced mathematical editor and presenter, using a combination of speech and 8-dot Braille output, and an enhanced, customized mathematical notation called LAMBDA code. One of the most noteworthy features of LAMBDA code is its compatibility with MathML, allowing sighted teachers to interpret LAMBDA code in a visually compatible format. The cross conversion from LAMBDA code to MathML means that it is compatible with LaTeX, TTS engines such as JAWS™ and SAPI™, and peripheral Braille hardware. Another important feature incorporated in the LAMBDA project, and one that reveals its EU-wide focus, is that the Braille output is localized for various national Braille formats (Karshmer, 2007). However, the system is fundamentally linear and does not exhibit non-speech sound support, spatial sound or 3D tactile features.

Several other software tools are worth mentioning in relation to mathematics presentation for blind students. The MATHS Project (Mathematical Access for TecHnology and Science for Visually Disabled People) (Stevens, 1996) consisted of a partnership between five European research institutes from 1994 to 1997 – the University of York (UK), University College Cork (Ireland), F.H. Papenmeier GmbH (Germany), Katholieke Universiteit Leuven (Belgium) and Grif S.A (France). Using a multimodal approach, the system incorporated tactile, speech and non-speech sound output. The system was SGML-based and placed an interesting emphasis on the non-speech component. The use of non-speech sound in the MATHS Project was an innovative approach at the time, and was primarily based on PhD work carried out by Robert Stevens (Stevens, 1996). Although some time was spent on exploring the use of non-speech sound in the spatial context, it wasn't implemented in the final release.

Similar in some respects to the MATHS Project, MAVIS (Mathematics Accessible to Visually Impaired Students) (Karshmer et al, 1998) incorporated speech, non-speech sound, tactile elements and visual translations for sighted users. It was developed by Arthur Karshmer's team at New Mexico State University in the late 1990's and was a significant contribution to the field in that it implemented a cross-translation mechanism from ASCII Nemeth code to LaTeX, ASCII Nemeth code and/or LaTeX to audio, and LaTeX to ASCII Nemeth code. It made good use of standard mouse clicks and keyboard spacebar input to control output parameters. In MAVIS, there were also attempts at giving the blind user an overview of the structure of an equation by

breaking it into chunks and sonifying the data. However, no spatial aspect was developed.

AsTeR (Audio System For Technical Readings) (Raman, 1994) was developed by a distinguished blind researcher, T.V. Raman, during his PhD studies at Cornell University in 1994. It was a system that used primarily speech to indicate precise content and some top-level structure information of equations (including trigonometry and matrices). Non-speech sound was employed to indicate upcoming events, but utilized to a much lesser degree than in the MATHS Project or MAVIS. One of its primary functions was to relay technical documents in LaTeX format to speech. The AsTeR system incorporated speech prosody, pitch variation, output volume variation and timbre variation to denote structural elements within mathematical equations.

Several other mathematics software packages exist for visually disabled student and are summarized in (Karshmer et al, 2007). However, the potential of spatial audio has not been fully explored in the most common mathematics packages available. Therefore, although many new solutions have been revealed through the development of these packages, a fundamental problem of relaying an overview to the listener without initiating cognitive overload remains. We believe that a spatial auditory environment, taking into account the perceptual constraints involved, is a promising approach to overcoming the issue of relaying overview structures of mathematics and spatial elements of certain types of mathematics to blind students.

ISSUES PERTAINING TO PRESENTING AN OVERVIEW OF MATHEMATICAL STRUCTURES AND SPATIAL REPRESENTATION TO BLIND STUDENTS

Consider the typical second-level mathematics textbook dealing with trigonometric problems.

The use of diagrammatic aids to help readers grasp the spatial and organizational attributes of the problem is very frequent (see Figure 6). Oftentimes, these diagrams are not suitable for efficient textual translation as they result in overly complex explanations when mapping spatial organization to what is essentially a linear format. Complex text generally means complex Braille, but this scenario has an even greater impact on the efficiency of Text-To-Speech systems. Such systems (i.e. TTS) do not provide an effective source of external memory due to their temporal nature (i.e. the diagram is always available to refer back to, but speech, once output, is gone). This makes Braille and TTS in their current format arduous and impractical for use as an effective mathematical relay tool for blind students.

One will find that in cases where a text equivalent is attempted (and subsequently TTS and Braille), it frequently needs to be lengthy and convoluted, and is rapidly deprived of the efficiency that the diagram itself provides (i.e. a fast overview of the problem). This is easily demonstrated if one were to delete the diagram in Figure 6 and attempt a text equivalent to explain the relatively simple trigonometric problem.

This is not only an issue when dealing with mathematics conveying inherent spatial attributes (such as in trigonometry) but is also of concern when dealing with complex linear mathematical structures where spatial placement of elements within an equation impacts on the interpretation of the problem. Simple algebraic equations are easily relayed using text, Braille or speech:

$4x+3 = 7$... find x.

But a small increase in complexity now introduces elements of structure and spatial relationship:

$(4x+3)(3x+4) = 7$

With further complexity, the textual and spoken description required to relay the equation becomes very complex and confusing for the listener:
Simplify the following:

$(3x-1)(1-2x)-5(x^2-x+1)-(3x-7)+(3x^3+5x^2+4x+3)(7x-1)$

What the visual spatial layout and context provides in these examples is an accurate, referable overview that is fundamental to the comprehension of the overall mathematical problem. This subsequently allows the student to prepare a series of methods whereby they can tackle and solve the

Figure 6. In the triangle abc, a = 10, b = 16 and A = 30°. i) Find B. (Hint is given in diagram) and ii) Find |ab|. Using the diagram as a visual aid, the student can gain a fast and effective overview of the problem, immediately interpret the spatial attributes of the problem, obtain a significant hint and refer back to two short, simple questions. Without the diagrammatic aid, try to formulate a text only equivalent!

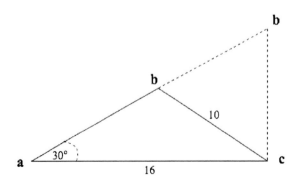

problem. The initial glance, or overview, is not only an important element in mathematics, but in many other areas where complex data is presented to the viewer or listener. Pie charts, graphs, and flowcharts are good examples where complex statistical characteristics of events, populations, etc. can be summarized and evaluated (for example, see Figure 7). This approach is a key element in the data visualization process.

Schneiderman (Schneiderman, 1996; Card et al, 1999) summarizes an effective visualization design structure as "Overview first, zoom and filter, then details-on-demand." A similar, if not identical, approach within the field of data auralization or sonification may be especially useful in terms of mathematics education for blind students.

Figure 7 presents the data in static 2D, which is still the most common method of data visualization. Current auditory graph technology is also predominantly non-spatial, although it does usually involve dynamic elements such as pitch movement. However, there are many instances in both the visual and auditory domains where 3D representation of data is advantageous. This is especially relevant for representing data that has intrinsic 3D qualities or data that entails movement (Mazza, 2009). Furthermore, the lack of 'external memory' (data on a screen) means that additional problems are encountered when presenting data via auditory means. If the listener misses a portion of the data, then this may seriously impinge on the quality of their interpretation of that data. The chances of this occurring within the auditory domain are compounded when the data requires several simultaneous sonic dimensions (pitch, intensity, rhythm etc.) to represent it (Peres & Lane, 2005). Additionally, given the temporal nature of current auditory graph designs, it is also difficult to compare past output with current output, such as directly comparing January's sales with October's in Figure 7.

Much research into the cognitive aspects of non-spatial data sonification is required for even the most trivial of data presentation (Nees & Walker, 2006; Flowers & Hauer, 1995; Nees & Walker, 2007). With the array of problems associated with non-spatial sound in this regard, it is clear that complex mathematical data could suffer a similar fate if non-spatial sound is utilized. Some mechanism is required that will lift the cognitive burden and allow some form of listener-control

Figure 7. Using some simple fictional data, we can see how effective visualization is in immediately giving the viewer a fast and simple overview. On the left a clustered column chart presents a clear indication that the summer months are the most lucrative for Product Z sales. On the right, a line graph is effective at presenting slightly more complex data, taking product sales from four different areas into account. It is very easy to immediately compare Product Z sale trends of each area, and we can immediately see that area 4 goes against the trend of the other three areas

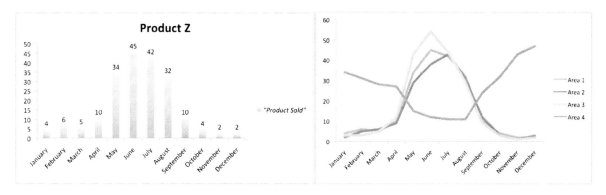

over the presentation. Direct TTS and Braille presentation of mathematical data does not provide the blind student with an effective equivalent allotted to sighted students, and non-spatial non-speech sound presents its own problems. Therefore, it is clear that an alternative method of representing the initial 'glance', or problem overview, is required, along with some form of user-control over how the data is navigated and explored. The authors believe that spatial sound developed in the game industry, or an educational audio game incorporating spatial sound and navigation control, is a useful tool in this regard.

Of course, as is the case in data visualization, not all scenarios require or benefit from spatial sound rendition. This is especially the case when unsophisticated data is being presented and typically consists of just one data series. However, with even just a slight increase in complexity (i.e. more than one data series), the hearing system is especially vulnerable to auditory scene clutter and auditory stream interference (Flowers, 2005). Careful choices with regard sonic dimensions and sound patterns are required on the part of the interface designer in order to maintain some sense of separation between data series. This is extremely difficult to achieve within a non-spatial context, and as the number of data series increases, the

auditory scene becomes extremely crowded for the listener. Spatial arrangement of sound streams can significantly accentuate the process of auditory stream segregation (Bregman, 1994). Using spatialization to clearly represent separate, but simultaneous, data series in an auditory graph is becoming a more popular method of data display. Brown et al (Brown et al, 2003) showed how the use of simple stereo separation (a rudimentary form of spatialization) helped listeners interpret simultaneous presentation of two data series. In further tests, they found significant benefit in 3D spatialization when presenting three data series (see figure 8 for illustration).

Experiencing sound in a non-spatial manner is a relatively recent and brief phenomenon, primarily introduced with the advent of telecommunication and sound amplification technologies. In contrast with this, 2D visual presentation of information has been part of human culture for thousands of years, from prehistoric cave-paintings to modern VDUs. Therefore, the success and relative ease at which complex data can be delivered using 2D visual tools may be simply down to evolutionary and cultural experience. Although surround sound and virtual binaural technologies (mostly within the entertainment and gaming industries) have now reverted our listening expe-

Figure 8. Each data series is virtually positioned triangularly around the listener via headphone output (Brown et al, 2003). Moving toward/away from a sonified data series allows the user to more accurately determine position and perceptually 'zoom' into a data series

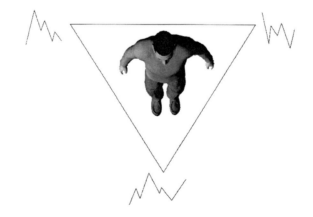

riences back to a more embracing spatial context, monaural output remains, by and large, the main presentation mode for assistive technology. If we lack the evolutionary and cultural experiences in this regard, then it may explain why the hearing system seems to be perceptually ill-equipped for tasks that are seemly trivial when relayed in the visual domain.

In addition to the potential uses of presenting simultaneous auditory streams and maintaining their perceptual segregation, spatialization encourages another very important facility – user-data interactivity. With interactivity comes a certain degree of user-control, allowing the user to self-evaluate the data at moments that correlate with their needs. In the 3D auditory graph environment developed by Brown et al (Brown et al, 2003), users could virtually navigate closer to one of the three data series for further investigation. This approach complies with Schneiderman's first and second visualization steps as mentioned above – 'overview first'; 'zoom and filter'. Although not implied in (Brown et al, 2003), the final step ('details on demand') could easily be implemented using speech output and activated by the user when required using a simple mouse click or other input device. User-data interaction is an important element in all sensory modes of complex data presentation as it is an effective method for avoiding or reducing cognitive overload (Mazza, 2009).

Therefore, non-visual presentation of complex mathematical information may benefit from an accurate auditory spatial rendition and interactive content navigation system. This concerns both mathematics that consist of inherent spatial attributes (for example trigonometry and matrices) and complex linear problems that may benefit from robust auditory stream segregation representing distinct, but related, chunks of data. Game technology offers not only a relatively accurate spatial sound render, but also incorporates established mechanisms of interacting with in-game content or data. The problems associated with

current approaches in presenting mathematical information to blind students may be overcome through gaming technology, given that it packages together both spatial sound and interactive navigation, potentially fulfilling the three elements (i) problem overview (ii) zoom and filter, and (iii) details on demand.

However, interface designers implementing a rich spatial audio environment must be mindful of the perceptual mechanisms of the human auditory system. Without a deep understanding, or without definitive guidelines in this respect, they may run into significant problems in terms of cluttered auditory scenes and cognitive overload. For example, decisions such as what sonic elements should be used need very careful consideration. Should the interface incorporate non-speech sound exclusively? Or should it contain speech? Or should it involve a multimodal approach? Decisions about the category of non-speech sound also require due consideration. Specific perceptual rules apply to different sonic structures and in different scenarios. In order to help auditory interface designers deal with such questions, we have developed a user interface model examining these perceptual issues.

PERCEPTUAL ISSUES RELATING TO SPATIAL AUDIO PRESENTATION

We have generated an Auditory User Interface Model (Neff, Keheo & Pitt, 2007; Neff, Pitt & Keheo, 2007) to guide the design process of developing an auditory interface that conforms to the perceptual traits of the human auditory system. The model outlines the auditory pathway from the most peripheral elements to the more central, higher cognitive mechanisms. We accept that many features of the human auditory system remain indeterminate but we believe that a viable model can be constructed for our purposes from contemporary perceptual theory (Vilimek & Hempel, 2005; Bregman, 1994; Jones & Macken, 1993; Jones et al, 1992; Baddeley, 1996; Wrigley

Figure 9. The auditory user interface model

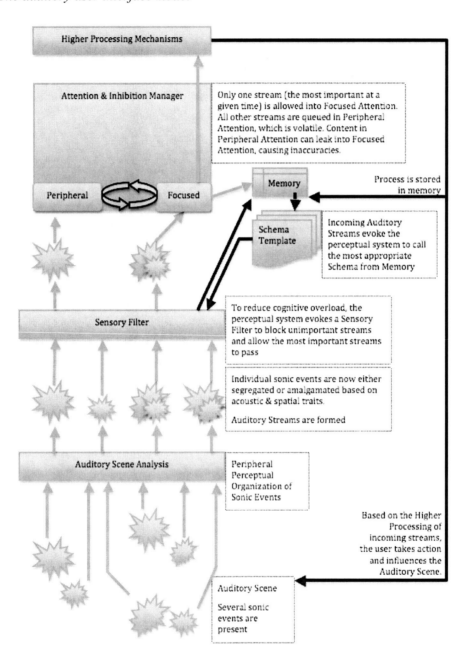

& Brown, 2000). The model comprises five main blocks—Auditory Scene Analysis, the Sensory Filter, Memory/Schema, the Attention and Inhibition Manager, and the Higher Processing Mechanism (see Figure 9).

In reference to Figure 9, the user is presented with an auditory scene, for example, consisting of several sonic events relaying mathematical information through spatial sound. A peripheral perceptual process organizes these sonic events into auditory streams by amalgamating some sonic events and segregating others. For example, we can hear an individual instrument, such as a flute, in a large ensemble despite the fact that many instruments are playing at the same time. Also, when the flute plays a series of notes (individual sonic events), we can determine that these sonic events are all from the same sound source – the flute. Particular acoustic structures and spatial arrangement are key criteria to how this primitive system works. Therefore, getting the structural design and spatial layout of sonic events wrong at this stage of the interface build will have an impact on the rest of the model's stages.

After the perceptual system organizes the sonic events into auditory streams, the Sensory Filter aims to simplify the auditory scene by allowing some auditory streams to pass while blocking many others. How the Sensory Filter determines which streams are allowed to pass is on a Schema template system stored in memory (discussed below). The Attention and Inhibition Manager further simplifies the scene by determining which stream, out of those allowed to pass by the Sensory Filter, is the most important and which streams can be queued in Peripheral Attention. The most important stream is allocated the best attention facilities (Focused Attention), and is subsequently given the most valuable Higher Processing resources. An example of a Higher Processing Mechanism is rehearsal where the sonic event is saved in memory and integrated into the Schema template system. Based on our model, the human auditory system needs to simplify a complex scene to determine the most vital information and subsequently choose the correct course of action. Without the various stages of filtering, a complex auditory scene would overwhelm the Higher Processing Mechanism.

The first stage of our model dealing with an auditory scene and subsequent auditory streams is based on the work of Bregman's Auditory Scene Analysis (Bregman, 1994). The segregation and amalgamation processes are the most peripheral of auditory perceptual mechanisms, and is autonomous. Although this primitive process simplifies the auditory scene somewhat, many streams may be generated and could still present a complex scenario for the Higher Processing Mechanism.

Therefore, the Sensory Filter will block many of the auditory streams produced during the autonomous process.

The Sensory Filter determines which streams to block and which to allow pass based on the user's experience of the particular task or environment in question. This information is stored at a higher level of the auditory system and is based on Schema Theory (Baddeley, 1996). In relation to our model, we describe this as a template of experiences, which are stored in long-term memory. The more exposure to a particular event/environment, the more refined the template becomes. This means that with more experience of the auditory task/environment at hand, the more accurate the Sensory Filter will be at determining the correct streams to pass and block. An inexperienced user, therefore, lacks the appropriate schema template and will apply a mismatched one, resulting in some important auditory streams being blocked while unimportant ones gaining access.

The Attention and Inhibition Manager further filters the auditory information by choosing which streams are allocated to Focused Attention and which are allocated to the volatile Peripheral Attention. Just one stream at a time is allowed access to Focused Attention and competition exists between streams for Focused Attention (Wrigley, 2000). Once again, particular acoustic traits of each stream play an important role in the process of Focused Attention allocation. It is therefore possible that unimportant streams may interfere with the allocation of the important stream to Focused Attention because of their acoustic makeup, such as sudden changes in pitch or volume. This is why we need to carefully consider the acoustic design of sonic events in the implementation of our system.

The rules of the memory component and the Higher Processing Mechanism in our model, is based on the Changing-State Hypothesis (Jones & Macken, 1993). The importance of this theory in relation to our model is that, although the Peripheral Loop is not directly linked to memory, streams in this loop can interfere with Higher Processing resources attending to the stream in memory. Jones et al (Jones & Macjen, 1993; Jones et al, 1922) have shown how an acoustically changing signal (stream) over time, whether speech based or non-speech based, can interfere with the rehearsal process attending to an important stream in memory – the Irrelevant Sound Effect. This again, has extremely important ramifications for the design of our interface where we have to balance between changes in a signal denoting changes of information over time, and yet avoid interfering with another stream. If possible, we aim to avoid any simultaneous audio instances.

EXPERIMENTAL STUDIES IN RELATION TO SPATIAL SONIC RENDERING OF TRIGONOMETRIC PROBLEMS

In a previous pilot study we examined various designs that complied to varying degrees with the rules of our model (Neff & Pitt, 2008). These tests (test 1) showed that three separate tones of varying pitch denoting angle size had weak results. We asserted that the three individual, but related, sine-tones were not perceived as one stream but rather three separate competing streams. This scenario, therefore, was not successful in simplifying the auditory scene. It also had an impact on the attention mechanism as a minimum of c.600ms (Wrigley & Brown, 2000) space between the offset of one stream and the onset of another is required for Focused Attention to recalibrate and align with a new stream. Also, we found that using pitch to denote angle size was redundant information as subjects concentrated on spatial position and made no use of the pitch information. We also found that subjects had difficulties in accurately locating sine-tones in 3D space. Refer to figure 10 for a summary of the results of these tests (test 1).

In a further pilot study (test 2), we designed a more compliant implementation using one single, traveling sound employing elements such as Doppler Shift and distance attenuation (Neff & Pitt, 2008). We also tested the use of white noise since its rich frequency spectrum helps in localization. We tested the following scenarios:

Figure 10. A summary of the results of a pilot study (test 1) examining various scenarios of individual sine-tones with varying pitch denoting angle size in 3D space. Some tests were not compliant to any of the rules of our model while others attempted to be compliant with only some of the rules of our model. Overall, accuracy levels needed much improvement

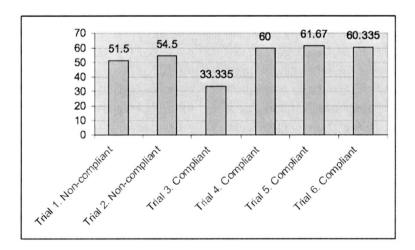

1. Using an unchanging sine-tone in the frontal hemisphere
2. Using an unchanging sinc-tone in surround sound
3. Using a sine-tone with slightly changing texture at points where an angle occurred in frontal hemisphere
4. Using a sine-tone with slightly changing texture at points where an angle occurred in surround sound
5. Using a sine-tone with emphasized change in texture at points where an angle occurred in frontal hemisphere
6. Using a sine-tone with emphasized change in texture at points where an angle occurred in surround sound
7. Using unchanging white noise in the frontal hemisphere
8. Using unchanging white noise in surround sound
9. Using white noise with slightly changing texture at points where an angle occurred in frontal hemisphere
10. Using white noise with slightly changing texture at points where an angle occurred in surround sound
11. Using white noise with emphasized change in texture at points where an angle occurred in frontal hemisphere
12. Using white noise with emphasized change in texture at points where an angle occurred in surround sound

Refer to Figure 11 for a summary of the results of these tests (test 2). These scenarios complied more faithfully with the model where only one stream was present in the auditory stream. Therefore, Focused Attention was allocated to the correct stream without interference from other streams. Also, this controlled competition at the Focal Buffer stage. Comparing results from both pilot studies, it is clear that accuracy levels were improved in most cases when employing this design. However, more improvement and model compliance was necessary.

We therefore decided to run more tests in an attempt to improve accuracy. The previous design was based on the ever-changing location of angles, whether frontal hemisphere or surround sound. Therefore, in order to simplify this process, we decided that a consistent position of the first angle occurrence would be more compliant with build-

Figure 11. A summary of the results of a pilot study (test 2) examining various scenarios of continuous sine-tone and white noise in denoting angle occurrence in 3D space. The best results where in fact a sine-tone in the frontal hemisphere with a textural variance of the tone at points where the angle occurred

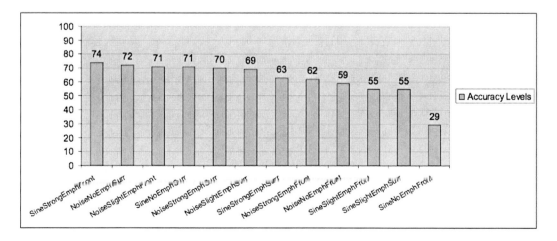

ing a simple schema template. Instead of an unexpected location, as in the previous studies and as illustrated in Figure 12a, we used the subject's head location as a consistent anchor point for the first angle (refer to Figure 12b).

New Pilot Study Overview

Based on our previous pilot studies (tests 1 & 2), we needed to implement a design that enacted the schema element in our model. Therefore, we structured our design so that it was consistent and whereby the user could easily build a schema template over time and experience. To achieve this, we always positioned the occurrence of the first angle (or change of sound direction) consistently at the subject's head location (test 3).

Once again we used both sine-tones and white noise, with and without textural variances. Refer to table 1 for a summary of the sound types used in test 3. Three sighted users performed each trial, presented randomly, and accuracy was measured for each scenario.

To assess user accuracy, each subject was required to draw the angle as accurately as pos-

sible after one rendition of each trial. No trial was repeated. The accuracy levels were evaluated by comparing the exact angle measurement produced by the system with that produced by the subject. This comparison was converted to accuracy percentages in an Excel spreadsheet.

The same spreadsheet formulas where used as in the previous pilot studies. Column A contained the angle size (in degrees) relayed by the subject and column B contained the correct angle size. Column C contained the difference between column A and B. Since only positive integers were required, we needed to include an IF ELSE statement that would determine whether the subjects' angle size was greater or less than the correct angle size. The following formula was used for column C:

$$=IF(A1>B1, A1-B1, B1-A1)$$

Column D contained the percentage equivalent of column C. Again, we required an IF ELSE statement since the largest angle between column A and B was regarded as 100 percent. Therefore, column D was the percentage by which the subject was inaccurate.

Figure 12. (a) In our previous pilot studies (tests 1 & 2), the angle or change of direction of the traveling sound could occur at any point in front or behind the subject. This led to inconsistencies for building a robust schema template for this scenario. (b) In the pilot studies described in this paper (test 3), we used the subject's head position as a consistent anchor point of where the first angle occurred. According to our model, this allows for a robust schema to be built over time and experience. The user will always know that the first angle occurs at their head

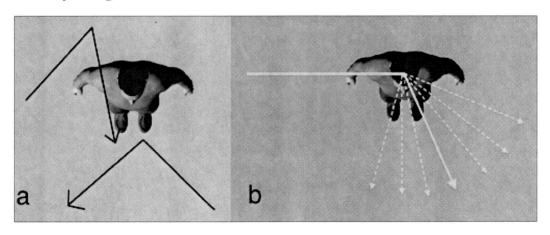

Table 1. Summary of sine-tones and white noise used during pilot study (test 3)

Description	Sine-tone	White noise
Without any angle indication	6 angles. No effect for angle	6 angles. No effect for angle
With angle indication	6 angles. Flanger effect denoting angle	6. angles. Flanger effect denoting angle
With emphasized angle indication	6. angles. Wahwah effect denoting angle	6 angles. Wahwah effect denoting angle

=IF(B1>A1, (100/B1)*C1, (100/1)*C1)

Column E contained the percentage accuracy of the subjects' angle compared with the correct angle. This was simply a case of subtracting the figure in column D from 100.

=100-D1

The host machine we used was a Dell® DIMC521 with a 1.9GHz AMD® Athlon™ Dual Core Processor with 1GB of RAM. To build our virtual environment we used Microsoft® XNA® Game Studio 2.0™ with its associated XACT™ audio engine and X3D Audio specialization helper library. This ran on Microsoft® Windows Vista® Home Basic edition. The 5.1 surround sound hardware used was Sigma® Tel 9227 audio card and Typhoon® speakers.

Pilot Study Accuracy Results

Figure 13 shows a summary of the results of the pilot studies conducted (test 3). The best scenario in this case was white noise with a slight indication of angle occurrence via a flanger effect. Overall, there was a further improvement compared with the previous pilot studies.

Figure 13. A summary of the results (test 3) showing a marked improvement on the previous pilot study. The most accurate scenario in this case was the use of white noise with a slight indication to angle occurrence

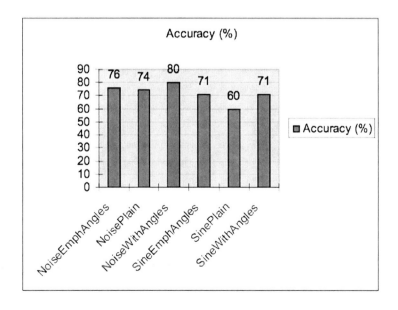

Comparison of Results between Previous Pilot Study and Current Pilot Study

In all scenarios except two (plain sine-tone and sine-tone with emphasized angle occurrence), the addition of applying schema rules to our implementation has further enhanced accuracy results. Figure 14 displays the comparison showing results from the previous pilot study (light grey) with results from the current pilot study (dark grey).

FUTURE RESEARCH DIRECTIONS

Further studies are necessary to examine more stages of the user model. These tests help to understand and further refine each stage of the model. Our eventual aim is to design a system that is truly multimodal and will allow the following services:

- The blind student will be able to comprehensively interpret the spatial and structural elements of mathematics, using spatial non-speech sound.

- The blind student will be able to rapidly observe an overview of the mathematical problem via non-speech sound.

- The blind student will be able to virtually navigate the system using a gamepad in order to zoom into certain mathematical elements and filter out other elements not currently required.

- The blind student will receive some form of haptic feedback (gamepad vibration) to let them know when they have reached a particular target.

- Once he/she has reached a target, they may trigger speech output to obtain specific information about the target, for example, exact unit details (details on demand).

Other applications are also being examined using this model, such as menu icon interpretation and navigation on mobile devices for blind users. We are again using spatial audio in conjunction with the model to build the interface, and we are

Figure 14. A summary of the results (test 1, 2 & 3) showing a marked improvement on the previous pilot study. The most accurate scenario (accuracy %) in this case was the use of white noise with a slight indication to angle occurrence

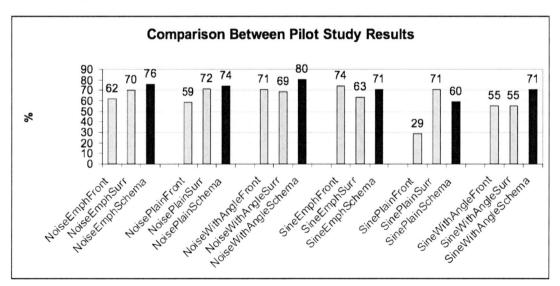

also incorporating accelerometer technology. We are using accelerometers to allow the blind user to 'roll' toward various sonic icons and perform accelerometer-based gestures when the icon target is reached so as to interact with the icon. We envisage that this approach will have important benefits for educational audio games for mobile devices.

CONCLUSION

In this chapter we discussed the problems encountered by blind students when attempting to interpret and interact with certain types of mathematical content. We discussed how many forms of mathematics are based on spatial attributes, structural relationships and abstract associations. Most current interfaces relaying mathematics to blind students are based on Braille and speech output, which are linear systems and do not conform well to inherently spatial mathematics, such as trigonometry and matrices, or to mathematics that imply complex structural relationships, such as algebra. Therefore, an alternative method of presenting these features is necessary.

Another problem associated with presenting mathematics to blind students is the lack of an efficient overview. Sighted users are informed of the overall structure of a mathematical problem via diagrams or visual summaries, which when translated to speech or Braille transform from being convenient overviews to complex, long-winded sentences. Many forms of mathematics are traditionally founded on descriptive visual aids, and without them, the problem is almost impossible to understand. Therefore, some method of providing the blind student with a fast overview that is comparable to a visual diagrammatic aid is required.

The final problem with regard to mathematics education for blind students is the process of retaining some form of control over the pace at which the problem is presented. Sighted users can read a problem at a rate that is comfortable, and at the same time very easily recap over a previous section that they didn't understand. This is because a page in the book, or the computer screen, acts as an external memory. The transient nature of speech means that blind students must rely on their own internal memory, which is sometimes inaccurate. It is also difficult to recall earlier steps, especially if a lengthy equation is being relayed to the student using speech alone. Therefore, some form of user-control is needed that would allow the blind student to skip back and forth at their own pace so that all elements of an equation are understood before the problem is tackled.

The problems mentioned above are not trivial, and much effort and innovation from researchers in the field have yielded some good progress and understanding of the issues. However, many of the fundamental problems persist, and mathematics education for many blind students remains a significant stumbling block to careers in science, technology and engineering. A robust, comprehensive solution has yet to be achieved, and many approaches rely on specialist, expensive equipment. We believe that mainstream technology should be utilized to tackle this issue head-on, as it will offer the most realistic and accessible solution to the problem. We feel that game technology offers such a solution.

Using standard hardware, game technology offers spatial audio, interactive navigation, content on demand, haptic feedback, and an element of fun. These ingredients, if utilized correctly, may offer the cheapest and most comprehensive solution to mathematics education for blind students. By employing a detailed user interface model, we are developing a system that is based on well-established theories of perception and cognition. Our goal is to provide a system that will allow spatial mathematics and structural relationships to be rendered to the listener using spatial audio mapping, will allow problem overviews to be relayed using non-speech sound, will allow the user to maintain control by providing virtual

3D navigation, will provide non-aural real-time feedback using gamepad haptics, and will provide precise content on demand via speech, activated only when required by the student.

Some key guidelines for designers of educational games when incorporating critical audio elements include:

- De-cluttering the auditory scene. Making the mistake of creating a large palette of sound at this stage of the interface will compromise the efficiency of all other perceptual stages in the chain. Only the most crucial data should be sonified and inexperienced designers may try to sonically represent many data elements at once.

- When important spoken content is being relayed, all other audio content should be greatly reduced. If some atmosphere is required during speech relay, then slow, unchanging sound content (such as long chord progressions on a synth pad) should be used instead.

- Not all data dimensions are used or interpreted by the listener. For example, in our pilot-studies, pitch was initially employed to represent angle size, but ended up being redundant. This was due to the subject not being able to easily interpret the pitch representation. They instead concentrating solely on angle position as represented by the spatial location of the emitting sound. In addition, incorporating this extra dimension only created a changeable element in the auditory stream, which goes against the rules of the *Changing-State Hypothesis* in the model, resulting in perceptual interference at higher levels.

- Unlike visual presentation of data where a form of external memory is available (the screen), the temporal nature of sound presentation means that the listener may easily miss some of the auditory streams. Therefore, some form of accessible "shelf life" for sonified data may be also useful. However, this cannot impact on current audio output either and remains a serious challenge for designers. Keyboard shortcuts may play a functional role where the listener can jump back to key moments of the stream. Other methods still under investigation are the rear spatialization of background sonic icons.

- If an auditory stream representing an emergency situation needs to be pulled to the forefront of the perceptual system, certain sonic dimensions can play a useful roll in grabbing attention. Sudden pitch and intensity variation easily grabs a listener's attention. A whistle sound, which is very common in many societies, is often used to call someone's attention. A human whistle sound employs these exact sonic features - rapid pitch and/or intensity change. If during game-play an error message requires the user's attention, then a sonic icon employing such features may be useful.

- If data incorporating two or three elements needs to be sonically represented, then forcing stream segregation may be the appropriate approach. This can be achieved by conforming to stream segregation rules in the model. Spatial location, separating sound in virtual space, is a very robust method for forcing stream segregation. Some other more subtle approaches can also be attempted, such as incorporating wide pitch gaps between sources, or significant textural differences. However, care must be taken as to how many sources you can represent at once, and sequential presentation of streams may yield better results.

- Building up the user's experience is also a key element. It is often useful to employ auditory icons over earcons for this very reason. Earcons tend to be abstract in design, and require more learning, but auditory icons readily map sounds already associated with real-world events. This is one major advantage over earcons, as the listener already has some form of memory template associated with the sounds. However, there is much less control over the sonic dimensions of auditory icons, and within a complex soundscape, auditory icons can easily cause havoc. This is a fundamental choice the designer has to make from the outset.

- In order to build schema templates (i.e. build the user's experience with the specific sounds used in the game), it would not be unreasonable for the designer to incorporate a sonic icon learning level for the user. This would help naturalize the user to the soundscape and to data elements the various sonic icons represent. As the schema becomes more mature, then the perceptual system will more readily deal with several auditory streams at once.

REFERENCES

Ahrens, J., & Spors, S. (2007). Rendering of virtual sound sources with arbitrary directivity in higher order Ambisonics. *Proceedings from the AES 123rd International Convention*, NY, USA.

Ahrens, J., & Spors, S. (2008). Focusing of virtual sound sources in higher order Ambisonics. *Proceedings from the AES 124th International Convention*, Amsterdam, Netherlands.

Algazi, R., Duda, R., Thompson, D., & Avendano, C. (2001). The CIPIC HRTF database. *Proceedings from the IEEE Workshop on Applications of Signal Processing to Audio and Acoustics*, NY, USA.

Baddeley, A. (1996). *Your memory–a user's guide*. London: Prion.

Batteau, D. (1967). The role of the pinna in human localization. [London.]. *Proceedings of the Royal Society of London. Series B. Biological Sciences, 168*(1011), 158–180. doi:10.1098/rspb.1967.0058

Bear, M., Connors, B., & Paradiso, M. (2007). *Neuroscience–exploring the brain* (3rd ed.). Lippincott, Williams & Wilkins.

Blackorby, J., Chorost, M., Garza, N., & Guzman, A. M. (2004). The academic performance of elementary and middle school students with disabilities. In Holden-Pitt, L. (Ed.), *Engagement, academics, social adjustment, and independence: The achievements of elementary And middle school students with disabilities*. USA: U.S. Department of Education.

Blauert, J. (1997). *Spatial hearing: The psychophysics of human sound localization*. Cambridge, MA: The MIT Press.

Breebaart, J. (2007). Analysis and synthesis of binaural parameters for efficient 3D audio rendering in MPEG surround. *Proceedings from the IEEE International Conference on Multimedia and Expo*. Beijing, China.

Breebaart, J., Herre, J., Faller, C., Rödén, J., Myburg, F., Disch, S., et al. (2005). MPEG spatial audio coding / MPEG surround: Overview and current status. *Proceedings from the AES 119ᵗʰ Convention*. NY, USA.

Breebaart, J., Herre, J., Villemoes, L., & Jin, C. (2006). Multi-channel goes mobile: MPEG surround binaural rendering. *Proceedings from the AES 29ᵗʰ International Conference*, Seoul, Korea.

Bregman, A. (1994). *Auditory scene analysis: The perceptual organization of sound*. Cambridge, MA: The MIT Press.

Brewster, S., Wright, P. C., & Edwards, A. D. N. (1994). A detailed investigation into the effectiveness of earcons. In G. Kramer (Ed.), *Proceedings of the International Conference on Auditory Display*, Santa Fe, NM: Addison Wesley Longman.

Brown, L., Brewster, S., Ramloll, R., Burton, M., & Riedel, B. (2003). Design guidelines for audio presentation of graphs and tables. *Proceedings from the 2003 International Conference on Auditory Display*. Boston, MA, USA.

Card, S., Mackinlay, J., & Schneiderman, B. (1999). *Readings in information visualization–using vision to think*. CA: Morgan Kaufmann.

Chapman, E. K., & Stone, J. M. (1988). *Special needs in ordinary schools: The visually handicapped child in your classroom*. UK: Cassell.

Chapman, M. (2008). New dimensions for Ambisonics. *Proceedings from the 124th Audio Engineering Society Convention*, Amsterdam.

Dick, T., & Kubiak, E. (1997). Issues and aids for teaching mathematics to the blind. *Mathematics Teacher, 90*(5).

Edwards, A., McCartney, H., & Fogarolo, F. (2006). Lambda: A multimodal approach to making mathematics accessible to blind students. *Proceedings from the 8th International ACM SIGACCESS Conference on Computers and Accessibility,* (pp. 48-54). Portland, OR, USA.

Edwards, A., & Stevens, R. (1993). Mathematical representations: Graphs, curves, and formulas. In Burger, D., & Sperandio, J. C. (Eds.), *Non-visual human-computer interactions* (pp. 181–193). London, Paris: Colloque INSERM/ John Libbey Eurotext Ltd.

Ernest, P. (1987). A model of the cognitive meaning of mathematical expressions. *The British Journal of Educational Psychology, 57*, 343–370.

Flowers, J. (2005). Thirteen years of reflection on auditory graphing: Promises, pitfalls, and potential new directions. *Proceedings from the International Conference on Auditory Display's 11th Meeting*, Limerick, Ireland.

Flowers, J., & Hauer, T. (1995). Musical versus visual graphs: Cross-modal equivalence in perception of time series data. *Human Factors, 37*, 553–569. doi:10.1518/001872095779049264

Furse, R. (2009). Building an OpenAL implementation using Ambisonics. *Proceedings from the AES 35th International Conference*, London, UK.

Gerzon, M. (1975). The design of precisely coincident microphone arrays for stereo and surround sound. *Proceedings from the 50th Convention of the Audio Engineering Society*, London, UK.

Goyal, V. (2006). *Pro Java ME MMAPI: Mobile Media API for Java micro edition*. CA, USA: Apress Press Inc.

Han, H. (1991). Measuring a dummy head in search of pinna cues. *Proceedings from the 90th AES Convention*, Paris.

Hiebert, G. (2007). *OpenAL programmer's guide OpenAL versions 1.0 and 1.1*. Creative Technology Limited.

Jansson, G., Petrie, H., Colwell, C., Kornbrot, D., Fänger, J., & König, H. (1999). Haptic virtual environments for blind people: Exploratory experiments with two devices. *The International Journal of Virtual Reality, 3*(4).

Jerrnigan Institute. (2009). *The Braille literacy crisis in America: Facing the truth, reversing the trend, empowering the blind*. Baltimore: National Federation of the Blind.

Jones, D., & Macken, W. (1993). Irrelevant tones produce an irrelevant speech effect: Implications for phonological coding in working memory. *Journal of Experimental Psychology. Learning, Memory, and Cognition, 19*(2), 369–381. doi:10.1037/0278-7393.19.2.369

Jones, D., Madden, C., & Miles, C. (1992). Privileged access by irrelevant speech to short-term memory: The role of changing state. *Quarterly Journal of Experimental Psychology, 44A*, 645–669.

Kahana, Y., & Nelson, P. (2000). Spatial acoustic mode shapes of the human pinna. *Proceedings from the 109th AES Convention*, Los Angeles, CA, USA.

Karshmer, A., Gupta, G., Geiiger, S., & Weaver, C. (1998). Reading and writing mathematics: The MAVIS project. *Proceedings from the 3rd International ACM Conference on Assistive Technologies*, (pp. 136-143). CA, USA

Karshmer, A., Gupta, G., & Pontelli, E. (2007). *Mathematics and accessibility: A survey. Technical report*. TX, USA: University of Texas at Dallas.

Kennedy, J. M., & Juricevic, I. (2006). Blind man draws using diminution in three dimensions. *Psychonomic Bulletin & Review, 13*(3), 506–509. doi:10.3758/BF03193877

Li, S., & Knudsen, J. (2005). *Beginning J2ME platform: From novice to professional*. CA, USA: Apress Press Inc.

Long, M., Levy, M., & Stern, R. (2005). *Architectural acoustics-applications of modern acoustics*. UT: Academic Press.

Magnusson, C., Rassmus-Gröhn, K., Sjöström, C., & Danielsson, H. (2002). *Navigation and recognition in complex haptic virtual environments–reports from an extensive study with blind users*. Edinburgh, UK: Proceedings from Eurohaptics.

Mazza, R. (2004). *Introduction to information visualisation*. Switzerland: Faculty of Communication Sciences, University of Lugano.

McCuskey, M., & Boer, J. (2003). *Beginning game audio programming*. Boston: Premier Press.

Moore, B. C. J. (2003). *An introduction to the psychology of hearing*. London: Emerald Group Pub Ltd.

Murphy, D., & Rumsey, F. (2001). A scalable spatial sound rendering system. *Proceedings from the 110th AES Convention*, Amsterdam, the Netherlands.

Nees, M. A., & Walker, B. N. (2006). Relative intensity of auditory context for auditory graph design. *Proceedings from the Twelfth International Conference on Auditory Display (ICAD06)*, London, UK.

Nees, M. A., & Walker, B. N. (2007). Listener, task, and auditory graph: Toward a conceptual model of auditory graph comprehension. *Proceedings from the International Conference on Auditory Display (ICAD2007)*. Montréal, Canada.

Neff, F., Kehoe, A., & Pitt, I. (2007). *User modeling to support the development of an auditory help system*. (LNCS 4629), (p. 390).

Neff, F., & Pitt, I. (2008). Using spatial non-speech sound to relay mathematical problems to visually disabled students. *Proceedings from the International Technology, Education and Development Conference*, Valencia, Spain.

Neff, F., & Pitt, I. (2008). A study toward the development of a spatial, non-speech auditory interface for trigonometric problem solving. *Proceedings from the 14th International Conference on Auditory Display*, Paris, France.

Neff, F., Pitt, I., & Kehoe, A. (2007). A consideration of perceptual interaction in an auditory prolific mobile device. *Proceedings from the Workshop on Spatial Audio for Mobile Devices, Mobile HCI*, Singapore.

Noordzij, M. L., Zuidhoek, S., & Postma, A. (2007). The influence of visual experience on visual and spatial imagery. *Perception, 36*(1), 101–112. doi:10.1068/p5390

OECD Publishing. (2005). Students with disabilities, learning difficulties and disadvantages: Statistics and indicators. *OECD Publishing, 17*, 1–154.

Parkes, D. (1991). Nomad: Enabling access to graphics and text- based information for blind and visually impaired and other disability groups. *Proceedings from the Conference Proceedings of the World Congress on Technology*, VA, USA.

Pereira, F. C., & Ebrahimi, T. (2002). *The MPEG-4 book*. Upper Saddle River, NJ: Prentice Hall PTR.

Peres, S. C., & Lane, D. M. (2005). Auditory graphs: The effects of redundant dimensions and divided attention. *Proceedings from the International Conference on Auditory Display (ICAD2005)*, Limerick, Ireland.

Raman, T. V. (1998). *Audio system for technical readings*. Berlin: Springer Verlag.

Rault, J. B. (1998). *Audio rendering of virtual room acoustics and perceptual description of the auditory scene*. (. *ISO, JTCI, SC29*(WG11), M4222.

Sánchez, J., & Sáenz, M. (2009). Video gaming for blind learners school integration in science classes. In Gross, T. (Eds.), *Proceedings from the 12th IFIP TC13 international conference on human-computer interaction: Part I* (pp. 36–49).

Santala, O., Vertanen, H., Pekonen, J., Oksanen, J., & Pulkki, V. (2009). Effect of listening room on audio quality in ambisonics reproduction. *Proceedings from the Audio Engineering Society 126th Convention*, Munich, Germany.

Schneidermann, B. (1996). The eyes have it: A task by data type taxonomy for information visualizations. *Proceedings from the 1996 IEEE symposium on visual languages, IEEE computer society*, Washington, DC.

Shaw, E. A. G., & Teranishi, R. (1968). Sound pressure generated in an external-ear replica and real human ears by a nearby point source. *The Journal of the Acoustical Society of America, 44*, 240. doi:10.1121/1.1911059

Sjöström, C. (2001). Designing haptic computer interfaces for blind people. *Proceedings from the Sixth International Symposium on Signal Processing and its Applications*.

Stevens, R. D. (1996). *Principles for the design of auditory interfaces to present complex information to blind people*. NY, USA: University of York, Department of Computer Science-Publications-YCST.

Stevens, R. D., Brewster, S. A., Wright, P. C., & Edwards, A. D. N. (1994). Design and evaluation of an auditory glance at algebra for blind readers. *Proceedings from the 2nd International Conference on Auditory Display*. Addison-Wesley.

Stevens, R. D., Wright, P. C., Edwards, A. D. N., & Brewster, S. A. (1996). *An audio glance at syntactic structure based on spoken form* (pp. 627–635). Proceedings from ICCHP.

Sugawara, M., Hamasaki, K. & Okano, F. (2004). Progress on large, wide-screen image presentation. 4000-scanning-line TV aims at a medium that is provocative yet pleasing to the senses. *Broadcast Technology, 18*.

Tanti, M. (2007). Teaching mathematics to a blind student-a case study. In Ernest, P. (Ed.), *Philosophy of Mathematics Education Journal, 20(1)*.

Toole, F. (2008). *Sound reproduction–loudspeakers and rooms*. MA, USA: Elsevier Ltd/Focal Press.

Väänänen, R. (1998). *Verification model of advanced BIFS* (Systems VM 4.0 subpart 2). (ISO/IEC JTCI/SC29/WG11 N2525).

Vilimek, R., & Hempel, T. (2005). Effects of speech and non-speech sounds on short-term memory and possible implications for in-vehicle use. *Proceedings from the International Conference of Auditory Design*, Limerick, Ireland.

Wang, W. T., Ma, W. C., Perng, K. L., Shieh, M. J., & Ouhyoung, M. (2001). A novel MPEG-4 based architecture for internet games. *Proceedings from the Game Technology Conference on SAR*.

Wrigley, S. N. & Brown, G. J. (2000). *A model of auditory attention*. University of Sheffield, Tech. Rep.

KEY TERMS AND DEFINITIONS

3/2: Used to denote the actual 5-channel surround sound standard. It signifies the use of three speakers in the frontal hemisphere of the listener and two surrounds. The usual commercial depiction is 5.1, but in fact the .1 (or the subwoofer) is regarded as optional in the standard. Other formats include 3/4 or 7.1, which signifies three speakers in front and four surrounds.

AC-3: Advanced Codec 3, Audio Codec 3. An audio coding algorithm developed by Dolby™.

Accelerometer: In the context of this chapter, it is a sensor in a device that determines orientation, vibration, and shock.

AMMS: (Advanced Multimedia Suppliments, JSR-234). The most advanced multimedia API extending the capabilities of MMAPI (Mobile Media API) for Java-enabled Symbian™ mobile devices. It allows the implementation of virtual binaural spatial sound via small Java applications on the highest spec devices (for example, the Nokia™ N97). A special type of Java environment (J2ME – Java 2 Micro Edition) is employed and is designed for devices with limited processing power, capacity and battery life.

ASCII Nemeth Code: Nemeth code is a form of Braille code for mathematics and scientific notation. ASCII Braille correlates Braille cells with the corresponding ASCII digits and characters.

Audio API: API is an acronym for Application Programming Interface. An API is a controlled and regulated interface allowing a programmer to create programming elements and to integrate these in an existing software system or framework. An audio API is a controlled programming environment specifically relating to creating and connecting audio elements to a games engine for example.

Audio Middleware: Middleware is software allowing developers to more easily integrate assets and implement various services in a larger software environment. Audio Middleware allows sound designers to easily attach sound files to a game environment and to readily determine the interaction of those files with existing, non-audio assets such as graphic sprites etc.

Auditory Graph: A graph whereby some, or all, of its data elements are presented using sound.

Auditory Pathway: An illustrative description of the capture and processing stages of sound information in the human hearing system.

Auditory Scene: A term used to describe the overall soundscape, or aural environment, where many independent and interactive sonic events/sources are present.

Auditory Stream Segregation: A primitive perceptual process of the human hearing system where sound that is present in the auditory scene is organized into individual streams, thereby associating one or more sounds with the same source in the environment. In a rich auditory scene, the perceptual system will segregate and associate various sonic elements so that it can formulate how many sources are present in the environment and determine what sonic elements are associated with each source. These different sources can have one or many individual auditory streams associated with them.

Azimuth: When referring to the spatial localization of sound, the azimuth represents the position of sound sources at approximately head height, 360°, around the listener.

Basilar Membrane: A component of the inner ear that vibrates as a function of pressure waves entering the inner ear structure. Sensory cells along its length are activated when particular movement of the membrane occurs, thereby encoding the pressure disturbances as neuro-chemical events. The Basilar membrane movement is representative of the incoming-signal's physical shape.

B-Format: A multi-channel audio recording format associated with the Ambisonic technique.

Crosstalk Cancellation: This is a method for eliminating an undesirable effect whereby a signal from one channel has a negative impact on the other. In terms of audio technology, this is primarily concerned with sound files already incorporating binaural filters being output via standard stereo speakers. The human auditory system filters for a second time the already filtered audio output (binaural encoding). Also, sound meant for one ear is also reaching the opposite ear causing undesirable effects. Crosstalk cancellation is another set of filters incorporated to reduce the above effects.

Decoder: A decoder interprets file formats that have been encoded in a particular format. In terms of audio technology, this often refers to software that can interpret compressed formats and output the file as sound playback. It also refers to encoded audio incorporating particular spatial cues and speaker matrixes.

DirectX: A collection of APIs (see description of API above) handling multimedia and game elements for Microsoft™ platforms, including the Xbox™.

Distance Attenuation: As an observer/listener moves farther away from a virtual sound-source, the sound-source's emitting sound gradually decreases in volume/loudness to simulate the increasing distance between source and listener.

Doppler Shift: Represents the frequency-change effect observed by a stationary listener as a sound-emitting source passes by. It also represents the frequency-change effect observed by a moving listener relative to the sound-emitting source.

Down-Mix: Where multi-channel audio is reduced in terms of its channel count.

Encoder: An encoder, in its simplest definition, is hardware or software that converts data from one format to another. In terms of audio technology, an encoder is predominantly used to describe software applications that compress raw audio files to a more compact format. It also refers to software applications that extract and format specific information relating to audio (such as spatial cues) that can be used for the purpose of an intermediary task, or for changing the final file format.

External Memory: Within the context of this chapter, this term represents the visual display. When using a GUI, users can keep much of the information onscreen without having to memorize it. At a later stage, they may then resort back to that information on screen.

Flanger: An audio effect created when two signals of the same frequency are mixed, but where the phase of one of the signals is slightly delayed.

Fuzzy Felt: Simple fabric shapes, used conventionally as toys, but also used as tactile representations of 3D shapes for the blind in education.

German Film: Plastic sheets that produce raised lines when a pen is applied to their surface. Used in the past for creating tactile drawings for the blind.

HRTF: An acronym for Head Related Transfer Function. This is a complex set of filters simulating the effect imposed by the head, shoulders and ears of the listener on a sound entering the auditory canal.

Interaural Level/Intensity Differences: The sound-wave pressure difference registered in the left and right ears. For example, a sound source on the left will have a higher sound pressure level when reaching the left ear compared to the right.

Interaural Time Difference: The temporal difference between a sound-wave reaching one ear before the other. For example, a sound source on the left will reach the left ear before it reaches the right.

Irrelevant Sound Effect: Derived from the Irrelevant Speech Effect whereby a person's visual recall of information is disrupted/corrupted/inaccurate because of concurrent irrelevant speech content being present in the environment. A similar effect can be observed when irrelevant non-speech sound is present, albeit to a lesser degree. It is also evident that speech and text content recall can be affected by concurrent irrelevant non-speech sound present in the environment. In the case of irrelevant non-speech sound, a link has been associated between the degree of impact the effect has on the recall process and the degree of variation of the irrelevant signal.

ISO/IEC: International Organization for Standardization / International Electrotechnical Commission. These are non-governmental international standards bodies, acting as umbrella organizations for many national standards authorities worldwide. The subcommittees of these bodies often encompass academic, commercial and industrial interests. They foster international collaboration between industry and academia, as well as promoting compatibility in software and hardware design and development. They also provide established and rigorous methodologies for the development of internationally compatible standards.

JAWS: Job Access With Speech. An advanced screen-reader developed by Freedom Scientific™ aimed at the Windows™ system and tightly integrated with common OS functions and applications.

LaTeX: A document markup language, formatting and typesetting system.

LFE: An acronym for Low Frequency Effect. This denotes the channel in surround sound that is dedicated to very low frequencies, usually below 120Hz. The subwoofer in a typical surround setup is the LFE.

Lossless Compression: A form of data compression where techniques are used to reduce the file size without deleting any information during the process. In audio, this involves predictive algorithms and other advanced processes. Examples of lossless audio compression are Free Lossless Audio Codec© and Apple™'s Apple Lossless©.

Lossy Compression: A form of data compression where elements of the data is deleted from the original file in order to reduce its file-size. In relation to audio technology, this is usually associated with compression techniques based on perceptual factors. Therefore, a lossy compression technique for audio incorporates some form of perceptual analysis to determine what elements can be permanently deleted without impacting on the perceived quality of the sound-file during playback. A prime example of this approach is MPEG-1, Layer 3 or .mp3.

MathML: Mathematical Markup Language. A standardized, XML-based description of mathematical notation, structure and content.

Multi-channel: In audio technology, multichannel refers to a system where sonic elements are output on discrete or shared speakers. Usually, it refers to systems incorporating more than two speakers and typically at least four.

Multimodal: A system that allows the user to interact with data and functionality using several different senses - vision, hearing, touch etc.

.NET Framework: This is a very large library of pre-coded elements for the Windows™ platform. It is also an environment that allows programmers to use several different compatible languages to create applications and services (virtual machine).

Notch Filter: A filter that blocks or attenuates frequencies that fall within the stop band of a particular center frequency. Frequencies above or below the band are not affected.

OpenAL: A cross-platform audio API (see API description above).

OpenGL: A cross-platform graphics API (see API description above).

OpenSL-ES: Open Sound Library for Embedded Systems. This is a cross-platform audio API capable of implementing spatial sound on mobile devices.

PCM file: Pulse Code Modulation. This is the raw, uncompressed digital representation of an analog signal. Typically, the analog signal is sampled several thousand times a second and represented in a binary format. Popular audio file formats, such as AIFF and WAV, employ PCM bitstream encoding.

Pinna Transfer Function: A mathematical representation of the filters imposed by the human pinna due to its physical structure.

Pinnae: *(singular: Pinna)*. The portion of the ear that is visible and protrudes from the head.

SAPI: Speech Application Programming Interface. An advanced speech recognition and synthesis API developed by Microsoft™. It is integrated into the Windows™ OS and other Microsoft™ applications.

Sonic Dimensions: Sound has several concurrent characteristics that can exist independently, yet interact with each other. These include rhythm, pitch, loudness, texture etc.

Sonify: *Sonification.* This is the process of representing events, structures and assets using non-speech sound. Sonification, in the context of computer interface design, is used to present GUI elements (such as icons) or events (such as alarms or warnings). Sonification is also used to convey scientific, mathematical and statistical data to the end-user. Sonification plays an increasingly important role for visually disabled users of technology.

Spatial Audio Coding: A process whereby spatial cues are extracted from a multi-channel recording and compiled as side/ancillary information. The actual audio is down-mixed (see description of down-mix). At the client side, the audio is up-mixed (see description of up-mix) in accordance with the side information.

Spatialization Cues: The attributes of a sound that determines its location in space. Various elements can impact or influence these attributes, such as immediate environmental surroundings (echo from walls etc.), the sound-source's distance from the observer, the sound-source's degree of angle relative to the observer etc.

Sweet spot: In a multi-speaker setup, the center-most location within the speaker configuration usually provides the best spatial sound experience for the listener. Outside the sweet spot results in a poorer spatial experience.

Text-To-Speech (TTS): A system that converts normal language text on a computer into audible speech output. The speech output may be prerecorded pieces of concatenated speech of the human voice stored in a database, or it may be purely synthetic based on synthesis techniques such as models of the human vocal chords, vocal tract and mouth. Visually disabled or impaired computer users rely heavily on this kind of technology for hearing emails, menu items, word documents etc.

Unreal Audio System: The cross-platform audio tool component of the Unreal Game Engine© developed by Epic Games™.

Up-mix: Where the channel count of an audio file is increased, usually in strict accordance with ancillary data containing precise spatial cue information.

VDU: Visual Display Unit. Technology that allows data to be presented in a medium that is accessible using vision.

Virtual Binaural: This is an approach to spatial audio rendering where filters and other spatial cues inherent in the human auditory system are utilized or simulated. Typically, the best results when listening to audio using this system is through standard headphones. With the addition of extra filters, this system can also be rendered on a stereo speaker setup as well.

VRML/X3D: Virtual Reality Modeling Language. A standard file format incorporating three-dimensional, vector graphics and limited spatial audio primarily for Web deployment. X3D is the XML-based replacement of VRML.

XACT: An audio library, audio engine and front-end GUI for incorporating audio elements into an XNA© Project. It is designed for Microsoft™ platforms.

XNA: A set of programming tools facilitating the development of games for Microsoft™ platforms (including the Xbox™).

Chapter 22
Mobile Gaming Environment:
Learning and Motivational Effects

Namsoo Shin
University of Michigan, USA

Cathleen Norris
University of North Texas, USA

Elliot Soloway
University of Michigan, USA

ABSTRACT

This study was conducted to investigate the relationship of students' attitude toward mathematics, attitude toward a game, gaming performance, gender, and ethnicity as they relate to learning in an educational gaming environment. During the four-month instructional period, fifty 2nd grade students from three classes used a mobile game. This study used a non-experimental, correlational analysis of the predictors of student performance in mathematics. Overall results showed that the performance of mobile gaming and attitude toward mathematics influence the learning of arithmetic skills regardless of gender and ethnic background. On the basis of these findings, the literature on games, and learning theories, this chapter discusses issues related to design, implementation, and research in order to develop effective mobile game-based learning environments.

INTRODUCTION

Individuals follow different paths as they progress toward expert understanding because they learn differently based on their gender, ethnicity, learning styles, previous knowledge and experience with content, strategies, and technology. Learning environments should be created to meet individual

differences for active engagement with learning tasks that result in meaningful learning. Educators have developed mobile game-based learning environments purported to attain individualized instruction to support learning, positive motivation toward learning and learning activities, and reflection of own learning.

Mobile technology in K-12 education has the potential to improve teaching and learning (Garris, Ahlers, & Driskell, 2002; Pillay, Brownlee, &

DOI: 10.4018/978-1-60960-495-0.ch022

Wilss, 1999; Rieber, Smith, & Noah, 1998; Rosas et al., 2002). Games in the classroom provide a flexible range of options from which students may individually choose. Games facilitate learners' active engagement through interaction with game systems that allow them to progress toward more expert performance. Educational games have been developed to achieve maximum benefits from mobile technology in learning activities. As opposed to traditional classroom environments, where students passively received information and content from teachers, mobile gaming creates an individualized learning environment that allows students to select their own learning paths based on their prior knowledge and learning progress. This flexible approach, linked to prior knowledge, leads to meaningful learning. Although some research has shown that there could be promising benefits to student learning in mobile gaming environments (Hennessy, 2000; Horton, Wiegert, & Niess, 2002; Staudt, 2002; Tatar et al., 2003), there are very few studies about the use of mobile games in classroom settings.

The main purpose of this study was to investigate the effects of mobile gaming on student learning in mathematics regardless of students' background, especially gender, ethnicity, and performance levels (e.g., high and low achievement). This chapter starts with a literature review about the effects of games on motivation and learning with mobile technology. Next, it discusses the empirical research about the effects of educational mobile gaming on motivation and student learning to illustrate the limitations and potentials of games in educational settings. Finally, it describes our study design, methodology, and results of educational mobile games on learning for elementary school students who were primarily upper middle class and Caucasian. We conclude by discussing design, research, and implementation issues for developing and using games in educational settings based on the literature review and our findings.

GAME FEATURES

Essential features in a game environment are rules/goals (de Felix & Johnston, 1993), learner control (Gredler, 1996; Thornton & Cleveland, 1990), challenge tasks (Malone, 1981; Baranauskas, Neto, & Borges, 1999), and no real-world consequences (Crookall, Oxford, & Saunders 1987; Thomas & Macredie, 1994). The following section describes each game feature and how the feature influences learning processes.

Rules/Goals

Games have clear learning goals and specific rules for guiding a learner to achieve learning outcomes. The clear learning goals specify what a player must reach to be successful. The rules of a game specify how a learner is to accomplish game goals within the limited game environment (Garris, Ahlers, & Driskell, 2002). Understanding goals and rules support student cognitive development, especially organization skills and abstract thinking. A learner needs to develop a mental structure to understand the underlying concepts of games including goals/rules, procedures, properties and conditions. The development of the mental structure facilitates the development of organization skills. In addition, playing games enhances abstract thinking because the learner needs to understand the symbolic use of objects in a game to become a successful "player" (Garris, Ahlers, & Driskell, 2002). Vigotsky states that the process of understanding the symbolization is considered the first step towards abstract thinking (1978). Research on motivation supports the notion that clear, specific, and difficult goals lead to enhanced performance (Locke & Latham, 1990).

Learner Control

Learner control is defined as players being able to regulate, direct, or command learning activities based on their learning styles, strategies, previous experience, and other factors (Crookall & Arai, 1995; Quintana, Shin, Norris, & Elliot, 2004). Because of individual differences, we cannot predict exactly how learners will play the games, or the optimal level of challenge for each learner. At the same time, although rules and goals may be specified and fixed, games allow learners to direct their own activity (Garris, Ahlers, & Driskell, 2002). Games evoke a sense of learner control when learners are allowed authority to regulate over elements of the game program such as selecting strategies, managing the direction of activity, and making decisions that directly affect learning outcomes. Learner control increases interest and enhances cognitive engagement (Blumenfield, Kempler, & Krajcik 2006). Learner control is an important aspect of effective learning, motivation and development of a positive attitude toward learning activities (Hannafin & Sullivan, 1996; Morrison, Ross, & Baldwin 1992). Research on learner control has yielded consistently positive results with regard to motivation and learning (Cordova & Lepper, 1996; Morrison, Ross, & Baldwin, 1992).

Challenge Task

Vygotsky advocates the importance of the Zone of Proximal Development (ZPD) in the learning processes. The main idea of ZPD is that learning is facilitated when individuals face activities that lay just outside of their ability (1978). Games offer challenging tasks that are not typically experienced in daily life. When learners face challenging tasks somewhat greater than their previous accomplishments, motivation to compete against their own previous scores to see how much better they can do increases (Malone, 1981). In addition, games also provide learners with feedback (i.e., embed expert guides) to reach established goals. When learners receive feedback, they are able to evaluate whether their current performance meets established goals (Kernan & Lord, 1990). Based on the feedback, they reflect on their previous

performance in order to determine how to reduce the discrepancy between goals and the performance (Baranauskas, Neto, & Borges, 1999). This learning process allows learners to keep track of their progress toward desired goals, and leads to increased effort and performance.

No Real-World Consequence

Games are created within imaginary environments. Activities within game are separate from real life in that decisions have no impact on the real world. Learners are engaged in repetitive play and continually return to the game activity over time (Crookall, Oxford, & Saunders 1987). This game feature leads to evaluation of performance based on trial-error strategies, and encourages persistence or intensity of effort to complete learning tasks (Thomas & Macredie, 1994). These repetitive activities guide experiential learning that can result in greater achievement (Garris, Ahlers, & Driskell, 2002).

EMPIRICAL EVIDENCE

Effects of Gaming on Motivation and Learning

Motivation is a self-determined behavior to engage in and to devote a persistent effort at a particular activity (Pintrich & Schrauben, 1992; Wolters, 1998). Motivation influences interest in, enjoyment of, and persistence on a task, and therefore enhances the quality of cognitive engagement (Keller, 1983; Malone, 1981). Highly motivated learners engage in an activity because it is interesting or enjoyable in itself and because achieving the goals is important (Deci & Ryan, 1985) to them. A number of studies provide evidence that student motivation, curiosity, attention and attitude towards learning increase in gaming environments (Garris, Ahlers, & Driskell, 2002; McFarlane, Sparowhawk, & Heald, 2002).

Whitehal and McDonald (1993) found that a game led to increased risk taking among students that resulted in greater persistence on the task. Based on research, it can be concluded that instruction that incorporates games seems to be effective at enhancing motivation and increasing student interest in subject matter (Druckman, 1995; Ricci, Salas, & Cannon-Bowers, 1996).

Moreover, there are a number of empirical studies that have examined the effects of game-based educational programs on learning. Research supports that game environments have positive effects on student performance and cognitive skills (Cordova & Lepper, 1996; Kenezek, 1997). The results of comparison game studies found that games improve student performance on algebra and mathematics problem solving (McFarlane, Sparowhawk, & Heald, 2002), reading comprehension, spelling and decoding of grammar (Rosas, et al., 2002). Some studies indicate that playing games enhances complex thinking skills including problem-solving, strategic planning, and self-regulated skills (Cordova & Lepper, 1996; Keller, 1992; Ricci, Salas, & Cannon-Bowers, 1996). However, research findings with regard to the effectiveness of educational computer games on learning are mixed. Randel, Morris, and Wetzel reported that only 32% of the research studies found positive effects of electronic simulation/games on student learning by comparing them to conventional classroom instruction (1992). This review also revealed that not all subject matter demonstrated beneficial effects of using games. Overall, the effectiveness of computer games may depend on how gaming environments are designed. To maximize the impact of games on teaching and learning, gaming environments need to be created by incorporating not only essential game features but also appropriate technology devices. Mobile technology has been used as a promising device to enhance the effects of gaming on student learning.

Effects of Mobile Technology on Motivation and Learning

Mobile technology may well enable K-12 education to provide every child with his or her own personal, powerful computer. The multiple and various features of mobile technology, including accessibility, flexibility, Internet connectivity, collaboration, and feasibility, can be applied for creative teaching and learning strategies. The key characteristic of the mobile devices such as Plam Pilots™, Pocket PC™, and GameBoy™, is their small size that makes it easy to handle. Mobile devices can be designed as a personal tool that each student can effectively use in and outside the classroom to support learning activities (Finn & Vandenham, 2004). For example, such devices provide students with more integral and spontaneous opportunities to more fully take advantage of "off-moments" from classroom activity (Crawford, Vahey, Lewis, & Toyama, 2002) to support learning. Research indicates that personal 'ownership' of technology increases levels of student engagement and motivation in classroom activities and assignments, and therefore enhances student learning (Russell, Bebell, & Higgins, 2004; Savill-Smith & Kent, 2003). Based on data from a snapshot survey (2003), Norris and Soloway claimed that sufficient and flexible access to technology is a primary condition for having a positive impact on learning and teaching. From a teacher perspective, research found that technology management was easier and less time consuming for the teachers when the classes had 1:1 students-to-mobile device ratio (Russell, Bebell, & Higgins, 2004). To this end, the teachers' attitude was positively changed for integrating technology into class activities.

Mobile technology can also extend individual activities into learning opportunities involving substantive discussion among group members and face-to-face interactions (Luchini, Quintana, & Soloway, 2002). Researchers have pointed out that flexibility, wirelessness, and instant accessibility of mobile technology allow students to get involved in highly collaborative activities anywhere and anytime (Jipping & Dieter, 2001; Soloway, 2001; Tinker & Vahey, 2002; Zurita & Nussbaum, 2004). The wireless communication capabilities of mobile technology enhance information sharing and collaborative work among students and teachers (Savill-Smith & Kent, 2003; Staudt, 2002). For example, teachers and students can easily share information by beaming files (Joyner, 2002). Various studies have shown that mobile technology increases student-teacher interaction, resulting in fewer behavioral problems, better attendance, and enhanced student commitment to classroom activities and school in general (Shin, Norris, & Soloway, 2006). In addition, mobile technology can facilitate parent-teacher communication (Strom & Strom, 2002). For example, students can store their work on an individual mobile device to demonstrate to their parents what they have been doing in school (Bauer & Ulrich, 2002; Greaves, 2000). Numerous research findings have observed that mobile technology supports collaborative work by enhancing coordination, communication, and interactivity among group members (Joyner, 2002; Savill-Smith & Kent, 2003; Tatar et al., 2003; Zurita & Nussbaum, 2004).

Many studies provide evidence that the use of mobile technology promote students' learning and achievement (Crawford, Vahey, Lewis, & Toyama, 2002; Joyner, 2002; Savill-Smith & Kent, 2003; Tinker & Vahey, 2002Rudy, 2003; van 't Hooft, Diaz, & Swan, 2004). Teachers have remarked that mobile technology has a positive influence on teaching and learning, increases students' engagement in the classroom activities, and improves the quality of learning activities (Rudy, 2003; Tatar et al., 2003). In addition, mobile technology can be a self-monitoring tool for students because they can record their accomplishments and track their academic progress throughout a semester (Norris & Soloway, 2003; Penuel & Yarnall, 2005; Savill-Smith & Kent, 2003).

Effects of Mobile Gaming on Motivation and Learning

From the literature review on games and mobile devices, we anticipate the ready-at-hand nature of mobile technology can enhance the effects of games on student learning. Games in mobile technology are more available than a desktop or laptop game because of their accessibility, flexibility, and Internet connectivity. They enable learners to play games with a high degree of frequency both independently and in parallel with peers. The features of mobile games allow teachers to make learning more interesting for students (Hennessy, 2000; Horton, Wiegert, & Niess, 2002; Staudt, 2002; Tatar et al., 2003). For example, Horton and colleagues designed a billiards game for mobile technology to teach geometry to secondary school students (2002). Staudt (2002) used mobile games to teach algebra to 6th – 8th grade students. In addition, researchers have reported that students with mobile gaming showed much more interest in problems, and tended to be more focused on solving problems (Staudt, 2002).

Although most agree that mobile games can engage student in learning activities, there is little consensus regarding the effectiveness of mobile games on learning (Druckman, 1995). Additional research regarding mobile games in classrooms is necessary to support the idea that mobile gaming has a substantial impact on teaching and learning. Based on the need for rigorous evidence for the use of mobile gaming to promote learning, we designed a study to investigate the effect of educational mobile games on student learning and motivation. The primary purpose of this study is to explore what aspects of learners' characteristics in a mobile gaming environment influence students learning of arithmetic skills. The specific research questions of this study is:

What aspects of learners' characteristics (attitude toward mathematics, attitude toward a mobile game, mobile gaming performance, gender, and ethnicity) influence student learning in a mobile gaming environment?

In the section that follows we describe our study design, methodology, and results of an educational mobile game on student learning.

METHODOLOGY

Participants

The participants of this study were 50 second graders from three classes attending an elementary school near a large city in the Midwest. The students were primarily upper middle class and Caucasian including 28 male and 22 female students. The ethnic composition of the participants was 31 Caucasians, eight Asians, six African Americans, four others and one Hispanic.

Game Content

An educational game program entitled *Skills Arena* was developed to teach students about basic arithmetic skills such as addition and subtraction. Although Internet accessibility is an essential feature of mobile technology, we did not use it in this study because the device we used, GameBoy™, does not have the function of wireless Internet connectivity. In addition, the learning tasks were designed for individual activities that do not require students to work in groups.

In *Skills Arena* students can create their own character with their name for playing the game, and are able to choose the game type and level based on their ability and learning goals. The game's six speed levels, from the easiest to the most difficult, are presented in the form of cartoon characters. There are three game types including mental, extension, and place games. The mental game deals with single digit numbers such as "___ + 3 = 10". The extension game includes only multiple digit numbers that include zeros. For instance,

"300 + 400 = _____, or 260 - 50 = _____". The place game uses multiple digit numbers without zeros such as "245 + 563 = _____, or 437 – 36 = ____." Each game type has three arithmetic tasks — addition, subtraction, and mixed addition and subtraction with one, two, three, and four digit numbers. Students have to solve the problems before the questions fade from the GameBoy™ screen. *Skills Arena* provides immediate feedback as to whether a student is correct or incorrect after a question is answered. The game displays the total number of problems solved, and the number of correctly solved problems as a performance summary after each game finishes. It also presents the total number of solved problems and correctly solved problems in the games the student has played over time (see Figure 1).

Instruments

Mathematic Scores

We developed a 70-item instrument to assess mathematics skills. The test items were directly aligned with the second grade mathematics curriculum standards of the participating school. The test had two parts. Part I consisted of 50 questions with 25 addition items and 25 subtraction items to measure basic arithmetic skills. Part II of the test had 20 questions including 10 addition and 10 subtraction items to assess advanced arithmetic skills. Face validity for this instrument was verified by the teachers at the participating school.

Figure 1. Skills arena game screen

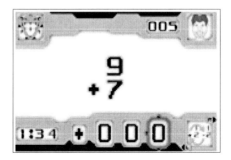

The students took Part I of the test in 15 minutes and Part II in 5 minutes.

Attitude toward Mathematics and Attitude toward Mobile Games

We used the Attitude Toward Math survey developed by Pearce, Lungren, and Wince (1998) to measure students' attitude toward mathematics. This survey has 23 items and includes an approximately equal number of positive and negative statements with respect to elementary students' attitudes toward mathematics. The teachers presented each statement orally to students. The students responded by marking "yes" or "no" to the statements on their answer sheets. We also developed an eight item questionnaire to examine students' attitude toward elements of the game such as the interface of the program, the usefulness of the feedback for learning math, the sounds and colors of the game, the likeability of the game, their attitude toward mobile games and additional comments. The items were a combination of "Yes or No" and open-ended questions. The participant teachers checked the readability of the items for second grade students. A researcher conducted an individual interview with all the students in order to get students' responses on each item.

Instruction and Procedures

The study was conducted for a four–month period. We conducted a one-hour training session for teachers and students on how to use the mobile game. Because most students had previous experience playing games on the GameBoy™, they were able to play the game with the basic guidelines we provided. The students used *Skills Arena* in a GameBoy™ following their teachers' directions. For example, depending on teacher class schedule, the students played the game for 15 minutes, twice, three times, or more than three times per week. The teachers and the investigators administered the posttest and the survey of students' attitudes toward mathematics in the three classes after the four-month mobile game instruction intervention. During the implementation stage of the mobile game, two researchers observed three classes twice a week to ensure that the *Skills Arena* game was implemented in the mobile game group as intended.

Research Design and Data Analysis

Multiple regression was used to test the relationship between mathematics scores and the predictor variables including attitude toward the mobile game, attitude toward mathematics, ethnicity, gender and performance with a mobile game (number of correctly solved problems over time). In order to detect multicollinearity among the independent variables, we computed Pearson correlation coefficients for the entire sample. There was no potential of multicollinearity among variables.

FINDINGS

To understand how students in the three classes performed on the mathematic test, descriptive analysis of each class were conducted (see Table 1).

All the predictor variables including attitude toward mathematics, attitude toward mobile games, scores of mobile gaming, gender and ethnicity were entered into the model simultaneously in the first step of the analysis (see Table 5). Mobile game scores, ß = .42, t = 3.61, p = .001, and attitude toward mathematics, ß = .39, t = 3.30, p = .002, emerged as significant predictors of mathematics test scores. In the second step of the analysis, we included only the significant predictors from the first regression analysis to reduce the error term associated with the inclusion of non-significant predictors in regression models. Attitude toward mathematics ß = .40, t = 3.52, p < .001, and mobile game scores ß = .48, t = 4.32, p < .000, were a significant predictor of mathematics test scores in this step. The two variables ac-

Table 1. Mean score of test, game and attitude

Group	Class One (n=20)		Class Two (*n* = 17)		Class Three (*n* = 9)	
	M [%]	(*SD*)	*M* [%]	(*SD*)	*M* [%]	(*SD*)
Math total (70)	47.60 [68]	(16.92)	45.53 [65]	(15.22)	46.78 [67]	(15.86)
Basic (50)	39.30 [79]	(11.48)	40.06 [80]	(11.57)	41.33 [83]	(12.10)
Advanced (20)	8.30 [42]	(6.05)	5.47 [27]	(5.21)	5.44 [27]	(5.05)
Game score						
Total[1]	3560.00	(2850.39)	3369.59	(1403.14)	4910.89	(2263.57)
Correct[2]	2371.03	(1677.05)	2790.82	(1408.22)	3286.33	(1806.89)
Ability						
Low	37.00 [53]	(15.92)	38.80 [55]	(16.22)		
High	60.56 [87]	(4.42)	55.14 [79]	(6.31)		
Gender						
Male	54.25 [78]	(11.46)	44.67 [64]	(17.05)	55 [79]	(6.06)
Female	37.63 [54]	(19.52)	46.50 [66]	(13.97)	40.20 [57]	(18.81)
Mobile game attitude	5.80 [97]	0.41	5.59 [93]	0.51	5.70 [95]	0.46
Mathmatics attitude	20.55 [89]	2.89	13.35 [58]	5.53	17.21 [75]	5.58

Note. 1. The total solved problems of the game. 2. The correct answers in the solved problem of the game.

counted for 45% (p < .000) of the variance in mathematics test scores (see Table 2). Attitude toward the mobile game, gender and ethnicity were not significant predictors of mathematics test scores.

The overall plot and normal probability plot of residuals were used to check violations of any assumptions of multiple regression analysis. Overall results of the residual graphs indicated that the samples of this study met the assumptions of multiple regression analysis to analyze the data

Table 2. First and second steps of regression analysis for four variables predicting mathematics scores

Variable (*N* = 50)	B	SEB	ß	*t*	*p*
Game scores	3.88	0.00	0.42	3.61	.001
Math attitude	1.11	0.34	0.39	3.30	.002
Gender	-5.87	3.55	-0.19	-1.65	.106
Game attitude	2.24	4.16	0.06	0.54	.592
Ethnicity	-2.54	1.42	0.00	-0.02	.986
Constant	13.17	24.47		0.54	.593
First step regression analysis. R^2 = .48 (*p* < .000)					
Game scores	4.52	0.00	0.48	4.32	.000
Math attitude	1.12	0.32	0.40	3.52	.001
Constant	15.04	6.04		2.49	.016
Second step regression analysis. R^2 = .45 (*p* < .000)					

of the mathematics test. Additionally, the results of the cross-validation technique confirmed that the prediction equation of the mathematics scores works for students other than those who were used to develop the equation.

Overall regression results from the first and second step analyses show that the cumulative number of problems solved correctly as indicated by the mobile game scores and the students' attitude toward mathematics significantly correlated to the students' scores on the mathematics final test. It can be interpreted that students who had higher attitudes toward mathematics and mobile game scores were more likely to achieve high scores on the mathematics test. Additionally, the students' scores on the mathematics test were not different based on ethnicity and gender. The t-test results of the attitude scores revealed that there was no significant attitude difference toward the mobile game between 21 male and 16 female students. It can be concluded that the mobile game would equally influence student learning regardless of gender and ethnic differences.

DISCUSSION AND CONCLUSION

From our research experience, the results of this study, and literature review, followings are our discussion about design, research and implementation issues for designing and implementing games in classroom to support rich, highly individualized learning experiences.

Design Issues

We proposed two design guidelines for creating a mobile game-based learning environment. First, a game designer should define specific learning goals for guiding to achieve targeted outcomes within a game environment. The learning goals are essential in order for game designers to develop activities that focus on a set of ideas for learners to study and be held accountable for understanding.

We recommend aligning learning goals with the standards that governments or states specify that students must achieve. Teachers should be more likely to implement mobile gaming if learning goals meet state or federally mandated standards for which teachers are already accountable. Second, ease of learning, ease of use, and reliability are critical for implementing mobile games successfully in classrooms. Because of limited time in K-12 classrooms, students and teachers cannot expend extensive effort learning how to use complex technology (Norris & Soloway, 2003). The interface of mobile gaming should contain only essential features without frills in order to help students and teachers focus on essential activities for teaching and learning.

Research Issues

Research is still needed to guide educators on how to design and implement games for meaningful learning. Studies in the area of mobile games are still relatively imprecise in presenting reliable information about the games' impact on learning. We suggest two important areas for further work. The first area is the importance of systematic research in mobile gaming. Most of the studies discussed in this chapter are initial trials rather than the kind of longitudinal, extensive work with scientifically developed instruments to investigate the effects of mobile games usage in education. It is also desirable to conduct randomized field trials, which would lend stronger support and generalizability to the conclusions. Quantitative studies need to be combined with qualitative research in order to explore the ways in which mobile games are used in practice and how they can be effective in the classroom. In particular, qualitative research is necessary to understand how each game feature impacts cognitive engagement and to provide more specific guidelines for designing games. The current study was designed to investigate the effects of a mobile gaming environment on student learning rather than relationships between individual game features and learning processes. Research should examine the extent to which specific features influence student interest and engagement in game activity.

Research also needed to examine how game features should be designed to enhance learning outcomes of complex cognitive tasks. Researchers need to explore the effectiveness of mobile gaming on higher-order thinking skills, such as creativity, problem solving, or decision-making rather than focusing on low-level understanding of subject matter. To do this, designers need to further develop games to promote higher-order thinking skills as target learning goals, and intensive research should follow to examine student learning. Such research requires understanding how classroom variables influence learner's engagement in game environments, and which circumstances are most advantageous for successfully implementing mobile games in classrooms. Classroom variables include teacher background (e.g., teaching style, experience of teaching and technology, attitude toward gaming), student background (e.g., gender, ethnicity, learning styles, strategies, prior experience of content, gaming, and technology), and aspects of the physical classroom setting (e.g., number of students, number of technology devices, type of technology). Identifying significant classroom variables is an important step in implementing games successfully in educational settings.

Implementation Issues

Almost every study about learning technology suggests that professional development plays a crucial role in the introduction of educational technologies (Finn & Vandenham, 2004; Spratt, Palmer & Coldwee, 2000). Well-designed professional development programs for classroom teachers must include technical training with basic skills as well as pedagogical training with regard to appropriate and successful integration of technology into the curriculum (Pownell

& Bailey, 2002; Rudy, 2003; Shin, Norris, & Soloway, 2008; Van'T Hooft, Diaz & Swan, 2004). Research suggests that peer mentoring has a great effect on the speed of acceptance for new technology and could help successfully disseminate new technology throughout the teachers' community (Finn & Vandenham, 2004). In addition to teacher training, principal leadership is an important factor that influences successful technology implementation in classrooms (Finn & Vandenham, 2004; Kincaid & Feldner, 2002). Leaders must have long-term dedication and full responsibility to change school and classroom culture for the successful implementation of new technology, such as mobile technology.

This study suggests that well-designed games that incorporate essential game features in mobile devices can provide individualized instructional materials to meet individual differences for active engagement on learning tasks that result in meaningful learning. The results of this study provide empirical evidence that mobile games could be an effective tool for facilitating student learning, particularly for elementary students learning arithmetic skills. Unfortunately, the small sample size might have influenced our results, so this general conclusion needs to be taken cautiously. A more extensive study with a larger sample size and randomized sampling procedure would make the results of this study about the effects of a mobile gaming environment on student learning more generalizable.

ACKNOWLEDGMENT

The authors thank to the two teachers, Anne Proctor and Donna Ramsey who gave us valuable feedback and continuous support to collect high quality data from their classes. The authors wish to acknowledge the helpful comments on this paper of Joseph Krajcik.

REFERENCES

Baranauskas, M., Neto, N., & Borges, M. (1999). Learning at work through a multi-user synchronous simulation game. In *Proceedings of the PEG'99 Conference, Exeter, UK,* (pp. 137-144). Exeter, UK: University of Exeter.

Bauer, A. M., & Ulrich, M. E. (2002). I've got a palm in my pocket. *Teaching Exceptional Children, 35*(2), 18–22.

Blick, A. (2005). *The impact of personal digital assistants an academic achievement.* Retrieved October 20, 2005, from http://learninginhand.com/links/research.html

Blumenfeld, P., Kempler, T. & Krajcik, J. (2006). *Motivation and cognitive engagement in learning.*

Bransford, J. D., Brown, A. L., & Cocking, R. R. (Eds.). (2000). *How people learn: Brain, mind, experience, and school* (Expanded ed.). Washington, DC: National Academy Press.

Carter, J. F. (1993). Self-management: Education's ultimate goal. *Teaching Exceptional Children, 25*(3), 28–32.

Cordova, D. I., & Lepper, M. R. (1996). Intrinsic motivation and the process of learning: Beneficial effects of contextualization, personalization, and choice. *Journal of Educational Psychology, 88,* 715–730. doi:10.1037/0022-0663.88.4.715

Crawford, V., Vahey, P., Lewis, A., & Toyama, Y. (2002*). Palm education pioneer program–March 2002 evaluation report.* Retrieved October 20, 2005, from http://www.palmgrants.sri.com/findings.html

Crookall, D., & Arai, K. (Eds.). (1995). *Simulation and gaming across disciplines and cultures: ISAGA at a watershed.* Thousand Oaks, CA: Sage.

Crookall, D., Oxford, R. & Saunders, D. (1987). Towards a reconceptualization of simulation: From representation to reality. *Simulation/Games for Learning, 17,* 147-171.

Danesh, A., Inkpen, K., Lau, F., Shu, K., & Booth, K. (2001). *GeneyTM: Designing a collaborative activity for the palm handheld computer.* Paper presented to the Human Factors in Computing Systems Conference. Seattle, WA.

de Felix, W., & Johnston, R. T. (1993). Learning from video games. *Computers in the Schools, 9,* 199–233.

Deci, E. L., & Ryan, R. M. (1985). *Intrinsic motivation and self-determination in human behavior.* New York: Plenum Publishing Co.

Dempsey, J., Haynes, L., Lucassen, B., & Casey, M. (2002). Forty simple computer games and what they could mean to educators. *Simulation & Gaming, 33*(2), 157–168. doi:10.1177/1046878102332003

Dewey, J. (1938). *Experience and education.* New York: Macmillan.

Druckman, D. (1995). The educational effectiveness of interactive games. In Crookall, D., & Arai, K. (Eds.), *Simulation and gaming across disciplines and cultures: ISAGA at a watershed* (pp. 178–187). Thousand Oaks, CA: Sage.

Duffy, T. M., & Jonassen, D. H. (1992). Constructivism: New implications for instructional technology. In Duffy, T., & Jonassen, D. (Eds.), *Constructivism and the technology of instruction* (pp. 1–16). Hillsdale, NJ: Erlbaum.

Duffy, T. M., & Jonassen, D. H. (Eds.), *Constructivism and the technology of instruction: A conversation.* Hillsdale, NJ: Lawrence Erlbaum.

Elliot, A. J., & Harackiewicz, J. M. (1994). Goal setting, achievement orientation, and intrinsic motivation: A mediational analysis. *Journal of Personality and Social Psychology, 66,* 968–980. doi:10.1037/0022-3514.66.5.968

Finn, M., & Vandenham, N. (2004). The handheld classroom; Educational implications of mobile computing. *Australian Journal of Emerging Technologies and Society, 2*(1), 1–15.

Fung, P., Hennessy, S., & O'Shea, T. (1998). Pocketbook computing: A paradigm shift? *Computers in the Schools, 14*, 109–118. doi:10.1300/J025v14n03_10

Garris, R., Ahlers, R., & Driskell, J. M. (2002). Games, motivation, and learning: A research and practice model. *Simulation & Gaming, 33*(4), 441–467. doi:10.1177/1046878102238607

Gay, G., Rieger, R., & Bennington, T. (2002). Using mobile computing to enhance field study. In Koschmann, T., Hall, R., & Miyaka, N. (Eds.), *CSCL 2: Carrying forward the conversation* (pp. 507–528). Mahwah, NJ: Lawrence Erlbaum Associates, Inc.

Gee, J. P. (2003). *What video games have to teach us about learning and literacy.* New York: Palgrave, MacMillan.

Greaves, T. (2000). One-to-one computing tools for life. *T.H.E. Journal, 27*(10), 54–56.

Gredler, M. (1996). Educational games and simulations: A technology in search of a (research) paradigm. In D.H.J. (Ed.), *Handbook of research on educational communications and technology.* (pp. 521-540). New York: Macmillan.

Hannafin, R. D., & Sullivan, H. J. (1996). Preferences and learner control over amount of instruction. *Journal of Educational Psychology, 88*, 162–173. doi:10.1037/0022-0663.88.1.162

Hennessy, S. (1999). The potential of portable technologies for supporting graphing investigations. *British Journal of Educational Technology, 30*(1), 57–60. doi:10.1111/1467-8535.00090

Hennessy, S. (2000). Graphing investigations using portable (palmtop) technology. *Journal of Computer Assisted Learning, 29*(8), 32–35.

Hill, J. R., Reeves, T. C., Grant, M. M., Wang, S.-K., & Han, S. (2002). The impact of portable technologies on teaching and learning: Year three report. Retrieved April 8, 2005, from http://lpsl.coe.uga.edu/Projects/aalaptop/pdf/aa3rd/Year-3ReportFinalVersion.pdf

Horton, B., Wiegert, E., & Niess, M. L. (2002). Using handhelds and billiards to teach reflection. *Learning and Leading with Technology, 29*(8), 33–35.

Jackson, L. (2004). *The 411 on one-to-one computing.* Retrieved October 20, 2005, from http://www.educationworld.com/a_tech/tech/tech194.shtml

Jipping, M. J., & Dieter, S. (2001). *Using handheld computers in the classroom: Laboratories and collaboration on handheld machines.* Paper presented at the 32nd Computer Science Education Conference, Charlotte, NC.

Johnson, D. W., & Johnson, R. (1989). Computer-assisted cooperative learning. *Educational Technology, 26*, 12–18.

Johnson, D. W., & Johnson, R. (1992). *Positive interdependence: Key to effective cooperation* (pp. 174–199). Cambridge, UK: Cambridge University Press.

Joyner, A. (2002). A foothold for handhelds. *American School Board Journal: Special Report.* Retrieved October 20, 2005, from http://www.asbj.com/specialreports/0903SpecialReports/S3.html

Kay, A. (2005). *The Dynabook revisited: A conversation with Alan Kay. The book and the computer: Exploring the future of the printed word in the digital age.* Retrieved May 26, 2005, from http://www.honco.net/os/kay.html

Keller, J. M. (1983). Motivational design of instruction. In Reigeluth, C. M. (Ed.), *Instructional-design theories and models: An overview of their current status* (pp. 383–434). Hillsdale, NJ: Lawrence Erlbaum.

Kernan, M. C., & Lord, R. G. (1990). Effects of valence, expectancies, and goal-performance discrepancies in single and multiple goal environments. *The Journal of Applied Psychology, 75*, 194–203. doi:10.1037/0021-9010.75.2.194

Kincaid, T., & Feldner, L. (2002). Leadership for technology integration: The role of principals and mentors. *Journal of Educational Technology & Society, 50*(1), 75–80.

Knezek, G. (1997). *Computers in education worldwide: Impact on students and teachers.* Retrieved from http://www.tcet.unt.edu/research/worldwd.htm

Lave, J., & Wenger, E. (1991). *Situated learning: Legitimate peripheral participation.* Cambridge, UK: Cambridge University Press.

Locke, E. A., & Latham, G. P. (1990). *A theory of goal setting and task performance.* Englewood Cliffs, NJ: Prentice Hall.

Luchini, K., Quintana, C., & Soloway, E. (2002). Designing learner-centered scaffolded tools for handheld computers. *Proceedings of the International Conference of the Learning Sciences.* (pp. 268-275). Seattle, WA.

Malone, T. W. (1981). What makes computer games fun? *Byte, 6*(12), 258–277.

Malone, T. W., & Lepper, M. R. (1987). Making learning fun: A taxonomy of intrinsic motivations for learning. In R.E. Snow & M.J. Farr (Eds.), *Aptitude, learning, and instruction: Vol. 3. Conative and affective process analyses.* (pp. 223-253). Hillsdale, NJ: Lawrence Erlbaum.

Mandryk, R. L., Inkpen, K. M., Bilezikjian, M., Klemmer, S. R., & Landay, J. A. (2001). *Supporting children's collaboration across handheld computers.* Paper presented at the Conference on Human Factors in Computing Systems (CHI). Seattle, WA. Retrieved June 11, 2005, from http://geney.juxta.com/chi2001_handheld.pdf

McClintock, R. (1999). *The educator's manifesto: Renewing the progressive bond with posterity through the social construction of digital learning communities.* New York: Institute For Learning Technologies, Teachers College, Columbia University. Retrieved March 21, 2005, from http://www.ilt.columbia.edu/publications/manifesto/contents.html

McFarlane, A., Sparowhawk, A., & Heald, Y. (2002). *Report on the educational use of games: An exploration by TEEM of the contribution which games can make to the education process.* Retrieved from http://reservoir.cent.jui.es/canals/octeto/es/440

Morrison, G. R., Ross, S. M., & Baldwin, W. (1992). Learner control of context and instructional support in learning elementary school mathematics. *Educational Technology Research and Development, 40,* 5–13. doi:10.1007/BF02296701

Norris, C., & Soloway, E. (2003). Handhelds impact K-12: The technology perspective. *Leadership, 3,* 55–70.

Norris, C., Sullivan, T., Poirot, J., & Soloway, E. (2003). No access, no use, no impact: Snapshot surveys of educational technology in K-12. *Journal of Research on Technology in Education, 36*(1), 15–28.

Papert, S. (1980). *Mindstorms: Children, computers and powerful ideas.* New York: Basic Books.

Parker, L. E., & Lepper, M. R. (1992). Effects of fantasy context on children's learning and motivation: Making learning more fun. *Journal of Personality and Social Psychology, 62,* 625–633. doi:10.1037/0022-3514.62.4.625

Pearce, K., Lungren, M., & Wince, A. (1998). *The effects of curriculum practices on first graders' attitudes, activity preference, and achievements in mathematics.* Retrieved from www.findarticles.com/p/articles/mi_qa3673/is_199810/ai_n8825517

Penuel, W. R., & Yarnall, L. (2005). Designing handheld software to support classroom assessment: An analysis of conditions for teacher adoption. *The Journal of Technology, Learning, and Assessment, 3*(5), 50–70.

Pfeifer, S., & Robb, R. (2001). Beaming your school into the 21st century. [Middle school education]. *Principal Leadership, 1*(9), 30–34.

Pillay, H., Brownlee, J., & Wilss, L. (1999). Cognition and recreational computer games: Implications for educational technology. *Journal of Research on Computing in Education, 32*(1), 203–216.

Pintrich, P. R., & Schrauben, B. (1992). Students' motivational beliefs and their cognitive engagement in classroom tasks. In Schunk, D., & Meece, J. (Eds.), *Student perceptions in the classroom: Causes and consequences* (pp. 149–183). Hillsdale, NJ: Lawrence Erlbaum.

Quintana, C., Shin, N., & Soloway, E. (2006). Learner-centered design: Reflections on the past and directions for the future. In Sawyer, R. K. (Ed.), *Cambridge handbook of the learning sciences.* Cambridge University.

Randel, J., Morris, B., Wetzel, C., & Whitehill, B. (1992). The effectiveness of games for educational purposes: A review of recent research. *Simulation & Gaming, 23*, 261–276. doi:10.1177/1046878192233001

Ricci, K., Salas, E., & Cannon-Bowers, J. A. (1996). Do computer-based games facilitate knowledge acquisition and retention? *Military Psychology, 8*(4), 295–307. doi:10.1207/s15327876mp0804_3

Rieber, L., Smith, L., & Noah, D. (1998). The value of serious play. *Educational Technology, 38*(6), 29–37.

Rieber, L. P. (1996). Seriously considering play: Designing interactive learning environments based on the blending of microworlds, simulations, and games. *Educational Technology Research and Development, 44*, 43–58. doi:10.1007/BF02300540

Rosas, R., Nussbaum, M., Cumsille, P., Marianov, V., Correa, M., & Flores, P. (2002). Beyond Nintendo: Design and assessment of educational video games for first and second grade students. *Computers & Education, 40*, 71–94. doi:10.1016/S0360-1315(02)00099-4

Roschelle, J., Penuel, W. R., & Abrahamson, L. (2004). The networked classroom. *Educational Leadership, 61*, 50–53.

Rudy, D. (2003). *Learning with handhelds.* Retrieved June 11, 2005, from http://www.remc11.k12.mi.us/lwl/pdf/BCLwHExecSum.pdf

Russell, M., Bebell, D., & Higgins, J. (2004). Laptop learning: A comparison of teaching and learning in upper elementary classrooms equipped with shared carts of laptops and permanent 1:1 laptops. *Journal of Educational Computing Research, 30*, 313–330. doi:10.2190/6E7K-F57M-6UY6-QAJJ

Sandholtz, J. H., Ringstaff, C., & Dwyer, D. C. (1997). *Teaching with technology: Creating student-centered classrooms.* New York: Teachers College Press.

Savill-Smith, C. & Kent, P. (2003*). The use of palmtop computers for learning: A review of the literature.* (ERIC Document Reproduction Service No. ED 481 345).

Shin, N., Norris, C., & Soloway, E. (2006). Findings from early research on one-to-one handheld use in K-12. In van't Hooft, M., & Swan, K. (Eds.), *Ubiquitous computing in education.* Lawrence Erlbaum Associates.

Smith, C. L., Wiser, M., Anderson, C. W., & Krajcik, J. (2006). Implications of research on children's learning for standards and assessment: A proposed learning progression for matter and the atomic molecular theory. *Measurement: Interdisciplinary Research and Perspectives, 4*(1), 1–98.

Soloway, E. (2001). *Supporting science inquiry in K-12 using Palm computers: A Palm manifesto.* Retrieved June 11, 2005, from http://www.pdaed.com/features/palmmanifesto.xml

Spratt, C., Palmer, S., & Coldwee, J. (2000). *Critical issues: Providing professional development for effective technology use.* Naperville, IL: North Central Regional Educational Laboratory. Retrieved June 11, 2005, from http://www.ncrel.org/sdrs/areas/issues/methods/technlgy/te1000.htm

Staudt, C. (2002). Understanding algebra through handhelds: Feedback beamed instantly helps a teacher identify students' misconceptions and correct them during a graphing lesson. *Learning and Leading with Technology, 30*(2), 36–39.

Stevens, S. Y., Delgado, C., & Krajcik, J. S. (in press). Developing a theoretical learning progression for atomic structure and inter-atomic interactions. *Journal of Research in Science Teaching.*

Strom, P. S., & Strom, R. D. (2002). Personal digital assistants and papers: A model for parent collaboration in school discipline. *Journal of Family Studies, 8*(2), 226–238. doi:10.5172/jfs.8.2.226

Tatar, D., Roschelle, J., Vahey, P., & Penuel, W. R. (2003). Handhelds go to school: Lessons learned. *IEEE Computer, 36*(9), 30–37.

Thomas, P., & Macredie, R. (1994). Games and the design of human-computer interfaces. *Educational and Training Technology International, 31*(2), 134–142.

Thornton, G., & Cleveland, J. (1990). Developing managerial talent through simulation. *The American Psychologist, 45*, 190–199. doi:10.1037/0003-066X.45.2.190

Tinker, R., & Vahey, P. (2002). CILT 2000: Ubiquitous computing, spanning the digital divide. *Journal of Science Education and Technology, 11*(3), 301–304. doi:10.1023/A:1016037022415

van 't Hooft, M., Diaz, S., & Swan, K. (2004). Examining the potential of handheld computers: Findings from the Ohio PEP project. *Journal of Educational Computing Research, 30*(4), 295–311. doi:10.2190/M1W6-A94D-3NKM-KBUU

Vygotsky, L. S. (1978). *Mind in society.* Cambridge, MA: Harvard University Press.

Wayne, A. J., & Youngs, P. (2003). Teacher characteristics and student achievement gains: A review. *Review of Educational Research, 73*(1), 89–122. doi:10.3102/00346543073001089

Whitehall, B., & McDonald, B. (1993). Improving learning persistence of military personnel by enhancing motivation in a technical training program. *Simulation & Gaming, 24*, 294–313. doi:10.1177/1046878193243002

Wolters, C. A. (1998). Self-regulated learning and college-students' regulation of motivation. *Journal of Educational Psychology, 90*, 224–235. doi:10.1037/0022-0663.90.2.224

Zurita, G., & Nussbaum, M. (2004). Computer supported collaborative learning using wirelessly interconnected handheld computers. *Computers & Education, 42*, 289–314. doi:10.1016/j.compedu.2003.08.005

KEY TERMS AND DEFINITIONS

Active Engagement: An interaction with a learning environment that allows students to progress toward more expert performance.

Individual Differences: Individuals follow different paths as they progress toward expert understanding because they learn differently based on their gender, ethnicity, learning styles, previous knowledge and experience with content, strategies, and technology.

Individualized Learning Environment: allows students to select their own learning paths based on their prior knowledge and learning progress.

Learner Control: Is defined as players being able to regulate, direct, or command learning activities based on their learning styles, strategies, previous experience, and other factors.

Learning Goals: A set of ideas for learners to study and be held accountable for understanding.

Mobile Technology: Such as Plam Pilots™, Pocket PC™, and GameBoy™, is a technology devise with small size that makes it easy to handle.

Motivation: Is a self-determined behavior to engage in and to devote a persistent effort at a particular activity

Chapter 23
Affective Gaming in Education, Training and Therapy:
Motivation, Requirements, Techniques

Eva Hudlicka
Psychometrix Associates, Inc., USA

ABSTRACT

Games are being increasingly used for educational and training purposes, because of their unique ability to engage students, and to provide customized learning and training protocols. In addition, games are being developed for health-related education and training, for cognitive and motor rehabilitation, and, more recently, for psychotherpy. Emotion plays a central role in learning, in the training of new cognitive and affective skills, and in the acquisition of new behaviors and motor skills, as well as in the elimina-tions of undesirable behaviors (e.g., addictions). This chapter discusses how the emerging discipline of affective gaming contributes to the design of more engaging and effective educational and training games, by explicitly integrating emotion into the gameplay. It focuses on the contributions from affective computing, and emphasizes the important role of emotion modeling. Emotion modeling is relevant both for modeling emotions in game characters, to enhance their believability and effectiveness, and for the development of affective user models, to enable real-time gameplay adaptation to the player's chang-ing affective state. The chapter introduces the notion of affect-centered games: games whose central objective is to train affective or social skills. It also discusses several concepts facilitating the design and evaluation of affect-centered games: affective player profile, affective gameplay profile and ideal affective player envelope. The chapter discusses approaches to modeling emotion in game characters, and concludes with a discussion of a tool that would facilitate the development of affect-centered games: an affective game engine.

DOI: 10.4018/978-1-60960-495-0.ch023

INTRODUCTION

Games are being increasingly used for educational and training purposes, for a variety of specific topics and domains (language, biology, mathematics, motor skills, cognitive skills, healthcare and medical training, military training). Games have a unique ability to engage students, and to provide customized learning and training protocols. This makes serious educational and training games a powerful tool for teaching and training. In addition, games are being developed for health-related education, training and cognitive and motor rehabilitation. Examples include games for education about healthy diet and exercise (e.g., Escape from Diab (archimage.com), Squire's Quest (http://www.squiresquest.com); and games for motor rehabilitation following stroke or brain trauma (e.g., (Burke, McNeill et al., 2009).

More recently, use of games has been suggested for psychotherapy (Brezinka and Hovestadt, 2007), and psychoeducation, for a variety of disorders, conditions and life-skills; e.g., stress reduction, smoking cessation, obesity prevention. Within the past few years, games have begun to emerge that directly address psychotherapy; e.g., a game designed to support cognitive-behavioral treatment in children (Treasure Hunt (Brezinka, 2008)); a game for children experiencing divorce, based on family therapy (Earthquake in Zipland (www.ziplandinteractive.com)); and a game designed to motivate adolescents for solution-focused therapy ("Personal Motivator" (Coyle, Matthews et al., 2005).

Emotion plays a central role in learning, in the training of new cognitive and affective skills, and in the acquisition of new motor skills. Emotion is also critical for the acquisition of new behavioral skills, as well as for the elimination of undesirable behaviors (e.g., addictions).

The emerging area of *affective gaming* (Sykes, 2004; Gilleade, Dix et al., 2005) is therefore directly relevant to the development of educational, training, and therapeutic games. Affective gaming focuses on the integration of emotion into game design and development, and includes the following areas: recognition of player emotions, adaptations of the gameplay to the players' affective states, and modeling and expression of emotions by non-playing characters

This chapter discusses how the emerging discipline of affective gaming contributes to the design of more engaging and effective educational, training and therapeutic games, by explicitly integrating emotion into the gameplay. The chapter focuses on the contributions from affective computing, and emphasizes the important role of emotion modeling. Emotion modeling is relevant both for modeling emotions in game characters, to enhance their believability and effectiveness, and for the development of affective user models, to enable real-time gameplay adaptation to the player's changing affective state.

The chapter focuses in particular on *affect-sensitive games*, which are capable of recognizing and adapting to the player's emotional state. It introduces the notion of *affect-centered games*, which are games where emotions play a central role, and whose explicit purpose is to train affective and social skills, or to aid in psychotherapy. The chapter also discusses several concepts that facilitate the design and development of educational, training, and therapeutic games, including the notions of *affective player profile*, *affective gameplay profile*, and the *optimal affective envelope* of the player. The chapter concludes with a discussion of an *affective game engine* (Hudlicka, 2009): a tool that would facilitate the development of affect-centered games, by providing the necessary embedded representational and knowledge primitives, and algorithms, to support more systematic affect-focused game design.

This chapter is organized as follows. *First*, the importance and role of emotion in learning and training is briefly discussed the next section. The affect-related constructs outlined above are then defined, and their relevance for the design of educational and training games in general, and affect-centered games in particular, are discussed in section "Affect-Related Constructs Useful for Educational Game Design". *Next,* the notion of affect-centered games is elaborated, and contrasted with more traditional educational and training games, in section "Affect-Sensitive and Affect-Centered Games", and some central issues for their design are highlighted in section "Affect-Focused Game Design". *Next,* background information on emotion research in psychology is provided in section "Emotion Research Background", followed by an introduction to the emerging area of affective gaming (section "Affective Gaming"), and a brief overview of affective computing, and its relevance for affective gaming (section "Affective Computing"). Some of the requirements for the development of affect-sensitive and affect-centered educational games are then discussed (section "Requirements for Developing Affect-Sensitive and Affect-Centered Games"), followed by a discussion of approaches available to model emotion generation and emotion effects in non-playing characters (section "Methods for Modeling Emotions in Game Characters and Player Models"). *Finally,* the notion of affective game engines is introduced, and the need for such a tool is discussed, along with some of its functionalities (section "Affective Game Engines"). Key design issues and choices are then highlighted and recommendations for researchers, practitioners and policy-makers are summarized (section "Summary and Recommendations"). The chapter concludes with a summary and discussion of the key challenges in the development of affective games for education, training and therapy.

A brief note on terminology. The term *affective states* covers emotions, moods and undifferentiated positive or negative affect. The term *emotion* refers to short-lasting, recognizable states with specific, known triggers (e.g., joy, anger, frustration or sadness). The term *mixed cognitive-affective states* covers states such as confusion, engagement, or flow, which cannot be considered purely affective but have a strong affective component.

Emotions and Personality in Learning and Training

Emotions play a critical role in motivation and exert strong effects on all aspects of cognition (LeDoux, 2000; Mineka, Rafael et al., 2003; Slovic, Finucane et al., 2004). Emotions and moods influence both the fundamental cognitive processes such as attention and memory (both encoding and recall), and higher-level cognitive processes such as situation assessment, problem-solving, planning, goal management and decision-making.

It is well established that some affective states, and mixed states, are conducive for learning; e.g., curiosity, excitement, engagement, and flow (Kort, Reilly et al., 2001). Research in affective biases on cognition provides evidence about the specific reasons why positive states improve learning. For example, happiness promotes more creativity in problem-solving, and more effective elaboration and encoding of memory (Mellers, Schwartz et al., 1998). In contrast, many affective states, such as boredom, frustration, fear and anxiety, are detrimental to learning. Interestingly, positive states aren't necessarily always good and negative states aren't necessarily always bad, providing their intensity is not extreme. For example, affective bias research suggests that negative emotions such as sadness are associated with increased analytical thinking, whereas positive emotions are associated with the use of heuristics and shortcuts (Mellers, Schwartz et al., 1998; Mineka, Rafael et al., 2003). While it would be bizarre to conclude that we should therefore induce sadness in students to promote analytical thinking, this finding does suggest that strong positive emotions may not always be the most desirable states for all aspects of learning or training.

To be effective, educational and training games need to track the student's mental state, particularly affective and mixed affective-cognitive states, identify states which are detrimental to learning, and modify the gameplay to reduce their intensity and frequency.

There is great individual variability in the affective states that particular students typically experience, in the triggers that induce these states, and in the manner in which these states dissipate and transform into other states. We discuss this below in the context of individual affective profiles. Learning and training games must take such individual profiles into considerations to ensure that the gameplay appropriately adapts to the students' individual and idiosyncratic affective needs. There are also differences in the general learning styles and motivational patterns among students, associated with their personality (which influences, indeed defines, the student's affective profile). For example, some individuals are motivated by reward, others by fear of failure (Matthews and Deary 1998). To be effective, educational games must take such individual differences into account and adapt the gameplay accordingly.

Affect-Related Constructs Useful for Educational Game Design

Several constructs are useful for the design and evaluation of affect-sensitive and affect-centered games for education, training and therapy:

- *affective player profile;*
- *affective gameplay profile* of the player during a particular gameplay; and
- *ideal affective envelope* for the student during the gameplay.

These constructs provide a basis for precise and quantitative descriptions of the players' affective states, as it relates to learning in general, and the gameplay in particular. Below we discuss these constructs, and their role in supporting the design of engaging games.

Affective player profile refers to the a description of the typical affective states the player experiences, typical triggers of these states, and typical behaviors associated with these states, all within the context of a particular game. The profile can be quite elaborate, and include also the associated cognitive biases and internal emotion effects, as they relate to the player's motivation and learning during gameplay. Different players will have different affective profiles, and the information in an affective profile is the basis for developing specific gameplays to meet the learning goals and needs of the student.

The related construct of an *affective gameplay profile* refers to the specific set of affective states experienced within a particular gameplay sequence, along with the specific triggers associated with transitions among states, and gameplay behaviors associated with each state. The affective gameplay profile is thus an instantiation of the more generic affective player profile discussed above, within a specific gameplay context. The same player can experience different affective gameplay profiles, depending on their mood, or their progression through the training protocol.

The affective player profile serves as a basis for designing optimal learning and training scenarios. The affective gameplay profiles then serve to track the actual affective states the player experiences during gameplay, and provide a basis for modifying the gameplay to meet the player's goals and needs. For example, if the affective gameplay profile consistently indicates that the player experiences significant amounts of frustration, the information in the profile (e.g., frustration triggers) can be used to modify the gameplay, to reduce these undesirable states.

An *ideal affective envelope* for a particular player-game interaction specifies the desired affective states, along with their intensities, for a particular set of learning or training goals, for a specific player-game context. The ideal affective envelope can be defined both in terms of the core dimensions of affect (typically arousal and valence), but also in terms of specific affective states, including both short-lasting emotions (e.g., joy, anger, sadness), and longer-lasting moods. Mixed states such as confusion, engagement and flow can also be included in the optimal affective envelopes. The ideal affective envelope then serves as a design goal for the game developer, and the game can be evaluated with respect to this goal, to assess how closely it meets the learning goals and needs of the student.

Affect-Sensitive and Affect-Centered Games

All games induce some emotions in players. When the gameplay is successful, these emotions are primarily positive, and encourage the player to continue engaging with the game. In the case of educational, training or therapeutic games, an additional benefit is that the player is acquiring new skills or knowledge, or experiencing a reduction in some undesirable symptoms.

When the games are not designed properly, or if there is a poor match between the game and the player interests and skills, games may induce negative emotions in the player (e.g., frustration, boredom, confusion), and the player abandons the game. In the case of educational games, little or no learning then takes place.

The degree of explicit focus on players' emotions in gaming and game design varies. Players' emotions may be a "side effect" of the game, with not much conscious thought given to emotion during design: as long as the game ends up being more 'fun' than 'frustrating', the players remain engaged and their emotions can be ignored by the designers.

The players' emotions can also function as a means-to-an-end, to control the players' engagement within the game. This requires more systematic attention to the players' affective reactions. This can be achieved through an "open-loop" approach. This approach does not require the game system sense the player's emotions, since the game can adapt through carefully structured levels, plot lines and sequences of increasingly difficult actions, required to achieve the ultimate game goal, or through game character behavior such as taunting or encouragement.

In contrast with this approach, the player's emotions can be incorporated into a game in a "closed-loop" manner, where they are sensed and recognized by the game system. Some aspect of the game is then modified, as a function of the player's state: the game is made less challenging if the player becomes frustrated, and more challenging if s/he becomes bored; the behavior of the game characters changes to accommodate the player's affective state; or the game situation is changed to adapt to the player's emotion (e.g., a shift to a less stressful 'place' within the game). Here, the player's emotion is a key factor, actively manipulated to ensure engagement. This type of dynamic affective adaptation (affective feedback (Bersak, McDarby et al., 2001)) is the focus of current affective gaming efforts (Becker, Nakasone et al., 2005; Gilleade, Dix et al., 2005). I refer to these types of games *affect-sensitive games*. The games are capable of actively detecting, recognizing and adapting to (some of) the player's affective states.

Finally, games can be developed for contexts that explicitly focus on affect. I refer to these as *affect-centered games*. Such games aim to train some affective skills: for example, emotional or social intelligence skills, such as recognition of emotion in self and others; learning coping strategies for negative emotions, such as re-appraisal, task-based problem-solving; and emotion regulation skills. Affect-centered games could also be used to help people in recognition of, and coping with, affective biases. For example, to recognize the anger-related hostility attribution bias, where hostility is attributed to someone whose behavior intereferes with one's goals; or fear and anxiety-related biases, such as threat and self bias in perception. Such games could be used to improve decision-making and perceptual skills. Affect-centered games could also be used as adjuncts in psychotherapy, to provide training and 'homework exercises', for highly-structured treatment protocols such as cognitive behavioral therapies; e.g., systematic de-sensitization. For a discussion of affect-centered games see Hudlicka (Hudlicka, 2009a).

Note that while the *ideal affective envelope* for an educational game may be rather simple (e.g., to maintain arousal and valence at an optimal level to ensure engagement, to minimize boredom and frustration, to induce curiosity and satisfaction), an affective envelope for a therapeutic game is likely to be quite complex. Such games may even necessitate the induction of negative emotions, to provide opportunities for the player to experience some undesirable emotion, in order to learn how recognize and cope with its effects. These games would then enable an implementation of protocols such as systematic desensitization. Similarly, the *affective gameplay profile* for such games may include negative emotions, so that coping and regulation strategies for managing these emotions can be trained.

In *affect-centered games*, the player's emotions are thus the *central* focus of the game; e.g., the achievement of a particular emotional state (e.g., happiness, pride) or the reduction of some undesirable state (e.g., fear, anger), or the induction of temporary negative state, for treatment purposes. Here the recognition of the players' emotions is essential to support the selection of appropriate gameplay, either affect-adaptive or affect-inducing. To enable the induction of the desired emotions in the players, the non-playing characters in affect-centered games will need to be more affectively- and socially-realistic. This will require deeper models of emotion in the NPCs, as discussed in the sections focusing on affective modeling below.

The notions of *affective envelope* and *affective profile* are even more important in the affect-centered games, where affective states are not just a byproduct, or a mediating factor, of the learning or training experience, but where they play a central role.

Affect-Focused Game Design

Affect-sensitive games, but especially affect-centered games, thus require an explicit focus on emotion during game design and evaluation. The constructs introduced above, *affective player profile, affective gameplay profile,* and *ideal affective envelope* for player-game interaction, provide the conceptual and representational structures that facilitate the central focus on player emotion during the game design process, and during the evaluation of the evolving game.

In addition to these constructs, which focus on the affective states of the players, we introduce another construct, which refers to game design in general: *affect-focused game design*. Affect-focused game design is an approach to game design that considers the student's affective state as a critical element of the gameplay. The player's emotion is thus not a side-effect of the game, which naturally occurs during the gameplay, and may at times include undesirable states, or states with undesirably high intensities. Rather, considerations of the player's desired affective state, defined in terms of the affective profiles and envelopes, guide the design choices for all aspects of the game. This includes the gameplay structure (e.g., definition of, and transition among, different levels), recognition of player emotions and moods, and modeling and expression of emotions and moods by non-playing characters.

Other aspects of the game design are also influenced, most notably the visual and auditory aspects of the game, which also greatly influence the player's affective state. Affect-inducing elements can be incorporated into multiple aspects of the game, including the look-and-feel and dynamics of the game environment, temporal and resource constraints on player behavior (e.g., requirements to complete a difficult task within a short timeframe designed to induce stress), choice of game tasks or situations provided to the player (e.g., easier tasks to build confidence, difficult task to challenge), and their integration within the overall plot or game narrative, as well as the appearance and behavior of the game characters or the players' avatars.

A range of issues must therefore be addressed by the game designer. In *game character* development, the game designer should be clear about the following:

- What emotions, moods and personality traits should they express, when, and how?
- Are deep models of emotion necessary?
- Do the characters need to affectively respond to all situations or can their affective behavior be scripted to respond to selected game and user events?
- How realistic do the affective expressions need to be to make the game characters believable and maintain player engagement?
- Which expressive modalities should be used (e.g., speech tone and content, behavior selection, gestures, facial expressions)?
- Should the game characters' behavior be directed to the player, other game characters or the game environment in general?

Regarding the *affect-adaptive gameplay*, the designer needs to be clear about the following:

- What role do the player's emotions play in the overall gameplay (e.g., side effect of the game vs. central focus in therapeutic games)?
- Which player emotions or moods need to be recognized and which modalities and signals are most appropriate for their recognition (e.g., physiological signals, facial expressions, player behavior within the game)?
- Does the player's personality need to be assessed?
- Which elements of the gameplay should be adapted (e.g., narrative and plot changes, game character behavior, game tasks)?

- What information about the player's affective makeup is necessary to enable these adaptations?

The remainder of this chapter discusses how the emerging discipline of affective computing, and existing research in the affective sciences (psychology and neuroscience), help provide answers to these questions, and thereby support affect-focused game design.

The discussion emphasizes the modeling of emotion in game characters and affective user modeling, as these are critical for the development of educational and training games, and essential for affect-centered games (e.g., games for the training of affective and social skills, and psychotherapeutic games).

EMOTION RESEARCH BACKGROUND

Emotion research in the affective sciences over the past 20 years has produced data, conceptual and computational models, and methods and techniques that are directly relevant to affective game design, including the development of affective game engines. The emerging findings inform sensing and recognition of user emotions by machines, computational affective modeling, and the generation of expressive affective behaviors in non-playing characters.

Definitions and Terminology

When searching for a definition of emotions, it is interesting to note that many definitions describe instead characteristics of affective processing (e.g., fast, undifferentiated processing), or the roles and functions of emotions. The latter are usefully divided into those involved in interpersonal, social behavior (e.g., communication of intent, coordination of group behavior, attachment), and those involved in intrapsychic regulation, adaptive behavior, and motivation (e.g., goal management, coordination of multiple systems necessary for action, selection of best adaptive behaviors). Nevertheless, many emotion researchers do agree on a high-level definition of emotions. For purposes of modeling, emotions can be defined as: the evaluative judgments of the environment, the self and other social agents, in light of the agent's goals and beliefs, and the associated distinct modes of functioning, reflected across multiple modalities (e.g., cognitive, physiological), and coordinating multiple subsystems (cognitive, behavioral), to achieve the agent's goals.

Multiple Modalities

A key characteristic of emotions is their multimodal nature, which has direct implications for both sensing and recognition of player emotion, and behavioral expression of emotions by game characters. The most visible is the *behavioral / expressive modality*; e.g., facial expressions, speech, gestures, posture, and behavioral choices. Closely related is the *somatic / physiological modality:* the neurophysiological substrate making behavior and cognition possible (e.g., neuroendocrine system manifestations, such as blood pressure and heart rate). The *cognitive / interpretive modality* is most directly associated with the evaluation-based definition of emotions above, and emphasized in the current cognitive appraisal theories of emotion generation. Finally, the *experiential/subjective modality* reflects the individual's conscious, idiosyncratic experience of emotions.

Taxonomies of Affective States and Traits

The term 'emotion' can often be used rather loosely, to denote a wide variety of affective states, each with different implications for sensing and recognition, modeling and expression. A brief taxonomy of affective states is provided below,

and their distinguishing features are highlighted. *Emotions* proper represent short states (lasting seconds to minutes), reflecting a particular affective assessment of the state of self or the world, and associated behavioral tendencies and cognitive biases. Emotions can be further differentiated into *basic* and *complex,* the latter including the important set of *social emotions,* based on their cognitive complexity, the universality of triggering stimuli and behavioral manifestations, and the degree to which an explicit representation of the agent's 'self' is required (Ekman and Davidson 1994; Lewis 1993). *Basic emotions* typically include fear, anger, joy, sadness, disgust, and surprise. *Complex emotions* such as guilt, pride, and shame have a much larger cognitive component and associated idiosyncrasies in both their triggering elicitors and their behavioral manifestations, which makes both their detection and their expression more challenging. *Moods* reflect less-focused and longer lasting states (hours to days to months). Finally, *affective personality traits* represent more or less permanent affective tendencies (e.g., extraversion vs. introversion, aggressiveness, positive vs. negative emotionality). There are also many mixed states, with strong cognitive and affective components. Some of these were already mentioned above and are important in learning; e.g., confusion, engagement, flow. Examples of longer-lasting mixed states that are also important for learning are attitudes. For example, a student may have a generally positive or negative attitude towards a particular topic (e.g., algebra) or a particular mode of instruction (e.g., rote learning vs. learning involving more creative elements).

Fundamental Processes of Emotions: Generation and Effects

In spite of the progress in emotion research over the past 20 years, emotions remain an elusive phenomenon. While some underlying circuitry has been elucidated for some emotions (e.g., amygdala-mediated processing of threatening stimuli, the role of orbitofrontal cortex in emotion regulation), much remains unknown about the mechanisms of emotions. Given the multiple-modalities of emotion, the complexity of the cross-modal interactions, and the fact that affective processes exist at multiple levels of aggregation, it may therefore seem futile, at best, to speak of 'fundamental processes of emotions'.

Nevertheless, for purposes of modeling emotions in game characters, as well as for the construction of affective user models, it is useful to divide emotions into two types of processes. Those responsible for the generation of emotions, and those which then mediate the effects of the activated emotions on cognition, expressive behavior (e.g., facial expressions, speech) and action selection.

While multiple modalities play a role in *emotion generation* (Izard, 1993), most existing theories (and computational models) emphasize the role of cognition, both conscious and unconscious, in emotion generation. These are termed the 'cognitive appraisal' theories of emotion (Ortony, Clore et al., 1988; Roseman and Smith, 2001; Scherer, Schorr et al., 2001), and are the most relevant for the modeling of emotions in game characters. We therefore focus on cognitive appraisal theories when discussing models of emotion generation later in this chapter.

Central component of most cognitive appraisal theories is a set of domain-independent *appraisal dimensions,* which capture aspects of the current situation or event, and its relationship to the perceiving agent. These include novelty, urgency, likelihood, goal relevance and goal congruence, responsible agent, and the agent's own ability to cope (Smith and Kirby, 2000; Ellsworth and Scherer, 2003). If the values of the dimensions can be determined, the resulting vector can be mapped onto the associated emotion space, defined by the appraisal dimensions, which provides a highly-differentiated set of possible emotions. (See figure 1).

Figure 1. Emotion generation via cognitive appraisal

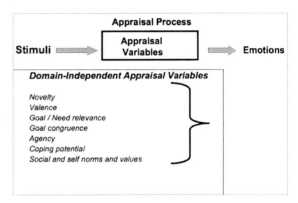

Less understood are the processes mediating the *effects of the triggered emotions.* The visible manifestations of specific emotions are certainly well documented, at least for the basic emotions; that is, the associated facial expressions, gestures, posture, nature of movement, speech content and tone characteristics. The appraisal dimension theories mentioned above have also been used to explain emotion effects on expressive behavior, with suggestions that specific values of particular dimensions (e.g., novelty, goal congruence) map onto specific features of the different expressive modalities (e.g., novelty induces raised eyebrows and opening of the eyes in facial expressions (Scherer, 1992)).

The effects of specific emotions on behavior are also known, again, primarily for the basic emotions; e.g., running or hiding associated with fear, aggression associated with anger, withdrawal with sadness. There is, of course, a high degree of individual and cultural variability for the more complex emotions.

Some effects of emotions on cognition are also known; e.g., fear reduces attentional capacity and biases attention toward threat detection (Isen, 1993; Mineka, Rafael et al., 2003). However, the mechanisms mediating these observed effects have not yet been identified, although several theories have been proposed, including *spreading activation* (Derryberry, 1988; Bower,

1992), and *parameter-based models*. Proposed independently by a number of researchers (e.g., (Matthews and Harley, 1993; Hudlicka, 1998; Ritter and Avramides, 2000; Ortony, Norman et al., 2005), parameter-based models suggest that affective states act as global parameters, inducing patterns of variations in cognitive processes. Different patterns then characterize different emotions, in terms of systemic changes in biases, and processing speeds and capacities.

Recently, some researchers have suggested that the individual appraisal dimensions can also be a basis for developing models of emotion effect on cognition. Specific values of particular appraisal dimensions are thought to be associated with a specific cognitive manifestation. For example, a high-value of the appraisal dimension of certainty may be associated with heuristics and short-cuts, and 'shallow' processing in general, whereas a low value may be associated with deeper, analytical thought (Lerner and Tiedens 2006). The individual appraisal dimensions can thus play a role not only in mediating cognitive appraisal, but also in mediating the effects of emotions on both expression and cognition.

Different Theoretical Views of Emotions

Emotions represent complex, and often poorly understood, phenomena. It is therefore not surprising that a number of distinct theories have evolved over time, to explain a specific subset of these phenomena, or to account for a particular subset of the observed data. Three of the most established theoretical perspectives, and those most relevant for computational affective modeling, are described below.

Discrete theories of emotions emphasize a small set of discrete or fundamental emotions. The underlying assumption of this approach is that these fundamental, discrete emotions are mediated by associated neural circuitry, with a large innate, 'hardwired' component. Different emotions are then characterized by stable patterns of triggers, behavioral expression, and associated distinct subjective experiences. The emotions addressed by these theories are typically the 'basic' emotions; joy, sadness, fear, anger, and disgust. Because of its emphasis on discrete categories of states, this approach is also termed the *categorical approach* (Panskepp, 1998). For modeling purposes, the 'semantic primitives' representing emotions in models would be the basic emotions themselves.

An alternative method of characterizing affective states is in terms of a small set of underlying factors, or dimensions, that define a space within which distinct emotions can be located. This *dimensional perspective* describes emotions in terms of two- or three-dimensions. The most frequent dimensional characterization of emotions uses two dimensions: valence and arousal. Valence reflects a positive or negative evaluation, and the associated felt state of pleasure vs. displeasure, as outlined in the context of undifferentiated affect above. Arousal reflects a general degree of intensity or activation of the organism. The degree of arousal reflects a general readiness to act: low arousal is associated with less energy, high arousal with more energy. Since this 2-dimensional space cannot easily differentiate among emotions that share the same values of arousal and valence, e.g., anger and fear, both characterized by high arousal and negative valence, a third dimension is often added. This is variously termed dominance or stance. The resulting 3-dimensional space is often referred to as the PAD space (Mehrabian, 1995) (pleasure (same as valence), arousal and dominance). The representational semantic primitives within this theoretical perspective are thus the 2 or 3 dimensions.

The third view emphasizes the distinct components of emotions, and is often termed the *componential perspective* (Leventhal and Scherer, 1987). The 'components' referred to in this view are both the distinct modalities of emotions (e.g., cognitive, physiological, behavioral, subjective) and also the components of the cognitive appraisal process. These are referred to as appraisal dimensions or appraisal variables. A stimulus, whether real or imagined, is analyzed in terms of its meaning and consequences for the agent, to determine the affective reaction. Several sets of appraisal variables have been proposed by different researchers, with the most comprehensive set proposed by Scherer, and consisting of the following: novelty (is the stimulus new), valence (is it inherently pleasant or unpleasant), goal relevance (does it represent a situation or event relevant to the agent's goals), responsible agent (who is responsible for the event or situation, and was it intentional or accidental), goal congruence (will the situation or event help or hinder the agent's goals), coping potential (what can the agent do about the situation or event), and norms and values (is the situation or event consistent with the agent's internal and cultural norms). Once the values of these dimensions are determined by the organism's evaluative processes, the resulting vector is mapped onto a particular emotion, within the n-dimensional space defined by the appraisal dimensions. The semantic primitives for representing emotions within this model are thus the individual appraisal dimensions.

Although generally not classified as a componential theory, the cognitive appraisal theory developed by Ortony and colleagues (Ortony, Clore et al., 1988), referred to as the OCC model, also offers a set of domain-independent evaluative features (e.g., desirability, goal congruence). The OCC model was the first computation-friendly theory of emotion generation, and is the most frequently implemented theory of cognitive appraisal in computational models of emotion.

It must be emphasized that these theoretical perspectives should not be viewed as competing for a single ground truth, but rather as distinct perspectives, each arising from a particular research tradition (e.g., biological vs. social psychology), focusing on different sets of affective phenomena, considering distinct levels of resolution and fundamental components (e.g., emotions as distinct primitives vs. appraisal dimensions as distinct primitives), and using different experimental methods (e.g., factor analysis of self-report data vs. neuroanatomical evidence for distinct processing pathways). The different perspectives also provide different degrees of support for the distinct processes of emotion; e.g., the componential theories provide extensive details about cognitive appraisal.

Until such time as emotions are fully understood and explained, it is best to view these theories as alternative explanations, each with its own set of explanatory powers and scope, and supporting data, analogously, perhaps, to the wave vs. particle theory of light, as suggested by Picard (Picard 1997).

AFFECTIVE GAMING

Affective gaming has received much attention lately, as the gaming community recognizes the importance of affect in the development of more engaging games (Sykes 2004; Gilleade, Dix et al., 2005). Affect plays a key role in the user experience, in entertainment, but especially in 'serious' games, developed for education, training, assessment, therapy or rehabilitation – that is, in the affect-sensitive and affect-centered games discussed above.

Current focus in affective gaming is primarily on the sensing and recognition of the players' emotions, and on tailoring the game responses to these emotions (Sykes and Brown, 2003; Gilleade and Dix, 2004). Progress is being made in emotion recognition in games, primarily in the recognition of arousal (a component of emotion), and several games have been developed in laboratories exploring the possibility of adapting the gameplay to the player's state; e.g., changing the difficulty of the levels or the reward structure if the player becomes too frustrated or bored (Becker, Nakasone et al., 2005; Gilleade, Dix et al., 2005).

A significant effort is also being devoted to generating 'affective behaviors' in the game characters, to enhance their realism and believability. This is made possible by the increasing sophistication of graphical techniques available for real-time rendering of the characters' expressive features, primarily facial expressions.

Less emphasis is placed on explicit models of emotions in game characters, both the dynamic generation of emotions in real time, and the modeling of their effects on the characters' expressive behavior, actions within the game, and emotion effects on the characters' perceptual and decision-making processes (Hudlicka, 2008).

Gilleade and colleagues captured the objectives of affective gaming in a succinct statement, describing a progression of functionalities an affective game should support: "Assist me, Challenge me, Emote me" (Gilleade, Dix et al., 2005). The last goal represents the type of enhanced engagement, perhaps even the induction of specific emotions, discussed above, in the context of affect-centered games.

In this chapter I suggest that advancing the state-of-the-art in gaming to effectively cover the "assist me, challenge me, emote me" spectrum will require increased emphasis on explicit models of emotions in non-playing game characters, as well as the development tools that directly support such models, such as the affective game engine discussed later in this chapter.

AFFECTIVE COMPUTING

Affective computing is a cross-disciplinary research and practice area that has been growing and evolving over the past 15 years. The term affective computing was coined by Picard in the eponymous book published in 1997 (Picard, 1997). Picard defined affective computing as "computing that relates to, arises from, or deliberately influences emotions" (Picard, 1997, p. 3).

Affective computing can be divided into four core areas: *emotion sensing and recognition by machines*; *affective models of users*; *computational models of emotion and cognitive-affective agent architectures, and emotion expression in synthetic agents and robots*. All of these areas are directly relevant to affective gaming, and for the development of educational and training games. Affective computing is of course even more relevant for affect-centered games, where inducing appropriate emotional states in the players, and adaptation to players' affective states, are essential.

The methods and techniques developed in the core areas of affective computing are directly applicable to the design of educational and training games, and especially relevant for the design of affect-centered games, such as therapeutic games. These four areas of affective computing are briefly introduced below.

Recognition of Emotion by Machines

Much progress has been made in machine recognition of emotion over the past 5 years. Multimodal approaches (facial expression, speech and physiological signals) are beginning to approach the accuracy rates of human observers (Pantic and Bartlett, 2007; Gunes, Piccardi et al., 2008). Significant advances are also being made in recognizing spontaneous emotion expressions, under more realistic circumstances (i.e., in real-life vs. controlled laboratory settings) (Zeng, Pantic et al., 2009), and attempts are being made to recognize more complex emotions, such as embarrassment (Cohn, Ambadar et al., 2005).

While impressive, these results don't translate into similar accuracy rates in more naturalistic settings, such as those required in gaming. In fact, accurate recognition of spontaneous emotions, in naturalistic settings, where the expressive manifestations of emotions are more subtle and have more variability, where the emotions are not limited to the basic emotions, and where the sensor data are noisy and incomplete, remains a major challenge in machine recognition of emotion (Zeng, Pantic et al., 2009).

Emotion recognition is best understood as a classification problem, where features extracted from the sensed data are mapped onto the categories of emotions to be recognized.

The major components of the emotion recognition process are therefore as follows:

- Obtain accurate signals that are most diagnostic of specific emotions.
- Identify most useful features within these signals to use as input into the classification algorithms.
- Select the most appropriate classification algorithm to obtain the best results.

The *multi-modal nature of emotions,* and their evolution over time, both facilitate and constrain recognition of emotions in players. Many emotions have characteristic multi-feature, multi-modal 'signatures' that serve as basis for both recognition and expression. For example, fear is characterized by raising of the eyebrows (facial expression), fast tempo and higher pitch (speech), threat bias in attention and perception (cognition), a range of physiological responses reflecting increased arousal and mobilizing the energy required for fast reactions, and, of course, characteristic behavior (flee vs. freeze). Identifying unique emotion signatures that provide the highly diagnostic signals necessary for recognition is a key challenge in machine emotion recognition. Once identified, the constituent features guide the selection of appropriate (non-intrusive) sensors, and the classification algorithms required to map the raw data onto a recognized emotion.

Recognition rates then depend greatly on the modality and channels used, on the quality of the sensed data, the feature sets used as input to the classification algorithm, and the classification algorithm itself. Increasingly, multi-modal approaches are being used, primarily visual (facial expression) and audio (speech content and prosody), to identify emotions. Physiological signals are also being incorporated to increase recognition accuracy, primarily signals reflecting the activity of the autonomic nervous systems. Contextual variables (e.g., state of the game) can also help to increase recognition rates.

However, not all of these promising results readily translate to the gaming context. Gaming presents a specific set of constraints and challenges for the recognition and expression of emotions. Broad game categories (e.g., entertainment vs. serious gaming), game genres (e.g., FPS vs. slower-tempo strategy games vs. games emphasizing social interaction, such as Sims), and delivery modes ranging from the Wii to iPhones, have different requirements for both the types of emotions that may need to be sensed and expressed, and the most appropriate channels and sensors for doing so.

Affective User Modeling

A key element in successful emotion recognition, and in adaptation to user emotion, is an affective model of the user. Affective user models are analogous to the traditional cognitive user models, used in learning and tutoring systems. However, as the name implies, affective user models are augmented to also include affective information about the user: a type of an *affective user profile*. Affective user modeling is concerned with the construction of such models, and affective adaptation addresses the ways in which a computer system, most often a learning or a training system, can then adapt to the user's emotional states.

Traditional 'cognitive' user models focus on representing the user's knowledge state, beliefs, preferences, general characteristics (e.g., age, gender, skill level), goals, plans, and, in learning environments, possible misconceptions about the domain of interest (Martinho, Machado et al., 2000). In contrast, an affective user model contains data about the types of emotions the user is likely to experience in a given human-machine context, and how those emotions are manifested by the user, within the modalities the system can sense. Such models can then be used as basis for emotion recognition, and to support affect-adaptive gameplay, by supporting reasoning about the likely triggers for particular user emotions (Hudlicka and McNeese, 2002).

Affective user models are thus representational structures that store information about the player's affective profile, and play a critical role in affect-adaptive gaming, supporting both emotion recognition, and the development of appropriate affect-adaptive strategy by the game system. Since affective behavior can be highly idiosyncratic, affective user models necessarily involve a learning component. These components enable the identification of characteristic affective patterns, extracted from player state and gameplay interaction, by tracking player's behavior over time. For example, Player A may express frustration by more forceful manipulation of the game controls, whereas Player B may exhibit increasing delays between game inputs.

Significant existing research in intelligent tutoring systems provides the knowledge and methods supporting affective user modeling (e.g., (D'Mello, Craig et al., 2008; Forbes-Riley, Rotaru et al., 2008; McQuiggan, Mott et al., 2008; Yannakakis, Hallam et al., 2008). This includes sensors and classification algorithms for identifying specific emotions that are relevant for both intelligent tutoring and gaming (e.g., frustration, interest, boredom, engagement) with reasonable rates of accuracy (70-80%). The algorithms used to associate specific user manifestations (e.g., increased heart rate, frown, speech quality) or user-system interaction patterns (e.g., type of input), with specific emotions range from simple correlations and multiple regression models (Witten & Frank, 2005; Forbes-Riley, Rotaru et al., 2008), to machine learning algorithms, both symbolic and connectionist, including tree induction algorithms and artificial neural nets (D'Mello, Craig et al., 2008). Many of these algorithms are available in the Waikato Environment for Knowledge Analysis (Witten and Frank, 2005).

Since affective user models are typically used in learning systems, other learning-relevant states are often of interest, in addition to emotions proper. These include boredom, uncertainty, confusion, interest, and flow (Carberry & de Rosis, 2008; D'Mello, Craig et al., 2008). Thus, for example, in a learning system which can detect boredom, frustration, and surprise, and tries to maintain an optimal level of engagement, the following information might be contained in an affective user model: signatures of boredom, frustration, surprise, interest, and a neutral state, in terms of the sensed channels (e.g., heart rate, galvanic skin response, mouse pressure); specific triggers in the user-system interactions that precede and follow each state (e.g., frustration occurs when user is unable to solve 2 tasks in a row, interest occurs when new information is presented to the user within his/her range of understanding); and user behavior when a specific state is entered (e.g., user stops working on a task when bored; makes mistakes when frustrated).

As discussed above, emotions are manifested along a number of expressive channels, including facial expressions, speech, physiological signals, posture, gestures, body movements, and, of course, actual behavioral choices. Any of these can potentially be sources of data for the construction of an affective user model.

Affective user models vary in the depth of the user's mental apparatus represented. They can be 'black box' models, where only the input-output patterns of the user's affective profile are represented.

For example, a black-box style affective user model might simply contain pairs of the form {<triggers><emotion>} and {<emotion>,<behavior>}, such as:

[{loss of points | unable to reach game goal | character dies}, frustration]

[frustration, {> 1 minute lag in input | mouse pressure > x | inputs insulting comments to computer system}]

and use these to support both emotion recognition (from user behavior), and the development of adaptive strategies (by using data about what system behavior or user-system interactions trigger which user emotions).

Alternatively, affective user models can attempt to reconstruct the user's mental apparatus, including internal constructs such as beliefs, expectations, goals, and plans, and attempt to simulate the user's actual cognitive-affective processing, within the context of the specific gameplay. Such models then provide 'deeper' representation of the user's mental architecture. In other words, the affective user model may try to simulate the user's own appraisal of the on-going situation, and infer his/her goals and beliefs. Such models then begin to resemble cognitive-affective architectures, and may be capable of simulating some of the user's own cognitive / affective processing; e.g., the cognitive appraisal processes resulting in a particular emotion.

Emotion Modeling and Cognitive-Affective Architectures

A number of computational emotion models have been developed for both research and applied purposes. These models typically focus on the basic emotions (e.g., joy, fear, anger, sadness), and use a variety of methods for implementing emotion generation via appraisal (Bates, Loyall et al., 1992; Andre, Klesen et al., 2000; Broekens & DeGroot, 2006; Reilly, 2006), or, less frequently, emotion effects on cognition, via parametric modeling (Hudlicka, 1998; Ritter & Avramides, 2000; Hudlicka, 2007; Hudlicka, 2008).

Models used as part of agent architectures also include the modeling of emotion effects on expressive behavior and action selection. These are typically implemented via direct mapping of a particular emotion onto specific behavior, or patterns of expression along one or more modalities; e.g., If 'happy' then 'jump' and 'smile'. Some models implement a mapping onto components of expressive behaviors, rather than fully-formed expressions; e.g., mapping values of individual appraisal dimensions onto elements of facial expressions, such as eye brow position (Scherer, 1992).

Most models of emotion focus on emotion generation, typically using cognitive appraisal.

Most of these appraisal models are based on either the OCC model (Ortony, Clore et al., 1988), or the explicit appraisal dimension theories developed by (Smith & Kirby 2000; Scherer, Schorr et al., 2001) (e.g., *novelty, valence, goal relevance and congruence, responsible agent, coping potential*). Typically, symbolic AI methods are used to implement the stimulus-to-emotion mapping, whether this is done via an intervening set of appraisal dimensions, or directly from the domain stimuli to the emotions. In general, the complexity of this process lies in analyzing the domain stimuli (e.g., features of a game situation, behavior of game characters, player behavior) and extracting the appraisal dimension values. This may require representation of complex mental structures, including the game characters' and players' goals, plans, beliefs and values, their current assessment of the evolving game situation, and expectations of future developments, as well as complex causal representation of the gameplay dynamics. Rules, semantic nets and Bayesian belief nets are some of the frequently used formalisms implementing this mapping.

Emotion Expression in Game Characters

The expression of emotions in synthetic agents and robots, and game characters, requires two distinct components, with associated distinct methods and technologies. The agent must not only depict the emotion in an appropriate manner, along its available expressive channels (e.g., face, speech, movement), appropriately synchronized, and depicting realistic affective dynamics, but it must also display an appropriate emotion for the specific context. Achieving these goals involves very different sets of methods and technologies, with the former closely linked to computer graphics (rendering and animation technologies) and robotics, and the latter involving emotion models and agent architectures, discussed above.

A critical factor in emotion expression of emotion is the identification of a set of *semantic primitives* for each expressive channel, whose distinct configurations characterize the different emotions (Hudlicka, 2005). An appropriate set of such primitives greatly facilitates both recognition and expression, by providing a unifying vocabulary of features. The most established example of such a vocabulary is the Facial Action Coding System (FACS) developed by Ekman and Friesen (1978). FACS describes in detail features such as shape of the lips and eyebrows, narrowing of the eyes, and raising of cheeks, to completely define a broad range of facial expressions. Specific configurations of these expressions then characterize different emotions; e.g., lips turned upward, raising of lower eyelid and narrowing of lids are associated with happiness. FACS has been successfully used to model facial expressions in synthetic characters. Semantic primitives for other modalities are also being developed, including speech (patterns of pitch and tonal variations used to identify basic emotions (Petrushin, 2000), and posture ('basic posture units' identified by Mota and Picard (Mota and Picard, 2004), used to identify boredom and engagement).

The semantic primitives then facilitate affective expression generation, by helping define the syntax and semantics of markup languages used to specify the expressive features of emotions, across different channels (face, body movement, speech) (Prendinger and Ishizuka, 2004). The identification of the most diagnostic emotion features also guides the selection of the best expressive channels to convey a particular emotion to the player, via game character behavior. In emotion expression, multiple modalities also present a challenge, by requiring that expression be coordinated and synchronized across multiple channels, to ensure character realism. For example, expression of anger must involve consistent signals in speech, movement and gesture quality, facial expression, body posture and specific action selection, evolving and decaying at appropriate rates.

REQUIREMENTS FOR DEVELOPING AFFECT-SENSITIVE AND AFFECT-CENTERED GAMES

To develop affect-sensitive and affect-centered games, all four of the categories of functionalities discussed above must be included.

Recognition of Player Emotions

The game needs to be able to recognize the player's emotions. Which emotions need to be recognized and which sensors are most appropriate, depends on the game and its context. For some games, it may be adequate to recognize levels of arousal and infer the associated emotion. This is relatively easy from physiological measures such as galvanic skin response or heart rate, and advances in non-intrusive sensors make detection of arousal increasingly feasible. To identify a specific emotion, an assessment of valence is also needed. This is more challenging, typically requiring machine vision or facial EMG, to detect the position and movement of facial muscles. Again, recent advances in EEG and other physiological sensors may make non-intrusive valence detection possible in the near future. Multimodal sensors are almost essential to achieve the desired accuracy. In gaming, there is the associated requirement for non-intrusive sensors. To this end, researchers have explored signals such as the manner in which players manipulate the game controls, to detect their affective state.

Affective Models of Players

The player's affective profile is essential for emotion recognition, and provides a basis for constructing a detailed affective user model. Such a model then supports both the recognition of player emotion, but also the selection of appropriate gameplay strategies, to adapt to the player's affective state. In affect-centered games, an affective user model allows the game to implement the best protocol for inducing specific emotion in the player, to achieve the game objectives. For example, to induce an emotion to allow the player to experience a particular affective bias, or to experience a negative emotion, for purposes of systematic desensitization in psychotherapeutic games.

Modeling Emotions in Non-Playing Characters

The more affectively and socially realistic the non-playing game characters are, the more effective the game can be in engaging the player, and in inducing the desired emotions in the player. To achieve these goals, the game characters need to have underlying models of emotion. Such models enable them to dynamically react to evolving game situations, or player-game interactions, and generate appropriate emotions in real-time. The NPCs in affect-sensitive and affect-centered games therefore need to have the capabilities to model emotion. This means modeling both *emotion generation,* and *emotion effects* on behavior and cognition. *Emotion generation* models are based on stimuli representing situations in the gameplay (e.g., behavior of another NPC, changes in the game environment, or player activity), and the characters' own internal goals and needs. *Emotion effects* models map the generated emotions onto their effects on cognition (affective biases), expressive behavior (e.g., facial expressions),

and specific behavioral choices (e.g., approach vs. withdraw).

The NPC emotion models may or may not need explicit models of the emotions on cognition. Such models provide additional richness and flexibility, and provide an efficient way to generate variability in behavior, thereby making the characters seem more lifelike. However, not all games require this type of complexity, and mapping emotions directly onto expressive behavior and action selection is often adequate.

Expression of Emotions by Non-Playing Characters

Finally, the NPCs should be able to express their emotions in a manner appropriate for the game context. This means selecting the most appropriate emotion-specific expressive behavior (e.g., smile, laugh, growl, etc.), and selecting a specific action that reflects the emotion (e.g., dance, hop and up and, attack, etc.). The specific choices depend on the deployment platform (e.g., a high-resolution large screen vs. an iPhone), and the modalities available for the character. For example, a low-resolution image on a mobile device, such as the iPhone, may make it difficult to express emotions via facial expressions, and may require instead displaying the emotion via body movements. Much progress has been made in the graphical support necessary to effectively convey realistic affective expression, and research in affective computing and social agents has much to contribute to emotion expression by NPCs.

Some of the affective computing methods for the sensing, recognition and expression of emotion are being explored in affective gaming (Sykes & Brown 2003). However, the area of affective user modeling and computational models of affect has, until very recently, been largely ignored (Hudlicka, 2008; Hudlicka and Broekens, 2009; Broekens & Hudlicka, 2010). The remainder of this chapter therefore emphasizes the importance of affective modeling, as a basis for more realistic behavior of game characters, and as a means of developing more realistic and complete affective models of the players. Both of these are necessary to support the design of and development of affect-sensitive and affect-centered educational, training and therapeutic games.

METHODS FOR MODELING EMOTIONS IN GAME CHARACTERS AND PLAYER MODELS

The complexity of models required to generate affective behavior in game characters varies with the complexity of the game plot, the characters, the available behavior repertoire of the player within the game, and of course the game objectives (e.g., entertainment vs. education vs. therapy). For many games, simple models are adequate. In these models, a small set of gameplay or player behavior features is mapped onto a limited set of game characters' emotions, which are then depicted in terms of simple manipulations of character features; e.g., player fails to find a treasure and the avatar shows a 'sad face', player loses to a game character and the character gloats (Broekens and Hudlicka, 2009; Hudlicka, and Broekens, 2009). Such simple models are termed *'black-box'* models, since they make no attempt to represent the underlying affective mechanisms. Data available from the affective sciences provide the basis for defining the necessary mappings (triggers-to-emotions, emotions-to-effects). However, as the complexity of the games increases, the need for more sophisticated affective modeling arises. This is due to more complex plots and narratives, and associated increase in the sophistication of the game characters, and richness of player interactions. This may require more complex *'process-models'*, which use explicit representations of some of the affective mechanisms, and allow a greater degree of generality and complexity.

In an effort to establish more systematic guidelines for affective model development, and to facilitate analysis of existing models, Hudlicka has recently suggested dividing the modeling processes into those responsible for emotion generation, and those responsible for implementing emotion effects (Hudlicka 2008a; 2008b). Each of these broad categories of processes are further divided into their constituent *computational tasks*. These computational tasks then serve as the building blocks for modeling the high-level affective processes.

For *emotion generation*, these computational tasks include defining the following:

- stimulus-to-emotion mapping;
- nature of the emotion dynamics; i.e., functions defining the emotion intensity calculation, and the ramp-up and decay of the emotion intensity over time; and
- methods for combining multiple emotions, necessary for combining existing emotions with newly derived emotions, and for selecting the most appropriate emotion when multiple emotions are generated.

For *emotion effects*, these computational tasks include defining the following:

- emotion-to-cognitive process mappings, to capture affective biases on cognition;
- emotion-to-behavior mappings, to capture emotion effects on expressive behavior and behavioral choices;
- magnitude of the associated effects on each affected process, and the dynamics of these effects; and
- methods for integration of the effects of multiple emotions, both in cases where a residual effect of a prior emotion is still in force, and in cases where multiple emotions are generated simultaneously, and their effects on cognition an behavior must be integrated.

Approaches to modeling these processes are discussed below.

Modeling Emotion Generation

Our understanding of emotion generation is best within the cognitive modality and most existing models of emotion generation implement *cognitive appraisal*, which is best suited for affective modeling in gaming. The discussion below is therefore limited to these theories and models.

Many researchers have contributed to the current versions of cognitive appraisal theories (Arnold, 1960; Lazarus, 1984; Mandler, 1984; Frijda, 1986; Roseman and Smith, 2001; Scherer, Schorr et al., 2001; Smith and Kirby, 2001). Most existing computational models of appraisal are based on either the OCC model (Ortony, Clore et al., 1988), or the explicit appraisal dimension theories developed by (Smith and Kirby, 2000; Scherer, Schorr et al., 2001), and outlined earlier in this chapter (e.g., *novelty, valence, goal relevance, goal congruence, responsible agent, coping potential*).

A number of computational appraisal models have been developed for both research and applied purposes (e.g., (Bates, Loyall et al., 1992; Andre, Klesen et al., 2000; Reilly, 2006). These models typically focus on the basic emotions (e.g., joy, fear, anger, sadness), and use a variety of methods for implementing a subset of the computational tasks outlined above. Most frequently, symbolic methods from artificial intelligence are used to implement the stimulus-to-emotion mapping, whether this is done via an intervening set of appraisal dimensions, or directly from the domain stimuli to the emotions.

In general, the complexity of this process lies in analyzing the domain stimuli (e.g., features of a game situation, behavior of game characters, player behavior), to evaluate their significance for the NPC, and enable the generation of a particular emotion. In situations where domain-independent appraisal dimensions are used,

the emotion generation process consists of two phases. First, the domain stimuli are analyzed to determine the values of the different appraisal dimensions (e.g., Is it new? Is it conducive to the NPC's goals? Who is responsible for it?). This analysis is likely to require the representation of a set of complex mental structures, including the game characters' and players' goals, plans, beliefs and values, their current assessment of the evolving game situation, and expectations of future developments, as well as complex causal representation of the gameplay dynamics. Rules, semantic nets and Bayesian belief nets are some of the most frequently used formalisms to implement this mapping. *Next*, the vector of appraisal dimensions is mapped onto the space of possible emotions, defined by the appraisal dimensions. This is typically done by designating certain regions within the n-dimensional emotion space as corresponding to specific emotions, and then identifying the emotion that is nearest the point represented by the appraisal vector. To determine closeness, some suitable measure of distance is then used, for example, Euclidean distance. The high-dimensionality of the space defined by the appraisal dimensions allows a high-degree of differentiation of affective states, e.g., delineating emotions of different intensity, from mild annoyance, through frustration, to anger and rage.

Emotion dynamics are generally limited to calculating emotion intensity, which is usually a relatively simple function of a limited set of the appraisal dimensions (e.g., absolute value of the desirability of an event or a situation multiplied by its likelihood (Reilly, 2006)), or some customized quantification of selected feature(s) of the stimuli (e.g., a linear combination of weighted factors that contribute to each emotion of interest).

The ramp-up and decay of emotion intensity may not be modeled at all, with the emotion simply appearing in its full intensity, lasting for some time interval, and then returning to zero or its baseline value for that character. Alternatively, the ramp-up and decay rates may follow some monotonically increasing or decreasing (respectively) function, to model the affective dynamics in a more realistic manner. A variety of functions have been used in appraisal models, including linear, exponential, sigmoid and logarithmic (Reilly, 2006; Hudlicka, 2008). In general, the theories and conceptual models developed by psychologists do not provide sufficient information to generate computational models of affective dynamics, and educated guess-work and model tuning are required during this phase of affective modeling.

The issue of integrating multiple emotions is the most neglected, both in existing psychological theories and conceptual models, and in computational models. Typically, very simple approaches are used to address this complex problem, which limits the realism of the resulting models in any but the most simple situations. In general, intensities of synergistic emotions (e.g., all positive or all negative emotions) are combined via a simple sum, average, or max functions. Recently, problems associated with these simple functions have been identified (Reilly, 2006), and other approaches have been suggested, including logarithmic and sigmoid functions (Reilly, 2006; Picard, 1997). In some cases, customized, domain-dependent weightings are used, so that a particular emotion is preferentially generated, as a function of the character's personality. For example, high-extraversion characters may be more likely to feel positive emotions, whereas high-neuroticism characters may be more likely to feel negative emotions (Hudlicka, 2007). A more problematic situation occurs when opposing or distinctly different emotions are derived (e.g., a particular situation brings both joy and sadness). Neither the available theories, nor existing empirical data, currently provide a basis for a principled approach to this problem. The computational solutions are therefore generally task- or domain- specific, and often ad hoc.

Modeling Emotion Effects

For modeling purposes, it is useful to divide emotion effects into two categories: the visible, often dramatic, behavioral expressions, and the internal, but no less dramatic, effects on attention, perception and cognition. The majority of existing models of emotion effects focus on the former. While technically challenging, the behavioral effects are easier from a modeling perspective. This is due to the large body of empirical data regarding the visible manifestations of particular emotions, and the established techniques for 3D dynamic graphical modeling and rendering required to display these expressions in virtual characters. We know, in general, how the basic emotions are expressed in terms of facial expressions, quality of movement and gestures, quality of speech, and behavioral choices. As with emotion generation, the degree of variability and complexity increases as we move from the fundamental emotions such as fear, joy, anger, to the more cognitively-complex emotions such as pride, shame, jealousy. The focus here will be on cognitive effects only. This is due in part to space limitations, but primarily because such models have been neglected in the emotion modeling literature, and are relevant for modeling emotions in NPCs in affect-sensitive and affect-centered games.

The internal effects that emotions exert on the perceptual and cognitive processes that mediate adaptive, intelligent behavior are less understood than those involved in emotion generation. This is true both for the fundamental processes (attention, working memory, long-term memory recall and encoding), and for higher-level processes such as situation assessment, problem-solving, goal management, decision-making, and learning. These processes are generally not modeled in existing game characters, and, indeed, may not be necessary. However, as the affective complexity of games increases, the need for these types of models will emerge. This is particularly the case in *affect-centered games*, where the assessment and triggering of specific emotions is the focus. For example, in games designed to support cognitive-behavioral therapies, and the associated cognitive restructuring, an ability to model the processes mediating affective biases would require explicit modeling of emotion effects on distinct perceptual and cognitive processes.

While data are available regarding some of the emotion effects on cognition, the mechanisms of these processes have not been identified. This presents challenges for the modeler, frequently resulting in black-box models rather than mechanism-based process models. Nevertheless, several recent efforts focus on process-models of emotion effects on cognition, most often in terms of parametric-modification of cognitive processes (e.g., (Hudlicka, 2003; Belavkin and Ritter, 2004; Hudlicka, 2007; Ritter, Reifers et al., 2007; Sehaba, Sabouret et al., 2007). For example, Hudlicka's MAMID model uses a series of parameters to control processing within individual modules in a cognitive-affective architecture, enabling the implementation of the observed emotion effects, such as speed and capacity changes in attention and working memory, as well as the implementation of specific biases in processing (e.g., threat and self-focus bias in anxiety). Several models of emotion effects on behavior selection use a decision-theoretic formalism, where emotions bias the utilities and weights assigned to different behaviors (Lisetti and Gmytrasiewicz, 2002; Busemeyer, Dimperio et al., 2007).

Modeling the magnitude and dynamics of emotion effect is problematic, as it requires going beyond the qualitative relationships typically available from empirical studies (e.g., anxiety biases attention towards threatening stimuli). In the majority of existing models, quantification of the available qualitative data is therefore more or less ad hoc, often involving some type of linear combination of the weighted factors, and requiring significant fine-tuning to adjust model performance. The same is true for modeling the integration of multiple emotions. Especially challenging for both of these tasks is the lack of data regarding the internal processes and structures (e.g., effects on goal prioritization, expectation generation, planning). The difficulties associated with characterizing these highly internal and transient states may indeed provide a limiting factor for process-level computational models of these phenomena.

The next section discusses how some of the techniques outlined above could be incorporated into a tool that would facilitate the development of *affect-sensitive* and *affect-centered games*: an *affective game engine*.

AFFECTIVE GAME ENGINES

Progress in gaming has been greatly aided by the emergence of game engines: development tools that facilitate the creation of games by providing realistic graphics and real-time simulation environments. Game engines exist for many game genres (e.g., FPS vs. serious games for training), and vary in complexity and cost (from the free Crystal Space, engines such as Unity (around USD200) to the popular Unreal engine (~USD300,000)) (Stang, 2003). However, to date, no engine has emerged that focuses explicitly on facilitating the development of affectively realistic game characters and avatars, and suitable for the development of affect-sensitive and affect-centered games. Availability of a high-level development tool, that would provide the primitives necessary to support development of affect-sensitive and affect-centered games, would greatly contribute to advancing the state-of-the-art in this area. Some requirements for such an affective game engine (Hudlicka, 2009b) are discussed below, in terms of the theories and methods offered by affective computing and affective modeling.

What types of capabilities would such an affective game engine need to have? To support the development of *affect-sensitive games*, the affective game engine would need to: (1) facilitate recognition of a broad range of player's emotions, in real-time, and within varied gaming contexts (e.g., from the Wii to iPhones); and (2) generate effective adaptations to these emotions, including changes in gameplay reward structure, and realistic portrayal of appropriate emotions by the game characters. To enable this type of emotion recognition and adaptation, the game engine would need to support the dynamic construction of an *affective user model* (Hudlicka and McNeese, 2002; Carberry and de Rosis, 2008); that is, a model of the user (i.e., the player) that contains information not only about his/her current level, skills, knowledge state, and game history, but also about the emotions typically experienced, their characteristic expression and behavioral manifestations, their triggers, and typical transitions among them.

To support the development of *socially complex and affectively realistic games,* the game engine would need to support the development of game characters capable of recognizing emotions in other game characters, and dynamically generating appropriate and affectively-realistic behavior. For example, one can imagine a next-generation of Sims, where the characters have sufficient affective complexity to react with pride, jealousy or embarrassment to some social situation. They could then realistically display the associated affective manifestations, across multiple modalities; e.g., facial expressions, head movement, hand gestures, gaze. To accomplish such level of realism, the game characters would need to incorporate a *computational model of emotion.* Such an emotion model would need to *dynamically generate emotions,* in real-time, in response to evolving gameplay, including the behavior of the player and the other game characters. The model would also need to *model the effects of these emotions* on the character's decision-making and behavior, the latter including both affective expression (e.g., changes in facial expressions, gestures and quality of movement), as well as specific emotion-dependent behavioral

choices (e.g., run or hide when fearful, approach when happy or helpful; attack when aggressive). The game engine would also need to support the development of affectively-realistic player avatars, capable of displaying the player's affective state in a manner consistent with the player's own expectations and needs.

The primary contributions to the development of an affective game engine would come from *affective computing* (Hudlicka, 2008), as discussed above. A number of specific requirements emerge for an affective game engine. These include a *central knowledge-base,* containing basic information about emotions in general, the affective profiles of both the player and the game characters, and representations of the currently active affective states, for both the player and the game characters (see Figure 2). The knowledge and data represented in this centralized information repository would be shared by the modules implementing the four core functionalities of an affective game engine: *emotion recognition* in the player, *emotion expression* by game characters and player avatars, *representation of the player's emotions* via dynamic affective user models, and *modeling of emotions within the game characters.*

The affective game engine would also provide templates and representational primitives to sup-

Figure 2. Role of a centralized emotion knowledge-base in the proposed affective game engine

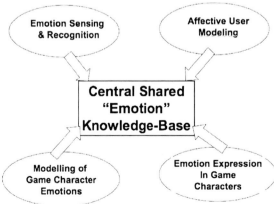

port the development of affective models of the player, and the structures discussed above, to facilitate the design and evaluation of affect-centered games: *affective player profile*, *affective gameplay profile*, and an *ideal affective envelope* of the player during the training or therapeutic gameplay.

The affective game engine would provide support for modeling both the emotion generation in game characters, and the subsequent effects of these emotions on the internal 'cognitive' processes within the NPCs' architecture, as well as their expressive behavior and actions in the game environment. The engine would offer alternatives for emotion generation in terms of either direct mapping of gameplay stimuli onto emotions, mappings via intervening appraisal dimensions, or via the 2 or 3 dimensions comprising the dimensional model of emotions (arousal, valence and dominance). The game engine would also provide functions for modeling affective dynamics, and enable the game designer to modify these. Analogous modeling primitives would be provided for modeling emotion effects on internal processes, as well as on the visible manifestations of emotions by the NPCs.

SUMMARY AND RECOMMENDATIONS

This chapter discussed a number of concepts, methods, techniques and tools, relevant for the development of affective serious games for education, training and therapy. The major design tasks are summarized below, along with some alternative design choices. The summary is organized in terms of the key functionalities that affect-sensitive and affect-centered games should provide, to be effective in training, education and therapy. The section concludes with some recommendations for researchers, practitioners and policy-makers.

Summary

To implement *recognition of player emotion*, the designer must identify the following:

- Player emotions that must be recognized by the game.
- Distinct, idiosyncratic signatures of these emotions in the player, across the available modalities and channels (e.g., facial expressions, autonomic nervous system signals, gameplay behavior).
- Most appropriate non-intrusive sensors, to detect the necessary signals, for a given game context and platform (e.g., desktop, stationary platform vs. mobile device platform).

To implement *affective models of players*, the designer must identify the following:

- Key elements and structure of the affective player profile (player affective and mixed states, their triggers, and associated behavioral characteristics; relevant personality traits).
- Most appropriate learning algorithms, and the gameplay and player features to use as inputs.
- Appropriate adaptation strategies, to ensure engagement and achieve game objectives.
- Best means to induce desired emotions within the game, via game characters' affective behavior, narrative and plot structure, music, and gameplay.

To model *emotion generation and emotion effects in non-playing characters*, the following must be identified:

- Non-playing character emotions that should be modeled, to ensure player engagement and achieve game objectives.

- Specific features of gameplay and non-playing characters to use as input for the emotion generation algorithm.
- Modeling resolution requirements for the necessary degree of affective realism and character believability, for a given game type and platform context.
- Selection of the appropriate model depth (black-box vs. process models); that is, the need for, and complexity of, the NPC agent architecture.
- Most appropriate theoretical perspective and representational primitives for modeling emotion (discrete, dimensional, componential).
- Most appropriate approach to emotion generation (e.g., cognitive appraisal alone vs. multimodal approaches), and the best algorithm for the given choice.
- Appropriate level of accuracy of affective dynamics to achieve desired character realism.
- Specific internal effects, if any, of emotion on cognition that must be modeled to achieve the desired character believability; that is, specific affective biases on attention, perception, decision-making in non-playing characters.

To model *expression of emotion in game characters*, the following must be identified:

- Degree of visual realism necessary to achieve the desired believability, for the given game objectives and platforms.
- Expressive features of non-playing characters, and their behavioral repertoire, available to depict different emotions, as a function of character appearance, game type, game objectives and platform.
- Distinct multi-modal signatures for the selected emotions, in terms of the expressive features available (depends on game type, degree of realism, platform).

- Most appropriate semantic primitives and markup language for the selected expressive modalities and channels, which can support the necessary cross-modal synchronization.

Recommendations

Successful implementation of the functionalities listed above has the potential to greatly advance the effectiveness of serious games. This will require advances in research and practice, as well as a commitment from policy makers and funding agencies. Some of the key challenges and recommendations are listed below.

Research

Tremendous progress has been made in both gaming and affective computing, that is directly relevant for the development of affect-sensitive and affect-centered serious games. However, many challenges remain, including the following:

- Improved understanding of the roles of emotion in serious gaming, to support design decisions about which emotions should be integrated, when, and in what manner.
- Improved understanding of affective dynamics to enable modeling of believable non-playing characters.
- Identification of the most useful player traits, for different gaming contexts, to develop useful affective user models; high-level traits such as the Five Factor model (e.g., extraversion, neuroticism, etc.) may not be the most productive for all serious gaming contexts.
- Identification of new mental states (affective and mixed affective-cognitive), which may be gameplay- and player-specific, to help improve gameplay adaptation and game effectiveness. (See, for example,

Picard's discussion of this issue in the context of emotion recognition (Picard, 2000).)

- Development of systematic guidelines for affect-focused game design, for a variety of serious game types, to develop the functionalities outlined above.
- Development of standards and sharable modules to facilitate rapid prototyping, sharing, and evaluation of games and game components.
- Development of tools with embedded semantic primitives at the appropriate level of abstraction, to support principled development of the functionalities outlined above (e.g., the affective game engine (Hudlicka, 2009b)).
- Addressing of any ethical issues that may arise as games become more effective in recognizing player emotions, and inducing emotions in players.

Practice

All of the research challenges above have direct implications for the development of fielded games. The development of standards, sharable modules, and high-level tools is particularly critical. In addition, the following will be necessary:

- Adherence to theoretically and empirically valid approaches to recognition, modeling and expression of emotion.
- Commitment to affect-focused design, where affective considerations are integrated into the design process, throughout the different stages of development and evaluation.
- Development of, and adherence to, systematic design guidelines to support affect-focused design.
- Development and use of affective envelopes and affective player profiles to guide game development and evaluation.

- Attention to any ethical issues that may arise, and development of appropriate ethical guidelines for the use of affect-centered games.

Policy Makers

The ambitious research challenges and goals outlined above will require a commitment on the part of policy-makers and funding agencies, as well as the management in game companies. All of the challenges listed in the bullets above would benefit from dedicated, long-term research programs. Areas that are particularly critical for advancing the state-of-the-art in serious affective games include support for the following.

- Research efforts to develop standards and sharable repositories of content and components.
- Research in affective computing within gaming, since games represent a distinct context and different requirements for emotion recognition, modeling and expression.
- Development of systematic design guidelines and developments tools.
- Cross-disciplinary workshops and collaborations.
- Development of educational programs and curricula to train researchers and developers of affective serious games in education, training and therapy.

CONCLUSION

The aim of this chapter was to discuss how the emerging discipline of affective computing contributes to *affect-focused game design* of serious games for education, training and therapy. The primary focus was on *affect-centered games*, whose objective is to train affective or social skills, or to provide therapy. In each case, such games need to induce particular affective states in the player and maintain appropriate level of engagement. These games therefore require more affectively-realistic and believable characters, as well as detailed affective models of the players.

Several concepts were introduced that would facilitate the design and evaluation of such games. These included the notion of *affect-focused game design*, where the actual or desired player emotion during gameplay plays a central role in the game design process, as well as *affective player profile, affective gameplay profile* and the *ideal affective envelope* for the player. Each of theses structures represents the actual or desired affective states of the player during a gameplay, and serves as a basis for an affective model of the player, and as a design specification of the types of emotions the gameplay should induce in the player.

The chapter provided information about existing data and theories from the *affective sciences.* These inform decisions about approaches to emotion sensing and recognition, generation of affective behavior in game characters, and computational affective modeling in affective gaming. A brief overview of the emerging discipline of *affective gaming* was also provided. This was followed by a more in-depth discussion of the requirements and approaches to modeling emotion in non-playing characters. The chapter discussed the notion of an *affective game engine:* a high-level game development tool that would provide the necessary modeling and representational primitives to support the design and development of *affect-sensitive* and *affect-centered* games. The chapter concluded with a summary of key design issues, and recommendations for researchers, practitioners and policy-makers, to help advance the state-of-the-are in serious affective gaming.

Affective gaming is emerging as a distinct subdiscipline. Its aim is to develop games that are more directly focused on the player's emotions, and capable of affect-based adaptations to the player's changing affective state, and affective needs. (More information about the emerging discipline of affective gaming can be found at:

www.affectivegaming.org) Today, the term 'affective gaming' generally means adapting to the player's emotions, to minimize frustration and ensure a challenging and enjoyable experience. The methods developed in affective computing provide many of the tools necessary to advance affective gaming to the next stage: where a variety of complex emotions can be induced in the player, for entertainment, but especially for training and therapeutic purposes.

Methods and techniques from affective computing directly support all three of the phases comprising affective gaming, as suggested by Gilleade and colleagues: "Assist Me, Challenge Me, Emote Me" (Gilleade, Dix et al., 2005). Tools that would directly provide these techniques and structures, such as the affective game engine proposed above, would serve as a foundation for systematic affect-focused game design, and would support the efficient development of affect-centered games for education, training and psychotherapy.

REFERENCES

Andre, E., Klesen, M., Gebhard, P., Allen, S., & Rist, T. (2000). Exploiting models of personality and emotions to control the behavior of animated interactive agents. *Proceedings of IWAI*, Siena, Italy.

Arnold, M. B. (1960). *Emotion and personality.* New York: Columbia University Press.

Bates, J., Loyall, A. B., & Reilly, W. S. (1992). Integrating reactivity, goals, and emotion in a broad agent. *Proceedings of the 14th Meeting of the Cognitive Science Society.*

Becker, C., Nakasone, A., Prendinger, H., Ishizuka, M., & Wachsmuth, I. (2005). *Physiologically interactive gaming with the 3D agent Max.* International Workshop on Conversational Informatics at JSAI-05, Kitakyushu, Japan.

Belavkin, R. V., & Ritter, F. E. (2004). OPTIMIST: A new conflict resolution algorithm for ACT-R. *Proceedings of the Sixth International Conference on Cognitive Modeling*. Pittsburgh: Lawrence Erlbaum.

Bersak, D., McDarby, G., Augenblick, N., McDarby, P., McDonnell, D., McDonald, B., et al. (2001). *Biofeedback using an immersive competitive environment*. Designing Ubiquitous Computing Games Workshop - Ubicomp 2001.

Bower, G. H. (1992). How might emotions affect memory? In Christianson, S. A. (Ed.), *Handbook of emotion and memory*. Hillsdale, NJ: Lawrence Erlbaum.

Brezinka, V. (2008). Treasure Hunt–a serious game to support psychotherapeutic treatment of children. In S.K. Andersen (Ed.), *e-health beyond the horizon–get IT there*. IOS Press.

Brezinka, V., & Hovestadt, L. (2007). *Serious games can support psychotherapy of children and adolescents. HCI and Usability for Medicine and Health Care*. Berlin: Springer.

Broekens, J., DeGroot, D., & Kosters, W. A. (2008). Formal models of appraisal: Theory, specification, and computational model. *Cognitive Systems Research*, *9*(3), 173–197. doi:10.1016/j.cogsys.2007.06.007

Broekens, J., & Hudlicka, E. (2010). *Hands-on guidelines and theoretical foundations for modeling emotions in NPCs and virtual characters*. Submitted to IEEE Conference on Computational Intelligence in Games, Copenhagen, Denmark.

Burke, J. W., McNeill, M. D. J., et al. (2009). *Serious games for upper limb rehabilitation following stroke*. IEEE International Conference in Games and Virtual Worlds for Serious Applications (VS Games '09).

Busemeyer, J. R., & Dimperio, E. (2007). Integrating emotional processes into decision-making models. In Gray, W. (Ed.), *Advances in cognitive models and cognitive architectures*. NY: Oxford University Press.

Carberry, S., & de Rosis, F. (2008). Introduction to special issue on affective modeling and adaptation. *User Modeling and User-Adapted Interaction*, *18*(1-2), 1–9. doi:10.1007/s11257-007-9044-7

Cohn, J. F., & Ambadar, Z. (2005). Observer-based measurement of facial expression with the facial action coding system. In Coan, J. A., & Allen, J. B. (Eds.), *The handbook of emotion elicitation and assessment*. NY: Oxford University Press.

Coyle, D., & Matthews, M. (2005). Personal investigator: A therapeutic 3D game for adolescent psychotherapy. *Journal of Interactive Technology and Smart Education*, *2*, 73–88. doi:10.1108/17415650580000034

D'Mello, S. K., & Craig, S. D. (2008). Automatic detection of learner's affect from conversational cues. *User Modeling and User-Adapted Interaction*, *18*(1-2), 45–80. doi:10.1007/s11257-007-9037-6

Derryberry, D. (1988). Emotional influences on evaluative judgments: Roles of arousal, attention, and spreading activation. *Motivation and Emotion*, *12*(1), 23–55. doi:10.1007/BF00992471

Ellsworth, P. C., & Scherer, K. R. (2003). Appraisal processes in emotion. In Davidson, R. J., Scherer, K. R., & Goldsmith, H. H. (Eds.), *Handbook of affective sciences*. NY: Oxford University Press.

Forbes-Riley, K., & Rotaru, M. (2008). The relative impact of student affect on performance models in a spoken dialogue tutoring system. *User Modeling and User-Adapted Interaction*, *18*(1-2), 11–43. doi:10.1007/s11257-007-9038-5

Frijda, N. H. (1986). *The emotions*. Cambridge, UK: Cambridge University Press.

Gilleade, K., & Dix, A. (2005). *Affective videogames and modes of affective gaming: Assist me, challenge me, emote me*. Vancouver, BC, Canada: DIGRA.

Gilleade, K. M., & Dix, A. (2004). *Using frustration in the design of adaptive videogames.* ACW 2004, Singapore.

Gunes, H., Piccardi, M., & Pantic, M. (2008). From the lab to the real world: Affect recognition using multiple cues and modalities. In Orr, J. (Ed.), *Affective computing, focus on emotion expression, synthesis and recognition.* InTech Education and Publishing.

Hudlicka, E. (1998). Modeling emotion in symbolic cognitive architectures. *Proceedings of the AAAI Fall Symposium: Emotional and Intelligent I.* Menlo Park, CA: AAAI Press.

Hudlicka, E. (2003). *Modeling effects of behavior moderators on performance: Evaluation of the MAMID methodology and architecture.* BRIMS-12, Phoenix, AZ.

Hudlicka, E. (2005). *Affect sensing, recognition and expression: State-of-the-art overview.* First International Conference on Augmented Cognition, Las Vegas, NV.

Hudlicka, E. (2007). Reasons for emotions. In Gray, W. (Ed.), *Advances in cognitive models and cognitive architectures.* NY: Oxford University Press.

Hudlicka, E. (2008). Affective computing and game design. *Proceedings of the 4th International North American Conference on Intelligent Games & Simulation,* McGill University, Montreal, Canada.

Hudlicka, E. (2008). Modeling the mechanisms of emotion effects on cognition. *Proceedings of the AAAI Fall Symposium: Biologically Inspired Cognitive Architectures.* Menlo Park, CA: AAAI Press. (TR FS-08-04 82-86).

Hudlicka, E. (2009a). *Affect-centered games: Using games to train affective skills.* (Technical Report 09-12). Blacksburg, VA: Psychometrix Associates, Inc.

Hudlicka, E. (2009b). *Affective game engines: Motivation and requirements.* 4th International Conference on Foundations of Digital Games. Orlando, FL: ACM.

Hudlicka, E., & Broekens, J. (2009). Foundations for modelling emotions in game characters: Modelling emotion effects on cognition. *Proceedings of the 3rd International Conference on Affective Computing and Intelligent Interaction.* Amsterdam, The Netherlands.

Hudlicka, E., & McNeese, M. (2002). User's affective & belief state: Assessment and GUI adaptation. *User Modeling and User-Adapted Interaction, 12*(1), 1–47. doi:10.1023/A:1013337427135

Isen, A. M. (1993). Positive affect and decision making. In Haviland, J. M., & Lewis, M. (Eds.), *Handbook of emotions.* NY: Guilford.

Kort, B., Reilly, R., et al. (2001). *An affective model of interplay between emotions and learning: Reengineering educational pedagogy—building a learning companion.* IEEE International Conference on Advanced Learning Technology: Issues, Achievements and Challenges. Madison, WI: IEEE Computer Society.

Lazarus, R. S. (1984). On the primacy of cognition. *The American Psychologist, 39*(2), 124–129. doi:10.1037/0003-066X.39.2.124

LeDoux, J. E. (2000). Cognitive-emotional interactions: Listen to the brain. R.D. Lane & L. Nadel (Eds.), *Cognitive neuroscience of emotion.* NY: Oxford University Press.

Leventhal, H., & Scherer, K. R. (1987). The relationship of emotion to cognition. *Cognition and Emotion, 1,* 3–28. doi:10.1080/02699938708408361

Lisetti, C., & Gmytrasiewicz, P. (2002). Can rational agents afford to be affectless? *Applied Artificial Intelligence, 16*(7-8), 577–609. doi:10.1080/08839510290030408

Mandler, G. (1984). *Mind and body: The psychology of emotion and stress*. New York: Norton.

Martinho, C., & Machado, I. (2000). A cognitive approach to affective user modeling. In Paiva, A. (Ed.), *Affective interactions: Towards a new generation of affective interfaces*. Berlin: Springer Verlag.

Matthews, G., & Deary, I. J. (1998). *Personality traits*. Cambridge, UK: Cambridge University Press.

Matthews, G. A., & Harley, T. A. (1993). Effects of extraversion and self-report arousal on semantic priming: A connectionist approach. *Journal of Personality and Social Psychology*, *65*(4), 735–756. doi:10.1037/0022-3514.65.4.735

McQuiggan, S. W., & Mott, B. W. (2008). Modeling self-efficacy in intelligent tutoring systems: An inductive approach. *User Modeling and User-Adapted Interaction*, *18*, 81–123. doi:10.1007/s11257-007-9040-y

Mehrabian, A. (1995). Framework for a comprehensive description and measurement of emotional states. *Genetic, Social, and General Psychology Monographs*, *121*, 339–361.

Mellers, B. A., & Schwartz, A. (1998). Judgment and decision making. *Annual Review of Psychology*, *49*, 447–477. doi:10.1146/annurev.psych.49.1.447

Mineka, S., & Rafael, E. (2003). Cognitive biases in emotional disorders: Information processing and social-cognitive perspectives. In Davidson, R. J., Scherer, K. R., & Goldsmith, H. H. (Eds.), *Handbook of affective sciences*. NY: Oxford University Press.

Mota, S., & Picard, R. W. (2004). *Automated posture analysis for detecting learner's interest level*. Cambridge, MA: MIT.

Ortony, A., & Clore, G. L. (1988). *The cognitive structure of emotions*. NY: Cambridge University Press.

Ortony, A., & Norman, D. (2005). Affect and proto-affect in effective functioning. In Fellous, J. M., & Arbib, M. A. (Eds.), *Who needs emotions? NY*. Oxford.

Pantic, M., & Bartlett, M. S. (2007). Machine analysis of facial expressions. In Delac, K., & Grgic, M. (Eds.), *Face recognition*. Vienna: I-Tech.

Petrushin, V. (2000). *Emotion recognition in speech signal*. 6th ICSLP.

Picard, R. (1997). *Affective computing*. Cambridge, MA: The MIT Press.

Picard, R. (2000). Toward computers that recognize and respond to user emotion. *IBM Systems Journal*, *39*(3-4), 705–719. doi:10.1147/sj.393.0705

Prendinger, H., & Ishizuka, M. (2004). *Life-like characters: Tools, affective functions, and applications*. NY: Springer.

Reilly, W. S. N. (2006). Modeling what happens between emotional antecedents and emotional consequents. *ACE 2006*, Vienna, Austria.

Ritter, F. E., & Avramides, M. N. (2000). *Steps towards including behavior moderators in human performance models in synthetic environments*. The Pennsylvania State University.

Ritter, F. E., & Reifers, A. L. (2007). Lessons from defining theories of stress for cognitive architectures. In Gray, W. (Ed.), *Advances in cognitive models and cognitive architectures*. NY: Oxford University Press.

Roseman, I. J., & Smith, C. A. (2001). Appraisal theory: Overview, assumptions, varieties, controversies. In Scherer, K. R., Schorr, A., & Johnstone, T. (Eds.), *Appraisal processes in emotion: Theory, methods, research*. NY: Oxford University Press.

Scherer, K., & Schorr, A. (2001). *Appraisal processes in emotion: Theory, methods, research.* NY: Oxford University Press.

Sehaba, K., & Sabouret, N. (2007). *An emotional model for synthetic characters with personality affective computing and intelligent interaction.* Lisbon, Portugal: ACII.

Slovic, P., & Finucane, M. L. (2004). Risk as analysis and risk as feelings: Some thoughts about affect, reason, risk, and rationality. *Risk Analysis, 24*(2), 311–322. doi:10.1111/j.0272-4332.2004.00433.x

Smith, C. A., & Kirby, L. (2000). Consequences require antecedents: Toward a process model of emotion elicitation. In Forgas, J. P. (Ed.), *Feeling and thinking: The role of affect in social cognition.* NY: Cambridge University Press.

Smith, C. A., & Kirby, L. D. (2001). Toward delivering on the promise of appraisal theory. In Scherer, K. R., Schorr, A., & Johnstone, T. (Eds.), *Appraisal processes in emotion.* NY: Oxford University Press.

Stang, B. (2003). *Game engines: Features and possibilities.* The Technical University of Denmark.

Sykes, J. (2004). *Affective gaming.* Retrieved May 2008, from http://www.jonsykes.com/Ivory.htm

Sykes, J., & Brown, S. (2003). *Affective gaming: Measuring emotion through the gamepad.* CHI.

Witten, I. H., & Frank, E. (2005). *Data mining: Practical machine learning tools and techniques.* San Francisco: Morgan Kaufmann.

Yannakakis, G. N., & Hallam, H. (2008). Entertainment capture through heart rate activity in physical interactive playgrounds. *User Modeling and User-Adapted Interaction, 18*(1-2), 207–243. doi:10.1007/s11257-007-9036-7

Zeng, Z., Pantic, M., Roisman, G. I., & Huang, T. S. (2009). A survey of affect recognition methods: Audio, visual, and spontaneous expressions. *IEEE Transactions on Pattern Analysis and Machine Intelligence-TPAMI, 31*(1), 39–58. doi:10.1109/TPAMI.2008.52

Chapter 24
Gestural Motivation, Learning and Evaluation using Interactive Game Design

Roman Danylak
Stockholm University, Sweden

ABSTRACT

Emerging game interface design increasingly incorporates human gestural learning. Electronic gestural games, when effectively designed, offer high levels of user engagement. The chapter to follow presents theatrical practice, an art form that manufactures expressive gestures in set paradigms, as a model for gestural game systems design. A rigorous definition of gesture is first developed from yoga practice as an exercise for performance preparation, emphasising the gesture as a still form executed within a narrative context. The theatrical model is then refigured into an interactive gestural film game design, To be or not be, based on a section of text from Shakespeare's play Hamlet (Danylak & Weakley, 2007). Evaluation of gestural learning is integrated into the system. The focus is on the generation of the physical aspect of the gesture as a movement.

INTRODUCTION

The Approach: Gestural Interaction using Theatre as a Game Model

The approach adopted uses text-based theatrical performance process as a model, refigured into an interactive gestural film game. Theatre is particularly well suited as a model because it has distinct developmental phases that eventually generate performed gestures in set paradigms and can be described as *text*, *rehearsal* and *performance*: the *text*, is in the form of a script written by a playwright, describes an imagined world of characters gesturing and talking and forms the blueprint of gesture and dialogue performance; next, there is the *rehearsal*, where directors and actors bring the textual world of the play onto the stage, interpreting how the characters should speak and move, building the play through gestural and speech reiteration following the text; and finally there is the *performance*, the fixed patterns of gesture and

DOI: 10.4018/978-1-60960-495-0.ch024

dialogue that make the theatrical work of art, the play, usually repeated as several performances. These three process elements – text, rehearsal and performance – are refigured into an electronic game format, appearing in a non-sequential manner to generate gestural learning as a game goal. From a gesture learning perspective, the design has three main characteristics. These are:

- a capacity to generate gestures
- a capacity to create continuity of user experience
- a capacity to capture the performed gestural data by the system for learning evaluation

Game: A Definition

A game may take many forms. In popular usage, if one was to say 'let us a play a game', then we would most likely understand that there is some tactical goal to achieve with there being an outcome of a single or team winner, the process including elements of probability. We would most likely expect to be amused in the process and that some sort of skill maybe tested or acquired. There, are of course, solitary games. In the discussion to follow 'a game' will mean probability-based play marked by the presence of a linear narrative within a technological interactive process (Frasca, 2007) (Schell, 2003). In following this definition an interactive game shows both a linear, story telling process, which can be cognitively apprehended, coupled with the unknown, probability-based outcomes, managed by computer program automation.

The word 'game' originates from Old English Word 'gamen' and is best contextualised as meaning 'fun' or 'amusement' (Dictionary, 2005). Game theory from a mathematical perspective is well developed; Von Neumann, who played a leading role in the evolution of modern computing in the decade of the 1950's, focused on game theory consistently in his work (Kuhn, 1997). Interactive games form an international industry that produces thousands of titles annually (Chesher, 2004). Such games as Sony's Eyetoy (Demming, 2004) are interactive games that use computational systems that respond to gamers' movements. The Wii (Schlömer et al. 2008) has also evolved an interface mostly of sporting narratives that allows gamers to engage in various competitive outcomes. The nature of gestural interaction included in game processes is increasing and has applications in a wide range of human functional and commercial activities that are extended or enhanced through computational interaction.

PART I: THE GESTURE

Obstacles and Potentials of Gestural Human-Computer Game Interaction

Bolt's (1980) work *Put That There,* was the first instance of demonstrating a practical outcome of gesture-based technology, combining voice response commands with deictic (pointing) instructions enabling movement of objects on a video screen. Hence, the potential of gestures as input in multimedia interactive systems became a matter of significant interest owing to the fact that when humans communicate in face-to-face interaction, gestures often communicate emotional states and associated intentions. The challenge was how to purposefully integrate gestures into an interactive system where coherency and continuity of an interactor experience could be created and measured.

From a design perspective, to isolate the gesture and to use the data in a constructive useable manner is problematic owing to the complexity of gestural communication. The variety of interpretations as to what constitutes a gesture amongst technology researchers is vast and varied, illustrating the fact that gestures are complex. Cadoz and Wanderley (2000) in a survey of gesture definitions used by researchers and artists in gesture technologies show great diversity, with no clear grammar for so called 'body-language' existing. The complexity present emerges from such fundamental design questions as: 'what categories of human sensory perception should be included, especially considering the increasing range of sensory input devices? What arrangement of devices will work, offering coherent and engaging usability?'

James and Seebe (2005) question the way in which multi-channel sensory options should be incorporated, establishing that the design combinations were characteristically complex. Audio and visual channels, it was stated, were processed independently, from which they drew a conclusion that fusion of the channels was 'still in its infancy'. How much information each channel delivered was difficult to ascertain, as was discerning if the input was emotional, intellectual or sensory. Oviatt (2003) has also stated that the interpretation of continuous movement is difficult, owing to the complexity of human movement, which does not readily lend itself to machine segmentation or interpretation as input data. Pantic (2005) offers a summary of such design challenges:

Realization of a human-like interpretation of sensed affective behaviour requires context dependent choices (i.e. environment – user and task profiled choices). Nonetheless, currently existing methods aimed at the automation of human-affect analysis are context insensitive. Although machine-context sensing, that is, answering questions like who is the user, where is (s)he, and what is (s)he doing, has witnessed recently a number of significant advances...the complexity of this problem makes context sensitive human-affect analysis a significant research challenge.

(Pantic et al., 2005)

Shamar's et al. (1988) four points on multi-modal integration, where a *modality* refers to the variety of human sensory inputs into a *multimedia* system – multimedia meaning a variety of media outputs - are a good general guide for the design process, responding to the complexity of the problem and will serve as a guide throughout this chapter. These are:

- Why integrate?
- Which modalities to integrate?
- When to integrate?
- How to integrate?
(Shamar, 1988)

Gestures in Theatre

Having established the potential and challenges of gestures as input / output in an interactive system, the approach is to focus on gesture formation in theatre, isolating the gesture as input data. Theatrical practice is an ideal model for the task in that text-based theatrical performance is an established paradigm of consciously created gestures. The performance of a play on Tuesday night and the subsequent performance of the play on Saturday night, have generally the same gestural patterns, communicating mostly the same message, making theatre a controlled, repeatable, gestural artefact.

How actors and directors assemble gestures for repeatable performance is a central concern to follow. There are two parts to the theatrical study: the first examines the individual body and gestures as the actor prepares for performance, evolving a definition of gesture, in particular examining yoga as a narrative-based gestural practice as employed by the theatrical director Grotowski (1969); the second looks at the directorial process and how the gestural art form is assembled from a text, following the theatrical techniques of Stanislavsky ([1936] 1981), establishing a model of media forms and process used in expressive gestural text-based theatre.

Gesture Vocabulary and Narrative

It is essential first to understand the nature of gestures. Kurtenbach and Hulteen (1990) state that a gesture is 'a movement of a body that contains information'. This definition is useful in that the designer of systems requires data in the form of information 'informing' us of the gestural act. From this perspective we can begin to build a picture where gestures are intentional. However, there has been conscious awareness of the role that gestures play in human communication for some time. St. Augustine of Hippo, a philosopher, stated the following regarding the relationship between language, emotions, learning and gestures, establishing an observed link between these elements. Simultaneously, it highlights a performed theatricality to gestures and the contexts in which they operate. He states that:

When they named any thing, and as they spoke turned towards it, I saw and remembered that they called what they would point out, by the name they uttered. And that they meant this thing and no other, was plain from the motion of their body, the natural language, as it were, of all nations, expressed by the countenance, glances of the eye, gestures of the limbs, and tones of the voice, indicating the affections of the mind, as it pursues, possesses, rejects and shuns. And thus by constantly hearing words, as they occurred in various sentences, I collected gradually for what they stood; and having broken in my mouth to these signs, I thereby gave enounciation to my will. Thus I exchanged with those about me these current signs of our wills, and so launched deeper into the stormy intercourse of human life, yet depending on parental authority and the beck of elders.

(Augustine [4ᵗʰ century A.D.] 1970)

Gestures can then be described as a *paralanguage*, that is they have a meaning that stands alongside spoken, verbal language and as such a contain meaning (Abercrombie, 1972). For instance, if we see someone slouching this may communicate that a person's emotional state is one of boredom or possible depression. Kendon offers a contemporary summation of the nature of gestures and describes them as having the same expressiveness as words, outlining the context in which gestures become meaningful:

Willingly or not, humans, when in co-presence, continuously inform one another about their intentions, interests, feelings and ideas by means of visible bodily action. For example, it is through orientation of the body and, especially through the orientation of the eyes, that information is provided about the direction and nature of a person's attention. How people arrange their bodies and how they orient them and place them in relation to each other or to features in the environment, provides important information about how they are engaged with one another and about the nature of their intentions and attitudes. Activities in which objects in the environment are being manipulated, modified or rearranged, are indispensable for grasping a person's aims and goals and interests. Of equal importance, however, are actions that are seen to be purely expressive... in other words, there is a wide range of ways in which visible bodily actions are employed in the accomplishment of expressions that, from a functional point of view, are similar to, or even the same as expressions in spoken language...These are the utterance uses of visible action...

(Kendon, 2004)

Ambiguity however underlies gestures and their interpretation. Darwin (Darwin, 1872) was the first to point out that a lateral shake of the head does not universally mean 'no' bringing attention to the fact that human gestures are learnt and not natural. Furthermore, gestures may simply be incidental and carry no emotional or expressive content (Barre, 1972). The person who slouches in a chair may simply have a bad chair. Similarly, we can easily imagine that a wave of hand may mean 'hello' or 'goodbye', 'come here', or may be testing practically for the presence of a breeze

Figure 1. Two named gestures used in yoga illustrating the dynamic range of the skeletal and muscular system. A dancer or actor may be called upon to employ such gestures. The naming of gestures establishes a vocabulary of gesture in the practice. Images: compliments of Nicole Walsh

Figure 1a Matsendrasana (spinal twist pose)

Figure 1b Bakasana (crane pose)

in the air, emphasising ambiguity. With the ever present potential for misinterpretation, a clear distinction needs to be made between gestures that are merely incidental versus gesture that are consciously expressive if the gesture is to be useful as input in an interactive system such as a game. The distinction is to differentiate between what will be termed *performed gestures* as different to *vernacular gestures*. The goal here is to motivate the user to generate gestures in a conscious, deliberate performed manner, to be generated in an interactive game system,

Performed and Vernacular Gestures

The particular distinction between *performed* and *vernacular* gestures (Danylak et.al 2007) reduces the volatility of gestural communication for the purposes of interactive design. The word vernacular means *the language or dialect spoken by the ordinary people* (Dictionary, 2005). The term *performed gesture* here denotes a gesture made consciously by the gesturer, the processes of which can be described in development of expert performance of dance, music and dramatic performance. *Vernacular gestures* are gestures made in everyday face to face conversation and may have performative elements but are not expert artistically.

Thus an actor in the theatre may reproduce *vernacular gestures* to appear *natural* by using an expert process of performed gesture, creating mimesis. Mimesis is the copied appearance of what is natural (Mathiijs and Mosselmans, 2000), that is a likeness, a key characteristic of the art form, in particular Stanislavskian theatre, where theatre makes us believe that what we see on stage is life as we know it, a copy of nature, and we relate to it as such. The performed gesture is consciously created and controlled as part of the art form; the vernacular gesture may or may not have conscious and expressive elements. Hence, the goal is the artificial generation of gestures as is the case in theatre.

Gesture: A Definition

Even with the above distinction between the vernacular, that is, everyday gestures – and the performed gesture, which is an expressive and conscious gestural action, the movement requires further final definition, again owing to its complexity. The purpose is to try to reduce ambiguity in the movement so as to isolate the gesture as an input in human-computer gestural interaction.

The notion adopted is to treat the motion of the body - that is, any part of the body - as a form *in the moment*. The approach is evolved from

Figure 2. A summary of media forms and processes used in text-based theatre to develop expressive gestures

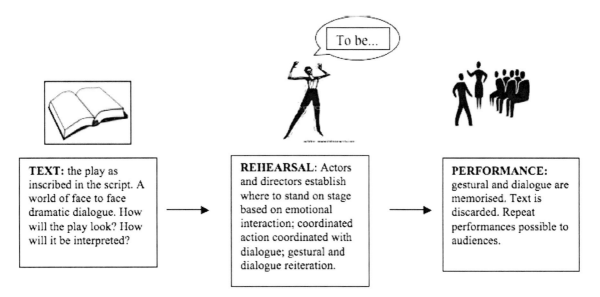

TEXT: the play as inscribed in the script. A world of face to face dramatic dialogue. How will the play look? How will it be interpreted?

REHEARSAL: Actors and directors establish where to stand on stage based on emotional interaction; coordinated action coordinated with dialogue; gestural and dialogue reiteration.

PERFORMANCE: gestural and dialogue are memorised. Text is discarded. Repeat performances possible to audiences.

the gestural training that both actors and dancers often receive, embodied in the ancient Hindu exercise practice known as Yoga (Iyengar, 1986). Grotowski (1969), a 20th century theatre director, employed yoga to increase the range and sensitivity of actors' bodies for the gesturally expressive art form of theatre.

Characteristic of such gestural preparation is the formation of a *still form*. The extension of the form, its shape, its strength, flexibility and ability to maintain the form is indicative of expressive control through self-awareness executed in a narrative progression of named positions. As such, the static bodily form is a test or a measure of the gesture. The formulation is highly useful as it allows the designer to think about what input and outputs can be utilised to capture specific gestures. Hence, gestural volatility is reduced. The definition for a gesture is as follows:

...a gesture is a bodily form, that may or may not have communicative intention, expressiveness or emotion attached to it. It may alter as a result of muscular and skeletal action occurring in any part of the human body. As such, a gesture is the momentary form of any part of the human body.

(Danylak, 2008)

PART II

The Theatre Model: Generating Gestures

Owing to the fact that a sustainable and useful definition of gesture was derived from yoga as a preparation to theatrical art, the notion emerged that other aspects of theatrical production could also be integrated into a multimedia system. The theatrical model was placed in a game configuration, the result being an interactive gestural film game entitled *To be or not to be,* based on text from Shakespeare's play *Hamlet,* Act III sc. i lines 55-61 where Hamlet speaks his famous soliloquy. The work was exhibited and evaluated in Sydney's Powerhouse Museum at The Creativity and Cog-

Figure 3. Theatre model indicating directorial interpretation and the key elements of text, rehearsal and performance in text-based theatre. The process is linear in that each step in the process is completed and then follows the next. Gestural expression in this way becomes fixed as an artefact for repetitive performance

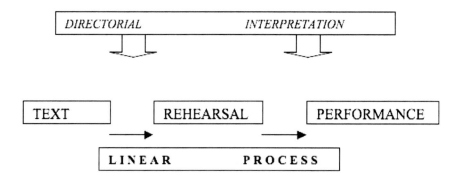

nition Studios immersive artwork testing facility *beta_space* (see www.betaspace.net.au/content/view/36/). A description of theatrical practice precedes the description of the design.

In theatrical practice, where realistic outcomes are desired by actors on a stage as is typical in a Stanislavskian ([1936] 1981) approach, directors interpret a world present in text, the script of a play, and bring the world as contained and described in that text to life. It is for this reason, that we are able to reproduce ancient Greek plays, the characters of the past living once again in contemporary theatre. Thus, the interpretation of the world in the text by the director happens long before any rehearsal.

The process by which directors and actors transfer text to a final performance can be described in the following three steps:

- text
- rehearsal
- performance

Text is the initial presence of a script, a world that has been designed and imagined by a playwright, where words encapsulate plot, character and action. The characters as yet do not have bodies by which to move and gesture but their written, verbal interactions with one another, give us strong suggestions of gestures and behaviour that we have learnt to associate with such language (see Figures 2 and 3).

Rehearsal is the process where spatial requirements are established, otherwise known as *blocking*. Blocking establishes where a character must stand at a particular point in time so as to then coordinate dialogue and emotional interactions with other actors. For example a character that has lost a comrade in battle will act grievously showing anxiety and pain and verbalise grief, as opposed to two characters that have a romantic interest in each other, the gestures of the lovers being typically gentle and considerate. The blocking in these two instances will be very different. The goal of rehearsal is gestural and dialogue reiteration, forming established patterns of gesture and dialogue on stage.

Finally, there is *performance*. Performance is the presentation of the established gestural paradigms along with associated dialogue. The combination of gesture and dialogue in reiterative patterns produces the illusion of *naturalism*, that is, we sit and watch a slice of life as written by the playwright and brought into reality by the director, actors and theatre technicians. The process is linear with the text being discarded after several

Figure 4. Drawing plan of To be or not to be

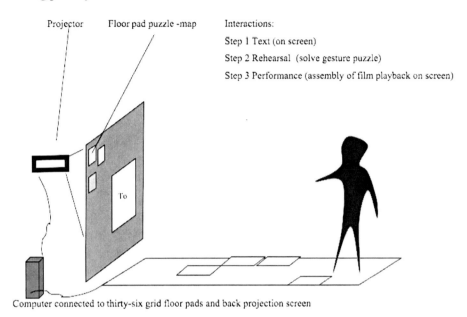

Figure 5. Theatrical model refigured as interactive gestural film game. Arrows indicate interactive non-linear game interactions. Performance (film) appears as linear construct, the goal of the game being to assemble the film by solving the gesture word puzzle

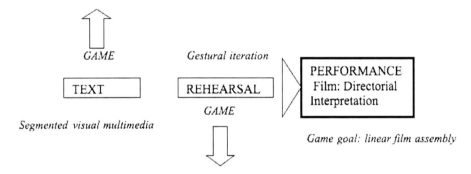

rehearsals, the gestures and lines memorised for performance (Brockett, 1987) (Nagler, 1952).

Refiguring the Theatrical Model as Interactive Gestural Film Game

The design plan was to convert the theatrical process into a game, capturing the gesture formation process. To enable this required that the elements text, rehearsal, and performance be refigured so as to be applicable in a multimedia interactive environment. The concept was to make a game where interactors would follow the syntactic patterns of the text to solve a gestural floor puzzle, thus generating gestures as if in rehearsal, with the outcome of assembling a film based on the Hamlet text, mirroring a final finished theatrical performance (see Figures 3 and 4). The capacity to generate the gesture in the first instance and then continuously were key considerations in generating gestural responses.

Figure 6. Interactor in two different gesture positions. The interactor engages with sections of the Hamlet text appearing on screen Simultaneously, the interactor position on the floor pad is indicated by the map in the upper left corner of the screen guiding the gesture puzzle game to a solution. The interactor can see his actual position (green squares) but moves to be in the blue square position to play the game. Once this is achieved the blue square turns red and a section of the Hamlet film plays. There are twenty-three gesture – word puzzles to assemble short the film playback as the game goal

Figure 6a

Figure 6b

Final Iteration: Construction Results

The final design comprised of a game where interactors walked upon a thirty-six square floor pad connected by computer program to a two metre by three metre back projected wall screen. The object of the game was for the user to solve particular game sequence puzzles that would appear as an interactive map on the left hand corner of the screen (see Figures 6a and 6b).

Interactors would set out to solve twenty-three word – gesture puzzles, the goal being to assemble the playback of the entire film by solving the walking gesture puzzle. Sections of the *Hamlet* text would appear on the centre of the screen, for example, frame one would have the words 'To be' appear, part of the phrase 'To be or not to be'. Simultaneously, the floor pad was programmed to indicate to the interactor their actual standing position through an illuminated green square appearing on a screen corner map. The effect was that the interactor could see where they were standing in the room on the floor pad grid. At the same time a blue target square would flash, encouraging the interactor to locate that position on the floor. In this way the interactor was moti-

vated to perform walking gestures, a key goal of the design.

Once having located the blue square place - the target square - the blue square would turn red indicating a hit. Having achieved this, a three to five second sequence of the Hamlet film would play. The film was pre-shot as an interpretation of the same the text which had appeared as the gesture-word puzzle, Act III, sc. i, lines 55 - 61 from Shakespeare's play *Hamlet,* the famous soliloquy by Hamlet, a reflection upon life and existence. The puzzle is based on the rhythm of the words. In this way both the syntax of the language and its semantic dimension, as interpreted by the director / designer of the film, are integrated into the work. There were twenty-three such puzzles to be performed in the work, the interactor then watching the entire film assembled in playback once achieving to solve all twenty-three game puzzles (see Table 1). The narrative of the *Hamlet* film features bored office workers, pirates and spirits and is intended as an examination of modern working life and choices that confront teenagers, the target interaction group.

The three main phases of the game that repeat with the solution of each gesture word puzzle,

Table 1. Word / gesture game map codes for To be or not to be

Blue	Green	Red
Target squares to be located by user. May be arranged in complex sequences	Shows location of user on one the 36 square floor pad	Target square has been achieved located by the user

based on the game model. Step 1 *Text* indicates the presentation of language as a syntactic puzzle of syllabic rhythms to be solved as standing gestures as shown on the main screen (see Figure 7a); Step 2 *Rehearsal* is the generation of standing positions on the floor pad grid that may solve the syntactic puzzle causing playback of film segments, a gesture puzzle to be solved by the interactor (see Figures 7b, d). The interactor engages with an interactive floor pad map of colour coded squares which they must chase to activate the right square in a correct position at a correct time; Step 3 *Performance* shows the interpretive use of language where the same script is used to create a film, guided by directorial intent (see Figure 7c). In this way, the theatrical model of text – rehearsal – performance has been refigured as interactive gestural film game. The interaction

Figure 7. 7a shows the screen with the first two syllables of the Hamlet text. Map code of position in upper right hand corner connected to floor pads showing interactor position. 7b is an exploded view of the map code showing blue square (left) as target square and green square (right) actual interactor position. 7c show a shot of the Hamlet film that will playback on achieving the gesture – word puzzle. The film is a narrative based on the selected Hamlet text. 7d is a map showing the floor pad positions activated in the first 'To be' sequence, twenty-three sequences in total, thirty - six square floor pad area.

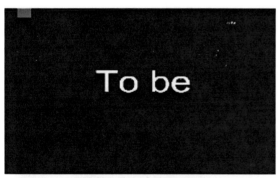

a) Multimedia text. First segment

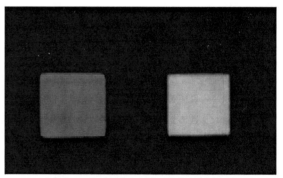

b) Map codes guiding gestural rehearsal game

c) Film playback, first segment. Bored office workers

d) Gesture movement floor plan

experience along with media forms are summarised in Table 2.

Evaluation of Gestural Responses

In keeping with the definition of a gesture being a static bodily form, the interactor performed a gestural goal to activate a floor pad in a specific place and time according to Virtual Reality testing specifications (Patel et.al 2006). The gesture involved was a still, standing, whole body gesture. The measure of gestures was the number of attempted gestures per syllabic unit of the text. The text was used as syntactic guide, establishing the rhythm of gestures to be performed, converting the target blue square as shown on the map to a red square showing that the gesture goal had been achieved (see Table 1). The game goal was to get to the target square with as few moves as possible.

To be or not to be was evaluated at Sydney's Powerhouse Museum at the Creativity and Cognition Studios public interactive art facility, *beta_space* (Danylak and Weakley, 2007). Nine

teenage participants were involved from mixed co-educational schools who were visiting as part of the museum's school's program. Both university ethical approval and parental consent were obtained before the testing. The selection process was random, the supervising teacher simply asking students who would like to volunteer to be involved in a research project. In the graph participants are labelled p1 to p9.

Participants were given no information about how the game worked as the game was designed as an independent artefact that would generate interest and gestural experience through purposeful design. Participants were instructed to interact for as long as they wished. Electronic log records of floor pad interactions were retained in the hard drive of the computer. Generating gestural responses was an integral part of the game design to serve research purposes.

Figure 8 and Figure 9 are two examples of the gestural performance of two participants' gestures marked against the syllabic unit. The performances were each different in that rehearsing the gesture

Table 2. Summary of interactor experience of first segment of game processes, showing media interactions, floor pad map and interaction functions as Text, Rehearsal or Performance

Interactor Experience	Function	Media Interaction
Sees text 'To be'. Narrative experience commences	Text	
Understands that on screen map of green squares shows actual position. Seeks to hit blue square position by walking about floor pad to find the place through gestural reiteration Gesture experience commences, rehearsal of gestures.	Rehearsal	
Map showing gesture positions on floor pad.	Rehearsal	
Gesture position achieved. Playback of film section as performance. Twenty three puzzles in total to to achieve single playback of film.	Performance	

Figure 8. Gesture response in interactive game To be or not to be, participant 9 - p(9) Note: Y axis is scaled accordingly to results of each participant. Back slash mark (/) indicates change of gesture / word puzzle frame

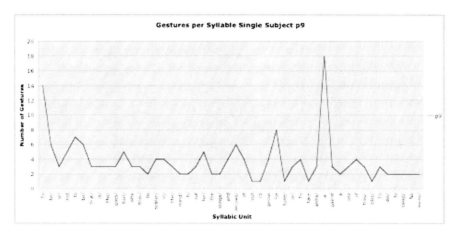

several times to activate the target square was at times necessary. A low achievement rate indicates rapid learning of the gesture.

In Figure 8, p9 showed initial difficulty in executing gesture / word puzzle. Rate drops quickly with consistent improvement in completing task. Cyclic behaviour of participant attempts as peaks and troughs. Difficulty was experienced at 'against' with the game process completed.

In Figure 9, p8 showed overall low gesture rate indicating successful execution of game process. Subject showed improvement in the execution of gesture word puzzle. Cyclic behaviour of participant attempts occurs as peaks and troughs. Game process completed.

Figure 9. Gesture response in interactive game To be or not to be, participant 8 - (p8) Note: Y axis is scaled according to results of each participant. Back slash mark (/) indicates change of gesture / word puzzle frame

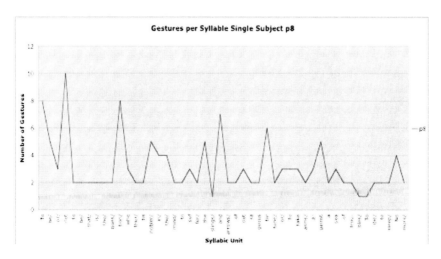

Figure 10. Total comparisons of all nine participants. Performed gestures per syllabic unit, comparison, nine participants in interactive game To be or not to be. Back slash mark (/) indicates change of gesture / word puzzle frame

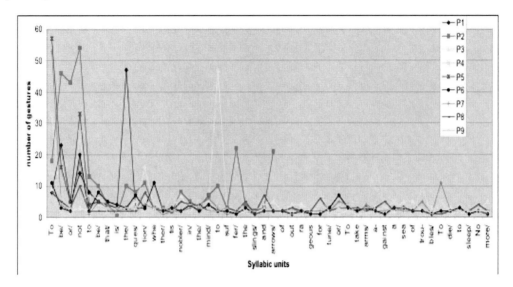

Totals of compared of gestural performance significantly show high completion rates with some variety in response (see Figure 10): p1 and p5 complete one third of the game. p2 completes half the game. The other six participants complete the entire game. p1 begins to show learning of the game as the rate declines but experiences difficulty at the syllables 'the ques' trebling the number of attempts and then abandoning the game after this spike. p5 starts with a high rate, declining rapidly, but abandons at the third frame 'to'. p2 also starts with a high rate and a rapid decline, which then rises again, but the game is abandoned midway at 'arrows'. p3 shows an unusually high number of gestures at 'mind'. p3, p4, p6, p7, p8 and p9 show relatively similar patterns of an average to low number of attempts. p7, p5 and p2 start with a very high number of gestures. p8 and p9 exhibit

Figure 11. Total number of performed gestures per syllabic unit, individual participants p1-p9 showing trendline for To be or not to be

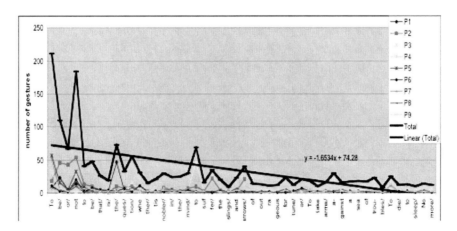

cyclic behaviour with high and low troughs occurring. At the syllable 'not', a peak is shared by all the nine participants.

Figure 11. shows the total trend of all gestures performed and the average fitted trendline with a minus slope. The minus slope of the average trendline means that the number of gestures performed decreased along the timeline of the interactive game experience. The participants showed an increased ability to perform fewer gestures, indicating that learning occurred as they used the system. The peaks and troughs indicate that difficulty and ease of the gesture puzzle sequence varied.

Data visualisations of tests in pre-evaluation trials (Figure 12, a & b) show gesture rates on the floor as a spatial distribution of gestures. These results are significant as they show that there are levels of predicted movement through interaction with the system yet with learning occurring. The participant of 12a has a much higher gesture rate but both show that have followed a similar path.

Design and Evaluation: Conclusion

A critical factor in the design of the work linking the theory of gesture derived from theatre practice, namely that a gesture is a still form, was the selection of the program to enable the experience. The Max / MSP program, which exhibits a high degree of design flexibility in delivering media objects, had a particular feature of split second timing - up to 1000th of a second. The timing characteristic of the program suited the definition of gesture and enabled an experience where the single standing gesture could then be generated as a multimedia game and measured. Hence, the rigour of the theoretical treatment of the theatrical practice served as a solid foundation for later technical design, accommodating the integration of sensory processes.

The learning of gestures was achieved by the design of *To be or not to be*. The interaction showed high levels of completion indicating that the configuration generated a gesture in the first instance, indicating a coherent design, then continued to generate continuously in most cases. The definition of a gesture derived from yoga / actor processes and the rigorous definition of gestures developed – the vernacular and the performed, was an effective basis by which the design could proceed based on the positive results. Furthermore, the negative slope shown in Table 6, reinforced that the reconfigured theatrical model was an effective design for gestural learning, effective primarily due to the creative choice of refiguring the theatrical process to suit interactive input and output requirements.

Constructing a film narrative based on the *Hamlet* text was an effective goal motivating the

Figure 12. Tables showing visualisation and tabulation of gesture hit rates per floor pad square, light squares indicating high levels of gestural interaction to solve gesture word puzzle. a) has much higher level of interaction meaning that; b) solve the puzzles in a shorter time. Frequency of gestural difficulty appears in similar areas. Data obtained in pre-evaluation trials

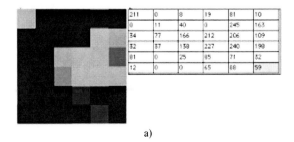

211	0	8	19	81	10
0	11	40	0	245	163
34	77	166	212	206	109
32	37	138	227	240	198
81	0	25	85	71	82
12	0	0	65	68	59

a)

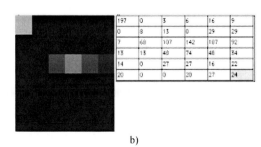

197	0	3	6	16	9
0	8	13	0	29	29
7	68	107	142	107	92
13	13	48	74	48	34
14	0	27	27	16	22
20	0	0	20	27	24

b)

interactor into continuous gestural game engagement. *To be or not to be* also exposes the interactor to a classical theatrical text, giving a different and novel means by which to present drama in what is often a core element in English school curricula. Data maps of the movements recorded by the program are significant in that the game exhibits a capacity to predict how a person may move in a given space. Hence intellectual and motivational engagement of an interactive narrative game that has a dramatic context, establishes a process by which gestural interaction can be generated.

RECOMMENDATIONS FOR INTERACTOR LEARNING IN GESTURAL GAME DESIGN

It is now possible to respond to Sharma's (1988) four points for multimodal integration (why integrate; which modalities to integrate; when to integrate, how to integrate?) followed by a design plan checklist:

- *Why integrate*: to generate a gesture in the first instance and then to continue generating gestures; to capture gesture generation data for learning evaluation.
- *How to integrate*: the integration concept *To be or not to be* is based on a refiguring of the theatrical model into a game format. The experience of the actor in gesture formation in the selected art form was central. Other models may be configured in a similar manner.
- *When to integrate:* The timing of the integration was defined by the game process and structure. The elements were programmed in such a manner using Max / MSP so as to be coherent and engaging to also create continuity of experience to reaching the game goal.
- *Which modalities:* the modalites – that is the sensory inputs and outputs – were

defined through an understanding of the theatrical process as a phenomenon of language. Hence the rhythmic aspect of the language, that is syntax, was used to generate the gestural pulse; simultaneously the semantic aspect, which builds narrative meaning, was used in the on-screen puzzle text and as a guide to make the Hamlet film, the playback reward. A detailed understanding of the sensory process developed in the early theatrical modelling guides the modality selection process.

The following points are offered as a design plan checklist when designing an interactive gestural game with projected learning outcomes:

- Define sensory input data in the human dynamic elements to reduce input volatility and uncertainty. Understand as best as possible the communicative and experiential aspects of the human actions.
- Select media defining the communication channels such as voice, text, image and similar and the role they might play in the human and machine interaction.
- Clearly establish the goals of the game, seeking a balance between challenge, pleasure and ease of comprehension and execution, making the goal outcome achievable.
- Select programs that match sensory input / output processes.
- Consider using a narrative context for games with probability outcomes - an established workable interactive format.
- Design the game with an evaluative outcome in mind.

ACKNOWLEDGMENT

The author wishes to thank: Dr Alistair Weakley for collaborative programming design; Dr Zafer

Bilda for collaborative evaluation design; Professor Ernest Edmonds, Director, Creativity and Cognition Studios, University of Technology, Sydney for supporting the work within the PhD program.

REFERENCES

Augustine,. (1970). *The confessions of St. Augustine* (pp. 8–9). London: Everyman.

Barre, W. (1972). The cultural basis of emotions and gestures. In Laver, J., & Hutcheson, S. (Eds.), *Communication in face to face interaction.* Middlesex, UK: Penguin.

Bolt, R. A. (1980). Put that there. *ACM, 14*(3), 262–270.

Brockett, O. G. (1987). *History of the theatre.* Boston: Allyn and Bacon.

Cadoz, C., & Wanderley, M. C. (2000). *Gesture-music* (pp. 71–93). Paris: IRCAM, Pompidou Centre.

Danylak, R. (2008). *A semiotic analysis of gesture and emotion in human-computer interaction.* Unpublished doctoral Thesis, University of Technology, Sydney, (p. 87).

Danylak, R., Bilda, Z., & Edmonds, E. (2007). Establishing research criteria for performed gestures and emotional interaction in an interactive gestural film game To be or not to be. In Fujita, H., & Pisanelli, D. (Eds.), *New trends in software methodologies, tools and techniques* (pp. 166–181). Rome: IOS Press.

Danylak, R., & Weakley, A. (2007). *To be or not to be.* Retrieved from http://www.youtube.com/watch?v=jKNvSpXG0Z0

Darwin, C. (1872). *The expression of emotions in man and animals.* Murray. doi:10.1037/10001-000

Demming, G. (2004). Sony eye toy. Developing mental models for 3-D interaction in a 2-D gaming environment. *Conference Proceedings APCHI,* (pp. 575-582).

Dictionary. (2005). *Electronic Oxford American dictionary,* Version 1.0.2.

Frasca, G. (2007). *Ludology meets narratology: Similitude and differences between video games and narrative.* Retrieved October 10, 2007, from http://www.Futurelab.org.uk/resources/publications-reports-articles/web-articles/Web-Article

Grotowski, J. (1969). *Towards a poor theatre.* London: Methuen.

Iyengar, B. K. S. (1986). *Light on yoga.* George, Allen and Unwin Ltd.

Kendon, A. (2004). *Visible action as utterance.* (p. 1). Cambridge, UK. Jaimes, A. & Sebe, N. (2005). *Multimodal human computer interaction: A survey.* (p. 11). IEEE International Workshop on Human Computer Interaction in Conjunction with ICCV 2005, Beijing.

Kurtenbach, G., & Hulteen, E. (1990). Gesture in human-computer interaction. In Laurel, B. (Ed.), *The art of human-computer interface design.*

Mathhijs, E., & Mosselmans, B. (2000). Mimesis and the representation of reality: A historical world view. [Springer Netherlands]. *Foundations of Science, 5*(1), 61–102. doi:10.1023/A:1026473504257

Nagler, A. (1952). *A source book in theatrical history.* New York: Dover.

Oviatt, S. (2003). Multimodal interfaces. In Jacko, J. A., & Sears, A. (Eds.), *Human-computer interaction handbook.* Mahwah, NJ: Lawrence Erbaum & Associates.

Pantic, M., Sebu, N., Cohn, J. F., & Huang, T. (2005). Affective multimodal human-computer interaction. *Conference Proceedings, Multimedia 05, ACM Singapore,* (pp. 669-676).

Patel, H., Cruz, M. D., Cobb, S., & Wilson, J. (2004). *Initial report on existing evaluation methodologies: VR and human factors best practice.* Information Society Technologies (IST) Program. Retrieved on January 8, 2006, from http://www. intuition-eunetwork.net/documents/deliverables.

Schell, J. (2003). Understanding entertainment: Story and gameplay are one. In Jacko, J. A., & Sears, A. (Eds.), *The human-computer interaction handbook* (p. 836). NJ: Lawrence Erlbaum & Associates.

Schlömer, T., Benjamin, P., Poppinga, B., Henze, N., & Boll, S. (2008). Gesture recognition with a Wii controller. In *Proceedings of the 2nd international conference on Tangible and Embedded Interaction,* (pp. 11-14).

Sharma, R., Pavlovic, V., & Huang, T. S. (1988). Toward multimodal human computer interface. *Proceedings of the IEEE, 86*(5), 853–869. doi:10.1109/5.664275

Stanislavsky, C. (1981). *Building a character.* UK: Methuen and Co.

KEY TERMS AND DEFINITIONS

Game: probability based play integrating linear narratives

Design: plan of organisation / building

Motivation: desire or willingness to act

Learning: acquisition of knowledge

Gesture: expressive use of the body or parts of the body

To be or not to be: Interactive gestural film game, designed by Roman Danylak / Alastair Weakley

Evaluation: to measure value or achievement of set goals

Performance: displayed capabilities of dramatic expression

Theatre: performance space for dramatic art

User: an individual engaging in a human computer interaction

Interaction: users having engaged a process in a computer system

Multimedia: more than media form appearing

Multimodal: the use of multiple sensory inputs / outputs in an interactive system.

Section 4
User-Centered Approach to Game-Based Learning:
Accounting for Users' Differences, Specificities and Disabilities

This section accounts for users' differences, specificities and disabilities in the design of GBL systems. The authors describe theoretical frameworks and guidelines that address issues and challenges such as improving motivation, providing tailored interventions with Intelligent Tutoring Systems (ITSs), accounting for gender differences, applying games to neuro-rehabilitation, or engaging children with attention deficit or intellectual disabilities.

Chapter 25
Hints for Improving Motivation in Game-Based Learning Environments

Jean-Charles Marty
University of Savoie, France

Thibault Carron
University of Savoie, France

ABSTRACT

In this chapter, the authors propose to address two main items contributing to motivation in Game-Based Learning Environments: the flexibility of the system and the immersion of the users in the system. The chapter is split into three sections. The first one deals with the need for adaptation from both the teacher's and the learners' point of view. The authors need to collect traces about pedagogical activities in order to propose observation features for updating a user model adapted for learning games. This user model is seen as an explicit collaborative object displayed in the game. The second section concerns the necessity of keeping the users immersed in the game and gives some guidelines for immersion concerning game design, game play and metaphorical support. The last part illustrates these points through a game-based learning environment called "learning adventure". The generation of a learning session in the environment is described and a real experiment is used as a support for explaining the concepts presented above.

PART 1: INTRODUCTION

Nowadays, compared to traditional teaching methods, Learning Management Systems (LMS) offer functionalities that are recognized as being valuable from different points of view. For instance, students can learn at their own speed. These environments also allow the teacher to evaluate specific activities in a uniform way. However, although they enable powerful features, they also receive major kinds of criticism (lack of awareness, few collaborative or *regulation* possibilities (Kian-Sam & Chee-Kiat, 2002)). Some students tend to consider LMS as unexciting (Prensky, 2000).

Concerning this particular point, and in agreement with Vygotsky's school of thought and ac-

DOI: 10.4018/978-1-60960-495-0.ch025

tivity theory (Vygotsky, 1934), we consider that the social dimension is crucial for the cognitive processes involved in the learning activity. Consequently, the question is how to enhance the social dimension in such environments. The emergence of learning games provides a possible answer to this problem and is seen as an evolution of "classical" LMS (Hijon, 2006). Learning Games have already been recommended as possessing several pedagogical qualities (Squire, 2003). For instance, they offer a specific and progressive learning curve adapted to each learner, they allow distance learning, and they can encourage specific usages in education such as collaborative learning or project pedagogy. More generally, videogames are even seen as providing a new form of rhetoric thanks to their basic "representational mode of procedurality" (Bogost, 2007) and may be a means by which to envisage programming or computation with a brand new view (Matheas, 2005).

Observing the emergence and success of online multiplayer games with our students, it was decided to experiment our own learning game approach, by developing a new game and by using it as a support for some learning sessions. We apply the metaphor of exploring a virtual world called "*Learning Adventure*", where each student embarks on a quest in order to collect knowledge related to a learning activity. We think that the way of acquiring knowledge during a learning session is similar to following an adventure in a Role-Playing Game (RPG). The combination of the two styles is called MMORPG and offers a good potential for learning (Galarneau, 2007; Yu, 2009) reformulated as MMOLE. On this point, we agree with (Buckingham, 2007) underlying affordance between Game and Educational practice by drawing attention to all the aspects of games that need to be addressed carefully.

A major factor in obtaining good results in the learning activity is the motivation of the learners, as reported in (Amory, 1999; Kirriemuir, 2004; Galarneau, 2007; Dondlinger, 2007). In this chapter, we would like to address two main

items contributing to motivation: the *flexibility* of the system and the *immersion* of the users in the system, also generally seen as a fundamental component of the game play (Ermi, 2005).

Flexibility

There is a need for adaptation both from the teacher's point of view (adaptation of the difficulty of the exercises, addition of new activities, splitting the group into sub groups) and from the learners' (motivation is sometimes related to novelty – the sequencing in the game should not be the same when one starts an adventure and when one has already completed some steps in the previous sessions).

These needs for adaptation can also be categorised into two groups: those that are related to adaptation during the activity (the need for dynamic adaptation) and those that are related to adaptation after the session, such as the necessary adaptation of the game for the next session or the items linked to a meta cognition process (the need for static adaptation).

Flexibility thus consists in adapting the environment according to a particular context. One key item in the context description is the current status of the learners, and we believe that the *flexibility* relies strongly on the use of a *user model*.

Immersion

We also focus on the concept of *immersion* because it is fundamental in keeping coherency between the pedagogical content and the game itself. As a matter of fact, even in recent learning games, our experience shows that one particular point is rarely taken into account: the whole game design is not linked to the learning concepts. Therefore, students/players do not feel immersed in a world that is consequently not coherent for them.

In this chapter, we first give attention to these central aspects for motivation: *Flexibility* and *Immersion*. We then describe their application in "*Learning Adventure*", our game-based environment.

PART 2: FLEXIBILITY AND USER MODEL

In LMS, the concept of learner profile or student model is used to represent the characteristics of a learner (Brusilovsky, 2001; Rueda, 2003; Vassileva, 2003). Naturally, it is even more important in a Learning Game with a Role Playing Game (RPG) approach, where the learner is represented directly in the game by an avatar.

Indeed in RPG, such an avatar representing the gamer includes individual characteristics; in a learning game, the student representation should also include pedagogical information in a specific object available both for the student and the teacher(s). Furthermore, it should be possible to use in other learning environments this information concerning both the knowledge acquired by the student and the behavioural aspects (talkative, cooperative, slow), and even civic characteristics as, shown in (Kahne, 2009) or found in (Salen, 2007) via the RPG Gamestar Mechanic. We thus consider that all this information should be gathered in a unique object (the *user model*) that should be persistent. On that point, we agree with Vassileva's idea: the *user model* is decentralised in new learning environments and belongs to the user (Vassileva, 2003). The *user model* can be a way of representing the student, bringing together the relevant characteristics for the learning aspects (skills, behaviours, preferences). This approach leads to systems where the *user model* is not directly integrated in the learning tools, but is accessible through inter-process communication. Kobsa demonstrates in (Kobsa, 2001) the advantages of such a distributed approach.

These numerous *characteristics* can be classified into several categories: common characteristics, preferences, skills, behaviours, or even special achievements. We thus set out in a first part what is inside the *user model* and a possible classification of the attributes (characteristics) of the user. As a matter of fact, previous works, experimentations and teachers' feedback have elicited several requirements concerning student representation in learning games. We also point out which improvements to the current *user model* require attention. Then, we describe a *graphical representation* of the *user model* taking into account the need for *flexibility* of such games.

2.1 Inside the User Model

A student is identified and represented by specific, generally static, information, especially in an academic domain. These common *characteristics* of the *user model* are important from an administrative point of view and are always present in a *user model* in order to identify a person individually.

A student is described by his/her name, student ID, past and current courses, diplomas, etc. Such information may be collected automatically from administrative services, or the system can explicitly ask the user him/herself when a new account is created in the learning game.

These characteristics are often used to adapt an application, making the system user-friendly (usage of the name, of the address to find local references, etc...).

The second category of User Characteristics deals with the user's preferences. In this category, we can find the User Interface Preferences (fonts, colours) or the subjects the user is keen on (if they are related to the application, of course).

Some preferences may be implemented in order to provide the student with adapted graphical interfaces or adapted modality of information presentation (text, image, sound, video) (Brusilovsky, 2001). This is particularly pertinent in pedagogical systems where knowledge acquisition is enhanced by a way of teaching that is adapted to the personal means of information memorization (Choukroun, 1985) of the user (visual, auditory, data format, etc.). This approach is however seldom used because the teacher needs to provide the same information in many formats or modalities, which is very time consuming.

The part of the *user model* containing information on the user skills refers to the knowledge acquired by a student. The characteristics contained in this part change more often than those described in the previous two parts. User skills are widely used to personalize the path for knowledge acquisition, and to adapt the form of presentation. (Brusilovsky, 2001) explains in detail how links can be extended or hidden according to the user's knowledge of a particular concept. In video games, especially RPG, the progression in the game is directly controlled by the skills of the avatar. For example, it is impossible to reach an island if your avatar cannot swim or does not have access to a boat... The "swim skill" has to be acquired in order to explore this island.

In order to make our Learning Games adaptable, and to make the activity requisites possible, we base our *user model* specifically adapted for Learning Games on the same concept: a learner is defined with skills (and different levels for each skill) that allow access to new exercises or to a part of the game world. As in traditional teaching, where some exercises require specific knowledge, the scheduling of exercises depends on the skills of the student and the game world is automatically adapted to each student according to his/her *user model*. It is possible to see a skill level as a key enabling the subsequent exercises (and following part of the world).

Finally, the fourth part contains characteristics deduced from the *behaviour of a user*. This part is particularly useful in new learning systems where the collaboration and the social aspects are central. It is therefore important for a teacher to be aware of the different behaviours of his/her students: collaborative, talkative, hesitant, etc.

These characteristics are crucial for regulating a learning activity (Marty, 2007). For instance, a teacher can define in his/her learning scenario (which gives the sequencing of the actions in the game) that an activity is available only if the cooperation within a group of students reaches a certain given threshold.

As we can see, the user's characteristics are numerous and it is a challenge for the game designer to present them to the users without obliging them to change their focus of attention. In addition to the current trends in the *user model* field, there is a real need for considering the *user model* as a real object, central to the system. This object is used to adapt the learning aspects in the game and the game itself. One should be able to easily update it according to the new knowledge or the new skills of the user. As a real object, we should also perform actions on it, such as *interaction* or *visualisation*. The interaction with the *user model* opens new perspectives in which the user can act on his/her own representation, expressing wishes on which skills s/he would like to enhance. The visualisation is directly linked with the visual representation of the *user model*: an adapted and user-friendly representation of the *user model* is important to keep the learner immersed in the game. We thus propose to link the standard *user model* formalization (text, xml) with a graphical one. In the following section, we explain how the different characteristics can be represented graphically according to the categories (defined above) and can be used to adapt the environment (the game) to the context.

2.2 Representing the User Model

In recent, conventional RPG video games (e.g. World of Warcraft, Dofus), certain pieces of information, characteristics or properties appear directly in the game, displayed on the avatar representation. In order to remain immersed in the game, it is crucial that the *user model* has a form related to the game. Figure 1 is an example where the model is represented on a scroll[1]. This approach is useful when the user needs to consult details on the *user model* (as when someone consults a map). However, it may be suitable to represent the main characteristics directly on the student avatar.

Figure 1. Example of user model for learning games

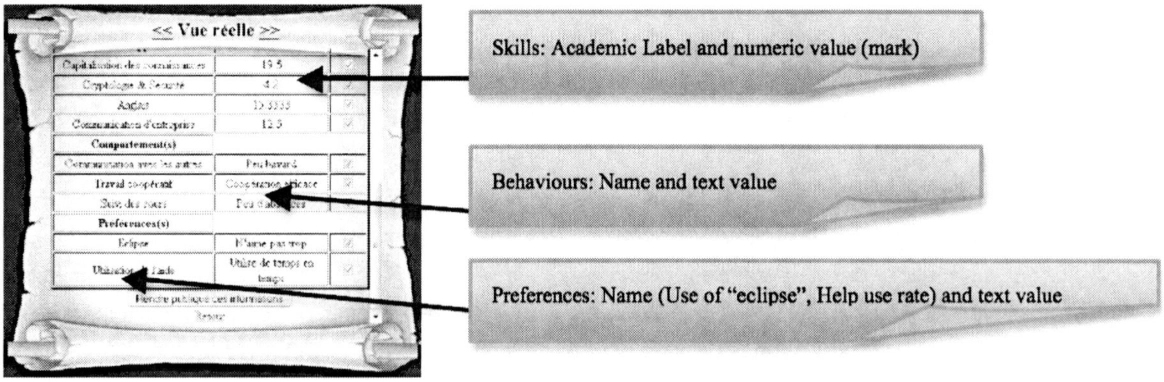

Here is an example of how we have represented certain student characteristics in the latest learning game (Carron, 2008) that we have developed. In this game, the teacher was interested mainly in the knowledge acquired by the student and in his/her behaviour. We have thus defined a graphical correspondence for the characteristics contained in the "skill" and "behaviour" parts. Some elements (sword, shield, helmet, etc.) gained or possessed explicitly by the avatar represent skills; we add a graphical representation to the *user model* for integration in the game. A certain number of elements are localized on the avatar representation to display selected and specific skills (In Figure 2, we have six parts represented

by question marks). As we will see in the second part of this chapter, for *immersion* and motivation purposes, real persons are represented directly in the game.

We can see in Figure 2 that there is a match between some characteristics in the textual *user model* (to be consulted when full details are needed) and in the graphical view corresponding to the avatar (displayed in the game). The same avatar is represented here with more impressive values on the right of the picture. Each part is represented with different displays (emphasis) in order to distinguish the levels of a given skill.

In some cases, it can be interesting to represent graphically the behaviours too. As with our col-

Figure 2. Example of graphical representation

Figure 3. Configuring elements that make up animations representing specific behaviours

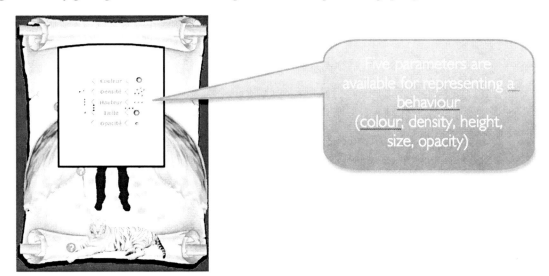

laborative indicators (Gendron, 2008), we chose to represent behaviours with different animations around the avatar. The form, the speed, the number (density), the height and the size of elements (see Figure 3) moving around the avatar representation may be used to give information concerning the behaviours highlighted for a direct representation in the game (see yellow balls around the avatar at the bottom of Figure 3).

Currently, the semantics associated to these visual indicators (concerning skills and behaviours) are free, chosen by and known to the administrator of the game and may require practice to be naturally or intuitively interpreted in the game.

The visualization of the *user model* is very useful for and attractive to the users. This is even more the case when the data are updated dynamically. In the following section we present how such a learner model is updated through *traces* left by the users.

2.3 Evolution of the User Model

With commercial websites or in collaborative platforms for knowledge management for ex-

ample, the main and well-known problem of a *user model* is to keep it updated (Fink, 2000). In this section, we will see how to take into account such an evolution in a learning game.

From our point of view, trace observation and Role Playing Games provide new possibilities to define a learner model. Our approach consists in taking advantage of the *digital traces* left by the players participating in the mediated learning activity to calculate awareness indicators for the learning game (Gendron, 2008). It is thus possible to implicitly identify skill progression but also the behaviours and preferences of the users (Carron, 2008) and interactive behaviour among learners (Dimitracopoulou, 2005; Dimitriadis, 2006). Consequently, defining and updating a specific *user model* is achievable. In a learning game and in our context of work, the problem is easier to solve because the *user model* is focused on the properties of a learner. A correct answer to a pedagogical activity or to an exercise in the game, or even the completion of a scenario in a learning game will give points, and will modify the value of corresponding skills in the learner model.

As shown in (Carron, 2008), it is possible to obtain information from *traces* left by the users

Figure 4. List of rules concerning the update of the skills

Nom	Règle de calcul				
Compétence(s) :					
Anglais	((('A_examen'+'A_particip')+'A_oral')/3)	Afficher	Editer	Dupliquer	Supprimer
Aspect qualité & Conduite de projet	'AQCP_projet'	Afficher	Editer	Dupliquer	Supprimer
Capitalisation des connaissances	('CC_projet')	Afficher	Editer	Dupliquer	Supprimer
Communication d'entreprise	('CE')	Afficher	Editer	Dupliquer	Supprimer
Cryptologie & Sécurité	(('CS_tp1'*3+'CS_tp2'*2)/5)	Afficher	Editer	Dupliquer	Supprimer
Génie Logiciel et IDM	(('GLIDM_tp'+('GLIDM_examen'*2))/3)	Afficher	Editer	Dupliquer	Supprimer
IHM	(('IHM_examen'*2+'IHM_tp')/3)	Afficher	Editer	Dupliquer	Supprimer
Mise à Niveau UML	('MNUML_examen')	Afficher	Editer	Dupliquer	Supprimer
Réseaux sociaux &					

when they play the learning game. The basic idea of our approach is to have probes that provide information on basic events occurring in the learning game (e.g. entering a room, chatting with someone) and to compose them in order to have more general assertions (e.g. this student answers correctly but works alone). The definition of specific rules will let the system use a specific trace to update one or several specific characteristics of the *user model* in the learning game (see Figure 4).

We generally equip our learning games with a tracing possibility based on a dedicated observation multi-agent architecture (see Figure 5) (Carron, 2006; Loghin, 2008). Actions such as correctly answering a quiz or using the instant messenger tool may be traced and thus collected by elementary probes. Each probe contains parameters and, depending on these, a particular aim in order to improve one or several characteristics appearing in the *user model*. For example, a threshold concerning talkative behaviour (x messages sent) is reached. The local part of the *user model* is updated thanks to rules[2] (see 1 in

Figure 5), then propagated to the full version on a server (see 2 in Figure 5) and to concerned clients (e.g. the teacher), possibly directly inside the game via indicators (see 3 in Figure 5).

Although a *user model* is generally considered as a private, more or less realistic view of a user, we propose to take advantage of observation in learning games and extend our vision of a *user model* for a learning game by adding another specific fundamental point of our learner model. It concerns the concept of interactive future views. As we will see presently, rules may be used to help the learner to reach goals proposed by the "virtual" views.

2.3.1 Considering the User Model as a Collaborative Object

From what we have described, it is clear that the *user model* is an important piece of information for the user. This model can serve in other learning environments to personalize them but also as data for expert research (we here approach

Figure 5. Observation multi-agent architecture

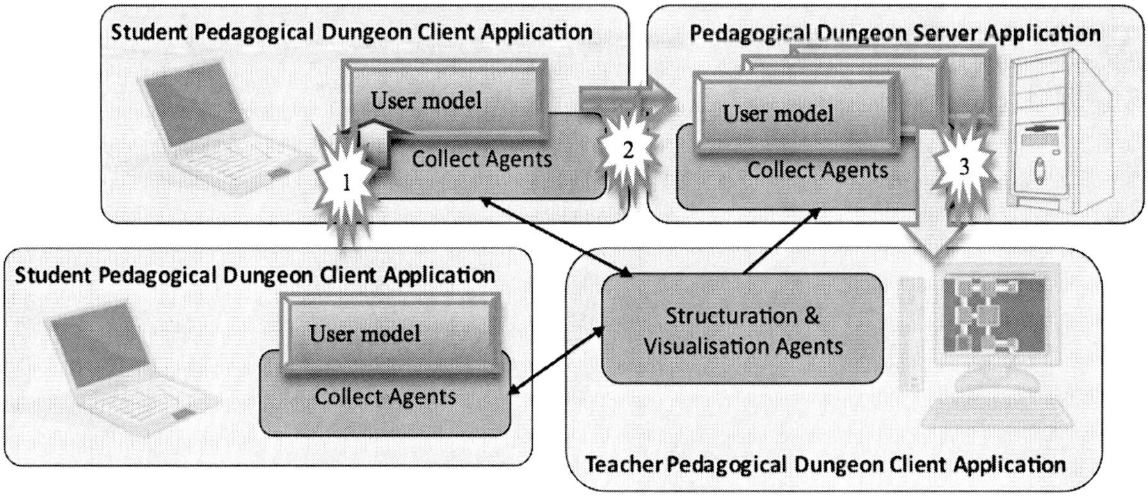

the field of knowledge capitalization). The user can see the *user model* of the learning game as a kind of passport describing his/her skills and behaviour. If s/he is interested in providing this passport to someone else, this object can be used as a real collaborative tool. In a pedagogical set-up, the teacher and the student both have a view as to how the student can improve his/her personal skills and behaviour. These views are not necessarily the same. A student may want to focus on one improvement such as "be even better in computer programming" whereas the teacher finds it more important for this student to "improve his/her foreign language ability" or to "adopt a more collaborative behaviour". All these considerations led us to extend our *user model* to include different views.

Starting from the current *user model* (real view) for a particular student (calculated as defined previously), the student would like to improve certain characteristics of his/her avatar (exactly as a user tries to make his/her avatar evolve in an RPG, which is a fundamental motivation point in such games). By defining these desired improvements, s/he defines his/her personal target, a future virtual *user model* view. In parallel, the teacher can have his/her own vision of the improvements needed

and defines the academic target, a future virtual *user model* view. This object can thus take several forms and can be a negotiation object for making an action plan for the improvement of a particular student. This is richer than a simple mark report, because the behavioural aspects are present, too.

We now describe how the actions are possible on the *user model*.

Personal Target

This view is interactive whereas the real one is static. In order to set personal goals (levels to reach), the learner is allowed to act on cursors, to tune the value of certain characteristics (see Figure 6). Such a view will help the learner to keep in mind his/her wishes and what to favour in terms of learning exercises in order to reach these objectives.

Academic Target

This other interactive view is dedicated to the learners but only modified by the teachers. Some cursors may be "pushed" in order to advise the student to make an effort especially on a particular characteristic (skill, behaviour or preference):

Figure 6. Example of "academic target" view on the left and example of "personal target" view[3] of the user model for learning games on the right

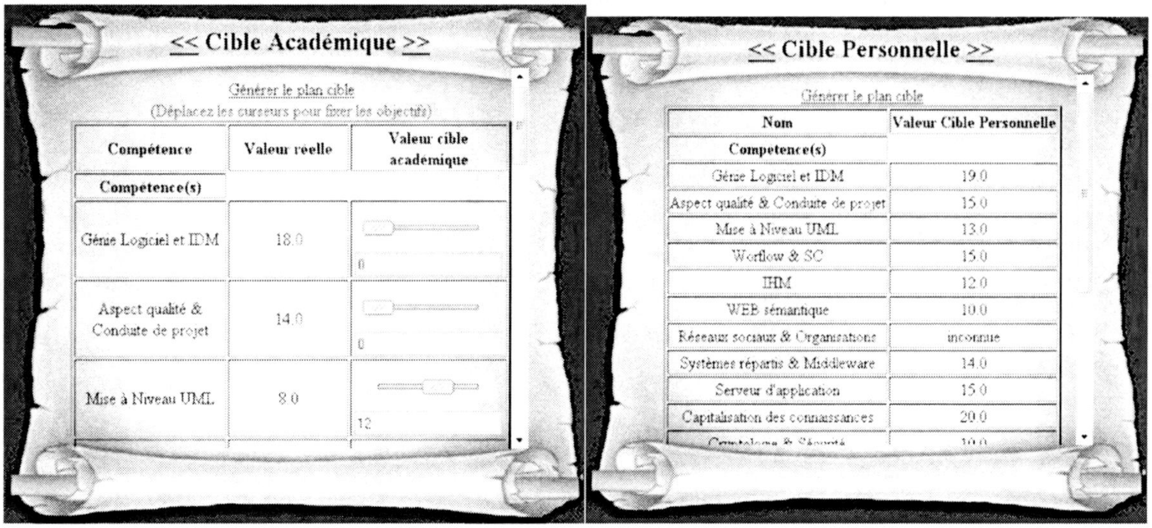

<< Cible Académique >>

Générer le plan cible
(Déplacez les curseurs pour fixer les objectifs)

Compétence	Valeur réelle	Valeur cible académique
Competence(s)		
Génie Logiciel et IDM	18.0	[slider] 0
Aspect qualité & Conduite de projet	14.0	[slider] 0
Mise à Niveau UML	8.0	[slider] 12

<< Cible Personnelle >>

Générer le plan cible

Nom	Valeur Cible Personnelle
Competence(s)	
Génie Logiciel et IDM	19.0
Aspect qualité & Conduite de projet	15.0
Mise à Niveau UML	13.0
Worflow & SC	15.0
IHM	12.0
WEB sémantique	10.0
Réseaux sociaux & Organisations	inconnue
Systèmes répartis & Middleware	14.0
Serveur d'application	15.0
Capitalisation des connaissances	20.0
Cryptologie & Sécurité	10.0

"reach this value in such a domain, be more co-operative, be less talkative, use the chat tool or this one more, improve your English, etc." (see the resulting view for the student in Figure 6).

Furthermore, the system is able to provide an action plan for reaching the objectives described in the targets by using the rules and values of the different characteristics (calculated as described in Figure 4).

Figure 7. Activity plan

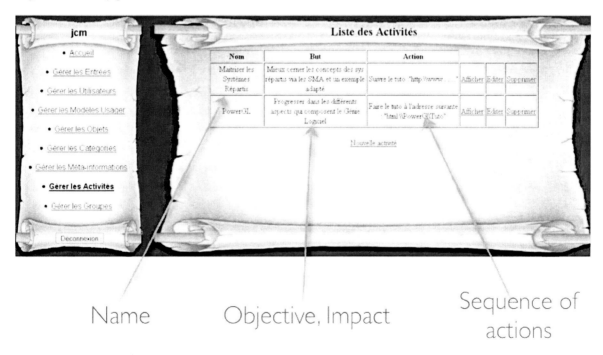

Name   Objective, Impact   Sequence of actions

PLAN GENERATION TO REACH VIRTUAL VIEWS

Metadata are associated to each pedagogical action (scenario, exercise, quiz or whatever similar learning action) available in the environment. These metadata describe which characteristics the pedagogical action is supposed to improve, and the application scope of the exercise. This last point allows us to take into account the level of difficulty of an exercise. If it is simple, and if the user is already an expert, s/he won't gain any experience by doing it. The situation is the same if an exercise is difficult and the user is a novice in the related field.

For each objective set in a virtual view, it is possible to add a plan of activities to carry out in order to reach it. For example, an activity plan may propose new scenarios selected in order to enhance a particular value concerning a skill or a behaviour that must be improved. As shown partially in Figure 7, an activity is composed of a description (name), a goal and a set of actions that allow this goal to be reached. The action plan is generated from the set of characteristics to be improved and from the description of the available pedagogical actions. Applicable exercises that en-

Figure 8. Example of group model

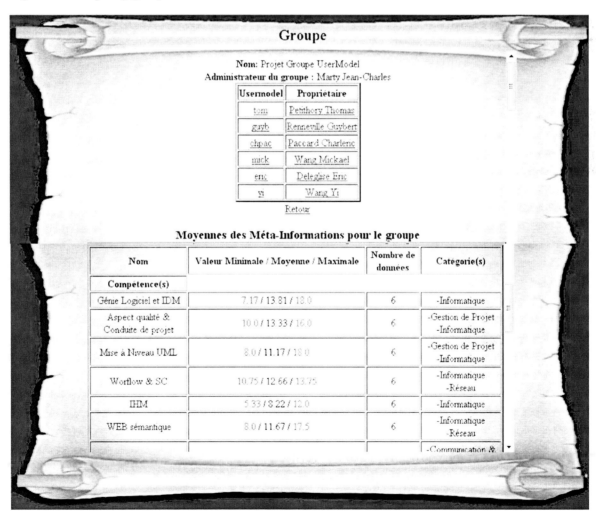

able the identified characteristics to be improved are added to the plan.

All the propositions we have made on user modelling apply to individual users. However, as already mentioned in the introduction, learning games allow collaboration in the learning process. We now propose to extend the *user model* concept to groups of learners.

Group Model

For the teacher and in the context of collaborative learning, we offer the possibility of managing the characteristics of groups of students. The administrator of the group is generally the teacher and for each characteristic chosen, s/he needs to know the minimum, the average and the maximum values. For instance, defining a specific *group model* is well suited for evaluating a project group in a project-based pedagogy (see Figure 8).

All the statements presented for individuals concerning their *user models* remain true for groups. It is therefore possible for a teacher to set objectives through the *group model*. However, generation of plans can be somewhat tricky because actions may be appropriate for some people and not for others. This means that new meta-data on pedagogical actions concerning group improvement should be defined.

As stated previously, Role-Playing Games focus on the player and her/his evolution in the game. Similarly, given that the learner is used to practising video games, it is natural for him/her to make his/her avatar progress. Nevertheless, even in recent learning games, our experience shows that one particular point is rarely taken into account: the whole game design is not linked to the learning concepts. Therefore, students/players do not feel immersed in a world that is coherent for them. Following the improvements through the *user model* constitutes an essential factor of *immersion* but as we will see in the following section, *immersion* should be seen in a wider and deeper way.

PART 3: GUIDELINES FOR IMMERSION

In this part, we explain how to support deep *immersion* in the game with the aim of increasing the focus on the pedagogical tasks as well as the collaboration between the actors. *Immersion*, a key point for motivation and collaboration in the game, is related to several concepts that can be found in many studies concerning video games (Woyatch, 2008; Crawford, 1984; Laurie, 2003). There is also another aspect that must be considered: when students learn something in a game, they need to transfer the acquired knowledge to real life. If the game includes elements that match the real situation, this transfer will be simplified. With this view, similarly to (Gee, 2007) concerning Video Games and Learning, we would like to give some guidelines *(indicated by* Gi *in italics)* in order to take the *immersion* feature into account as much as possible while designing the educational game. We have chosen to focus on three concepts that can be generally found in classical video game theory: Game Design, Game Play and coherent metaphors.

3.1 Game Design

A learning RPG usually proposes to transfer the student to a virtual world. First of all, it is not always possible (time, cost) for the game designers to develop an up-to-date and graphically very realistic world. Nevertheless, it is important to propose a consistent and coherent environment. From our point of view, a well-known environment, similar to established famous games or styles of game (Zelda or Mario world, Final Fantasy) will help the students to immerse in the game. Many references, clues or jokes added by the game design are useful to enhance this aspect. The idea is to provoke the desire to go further, to explore the world and find other funny or pleasant references. As shown by the success of the

Wii console (Nintendo), the quality of graphics is not a key point.

G1: Develop a coherent world. For cost reasons, it may be helpful to reuse the look and feel of well-known games.

The game design also deals with the map of the game. In order to make links between the real and the virtual worlds, this map should correspond as much as possible to the real premises where the learning sessions usually take place (classrooms, buildings).

G2: Find the real places or people usually involved in the learning process that you would like to integrate into the game. Think of "funny little stories" that are part of the learning context.

Concerning the educational domain, it is even more important to focus on the game play and "break the game rules".

3.2 Game Play

The game play may be understood as the set of rules of the game (Djaouti, 2008). Here, the idea is to create a surprising effect by changing the rules both with the educational domain and the game. For example, when we first experimented our learning game, our students were really surprised to be together in the same game world, to see their friends' actions and to be allowed/encouraged to exchange ideas in the game with a chat tool (Carron, 2007). All the rules of the game can be derived from a general scenario, a coherent story representing the general pedagogical goal.

G3: Design an overall pedagogical scenario, a story, taking place in the premises defined in the game design.

Again, we need to show explicitly that this game is adapted or designed for the particular

actors that will learn in this environment. The quests and designed objects/NPCs should explicitly reference the corresponding ones in the real world. For example, the cafeteria is closed for a while because people did not respect the work of cleaning agents! (a real event). As we will see in the following section, one of the most successful examples is to bring the teacher directly inside the game and give the students the possibility of interacting (requesting some help) directly with her/him by chat. Other teachers (not directly involved in the learning process) may also be added as NPCs.

G4: Find out which rules from the real world you need to reproduce in the game. Some can be there to improve the credibility of the virtual world, others are directly linked to the learning process (degree of collaboration allowed, for instance).

3.3 Coherent Metaphors

The last point concerns the coherence of the game world itself. Generally, a specific world, often dream-related, is designed and used as a support for all the learning concepts. The result is that the game is filled with a pedagogical content which is not adapted to the environment of the game itself. We want to stress the fact that the game design and the game play have to be linked to the learning concepts in order to create a more coherent game and to keep the player immersed.

Metaphors are a powerful way of keeping a strong coherence in the environment, because the different learners can understand them easily. For example, a Learning Management System developed in a French university was called the electronic schoolbag (Chabert, 2005); an "electronic pigeon-hole" was proposed to store "big" documents, the satellite to observe what is going on in the LMS, and this helped a lot for an easy introduction of the environment to new users. We believe that the same kind of metaphors must be inserted in the game in order to link the learning content to the environment of the game. For example, if you want to teach a foreign language, players will discover a new country (a specific part of the game map) where all the corresponding NPCs speak in the foreign language. Some clues symbolizing the country may be added to the world in order to reinforce the feeling of coherence. Moreover, concerning the general game play, a correct answer to an exercise can give the key to another place. This is simpler than explaining that "the knowledge to be acquired in this activity is a prerequisite for the next concept to learn in the pedagogical session". The player is therefore not disconnected from the game world by switching from the game to a specific learning feature. This enables us to keep the player immersed in the game.

G5: Define metaphors linked with the general story (G3) and with the different learning objects.

In the next part, we explain how we have implemented these features in a *Game-Based Learning Environment* and we describe how we have conducted an experiment with this environment.

PART 4: LEARNING ADVENTURE AND EXPERIMENTS

Description of Learning Adventure (L.A.)

In this part, we first describe a *Game-Based Learning Environment* that we have developed. This environment will serve as an example for illustrating the ideas described in parts 2 and 3. We explain the links between a learning session and the objects in the Game and we give details on the enactment of a learning session with students. We then describe how the collaboration takes place in L.A. We provide the user with hints on how to use User Modelling in this game for adapting the

scenario used by the learners. We reinforce the function of the *user model* by also considering it as an interactive object, on which we can perform actions, such as *interaction* or *visualisation*. The interaction with the *user model* opens new perspectives in which the user can act on his/her own representation, expressing wishes concerning the skills that s/he would like to enhance.

Learning Adventure (LA) is a Game-Based Learning Management System representing a 3D environment where the learning session takes place (see Figure 10). A particular map (environment with lakes, mountains and hills – guideline G1-) is dedicated to a particular learning activity, for a particular subject. Each part of the map represents the place where a given (sub) activity can be performed. The map topology represents the overall scenario of the learning session, i.e. the sequencing between activities. There are as many regions as actual activities, and the regions are linked together through paths and NPC guards, showing the attainability of an activity from other ones. An example of a scenario seen as a map topology is presented in figure 10. Similar models that link pedagogical issues with game elements can be found with a more general point of view in (Amory, 1999) and more precisely concerning this approach in (Carron, 2008).

Figure 9. An example of a scenario seen as a map topology

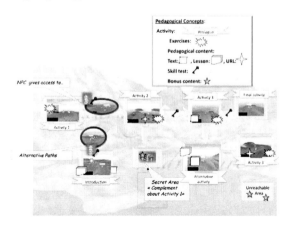

Figure 10. Screenshot of Learning Adventure: Teleporting a book in the game via a linux system command

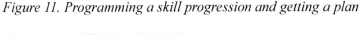

Players (students or teachers) possibly represented by their own avatars (G2), can move through the environment, performing a sequence of sub activities in order to acquire knowledge (see Figure 10). Activities can be carried out in a personal or collaborative way (see (Dillenbourg, 1996) for a list of cooperation abilities): one can access knowledge through objects available in the world, via help from the teachers, or from work with other students. When needed, it is easy to have a summary of the knowledge already acquired and of the general behaviour in the environment. Indeed, one can easily reach one's *user model* through the bag icon at the bottom right-hand part of the screen.

Similarly to (Egenfeldt-Nielsen, 2003), our approach is very pragmatic and mainly based on empirical experiments.

An Experiment with L.A.

We now illustrate how a training session can be immersive and flexible in such an environment, through an experiment in L.A.

Conditions and Methodology of the Experiment

This experiment was carried out in 2009 in our university with co-located settings. During the experiment, six groups of fifteen students with their teacher were present successively in the

Figure 11. Programming a skill progression and getting a plan

classroom equipped with 15 computers. Concerning the social presence perception (see (de Kort, 2008)), players were oriented away from each other, limiting mutual eye contact, natural reciprocation of approach or avoidance cues and mirroring. The students were 18 years old and familiar with computer use. In the six groups, there was an almost equal distribution between male and female. Each student accessed the virtual environment through his/her workstation, and had a personal (adapted) view on the world. These students used the environment for approximately one hour and half.

They were explicitly allowed to communicate through the chat tool provided with the system (integrated in L.A.) and were warned that they would be observed concerning the use of the system. Two observers were present in the classroom. The students were free to refuse this observation (the same practical work was available outside the learning environment), but everyone agreed to follow the proposed protocol. Finally, absolutely no clue was given concerning the use of the game (what an avatar is, how to move one's own avatar, how to interact with NPCs, objects and other players).

Pedagogical Objectives

The course was dedicated to the Operating Systems field. The learning content dealt with "Unix basic shell commands[4]". The aim of the session (role playing game) was to assess the knowledge and know-how of the students about the latter. A story guided the knowledge quest thanks to metaphors (G5): teleporting, cloning and destroying objects in the world representing respectively moving, copying and deleting files in the file system. The challenge is encouraged through NPCs who propose a coherent contest, here to test new futuristic developments (G3). *Immersion* is reinforced when the users' actions have a direct impact on the objects of the world. In this experiment, an artefact corresponding to

the system console was present in the game (see Figure 11). Actions correctly achieved on the file system were visible in the game: a book (object) was moved, duplicated or deleted in the game thanks to effective actions on the file system book (file) (G4). Finally, the teacher was present in the game via an avatar (G4): it was possible to chat with him, to ask for help for example.

Technical Considerations

The whole environment is coded in JAVA developed with the help of an engineer and students on placement (internship). The network part relies on the Red Dwarf[5] project. The whole environment is based on client-server architecture. The initial development of the *user model* was done in ruby and ruby on rails for the *user model* management (creation and consultation), but is currently integrated in L.A. in java, as shown in figure 11.

Correct actions are automatically rewarded with the relevant skill level up. The learner's *user model* is consequently updated in the game.

As explained in part 2, it is also possible to act on the *user model*, to set up new values in this model, representing a concrete objective to reach. In that case, one can expect from the system a generated plan composed of several activities contributing to this objective. The system must therefore be able to detect if an existing exercise is relevant to the given objective (see Figure 11 for such a process).

Technically, plans are currently described in a simple xml format as shown in Box 1.

EVALUATION AND RESULTS

At the end of the experiment, the students were asked to fill in questionnaires to give feed back about their feelings concerning their work session. Twelve questions (ranking and open-ended) were used. The questionnaire evaluated aspects relating to several parts of the learning game (pedagogical

Box 1.

```
<attribut default="0" end="7" name="linux-command" semantic="competency" start="0" teacher-
default="" type="int-interval" visible="true">
 <plan action="void" description="Go East, succeed in Navéca's Exercises" need="2" to="6"/>
  <plan action="void" description="Go talk to Domanec" need="0" to="2"/>
  <plan action="void" description="Go talk to Napram" need="6" to="7"/>
</attribut>
```

content, scenario-story, collaborative activities, and accessibility of the user interface).

The final question let the students propose improvements concerning weak and strong points of the game.

The initial objective concerning motivation was reached. The students were unanimous in preferring to work with this environment rather than do conventional practical work on workstations, and more generally were very enthusiastic about this kind of experiment.

In a 5-level ranking (ranging from *definitely not* -1- to *strongly agree* -5-), the results were mainly *agree* -4- or even -5-, concerning the addition of more collaborative aspects. We must say that the chosen activities matched very well with the game. The results obtained from the questionnaires were confirmed by the fact that the students did not take a break. Contrary to some preliminary experiments with videogames, our pedagogical resources or *background information* (Egelfeldt-Nielsen, 2003) were well integrated in the game and adapted for the game experience. Nevertheless, some questionnaires suggest possible improvements, mainly linked to the interface or to the scenario (girls did not like the scenario very much). Concerning the augmentation of the story part, 33.3% disagree, 41.7% have no opinion about this and 25% agree.

Apart from their perception of the scenario, male and female students appear to react similarly to this learning game, but this may be due to the small sample size which is not a true representation of the population, as it is now well known that specific gender aspects have to be taken into account (Hayes, 2008).

It was also important to interview the teacher. From his point of view, in the light of a previous experiment (Marty, 2009), it was mandatory to have tools supporting him in the monitoring task. Several indicators or widgets were therefore set up in our environments in order to meet this requirement.

One important point concerning *flexibility* is linked to the adaptation of observation of the on-going activity. Facts obtained from observation are relevant only if what is observable refers to an objective. The teacher may need to change this objective. In our experiment, an overall view widget was activated at the beginning of the learning session: each student's progression was monitored at a high level of granularity. The teacher needed a general view of the on- going activity: the former was then able to obtain more accurate information about a specific student having difficulties, thanks to the information included in this learner's *user model* (see Figure 12 – small picture- lower widget: connected student list; upper widget: skills).

We can even go one step further and use these indicators to regulate the activity (if the indicators relate to collaboration in the environment) or to perform remediation actions when a learner needs help. This feature can for instance be applied to a situation related to that shown in figure 12. We may observe that the mark associated to file rights ("droit-fichier") is very low. This means that this student is unable to change the rights of a file, and that this skill was particularly central in the experiment, for instance to act on newly discovered objects. To achieve the quest and for an accurate learning assessment, it is important that

Figure 12. Indicators and possible reactions concerning a specific student

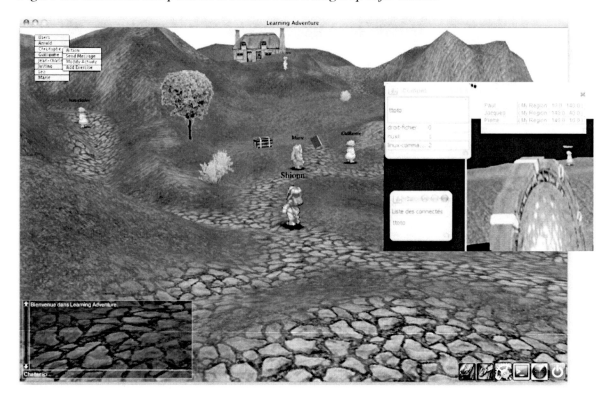

the teacher detect this problem and react to it quickly.

In order to enhance learning concerning this skill, the system proposes three remediation actions to the teacher: add new NPC (exercise), add new objects (resources), and send a message for direct help (communication between roles) as shown in the upper left corner of figure 12. These facilities help the *immersion* of the teacher in the game. However, this objective is quite ambitious and needs a complete classification of the actions in terms of remediation. This huge task can currently only be done for a tiny world.

It may be noted that such environments are very generic and make it possible to play at any time, from anywhere, and on different learning topics. Several students asked us to be able to complete or redo a quest later. It is therefore important to include persistent features to construct composite knowledge over time. The *user model* is a key concept that allows us to declare the skills and

behaviours of a particular learner. We are currently adapting the *Learning Adventure* environment in order to obtain a persistent world.

CONCLUSION

In this chapter, we have presented our work around a *User Model* adapted for Learning Games. As seen in the first section, the introduction of such a model in a learning game raises a certain number of questions: what is inside a user model adapted for Learning Games? Can this information be classified, and how? How to make this information available to the users inside the game? Through which graphical ways is it possible? How to update the *user model* dynamically? Can the *user model* serve as a *collaborative object* between the students and the teacher to negotiate pedagogical objectives? All these questions have been answered in this section, illustrating the need for a specific and flexible *user model* adapted for learning games. We have even proposed a *group model*, consolidating our belief that the next generation of *Game-Based Learning Environments* will take into account the social dimension. But as shown in the second section, *immersion* is another key concept that has to be taken into account when designing a learning game. Guidelines have thus been proposed in order to meet this other requirement. Furthermore, it is important to set up visual indicators of collaboration, in order to have a better awareness of what is occurring in a collaborative learning session, in order in turn to regulate the social interactions between actors.

REFERENCES

Amory, A., Naicker, K., Vincent, J., & Adams, C. (1999). The use of computer games as an educational tool: Identification of appropriate game types and game elements. *British Journal of Educational Technology*, *30*(4), 311–321. doi:10.1111/1467-8535.00121

Bogost, I. (2007). *Persuasive games: The expressive power of videogames*. Cambridge: MIT Press.

Brusilovsky, P. (2001). Adaptive hypermedia. *User Modeling and User-Adapted Interaction*, *11*(1/2), 87–110. doi:10.1023/A:1011143116306

Buckingham, D., & Burn, A. (2007). Game literacy in theory and practice. *Journal of Educational Multimedia and Hypermedia*, *16*(3), 323–349.

Carron, T., Marty, J.-C. & Heraud, J.-M. (2008). Teaching with game based learning management systems: Exploring and observing a pedagogical dungeon. *Simulation & Gaming Special issue on eGames and Adaptive eLearning*.

Carron, T., Marty, J. C., Heraud, J. M., & France, L. (2006). *Helping the teacher to re-organize tasks in a collaborative learning activity: An agent based approach*. Sixth IEEE International Conference on Advanced Learning, ICALT'06, (pp. 552-554). Kerkrade, Netherlands.

Carron, T., Marty, J. C., Heraud, J. M., & France, L. (2007). *Games as learning scenarios: Are you serious?* European Conference on Games Based Learning (Scotland).

Chabert G., Marty, J.-C., Caron, B., Carron, T., Vignollet, L. & Ferraris C. (2005). The electronic schoolbag: A CSCW workspace. *AI & Society: The Journal of Human-Centred Systems and Machine Intelligence*.

Choukroun, J., & Lieury, A. (1985). Rôle du mode de présentation (visuel, auditif, audio-visuel) dans la mémorisation d'instructions. *L'Année Psychologique*, (4): 503–516.

Crawford, C. (1984). *The art of computer game design*. Osborne/McGraw-Hill.

De Kort, Y.A.W. & Ijsselsteijn, W.A. (2008). People, places, and play: Player experience in a socio-spatial context. *Computers in Entertainment*, *6*(2).

Dillenbourg, P., Baker, M., Blaye, A., & O'Malley, C. (1996). The evolution of research on collaborative learning. In *Learning in humans and machine: Towards an interdisciplinary learning science*. (pp. 189-211).

Dimitracopoulou, A., Bollen, L., Dimitriadis, Y., Harrer, A., Jermann, P., & Kollias, V. (2005). *State of the art of interaction analysis for metacognitive support & diagnosis*. In IAJEIRP.

Dimitriadis, Y., Antonio Marcos, J., Martínez, A., & Anguita, R. (2006). *Interaction analysis for the detection and support of participatory roles in CSCL* (pp. 155–162). CRIWG.

Djaouti, D., Alvarez, J., Jessel, J-P, Methel, G. & Molinier, P. (2008). A gameplay definition through videogame classification. *International Journal of Computer Game Technology*. Hindawi Publishing Corporation.

Dondlinger, M. J. (2007). Educational video game design: A review of the literature. *Journal of Applied Educational Technology*, *4*(1), 21–31.

Egenfeldt-Nielsen, S. (2004). Practical barriers in using educational computer games. *Horizon, 12*(1), 18–21. doi:10.1108/10748120410540454

Ermi, L., & Mäyrä, F. (2005). Fundamental components of the gameplay experience: Analysing immersion. In *Print Proceedings, Changing Views: Worlds in Play, Digital Games Research Association Conference*. Tampere: University of Tampere Press.

Fink, J., & Kobsa, A. (2000). A review and analysis of commercial user modeling servers for personalization on the World Wide Web. *User Modeling and User-Adapted Interaction, 10*(2-3), 209–249. doi:10.1023/A:1026597308943

Galarneau, L., & Zibit, M. (2007). Online game for 21st century skills. In Gibson, D., Aldrich, C., & Prensky, M. (Eds.), *Games and simulations in online learning: Research and development frameworks* (pp. 59–88). Hersey, PA: Information Science Publishing.

Gee, J. P. (2007). *Good video game + good learning: Collected essays on video games, learning, and literacy*. New York: Palgrave MacMillan.

Gendron, E., Carron, T., & Marty, J.-C. (2008). *Collaborative indicators in learning games: An immersive factor*. 2nd European Conference on Games Based Learning, Barcelona, Spain, 16-17 October.

Hayes, E. (2008). Girls, gaming and trajectories of IT experience. In Kafai, Y., Heeter, C., Denner, J., & Sun, J. (Eds.), *Beyond Barbie and Mortal Kombat: New perspectives on gender and gaming* (pp. 217–230). Cambridge, MA: MIT Press.

Hijon, R., & Carlos, R. (2006). E-learning platforms analysis and development of students tracking functionality. In *Proceedings of the 18th World Conference on Educational Multimedia, Hypermedia & Telecomunications*, (pp. 2823-2828).

Kahne, J., Middaugh, E., & Evans, C. (2009). *The civic potential of video games*. Cambridge, MA: MIT Press.

Kian-Sam, H., & Chee-Kiat, K. (2002). Computer anxiety and attitudes toward computers among rural secondary school teachers: A Malaysian perspective. *Journal of Research on Technology in Education, 35*(1), 27–49.

Kirriemuir, J., & MacFarland, A. (2004). *Literature review in games and learning*. Retrieved April 6, 2010, from http://hal.archives-ouvertes.fr/docs/00/19/04/53/PDF/kirriemuir-j-2004-r8.pdf

Kobsa, A. (2001). Generic user modeling systems. *User Modeling and User-Adapted Interaction, 11*(1-2), 49–63. doi:10.1023/A:1011187500863

Loghin, G., Marty, J.-C., & Carron, T. (2008). *A flexible agent-based observation solution for educational platforms*. In IEEE International Conference on Advanced Learning, ICALT'08.

Marty, J.-C., Carron, T., & Heraud, J.-M. (2009). Observation as a requisite for games based learning environments. In *Games based learning advancements for multisensory human computer interfaces: Techniques and effective practices*. (pp. 51-71).

Marty, J.-C., Heraud, J.-M., France, L., & Carron, T. (2007). Matching the performed activity on an educational platform with a recommended pedagogical scenario: a multi source approach. *Journal of Interactive Learning Research, 18*(2), 27.

Matheas, M. (2005). Procedural literacy: Educating the new media practitioner. *Horizon, 13*(2), 101–111. doi:10.1108/10748120510608133

Prensky, M. (2000). *Digital game-based learning*. New York: MacGraw Hill.

Rueda, U., Larranaga, M., Arruarte, A., & Elorriaga, J. A. (2003). Dynamic visualization of student models using concept maps. *Proceedings of the 11th International Conference on Artificial Intelligence in Education*, (pp. 89-96).

Salen, K. (2007). Gaming literacies: A game design study in action. *Journal of Educational Multimedia and Hypermedia, 16*(3), 301–322.

Squire, K. (2003). Videogames in education. *International Journal of Intelligent Games & Simulations, 2*(1), 49–62.

Taylor, L. N. (2003). *Video games: Perspective, point-of-view, and immersion.* Retrieved from http://www. gamasutra.com/education/ theses/20030818/taylor_01.shtml# Vassileva, J., McCalla, G. & Greer, J. (2003). Multi-agent multi-user modeling. *User Modeling and User-Adapted Interaction, 13*(1), 179-210.

Vygotsky, L. S. (1934). *Language and thought.* Moscow: Gosizdat.

Woyach, S. (2008). Immersion through video games. *Illumin Review of Engineering in Everyday Life, 4*(5).

Yu, T.W. (2009). Learning in the virtual world: The pedagogical potentials of massively multiplayer online role playing games. *International Education Studies, 2*(1).

ENDNOTES

[1] To illustrate our purpose, we present pictures of a user model, applied to another learning game that we have developed called "pedagogical dungeon", in which a « heroic fantasy style » is used.

[2] For example: Rule::'MessageNumber > 20' => behaviour(talkative, high)

[3] NB: Here, non interactive because logged as owner and not as teacher.

[4] Most Operating Systems may be directly controlled by inserting text commands into a specific tool called « shell interpreter ». Examples of commands: file copy, move, delete, etc.

[5] See http://www.reddwarfserver.org/

Chapter 26
Exploring the Gender Differences between Student Teachers when Using an Educational Game to Learn Programming Concepts

Eugenia M. W. Ng
The Hong Kong Institute of Education, Hong Kong SAR, China

ABSTRACT

The gender differences have long been an issue in computer games, but there is very little empirical research on the behavior and performance of females and males when playing computer games. This chapter discusses an exploratory study that aimed to examine the gender differences between female and male student teachers who played an educational game to learn programming concepts. This study we adopted a self-made educational game called "Game". Fifteen males and eighteen females finished playing a level of the Game. Female participants spent more time in the Game but their scores were lower. Female and male students also employed different strategies when playing the Game. The findings call for larger and longer research studies and perhaps a re-design of the Game to make it more appealing to females, in order to have a thorough examination on the gender differences when using an educational game to learn.

INTRODUCTION

Computer games are very popular for the young generation due to its interactivity and multimedia features. Gee (2003) elaborates video games as a semiotic domain and he believes that when people learn to play games, they are learning a new literacy. Malone (1981) suggests challenge, fantasy, and curiosity are the three main elements that "make video games fun". Apart from playing

DOI: 10.4018/978-1-60960-495-0.ch026

games for fun, games are useful for improving learning skills in practical reasoning (Wood & Stewart, 1987), making inferences and engaging in inductive reasoning (Mayer & Sims, 1994), solving complex problem (Hayes, 1981), enhance spatial skills performances (Baenninger & Newcomber, 1989) and cognitive process (Pillay, Brown, & Wilss, 1999; Quinn, 1996).

The gender differences have long been a problem in the area of computing. There are a number of studies on gender differences in computer experiences, skills and adoptions. Females were likely to be computer phobic than males (Igbaria & Chakrabarti, 1990; Rosen & Maguire, 1990). Morahan-Martin, Olinsky & Schmacher (1992) found that there were a significant gender differences between male and females where the former had greater experience skills with computers. Females were slower to adopt Internet than males (Weil & Rosen, 1995, 1997), and females reported higher levels of discomfort and incompetence of using computers (Schumacher & Morahan-Martin, 2001). More recently, Schumacher & Morahan-Martin (2001) conducted a survey to university students and found that females reported higher levels of discomfort and incompetence in using computers. Males were also more experienced and possessed higher levels of skills in using Internet. Moreover, Wilson (2002) found that there was no difference between female and male undergraduate computer science students in terms of comfort level, mathematics background and attribution to luck but there was a significant gender difference in game playing as males had much more experiences.

The usefulness of using games to enhance learning and the lack of gender difference empirical research in this area instill the author to investigate whether there is any difference between female and male students when using an educational game to learn programming. The following section described the pertinent literature review related to using computer games for learning. The review will be followed by a discussion of the

research methodology and findings. Finally, the conclusion of the research and future directions in research and game design will also be discussed.

BACKGROUND

Computer games are broadly divided into two categories, namely action games and strategy games. Action games mainly require better eye-hand coordination to win whilst strategy games require better planning and critical thinking skills. Examples of action games include Super Mario and Half Life whilst strategy games include Sim-City and Age of Empire. When playing games, players interact with the objects in the game and sometimes other players and to manipulate variables to solve specific problems. Educational games are one form of serious games as they are designed to address specific learning outcomes such as reinforcing some concepts or recalling of some facts. Sometimes, educational games are called edutainment.

Garris, Ahlers & Driskell (2002) reviewed a number of articles on the characteristics of computer games and suggested that games could be grouped into the following dimensions: (1) fantasy, (2) rules/goals, (3) sensory/stimuli, (4) challenge, (5) mystery and (6) control. The factors that affect players are: (1) interest, (2) enjoyment, (3) task involvement and (4) confidence. Moreover, the learning outcomes could be grouped into skilled, cognitive and affective based. Under the cognitive learning outcomes, it includes declarative, procedural, strategy knowledge. Soukup (2007) reviewed a number of video games and found that most popular video games embrace mastery and dominations via violence and aggressive competition which should be challenged by feminist.

Boys and girls are equally interested in playing games at the young age but girls tend to have reduced interests in game playing as they grow (Agosto, 2004). Beasley & Collins Standley (2002) found that most popular video games are primarily targeted to young men which consists of male protagonists and some of the action games are attractive to boys but not to girls (Quaiser-Pohl, Geiser, & Lehmann, 2006; Terlecki & Newcombe, 2005). When children were designing video games, it was found that boys and girls designed very different games in terms of the game nature, the spaces, characters, interaction and feedback (Kafai, 1996). There were research findings on the exposure of violent videos games affecting young women's behavior (Anderson and Dill, 2000; Anderson, 2002; Anderson and Murphy, 2003) and males were more likely video players and they spent much more time in playing video games than females (Cherney & London, 2006; Lucas & Sherry, 2004).

Gee (2003) has addressed many aspects of video game in his book and yet he did not discuss anything related to gender differences and claimed that it has been "well discussed elsewhere" (p.10). Bryce and Butter (2002) reviewed research related to gender and gaming and they found that much of the discussion is related to the contents of the games rather than on the analysis of female and male gaming experiences. Chou & Tsai (2007) conducted a survey on high school students on their opinions on computer games. It was found that boys spent more time in playing computer games and they were also more motivated and enjoyed computer games more. Similarly, Takayoshi (2007) conducted a case study of her female relatives on video gaming and concluded that (1) the gamers had virtually no female role models; (2) female games regularly received the message that gaming was male territory and they turned to their female counterparts for support; (3) they did not identify themselves as gamers and were disconnected from the gaming culture.

There are many reasons for using computer games for education. Firstly, learning had changed from rote learning to search and use information (Simon, 1996). Secondly, research findings suggested that games could enhance learning and understand difficult subject matters (Ricci, Salas,

& Cannon-Bowers, 1996; Simon, 1996; White-hall & McDonald, 1993). Thirdly, playing games provided compelling and rewarding experiences. However, there had not been any agreement on the types of features that supported learning (Garris, et al., 2002).

A number of researchers have conducted research investigating the value of computer games in enhancing learning in a number of disciplines such as mathematics, geography, engineering, sex education and history (Egenfeldt-Nielsen, 2007). Most findings supported the notion that computer games could enhance learning (Becker, 2001; Buch & Egenfeldt-Nielsen, 2006; Gander, 2002) but some findings found the oppositie (McFarlane, Sparrowhawk, & Heald, 2002; McMullen, 1987; Wiebe & Martin, 1994). However, O'Neil, Wainess and Baker (2005) found only 19 out of several thousand articles related to games met their standards of empirical research when they searched databases for articles published in the last 15 years. The educational benefits of games are mixed and the positive findings are attributed to instructional design rather than the nature of the games. Egenfeldt-Nielsen (2007) reviewed related articles and found that some of positive claims of using computer games to enhance learning were faulty. The main faults were: without control groups, using computer games as additional teaching resources rather than comparing it to other teaching methods; studies were one-shot studies and there were no pretests and post–tests to support the claims. He further substantiated some problems of using computer for education. Problems included: (1) players had little intrinsic motivation, (2) no integrated learning experience, (3) concentrated on drill-and-practice, (4) simple game design, (5) small budget, (6) no teacher presence during gaming and (6) distribution and marketing different from commercial games.

There had been many studies on the usefulness of using computer games for learning and yet not much research on the gender issues had been done. Much of the research related to using computer games to learn is related to spatial attention. For example, Green & Bavelier's (2003) found that females benefitted more in enhancing their spatial attention when playing an action game but they did not attain the same higher levels of their male counterparts. Similarly, Feng, Spencer and Pratt (2007) found that females had substantial gains in spatial attention and mental rotation when they played an action video game for 10 hours. There had been very little research on the behavior and performance of females and males when playing computer games. The lack of empirical research findings lead us to investigate if there are any gender differences between female and male student when they are engaged in using educational games to learn programming concepts.

MAIN FOCUS OF THE CHAPTER

1. The Study

The author has taught programming languages to student teachers for a number of years and it was found that most of them were rather weak in programming concepts and this was not unique to the author's classes (Feldgen & Clua, 2004). In order to enhance their programming concept, a self-developed educational game was developed. The rationale of designing an educational game was to motivate student teachers to learn with computers (Kinzer, Sherwood, & Bransford, 1986), in particular, to learn programming concepts in a visual and engaging environment. The design of this game followed the rationale of Logo which was intended to provide children with a new way of "playing" with (and learning) mathematical ideas by controlling a turtle's motion (Papert, 1980). The simple commands of Logo also enabled players to learn programming concepts more easily. There were two objectives of the "Game" - the first objective was to scaffold students' logic and programming concepts (such as scripting) and the second objective was

to facilitate students to learn control technology concepts through visualizations. However, the main objective of this study was to investigate whether there were any differences between female and male student teachers when using an educational game to learn programming.

Three hypotheses are formulated to answer the research question:

H1: there is no difference between males and females in their mean gaming time

H2: there is no difference between males and females in their mean gaming score

H3: there is no difference between males and females in their gaming strategies

2. The Game

2.1 Stages

The "Game" has ten stages with increasing difficulties and variations of tasks. Players of the game are asked to guide the little Plane in the game to arrive at the destination which is denoted by a red tile. The stages are grouped into three levels: Beginner (Stages 1-4), Intermediate (Stages 5-7) and Advanced (Stages 8-10). Players can select to play any level or to choose a random mode. It is expected that players will learn Logo programming scripting and to familiarize with the interface of the game in the beginner stages. Players are required to tackle three dimensional (3-D) movements such as to guide the Plane to get a ball which is placed on a different level in the "Intermediate" stages. These first two levels are meant to meet the first objective of developing the game. In the stages of "Advanced" level, players are required to use the concepts of logic gates such as "or", "and" and "not" to guide the Plane through various hurdles in the scene. Students are also expected to consolidate the concepts and skills they had

Figure 1. Control mode

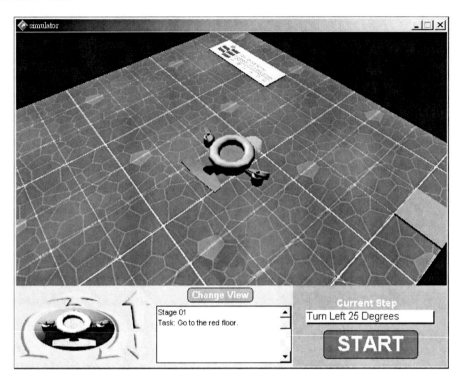

acquired in the first two levels. Players should have achieved the second objective of the design of the game if they could tackle the problems in the advanced stages.

2.2 Interfaces

There are two types of interfaces which cater for individual preferences. In the "Control" mode, players can control the Plane by selecting the arrow keys using a mouse (see Figure 1). They are not required to write any scripts or to complete any tasks in this mode. The purpose of this mode is to give players an idea of a stage and to manipulate the little Plane without worrying about the scripting. In fact, the scripts that are equivalent to the current Plane movements are displayed in the field "Current Step" so the players can get a rough idea of scripting.

Another interface is called "Scripting" mode (see Figure 2). In this mode, players are required

to input scripts and then execute them in order to manipulate the Plane. When a player believes he/she has enough preparation on scripting, he/she can click the "Start" button at the right bottom of the scene and the game will be changed from "Control" mode to "Scripting Mode". If a player is unsure at the "Scripting" mode and would like to get familiar with the stages again, he/she can click "Control Mode" button at any time and vice versa, i.e., the interface of game can be changed to the selected mode instantly.

2.3 Manipulations

In the Logo programming environment, the learners have to follow the syntax and to input all scripts such as "LT 90" using a keyboard to manipulate a turtle. In this Game, scripts are divided into two parts, namely, actions and units. Actions scripts include commands like "Turn Left", "Turn Right", "Move Up" and "Move Down" whilst units include

Figure 2. Scripting mode

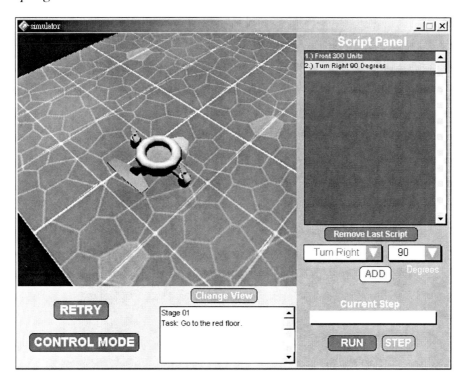

the number of steps and turning angles such as "100 units" and "45 degrees". Figure 3 shows that the two parts are placed in two separate drop-down menus. With these drop-down menus, players are required to select the appropriate scripts using a mouse only so that it is much easier and faster to operate than keying in and remembering the syntaxes. Therefore, the Game is used as cognitive tools rather than a training device (Brehmer & Dorner, 1993).

2.4 Playing Strategies

At first glance, the Game appears to be an action game but in fact it is a strategy game. As the scene of the stages becomes more complicated, players should be aware that there are many different approaches to completing a task. This variation affects the number of scripts used and distance that the Plane travels which is similar to composing the scripts when programming. The player has

Figure 3. Control interface

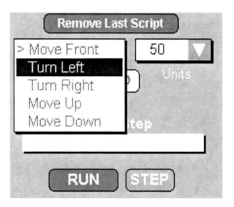

to decide how to guide the Plane to the red tile by thinking of the appropriate actions and units. Take Figure 4 which is at stage one as an example. When the game starts, the Plane faces north and there are at least two routes to arrive at the red tile. The traveling distance is the same between Route 1 and Route 2. If Route 2 is chosen, we can obtain higher score because Route 1 requires

Figure 4. Scene of Stage 1

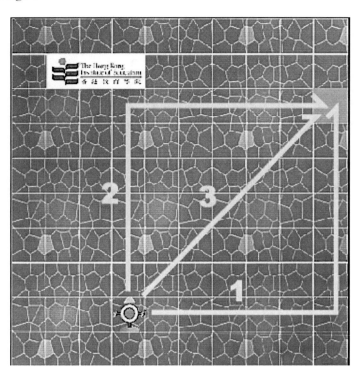

one more script. The Plane has to "Turn Right 90 degrees" first before proceeding to the other movements, i.e., move Front 600 units (100 Units is equivalent for 1 tile), Turn Left (Turn Right for Route 2) 90 degrees and Move Front 600 units to reach the red tile.

Apart from Route 1 and Route 2, there are other possible routes for the Plane to arrive at the destination. In fact, the best solution of this example is to manipulate the Plane to turn right 45 degrees and then move diagonally (Route 3) to the destination. It is clear that the player has to know some mathematical theories such as Pythagorean Theorem in order to find the shortest distance of the path which is the aim of learning Logo programming. This example shows that there are many routes for the Plane for simple stages and it is not difficult to imagine that much more routes are possible in later stages of the game when the Plane has to escape from obstacles at 3D environments and also to solve problems using logic gates knowledge. Figure 5 shows a

Stage 9 scene, which aims to complete the logic circuit by bringing appropriate binaries on the red tile. The players are required to have a good understanding of control technology to tackle this task.

2.5 Net Ranking

Apart from its basic features, the Game has another feature called "Net Ranking". After finishing each required task, there is a summary screen showing the number of steps (scripts) used, the total distance traveled and the score (fewer steps and shorter distance yields higher score). Players could choose to submit the results for "Net Ranking" or just proceed to the next stage. If a player chooses to submit his/her result, this will be compared with other submitted results stored in the server. The results will be displayed if the result of that player is within rank 1 to 10. This feature should give the players the sense of control which in turn intrinsically motivated them to adjust their actions

Figure 5. Screen shot of Stage 9

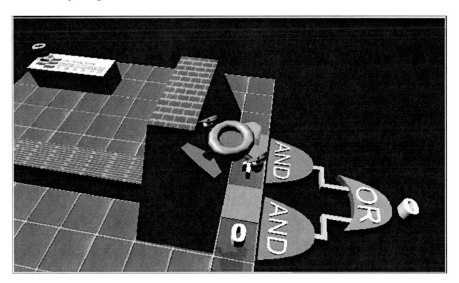

to reach the goal. Furthermore, there is also a random mode which displays the starting position of the Plane, obstacle positions and difficulty level randomly and these features should provide flexibility and additional challenges for players.

3. The Participants

A group of forty seven pre-service student teachers participated in this study. They were information technology minor students who might have Logo programming during secondary school or university education. They have learnt the Truth Table in the programming module that they took with the author. They were told that the Game was to consolidate their programming and control technology concepts after a few weeks of classes. After a brief introduction to the game, they were asked to play "Game" freely during their leisure time. Students recorded their entire playing process as digital video files (wmv file format) and to upload their playing process upon completion. The participation in the Game would be counted as part of the class participation marks.

4. Findings and Discussions

To answer the research question - if there are any gender differences between female and male student teachers when they are engaged in using educational games to learn programming concepts, the video recordings of student teachers' game playing performances were viewed and analyzed by a research assistant. There were 15 males and 18 females who have finished playing at least one level (3 stages) of the Game. Most students (45%) finished playing the beginner level, 30.8% and 24.2% the intermediate and advanced level respectively (see Figure 6).

The average number of attempts of each stage was 1.91. 90% of students completed the game within 3 attempts. For stage 5, 60% of students attempted more than 3 times to finish the task. There was a special case in stage 1, 17 students completed it in one attempt but one student had attempted 13 times (see Figure 7). Perhaps that person was so unfamiliar with playing, he/she had to try many times. Figure 7 also showed that players required more attempts to complete the tasks after stages 2 as the stages were getting more complex.

Figure 6. Level of Game played

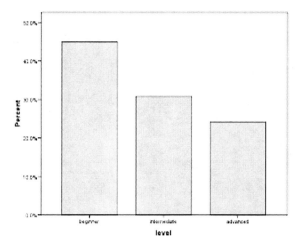

The average number of steps required to complete the task was 7.25 and the least and most steps were 2 and 23 respectively. Generally, 80.8% of students completed the task by using less than 10 steps. Figure 8 showed that the number of steps required to complete the task was somewhat proportional to the level of difficulties of the game. For stages 1 to 6, about 90.1% of students completed the task in 10 steps or less. For example, stage 7 which required opening a logical gate, students spent at least 15 steps to finish the game. However, they had learnt the concepts quickly and spent less time in the following stages.

The 33 students played 120 games in total, i.e., each player played about 3.63 games. On average, male students should have played 55.55 games and female students should have played 65.45 games. However, it was found that 15 male students played 41 games (34.2%) and each male played 2.73 games on average whereas 18 female students played 79 games (65.8%) and 4.39 games were played per female on average. It was very clear that female students played more games than male students.

4.1 Gaming Time

The game time started at Control Mode. The shortest and longest game time were 9 seconds and 17 minutes respectively and the mean of the game time that participants spent in each stage was about 2 minutes. In fact, most of the games

Figure 7. Number of attempts for different stages

Count											
					stage						
		1	2	3	4	5	6	7	8	9	10	Total
attempt	1	17	16	9	7	4	5	3	5	5	3	74
	2	0	3	5	6	0	3	4	3	2	1	27
	3	0	1	2	1	0	2	1	0	0	0	7
	4	0	0	0	0	1	0	0	0	0	1	2
	5	0	1	0	2	2	0	0	0	0	0	5
	6	0	0	0	0	1	0	0	0	0	0	1
	7	0	0	0	0	1	0	0	0	0	0	1
	10	0	0	0	0	0	0	1	0	0	0	1
	11	0	0	0	0	1	0	0	0	0	0	1
	13	1	0	0	0	0	0	0	0	0	0	1
Total		18	20	16	16	10	11	9	8	7	5	120

Figure 8. Frequency of number of steps in each stage

			stage 1	2	3	4	5	6	7	8	9	10	Total
step_range	less than 5 steps	Count	17	17	10	2	0	0	0	7	5	0	58
		% within stage	94.4%	85.0%	62.5%	12.5%	.0%	.0%	.0%	87.5%	71.4%	.0%	48.3%
	5 to 10 steps	Count	0	3	6	11	5	11	0	1	2	0	39
		% within stage	0%	15.0%	37.5%	68.8%	50.0%	100.0%	.0%	12.5%	28.6%	.0%	32.5%
	10 to 15 steps	Count	1	0	0	3	5	0	0	0	0	1	10
		% within stage	5.6%	0%	0%	18.8%	50.0%	0%	0%	0%	0%	20.0%	8.3%
	15 to 20 steps	Count	0	0	0	0	0	0	5	0	0	4	9
		% within stage	.0%	0%	0%	.0%	.0%	.0%	55.6%	0%	0%	80.0%	7.5%
	more than 20 steps	Count	0	0	0	0	0	0	4	0	0	0	4
		% within stage	.0%	0%	0%	.0%	.0%	.0%	44.4%	0%	0%	.0%	3.3%
Total		Count	18	20	16	16	10	11	9	8	7	5	120
		% within stage	100.0%	100.0%	100.0%	100.0%	100.0%	100.0%	100.0%	100.0%	100.0%	100.0%	100.0%

were completed within 2 minutes (66.7%), only 5% of games were finished after 6 minutes (see Figure 9). At the beginner level, 90.7% of games were completed within 2 minutes; in the intermediate level, only 40.5% of games were completed within 2 minutes. Especially in stage 5, 30% of games were finished after 6 minutes. However, in the advanced level, 55.17% of games were completed within 2 minutes. The plausible reason that games were completed slower in the intermediate level suggested that students needed more time to tackle the 3D challenges. As mentioned above, students took most steps to complete the game but the time that they spent on it had the widest range. Similarly, they spent much less time in the following stages once they were able to learn and grasp such a technique in the advanced stages to solve logic gate problems.

Male students spent much shorter time in completing stages than female students. The means of the gaming time for each stage for male and female students were 1 minute 48 second and 2 minutes 32 second respectively (see Figure 10). By performing t-test (p-value=0.044), the result showed that there was a difference between males and females in their means of gaming time at 5% significance level and thus H1 is not supported. Perhaps male students had more experiences and spent more time in gaming and the experiences allowed them to complete the tasks faster (Cherney & London, 2006; Lucas & Sherry, 2004) and they also had better spatial attention (Feng, et al., 2007; Green & Bavelier, 2003)

Figure 9. Frequency of game time in each stage

			stage 1	2	3	4	5	6	7	8	9	10	Total
dur_range	less than 1 min	Count	16	12	5	2	2	3	1	4	2	0	47
		% within stage	88.9%	60.0%	31.3%	12.5%	20.0%	27.3%	11.1%	50.0%	28.6%	0%	39.2%
	within 1 and 2 min	Count	1	6	9	4	0	4	1	2	5	1	33
		% within stage	5.6%	30.0%	56.3%	25.0%	.0%	36.4%	11.1%	25.0%	71.4%	20.0%	27.5%
	within 2 and 3 min	Count	0	1	2	6	2	3	1	2	0	1	18
		% within stage	.0%	5.0%	12.5%	37.5%	20.0%	27.3%	11.1%	25.0%	0%	20.0%	15.0%
	within 3 and 4 min	Count	0	1	0	2	0	1	1	0	0	2	7
		% within stage	.0%	5.0%	.0%	12.5%	.0%	9.1%	11.1%	0%	0%	40.0%	5.8%
	within 4 and 5 min	Count	0	0	0	1	1	0	3	0	0	0	5
		% within stage	.0%	.0%	.0%	6.3%	10.0%	0%	33.3%	0%	0%	0%	4.2%
	within 5 and 6 min	Count	0	0	0	1	2	0	1	0	0	0	4
		% within stage	.0%	.0%	.0%	6.3%	20.0%	0%	11.1%	0%	0%	0%	3.3%
	more than 6 min	Count	1	0	0	0	3	0	1	0	0	1	6
		% within stage	5.6%	.0%	.0%	.0%	30.0%	0%	11.1%	0%	0%	20.0%	5.0%
Total		Count	18	20	16	16	10	11	9	8	7	5	120
		% within stage	100.0%	100.0%	100.0%	100.0%	100.0%	100.0%	100.0%	100.0%	100.0%	100.0%	100.0%

Figure 10. Game time played by different gender

	gender	N	Mean	Std. Deviation	Std. Error Mean
duration_sec	Male	41	88.85	85.038	13.281
	Female	79	139.42	146.559	16.489

4.2 Score

The mean score for the participants was 8582.41 but the mean scores of male and female students were 9491.88 and 8110.41 respectively (see Figure 11). Male students achieved higher scores and yet they spent much shorter time in playing the Game. By performing t-test (p-value=0.025), the result showed that there was a difference between males and females in their mean gaming score at 5% significance level and thus H2 is not supported. Perhaps the objects in the Game was more "masculine" which were favored by male students as males demonstrated better visual memory of "masculine" and "neutral" items than females (Ferguson, Cruz, & Rueda, 2008; Kafai, 1996).

4.3 Strategy

After reviewing the computer recordings of the players playing the game, we had grouped the different strategies employed by the gamers into 3 broad categories, namely, "calculation", "step by step" and "trial and error". "Calculation" strategy was to plan the route in advance and achieved the goal at first attempt. "Step by step" strategy was similar to "calculation" strategy but to divide the route into several parts to achieve the goal at one go. "Trial and error" strategy was trying different ways until the goal was achieved. Most of the tasks were solved by "calculation" (62.5%) approach, followed by "trial and error" (30.8%) and only 8 games (6.7%) were solved by "step by step" approach (Figure 12).

Comparing the strategies used in each stage, the number of times of using "calculation" decreased as the level went up. Figure 13 showed that most of the students used "calculation", except for stage 4, 5 and 7 when a high ratio of them used "trial and error". "Trial and error" approach was frequently used (50%) in the intermediate level but 34.48% was used in the advanced level.

Figure 11. Mean scores between female and male participants

	gender	N	Mean	Std. Deviation	Std. Error Mean
score	Male	41	9491.88	3365.126	525.544
	Female	79	8110.41	3038.016	341.803

Figure 12. Frequency of different strategies used

		Frequency	Percent	Valid Percent	Cumulative Percent
Valid	calculation	75	62.5	62.5	62.5
	step by step	8	6.7	6.7	69.2
	trial and error	37	30.8	30.8	100.0
	Total	120	100.0	100.0	

Figure 13. Strategy adopted for different stages

			strategy			
			calculation	step by step	try and error	Total
stage	1	Count	17	0	1	18
		% within stage	94.4%	.0%	5.6%	100.0%
	2	Count	15	1	4	20
		% within stage	75.0%	5.0%	20.0%	100.0%
	3	Count	10	2	4	16
		% within stage	62.5%	12.5%	25.0%	100.0%
	4	Count	7	1	8	16
		% within stage	43.8%	6.3%	50.0%	100.0%
	5	Count	4	1	5	10
		% within stage	40.0%	10.0%	50.0%	100.0%
	6	Count	6	0	5	11
		% within stage	54.5%	.0%	45.5%	100.0%
	7	Count	3	2	4	9
		% within stage	33.3%	22.2%	44.4%	100.0%
	8	Count	5	0	3	8
		% within stage	62.5%	.0%	37.5%	100.0%
	9	Count	5	0	2	7
		% within stage	71.4%	.0%	28.6%	100.0%
	10	Count	3	1	1	5
		% within stage	60.0%	20.0%	20.0%	100.0%
Total		Count	75	8	37	120
		% within stage	62.5%	6.7%	30.8%	100.0%

In fact, 55.17% of students used "calculation" again in the advanced level. This could reflect that students had learnt quickly through playing with the Game in the intermediate level.

Comparing different strategies used by different genders, no male students and about 10% of female students used the "step by step" strategy (see Figure 14). The finding suggested that female students were more eager to achieve the goal even though they could not achieve the goal in one attempt. In the beginner level, the percentages of using different strategies for males and females were very similar. However, in the intermediate level, 63.6% of males and only 37.9% females used "calculation" approach whilst 36.4% males and 55.2% females used "trial and error" approach. In the advanced level, 80% of males and only 42.1% females used "calculation" whilst 20%

males and 42.1% females used "trial and error". It was very clear that female and male students adopted different approaches and male students adopted more "calculation" approach throughout different stages and thus H3 is not supported. The findings indicated that male students were better in logical thinking and could deal with different level of problems more easily.

CONCLUSION

This chapter discussed the features of an educational game and explored the behavior of student teachers when using it to learn programming concept after classes. It was found that 15 male and 18 female participants performed differently despite the fact that their formal education

Figure 14. Frequency of gender in different strategies

level					gender		Total
					Male	Female	
beginner	strategy	calculation	Count		18	24	42
			% within strategy		42.9%	57.1%	100.0%
			% within gender		85.7%	72.7%	77.8%
		step by step	Count		0	3	3
			% within strategy		.0%	100.0%	100.0%
			% within gender		.0%	9.1%	5.6%
		try and error	Count		3	6	9
			% within strategy		33.3%	66.7%	100.0%
			% within gender		14.3%	18.2%	16.7%
	Total		Count		21	33	54
			% within strategy		38.9%	61.1%	100.0%
			% within gender		100.0%	100.0%	100.0%
intermediate	strategy	calculation	Count		7	10	17
			% within strategy		41.2%	58.8%	100.0%
			% within gender		70.0%	37.0%	45.9%
		step by step	Count		0	2	2
			% within strategy		.0%	100.0%	100.0%
			% within gender		.0%	7.4%	5.4%
		try and error	Count		3	15	18
			% within strategy		16.7%	83.3%	100.0%
			% within gender		30.0%	55.6%	48.6%
	Total		Count		10	27	37
			% within strategy		27.0%	73.0%	100.0%
			% within gender		100.0%	100.0%	100.0%
advanced	strategy	calculation	Count		8	8	16
			% within strategy		50.0%	50.0%	100.0%
			% within gender		80.0%	42.1%	55.2%
		step by step	Count		0	3	3
			% within strategy		.0%	100.0%	100.0%
			% within gender		.0%	15.8%	10.3%
		try and error	Count		2	8	10
			% within strategy		20.0%	80.0%	100.0%
			% within gender		20.0%	42.1%	34.5%
	Total		Count		10	19	29
			% within strategy		34.5%	65.5%	100.0%
			% within gender		100.0%	100.0%	100.0%

background had been very similar. All the three formulated hypotheses: H1- there is no difference between males and females in their mean gaming time, H2 - there is no difference between males and females in their mean gaming score, and H3 - there is no difference between males and females in their gaming strategies, had been rejected. Male students spent shorter time and yet scored better than female students. Male students had a tendency to adopt "calculation" strategy for different stages whereas female students adopted "trial and error" approaches for the intermediate level. The differences of female and male students'

performance were also statistically significant and thus the three set of formulated hypotheses were not supported. The findings, certainly provide an empirical evidence to answer the research question that there is a gender difference between female and male student teachers when using an educational game to learn programming.

FUTURE DIRECTIONS

Using the educational game to enhance students' programming concepts was the main educational goal and exploring the behavior of female and male game playing is only a by-product of the educational goal. There are three possible future directions: (1) for teaching and learning using video games; (2) for educational game development; and (3) for more research into gender differences.

The findings indicate that all the participants who completed the Game were able to use the video game to learn but about 30% of the participants did not complete the Game. There are various approaches to motivate students to use video games to learn and to narrow the gender differences.

1. Teachers can do a demonstration on how to play some stages of the game so that students can have a better idea of how to tackle the problems especially for female students who have less video games experiences.
2. The students could play the video games in pair, preferably, a male student to team up with a female student, so that they could collaborate and complement each other.
3. Some extrinsic rewards such as extra marks or certificate of completion can be given to gamers to recognize their successful completion of the video games.
4. As students like the idea of using video games to learn, video games can also be used for learning different disciplinary knowledge.

Regarding the future game design direction, there are some possibilities to cater for females' preferences as the present design is rather masculine and it was found that different genders have different preferences (Kafai, 1996).

1. Instead of having a default Plane, scenes and interfaces, the future development of the game could include giving players a choice of more feminine objects, scenes and obstacles. For example, the choice of objects can be pets, toys or people, the

destination could be food or a rose garden and the obstacles could be houses, animals and trees. Female players might perform better in a more feminine environment as they tend to remember "feminine" objects better (Ferguson, et al., 2008).
2. Females tend to prefer collaboration more than competition. The Internet provides a friendly environment for social networking. The game could include some social functions such as collaboration between players.
3. Instead of manipulating the objects using mouse, perhaps the game can accept input verbally as females sometimes tend to prefer speaking rather than doing.

Given the popularity of video games and usefulness of video games in supporting learning, perhaps it is high time for policy makers to set directions for developing educational video games as part of the learning resources, especially since it is very expensive for teachers to develop interesting and effective video games on their own.

This study presented a small-scale research in this area and it is inappropriate to generalize the findings. There are different approaches to conduct further research in this area. Firstly, we should enlarge the sample size of the participants. Given the fact that we do not have many student teachers taking IT as a minor discipline, perhaps we can cooperate with other researchers to conduct larger scale research together. Secondly, it is unclear if playing the Game can enhance student teachers' programming knowledge and skills. The result would be more convincing if we could conduct pre-tests and post-tests and to find out the effectiveness of game playing to learning. Thirdly, the finding is based on one snap-shot study. It may be helpful for the participants to play computer games and to use computer games to learn for a longer period of time, as it was found that improvements were made when females were engaged in 10 hours of action-video-game (Feng, et al., 2007). Fourthly, we are not too sure if educational games can enhance other disciplinary learning or not. It would be useful to develop computer games and conduct research for the same participants to explore if computer games can enhance learning in general. It would be more convincing to conduct longitudinal research to evaluate the long-term effect of gender differences of using educational games to learn different disciplinary knowledge. Fifthly, it is unclear if the gender differences or other factors affected student teachers' gaming performances. We could ask students of their experiences of gaming and their programming experiences and do some statistical analysis on different factors which might contribute to the differences. Last but not least, there is a great need to include some controlled groups in the research to find out the impact of different factors on using computer games to enhance learning.

ACKNOWLEDGMENT

The authors would like to thank BEd(S) and BEd(P) participants for participating in this study and providing us with comments on how to improve "Game". Research assistance from Wilson Chung and Rita Wan are also acknowledged.

REFERENCES

Agosto, D. E. (2004). Girls and gaming: A summary of the research with implications for practice. *Teacher Librarian, 31*(3), 8–14.

Baenninger, M., & Newcomber, N. (1989). The role of experience in spatial test performances: A meta-analysis. *Sex Roles, 20*, 327–344. doi:10.1007/BF00287729

Beasley, B., & Collins Standley, T. (2002). Shirts vs. skins: Clothing as an indicator of gender role stereotypig in video games. *Mass Communication & Society, 5*, 279–293. doi:10.1207/S15327825MCS0503_3

Becker, K. (2001). Teaching with fames-the Minesweeper and Asteroids experience. *The Journal of Computing in Small Colleges, 17*(2), 22–32.

Brehmer, B., & Dorner, D. (1993). Experiments with computer-simulated microworlds: Escaping both the narrow straits of the laboratory and the deep blue sea of the field study. *Computers in Human Behavior, 9*(2-3), 171–184. doi:10.1016/0747-5632(93)90005-D

Bryce, J., & Rutter, J. (2002). *Killing like a girl: Gendered gaming and girl gamers' visibility.* Paper presented at the Computer Games and Digital Cultures, Tampere, Finland.

Buch, T., & Egenfeldt-Nielsen, S. (2006). *The learning effect of global conflicts: Palestine.* Paper presented at the Conference Proceedings Media@Terra, Athens.

Cherney, I. D., & London, K. (2006). Gender-linked differences in the toys, television shows, computer games, and outdoor activities of 5 to 13 year old children. *Sex Roles, 54*(9-10), 717. doi:10.1007/s11199-006-9037-8

Chou, C., & Tsai, M.-J. (2007). Gender differences in Taiwan high school students' computer game playing. *Computers in Human Behavior, 23*, 821–824. doi:10.1016/j.chb.2004.11.011

Egenfeldt-Nielsen, S. (2007). Third generation educational use of computer games. *Educational Multimedia and Hypermedia, 16*(3), 263–281.

Feldgen, M., & Clua, O. (2004). *Games as a motivation for freshman students to learn programming.* Paper presented at the 34th ASEE/IEEE Frontiers in Education Conference.

Feng, J., Spence, I., & Pratt, J. (2007). Playing an action video game reduces gender differences in spatial cognition. *Psychological Science, 18*(10), 850. doi:10.1111/j.1467-9280.2007.01990.x

Ferguson, C. J., Cruz, A. M., & Rueda, S. M. (2008). Gender, video game playing habits and visual memory tasks. *Sex Roles, 58*(3-4), 279–286. doi:10.1007/s11199-007-9332-z

Gander, S. (2002). Does learning occur through gaming. *Electronic Journal of Instructional Science and Technology, 3*(2).

Garris, R., Ahlers, R., & Driskell, J. E. (2002). Games, motivation, and learning: A research and practice model. *Simulation & Gaming, 33*(4), 441–467. doi:10.1177/1046878102238607

Gee, J. P. (2003). *What video games have to teach us about learning and literacy*. New York: Palgrave Macmillan.

Green, C. S., & Bavelier, D. (2003). Action video game modifies visual selective attention. *Nature, 423*, 534–537. doi:10.1038/nature01647

Hayes, J. R. (1981). *The computer problem solver*. Philadelphia: Franklin Institute Press.

Igbaria, M., & Chakrabarti, A. (1990). Computer anxiety and attitudes towards microcomputer use. *Behaviour & Information Technology, 9*, 229–241. doi:10.1080/01449299008924239

Kafai, Y. B. (1996). Electronic play worlds-gender differences in children's construction of video games. In Kafai, Y. B., & Resnick, M. (Eds.), *Constructionism in practice-designing, thinking, and learning in a digital world*. Mahwah, NJ: Lawrence Erlbaum Associates.

Kinzer, C. K., Sherwood, R., & Bransford, J. D. (1986). *Computer strategies for education: Foundations and content-area applications*. Merrill Publishing Company.

Lucas, K., & Sherry, J. L. (2004). Sex differences in video game play: A communication-based explanation. *Communication Research, 31*(5), 499–523. doi:10.1177/0093650204267930

Malone, T. W. (1981). Towards a theory of intrinsically motivating instruction. *Cognitive Science, 5*(4), 333–369. doi:10.1207/s15516709cog0504_2

Mayer, R. E., & Sims, V. K. (1994). For whom is a picture worth a thousand words? Extensions of a dual-coding theory of multimedia learning. *Journal of Educational Psychology, 86*(3), 389–401. doi:10.1037/0022-0663.86.3.389

McFarlane, A., Sparrowhawk, A., & Heald, Y. (2002). *Report on the educational use of games*. Cambridge.

McMullen, D. (1987). *Drills vs. games-any differences? A pilot study*. ERIC.

Morahan-Martin, J., Olinsky, A., & Schumacher, P. (1992). Gender differences in computer experience, skills, and attitudes among incoming college students. *Collegiate Microcomputer, 10*, 1–8.

O'Neil, H. F., Wainess, R., & Baker, E. L. (2005). Classification of learning outcomes: Evidence from the computer games literature. *Curriculum Journal, 16*(4), 455–474. doi:10.1080/09585170500384529

Papert, S. (1980). *Mindstorms: Children, computers, and powerful ideas*. Sussex, UK: The Harvester Press Limited.

Pillay, H., Brown, J., & Wilss, L. (1999). Cognition and recreational computer games: Implications for education technology. *Journal of Research on Computing in Education, 32*(1), 203–216.

Quaiser-Pohl, C., Geiser, C., & Lehmann, W. (2006). The relationship between computer-game preference, gender and mental-rotation ability. *Personality and Individual Differences, 40*, 609–619. doi:10.1016/j.paid.2005.07.015

Quinn, C. N. (1996). Designing an instructional game: Reflections on quest for independence. *Education and Information Technologies, 1*, 251–269. doi:10.1007/BF02350662

Ricci, K., Salas, E., & Cannon-Bowers, J. A. (1996). Do computer-based games facilitate knowledge acquisition and retention? *Military Psychology*, *8*(4), 294–307. doi:10.1207/s15327876mp0804_3

Rosen, L., & Maguire, P. (1990). Myths and realities of computerphobia: A meta-analysis. *Anxiety Research*, *3*, 167–179.

Schumacher, P., & Morahan-Martin, J. (2001). Gender, Internet and computer attitudes and experiences. *Computers in Human Behavior*, *17*, 95–110. doi:10.1016/S0747-5632(00)00032-7

Simon, H. A. (1996). *Observations on the sciences of science learning*. Paper presented at the Committee on Developments in the Science of Learning for the Sciences of Science Learning: An Interdisciplinary Discussion, Carnegie Mellon University, Department of Psychology.

Soukup, C. (2007). Mastering the game: Gender and the Entelechial motivational system of video game. *Women's*. *Studies in Communications*, *30*(2), 157–178.

Takayoshi, P. (2007). Gender matters: Literacy, learning, and gaming in one American family. In Selfe, C. L., & Hawisher, G. E. (Eds.), *Gaming lives in the twenty-first century-literate connections* (pp. 229–249). Hampshire, UK: Palgrave Macmillan.

Terlecki, M. S., & Newcombe, N. S. (2005). How important is the digital divide? The relation of computer and videogame usage to gender differences in mental rotation ability. *Sex Roles*, *53*, 433–441. doi:10.1007/s11199-005-6765-0

Weil, M., & Rosen, L. (1995). The psychological impact of technology from a global perspective: A study of technological sophistication and technophobia. *Computers in Human Behavior*, *11*, 95–133. doi:10.1016/0747-5632(94)00026-E

Weil, M., & Rosen, L. (1997). *Technostress: Coping with technology @ work, @ home, @ play*. NY: Wiley.

Whitehall, B., & McDonald, B. (1993). Improving learning persistence of military personnel by enhancing motivation in a technical training program. *Simulation & Gaming*, *24*, 294–313. doi:10.1177/1046878193243002

Wiebe, J. H., & Martin, N. J. (1994). The impact of a computer-based adventure game on achievement and attitudes in geography. *Journal of Computing in Childhood Education*, *5*, 61–71.

Wilson, B. C. (2002). A study of factors promoting success in computer science including gender differences. *Computer Science Education*, *12*(1-2), 141–164. doi:10.1076/csed.12.1.141.8211

Wood, L. E., & Stewart, R. W. (1987). Improvement of practical reasoning skills with computer skills. *Journal of Computer-Based Instruction*, *14*(2), 49–53.

Chapter 27
Designing Games to Motivate Student Cohorts through Targeted Game Genre Selection

Penny de Byl
Bond University, Australia

Jeffrey E. Brand
Bond University, Australia

ABSTRACT

The objective of this chapter is to develop guidelines for targeted use of games in educational settings by presenting a typology of learning styles, motivations, game genres, and learning outcomes within disciplinary student cohorts. By identifying which academic outcomes best align with the motivations and learning styles of students and which game genres are best suited to those motivations and outcomes, the authors elucidate a typology to assist serious game designers' and educators' pursuits of games that both engage and instruct. The result will guide the implementation of games in the classroom by linking game genre and game mechanics with learning objectives, and therefore enhance learning and maximise education outcomes through targeted activity.

GAMES AS MOTIVATORS

The notion of using games as motivators to facilitate learning is a key driver for the design of *Serious Games,* as computer games inherently motivate players to meet their objectives (Malone, 1981; Malone & Lepper, 1987; Tychsen, Hitchens et al., 2008). Research has shown that the use of games in the classroom improves student motivation (Baltra, 1990; Gee, 2007) and participation

(McGonigal, 2007; Rigby & Prysbylski, 2009; Werner, Hanks et al., 2004). Moreover, different game genres (Wolf & Baer, 2002) have been found to be effective for different types of learning (Garris, Ahlers et al., 2002) and may work for different personality types (Rapeepisarn, Wong et al., 2008).

Despite the evidence that learning styles, motivation, personality and game genre are diverse, *Serious Games* tend to be used in the classroom with a one-size fits all approach. This is understandable because games development is

DOI: 10.4018/978-1-60960-495-0.ch027

expensive and resource-intensive to develop. As such, creating different games for a single type of player to meet the needs of all learning styles would be an unsustainable commercial model. A more targeted approach would be to consider the learning styles of a particular student cohort based on field of study and assessment types and develop and select games which are most effective in meeting their learning objectives. For example, engineering students likely have a common learning style (c.f., Feldman, 1974) in which the average differs from that of media students; law students must learn laws and policies which require memorization and questioning learning activities as opposed to psychology students who learn about behavior through interviews, coaching and practice.

LEARNING ACTIVITIES AND LINKS TO GAME MECHANICS

Differing experiential learning methods are applied across different professions and academic disciplines in higher education. From empirical evidence, Kolb and others (Kolb, 1981; Honey & Mumford, 1982; Kolb & Kolb, 2005) have discovered that broadly speaking:

- practitioners of creative disciplines, such as the arts, have a "try it and see" attitude towards learning and prefer to innovatively experiment to see how and if things work;

- pure scientists and mathematicians are best at processing abstract ideas and prefer problem-solving activities;
- applied scientists prefer to use a scientific approach to solve practical problems while lawyers respect scientific evidence; and
- professionals who have to operate more intuitively, such as teachers, prefer learning situations in which they are required to take risks and partake in new experiences.

In addition, Prensky (Prensky, 2005) recognises the need to deliver educational content and assessment with differing game genres and mechanics because different types of content and learning require different pedagogical approaches. Some examples are given in Table 1.

This chapter is designed to better connect the heretofore disjointed dots from literature on learning through games, motivation, educational activities, and personality psychology. It begins by examining learning style and how it affects the suitability of learning activities across disciplines. Following this, personality types across the student cohort will be investigated as this too has been linked with learning style, discipline and game genre choice and links learning and motivation in a critical relationship that also focuses attention on learning objects and learning environments, such as games. Next, the concept of motivation is discussed with respect to the most effective ways to stimulate disciplinary specific student cohorts to engage with their educational content. Motivation will also be explored with respect to

Table 1. Educational content associated learning activities and games. Extracted from Prensky (2005)

Content	Examples	Learning Activities	Games
Facts	Laws, procedures, product specifications, policies, chemical elements	Questions, practice and drill, memorisation	Flash cards, Detective Games
Language	Acronyms, foreign languages	Imitation, immersion, practice	Role playing Games, Flash cards, Simulation Games
Creativity	Invention, product design	play	Puzzles, Invention Games

learning styles and personality traits. These will be used later in the chapter to match suitable game mechanics to study domains. After this, an elucidation of game genre and mechanics will be provided to explain the learning opportunities available in action games, adventure games, strategy games and process-orientated games. Finally, a typology will be presented which provides clear guidelines for matching disciplinary student groups with the most appropriate types of games for delivering educational content relevant to their vocation.

LEARNING STYLES

Learning style refers to the way a student processes information. They are often referenced with respect to how different learning and teaching approaches motivate different students. One of the most frequently cited models based on Experiential Learning Theory (ELT) is Kolb's (1981) research on learning styles and Kolb and Kolb's (2005) Learning Style Inventory (LSI). The inventory has evolved since it was introduced in the early 1970s, based on repeated trials with different large samples drawn from a wide range of different populations.

Another and related model of four learning styles provides a simplified structure to understand learners' approaches to acquiring and using new information (Busato, Prins et al., 2000) and these are predictably covariate with personality traits. The first learning style is *undirected* in which learners struggle to process study information, manage the volume of information and fail to prioritise important information and filter out unimportant information. *Reproduction directed* students are instrumentalists who reproduce content to pass examinations. *Application directed* students attempt to apply new information to real-world settings and their own experiences. The last learning style is *meaning directed* in which students seek to analyse new information to form their own view

and definitions or applications while allowing for critical rejection of some or all of the information they are given. In this section we posit the ways in which different learners, perhaps in different discipline cohorts (Brauer & Delemeester, 2001) likely learn from computer games generally and we base this analysis on Kolb and Kolb (2005) who note, "...previous research with the LSI shows that student learning style distributions differ significantly by academic fields, as predicted by ELT," (p. 26).

The Learning Style Inventory

The LSI examines strengths and weaknesses of a learner based on experiential learning theory. Experiential learning is considered a four-stage cycle for (1) immediate concrete experience; (2) observation and reflection; (3) formation of abstract concepts and generalisations; and (4) testing hypotheses to create new experiences. Thus, the effective learner possesses four different learning modes: Concrete Experience (CE), Reflective Observation (RO), Abstract Conceptualization (AC), and Active Experimentation (AE). This means, they must be able to involve themselves fully, openly, and without prejudice in novel experiences (CE), reflect on and notice these experiences from multiple perspectives (RO), create concepts that link observations with logically sound ideas (AC), and use these ideas in decision making and problem solving (AE). The extent to which a student engages with these learning modes determines their learning styles; *Diverger*, *Assimilator*, *Converger* or *Accomodator*. For each style, researchers Honey and Mumford (1982) recommend different teaching methods that best suit these classifications.

Divergers

Divergers are reflective learners. They learn best by listening and sharing ideas. They are imaginative and insightful thinkers. The strengths of these students include innovative and creative work, perceptive thinking, ability to function in a team environment as well as alone and the ability to analyse problems from different perspectives. Recommended careers for divergers mostly focus on working with people in occupations such as teachers, counselors or public relations.

These students learn best in situations when they can observe others at work and review conditions of that work. Accordingly, comparative analysis and other types of reports are the preferred types of assignment. However, these reflective learners do not respond well to tight deadlines, role-playing and being thrown in at the deep end.

Assimilators

Assimilators are theorists. As learners, they excel at processing abstract ideas such as those presented in mathematics and the sciences. They prefer to think through ideas and to solve problems rationally with sequential thinking and detailed information. These types fit well in occupations involving natural science, mathematics and research.

Theorists benefit the most from teaching and learning exercises when they are put in situations that require them to use their knowledge and skills to solve complex problems. They prefer structured instruction which can be linked to their specific interests and learning objectives. In addition, these types of learners excel at discovering the reasoning behind ideas. They like to know how things work. Less popular with these types of students are emotional situations, unstructured lessons, incomplete information and being asked to complete a task without knowing the *whole picture*.

Convergers

Convergers are pragmatists. They learn through testing theories and applying common sense to real world problems. They have a practical approach to problem solving and prefer to use scientific

evidence and facts. They dislike imprecision or extravagance. Occupations that would suit them include engineering, surveying and applied sciences.

Pragmatists prefer learning about topics, that help them achieve their goals. They do not shy away from role-playing and possess a need to learn through mimicking either role models or the work of others. They are less interested in learning about things that they cannot see have an immediate benefit to themselves personally and have no previously devised set of guidelines.

Accommodators

Accommodators are activists in that they learn by doing, through the experimentation of trial and error. They excel at taking risks, being flexible and self-discovery. They are energetic and good at engaging and motivating others. Accommodators are highly suited for careers in marketing, sales, education and professions involving the community.

These activists' paramount learning experiences lie in being involved in new experiences, problem-solving and experiential opportunities. They particularly enjoy working with others and being faced with difficult tasks. These types of learners prefer to be leading discussions in class and directing other students in problem solving tasks. To best accommodate these types, lectures, long reading and writing exercises and precise instructive tasks should be avoided.

Learning Styles and Academic Discipline Relationships

There have been many studies performed within educational institutions to determine if learning styles differ among academic discipline (Biglan, 1973; Feldman, 1974; Kolb & Kolb, 2005; Vermunt, 2005; Lindblom-Ylanne, Trigwell et al., 2006). Significant variation has been found as shown in Figure 1. For example, Business stu-

Figure 1. Learning style differences among academic disciplines adapted from Biglan 1973, Feldman 1974, Kolb 1981 and de Byl 2010

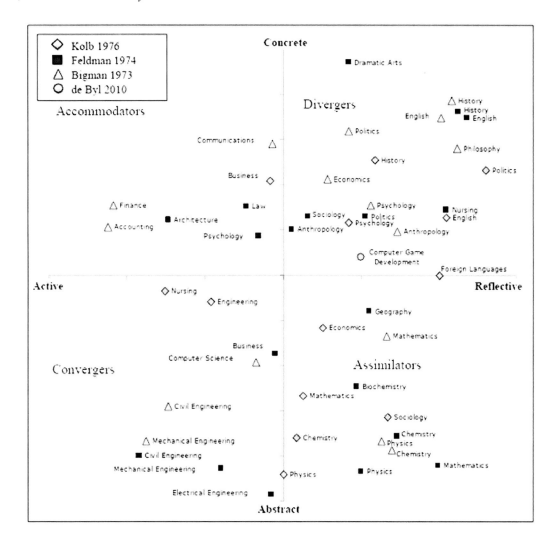

dents were observed by Feldman (1974) and Kolb (1976) at different ends of the Abstract-Concrete dimension of learning with Feldman observing them as more Concrete learners and Kolb finding Business students tending toward Abstract learners. However, Feldman (1974) and Kolb (1976) observed business students at the same position on the Active-Reflective dimension of learning with both observing them to balance Reflective and Active. This suggests that more variables need to be considered to understanding of how different people learn. For example, at the individual level, personality factors are implicit in the four studies represented in Figure 1. At a broader level divergent outcomes in these studies are explained by definitions of disciplines which vary among educational institutions and discipline boundaries where some fields may naturally represent a more diverse range of knowledge domains (for example, Business compared with Chemistry).

This information is being used by many educators to design curriculum and teaching activities which best fit their students' learning styles to enhance academic performance. Rather than a one size fits all approach or a customised and personalised approach through use of analysis of student cohorts within disciplines, educators can better spend their time developing and delivering targeted teaching and learning activities which best suit their students needs.

Educational Implications for Learning Styles and Motivating Students with Games

In recent years Serious Games have become more accepted in the classroom. The initial assumption being that because students find games engaging, an educational game should be an effective way of learning. Serious Games, however, deliver interaction and educational content in many and varied ways (as discussed later in the chapter). Of course, the game format might not suit all students. In addition, different types of learning content are better delivered with certain game mechanics than others. For example, Prensky (2005) suggests facts learned through questioning, memorisation and drilling are best delivered in game show competitions and flashcard type games. Furthermore, the player's interaction and experience with a game environment differs according to their learning style (Chong, Wong et al. 2005). For example, Chong et al. found Convergers to dislike playing *Counter Strike* while Accommodators enjoyed it and Assimilators did not like puzzle games while Convergers thrived on them.

Educators who consider the learning styles of their students may implement more effective teaching methodologies which are more student-centred than traditional methods. These different approaches to learning naturally are likely to depend too on personality differences which also relate to individual learning styles. A relationship among these factors may allow serious game designers to predict the way learners react and feel in different gaming situations.

PERSONALITY FACTORS

Personality is thought to underpin much of the cognitive functioning of learners (Busato, Prins et al. 2000). The most universally demonstrated and simplistic structure for personality traits is widely described as "the Big Five" validated by Goldberg (Goldberg, 1990). Also known as the five-factor approach (FFA), these five factors are orthogonal to one another, meaning that each one is a continuum of low to high for every individual. The five factors are *openness, conscientiousness, extraversion, agreeableness*, and *neuroticism*. The first three are most commonly associated with learning motivation (Busato, Prins et al., 2000) and neuroticism being least associated with generalised learning motivations.

Importantly, these five factors are associated in different ways when compared with other social phenomena and not all parallel particular learning styles. A number of researchers have linked personality factors with learning styles (Kolb, 1981; Busato, Prins et al., 2000), motivation and achievement (Goldberg, 1990), and performance (Garris, Ahlers et al. 2002; Hu, 2004). Thus personality factors may link learning and motivation in a critical, but complex, relationship that also focuses attention on learning objects and learning environments, such as games and their many genres.

Openness

Having a higher level (or measured score) on openness has been related to being curious, imaginative, autonomous, and unconventional. At the level of face validity, an open personality would be naturally pre-disposed to the diverse worlds of computer games and particularly those that have a more exploratory and open objective structure. Learning in such an environment would be guided by those environments that present a sense of mystery and allow for free-form exploration. Busato et al. (1999) found that openness correlated positively with meaning and application directed learning styles and related these to Honey and Mumford's (1982) learning styles of activists and pragmatists and Kolb's (1981) corresponding learning styles accommodators and Convergers.

Conscientiousness

People who score highly on conscientiousness are associated with being dependable, having self-discipline, being planners, holding a sense of duty, and being achievement-oriented. For conscientious learner-players, games that are "on rails" and present the player with clear and defined achievement objectives would be best suited. Moreover, games with frequent reward schedules and competitive scoring ladders would likely appeal. Conscientious personality traits correlate positively with meaning, reproduction and application directed learning style according to Busato et al. (1999) and therefore Kolb's (1981) Accommodator.

Extraversion

High scorers on the extraversion personality dimension tend to be sociable, demonstrate positive attitudes and enthusiasm and are willing to assert their interests in the presence of others. Therefore, multiplayer, competitive and cooperative games would presumably be most effective in contributing to learning outcomes and motivation. Busato et al. (1999) found that extraversion correlated positively with meaning directed, reproduction directed and application directed learning styles on a par with Converger and Accommodators, but noted that it correlated negatively with the Reflector/Diverger learning style.

Agreeableness

Agreeableness is related to trusting others, being cooperative, even acquiescent, gentle and nurturing. As gamers, agreeable learners are likely to enjoy role-playing games, cooperative play and non-combat simulations. Busato et al. (1999) reported positive correlations between agreeableness and reproduction and application directed learning styles and the accommodator/activist learning style.

Neuroticism

Those who score high on the dimension of neuroticism tend to display negative affects such as hostility and anxiety and are least likely to adjust easily to wide-ranging situations. Although neuroticism can be seen as a pejorative and maladaptive personality trait, one expects that games offering routine problem-solving, reality-based simulations and puzzles would appeal to such personalities. Neuroticism correlates negatively with Assimilator and Accommodator learning styles and positively with Diverger/Reflector learning styles (Busato et al., 1999).

The literature provides sufficient evidence of a non-linear relationship between learning style and personality trait. Indeed, Busato et al., (1999) have suggested only modest utility from measuring both learning style and personality trait. However, for the purposes of this typology, we suggest retaining the Big Five personality traits for explanatory and heuristic value in better understanding how to design serious games for different learners. Moreover, because learning style fails to account for all the variance observed in personality trait measures, we understand that designers will likely be able to predict game success by considering the multiple dimensions of their student audience. Game developers already identify player types in relation to game objectives (Bartle, 2005). However, research is needed particularly in the context of serious games to test different ludic dimensions (c.f., Aarseth, Smedstad & Sunnana, 2003) of games (including objectives) with personality types identified by Goldberg (1990) and may need to include motivations for learning.

MOTIVATIONS

Encouraging student motivation is an age old challenge for educators. While most students are inherently eager to learn many others require external stimulation from their teachers. The reaction to Prensky's "Digital Natives" description (Prensky 2000) has seen many educators challenge traditional teaching methods and has them scrambling to design, develop and integrate the latest technologies into the classroom in unconventional ways. Because students today demand more from their educational experiences than flat pages of content, noninteractive videos and text based communication software, materials deemed acceptable in the past now fail to engage students who are more attuned to the high quality 3D entertainment software such as computer games.

Although many educators and game developers have assumed computer games to be motivational for learning and teaching, because in general many students spend a lot of time playing computers games, this in itself does not guarantee games will produce the same level of motivation and engagement in the classroom. Studies have found that some individuals do not necessarily find educational games to be motivational even within the key demographic of game players (Whitton, 2007). This may be due to poor design or more importantly because the game genre and mechanics don't *speak* to the player.

Many factors influence individual student motivation. These include an interest in the subject matter, perception of topic relevance, a desire to perform well, patience and persistence. Furthermore students are motivated by a variety of diverse values, needs and desires. Fortunately, research has revealed correlations between motivational factors and learning styles across disciplines.

According to Shih and Gamon (2001), motivation is related to a student's learning style and influences their engagement, cognitive processing habits and metacognitive skills. Kellar, Watters et al. (2005) suggest a framework of positive and negative motivational factors in educational situations which includes:

- **Control:** the level of a student's autonomy within an environment which allows for interaction, innovation, personalization and decision making;
- **Context:** the relevance, completeness and believability of feedback and storylines,
- **Competency:** the provision and attainability of appropriate tasks and problem solving challenges; and,
- **Engagement:** the level of immersion within an activity given social interactions, methods of communication and rewards.

These factors when cross referenced with the pedagogical approaches given by Honey and

Table 2. Suggested pedagogical approaches for motivating students based on learning style

	Divergers	**Assimilators**	**Convergers**	**Accommodators**
Control	High level of control over environment to personalise and innovate.	Highly pre-defined and structured lessons.	High control over manipulation of environment in order to test hypotheses	Require an environment where they can trial ideas and learn from mistakes
Context	Observation and Reviewing of Others	Require holistic view of learning situation (e.g. all the facts). Abstract problems	Relevant real world problems	New opportunities, highly challenging tasks
Competency	Approaching problem-solving from multiple perspectives.	Solving problems requiring sequential thinking.	Mimicking	Risk-taking, Flexible
Engagement	Team environments.	Rational situations, working alone	Role-playing with others.	Engaging with and leading others

Mumford 1982 for each of Kolb's four learning styles produces the matrix of appropriate motivating pedagogical approaches for differing student cohorts shown in Table 2.

Computer games inherently address each of these factors. The degree to which they achieve these for an individual influences the learner's motivation to continue playing the game. Rather than considering how motivated a particular student group is towards their chosen areas of expertise, we should investigate what it is about the individual disciplines, their educational content and the way they are taught which produce this motivation. Moreover, research is necessary to better understand how games within particular genres can be designed to meet a wide range of motivations.

Mass entertainment games have large audiences because they match a wide range of motivators. The challenge for serious games is to embody a range of motivators that address all people from a disciple. Only then can we design targeted serious games which address student's learning needs.

GAME GENRE

Rapeepisarn et al (2008) argue that genres within educational computer games may present an important set of considerations for game designers. Early work in this area began in earnest by Papert in his work on *Mindstorms* (Papert, 1980) in which he considered children's developmental stages and therefore different processing routes for learning. He wrote,

... the computer can concretize (and personalize) the formal... it is not just another powerful educational tool. It is unique in providing us with the means for addressing ... the obstacle which is overcome in the passage from child to adult thinking. ... it can allow us to shift the boundary separating concrete and formal. Knowledge that was accessible only through formal processes can now be approached concretely. And the real magic comes from the fact that this knowledge includes those elements one needs to become a formal thinker. (p. 21).

Indeed, the intersection of learning styles, personality factors and motivations may well be concretised in player attachments to particular game genres. Although many observers value the utility of categorizing games (and other media) by genre, agreement on genres for games has not been easy. Wolf (2002) was among the first to give the matter detailed academic attention and he observed, "The idea of genres has not been without difficulties, such as defining what exactly constitutes a genre, overlaps between genres, and the fact that genres are always in flux..." (p. 113). The interactive nature of games has added a layer of complexity on top of the common elements that have characterized mainstream commercial cinema including formal features, story structure and theme. As genre is meant to provide a simple structure, the intersection between traditional genre elements and interactivity has made the formulation of genres for games more complex. Wolf, for example, concluded with 42 genre labels, one of which was *educational*. Wolf acknowledged the limitations of this unwieldy list observing that not all his labels represented mutually exclusive outcomes and noting that among the labels were applications that were not, strictly speaking, games. Yet Wolf's contribution borrowed from and has contributed to the commercial industrial labels often associated with game publishers' labels and those used by games reviews and journalism.

Subsequent research has refined and simplified the list of genres for game. Parsimony is essential in applying game genres to learning from games, particularly when cross tabulating these with other factors such as learning style, personality and motivation.

A simplified system of four genres based on a game's criteria for success such as that proposed

Table 3. Game genres, actions and success. Adapted from Egenfeldt-Nielsen et al. (2008)

	Action games	**Adventure games**	**Strategy games**	**Process-oriented games**
Typical action (interactivity)	Battle	Solving mystery	Build nation in competition with others	Exploration and/or mastery
Criterion of success	Fast reflexes	Logic ability	Analysing interdependent variables	Varies widely, often non-existent
Sub-genres	FPS, Combat, Race, Rhythm	Platformer, Flyers, Puzzle, Quiz	RTS, Gambling, Board, Card,	Sims, RPG, MMORPG
Archetypal titles	*Counter-Srike*	*Myst*	*Civilization*	*Sim-City*

by Egenfeldt-Nielsen, et al. (2008) fits well in the context of games for learning in which action, thinking and systemic understanding are clear goals aligned with learning styles. After we consider these four over-arching genres, we will then further align them with commonly understood genres along the lines of Wolf (2002) and commercial game publishing.

The criterion for a *success model* proposed by Egenfeldt-Nielsen at al. (2008) embeds within it Wolf's observation that games add to traditional media of cinema and television the element of interactivity. Thus, in addition to identifying a criterion for success, the model also accounts for the "typical action" a player performs in order to achieve success. For simplicity, we will focus on one discipline, health science, to demonstrate.

Action

The first of the four genres is *action games* in which "motor skill and hand-eye coordination" are essential in order to achieve success which is determined by the criterion of employing fast reflexes. Thus, for laparoscopic surgeons, superior motor skill and shorter surgical times have been linked with playing action games (Rosser, Lynch et al. 2007).

Adventure

Adventure games require "deep thinking and great patience," often found in solving mysteries or complex puzzles (c.f., Egenfeldt-Nielsen et al., 2008). The application of logic and clear thinking determines how a player succeeds in adventure games. Keeping with the theme of educating medical students, general practice is a panoptic field requiring investigation-based evaluation of patient presentations. An adventure inside the blood stream looking for pathogens attacking healthy cells would be consistent with this genre.

Strategy

Strategy games typically engage players in building nations or empires. They succeed at this by managing "large numbers of interdependent variables" and balancing a range of competing priorities. In medicine, the management of large patient caseloads, particularly in hospital wards might be well suited. Rather than seeking to train surgeons or oncologists, strategy games might be ideally suited to training hospital administrators and managers.

Process-Oriented

Finally *process-oriented games* centre on exploration of vast environments and even mastery of a detailed environment. By offering the player "a system to play with" growing skill and understanding, indeed mastering the complexities of the system or interface, is the criterion for success. In the early stages of medical education, a process-oriented game would suit anatomy, developing knowledge of complex organs and coming to understand the inter-relationships among different systems. Table 3 shows the relationship between the four-genre structure and interactivity and success.

Kolb's (1981) learning styles focus on process (activity) and outcomes (success). Egenfeldt-Nielsen et al.'s (2008) genre classes, based on activity and outcomes provides a symmetrical heuristic with which to begin understanding the place of serious games in learning.

PUTTING IT ALL TOGETHER

Learning styles, personality factors, motivations and game genres are four fundamental elements that we propose make up a model for informed educational game design. In much the same way as commercial entertainment game designers target specific audiences with their products, serious game designers are able to use a relatively simple and yet highly predictive model by which to target student cohorts, particularly within disciplines, by matching game genres to learning styles, personality factors and motivations underlying specific learning objectives. For example, Nursing students might have an Active/Concrete (CE/AE) Converger learning style. When they need to learn mathematics for nursing the type of game most appropriate (e.g. role playing/hospital simulation as opposed to other forms of learning mathematics (for example by rote). Concretely, time trials might work well with nursing where a drug dose has to be delivered within a timeframe ... for 12 patients at once!... but would work very poorly in a job that requires meticulous problem solving such as Human Resource Management in which puzzles might better suit. Thus, we are differentiating game play factors from game genres. Meanwhile, a deeply narrative game might be better for ethics training than time-management training because stories may be needed to express

dilemmas, present context and consequences of actions along a story arc.

Student Gaming Motivations Matrix

Table 4 includes a summary of the information presented in this chapter matching learning style, disciplines, personality and learning motivators with suitable game genres. The variables considered in this chapter, summarized in Table 4 represent orthogonal combinations that require further investigation. Indeed, each combination deserves more detailed treatment than we present here. Borrowing from cognitive psychology and using this matrix as a heuristic, further research will likely produce better understanding for both educators and developers.

For example, cognitive psychology refers to a strategy for information recoding in short-term memory as chunking. Chase and Simon (1973) extended the use of the concept to indicate units of perception and meaning as long-term memory structures. In general, the term chunking has come to be understood as a learning mechanism. Miller (1956) found that people can hold $7 +/- 2$ chunks of knowledge in their minds at any given time. If the chunks simply contain unrelated facts, the knowledge obtained is restricted compared to chunks of interconnected facts. Domain experts chunk information to find meaningful patterns within a problem space. This concept is recognized across multiple areas of expertise (DeGroot, 1965; Egan & Schwartz, 1979; Lesgold, 1988).

Learning researchers are increasingly making the same distinction in teaching and learning environments. Where rote memorisation techniques deliver disconnected chunks, chunks connected and organized around a concept provide a deeper level of understanding and the potential to transfer to other knowledge areas (Bransford et al., 2009).

This notion is at the very heart of the effective use of computer games for education. Games have the potential to provide learning in a meaningful context in which players learn to recognise inter-

Table 4. Guideline for development of serious games for specific learning styles(*Honey and Mumford 1982)

Learning Styles	Disciplines	Personality	Learning Motivators	Game Genres
Divergers (Reflectors)*	Dramatic Arts, History, English, Philosophy, Politics, Communications, Economics, Psychology, Anthropology, Computer Games Development	High Neuroticism	Observational Situations, Time for Contemplation, Thinking things through before acting, Detailed Researching and Analysis, No strict deadlines, Can freely exchange opinions without threat of backlash.	Strategy games (featuring world-building real-time strategy-not too pressured)
Assimilators (Theorists)*	Geography, Economics, Mathematics, Biochemistry, Chemistry, Physics	Low Neuroticism High Extraversion	Can understand educational content in the context of a larger system: • Methodical exploration • Hypothesising and Testing • Intellectually Challenging • Highly Structured • Extra-curriculum knowledge	Adventure games (platformers, puzzles, quizzes that reward trial and error)
Convergers (Pragmatists)*	Nursing, Engineering, Computer Science	High Openness, High Extraversion	Relevant links with real world issues, problems and their own lives. Techniques with practical advantages, Apprenticeships and/or on the job training, Imitation, Immediate implementation, Getting on with the job	Process-oriented games (featuring life simulation, role-playing and online social environments)
Accomodators (Activists)*	Business, Finance, Architecture, Accounting, Law	High Openness, High Conscientiousness, High Extraversion, High Agreeableness	Challenges, Relevant competitive teamwork, Variety and excitement, Leadership and high visibility tasks, Brainstorming sessions, Entrepreneur	Action games (tapping into on-rail and achievement oriented score ladders)

related chunks of information in realistic situations and problem spaces. Indeed, the premise of this chapter supports the many studies that have concluded that experiential learning is a fundamental human process (Kolb, 1984).

The divergence of game genre between disciplines is a product of differing learning styles that correlate with personality and career/study choice of individuals. The goal of all games is to teach the player. The chunks within the game are identified by the player and thus 'speak' to their preferred way of learning. In addition, these chunks must be presented as interrelated facts and delivered through the appropriate game mechanics. For example, Divergers learn best through observation and analysis of underlying cause and effect;

strategy games deliver a game mechanic which best fits this requirement. Furthermore, Divergers better assimilate knowledge when it is presented as interconnected material related to the bigger picture, rather than unrelated chunks which are perceived as merely information. In contrast, the more extraverted learning styles prefer to control what knowledge chunks contain and determine how they are related.

To this end, Table 4, identifies how learning styles could be best matched in terms of game-genre and game mechanics.

The classification of motivators in Table 4 also relates directly to the game genre and thus game mechanics. Motivation during game play is linked to Flow Theory (Csikszentmihalyi, 1975) which describes how the game challenge at hand must not be too difficult or too easy to keep the player interested. For a student to attain flow in a learning activity a balance between external complexity and the internal mental model of the learner must be found. This internal mental model is a direct result of how the game chunks the content and presents it to the player. As such, game genre and game mechanics are most relevant in delivering game content to achieve flow for different learning styles whether it be for an individual or an entire student cohort within a discipline.

In developing this overview, we also understand that students are presented with a wide diversity of teaching and learning activities at tertiary institutions which may require the use of a variety of game genres to best deliver content. As such, the typology presented here relates to the fundamental learning activities and professional situations encountered by differing student cohorts. For example, although nurses are required to learn mathematics (the domain of the Assimilator), their principle assignment is in dealing with and managing people. Having said this, it is also worth considering that subjects which are cross-disciplinary require different teaching approaches across student cohorts and appropriate games and pedagogy needs to match learning styles. For example, a practical role-playing based game in which students measure and administer medicines for learning mathematics would be more suitable than mathematical puzzles for nurses.

SOME FINAL WORDS

Educators who integrate knowledge about their students' learning styles with their use of computer games in the classroom can greatly improve student motivation in the use and educational effectiveness of the games. Narrowing the focus of which games are the most appropriate further assists teachers in creating a more student-centred classroom.

The first stage in implementing learning style-based serious games is in understanding disciplinary characteristics by either conducting the LSI questionnaire in class or referring to previous studies. Following this it is necessary to understand the nature of the learning objectives with the discipline in order to select and/or develop an effective and motivational game. Finally, educators should assess their current instructional methods and evaluate them against recommendations from learning style literature to develop and adapt them to conform.

This chapter has identified the need for both empirical and conceptual clarity on the most effective way to use games to teach to ensure maximised learning outcomes. The scope and focus of contributes to the understanding of *Serious Games* by clarifying and adding precision to the acceptance of particular games for motivating particular student cohorts. This chapter also provides best practice advice to developers to assist them in creating maximally motivating games. Our intention has been to provide concrete examples that serve as take-away guidance for developers and educators alike. The authors bring backgrounds to the book from software engineering education and social psychology education and understand the need to communicate clearly to the target audience of practitioners, researchers and educators in a diverse range of fields.

The pedagogical reasons for deploying computer game-based learning is that they have the potential to act as experiential, problem-based and collaborative environments which include characteristics of constructivist learning opportunities. However, it should not be assumed that games always motivate because learning style and personalities are diverse across disciplinary study areas and as such differing student cohorts are motivated and engaged through a variety of differing pedagogical activities.

Through the presentation of the typology herein, we suggest a targeted approach to the use of computer games in the classroom. If the games are to motivate the students then they must address the learning style and personality needs within different disciplines. Only then can we be sure we are using the correct match of effective teaching motivations and principles with student needs and not relying solely on the computer game as a new medium to inherently talk to learners.

REFERENCES

Aarseth, E., Smedstad, S. M., & Sunnana, L. (2003). A multi-dimensional typology of games. In M. Copier & J. Raessens (Eds.), *Proceedings of the First Annual Digital Games and Research Association Conference*, Utrecht, 4-6 November, (pp. 48-53).

Baltra, A. (1990). Language learning through computer adventure games. *Simulation & Gaming, 21*(4), 445–452. doi:10.1177/104687819002100408

Bartle, R. (2005). Virtual worlds: Why people play. In Alexander, T. (Ed.), *Massively multiplayer game development* (2nd ed., pp. 3–18). MA: Charles River Media.

Biglan, A. (1973). The characteristics of subject matter in different academic areas. *The Journal of Applied Psychology, 57*, 195–203. doi:10.1037/h0034701

Bransford, J. D., Sherwood, R. D., Hasselbring, T. S., Kinzer, C. K., & Williams, S. M. (1990). Anchored instruction: Why we need it and how technology can help. In Nix, D., & Spiro, R. J. (Eds.), *Cognition education, and multimedia: Exploring ideas in high technology* (pp. 115–141). Hillsdale, NJ: Lawrence Erlbaum Associates.

Brauer, J., & Delemeester, G. (2001). Games economists play: A survey of non-computerized classroom-games for college economics. *Economic Surveys, 15*, 221–236. doi:10.1111/1467-6419.00137

Busato, V., Prins, F. J., Elshout, J. J., & Hamaker, C. (2000). Intellectual ability, learning style, personality, achievement motivation and academic success of psychology students in higher education. *Personality and Individual Differences, 29*(6), 1057–1068. doi:10.1016/S0191-8869(99)00253-6

Chase, W. G., & Simon, H. A. (1973). Perception in chess. *Cognitive Psychology, 4*, 55–81. doi:10.1016/0010-0285(73)90004-2

Chong, Y., & Wong, M. (2005). *The impact of learning styles on the effectiveness of digital games in education*. Symposium on Information Technology in Education. Malaysia, KDU College, Patailing Java.

Csikszentmihalyi, M. (1975). Play and intrinsic rewards. *Journal of Humanistic Psychology, 15*, 41–63. doi:10.1177/002216787501500306

de Byl, P. (2010). The learning styles of computer game development students and implications for teaching style. *Game Education Review, 1*.

DeGroot, A. (1965). *Thought and choice in chess*. The Hague: Mouton.

Egan, D. E., & Schwartz, B. J. (1979). Chunking in recall of symbolic drawings. *Memory & Cognition, 7*, 149–158. doi:10.3758/BF03197595

Egenfeldt-Nielsen, S., Smith, J. H., & Tosca, S. P. (2008). *Understanding video games: The essential introduction*. New York: Tayor & Francis.

Feldman, S. (1974). *Escape from the doll's house*. New York: McGraw-Hill.

Garris, R., Ahlers, R., & Driskell, J. E. (2002). Games, motivation and learning: A research and practice model. *Simulation & Gaming, 33*(4), 441–467. doi:10.1177/1046878102238607

Gee, J.P. (2007). Learning and games. *Digital Media and Learning*, 21-40.

Goldberg, L. R. (1990). An alternative description of personality: The big-five factor structure. *Journal of Personality and Social Psychology, 59,* 1216–1229. doi:10.1037/0022-3514.59.6.1216

Honey, P., & Mumford, A. (1982). *Manual of learning styles*. London: P. Honey.

Hu, M. (2004). *The relationship between big five personality traits: Learning motivations and learning performance of the hospitality students in Taiwan.* Paper presented at the 10th Annual Asia Pacific Tourism Association (APTA) Conference, July 4-7 2004, Nagasaki, Japan.

Kellar, M., Watters, C., & Duffy, J. (2005). *Motivational factors in game play in two user groups. DIGRA 2005: Changing Views-Worlds in Play.* Authors & Digital Games Research Association.

Kolb, D. A. (1981). Learning styles and disciplinary differences. A.W. Chickering (Ed.), *The modern American college*. San Francisco: Jossey-Bass.

Kolb, D. A., & Kolb, A. Y. (2005). *The Kolb learning style inventory-version 3.1*. Case Western Reserve University, HayGroup.

Lesgold, A. (1988). Toward a theory of curriculum for use in designing intelligent instructional systems. In Mandl, H., & Lesgold, A. (Eds.), *Learning issues for intelligent tutoring systems* (pp. 114–137). New York: Springer-Verlag.

Lindblom-Ylanne, S., & Trigwell, K. (2006). How approaches to teaching are affected by discipline and teaching context. [Routledge.]. *Studies in Higher Education,* •••, 31.

Malone, T.W. (1981). Toward a theory of intrinsically motivating instruction. *Cognitive Science: A Multidisciplinary Journal, 5*(4), 333-369.

Malone, T. W., & Lepper, M. R. (1987). Making learning fun: A taxonomy of intrinsic motivations for learning. In Snow, R. E., & Farr, M. J. (Eds.), *Aptitude, learning and instruction: III. Conative and affective process analyses* (pp. 223–253). Hillsdale, NJ: Erlbaum.

McGonigal, J. (2007). Why I love bees: A case study in collective intelligence gaming. *Digital Media and Learning,* 199-227.

Miller, G. A. (1956). The magical number seven, plus or minus two: Some limits on our capacity for processing information. *Psychological Review, 63,* 81–97. doi:10.1037/h0043158

Papert, S. (1980). *Mindstorms: Children, computers and powerful ideas*. Cambridge: ACM.

Prensky, M. (2000). *Digital game-based learning*. McGraw-Hill Companies.

Prensky, M. (2005). Computer games and learning: Digital game-based learning. In Raessens, J., & Goldstein, J. (Eds.), *Handbook of computer game studies*. Cambridge, MA: MIT Press.

Rapeepisarn, K., Wong, K. W., Fung, C. C., & Khine, M. S. (2008). *The relationship between game genres, learning techniques and learning styles in educational computer games*. Technologies for E-Learning and Digital Entertainment, Third International Conference, Edutainment 2008, Nanjing, China, Springer-Verlag.

Rigby, C. S., & Prysbylski, A. K. (2009). Virtual worlds and the learner hero: How today's video games can inform tomorrow's digital learning environments. *Theory and Research in Education, 7*(2), 214–223. doi:10.1177/1477878509104326

Rosser, J. C. Jr, Lynch, P. J., Cuddihy, L., Gentile, G. A., Klonsky, J., & Merrell, R. (2007). The impact of video games on training surgeons in the 21st century. *Archives of Surgery, 142*(2), 181–186. doi:10.1001/archsurg.142.2.181

Shih, C., & Gamon, J. (2001). Web-based learning: Relationships among student motivation, attitude, learning styles and achievement. *Journal of Agricultural Education, 42*(4). doi:10.5032/jae.2001.04012

Tychsen, A., Hitchens, M., & Brolund, T. (2008). *Motivations for play in computer role-playing games. Future play: Research, play, share*. Toronto, Ontario.

Vermunt, J. D. (2005). Relations between student learning patterns and personal and contextual factors and academic performance. [Netherlands: Springer]. *Higher Education*, *49*, 205–234. doi:10.1007/s10734-004-6664-2

Werner, L., Hanks, B., & McDowell, C. (2004). Pair-programming helps female computer science students. *ACM Journal of Educational Resources in Computing*, *4*(1), 1–8.

Whitton, N. (2007). *Motivation and computer game based learning*. ASCILITE 2007. Singapore.

Wolf, M. J. P., & Baer, R. H. (2002). Genre and the video game. In *The medium of the video game* (pp. 114–134). Austin: University of Texas Press.

KEY TERMS AND DEFINITIONS

Game Mechanics: The fundamental rules that define the play, objective and challenge to which the player works in order to win; common mechanics include taking turns, random chance, capture and eliminate, bidding in an auction, racing the clock and so on.

Genre: Categories of different types within the same medium; computer games genres class games according to the actions and objectives set out for the player to reach a win our outcome such as action, adventure, strategy and role-playing games. Some games are characterized by the visual perspective of the player in relation to the character in the game, such as first-person shooter games.

Learning Activity: Exercises and experiences designed by teachers to facilitate learning; learning activities often match a learning style.

Learning Style: Different ways students processes information and thereby learn optimally; learning styles include concrete experience, reflective observation, abstract conceptualization and active experimentation.

Motivation: The initiation of behavior for achieving a goal, motivation can be achieved either from within the learner or from outside the learner by a stimulus such as a teacher or a game.

Participation: Involvement of a person in an activity either with others or in an experience designed by others.

Personality: The combination of characteristics that define the way the person thinks and behaves; it is believed that all people have every type of personality trait but that some have low levels and others high levels on each trait.

Serious Game: Serious games are games that serve a purpose beyond leisure; serious games are designed to be entertaining and to educate or demonstrate, persuade or communicate.

Chapter 28
Game–Based Learning:
Current Research in Games for Health, a Focus on Biofeedback Video Games as Treatment for AD/HD

Krestina L. Amon
The University of Sydney, Australia

Andrew J. Campbell
The University of Sydney, Australia

ABSTRACT

Sensor technology and its use in games control is a new area of video games development, and has demonstrated great application in the field of 'serious games' for edu-tainment and behaviour health. Attention-Deficit/Hyperactivity Disorder (AD/HD) is amongst one of the highest ranked mental health disorders in children and young adolescents. Children diagnosed with AD/HD frequently demonstrate a continuous pattern of inattention and/or hyperactivity-impulsivity, which are more frequent or serious than is typically observed in individuals of the same developmental level (APA, 2000).

This chapter outlines the rapid uptake of video games with new interface technology and how current research is providing evidence of the success of these modalities to influence academic abilities and remediate common attention problems, such as AD/HD. The authors pay special focus to their own leading research in biofeedback technology. With support from previous research on biofeedback technology, the findings from this study show that as a biofeedback system, The Journey to Wild Divine video game has the potential to produce positive changes for disruptive behaviours, with minimal side effects. It has shown the ability to teach children breathing and relaxation techniques, which helped reduce core symptoms in children with AD/HD aged between 5 and 15 years, and improve parental depression, anxiety, and stress levels.

DOI: 10.4018/978-1-60960-495-0.ch028

Whilst biofeedback video games are still new to AD/HD treatment options, this Chapter demonstrates that with children growing up in a technologically advanced world, it is not surprising that the prospect of learning relaxation skills to clear the mind, and calm anxiety or frustration, and receive treatment through a video game would increase a child's interest and cooperate with biofeedback treatment.

INTRODUCTION

Computer and video games provide players with a medium that engages and, in some instances, cognitively immerses them for certain periods of time. By balancing numerous game components including game narrative, character traits, obstacles and challenges, game rewards, competition and collaboration with other human gamers. Video games draw out powerful emotional reactions in their players. These emotions include wonder and elation, power, fear, aggression, and joy (Squire, n.d.). Research studies conducted on computer and video games are increasing in number. Malone (1981) and Bekhtina (2002, cited in Cole & Griffiths, 2007) suggests that the basic motivations for playing video games are curiosity and interest, mastery and control, challenge, cognitive stimulation, as well as indulgence in fantasy and enjoyment of attending to life in a virtual world.

More recently, research has investigated the different 'affective' avenues video games can manipulate. As an entertainment source, video games have been produced that guide the player to focus, relax, be challenged, and become immersed in another world. As an education tool, video games have been shown to teach a range of technical and cognitive skills in increasing perception and stimulation, problem solving, strategic thinking and assessment, organising and discovering answers (Subrahmanyam, Greenfield, Kraut, & Gross, 2001; Wan Rozali, Hamid, & Sabri, 2007). Over the years, video games have evolved from basic sources of entertainment into a completely new level of fun, socialising, and education using advanced technology – which are frequently referred to as, serious games.

Serious games are associated with games which aim to achieve something more than just entertainment. Game-based learning deals with applications with defined learning outcomes and include the teaching, training, and informing features of education (Susi, Johannesson, & Backlund; 2007). Serious games are "…about leveraging the power of computer games to captivate and engage end-users for a specific purpose, such as to develop new knowledge and skills" (Corti, 2006, p.1; cited in Susi, Johannesson, & Backlund; 2007).

This Chapter will focus on the serious games of health, with particular focus on biofeedback technology for AD/HD.

Serious Games in Health

Serious games have been noted to support the development of a number of different skills including strategic and planning skills, insight, analytical and spatial abilities, learning and recollection proficiency, psychomotor capabilities, group collaboration, communication, negotiation, and decision making skills (Mitchell & Savill-Smith, 2004; Squire & Jenkins, 2003; Susi, Johannesson, & Backlund, 2007).

Serious games in health can have both a direct and indirect positive physiological and psychological effect on individuals. Susi, Johannesson, & Backlund (2007) provide a number of examples related to physical and mental health topics that have been developed for games. They focus on a number of *Wii* sport games such as *Wii fitness,* and others like *Dance Dance Revolution* for physical fitness. Education video game range in topics from self-directed care such as the *Hungry Red Planet,* which teaches children nutrition and healthy eating habits; to games such as *S.M.A.R.T*

BrainGames that help improve attention and focus in children diagnosed with AD/HD. On the market there are other games to aid in distraction therapy, recovery and rehabilitation, training and simulation, cognitive functioning, and control. The serious games market is expanding rapidly and is estimated to branch into many areas of health and healthy development across cultures over the coming decade.

One particular area of rapid development in serious games is that of sensor technology. This technology involves reading the biological signals from the gamer, which will in turn influence the game play. One popular sensor technology is that of biofeedback. It is a training technique by which individuals are taught to gain conscious control over autonomic body functions (e.g. breathing, blood pressure, heart rate, etc) to improve health and performance, by using physiological signals from their bodies (M. Schwartz & Andrasik, 2003; Yates, 1980). Research utilising neurofeedback therapy (the harnessing and measurement of brain activity) has demonstrated positive outcomes for anxiety and affective disorders, as well as showing behavioural and cognitive improvements in children with learning disabilities (Fernández et al., 2007; Hammond, 2005). More specifically, recent studies (Butnik, 2005; Fox, Tharp, & Fox, 2005; Monastra et al., 2005) support former findings (Alhambra, Fowler, & Alhambra, 1995; Boyd & Campbell, 1998; Rossiter & LaVaque, 1995) that neurofeedback, as one form of biofeedback, continue to report noticeable improvements of AD/HD symptoms, cognitive performance and behaviour.

Attention-Deficit/Hyperactivity Disorder (AD/HD)

Reported to be a developmental disorder, AD/HD is prevalent in young children. With a prevalence rate of 7.5 percent in 6-17 year olds (Australian Institute of Health and Welfare [AIHW], 2003; Graetz et al., 2001), children with AD/HD have higher levels of inattention, hyperactivity, and impulsivity compared to children of the same developmental age. Affected with an inability to sit still, failure to concentrate and a lack of self-control, children with AD/HD are often lacking important social skills and found to be at the bottom end of the academic scale (Barkley, 2006).

Literature has demonstrated that children with AD/HD have difficulty staying focused and sustaining attention, and are highly distractible, which often leads to difficulties learning in the classroom and staying on tasks set, leading to academic underachievement (Barkley, 2006; Forness & Kavale, 2001). Children with AD/HD have also been reported to display an inability to delay gratification, demonstrating unpredictable behaviour and problems with self-regulation (Barkley, 2005b). Due to these elements, children with AD/HD frequently have difficulty socialising with peers. Subject to peer rejection, children with AD/HD are often found to have fewer pro-social friends, are involved in antisocial behaviour, and associate more with children who are socially similar to them, reinforcing problem behaviour (Bagwell, Molina, Pelham, & Hoza, 2001).

A suitable treatment plan can significantly aid in reducing the impact of AD/HD symptoms. Several management options include; pharmacological therapy, behavioural therapy, cognitive therapy, nutritional diets and supplements, exercise, yoga, and biofeedback. Much research has been conducted on the effectiveness, and inadequacies of each of these treatments for AD/HD. It has been reported however, that some form of treatment is better than no treatment at all (Barkley, 2006).

Biofeedback: Neurofeedback Behavioural Training

AD/HD is linked to neurological causes, thus, neurofeedback training has shown merit in its ability to train the brain to establish control over a desired response. It does this by making the subject aware of the actions associated with the occurrence of the response. As a form of behavioural training, neurofeedback aims at developing skills for self regulation of brain wave activity. This process specifically involves the training of brain activity where brain frequencies are in excess, or in deficit. Neurotherapy helps modify these frequencies to appropriate levels (Gunkelman & Johnstone, 2005; Heinrich, Gevensleben, & Strehl, 2007). Children with AD/HD have predominantly shown to have greater slow wave (theta band) activity (associated with emotions, feelings, drives, and impulses) and lower fast wave (beta band) activity (related to concentration, perception, alertness, and attention) than children without AD/HD (Butnik, 2005; Clarke, Barry, McCarthy, & Selikowitz, 2001b). Some studies have also revealed that some children with AD/HD have excess beta activity, which have reported to be found in children with an AD/HD-C (combined type) diagnosis, who were more prone to temper tantrums and mood swings (Clarke, Barry, McCarthy, & Selikowitz, 2001a; Clarke et al., 2001b).

Neurofeedback involves attaching electrodes to the scalp of the participant. These electrodes measure electrical activity of the brain (or electroencephalogram – EEG) which is sent and processed to a computer and an electroencephalograph. Modern technology has enabled data of the participant's EEG to be translated into displays in a video game. The participant manoeuvres through the game by being rewarded or hindered depending on whether they are able to meet the criteria for positive feedback. Over a series of sessions the participant learns to use their EEG to control the game. The game is able to give the participant continuous visual, and sometimes auditory feedback (depending on the neurofeedback software used) during the game, which provides continuous information about their attention and state of consciousness. When a participant successfully shifts their EEG to meet certain criteria, they are automatically rewarded on screen. As participants learn to regulate their mental activity in this way, the symptoms of AD/HD are reported to normalise (Butnik, 2005; Gunkelman & Johnstone, 2005; Heinrich, et al., 2007).

Despite findings demonstrating neurofeedback as a viable treatment option for AD/HD, it is a controversial issue as other researchers and professionals have dismissed its credibility. Some researchers suggest that EEG biofeedback cannot be considered a scientifically established effective treatment option for AD/HD (Barkley, 2005a; DuPaul & Stoner, 2003). Neurofeedback studies for AD/HD have been criticised for its flaws with its generally small sample sizes, failure to randomly assign participants to treatment groups, and neglect to use placebo control groups (T. E. Brown, 2005). Other doubtful researchers have also raised the issue that to obtain a desired outcome, children would need to attend roughly 40-80 sessions for a minimum of 3 months, which would be a heavy cost to parents (Barkley, 2005a).

Neurofeedback researchers have not discounted these issues, but argue that neurofeedback is a cost-effective option in the long term (Fox et al., 2005). With studies showing sustained improvements even after treatment with the application of neurofeedback (Monastra et al., 2002), and providing evidence that it is a safe alternative treatment option to medication with generally no side effects, it has also shown promise for children who did not respond to medication (Butnik, 2005; Heinrich et al., 2007).

Alternative treatment options to help manage AD/HD symptoms have shown to be of increasing interest to parents and families who care for children with AD/HD (Concannon & Tang, 2005; Sinha & Efron, 2005). Whilst Neurofeedback is one form of biofeedback, another form of biofeedback is through heart rate and skin temperature measurements.

Biofeedback: Heart Rate Variable (HRV) and Skin Conductance Level (SCL)

An emerging area of biofeedback is the measurement of an individual's heart rate variable (HRV) and skin conductance levels (SCL). HRV is the measure of a person's natural changes between heart beats (McCraty & Tomasino, 2004). SCL is the measure of electrical conductance in the skin associated with the activity of sweat glands (Peek, 2003). Like neurofeedback, HRV and SCL biofeedback involves placing sensors on the patient's body, fingertips or earlobes, which measures their heart rate, pulse, and peripheral skin temperature. Results are similarly fed back to the patient via a computer through graphs, audio tones, or video games (Patrick, 2002). Using less stringent equipment than EEG biofeedback, biofeedback video games measuring heart rate and skin temperature may have the ability to be used for AD/HD management in the home. Coupled with the right setting and use, off the shelf biofeedback video games, such as HeartMath's *Freeze Framer*, or *The Journey to Wild Divine*, may have the potential to be used at home as treatment to help teach breathing and relaxation skills through a more entertaining medium, which may in turn help manage AD/HD symptoms.

Literature on HRV biofeedback illustrates positive results for disorders such as stress, asthma, coronary heart disease, fibromyalgia syndrome, Raynaud's disease, and depression (Blasé, 2005; Del Pozo, Gevirtz, Scher & Guarneri, 2004; Freedman, Lynn, Ianni & Hale, 1981; Gervirtz, 2005; Lehrer et al., 2004). Previous research has shown that HRV and SCL measurements are able to detect changes in children when using relaxation techniques (Lohaus et al., 2001). However, studies in this area of biofeedback for child and adolescent health and learning, are limited, and have only begun to emerge in recent years. Research studies have demonstrated the ability of biofeed-

back equipment using *HeartMath* learning tools to reduce student stress, decrease distractibility, increase calmness and positive emotions, improve attention, learning and academic performance, and have created noticeable shifts towards positive classroom dynamics and cooperation (Arguelles, McCraty, & Rees, 2003; HunterKane, 2003; McCraty, 2001, 2003, 2005; McCraty, Atkinson, Tomasino, Goelitz, & Mayrovitz, 1999; McCraty, Tomasino, Atkinson, Aasen, & Thurik, 2000).

Studies at the Institute of HeartMath in the United States of America, have explored the use of heart rhythm coherence biofeedback in a classroom setting to teach students important skills in increasing emotional self-management, self-awareness, promoting effective communication, and practicing responsible behaviours, by managing their physiological internal states (McCraty, 2005; McCraty et al., 2000). There are important connections between emotions, learning, and performance. When emotional stress negatively affects learning and performance, the connection between nervous system activity and the brain is distorted, limiting important cognitive processes essential for clear thinking, memory, problem solving and reasoning, and attention (Arguelles et al., 2003; McCraty, 2005). Thus, an association between positive emotions and cognitive functions demonstrates that during positive emotional states, rational and consistent signals are sent to the brain coordinating nervous system activity, generating high cognitive states, termed *physiological coherence* (McCraty & Tomasino, 2006). Individuals create a harmonious state between the body, brain, and nervous system. Evidently, this can be done through the use of HeartMath learning tools. These tools enable individuals to recognise stress reactions in order for them to intercept and modify their responses to these situations, and develop their ability to maintain positive emotions and physiological coherence for longer periods (Arguelles et al., 2003; McCraty & Tomasino, 2006).

One of the HeartMath tools is the *Freeze-Framer* (McCraty & Tomasino, 2006). It uses a small finger indicator to measure an individual's heart rate and pulse. In a similar fashion to neurobiofeedback, measurements are fed back to the individual through a computer screen. The *Freeze-Framer* uses three games to teach an individual to make connections between their heart rate levels, and their success in the game. For example, a hot air balloon activity requires the individual to float a hot air balloon through a number of obstacles. The player's heart rate determines how high the balloon will fly. That is, if the individual's heart rate is too low, the balloon will return to the ground ceasing movement (McCraty, 2001, 2005). A high heart rate will thus have the opposite effect.

Research demonstrates the ability of HRV and SCL biofeedback in helping students better their interpersonal skills, classroom behaviour, and academic performance. Biofeedback studies have shown significant improvements in children and adolescents without AD/HD in cognitive and behavioural performance following biofeedback intervention (Hunter Kane, 2003; McCraty et al., 1999; McCraty et al., 2000). Researchers at the HearthMath Institute and Hunter Kane Ltd. are at the forefront of research into biofeedback of this nature. Further scientific research into the use of HRV and SCL biofeedback, particularly for AD/HD is needed, as observations (St. Martin, 2005), and preliminary studies (Hunter Kane, 2006a, 2006b) have shown it capable of helping children manage AD/HD symptoms and improve physiological coherence and cognitive performance.

These research studies show that biofeedback video games are an attractive avenue to immerse a child in therapy while providing positive outcomes at the same time. However, it is also important to examine why children connect so well with the technology, evaluate the research on other positive impacts games can have, along with the risks of prolonged video game use.

Biofeedback as Learning

Biofeedback is a technique that teaches individuals to use physiological signals from their bodies to recognise and change internal states, and eventually learn to control them (M. Schwartz & Andrasik, 2003). According to Budzynski (1973), there are three main goals to biofeedback; (1) to develop an increased awareness of relevant internal physiological functions, (2) to establish control over these functions, and (3) to use this learned control in other areas in their life, away from the training site. Biofeedback training involves connecting an individual and biofeedback equipment, that is used to show them one or a number of their body functions which are translated into observable signals, including; graphs, tones, or successful movement in a computer game. Once an individual is able to recognise their body's inner movements, they can learn to slowly control them at will, and in time, be able to continue to do so without mechanical aids.

An underlying process of biofeedback is learning (Heinrich, et al., 2007). It is a strategy derived from psychological learning theory. Many writers have reported on the role learning has in biofeedback (G. Schwartz & Beaty, 1977; M. Schwartz & Olsen, 2003; Yates, 1980). The earliest learning theory of behaviour change is *classical conditioning*, which was first identified by Ivan Pavlov in the 1900's. He described this as the pairing of a previously automatic unconditioned response, or reflex, with a new unconditioned stimulus, that produces a conditioned response or reflex. Conditioning has occurred if there is a change in an individual's behaviour as a consequence of their exposure to the stimulus (Mackintosh, 1983).

Biofeedback has often been described as an operant learning process. The particular learning theory concerned is *operant conditioning*. Burrhus Skinner emphasised the connection between the effects of the consequence on the future probability of the behaviour. Skinner categorised behaviour into two; (1) involuntary behaviours, demonstrated through classically conditioned situations, which he called respondent behaviour; and (2) voluntary behaviours he called operant behaviours (Davey & Cullen, 1988; Henton & Iversen, 1978). He believed these behaviours, unlike the involuntary reflexive-type, were controlled by their consequences rather than by the stimuli that preceded them. In contrast to Pavlov's classical conditioning, operant conditioning is the pairing of voluntary behaviour with systematic consequences. An important component is the consequence which will either increase or decrease the frequency of the behaviour. Operant conditioning creates a relationship between a response performed in a certain situation, and the reward or punishment that follows it. The individual will learn that obtaining a reward or punishment depends on their actions. The key to operant conditioning therefore, is reinforcement. Reinforcement is necessary as it provides an individual with information as to whether their response was correct or not (Blanchard & Epstein, 1978). When an individual performs a behaviour that is followed by *positive reinforcement*, or a pleasant reward, the behaviour is more likely to occur again. Similarly, if an individual performs a behaviour that is then presented with a *negative reinforcement* such as a punishment, or the reward removed, the less likely it is that the behaviour will be repeated (Catania, 1968; Michael, 1975). Over time, these contingencies reinforce the behaviours paired with positive reinforcements, and behaviours that are punished or not rewarded, decline.

As an operant conditioning process, biofeedback uses instruments to detect physiological responses and to feed back to an individual information concerning these responses, so that they can become aware of them, and modify them. Individuals learn through trial and error, to manipulate certain physiological functions. When they are able to create the change, the behaviour conducted is positively reinforced by being rewarded with auditory feedback, such as a beep or ring of a bell, or visual feedback, through a light bulb lighting

up, or successful movement through a video game (Heinrich et al., 2007). Until they reach the desired physiological state, individuals are hindered from the reward of ringing the bell, lighting the bulb, or moving on in the game. Depending on the biofeedback system used, individuals may also be given negative feedback such as a harsh tone, or regression in their movement in the video game. Thus, individuals positively rewarded when they successfully manipulate a desired physiological state, are more likely to continue the behaviour they were doing to obtain the positive feedback, rather than continue with the behaviour that would produce negative feedback or punish them. The reward reinforces, but does not elicit the response. It simply increases the frequency for which the response was to occur again.

For example, individuals using biofeedback to reduce stress may receive positive feedback when they are able relax their muscles and lower their heart rate levels, and may receive negative feedback when they are doing the opposite, increasing heart rate and tensing their muscles. In accordance with the operant conditioning learning theory, individuals would be more likely to practice slowing their heart rate and relaxing their muscles to reduce stress following positive feedback, as opposed to increasing their heart rate and muscle tension.

According to G. Schwartz and Beaty (1977), biofeedback is a powerful research tool. It need not necessarily produce large degrees of changes, but it provides a means of achieving experimental manipulation over specific physiological processes that explore the relationship between other processes associated with environmental and behavioural conditions.

Teaching Children Relaxation Skills

Relaxation is characterised by a weakened state of physiological arousal, and peaceful state of mental well-being (Chang, 1991; Payne, 2005). Relaxation training has long been found to be useful for adults when managing a number of psychological conditions such as stress, anxiety, and depression (Holmes & Roth, 1988; Kessler et al., 2001; Roth & Holmes, 1987), as well as physical conditions such as headache, muscle tension, and irritable bowel syndrome (Blanchard, Greene, Scharff, & Schwarz-McMorris, 1993; Haynes, Moseley, & McGowan, 1975; Holroyd & Penzien, 1990; Tobin, Holroyd, Baker, Reynolds, & Holm, 1988). Research has also shown positive effects from teaching children and adolescents' relaxation skills (Chang, 1991; Donney & Poppen, 1989; Goldbeck & Schmid, 2003; Margolis, 1990).

Chang (1991) and Margolis (1990) discussed relaxation methods that can be used to train children in child and youth care settings, which included meditation procedures, autogenic training, progressive relaxation, biofeedback training, abbreviated relaxation methods, and visual imagery. They reported that, when conducted appropriately, such techniques are useful skills in minimising dysfunctional behaviour, reducing stress and anxiety levels, treating headaches, encouraging reading achievement, improving self-concepts, and enhancing self-esteem.

Findings from studies (Raymer & Poppen, 1985; Donney & Poppen, 1989; Goldbeck & Schmid, 2003; Beauchemin, Hutchins, & Patterson, 2008) demonstrate that children as young as 6 years of age (Goldbeck & Schmid, 2003) can be taught relaxation techniques, and measurements through various questionnaires, and physiological effects through Heart Rate (HR), Skin Conductance Levels (SCL) and Skin Temperature (ST) (Lohaus, Klein-Heßling, Vögele, & Kuhn-Henninghausen, 2001; Shilling & Poppen, 1983), and EMG (Shilling & Poppen, 1983) measures support the changes in the children's behaviours, and emotional developments. In particular, Donney and Poppen (1989) make note that the positive results from relaxation training studies demonstrate that as a "non-chemical" (p. 319) alternative, the effects of the skills learnt and utilised has shown the potential to reduce disrup-

tive behaviour and increase adaptive behaviour in children with hyperactive tendencies, as found in children with AD/HD.

Findings from these relaxation studies combined with the results from biofeedback research helps support the rationale of how and why the following research would provide positive effects as a serious game for health.

CURRENT BIOFEEDBACK RESEARCH

Research at The University of Sydney, Australia recently completed a study on *"Exploring the use of biofeedback video games to help children diagnosed with Attention-Deficit/Hyperactivity Disorder (AD/HD)"*. The purpose of the study was to determine the effectiveness of *The Journey to Wild Divine* as a suitable biofeedback management program for children diagnosed with AD/HD, compared with children without AD/HD. The study measured changes in the children's behaviour through questionnaires completed by parents at certain intervals of the study, combined with observations of heart rate graphs of the children's progression through the game. It was believed that *The Journey to Wild Divine* may be an effective biofeedback program that may help reduce the primary symptoms of AD/HD in children and young adolescents, and produce little to no side effects following its use.

As an exploratory study (Amon & Campbell, 2008a, 2008b), researchers aimed to contribute to this new area in AD/HD research by raising the following questions; (1) how effective is *The Journey to Wild Divine* as a biofeedback video game for children with and without AD/HD? (2) is there a difference in treatment outcomes between session frequency? (3) are there any side effects? and (4) what are the effects on parents mental health status throughout their children's biofeedback sessions?

The Journey to Wild Divine

This research study used a biofeedback system created by scientist Kurt Smith and game computer graphics artist Corwin Bell (Goldner, 2003), called *The Journey to Wild Divine*. *The Journey to Wild Divine* is an interactive computer game that uses three biofeedback finger sensors, called 'Magic Rings', to measure the player's heart rate variability (HRV) and skin conductance levels (SCL). Measurements from the sensors are registered through the Wild Divine 'Light Stone' and fed back to the player through visual biofeedback activities, called 'events', on the computer screen. The equipment monitors the player's internal physiological states and uses visual feedback to help the player learn how to control these states, by balancing, releasing, or recovering from the situation they find themselves in.

The Journey to Wild Divine involves two 'Journeys'. The first is *The Journey to Wild Divine: The Passage* and the second is *The Journey to Wild Divine: Wisdom Quest*. Part two of the Journey provides players with more events to practice their skills learnt in *The Passage*, and an extended ability to vary difficulty levels to advance their breathing skills and manage their physiological states. The participants in the study began with *The Passage*, and then continued with *Wisdom Quest* upon completion of the first.

Measures

To measure any changes, parents were required to complete online questionnaires as part of their Diary at four stages of the study. Baseline scores were measured at pre-intervention, in Diary 1, Diary 2 was to be completed after the first month of session, Diary 3 was to be completed after the second month of sessions, and Diary 4 was to be completed after the third month of biofeedback sessions to measure post-intervention scores.

The Diary entries included (1) a non-standardised 13-item *Demographic Questionnaire* created by the researcher to focus on the background of the parent filling out the questionnaire and their children. These questions would help provide a demographic outline of the participants involved in the study. (2) An *AD/HD Symptoms Questionnaire*. Researchers created this non-standardised questionnaire involving questions targeting specific AD/HD symptoms. This AD/HD Symptoms Questionnaire incorporated 18-items which presented parents with AD/HD symptoms derived from the Text Revision of the Diagnostic and Statistical Manual for Mental Disorders (DSM-IV-TR) (APA, 2000) regarding inattention, hyperactivity, and impulsivity. (3) The *Strengths and Difficulties Questionnaire* (SDQ; Goodman, 1997), which measured social, emotional, and behavioural functioning in children and adolescents. (4) A questionnaire on the *Journey to Wild Divine* game. A 7-item non-standardised questionnaire was created based on the experience of the Wild Divine game as a biofeedback system following sessions, and (5) the *Depression, Anxiety, and Stress Scale* (DASS; Lovibond & Lovibond, 1995) which incorporated subscales for each of the negative emotional states of depression, anxiety, and stress.

Participants

The experimental group included a total of 24 children with AD/HD (15 males, and 9 females; mean age 9.50 years), and their parents (1 male, and 18 female; mean age = 38.79 years). Groups were further divided into two groups – Group One, attended biofeedback sessions once a week for 12 weeks (12 sessions), and Group Two, attended more than once a week, either twice a week (24 sessions) or three times a week (36 sessions) over 12 weeks. This separation would help determine whether a difference between the amount and frequency of sessions attended would arise. To ensure a high attendance rate, parents chose which group they wished to attend. Group One (once a week) included 17 children and Group Two (more than once a week) included 7 children. Parents provided written reports and psychological tests conducted with their children, which demonstrated that 83.3 percent of children were diagnosed with AD/HD by a primary health care professional (general practitioners, and paediatricians), and 16.7 percent were diagnosed by allied health care professionals (psychologists and psychiatrists). 62.5 percent of children were taking medication for AD/HD, 92.3 percent of which were taking stimulant medications (e.g. Ritalin), and 7.7 percent were taking non-stimulants (e.g. Straterra). The control group included 12 children not diagnosed with AD/HD (9 males, and 3 females; mean age = 8.75 years), and their parents (8 female; mean age = 38.38 years). Group One included 10 children and Group Two included 2 children.

The control group in the study included children who were not diagnosed with AD/HD, this was decided over using a control group with children diagnosed AD/HD for a number of reasons. Firstly, a wait list control group with children diagnosed with AD/HD would have been unethical, as there is a standard pharmacological treatment for the disorder. Parents may not be willing to be part of a waitlist group for 3 months without treatment when they are seeking help for their child. Secondly, to use a control group with children diagnosed with AD/HD with a placebo treatment, such as an imitation biofeedback game, would not be appropriate as the researcher and participants would be able to distinguish between the use of the biofeedback equipment, and an imitation. Previous literature on the effects of breathing and relaxation skills, as well as neurofeedback technology, has shown that these skills and techniques have been able to improve academic performance, effective communication, and emotional functioning, in children without AD/HD (McCraty, 2005; Mc-Craty & Tomasino, 2006). Thus, the purpose of recruiting children without AD/HD as part of our control group was to determine whether this type of biofeedback could also improve behaviour and functioning in typically developed children, as well

as establish its potential as a treatment option for children with AD/HD.

More importantly, as an exploratory study, researchers sought to trial the biofeedback program on these groups of children while observing and taking note of the technology's potential to benefit the children. Without previous scientific research in this specific area of biofeedback with this program, researchers found it fit for the experimental group to consist of children diagnosed with AD/HD, and children without AD/HD to form the control group, and record its impact.

RESULTS

AD/HD Symptoms Questionnaire

T-tests were able to indicate change in the children's behaviour during intervention. A paired samples t-test demonstrated a statistically significant decrease in the AD/HD Symptoms Questionnaire between Diaries 1 and 2, $t(23) = 3.02$, and Diaries 2 and 3, $t(23) = 3.55$, but whilst there continued to be reductions in scores, they were not found significant between Diaries 3 and 4, $t(23) = 1.77$.

An analysis of variance (ANOVA) assessed the impact of attending biofeedback sessions once a week or more than once a week across the four time intervals at Diary 1, Diary 2, Diary 3, and Diary 4. Multivariate tests show a significant main effect for time between Diaries, Wilks' Lambda = .40, $F(3,20) = 9.74$, partial eta squared = .59, with both groups showing a reduction in AD/HD Symptoms Questionnaire scores over time. There was however, no significant interaction between frequency of sessions attended and time, Wilks' Lambda = .95, $F(3,20) = .32$, partial eta squared = .04. The main effect comparing the frequency of sessions attended was non-significant, $F(1,22) = 1.52$, partial eta squared = .06, suggesting no difference between participants who attended sessions once a week, to those who attended sessions more than once a week.

Both experimental and control groups demonstrated significant reductions in AD/HD Symptoms Questionnaire scores, and multivariate tests show that the difference in the changes between groups were also significant over time, Wilks' Lambda = .80, $F(1, 24) = 8.46$, partial eta squared = .20. There was a significant impact of having AD/HD (experimental group) or not (control group) on the AD/HD Symptoms Questionnaire scores, $F(1, 34) = 49.33$, partial eta squared = .59.

Strengths and Difficulties Questionnaire

A paired samples t-test of the complete sample was conducted to evaluate the impact of biofeedback on the children's behaviours. Mean baseline scores at pre-intervention ($M = 26.29$, $SD = 6.06$) placed the children under the "abnormal" band. Results show a statistically significant improvement in behaviours from pre-intervention scores in Diary 1 to post-intervention scores in Diary 4, $t(23) = 4.31$. Post-intervention scores reduced, but the children remained in the "abnormal" band ($M = 22.75$, $SD = 3.38$).

Independent samples t-test scores found no significant difference between scores from participants who attended sessions once a week ($n = 17$, $M = 26.82$, $SD = 5.18$), to those who participated in sessions more than once a week ($n = 7$, $M = 25.00$, $SD = 8.14$), $t(22) = .66$ which suggests no difference in the effectiveness of attending sessions more than once a week, than attending only once a week.

Between the experimental group and the control group, independent samples t-test show that the difference in scores are significantly different at both pre-intervention $t(34) = 5.81$, and post-intervention $t(34) = 3.31$. The control group did not reveal a significant reduction in pre- and post-intervention scores as the experimental group had. Multivariate test results show a significant impact of being in the experimental group compared to being in the control group on SDQ scores,

Wilks' Lambda - .84, $F(1,34) = 6.24$, partial eta squared = .15.

Wild Divine Questionnaire

Results demonstrated that all children (both experimental and control groups) experienced the same level of difficulty throughout the study. Results show that by the end of the biofeedback sessions, majority of parents in the experimental groups (58.3%) reported their children to have experienced the game to still be "Somewhat difficult", whereas majority of parents in the control group (58.3%) reported their children to have experienced the game to only be a "Little bit difficult" by the end of the sessions. Despite this, analysis demonstrated no significant difference on the difficulty levels reported between the experimental and control groups. This demonstrates that children as young as 5 years of age, with or without AD/HD diagnosis can learn and use breathing techniques through *The Journey to Wild Divine* biofeedback video game.

There was however, a significant difference between the changes in children's behaviour following sessions as reported by parents. Multivariate tests reveal a significant difference between experimental and control groups across the three Diaries on reported change in behaviour, Wilks' Lambda = .82, $F(2,33) = 3.63$, partial eta squared = .18.

Results from Group One and Group Two demonstrate a significant difference between experimental and control group across Diaries on reported changes in behaviour for participants who attended sessions once a week, Wilks' Lambda = .76, $F(2,24) = 3.64$, partial eta squared = .23. However, there was no significant difference between experimental and control groups on reported changes in behaviour for participants who attended sessions more than once a week, Wilks' Lambda = .89, $F(2,6) = .34$, partial eta squared = .10. This suggests that attending sessions more than once a week was not of greater benefit to either experimental or control group.

Depression, Anxiety, and Stress Scale

Parents in both the experimental and control groups demonstrated reductions in scores, but with no significant main effect. Independent samples t-test results from post-intervention scores show significant difference in depression levels, $t(33.64) - 2.12$, as well as stress levels $t(33.96) = 3.58$, with no difference in anxiety levels $t(34) = .92$. This suggests that by the end of the sessions, parents in the experimental group still had higher depression ($M = 4.83$, $SD = 6.87$), and stress levels ($M = 10.00$, $SD = 7.77$), compared to the control group depression ($M = 1.33$, $SD = 2.99$) and stress levels ($M = 3.16$, $SD = 3.66$), though reductions in symptomology for the experimental group parents was evident.

DISCUSSION

Previous research has shown that teaching children relaxation skills has the ability to reduce stress and anxiety levels, encourage reading achievement, improve self-concepts, and enhance self-esteem (Chang, 1991; Margolis, 1990). For children with AD/HD, being taught breathing and relaxation skills has shown to reduce hyperactive levels, minimise dysfunctional behaviour, and improve emotional development (Donney & Poppen, 1989; Raymer & Poppen, 1985). Biofeedback technology provides an opportunity to teach children breathing skills through a modern medium that children and adolescents of contemporary society are cultivated in. This research study aimed to explore the use of biofeedback video games to help children diagnosed with AD/HD to manage symptoms. Following biofeedback sessions, results from 24 children diagnosed with AD/HD, their parents and 12 children not diagnosed with AD/HD along with their parents, show that as a

biofeedback program, *The Journey to Wild Divine* has the potential to teach children breathing and relaxation techniques, which helps reduce disruptive behaviour and, in turn, reduce parental stress.

Results from the study demonstrated that following biofeedback sessions, children with AD/HD had significantly reduced inattention, hyperactivity, and impulsivity levels. The significant decrease shown from pre- to post-intervention in the study demonstrated that the children's behaviour in their home life, friendships, classroom learning, and leisure activities, had significant improvements following biofeedback sessions.

Biofeedback was explored as an operant learning process. Operant conditioning creates a relationship between a preformed response and the reward or punishment that follows it (Blanchard & Epstein, 1978). Through this operant conditioning process, *The Journey to Wild Divine* video game was used as a biofeedback instrument to detect physiological responses to feed information back to the player concerning these responses to become aware of them, and modify them. Through the game, the children were taught breathing techniques to help them succeed in the activities. The operant conditioning theory states that reinforcement is important to provide an individual with information as to whether or not what they are doing is correct. The children had to apply breathing techniques in the activities, and if they met the correct breathing states, they were positively rewarded with continued progress and success in the activity. To positively reinforce the use of calm breathing, the children were positively rewarded with forward movement along the game. However, if the children became frustrated, entering into uneven breathing, the children were negatively reinforced and presented with a punishment of not being allowed to proceed in the game.

For example, one activity required the child to practice the 'Heart Breath' to bring up stones from under water to allow them to walk on the stones to proceed to the other side. Continued use of the

'Heart Breath' brought up the stones one or two at a time from under the water. However, if mid-way through the activity the child lost concentration, or became frustrated or agitated and their breathing changed, slowly the stones reverted back under water to hinder further movement in the game. If the children managed to get their breathing back to a 'Heart Breath' pattern and level, they were rewarded by the stones rising from under water again. Through these reinforcements, the children learn that stable and calm breathing rewards them with progress through the game. To which the learning theory states that individuals who are positively rewarded when they successfully manipulate a desired physiological state are more likely to continue this behaviour to obtain the positive feedback, rather than practice the behaviour that would produce the negative feedback and punish them. As such, following biofeedback sessions, children learnt that manipulating their breathing to calmer states will help bring positive rewards, whereas frustration and uneven breathing will present negative punishments. Given this, the children are taught skills to recognise the difference in their physiological states and are thus able identify when they are frustrated - therefore leading them to relaxation techniques to modify this state. It was anticipated that the children would learn these skills and use the breathing techniques away from the computer in other situations such as having difficulty and becoming frustrated with homework, or becoming involved in an argument.

The onscreen mentors in the video game taught the children breathing techniques that would in turn modify heart rate and skin temperature for the biofeedback equipment to measure. However, as the children were only given direct instructions on heart rate movements using breathing techniques, no instructions or connections between breathing and skin temperature were provided or taught to the children. The focus was therefore kept on breathing techniques for heart rate changes to keep to the simplistic nature of the game for the children.

Findings and Conclusions from the Study: Directions for Future Research

AD/HD and Comorbid Disorders

This present study did not identify any participants who had comorbid disorders to their AD/HD diagnosis. As such, it cannot be addressed whether the biofeedback was able to help children with a sole diagnosis of AD/HD, to those who have comorbid disorders, such as oppositional defiant disorder (ODD), conduct disorder (CD), anxiety disorders, and learning disabilities (LD), which are commonly linked with AD/HD. This is an important area for future research studies to include in the screening and testing process, as it could help identify which internal and external behaviours are specifically being improved through the treatment. Especially for AD/HD comorbid with anxiety disorders, the breathing techniques taught through the video game may be a highly useful strategy in helping reduce heart rate and teaching the children to modify their own anxiety levels as recent research has shown that meditative techniques can positively improve anxiety levels in children (Beauchemin, Hutchins, & Patterson, 2008). The biofeedback trials of this present study have shown that it can help improve AD/HD behaviours, however further research with the comorbidities of AD/HD would be an insightful direction towards the technology's potential to determine whether it can also help with learning, as Beauchemin, Hutchins, and Patterson's (2008) study shows, the practice of meditative techniques helps improve concentration and attention consequently improving academic performance and social skills.

There is currently no literature on biofeedback video games to help manage AD/HD comorbid with other disorders. The research studies presented and discussed in this Chapter, on breathing and relaxation skills, and neurofeedback technology, establishes a noteworthy rationale towards the potential of the biofeedback technology trialled in the present study to improve not only AD/HD related behaviours, but also symptoms of other related disorders such as apprehensive symptoms characterised in anxiety disorders, heightened unruly behaviour noted in ODD/CD, and processing disabilities in LD. It is suggested that future research also note comorbid disorders with AD/HD when identifying improvements from biofeedback video games, to identify specific areas, symptoms, and characteristics, which are improved or modified from the technology.

Cues

Abbreviated relaxation methods included the use of cues paired with a relaxation state (Chang, 1991). This biofeedback video game uses two types of cues to initiate the use of certain breathing techniques to evoke related states for success in the game. The first, is the use of cue words. Cue words such as "Heart Breath" and "Peaceful Breath", is used to initiate the type of breathing technique to use. Second is the use of visual cues. Most activities in *The Journey to Wild Divine* do not verbally instruct the player on which breathing to use. Instead, the game often uses a set of coloured eyes to cue the breathing technique to be used. That is, a pair of blue coloured eyes represents slow calm breathing, similar to the Heart Breath, and a pair of magenta eyes symbolises deeper and quicker breathing for a faster heart rate measurement. These coloured eyes act as cues to direct the child towards which type of breathing is required for the activity. It would be a useful proposal to use these coloured eyes as cues away from the sessions. As the children learn to pair cue words and images, they can learn to use these breathing techniques whenever they hear a cue word, or see the coloured eyes.

Future research should look to use these cues to help increase the use of the breathing techniques away from the sessions. For example, in combination with parent involvement, each child could

be given a pair of blue coloured eyes to stick in the child's bed room or somewhere around the house, possibly even at school, for the child to see, which would prompt the child to use their calm breathing. Or, when a parent believes a child needs calming down from being over active, or feeling frustrated, they could use the cue words - Heart Breath or Peaceful Breath, for the child to exercise their calm breathing. These cues prompt the relaxation technique and helps shift the child's tense physiological state into a more relaxed and calm one.

Involving Parents

A great number of participants in both the experimental and control groups exercised the breathing techniques they learnt through the video game either at home, at school, or elsewhere away from the sessions. However, while results showed that parents from both the experimental and control groups felt that it helped improve their children's behaviour following the first month of sessions, by the end of the study parents from the control group did not feel it was as beneficial as the parents in the experimental group. Therefore, whilst the children were able to learn breathing and relaxation skills through the video game, future research should consider a way to involve teaching the parents the skills also. This would educate them with the knowledge of how to link the breathing techniques with situations in which they could initiate the use of controlled breathing to help manage the behaviour and/or the situation. Previous research studies on breathing and relaxation, yoga, and cognitive therapy, have shown that parent involvement and practice of AD/HD treatment in the home, have been beneficial for desired outcomes (Harrison, Manocha, & Rubia, 2004; Jensen & Kenny, 2004; Raymer & Poppen, 1985). By involving parents, the skills learnt from the video game are extended beyond its use during the sessions to external use in their home life, school and after school social activities. The extent of parent involvement in this current study was limited. It was suggested to the parents to remind their children to use the breathing techniques they learnt when they feel their child needed calming down. Further parent involvement, such as teaching the parents what the breathing techniques actually involve, as well as specific scenarios they can use them in, will allow for the children and parents to work together to ensure practice and use of the skills. Also, by teaching the parents the information and skills that the children are taught, the parents are able to understand when they can suggest the use of the breathing techniques if the children forget, and they will also be able to recognise when the children initiate the use of the relaxation skill on their own that the child may need those few minutes just to calm themselves on their own.

By involving parents, this may also help reduce the negative effects of the behaviour on parents. Wells et al. (2000) reported that reductions in the primary and comorbid symptoms of AD/HD may help relieve the negative stress and depressive experiences faced by families. Using results from the MTA Study, Wells et al.'s (2000) analysis showed that treating AD/HD solely with medication, solely with behavioural treatment, or a combination of the two, demonstrated the same levels of improvements in maternal depression, marital conflict and parenting stress. This reveals that treating AD/HD has significant positive effects on the mental and emotional health statuses of parents and families. Researchers of the present study hypothesised that parent's stress levels from their children's behaviour would decline with session progression. Supporting previous research for treating children with AD/HD, analysis of the current study found significant reductions in depression, anxiety and stress scores at post-intervention for parents in the experimental groups. The control group parents were found only to have a significant reduction in depression and stress scores. At post-intervention, parents of children with AD/HD still had higher depression and stress levels in comparison to parents of typi-

cally developed children. That is, whilst children were attending biofeedback sessions, not only did parents report improvements in their children's behaviour, but also improvements in their own depression, anxiety, and stress levels throughout the study. Specific analysis of the results between the children's behaviour and the parent's mental health levels were not conducted in the present study, however, future analysis of data could look at the relationship between the improvements in the children's behaviour and improvements in the parent's mental health states, and distinguish any direct links.

Side Effects

There is significantly limited scientific literature on the use of HRV biofeedback as treatment for AD/HD. Due to the lack of evidence of this therapy; no side effects have been reported from the use biofeedback video games measuring heart rate or skin temperature with children or young adolescents. The current study reported similar side effects to that found in neurofeedback studies, including hyperactivity, dizziness, headaches, and irritability. Other side effects reported from this study included lack of appetite, feeling emotional and/or teary, and feeling tired. Of the participants who experienced side effects after the final session, 75 percent were reported to be taking medication. However, there were no significant difference between participants in the experimental group who were taking medication to those who were not. The side effects listed by parents are not only similar to that of research with neurofeedback, but also similar to the reports in literature linked to the side effects frequently experienced with the use of medications (Greydanus, 2005). Thus, whilst no participants in the control group were reported to have experienced side effects, the side effects reported in the experimental group may or may not have been the effect of the biofeedback intervention, the medication, or a combination of both. As noted by Monastra et al. (2005), a reduction in medication doses aided in eliminating several side effects. Whilst this study did not suggest decreases in medication doses to parents, future research may look more closely at the relationship between the combination of biofeedback and medication, and the effects of dosage levels, particularly when no participants in the control group, who were not taking medications, did not report any experience of side effects.

Previous research has demonstrated that families with children diagnosed with AD/HD are more frequently turning to alternative treatments for reasons such as experiencing aversive side effects from taking medications (Brue & Oakland, 2002; Chan, Rappaport, & Kemper, 2003; Sinha & Efron, 2005). This current research has shown that whilst some side effects were noted following biofeedback sessions, these were only reported in the experimental group, of which 90 percent of participants were taking stimulant medications, and 7.7 percent reported to be taking non-stimulant medications. No participants in the control group were reported to be taking medication, and no side effects were recorded. Further research comparing only biofeedback with biofeedback in combination with medication will be able to determine the origin of the side effects. At this stage, this type of biofeedback can be said to be a reasonable alternative treatment for children without aversive side effects.

Recommendations

Researchers propose that the combination of new stimulation through the video game, and meditation-style breathing techniques brought about motivating factors and physiological change, which helped generate improvements in AD/HD symptoms. Despite the significant changes demonstrated from pre- to post-intervention, closer analysis has shown that whilst there was a significant change between Diaries 1 and 2, Diaries 2 and 3, there was no significant change during the last month of biofeedback sessions reported in

Diaries 3 and 4, demonstrating a plateau period. This suggests that after an initial improvement on AD/HD symptoms, the effect of biofeedback training plateaus. Similar findings were reported in Raymer and Poppen's (1985) study teaching hyperactive boys Behavioural Relaxation Training (BRT). Where this previous study involved 25 minute weekly sessions, they experienced a plateau period following the seventh session (7 weeks), this current study experienced a plateau period sometime following the second month (8 weeks) of sessions. Towards the final few weeks of sessions, many children in this current study had completed both parts of *The Journey to Wild Divine* game and were returning to previous activities they had either not completed, or found difficult to complete, to attempt it again or to test improvement in skills learnt. Researchers believe that having to return to past activities had decreased the children's interest in the game, as they were no longer stimulated with having to repeat old activities. This in effect may have reduced the efficacy of biofeedback, causing the plateau. Future research should look at how the video game can produce greater stimulation to extend beyond 12 weeks.

Researchers speculate that if there were more activities for the children to continue playing, or a way to change the outcomes of activities based on the children's responses to prolong the length of the game, the plateau may not have occurred. Based on this phenomenon it is important to look at what future biofeedback technology can do to keep children engaged in the video game play that is beneficial to them, so they continue to improve and manage their AD/HD symptoms. Research in this area is still new, but ultimately has the opportunity to take several different avenues.

CONCLUSION

This Chapter aimed to examine a therapy that is not a mainstream form of treatment for AD/HD, to demonstrate the potential of serious games in health. Biofeedback video games are an area that is still fairly new to AD/HD treatment. As such there is a severe lack of scientific evidence of its potential. The literature highlighted in this Chapter provided a strong rationale towards the importance of the study and justification for the scientific merit of the technology for AD/HD treatment. Following the trials of *The Journey to Wild Divine*, results demonstrated that biofeedback video games have the potential to teach children and young adolescents breathing and relaxation techniques, as well as help improve behaviour and emotional functioning in several situations. Analysis of results demonstrated that a significant number of participants were reported to show improvements in AD/HD symptoms and other disruptive, emotional behaviours, which have also shown to help improve parental depression, anxiety and stress levels.

No common features were found between the sexes or age groups of the children and their experience with *The Journey to Wild Divine* video game, in either the experimental or control groups. Future research into this area should take note of any common elements found. For example, if older children found the game easier than the younger children, or if more females than males were reported to show greater improvements and vice versa. These traits will help provide further insight into the potential of the treatment to help children with AD/HD, as well as helping to refine the ability of the technology to manage the disorder.

Upon analysis and interpretation of results, a number of suggestions have been made to improve the methods for future studies in this area, as well as recommendations for ways the biofeedback software can be expanded to become more appropriate for AD/HD treatment. Further research needs to investigate long term effects of biofeedback on a greater number of participants. Future research should also aim to measure changes over a longitudinal period that includes tasks that do not repeat themselves, thus enhancing rewards and reinforcement for breathing and relaxation techniques that will produce positive learning behaviour.

The trivial nature of the biofeedback video game allows for its use in the home. Where neurofeedback video games require the use of electrodes to be attached to the scalp of the player, it also uses complex equipment to measure and interpret brain wave movement through the video game. *The Journey to Wild Divine* on the other hand was purchased as an off the shelf product designed for personal use, that only involves the use of connecting the biofeedback light stone and sensor rings to a desktop computer or laptop.

Given this, future research should validate frequency of use and evaluate the development of activities for longer, to extend opportunities for improvements. With an appropriate therapeutic schedule, and rigorous guidelines on its use, coupled with the simplistic features of the technology, biofeedback video games can be a positive management tool for AD/HD symptoms as a complementary or alternative treatment that can be used in the privacy of the family home. This would be beneficial in relating the practice of breathing techniques from the biofeedback activities to other parts of the child's life, as the technology has shown to have the ability to help teach skills that can help improve concentration and attention to tasks that would ultimately aim to reduce the core symptoms of AD/HD. The positive findings from this current study add to the body of knowledge on biofeedback video games through heart rate measurements. It also provides direction for further, more specific, investigations into AD/HD treatment utilising this technology.

REFERENCES

Alhambra, M. A., Fowler, T. P., & Alhambra, A. A. (1995). EEG biofeedback: A new treatment option for ADD/ADHD. *Journal of Neurotherapy*, *1*(2), 39–43. doi:10.1300/J184v01n02_03

American Psychological Association (APA). (2000). *Diagnostic and statistical manual of mental disorders-Text revision* (4th ed.) (DSM-IV-TR). Washington DC: American Psychiatric Association.

Amon, K. L., & Campbell, A. J. (2008a). Biofeedback video games to teach AD/HD children relaxation skills to help manage symptoms. *The Journal of the Professional Association of Teachers of Students with Specific Learning Difficulties, 21*, 34–38.

Amon, K. L., & Campbell, A. J. (2008b). Can children with AD/HD learn relaxation and breathing techniques through biofeedback video games? *Australian Journal of Educational and Developmental Psychology, 8*, 72–84.

Arguelles, L., McCraty, R., & Rees, R. A. (2003). The heart in holistic education. *Encounter: Education for Meaning and Social Justice, 16*(3), 13–21.

Australian Institute of Health and Welfare (AIHW). (2003). Australia's young people: Their health and wellbeing. Retrieved March 8, 2009, from http://152.91.62.50/publications/phe/ayp03/ayp03-c08.pdf

Bagwell, C. L., Molina, B., Pelham, W., & Hoza, B. (2001). Attention-Deficit Hyperactivity Disorder and problems in peer relations: Predictions from childhood to adolescence. *Journal of the American Academy of Child and Adolescent Psychiatry, 40*, 1285–1292. doi:10.1097/00004583-200111000-00008

Barkley, R. A. (2005a). *Take charge of ADHD: The complete authoritative guide for parents*. Victoria, Australia: Hinkler Books Pty. Ltd.

Barkley, R. A. (2005b). *ADHD and the nature of self control*. New York: The Guilford Press.

Barkley, R. A. (2006). *Attention Deficit Hyperactivity Disorder: A handbook for diagnosis and treatment* (3rd ed.). New York: Guilford Publications.

Beauchemin, J., Hutchins, T. L., & Patterson, F. (2008). Mindfulness meditation may lessen anxiety, promote social skills, and improve academic performance among adolescents with learning disabilities. *Complementary Health Practice Review, 13*, 34–45. doi:10.1177/1533210107311624

Blanchard, E. B., & Epstein, L. H. (1978). *A biofeedback primer*. Massachusetts: Wesley Publishing Company.

Blanchard, E. B., Greene, B., Scharff, L., & Schwarz-McMorris, S. P. (1993). Relaxation training as a treatment of irritable bowel syndrome. *Biofeedback and Self-Regulation, 18*(3), 125–132. doi:10.1007/BF00999789

Boyd, W. D., & Campbell, S. E. (1998). EEG biofeedback in the schools: The use of EEG biofeedback to treat ADHD in a school setting. *Journal of Neurotherapy, 2*(4), 65–71. doi:10.1300/J184v02n04_05

Brown, T. E. (2005). *Attention Deficit Disorder: The unfocused mind in children and adults*. New Haven, CT: Yale University Press.

Brue, A. W., & Oakland, T. D. (2002). Alternative treatments for Attention-Deficit/Hyperactivity Disorder: Does evidence support their use? *Alternative Therapies in Health and Medicine, 8*, 68–74.

Budzynski, T. H. (1973). Biofeedback procedures in the clinic. In Birk, L. (Ed.), *Biofeedback: Behavioural medicine* (pp. 177–187). New York: Grune and Stratton.

Butnik, S. M. (2005). Neurofeedback in adolescents and adults with Attention Deficit Hyperactivity Disorder. *Journal of Clinical Psychology, 61*, 621–625. doi:10.1002/jclp.20124

Catania, C. (Ed.). (1968). *Contemporary research in operant behaviour*. Illinois: Scott, Foresman and Company.

Chan, E., Rappaport, L. A., & Kemper, K. J. (2003). Complementary and alternative therapies in childhood attention and hyperactivity problems. *Developmental and Behavioural Pediatrics*, *24*, 4–8.

Chang, J. (1991). Using relaxation strategies in child and youth care practice. *Child and Youth Care Forum*, *20*, 155–169. doi:10.1007/BF00757198

Clarke, A. R., Barry, R. J., McCarthy, R., & Selikowitz, M. (2001a). Electroencephalogram differences in two subtypes of Attention-Deficit/Hyperactivity Disorder. *Psychophysiology*, *38*, 212–221. doi:10.1111/1469-8986.3820212

Clarke, A. R., Barry, R. J., McCarthy, R., & Selikowitz, M. (2001b). Excess beta activity in children with attention-deficit/hyperactivity disorder: An atypical electrophysiological group. *Psychiatry Research*, *103*, 205–218. doi:10.1016/S0165-1781(01)00277-3

Cole, H., & Griffiths, M. D. (2007). Social interactions in massively multiplayer online role-playing gamers. *Cyberpsychology & Behavior*, *10*, 575–583. doi:10.1089/cpb.2007.9988

Concannon, P. E., & Tang, Y. P. (2005). Management of attention deficit hyperactivity disorder: A parental perspective. *Journal of Paediatrics and Child Health*, *41*, 625–630. doi:10.1111/j.1440-1754.2005.00771.x

Davey, G., & Cullen, C. (Eds.). (1988). *Human operant conditioning and behaviour modification*. New York: John Whiley & Sons.

Del Pozo, J. M., Gevirtz, R. N., Scher, B., & Guarneri, E. (2004). Biofeedback treatment increases heart rate variability in patients with known coronary artery disease. *American Heart Journal*, *147*(3), G1–G6. doi:10.1016/j.ahj.2003.08.013

Donney, V. K., & Poppen, R. (1989). Teaching parents to conduct behavioural relaxation training with their hyperactive children. *Journal of Behavior Therapy and Experimental Psychiatry*, *20*, 319–325. doi:10.1016/0005-7916(89)90063-3

DuPaul, G., & Stoner, G. (2003). *ADHD in the schools: Assessment and intervention strategies* (2nd ed.). New York: The Guilford Press.

Fernández, T., Harmony, T., Fernández-Bouzas, A., Díaz-Comas, L., Prado-Alcalá, R. A., & Valdés-Sosa, P. (2007). Changes in EEG current sources induced by neurofeedback in learning disabled children. An exploratory study. *Applied Psychophysiology and Biofeedback*, *32*, 69–183. doi:10.1007/s10484-007-9044-8

Forness, S. R., & Kavale, K. A. (2001). ADHD and a return to the medical model of special education. *Education & Treatment of Children*, *24*, 224–247.

Fox, D. J., Tharp, D. F., & Fox, L. C. (2005). Neurofeedback: An alternative and efficacious treatment for Attention Deficit Hyperactivity Disorder. *Applied Psychophysiology and Biofeedback*, *30*, 365–373. doi:10.1007/s10484-005-8422-3

Freedman, R. R., Lynn, S. J., Ianni, P., & Hale, P. A. (1981). Biofeedback treatment of Raynaud's disease and phenomenon. *Biofeedback and Self-Regulation*, *6*, 355–365. doi:10.1007/BF01000660

Gervirtz, R. (2005). Symposium: Heart rate variability biofeedback: Emotions and the Heart. Paper presented at the 9th Annual Meeting of the Biofeedback Foundation of Europe, Hasselt, Belgium. *Applied Psychophysiology and Biofeedback*, *30*, 159–161.

Goldbeck, L., & Schmid, K. (2003). Effectiveness of autogenic relaxation training on children and adolescents with behavioural and emotional problems. *Journal of the American Academy of Child and Adolescent Psychiatry*, *42*, 1046–1054. doi:10.1097/01.CHI.0000070244.24125.F

Goodman, R. (1997). The strengths and difficulties questionnaire: A research note. *Journal of Clinical Child Psychology and Psychiatry*, *38*, 581–586. doi:10.1111/j.1469-7610.1997.tb01545.x

Greydanus, D. E. (2005). Pharmacologic treatment of Attention-Deficit Hyperactivity Disorder. *Indian Journal of Pediatrics, 72*, 953–960. doi:10.1007/BF02731672

Gunkelman, J. D., & Johnstone, J. (2005). Neurofeedback and the brain. *Journal of Adult Development, 12*(2/3), 93–98. doi:10.1007/s10804-005-7024-x

Hammond, D. C. (2005). Neurofeedback with anxiety and affective disorders. *Child and Adolescent Psychiatric Clinics of North America, 14*, 105–123. doi:10.1016/j.chc.2004.07.008

Harrison, L. J., Manocha, R., & Rubia, K. (2004). Sahaja yoga meditation as a family treatment programme for children with Attention Deficit-Hyperactivity Disorder. *Clinical Child Psychology and Psychiatry, 9*, 479–497. doi:10.1177/1359104504046155

Haynes, S. N., Moseley, D., & McGowan, W. T. (1975). Relaxation training and biofeedback in the reduction of frontalis muscle tension. *Psychophysiology, 12*, 547–552. doi:10.1111/j.1469-8986.1975.tb00044.x

Heinrich, H., Gevensleben, H., & Strehl, U. (2007). Annotation: Neurofeedback-train your brain to train behaviour. *Journal of Child Psychology and Psychiatry, and Allied Disciplines, 48*, 3–16. doi:10.1111/j.1469-7610.2006.01665.x

Henton, W. W., & Iversen, I. H. (1978). *Classical conditioning and operant conditioning.* New York: Springer-Verlag.

Holmes, D. S., & Roth, D. L. (1988). Effects of aerobic exercise training and relaxation training on cardiovascular activity during psychological stress. *Journal of Psychosomatic Research, 32*, 469–474. doi:10.1016/0022-3999(88)90031-1

Holroyd, K., & Penzien, D. B. (1990). Pharmacological versus non-pharmacological prophylaxis or recurrent migraine headache: A meta-analytic review of clinical trials. *Pain, 42*, 1–13. doi:10.1016/0304-3959(90)91085-W

Hunter Kane. (2003). *Discovery project-Portsmouth schools. Benefits of peak performance presentation and coaching.* Retrieved March 6, 2009, from http://www.hunterkane.com/heartmath/heartmath_in_education/case_studies/Discovery.pdf

Hunter Kane. (2006a). *The effects of peak performance training on a group of students statemented with AD(H)D.* Unpublished research project. Hunter Kane Ltd. Retrieved March 6, 2009, from http://www.hunterkane.com/heartmath/heartmath_research/ADHD%20Summary%20Results%20(pre%20publication).pdf

Hunter Kane. (2006b). *HeartMath research: The effects on children with AD/HD.* Retrieved March 6, 2009, from http://www.hunterkane.com/heartmath_research/children_with_ADHD.htm

Jensen, P. S., & Kenny, D. T. (2004). The effect of yoga on the attention and behaviour of boys with Attention-Deficit/Hyperactivity Disorder (ADHD). *Journal of Attention Disorders, 7*, 205–216. doi:10.1177/108705470400700403

Kessler, R. C., Soulkup, J., Davis, R. B., Foster, D., Wilkey, S. A., & Rompay, M. I. V. (2001). The use of complementary and alternative therapies to treat anxiety and depression in the United States. *The American Journal of Psychiatry, 158*, 289–294. doi:10.1176/appi.ajp.158.2.289

Lehrer, P. M., Vaschillo, E., Vaschillo, B., Lu, S., Scardella, A., & Siddique, M. (2004). Biofeedback treatment for asthma. *Chest, 126*, 352–361. doi:10.1378/chest.126.2.352

Lohaus, A., Klein-Heßling, J., Vögele, C., & Kuhn-Henninghausen, C. (2001). Psychophysiological effects of relaxation training in children. *British Journal of Health Psychology, 6*, 197–206. doi:10.1348/135910701169151

Mackintosh, N. J. (1983). *Conditioning and associative learning.* Oxford: Oxford University Press.

Margolis, H. (1990). Relaxation training: A promising approach for helping exceptional learners. *International Journal of Disability, 37*, 215–234. doi:10.1080/0156655900370306

McCraty, R. (2001). *The Freeze-Framer: A stress management and performance enhancement system that increases physiological coherence*. Paper presented at the Futurehealth Winter Brain Meeting, Miami, Florida.

McCraty, R. (2003). *Scientific role of the heart in learning and performance*. Retrieved March 6, 2009, from http://www.heartmath.org/education/scientific-role-heart.pdf

McCraty, R. (2005). Enhancing emotional, social, and academic learning with heart rhythm coherence feedback. *Biofeedback, 33*, 130–134.

McCraty, R., Atkinson, M., Tomasino, D., Goelitz, J., & Mayrovitz, H. N. (1999). The impact of an emotional self-management skills course on psychosocial functioning and autonomic recovery to stress in middle school children. *Integrative Physiological and Behavioral Science, 34*, 246–268. doi:10.1007/BF02688693

McCraty, R., & Tomasino, D. (2004). *Heart rhythm coherence feedback: A new tool for stress reduction, rehabilitation, and performance enhancement*. (pp. 1-6). Retrieved 2009, from http://www.heartmath.org/research/research-papers/HRV_Biofeedback2.pdf

McCraty, R., & Tomasino, D. (2006). Emotional stress, positive emotions, and psychophysiological coherence. In Arnetz, B. B., & Ekman, R. (Eds.), *Stress in health and disease* (pp. 342–365). Weinheim: Wiley. doi:10.1002/3527609156.ch21

McCraty, R., Tomasino, D., Atkinson, M., Aasen, P., & Thurik, S. J. (2000). *Improving test-taking skills and academic performance in high school students using HeartMath learning enhancement tools*. Retrieved March 6, 2009, from http://www.heartmath.org/research/research-papers/improving-test-taking.html

Michael, J. (1975). Positive and negative reinforcement, a distinction that is no longer necessary. Or a better way to talk about bad things. *Behaviorism, 3*. Retrieved November 19, 2009, from http://www.behavior.org/journals_BP/2000/JackMichael.pdf

Mitchell, A., & Savill-Smith, C. (2004). *The use of computer and video games for learning*. London: Learning and Skills Development Agency.

Monastra, V. J., Lynn, S., Linden, M., Lubar, J. F., Gruzelier, J., & LaVaque, T. J. (2005). Electroencephalographic biofeedback in the treatment of Attention-Deficit/Hyperactivity Disorder. *Applied Psychophysiology and Biofeedback, 30*, 95–113. doi:10.1007/s10484-005-4305-x

Monastra, V. J., Monastra, D. M., & George, S. (2002). The effects of stimulant therapy, EEG biofeedback, and parenting style on the primary symptoms of Attention-Deficit/Hyperacitivity Disorder. *Applied Psychophysiology and Biofeedback, 27*, 231–249. doi:10.1023/A:1021018700609

Patrick, G. J. (2002). Biofeedback applications for psychiatric nursing. *Journal of the American Psychiatric Nurses Association, 8*, 109–113. doi:10.1067/mpn.2002.126887

Payne, R. A. (2005). *Relaxation techniques: A practical handbook for the health care professional*. Edinburgh: Elsevier.

Peek, C. J. (2003). A primer of biofeedback instrumentation. In Schwartz, M., & Andrasik, F. (Eds.), *Biofeedback: A practitioner's guide* (3rd ed.). New York: The Guilford Press.

Raymer, R., & Poppen, R. (1985). Behavioural relaxation training with hyperactive children. *Journal of Behavior Therapy and Experimental Psychiatry, 16*, 309–316. doi:10.1016/0005-7916(85)90005-9

Rossiter, T. R., & LaVaque, T. J. (1995). A comparison of EEG biofeedback and psychostimulants in treating Attention Deficit/Hyperactivity Disorders. *Journal of Neurotherapy, 1*, 1–12. doi:10.1300/J184v01n01_07

Roth, D. L., & Holmes, D. S. (1987). Influence of aerobic exercise training and relaxation training on physical and psychologic health following stressful life events. *Psychosomatic Medicine, 49*, 355–365.

Schwartz, G., & Beaty, J. (1977). *Biofeedback: Theory and research*. New York: Academic Press.

Schwartz, M., & Olsen, R. P. (2003). A historical perspective on the field of biofeedback and applied psychophysiology. In Schwartz, M. S., & Andrasik, F. (Eds.), *Biofeedback: A practitioner's guide* (3rd ed.). New York: Guilfords Press.

Schwartz, M. S., & Andrasik, F. (Eds.). (2003). *Biofeedback: A practitioner's guide* (3rd ed.). New York: The Guilford Press.

Shilling, D., & Poppen, R. (1983). Behavioural relaxation training and assessment. *Journal of Behavior Therapy and Experimental Psychiatry, 14*, 99–107. doi:10.1016/0005-7916(83)90027-7

Sinha, D., & Efron, D. (2005). Complementary and alternative medicine use in children with attention deficit hyperactivity disorder. *Journal of Paediatrics and Child Health, 41*(1-2), 23–26. doi:10.1111/j.1440-1754.2005.00530.x

Squire, K. (2009). *Video games in education*. Retrieved October 7, 2009, from http://www.cyberfest.us/Education/Video_Games_in_Education-MIT_Study.pdf

Squire, K., & Jenkins, H. (2003). Harnessing the power of games in education. *Insight (American Society of Ophthalmic Registered Nurses), 3*, 5–33.

St. Martin, C. (2005). *The garden of the heart: HeartMath-the new biotechnology for treating children with ADD/ADHD and arrhythmia*. Retrieved March 6, 2009, from http://www.heartmath.org/research/research-papers/HeartMath_and_ADHD.pdf

Subrahmanyam, K., Greenfield, P., Kraut, R., & Gross, E. (2001). The impact of computer use on children's and adolescents' development. *Applied Developmental Psychology, 22*, 7–30. doi:10.1016/S0193-3973(00)00063-0

Susi, T., Johannesson, M., & Backlund, P. (2007). *Serious games–an overview*. (Technical Report HS-IKI-TR-07-001). Retrieved October 6, 2009, from http://citeseerx.ist.psu.edu/viewdoc/download?doi=10.1.1.105.7828&rep=rep1&type=pdf

Tobin, D. L., Holroyd, K. A., Baker, A., Reynolds, R. V. C., & Holm, J. E. (1988). Development and clinical trial of a minimal contact, cognitive-behavioural treatment for tension headache. *Cognitive Therapy and Research, 12*, 325. doi:10.1007/BF01173301

Wan Rozali, W. A., Hamid, X. H. A., & Sabri, M. I. M. (2007). *Video games: Issues and problems*. Paper presented at the International Conference on Information and Communications Technology, Cairo.

Wells, K. C., Epstein, J. N., Hinshaw, S. P., Conners, C. K., Klaric, J., & Abikoff, H. B. (2000). Parenting and family stress treatment outcomes in Attention Deficit Hyperactivity Disorder (ADHD): An empirical analysis in the MTA study. *Journal of Abnormal Child Psychology, 28*, 543–553. doi:10.1023/A:1005131131159

Yates, A. J. (1980). *Biofeedback and the modification of behaviour*. New York: Plenum Press.

KEY TERMS AND DEFINITIONS

Attention-Deficit/Hyperactivity Disorder (AD/HD): A developmental disorder the essential features of AD/HD is a continual pattern of inattention and/or hyperactivity-impulsivity, comparable to what is typically observed in individuals of the same developmental level. To be diagnosed with AD/HD, a minimum of 12 symptoms listed in the

DSM-IV-TR (APA, 2000) must have persisted for at least six months to a degree that is inconsistent with the appropriate developmental level, and have been present before the age of seven years. Symptoms should be observed as present in two or more settings (e.g., at school and at home), and must demonstrate clear evidence of significant impairment of functioning in social and academic environments.

Biofeedback: Individuals use biofeedback as a training technique using their physiological signals to gain conscious control over their body's functions to improve health and performance.

Classical Conditioning: It is learning to respond in a desired manner whereby a neutral stimulus (known as a conditioned stimulus) is repeatedly presented in association with a stimulus (unconditioned stimulus) eliciting a natural response or reflex (unconditioned response) until the neutral stimulus alone produces the same response (now called the conditioned response).

Heart Rate Variability (HRV): The measure of a person's natural changes between heart beats.

Neurofeedback: Neurofeedback training aims to develop skills for self regulation of brain wave activity, using real time EEG measurements. Individuals learn to train their brain activity to establish control over a desired response by making themselves aware of the sensations associated with the occurrence of a response.

Operant Conditioning: It is the likelihood of whether a specific behaviour is increased or decreased through positive or negative reinforcement. The behaviour becomes associated with the pleasure or displeasure of the reinforcement.

Relaxation: Relaxation is characterised by a weakened state of physiological arousal and peaceful state of mental well-being. Relaxation training involves a number of methods such as meditation procedures, autogenic training, progressive relaxation, visual imagery etc., useful for managing a number of physiological and psychological conditions.

Skin Conductance Level (SCL): The measure of electrical conductance in the skin associated with the activity of sweat glands.

***The Journey To Wild Divine*:** Created by scientist Kurt Smith and game computer graphics artist Corwin Bell, The Journey to Wild Divine is an interactive computer game that uses three biofeedback finger sensors, called 'Magic Rings', to measure the player's heart rate variability (HRV) and skin conductance levels (SCL). Measurements from the sensors are registered through the Wild Divine 'Light Stone' and fed back to the player through visual biofeedback activities, called 'events', on the computer screen.

Chapter 29
As You Like It:
What Media Psychology Can Tell Us About Educational Game Design

Stephanie B. Linek

German National Library of Economics (ZBW), Germany

ABSTRACT

Game-based learning is based on the idea of using the motivational potential of video games within the educational context. Thus, when designing an educational game, not only the fun and game play but also the instructional efficiency of the educational game is of pivotal importance. This chapter provides an overview on media psychological approaches and findings that could be helpful for understanding and creating an educational game. Thereby, a special focus lies on the benefit of an interdisciplinary approach that allows for the integration of an appropriate scientific base from psychology with best-practice game design.

INTRODUCTION AND GENERAL OVERVIEW

There are many general remarks in literature regarding instructional design as well as game design. However, most of them are very general assumptions and lack scientific-empirical proof.

Concrete design recommendations with respect to educational games are rather spare.

This chapter points out, how psychological meaningful recommendations could be derived from theories and empirical findings from the research field of media psychology.

Media psychology is a subfield of psychology. The American Psychological Association defines Media Psychology (Division 46) as follows: "Media Psychology focuses on the role psychologists

DOI: 10.4018/978-1-60960-495-0.ch029

play in various aspects of the media, including, but not limited to, radio, television, film, video, newsprint, magazines, and newer technologies. It seeks to promote research into the impact of media on human behavior; to facilitate interaction between psychology and media representatives; to enrich the teaching, training and practice of media psychology; and to prepare psychologists to interpret psychological research to the lay public and to other professions" (http://www.apa.org/divisions/div46/)

Shortly spoken, Media Psychology applies psychological theories, methods and findings to investigate the intra- and inter-individual psychological processes underlying the perception and behavior of humans in the context of media. (The definition also implies that every *psychological* research on games and game-based learning can be classified as media psychological research.)

From a media psychological perspective the educational game design should be appropriate for the cognitive as well as the affective and motivational demands of the user. Especially the close interconnection and interdependencies between cognition, emotion and motivation should be considered when designing an educational game.

An educational game can be defined as "applications using characteristics of video and computer games to create engaging and immersive learning experiences for delivering specified learning goals, outcomes and experiences" (De Freitas, 2006). From a design perspective, there are three main core elements which are closely interconnected: Multimedia design of the game (including sound and graphics), the design of the narratives of the game (including dialogues, socio-motivational appeal) and the design of the characters within the game (NPCs and avatars). These elements are not exclusively used in (educational) games, but also aspects of other media (e.g., television or conventional e-learning environments). Consequently, not only (media) psychological findings on games and game-based learning but also related media psychological research could

be helpful for providing psychologically founded recommendations on concrete design questions, namely findings on multimedia design, insights on the cognitive and socio-motivational impact of media in general as well as research on media characters in a broader sense (e. g. in television or learning environments).

The following chapter aims to provide scientific-based answers on important design questions one is confronted with when designing a game, namely the multimedia design as well as the socio-motivational appeal of narratives and game characters.

After a short introduction the chapter starts with a description of the most popular and well founded cognitive theories on instructional design. Thereby, also findings are reported that suggests severe shortcomings of such a pure cognitive view. Subsequently, a socio-motivational enhanced view of human-computer interaction is outlined that provides the appropriate psychological-theoretical base for the design of educational games. Thereby, it will be pointed out, how the findings could be used for concrete game design decisions. In a next step games in general and educational games in specific are disputed and the joy of gaming is explored from a media psychological point of view. The chapter finishes with a framework for designing educational games and a short summary of the reported research and its applicability.

COGNITIVE EDUCATIONAL APPROACHES AND INSTRUCTIONAL DESIGN

When designing an educational game, one is confronted with a lot of *multimedia design decisions* that are related to the explanatory parts and the learning elements. Mayer (2003) states "multimedia learning occurs when students build mental representations from words and pictures that are presented to them" (p. 125). Following this definition, also game based-learning can be seen as a kind of multimedia learning since the learning contents of an educational game are often explained by multimedia messages respectively (narrated) animations.

Imagine for example an educational adventure game on a medical training where the student/player (in the role of the avatar) should learn about a bullet wound or injury to the head by the advisory of an experienced medical (medical NPC). Now, the question arises, how to design the explanatory learning parts presented by the NPC: Should the NPC deliver just verbal explanations? Or should the medical NPC show what to do, i.e. healing a wounded other NPC? Or both, i.e. should the visible procedure be commented by the medical NPC? How should this verbal comments of the NPC formulated?

Such questions could be easily answered by applying research on multimedia design that will be described in this section. Thereby, the most popular cognitive psychological approaches on multimedia learning are explained and the theoretically derived and empirically proved multimedia design principles are described. Additional, shortcomings of pure cognitive approaches are demonstrated (by selected research findings) and the impact for educational game design is disputed.

Cognitive Approaches on Multimedia Design

Theoretical Assumptions

The currently most prominent cognitive theories on multimedia design are the cognitive theory of multimedia learning (Mayer, 2001; Clark, & Mayer, 2003) and the cognitive load theory (Sweller, van Merriënboer, & Paas, 1998). These two approaches can be seen as alternative theories that are based on the same theoretical assumptions regarding the human cognitive architecture and lead to analogous design principles (with slightly different argumentations). The following explanations relate to the cognitive theory of multimedia

learning (CTML) because this theory has some advantages for our purpose since it is also extended with respect to socio-motivational factors.

The CTML is based on three pivotal assumptions regarding the human cognitive architecture: the dual-channel assumption, the limited capacity assumption, and the active processing assumption.

Accordingly the *dual-channel assumption* that traces back to the approach of Baddeley (Baddeley, 1992; Baddeley & Logie, 1999) the human information processing system consists of two separate channels: One channel for the processing of visual/pictorial information/representations and one channel for the processing of verbal/auditory information/representations.

The two channels described above are both limited with respect to the amount of information that can be processed at one time (*limited capacity assumption*). The capacity of each channel is independent from each other, i.e., if the capacity of one channel is overloaded this doesn't affect the capacity of the other channel. (In contrast to the working memory, the long-term memory is not limited in its capacity and comprises schemata that that can be used to overcome the limitations of the working memory.)

The *active processing* assumption stresses the importance of sense-making activities and deeper cognitive processing of the incoming information for meaningful learning. Active processing includes the selection of relevant information, the organization of the selected information into coherent meaningful representations as well as the integration of the verbal and pictorial representation.

Principles of Multimedia Learning

Multimedia learning according to Mayer (2003) includes learning with pictures and text (e.g., in books) as well as computer-based learning and learning with dynamic visualizations (animations), auditory/spoken text (narrations), and on-screen text, respectively. The assumptions of the CTML have allowed deriving several design guidelines for multimedia learning which have been supported by numerous empirical investigations (for an overview see Mayer, 2001; Mayer & Moreno, 2002; Sweller, Van Merriënboer, & Paas, 1998). These principles of multimedia learning will be explained in the following:

- **Multimedia principle:** Using dynamic visualization accompanied by spoken/auditory text (= narrated animation) results in higher learning success compared to using a narration alone.
- **Modality-Principle:** When presenting visual graphical representations (pictures, animation) with explanatory text, one should use spoken/auditory text instead of written text. (Theoretical explanation: In the case of spoken text, the pictorial and verbal information is equally spread over the visual and the auditory channel and thus, overload of one of the channels is avoided.)
- **Redundancy principle:** It's more advantageously for learning to present an animation (or picture) and narration alone compared to presenting animation, narration and (identical) on-screen text. (Theoretical explanation: On-screen text is redundant, but requires capacities of the visual channel.)
- **Temporal contiguity principle:** Verbal explanations should be presented just in time, i.e., simultaneously with the corresponding pictures. (Theoretical explanation: Successively presentation would result in a temporal split-attention effect.)
- **Spatial contiguity principle (see also split-attention effect):** If written labels or written short explanations are necessary, they should be presented near the feature that is denominated (in order to avoid visual search or visual split-attention, respectively.)

- **Coherency principle:** Interesting but extraneous (i.e., irrelevant for learning) words, sounds and/or video should be avoided since they require cognitive capacity that is no longer available for learning.

These multimedia principles answered a lot of the questions in the context of the game-based medical training example in the beginning. Now we know, that the medical NPC should deliver his verbal explanations in a spoken way (*modality principle*) while he simultaneously (*temporal contiguity principle*) shows the procedure with a wounded NPC (*multimedia principle*). Additionally we have learned that the medical NPC should not make jokes (or something else) that has nothing to do with the healing procedure itself while explaining it to the learner/avatar (*coherency principle*).

Restrictions of Pure Cognitive Approaches

Although there is broad empirical evidence in favor of the described multimedia design principles there are also some findings that demonstrate several limitations and restrictions.

One prominent example is the so-called *expertise reversal effect* (for an overview see Kalyuga, Ayres, Chandler, & Sweller, 2003) that demonstrates the moderating role of learner characteristics for nearly all of the described multimedia principles (aptitude-treatment interaction). The expertise reversal effect regards to the influence of prior knowledge and was empirically obtained in the comparison of experts versus novices (i.e., inexperienced learners with no or low prior knowledge). Kalyuga and colleagues (2003) provide a cognitive explanation for the expertise reversal effect in the form that the instructional guidance produces a redundancy-effect for experts due to their higher prior knowledge.

For our game-example that means that we have to adapt the verbal explanations to the prior knowledge of the player. This can be easily done by game-level: For the beginners level, the medical NPC should give additional verbal explanations. For the higher levels (when the learner has more prior knowledge), the medical NPC should be silent.

Besides the mentioned restrictions of the cognitive multimedia principles, there are also some first approaches to take also socio-motivational aspects into account which leads to additional design recommendations:

Personalization principle: Verbal explanations should be presented in a personalized style, i.e., using first and second person ("I", "we", "you") rather than a formalized text style, i.e., using third person ("it"). The personalization principle is theoretically explained by the higher involvement of learners when using a personalized text style (Moreno & Mayer, 2000). This explanation goes beyond pure cognitive considerations and takes also socio-motivational aspects into account. Similar statements on the close connection between emotions and cognitions can also be found in the context of research on affective learning (see Picard, Papert, Bender, Blumberg, Breazeal, Cavallo, Machover, Resnick, Roy, & Strohecker, 2004).

Voice principle: The auditory text should be presented with a human standard-accent voice rather than a machine-synthesized foreign-accent voice. This principle is based on two experimental studies and can theoretically be explained by the so-called social agency theory (Mayer, Sobko, & Mautone, 2003) which will be explained below.

Applying the voice principle and personalization principle to our game example, the medical NPC should speak in standard-accent human voice and give the explanations in a personal style, directly addressing the player (i.e. "You have to disinfect the wound first" instead of "One have to disinfect the wound first")

Additionally, there are other approaches on instructional design that directly use socio-motivational factors and could partly be seen as early attempts to playful learning, namely discovery learning and anchored instruction.

Discovery learning is a constructivist learning approach that goes mainly back to the work of Bruner (1967). According to this approach, the best way to learn something is discovery. Within this view, the learner is a problem solver who explores his/her environment like a naïve scientist by testing hypothesis and deriving rules and generalizations. Thus, the goal of education and the role of the teacher aim mainly at supporting these discovery activities of the learner. The discovery learning approach has four core elements, namely curiosity/uncertainty, structure of knowledge, sequencing and motivation.

The *anchored instruction approach* (Bransford, Sherwood, Hasselbring, Kinzer & Williams, 1990) is close related to discovery learning and in several aspects very similar to game-based learning. Anchored instruction has been developed by the Cognition & Technology Group at Vanderbilt (1993) by creating a set of interactive videodiscs which represent the program called "Jasper Woodbury Problem Solving Series". In these videodisc series mathematical concepts should be used to solve problems in the context of several adventures of Jasper Woodbury (which is the protagonist/hero of the story/serial). The video materials include the "narrative anchor": The mathematical problems are embedded in a (adventure) story that serves as an anchor for all subsequent learning and instruction. This narrative anchor is thought to create an interesting, creative, realistic context that engages learners in active constructive learning.

Within these instructional design approaches different methods are used (e.g., coaching, fading, metacognition, structuring of knowledge), that can be easily adapted on game based learning.

In our game-scenario, a discovery learning approach would propagate for example, that the player can discover some complications like a hidden bullet in the wound that is only visible from a specific angle. Following an anchored instruction approach the medical NPC could coach the player while removing the bullet without violating important blood vessels.

Discovery learning and anchored instruction are only two examples for possible pedagogical foundations of games. A meta-analysis of different pedagogical foundations of available educational games is given by Kebritchi and Hirumi (2008).

INTERACTING WITH MEDIA: SOCIO-MOTIVATIONAL ENHANCED VIEW

The described findings and theories above regard mainly to multimedia learning. However, they can also be used for the design of educational games, especially the design of learning situations like pointed out above.

Although there are first attempts to include also socio-motivational aspects in the theoretical approaches on multimedia learning, we must keep in mind that CTML as well as other approaches on instructional design concentrates mainly on cognitive factors. In the following we turn to approaches that focus stronger on socio-motivational aspects and their interconnection with cognitive factors. The essential theoretical (media psychological) approaches that provide the backbone for this view are the media equation theory, the social agency theory as well as research on identification and parasocial interaction with media characters. These approaches allow us to give additional recommendations for the design of the narratives and the game characters.

Media Equation Theory

Basic Assumptions

The so-called media equation theory states "media equal real life" (Reeves & Nass, 1996, p. 5). People behave towards media just in the same way like they behave in real life, i.e., they apply the same social and natural rules of the real world on media.

Thus, the interaction with media "is fundamental social and natural" (Reeves & Nass, 1996, p. 5) including several social principles like gender stereotypes, politeness rules, or similarity-attraction.

It's worth noting, that the media equation (ME) is a *ubiquitous* phenomenon. ME applies not only to specific individuals but rather every type of media user. The studies on ME included experienced (even computer specialists) as well as inexperienced computer user as participants. Normally, the social and natural reactions towards media are *automatic and unconscious*, i.e., users deny behaving in a social way towards media. Reactions in the sense of ME are not an exceptional behavior; rather they are *wide spread* and were found with respect to *different media* (television, computers, pictures). Accordingly, media must not be very sophisticated; also simple features (e.g., line drawings and even the color of a screen-coverage) are apt to elicit social and natural behavior towards media.

Empirical Evidence: Selected Findings

There is broad empirical evidence in favor of the media equation approach that proves the application of several social and natural principles to media (for an overview see Reeves & Nass, 1996). For example, it was found, that people react positively to *flattery* given by computers and that computers easily accepted as *teammates* (Nass, Fogg, & Moon, 1996).

Additionally, people apply *politeness rules* to computers. For example, when someone is asked for a feedback regarding a presentation, he/she (as a polite person) gives more positive answers when asked by the presenter himself. Contrariwise, one gives more honest, less positive answers if someone else (from the auditory) asks for his/her evaluation. Similar, computer users give more positive (polite) evaluations regarding a computer program when the evaluation was given to the same computer whereas less positive (more honest) evaluations were given when another computer ask for the evaluation (or the evaluation was given paper-pencil based). This latter finding is especially important for the assessment of an accurate (not polite) evaluation of a computer program or a game.

Moreover, Moon (2000) proved principles of intimate exchange in the form of *reciprocal self-disclosure* in human-computer interaction: After the computer provided some information about itself (his system properties etc.) the users show greater willingness to give private information. (One can exploit this phenomenon when e.g., assessing the players personal data.)

Research on media equation has also shown that people ascribe *personality* to a computer based on the verbal and visual cues it deliver and prefer computers that resemble their own personality (Nass & Lee, 2001; Linek, Schwarz, Hirschberg, Kickmeier-Rust, & Albert, 2007). However, there was not only evidence in favor of *similiarity-attraction* but also for *complementary-attraction* towards interactive computer characters (Isbister & Nass, 2000). This inconsistency of results matches the inconsistent findings in human-human interaction. Which of the two principles will be applied depends probably on the concrete context (e.g. Amodio & Showers, 2005).

In accordance with *consistency-attraction* of human-human interaction people prefer consistent computer characters (Isbister & Nass, 2000; Stern, Mullenix & Yaroslavsky, 2006), i.e., characters that behave and appear in a consistent way (e.g. dominant gesture together with dominant voice compared to a submissive voice).

There was also evidence for *gender-stereotyping* towards media. For instance, computers with female voices were seen as more competent regarding female topics like love & relationships whereas male-voice computers were ascribed a higher competence regarding male topics like math and technical issues (Nass, Moon, Green, 1997). Similar, if one TV-program was labeled as a "*specialist*" its contents received higher competence

ratings compared to an identical program without such a label (Reeves & Nass, 1996).

Besides social rules, also *natural rules* are important for human-computer interaction. For example, in real life it is quite natural to have a blurry view because of fog or dust. (Additionally, because of the anatomy of the human visual system we have only a very sharp view in the fovea.) However, to hear a blurry sound is rather unusual in the real world. Moreover, normally speech and lip movement appear synchronized. Especially, in real life it is impossible to get sound before perception of the visual scene. (The other way round is in some cases possible because of the different speed of light and sound.) In concordance with these natural experiences it was found, that the fidelity of graphics has only little effects on attention, memory, and evaluation of experience whereas audio fidelity has rather strong effects on these variables (Reeves & Nass, 1996, chapter 18). Additionally, also the asynchronicity of sound/speech and lip movements in media presentations has strong negative effects on the evaluations of the speaker – even so the users didn't recognize the asynchronicity (Reeves & Nass, 1996, chapter 19).

The ME and the reported findings give us important information on the design of the narratives, i.e. we can directly apply the natural and social rules on our game design. For example, according to the consistency principle the game characters should be behave in a consistent way; this in turn requires that we need a consistent personality for each character. If we design the medical NPC as an extraverted character, he should behave in an extraverted way all through the different game scenarios, i.e. the NPC should speak a lot and seeking for companionship no matter if the situation is sad or funny.

The findings on ME (on natural rules) provide also information that the quality of sound within a game is of even higher importance than the graphics. Especially, the synchronicity of voices with the lip movements of the NPC and the avatar is necessary to create authentic game characters.

Social Agency Theory

The ME approach relates mainly to affective, motivational and social variables. Thus, the question arises if and how such social and natural behavior towards media might affect computer-based learning. This issue was addressed by the so-called social agency theory which will be described in the following.

The social agency theory (Mayer, Sobko & Mautone, 2003) is based on the idea (borrowed from ME) that multimedia messages can also incorporate social cues, e.g., in forms of pictures or voices. Because of these social cues subjects interpret the multimedia message as a kind of social communication and not a pure information delivery. Social cues result in learners being more motivated and investing more effort to understand the spoken words. Or in other words, because of social cues the learners engage in a sense-making activities and deeper cognitive processing which in turn should improve learning outcomes.

To support this assumptions Mayer and his colleagues (2003) compared a human voice with a computer-synthesized voice and a standard-accent with a foreign-accented voice. In accordance with their theoretical assumptions they found that people learned better with a human, standard-accent voice (*voice principle*). Further support for the greater effectiveness of a human voice was also provided by Atkinson, Mayer & Merrill (2005).

Research on the impact of other social principles like gender-stereotyping and interpersonal attraction provided additional evidence for the influence of socio-motivational aspects in multimedia learning by demonstrating greater effectiveness of female voices within a male/mathematical domain (speaker/gender effect; Linek, 2007b). However, the causal chain assumed by the social agency theory (via motivation) was not fully sup-

ported. Rather the results suggest the relevance of other, additional variables beside motivation.

In this line of reasoning it can be assumed that also other specific features of a human voice (besides accent and gender) may influence learning since also other social principles/stereotypes were applied towards voices, like for example the attractiveness stereotype: Visual attractive people were judged as being more intelligent, nicer and likeable (Dion, Berscheid & Walster, 1972). The same is true for the so-called vocal attractiveness (Zuckerman & Driver, 1989).

Applying the social agency theory to educational games, it is of essential importance getting the player involved in the explanations given on the learning content. This could be done by designing a strong relationship between the medical NPC and the player, e.g. the medical NPC can be designed as an old friend of the player's character. Taking the speaker/gender principle into account the medical NPC should be designed as a female character and in the case of a male player, flattery could used to establish a strong involvement.

Learning with Pedagogical Agents

The social agency theory and ME can be also suggested the main theoretical background for research on learning with pedagogical agents. Pedagogical agents (PAs) or animated interface agents are embodied figures with human-like behavior that aid users through a computer program (Baylor & Kim, 2009). Thus, the function an animated interface agent in a "normal" (multimedia, hypermedia) learning environment seems to be quite similar to the role of the NPC that gives guidance and advices in an educational game. Because of this similarity, research on PAs is also insightful for the design of game characters that serve as advisors and guide the player through the game.

PAs are discussed controversially and have their advocates as well as their opponents. Advocates of PAs claimed their positive impact on motivation, engagement, usability, entertainment and learning success. However, opponents of PAs regard to quite similar aspects and argue that PAs might obstruct human-computer interaction, induce false mental models of the system or distract the user from learning.

Empirical research on the value of PAs provided partly inconsistent finding (Woo, 2009). But despite the inconsistencies in research, an overall view of the field leads to the following conclusions (see Dehn & Van Mulken, 2000): PAs *can* improve subjective experience and enjoyment as well as the usability of the system and performance. The improvement of usability and performance might partially be due to the social presence (persona effect; see Lester, Converse, Kahler, Barlow, Stone & Bhogal, 1997) respectively the social appeal of the agent (Beale & Creed, 2009). Besides, it might partially be caused by the surplus information a PA delivers, e.g. by signaling or hightlighting important information (e.g., Cassell & Thórisson, 1999; Ozcelik, Arslan-Ari, & Cagiltay, 2010), a functionality, that can be easily used in educational games as well.

With respect to concrete design features of PAs the findings on media equation described above can be used for PAs in conventional e-learning environments as well as for characters in educational games. Additional, research findings on PAs in particular provide further insights regarding some specific design features:

- **Realism/naturalism and color:** According to Baylor (2005) realistic images are more apt compared to cartoon images, especially for male students. However, the findings of Gulz and Haake (2005) suggest that an iconic visual representation might be more supportive. Recent findings from Groom and colleagues (2009) provide evidence that a moderate level of realism should be used. Regarding games in specific, the results of a design-study proved the users'

preference for a naturalistic and colored non-player character (Linek et al., 2007).

- **Stereotypes:** Research on ME showed, that stereotypes are applied to computer characters, e.g., a male character is seen as an expert for a male domain. However, the fact that stereotypes are applied doesn't mean that stereotyped characters are preferable. For example, Baylor (2005) found, that PAs with *non*-stereotypical roles are supportive for motivation as well as for learning success. This finding fits also with the speaker/gender effect (Linek, 2007b) according to which a female voice is advantageously in a mathematical male domain. Accordingly, the speaker/gender effect is explained by schema-incongruity between math as a masculine content and female voice as a feminine presentation format.

- **Ethnicity and similarity-attraction:** With respect to ethnicity for African-American students an African-American PA should be used. This design recommendation is in line with research of ME on similarity-attraction. However, the findings of Moreno and Flowerday (2006) show that learning with a same-ethnicity PA chosen by the users themselves can also corrupt learning because of cognitive distraction, i.e., learners concentrate more on how the PA represents their own ethnicity than on learning contents.

- **Choice:** The possibility to choose a PA by the users themselves is assumed to be the optimal way to serve users preferences and thus, enhances motivation (see e.g., Ryan & Deci, 2000). However, empirical studies take this putative advantage of choice into question. Moreno and Flowerday (2006) found no positive effect of choosing a PA (neither for learning nor for the evaluation of the program). Similar, the findings of Linek (2007b) suggest that the possibility of choosing a specific speaker/voice may enhance motivation but has no impact on learning.

The research on PAs gives further evidence for applying social rules. However, it is important to not, that non-stereotypical roles are advantageously, e.g. to have a female doctor and a male nurse as NPCs. Additionally, the findings imply that it is essential being adaptive to the player's characteristics, i.e. provide game characters of the same ethnicity or similar personality. Another important point is to give the player (at least to some extend) the possibility to choose, e.g. in our medical training example the choice between different medical NPCs as mentor/companion throughout the game.

Last but not least, research on PAs provides important information on the overall graphical design in the sense that a colored, naturalistic design is preferable.

Media Characters: Parasocial Interaction and Identification

Like pointed out, research on PAs and ME could be easily used for designing the non-player character (NPC) that provides guidance and takes the role of the teacher within an educational game. However, regarding the design of the other NPCs and the avatar(s) within an educational game, other field within media psychology, namely research on parasocial interaction and identification provide deeper insights in optimizing the educational game- design.

Parasocial Interaction

The phenomenon of parasocial interaction (PSI) was first mentioned by Horton and Wohl (1956) who regard to the interaction of mass media users with human media figures (such like presentators, anchor man, or newscaster). They called this kind of interaction *parasocial*, because on the one hand

the interaction is *social* since the mass media users act in way typical for normal social relationships, however on the other hand it is only *para*-social because it is not reciprocal - since the media figure doesn't really participate in the interaction and his/her behavior is not (directly) related to the user. A consistent repeated PSI could also result in a parasocial relationship (Giles, 2002; Gleich, 1997; Sanderson, 2009). PSI is not necessary positive but could also be hostile in its nature (Konjin & Horn, 2005; Sanderson, 2008).

Giles (2002) identifies three key aspects for PSI: Authenticity/realism, representation across different media outlets, and user contexts. Additionally, he describes four qualities of social encounters: Number of persons involved, physical distance, social conventions, and potential relationship. Based on these qualities Giles develops an extended model according to which there is a continuum of social to parasocial interaction.

Recently, Klimmt, Hartmann & Schramm (2006) provided a theoretical model with a more process-based view of PSI. Thereby the authors differentiate between cognitive, emotional and behavioral phenomenon as PSI (sub-) processes. In the case of low personal involvement or "low-level PSI", respectively all three subcomponents are of low intensity. Contrariwise, "high-level PSI" occurs if at least some PSI components are of high intensity. The process-oriented view suggests that the intensity of the personal involvement might dynamically change in the course of the viewing process.

Research on PSI is strongly connected with the ME approach and is of high relevance for the conceptualization of game-characters, especially the NPC-design. Focused research on the design of game-characters provided additional insights. For example it was found, that there was also similarity-attraction regarding the personality-characteristics of the NPC (Linek et al., 2007) Accordingly, it could be suggested, that the personality characteristics of the NPC and the PSI within the educational game should be adaptive to the players preferences. For example, if the player likes a snappy, yoking style of conversation and some romantic relationship within the game then we should implement some accordingly NPC, e.g. to have another NPC. This could be a (male/female – depending on the player's gender) medical student, nurse, or relative of the wounded NPC that uses this conversation-style and thus, strengthened the player's involvement by providing an additional incentive in the form of an interesting PSI.

First attempts to create believable, adaptive game characters were made by the PLEASE Model (Felicia & Pitt, 2007) and the BASIC Model (Romano, Sheppard, Hall, Miller, & Ma, 2005).

Identification with Media Characters

An avatar is the game character our player is thought to identify with (Hoffner & Buchanan, 2005; Klimmt, Hefner, & Vorderer, 2009). Thus, the avatar should be designed in a way that eases this process of identification or the user should have the option to create the avatar by his/her own (like for example in the virtual 3D world "Second Life", see http://secondlife.com). In this line of reasoning research on wishful identification with television characters might be useful. Wishful identification can be described as the wish to behave and become like a specific media character.

In a study with 208 adults at the average age of 20 years, Hoffner & Buchanan (2005) found that wishful identification is more likely with characters that have attitudes similar to the viewer and with same-gender characters. This is in line with prior studies that found higher wishful identification with same-gender characters, whereby several studies with children reveal that this tendency was stronger for boys compared to girls (e.g., Hoffner, 1996; Miller & Reeves, 1976). One possible explanation could be that it is more socially acceptable for girls to take a male role than for boys to behave in a feminine way (Deaux & Lafrance, 1998).

Further findings of Hoffner & Buchanan (2005) showed, that for wishful identification with same-gender characters, male viewers prefer male characters that were successful, intelligent, and violent. Contrariwise, female viewers identify more likely with female characters that are successful, intelligent, admired and attractive. However, regarding identification with characters of the opposite gender, both, males and females show higher wishful identification with successful and admired characters. Additionally, it was found that most respondents prefer a character of their own race whereby this preference was much higher among white participants. It is worth noting that humor was the only variable not correlated with wishful identification.

The reported findings can be directly applied to the design of the player's avatar, which in turn means, that we (again) have to be adaptive to the player's characteristics, not only to the player's gender but also gender-related preferences. Again, it is advantageously to provide some choice, not only choice between a female or male avatar but also the possibility to create an avatar with the preferred attributes (visible appearance as well as personality).

The Dark Side of Entertainment

So far we concentrated on features that enhance the attraction towards a media character. However, to be fair we should also have a look at the other side of entertainment and avert our eyes from comedies and romances with beauty queens and sunny boys. Let's consider splatters and thrillers with their ugly monsters, nasty girls and brutal men ;-)

Normally, games include not only good, beautiful and likeable characters. Contrariwise, sometimes the evil, bad guys are the secret heroes that are crucial for a good storytelling (Imagine "Star Wars" without Darth Vader or "Quake" without monsters – wouldn't it be boring?) Accordingly, the PEFiC (perceiving and experiencing fictional characters) approach of Konjin and Hoorn (2005), assumes that involvement and distance are two independent sources for the appreciation of fictional characters. That means that involvement with a character is independent from the distance to a character. For example, on can feel very distant to a (bad, ugly) character and simultaneously be very involved with this (distant) character. This empirical study (on movie characters) provides some first evidence, that involvement and distance in fact have independent effects. Additionally, it is worth noting, that feelings of ambivalence or imbalance, which are perceived as a negative emotional state in real life, may enhance enjoyment in fictional experiences. Thus, the interaction with an evil or complicated, ambivalent character might be seen as a kind of social challenge (social challenging situation) which in turn could enhance motivation and enjoyment.

For our game scenario this means that we need also some evil, disliked NPCs, for example a nasty other doctor or a criminal NPC who has shot the wounded patient. The evil NPC can also be used to add some special educational/training aspects of the game scenario. For example, to train stress-resistance, the criminal NPC might menace the player while he/she vet the wounded NPC.

GAMES AND GAME-BASED LEARNING: WHAT MAKES THE DIFFERENCE?

So far we have constructed an educational game scenario by applying findings of other conventional media. In this section the essential differences between games and game-based learning in contrast to conventional media use and technology-enhanced learning are outlined. These differences lead to additional design recommendations and provide a deeper insight in the joy of gaming and the benefits of game-based learning.

New Generation of Learners

Besides the motivational potential of educational games via gameplay there are also other arguments for the propagation of game-based learning that refer to the learner itself. As Prensky (2005) pointed out, there are two pivotal reasons for using game-based learning: First, the learners nowadays are different from former generations and thus, second, we need new ways to motivate this new generation of learners. According to the considerations of Prensky (2001, 2005, 2006), the learners nowadays have completely different media socialization since they grow up with the digital technology. From the very beginning they are used to the new kinds of media experiences provided by e.g., computers, video games, cell phones and other digital tools. Prensky (2005) named these learners Digital Natives, because "our students today are all native speakers of the digital language of computers, video games, and the Internet" (p. 98). Due to these new kinds of experiences "thinking patterns" have changed.

Accordingly, Prensky (2005, p.102) describes the unique pattern of motivating elements inherent to games that he supposed as excellent facilities for teaching Digital Natives:

The fun of games gives *enjoyment and pleasure* and the play itself provides *intense and passionate involvement*. The rules within games deliver *structure* whereas the goals of the game incorporate *motivation*. The interactivity within games gives *doing* and the game's adaptivity foster *flow*. The outcomes and feedback of games are related to learning and the win states deliver *ego gratification*. Furthermore, players get *adrenalin* by the conflict and competition elements and their *creativity* is activated by problem solving. Additionally, games provide also *social groups* by interaction as well as *emotion* by characters and story.

Prensky (2005) pointed out that gaming is continuous and constantly learning and thus, digital game-based learning should consist of high gameplay as well as of high learning. Ideally, these two components are equally balanced. Overall, the game and the gameplay have priority or like Prensky stated "Fun (i.e., gameplay) first, learning second" (p. 119). To refine these very general guidelines he explained the most important points of this creation process in more detail (p. 111ff), i.e., the understanding of the player's individual characteristics and preferences, the selection of the appropriate game style and game elements, the understanding of the learning content and the accordingly careful choice of learning activities and techniques. (Analogous argumentation could be found by Mitchell and Savaill-Smith (2004) based on a literature review.)

Game-Based Learning: Mission Impossible or a Matter of Course?

From the perspective of a practical game designer (e.g., Crawford, 1997, Salen & Zimmerman, 2004) similar design recommendations can be drawn. For example, the game designer Chris Crawford (1997) claims not only that computer games are a new form of art but also states that learning is the core motivation for all gaming activities. With regard to gameplay of young animals (that trained their survival abilities in a playful way) he claims, that playing is the oldest and most original form of learning and preparation for real life. According to Crawford (1997) there are also other motivations for playing games like fantasy/exploration (whereby games especially apt for escapism because they are participatory), nose-thumbing (i.e., breaking social rules and conventions in a safety setting), proving oneself (i.e., to be a hero; this aspect regards to the risk and safeness of a game respectively winning by chance versus winning by skills/power), social lubrication (i.e., games fostering social interactions with other players), exercise (i.e., play as a funny way of training) and need for acknowledgement.

However, these general motivations for playing games have to be differentiated from the reasons for choosing/playing a specific game which depends mainly on enjoyment aspects like gameplay and sensory gratification as well as on the individual preferences.

An affirmative argumentation can be found by Koubek and Macleod (2004) who state that "playing is not necessary funny" and "learning is not necessarily educational" (p. 15). They see playing activities as natural learning since their original function in animal world is "experimental preparation for adult life" (p17). Thus, it is quite natural to use games and playing activities in the educational context.

However, neither Prensky's argumentation nor the argumentation by practical game designers is based on hard empirical evidence. Even though there are some studies and meta-studies that provide first evidence on the effectiveness of educational games (e.g., Papastergiou, 2009), most of the data are on a general level and don't focus on the single elements of the surface design. More specific examinations like the study of Ritterfeld, Shen, Wang, Nocera, and Wong (2009), that support the effectiveness of multimodality ad interactivity, provide deeper insights but also on a rather abstract level, i.e. there are various practical ways how multimodality and interactivity can be integrated in a game.

In the sections above several concrete design recommendations were derived from empirical findings on conventional media and an accordingly practical example was provided. However, what we have created so far was mostly a pleasurable learning scenario with interesting characters and dialogues. What is still missing is the overall "frame", i.e. what makes the educational game as such enjoyable. Subsequently, the core features of an enjoyable gaming experience and its connection to learning will be outlined.

The Joy of Gaming

The joy of gaming is a composition of different aspects which are closely interconnected. These different aspects and pivotal concepts of enjoyable gaming and playful learning are described and integrated. Thereby, intrinsically motivating instruction and rather blurry concepts like "enjoyment" will be explored. Additionally, the so called flow-theory is outlined as an approach that conceptualizes the challenges (including learning) within a (game-) scenario as a crucial element for the pleasurable so-called flow-experience. Thereby, a special issue is the need for an adaptive game design that is accomplished not only by different "levels" but also by the consideration of different user subgroups. In this context, also gender-specific aspects of enjoyable gaming are described.

Intrinsically Motivating Instruction and Enjoyment

In talking about the reasons why people play computer games, the terms enjoyment, immersion, and flow are popular starting points. If one takes a closer look at the different motivations for playing games identified in the literature (Crawford, 1997; Dondi, Edvinsson, & Moretti, 2004; Grodal, 2000; Linek, 2007a; Ritterfeld, Cody & Vorderer, 2009; Vorderer & Bryant, 2006) it becomes obvious, that there are multiple aspects that attract players, for example active participation, social and parasocial interaction, fantasy, escapism, collaborative interaction, pleasure of control, and/or breaking social rules and conventions in a safety setting.

A first systematic framework regarding the motivation of players is provided by Malone (1981) who proposes a theory of intrinsically motivating instruction. This approach is based on a review of prior work on intrinsic motivation as well as on studies on highly motivating computer games. The core concepts of Mallone's (1981) approach are challenge, fantasy and curiosity.

Challenge is constituted by a goal with uncertain outcome. According to Malone (1981) the goal should be personally meaningful and obvious or easy to identify. Additionally, to enhance the

motivation to reach a specific goal there should be clear performance feedback. The uncertain outcome can be constituted by variable difficulty levels of the game itself and/or by multiple level goals, i.e., the goal vary in difficulty (e.g., by speeded responses). Additionally, also hidden information and randomness can constitute uncertain outcomes.

Fantasy is another important element for fostering intrinsic motivation in games. Many of the "natural" games of children include fantasy elements (e.g. playing ghosts, pirates, knights, monsters…) and thus, it seems to be plausible that the same kinds of fantasy-aspects are important for the appeal of external game environments.

Curiosity is constituted by novelty, complexity, surprise, and incongruity. The potential of a gaming environment to provoke and satisfy our curiosity is essential for intrinsic motivation.

The approach of Malone on intrinsically motivating instruction is very similar to the enjoyment of media in general. Vorderer, Klimmt, and Ritterfeld (2004) conceptualize "media-related enjoyment as a complex construct that includes references to physiological, affective, and cognitive dimensions" (p. 389). In their view, enjoyment is the heart of media entertainment whereby entertainment is defined as the user's response to media. They listed three main motives for being entertained: Escapism, mood management, and competition.

Escapism an be described as the tendency to escape from the actual real word or the social environment, respectively, in which the person experienced frustration or is somehow underprivileged (e.g., Henning & Vorderer, 2001; Katz & Foulkes, 1962)

Mood management relates to the so-called mood-management theory by Zillmann (1988, 2006) which states that people use the media experiences for optimizing their emotional state and their arousal level, respectively. For example, if a person is under-stimulated (i.e., in a low level of arousal), he/she will choose an exciting action film in order to higher his/her arousal near to the optimal level. Thus, media (experiences) are used for regulation of one's own mood (by means of optimizing the stimulus environment).

Competition relates mainly to interactive media use. Whereas the use of traditional media is an activity that (normally) requires not much effort, interactive media offer challenging opportunities. Thus, people who seek for achievement and competition within the media use will mainly choose interactive media. In this line of reasoning, Vorderer and his colleagues assume that "the most important motive for interactively entertaining oneself" is "the wish to be challenged, though, to compete with others, with a program, or even with one's own previous achievements (i.e., score)" (Vorderer et al., 2004, p. 400; see also Vorderer, Hartmann, & Klimmt, 2003). This might be the important difference between traditional and interactive media. Whereas feedback on success and failure or even the notion of achievement is often seen as detrimental to entertainment through traditional media, the absence of challenge, competition and achievement seems to be fatal for the entertainment through interactive media (Vorderer et al., 2003, 2004).

Based on the described theoretical considerations, an educational game should be designed in a *challenging* way, i.e. in our medical example the background story should give an extraordinary important reason for healing the wounded NPC, e.g. the wounded NPC is the father of the player's avatar or a scientist who possess the formula for stop global warming. Regarding *fantasy* there are unlimited possibilities: We could add some evil NPC as pirates or put the medical scenario in the middle of the jungle with bad hygienic conditions (which in turn can be used for teaching some knowledge about parasites or sepsis). These fantasy elements can build also the basis for *curiosity*, e.g. to find a healing plant in the jungle. Fantastic elements are also closely connected to *escapism*, i.e., being in a jungle with a good companionship instead of being alone in a high-rise building. The challenging situations in the game can provide also the accurate stimulation for *mood management*, e.g. the player is stimulated by facing a danger like a wild tiger in the jungle or by being menaced by the evil NPC. *Competition* as a main element for entertainment can be easily implemented by another competing NPC or in the case of a multiplayer game also by other players.

Moreover, competition and achievement can also be provided in the form of the challenging situation itself and the progress of the player in the face of his growing skills like it is pointed out by the so-called flow theory which will be described in the next section.

Flow Theory

As mentioned above, challenge is one core element for motivation in games (Malone, 1981). Challenge is also a key concept of the flow theory (Csikszentmihalyi, 1975, 1990; Moneta & Csikszentmihalyi, 1996). The flow theory is a unified framework on subjective experience in the course of mastering everyday challenges. According to the flow theory, the quality of subjective experience is determined by the balance between the perceived challenges (intrinsic demands) on the one hand and the perceived skills (self-perceived capacity to meet demands) on the other hand. If challenges and skills are both at a low level, the person experiences apathy. If the perceived challenges are lower than the perceived skills, the person is bored. If the perceived challenges overrun the perceived skills, the person feels anxiety. If the perceived challenges as well as the perceived skills are simultaneously high, the person experiences flow or flow in consciousness, respectively, and this represents the highest quality of subjective experience. Thus, according to the flow theory the balance between challenges and skills is crucial for intrinsic motivation and enjoyment of the activity. In general, research supports this assumption (Asakawa 2004; Moneta

620

& Csikszentmihalyi, 1996; Schweinle, Meyer & Turner, 2006).

The experience of flow or being immersed the activity, is intrinsically rewarding and can be seen as a hedonic state. This implies two dynamics (assumed that the person tries to reach this marvelous state): If the person is bored (skills > challenges) then he/she should seek new challenges. On the other hand, if the person is overloaded and anxious (skills < challenges) he/she should try to enhance his/her skills and knowledge, or in other words he/she will engage in learning activities.

Overall, the so-called flow-experience can be characterized by intense, focused concentration, clear goals, direct, immediate feedback (success and failures are apparent), balance between the perceived challenges and the perceived skills, feeling of control, distortion of the sense of time, loss of self-consciousness (because of being immersed in the activity), and hedonic quality of the experience (intrinsically rewarding).

Thereby the flow theory states that there are several conditions that facilitate the experience of flow: Structured activities with manageable rules and clear goals, the possibility to adjust the required actions in respect to one's own abilities, the provision of clear feedback, as well as the elimination of distraction and the provision of the possibility for concentrated work.

The mentioned conditions for facilitation the flow-experience (that are suggested as a core experience of successful conventional video games), are often inherent elements of video games. A game itself can be defined as a rule-based play (Salen & Zimmermann, 2004) which in turn implies (at least partly) structured activities and manageable rules with clear goals. In our medical training example, the rescue of the wounded NPC is the goal and the rules traces back to the (medical) possibilities within the game environment (jungle versus a hospital) and the physiological laws of the body. Feedback could be provided either by the medical NPC (saying if an action is helpful or stupid) or the reaction of the wounded NPC (e.g.,

dying). One core feature for balancing challenges and skills and thus, enhancing the flow-experience, is (again) adaptivity. In a rough way, this can be done by the different levels within the game: On first level just one NPC with a light wound is presented; on higher levels the player has to manage more severe wounds or has to rescue more than one wounded NPC. Thereby, it becomes clear, that learning and gaming are in principle two sides of the same medal: The challenge of the training situation/game scenario is the main vehicle for experiencing flow (as an intrinsically rewarding state).

The conception of flow theory is not completely new (see also Moneta & Csikszentmihalyi, 1996). Similar theoretical conceptions are e.g., the Yerkes-Dodson-law (Yerkes & Dodson, 1908; Hebb, 1955) or the theoretical conception of Berlyne (1970) regarding stimulus complexity. Roughly spoken, the common denominator of these approaches is, that pleasure as well as learning is optimized in an medium level (of arousal, challenge, complexity) that neither bores nor overwhelmed the subject whereby the absolute level (what is "medium") depends on the person's individual abilities/characteristics. It is worth noting that these approaches partly regard to physiological, partly to affective and partly to cognitive aspects.

With respect to (educational) games it can be assumed that the challenges in the game should be adaptive with respect to the gamer's skills – not only in order to enhance learning but also to foster enjoyment of the gamer. However, besides this cognitive adaptivity, one can also ask for sensory adaptivity (in parallel to sensory curiosity) or generally spoken physical adaptivity which may be influenced for example by the speed of gaming and/or perceptual challenges like music. Additionally, also the parasocial situations included in a game, i.e. the interaction with the NPC and other gaming characters or social conflicts, can be challenging and may evoke curiosity. Thus, one can also think of socio-affective adaptivity (see

Linek, 2007a). This threefold conception of flow is very well in line with newer conceptualizations of (media) enjoyment like explained above.

With respect to game design, this means, that we have to go beyond providing just different game levels of cognitive difficulty, e.g. in the form of more or less difficult medical situations, but also provide different levels of socio-affective and physiological challenge. Socio-affective challenge can be implemented by the game characters and the dialogues, e.g. having on the easiest level a very nice patient medical NPC and on higher levels an inpatient, harsh doctor who gives advisory. Different physical levels can be accomplished by different properties of the gaming environment like speed, e.g. escape from an old slow tiger versus an adult very fast tiger. But also other physical attributes like noise or light can be used and implemented in the game, e.g. by having a quiet place with sonny weather or a jungle camp in the middle of an earthquake.

Gendered Gaming and the Influence of Cognitive Styles

It is often claimed, that computer games are a male domain. However, recently there is an increasing number of female players (see e.g., ESA, 2007) whereby first research findings (e.g., Hartmann & Klimmt, 2006) suggest very different reasons for males and females to play games. With respect to existing video games, female player claim a lack of meaningful social interaction and are discourage by violence and stereotyped gender roles of female game characters. Additionally, the findings suggests that female players are less keen of competitive elements but rather attracted by the (para)social appeal of video games.

This is in line with Dickey's (2006) review on girl gamers, according to which collaboration and community is one of the most important elements for female gamers. This regards to Tailors (2003) notion that Massively Multiplayer Online Role-Playing Games (MMORPGs) comprise several female-appropriate game-characteristics. However, one should keep in mind, that there are also gender-dependent motivations for taking part in MMORPGs (Yee, 2006a, and b). Whereas males indicate higher scores on the motivational factors "achievement" and "manipulation", female gamers score higher on the motivational factors "relationship", "immersion", and "escapism".

However, until now it is not yet clear how to address these different needs of female versus male players. A possible starting point is given by Sherry (2004) who points out that those general gender-dependent differences in cognition and behavior fits very well with the found gender-dependent preferences for different game-genres like puzzles, adventure-games, or card games.

In a set of studies Sherry and his colleagues (cited in Sherry, 2004) provided empirical support for the conceptualization of enjoyment as media flow since challenge was one of the top motives for playing games. Additionally, regarding individual preferences, Sherry (2004) pointed out that the preferences of girls and boys for different types of video games match their gender-related abilities. For example, empirical findings reveal an advantage for boys in spatial vision which is in line with the male preference for shooters that often requires 3D rotation. On the other hand, females normally have higher abilities in color memory and verbal fluency which matches their preference for puzzles and classic board games.

Recent research provides not only support to the general effectiveness of game based learning, but also suggests that the cognitive style of the gamer is of special importance (Milovanović, Minović, Kovačević, Minović, & Starčević, 2009; Sherry, 2004). Following the argumentation of Sherry (2004) who combines the conception of media enjoyment and flow theory, media enjoyment is a result of the balance between the complexity of the media content and the user's abilities to interpret/understand this content. The difficulty to understand the media content can result either from formal characteristics or from the story content.

The user's abilities to interpret the media content are individually different (depending for e.g., on age, gender, media experience) and thus, can result in individual different media preferences.

Sherry (2004) argues that video games matches activities that are likely to create flow since the majority of games have concrete rules and defined goals, provide clear and immediate feedback, offer the opportunity to adjust game difficulty (by means of difficulty level), and have visual and auditory features that supports focusing the users concentration.

Also Grodal (2000) strengthened the argumentations above by referring to another key element of flow, namely the feeling of control (which results from the balance between challenges and skills). In his view, video games can act as mood managers since they provide the opportunity of a "self-controlled arousing experience" (Grodal, 2000, p. 209). Games contain cognitive, emotional and physically demands whereby the player himself can choose individually his/her appropriate level of difficulty. Additionally, also the time spent on the game is self-controlled and the player can engage in gaming until he/she has reached his/her individual optimal level of arousal.

Taking these findings together, again the claim for an adaptive game design arises. Especially for female players a female avatar and more female game characters should be implemented, e.g. having a female doctor and/or female pirates. Additionally, it became clear that the PSI with the other game characters is more important for female players, and thus, there should be more cooperative relationship and less competition with the other NPCs. With respect to the cognitive style of the player the game should adapt to the preferred way, e.g. to give either verbally or visually based explanations. Besides, again the different game levels and the adaptivity within the gaming-session are of special importance. This is very well in line with the flow-theory explained above. Practically, this could be not only accomplished by providing the gaming levels of increasing difficulty but also by analyzing the player's behavior. If a player consistently asks the medical NPC for (additional) verbal explanations this is also a sign for the need of verbal support.

Parents' Dilemma: Choosing the Right Game for Children

So far the chapter has concentrated how to use the motivational potential of games for educational purpose. For some parents who are unfamiliar with games and are mostly confronted with this topic by the discussion on violent games, this idea might seem a bit strange.

In fact, there is a broad field of research on the effects of violent video games and accordingly meta-analyses lead to the well known General Affective Aggression Model (Anderson, & Bushman, 2001). Additionally, there are also findings that sexual harassment or gender stereotypes could be a problem (Hartmann & Klimmt, 2006). But violence and sexual harassment are normally only problems of conventional video games, but not in educational games.

However, following Prenskys (2005, 2006) considerations children can learn not only from the educational games, but also from conventional video games. Even though it is discussionable if one should follow the very optimistic view of Prensky, nevertheless his considerations about the differences between Digital Natives and Digital Immigrants are a good starting point for parents when selecting an appropriate (educational) game for their children. Contrariwise to their parents, children are Digital Natives and thus, have a completely different view of media in general and games in specific. That means not only that "fun" have another meaning but also that "learning" is done in a completely different way. Additionally, research on games and educational games underlie the importance of individual differences. Thus, it is really hart or nearly impossible for parents to choose a general appropriate game for their kids. The better way to select an (educational) game is to do it together with your children. If your children don't like the game, they'll never play it. Many educational games fail in attracting young children, but there are also some conventional games that might serve the same purpose. Some popular examples are given on the webpage www.gamesparentsteachers.com. Furthermore, most games have free demo-version and nowadays critiques and recommendations could be easily found. Thus, test together with your children different games and then choose which on is the best option in the individual case.

TO PLAY OR NOT TO PLAY: DESIGNING EDUCATIONAL GAMES

The final section of this chapter addresses mainly developers of educational games and highlights the most important psychological factors that should be keep in mind when developing an educational game. Since the process of creating educational games is rather complex, first a framework for designing educational games is presented. Afterwards an overall symbiosis and summary of the described research and it applicability is provided. The accordingly literature and the derived concrete practical examples were already explained in the accordingly sections above. The summary is conceptualized as a kind of checklist. The systematically listed recommendations regard on the multimedia elements in the game, the narratives as well as the game characters.

Conceptual Framework for Designing Educational Games

Even though some general theories from the field of game design are available (e.g., Salen & Zimmerman, 2004), it seems to be advantageously to combine insights from psycho-pedagogy with the experience and creativity of game-designers and developers. A successful example for such an interdisciplinary approach was the EC-project

ELEKTRA (www.elektra-project.org). Within this project a general methodology about the conceptual design and production of digital learning games was established. This conceptual framework will be exemplarily described as a basis for structuring the general workflow within a interdisciplinary collaboration in creating educational games. The methodology shares a lot of elements with usual instructional design models that many readers might be familiar with (e.g., Brown & Green, 2006). In particular the proposed methodology can be seen as an adaptation of the Dick and Carey System Approach Model (Dick, Carey & Carey, 2005) – revised for the purpose of making a state-of-the-art digital learning game.

The base of the developed methodology can be summarized by the ELEKTRA's 4Ms, namely macroadaptivity, microadaptivity, metacognition, and motivation, that were identified as the pivotal elements of an (exciting) educational game (independent of the concrete learning content and storyline/genre of the game). In order to manage the workflow within the interdisciplinary collaboration a framework with eight phases was developed.

- **Phase 1:** Identify instructional goals
- **Phase 2:** Instructional analysis
- **Phase 3:** Analyze learners and context of learning
- **Phase 4:** Write performance objectives and overall structure of the game
- **Phase 5:** Learning game design
- **Phase 6:** Production and development
- **Phase 7:** Evaluation of learning
- **Phase 8:** Revise instruction

Even though these phases are numbered from one to eight, they do not follow a linear order but have several interconnections and feedback cycles.

The ELEKTRA's 4Ms are mainly addressed in phase 5 which can be suggested as the core of the methodology: the learning game design. Regarding this very heart of an educational game, the following chapter will give a summary on design recommendations that could be derived from the described media psychological research. (A detailed description of the conceptual framework, including its empirical evaluation, can be found in Linek, Schwarz, Bopp, & Albert (in press).

This interdisciplinary framework is open for new approaches and can be combined with related work on game design that focus on specific aspects like for example the framework for reducing design complexity by Westera, Nadolski, Hummel, and Wopereis (2008) or the techniques for designing narratives provided by Dickey (2006).

Summary: Recommendations for Educational Game Design

In this section, several educated guesses based on what we have learned so far from research on conventional media as well as from literature on games will be given. These recommendations are a very short summary; for the related details, more concrete information (including cited literature) and the practical examples how research findings can be applied please see the accordingly mentioned sections above.

Design of Multimedia Elements

- *Multimedia design of learning situations.* For the construction of learning situations one can rely on the existing instructional design theories and multimedia principles as far as they don't destroy enjoyment and beware of the nature of Digital Natives. Additionally, one has to remind the expertise-reversal effect which implies an adaptive design for experts versus novices.
- *Quality of sound should be equal or even higher than graphical quality.* According to the findings on media equation (regarding natural rules), users are more disturbed by bad sound compared to bad graphics.

Thereby, it is also of crucial importance to synchronize sound and pictures.
- *Use a naturalistic, colored design.* Based on empirical findings on PAs we can recommend using a colored, naturalistic graphical design.

Design of Narratives

- *Use social principles to establish interesting dialogues.* The PSI with the game characters is a main vehicle for creating an interesting playing experience. The ME theory provides evidence on numerous social principles that can be applied within the storyline.
- *Provide choice.* People like to have the choice not only about the attributes of game characters but also about the story elements (e.g. challenges within the game or selection of different paths and companionships).
- *Create fantasy.* A main element for enjoyment is fantasy that allows for escapism, mood managements and curiosity. This can be accomplished by means of the game environment/setting as well as be the game characters and the dialogues.
- *Be adaptive and challenging.* Adaptivity to the player's skills is not only crucial for the optimization of learning but also for the experience of flow. Adaptivity should regard not only to cognitive abilities of the player but also consider socio-affective and physiological factors. Thereby, it is important not only avoiding too difficult tasks but also too simple (and thus boring) situations without challenge for the player.
- *Provide clear goals, rules and feedback.* Like pointed out in the context of the flow-theory, clear goals, rules and accordingly feedback are essential intrinsic motivation of the player. Although one might worry about frustrating the players by confront

them with their failures there are good reasons for giving the players direct feedback regarding their achievement, because this will not only optimize learning but also motivation and enjoyment. Thereby goals, rules and feedback can provided by means of the story elements (including characters)

- *Be aware of individual differences.* Different subpopulations of learner's have different preferences and abilities. Especially, gender-related differences should be addressed, e.g., when selecting the game-type, creating the characters or providing hints.

Design of Game Characters

- *The avatar should be designed similar to the users' characteristics.* Based on the research on identification, it can be suggested that the avatar should possess similar characteristics like the player, especially with respect to gender. This implies an adaptive avatar or the choice over different avatars.
- *Design of the gaming characters should make use of social principles.* Based on research on ME and PAs it can be suggested that especially similarity-attraction (which implies adaptivity to the user's characteristics) and consistency-attraction are of special importance – at least for the nice, likeable characters. However, also distance to characters could be used for creating an interesting enjoyable storyline.
- *Bad guys and good guys.* Research on PSI has shown that evil characters (that are disliked but although very involving) are also essential for game play and involvement. The evil characters within a game can also be used as a (learning) challenge in the sense of the flow-theory.
- *Be aware of user's preferences.* When designing the game characters we should not only care of general social principles but also of individual preferences. This traces also back to the recommendation given for narratives "provide choice". This is the best way to address user's individual preferences.

RESUME: PLAYING IS LEARNING

This chapter provided a summarized overview of the different fields of media psychology and related fields of research that can be exploited for creating educational games. Even though there are several media psychological approaches and research on (educational) games that can be applied on educational game design, many questions remain unanswered. Further research is needed and we as scientists and parents have to learn from the new generations of Digital Natives. Thus, remember the core idea of game-based learning: learning and playing are the two sides of the same medal. Or in other words: Playing is learning and we are all "homo ludens" (Huizinga, 1950). So let's have fun!

REFERENCES

Amodio, D. M., & Showers, C. J. (2005). Similarity breeds liking revisited: The moderating role of commitment. *Journal of Social and Personal Relationships*, 22, 817–836. doi:10.1177/0265407505058701

Anderson, C. A., & Bushman, B. J. (2001). Effects of violent video games on aggressive behavior, aggressive cognition, aggressive affect, physiological arousal, and prosocial behavior: A meta-analytic review of the scientific literature. *Psychological Science*, 12, 353–359. doi:10.1111/1467-9280.00366

Asakawa, K. (2004). Flow experience and autotelic personality in Japanese college students: How do they experience challenges in daily life? *Journal of Happiness Studies*, 5(2), 123–154. doi:10.1023/B:JOHS.0000035915.97836.89

Atkinson, R. K., Mayer, R. E., & Merrill, M. M. (2005). Fostering social agency in multimedia learning: Examining the impact of an animated agent's voice. *Contemporary Educational Psychology, 30,* 117–139. doi:10.1016/j.cedpsych.2004.07.001

Baddeley, A. (1992). Working memory. *Science, 255*(5044), 556–559. doi:10.1126/science.1736359

Baddeley, A. D., & Logie, R. H. (1999). The multiple-component model. In Miyake, A., & Shah, P. (Eds.), *Models of working memory. Mechanisms of active maintenance and executive control* (pp. 28–61). Cambridge University Press.

Baylor, A., & Kim, S. (2009). Designing nonverbal communication for pedagogical agents: When less is more. *Computers in Human Behavior, 25*(2), 450–457. doi:10.1016/j.chb.2008.10.008

Baylor, A. L. (2005). Preliminary design guidelines for pedagogical agent interface image. *Proceedings of the International Conference on Intelligent User Interfaces, 10,* 249–250.

Beale, R., & Creed, C. (2009). Affective interaction: How emotional agents affect users. *International Journal of Human-Computer Studies, 67*(9), 755–776. doi:10.1016/j.ijhcs.2009.05.001

Berlyne, D. E. (1970). Novelty, complexity, and hedonic value. *Perception & Psychophysics, 8,* 279–286. doi:10.3758/BF03212593

Bransford, J. D., Sherwood, R. D., Hasselbring, T. S., Kinzer, C. K., & Williams, S. M. (1990). Anchored instruction: Why we need it and how technology can help. In Nix, D., & Spiro, R. J. (Eds.), *Cognition, education, and multimedia* (pp. 115–141). Hillsdale, NJ: Erlbaum.

Brown, A., & Green, T. D. (2006). *The essentials of instructional design. Connecting fundamental principles with process and practice.* Upper Saddle River, NJ: Pearson/Merrill Prentice Hall.

Bruner, J. S. (1967). *Toward a theory of instruction.* Cambridge, MA: Harvard University Press.

Cassell, J., & Thórisson, K. R. (1999). The power of a nod and a glance: Envelope vs. emotional feedback in animated conversational agents. *Applied Artificial Intelligence, 13,* 519–538. doi:10.1080/088395199117360

Clark, R. C., & Mayer, R. E. (2003). *E-learning and the science of instruction. Proven guidelines for consumers and designers of multimedia learning.* San Francisco: Pfeiffer.

Cognition and Technology Group at Vanderbilt. (1993). Designing learning environments that support thinking: The Jaspers series as a case study. In Duffy, T. M., Lowyck, J., & Jonassen, D. H. (Eds.), *Designing environments for constructive learning* (pp. 3–36). Berlin: Springer.

Crawford, C. (1997). *The art of computer game design.* Retrieved Ocober 3, 2006, from http://www.vancouver.wsu.edu/fac/peabody/game-book/Coverpage.html

Csikszentmihalyi, M. (1975). *Beyond boredom and anxiety.* San Francisco: Jossey-Bass.

Csikszentmihalyi, M. (1990). *Flow: The psychology of optimal experience.* New York: Harper & Collins.

De Freitas, S. (2006). Learning in immersive worlds. A review of game-based learning. Retrieved April 23, 2010, from http://www.jisc.ac.uk/media/documents/programmes/elearninginnovation/gamingreport_v3.pdf

Deaux, K., & Lafrance, M. (1998). Gender. In Gilbert, D. T., Fiske, S. T., & Lindzey, G. (Eds.), *The handbook of social psychology* (pp. 788–827). New York: McGraw-Hill.

Dehn, D. M., & van Mulken, S. (2000). The impact of animated interface agents: A review of empirical research. *International Journal of Human-Computer Studies, 52,* 1–22. doi:10.1006/ijhc.1999.0325

Dick, W., Carey, L., & Carey, J. O. (2005). *The systematic design of instruction* (6th ed.). Boston: Pearson/Allyn & Bacon.

Dickey, M. D. (2006). Game design narrative for learning: Appropriate adventure game design narrative devices and techniques for the design of interactive learning environments. *Educational Technology Research and Development*, *54*(3), 245–263. doi:10.1007/s11423-006-8806-y

Dickey, M. D. (2006). Girl gamers: The controversy of girl games and the relevance of female-oriented game design for instructional design. *British Journal of Educational Technology*, *37*(5), 785–793. doi:10.1111/j.1467-8535.2006.00561.x

Dion, K., Berschied, E., & Walster, E. (1972). What is beautiful is good. *Journal of Personality and Social Psychology*, *24*, 285–290. doi:10.1037/h0033731

Dondi, C., Edvinsson, B., & Moretti, M. (2004). Why choosing a game for improving learning and teaching processes? In Pivec, M., Koubek, A., & Dondi, C. (Eds.), *Guidelines for game-based learning* (pp. 20–76). Lengrich, Germany: Pabst Science Publisher.

ESA. (2007). *Gamer data*. Retrieved from http://www.theesa.com/facts/gamer_data.php

Felicia, P., & Pitt, I. J. (2007). The PLEASE model: An emotional and cognitive approach to learn in video games. *Proceedings of the International Technology, Education and Development Conference (INTED)*, *7th-9th March, 2007, Valencia, Spain*.

Giles, D. C. (2002). Parasocial interaction: A review of the literature and a model for future research. *Media Psychology*, *4*, 279–305. doi:10.1207/S1532785XMEP0403_04

Gleich, U. (1997). Parasocial interaction with people on the screen. In Winterhoff-Spurk & T.H.A. Van der Voort (Eds.), *New horizons in media psychology: Research cooperation and projects in Europe*. (pp. 35-55). Opladen, Germany: Westdeutscher Verlag.

Grodal, T. (2000). Video games and the pleasure of control. In Zillmann, D., & Vorderer, P. (Eds.), *Media entertainment: The psychology of its appeal* (pp. 197–213). Mahwah, N.J.: Erlbaum.

Groom, V., Nass, C., Chen, T., Nielsen, A., Scarborough, J. K., & Robles, E. (2009). Evaluating the effects of behavioural realism in embodied agents. *International Journal of Human-Computer Studies*, *67*(10), 842–849. doi:10.1016/j.ijhcs.2009.07.001

Gulz, A., & Haake, M. (2005). *Social and visual style in virtual pedagogical agents*. 10th International Conference on User Modeling. UM05. Retrieved October 19, 2006, from http://www.di.uniba.it/intint/UM05/list-ws-um05.html

Hartmann, T., & Klimmt, C. (2006). Gender and computer games: Exploring females' dislikes. *Journal of Computer-Mediated Communication*, *11*(4), 910–931. doi:10.1111/j.1083-6101.2006.00301.x

Hebb, D. O. (1955). Drives and the C.N.S. (conceptual nervous system). *Psychological Review*, *62*, 243–254. doi:10.1037/h0041823

Henning, B., & Vorderer, P. (2001). Psychological escapism: Predicting the amount of television viewing by need for cognition. *The Journal of Communication*, *51*, 100–120. doi:10.1111/j.1460-2466.2001.tb02874.x

Hoffner, C. (1996). Children's wishful identification and parasocial interaction with favorite television characters. *Journal of Broadcasting & Electronic Media*, *40*, 389–402.

Hoffner, C., & Buchanan, M. (2005). Young adults' wishful identification with television characters: The role of perceived similarity and character attributes. *Media Psychology*, *7*, 325–351. doi:10.1207/S1532785XMEP0704_2

Horton, D., & Wohl, R. R. (1956). Mass communication and para-social interaction. *Psychiatry*, *19*, 215–229.

Huizinga, J. (1950). *Homo Ludens: A study of the play element in culture*. New York: Roy Publishers.

Isbister, K., & Nass, C. (2000). Consistency of personality in interactive characters: Verbal cues, non-verbal cues and user characteristics. *International Journal of Human-Computer Studies*, *53*, 251–267. doi:10.1006/ijhc.2000.0368

Kalyuga, S., Ayres, P., Chandler, P., & Sweller, J. (2003). The expertise reversal effect. *Educational Psychologist*, *38*, 23–31. doi:10.1207/S15326985EP3801_4

Katz, E., & Foulkes, D. (1962). On the use of mass media for escape: Clarification of a concept. *Public Opinion Quarterly*, *26*, 377–388. doi:10.1086/267111

Kebritchi, M., & Hirumi, A. (2008). Examining the pedagogical foundations of modern educational computer games. *Computers & Education*, *51*, 1729–1743. doi:10.1016/j.compedu.2008.05.004

Klimmt, C., Hartmann, T., & Schramm, H. (2006). Parasocial interactions and relationships. In Bryant, J., & Vorderer, P. (Eds.), *Psychology of entertainment* (pp. 291–313). Mahwah, NJ: LAS.

Klimmt, C., Hefner, D., & Vorderer, P. (2009). The video game experience as true identification: A theory of enjoyable alterations of player's self-perception. *Communication Theory*, *19*(4), 351–373. doi:10.1111/j.1468-2885.2009.01347.x

Konijn, E. A., & Hoorn, J. F. (2005). Some like it bad: Testing a model for perceiving and experiencing fictional characters. *Media Psychology*, *7*, 107–144. doi:10.1207/S1532785XMEP0702_1

Koubek, A., & Macleod, H. (2004). Game-based learning. In Pivec, M., Koubek, A., & Dondi, C. (Eds.), *Guidelines for game-based learning* (pp. 15–19). Lengrich, Germany: Pabst Science Publisher.

Lester, J. C., Converse, S. A., Kahler, S. E., Todd Barlow, S., Stone, B. A., & Bhogal, R. S. (1997). The persona effect: Affective impact of animated pedagogical agents. In Pemberton, S. (Ed.), *Human factors in computing systems: Looking to the future* (pp. 359–368). Reading, MA: Addison-Wesley. doi:10.1145/258549.258797

Linek, S. B. (2007a). Creating flow in game-based learning: Threefold conception of challenges and skills. *Proceedings of the International Technology, Education and Development Conference (INTED), 7th-9th March, 2007 Valencia, Spain.*

Linek, S. B. (2007b). Speaker/gender effect: Effects of using female voices for auditory explanatory text. In Zauchner, S., Siebenhandl, K., & Wagner, M. (Eds.), *Gender in e-learning and educational games. A reader* (pp. 53–70). Innsbruck: Studienverlag.

Linek, S. B., Schwarz, D., Bopp, M., & Albert, D. (In press). When playing meets learning: Methodological framework for designing educational games. In J. Cordeiro & J. Filipe (Eds.), *WEBIST 2009 Revised best papers*. Berlin, Heidelberg: Springer-Verlag GmbH.

Linek, S. B., Schwarz, D., Hirschberg, G., Kickmeier-Rust, M., & Albert, D. (2007). Designing the non-player character of an educational adventure-game: The role of personality, naturalism, and color. *Proceedings of the International Technology, Education and Development Conference (INTED), 7th-9th March, 2007, Valencia, Spain.*

Malone, T. W. (1981). Toward a theory of intrinsically motivating instruction. *Cognitive Science*, *5*, 333–369. doi:10.1207/s15516709cog0504_2

Mayer, R. E. (2001). *Multimedia learning*. New York: Cambridge University Press.

Mayer, R. E. (2003). The promise of multimedia learning: Using the same instructional design methods across different media. *Learning and Instruction*, *13*, 125–139. doi:10.1016/S0959-4752(02)00016-6

Mayer, R. E., & Moreno, R. (2002). Animation as an aid to multimedia learning. *Educational Psychology Review, 14*, 87–99. doi:10.1023/A:1013184611077

Mayer, R. E., Sobko, K., & Mautone, P. D. (2003). Social cues in multimedia learning: Role of speaker's voice. *Journal of Educational Psychology, 95*, 419–425. doi:10.1037/0022-0663.95.2.419

Miller, M., & Reeves, B. (1976). Dramatic TV content and children's sex-role stereotypes. *Journal of Broadcasting, 20*, 35–50.

Milovanović, M., Minović, M., Kovačević, I., Minović, J., & Starčević, D. (2009). Effectiveness of game-based learning: Influence of cognitive style. In M.D. Lytras, P. Ordóñez de Pablos, E. Damiani, D. Avison, A. Naeve, & D.G. Horner (Eds.), *Best practices for the knowledge society. Knowledge, learning, development and technology for all. Proceedings of WSKS 2009*, CCIS 49, (pp. 87-96). Heidelberg: Springer-Verlag.

Mitchel, A., & Savill-Smith, C. (2004). *The use of computer and video games for learning.* London: LSDA (Learning and Skills Development Agency). Retrieved August 25, 2006, from http://www.lsda.org.uk/files/PDF/1529.pdf

Moneta, G. B., & Csikszentmihalyi, M. (1996). The effect of perceived challenges and skills on the quality of subjective experience. *Journal of Personality, 64*, 275–310. doi:10.1111/j.1467-6494.1996.tb00512.x

Moneta, G. B., & Csikszentmihalyi, M. (1996). The effect of perceived challenges and skills on the quality of subjective experience. *Journal of Personality, 64*, 275–310. doi:10.1111/j.1467-6494.1996.tb00512.x

Moon, Y. (2000). Intimate exchanges: Using computers to elicit self-disclosure from consumers. *The Journal of Consumer Research, 26*, 323–339. doi:10.1086/209566

Moreno, R., & Flowerday, T. (2006). Students' choice of animated pedagogical agents in science learning: A test of the similarity-attraction hypothesis on gender and ethnicity. *Contemporary Educational Psychology, 31*, 186–207. doi:10.1016/j.cedpsych.2005.05.002

Nass, C., Fogg, B. J., & Moon, Y. (1996). Can computers be teammates? *International Journal of Human-Computer Studies, 45*, 669–678. doi:10.1006/ijhc.1996.0073

Nass, C., & Lee, K. M. (2001). Does computer-synthesized speech manifest personality? Experimental tests of recognition, similarity-attraction, and consistency attraction. *Journal of Experimental Psychology, 7*, 171–181.

Nass, C., Moon, Y., & Green, N. (1997). Are machines gender-neutral? Gender stereotypic responses to computers. *Journal of Applied Social Psychology, 27*, 864–876. doi:10.1111/j.1559-1816.1997.tb00275.x

Ozcelik, E., Arslan-Ari, I., & Cagiltay, K. (2010). Why does signaling enhance multimedia learning? Evidence from eye-movements. *Computers in Human Behavior, 26*(1), 110–117. doi:10.1016/j.chb.2009.09.001

Papastergiou, M. (2009). Exploring the potential of computer and video games for health and physical education: A literature review. *Computers & Education, 53*, 603–622. doi:10.1016/j.compedu.2009.04.001

Picard, R. W., Papert, S., Bender, W., Blumberg, B., Breazeal, C., & Cavallo, D. (2004). Affective learning–a manifesto. *BT Technology Journal, 22*(4), 253–269. doi:10.1023/B:BTTJ.0000047603.37042.33

Prensky, M. (2001). *Digital game-based learning.* New York: McGraw-Hill.

Prensky, M. (2005). Computer games and learning: Digital game-based learning. In Raessens, J., & Goldstein, J. (Eds.), *Handbook of computer game studies* (pp. 97–122). Cambridge, MA/London: MIT Press.

Prensky, M. (2006). *Don't bother me Mom, I'm learning*. Paragon House Publishers.

Reeves, B., & Nass, C. (1996). *The media equation*. Stanford, CA: CSLI Publications.

Ritterfeld, U., Cody, M. J., & Vorderer, P. (2009). *Serious games: Mechanisms and effects*. USA: Routledge.

Ritterfeld, U., Shen, C., Wang, H., Nocera, L., & Wong, W. L. (2009). Multimodality and interactivity: Connecting properties of serious games with educational outcomes. *CyberPsychology & Behaviour*, *12*(6), 691–697. doi:10.1089/cpb.2009.0099

Romano, D. M., & Sheppard, G. (2005). Hall, J., Miller, A. & Ma, Z. (2005). BASIC: A believable adaptable socially intelligent character for social presence. *Presence (Cambridge, Mass.)*, 81–95.

Roseman, I. J., & Evdokas, A. (2004). Appraisal cause experience emotions: Experimental evidence. *Cognition and Emotion*, *18*, 1–28. doi:10.1080/02699930244000390

Ryan, R. L., & Deci, E. M. (2000). Self-determination theory and the facilitation of intrinsic motivation, social development, and well being. *The American Psychologist*, *55*, 68–78. doi:10.1037/0003-066X.55.1.68

Salen, K., & Zimmerman, E. (2004). *Rules of play. Game design fundamentals*. Cambridge, MA: MIT Press.

Sanderson, J. (2008). You are the type of person that children should look up as a hero: Parasocial interaction on 38pitch.com. *International Journal of Sport Communication*, *1*, 337–360.

Sanderson, J. (2009). You are all loved so much: Exploring relational maintenance within the context of parasocial relationships. *Journal of Media Psychology*, *21*(4), 171–182. doi:10.1027/1864-1105.21.4.171

Schweinle, A., Meyer, D. K., & Turner, J. C. (2006). Striking the right balance: Students' motivation and affect in elementary mathematics. *The Journal of Educational Research*, *99*(5), 271–293. doi:10.3200/JOER.99.5.271-294

Sherry, J. L. (2004). Flow and media enjoyment. *Communication Theory*, *14*, 328–347. doi:10.1111/j.1468-2885.2004.tb00318.x

Stern, E. S., Mullennix, J. W., & Yaroslavsky, I. (2006). Persuasion and social perception of human vs. synthetic voice across person as source and computer as source conditions. *International Journal of Human-Computer Studies*, *64*, 43–52. doi:10.1016/j.ijhcs.2005.07.002

Sweller, J., van Merriënboer, J. J. G., & Paas, F. G. W. C. (1998). Cognitive architecture and instructional design. *Educational Psychology Review*, *10*, 251–296. doi:10.1023/A:1022193728205

Taylor, T. L. (2003). Multiple pleasures: Women and online gaming. *Convergence*, *9*(1), 21–46.

Vorderer, P., & Bryant, J. (2006). *Playing video games: Motives, responses, and consequences*. Mahwah, NJ: Lawrence Erlbaum.

Vorderer, P., Hartmann, T., & Klimmt, C. (2003). Explaining the enjoyment of playing video games: The role of competition. In D. Marinelli (Ed.), *Proceedings of the 2nd International Conference of Entertainment Computing (ICEC 2003)*, Pittsburgh. (pp. 1-8). New York: ACM.

Vorderer, P., Klimmt, C., & Ritterfeld, U. (2004). Enjoyment: At the heart of media entertainment. *Communication Theory*, *14*, 388–408. doi:10.1111/j.1468-2885.2004.tb00321.x

Westera, W., Nadolsky, R. J., Hummel, H. G. K., & Wopereis, L. G. J. H. (2008). Serious games for higher eduction: A framework for reducing design complexity. *Journal of Computer Assisted Learning*, 24(5), 420–432. doi:10.1111/j.1365-2729.2008.00279.x

Woo, H. L. (2009). Designing multimedia learning environments using animated pedagogical agents: Factors and issues. *Journal of Computer Assisted Learning*, 25(3), 203–218. doi:10.1111/j.1365-2729.2008.00299.x

Yee, N. (2006a). The demographics, motivations, and derived experiences of users of massively multi-user online graphical environments. *Presence (Cambridge, Mass.)*, 15(3), 309–329. doi:10.1162/pres.15.3.309

Yee, N. (2006b). The psychology of MMORPGs: Emotional investment, motivations, relationship formation, and problematic usage. In Schroeder, R., & Axelsson, A. (Eds.), *Avatars at work and play: Collaboration and interaction in shared virtual environments* (pp. 187–207). London: Springer-Verlag.

Yerkes, R. M., & Dodson, J. D. (1908). The relation of strength of stimulus to rapidity of habit-formation. *The Journal of Comparative Neurology and Psychology*, 18, 459–482. doi:10.1002/cne.920180503

Zillmann, D. (1988). Mood management through communication choices. *The American Behavioral Scientist*, 31, 327–340. doi:10.1177/000276488031003005

Zillmann, D. (2006). Dramaturgy for emotions from fictional narration. In J. Bryant & P. Vorderer (Eds.), *Psychology of entertainment.* (215-238). Mahwah, NJ: Lawrence Erlbaum Associates.

Zuckerman, M., & Driver, R. (1989). What sounds beautiful is good: The vocal attractiveness stereotype. *Journal of Nonverbal Behavior*, 13, 67–82. doi:10.1007/BF00990791

KEY TERMS AND DEFINITIONS

Flow-Experience: The so-called flow-experience can be characterized by intense, focused concentration, clear goals, direct, immediate feedback (success and failures are apparent), balance between the perceived challenges and the perceived skills, feeling of control, distortion of the sense of time, loss of self-consciousness (because of being immersed in the activity), and hedonic quality of the experience (intrinsically rewarding).

Identification: Identification is a psychological process that allows media users/players to feel like they experience the same like the media/game character they identify with.

Media Character: A media character (e.g., game character) is a (social) actor that appear in a specific media (e.g., in a game).

Media Psychology: Media Psychology is a subsection of Psychology that applies psychological theories, methods and findings to investigate the intra- and interindividual psychological processes underlying the perception and behavior of humans in the context of media.

Multimedia Design: Multimedia design (in a broader sense) regards to every combination of words and pictures presented by media.

Narratives: The narratives of a game describe the sequence of scenes and events as well as the construction of single scenes (including the behavior of the game characters and the options the user has).

Parasocial Interaction: Parasocial interaction is the interaction between a media character (artificial or human) and the media user. This kind of interaction is called parasocial, because on the one hand the interaction is social since the mass media users act in way typical for normal social relationships, however on the other hand it is only para-social because it is not reciprocal – since the media figure doesn't really participate in the interaction and his/her behavior is not (directly) related to the user.

Chapter 30
Engaging the Un–Engageable

John Carr
University of Nottingham, UK

Peter Blanchfield
University of Nottingham, UK

ABSTRACT

Computer games offer an extremely engaging experience and are an overwhelmingly popular pastime for today's youth. As such, they make an attractive medium for educators seeking to utilise new media to create new engaging learning experiences and provide for those with special needs. Effective integration of game-play and education is extremely difficult to achieve. This problem has plagued the educational games industry since its inception. This chapter will examine this problem with reference to a study which attempts to utilise the motivational power of computer games to aid the education of some of the most challenging students; children who are exhibiting behavioural disorders (oppositional defiant behaviour, attention deficit). Such children can find it almost impossible to focus on traditional educational activities but will give the right computer game their full attention for extended periods. Computer games can engage these children, but can this power be utilised for more than entertainment?

1. INTRODUCTION

Behavioural, emotional and social difficulties (BESD) have been an increasing problem amongst school children throughout the UK in recent years. The Special Educational Needs Code of Practice issued by the Department for Education and Skills defines BESD as:

"A learning difficulty where children and young people demonstrate features of emotional and behavioural difficulties such as: being withdrawn or isolated, disruptive and disturbing; being hyperactive and lacking concentration; having immature social skills; or presenting challenging behaviours arising from other complex special needs. Learning difficulties can arise for children and young people with BESD because their difficulties can affect their ability to cope with school routines and relationships." (DfES, 2001)

DOI: 10.4018/978-1-60960-495-0.ch030

The number of children affected has been steadily increasing. Pupil level annual school census data for the UK in 2006/7, showed the overall numbers of children reported as suffering some form of BESD increasing from 134,810 to 139,410 (DCSF, 2007). At the same time there is evidence indicating that those exhibiting behavioural difficulties during childhood are significantly more likely to develop serious and often criminal behavioural patterns later in life (Robins & Price, 1991; Offord & Bennett, 1994; Babinski, Hartsough & Lambert, 1999).

The SEAL (Social and Emotional Aspects of Learning) program is a recent initiative developed by UK government agencies to combat the growing incidence of BESD in children and to put the development of social and emotional skills into the curriculum of every student, not just those exhibiting difficulties in this regard. It is these students however, those suffering from difficulties, who represent the greatest challenge for educators. These children tend to be difficult and disruptive if not overtly aggressive, often suffer from Attention Deficit Hyperactivity Disorder (ADHD) and possess poor social skills. They are often excluded from mainstream classes because of their disruptive behaviour and as such are often unable to participate in group based exercises. For these reasons it is often very difficult for teachers and helpers to develop good working relationships with such students. It is a common assumption that these children are simply incapable of working on task for more than a few minutes at a time. Experiments carried out at the University of Nottingham using computer games of several different genres with a group of children all suffering from a variety of behavioural problems, including ADHD, indicated that these children could retain focus and attention on a particular game task for long periods of time provided it was sufficiently interesting and engaging. Games *can* be a useful tool for engaging these children, but can they provide serious educational as well as motivational benefits?

The Dual Purpose of Learning Games

The study of educational and serious games has developed into a thriving field in its own right. One only has to glimpse the levels to which young people will engage with commercial computer games to understand the effort educators put in to attempting to harness games as tools for constructive learning. Computer games offer exciting potential as a tool to help educators engage with children who are particularly difficult to connect with. This potential comes with many pitfalls however. The development of educational games requires the blending of serious educational content with game play concepts that were usually developed purely for entertainment purposes. In striving to create something genuinely educational it is all too easy to forgo the essence of what makes computer games engaging and enjoyable in the first place. Conversely, it is equally easy to create a good computer game where the educational content can be ignored or skipped entirely; the game may be engaging but it is such only in the non-educational aspects of game-play. Educational games have a dual purpose, to be engaging and enjoyable but also genuinely educational. If they fail in either regard they fail to deliver that which they were created for. A good game that fails to be genuinely educational is, in the worst case, no more than entertainment - an educational title lacking the engagement and enjoyment associated with games can still be a useful tool for education but forgoes the essence and value of the medium.

This chapter will examine these issues with reference to an ongoing project to develop an educational computer game based around the SEAL program that aims to aid the social, emotional and behavioural development of children suffering from BESD in schools. The development process has highlighted issues effecting educational games, particularly those in this subject area. There is a marked tendency for such games to focus on education while often neglecting game-play. The resulting software often resembles traditional educational materials wrapped in a game-like interface. While such software can be sufficient for use with motivated learners, children suffering from BESD are notoriously difficult to engage with and are unlikely to be satisfied. More and more children play games as a primary pastime and as such have concrete expectations of what a computer game should be. In order to be effective working with this group it is vital that such software is recognisable to them as a game as well as being useful educationally. The project detailed is aimed at a particularly challenging and vulnerable group but the problems encountered are relevant for any who would make educational games for engagement purposes.

2. BESD IN SCHOOL AGED CHILDREN: A CHALLENGE OF ENGAGEMENT

"Behavioural, emotional and social difficulties" is an educational term and is to be understood in such a context. Problematic behaviour exhibited by some children can interfere with their educational development and normal schooling. These behavioural problems can be symptomatic of underlying mental health issues. A disruptive and aggressive child might be defined as having an emotional and behavioural problem within an educational context but a medical practitioner may describe the same child as having a clinical conduct disorder (DfEE, 2001).

There are a myriad of internal and external factors that can negatively affect a child's mental health. External problems such as those in the home, family or community are difficult to deal with as they are outside the influence of those working with the child. According to UK Department for Education and Employment guidelines there is a complex interplay between factors of risk to a child's mental health and those affecting their resilience. Resilient children are more likely

to find ways of coping with problems and difficult situations. The guidance lists the following factors specific to the child as positive regarding resiliency (DfEE, 2001):

- Secure early relationships
- Being female
- Higher intelligence
- Easy temperament when an infant
- Positive attitude, problem-solving approach
- Good communication skills
- Planner, belief in control
- Humour
- Religious faith
- Capacity to reflect

SEAL: Social and Emotional Aspects of Learning

Focus on these issues in the educational world has continued to increase. There are now considerable resources directed towards promoting mental health and emotional well-being in young children. SEAL is one such program and represents an explicit, structured whole-curriculum framework for developing children's social, emotional and behavioural skills (SEAL Materials, 2005). The five key principles of SEAL are self-awareness, empathy, managing feelings, motivation and social skills. The framework is designed to be implemented school wide with these concepts being taught to every pupil. The aim is to facilitate a systematic and spiral approach to learning with core topics revisited and developed each year as students progress though the school. They are encouraged to become familiar with both the principles and vocabulary that surround each theme in an incremental fashion as they develop and grow.

SEAL recommends a multi-tiered approach to ensure that children who suffer from difficulties such as those classified with BESD get the extra help they need. At the basic level there is teaching of social, emotional and behavioural skills to all children, then small-group intervention for children who need additional help in developing skills. At the top of the hierarchy there is individual support for children with more severe difficulties.

There are many different kinds of intervention and treatment for children suffering from such difficulties. There are often emotional literacy classes run for small groups of children whose teachers, for whatever reason, feel extra help in this regard would be beneficial. Children with more serious problems often receive more focused support. It is common for children who exhibit particularly disruptive behaviour to be taught temporarily or full time in units separate from other classrooms. These units generally cater for small numbers and have a high ratio of teachers and assistants to children.

BESD is a broad term and can encompass many different underlying problems and resulting behaviours. However, there is a tendency for children in this group towards difficult, defiant and sometimes aggressive behaviour. They are more likely to be male and from a poor socio-economic background. Children fitting this pattern are often disruptive and unresponsive, and as such they are some of the most challenging students to teach. Their behaviour often necessitates their exclusion from mainstream classes. They often have a poor working relationship with their teachers and suffer from attention deficit disorders. These children are notoriously difficult to motivate and engage with traditional educational materials. Low attention spans make it challenging to keep them "on task" for more than a trivial amount of time. Children with particularly severe behavioural problems can ensure that it is virtually impossible for educators and teaching assistants to devote any time at all towards actual education, instead forcing them to focus on management of problematic behaviour. In meetings with therapists and care workers with long experience treating such children, a specific problem that arises is that the child sometimes sees the teacher as "the bad guy" who is only interested in punishing them. In this situation it is particularly difficult for educators to establish a positive relationship with the child.

Computer Games: A Tool to Engage the Un-Engageable

There are many tools teachers can use to attempt to engage with children with defiant behaviour. Stories and game-playing are widely utilised. An educational computer game based on SEAL principles could offer a powerful tool for engaging with this challenging group. Commercial computer games are a wildly popular pastime among school aged children. The potential these games could have for motivating learners has been well theorised in popular literature. (Gee, 2003; Prensky, 2001; Shaffer, 2006). A recent experiment conducted at the University of Nottingham attempted to gauge the levels to which children who suffer from behavioural problems can engage with computer games using commercial titles. (Alshanqiti, Blanchfield & Carr, 2008) The participants were all being treated at a day centre for children who suffer from relatively severe conduct related problems. The group consisted of mostly boys with a small minority of girls; which is in line with the general demographic. Many were diagnosed with ADHD and their carers stated that they were generally unable to stay on task in any activity without constant supervision. Several different titles were chosen for the group to play; these encompassed many different genres and play styles. In the experiment there were occasional frustrated outbursts and lack of focus when the children were not particularly impressed with the game they were playing. As the children experimented with the different titles available many found one they liked and settled into it with remarkable ease. Once engrossed in playing a game, many continued to focus for around 40 minutes until the experiment ended. One child spent the entire session quietly engrossed in a simple bus driving simulation. The right computer game does have the power to capture the full attention and imagination of children, even those considered notoriously difficult to engage.

There are other possible benefits of the platform that extend beyond the motivational. A computer game can offer an activity where the child takes the lead; children who play games at home could consider game-based activities to be more in their own domain than that of the school and teachers. Computer games and simulations also have the potential to offer a uniquely interactive experience. They can provide children with a presence in an interactive, virtual world filled with characters and activities to discover and explore. This world can provide a unique opportunity for them to interact with and think about topics which can be difficult and often embarrassing without any fear of judgement from their peers, and without the stigma that comes with the teacher student relationship. Understanding of empathy is not something that can truly be gained from instruction alone. It is an emotional response, and as such must be developed over time. Education aimed at developing emotional literacy must help the pupil to think about the relevant issues in an appropriate way. An individual immersed in playing a computer game can experience a powerful sense of presence in the virtual world of the game, something that has been described as the "*perceptual illusion of non-mediation*" (Lombard & Ditton, 1997). The player can feel like they have real substance in that world and that this is an extension of themselves. This effect can be augmented by role play. The player can take on the role of his character, which could be something fantastic or different to the way they perceive themselves. This further enhances the feeling that the player is a real part of the world they are exploring. We believe the events the player encounters while exploring this world can be experiential rather than instructional in a way that no other medium could hope to achieve. In this there could be the opportunity for a powerful and unique educational experience in itself.

An Overview of Games for Engagement with Social Learning and Behaviour

Attempts have been made to harness the power of the computer game to engage and to motivate young people for serious therapy and social/behavioural education since the early 1980's when home computers first became widespread. This work has been undertaken in both academic and commercial circles. In 1984 Richard Schoech, then Professor at the School of Social Work at the University of Arlington, Texas along with psychological assistant Betty Clark published details of their therapeutically focused computer game titled "Adventures of Lost Loch" (Clark & Schoech, 1984). The game was entirely text based (in fact it was played with no display, output was instead via teletype printing machine as they had no access to a CRT monitor at the time) and involved a fantasy quest to lead a band of adventurers though a dangerous cave in search of the stolen crown of the King. It was designed to aid adolescents in active therapy for issues relating to low impulse control. Adventures of Lost Loch was evaluated by adolescents receiving therapy for impulse related problems. Results indicated increased engagement with therapy concepts as well as a significant increase in session attendance amongst adolescents involved. Despite promising results in initial testing the software was never completed.

Hy Resnick published initial details of his purpose designed computer game in 1986 (Resnick, 1986). The game, entitled BUSTED, was designed to increase consequence awareness to combat antisocial behaviour in young offenders. BUSTED was designed as a computerised dice based board game with a layout similar to a Monopoly board. Around the board were situation squares. Players landing on such squares would be given a random situation and a number of possible actions they could take in response. The outcome of the scenario was then generated randomly from a small pool of positive or negative results based on the choice of response. BUSTED, only a prototype at the time of publication, was evaluated in small scale trials over a six week period. These tests yielded promising results with teachers and students describing the system as an "enjoyable and useful addition to the classroom". Despite this, BUSTED, was shelved and remained unfinished for a further 15 years when it was eventually passed on to and completed by Les Cowan. At the time, however, Cowan was working on his own game - The Optex Adventure system (Cowan, 1994).

Cowan designed the Optex system while employed as a social worker. It was a computerised alternative to paper based activities used with young clients involved in adoption breakdown. These activities included a number of short scenarios involving characters experiencing difficulties regarding their adoption. The children would be asked to consider the outcomes and repercussions of a selection of choices the character could make in each scenario. In computerisation of this process Cowan hoped to provide an experience similar to text based adventure games as well as offering social workers an authoring system with which to easily create new scenarios. He later formed Information Plus, a company which produced "social learning software". In 1999 he updated the original premise behind OPTEX into a full multimedia adventure called "Billy Breaks the Rules" (Cowan, 2002). This developed into a series of titles, all featuring protagonist "Billy" in a variety of problematic situations. Cowan's work in this area is especially notable as commercialised titles are exceedingly rare.

Some work has attempted to use commercial computer games as tools to aid youngsters receiving psychotherapy. Gardener experimented with the Nintendo hit Super Mario Brothers (Gardener 1991). Child practitioner Ron Kokish, inspired by work on Adventures of Lost Loch, experimented with using the early role playing game Ultima for use in play therapy (Kokish, 1994). Both concluded that the computerised games could be very helpful

as third objects in therapy and experienced excellent results in engaging the children's attention.

A more recent bespoke commercial title was released in 2006 by Zipland Interactive. Earthquake in Zipland is a research based psychological computer game designed by child therapist Chaya Harash to help children deal with emotional distress stemming from parental divorce (Ziplandinteractive, 2008). The game was designed to implement Strategic Paradoxical and Solution Focused principles in therapy. It followed the style and feel of point and click graphical adventure games. No specific mention of divorce itself is made during the game, which, instead, focuses on metaphors, initially an earthquake which separates the two continents with each parent on one side. The player then embarks on a quest to reunite the continents and thus the two separated parents. As the story unfolds it becomes apparent that this is an unrealistic and unachievable goal. As a commercial title there is a lack of formal evaluation of Earthquake in Zipland. It has been at least moderately successful in the commercial market as it is still available at the time of writing and has received positive feedback from various non scientific publications (Obley, 2008).

Recent academic work includes "Personal Investigator", a game designed to implement "Computer Mediated Adolescent Psychotherapy" (Mathews, Coyle, Sharry, Nisbet & Doherty, 2004). Personal Investigator follows the framework laid out in Solution Focused Therapy, focusing on development of coping strategies rather than examining the root cause of the symptoms. The player takes on the role of a trainee detective who must search for solutions to personal problems. Personal Investigator has been used in a pilot scheme involving 4 patients and 3 therapists. All three therapists rated the software highly as a tool for opening up lines of communication with adolescents and for keeping them focused on the therapeutic task for an extended period. The authors argue that the less direct and confrontational communication between therapist and adolescent helped reduce client stress and aided in development of the therapeutic relationship. The four adolescents involved in the trial rated the game as very helpful in assisting them to think about and solve personal problems. The video testimonies of other adolescents were marked out as particularly memorable. Paul Stallard, author of the widely acclaimed book on child focused cognitive behavioural therapy "Think Good, Feel Good" has also undertaken some therapeutic work with computer games (Stallard, 2005). A team at Nottingham Trent University have developed a game aimed at adolescents who are considered to be at risk of social exclusion (Brown, Shopland, Battersby, Lewis & Evett, 2007). The game places the player on a volcanic island in danger due to an imminent eruption. In order to escape, the player must acquire crew members who are recruited as the player completes personal development tasks. The developers both extol computer games as a tool for engagement of adolescents but also are keen to stress the strengths of computer games as a unique platform for learning. Another cognitive behavioural therapy based game, "Treasure Hunt", has been developed by a partnership between the Departments of Child and Adolescent Psychiatry and Computer Aided Architectural Design, at the University and ETH in Zurich, Switzerland (Brezinka & Hovestadt, 2007). The game is designed for eight to twelve year olds to use in active therapy sessions.

Summary

There is a tendency with the academic software in this area to remain unfinished. Although many of the small scale evaluations undertaken reported positive findings, there is a lack of substantial empirical evidence suggesting the efficacy of these games and few have ever been used in a real world setting. Many of the bespoke educational titles described are particularly sparse in terms of game-play mechanisms. Some are described as games but could be more accurately referred

to as virtual learning environments. It is possible with some titles that the "novelty factor" associated with computer games was responsible for some of the increased interest and engagement reported in trials. Early work was particularly vulnerable to such bias as computers were often a rare and exciting piece of technology. The work conducted with commercial titles such as Mario and Ultima show that positive results are possible just from the act of playing games with children in therapeutic settings.

3. EDUCATIONAL GAMES: ENTERTAINMENT VS. LEARNING

The popularity of commercial computer games has expanded at a phenomenal rate over the past few decades. Once considered a niche market, games are now breaking entertainment sales records industry wide. In recent years several games have broken launch records traditionally held by the motion picture industry. Like big budget motion pictures, top games represent a massive investment of both money and man hours. It is normal for teams consisting of hundreds of programmers, artists, writers and designers to spend several years meticulously crafting the final product. Overall budgets can reach into the hundreds of millions. Children today who grow up with access to modern games have some of the most expensive, intricately crafted and above all else engrossing, exciting and engaging entertainment experiences ever created in their homes and at their fingertips. Playing electronic games is now one of the most popular activities for young people. The 2009 National Gamers Survey found that among 8 to 12 year olds, 99% of boys and 96% of girls surveyed played computer games (National Gamer Survey, 2009). Many classified playing games as their favourite pastime, ahead of watching television and browsing the internet.

It is easy to see why educators have attempted to utilise computer games for learning. One only has to observe a child playing a game for a short time to see not only the staggering level of engagement that can be achieved, but also the sheer concentration, thought and effort that is put into this "play". Malone and Lepper conducted pioneering work on educational game theory in 1987. They set out 3 key characteristics of learning games as challenge, curiosity and control (Malone & Lepper, 1987). Despite academic work towards a framework for learning games the educational computer games industry did not enjoy the success associated with entertainment games. This generation of titles, dubbed "edutainment", was criticised for taking the worst aspects of both education and of games (Papert, 1998). It has been argued that most products attempting to be both fun and educational ended up being neither. Amy Bruckman succinctly agues this failure was due to educational games treating fun like a sugar coating for an educational core, something which "*makes about as much sense as chocolate dipped broccoli*" (Bruckman, 1999).

The problem with the edutainment approach was that the game aspect of the software was often entirely distinct from the educational content. Sometimes there was a game included with an educational system which could only be played as reward for completing a certain amount of the educational work - answer 20 questions correctly and you get to play a shooting game for five minutes. This approach fails to make learning any more interesting, merely attempting to sweeten the bitter pill of boring and repetitive study.

There has been renewed interest in using games to teach in recent years. Modern serious games aim to be genuinely educational while avoiding the flaws of early edutainment. There are still many pitfalls into which modern educational games often fall. While designers recognise the benefits of intrinsic integration of game concept with the educational subject matter, the mechanisms by which the game is actually played - the game-play mechanics, are often overlooked. It has been argued that game mechanics play a pivotal role in

the educational effectiveness of learning games (Habgood, 2007). The key aspect is the skills or knowledge which the player must develop in order to succeed in the game. Educational games often attempt to blend educational themes with play styles lifted straight from commercial titles. If successful this would surely be the best of both worlds, the game would retain the fun elements of its commercial counterpart and the player would learn something while playing.

Game Skills in the Real World

Recent studies have examined the potential educational benefits of playing historically themed commercial strategy games. The studies were based on the commercially successful title Civilization 3 (Squire 2005) and Europa Universalis II (Egenfeldt-Nielsen, 2005). Both games were designed for entertainment rather than education but were based upon accurate historical information. Both studies reported difficulties in developing students' understanding of history. Part of the problem is due to the nature of the strategy genre. Civilisation 3 requires the player to become the leader of a historical tribe and guide their progress using trade, technology, diplomacy and combat. One might expect that in playing a game so entrenched in history that it would be difficult to avoid learning some useful historical information. In terms of game-play mechanics however, Civilization 3 is broadly in-line with other strategy games. Gamers experienced in playing similar games would expect to do well playing Civilization 3 for the first time as they are already familiar with the core concepts and strategies. The goals and challenges of the game would be largely unchanged if the player controlled robots or aliens instead of historical troops. The context and the feel of the game would certainly change, but the core experience of playing a strategy game would not. The player would still win or lose based on the same strategies, as these do not rely on knowledge of history the intended focus is easily overlooked.

Modern computer games often require a highly significant skill set if experienced players are to complete the harder challenges of the game world. Good games teach the player to develop these skills very effectively. An ideal educational game would develop useful skills in this way and these would continue to be useful outside of the game world. It is important to note the separation that often exists between the theme of the game and the skills required by the game mechanics. Playing sports themed games can teach the player about the rules and strategies involved but few if any of the skills learned by playing would transfer to their real world equivalents. A realistic racing game may give the player a sensation similar to being behind the wheel of a vehicle but does not teach them to drive. A skilled player of Olympic themed game Beijing 2008 (Sega™) must be adept at pressing alternate buttons rapidly, a skill entirely distinct from the real world of athletics. While the theme of a game is not enough to ensure transfer of useful skills it remains an important in motivational context. Students who enjoy playing a historically themed game may be motivated to learn more about the subject.

Games Made for Gamers by Gamers

Computer games are full of conventions. Each of the different genres has a distinct play style with themes and features shared between similar titles. Experienced Halo (Microsoft™) players could expect most of their skills to transfer directly to similar games such as Call of Duty (Activision™) due to the similarity in game-play and control scheme. The same is true for other game types such as racing titles. Control layouts for each genre are to some extent deliberately standardised by game designers to ensure their games are accessible and intuitive to experienced gamers. Some educational game projects undertaken by academics suffer from a lack of familiarity of how games work. This

can be due to a lack of experience in game design and development, but fundamentally some who develop educational games are not experienced game *players*. Educators who seek to utilise games without understanding the conventions engrained in the industry and without a real appreciation of the way games work at a fundamental level will struggle to create products that work in terms of game-play. Some educational games developers freely admit to not playing games at all. The software they create often looks game-like in terms of interface, but game-play elements have been completely overlooked and in some cases omitted entirely. The following quote was published by games and television pundit Charlie Brooker who attempts to describe his frustration at the difficulties involved with sharing his enjoyment of computer games with non-gamers:

"Veteran players have years of experience. We're schooled in the way games work. It's as if we have learned a new man-made language, like Esperanto. And games are the equivalent of Esperanto-language movies – except they're better than movies. They're engrossing and exciting, playful and challenging, constantly evolving, constantly surprising. They're interactive and, thanks to the rise of modern multiplayer, infinitely more social than mere television. But because they're in Esperanto, it's hard for non-speakers to appreciate them." (Brooker, 2009)

The vast majority of today's children, especially the male demographic, spend a significant amount of time playing games (National Gamer Survey, 2009). They are *experienced gamers*. They spend countless hour playing games, they understand them, what conventions to expect and what makes them enjoyable or boring. If we, as educators, expect to utilise games as a medium for engagement of experienced gamers then the importance of understanding these issues ourselves simply cannot be overstated. A solid appreciation of the elements that contribute to making games fun and engaging can be gained simply by playing them. While it should not be implied that game players are intrinsically able to make good games, it is reasonable to suggest an appreciation of gaming fundamentals is a prerequisite for any who would hope to utilise the medium with any degree of success.

4. DEVELOPING A ROLE PLAYING GAME FOR BEHAVIOURAL EDUCATION

This section explores a study being undertaken at the University of Nottingham to develop an educational computer game to aid the development of emotional and behavioural literacy in school aged children. Two playable prototype games have been developed using Microsoft's XNA framework. Video clips from both versions can be obtained from: http://www.cs.nott.ac.uk/~jxc/gv.html

The games are intended for use by eight to twelve year olds receiving extra help from educational institutions for behavioural emotional or social difficulties. The initial design attempts to avoid some of the problems described in section 3 by following a framework from a commercial genre that allows close integration of game-play and educational content. This is implemented with a control layout and game-play conventions that should be both familiar to experienced game players and as accessible as possible to non gamers. The nature of the subject matter limits the choice of game genre substantially. Emotional and behavioural topics are open-ended, complex and deeply personal. Rich characters and extensive dialogue are required in order to address the subject matter with any degree of depth. There is however one established game genre which allows game-play to focus on story, characters and dialogue – the RPG or Role Playing Game.

The team working on the project is small as is common in the research environment. They include an experienced game player and a member who has been developing games for a number of years. In addition others in the research group have been developing other related games. As a result a large number of experts in the treatment of children with behavioural disorders have been involved in the design – both in assessing their working and providing functional requirements. In addition to this the game play behaviour of a group of children of the appropriate age has been studied, both playing the games that have been developed and in using other commercial games of different genre.

The Role of Narrative and Empathy

Narrative has an important role in learning. Tooby and Cosmides argue that human beings are predisposed to engage with narrative out of evolutionary necessity (Tooby & Cosmides, 2001). We accumulate knowledge from experience. Our ability to engage with narrative worlds - to use our imaginations and place ourselves inside them gives us the ability to learn from "surrogate experience".

"Fictional worlds engage emotion systems while disengaging action systems (just as dreams do). An absorbing series of fictional events will draw out of our mental mechanisms a rich array of emotional responses—the same responses that would be appropriate to those same events and persons if they were real. We care about the people involved, we identify our welfare with one or more of the characters, we may be afraid, or disgusted, or shattered, as if (in the emotional channel) those events were happening to us." (Tooby & Cosmides, 2001:p 8-9)

Narrative based education is also well suited to the learning goals of the game. The SEAL materials contain many stories relating to different core principles. These stories use the power of narrative to promote empathetic reactions and promote the understanding of topics such as feelings and emotions.

Empathy development is an important aspect of the SEAL approach. Studies utilising virtual learning environments to explore issues such as bullying indicate that empathetic engagement is increased if the participants believe they can affect characters through interactions within the environment (Hall, Woods, Aylett, Newall & Paiva, 2005). An RPG featuring interactive branching storylines and character interaction where the player has real influence to affect the story's characters could be a powerful learning environment as well as an engaging game experience.

Role Playing Game Dynamics

RPGs can be described as interactive narratives where the player takes control of an in-game character which develops over time. A detailed story is often crucially important and is interwoven with other game mechanics to aid in-game motivation. RPGs conventionally begin with the player customising some kind of avatar which they will use to explore the virtual world of the game. This customisation aids the immersive properties of the game and adds to the feeling of direct control. Throughout the game this character advances and progresses in a way directed by player choice, either directly or indirectly through their play style. For example, the character could gain new abilities based around tactics employed by the player in the game. The story serves as the foundation of the game world. This will typically advance in line with the player's character level. Good role playing games combine an engrossing story with a believable virtual world in which the player has real presence and effect.

Symbolic Modelling

The educational theory underpinning the design is based on symbolic modelling, a technique derived from cognitive behavioural therapy. This form of therapy has been shown to be effective in the treatment of children suffering behavioural and conduct related disorders (Sukhodolsky, Kassinove & Gorman, 2004). It attempts to influence dysfunctional emotions, behaviour and thoughts through a goal-oriented, psychotherapeutic procedure. In therapist led cognitive behavioural therapy, problematic situations are modelled by live or recorded actors, these situations are then analysed with the client and dysfunctional cognitions, emotions and behaviours discussed. The situations can then be re-modelled using specific coping strategies to examine how better outcomes might be achieved if a different approach is taken. This allows the child to examine coping strategies in a non-threatening and supportive environment.

Symbolic Modelling in-game is achieved through non-player characters (NPCs). These characters exhibit common behavioural and thinking dysfunctions. The player can then take on a role where they become part of the solution, helping to find appropriate coping strategies based on the problems exhibited by the NPCs. Another advantage of using this technique to explore issues of dysfunctional behaviour is that it avoids classifying the child as being the source of the problem. Observing and actively participating in the journey of a character with similar difficulties to the player as they learn and develop coping skills that make an evident positive change could be extremely beneficial and motivating. In section 2, certain factors were listed that are considered to aid resiliency against mental health problems in children. The design focuses on content which fosters these traits in the following ways:

- Positive attitude, problem-solving approach
  - Problem solving will be central to progress through the game, often the player will be faced with choices where there are no clear right and wrong answer
  - Positive thinking and the problems that can be caused by a negative outlook are central themes throughout

- Good communication skills
  - There will be numerous opportunities to interact with other characters throughout the game
  - These will include many good and bad ways of communicating with people and the consequences of both will be explored in the storyline
- Planner, belief in control
  - The concept that behaviour can be changed with a little knowledge and effort is again a central theme
  - The message that we are each largely in control of our own destinies is explored through observation of the different choices made by both player and characters and the consequences of these choices
- Humour
  - Humour can be an important part of a fun gaming experience, as such there will be things purely designed to be light-hearted and humorous
- Capacity to reflect
  - The ability to reflect on events and consider the meaning of the characters stories will be critical to progressing through the game, without reflection it will not be possible to win

Version 1: Overview

The first game prototype is a 3D, super hero themed role-playing adventure based on exploration, collection and interaction with in-game characters. The design follows the formula laid out by commercial RPGs. Most examples of such utilise some kind of combat mechanic which is central to game-play. Enemy difficulty typically increases as the player becomes more powerful thus maintaining a good element of challenge. However, combat or violence of any kind is entirely unsuitable for a game aimed at development of

good behavioural skills and emotional literacy. To provide a non-violent substitute for this game-play mechanic a trading card style game was designed. The card game incorporates the same principles found in RPG combat but in a non-violent way. Each card has certain values attached to it, some are stronger than others. The player must build a collection of good cards in order to be able to continue to win against stronger opponents. To attempt to ensure that important game mechanics are not distinct from educational elements both battles and cards were themed based on specific concepts. If the player chose cards that relate in an appropriate way with the theme of the battle then these cards will receive a bonus in play. This links educational goals with game play in a way that makes knowledge of subject matter beneficial in-game. Players who consider the meaning of the themes will have a definite advantage in card battles.

The control scheme attempts to cater for both experienced and inexperienced gamers, utilising an Xbox 360 controller. The layout is kept as simple as possible while conforming to industry standards. On the game pad the analogue sticks control both character movement and menu selection and a single button is used to select or interact. Each level contains a large amount of dialogue. There is a tendency in the target group towards poor literacy and reading skills, so to remain accessible it was necessary to ensure that the game did not rely on such skills. All text based content is also voiced by actors alongside a scrolling text display.

The narrative sees the player take on the role of a trainee superhero attempting to join the "Hero League", a group sworn to protect children everywhere. They must rise through the ranks by helping others; each rank will allow the player to choose a superpower which will allow them to progress further in the game. The story begins as the player arrives at "Hero League" headquarters, figure 1, a mysterious place filled with glowing crystals.

The player is then recruited into the league as an apprentice hero. Their first task will be to assist

Figure 1. Introductory screen – arrival at the "Hero League"

a veteran hero, "Captain Concept", in his mission to help some children at a nearby school. Gary is about to be expelled from school for hurting another child. Captain Concept uses his powers to look into the future and show the player a situation that will lead Gary to lose his temper and lash out. A number of children in the playground are teasing Gary and being quite cruel, Gary eventually loses his temper and kicks one of the girls, Figure 2.

Captain Concept then analyses the scene pointing out what Gary was thinking and feeling throughout. In order to help Gary deal with the situation better the player must learn more about him and the kind of problems he suffers from. Captain Concept gives the player the task of retrieving several specially themed cards from the "Chaos Agents" sworn enemies of the Hero League. These cards hold the power the he needs to learn more about Gary's problems and discover some ways to help him.

The player then explores the environment and interacts with various characters and searches for Chaos Agents. When the player encounters one

they must select a set of cards with which to battle the agent, Figure 3.

When the player successfully wins the battle they receive a special card. Returning this to Captain Concept will reveal a further scenario detailing Gary's difficulties at school. Each card gained is transformed into a lesson that can be given to Gary which will show him coping strategies and better ways to deal with the situations he has faced. They also correspond to thinking errors Gary makes in the final altercation that leads to his expulsion. When all the cards are collected the player must revisit this final altercation and identify which of the special cards has a theme which corresponds to Gary's situation. For each choice they make correctly Gary is teleported out of the situation and the corresponding lesson is delivered by Captain Concept. One such lesson concerns anger management. In this lesson Gary is taught to recognise the feelings that lead up to him losing his temper and to try counting to ten and to think of something relaxing when he first feels this way. After this lesson Gary does not lose his temper when the other children tease

Figure 2. An example scene from within the game – Gary loses his temper

Figure 3. A chaos agent

him, instead he counts slowly to ten and takes deep breaths. At this point a teacher arrives and breaks up the situation, the girl responsible for most of the teasing gets in trouble instead of Gary.

The player is then rewarded at the Hero League headquarters for successful completion of the mission with a promotion and a new superpower to be utilised in later missions

Testing Version 1

Ethical constraints demanded a process of significant feedback from childcare workers and field experts as well as testing with healthy children in the target age group before progressing to more significant trials using more vulnerable school children with difficulties.

A small number of children in the target age group were selected to evaluate the game. All were experienced gamers and played high level commercial games as a primary pastime. These evaluations found that the interface and control scheme were immediately intuitive. The concept and language used was suitable for the age group. The children enjoyed the game world and remained engaged during both educational and game-play portions of the level. Despite this, problems were identified during feedback with experts in educating children with behavioural difficulties. The children used in testing were experienced gamers but also motivated learners. Several issues were identified that were likely to be problematic when dealing with students who are difficult to engage with. Despite efforts to ensure the trading card game was relevant to educational content it remained too distinct from the main story and characters to be especially useful educationally. This game implementation had failed to effectively blend the core game-play mechanisms with the educational content. In particular cut scenes delivering educational subject matter were considerably too long and un-interactive, something likely to lead to students becoming bored and frustrated. Despite the efforts of the designers the first implementation would likely fail to achieve the engagement for which it was created and because of the distinction in game-play and subject matter could fail educationally as well. The resulting software looked game like and proved acceptable to motivated learners but had become a piece of educational software with distinct game-play elements.

Problems and Revisions: Version 2

The second prototype was redesigned to address the issues identified above and reflect the evolution of continuing research into behavioural education. This resulted in a switch in pedagogy to an approach based on SEAL materials rather than derivatives of the highly specialised and less accessible cognitive behavioural therapy framework. While educational goals remain unaltered, the change in methodology avoids many pitfalls inherent with the previous implementation as well as allowing a vastly increased potential user base. The underlying game engine is similar to the first version and uses identical graphics and models. The superhero theme is retained but the level model, game-play and story structure have all been completely redesigned in an attempt to increase interactivity and engagement and to further integrate the subject matter with game-play.

The pilot version contains a single level, the story for which was derived directly from material on bullying and empathy development in the SEAL guidelines. Additional levels build on these principles and introduce further topics like self esteem and managing feelings. Game-play mechanics function in an entirely different way to the original. Both versions follow the general framework of the RPG genre. The original implementation relied upon a trading card game as the core game-play mechanic. This proved to be difficult to integrate in a meaningful way with the educational themes of the game. The role of narrative is central to our pedagogy; as such the redesign places the interactivity of narrative central to game-play itself. This type of mechanic has been used successfully in several commercial RPGs, for example Mass Effect™ (BioWare, 2008) and Dragons Age Origins™ (BioWare, 2009). The player develops the story by exploring the environment and interacting directly with important characters. They are also given much more control over the manner in which the story develops. In each character encounter the player is given several different options of how the interaction should proceed. Their choices change the narrative as they proceed through the game. These choices also affect subsequent encounters with in-game characters in a persistent way. The manner in which the player decides to handle any given situation will dictate both how other characters react to them and the manner in which the story progresses. Missions based on these interactive narrative driven encounters are now the core mechanic of the game. The player completes missions successfully or unsuccessfully based on the choices they make as they explore the game world. This approach keeps the educational aspects central to the activity and makes for a more involved experience as the player is given meaningful presence and control in the world of the game.

This change also ensures the educational content can be explored in a more interactive way. The first version had long cut scenes lasting several minutes and covered a large amount of dialogue in a very dictatorial style. The interactivity of the narrative now allows information to be examined in much smaller doses while encouraging the player to consider the meaning behind the dialogue. This approach also presents an interface dilemma. Commercial RPGs which follow a similar framework for providing interactivity in narrative provide the player with interactive options in text only format, even if voice acting is used after the selection is made. Voice acting for this text would assign audible identity which should belong to the player rather than his character. This methodology requires good basic literacy in the player - even if they don't have to read the dialogue in text form they must read their available options. Because of the limited reading skills which are common in the target demographic it is necessary to have an audible explanation of the options available to the player at any given point. To address this issue a generic game construct was designed to handle all interactions in game. This comes in the shape of an on-screen mobile phone type gadget

called the "Gizmotron". This device enhances the fantasy setting of the game and allows the user to perform various interactions within the game world. The player is granted the Gizmotron upon gaining entry to the Hero League. The device then pops up on screen whenever the user has the option to interact with characters or the environment. It can also used to save and load the game, contact allies at the hero league and manage superpowers. Specific options available to the player during interactions with characters and interactive objects are dictated audibly by the device in a robotic style voice. This keeps with the requirement that the game should be accessible to children with poor literacy skills without encroaching too far into the sense of identity and control given to the player.

The control scheme is almost identical to the previous version, but features some additional controls to allow the player to control the Gizmotron device. The start button now toggles the device off or on. While using the device the player is able to select different options relevant to their position in the game as well as saving or loading the game, activating superpowers or viewing statistics on their character. The general storyline follows the same theme as the first version. The player is an apprentice in a league of superheroes. They must gain ranks and develop their character in order to unlock superpowers. The first level was derived from a short story in the SEAL materials which concerns bullying. It explores the issue of empathy focusing on the feelings of a young girl who is alienated and teased at school, Figure 4.

The teacher plays a critical role inside the game world as well as in the real world implementation of the project. Teacher NPCs in game are available for the player to interact with and ask for advice. The player, despite super hero status, is not treated by child NPCs as an authority figure in the same way as a teacher is. The player will be able to go to teacher characters for help in certain in-game situations, Figure 5.

The Chaos Agents now feature more prominently in the story, moving around the level and

Figure 4. Laura has problems at school

causing mischief instead of simply serving as guardians of special cards. The ultimate goal is for the player to interact with the teachers and children who make up the level and attempt to help the bullied child. The correct way to go about this is through exploring and understanding empathy and attempting to relay these lessons to the children responsible for the bullying. A Chaos Agent makes several appearances in order to hamper the player's progress. In order to complete

Figure 5. The teacher intervenes

Figure 6. Chaos agents - Now more prominent

the level the player will have to capture the Agent. The player will then interact with the Chaos Agent and have an opportunity to reform them. This is done using a highly interactive branching dialogue structure. There are many different arguments that lead to many different outcomes. In order to succeed in this task genuine understanding of the meaning of empathy and the events of the level is required. The player is given the opportunity to return to the Agent multiple times and try again if they fail, but not immediately, to prevent any attempt to solve the problem in a combinatorial way by simply trying all the different options without considering their meaning. This is in order to make it impossible for the player to succeed in this task without some understanding of the core topics and some deliberation on their meaning in this context.

The end of each level will feature a mission report from the players in game mentor, Captain Concept. This will detail the major choices the player has made in the game and attribute points accordingly. Bad decisions can lead to points being taken away. This is intended to give the

player an opportunity to reflect on the events of the level and discuss the individual issues with a teacher or supervisor outside of the game. This offers teachers an opportunity to discuss issues from a useful context as well as discussing the players motivations for choosing a specific responses to the problems they encountered. The objective of the game is for the player to be a positive influence in the game world and to help others deal with their problems. It is hoped that the ability to discuss behaviour with a teacher, from this positive standpoint, will remove the barriers that sometimes develop in children who are used to being considered the source of problematic behaviour themselves.

The issue of negative feedback can be problematic considering the target demographic. Some child therapists state that all feedback should be positive when dealing with conduct related problems. This idea is contrary to the way traditional games work - to be able to win one must also be able to lose. Another study taking place at the University of Nottingham attempts to implement game mechanics without use of negative feedback

Figure 7. Captain Concept, an in-game mentor

systems. The study detailed here, however, currently allows players to make negative choices and penalises them points when they do so. This has proved effective in tests with healthy children. Upon losing points they tend to focus harder on making better choices in future. This issue may present engagement problems when evaluation begins with children suffering from BESD. This important issue will be monitored and discussed in subsequent findings of the study.

Testing Version 2

The modified game was evaluated by individual children and groups of two. All participants were again experienced gamers in the target age group. The alterations in game-play dynamics appeared to have positive effects on involvement levels. In particular, the heightened involvement of the Chaos Agents was popular with the children who enjoyed the idea of facing up to them. The encounter style format in which information is delivered allowed supervisors to discuss topics with the player as different facets of the problem

develop without having to pause the action. Small group testing also gave interesting results. Two children sharing the controls were encouraged to discuss the options available to them before proceeding. This resulted in some interesting and highly productive dialogue between players. There seemed to be a tendency for children playing co-operatively to take more aggressive options in dealing with the problems presented to them. Supervisors close to the children suspected they would have played in a different way individually. The second prototype is considered more likely to be successful in working with the most challenging students. Further research is required, however, in order to measure its effectiveness as a learning aid for the un-engageable.

5. RECOMMENDATIONS AND FUTURE WORK

The importance of promoting development of behavioural and emotional skills in children is now well recognised. The SEAL program, now part of the primary national strategy for UK schools, recommends the development of such skills be given school-wide prominence. It remains a particularly stiff challenge however, for educational institutions to aid the children who have special needs in this regard. As a group they are some of the most challenging children to motivate and engage with. Educational computer games could offer a powerful tool with which to involve such children with SEAL topics. Game playing is now a massively popular pastime for primary aged school children. These games can engage the un-engageable, even those who suffer from serious behavioural problems and attention deficit disorders can concentrate for considerable lengths of time given the right game to play. This motivational power alone makes a strong argument for the potential of learning games for children with behavioural problems and attention deficit disorders. Development of behavioural emotional and social skills cannot be achieved through instructional education alone; experience and reflection is also required. Computer games can offer the player a presence inside of a virtual world which they have the power to shape with their actions. The immersive properties of a well made computer game coupled with a role play element offers an activity based on an *experience* in a way that no other medium can achieve. This experience allows for the connection of ideas with the reality they represent, something that has been referred to as situated understanding (Gee &Shafer 2005). Experiences in this virtual world are also unique as they come without judgement from peer groups. This world could act as a sandbox for children to play in and practice thinking about important concepts like how people see themselves and interact with each other. In this there is enormous potential, both educational and motivational. The challenges facing a successful implementation are stiff however. All educational games attempt to integrate learning with game-play. Failure in this regard is more dangerous than usual considering the needs of the target demographic.

Play to Win or Play to Learn

The educational games industry has long attempted to utilise the motivational aspects of computer games to aid in the learning process. Many early titles kept educational and game-play elements entirely separate, using the game as a reward for completion of educational tasks. More recent educational games try to integrate learning and game concepts closely to enhance motivational properties and the learning experience. Despite the advances, there are still issues of separation between the educational content and game mechanics. These issues are intrinsically related to the nature of the computer game as a medium and the ways in which people play them. Studies attempting to utilise commercial strategy games to teach history highlight the difficulties involved (Egenfeldt-Nielsen, 2005; Squire, 2005). It is easy for players to focus on developing the strategies that will allow them to win the game while ignoring the context of on screen events. Retaining knowledge pertaining to the historical themes will not improve the player's performance in-game in any way. Game players will inevitably focus on what is required in order to win; this is the key to the motivation of games - no one plays to lose.

It is surely vital for educational games to ensure that, unlike in commercial titles, some knowledge of the educational content is required before the player can progress or win. This is a relevant issue for any who would attempt to utilise games for enhanced motivation in learning. Experienced gamers are skilled at finding the boundaries in a game while working out exactly what actions are required for them to win. If winning is possible without learning the educational content then that is all that will be will learned. Ideally educational content should be intertwined with game-play such that there is no significant separation. This is especially important when considering the target demographic of this study. Young children suffering from behavioural problems such as attention deficit or oppositional defiant disorders represent a significant challenge to educational establishments. To provide an activity which these children can really connect with and learn from, the best aspects of both games and education must be utilised. These children will become frustrated, distracted - disengaged immediately if the focus shifts from game-play to education. If a game is to be an effective and engaging learning tool for these children it is not sufficient to package traditional education into a game-like interface, or to trivially integrate educational content with game mechanics designed for entertainment. The core game-play itself must both be genuinely entertaining and also educational.

Educational Games: Potential Not Yet Fully Realised

This chapter has detailed the development of two game prototypes to examine these problems. The flaws inherent in the first design demonstrate pitfalls that can all too easily afflict educational games. To provide a genuinely educational experience through a game based format is extremely challenging. It is all too easy for developers to focus on educational challenges while neglecting to ensure that game-play aspects work and are effectively integrated. The initial prototype was guilty of relying on game-play mechanics that were too distinct from the subject matter to aid with educational goals or provide an engaging game-like experience. During the development process it became apparent that the first prototype was becoming a piece of educational software with game-play elements superficially "tacked on". A complete redesign was undertaken in order to rectify these issues. In the second prototype, the child discovers the facts needed by exploration of the game environment and passing tests at different stages. Involvement in the game is sustained as the character wins powers that can improve their ability to get the right outcomes. At the same time the teaching element is retained because it is impossible to win unless you recognise

the purpose of the lesson. Small scale evaluation of both versions indicate the improved game-play experience in the second version results in heightened levels of immersion and involvement.

Further research is required in order to evaluate the real effectiveness of this approach with the most challenging children. The problems inherent in using games for education however have been highlighted. The study detailed is aimed at a small and vulnerable group, these issues however, are of potential relevance to any who would develop educational games for motivational purposes. It is more and more likely that educational games aimed at children will be used by experienced game players. Those seeking to engage these children using games as a medium for learning must understand the conventions and game-play mechanics normal to the commercial games they play on a daily basis. Failure in this regard will result in a less effective piece of software when used by an experienced gamer. The language of games is complex and constantly evolving. If games are to realise their full potential as a medium for learning as well as engagement we, as educators, must seek to understand the language of games in order to best utilise them for educational means. The perspective and understanding of an experienced game player could be invaluable for educators seeking to design educational activities that integrate effectively with game-play. This is something that can only truly be gained from playing and enjoying games firsthand. Partnerships between educators and game designers are important, however, a mutual understanding of game-play and education fundamentals is vital.

Game and Education United

For educational games to realise their full potential as engaging educational tools they must do more than merely look game-like, they must harness the full power of the medium. Game-play mechanics must be carefully constructed to be recognisable and enjoyable to experienced gamers. Educational content must be linked with game-play in a meaningful way and must be central to the success of the player. This remains a particularly challenging problem and one that has yet to be solved. The systems and mechanisms that traditional games are based around do not integrate easily with education. If this close integration of game-play and education is to be fully realised, innovative solutions to the incompatibilities in traditional incarnations of both games and education must be found. This surely requires new approaches to both game-play and education.

Computer games can engage children for whom traditional educational material is of little use. These challenges, however, must be overcome if educational computer games are to be successful in achieving educational goals while maintaining their ability to engage the un-engagable.

REFERENCES

Alshanqiti, H., Blanchfield, P., & Carr, J. (2008). Study to inform the design of a psycho-educational game: Children and the magical do better. In *Proceedings of the 2nd European Conference on Game Based Learning* (ECGBL), 16-17 October 2008, Barcelona, Spain.

Babinski, L., Hartsough, C., & Lambert, N. (1999). Childhood conduct problems, hyperactivity-impulsivity and inattention as predictors of adult criminal activity. *Journal of Child Psychology and Psychiatry, and Allied Disciplines, 40*, 347–355. doi:10.1111/1469-7610.00452

Brezinka, V., & Hovestadt, L. (2007). *Serious games can support psychotherapy of children and adolescents*. Springer-Verlag.

Brooker, C. (2009). *Why I love video games*. Retrieved January 7, 2010, from http://www.guardian.co.uk/technology/2009/dec/11/charlie-brooker-i-love-videogames

Brown, D., Shopland, N., Battersby, S., Lewis, J., & Evett, L. (2007). Can serious games engage the disengaged? In *Proceedings of 1st European Conference on Games Based Learning.* (ECGBL), 25-26 October, 2007, Paisley, Scotland.

Bruckman, A. (1999). *Can educational be fun?* Paper presented at the Game Developers Conference '99, San Jose, CA.

Clark, B., & Schoech, D. (1984). *A computer assisted therapeutic game for adolescents: Using computers in clinical practice*. Howarth Press Inc.

Cowan, L. (1994). OPTEXT adventure system, software development in practice [Howarth Press Inc]. *Computers in Human Services, 11*.

Cowan, L. *(2002)*. Interactive media for child care and counselling: New resources, new opportunities: Electronic technology for social work education and practice, *2nd ed.*

DCSF. (2008). *The education of children and young people with behavioural, emotional and social difficulties as a special educational need.* Retrieved April 10, 2009, from http://www.teachernet.gov.uk/_doc/12604/ACFD633.doc

DCSF - Department for Children Schools and Families. (2007). *Planning provision for pupils with BESD*. Retrieved December 15, 2009, from http://nationalstrategies.standards.dcsf.gov.uk/downloader/6edb967e04fbf97c80624d275b66d7ff.ppt

DfEE. (2001). Promoting children's mental health within early years and school settings.

DfES. (2001). *Special educational needs code of practice.*

Egenfeldt-Nielsen, S. (2005). *Beyond edutainment: Exploring the educational potential of computer games*. Unpublished doctoral dissertation, IT-University of Copenhagen.

Gardener, J. E. (1991). Can the Mario Bros help? Nintendo games as an adjunct in therapy with children. *Psychotherapy (Chicago, Ill.), 28*(4).

Gee, J. P. (2003). *What video games have to teach us about learning and literacy.* New York: Palgrave/Macmillan.

Habgood, M. P. J. (2007). *The effective integration of digital games and learning content.* Unpublished doctoral dissertation, University of Nottingham.

Hall, L., Woods, S., Aylett, R., Newall, L., & Paiva, A. (2005). Achieving empathic engagement through affective interaction with synthetic characters. In *Proceedings of Affective Computing and Intelligent Interaction,* Bejing, China October 22-24, 2005. (LNCS 3784), (pp. 731-731). Springer.

Kokish, R. (1994). *Experiences using a PC in play therapy with children: Electronic technology for social work education and practice.* Howarth Press.

Malone, T. W., & Lepper, M. R. (1987). Making learning fun: A taxonomy of intrinsic motivations for learning. In Snow, R. E., & Farr, M. J. (Eds.), *Aptitude, learning and instruction: III. Conative and affective process analyses* (pp. 223–253). Hilsdale, NJ: Erlbaum.

Matthews, M., Coyle, D., Sharry, J., Nisbet, A., & Doherty, G. (2004). *Personal investigator: Computer mediated adolescent psychotherapy using an interactive 3D game.* NILE 2004 3rd International Conference for Narrative in Interactive Learning Environments National Gamers Survey. (2009). *Percentage of UK population playing games and time spent.* Retrieved on November 20, 2009, from www.nationalgamerssurvey.co.uk

Obley, S. (2008). Earthquake in Zipland addresses fears of children whose parents get divorced. Retrieved April 13, 2010, from http://www.divorce360.com/divorce-articles/news/trends/video-game-divorce-therapy.aspx?artid=977

Offord, D. R., & Bennett, K. J. (1994). Conduct disorder: Long-term outcomes and intervention effectiveness. *Journal of the American Academy of Child and Adolescent Psychiatry, 33,* 1069–1078. doi:10.1097/00004583-199410000-00001

Papert, S. (1998). Does easy do it? Children, games and learning. *Game Developer,* 87-88.

Prensky, M. (2001). *Digital game-based learning.* New York: McGraw-Hill.

Resnick, H. (1986). *Electronic technology and rehabilitation, a computerised simulation game for youthful offenders. Simulations and Games, 17(4).* Sage Publishing.

Robins, L. N., & Price, R. K. (1991). Adult disorders predicted by childhood conduct problems: Results from the NIMH Epidemiologic Catchment Area project. *Psychiatry, 54,* 116–132.

Seal Materials. (2005). *Excellence and enjoyment: Social and emotional aspects of learning.* Retrieved November 7, 2008, from http://www.standards.dfes.gov.uk/primary/publications/banda/seal/pns_seal137805_guidance.pdf

Shaffer, D. W. (2006). *How computer games help children learn.* New York: Palgrave Macmillan. doi:10.1057/9780230601994

Squire, K. D. (2004). *Replaying history: Learning world history through playing Civilization III.* Bloomington, IN: Indiana University.

Stallard, P. (2002). *Think good-feel good: A cognitive behaviour therapy workbook for children and young people.* John Wiley & Sons Ltd.

Sukhodolsky, D., Kassinove, H., & Gorman, S. (2004). Cognitive behavioural therapy for anger in children and adolescents: A meta-analysis. [Pergamon.]. *Aggression and Violent Behavior, 9,* 247–269. doi:10.1016/j.avb.2003.08.005

Tooby, J., & Cosmides, L. (2001). Does beauty build adapted minds? Towards an evolutionary theory of aesthetics, fiction and the arts. *SubStance, 94/95*(30), 6–27.

Ziplandinteractive. (2008). *Home page*. Retrieved September 21, 2008, from http://www.ziplandinteractive.com

ADDITIONAL READING

Aldrich, C. (2004). *Simulations and the future of learning*. San Francisco: Pfeiffer.

Crawford, C. (1982). *The art of computer game design*. Retrieved 13th Jan, 2010, from http://www.erasmatazz.com/free/AoCGD.pdf

DCSF. (2008) *The Education of Children and Young People with Behavioural, Emotional and Social Difficulties as a Special Educational Need*. Retrieved 10/04/2009 from http://www.teachernet.gov.uk/_doc/12604/ACFD633.doc

DfEE (2001) - *Promoting Children's Mental Health within Early Years and School Settings*. Document Reference DfES/0121/2001

DfES (2001) *Special Educational Needs Code of Practice:* Document Reference: DfES/581/2001

Gee, J. P. (2003). *What video games have to teach us about learning and literacy*. New York: Palgrave Macmillan.

Gee, J. P. (2005). Learning by design: Good video games as learning machines. *E-learning, 2*(1), 5–16. doi:10.2304/elea.2005.2.1.5

Habgood, M. P. J., Ainsworth, S., & Benford, S. (2005b). *Endogenous fantasy and learning in digital games*. Simulation and Gaming, 36(4). Kafai & M. Resnick (Eds.), *Constructionism in practice: Designing, thinking and learning in a digital world* (pp. 71-96). Mahwah, NJ: Lawrence Erlbaum Associates.

Kafai, Y. B. (2001). *The educational potential of electronic games: From games-to-teach to games-to-learn*. Retrieved 3rd January, 2010, from http://www.savie.ca/SAGE/Articles/1182_1232-KAFAi-2001.pdf

Koster, R. (2005). *A theory of fun for game design*. Scottsdale, AZ: Paraglyph Press.

Laurillard, D., Stratfold, M., Luckin, R., Plowman, L., & Taylor, J. (2000). Affordences for learning in a non-linear narrative medium. *Journal of Interactive Media in Education, 2*.

Lepper, M. R. (1985). Microcomputers in Education - Motivational and Social-Issues. *The American Psychologist, 40*(1), 1–18. doi:10.1037/0003-066X.40.1.1

Malone, T. W. (1981). Toward *a theory of intrinsically motivating instruction*. Cognitive Science, 5(4), 333–369. doi:10.1207/s15516709cog0504_2

Malone, T. W., & Lepper, M. R. (1987). Making learning fun: A taxonomy of intrinsic motivations for learning. In Snow, R. E., & Farr, M. J. (Eds.), *Aptitude, Learning and Instruction: III. Cognitive and affective process analyses* (pp. 223–253).

Papert, S. (1998). *Does easy do it? Children, games and learning*. Game Developer, June 1998, 87-88.

Papert, S., & Talcott, J. (1997). The children's machine. *Technology Review, 96*(5), 29–36.

Parker, L. E., & Lepper, M. R. (1992). Effects of fantasy contexts on childrens learning and motivation: Making learning more fun. *Journal of Personality and Social Psychology, 62*(4), 625–633. doi:10.1037/0022-3514.62.4.625

Pearce, C. (2004). Story as play space: narrative in games. In King, L. (Ed.), *Game on: The history and culture of video games* (pp. 112–116). London: Lawrence King.

Prensky, M. (2001). *Digital game-based learning*. New York: McGraw-Hill.

Reiber, L. P. (1996). Seriously considering play: Designing interactive learning environments based on the blending of microworlds, simulations, and games. *Educational Technology Research and Development, 44*(2), 43–58. doi:10.1007/BF02300540

Rouse, R. (2001). *Game design: Theory and practice*. Plano, TX: Wordware.

Salen, K., & Zimmerman, E. (2004). *Rules of play: Game design fundamentals*. Cambridge, MA: The MIT Press.

Sandford, R., Ulicsak, M., Facer, K., & Rudd, T. (2006). *Teaching with games: Using commercial off-the-shelf computer games in formal education*. Bristol, UK: Futurelab.

Sandford, R., & Williamson, B. (2005). *Handbook on games and learning*. Bristol: Futurelab.

Schott, G., & Kambouri, M. (2006). Social play and learning. In Carr, D., Buckingham, D., Burn, A., & Schott, G. (Eds.), *Computer Games: Text, Narrative and Play* (pp. 119–132). Cambridge, UK: Polity Press.

Seal Materials. (2005) *Excellence and Enjoyment: social and emotional aspects of learning*. Retrieved 07/11/2008 from http://www.standards. dfes.gov.uk/primary/publications/banda/seal/ pns_seal137805_guidance.pdf

Shaffer, D. W. (2006). *How computer games help children learn*. New York: Palgrave Macmillan. doi:10.1057/9780230601994

Tooby, J., & Cosmides, L. (2001) *Does Beauty Build Adapted Minds? Towards an Evolutionary Theory of Aesthetics, Fiction and the Arts*, Sub-Stance 94/95, vol. 30

Vollmeyer, R., & Rheinberg, F. (2005). A surprising effect of feedback on learning. *Learning and Instruction, 15*(6), 589–602. doi:10.1016/j. learninstruc.2005.08.001

Wood, D. (1998). *How children think and learn* (2nd ed.). Oxford, UK: Blackwell Publishing.

About the Contributors

Patrick Felicia, PhD, is a lecturer, course leader, and researcher at Waterford Institute of Technology, where he teaches and supervises postgraduate students. He obtained his MSc in Multimedia Technology in 2003 and PhD in Computer Science in 2009 from University College Cork, Ireland. His research interests and expertise are mainly in Game-Based Learning, Multimedia, Educational Psychology, and Instructional Design. He has served on program committees for international Game-Based Learning and Technology-Enhanced Learning conferences, and is also Editor-In-Chief of the *International Journal of Game-Based Learning* (IJGBL).

* * *

Martin Acosta was born in Bogota in 1965. He got Bachelor's degree in Educational Science at the Pontificia Universidad Javeriana of Bogota in1988. After that he worked in different secondary schools in Bogota as a math teacher till 1992. From 1992 to 1996 he continued his study in language and translation, specializing in technology for teaching and learning at the University of Geneva. When he returned to Bogota, he began to work at the Ministry of Education, with a project integrating technology into mathematics teaching. In 2000, he went to Europe for his Master and PhD studies in Mathematics Education at the University Joseph Fourier of Grenoble and the University of Geneva. He obtained his PhD in 2008. He is professor at the Universidad Industrial de Santander (Escuela de Matemáticas) and is expert in Theory of Didactic Situations and in use of dynamic geometry software for teaching and learning geometry. As a part of his interest and research on the use of technology to teach and learn mathematics, he studies educational computer games.

Brian D. Agnew is Director of Development for the Faculty of Arts and Sciences, Newark, at Rutgers, The State University of New Jersey. He is responsible for strategic oversight of development efforts and communication for the largest of seven schools that constitute Rutgers–Newark. Mr. Agnew is currently pursuing his Doctorate in Organizational Communication with focus on Leadership at the School of Communication and Information at Rutgers University. Mr. Agnew received his undergraduate degree in Public Relations and Journalism from Utica College and a Masters in Business Administration from the Martin J. Whitman School of Management at Syracuse University.

Anna Åkerfeldt is a PhD student at Stockholm University, Sweden. Åkerfeldt has a background as a producer of custom made digital learning resources and her research interest is digital learning environment in educational settings. She is currently involved in a project called "Observation of 1:1. Learning in a digital environment". The project studies how teachers use and implement laptops in their teaching and how pupils use them for their learning. The project also studies what challenges the headmasters are faced with when it comes to organise education when implementing 1:1. Åkerfeldt is also one of the editors of the on-line journal *Designs for learning*.

Julian Alvarez obtained a PhD in communication and video game at IRIT (Institute of Computer Researh of Toulouse) and LARA (Laboratory of audiovisuel Reseach) of the Universities of Toulouse II & III (France). His research focuses on the way to use video games as tools for communications.

Krestina Amon graduated from The University of Sydney, Australia, with Honours in Behavioural and Community Health Sciences focusing on parental stress and coping with children diagnosed with Attention-Deficit/Hyperactivity Disorder (AD/HD) in 2005. She graduated with her Doctorate of Philosophy on Biofeedback video games for children with AD/HD in 2009. Part of the Prometheus Research Team at The University of Sydney, she has attended and presented at a number of national and international conferences, published in peer reviewed journals, and been invited to present her project in news media. She is currently working in children's services.

Kostas Anagnostou has a PhD in Computer Graphics and has worked in the videogame industry (Microsoft Game Studios) for several years. He has taken part in the development of one Xbox and three Xbox360 games. He is an adjunct Lecturer at the Department of Informatics, Ionian University, Greece, where he teaches courses on the Videogame Industry and Development as well as courses on Virtual Reality and Computer Graphics. His research interests include videogame and virtual world technologies and their application in education and training. He has written a book in Greek on the videogame industry and development and is running two blogs (in Greek) on these subjects.

Neil Anderson holds the 'Pearl Logan Chair in Rural Education' at James Cook University, Australia and is a senior research fellow at the Cairns Institute. His research has focused on rural education, e-learning and ICT equity themes. Current research interests include leading an Australian Research Council (ARC) funded study that involves collaborative research to examine issues associated with middle schooling and ICT. Other ARC funded studies have focused on the low rates of female participation in professional ICT occupations and education pathways. Professor Neil Anderson is the chair of SiMERR Australia executive (Science, ICT and Mathematics Education for Rural and Regional Australia) and leads the 'Wired' research community within the multi-university consortium, The Eidos Institute (http://www.eidos.org.au). He serves on the editorial board of 'Australian Educational Researcher', 'Australian Educational Computing' and 'Knowledge-based Innovation in China' and 'E-Tropic'. He is a member of the advisory board and conference committee for the Asia Pacific Professional Leaders in Education Conference (QSAPPLE) (http://www.qsapple.org).

Julien Andureu is a research engineer in the Biorobotics Department at Fatronik-Tecnalia. His main research focus concerns usability and the use of gaming for stroke rehabilitation. He received his M.Sc. degree in human factor engineering from the Ecole Nationale Supérieure de Cognitique in Bordeaux (France) in 2009. His research interests are in the field of human factors, usability, human-machine interfaces, game design, and neurorehabilitation.

Leonard Annetta, an associate professor of Science Education at North Carolina State University, Dr. Annetta's research has focused on distance learning and the effect of instructional technology on science learning of teachers and students in rural and underserved populations. His research vigorously began to parlay the results of his dissertation into a pursuit of how synchronous interaction over the Web could propel distance learning in formal and informal settings. Understanding the popularity of online, multiuser video game play, Dr. Annetta began to use his past programming knowledge to build a virtual environment that became the platform for his current research agenda. Dr. Annetta has been awarded over $5 million in grants to support his work on distance learning and the use of Serious Educational Games as a vehicle for learning STEM content and STEM career awareness.

Daniel Aranda is Associate Professor at the Open University of Catalonia (Universitat Oberta de Catalunya) where he coordinates and teaches on Mass Communication Sociology, Media Script and Media Studies. He has achieved a PhD in Media Studies (University Ramon Llull) and a Master in Education and Communication (Universidad Autónoma de Barcelona). He is currently involved in a project which is researching into youth, digital tools and devices (such as cell phones, GPS, social networks or videogames) and their use and application in leisure settings managed by non-formal education bodies, such as leisure associations for young people. Among other activities, he collaborates with the research groups SPIDER (Smarter People through Interactive Digital Entertainment Resources- http://spider-uoc.blogspot.com) and Communication & New Media (at the Internet Interdisciplinary Institute IN3).

Helen Axe, Holding a BA (Hons) in Communication Culture and Media from Coventry University, Helen has gathered over four year's experience of working with innovative forms of technology. Working for PIXELearning for the past two years she has taken a lead Instructional Design and Project Management role on projects for a process awareness game for Shell, an EU funded project, and educational projects aimed at bringing games into education. With this, Helen has first handedly seen students and teachers respond to games as a valued medium of learning. Further, to her involvement in projects, Helen has been aiding PIXELearning in their marketing activities with the intention of spreading a positive outlook on Serious Games.

Jessica D. Bayliss received her Ph.D. in Computer Science from the University of Rochester in 2001. Her background is in Artificial Intelligence, where she has done research on the design and implementation of brain-computer interfaces as well as hyperspectral data analysis for the NASA Goddard Space Flight Centre. She joined the faculty of Computer Science at the Rochester Institute of Technology in 2001. Jessica's research interests focus around using technology to help people and in 2005 she received a grant from Microsoft Research for using games as a context in order to teach computer programming concepts. Games turned out to be a very strong motivator for learning computing and in 2009 Jessica became a founding member of the Department of Interactive Games and Media at the Rochester Institute of Technology.

Robert Biddle is Professor of Human-Computer Interaction at Carleton University in Ottawa Canada. His research is on "the secret life of software," meaning how software design can influence users and usage. His primary research projects are on improving computer security, and on learning and collaboration in computer games and other new media environments. He has worked in the software industry and studied in Canada and in New Zealand; he holds a diploma in education, and degrees in mathematics and computer science.

Peter Blanchfield is Senior Tutor in the School of Computer Science at the University of Nottingham. His main research areas are in the educational use of computer games and particularly in developing these games–what makes them games and whether the education really be integrated into the games. He has a number of research students working with him on several aspects of this subject including games for behaviour education and aspects of group collaboration.

Brandy Bowling is currently a doctoral student in Science Education at North Carolina State University. She obtained a Master of Science degree in Biology from the University of North Carolina at Greensboro and a Bachelor of Science degree in Biology from the University of North Carolina at Chapel Hill. Prior to pursuing her doctorate, Brandy worked in medical genetics research laboratories at Duke University, studying both hereditary kidney and corneal diseases.

Liz Boyle is a Lecturer in Psychology in the School of Social Sciences at the University of the West of Scotland. She has published papers on approaches to learning, learning styles and personality, motivation and games-based learning.

Jeffrey E. Brand (PhD, MSU; MA, UM) is Associate Professor of Communication and Media at Bond University and Director of the Centre for New Media Research. His teaching focuses on emerging media, interactive media industries, and research methods. His research explores the social psychology of audiences, their use of interactive media and the content regulation imperatives that arise from presumed media effects. His current work explores interactive media audiences, and he serves as consultant to the Australian Communications and Media Authority, the Australian Classification Board, the Special Broadcasting Service, and the Interactive Games and Entertainment Association. He is author of the Interactive Australia series of national studies on game audiences.

Karen Butler-Purry is a Professor in the Department of Electrical Engineering at Texas A&M University. Her research interests are in the areas of distribution automation and intelligent systems for power quality, equipment deterioration and fault diagnosis, and engineering education. She has received awards for outstanding teaching from her students and her college and is interested in the impact of teaching materials by gender and ethnicity.

Wolfgang Bösche (born 1971) is research assistant and lecturer at the Department of Psychology, Technische Universität Darmstadt, Germany. He received his doctorate in 2002 for his dissertation on adaptive network models of classification learning. His research and teaching interests encompass media psychology (with focus on the effects of violent video games), cognitive and mathematical psychology, and methodology.

Andrew Campbell is a Senior Lecturer in Psychology at The University of Sydney and has been researching the use of the Internet, mobile phones and computer games and their impact on human behaviour for more than 10 years. Andrew is the Director of Prometheus (www.prometheus.net.au), a research group dedicated to the study and application of technology towards the advancement of mental health treatments in such disorders as Attention Deficit/Hyperactivity Disorder (ADHD), depression, anxiety, stress, self-esteem and learning difficulties. Prometheus research groups are located at The University of Sydney and University of Western Ontario. He is also a practicing child, adolescent, and family psychologist at the Brain and Mind Research Institute Clinical Centre in Sydney.

Stefan Carmien is a research scientist in Fundación Fatronik, San Sebastian, Spain. He has a MS in Computer Science (University of Colorado, 2002) and a PhD in Computer Science with a certificate in Cognitive Science (University of Colorado, 2006). His PhD work at the Centre for Lifelong Learning and Design centred on the design and evaluation of active task support for persons with cognitive disabilities and caregivers. From 2006 till 2008 he was a senior researcher in the Fraunhofer Institute for Applied Information Technology; while there, Dr. Carmien was a research partner in several European Commission projects. Since 2008 he has been working on health and gerontology related projects in the Health Unit of Fatronik-Tecnalia. Dr. Carmien has contributed 10 peer-reviewed articles, five book chapters, and is the author of the book "Leveraging Skills into Independent Living – Distributed Cognition and Cognitive Disability".

John Carr is Senior Tutor in the School of Computer Science at the University of Nottingham. His main research areas are in the educational use of computer games and particularly in developing these games–what makes them games and whether the education really be integrated into the games. He has a number of research students working with him on several aspects of this subject including games for behaviour education and aspects of group collaboration.

Thibault Carron is an associate professor of computer science at the University of Savoie. He is a member of the Syscom laboratory. He obtained his PhD in computer science at the "Ecole Nationale Supérieure des Mines de Saint-Etienne" in 2001. His current research interests deal with the study of collaborative activity observation and with learning games (Projects: Learning Adventure, Learning Games Factory, Serious Lab for Innovation, Pegase).

Francesca Irene Cavallaro is a research scientist in the Health Unit of Fatronik-Tecnalia. Her main research focus concerns the link between attentional skills, multisensory integration, and motor control. She obtained a Ph.D. in cognitive science from the University of Siena (Italy) in 2007 and received an excellence mention for her PhD thesis on cognitive modulation of sensorimotor integration. Her expertise ranges from acquisition and analysis of postural signals, EEG acquisition, to neuropsychological evaluation of attentional and imagery skills. Before joining the Health Unit's team in Fundación Fatronik, she worked at Centro Piaggio, Pisa University (Italy), focusing on multisensory integration in haptics. She has formally studied geriatrics and computer based neuro-psychological assessment of cognitive impaired individuals. As a research scientist in Fatronik, she joined projects aimed at 1) improving quality of life of individuals suffering from mild cognitive impairments and Alzheimer's, as well as 2) improving gaming design in motor rehabilitation for elders.

Dimitrina Chakinska, BSc, is currently a student at the VU University Amsterdam, pursuing two Master of Science degrees: Work and Organizational Psychology and Communication Science. She is also holding a part-time position as a research assistant within the Centre of Advanced Media Research Amsterdam at the VU University. She has previous research experience with the subjects of intergroup processes and communication; (inter)personal motivation; personality, motivation and job performance; HEXACO personality and social relations analysis; and social desirability of personality questionnaires. Her special interests lay in the subjects of (trait) personality and work; (new) technology mediated interpersonal communication; new media applications and effects on people; serious games and health applications; and health communication. Her current work is in communication instruments for climate change policies; personality and ethical leadership; and happy slapping phenomenon. Her academic achievements include: co-authorship in scientific documents currently under peer review, three international conference submissions, and presentations.

Rebecca Cheng is a doctoral student in science education at the North Carolina State University. Her major research interests are in the area of science learning in virtual environments, emphasis on cognitive processes, personality and individual differences. She worked as an environmental educator at a zoo and aquarium in Hong Kong for eight years and dedicated to examining the role of informal contexts in STEM literacy, environmental education, and lifelong learning.

Arul Chib is an assistant professor in the Public and Promotional Communication division at Nanyang Technological University, and is the assistant director of the Singapore Internet Research Centre. Programmatically, Dr. Chib pursues action-oriented research with marginalized communities, in varied cross-cultural and socio-economic contexts, studying the impact of information and communication technologies. He has proposed theoretical frameworks of analysis, including the ICT for healthcare development and the Technology-Community-Management models. His work can be found in international refereed publications, such as the International Journal of Communication, the Journal of Computer-mediated Communication, the Asian Journal of Communication, and International Communication Association Conference theme books, and he has received top paper awards at major international refereed conferences, such as the International Communication Association, and the Telecommunications Policy and Research conference. Arul has lived and worked extensively in China, India, Indonesia, Nepal, Peru, Singapore, Thailand, and the United States of America.

Thomas Connolly is Chair of the ICT in Education Research Group at the University of the West of Scotland and is Director of the Scottish Centre for Enabling Technologies and Director for the Centre of Excellence in Games-based Learning. His specialities are online learning, games-based learning and database systems. He has published papers in a number of international journals as well as authoring the highly acclaimed books 'Database Systems: A Practical Approach to Design, Implementation, and Management', 'Database Solutions' and Business Database Systems, all published by Addison Wesley Longman. Professor Connolly also serves on the editorial boards of many international journals, as well as managing several large-scale externally funded research projects.

Andrea Corradini studied mathematics at the University of Trento, Italy. He received his Ph.D. in computer science from the Department of Neuroinformatics and Cognitive Robotics at the Technical University of Ilmenau, Germany. After his PhD, Dr. Corradini held the position of senior research associate at the Centre for Human-Computer Communication at the Oregon Graduate Institute of Science and Technology, Oregon, USA. Later, he took take on a faculty position at the Assistant Professor level at the Natural Interactive Systems Laboratory at the University of Southern Denmark in Odense. For two years, he was funded by a Marie Curie Fellowship to work at the Department of Computational Linguistics at the University of Potsdam in Germany. Currently, he is an Associate Professor at the Institute of Business Communication and Information Science at the University of Southern Denmark in Kolding. His research interests include multimodal interaction, natural language processing, gesture/face recognition and analysis, embodied conversational characters, and interactive computer games.

Lyn Courtney, Psychologist, BPsych(Hons), is nearing completion of a PhD, James Cook University (JCU), investigating successful ageing of Australian baby boom career women. Lyn, a Senior Researcher, has worked for the past six years with Prof Neil Anderson and Prof Colin Lankshear on ARC Linkage grants investigating the declining rate of girls entering Information and Communication Technology (ICT) career pathways. As ICT Coordinator of the Queensland Centre of Science, ICT and Mathematics Education for Rural and Regional Australia (SiMERR), Lyn has also worked on 12 funded projects, and has a strong publication record including four publication awards. Recently, Lyn and Prof Anderson have undertaken research on developing design thinking skills in indigenous high school students through an intervention program whereby students develop computer video games with indigenous content. Lyn is also a Lecturer and Subject Coordinator for the Masters of Guidance and Counselling teaching at JCU Singapore and JCU Cairns/Townsville.

Boaventura DaCosta is a researcher with Solers Research Group in Orlando, FL. He holds a B.S. in computer science and an M.A. and Ph.D. in instructional systems design. In addition to his research interests in cognitive psychology and information and communication technology innovations, Dr. DaCosta is also interested in how games can be used in learning. Complementing his work as a researcher, Dr. DaCosta has worked in the commercial and government training sectors for the past 15 years as a software engineer and has been involved in a number of defense programs.

Vasiliki Dai graduated from the School of English Language and Literature in the Aristotle University of Thessaloniki in 1995. She worked in private schools teaching English for 9 years. She has worked in both primary and secondary public schools. Today, she is appointed in the High School of Vartholomio, Ileia. She is also a postgraduate student at the M.Ed. in TESOL, Hellenic Open University.

Vasilis Daloukas has an MSc in Computer Science (2009, "The use of Games in the Teaching Process"), during which he created the Moodle's module named 'Game' for the use of games, such as hangman, crossword, snakes 'n' ladders through moodle. He graduated from the Department of Computer Engineering and Informatics in the University of Patras in 1999. He worked in the private sector for 5 years, and since 2003, has been a teacher in secondary education.

Roman Danylak is an artist who conducts research into Interactive Systems Design. He completed a PhD in Human-Computer Interaction in 2008 using theatre art and semiotics-a novel process for creating innovation-to research emotion and gestural system design. He has lectured in Interactive Art at Stockholm University and has presented papers at numerous international conferences on software design, gaming, and interactive art. Danylak has also worked in film, television, and theatre as both writer and performer. He has worked in collaborative art and technology since 1996.

Penny de Byl (Ph.D.) is Associate Professor of Games and Multimedia at Bond University. In 2005, Dr de Byl co-founded the ALIVE (Advanced Learning and Immersive Virtual Environments) Research and Development laboratory at USQ, which employs 3 full-time associates. This project received a $215K grant from the Carrick Institute in 2006 and won Dr de Byl the 2007 Qld government Smart State Women in ICT award. Dr de Byl also initiated the study, as Project Manager, for the uptake of Moodle at USQ. Recently, Penny recently worked as Associate Professor of Serious Games in the Netherlands and collaborating with Augmented Reality industry partners. She completed her PhD in 2002 in the area of intelligent character creation for computer games and has since published two text books with a focus on this area.

Rosario De Chiara got a Ph.D. in Computer Science in 2005 from Università degli Studi di Salerno, Italy. He currently works as Post-doctoral Research Fellow at Dipartimento di Informatica ed Applica-zioni "R.M. Capocelli" at Università degli Studi di Salerno. He co-authored about 20 scientific papers in international peer-reviewed conferences and journals. His main scientific interests concern visualization, parallel computing, and computer graphics.

Sara De Freitas (BA (Hons), MA, PhD, FRSA) is Director of Research and Professor of Virtual Environments at the Serious Games Institute at the University of Coventry where she leads an applied research team working closely with industry. Sara holds a visiting fellowship at the University of London, is elected Chair of the Lab Group, and is a Fellow of the Royal Society of Arts. Voted the Most Influential Woman in Technology 2009 and 2010 by US Fast Company, Sara also chairs the IEEE Serious Games and Virtual Worlds conferences (VS-Games) and is a regular speaker at international conferences. Sara currently holds 12 funded projects, funded through European, regional, and national agencies. Her current research includes multimodal interfaces, experience design,n and perceptual modelling in games and virtual worlds. Sara publishes widely with over 90 publications (reports, journal articles, conference papers and books) in the areas of: pedagogy and e-learning, change management, and serious games and virtual worlds for supporting training and learning.

Menno Deen graduated as a (BA) designer at the Utrecht School of Arts and subsequently as (MA) cultural researcher at Utrecht University. His design and research is on virtual citizenship, homosexuality, and the educational potential of video games. Deen wrote his MA thesis on the correspondence between learning styles and playing styles. Subsequently he works as Ranj's game researcher, validating the learning outcome of a second language learning game called CheckOut! Since 2009, Deen has been a PhD candidate at Fontys University of Applied Sciences. He has published about serious games and education (OSG), co-authored a report about the attractiveness of casual games (My Child Online Foundation), and co-authored a chapter on online casual games in Contact! Children and New Media (2010). Deen's PhD research is on motivations for games and learning. He works on a serious game design method for educational games that may change students' motivation towards learning for the better.

Damien Djaouti. His main interest lies in multidisciplinary approaches that can help to analyse videogames whose purpose isn't solely entertainment (Serious Games, Art Games, Edugames...). He is currently studying design methodologies and tools that could help "non-professional" designers to create such videogames. Alongside with his research, he designs and develops Serious Games and Casual Games.

Claire Dormann is an Assistant Professor at the University of Ottawa, in the School of Information Studies. She has a multi-disciplinary background in Psychology, Computer Science and Multimedia Design. Her research is dedicated to investigating new technologies for lifelong learning through the study and design of novel forms of play and learning. Current projects relate to affective learning and computer games, serious games, humour, as well as urban games and communities. Her expertise includes computer games, educational technology, and human-computer interaction. Research interests also pertain to persuasive technology, affective design, and visual rhetoric.

Ian Dunwell is a postdoctoral researcher at the Serious Games Institute, currently leading the area of games for health. Having obtained his PhD in Computer Science from the University of Hull, he also holds a degree in Physics from Imperial College London, and is an Associate of the Royal College of Science. His research interests lie primarily in the application of an understanding of cognitive processes within virtual environments as a means for providing optimised and effective learning experiences to users, and the use and evaluation of novel HCI interface technologies (such as the NeuroSky and Emotiv headsets) to enable more meaningful and affect-based interactions between humans and machines. In the domain of serious games, he has consulted with a number of leading serious game companies including Blitz Games and PlayGen to design and develop evaluation strategies for serious games such as Patient Rescue, Ward Off Infection, i-Seed and Parent Know-How, and worked extensively with games aimed at reaching difficult demographics as well as changing the affect and motivation of learners.

Manuel Ecker is a research assistant at the University of Education Weingarten, Germany. He is member of the Media Education and Visualization Group and teaches in the Bachelor/Master program 'Media and Education Management' the topics media production and media design, and supports several IT projects in educational context. After his studies in Media and Computing, he received his diploma and Master's degree in Computer Science at University of Applied Science Heidelberg, Germany in 2005 and 2007. His research work is focused on learning and teaching with digital media. He engages in the fields of E-Learning, Game-based Learning, Human-Computer Interaction, and Video-based Learning, as well as Mobile Learning. Manuel Ecker works as a consultant in several projects in the field of Information Technology, multimedia, and education in cooperation with educational institutions as well industry partners.

Monica Evans is an assistant professor of computer game design in the Arts and Technology Program at the University of Texas at Dallas. Dr. Evans received her Ph.D. from the UT Dallas in 2007, and has designed and developed serious games with numerous university partners, including the Dallas Museum of Art, Alcatel, Nortel, U.S. Army Training Doctrine and Command (TRADOC), Joint Forces Command (JFCOM), the Smart Hospital at UT Arlington, and Children's Medical Centre of Dallas. She is affiliated with the Mobile Innovations Lab, the Virtual Worlds Lab, and the Institute for Interactive Arts and Engineering at UT Dallas, and with the Serious Games Initiative within the University of Texas System.

Dr. Evans is the principal investigator for the Digital Calculus Coach, and the project lead for the Values Games Initiative within the Centre for Values in Science, Medicine, and Technology at UT Dallas.

Ernesto Fabiani is associate professor of Civil Procedure Law at the University of Benevento and president of the degree course in Law at the Law and Economics Faculty of the University of Benevento. He authored numerous articles and monographs in the field of civil adjective law. In the last few years, he started to be interested in the use of simulation environments in legal education and established an experimental course in civil adjective law based on the serious game "Simulex."

Ryan Flynn is a Senior Lecturer at the University of Greenwich in Games and Multimedia Technologies. He teaches how to design and develop computer and video games for a number of different platforms, including Flash, XNA and iPhone/iPod Touch. He is also currently studying for a PhD, where he is investigating the link between games and education.

Thomas Hainey is a researcher in the School of Computing at the University of the West of Scotland specialising in games-based learning and particularly evaluation of games-based learning. He has a number of journal and conference publications in this area.

Priscilla Haring, MSc, studied Marketing Management (Hogeschool Schoevers) before turning to Communication Science, and eventually specializing in Media Psychology (VU University Amsterdam) with additional minors in English Linguistics and Journalism. She wrote her Master thesis on the different media realities of two gaming genres; Alternate Reality Games and Massively Multiplayer Online Role Playing Games. During her studies, she held the position of student-assistant for several lecturers and the interfaculty institute of CAMeRA (Centre of Advanced Media Research Amsterdam) before joining the European a2e2 project (Adaptive Ambient Empowerment of the Elderly). Within this project, her research focus is on motivation and feedback. She has a very broad understanding of gaming in all its (social) aspects.

Sonia Hetzner, Institute for Innovation in Learning (FIM NewLearning), University of Erlangen-Nuremberg, Germany. Sonia Hetzner studied politics, sociology, and biology and graduated in Geography. She is senior researcher and project manager. She is responsible for conceptualisation, development, management, and evaluation of e-learning course environments for different target groups. She is author of self-learning materials for different target groups. She is an experienced manager of European projects and has participated in several regional, national, and European projects.

Stephen Howell received a BSc (Hons) in Computer Applications from Dublin City University (Ireland, 1998) and is currently undertaking PhD research in University College Dublin. As a graduate, he worked as a software engineer for companies such as Sapient and IBM. He is currently a lecturer in the Institute of Technology Tallaght Dublin, where he teaches software development and interactive media design & development. He has a strong interest in innovative teaching strategies, and has received funding for several projects to explore this area.

Eva Hudlicka is a Principal Scientist and President at Psychometrix Associates, Blacksburg, VA. Her primary research focus is the development of computational models of emotion, aimed at elucidating the mechanisms mediating affective biases. She is currently exploring the applications of this research to the development of serious games for psychotherapy. Prior to founding Psychometrix, she was a Senior Scientist at Bolt Beranek & Newman in Cambridge, MA. Dr. Hudlicka was recently a member of the National Research Council committee on "Behavioral Modeling and Simulation". She has taught courses in "Affective Computing" and "Affective Modeling", and authored a number of book chapters and articles in this research area. She is currently writing a book entitled "Affective Computing: Theory, Methods and Applications", to be published by Taylor and Francis. Dr. Hudlicka received her BS in Biochemistry (Virginia Tech), MS in Computer Science (Ohio State University), and PhD in Computer Science (University of Massachusetts-Amherst).

Kathleen M. Immordino is the Director of Organizational Research and Assessment for the University Centre for Organizational Development and Leadership at Rutgers, The State University of New Jersey. Prior to joining Rutgers in 2007, she was a career public administrator and Certified Public Manager, including appointments as the Assistant Commissioner for Administration in the New Jersey Department of Transportation, Executive Administrator for Planning and Development in the New Jersey Department of Labor and Assistant Commissioner for Planning and Research in the New Jersey Department of Personnel. Dr. Immordino is a past president of the New Jersey Chapter of the American Society for Public Administration. She was a member of the Publications Advisory Board of the International Public Management Association for Human Resources. She is the author of Organizational Assessment and Improvement in the Public Sector (Taylor and Francis, 2009). She received her undergraduate degree from Dickinson College, a Masters in Administration from Rider University, and a Ph.D. in Organizational Communication from Rutgers University.

Jean-Pierre Jessel. After a Master in Computer Science, he obtained a PhD in Computer Graphics in 1992, and a Habilitation in 2000. He is head of the VORTEX Group (Computer Graphics, Augmented / Virtual Reality) at IRIT laboratory. His current research interests include distributed virtual reality applied to virtual prototyping, cultural heritage, and serious games. He is also chair of the French Computer Graphics Association.

Sue Johnston-Wilder. Originally a secondary mathematics teacher, Sue has worked to develop and improve the use of ICT for teaching and learning mathematics since the BBC microcomputer. She was joint-editor of Micromath, a journal of the Association of Teachers of Mathematics. She was Deputy Director of Nuffield Advanced Mathematics, integrating ICT into the 16-19 math's curriculum. She was Director of NOF-funded ICT training in Bedfordshire and Hertfordshire. Sue's work includes 'Teaching Secondary Mathematics with ICT' and 'Developing Thinking with Geometry' which includes a CD of applets. She was a member of the team which developed Grid Algebra and the Bowland Mathematics materials.

Florian Kattner (born 1982) is a PhD student and lecturer at the Department of Psychology, Technische Universität Darmstadt, Germany, since 2007. His research mainly focuses on (associative) learning processes, working memory, and the interplay of cognition and emotion. He has given classes in general psychology, cognitive psychology, and methodology.

Caroline Kearney is an Education Analyst within the Knowledge-building Team at European Schoolnet (www.europeanschoolnet.org) - a network of 31 Ministries of Education in Europe and beyond. She works on European comparative studies and issues of knowledge management and policy analysis, particularly in the fields of ICT, creativity, and innovation in education. Previous to this post she was a Research Analyst at Eurydice's Headquarters–the European Commission's Information Network on Education in Europe. She holds a BA Honours Degree in Philosophy and History of Art, and has a Masters with Distinction in Comparative Education, from London's Institute of Education. Caroline has had teaching experience in France, and in EU project management in Prague, as well as policy experience as a trainee in the European Commission's Directorate General for Education and Culture, in the unit for Lifelong Learning Policies.

Thierry Keller received his Dipl. Ing. degree in electrical engineering (M.Sc.E.E.) and his Doctorate (Dr. sc. Techn.) from the ETH Zurich, Switzerland in 1995 and 2001, respectively. He is currently the head of the Biorobotics Department at Fatronik-Tecnalia, a technological centre in Spain. From 2002 to 2007 he led the Electrical Stimulation Group at the Automatic Control Laboratory, ETH Zurich and the Paraplegic Centre of University Hospital Balgrist, Zurich. He developed various neuroprostheses that help improve walking and grasp functions in spinal cord injured and stroke subjects. His research interests are in the fields of rehabilitation engineering and robotics, neural prostheses, signal processing, and human-machine interaction. His research focused on the development of novel technologies for transcutaneous functional electrical stimulation (FES) and rehabilitation robotics for clinical and domestic use, tele-rehabilitation, technology transfer to industry, and biomedical modelling. Dr. Keller is member and board director of the International Functional Electrical Stimulation Society (IFESS) and member of the IFESS Upper Limb Assessment Group.

Carolyn Kinsell holds a Ph.D. in instructional technology and a certificate in human performance. Her career spans 18 years, during which, she has focused on the application of training, ranging from analysis, to the development of virtual environments, to defining requirements and solutions for human performance standards; and, more recently, continuous investigation to determine links between blending training, gaming, and simulation techniques to establish exemplar training conditions and methods. She has worked closely with the military to include Cryptologists, Intelligence Specialists, Naval Diving and Salvage experts, and Force XXI Battle Command Brigade and Below (FBCB2) Joint Capabilities Release (JCR). She has also supported commercial clients such as Cingular and North America Honda, to name a few.

Vassilis Komis holds a degree in Mathematics from the University of Crete (1987), DEA (1989) and doctoral degrees (1993) in Teaching of Computer Science (Didactique de l'Informatique) from the University of Paris 7 - Denis Diderot (Jussieu). He is currently an Associate Professor of ICT applications in Education in the Department of Educational Sciences and Early Childhood Education at the University of Patras (Greece). He is also the founder and head of Information and Communications Technologies in Education Group at the University of Patras. His publications and research interests concern the conception and the development of educational software, the implementation of collaborative systems, the teaching of computer science and the integration of ICT applications in education.

Richard Lamb came to North Carolina State University as a Ph.D. student after several years teaching high school science. Richard is currently a technical writer at the Centre for Child and Family Policy, Duke University and an adjunct professor of Education at Campbell University. His areas of research interest are integration of educational technology into the science classroom and instrument development. Working with his mentor, Len Annetta he has sought to provide meaningful and interesting additions to the field of Science Education. An important aspect of his life is his two children and his loving family.

Nicola Lettieri is researcher at Italian Institute for the development of the vocational training of Rome, and contract professor of Legal Informatics at the Law School of the University of Benevento. He has a degree in Law and got a Ph.D. in Legal Informatics from the University of Florence. He worked at the Institute of Legal Information Theory and Techniques of the Italian National Research Council. His main research interests concern agent based social simulations and their applications in the analysis of socio-legal dynamics, artificial intelligence and law, serious games and learning simulations, and models for the representation of legal knowledge.

Stephanie B. Linek graduated from the University of Wuerzburg in 1997 with a diploma (MS) in Psychology. From 1998 to 1999, she worked as a postgraduate researcher at the University of Heidelberg. After postgraduate studies at the University of Koblenz-Landau, in 2002, she received the Certificate "Media- and Communication Psychologist". From 2003 to 2006, she was a postgraduate researcher at the Knowledge Media Research Centre in Tuebingen (Germany) and worked on her PhD thesis on "Gender-specific design of narrated animations: Speaker/Gender Effect and the schema-incongruity of information". In 2007, she received her Dr. rer. nat (D.Sc.) from the University of Tuebingen. Since 2006, she has worked in the Cognitive Science Section University of Graz in several EC-research projects and (since 2008) also as university assistant. Her research interests are in several areas of games and game-based learning, as well as in evaluation and methodology.

Dennis Maciuszek, Dipl.-Inform., Lic., M.A., studied Computer Science, Psychology, and Media Author in Braunschweig (Germany), Linkˆping (Sweden), and Stuttgart (Germany). Previous work included research on Intelligent Tutoring Systems, natural language processing, assistive technology, film studies, and the development of several computer games. He is currently employed as a doctoral student and researcher at the University of Rostock (Germany), Department of Computer Science and Electrical Engineering, e-Learning and Cognitive Systems group, where he is working in the area of game-based learning. Current research interests cover the design of digital educational games from three directions: software design, instructional design, and game design.

Alke Martens is Professor at the Department of Computer Science and Electrical Engineering at the University of Rostock, Germany. She is the leader of the research group "eLearning and Cognitive Systems". She received her PhD in Computer Science from the University of Rostock in the research field of Artificial Intelligence in the context of Intelligent Tutoring Systems. Her current research interests are formal methods, software engineering, modelling and simulation, artificial intelligence, teaching and training systems, and a combination thereof, e.g. in game-based learning. Current application domains of her research and her projects are systems biology, medicine, and education of computer scientists.

Jean-Charles Marty is an associate professor at University of Savoie (France). He leads the "Traces and Observation" group at the SysCom laboratory. His research interests are in the observation of collaborative activities, through the traces of these activities. The results of his research are applied to Technology Enhanced Learning, and more recently to Game-Based Learning environments. Jean-Charles Marty participates in several projects in this field (Learning Adventure, Learning Games Factory, Serious Lab for Innovation, Pegase). He is organizing an international school on Learning Games that will take place in France in July 2011.

Costas Mourlas is Assistant Professor in the National and Kapodistrian University of Athens (Greece), Department of Communication and Media Studies since 2002. He obtained his PhD from the Department of Informatics, University of Athens in 1995 and graduated from the University of Crete in 1988 with a Diploma in Computer Science. In 1998, he was an ERCIM fellow for post-doctoral studies through research in STFC, UK. He was employed as Lecturer at the University of Cyprus, Department of Computer Science from 1999 till 2002. His previous research work focused on distributed multimedia systems with adaptive behaviour, Quality of Service issues, streaming media, and the Internet. His current main research interest is in the design and the development of intelligent environments that provide adaptive and personalized context to the users according to their preferences, cognitive characteristics, and emotional state. He has several publications including edited books, chapters, and articles in journals and conference contributions. Dr. C. Mourlas has taught various undergraduate as well as postgraduate courses in the Dept. of Computer Science of the University of Cyprus and the Dept. of Communication and Media Studies of the University of Athens. Furthermore, he has coordinated and actively participated in numerous national and EU funded projects.

Wolfgang Müller is Professor for Media Education at the University of Education Weingarten, Germany. There he is leading the Media Education and Visualization Group, fostering research in the fields of E-Learning, Game-based Learning, Human-Computer Interaction, and Visualization. He received his diploma and doctorate in Computer Science from Darmstadt University of Technology in 1990 and 1997, respectively. Before joining the University of Education Weingarten, he held lecturer and research positions amongst others with Anhalt University of Applied Sciences, the University of Frankfurt, and with the Fraunhofer Computer Graphics Research Group. Wolfgang Müller has published several papers in international magazines and at international conferences in the fields of Interactive Storytelling, E-Learning, Multimedia, and Visualization, and Computer Graphics, and also contributed two books in these fields. Moreover, Wolfgang Müller served as in the program committee and as a reviewer for various international conferences and magazines. Currently, he serves as a Co-Editor in Chief for the Springer Journal Transactions on Edutainment. Wolfgang Müller is a member of IEEE Computer Society, ACM, ACM SIGCHI, and the German Informatics Society (GI). Furthermore, he is a German delegate to IFIP WG 3.3.

Angelique Nasah is a partner and researcher with Solers Research Group in Orlando, FL, and she holds a Ph.D. in instructional technology. Her research interests include the reduction of cognitive load through instructional design principles. Dr. Nasah is also interested in how information and communication technology innovation and usage impacts learning outcomes for various learning audiences. In addition to her work as a researcher, Dr. Nasah has worked in the education and training sector for more than 17 years; she has experience in secondary and higher education settings, as well as in the area of defense training.

Flaithrí Neff is a lecturer and researcher at the Department of Electrical & Electronic Engineering, Limerick Institute of Technology, Ireland. He is also a research member of the IDEAS Research Group at the Department of Computer Science, University College Cork, Ireland, where he is currently completing his PhD studies. In 2002 he attained a first class honours MSc degree at the University of Limerick, Ireland specializing in Audio Technology. His research interests are in virtual sonic interface design and intelligent hearing systems. He is particularly focused on applying his research to issues encountered by visually-disabled users of technology.

Sean Neill originally studied animal behaviour before researching adolescent fighting; he continues to research disruptive behaviour, most recently in surveys for the National Union of Teachers. He specialises in quantitative analysis and the function of behaviour, including play. He has worked on projects on the educational applications of computers since the 1990s, including four European Union financed international collaborative projects on IT based learning.

Eugenia M. W. Ng is an Associate Professor in the Mathematics and Information Technology Department and Associate Dean of Graduate School at the Hong Kong Institute of Education. She has had over seventy articles published in conference proceedings, journals, newspapers and as book chapters. Her publications have appeared in Issues in Informing Science and Information Technology, Journal of Interactive Instruction Development, of Information Systems Education, Journal of Quality School Education and Annals of Cases on Information Technology. Her book chapters have appeared in Subject Teaching and Teacher Education in the New Century: Research and Innovation, and Improving student learning: Learning-oriented assessment in action, Encyclopaedia of Information Technology Curriculum Integration, Encyclopaedia of Information Communications and Technology and Encyclopaedia of Networked and Virtual Organizations. She is the editor of Comparative blended learning practices and environments, and Co-editor-in-Chief of International Journal of Web-based Learning and Teaching Technologies.

Elisabet M. Nilsson holds a Ph.D. in Educational Sciences from the School of Education, Malmö University in Sweden. Her research interest concerns how new tools and technologies, such as computer games, influence activities in society and evoke new patterns of behaviour and thinking. Two tendencies are important as a background to her work. Firstly, the rapidly increased use of digital media among young people. Secondly, the challenge digital media pose for education. The research projects presented in her doctoral dissertation "Simulated 'real' worlds: Actions mediated through computer game play in science education" empirically explore what happens in situ when students collaboratively play and reflect on their computer game play in a science learning context.

Cathleen Norris is a Regents Professor in the College of Information, Department of Learning Technologies at the University of North Texas. Cathie's 14 years in K-12 classrooms–and receiving Dallas' Golden Apple Award–has shaped her university research agenda: helping K-12 teachers move from the 19th century into the 21st century. Cathie has been President of the International Society for Technology in Education (ISTE), the leading international organization for technology-minded educators. From 1996 through 2001, she was the President of the National Educational Computing Association (NECA), the association that organized NECC, the premier conference on technology in K-12. Cathie is co-founder of GoKnow, Inc. the premier mobile learning company.

Lucia Pannese, Italian, graduated in Mathematics, has extended experience in research projects with special attention to technology enhanced learning solutions, particularly based on the use of serious games. After working for more than 10 years in mainly technology companies with training and research/innovation responsibilities, in February 2004, together with 2 partners, she founded imaginary s.r.l., a company belonging to the Innovation Network of the university Politecnico di Milano. Imaginary specialises in the design and development of Serious Games and simulation systems for different business market sectors and is currently entering the educational sector. At present, she is covering the position of CEO and manager for international (research) activities. In October 2008 she founded Games2Growth Ltd based at the Serious Games Institute, Coventry University Technology Park, another SME specialising in design and development of serious games.

Anastasia Pappa has a PhD in Astrophysics. Her research interests focus on the use of virtual worlds and videogames in science communication and physics education. She is currently involved in the designing of a physics videogame for secondary school children. She also develops educational workshops for schoolchildren and is an active science communicator. She is a regular contributor to Greek publications and runs a blog (in Greek) which discusses issues of new technologies in science education as well as science communication.

Dimitra Pappa, holds a degree in Electrical Engineering from the National Technical University of Athens Greece (NTUA), specialising in telecommunication technologies. Since the late 1990's she has taken part in a number of European and national research and development projects in the fields of e-Learning, e-Health, e-Government and e-Commerce (under FP5 & FP6, eContentPlus, Lifelong Learning, eTEN, Ten-Telecom, ADAPT, ACTS, eLearning Initiative & EUMEDIS programmes), as scientific supervisor, project manager and/or member of the work team. The list of projects includes: OpenScout, PROLIX, PROLEARN, e-VITA, TEN-A, LIVIUS, ADAPT, GALENOS, MEDASHIP, EMISPHER, eGOV, PRAXIS. She has published several papers in refereed international scientific journals and conferences. Her current research interests revolve around the various facets of technology-enhanced learning.

Susan Pedersen joined the educational technology faculty in 2000 after completing her doctorate in Curriculum and Instruction at the University of Texas at Austin. She teaches graduate level classes in educational video, interface design, and computer-assisted instruction. Her research focuses on the use of technology to bring student-centred learning approaches, such as problem-based learning and student-directed inquiry, to K-12 environments. She was the lead instructional designer of "Alien Rescue", winner of the 2001 Learning Software Design Competition.

Joel Christopher Perry is a research engineer in the Biorobotics Department at Fatronik-Tecnalia and lead researcher for upper limb rehabilitation. He received his B.Sc. degree in mechanical engineering from Gonzaga University in 2000, and M.Sc. and Ph.D. degrees in mechanical engineering from the University of Washington, Seattle, Washington, in 2002 and 2006. Before joining Fatronik, Dr. Perry was involved in the development of various robotic devices for rehabilitation, surgery, and surgery simulation including a 7 degree-of-freedom (dof) arm exoskeleton, a 5-dof high precision positioning robot, a 5-dof surgical simulator, a novel 2-dof surgical grasper, and a 1-dof powered prosthesis in collaborative projects between the University of Washington (Seattle, USA), University of Washington Medical Centre, and the VA Puget Sound Health Care System (Seattle, USA). His research interests include enabling technologies for disability and human assistance, as well as robotic devices for surgical and rehabilitation applications.

Ian Pitt lectures in Usability Engineering and Interactive Media at University College, Cork, Ireland. He took his D.Phil at the University of York, UK, then worked as a research fellow at Otto-von-Guericke University, Magdeburg, Germany, before moving to Cork in 1997. He is the leader of the Interaction Design, E-learning and Speech (IDEAS) Research Group at UCC, which is currently working on a variety of projects relating to multi-modal human-computer interaction across various application domains. His own research interests centre around the use of speech and non-speech sound in computer interfaces, and the design of computer systems for use by blind and visually-impaired people

Aristidis Protopsaltis is a researcher at The Serious Games Institute at the Coventry University working on a number European projects. He holds a PhD and an MSc in Cognitive Science from the University of Westminster, where he studied with a scholarship from the Greek Foundation of Scholarships (IKY). He also holds a BSc in Primary Education from the University of Crete. Aristidis has spent several years as a visiting lecturer and teaching assistant at the University of Westminster and the CITY University London respectively. He has also worked as post doc researcher at the Reading University in the department of Education. He has published a number of peer-reviewed conference and journal papers, and served as a program committee member and program and general co-chair in several conferences. He is the vice-chair of the ACM SIGDOC European chapter. He research interests focus on Serious Games and Virtual Worlds and Education, Human Computer Interaction, Technology and Education.

Genaro Rebolledo-Mendez is a full time researcher at the Faculty of Informatics, University of Veracruz Mexico. He has been a researcher at Serious Games Institute, the University of Coventry, a Research Fellow at the London Knowledge Lab, University of London and the IDEAS Lab, Sussex University. Genaro's interest is the design and evaluation of educational technology that adapts sensitively to affective and cognitive differences among students. To do so, he studies how cognitive and affective differences impact students' behaviour while interacting with educational technology and how, in turn, technology impacts students' learning. To that end, he uses techniques from Artificial Intelligence, Computer Science, Education and Psychology.

Maria Rigou, PhD in Computer Science (2005, Web Personalization), has been a scientific collaborator of CTI Research Unit 5 (Internet and Multimedia Technologies) since 1998. Today, she is the technical manager of 4 IT projects (3 of which relate e-learning software) and is also a lecturer (subject: e-business) at the Technological Educational Institution of Messolonghi, Department of Applied Informatics in Administration and Economy and the University of Patras, Department of Computer Engineering and Informatics. She has worked in more than 20 IT projects of national and international funding and has more than 60 scientific publications in journals and conference proceedings. She is to receive (2010) an MSc in Graphic Arts and Multimedia from the Hellenic Open University where she is also a lecturer in the post-graduate course "Information Systems" (course: Design and Management of Information Systems).

Ute Ritterfeld, Ph.D., is heading the department of Language and Communication of the Technical University Dortmund. Her expertise includes applications for health and life style changes especially tailored towards seniors and individuals with special needs, and tools to motivate and facilitate deeper learning in all age groups. Ritterfeld received her education in the Health Sciences (Academy of Rehabilitation in Heidelberg 1983) and in Psychology (University of Heidelberg 1986), completed her Ph.D. in Psychology (Technical University of Berlin 1995), and habilitated at the University of Magdeburg, Germany (Dr. phil. habil. 2004) within the disciplines of psychology, communication and health sciences. She was Assistant Professor at the University of Magdeburg/Germany, Associate Professor at the University of Southern California in Los Angeles, and full professor at the VU University Amsterdam.

Eleni Rossiou is a Mathematician with M.Sc. in Computer Science and Ph.D. in Applied Informatics. She has Postgraduate studies in Distance Education and Adults Education, as well. Her research area includes blended learning methods with synchronous and asynchronous e-tools, cooperative learning, game-based learning and ICT exploitation in Secondary and Higher Education. She is a teacher of Informatics in Secondary Education, member of Algorithmic Operations Research Group of the University of Macedonia, member of Hellenic Network of Open and Distance Education, and member of Hellenic Scientific Association of Information and communication technologies. She authored and co-authored in various research papers published in national, European and international and journals and conference proceedings. She has extended experience in distance education, adult education, teaching and learning in virtual learning environments, and development of eLearning materials.

Helen Routledge is PIXELearning's Instructional System Designer Manager and specialises in designing serious games for corporate training and education. With 8 years market experience and a background in Behavioural Sciences (Psychology) Helen has helped create, promote and evaluate games for learning in various corporate sector companies such as Comcast and HP and public sector organisations such as the Scottish Institute for Sport Foundation. Helen's experience has gained her credibility and a name within the industry, as one of the leaders, innovators and entrepreneurs shaping and leading the industry. Her experience has resulted in her becoming a recognised figure on the international speaking circuit on the topics of games for learning in corporate and education.

Brent Ruben is Professor II (distinguished professor) of communication, executive director of the University Centre for Organizational Development and Leadership, and an associate member of the faculty of the Graduate School of Education at Rutgers University. Professor Ruben conducts research, teaches, publishes, and provides professional consultation nationally and internationally in the areas of communication and higher education leadership, assessment, planning and change. His recent books include: A Guide to Excellence in Higher Education: An Integrated Approach to Assessment, Planning, and Improvement in Colleges and Universities (2009), Understanding, Planning and Leading Organizational Change (2009), What Leaders Need to Know and Do: A Leadership Competencies Scorecard (2006); Communication and Human Behavior. Fifth Edition (with L. Stewart, 2006); and Pursuing Excellence in Higher Education: Eight Fundamental Challenges (2004). Dr. Ruben is author of 40 books, and 200 book chapters and articles.

Richard Sandford is a Senior Researcher at Futurelab in the UK. He is currently based in Singapore, working with the Media Development Authority and Republic Polytechnic to develop and evaluate computer games to support learning. Previously, he led the research and scenario development phases of the Beyond Current Horizons programme, a UK government-funded foresight programme investigating possible educational futures and their implications for current policy and practice. His research focuses on mobility, play, and digital games, and how these relate to learning.

Maria Saridaki is a Research Associate at the Laboratory of New Technologies at the Faculty of Communication & Media Studies of the National & Kapodistrian University of Athens. Her research interest lies on Digital Games and New Multimedia Social Environments with a special interest on Computer Games as an educational, motivational and recreational tool for people with cognitive disabilities. She obtained a Masters Degree in Information Management from the University of Strathclyde and a Bachelor in Media and Communication Studies at the University of Athens. She also has diplomas in Counseling and Play therapy with a focus on young people with special needs. She has taught workshops on Applied Gaming and Digital Media awareness targeted at students with disabilities, educators, journalists and communication managers. She has also been involved, or is currently participating in various EU and National projects as a researcher, game based learning specialist and project manager.

Vittorio Scarano is Associate Professor at Università di Salerno. He is a member of the Dipartimento di Informatica ed Applicazioni "R.M. Capocelli" of the Università di Salerno and is one of the founders of ISISLab. His research was first directed at the parallel architectures and algorithms. More recently, his interests in this area were expanded to cover to use the World Wide Web as a platform to offer advanced and interactive services to users. His research interest is also devoted to information visualization and interactive virtual environments. In this area, his interests are mainly on the applications of the videogame engines to non-ludic contexts (so called "serious games"). He is co-author of more than 100 papers in internationally refereed journals and conferences of IEEE, ACM, et cetera, and he has been the PhD supervisor of 6 PhD students of Computer Science PhD program at the University of Salerno.

Gareth Schott is a Senior Lecturer at the School of Arts, University of Waikato, New Zealand. He has published extensively in the emerging field of game studies over the last decade, contributing research on the topics of female gaming, game fandom and participatory cultures, the application of multi-modality theory to analysing game texts, metrics of violence and research into players, player cultures and player experience. His research has been funded by the Arts and Humanities Research Board (AHRB) and University for Industry (UfI) in the UK and Royal Society of New Zealand in NZ. He is one of the authors of Computer Games: Text, narrative and play published by Polity Press.

David I. Schwartz, Ph.D, published two textbooks while completing his dissertation in civil engineering, which sparked Cornell University's interest. So, in 1999, Schwartz accepted a lecturer position in the Department of Computer Science to teach computer programming. Recognizing the academic potential of games, Schwartz founded the Game Design Initiative at Cornell (GDIAC) in 2001. By 2006 Cornell offered a Minor in Game Design, the first formal undergraduate Ivy-League games program. In 2007, Schwartz joined the Rochester Institute of Technology's Game Design & Development program as an assistant professor. In 2009, he joined his new colleagues in founding RIT's Department of Interactive Games and Media, in which Schwartz's engineering and computer science experience paved the way for him to teach game programming, prototyping, design, and physical modeling. Dr. Schwartz currently researches a range of applications: instructional design and sustainability, ethics education, wargame design, and alternative interfaces.

Staffan Selander is professor in Didactic Science at Stockholm University, Sweden. Selander's research has focused learning from hermeneutic, socio-cultural and semiotic perspectives, especially on questions concerning interpretation, transformation and representation. In recent years he (and his research team) has developed the approach called *designs for learning*. Staffan Selander has been in charge of various research projects concerning multimodal texts, toys, aesthetic learning processes, digital learning resources and learning in various contexts. He has also for many years been the president of IARTEM (www.iartem.no). Among his recent publications (in English) are Designs for learning and ludic engagement (2008), Socio-cultural theories as ideology? The need for a design-theoretic, multimodal approach to learning (2008), Coordinating multimodal social semiotics and an institutional perspective in studying assessment actions in mathematics classrooms (with Lisa Boistrup-Björklund, 2009) and Nordic identities in transition – as reflected in pedagogic texts and cultural contexts (ed. with Bente Aamotsbakken, 2009).

Neil Selwyn is a Senior Lecturer at the London Knowledge Lab (University of London, UK). His research and teaching focuses on the place of digital media in everyday life, and the sociology of technology (non)use in educational settings. He has written extensively on a number of issues, including digital exclusion, education technology policymaking and the student experience of technology-based learning. He has carried out funded research on Information Technology, society, and education for the Economic and Social Research Council (ESRC), the BBC, Nuffield Foundation, the Spencer Foundation, Becta, Centre for Distance Education, the Welsh Office, National Assembly of Wales and various local authorities.

Soonhwa Seok has an M.A. and Ph.D. in curriculum and instruction. Dr. Seok has interests in educational communication and technology with applications for teaching English as a second language and special education. Most recently, as a postdoctoral researcher, Dr. Seok examined intersensory learning models, assistive technology, and motivation and feedback for students with learning disabilities. Additionally, she has served as a peer reviewer for conference proposals, presented on Web accessibility, and published articles on distance education and special education technology.

Sahar Shabanah received a Bachelor of Science in Computer Science from King Abdulaziz University in 1990. Since 1992, she has joined the Computer Science Department at King Abdulaziz University as a faculty member. She received a Master of Science M.S. in Computer Science (Multimedia and Computer Graphics) from George Washington University in 2001 and a Doctor of Philosophy in Computer Science (Computer Graphics and Games) from George Mason University in 2010. Currently, she is an assistant professor at the Computer Science Department/King Abdulaziz University. Her research interests include computer graphics, animation, computer games design, human computer interaction, educational games, algorithm visualization, and computer science education.

Namsoo Shin, Ph.D., is a research scientist in the School of Education at the University of Michigan. Her interests are focused on the impact of constructivist learning environments on student learning, especially everyday problem-solving skills, among K-12 students. The theoretical framework of her research focuses on the technology that must be used as a cognitive tool based on constructivist philosophy (e.g., inquiry learning, problem-based learning). She has researched problem-solving skills, argumentation skills, social interaction, gender differences, and cooperative learning in multimedia simulation context. She specializes in using quantitative methods to document the effectiveness of instructional materials. Her expertise is in developing instruments to assess students' problem solving skills and argumentation skills.

Ben Schouten graduated from the Rietveld Art Academy and worked as a professional artist for more than twenty years. He founded Desk.nl, an Application Software Provider (ASP), providing innovative Internet related solutions. Together with the Dutch Design Institute, Desk was internationally awarded a Webby award in gaming. In 2001, he received his PhD on content based image retrieval interfaces that express in an adaptive and intuitive way image similarities according to human perception. In the same year, he resumed teaching at the Utrecht School of Art & Technology (HKU) in interaction design, supervising Masters and Bachelors in interaction design and gaming. He is an advisor for the Dutch Media Fund, supporting e-culture for national broadcasting companies. Since 2010, he has been Professor Playful Interaction at the Faculty of Industrial Design at Eindhoven University of Technology as well as Lector Serious Game Design at Fontys University of Applied Sciences

Spiros Sirmakessis, PhD in Computer Science (1997, Computational Geometry and Multi-dimensional Data Structures), has been a scientific collaborator of CTI since 1992. Today, he is the manager of Research Unit 5 (Internet and Multimedia Technologies) and is also an Assisting Professor at the Technological Educational Institution of Messolonghi, Department of Applied Informatics in Administration and Economy. He has worked as project leader in 3 major international IT projects, has technically coordinated more than 30 IT projects of national and international funding as well as of the private sector (12 of which concerned e-learning related software) and has more than 100 scientific publications in journals and conference proceedings and more than 20 technical reports. He is the founder and coordinator of hci.gr, a team of usability consultants specialized in Web applications.

Elliot Soloway is an Arthur F. Thurnau Professor in the Dept of CSE, College of Engineering, School of Education and School of Information, University of Michigan. For the past 10 years, Soloway's research has been guided by the vision that mobile, handheld, and very low-cost networked devices are the only way to truly achieve universal 1:1 in schools all across the globe. In 2001, the undergraduates selected him to receive the "Golden Apple Award" as the Outstanding Teacher of the Year. In 2004, the

EECS College of Engineering HKN Honor Society awarded Elliot the "Distinguished Teacher of the Year Award." Elliot is a co-founder of GoKnow, Inc.

Vinod Srinivasan is a faculty member in the Department of Visualization at Texas A&M University. His primary research is in the area of applied gaming, particularly applications in education. His other research interests include applications of interactive visualization in 3D modeling, simulation, and design. He teaches game design and development, graphics programming, and 3D modeling. His current research projects include PlanetK, a game to teach digital logic design to undergraduate engineering majors, and an upcoming game to teach nutrition concepts to middle-school children. He is also the lead designer, architect, and developer of TopMod, a popular open source topological mesh modeler.

René Saint-Pierre has been developing and applying a research/design methodology involving digital technologies for more than twenty years. In 1999, he completed his Masters in Communications at UQAM with an interactive multimedia project on the life and work of French sculptor Armand Vaillancourt. In 2007, he obtained a Doctorate in Art Studies and Practices from the UQAM School of Visual and Media Arts. René Saint-Pierre has also taught design and multimedia development and production techniques at the college and university level for 8 years. He is currently involved in post-doctoral studies to further develop and share his research hypotheses with the international community of researchers and practitioners working in the emerging field of serious games for education.

Jan-Paul van Staalduinen (1980) is a PhD researcher in the Systems Engineering Group of the Faculty of Technology, Policy and Management of Delft University of Technology (TU Delft). His research interests are education, social software, and serious games. His PhD research focuses on the integration of educational theory and game design methods. In 2004 he got his Masters in Systems Engineering & Policy Analysis at the TU Delft, with a thesis on scenarios for education support infrastructures. After graduating, he worked as an e-learning consultant for the TU Delft. After that, he worked at Unisys Netherlands, as a process analyst and trainer. From 2006 to 2008, he worked for the consultancy firm Verdonck, Klooster & Associates, where he helped governmental bodies with projects on ICT policy and strategy, information management and quality management. He is a fulltime PhD researcher since July 2008.

Mark Stansfield is a Senior Lecturer in the School of Computing at the University of the West of Scotland. He has written and co-written more than 80 refereed papers in areas that include e-learning, games-based e-learning and virtual campuses. He also serves on the editorial boards of several international journals that include the International Journal of Information Management, Journal of Information Systems Education, ALT-J, and the Journal of IT Education, as well as being an Editor of the Interdisciplinary Journal of E-Learning and Learning Objects. He was Project Coordinator of the European Commission co-financed project 'Promoting Best Practice in Virtual Campuses' and is currently working on the Web 2.0 European Resource Centre project.

Gunilla Svingby is Professor at the School of Education, Malmö University, Nature, Mathematics and Society. She initiated Malmö University Centre for Games Studies and the research group on Simulations and Games for Learning, Assessment, and Competency. Dr. Svingby's research focus is formative assessment, computer supported collaborative learning, and simulations and games. Among her projects are "Accessibility and Learning in Higher Education" where the social dynamic of group work on the net is studied. In "The interactive examination", students from three programs are assessed by simulated, video filmed, authentic situations, which students describe, analyse, and act on. In an ongoing project "Teachers as professionals", a simulation game is developed to assess and support teacher students' professional development. Dr. Svingby has worked as professor at the universities of Oslo, Tromso, Norway, Monash, Australia, Gothenburg and Lund, Sweden. She has supervised 18 Ph.D. students.

Nicolas Szilas has been working in the field of Cognitive Science for fifteen years till now. From research to industry, and from industry to research, he has been aiming at being at the heart of innovation, in the various domains that he works. After the completion of his Ph.D in 1995 and two postdoctoral positions in Montreal, he entered a video game studio in 1997, in order to manage the newly created R&D program on AI for video games. From 1999, he conducted his own research program on Interactive Drama, named IDtension. Since 2003, he has been working on this project in French, Australian and Swiss Universities. He is now associate professor at TECFA, University of Geneva, working at the intersection of games, narrative, learning, and technology. He is now involved in Swiss and European projects related to Interactive Narrative in which IDtension narrative engine is employed for both entertainment and educational applications.

Jordi Sánchez-Navarro is Associate Professor at the Department of Information and Communication Sciences at the Open University of Catalonia (Universitat Oberta de Catalunya) where he coordinates the Graduate Studies area. He has widely written on film, television, and videogames and worked as a consultant and curator in exhibitions, festivals, and conferences. He holds a PhD in Film and Media Studies (Universitat Ramon Llull). Currently he is researching on the forms of innovation in the audiovisual entertainment and how these forms interact with the new practices of cultural consumption in the contemporary media landscape. Among other activities, he collaborates with the research groups SPIDER (Smarter People through Interactive Digital Entertainment Resources-http://spider-uoc.blogspot.com) and Communicationa nd New Media (at the Internet Interdisciplinary Institute- IN3). Recent publications include Aprovecha el tiempo y juega. Algunas claves para entender los videojuegos (Editorial UOC, 2009) and Jóvenes y ocio digital.

Wee Hoe Tan. Formerly a 3D animator, Wee Hoe joined academia in mid 2004 to teach and develop multimedia courses in Malaysia. He was the R&D Coordinator of Malaysian Institute of Information Technology, a subsidiary of Universiti Kuala Lumpur. He is a member of the international editorial board of the International Journal of Game-Based Learning. He is at the end of his doctoral research, studying game-based learning (GBL) in the Institute of Education, University of Warwick, UK. The research concerns with issues related to how subject matter experts and game experts can collaborate to design and develop GBL for use in formal education contexts. This research is funded by the Malaysian Ministry of Higher Education and Universiti Pendidikan Sultan Idris, Malaysia.

Antonella Tartaglia Polcini is full professor of Civil Law and head of the Department "Persona, Mercato, Istituzioni" at the Law and Economics Faculty of the University of Benevento. He authored numerous articles and monographs in the field of civil law with special regard to arbitration. Beside strictly legal subjects, her research interests have involved, for a few years, computer law and the use of ICT in legal education.

Paul Toprac is a lecturer at The Guildhall at Southern Methodist University, where he focuses on teaching and the research, design, and implementation of game technology based applications. He has more than the twenty years of experience in the software industry, in roles ranging from CEO to product manager to consultant. During his studies at the University of Texas at Austin, Paul was the producer and designer of a science-based computer game called Alien Rescue: The Game, which was used in his dissertation, entitled "The Effects of a Problem Based Learning Computer Game on Continuing Motivation to Learn Science." He holds a Bachelor's of Science in Engineering, a Master's of Business Administration, and a Ph.D. in Curriculum and Instruction from The University of Texas at Austin. In his spare time, Paul hopes to convince universities and schools that students can have fun and learn at the same time.

Sherrie Tromp is Associate Director of the University Centre for Organizational Development and Leadership at Rutgers, The State University of New Jersey. Ms. Tromp is co-author (with Brent Ruben) of Strategic Planning in Higher Education: A Guide for Leaders, 2nd Edition (NACUBO, 2010) and primary author of Process Improvement in Higher Education (Dubuque, IA: Kendall-Hunt, 1997), The Process Improvement Instructor's Guide, and Root Cause Analysis in Higher Education (Dubuque, IA: Kendall-Hunt, 1997). Ms. Tromp received her undergraduate degree in bilingual education from Arizona State University and her Masters in cultural anthropology from Rutgers University. During her tenure at Rutgers she has also held the positions of Associate Director of Admissions and University Data Administrator. She has served as a consultant to higher education organizations, and is a member of the American Association of Higher Education, and the National Consortium for Continuous Improvement. She also served on the Rutgers Advisory Board for the Kellogg Leadership for Institutional Change Initiative.

Tony Veale is a lecturer in the department of Computer Science at University College Dublin (UCD), Ireland. He has been a researcher in the areas of Computational Linguistics, Cognitive Science, Cognitive Linguistics and Artificial Intelligence since 1988, both in industry and in academia. He obtained a B.Sc (hons) in Computer Science from University College Cork (UCC) in 1988, and an M.Sc in Computer Science in 1990, before joining Hitachi Dublin Laboratory in 1990. He received his Ph.D in Computer Science from Trinity College, Dublin in 1996. He has divided his career between academia and industry. In the latter, he has developed text-understanding and machine translation systems for Hitachi (in particular, the translation of English into American Sign language, ASL), as well as analogical reasoning tools for the CYC project in Cycorp at Austin, Texas, and patented Web-based question-answering technology for Intelliseek (Cincinnati, Ohio) and Coreintellect (Dallas, Texas), where he held the position of Chief Scientist. During his tenure on the CYC project in Cycorp Inc., he developed a model of analogical reasoning for CYC and contributed to the DARPA-funded, High-Performance-Knowledge-Bases (HPKB) and Rapid-Knowledge-Formation (RKF) projects. He was, from 2002-2007, the academic coordinator for UCD's unique international degree programme in Software Engineering, which UCD delivers in Shanghai at Fudan University; he continues to deliver courses on this degree.

Jan Veneman holds an Engineering degree in Mechanical Engineering and a Master of Science degree in Philosophy of Science, Technology and Society, both from the University of Twente (The Netherlands). He obtained a Dr. degree from the same university in December 2007 for work on the development and evaluation of an impedance controlled robotic system for providing gait training for post-stroke patients, called LOPES. He subsequently joined Roessingh Research and Development (RRD, Enschede, the Netherlands), where he worked on the monitoring of gait recovery. His primary interests are conceptual and mechanism design, (compliant) actuation technology, haptic or mechanical human-robot interaction, technology for neurorehabilitation, and gait measurement. In October 2008, he joined the Biorobotics department of Fatronik-Tecnalia as research engineer/project manager. He has published and contributed to 5 peer reviewed journal articles, one book chapter and many conference proceedings.

Iro Voulgari is a PhD candidate at the Department of Educational Sciences and Early Childhood Education at the University of Patras (Greece). She has studied Education Sciences in Pre-School Age at the Democritus University of Thrace (Greece) and holds an M.Ed. in Information Technology, Multimedia and Education from the University of Leeds (UK), School of Education and Computer Based Learning Unit. She has worked in a number of Research and Development projects relevant to e-learning and the development of online educational content. Her publications concern the educational and social aspect of multiplayer games, and her research interests include educational computer games, educational software, virtual worlds, computer-mediated communication and collaboration, e-learning, and collaborative problem solving.

Jennifer R. Whitson is a Sociology PhD candidate at Carleton University. Her current research interests include social influences on game software development processes, governance in online domains, and digital identity management. Her most recent work includes an article on governance in games in the May 2010 issue of fibreculture, a feature article on identity theft in the March/April 2009 edition of ACM's Interactions magazine, a chapter on virtual world governance, co-authored with Aaron Doyle, in Stéphane Leman-Langlois' edited collection, Technocrime, and an article on identity theft, co-authored with Kevin Haggerty, in the November 2008 issue of Economy & Society.

Nicola Whitton works as a Research Fellow in the Institute of Education at Manchester Metropolitan University. Her background is in Information Technology and online learning, and she is interested in pedagogic and technological innovation, particularly in the areas of collaborative and problem-based learning. Her research focuses on the use of computer games in Higher Education and in the context of lifelong learning, and she is particularly interested in the nature of motivation and engagement with games.

Ben Williamson is a Senior Researcher at Futurelab and a Research Fellow at the University of Exeter in the UK. His research focuses on curriculum innovation related to ICT in schools, on the role of videogames and creative software in young people's social and educational experiences, and on the development of young people's digital media literacy. Ben's recent publications have concentrated on the use of videogames in school, curriculum innovation, teacher professional development, and children's science-fiction literature. Ben also has a PhD in American literature, critical theory and pragmatist philosophy.

Johannes Zylka studied teaching for secondary schools in the subjects of geography, mathematics, and computer science, and is a PhD student at the University of Education Weingarten since May 2010. He received his diploma from University of Education Weingarten in media pedagogics. As a member of the Media Education and Visualization Group, he deals with the topics of media education, media literacy education, and the measurement of media- and especially computer-related skills, as well as with video game-related topics, such as Serious Games and Game-based Learning.

Index

H

S

W

X

Y

Z

CPSIA information can be obtained at www.ICGtesting.com
Printed in the USA
BVOW070925200911

271623BV00002B/13/P